THE
RANGE
OF
LITERATURE

THE
RANGE
OF
LITERATURE

An Introduction to Prose and Verse

Elisabeth W. Schneider
TEMPLE UNIVERSITY

Albert L. Walker
IOWA STATE UNIVERSITY

Herbert E. Childs
OREGON STATE COLLEGE

AMERICAN BOOK COMPANY

New York

ACKNOWLEDGMENTS

Grateful acknowledgment is made to the following publishers and individuals for permission to reprint material which is in copyright or of which they are the authorized publishers:

GEORGE ALLEN AND UNWIN LTD: For "A Free Man's Worship" from *Mysticism and Logic* by Bertrand Russell. By permission of the publishers.

THE ATLANTIC MONTHLY: For "A Sick Call" by Morley Callaghan.

MISS OONE AULT: For "Who Would Have Thought" by Thomas Howell, "Why Do We Love" by Sir Benjamin Rudyerd, "Brown is My Love" Anonymous, "Thou Sleepest Fast" Anonymous, "To a Lady to Answer Directly With Yea or Nay" by Sir Thomas Wyatt, "The Lover Showeth How He Is Forsaken of Such as He Sometime Enjoyed" by Sir Thomas Wyatt, and "Song" by George Peele from *Elizabethan Lyrics,* 3rd ed., 1949, edited by Norman Ault.

THE BELKNAP PRESS OF HARVARD UNIVERSITY PRESS: For "What shall I do when the Summer troubles," "The Soul selects," "I like to see it lap the miles," "A loss of something ever felt I," and "Finding is the first Act" from *The Poems of Emily Dickinson,* edited by Thomas H. Johnson, copyright 1955 by The President and Fellows of Harvard College. Reprinted by permission of the publishers.

BRANDT & BRANDT: For the Harper's Ferry episode from *John Brown's Body* by Stephen Vincent Bénet, Rinehart & Company, Inc., copyright 1927, 1928 by Stephen Vincent Bénet, copyright renewed 1955, 1956 by Rosemary Carr Bénet.

THE CLARENDON PRESS, OXFORD: For "Sonnet No. 23," "Triolet," "Nightingales," and "November" from *The Shorter Poems of Robert Bridges,* published by the Clarendon Press, Oxford. For selections from Aristotle's *Poetics,* translated by Ingram Bywater in *The Student's Oxford Aristotle,* edited by W. D. Ross. By permission of the publishers and Oxford University Press, Inc.

THE CITADEL PRESS: For selections from *The Devil's Dictionary* by Ambrose Bierce. By permission of the publisher.

JONATHAN CAPE AND HARRISON SMITH, INC.: For "The Hermit" from *Collected Poems* by W. H. Davies.

COWARD-MCCANN, INC.: For *The Cherry Orchard* by Anton Chekhov translated by Jennie Covan, copyright, 1923, 1933 by Coward-McCann, Inc.

DODD, MEAD AND COMPANY, INC.: For "On the Need for a Quiet College" from Stephen Leacock's Laugh Parade, copyright © 1940 by Dodd, Mead and Company, Inc. Reprinted by permission of the publishers.

J. M. DENT AND SONS LTD.: For "Heart of Darkness" from *Youth* by Joseph Conrad.

JOHN DOS PASSOS: For "Tin Lizzie" from U.S.A. by John Dos Passos, copyright by John Dos Passos, published by Houghton Mifflin Company.

DOUBLEDAY AND COMPANY, INC.: For "The Outstation" from *The Casuarina Tree* by W. Somerset Maugham, copyright © 1924 by International Magazine Company, For "He Don't Plant Cotton" from *The Prince of Darkness and Other Stories* by J. F. Powers, copyright © 1943 by J. F. Powers. For "Stickman's Laughter" from *Neon Wilderness* by Nelson Algren, copyright © 1942 by Nelson Algren. For "Like the Noise of Great Thunders" from *A Stillness at Appomattox* by Bruce Catton, copyright 1953 by Bruce Catton. All the above reprinted by permission of Doubleday and Company, Inc.

ENCYCLOPÆDIA BRITANNICA: For "James Boswell" by Thomas Seccombe, from *Encyclopædia Britannica,* 11th ed. By permission.

FUNK & WAGNALLS COMPANY: For "The Enormous Radio" from *The Enormous Radio and Other Stories* by John Cheever, Funk & Wagnalls Company, New York. Reprinted by permission of the publishers.

HARCOURT, BRACE AND COMPANY, INC.: For "Flowering Judas" from *Flowering Judas and Other Stories* by Katherine Anne Porter, copyright 1930, 1935, 1958 by Katherine Anne Porter. For *The Oedipus Rex of Sophocles:* An English Version by Dudley Fitts and Robert Fitzgerald, copyright 1949 by Harcourt, Brace and Company, Inc. For "Autumn" and "Embankment" from *Speculations* by T. E. Hulme. For "The Love Song of J. Alfred Prufrock" and "Journey of the Magi" from *Collected Poems 1909–1935* by T. S. Eliot, copyright 1936 by Harcourt, Brace and Company, Inc. For "nobody loses all the time," copyright 1926 by Horace Liveright, renewed 1953 by E. E. Cummings, reprinted from *Poems 1923–1954* by E. E. Cummings. For "a pretty day," copyright 1940 by E. E. Cummings, reprinted from *Poems 1923–1954* by E. E. Cummings. For "O sweet spontaneous" and "Chansons Innocentes: I," copyright 1923, 1950 by E. E. Cummings, reprinted from *Poems 1923–1954* by E. E. Cummings. All the above reprinted by permission of Harcourt, Brace and Company, Inc.

HARPER AND BROTHERS: For "The Door" from *The Second Tree from the Corner* by E. B. White, copyright 1939 by E. B. White, originally published in *The New Yorker.* For "Under Cover" from *Outcrop* by Abbie Huston Evans, copyright 1928 by Harper and Brothers, copyright 1956 by Abbie Huston Evans. For "My Uncle's Farm" from *Mark Twain's Autobiography,* copyright 1924 by Clara Gabrilowitsch, copyright 1952 by Clara Clemens Samossoud. For "Letter from the Recording Angel" from *Captain Stormfield's Visit to Heaven* by Mark Twain, copyright 1946 by the Mark Twain Company.

HENRY HOLT AND COMPANY, INC.: For "The Death of the Hired Man," "After Apple-Picking," "The Runaway," "Mending Wall," "Dust of Snow," "Nothing Gold Can Stay," "Fire and Ice," and "Desert Places" from *Complete Poems of Robert Frost,* copyright 1930, 1949 by Henry Holt and Company, Inc. For "When smoke stood up from Ludlow," "Bredon Hill," "The rain, it streams on stone and hillock," "To an Athlete Dying Young," and "Easter Humn" from *Complete Poems* by A. E. Housman, copyright 1940 by Henry Holt and Company, Inc., copyright © 1959 by Henry Holt and Company, Inc. For "Fog" and "Limited" from *Chicago Poems* by Carl Sandburg, copyright 1916 by Henry Holt and Company, Inc., copyright 1944 by Carl Sandburg. All the above reprinted by permission of the publishers.

HOUGHTON MIFFLIN COMPANY: For "The Fall of the Government" from *The Gathering Storm* by Sir Winston Churchill. For "You, Andrew Marvell" from *Poems* by Archibald MacLeish. The above selections reprinted by permission of and arrangement with Houghton Mifflin Company, the authorized publishers.

ALFRED A. KNOPF, INC.: For "The Wayfarer" and "A Man Said to the Universe" from *The Collected Poems of Stephen Crane.* For "Blue Girls" from *Selected Poems* by John Crowe Ransom, copyright 1927, 1945 by Alfred A. Knopf, Inc. For "The Death of a Soldier" from *The Collected Poems of Wallace Stevens,* copyright 1931, 1954 by Wallace Stevens. For "The Blue Hotel" from *Stephen Crane: An Omnibus,* edited by Robert Wooster Stallman, copyright 1952 by Alfred A. Knopf, Inc. For "Guests of the Nation" from *More Stories of Frank O'Connor,* copyright 1954 by Frank O'Connor. For "The Daughters of the Late Colonel" from *The Short Stories of Katherine Mansfield,* copyright 1922, 1937 by Alfred A. Knopf, Inc. For "The Fight Between Jappe and Do Escobar" from *Stories of Three Decades* by Thomas Mann, translated from the German by H. T. Lowe-Porter, copyright 1936 by Alfred A. Knopf, Inc. All the above reprinted by permission of Alfred A. Knopf, Inc.

THE MACMILLAN COMPANY: For "The New Villa" from *The Witch and Other Stories* by Anton Chekhov, translated by Constance Garnett. For "To My Mother" from *Selected Poems* by George Barker. For "Birds at Winter Nightfall," "By the Earth's Corpse," "The Convergence of the Twain," and "Waiting Both" from *Collected Poems* by Thomas Hardy. For "Mr. Flood's Party" from *Collected Poems* by Edwin Arlington Robinson. For "Her Praise," "No Second Troy," "That the Night Come," "The Host of the Air," "The Three Beggars," "The Balloon of the Mind," "The Cold Heaven," "The Second Coming," "The Magi," and "Among School Children" from *Collected Poems* by William Butler Yeats. All the above reprinted by permission of The Macmillan Company.

MRS. ELLEN C. MASTERS: For "Lucinda Matlock" from *Spoon River Anthology* by Edgar Lee Masters, published by The Macmillan Company.

WILLIAM MORROW AND COMPANY, INC.: For "The Homestead Orchard" from *Team Bells Woke Me and Other Stories* by H. L. Davis, copyright 1939 by the Curtis Publishing Company, reprinted by permission of William Morrow and Company, Inc.

NEW DIRECTIONS: For "The River-Merchant's Wife: A Letter" and "Ancient Music" from *Personae* by Ezra Pound, copyright 1926, 1952 by Ezra Pound. For "Overture to a Dance of Locomotives" from *Collected Earlier Poems* by William Carlos Williams, copyright 1938, 1951 by William Carlos Williams. For "After the Funeral" and "Fern Hill" from *Collected Poems* by Dylan Thomas, copyright 1953 by Dylan Thomas. All the above reprinted by permission of the publisher, New Directions.

THE NATION: For "Euroclydon" by Abbie Huston Evans, printed in *The Nation* for December 27, 1952.

HAROLD OBER ASSOCIATES: For "The Sad Horn Blowers" by Sherwood Anderson from *Harper's,* February, 1923, and from *Horses and Men* (B. W. Huebsch), copyright © 1923 by Eleanor Anderson, reprinted by permission of Harold Ober Associates Incorporated.

OXFORD UNIVERSITY PRESS: For "No worst, there is none," "Pied Beauty," and "The Windhover" from *Poems of Gerard Manley Hopkins.*

NORMAN HOLMES PEARSON: For "Lethe" from *Collected Poems* by H. D. By permission of Norman Holmes Pearson.

RANDOM HOUSE, INC.: For "Two Soldiers" from *Collected Stories of William Faulkner,* copyright 1942 by William Faulkner. For "Delta Autumn" from *Go Down Moses and Other Stories* by William Faulkner. For "The Lift That Went Down into Hell" from *The Eternal Smile and Other Stories* by Pär Lagerkvist, copyright 1954 by Random House, Inc. For "O What is that Sound," copyright 1937 by Random House, Inc., reprinted from *The Collected Poetry of W. H. Auden.* For "The Unknown Citizen," "In Memory of W. B. Yeats," and "Musée des Beaux Arts," copyright 1940 by W. H. Auden, reprinted from *The Collected Poetry of W. H. Auden.* For "The Inquisitors," copyright 1948 by Robinson Jeffers, reprinted from *The Double Axe and Other Poems* by Robinson Jeffers. For "What I Expected," "I hear the Cries of Evening," and "The Express," copyright 1934 by The Modern Library, Inc., reprinted from *Collected Poems 1928–1953* by Stephen Spender. For "Museums," "Bagpipe Music," and "Sunday Morning" from *Poems* by Louis MacNeice, copyright 1937 by Louis MacNeice. For "Precursors" from *Springboard 1941–1944* by Louis MacNeice, copyright 1944 by Louis MacNeice. All the above reprinted by permission of Random House, Inc.

ELMER RICE: For *The Adding Machine,* including previously-unpublished Prison Scene, copyright 1922, 1929 by Elmer Rice.

SCHOCKEN BOOKS, INC.: For "A Country Doctor" from *The Penal Colony* by Franz Kafka. Reprinted by the publishers' permission.

CHARLES SCRIBNER'S SONS: For "In Another Country," copyright 1927 by Charles Scribner's Sons, renewal copyright 1955, reprinted from *Men Without Women* by Ernest Hemingway. For "Haircut," copyright 1925 by Ellis A. Lardner, renewal copyright 1953, reprinted from *The Love Nest and Other Stories* by Ring Lardner. For "Question" from *Poets of Today* by May Swenson, copyright 1954 by May Swenson. For "Miniver Cheevy" from *The Town Down the River* by E. A. Robinson, copyright 1910 by Charles Scribner's Sons, 1938 by Ruth Nivison. All the above reprinted by permission of Charles Scribner's Sons.

THE SOCIETY OF AUTHORS: For "The House" from *Collected Poems, 1919–1934,* by Walter de la Mare, copyright 1941. For "The Ghost," Book 1; "The Mocking Fairy," Book 2; "At the Keyhole," Book 2; "The Old Man," Book 1; and "The Listeners," Book 1 from *Collected Poems, 1901–1918* by Walter de la Mare. All the above reprinted by permission of the Literary Trustees of Walter de la Mare and The Society of Authors as their representative.

MRS. HELEN THOMAS: For "Gallows" from *Poems* by Edward Thomas. For "Out in the Dark" and "The New House" from *Collected Poems* by Edward Thomas.

JAMES THURBER: For "Death in the Zoo" and "Interview with a Lemming" from *My World and Welcome To It,* copyright 1937, 1938, 1939, 1940, 1941 by James Thurber.

THE VANGUARD PRESS, INC.: For "Colonel Fantock" from *The Collected Poems of Edith Sitwell,* copyright 1954 by Edith Sitwell. Reprinted by permission of the publishers, The Vanguard Press, Inc.

THE VIKING PRESS, INC.: For "The Boarding House" from *Dubliners* in *The Portable James Joyce,* copyright 1946, 1947 by The Viking Press, Inc., New York. For "Pot-Luck Among the Casuals" and "Squirrel" from *Selected Poems* by Marsden Hartley, copyright 1945 by Norma Berger. All the above reprinted by permission of The Viking Press, Inc., New York.

PREFATORY NOTE

We have been guided in the preparation of this anthology by the conviction that most instructors have two principal objectives in giving the student his first college experience with literature.

The first objective is to give the student mastery of the elements of literature, without which he usually must remain merely a story hunter, rather than becoming a reader. It is a relatively easy thing to set down one's own theories and then attach the literature to them. This has been done more than once, and it is wonderful to see how rigidity sets in, with the student (or instructor) given never a chance to think for himself about the literature. In every line of our analytical and informational apparatus, we have tried to avoid standing between student and literature or between student and instructor. The apparatus is ammunition for the student's arsenal, not directions for firing.

The second objective is to give the student some sense of the resources of the various literary forms and to place before him worthy examples of those resources. We have tried to represent the full range of each form, modifying, to that end, our personal penchants, and remembering how the student learns and what kinds of representative pieces he can best begin with.

Our desire for full representation has led to what we hope is a pleasing balance of older and newer literature. Many traditional favorites are here, of course, but we include also quite a few pieces that have been anthologized seldom or never.

Some may wish to start the course with the last section of the book, "The Nature and Functions of Literature," which offers samples of some theoretical statements about the *raison d'etre* of all literature. But since others may prefer to postpone considerations of general philosophic import until later, we have set these selections in the final, neutral position. We include what we believe will be enough to initiate good class discussion and perhaps to entice the student into further reading, but not so much as to scare him away.

E. W. S.
A. L. W.
H. E. C.

CONTENTS

THE ART OF READING POETRY   259

THE ART OF READING DRAMA   406

THE FURTHER RANGE OF PROSE   *611*

THE FURTHER RANGE OF PROSE: BIOGRAPHY   *664*

THE NATURE AND FUNCTIONS OF LITERATURE   698

The Art of Reading Fiction

The reading of fiction can be an almost passive occurrence or it can be active—an art, a skill used with purpose and based on knowledge. Reading is a psychological transaction between the reader and the story. Little of value ever arises from the act of reading unless the individual reader wants it to. Reading is a highly personal matter, and the rewards are personal rewards.

The most passive kind of reading probably occurs when we "consume" commercial fiction, the kind that typically appears in mass-circulation magazines. No one needs instruction in reading at this level: the mental age required is about 8 to 12 years; words that might be strange are carefully screened out; the ideas are familiar to everyone and are there for that reason. Fiction at this level constitutes, let us guess, 97.333 per cent of the yearly output, and the consumer typically says that he reads to pass the time, to relax, to get his mind off his troubles, which we must assume are numerous. It makes no difference whether the escape-hatch is labeled *Larcenous Love, Death at Six-Gun Mesa*, or *Dr. Quantum's Misadventures in Space*—the reader of commercial fiction knows exactly what rewards are offered, and he gets them easily, passively.

To approach better fiction with the expectations that apply to commercial fiction is to invite disappointment, for the reading of good fiction cannot be entirely passive. Many readers do, however, approach good fiction with wrong expectations. That is why, in this introduction, we shall talk directly and specifically about things that can happen, and do happen, when people read good fiction skillfully.

The following is a list showing topics to be discussed in connection with three stories used as examples. It is advisable not to try to read all the discussion at one sitting, for fiction is a complex art which is best understood by degrees. At key points in the discussion, problems or questions are given which should aid the student in fixing his understanding of fundamentals. (A "problem" we regard as something that should be investigated over a period of time, resulting perhaps in a written report; a "question" can be discussed in class and answered with relative speed.)

Some Characteristics of Fiction
Story: "Two Soldiers," by William Faulkner.
Public and private fact; the subjective world; why authors sometimes write about trouble; functions of humor.   (Problems and Questions)

Some Problems of Reading
Story: "A Sick Call," by Morley Callaghan.
Finding the center of emphasis; immediate and delayed reactions; types of

I

"wrong" reading. The problem of implied meanings. "Easy" and "difficult" reading.   (Problems and Questions)

Fiction and "Truth"

Fiction compared with other reports of experience—social statistics, psychology, history.

Major Effects of Reading Fiction

Reading as an experience involving emotion: comments on the psychology of art.

Reading as an experience involving emotion: functions of curiosity and "caring" in the reading of fiction.

Fiction as a source of ideas and beliefs.

Fiction as a source of information: the question of whether "believability" is important.

Fiction as art: story elements and their interrelationships; art as an ordering of experience; science, religion, and art.

Nonrealistic Fiction; Symbolism

Story: "The Lift That Went Down into Hell," by Pär Lagerkvist.

Symbolism in fiction; reasons for the use of nonrealistic elements in a story; discussion of "Lift"; special uses of symbols.   (Problems)

Technical Information for Readers of Fiction

Point of view and focus; author's comment; "objective" technique; wording, sentence structure and rhythm; paraphrases; conflict; main character; title; kinds of fiction; strategy for readers.   (Problems)

For Exploration and Discovery

See Table of Contents: *Far Places, Before the Wars; Contrasts of Character in Time and Place; Twentieth-Century Causes and Loyalties.*

Instructors will quickly see that the topics shown above, with the examples, are designed to lead the student by easy stages from a view of art as realistic representation only—an idea widely current among beginning students—to a view of art as symbol. The brief discussions of the relations between fiction and "truth" are an essential part of this progressive development of understanding. Each of the first six major parts would make an assignment of a convenient size.

SOME CHARACTERISTICS OF FICTION

In order to have an example of fiction in mind from the beginning, we present the story "Two Soldiers," by William Faulkner, a winner of the Nobel Prize for Literature. We suggest that the reader begin his practice in the art of reading by taking time to get the flavor and meaning of small details in this story, which a hurried reading may obscure.

TWO SOLDIERS

William Faulkner
(1897–   )

Me and Pete would go down to Old Man Killegrew's and listen to his radio. We would wait until after supper, after dark, and we would stand outside Old Man Killegrew's parlor window, and we could hear it because Old Man Killegrew's wife was deaf, and so he run the radio as loud as it would run, and so me and Pete could hear it plain as Old Man Killegrew's wife could, I reckon, even standing outside with the window closed.

And that night I said, "What? Japanese? What's a pearl harbor?" and Pete said, "Hush."

And so we stood there, it was cold, listening to the fellow in the radio talking, only I couldn't make no heads nor tails neither out of it. Then the fellow said that would be all for a while, and me and Pete walked back up the road to home, and Pete told me what it was. Because he was nigh twenty and he had done finished the Consolidated last June and he knowed a heap: about them Japanese dropping bombs on Pearl Harbor and that Pearl Harbor was across the water.

"Across what water?" I said. "Across that Government reservoy up at Oxford?"

"Naw," Pete said. "Across the big water. The Pacific Ocean."

We went home. Maw and pap was already asleep, and me and Pete laid in the bed, and I still couldn't understand where it was, and Pete told me again—the Pacific Ocean.

"What's the matter with you?" Pete said. "You're going on nine years old. You been in school now ever since September. Ain't you learned nothing yet?"

"I reckon we ain't got as fer as the Pacific Ocean yet," I said.

We was still sowing the vetch then that ought to been all finished by the fifteenth of November, because pap was still behind, just like he had been ever since me and Pete had knowed him. And we had firewood to git in, too, but every night me and Pete would go down to Old Man Killegrew's and stand outside his parlor window in the cold and listen to his radio; then we would come back home and lay in the bed and Pete would tell me what it was. That is, he would tell me for a while. Then he wouldn't tell me. It was like he didn't want to talk about it no more. He would tell me to shut up because he wanted to go to sleep, but he never wanted to go to sleep.

He would lay there, a heap stiller than if he was asleep, and it would be something, I could feel it coming out of him, like he was mad at me even, only I knowed he wasn't thinking about me, or like he was worried about something, and it wasn't that neither, because he never had nothing to worry about. He never got behind like pap, let alone stayed behind. Pap give him ten acres when he graduated from the Consolidated, and me and Pete both reckoned pap was durn glad to get shut of at least ten acres, less to have to worry with himself; and Pete had them ten acres all sowed to vetch and busted out and bedded for the winter, and so it wasn't that. But it was something. And still we would go down to Old Man Killegrew's every night and listen to his radio, and they was at it in the Philippines now, but General MacArthur was holding um. Then we would come back home and lay in the bed, and Pete wouldn't tell me nothing or talk at all. He would just lay there still as a ambush and when I would touch him, his side or his leg would feel hard and still as iron, until after a while I would go to sleep.

Then one night—it was the first time he had said nothing to me except to jump on me about not chopping enough wood at the wood tree where we was cutting—he said, "I got to go."

"Go where?" I said.

"To that war," Pete said.

"Before we even finish gittin' in the firewood?"

"Firewood, hell," Pete said.

"All right," I said. "When we going to start?"

3

But he wasn't even listening. He laid there, hard and still as iron in the dark. "I got to go," he said. "I jest ain't going to put up with no folks treating the Unity States that way."

"Yes," I said. "Firewood or no firewood, I reckon we got to go."

This time he heard me. He laid still again, but it was a different kind of still.

"You?" he said. "To a war?"

"You'll whup the big uns and I'll whup the little uns," I said.

Then he told me I couldn't go. At first I thought he just never wanted me tagging after him, like he wouldn't leave me go with him when he went sparking them girls of Tull's. Then he told me the Army wouldn't leave me go because I was too little, and then I knowed he really meant it and that I couldn't go nohow noways. And somehow I hadn't believed until then that he was going himself, but now I knowed he was and that he wasn't going to leave me go with him a-tall.

"I'll chop the wood and tote the water for you-all then!" I said. "You got to have wood and water!"

Anyway, he was listening to me now. He wasn't like iron now.

He turned onto his side and put his hand on my chest because it was me that was laying straight and hard on my back now.

"No," he said. "You got to stay here and help pap."

"Help him what?" I said. "He ain't never caught up nohow. He can't get no further behind. He can sholy take care of this little shirttail of a farm while me and you are whupping them Japanese. I got to go too. If you got to go, then so have I."

"No," Pete said. "Hush now. Hush." And he meant it, and I knowed he did. Only I made sho from his own mouth. I quit.

"So I just can't go then," I said.

"No," Pete said. "You just can't go. You're too little, in the first place, and in the second place ——"

"All right," I said. "Then shut up and leave me go to sleep."

So he hushed then and laid back. And I laid there like I was already asleep, and pretty soon he was asleep and I knowed it was the wanting to go to the war that had worried him and kept him awake, and now that he had decided to go, he wasn't worried any more.

The next morning he told maw and pap. Maw was all right. She cried.

"No," she said, crying, "I don't want him to go. I would rather go myself in his place, if I could. I don't want to save the country. Them Japanese could take it and keep it, so long as they left me and my family and my children alone. But I remember my brother Marsh in that other war. He had to go to that one when he wasn't but nineteen, and our mother couldn't understand it then any more than I can now. But she told Marsh if he had to go, he had to go. And so, if Pete's got to go to this one, he's got to go to it. Jest don't ask me to understand why."

But pap was the one. He was the feller. "To the war?" he said. "Why, I just don't see a bit of use in that. You ain't old enough for the draft, and the country ain't being invaded. Our President in Washington, D.C., is watching the conditions and he will notify us. Besides, in that other war your ma just mentioned, I was drafted and sent clean to Texas and was held there nigh eight months until they finally quit fighting. It seems to me that that, along with your Uncle Marsh who received a actual wound on the battle-fields of France, is enough for me and mine to have to do to protect the country, at least in my lifetime. Besides, what'll I do for help on the farm with you gone? It seems to me I'll get mighty far behind."

"You been behind as long as I can re-member," Pete said. "Anyway, I'm going. I got to."

"Of course he's got to go," I said. "Them Japanese ——"

"You hush your mouth!" maw said, crying. "Nobody's talking to you! Go and get me a armful of wood! That's what you can do!"

So I got the wood. And all the next day, while me and Pete and pap was getting in as much wood as we could in that time because Pete said how pap's idea of plenty of wood was one more stick laying against the wall that maw ain't put on the fire yet, Maw was getting Pete ready to go. She washed and mended his clothes and cooked him a shoe box of vittles. And that night me and Pete laid in the bed and listened to her packing his grip and crying, until after a while Pete got up in his nightshirt and went back there, and I could hear them talking, until at last maw said, "You got to go, and so I want you to go. But I don't understand it, and I won't never, and so don't expect me to." And Pete come back and got into the bed again and laid again still and hard as iron on his back, and then he said, and he wasn't talking to me, he wasn't talking to nobody: "I got to go. I just got to."

"Sho you got to," I said. "Them Japanese ———" He turned over hard, he kind of surged over onto his side, looking at me in the dark.

"Anyway, you're all right," he said. "I expected to have more trouble with you than with all the rest of them put together."

"I reckon I can't help it neither," I said. "But maybe it will run a few years longer and I can get there. Maybe someday I will jest walk in on you."

"I hope not," Pete said. "Folks don't go to wars for fun. A man don't leave his maw crying just for fun."

"Then why are you going?" I said.

"I got to," he said. "I just got to. Now you go on to sleep. I got to ketch that early bus in the morning."

"All right," I said. "I hear tell Memphis is a big place. How will you find where the Army's at?"

"I'll ask somebody where to go to join it," Pete said. "Go on to sleep now."

"Is that what you'll ask for? Where to join the Army?" I said.

"Yes," Pete said. He turned onto his back again. "Shut up and go to sleep."

We went to sleep. The next morning we et breakfast by lamplight because the bus would pass at six o'clock. Maw wasn't crying now. She jest looked grim and busy, putting breakfast on the table while we et it. Then she finished packing Pete's grip, except he

never wanted to take no grip to the war, but maw said decent folks never went nowhere, not even to a war, without a change of clothes and something to tote them in. She put in the shoe box of fried chicken and biscuits and she put the Bible in, too, and then it was time to go. We didn't know until then that maw wasn't going to the bus. She jest brought Pete's cap and overcoat, and still she didn't cry no more, she jest stood with her hands on Pete's shoulders and she didn't move, but somehow, and just holding Pete's shoulders, she looked as hard and fierce as when Pete had turned toward me in the bed last night and tole me that anyway I was all right.

"They could take the country and keep the country, so long as they never bothered me and mine," she said. Then she said, "Don't never forget who you are. You ain't rich and the rest of the world outside of Frenchman's Bend never heard of you. But your blood is good as any blood anywhere, and don't you never forget it."

Then she kissed him, and then we was out of the house, with pap toting Pete's grip whether Pete wanted him to or not. There wasn't no dawn even yet, not even after we had stood on the highway by the mailbox, a while. Then we seen the lights of the bus coming and I was watching the bus until it come up and Pete flagged it, and then, sho enough, there was daylight—it had started while I wasn't watching. And now me and Pete expected pap to say something else foolish, like he done before, about how Uncle Marsh getting wounded in France and that trip to Texas pap taken in 1918 ought to be enough to save the Unity States in 1942, but he never. He done all right too. He jest said, "Good-by, son. Always remember what your ma told you and write her whenever you find the time." Then he shaken Pete's hand, and Pete looked at me a minute and put his hand on my head and rubbed my head durn nigh hard enough to wring my neck off and jumped into the bus, and the feller wound the door shut and the bus begun to hum; then it was moving, humming and grinding and whining louder and louder; it was going fast, with two little red lights behind it that never seemed to get no littler, but jest seemed to be running together until pretty soon they would touch and jest be one light. But they never did, and then the bus was gone, and even like it was, I could have pretty nigh busted out crying, nigh to nine years old and all.

Me and pap went back to the house. All that day we worked at the wood tree, and so I never had no good chance until about middle of the afternoon. Then I taken my slingshot and I would have liked to took all my bird eggs, too, because Pete had give me his collection and he help me with mine, and he would like to git the box out and look at them as good as I would, even if he was nigh twenty years old. But the box was too big to tote a long ways and have to worry with, so I just taken the shikepoke egg, because it was the best un, and wropped it up good into a matchbox and hid it and the slingshot under the corner of the barn. Then we et supper and went to bed, and I thought then how if I would 'a' had to stayed in that room and that bed like that even for one more night, I jest couldn't 'a' stood it. Then I could hear pap snoring, but I never heard no sound from maw, whether she was asleep or not, and I don't reckon she was. So I taken my shoes and drapped them out the window, and then I clumb out like I used to watch Pete do when he was still jest seventeen and pap held that he was too young yet to be tomcatting around at night, and wouldn't leave him out, and I put on my shoes and went to the barn and got the slingshot and the shikepoke egg and went to the highway.

It wasn't cold, it was jest durn confounded dark, and that highway stretched on in front of me like, without nobody using it, it had stretched out half again as fer just like a man does when he lays down, so that for a time it looked like full sun was going to ketch me before I had finished them twenty-two miles to Jefferson. But it didn't. Daybreak was jest starting when I walked up the hill into town. I could smell breakfast cooking in the cabins and I wished I had thought to brought me a cold biscuit, but that was too late now. And Pete had told me Memphis was a piece beyond Jefferson, but I never knowed it was no eighty miles. So I stood there on that empty square, with daylight coming and coming and the street lights still burning and that Law looking down at me, and me still eighty miles from Memphis, and it had took me all night to walk jest twenty-two miles, and so, by the time I got to Memphis at that rate, Pete would 'a' done already started for Pearl Harbor.

"Where do you come from?" the Law said.

And I told him again. "I got to get to Memphis. My brother's there."

"You mean you ain't got any folks around here?" the Law said. "Nobody but that brother? What are you doing way off down here and your brother in Memphis?"

And I told him again, "I got to get to Memphis. I ain't got no time to waste talking about it and I ain't got time to walk it. I got to git there today."

"Come on here," the Law said.

We went down another street. And there was the bus, jest like when Pete got into it yestiddy morning, except there wasn't no lights on it now and it was empty. There was a regular bus dee-po like a railroad dee-po, with a ticket counter and a feller behind it, and the Law said, "Set down over there," and I set down on the bench, and the Law said, "I want to use your telephone," and he talked in the telephone a minute and put it down and said to the feller behind the ticket counter, "Keep your eye on him. I'll be back as soon as Mrs. Habersham can arrange to get herself up and dressed." He went out. I got up and went to the ticket counter.

"I want to go to Memphis," I said.

"You bet," the feller said. "You set down on the bench now. Mr. Foote will be back in a minute."

"I don't know no Mr. Foote," I said. "I want to ride that bus to Memphis."

"You got some money?" he said. "It'll cost you seventy-two cents."

I taken out the matchbox and unwropped the shikepoke egg. "I'll swap you this for a ticket to Memphis," I said.

"What's that?" he said.

"It's a shikepoke egg," I said. "You never seen one before. It's worth a dollar. I'll take seventy-two cents fer it."

"No," he said, "the fellers that own that bus insist on a cash basis. If I started swapping tickets for bird eggs and livestock and such, they would fire me. You go and set down on the bench now, like Mr. Foote ———"

I started for the door, but he caught me, he put one hand on the ticket counter and jumped over it and caught up with me and reached his hand out to ketch my shirt. I whupped out my pocketknife and snapped it open.

"You put a hand on me and I'll cut it off," I said.

I tried to dodge him and run at the door, but he could move quicker than any grown man I ever see, quick as Pete almost. He cut me off and stood with his back against the door and one foot raised a little, and there wasn't no other way to get out. "Get back on that bench and stay there," he said.

And there wasn't no other way out. And he stood there with his back against the door. So I went back to the bench. And then it seemed like to me that dee-po was full of folks. There was that Law again, and there was two ladies in fur coats and their faces already painted. But they still looked like they had got up in a hurry and they still never liked it, a old one and a young one, looking down at me.

"He hasn't got a overcoat!" the old one said. "How in the world did he ever get down here by himself?"

"I ask you," the Law said. "I couldn't get nothing out of him except his brother is in Memphis and he wants to get back up there."

"That's right," I said. "I got to git to Memphis today."

"Of course you must," the old one said. "Are you sure you can find your brother when you get to Memphis?"

"I reckon I can," I said. "I ain't got but one and I have knowed him all my life. I reckon I will know him again when I see him."

The old one looked at me. "Somehow he doesn't look like he lives in Memphis," she said.

"He probably don't," the Law said. "You can't tell though. He might live anywhere, overhalls or not. This day and time they get scattered overnight from he—— hope to breakfast; boys and girls, too, almost before they can walk good. He might have been in Missouri or Texas either yestiddy, for all we know. But he don't seem to have any doubt his brother is in Memphis. All I know to do is send him up there and leave him look."

"Yes," the old one said.

The young one set down on the bench by me and opened a hand satchel and taken out a artermatic writing pen and some papers.

"Now, honey," the old one said, "we're going to see that you find your brother, but we must have a case history for our files first. We want to know your name and your brother's name and where you were born and when your parents died."

"I don't need no case history neither," I said. "All I want is to get to Memphis. I got to get there today."

"You see?" the Law said. He said it almost like he enjoyed it. "That's what I told you."

"You're lucky, at that, Mrs. Habersham," the bus feller said. "I don't think he's got a gun on him, but he can open that knife da—— I mean, fast enough to suit any man."

But the old one just stood there looking at me.

"Well," she said. "Well. I really don't know what to do."

"I do," the bus feller said. "I'm going to give him a ticket out of my own pocket, as a measure of protecting the company against riot and bloodshed. And when Mr. Foote tells the city board about it, it will be a civic matter and they will not only reimburse me, they will give me a medal too. Hey, Mr. Foote?"

But never nobody paid him no mind. The old one still stood looking down at me. She said "Well," again. Then she taken a dollar from her purse and give it to the bus feller. "I suppose he will travel on a child's ticket, won't he?"

"Wellum," the bus feller said, "I just don't

know what the regulations would be. Likely I will be fired for not crating him and marking the crate Poison. But I'll risk it."

Then they were gone. Then the Law come back with a sandwich and give it to me.

"You're sure you can find that brother?" he said.

"I ain't yet convinced why not," I said. "If I don't see Pete first, he'll see me. He knows me too."

Then the Law went out for good, too, and I et the sandwich. Then more folks come in and bought tickets, and then the bus feller said it was time to go, and I got into the bus just like Pete done, and we was gone.

I seen all the towns. I seen all of them. When the bus got to going good, I found out I was jest about wore out for sleep. But there was too much I hadn't never saw before. We run out of Jefferson and run past fields and woods, then we would run into another town and out of that un and past fields and woods again, and then into another town with stores and gins and water tanks, and we run along by the railroad for a spell and I seen the signal arm move, and then I seen the train and then some more towns, and I was jest about plumb wore out for sleep, but I couldn't resk it. Then Memphis begun. It seemed like, to me, it went on for miles. We would pass a patch of stores and I would think that was sholy it and the bus would even stop. But it wouldn't be Memphis yet and we would go on again past water tanks and smokestacks on top of the mills, and if they was gins and sawmills, I never knowed there was that many and I never seen any that big, and where they got enough cotton and logs to run um I don't know.

Then I seen Memphis. I knowed I was right this time. It was standing up into the air. It looked like about a dozen whole towns bigger than Jefferson was set up on one edge in a field, standing up into the air higher than ara hill in all Yoknapatawpha County. Then we was in it, with the bus stopping ever' few feet, it seemed like to me, and cars rushing past on both sides of it and the street crowded with folks from ever'- where in town that day, until I didn't see how

there could 'a' been nobody left in Mis'sippi a-tall to even sell me a bus ticket, let alone write out no case histories. Then the bus stopped. It was another bus dee-po, a heap bigger than the one in Jefferson. And I said, "All right. Where do folks join the Army?"

"What?" the bus feller said.

And I said it again, "Where do folks join the Army?"

"Oh," he said. Then he told me how to get there. I was afraid at first I wouldn't ketch on how to do in a town big as Memphis. But I caught on all right. I never had to ask but twice more. Then I was there, and I was durn glad to git out of all them rushing cars and shoving folks and all that racket fer a spell, and I thought, It won't be long now, and I thought how if there was any kind of a crowd there that had done already joined the Army, too, Pete would likely see me before I seen him. And so I walked into the room. And Pete wasn't there.

He wasn't even there. There was a soldier with a big arrerhead on his sleeve, writing, and two fellers standing in front of him, and there was some more folks there, I reckon. It seems to me I remember some more folks there.

I went to the table where the soldier was writing, and I said, "Where's Pete?" and he looked up and I said, "My brother. Pete Grier. Where is he?"

"What?" the soldier said. "Who?"

And I told him again. "He joined the Army yestiddy. He's going to Pearl Harbor. So am I. I want to ketch him. Where you all got him?" Now they were all looking at me, but I never paid them no mind. "Come on," I said. "Where is he?"

The soldier had quit writing. He had both hands spraddled out on the table. "Oh," he said. "You're going, too, hah?"

"Yes," I said. "They got to have wood and water. I can chop it and tote it. Come on. Where's Pete?"

The soldier stood up. "Who let you in here?" he said. "Go on. Beat it."

"Durn that," I said. "You tell me where Pete ———"

I be dog if he couldn't move faster than

the bus feller even. He never come over the table, he come around it, he was on me almost before I knowed it, so that I jest had time to jump back and whup out my pocket-knife and snap it open and hit one lick, and he hollered and jumped back and grabbed one hand with the other and stood there cussing and hollering.

One of the other fellers grabbed me from behind, and I hit at him with the knife, but I couldn't reach him.

Then both of the fellers had me from behind, and then another soldier come out of a door at the back. He had on a belt with a britching strop over one shoulder.

"What the hell is this?" he said.

"That little son cut me with a knife!" the first soldier hollered. When he said that I tried to git at him again, but both them fellers was holding me, two against one, and the soldier with the backing strop said, "Here, here. Put your knife up, feller. None of us are armed. A man don't knife-fight folks that are barehanded." I could begin to hear him then. He sounded jest like Pete talked to me. "Let him go," he said. They let me go. "Now what's all the trouble about?" And I told him. "I see," he said. "And you come up to see if he was all right before he left."

"No," I said. "I came to ——"

But he had already turned to where the first soldier was wropping a handkerchief around his hand.

"Have you got him?" he said. The first soldier went back to the table and looked at some papers.

"Here he is," he said. "He enlisted yestiddy. He's in a detachment leaving this morning for Little Rock." He had a watch stropped on his arm. He looked at it. "The train leaves in about fifty minutes. If I know country boys, they're probably all down there at the station right now."

"Get him up here," the one with the backing strop said. "Phone the station. Tell the porter to get him a cab. And you come with me," he said.

It was another office behind that un, with jest a table and some chairs. We sat there while the soldier smoked, and it wasn't long;

I knowed Pete's feet soon as I heard them. Then the first soldier opened the door and Pete come in. He never had no soldier clothes on. He looked jest like he did when he got on the bus yestiddy morning, except it seemed to me like it was at least a week, so much had happened, and I had done had to do so much traveling. He come in and there he was, looking at me like he hadn't never left home, except that here we was in Memphis, on the way to Pearl Harbor.

"What in durnation are you doing here?" he said.

And I told him, "You got to have wood and water to cook with. I can chop it and tote it for you-all."

"No," Pete said. "You're going back home."

"No, Pete," I said. "I got to go too. I got to. It hurts my heart, Pete."

"No," Pete said. He looked at the soldier. "I jest don't know what could have happened to him, lootenant," he said. "He never drawed a knife on anybody before in his life." He looked at me. "What did you do it for?"

"I don't know," I said. "I jest had to. I jest had to git here. I jest had to find you."

"Well, don't you never do it again, you hear?" Pete said. "You put that knife in your pocket and you keep it there. If I ever again hear of you drawing it on anybody, I'm coming back from wherever I am at and whup the fire out of you. You hear me?"

"I would pure cut a throat if it would bring you back to stay," I said. "Pete," I said. "Pete."

"No," Pete said. Now his voice wasn't hard and quick no more, it was almost quiet, and I knowed now I wouldn't never change him. "You must go home. You must look after maw, and I am depending on you to look after my ten acres. I want you to go back home. Today. Do you hear?"

"I hear," I said.

"Can he get back home by himself?" the soldier said.

"He come up here by himself," Pete said.

"I can get back, I reckon," I said. "I don't live in but one place. I don't reckon it's moved."

Pete taken a dollar out of his pocket and give it to me. "That'll buy your bus ticket right to our mailbox," he said. "I want you to mind the lootenant. He'll send you to the bus. And you go back home and you take care of maw and look after my ten acres and keep that durn knife in your pocket. You hear me?"

"Yes, Pete," I said.

"All right," Pete said. "Now I got to go." He put his hand on my head again. But this time he never wrung my neck. He just laid his hand on my head a minute. And then I be dog if he didn't lean down and kiss me, and I heard his feet and then the door, and I never looked up and that was all, me setting there, rubbing the place where Pete kissed me and the soldier throwed back in his chair, looking out the window and coughing. He reached into his pocket and handed something to me without looking around. It was a piece of chewing gum.

"Much obliged," I said. "Well, I reckon I might as well start back. I got a right fer piece to go."

"Wait," the soldier said. Then he telephoned again and I said again I better start back, and he said again, "Wait. Remember what Pete told you."

So we waited, and then another lady come in, old, too, in a fur coat, too, but she smelled all right, she never had no artermatic writing pen nor no case history neither. She come in and the soldier got up, and she looked around quick until she saw me, and come and put her hand on my shoulder light and quick and easy as maw herself might 'a' done it.

"Come on," she said. "Let's go home to dinner."

"Nome," I said. "I got to ketch the bus to Jefferson."

"I know. There's plenty of time. We'll go home and eat dinner first."

She had a car. And now we was right down in the middle of all them other cars. We was almost under the busses, and all them crowds of people on the street close enough to where I could have talked to them if I had knowed who they was. After a while she stopped the car. "Here we are," she said, and I looked at it, and if all that was her house, she sho had a big family. But all of it wasn't. We crossed a hall with trees growing in it and went into a

little room without nothing in it but a nigger dressed up in a uniform a heap shinier than them soldiers had, and the nigger shut the door, and then I hollered, "Look out!" and grabbed, but it was all right; that whole little room jest went right on up and stopped and the door opened and we was in another hall, and the lady unlocked a door and we went in, and there was another soldier, a old feller, with a britching strop, too, and a silver-colored bird on each shoulder.

"Here we are," the lady said. "This is Colonel McKellogg. Now, what would you like for dinner?"

"I reckon I'll jest have some ham and eggs and coffee," I said.

She had done started to pick up the telephone. She stopped. "Coffee?" she said. "When did you start drinking coffee?"

"I don't know," I said. "I reckon it was before I could remember."

"You're about eight, aren't you?" she said.

"Nome," I said. "I'm eight and ten months. Going on eleven months."

She telephoned then. Then we set there and I told them how Pete had jest left that morning for Pearl Harbor and I had aimed to go with him, but I would have to go back home to take care of maw and look after Pete's ten acres, and she said how they had a little boy about my size, too, in a school in the East. Then a nigger, another one, in a short kind of shirttail coat, rolled a kind of wheelbarrer in. It had my ham and eggs and a glass of milk and a piece of pie, too, and I thought I was hungry. But when I taken the first bite I found out I couldn't swallow it, and I got up quick.

"I got to go," I said.

"Wait," she said.

"I got to go," I said.

"Just a minute," she said. "I've already telephoned for the car. It won't be but a minute now. Can't you drink the milk even? Or maybe some of your coffee?"

"Nome," I said. "I ain't hungry. I'll eat when I git home." Then the telephone rung. She never even answered it.

"There," she said. "There's the car." And we went back down in that 'ere little moving room with the dressed-up nigger. This time it was a big car with a soldier driving it. I got into the front with him. She give the soldier a dollar. "He might get hungry," she said. "Try to find a decent place for him."

"O.K., Mrs. McKellogg," the soldier said.

Then we was gone again. And now I could see Memphis good, bright in the sunshine, while we was swinging around it. And first thing I knowed, we was back on the same highway the bus run on this morning—the patches of stores and them big gins and saw-mills, and Memphis running on for miles, it seemed like to me, before it begun to give out. Then we was running again between the fields and woods, running fast now, and except for that soldier, it was like I hadn't never been to Memphis a-tall. We was going fast now. At this rate, before I knowed it we would be home again, and I thought about me riding up to Frenchman's Bend in this big car with a soldier running it, and all of a sudden I begun to cry. I never knowed I was fixing to, and I couldn't stop it. I set there by that soldier, crying. We was going fast.

Discussion: public and private fact; the subjective world; why authors sometimes write about trouble; functions of humor

Though "Two Soldiers" must be classified as good fiction, it is easy to read, as much other good fiction is. Quality does not necessarily mean difficulty.

World War II and the attack on Pearl Harbor were facts—large, disagreeable, public facts. All sorts of people could take all sorts of attitudes toward Pearl Harbor, and did. Some saw a chance to make money or be promoted, some a problem of getting into the right branch of the service, some a chance of adventure, some a problem of living or dying. These human reactions were as "real" as the fact of war itself. In "Two Soldiers" Faulkner represents still another reaction. To understand what fiction does, we need to realize that an author deals with both public, objective fact and with inner, subjective fact—and that the second is as real a force in life as the first. It is the force which leads to decisions and sets directions. It is the part of our human nature which sets a *value* on things and people and events, with consequent results in action.

The two brothers in Faulkner's story are not confused, or cynical, or self-seeking, or doubtful about personal values. They are not ashamed of affection, or afraid of the big world, or afraid of being laughed at. They know nothing about cities, or colleges, or the Reserve Officers' Training Corps. Faulkner presents them with respect and affection. They can be unhappy or have misfortune (in the sequel to this story, the older brother is killed); but they are whole, sound, secure in their values.

Readers have remarked that "Two Soldiers" is a strangely "comforting" story, in spite of the fact that it deals with human trouble. The reason is easy to see, and the "comfort" does not lie in the humor of the story. The two brothers are images of human soundness. They represent a kind of balance and surety which every living person would like to possess, which war and misfortune cannot destroy. This story is a clear example of why good authors will often write about trouble, for trouble can reveal human quality. The "comfort" or "consolation" which some readers receive from such an account of human quality is different from the fake reassurance about life which the usual "happy ending" of the commercial story provides. The problem here is real. There is no false "solution."

The humor in "Two Soldiers" is enjoyable itself, and it relieves the more serious emotion from time to time, allowing the author to build the emotion still higher. This is a classic function of humor. If you will notice the points at which humor occurs, in relation to the serious emotional climaxes, you will begin to appreciate the skill, the art, with which the story is written. There are three or four kinds or causes of humor in "Two Soldiers." We leave discovery of these to the reader, with the assurance that the story is worth rereading for that purpose. Since humor, like other effects, depends on the reader as well as on the story, it is profitable to ask whether this story would seem humorous to two *real* persons like the two brothers, and to think over the meaning of the answer. Something about the nature of humor will be discovered.

> *Problem:* Do the rereading and analysis described in the preceding paragraph. A good story will not be ruined by rereading or by a reasonable amount of analysis. The reader's skill in noticing various qualities will increase in the only way such skill *can* increase.
>
> *Problem:* "Two Soldiers" contains relatively little "action" in the first part. "Action" picks up when the younger brother leaves home. Is the first part necessary, then? If it were omitted or reduced, what difference would such a change make? To answer this question it is necessary to ask what is achieved in the first part of the story and to ask whether this is necessary for effects achieved later.
>
> *Question:* Can you find in this story an example of (a) humor arising from situation alone, (b) humor arising from character?

Some Problems of Reading

A second example of fiction is the story "A Sick Call," by Morley Callaghan. It is in some ways more difficult to read than "Two Soldiers," but it has never, to our knowledge, left a reader indifferent. One difficulty of reading lies in the fact that the story touches emotional allegiances among readers.

A SICK CALL

Morley Callaghan
(1903–   )

I

Sometimes Father Macdowell mumbled out loud and took a deep wheezy breath as he walked up and down the room and read his office. He was a huge old priest, white-headed except for a shiny baby-pink bald spot on the top of his head, and he was a bit deaf in one ear. His florid face had many fine red interlacing vein lines. For hours he had been hearing confessions and he was tired, for he always had to hear more confessions than any other priest at the cathedral; young girls who were in trouble, and wild but at times repentant young men, always wanted to tell their confessions to Father Macdowell, because nothing seemed to shock or excite him, or make him really angry, and he was even tender with those who thought they were most guilty.

While he was mumbling and reading and trying to keep his glasses on his nose, the house girl knocked on the door and said, "There's a young lady here to see you, Father. I think it's about a sick call."

"Did she ask for me especially?" he said in a deep but slightly cracked voice.

"Indeed she did, Father. She wanted Father Macdowell and nobody else."

So he went out to the waiting room, where a girl about thirty years of age, with fine brown eyes, fine cheek bones, and rather square shoulders, was sitting daubing her eyes with a handkerchief. She was wearing a dark coat with a gray wolf collar. "Good evening, Father," she said. "My sister is sick. I wanted you to come and see her. We think she's dying."

"Be easy, child; what's the matter with her? Speak louder. I can hardly hear you."

"My sister's had pneumonia. The doctor's coming back to see her in an hour. I wanted you to anoint her, Father."

"I see, I see. But she's not lost yet. I'll not give her extreme unction now. That may not be necessary. I'll go with you and hear her confession."

"Father, I ought to let you know, maybe. Her husband won't want to let you see her. He's not a Catholic, and my sister hasn't been to church in a long time."

"Oh, don't mind that. He'll let me see her," Father Macdowell said, and he left the room to put on his hat and coat.

2

When he returned, the girl explained that her name was Jane Stanhope, and her sister lived only a few blocks away. "We'll walk and you tell me about your sister," he said. He put his black hat square on the top of his head, and pieces of white hair stuck out awkwardly at the sides. They went to the avenue together.

The night was mild and clear. Miss Stanhope began to walk slowly, because Father Macdowell's rolling gait didn't get him along the street very quickly. He walked as if his feet hurt him, though he wore a pair of large, soft, specially constructed shapeless shoes. "Now, my child, you go ahead and tell me about your sister," he said, breathing with difficulty, yet giving the impression that nothing could have happened to the sister which would make him feel indignant.

There wasn't much to say, Miss Stanhope replied. Her sister had married John Williams two years ago, and he was a good, hardworking fellow, only he was very bigoted and hated all church people. "My family wouldn't have anything to do with Elsa after she married him, though I kept going to see her," she said. She was talking in a loud voice to Father Macdowell so he could hear her.

"Is she happy with her husband?"

"She's been very happy, Father. I must say that."

"Where is he now?"

"He was sitting beside her bed. I ran out because I thought he was going to cry. He said if I brought a priest near the place he'd break the priest's head."

"My goodness. Never mind, though. Does your sister want to see me?"

"She asked me to go and get a priest, but she doesn't want John to know she did it."

3

Turning into a side street, they stopped at the first apartment house, and the old priest followed Miss Stanhope up the stairs. His breath came with great difficulty. "Oh dear, I'm not getting any younger, not one day younger. It's a caution how a man's legs go back on him," he said. As Miss Stanhope rapped on the door, she looked pleadingly at the old priest, trying to ask him not to be offended at anything that might happen, but he was smiling and looking huge in the narrow hallway. He wiped his head with his handkerchief.

The door was opened by a young man in a white shirt with no collar, with a head of thick black wavy hair. At first he looked dazed, then his eyes got bright with excitement when he saw the priest, as though he were glad to see someone he could destroy with pent-up energy. "What do you mean, Jane?" he said. "I told you not to bring a priest around here. My wife doesn't want to see a priest."

"What's that you're saying, young man?"

"No one wants you here."

"Speak up. Don't be afraid. I'm a bit hard of hearing." Father Macdowell smiled rosily. John Williams was confused by the unexpected deafness in the priest, but he stood there, blocking the door with sullen resolution as if waiting for the priest to try to launch a curse at him.

"Speak to him, Father," Miss Stanhope said,

but the priest didn't seem to hear her; he was still smiling as he pushed past the young man, saying, "I'll go in and sit down, if you don't mind, son. I'm here on God's errand, but I don't mind saying I'm all out of breath from climbing those stairs."

John was dreadfully uneasy to see he had been brushed aside, and he followed the priest into the apartment and said loudly, "I don't want you here."

Father Macdowell said, "Eh, eh?" Then he smiled sadly. "Don't be angry with me, son," he said. "I'm too old to try and be fierce and threatening." Looking around, he said, "Where's your wife?" and he started to walk along the hall, looking for the bedroom.

John followed him and took hold of his arm. "There's no sense in your wasting your time talking to my wife, do you hear?" he said angrily.

Miss Stanhope called out suddenly, "Don't be rude, John."

"It's he that's being rude. You mind your business," John said.

"For the love of God let me sit down a moment with her, anyway. I'm tired," the priest said.

"What do you want to say to her? Say it to me, why don't you?"

4

Then they both heard someone moan softly in the adjoining room, as if the sick woman had heard them. Father Macdowell, forgetting that the young man had hold of his arm, said, "I'll go in and see her for a moment, if you don't mind," and he began to open the door.

"You're not going to be alone with her, that's all," John said, following him into the bedroom.

Lying on the bed was a white-faced, fair girl, whose skin was so delicate that her cheek bones stood out sharply. She was feverish, but her eyes rolled toward the door, and she watched them coming in. Father Macdowell took off his coat, and as he mumbled to himself he looked around the room at the mauve-silk bed light and the light wallpaper with the tiny birds in flight. It looked like a little

girl's room. "Good evening, Father," Mrs. Williams whispered. She looked scared. She didn't glance at her husband. The notion of dying had made her afraid. She loved her husband and wanted to die loving him, but she was afraid, and she looked up at the priest.

"You're going to get well, child," Father Macdowell said, smiling and patting her hand gently.

John, who was standing stiffly by the door, suddenly moved around the big priest, and he bent down over the bed and took his wife's hand and began to caress her forehead.

"Now if you don't mind, my son, I'll hear your wife's confession," the priest said.

"No, you won't," John said abruptly. "Her people didn't want her, and they left us together, and they're not going to separate us now. She's satisfied with me." He kept looking down at her face as if he could not bear to turn away.

Father Macdowell nodded his head up and down and sighed. "Poor boy," he said. "God bless you." Then he looked at Mrs. Williams, who had closed her eyes, and he saw a faint tear on her cheek. "Be sensible, my boy," he said. "You'll have to let me hear your wife's confession. Leave us alone awhile."

"I'm going to stay right here," John said, and he sat down on the end of the bed. He was working himself up and staring savagely at the priest. All of a sudden he noticed the tears on his wife's cheeks, and he muttered as though bewildered, "What's the matter, Elsa? What's the matter, darling? Are we bothering you? Just open your eyes and we'll go out of the room and leave you alone till the doctor comes." Then he turned and said to the priest, "I'm not going to leave you here with her, can't you see that? Why don't you go?"

"I could revile you, my son. I could threaten you; but I ask you, for the peace of your wife's soul, leave us alone." Father Macdowell spoke with patient tenderness. He looked very big and solid and immovable as he stood by the bed. "I liked your face as soon as I saw you," he said to John. "You're a good fellow."

John still held his wife's wrist, but he rubbed one hand through his thick hair and said angrily, "You don't get the point, sir. My wife and I were always left alone, and we merely want to be left alone now. Nothing is going to separate us. She's been content with me. I'm sorry, sir; you'll have to speak to her with me here, or you'll have to go."

"No, you'll have to go for a while," the priest said patiently.

5

Then Mrs. Williams moved her head on the pillow and said jerkily, "Pray for me, Father."

So the old priest knelt down by the bed, and with a sweet unruffled expression on his florid face he began to pray. At times his breath came with a whistling noise as though a rumbling were inside him, and at other times he sighed and was full of sorrow. He was praying that young Mrs. Williams might get better, and while he prayed he knew that her husband was more afraid of losing her to the Church than losing her to death.

All the time Father Macdowell was on his knees, with his heavy prayer book in his two hands, John kept staring at him. John couldn't understand the old priest's patience and tolerance. He wanted to quarrel with him, but he kept on watching the light from overhead shining on the one baby-pink bald spot on the smooth white head, and at last he burst out, "You don't understand, sir! We've been very happy together. Neither you nor her people came near her when she was in good health, so why should you bother her now? I don't want anything to separate us now; neither does she. She came with me. You see you'd be separating us, don't you?" He was trying to talk like a reasonable man who had no prejudices.

Father Macdowell got up clumsily. His knees hurt him, for the floor was hard. He said to Mrs. Williams in quite a loud voice, "Did you really intend to give up everything for this young fellow?" and he bent down close to her so he could hear.

"Yes, Father," she whispered.

"In Heaven's name, child, you couldn't have known what you were doing."

"We loved each other, Father. We've been very happy."

"All right. Supposing you were. What now? What about all eternity, child?"

"Oh, Father, I'm very sick and I'm afraid." She looked up to try to show him how scared she was, and how much she wanted him to give her peace.

He sighed and seemed distressed, and at last he said to John, "Were you married in the church?"

"No, we weren't. Look here, we're talking pretty loud and it upsets her."

"Ah, it's a crime that I'm hard of hearing, I know. Never mind, I'll go." Picking up his coat, he put it over his arm; then he sighed as if he were very tired, and he said, "I wonder if you'd just fetch me a glass of water. I'd thank you for it."

John hesitated, glancing at the tired old priest, who looked so pink and white and almost cherubic in his utter lack of guile.

"What's the matter?" Father Macdowell said.

John was ashamed of himself for appearing so sullen, so he said hastily, "Nothing's the matter. Just a moment. I won't be a moment." He hurried out of the room.

6

The old priest looked down at the floor and shook his head; and then, sighing and feeling uneasy, he bent over Mrs. Williams, with his good ear down to her, and he said, "I'll just ask you a few questions in a hurry, my child. You answer them quickly and I'll give you absolution." He made the sign of the cross over her and asked if she repented for having strayed from the Church, and if she had often been angry, and whether she had always been faithful, and if she had ever lied or stolen—all so casually and quickly as if it hadn't occurred to him that such a young woman could have serious sins. In the same breath he muttered, "Say a good act of contrition to yourself and that will be all, my dear." He had hardly taken a minute.

When John returned to the room with the

glass of water in his hand, he saw the old priest making the sign of the cross. Father Macdowell went on praying without even looking up at John. When he had finished, he turned and said, "Oh, there you are. Thanks for the water. I needed it. Well, my boy, I'm sorry if I worried you."

John hardly said anything. He looked at his wife, who had closed her eyes, and he sat down on the end of the bed. He was too disappointed to speak.

Father Macdowell, who was expecting trouble said, "Don't be harsh, lad."

"I'm not harsh," he said mildly, looking up at the priest. "But you weren't quite fair. And it's as though she turned away from me at the last moment. I didn't think she needed you."

"God bless you, bless the both of you. She'll get better," Father Macdowell said. But he felt ill at ease as he put on his coat, and he couldn't look directly at John.

7

Going along the hall, he spoke to Miss Stanhope, who wanted to apologize for her brother-in-law's attitude. "I'm sorry if it was unpleasant for you, Father," she said.

"It wasn't unpleasant," he said. "I was glad to meet John. He's a fine fellow. It's a great pity he isn't a Catholic. I don't know as I played fair with him."

As he went down the stairs, puffing and sighing, he pondered the question of whether he had played fair with the young man. But by the time he reached the street he was rejoicing amiably to think he had so successfully ministered to one who had strayed from the faith and had called out to him at the last moment. Walking along with the rolling motion as if his feet hurt him, he muttered, "Of course they were happy as they were . . . in a worldly way. I wonder if I did come between them?"

He shuffled along, feeling very tired, but he couldn't help thinking, "What beauty there was to his staunch love for her!" Then he added quickly, "But it was just a pagan beauty, of course."

As he began to wonder about the nature of this beauty, for some reason he felt inexpressibly sad.

Discussion 1 : finding the center of emphasis in a story; immediate and delayed reactions; types of "wrong" readings

On one campus, written comments on "A Sick Call" were made by more than three hundred college students, both men and women, immediately after the reading. These first quick responses were obviously influenced by beliefs about religion. Some Protestants, and a few readers who described themselves as skeptics, resented Father Macdowell and said that he was "dishonest" or "hypocritical." One self-styled agnostic said, "It is a pity that unhappiness has to be caused by mere matters of belief." Other readers, both Protestant and Catholic, said that Father Macdowell was doing his duty as he saw it, and that the young husband would "get over" his disappointment.

The remarks quoted above show what *can* happen first when people read fiction which touches emotion or belief. These first quick responses, which may be called Phase No. 1 in the reading of some stories, may or may not be appropriate to the total content of a story or to the author's apparent intentions, just as first impressions of real people or problems may be accurate or inaccurate. One of the convenient things about reading is the fact that we can respond freely and then think it over. All-out reactions to people and problems in real life can cause trouble, and they are sometimes hard to modify because of pride. Reading is safer, yet it provides the material for reflection, for seeing what is marginal and what is central in a human problem or human character.

Phase No. 2 in skilled reading may therefore include reflection, which often involves

rereading. A good way to begin this process of reflection is to ask what the author emphasizes, what seem to be his attitudes toward the fictional persons and situations he presents
as "real." Or we can ask the same question in another way: What does the author do with
each of the story elements—action (including conflict and plot), characters, setting,
words? It is apparent immediately that action and character will provide the main clues
in "A Sick Call," since little depends on setting or environment in this story and since
the "wording" reveals the author's attitudes only slightly.

Why should we indulge in deliberate reflection about a piece of reading? Simply because
meanings will be missed if we don't. Why do we ever reflect about anything, rethink
anything? We do so to improve our grasp of ideas or problems, to refine our powers of
observation and judgment. Therefore, some reflection about this story is in order.

First of all, the author gives most of his attention to Father Macdowell. The very title
of the story names a duty of clergymen: to make emergency calls on the dangerously ill.
The story begins with Father Macdowell and ends with him. At the beginning, in addition
to details of a favorable kind, there is emphasis on Father Macdowell's reputation for
tolerance. At the end, he admits a doubt about his own action: "I don't know as I played
fair with him." This is favorable characterization again: we find it more attractive in a
person to admit a doubt or a fault than to brazen it out or conceal it. At the end, Father
Macdowell recognizes the young man's integrity and love and indulges in a piece of self-
reassurance that doesn't work very well: "But it was just a pagan beauty, of course. . . .
As he thought of the nature of this beauty, he was for some reason inexpressibly sad."

So we have part of the answer to the question "What is emphasized?" It is Father
Macdowell's story. Since he cannot be characterized in a vacuum, his character appears
in action as he deals with a real and important problem. John's attitude is a reality, a
determined policy arising from a time when the young couple were all-sufficient for each
other. The characterization of John is thus a means to an end. The end is (1) clear characterization of Father Macdowell, and (2) a quick but not superficial view of the ethical
problem created by John's attitude and action.

As to the author's attitude, it is easy to recognize that this is not the kind of story in
which the author takes sides, in the sense of approving one character to the limit and
disapproving another. He presents Father Macdowell as sincere in his vocation, to the
point of using an undeniable trick as a means to an end. (Who would respect a clergyman
who would fail to help the sick and thus abandon a duty at a moment's notice?) The
author further portrays Father Macdowell as honest with himself—up to that familiar
human point at which most people will resist anything that seems to challenge a belief
or a way of life. At this point Father Macdowell experiences a sadness he doesn't wholly
understand. He has glimpsed, in John and the marriage, an apparently true value, the
"nature" of which saddens him. This value seems to be independent of religion and apparently is not caused by religion. No wonder he feels sad, without quite understanding
the reason. Like many another human being, he wants to believe that his action is "right."
Thus the author respects Father Macdowell but nevertheless shows him as vulnerable,
human.

The young man is presented with equal respect. Much of this favorable characterization
is achieved through the mind of the priest. The suggestion is made, however, that John's

admirable desire to be everything to his wife carries with it a preoccupation with self, an unwillingness to believe that his wife can possibly need anything he cannot offer. The wife's need to see a priest—whether John thinks it sensible or not—is presented as a reality which John is about to ignore. John and Father Macdowell are thus more alike than may at first appear. Each has a direction in life. Each is capable of over-riding other values or principles as he persists in the direction chosen—Father Macdowell consciously, John unknowingly. Each will work hard to believe what he wants to believe. Each is capable of an impressive amount of honesty when the facts *have* to be faced.

So the author presents both characters with respect. The moment we realize this fact, we see that it is a means to still another end: the author is dramatizing a truth of human experience—that all-out devotion to a cause or a settled objective may finally force an individual to give up the objective or take some other action that in itself is far from desirable or admirable. This, in capsule form, is part of the history of most all-out causes and programs of action. If the author had tried to present one character as wholly "right" and the other as wholly "wrong," he would not have been able to emphasize this important fact of experience with the same effect, for the story would then present a battle between causes, with one cause "winning." To get the effect he wants, the author presents both characters as persons whose steadiness of purpose forces them into awkward choices. The story is thus a far cry from inferior fiction, with its wholly "right" and "wrong" characters and its problems that are "solved" so much more easily than are the genuine dilemmas of life. (The author is—deliberately?—vague about the degree of the wife's danger, and the priest makes no preparation to give the regular service for the dying. This may be a sign of a careless "tolerance" or optimism, a note which is struck at the beginning of the story. Father Macdowell is a vulnerable human being who comforts a sick woman.)

It was apparent, in the study of readers' responses we referred to earlier, that many readers did not begin to see the central meanings of the story under discussion, for the clear reason that emotions got in the way. Those who said that John would eventually get over his disappointment were not even talking about the story before them; they were writing one of their own, in their own minds, with a happier ending. Those who used the story as "proof" of fixed personal ideas about religion were not reading what is there either, for the author of this story could hold any religious point of view we might care to name and still say exactly what he says—*if* he were sufficiently observant. The story is not an argument about religion. It is a representation of a common and important human problem—or rather, of several problems. The story happens to deal with religion, but the same major ethical problems—ends-means, self-absorption, possessiveness—occur in many other situations, with similar human reactions. These problems, these human dilemmas are the center of emphasis.

It seems desirable to make an effort to see what a good author is trying to do. Otherwise, we use a story merely as a stimulus for our own familiar ideas and never meet a new idea.

Discussion 2: the problem of implied meanings

It is easy to read and enjoy a story like "Two Soldiers," for action and humor carry the reader along while other effects are achieved in the realm of characterization and deeper feeling. Much good fiction is fully as easy.

"A Sick Call" is slightly more difficult, for reasons other than the fact, already shown, that readers can be deceived by their emotions into misinterpretation. The reader of "A Sick Call" is in the position of receiving various bits of information which finally form a conclusion. We read such a story for *implied* meanings rather than for meanings stated directly and literally. This problem nearly always puzzles the reader who is meeting it for the first time, though an expert reader would notice that the author's attitude toward Father Macdowell is suggested within fifty to a hundred words of the opening of the story. The following questions occur to many inexperienced readers.

(1) Why don't these authors come right out and say what they mean? Why convey meaning in such an indirect way?

These are natural questions. They express genuine puzzlement and perhaps a certain amount of resentment of the author's method. Both questions rest on a misunderstanding of human communication, a failure to realize that we pick implied meanings out of experience every day of our lives.

Real people seldom describe themselves as honest or dishonest, as saints, sinners, or hypocrites. They *reveal* such things by what they say and do, indirectly, and we note the implication. Some authors want as much "reality" as they can get, and so do not want to insert morals or state meanings in literal terms. When we read such an author, we interpret what his characters say and do, just as we interpret real events. There is nothing unnatural about the process.

The indirect, dramatic method of writing a story is actually a compliment to the reader, who is assumed to be as good an observer when he reads as when he notes the behavior of people he knows. One reader remarked that he liked Hemingway's fiction because "he isn't always telling me what to think; he presents the characters and lets me draw my own conclusions."

Such a reader, far from resenting the indirect method, likes it. Strictly speaking, authors who use the indirect, dramatic method just *seem* not to guide the reader, for they employ many signs of attitude and emphasis. Authors will always want to communicate their judgments. But outright moralizing in the manner of the nineteenth century is out of fashion today, and is thus relatively ineffective with many readers.

Finally, there are some meanings which *cannot* be stated directly, and certain other meanings lose force when stated directly. If the author of "Two Soldiers" had said, at every opportunity, "These are fine boys; I admire these boys," that would insult the reader, lessen the force of the story, *and not really convey the author's attitudes.* The experience of reading fiction is not that of reading generalizations or lectures or sermons. It is, rather, an experience during which a good reader will feel the impact of characters, action, setting, and words, and will grasp essential meanings. (See the comments on symbolism, pp. 38–44).

(2) Do I have to make a time-consuming analysis every time I read good fiction?

The answer is No, but the inexperienced reader may easily believe it is surely Yes.

First, much good fiction is not as difficult as the question assumes.

Second, the problem is simply that of developing a new reading habit—
the habit, or skill, of noticing implied meanings, including the implications
of action and event. This skill develops quickly once the problem is recognized. A reader who will give sharp attention to detail in just a few stories
will find that he begins to notice much more with little or no special effort.
It is mainly a matter of realizing that the author *is* using details of speech,
description, or action to *suggest* meanings.

The person who learns to be more aware of implied meanings will develop a power that
is useful quite apart from reading. It is like adding an extra-sensitive tube or circuit to a
radio receiver. The ability to understand implied meaning is involved in all verbal communication except at the simplest and most literal level. This ability is used in all first-class
observation of human character and action, for actions have meanings and implications,
whether reported in fiction or observed in life. The person who is steadily unaware of the
implications of what he sees, hears, says, and does is the person who "can't take a hint,"
the person who lives in a naïve, over-simple world of literal meaning. We can of course
observe people and events in a crude manner, without reflection or insight, as the history
of human error proves. But we cannot read first-class literature skillfully without using
our full human powers.

Discussion 3: the problem of "easy" and "difficult" reading

There is still another interference with expert reading which may as well be mentioned
now. It is caused by wishes that lie deep in human nature and affect our choice of *what*
we read. These well-concealed wishes often reveal themselves as a process of thought, a
set of ideas familiar to everyone. Here is one such idea:

All pleasure must be easy; if it isn't easy, it can't be pleasure.

This is well-loved and cherished nonsense. All major forms of personal achievement are
difficult in some way (self-knowledge, for example), but they produce special satisfactions
or "pleasures" as a result, often as a by-product. "Pleasure" in reading some fiction can obviously mean pure escape from thought or knowledge of any kind. But it can also mean
a sounder view of experience, a cure for provinciality or stereotyped thought. This
second kind of "pleasure" isn't always "easy," but it is infinitely more valuable.

A second idea, equally inaccurate, is urged sometimes by those who like to regard
themselves as "practical" people with no time for nonsense:

The purpose of literature is to provide pleasure for the
lighter hours. It is one of the decorations or frills of living,
with no practical value.

Entertainment and easy pleasure are indeed obtained from some very good literature,
with such definite effects on the way we feel that these effects are valuable in a real sense.
But to classify literature as "mere" entertainment is to reveal something like an absolute
lack of knowledge—if the idea is stated seriously. The idea is not often meant seriously.
It is just one of those notions we wouldn't think of trying to defend, because we know it
can't be done. We are determined nevertheless to *use* the idea, for the "mere entertain-

ment, no practical value" line of thought conceals something—a personal unwillingness to use mind or emotion for exploration and discovery, especially self-discovery. The results might be disturbing.

The fear of being disturbed is revealed in a third idea, also taking the form of a judgment about "practicality":

> Serious literature is too serious; problems are always being presented that stir people up. Authors are always writing about trouble, and we have enough trouble anyway.

This judgment is a far cry from the notion that literature is "merely" a decoration or a frill of living. But the three ideas taken together make a convenient excuse for avoiding any reading more meaningful than the latest commerical story.

It is tempting and natural to use one or more of these excuses when we think about reading. If there is one desire common to people in their reflective moments, it is the desire for a simple, neat view of life. We like to believe that existence is simple rather than complex, and that "answers" and "solutions" are easy. Good literature, taken as a whole, will not support so naïve a view and is bound to disturb the reader who insists on simple views as his equipment for living.

But when we are tempted never to read good literature if we can avoid it, we overlook the fact that good literature offers its own kind of reassurance, as was indicated in the discussion of "Two Soldiers." It doesn't always "stir people up"; frequently it consoles, without falsifying problems. Frequently it increases our respect for the potentialities of other men and women, and thus our respect for ourselves. Equally important, good literature presents attitudes, choices, and decisions that men have found useful in their efforts to live happily—or with courage and dignity—in the real world.

There are problems in everyone's life, of course. But the "practical" man overlooks the only practical thing he can do—that is, find a realistic way of living with a problem or of solving it. Pretending that a problem doesn't exist is not a solution. Good authors do not agree about everything, of course, nor do they all have ready-made philosophies to offer. But the individual reader is likely to find, almost any day, just the insight he needs into causes, just the attitude he needs as a source of balance, a preparation against surprise, a cure for over-simple views. Inferior literature is the only place in the world where problems are "solved" quickly, easily, and forever. In a sense, the reading we do is somewhat like fishing. Why fish in poor water?

It is true that an individual human being, a given reader, can stand only so much "reality," only so much thought about "problems," and everyone has his own private stopping point. Every reader, as we have said from the beginning, makes his own decisions. Our purpose in talking about the desire *not to know, not to look*, and the wishful logic that results, is to describe the nature of the choice every person makes when he decides what to read or not read, and to suggest that good literature is neither so difficult nor so impractical as wishful thinking may say it is. The choice is not usually between easy pleasure and no pleasure at all. More often it is a choice between dreaming and thinking, between a dangerously unreal view of human affairs and a beginning of knowledge.

"A Sick Call" puts pressure on the reader, as much good literature does. The story presses questions that involve the reader's own attitudes and knowledge of himself:

> *Questions:* Is it ever really possible to respect a person whose beliefs on an important matter are different from mine?
>
> Do I ordinarily judge other people by the *labels* they wear ("priest," "young husband") or by their single acts, or by their total behavior as far as I know it?
>
> Is it ever true that the end justifies the means? If so, under what conditions? If not, why not?
>
> Do I prefer an ethically complex or ethically simple view of life?
>
> Do I ever insist on the ethically simple view with little reason?
>
> What capacity do I possess for being objective about people whose actions or opinions differ from mine?

Fiction and "Truth"

We live in an age in which science increasingly assembles objective, quantitative data, and we respect scientific method as a means of getting knowledge, a means which has its own power of self-correction. A reader who happens to know the way in which science works, and who reads habitually for information alone, is often tempted to classify fiction (short stories, novels, and plays) as "mere" entertainment, not as a source of knowledge at all. Obviously, stories and novels and plays do not come to the reader with experimental data attached, but there are ways in which fiction does convey information or "knowledge." These, however, are the ways of art, not of science.

There is a kind of novel—the "social problem" novel—which often raises in our minds the question of factual accuracy, for this kind of novel is tied more closely to particular social problems at particular times than most other realistic fiction is. Examples are the novels of Dickens, Balzac, Steinbeck, Farrell, Dreiser, Tolstoy, or Paton. Many authors of such novels assert, for example, that there is a causal relationship between bad social conditions and crime, a thesis which appeared first in literature and has since been explored by sociology. Much time is spent, in some novels, in describing the causalities which seem to operate. Without exception, however, the novelists named above reveal an awareness that there are causes of crime—and of human decency—which are not attributable to external environment, bad or good. (No one, of course, has yet found a human being who has no environment, who is, so to speak, just a walking and talking instance of heredity.)

The implications of all this for the question of "truth" in fiction seem clear. There are today sets of statistics, arrays of percentages, showing the frequency of crimes of various kinds in "bad" and "good" areas. Any author can obtain this information in ten minutes by consulting the latest statistical report. A capable author, however, can obtain the same general idea in another way—by diversified personal observation, the method of Dickens or Balzac. But the general fact or "truth," however obtained, will never by itself make a novel. Consider how little force the story "Two Soldiers" would possess if merely summarized: "Latest researches show that patriotism exists among siblings in non-urban areas of the Deep South."

Good realistic fiction attempts to represent the concrete reality of village or farm or city neighborhood, with that complex of desire, thought, feeling, and action which is the specific content of individual awareness and individual experience. Fiction of that kind tries to represent experience as individual persons know it and feel it. Such fiction is in this way more whole, more complete, than any table of percentages or collection of generalities. (Many social statistics, incidentally, have their source in personal observation.)

A fictional report is thus a *different kind* of report on human experience. It is not "better" or "worse" absolutely; it is simply different. When we say that one report is better than another, we have to indicate the use the report is to be put to, what it is better *for*. Otherwise, the statement about "better" is meaningless. A map constructed by means of a polar projection will be more useful in plotting certain air routes than a Mercator projection will be. Neither map would be much help in plotting soil erosion in Kansas. There are many good maps, but they serve different purposes. A general "truth" about crime—or about anything else—may appear in either fiction, on the one hand, or in history, sociology, biology, anthropology, or psychology, on the other. The idea or "truth" may be correct or incorrect. It may be tested through careful observation, and it should be tested wherever it appears. It is thus important to realize that the problem of "truth" is not a simple either-or alternative, with quantitative observations being always RIGHT and all other observations being always WRONG. Actually, we obtain knowledge of many kinds from many sources, and much of the complex knowledge we need, particularly the understanding of human beings and of moral or ethical judgment, is not yet in quantitative form and may never be.

The writer of realistic fiction may thus know as much abstract theory as the psychologist does, or more, or less. He may even *be* a psychologist. But he gets most of his material in a different way and presents it in a different form for different purposes. There is nothing to keep him from being well-informed except the limits of his natural ability—but, again, a psychological theory does not make a novel or story or play. Nor do the detailed facts of history. Art is not science.

It is important for any twentieth-century person to understand that what we call "reality" is complex. Each kind of observer approaches "reality" in his own way and for his own purposes. Each may obtain in his own way a piece of that rare commodity "truth." The scientist concentrates on building ever-more-accurate theory, with a view to control or prediction. The realistic novelist concentrates on exact personal observation. He may give much thought to the "typicality" of his fictional character or give it no thought whatever; it is the *reader* who must decide when generalization is appropriate. The realistic novelist or story writer will give thought to human behavior and motivation because he must. The result may be very accurate or very thin indeed, depending on the writer's powers and purposes. The best realistic fiction reports nuances of individual feeling and judgment which have never yet been conveyed as accurately in any other way except in poetry. This kind of "truth," of course, is not the sole purpose of fiction, not even the most important purpose, but it is often one purpose (or, if you prefer, it is one thing that happens).

In this brief comment on fiction and "truth," we have discussed the content of fiction on the plane of information, or truth to the causalities in people and in nature. We have said nothing here about fiction as a carrier of value judgments, which in an older day were called "moral truths." It is enough now to say that fiction can convey a knowledge of what man's problems and dilemmas have been, together with a knowledge of what man has valued. In order to achieve perspective on this whole question of the relation of fiction to "truths" of various kinds, it is necessary now to ask what actually happens when people read fiction and to discuss what it means to say that fiction is a form of imaginative art.

MAJOR EFFECTS OF READING FICTION

What typically happens when people read fiction? What happens, that is, which can be stated specifically enough to be used by readers who wish to increase their personal awareness and competence?

We do not have to guess about the major kinds of effect, for we have reports from scores of college-age readers containing reactions to the two stories already printed here and to other stories and novels. Obviously, no two readers will have exactly the same experience in detail. But it is no accident, in a theatre for example, or when a story is read aloud, that whole audiences often respond at the same instant in identifiable ways.

(A) Reading as an experience involving emotion: comments on the psychology of art.

The reading of fiction is, first of all, an experience which involves the reader's capacities in several ways. A frequent part of this experience is a degree of emotional involvement. The reaction to "A Sick Call" is, as we have shown, partly a response to labels ("priest," "young husband," "young wife") and to a problem which stirs religious allegiances in some readers. Emotional involvement in "Two Soldiers" includes the reader's amusement and, more important, a degree of sympathy and respect for the two brothers—indeed, for the family. The coming of war is no light matter for them, and they behave well.

There is no need to classify these emotional results as either "identification" or "empathy," for the causes and nature of the results vary widely. Often the most accurate way of describing what happens when we read certain stories is to say that, at certain levels, we "take sides" in a conflict, as many readers of "A Sick Call" did. In that story the author was not "taking sides" but was regarding both main characters with sympathy. The reader had to discover that fact for himself, and such a discovery is often an element in the art of reading. In some other stories, the author *does* take sides, in the sense of disposing his respect or sympathy in one direction rather than another. But the basic and general fact is that reading is an experience which often involves the reader's emotions and that readers frequently describe such an experience as "pleasurable."

Emotion aroused directly in a life situation is not always pleasurable—fear, for example. Emotion aroused by a work of art usually is pleasurable. Why this should be so is a question which theorists from the ancient Greeks forward have tried to answer—but there is no doubt whatever that it is so. A reader is partly an observer and partly—at a safe distance—

a participant, vicariously. A story itself is not, of course, the events it represents. As Kenneth Burke has said, it is symbolic action, but it can stir emotion. (Some theorists have said that the pleasure arises from the fact of imitation, the medium of art being used to imitate human experience.)

Occasionally a writer tries to make his story carry more emotion than we feel is appropriate. We call the story a "tear-jerker" and accuse the writer of sentimentality. We mean that he is asking for a stronger response than the story, *as presented*, seems to justify. This may mean that the writer lacks art—skill in handling his materials, in conveying what they mean to him. It may be that he is confused, or doesn't know his subject intimately, or is insincere. Any one of these causes can produce writing which we call "unconvincing," and this leads to the charge of sentimentality, for we cannot take the emotion seriously if the story as a whole is unconvincing.

The younger brother in "Two Soldiers" is a ready object of sympathy and respect for many readers. He has courage and purpose; he is young and naïve. Such a character could be presented in a general or stereotyped manner—and fail to move the experienced reader. The treatment in "Two Soldiers" is specific—in the detail of the familiar environment, in the attitudes of all the characters, in the impact of the city, and especially in the thoughts, feelings, actions, and language of the younger brother. No character in "A Sick Call" is presented in as complete or individual a way, and the feeling aroused is of a different kind, somewhat closer to one's reaction to a stereotyped presentation. However, "A Sick Call" is so condensed, so economical in its use of detail, that it is a distinct achievement, and Father Macdowell is almost an individual.

Inferior fiction does not differ from better fiction in the *general* subjects or situations presented. Some of the worst stories and novels ever written deal with "universal" subjects like father-love, mother-love, and just plain love, as a glance at any pulp magazine will demonstrate. Inexperienced or immature readers will respond to stereotyped fiction that leaves other readers cold, just as the inexperienced or the immature will be less acute in sizing up people and events in real life. Our response to anything outside us—a book, another person, a problem, an idea—depends on (1) the nature of that thing, and (2) our own experience and maturity. Probably the best way for a reader to learn the differences between first-rate and mediocre fiction is to refine his judgments through wide reading and specific comparisons. These comparisons must include the effects achieved and the way in which they are achieved. If we know what effects are typical, such as the effects being described here, we read more alertly. To summarize: The reading of fiction is an experience that can involve emotion, and we read for this effect among others. When emotion is touched, an experienced reader can keep an eye on himself. He can learn the nature of his own reactions, his emotional allegiances, his judgments. Emotional self-knowledge is gained only through experiences which *do* involve emotion. Reading is one such experience.

(B) *Reading as an experience involving emotion: functions of curiosity and "caring" in the reading of fiction.*

Curiosity about "what will happen next" in a story or novel is probably the commonest effect of reading fiction—at the time of reading. Even the thinnest story makes this appeal in some degree. Often we think we know how a story will end, and yet we read on to make sure. Often we are sure that a character will solve his problem, but we read on to find out how. We know in advance, for example, that the younger brother in "Two Soldiers" will not be permitted to join the Army. But curiosity remains as to how he will be persuaded to go home, and there is additional curiosity as to how he will feel, how he will take the final No, the *realized* separation from his older brother. Interest of this kind approaches a "caring" about what happens to the fictional character. This sort of interest arises usually when we have been led by the story to know the character as an individual, in the same second-by-second way we know ourselves and other real people. Such an interest, once aroused, causes us to make demands on the story and on the author. The author of "Two Soldiers" has to do something to satisfy the interest in the younger brother's final state of mind and feeling, or the story will lack an element which belongs in it organically, functionally, a lack which would make the reader feel cheated.

When we say that a story is, as the phrase goes, "a work of art," we mean partly this functional, organic kind of thing, for a genuine work of art—by the commonest definition—contains everything it needs to be complete, and nothing extra, nothing unrelated or out of proportion. If a story arouses definite curiosity or definite emotion, that fact shapes our sense of what "completeness" means. A good writer is aware of this problem. He provides, in a way, a complete mental and emotional journey for the reader. As T. S. Eliot has said, we go "into and out of" the situation or problem raised in the story or through its characters. If "Two Soldiers" had ended when the older brother said, "You must go home. . . . I am depending on you to look after my ten acres," it would have been incomplete functionally and therefore artistically.

A skilled reader will notice the rise of curiosity *and the forms it takes*, especially when some degree of "caring" is attached to action or characters. A skilled reader knows that curiosity about what will happen next is a kind of bait to keep his attention while deeper things happen, such as understanding of human character or ideas or problems. A deliberate comparison of even two or three stories in respect to the functioning of curiosity and "caring" will increase alertness and enjoyment, through increased knowledge of what is possible and valuable in fiction.

> *Problem:* Curiosity in a story is somewhat like a Chinese box. Each question gives way to a new question: First the brothers hear about Pearl Harbor, then the older brother is worried and the younger is puzzled, then the older brother leaves, and then the younger acts. At each stage, the reader is curious about a new event which is related causally to earlier events and earlier knowledge. Gradually we are led to the heart of the story. The questions which a story thus places in the reader's mind in sequence are called "narrative" questions. Compare the functions of curiosity and "caring" in two other stories.

> *Problem:* Can you find a fictional character who is definitely more individualized —you know more about him—than other characters in these same two stories?

(C) Fiction as a source of ideas and beliefs.

A reader of fiction always receives an *as if* picture of "reality." This effect is especially strong in fiction written in the so-called realistic mode. For example, from "Two Soldiers" we receive a picture of the external environment in which the boys have grown up, and of the mental environment—attitudes of father, mother, their views of past history as it has touched them, attitudes toward work, toward the new war, toward the land. We receive also a picture of the inner working of the younger brother's mind, and we learn what the older brother feels through what he says and does. All such elements constitute the basic "reality" in a work of fiction. This "reality" is "given," assumed for the purposes of the story. We read *as if* all the details are real and correct, and they range all the way from the fact that the family burns wood to major events in the younger brother's mind.

On the basis of the "reality" in a story we can and do form general beliefs, justified or not, which can be phrased in dozens of ways: there are patriotic people in the Deep South; mothers can teach their children self-respect ("your blood is good as any blood anywhere, and don't you never forget it"); Hitler, who thought us to be decadent in 1943, could have learned something to his profit from this story; and so on. Social-problem novels often convey to the reader inclusive beliefs or general ideas about fact, such as the idea that bad conditions in one segment of society will cause eventual harm to people living in "better" segments of society. Such beliefs about fact arise from the highly detailed "reality" in some novels.

In addition to the *as if* or symbolic picture of "reality" in fiction, there is also a view of human values. These values are "realities" too, in fiction and in life, in the sense that people believe in them and live by them. In addition to showing the reader of "Two Soldiers" that the older brother is patriotic ("I jest ain't going to put up with no folks treating the Unity States that way") or that the brothers both have courage, the story clearly implies value judgments: patriotism is a good and admirable thing; courage is to be respected. These are judgments as to what *should be*, what is good or bad, desirable or undesirable. The value picture grows when the father states his characteristic view of military service, and the mother has *her* distinct view ("They could take the country and keep the country, so long as they never bothered me and mine").

To understand fiction—or indeed human communication—it is essential to recognize the double effect which has been described:

(1) There is in every story an *as if* picture of "reality"—for the purposes of the story. This "reality" includes, first, all the detail of the setting and of the characters and their actions. It includes, second, what the characters desire, want, value. The values, dramatized, are part of the story, part of the total picture we receive as readers. The mother's attitude toward the war, in "Two Soldiers," is just as clearly a "fact" as is her preparing a lunch for the son to take with him.

(2) We discover from the story what it is that the author wants to emphasize, and especially what he approves of, laughs at, disapproves. Such elements come close to being what the author wants to "say," if we wish to think in such terms.

Any piece of fiction—indeed, any fragment of experience—should show us that events in themselves are uninteresting and unimportant and neutral except as human beings attach value to them. If an unknown man wanders through the neighborhood tomorrow, that will be a matter of relative indifference in itself. But if we happen to be afraid of strangers, we will immediately attach a value to the event; we do not want these strangers in the neighborhood. We are valuing beings, with capacity for infinite variety in judgment. Literature is the most complete and forceful record of this human capacity. Though the symbolic report of external "fact" which appears in fiction is sometimes very important, the record of man's values is more important and more abiding.

The basic duality of fiction—that it presents both events and a valuing of events—has a definite bearing on what has been called "emotional involvment." If we admire or dislike a fictional character, it is largely because he represents values of which we approve or disapprove; we may even disapprove of his actions but value *him*, a reaction which occurs often enough in daily life. The values emphasized in a story through its characters are often the basis and strongest source of emotional appeal. *Responses at this level are much more lasting than are the momentary stirrings of curiosity.*

Values do not affect us much, however, when they are merely stated in abstract language. They have to be presented in dramatic, concrete form to be moving—and this is what the detailed "reality" in fiction can do. A word like "justice" is relatively uninteresting and unexciting in the abstract. But in the context of a historical situation like the American Revolution, or the human action in a novel, such an idea can be felt so powerfully as to change the lives or purposes of real people. The philosopher Plato knew this. He feared the influence of "wrong" ideas powerfully presented, especially ideas of value, and he would have outlawed poetry in his ideal Republic. If we assume, then, that reading is solely a matter of "admiring" various works of literature, we will overlook the elements that keep good literature alive in the minds of men and that cause it to be read as an important account of human experience.

> *Problem:* Read a story that has not been discussed in this section and identify the elements of "fact" and "value" in it. Try to see what the author emphasizes. Remember that the author's attitudes may appear in small details, and that what a fictional character is allowed to do or *not* do can be a major sign of the author's attitude.

Commercial fiction lodges beliefs in our minds as readily as better fiction does. We read commerical fiction without serious purpose, for entertainment or relaxation, and we rarely notice what is happening in the realm of belief. As a quick example, almost all "Western" novels feature a blue-eyed hero built like an isosceles triangle standing on its tip. He never has a mother. Neither does his true love, who also has blue eyes. Inferior or outright bad characters in this fiction usually have brown or black eyes, plus a hint of "something in the blood" that comes from "below the border." (The major exception to this rule is a conventional species of pale-blue-eyed killer. "You can tell it by his eyes.") There is no need to make a heavy case for all this; it is one of several conventions of "Western" fiction, with origins in a real historical struggle between racial elements in the Southwest and West in early days. The point is that general ideas and attitudes are delivered steadily through commercial fiction without attracting much notice, if any.

The author of commercial fiction is certainly not trying to convey deeply held beliefs of his own, for his principal way of judging an idea is by the convention he writes in or by saleability. A degree above this level is the writer who actually knows the Western country and develops his characters more carefully, especially their motivations and their attitudes toward problems. If what has been said leaves the impression that there is a fixed line between "commercial" and "better" fiction, that is not the intention. There are many gradations in quality which can be known only through specific comparisons. General ideas and beliefs appear at all levels of quality, however, ready to take their place as part of our mental equipment, whether we like this fact or not, whether or not we feel that we are reading "just for entertainment."

The fact that fiction is written at many levels of quality and for purposes which range from mere entertainment to an attempt to present deeply held ideas or attitudes places a genuine burden on the reader who wishes to develop his powers of discrimination. It has already been suggested that one difference between inferior and better fiction may lie in the degree to which the characters are individualized, or in the avoidance of stereotypes which represent experience crudely. It has also been suggested that the same general problems or the same *types* of character may appear in fiction at any level. The differences then, including those already mentioned, can be best understood in several ways:

> What seem to be the writer's general motives—that is, the reasons why he writes at all? Is he a "serious" writer or a commercialist?
>
> How specific and complex are the handling of detail and the dramatization of ideas, problems, attitudes, values?
>
> What degree of skill, of artistry, is attained?

These questions are related. A high degree of artistry is usually evidence that the writer is serious in what he attempts and is not simply a commercialist; but artistry in itself is no guarantee that the writer will have important things to say. Too, some of the greatest writers, Tolstoy for example, have not been heavily occupied with the art of what they produced. However, it is impossible in many instances to distinguish between *what* is said (the content) and the *way* it is said. General, abstract ideas may indeed be picked out of most stories, but the author's exact understanding of an idea—and thus the reader's— is inseparable from the concrete form in which the idea is conveyed, the *total* story or novel with all its detail. The form controls the way in which the reader will experience and understand what the author is presenting.

As to the writer's motives, we must understand that the general reason why a man writes at all is not the same as his purpose or intention in a particular piece of writing, which we infer mainly from the writing itself. Most writers, of course, need to make enough money, in some way, for food and shelter. But the commercial motive may not be the only one, or even the main one. Motives other than the commercial are always involved in the best writing. There is, for example, the desire for achievement. There is the desire to convey with force that which the writer holds to be true or valuable. There is the desire to use a talent, to do perfectly the thing one's powers enable him to try. A person with unusual ability is almost compelled to use it in order to complete himself, to be a whole person. The purely commercial motive is insufficient for production of the finest art or the best scientific research. Any reader can prove for himself the truth of this assertion by talking with people of genuine achievement, whether in the arts or in the sciences.

Fiction supplies, then, a vast array of pictures of "reality" and of ideas and beliefs. On these we use our minds and emotions. Some of these pictures are so incomplete, so hastily contrived, as to be useless or even dangerous. Other artistic accounts of experience are the most accurate and subtle that serious and gifted men and women can produce. We cannot prevent or stop the influence of the arts—popular or otherwise—unless we live in caves and agree not to draw on the walls or tell each other stories. What we *can* do is develop awareness of what is going on when we read, including awareness of what it means to say, "This is a work of art." The critical happenings occur in our own minds and are based on knowledge and experience. A wise man once said that a major result of education is the ability to recognize excellence when we see it.

(D) *Fiction as a source of information; the question of whether "believability" is important.*

A work of fiction, depending on its calibre and purposes, may stand in *any relation whatever* to what may be called "total reality," which no man has ever known. Fictional accounts of current social conditions should be checked, just as we check any report, if we intend to use these accounts as a source of belief or action. To subject a work of fiction to this sort of external test is not at all to be a non-appreciator of literary art.

There is a sense, however, in which the accuracy of a fictional account of historical or social "reality" does not matter at all. Good fiction in the realistic mode is concerned primarily with human character and motives and with human values as these have always existed. These elements, *if well enough presented*, are more important in the long run than any account of social conditions, for the characters, their actions, and their values remain meaningful long after particular social conditions have changed. It is in this sense, among others, that the novels of Dickens or Balzac or Tolstoy or Henry James have a life never achieved by such a novel as *Uncle Tom's Cabin*, influential as that novel was in its time as a work of propaganda.

Art is not photography—or sociology or history. An author selects details of many kinds in order to produce the effects he wants. Once we understand that art means selection and that fiction is symbolic action which has its own purposes, its own powers as a means of communication, then we are not concerned in quite the same way about exact correspondences between a story and what we naïvely think of as "the facts." An author can make an important comment on reality by means of a story which is admittedly a pure fable.

There is much good fiction, of course, which represents life in many parts of the world and in many professions with admirable accuracy. For those who are curious about the big world of the past or the present, such fiction is a resource for increasing one's store of knowledge in a very agreeable way. This development of factual interests is not, however, the essential business of a course in literature, which has enough to do in revealing what the various literary values are and in showing the range of quality available to readers. But unless education is to be rigidly compartmentalized, there is no good reason why one interest should not lead to another, even in college.

There is one further way of stating the fiction-truth problem which may be useful. A dozen commercially written stories dealing with any one subject or type of problem will convey about the same stereotyped and wholly expected ideas. A dozen stories by better writers on exactly the same subject or problem will show it in a dozen truly individual ways, for a good writer speaks as an individual. Viewed collectively, the better fiction will offer (1) wider knowledge of the subject or problem, with relative freedom from stock conclusions; (2) more knowledge of the alternatives in personal decision and value judgment which do in fact exist. This is not to say that good authors cannot agree or may not have their own prejudices. It is to say that the level of representative accuracy in good fiction will be high because of the integrity and skill of the whole operation—the writer's own seriousness, the detailed content, the art or skill brought into play. The area of agreement will include the fact that good writers tend to recognize the complexity of life and the variety of attitude to a degree that should be a warning to other observers of human behavior.

The effects of reading fiction which have been mentioned thus far are quite apparent once we stop to ask what does happen when we read. What is not always so apparent is the way in which we can use this awareness, either to read more skillfully, or to learn more about ourselves, or to reduce naïveté and refine judgments in the direction of depth and accuracy.

(E) *Fiction as art; story elements and their interrelationships; art as an ordering of experience.*

Few untrained readers, when questioned without preparation, will name "pleasure from appreciation of artistry" as a major source of satisfaction in reading. Readers are much more likely to talk about other rewards, such as interest in action, suspense, characters, humor, even ideas and problems. The art, the skill, of a story is not the first thing most people mention or think of. Yet the art of the thing is what causes the more obvious effects; when a reader says that a story or novel has more than average power, he is usually making an indirect comment on the art or skill of the author. Such a reader, quite soundly, views the art of the thing as a *means* to various *ends*. He does not regard art as a special source of pleasure, and yet it is, or can be. As experience grows, most readers begin to see that major effects in the realm of emotion or idea or "reality" are indeed inseparable from the writer's powers as an artist, and they begin to develop this final form of appreciation and knowledge.

A writer of fiction has a limited number of devices or story elements to work with:

> The action, including what are called "plot" and "conflict."
>
> One or more fictional characters—with all that any one of them may be represented as thinking, saying, feeling, doing, which returns us to the idea of action.
>
> The setting, or environment.
>
> Words, language, through which all the foregoing is presented; or language used directly for remarks or comments by the author, speaking in his own person and not through the dramatic action. *Words are the basic medium.*

The writer uses these story elements and only these, including what he can manage to *suggest* through them, to produce such effects as the following, singly and in combination:

> The reader sees an *as if* picture of "reality" at some level of detail—and on this picture a number of other effects depend.
>
> The reader is amused or moved emotionally, from causes which have been indicated, especially by the values which are dramatized.
>
> The reader is curious—mainly about what will happen, and why and how; sometimes curiosity develops as to the nature of a problem, a phase of experience, the meaning of an idea.
>
> The reader understands—and often shares—a belief about fact or a value judgment (this includes moral and ethical judgments).
>
> The reader is informed.
>
> The reader receives aesthetic satisfaction.

The art of fiction, like the other arts, is complex. Complexity arises from the fact that the author may intend only one major effect but achieve it through other effects which serve as means to the main end. The humor in "Two Soldiers" is not the main effect in that story, but it is nevertheless a *genuine* effect, which the author achieves deliberately as an aid in producing still other effects.

One specific problem of reading is therefore to discover what the various effects of a story or novel are and to see clearly their relationship. The act of noticing the various effects intended or attempted leads also to criticism of a practical kind. "Two Soldiers," for example, carries a stronger appeal to both humor and curiosity in the last half or two-thirds. This raises the question of whether the first third is needed, and this in turn raises the further question of what *is* achieved in the early pages of the story. As soon as we ask this question, we become aware of certain facts: (1) The two brothers and their relationship are made very real in the quiet opening of the story. (2) The mother's attitude is made real and believable, with the result that we can believe in the older brother's decision as both difficult and serious. (3) The customary way of life is made clear. (4) The main narrative question is stated. Without these elements, the remainder of the story would lose much of the force it finally develops. Thinking *into* a story in this manner brings a clearer appreciation of what the author has achieved.

The elements in a story—action or plot, character, setting, wording—are related and interdependent just as the effects are, for these elements are the tools the author uses in producing the various related effects. For example, even a bare outline of action can convey meaning. A man from a "poor" area kills a man from a "good" area while robbing a house. This action in itself conveys the idea that bad conditions in one segment of society will harm the rest of society. But the bare record of action does little to create understanding or arouse feeling and judgment. The moment we add the "reality" of the characters involved, in such a way that the reader begins to "know" them as human beings, as individuals, in that moment other effects are achieved. It is much like the difference between hearing that an unidentified person has been hurt in an accident and hearing that someone we know has been hurt. The second report has an extra dimension, which involves "caring."

Each story element, therefore, has its own work to do, and each adds meaning to the others. Characterization amounts to little without action, and action is made far more meaningful by characterization. Setting, or environment, is slightly different. It may be used heavily for special purposes, or lightly as minimum information, minimum "reality." In thinking about "action," however, it is necessary to realize that overt or external action is only one kind; subjective action—events in the mind—is obviously important.

The definition of story elements need not be labored here, for they are known to most students and have been part of our vocabulary from the start. The words "conflict" and "plot," however, may deserve brief attention, as parts of the larger concept "action."

We can find what the "conflict" is in a story by asking one question: "What is opposed to what in this story?" Two characters may be in opposition, as in "A Sick Call." There may be a conflict in a character's mind, or the fictional character may be in conflict with something outside himself, such as the social judgment that very young boys are not permitted to join the Army. There may be a conflict with some phase of external nature, or a conflict of ideas. Perhaps the most functional way of thinking about conflict is to ask what *values* are opposed. If one feels that he can represent the story fairly by naming the subject of the conflict or by stating an especially prominent idea, what he states as a result is often called the "theme" of the story. For example, we may say that the theme of "A Sick Call" is the problem of ethical judgment, or of ends and means, or of human unawareness of motives. The trouble with trying to state the so-called theme of a story is that what we finally get is likely to be rather barren. A stated theme is often an over-simplification and is usually abstract and uninteresting compared with the much richer experience which is the story itself.

In the modern period many "slice-of-life" stories have been written which seem to contain no very definite conflict; they seem to be just series of incidents, like sequences of events in daily life. These stories are written in such a way because the authors believe that the result is more like life, more "real." If we search a "slice-of-life" story carefully enough, however, we will usually find that values of some kind are in conflict.

"Plot" means a bit more than "conflict." The plot of a story is its plan, which includes the development of the conflict or the development of any series of events which is supposed to carry meaning. We may know that the major conflict in "Two Soldiers" is that of the younger brother's desire *versus* a social rule, but the plot consists of *all* the steps, small and large, which are needed to show the reality and meaning of the major conflict. The plot thus includes all the separate events of the story, arranged in order. Choice of events for major and minor emphasis is an element in the *art* the writer employs. (Some events in certain stories are merely summarized; others are developed in detail.)

What has been said about story elements and the various effects produced through their use has important applications to skillful reading. The careful reading of a story can be approached in at least two ways:

(1) Knowing already what the major effects can be, a reader can watch for these effects and try to be more and more aware of their relationships. Increased satisfaction in reading is usually the result.

(2) Knowing what the essential story elements are, we can ask what elements the author depends on in a story, including a possible dependence on the suggestive power of words. We can ask what the implications of characters and action are. Increased accuracy in seeing meanings is usually the result. A good way to begin is to try to retell a story by relating the action alone. It will usually become apparent that this is not the "whole" story, or even the real story. Attention will thus be drawn to other meanings.

Enjoyment of the art of a story is partly a pleasure in the fine and effective working together of all elements, from language to action. It is the same pleasure we receive from an expert, near-perfect performance of any kind. It is partly an appreciation of technique, as we slowly learn more about technique. (See the discussion of technique, pp. 44–48.) Finally, this enjoyment arises because experience viewed through a work of literary art is *ordered* experience. Everything in the story is seen in relation to everything else, and it all makes its own kind of sense. Life itself, the daily drag of people and events, does not seem as orderly, for it contains distractions, puzzles, elements that seem not to fit, connections and causalities that are obscure. The artist imposes his own kind of order on the raw materials of experience. He shows parts of experience in relation to one another, and reveals all sorts of connections and meanings. By so doing, he deeply influences our views of life. A work of art is thus an image or symbol of completeness, with no loose ends, no functionless parts or details, with things of importance highlighted. We like this effect, sometimes without quite knowing why, for we deeply prefer order to disorder, "point" to pointlessness. Science provides a somewhat similar satisfaction by reporting the regular, orderly causalities in nature, in its own way and for its own purposes. The great world religions assert pattern and purpose in life, thus ordering experience in *their* own way. These three—art, science, religion—are indeed major sources of order and purpose in man's life and thought.

The literary artist, however, is not the representative of any fixed system. He speaks as an individual, ordering experience in his own way, coming to terms with those phases of experience that are important to him. If he does this with sufficient insight and skill, other people find his report valuable. The thing he does with special power is to dramatize those human values which are forces in all our lives, sources of purpose and order and continuity.

Nonrealistic Fiction

The final story in this section is "The Lift That Went Down into Hell," by Pär Lagerkvist, another winner of the Nobel Prize for Literature. *Lift* is the common word in England for *elevator*. Since elevators do not actually go down into Hell, the story is understood at once to be an example of nonrealistic fiction, at least in part. The central facts to hold in mind about a story that contains nonrealistic elements are these: (1) the author is probably trying to represent problems or ideas or attitudes that *are* real; (2) the nonrealistic machinery is a means to that end. The reader has to decide what the strange or unusual elements in the story *do*.

THE LIFT THAT WENT DOWN INTO HELL

Pär Lagerkvist
(1891–   )

Mr. Smith, a prosperous businessman, opened the elegant hotel lift and amorously handed in a gracile creature smelling of furs and powder. They nestled together on the soft seat and the lift started downward. The little lady extended her half-open mouth, which was moist with wine, and they kissed. They had dined up on the terrace, under the stars; now they were going out to amuse themselves.

"Darling, how divine it was up there," she whispered. "So poetic sitting there with you, like being up among the stars. That's when you really know what love is. You do love me, don't you?"

Mr. Smith answered with a kiss that lasted still longer; the lift went down.

"A good thing you came, my darling," he said; "otherwise I'd have been in an awful state."

"Yes, but you can just imagine how insufferable he was. The second I started getting ready he asked where I was going. 'I'll go where I please,' I said. 'I'm no prisoner.' Then he deliberately sat and stared at me the whole time I was changing, putting on my new beige—do you think it's becoming? What do you think looks best, by the way, perhaps pink after all?"

"Everything becomes you, darling," the man said, "but I've never seen you so lovely as this evening."

She opened her fur coat with a gratified

smile, they kissed for a long time, the lift went down.

"Then when I was ready to go he took my hand and squeezed it so that it still hurts, and didn't say a word. He's so brutal, you've no idea! 'Well, good-bye,' I said. But not a word from him. He's so unreasonable, so frightfully, I can't stand it."

"Poor little thing," said Mr. Smith.

"As though I can't go out for a bit and enjoy myself. But then he's so deadly serious, you've no idea. He can't take anything simply and naturally. It's as though it were a matter of life and death the whole time."

"Poor pet, what you must have gone through."

"Oh, I've suffered terribly. Terribly. No one has suffered as I have. Not until I met you did I know what love is."

"Sweetheart," Smith said, hugging her; the lift went down.

"Fancy," she said, when she had got her breath after the embrace, "sitting with you up there gazing at the stars and dreaming—oh, I'll never forget it. You see, the thing is— Arvid is impossible, he's so everlastingly solemn, he hasn't a scrap of poetry in him, he has no feeling for it."

"Darling, it's intolerable."

"Yes, isn't it—intolerable. But," she went on, giving him her hand with a smile, "let's not sit thinking of all that. We're out to enjoy ourselves. You do really love me?"

"Do I!" he said, bending her back so that she gasped; the lift went down. Leaning over her he fondled her; she blushed.

"Let us make love tonight—as never before. Hm?" he whispered.

She pressed him to her and closed her eyes; the lift went down.

Down and down it went.

At last Smith got to his feet, his face flushed.

"But what's the matter with the lift?" he exclaimed. "Why doesn't it stop? We've been sitting here for ever so long talking, haven't we?"

"Yes, darling, I suppose we have, time goes so quickly."

"Good Heavens, we've been sitting here for ages! What's the idea?"

He glanced out through the grill. Nothing but pitch darkness. And the lift went on and on at a good, even pace, deeper and deeper down.

"Heavens alive, what's the idea? It's like dropping down into an empty pit. And we've been doing this for God knows how long."

They tried to peep down into the abyss. It was pitch dark. They just sank and sank down into it.

"This is all going to hell," Smith said.

"Oh dear," the woman wailed, clinging to his arm, "I'm so nervous. You'll have to pull the emergency brake."

Smith pulled for all he was worth. It was no good. The lift merely plunged down and down interminably.

"It's frightful," she cried. "What are we going to do!"

"Yes, what the devil is one to do?" Smith said. "This is crazy."

The little lady was in despair and burst into tears.

"There, there, my sweet, don't cry, we must be sensible. There's nothing we can do. There now, sit down. That's right, now we'll sit here quietly both of us, close together, and see what happens. It must stop some time or there'll be the devil to pay."

They sat and waited.

"Just think of something like this happening," the woman said. "And we were going out to have fun."

"Yes, it's the very devil," Smith said.

"You do love me, don't you?"

"Darling," Smith said, putting his arms around her; the lift went down.

At last it stopped abruptly. There was such a bright light all around that it hurt the eyes. They were in hell. The Devil slid the grill aside politely.

"Good evening," he said with a deep bow. He was stylishly dressed in tails that hung on the hairy top vertebra as on a rusty nail.

Smith and the woman tottered out in a daze. "Where in God's name are we?" they exclaimed, terrified by the weird apparition. The Devil, a shade embarrassed, enlightened them.

"But it's not as bad as it sounds," he hastened to add. "I hope you will have quite a pleasant time. I gather it's just for the night?"

"Yes, yes!" Smith assented eagerly, "it's just for the night. We're not going to stay, oh no!"

The little lady clung tremblingly to his arm. The light was so corrosive and yellow green that they could hardly see, and there was a hot smell, they thought. When they had grown a little more used to it they discovered they were standing as it were in a square, around which houses with glowing doorways towered up in the darkness; the curtains were drawn but they could see through the chinks that something was burning inside.

"You are the two who love each other?" the Devil inquired.

"Yes, madly," the lady answered, giving him a look with her lovely eyes.

"Then this is the way," he said, and asked them to follow please. They slunk into a murky side street leading out of the square. An old cracked lantern was hanging outside a filthy, grease-stained doorway.

"Here it is." He opened the door and retired discreetly.

They went in. A new devil, fat, fawning, with large breasts and purple powder caked on the moustache around her mouth, received them. She smiled wheezily, a good-natured, knowing look in her beady eyes; around the horns in her forehead she had twined tufts of hair and fastened them with small blue silk ribbons.

"Oh, is it Mr. Smith and the little lady?" she said. "It's in number eight then." And she gave them a large key.

They climbed the dim, greasy staircase. The stairs were slippery with fat; it was two flights up. Smith found number eight and went in. It was a fairly large, musty room. In the middle was a table with a grubby cloth; by the wall a bed with smoothed-down sheets. They thought it all very nice. They took off their coats and kissed for a long time.

A man came in unobtrusively from another door. He was dressed like a waiter but his dinner jacket was well cut and his shirt-front so clean that it gleamed ghostlike in the semidarkness. He walked silently, his feet making no sound, and his movements were mechanical, unconscious almost. His features were stern, the eyes looking fixedly straight ahead. He was deathly pale; in one temple he had a bullet wound. He got the room ready, wiped the dressing table, brought in a chamberpot and a slop pail.

They didn't take much notice of him, but as he was about to go Smith said, "I think we'll have some wine. Bring us half a bottle of Madeira." The man bowed and disappeared.

Smith started getting undressed. The woman hesitated.

"He's coming back," she said.

"Pshaw, in a place like this you needn't mind. Just take your things off." She got out of her dress, pulled up her panties coquettishly and sat on his knee. It was lovely.

"Just think," she whispered, "sitting here together, you and I, alone, in such a queer, romantic place. So poetic, I'll never forget it." "Sweetheart," he said. They kissed for a long time.

The man came in again, soundlessly. Softly, mechanically, he put down the glasses, poured out the wine. The light from the table lamp fell on his face. There was nothing special about him except that he was deathly pale and had a bullet wound in his temple.

The woman leaped up with a scream.

"Oh my God! Arvid! Is it you? Is it you? Oh God in Heaven, he's dead! He's shot himself!"

The man stood motionless, just staring in front of him. His face showed no suffering; it was merely stern, very grave.

"But Arvid, what have you done, what have you done! How could you! My dear, if I'd suspected anything like that, you know I'd have stayed at home. But you never tell me anything. You never said anything about it, not a word! How was I to know when you never told me! Oh my God . . ."

Her whole body was shaking. The man looked at her as at a stranger; his gaze was icy and gray, just went straight through everything. The sallow face gleamed, no blood came from the wound, there was just a hole there.

"Oh, it's ghastly, ghastly!" she cried. "I won't stay here! Let's go at once. I can't stand it."

She grabbed her dress, hat and fur coat and rushed out, followed by Smith. They slipped going down the stairs, she sat down, got spittle and cigarette ash on her behind. Downstairs the woman with the moustache was standing, smiling good-naturedly and knowingly and nodding her horns.

Out in the street they calmed down a little. The woman put on her clothes, straightened herself, powdered her nose. Smith put his arm protectingly round her waist, kissed away the tears that were on the point of falling—he was so good. They walked up into the square.

The head devil was walking about there, they ran into him again. "You *have* been quick," he said. "I hope you've been comfortable."

"Oh, it was dreadful," the lady said.

"No, don't say that, you can't think that. You should have been here in the old days, it was different then. Hell is nothing to complain of now. We do all we can not to make it too obvious, on the contrary to make it enjoyable."

"Yes," Mr. Smith said, "I must say it's a little more humane anyway, that's true."

"Oh," the Devil said, "we've had everything modernized, completely rearranged, as it should be."

"Yes, of course, you must keep up with the times."

"Yes, it's only the soul that suffers nowadays."

"Thank God for that," said the lady.

The Devil conducted them politely to the lift. "Good evening," he said with a deep bow, "welcome back." He shut the grill after them, the lift went up.

"Thank God that's over," they both said, relieved, and nestled up to one another on the seat.

"I should never have got through it without you," she whispered. He drew her to him, they kissed for a long time. "Fancy," she said, when she had got her breath after the embrace, "his doing such a thing! But he's always had such queer notions. He's never been able to take things simply and naturally, as they are. It's as though it were a matter of life and death the whole time."

"It's absurd," Smith said.

"He might have *told* me! Then I'd have stayed. We could have gone out another evening instead."

"Yes, of course," Smith said, "of course we could."

"But, darling, let's not sit thinking of that," she whispered, putting her arms around his neck. "It's over now."

"Yes, little darling, it's over now." He clasped her in his arms; the lift went up.

Discussion 1: symbolism in fiction

We hear much these days about "symbolism" in fiction and about something called "nonrepresentational" or "abstract" art. This is not the place to discuss the latter, except to say that a good work of art will satisfy basic human needs, however strange the artistic method may seem to be. But a brief comment on symbolism is necessary before we discuss "The Lift That Went Down into Hell."

The number 3 is a symbol, used to represent three objects, ideas, parts, functions, and so forth. The number is not the things it represents or refers to. In the same way, the word *tree* or *house* is a symbol, not the real thing. Language itself is symbolic. The "characters" in a story, thus, are not real people, but are collections of detail reported by means of words. The most "realistic" story is symbolic, in the sense that any story is a representation, an *image*, of people and places and events. A story exists in the mind of the author and reaches the mind of the reader through the medium of words, which in turn may refer to things we know in the world of actuality or even the world of dreams.

We do most of our thinking with symbols—mathematical, verbal, rhythmic, pictorial, and so on. These symbols have various relations to so-called "real" events—such events as Pearl Harbor, wood-cutting, clergymen, husbands and wives. Symbols refer also to such things as the motions of our minds, or the causalities in test tubes and nuclear reactors. We represent all things, from the most objective to the most subjective, by means of symbols. We *have* to do this in order to talk or think about our experience. If the experience is complex, then the symbols we use are likely to have complex interrelationships.

The people and events and settings in a story are likely to be interesting in themselves. They are likely also to suggest still other people or events or places or problems, which we often know about or can imagine. "Two Soldiers," for example, is interesting just as a story; but it is also a symbol of wholly possible reactions to war, and of a way of life in a specific environment. "A Sick Call" too is interesting just as a story, but it symbolizes certain realities in human wishing and thinking and loving; further, it is a symbol of the universal and never-ceasing problem of ends and means. The student should note that such a story, involving characters in action, is itself rather concrete, but the concrete symbol, through its power of suggestion, can refer to abstract matters, such as love, or loyalty, or "the problem of ends and means." The symbolism mentioned thus far is in general "realistic"—that is, the symbols refer to people and events and problems that we can recognize easily as probable elements in human experience.

There is a more special way, also, in which symbols are used—that is, the symbol may have traditional meanings. For example, the number 3 has been used throughout much of history, in particular contexts, to represent the Trinity, or combinations of gods in the Hindu religion, or broad divisions of nature, or cardinal colors, and so on. If a young woman should be named Athene, in life or in fiction, the very name would symbolize wisdom or mental brilliance—to anyone who knew the traditional, abstract qualities associated with the goddess Athene. We will return later to this question of the special uses of symbols.

Some writers of fiction pose unnecessary problems for the reader by what amounts to a pointless and cluttered multiplication of special symbols. But the present author, Lagerkvist, does not belong in the class of writers who play with symbols as substitutes for meaning. Instead, he uses symbolism—in both a general and a special way—to communicate meaning.

Discussion 2: reasons for the use of nonrealistic elements in a story

Why would a serious writer include in a story such an element as the hell-destined elevator in "Lift"?

> To attract attention? Possibly, for it does so.
>
> To help convey briefly, intensely, an aspect of life that otherwise would have to be spelled out at length and with less interest? Very probably, for an artist wants economy of method with maximum effect. As you will see later, the elevator makes it possible to express with great brevity some meanings which are important.
>
> To suggest a reality of experience for which the author cannot find a better expression? Very probably. Many things cannot be said directly, literally. Many more cannot be said as well directly. It is a reality, in "Lift," that the man and woman are "going down," morally. Their first trip in the elevator is a symbol of this and a basic aid in conveying still other meanings, as the analysis of the story will show.

The use of a nonrealistic device is almost a promise to the reader that special meanings will arise from it, though the reader may at times have to work harder at interpretation than in a wholly realistic story. The basic thing to remember is that nonrealistic symbolism has exactly the same functions as the more familiar symbolism of a story in the realistic mode: to help the writer with the effective expression or communication of *meaning*.

In discussing what we have called "emotional involvment" we suggested that a concrete presentation of "reality" often sharpens the reader's emotional response, and that abstractions alone are not very moving. It is easy to see that "Lift" retains the advantage of concreteness, even in its nonrealistic material. An elevator is real enough; it is the *journey* of this particular elevator which takes us away from ordinary "reality."

Discussion 3: "The Lift That Went Down into Hell"

We have been emphasizing the fact that all language is symbolic and that the most interesting symbols are likely to be concrete—that is, things as definite and as available to our senses as The Flag, or the sensory reality of a man, a woman, a field in sunlight, all represented by means of words. But there is more to the use of concrete symbolism than interest. There is the fact that some ideas and feelings cannot be conveyed directly, literally, but must be conveyed by means of concrete symbols which suggest realities of a more abstract kind.

As an approach to the discussion of "Lift," consider for a moment what happens when people read or see such a drama as Shakespeare's *Othello*, reprinted later in this book. Othello is a famous general who comes to believe certain lies about the behavior of his wife, Desdemona. The person seeing or reading this play finds himself in a special position, for he knows that the lies *are* lies, though Othello (the fictional character) does not. Othello sees motives and meanings in his wife's behavior that are not really there at all, and a complex of misunderstanding and jealousy develops in a seemingly uncheckable manner. The reader or viewer is slowly impressed with a fatality in the whole sequence of events, for the motives of the characters are as real as anything in the world and apparently will not change. The special, ironic knowledge begins to arouse definite feelings in the reader or viewer. There is the sense of fatality, already mentioned, somewhat like the feeling we have when we see an accident about to happen that we cannot prevent. There is also fear, because the uncheckable forces in this play are human passions and motives and beliefs. All this is frightening, because men and women are supposed to be in command of themselves—that is, we like to think we are. Yet in this play a terrible action (murder and suicide) is prepared and committed simply because one man believes what a "friend" tells him—and Othello is the wrong kind of man to be told such things. It does little good to ask why Othello was so foolish as to believe the lies he was told, for we know in our hearts that we *do* believe those we love and trust. Therefore we pity him, a victim of trust and of his own passion. The play is thus a symbol of wholly possible human behavior, with the results for the reader or viewer that have been mentioned: ironic knowledge, pity, fear. The moment we dare to think of human life as containing motives and misunderstandings that grow in force until they cannot be stopped or changed, in that moment we fear. No amount of abstract talk will produce this effect, but a story will—through the power of concrete symbolism. The story is of course interesting in itself, but a further level of interest and feeling lies in the fact that the concrete symbol— the story with all its elements—causes us to recognize the deeper meanings, the universal application and truth.

So with "The Lift That Went Down into Hell." In trying to read "A Sick Call" carefully, we began by asking what the author seemed to be emphasizing, and we found the answer in a combination of characters and action, plus a small amount of descriptive language that suggested the author's attitudes. In "Lift" there are certainly characters (the man, the woman—unnamed, we observe—and the denizens of Hell). The action of the man and woman is pointed in the direction of a "good time." But something unexpected happens (the elevator) and because of this still other things happen which the man and woman must adjust to in their own way, whatever that way is to be and mean. If we look for signs of the author's attitude toward the man and woman, it begins to seem that the elevator, with the action and characterization it makes possible, is one sign: the man and woman *do not know where they are going; events have taken them in charge, unexpected events.* Thus, the elevator is already beginning to convey meaning, the proper function of any symbol, realistic or unrealistic. At first, physically, the man and woman are going *down*, and later we find that they *are* going down, in a moral sense. Later, they think they are going *up*, and physically they are, but we know better, for the trips down and back, with the events in Hell and the Devil's comments, have thrown an ironic light on everything the man and woman say and do and think.

In other words, we receive a view of the characters *that the characters themselves do not have*, and this view—the author's attitude—arises from special ironic knowledge which has been provided. This knowledge comes from (1) the elevator, (2) the comments made by the Devil, (3) the events in Hell, including the description, and (4) what the man and woman say and do *in the context of the other elements of the story*. When the Devil shows that he is sure he will see the man and woman again, for example, we know that it is only a matter of time until "soul torture" occurs. From many other signs, we know what is fated to happen. The husband, whether "really" shot in the head or not, might just as well be as far as his marriage is concerned: he is married to a woman who can say that he is too "serious" about marriage. In not replying, the husband shows his knowledge that the marriage is "dead," that no message from him can now reach his wife, that she is bound on her course. The Devil's early reference to the man and woman, "You are the two who love each other?" is an ironic comment which keys everything else he says. Once we see the communicative purpose of the trip to Hell, including the Devil and the "apartment" and its caretaker and the action there, the various details of the story fall into place, and there is no lost motion, no meaningless act or word. The basic characteristic of the wife—and of her escort—is unknowingness, or unawareness. She is unaware of the nature of the journey—a symbol of life—which starts as the elevator goes down; she learns nothing from the incidents of the journey itself; she has a blind and selfish expectation that life will continue to be pleasant and amusing, in spite of the terrible symbolic meanings the journey assumes for the observer—the reader of the story.

The story "Lift" can thus be read as a plain moral story, for it is certainly that—at a minimum level. But the story is also much more. The reader who once sees the elevator and the trip to Hell as a source of ironic knowledge—knowledge that the man and woman are fatally unable to share—will receive a twist of feeling somewhat similar to that delivered by the play *Othello*. But sympathy and respect are not developed for the man and woman in "Lift" as they are for the main characters in *Othello;* therefore, the elements of "caring" and of pity and fear cannot be as strong in the reader of "Lift." The attitude is one of sardonic amusement rather than sympathy and respect, and it is revealed mainly through the Devil's comments. The Devil is indeed a major device by means of which the author's attitudes can enter the story. Other means, of course, are the descriptive details and the action in Hell. The Devil knows what sin is, and by the same token knows what good is, which the man and woman are destroying. The Devil is amused. So is the author, in a grim kind of way.

"Lift" can also be read as a realistic statement—through the power of symbol—that a special trip to Hell, with reservations in advance, would not deter some people from their usual course of action. It is also a symbol of the ingenuity and determination a human being can exert in fooling himself, the excuses he can invent, his human capacity to forget, or refuse to see, the sure consequences of action and attitude. So the whole is a moral story at several levels. Though it contains nonrealistic elements, it is a symbol of various possible realities in human life.

Discussion 4: special uses of symbols

Throughout the discussion of "Lift" an obvious point was omitted deliberately—that the meaning of the story, the fact that it can work at all as a story, depends on the use of the familiar Christian symbols of Hell and the Devil. These symbols work so well that we are hardly aware of the fact as we read, but these symbols are, of course, another example of what was referred to earlier as traditional symbolism. Such symbols work because they are widely known and because their connotations are understood. In a culture unfamiliar with Christianity, these symbols might not be effective at all.

Symbols can be used, however, in a still more special way, as something more than well-established representations whose meanings can be translated directly and easily. There are authors who develop through repeated use their own private sets of symbols, which can be recognized and interpreted correctly only if the repeated uses are studied. An example is a rather special use the writer Sherwood Anderson makes of the symbol of race horses. A race horse, in Anderson's work, runs the best race it can, whereas men often lack this admirable, all-out quality. Only a dishonest rider or "fixer" can cause a race horse to do less than its best; men, however, often carry hidden controllers in their minds, which interfere with dedicated, all-out effort. Thus the race horse becomes, in Anderson's work, a special symbol of an attitude toward achievement and toward mankind.

From this brief analysis of the possibilities, it is apparent that symbols have a wide range of functions in fiction, somewhat as follows:

(1) Every word is a symbol, and language itself is symbolic. Thus, any story is symbolic in that the characters and events symbolize human experience.

(2) There are traditional symbols well known within a given culture, such as the symbols of a widely known religion or nation or profession or way of life. Such symbols, as we have seen, can have the effect of adding a universal significance to an otherwise plain story.

(3) Some symbols are so treated as to be almost private, esoteric. New symbols can be invented. Storytellers who have built their own special meanings into symbols of a more general or even traditional nature have perhaps been better communicators of meaning than have those who have tried to create entirely new symbol systems. There is nothing new about the idea of a race horse, but Anderson, as we have indicated, built new meanings into it. If we should examine various fictional presentations of Hell and Satan, we

would find that Lagerkvist has in part used the traditional meanings but has also built special meanings of his own into the character of Satan and the geography and mechanism of Hell. Whatever new interpretation Lagerkvist has added would be called a special use of these symbols. Whatever established meanings he has used would be called traditional.

The reasons suggested earlier as to why an author may use nonrealistic elements in a story are, we believe, sound. The story "Lift" is less than 2,500 words in length; yet no reader is likely to forget it. Meanings which apply to much human experience have been conveyed powerfully and economically through the use of symbols. In this connection, later, the reader should examine the uses of symbolism in "Delta Autumn," by William Faulkner; "Flowering Judas," by Katherine Anne Porter; "A Country Doctor," by Franz Kafka; "The Sad Horn-Blowers," by Sherwood Anderson; and "Heart of Darkness," by Joseph Conrad.

We have come a long way from relatively simple though effective stories such as "Two Soldiers." The approach to questions concerning symbols and to the interrelationships among elements in a work of art has been deliberately slow. The student who will reflect on these matters, however, will begin to develop a more complex understanding of the ways in which imaginative art works, and he will be less concerned about exact correspondences between the symbols in a work of art and what may be thought of as "the facts" of either life or history.

Problems: (1) If you will recall now the three stories in this section, you will see that in each instance you—as reader—came to know and understand things which the characters themselves did not know or understand. This ironic knowledge was the source not only of pleasure but also of specific meanings carried by the story. Such meanings are not "read into" the story, but are there by intention, for the skilled reader to discover.

Read one story not discussed in this introductory section. Make notes on the first signs of the author's attitude you can find, and notes on the things you are led to know or understand which the characters in the story do not know or understand. Read another story, making notes of the same kind. Then write a report in which you discuss the means by which the author's attitudes are revealed and the nature and extent of the dramatic irony in each story. Add a comment as to which story, in your opinion, makes the most forceful use of dramatic irony.

(2) Write a brief report in which you attempt to define, through fresh examples, (a) traditional symbolism; (b) traditional symbolism modified in a special way by the author, as Lagerkvist makes his own special characterization of the Devil in "Lift."

(3) Write a brief report on the speech (language) and thought of the younger brother in "Two Soldiers." His use of language is the most fundamental source of concrete reality in that story. In your report, then, try to discover how it is that the younger brother is able, with seeming naturalness, to mention so very many details of his environment and his experiences. This project will reveal more about the uses of first-person narrative than will any amount of theory.

(4) The environment of Hell in "Lift" provides an ironic meaning for many descriptive details that would otherwise be commonplace realism. Find a dozen

details in that story which take on an edge of ironic meaning simply because of the environment.

(5) Choose a story not discussed in this introductory section. Then write a brief report on the whole story as a symbol of meanings which lie outside the story. That is, what bearings does the story have on phases of human experience you know about or can think of, on human problems and issues and values?

Technical Information for Readers of Fiction

Much information that is "technical" in a broad sense has already been presented:

Implied meanings in fiction	pp. 18–20
Major effects of reading fiction	pp. 24–34
Fiction as art: interdependence of elements	pp. 31–34
Story elements: action, characters, setting, words; conflict; plot; theme	pp. 32–34
Realistic and nonrealistic elements in fiction	pp. 34–44
Fiction as symbol; levels of symbolism	pp. 38–43

Without an understanding of these larger matters, any reader is likely to miss valuable experiences. But the reader who is making his first serious attempt to understand the workings of fiction needs, also, some information about smaller points of technique.

Discussion 1: point of view and focus; author's comment; "objective" technique

Within the first fifty to two hundred words of most stories, a trained reader can identify the author's general method or technique. A major technique is easy to recognize; yet the reader who does not trouble to do so will miss major and minor meanings. A prominent feature of technique is the *focus* or *point of view* that an author uses.

Is the story told, for example, as a *first-person narrative*, like "Two Soldiers," in which a major character reports what he sees, thinks, feels, does—all in his own natural speech? If this is the method, the reader can expect one or more of several results. The narrator (speaker) may reveal his own character without knowing he does, producing for the reader a pleasure in noting these revelations (a form of dramatic irony). Second, the first-person method may carry an overtone of humor. Third, the first-person narrative may be used to increase the believability of what the narrator says: that is, the authority of the narrator—as one who says, "I was there, I saw, I know"—is felt. The authoritative first-person narrator is seen in *True Confession* stories, in such a novel as Defoe's *Moll Flanders*, or in Poe's familiar story "The Cask of Amontillado," in which the believability arises from a narrator who is the sole living witness of the events he reports.

If a story happens to be told through first-person narrative by a minor character, the reader has a clear question to answer: Is the narrator merely a convenience for getting the story told, or is he chosen for some emphasis or effect which only a narration by this particular minor character can produce? The answer will usually be found if we ask what would be missing from the story if that narrator were not used. (This question should be applied to Ring Lardner's story "Haircut" reprinted later in this book.) Sometimes a minor character who narrates a story is simply a stand-in for the author; sometimes the minor character has special knowledge which makes for believability, or a special attitude of mind. The reader who will try to see the function of such a narrator will come much closer to a total reading of the story.

A special form of first-person narrative is the *dramatic monologue*, in which one character speaks to a listener or listeners who are assumed to be present but do not themselves speak. For the reader, the effect is like that of listening to one end of a telephone conversation. The emphasis may be on character revelation or on the story the narrator tells, or both. Humor is a frequent effect of the dramatic monologue, satirical humor especially, arising from *dramatic irony*.

Stories told from a third-person point of view include several technical variations, each of which has its own advantages:

> third-person narrative with *unity of focus*
> third-person narrative with *shifting focus*
> third-person narrative with *author's comment*
> third-person narrative with *"objective" view* of persons and
> events
> combinations of the techniques named above

Unity of focus means that everything in the story is viewed through the senses and mind and emotion of *one* character, who is spoken of by the author in the third person (He or she saw, did, said, thought, felt, remembered, and so on). This rather strict method is close in some of its effects to a second-by-second narration in the first person, for events reported in this way seem real and immediate. But there are some things a first-person narrator probably would not talk about which seem quite natural if reported as occurring in the mind of a character presented in the third person. Some detail of sensation and thought appears natural in the third person which would not be natural in conversation. Much detail presented in the third person would seem labored or dull in the first person, especially stream-of-consciousness detail. Thus the third-person point of view, with unity of focus, is a major tool for presenting the reality of thought, observation, feeling—man's inner life.

Shift of focus means that events are reported as if seen first by one character and then by another. Here the author assumes omniscience—that is, full knowledge of what goes on in the mind and experience of each character. This method is useful for showing *the grounds of human difference*—the dramatic fact that events may not be understood or valued in the same way by different persons. Differences between people can be presented in other ways, of course, but a shift of focus often has special power in causing the reader to share the inner experience of contrasting characters. Though the focus in "A Sick Call" is mainly that of the mind of Father Macdowell, it does shift briefly to the mind of the young husband.

Author's comment is often used in third-person stories, and it is used in "A Sick Call" in one form. Early in the story, these words appear:

> He was a huge old priest, white-headed except for a shiny
> baby-pink bald spot on the top of his head . . . nothing
> seemed to shock or excite him or make him really angry,
> and he was even tender with those who thought they were
> most guilty.

This is the author speaking—describing, giving information directly. If the author describes things which can be known or seen also by some character in the story, the whole amounts to a kind of borderline point of view which could be the author's or the character's, or both. The final part of the author's comment just cited has another characteristic also. It is *summary narrative*, summarizing the priest's nature and actions over a period of time, months or years ("nothing seemed to shock or excite him . . .").

Author's comment of a second kind—more overt and noticeable—occurs when the author, in his own person, takes time out from the story to reflect, philosophize, or moralize. This device was much more popular in the nineteenth century—in the novels of Charles Dickens, for example—than it is now, and it does not occur in "A Sick Call."

The so-called *objective point of view* in fiction means that actions, events, speech, and so forth, are reported as if seen not by any character in the story but by an unnamed observer outside the story. Nothing is said of what goes on in the mind or feeling of any character. The unnamed observer is of course the author, who reports events much as he might see them acted out on a stage, or in the street. The author who uses this technique in its strictest form must rely on the behavior of the characters to suggest his central meanings, must never report their inner thoughts or feelings, and must avoid author's comment. If he uses the technique strictly, he must be especially careful with description—careful, that is, not to use "loaded" or connotative words. "Lift" is an example of fiction written in a relatively objective manner, for the reader of "Lift" must rely on what the characters say or do; he is not admitted into the mind of any character, and is given no outright author's comment as an aid. "Lift" is not completely objective in technique, however, because the description is heavily connotative at certain points, suggesting the author's attitudes. A pure and consistent objective technique is probably nonexistent in fiction.

It is important to realize that the term "objective point of view" as applied to fiction refers *only* to a particular way of telling a story. It does *not* mean that the author is trying to conceal his attitudes or be truly dispassionate, for value judgments are a major ingredient in fiction. Some authors—James Joyce, for example—have tried on occasion to be objective in attitude as well as in technique and have found it impossible, for judgments are revealed by the very materials selected for a story, if in no other way. The important point, for the reader, is that a relatively objective story, in the technical sense, is often a tool for conveying a sense of implacable, on-going, relentless process, as in many stories by Hemingway.

Obviously, the major points of view in story-telling that have been mentioned here are subject to adaptations and combinations by individual authors. A capable author will always adapt major techniques to his own purposes.

What we have been saying about point of view means simply that an author can communicate his meanings or attitudes in several ways, at several levels, ranging from the dramatic to the deliberately expository. The experienced reader notices the *way* a story is told and makes the most of it, realizing that each method has its own uses and limitations.

Discussion 2: diction; sentence structure and rhythm; paraphrases

Early in a story, a good reader will notice whether there is anything distinctive about the way the author uses his basic tool—words. In describing settings or characters, some authors rely heavily on the suggestive power of words, the connotations. The opening description of Father Macdowell is favorable description, connotative in some degree; but only "Two Soldiers," among the three stories in this introductory section, achieves dominant and ever-present tonal effects through language alone. The younger brother's talk is a prime source of reality and humor. In the main, neither the language in "A Sick Call" nor that in "Lift," in the English translation at least, produces special effects beyond the basic appropriateness to be expected in a good writer.

It is sometimes difficult, as indicated earlier, to distinguish between *what* is said and the *way* it is said, for the suggestive power of words is responsible for much meaning over and beyond literal statement. We can rewrite a statement or a descriptive detail—that is, paraphrase it—and though part of the original meaning remains in the paraphrase, something is usually missing. The "something" is very often the author's *attitude;* other qualities of feeling may disappear also when we paraphrase, and related ideas or feelings which the original would suggest are not suggested by the paraphrase. The more an author depends on the suggestiveness of words, the more difficult it is to make a paraphrase or to distinguish between what is said and the way it is said. Authors differ widely in this way, and they also differ in their use of sentence structure and rhythm, which are closely related to the heaviness or lightness of the language used. *Everything* in a good story contributes to the total effect. Summaries of whole stories or novels, or statements of "theme," deliver to the reader only the most crude and obvious of the author's meanings and often distort them.

Discussion 3: conflict; main character; title

A good reader can notice a few more things early in a story, obvious but sometimes overlooked. These can be indicated without explanation:

> What are the early signs of the conflict or human problem which will be the center of the story?

> Who seems to be the main character, or the chief carrier of meaning?

> Does the title of the story offer any clues to these matters?

There is really no substitute for early awareness of these things. With experience, no reader will need to lose time on them, for he will be using *technical* knowledge to speed understanding. If a story offers only meager clues at the beginning, the inexperienced reader will do well to control his natural impatience. We know that most commercial fiction makes sure of having a "man in motion" close to the beginning, to provide some appearance of action and to show who the main character is and what his problem is. If such elements are not present early in a story, the experienced reader will realize that the material which *is* being presented may be important later for full understanding, and he will wait with some patience. If he notices, at the same time, that words are being used with precision and skill, he will wait confidently.

Discussion 4: kinds of fiction; strategy for readers

Fiction includes stories as simple as Aesop's *Fables* and as complex as the novels of Joyce or Faulkner. In addition to learning to notice small things early, a reader always needs to recognize what general kind of fiction he is reading.

Most fiction is written in the realistic mode—*as if* the persons and events represent probable or possible "realities." We have seen that some fiction is based on particular social or historical events, with an almost perfect relationship between fiction and certain kinds of factual detail. But we have observed also that much fiction does not concern itself with "reality" of this type at all, and aims at a more universal significance. Some, as we have seen, employs nonrealistic elements in order to communicate meanings which apply to the real world. Such fiction, by its very tone and method, often seems close to the outright fable. So-called "science" fiction, which has not been discussed here, ordinarily uses strange settings or strange gadgets, genuine scientific information at some level—and human beings superficially portrayed. Science fiction, as a form, has yet to achieve in most instances the depth and complexity which are characteristic of more traditional forms, and its main appeals are to speculative curiosity, or to interest in gadgetry, new information, or occasional dramatization of social ideas and problems—again, at a rather elementary level. We have seen also that commercial fiction, such as the Western or the detective story, has its own characteristics, and there is no trouble in realizing that its main business is entertainment.

The broad categories or kinds of fiction that have just been named are quite easy to recognize. The most important distinction is probably that between the author who is frankly trying to entertain and the one who is using fictional methods seriously as a means of communicating matters that seem important to him. The serious writer can usually be recognized by his artistry: wording, sentence structure, interdependence of elements, clarity of emphasis, economy of means.

Knowing that a story is, in general, "realistic" or "nonrealistic," or that it is "commercial" or relatively "serious" in its intent is often useful in helping the reader to a correct set of expectations. But suppose the author is writing realistic satire—a story with seemingly "real" characters whom the author intends to laugh at, good-humoredly or bitterly? True, the author may use exaggeration to the point that we cannot miss his intention, or he may use overt author-comment with the same result. Many a satirist, however, in speaking or in writing, uses a deadpan manner. His attitude and intention may dawn on us slowly, but without this knowledge we cannot read him correctly.

What to do? A reader can usually secure one anchor, one fundamental clue, by noting *every* sign of the author's attitude toward events and especially toward characters. This point has been emphasized throughout the present discussion. The signs of an author's attitude are often small but cumulative. Once a general direction is apparent, it is possible to read with pleasure and understanding.

GROUP 1: FAR PLACES, BEFORE THE WARS

In the long story by Somerset Maugham and in the short novel by Joseph Conrad, the reader will find a symbolic record of places and human occupations and social groupings and attitudes as these existed in both "civilized" and "undeveloped" countries before the great wars of our century affected colonial structures. If our understanding of the present depends in any important way on an understanding of the immediate past, then these two works of fiction have a clear function as records of causality, psychological causality in particular. Beyond this semihistorical function, each of these works addresses itself to a basic and continuing concern of good fiction—the representation of human character in action. "Heart of Darkness," in addition to its representational function, is of particular interest because of its complex symbolic structure.

THE OUTSTATION

W. Somerset Maugham
(1874–   )

The new assistant arrived in the afternoon. When the Resident, Mr. Warburton, was told that the prahu was in sight he put on his solar topee and went down to the landing-stage. The guard, eight little Dyak soldiers, stood to attention as he passed. He noted with satisfaction that their bearing was martial, their uniforms neat and clean, and their guns shining. They were a credit to him. From the landing-stage he watched the bend of the river round which in a moment the boat would sweep. He looked very smart in his spotless ducks and white shoes. He held under his arm a gold-headed Malacca cane which had been given him by the Sultan of Perak. He awaited the newcomer with mingled feelings. There was more work in the district than one man could properly do, and during his periodical tours of the country under his charge it had been inconvenient to leave the station in the hands of a native clerk, but he had been so long the only white man there that he could not face the arrival of another without misgiving. He was accustomed to loneliness. During the war he had not seen an English face for three years; and once when he was instructed to put up an afforestation officer he was seized with panic, so that when the stranger was due to arrive, having arranged everything for his reception, he wrote a note telling him he was obliged to go up-river, and fled; he remained away till he was informed by a messenger that his guest had left.

Now the prahu appeared in the broad reach. It was manned by prisoners, Dyaks under various sentences, and a couple of warders were waiting on the landing-stage to take them back to jail. They were sturdy fellows, used to the river, and they rowed with a powerful stroke. As the boat reached the side a man got out from under the attap awning and stepped on shore. The guard presented arms.

"Here we are at last. By God, I'm as cramped as the devil. I've brought you your mail."

He spoke with exuberant joviality. Mr. Warburton politely held out his hand.

"Mr. Cooper, I presume?"

"That's right. Were you expecting any one else?"

The question had a facetious intent, but the Resident did not smile.

"My name is Warburton. I'll show you your quarters. They'll bring your kit along."

He preceded Cooper along the narrow pathway and they entered a compound in which stood a small bungalow.

"I've had it made as habitable as I could, but of course no one has lived in it for a good many years."

It was built on piles. It consisted of a long living-room which opened on to a broad verandah, and behind, on each side of a passage, were two bedrooms.

"This'll do me all right," said Cooper.

"I daresay you want to have a bath and a change. I shall be very much pleased if you'll dine with me to-night. Will eight o'clock suit you?"

"Any old time will do for me."

The Resident gave a polite, but slightly disconcerted, smile and withdrew. He returned to the Fort where his own residence was. The impression which Allen Cooper had given him was not very favourable, but he was a fair man, and he knew that it was unjust to form an opinion on so brief a glimpse. Cooper seemed to be about thirty. He was a tall, thin fellow, with a sallow face in which there was not a spot of colour. It was a face all in one tone. He had a large, hooked nose and blue eyes. When entering the bungalow, he had taken off his topee and flung it to a waiting boy, Mr. Warburton noticed that his large skull, covered with short, brown hair, contrasted somewhat oddly with a weak, small chin. He was dressed in khaki shorts and a khaki shirt, but they were shabby and soiled; and his battered topee had not been cleaned for days. Mr. Warburton reflected that the young man had spent a week on a coasting steamer and had passed the last forty-eight hours lying in the bottom of a prahu.

"We'll see what he looks like when he comes in to dinner."

He went into his room where his things were as neatly laid out as if he had an English valet, undressed, and, walking down the stairs to the bath-house, sluiced himself with cool water. The only concession he made to the climate was to wear a white dinner-jacket; but otherwise, in a boiled shirt and a high collar, silk socks and patent-leather shoes, he dressed as formally as though he were dining at his club in Pall Mall. A careful host, he went into the dining-room to see that the table was properly laid. It was gay with orchids and the silver shone brightly. The napkins were folded into elaborate shapes. Shaded candles in silver candlesticks shed a soft light. Mr. Warburton smiled his approval and returned to the sitting-room to await his guest. Presently he appeared. Cooper was wearing the khaki shorts, the khaki shirt, and the ragged jacket in which he had landed. Mr. Warburton's smile of greeting froze on his face.

"Hulloa, you're all dressed up," said Cooper. "I didn't know you were going to do that. I very nearly put on a sarong."

"It doesn't matter at all. I daresay your boys were busy."

"You needn't have bothered to dress on my account, you know."

"I didn't. I always dress for dinner."

"Even when you're alone?"

"Especially when I'm alone," replied Mr. Warburton, with a frigid stare.

He saw a twinkle of amusement in Cooper's eyes, and he flushed an angry red. Mr. Warburton was a hot-tempered man; you might have guessed that from his red face with its pugnacious features and from his red hair, now growing white; his blue eyes, cold as a rule and observing, could flush with sudden wrath; but he was a man of the world and he hoped a just one. He must do his best to get on with this fellow.

"When I lived in London I moved in circles in which it would have been just as eccentric not to dress for dinner every night as not to have a bath every morning. When I came to Borneo I saw no reason to discontinue so good a habit. For three years, during the war, I never saw a white man. I never omitted to dress on a single occasion on which I was well enough to come in to dinner. You have not been very long in this country; believe me, there is no better way to maintain the proper pride which you should have in yourself. When a white man surrenders in the slightest degree to the influences that surround him he very soon loses his self-respect, and when he loses his self-respect you may be quite sure that the natives will soon cease to respect him."

"Well, if you expect me to put on a boiled shirt and a stiff collar in this heat I'm afraid you'll be disappointed."

"When you are dining in your own bungalow you will, of course, dress as you think fit, but when you do me the pleasure of dining with me, perhaps you will come to the conclusion that it is only polite to wear the costume usual in civilized society."

Two Malay boys, in sarongs and songkoks, with smart white coats and brass buttons, came in, one bearing gin pahits, and the other a tray on which were olives and anchovies. Then they went in to dinner. Mr. Warburton flattered himself that he had the best cook, a Chinese, in Borneo, and he took great trouble to have as good food as in the difficult circumstances was possible. He exercised much ingenuity in making the best of his materials.

"Would you care to look at the menu?" he said, handing it to Cooper.

It was written in French and the dishes had resounding names. They were waited on by the two boys. In opposite corners of the room two more waved immense fans, and so gave movement to the sultry air. The fare was sumptuous and the champagne excellent.

"Do you do yourself like this every day?" said Cooper.

Mr. Warburton gave the menu a careless glance.

"I have not noticed that the dinner is any different from usual," he said. "I eat very little myself, but I make a point of having a proper dinner served to me every night. It keeps the cook in practice and it's good discipline for the boys."

The conversation proceeded with effort. Mr. Warburton was elaborately courteous, and it may be that he found a slightly malicious amusement in the embarrassment which he thereby occasioned in his companion. Cooper had not been more than a

few months in Sembulu, and Mr. Warburton's enquiries about friends of his in Kuala Solor were soon exhausted.

"By the way," he said presently, "did you meet a lad called Hennerley? He's come out recently, I believe."

"Oh, yes, he's in the police. A rotten bounder."

"I should hardly have expected him to be that. His uncle is my friend Lord Barraclough. I had a letter from Lady Barraclough only the other day asking me to look out for him."

"I heard he was related to somebody or other. I suppose that's how he got the job. He's been to Eton and Oxford and he doesn't forget to let you know it."

"You surprise me," said Mr. Warburton. "All his family have been at Eton and Oxford for a couple of hundred years. I should have expected him to take it as a matter of course."

"I thought him a damned prig."

"To what school did you go?"

"I was born in Barbadoes. I was educated there."

"Oh, I see."

Mr. Warburton managed to put so much offensiveness into his brief reply that Cooper flushed. For a moment he was silent.

"I've had two or three letters from Kuala Solor," continued Mr. Warburton, "and my impression was that young Hennerley was a great success. They say he's a first-rate sportsman."

"Oh, yes, he's very popular. He's just the sort of fellow they would like in K.S. I haven't got much use for the first-rate sportsman myself. What does it amount to in the long run that a man can play golf and tennis better than other people? And who cares if he can make a break of seventy-five at billiards? They attach a damned sight too much importance to that sort of thing in England."

"Do you think so? I was under the impression that the first-rate sportsman had come out of the war certainly no worse than any one else."

"Oh, if you're going to talk of the war then I do know what I'm talking about. I was in the same regiment as Hennerley and I can tell you that the men couldn't stick him at any price."

"How do you know?"

"Because I was one of the men."

"Oh, you hadn't got a commission."

"A fat chance I had of getting a commission. I was what was called a Colonial. I hadn't been to a public school and I had no influence. I was in the ranks the whole damned time."

Cooper frowned. He seemed to have difficulty in preventing himself from breaking into violent invective. Mr. Warburton watched him, his little blue eyes narrowed, watched him and formed his opinion. Changing the conversation, he began to speak to Cooper about the work that would be required of him, and as the clock struck ten he rose.

"Well, I won't keep you any more. I daresay you're tired by your journey."

They shook hands.

"Oh, I say, look here," said Cooper, "I wonder if you can find me a boy. The boy I had before never turned up when I was starting from K.S. He took my kit on board and all that and then disappeared. I didn't know he wasn't there till we were out of the river."

"I'll ask my head-boy. I have no doubt he can find you some one."

"All right. Just tell him to send the boy along and if I like the look of him I'll take him."

There was a moon, so that no lantern was needed. Cooper walked across from the Fort to his bungalow.

"I wonder why on earth they've sent me a fellow like that?" reflected Mr. Warburton. "If that's the kind of man they're going to get out now I don't think much of it."

He strolled down his garden. The Fort was built on the top of a little hill and the garden ran down to the river's edge; on the bank was an arbour, and hither it was his habit to come after dinner to smoke a cheroot. And often from the river that flowed below him a voice was heard, the voice of some Malay too timorous to venture into the light of day, and a complaint or an accusation was softly wafted to his ears, a piece of information

was whispered to him or a useful hint, which otherwise would never have come into his official ken. He threw himself heavily into a long rattan chair. Cooper! An envious, ill-bred fellow, bumptious, self-assertive and vain. But Mr. Warburton's irritation could not withstand the silent beauty of the night. The air was scented with the sweet-smelling flowers of a tree that grew at the entrance to the arbour, and the fireflies, sparkling dimly, flew with their slow and silvery flight. The moon made a pathway on the broad river for the light feet of Siva's bride, and on the further bank a row of palm trees was delicately silhouetted against the sky. Peace stole into the soul of Mr. Warburton.

He was a queer creature and he had had a singular career. At the age of twenty-one he had inherited a considerable fortune, a hundred thousand pounds, and when he left Oxford he threw himself into the gay life which in those days (now Mr. Warburton was a man of four and fifty) offered itself to the young man of good family. He had his flat in Mount Street, his private hansom, and his hunting-box in Warwickshire. He went to all the places where the fashionable congregate. He was handsome, amusing and generous. He was a figure in the society of London in the early nineties, and society then had not lost its exclusiveness nor its brilliance. The Boer War which shook it was unthought of; the Great War which destroyed it was prophesied only by the pessimists. It was no unpleasant thing to be a rich young man in those days, and Mr. Warburton's chimney-piece during the season was packed with cards for one great function after another. Mr. Warburton displayed them with complacency. For Mr. Warburton was a snob. He was not a timid snob, a little ashamed of being impressed by his betters, nor a snob who sought the intimacy of persons who had acquired celebrity in politics or notoriety in the arts, nor the snob who was dazzled by riches; he was the naked, unadulterated common snob who dearly loved a lord. He was touchy and quick-tempered, but he would much rather have been snubbed by a person of quality than flattered by a commoner. His name figured insignificantly in Burke's Peerage, and it was marvellous to watch the ingenuity he used to mention his distant relationship to the noble family he belonged to; but never a word did he say of the honest Liverpool manufacturer from whom, through his mother, a Miss Gubbins, he had come by his fortune. It was the terror of his fashionable life that at Cowes, maybe, or at Ascot, when he was with a duchess or even with a prince of the blood, one of these relatives would claim acquaintance with him.

His failing was too obvious not soon to become notorious, but its extravagance saved it from being merely despicable. The great whom he adored laughed at him, but in their hearts felt his adoration not unnatural. Poor Warburton was a dreadful snob, of course, but after all he was a good fellow. He was always ready to back a bill for an impecunious nobleman, and if you were in a tight corner you could safely count on him for a hundred pounds. He gave good dinners. He played whist badly, but never minded how much he lost if the company was select. He happened to be a gambler, an unlucky one, but he was a good loser, and it was impossible not to admire the coolness with which he lost five hundred pounds at a sitting. His passion for cards, almost as strong as his passion for titles, was the cause of his undoing. The life he led was expensive and his gambling losses were formidable. He began to plunge more heavily, first on horses, and then on the Stock Exchange. He had a certain simplicity of character and the unscrupulous found him an ingenuous prey. I do not know if he ever realized that his smart friends laughed at him behind his back, but I think he had an obscure instinct that he could not afford to appear other than careless of his money. He got into the hands of moneylenders. At the age of thirty-four he was ruined.

He was too much imbued with the spirit of his class to hesitate in the choice of his next step. When a man in his set had run through his money he went out to the colonies. No one heard Mr. Warburton repine. He made no complaint because a noble friend had advised a disastrous speculation, he pressed nobody to whom he had lent money to repay it, he paid his debts (if he had only known it, the despised blood of the Liverpool manufacturer came out in him there), sought help from no one, and, never having done a stroke of work in his life, looked for a means of livelihood. He remained cheerful, unconcerned and full of humour. He had no wish to make any one with whom he happened to be uncomfortable by the recital of his misfortune. Mr. Warburton was a snob, but he was also a gentleman.

The only favour he asked of any of the great friends in whose daily company he had lived for years was a recommendation. The able man who was at that time Sultan of Sembulu took him into his service. The night before he sailed he dined for the last time at his club.

"I hear you're going away, Warburton," the old Duke of Hereford said to him.

"Yes, I'm going to Borneo."

"Good God, what are you going there for?"

"Oh, I'm broke."

"Are you? I'm sorry. Well, let us know when you come back. I hope you have a good time."

"Oh, yes. Lots of shooting, you know."

The Duke nodded and passed on. A few hours later Mr. Warburton watched the coast of England recede into the mist, and he left behind everything which to him made life worth living.

Twenty years had passed since then. He kept up a busy correspondence with various great ladies and his letters were amusing and chatty. He never lost his love for titled persons and paid careful attention to the announcements in The Times (which reached him six weeks after publication) of their comings and goings. He perused the column which records births, deaths, and marriages, and he was always ready with his letter of congratulation or condolence. The illustrated papers told him how people looked and on his periodical visits to England, able to take up the threads as though they had never been broken, he knew all about any new person who might have appeared on the social surface. His interest in the world of fashion was as vivid as when himself had been a figure in it. It still seemed to him the only thing that mattered.

But insensibly another interest had entered into his life. The position he found himself in flattered his vanity; he was no longer the sycophant craving the smiles of the great, he was the master whose word was law. He was gratified by the guard of Dyak soldiers who presented arms as he passed. He liked to sit in judgment on his fellow men. It pleased him to compose quarrels between rival chiefs. When the head-hunters were troublesome in the old days he set out to chastise them with a thrill of pride in his own behaviour. He was too vain not to be of dauntless courage, and a pretty story was told of his coolness in adventuring single-handed into a stockaded village and demanding the surrender of a bloodthirsty pirate. He became a skillful administrator. He was strict, just and honest.

And little by little he conceived a deep love for the Malays. He interested himself in their habits and customs. He was never tired of listening to their talk. He admired their virtues, and with a smile and a shrug of the shoulders condoned their vices.

"In my day," he would say, "I have been on intimate terms with some of the greatest gentlemen in England, but I have never known finer gentlemen than some well-born Malays whom I am proud to call my friends."

He liked their courtesy and their distinguished manners, their gentleness and their sudden passions. He knew by instinct exactly how to treat them. He had a genuine tenderness for them. But he never forgot that he was an English gentleman and he had no patience with the white men who yielded to native customs. He made no surrenders. And he did not imitate so many of the white men in taking a native woman to wife, for an intrigue of this nature, however sanctified by custom, seemed to him not only shocking but undignified. A man who had been called

George by Albert Edward, Prince of Wales, could hardly be expected to have any connection with a native. And when he returned to Borneo from his visits to England it was now with something like relief. His friends, like himself, were no longer young, and there was a new generation which looked upon him as a tiresome old man. It seemed to him that the England of to-day had lost a good deal of what he had loved in the England of his youth. But Borneo remained the same. It was home to him now. He meant to remain in the service as long as was possible, and the hope in his heart was that he would die before at last he was forced to retire. He had stated in his will that wherever he died he wished his body to be brought back to Sembulu and buried among the people he loved within sound of the softly flowing river.

But these emotions he kept hidden from the eyes of men; and no one, seeing this spruce, stout, well-set-up man, with his clean-shaven strong face and his whitening hair, would have dreamed that he cherished so profound a sentiment.

He knew how the work of the station should be done, and during the next few days he kept a suspicious eye on his assistant. He saw very soon that he was painstaking and competent. The only fault he had to find with him was that he was brusque with the natives.

"The Malays are shy and very sensitive," he said to him. "I think you will find that you will get much better results if you take care always to be polite, patient and kindly."

Cooper gave a short, grating laugh.

"I was born in Barbadoes and I was in Africa in the war. I don't think there's much about niggers that I don't know."

"I know nothing," said Mr. Warburton acidly. "But we were not talking of them. We were talking of Malays."

"Aren't they niggers?"

"You are very ignorant," replied Mr. Warburton.

He said no more.

On the first Sunday after Cooper's arrival

he asked him to dinner. He did everything ceremoniously, and though they had met on the previous day in the office and later, on the Fort verandah where they drank a gin and bitters together at six o'clock, he sent a polite note across to the bungalow by a boy. Cooper, however unwillingly, came in evening dress and Mr. Warburton, though gratified that his wish was respected, noticed with disdain that the young man's clothes were badly cut and his shirt ill-fitting. But Mr. Warburton was in a good temper that evening.

"By the way," he said to him, as he shook hands, "I've talked to my head-boy about finding you some one and he recommends his nephew. I've seen him and he seems a bright and willing lad. Would you like to see him?"

"I don't mind."

"He's waiting now."

Mr. Warburton called his boy and told him to send for his nephew. In a moment a tall, slender youth of twenty appeared. He had large dark eyes and a good profile. He was very neat in his sarong, a little white coat, and a fez, without a tassel, of plum-coloured velvet. He answered to the name of Abas. Mr. Warburton looked on him with approval, and his manner insensibly softened as he spoke to him in fluent and idiomatic Malay. He was inclined to be sarcastic with white people, but with the Malays he had a happy mixture of condescension and kindliness. He stood in the place of the Sultan. He knew perfectly how to preserve his own dignity, and at the same time put a native at his ease.

"Will he do?" said Mr. Warburton, turning to Cooper.

"Yes, I daresay he's no more of a scoundrel than any of the rest of them."

Mr. Warburton informed the boy that he was engaged and dismissed him.

"You're very lucky to get a boy like that," he told Cooper. "He belongs to a very good family. They came over from Malacca nearly a hundred years ago."

"I don't much mind if the boy who cleans my shoes and brings me a drink when I want it has blue blood in his veins or not. All I ask is that he should do what I tell him and look sharp about it."

Mr. Warburton pursed his lips, but made no reply.

They went in to dinner. It was excellent, and the wine was good. Its influence presently had its effect on them and they talked not only without acrimony, but even with friendliness. Mr. Warburton liked to do himself well, and on Sunday night he made it a habit to do himself even a little better than usual. He began to think he was unfair to Cooper. Of course he was not a gentleman, but that was not his fault, and when you got to know him it might be that he would turn out a very good fellow. His faults, perhaps, were faults of manner. And he was certainly good at his work, quick, conscientious and thorough. When they reached the dessert Mr. Warburton was feeling kindly disposed towards all mankind.

"This is your first Sunday and I'm going to give you a very special glass of port. I've only got about two dozen of it left and I keep it for special occasions."

He gave his boy instructions and presently the bottle was brought. Mr. Warburton watched the boy open it.

"I got this port from my old friend Charles Hollington. He'd had it for forty years and I've had it for a good many. He was well known to have the best cellar in England."

"Is he a wine merchant?"

"Not exactly," smiled Mr. Warburton. "I was speaking of Lord Hollington of Castle Reagh. He's one of the richest peers in England. A very old friend of mine. I was at Eton with his brother."

This was an opportunity that Mr. Warburton could never resist and he told a little anecdote of which the only point seemed to be that he knew an earl. The port was certainly very good; he drank a glass and then a second. He lost all caution. He had not talked to a white man for months. He began to tell stories. He showed himself in the company of the great. Hearing him you would have thought that at one time ministries were formed and policies decided on his suggestion whispered into the ear of a duchess or thrown over the dinner-table to be gratefully acted on by the confidential adviser of the sovereign. The old days at Ascot, Goodwood and Cowes lived again for him. Another glass of port. There were the great house-parties in Yorkshire and in Scotland to which he went every year.

"I had a man called Foreman then, the best valet I ever had, and why do you think he gave me notice? You know in the House-keeper's Room the ladies' maids and the gentlemen's gentlemen sit according to the precedence of their masters. He told me he was sick of going to party after party at which I was the only commoner. It meant that he always had to sit at the bottom of the table and all the best bits were taken before a dish reached him. I told the story to the old Duke of Hereford and he roared. 'By God, sir,' he said, 'if I were King of England I'd make you a viscount just to give your man a chance.' 'Take him yourself, Duke,' I said. 'He's the best valet I've ever had.' 'Well, Warburton,' he said, 'if he's good enough for you he's good enough for me. Send him along.'"

Then there was Monte Carlo where Mr. Warburton and the Grand Duke Fyodor, playing in partnership, had broken the bank one evening; and there was Marienbad. At Marienbad Mr. Warburton had played bac-carat with Edward VII.

"He was only Prince of Wales then, of course. I remember him saying to me, 'George, if you draw on a five you'll lose your shirt.' He was right; I don't think he ever said a truer word in his life. He was a wonderful man. I always said he was the greatest diplomatist in Europe. But I was a young fool in those days, I hadn't the sense to take his advice. If I had, if I'd never drawn on a five, I daresay I shouldn't be here to-day."

Cooper was watching him. His blue eyes, deep in their sockets, were hard and super-cilious, and on his lips was a mocking smile. He had heard a good deal about Mr. War-burton in Kuala Solor. Not a bad sort, and he

ran his district like clockwork, they said, but by heaven, what a snob! They laughed at him good-naturedly, for it was impossible to dis-like a man who was so generous and so kindly, and Cooper had already heard the story of the Prince of Wales and the game of baccarat. But Cooper listened without in-dulgence. From the beginning he had re-sented the Resident's manner. He was very sensitive and he writhed under Mr. War-burton's polite sarcasms. Mr. Warburton had a knack of receiving a remark of which he disapproved with a devastating silence. Cooper had lived little in England and he had a peculiar dislike of the English. He resented especially the public-school boy since he always feared that he was going to patronize him. He was so much afraid of others putting on airs with him that, in order as it were to get in first, he put on such airs as to make every one think him insufferably conceited.

"Well, at all events the war has done one good thing for us," he said at last. "It's smashed up the power of the aristocracy. The Boer War started it, and 1914 put the lid on."

"The great families of England are doomed," said Mr. Warburton with the com-placent melancholy of an *émigré* who re-membered the court of Louis XV. "They can-not afford any longer to live in their splendid palaces and their princely hospitality will soon be nothing but a memory."

"And a damned good job too in my opin-ion."

"My poor Cooper, what can you know of the glory that was Greece and the grandeur that was Rome?"

Mr. Warburton made an ample gesture. His eyes for an instant grew dreamy with a vision of the past.

"Well, believe me, we're fed up with all that rot. What we want is a business govern-ment by business men. I was born in a Crown Colony and I've lived practically all my life in the colonies. I don't give a row of pins for a lord. What's wrong with England is snob-bishness. And if there's anything that gets my goat it's a snob."

A snob! Mr. Warburton's face grew purple and his eyes blazed with anger. That was a word that had pursued him all his life. The great ladies whose society he had enjoyed in his youth were not inclined to look upon his appreciation of themselves as unworthy, but even great ladies are sometimes out of temper and more than once Mr. Warburton had had the dreadful word flung in his teeth. He knew, he could not help knowing, that there were odious people who called him a snob. How unfair it was! Why, there was no vice he found so detestable as snobbishness. After all, he liked to mix with people of his own class, he was only at home in their company, and how in heaven's name could any one say that was snobbish? Birds of a feather.

"I quite agree with you," he answered. "A snob is a man who admires or despises another because he is of a higher social rank than his own. It is the most vulgar failing of our English middle class."

He saw a flicker of amusement in Cooper's eyes. Cooper put up his hand to hide the broad smile that rose to his lips, and so made it more noticeable. Mr. Warburton's hands trembled a little.

Probably Cooper never knew how greatly he had offended his chief. A sensitive man himself he was strangely insensitive to the feelings of others.

Their work forced them to see one another for a few minutes now and then during the day, and they met at six to have a drink on Mr. Warburton's verandah. This was an old-established custom of the country which Mr. Warburton would not for the world have broken. But they ate their meals separately, Cooper in his bungalow and Mr. Warburton at the Fort. After the office work was over they walked till dusk fell, but they walked apart. There were but few paths in this country, where the jungle pressed close upon the plantations of the village, and when Mr. Warburton caught sight of his assistant passing along with his loose stride, he would make a circuit in order to avoid him. Cooper, with his bad manners, his conceit in his own judgment and his intolerance, had already got on his nerves; but it was not

till Cooper had been on the station for a couple of months that an incident happened which turned the Resident's dislike into bitter hatred.

Mr. Warburton was obliged to go up-country on a tour of inspection, and he left the station in Cooper's charge with more confidence, since he had definitely come to the conclusion that he was a capable fellow. The only thing he did not like was that he had no indulgence. He was honest, just and painstaking, but he had no sympathy for the natives. It bitterly amused Mr. Warburton to observe that this man, who looked upon himself as every man's equal, should look upon so many men as his own inferiors. He was hard, he had no patience with the native mind, and he was a bully. Mr. Warburton very quickly realized that the Malays disliked and feared him. He was not altogether displeased. He would not have liked it very much if his assistant had enjoyed a popularity which might rival his own. Mr. Warburton made his elaborate preparations, set out on his expedition, and in three weeks returned. Meanwhile the mail had arrived. The first thing that struck his eyes when he entered his sitting-room was a great pile of open newspapers. Cooper had met him, and they went into the room together. Mr. Warburton turned to one of the servants who had been left behind and sternly asked him what was the meaning of those open papers. Cooper hastened to explain.

"I wanted to read all about the Wolverhampton murder and so I borrowed your Times. I brought them back again. I knew you wouldn't mind."

Mr. Warburton turned on him, white with anger.

"But I do mind. I mind very much."

"I'm sorry," said Cooper, with composure. "The fact is, I simply couldn't wait till you came back."

"I wonder you didn't open my letters as well."

Cooper, unmoved, smiled at his chief's exasperation.

"Oh, that's not quite the same thing. After all, I couldn't imagine you'd mind my looking at your newspapers. There's nothing private in them."

"I very much object to any one reading my paper before me." He went up to the pile. There were nearly thirty numbers there. "I think it extremely impertinent of you. They're all mixed up."

"We can easily put them in order," said Cooper, joining him at the table.

"Don't touch them," cried Mr. Warburton.

"I say, it's childish to make a scene about a little thing like that."

"How dare you speak to me like that?"

"Oh, go to hell," said Cooper, and he flung out of the room.

Mr. Warburton, trembling with passion, was left contemplating his papers. His greatest pleasure in life had been destroyed by those callous, brutal hands. Most people living in out-of-the-way places when the mail comes tear open impatiently their papers and taking the last ones first glance at the latest news from home. Not so Mr. Warburton. His newsagent had instructions to write on the outside of the wrapper the date of each paper he despatched and when the great bundle arrived Mr. Warburton looked at these dates and with his blue pencil numbered them. His head-boy's orders were to place one on the table every morning in the verandah with the early cup of tea, and it was Mr. Warburton's especial delight to break the wrapper as he sipped his tea, and read the morning paper. It gave him the illusion of living at home. Every Monday morning he read the Monday Times of six weeks back and so went through the week. On Sunday he read The Observer. Like his habit of dressing for dinner it was a tie to civilization. And it was his pride that no matter how exciting the news was he had never yielded to the temptation of opening a paper before its allotted time. During the war the suspense sometimes had been intolerable, and when he read one day that a push was begun he had undergone agonies of suspense which he might have saved himself by the simple expedient of opening a later paper which lay waiting for him on a shelf. It had been the severest

trial to which he had ever exposed himself, but he victoriously surmounted it. And that clumsy fool had broken open those neat tight packages because he wanted to know whether some horrid woman had murdered her odious husband.

Mr. Warburton sent for his boy and told him to bring wrappers. He folded up the papers as neatly as he could, placed a wrapper round each and numbered it. But it was a melancholy task.

"I shall never forgive him," he said. "Never."

Of course his boy had been with him on his expedition; he never travelled without him, for his boy knew exactly how he liked things, and Mr. Warburton was not the kind of jungle traveller who was prepared to dispense with his comforts; but in the interval since their arrival he had been gossiping in the servants' quarters. He had learnt that Cooper had had trouble with his boys. All but the youth Abas had left him. Abas had desired to go too, but his uncle had placed him there on the instructions of the Resident, and he was afraid to leave without his uncle's permission.

"I told him he had done well, Tuan," said the boy. "But he is unhappy. He says it is not a good house and he wishes to know if he may go as the others have gone."

"No, he must stay. The tuan must have servants. Have those who went been replaced?"

"No, Tuan, no one will go."

Mr. Warburton frowned. Cooper was an insolent fool, but he had an official position and must be suitably provided with servants. It was seemly that his house should be improperly conducted.

"Where are the boys who ran away?"

"They are in the kampong, Tuan."

"Go and see them to-night and tell them that I expect them to be back at Tuan Cooper's house at dawn tomorrow."

"They say they will not go, Tuan."

"On my order?"

The boy had been with Mr. Warburton for fifteen years, and he knew every intonation of his master's voice. He was not afraid of him, they had gone through too much together, once in the jungle the Resident had saved his life and once, upset in some rapids, but for him the Resident would have been drowned; but he knew when the Resident must be obeyed without question.

"I will go to the kampong," he said.

Mr. Warburton expected that his subordinate would take the first opportunity to apologize for his rudeness, but Cooper had the ill-bred man's inability to express regret; and when they met next morning in the office he ignored the incident. Since Mr. Warburton had been away for three weeks it was necessary for them to have a somewhat prolonged interview. At the end of it Mr. Warburton dismissed him.

"I don't think there's anything else, thank you." Cooper turned to go, but Mr. Warburton stopped him. "I understand you've been having some trouble with your boys."

Cooper gave a harsh laugh.

"They tried to blackmail me. They had the damned cheek to run away, all except that incompetent fellow Abas—he knew when he was well off—but I just sat tight. They've all come to heel again."

"What do you mean by that?"

"This morning they were all back on their jobs, the Chinese cook and all. There they were, as cool as cucumbers; you would have thought they owned the place. I suppose they'd come to the conclusion that I wasn't such a fool as I looked."

"By no means. They came back on my express order."

Cooper flushed slightly.

"I should be obliged if you wouldn't interfere with my private concerns."

"They're not your private concerns. When your servants run away it makes you ridiculous. You are perfectly free to make a fool of yourself, but I cannot allow you to be made a fool of. It is unseemly that your house should not be properly staffed. As soon as I heard that your boys had left you, I had them told to be back in their place at dawn. That'll do."

Mr. Warburton nodded to signify that the interview was at an end. Cooper took no notice.

"Shall I tell you what I did? I called them and gave the whole bally lot the sack. I gave them ten minutes to get out of the compound."

Mr. Warburton shrugged his shoulders.

"What makes you think you can get others?"

"I've told my own clerk to see about it."

Mr. Warburton reflected for a moment.

"I think you behaved very foolishly. You will do well to remember in future that good masters make good servants."

"Is there anything else you want to teach me?"

"I should like to teach you manners, but it would be an arduous task, and I have not the time to waste. I will see that you get boys."

"Please don't put yourself to any trouble on my account. I'm quite capable of getting them for myself."

Mr. Warburton smiled acidly. He had an inkling that Cooper disliked him as much as he disliked Cooper, and he knew that nothing is more galling than to be forced to accept the favours of a man you detest.

"Allow me to tell you that you have no more chance of getting Malay or Chinese servants here now than you have of getting an English butler or a French chef. No one will come to you except on an order from me. Would you like me to give it?"

"No."

"As you please. Good morning."

Mr. Warburton watched the development of the situation with acrid humour. Cooper's clerk was unable to persuade Malay, Dyak or Chinese to enter the house of such a master. Abas, the boy who remained faithful to him, knew how to cook only native food, and Cooper, a coarse feeder, found his gorge rise against the everlasting rice. There was no water-carrier, and in that great heat he needed several baths a day. He cursed Abas, but Abas opposed him with sullen resistance and would not do more than he chose. It was galling to know that the lad stayed with him only because the Resident insisted. This went on for a fortnight and then, one morning, he found in his house the very servants whom he had previously dismissed. He fell into a violent rage, but he had learnt a little sense, and this time, without a word, he let them stay. He swallowed his humiliation, but the impatient contempt he had felt for Mr. Warburton's idiosyncrasies changed into a sullen hatred; the Resident with this malicious stroke had made him the laughing-stock of all the natives.

The two men now held no communication with one another. They broke the time-honoured custom of sharing, notwithstanding personal dislike, a drink at six o'clock with any white man who happened to be at the station. Each lived in his own house as though the other did not exist. Now that Cooper had fallen into the work, it was necessary for them to have little to do with one another in the office. Mr. Warburton used his orderly to send any message he had to give his assistant, and his instructions he sent by formal letter. They saw one another constantly, that was inevitable, but did not exchange half a dozen words in a week. The fact that they could not avoid catching sight of one another got on their nerves. They brooded over their antagonism and Mr. Warburton, taking his daily walk, could think of nothing but how much he detested his assistant.

And the dreadful thing was that in all probability they would remain thus, facing each other in deadly enmity, till Mr. Warburton went on leave. It might be three years. He had no reason to send in a complaint to headquarters: Cooper did his work very well, and at that time men were hard to get. True, vague complaints reached him and hints that the natives found Cooper harsh. There was certainly a feeling of dissatisfaction among them. But when Mr. Warburton looked into specific cases, all he could say was that Cooper had shown severity where mildness would not have been misplaced and had been unfeeling when himself would have been sympathetic. He had done nothing for which he could be taken to task. But Mr. Warburton watched him. Hatred will often

make a man clear-sighted, and he had a suspicion that Cooper was using the natives without consideration, yet keeping within the law, because he felt that thus he could exasperate his chief. One day perhaps he would go too far. None knew better than Mr. Warburton how irritable the incessant heat could make a man and how difficult it was to keep one's self-control after a sleepless night. He smiled softly to himself. Sooner or later Cooper would deliver himself into his hand.

When at last the opportunity came Mr. Warburton laughed aloud. Cooper had charge of the prisoners; they made roads, built sheds, rowed when it was necessary to send the prahu up- or down-stream, kept the town clean and otherwise usefully employed themselves. If well-behaved they even on occasion served as house-boys. Cooper kept them hard at it. He liked to see them work. He took pleasure in devising tasks for them; and seeing quickly enough that they were being made to do useless things the prisoners worked badly. He punished them by lengthening their hours. This was contrary to the regulations, and as soon as it was brought to the attention of Mr. Warburton, without referring the matter back to his subordinate, he gave instructions that the old hours should be kept; Cooper, going out for his walk, was astounded to see the prisoners strolling back to the jail; he had given instructions that they were not to knock off till dusk. When he asked the warder in charge why they had left off work he was told that it was the Resident's bidding.

White with rage he strode to the Fort. Mr. Warburton, in his spotless white ducks and his neat topee, with a walking-stick in his hand, followed by his dogs, was on the point of starting out on his afternoon stroll. He had watched Cooper go and knew that he had taken the road by the river. Cooper jumped up the steps and went straight up to the Resident.

"I want to know what the hell you mean by countermanding my order that the prisoners were to work till six," he burst out, beside himself with fury.

Mr. Warburton opened his cold blue eyes very wide and assumed an expression of great surprise.

"Are you out of your mind? Are you so ignorant that you do not know that that is not the way to speak to your official superior?"

"Oh go to hell. The prisoners are my pidgin and you've got no right to interfere. You mind your business and I'll mind mine. I want to know what the devil you mean by making a damned fool of me. Every one in the place will know that you've countermanded my order."

Mr. Warburton kept very cool.

"You had no power to give the order you did. I countermanded it because it was harsh and tyrannical. Believe me, I have not made half such a damned fool of you as you have made of yourself."

"You disliked me from the first moment I came here. You've done everything you could to make the place impossible for me because I wouldn't lick your boots for you. You got your knife into me because I wouldn't flatter you."

Cooper, spluttering with rage, was nearing dangerous ground, and Mr. Warburton's eyes grew on a sudden colder and more piercing.

"You are wrong. I thought you were a cad, but I was perfectly satisfied with the way you did your work."

"You snob. You damned snob. You thought me a cad because I hadn't been to Eton. Oh, they told me in K.S. what to expect. Why, don't you know that you're the laughing-stock of the whole country? I could hardly help bursting into a roar of laughter when you told your celebrated story about the Prince of Wales. My God, how they shouted at the club when they told it. By God, I'd rather be the cad I am than the snob you are."

He got Mr. Warburton on the raw.

"If you don't get out of my house this minute I shall knock you down," he cried.

The other came a little closer to him and put his face in his.

"Touch me, touch me," he said. "By God, I'd like to see you hit me. Do you want me to say it again? Snob. Snob."

Cooper was three inches taller than Mr. Warburton, a strong, muscular young man. Mr. Warburton was fat and fifty-four. His clenched fist shot out. Cooper caught him by the arm and pushed him back.

"Don't be a damned fool. Remember I'm not a gentleman, I know how to use my hands."

He gave a sort of hoot, and, grinning all over his pale, sharp face, jumped down the verandah steps. Mr. Warburton, his heart in his anger pounding against his ribs, sank exhausted into a chair. His body tingled as though he had prickly heat. For one horrible moment he thought he was going to cry. But suddenly he was conscious that his head-boy was on the verandah and instinctively regained control of himself. The boy came forward and filled him a glass of whisky and soda. Without a word Mr. Warburton took it and drank it to the dregs.

"What do you want to say to me?" asked Mr. Warburton, trying to force a smile on to his strained lips.

"Tuan, the assistant tuan is a bad man. Abas wishes again to leave him."

"Let him wait a little. I shall write to Kuala Solor and ask that Tuan Cooper should go elsewhere."

"Tuan Cooper is not good with the Malays."

"Leave me."

The boy silently withdrew. Mr. Warburton was left alone with his thoughts. He saw the club at Kuala Solor, the men sitting round the table in the window in their flannels, when the night had driven them in from golf and tennis, drinking whiskies and gin pahits and laughing when they told the celebrated story of the Prince of Wales and himself at Marienbad. He was hot with shame and misery. A snob! They all thought him a snob. And he had always thought them very good fellows, he had always been gentleman enough to let it make no difference to him that they were of very second-rate position. He hated them now. But his hatred for them was nothing compared with his hatred for Cooper. And if it had come to blows Cooper could have thrashed him. Tears of mortification ran down his red, fat face. He sat there for a couple of hours smoking cigarette after cigarette, and he wished he were dead.

At last the boy came back and asked him if he would dress for dinner. Of course! He always dressed for dinner. He rose wearily from his chair and put on his stiff shirt and the high collar. He sat down at the prettily decorated table and was waited on as usual by the two boys while two others waved their great fans. Over there in the bungalow, two hundred yards away, Cooper was eating a filthy meal clad only in a sarong and a baju. His feet were bare and while he ate he probably read a detective story. After dinner Mr. Warburton sat down to write a letter. The Sultan was away, but he wrote, privately and confidentially, to his representative. Cooper did his work very well, he said, but the fact was that he couldn't get on with him. They were getting dreadfully on each other's nerves and he would look upon it as a very great favour if Cooper could be transferred to another post.

He despatched the letter next morning by special messenger. The answer came a fortnight later with the month's mail. It was a private note and ran as follows:

My dear Warburton:—

I do not want to answer your letter officially and so I am writing you a few lines myself. Of course if you insist I will put the matter up to the Sultan, but I think you would be much wiser to drop it. I know Cooper is a rough diamond, but he is capable, and he had a pretty thin time in the war, and I think he should be given every chance. I think you are a little too much inclined to attach importance to a man's social position. You must remember that times have changed. Of course it's a very good thing for a man to be a gentleman, but it's better that he should be competent and hard-working. I think if you'll exercise a little tolerance you'll get on very well with Cooper.

> *Yours very sincerely*
> *Richard Temple.*

The letter dropped from Mr. Warburton's hand. It was easy to read between the lines. Dick Temple, whom he had known for twenty years, Dick Temple, who came from quite a good county family, thought him a snob and for that reason had no patience with his request. Mr. Warburton felt on a sudden discouraged with life. The world of which he was a part had passed away, and the future belonged to a meaner generation. Cooper represented it and Cooper he hated with all his heart. He stretched out his hand to fill his glass and at the gesture his head-boy stepped forward.

"I didn't know you were there."

The boy picked up the official letter. Ah, that was why he was waiting.

"Does Tuan Cooper go, Tuan?"

"No."

"There will be a misfortune."

For a moment the words conveyed nothing to his lassitude. But only for a moment. He sat up in his chair and looked at the boy. He was all attention.

"What do you mean by that?"

"Tuan Cooper is not behaving rightly with Abas."

Mr. Warburton shrugged his shoulders. How should a man like Cooper know how to treat servants? Mr. Warburton knew the type: he would be grossly familiar with them at one moment and rude and inconsiderate the next.

"Let Abas go back to his family."

"Tuan Cooper holds back his wages so that he may not run away. He has paid him nothing for three months. I tell him to be patient. But he is angry, he will not listen to reason. If the tuan continues to use him ill there will be a misfortune."

"You were right to tell me."

The fool! Did he know so little of the Malays as to think he could safely injure them? It would serve him damned well right if he got a kris in his back. A kris. Mr. Warburton's heart seemed on a sudden to miss a beat. He had only to let things take their course and one fine day he would be rid of Cooper. He smiled faintly as the phrase, a masterly inactivity, crossed his mind. And now his heart beat a little quicker, for he saw the man he hated lying on his face in a pathway of the jungle with a knife in his back. A fit end for the cad and the bully. Mr. Warburton sighed. It was his duty to warn him and of course he must do it. He wrote a brief and formal note to Cooper asking him to come to the Fort at once.

In ten minutes Cooper stood before him. They had not spoken to one another since the day when Mr. Warburton had nearly struck him. He did not now ask him to sit down.

"Did you wish to see me?" Cooper asked.

He was untidy and none too clean. His face and hands were covered with little red blotches where mosquitoes had bitten him and he had scratched himself till the blood came. His long, thin face bore a sullen look.

"I understand that you are again having trouble with your servants. Abas, my head-boy's nephew, complains that you have held back his wages for three months. I consider it a most arbitrary proceeding. The lad wishes to leave you, and I certainly do not blame him. I must insist on your paying what is due to him."

"I don't choose that he should leave me. I am holding back his wages as a pledge of his good behaviour."

"You do not know the Malay character. The Malays are very sensitive to injury and ridicule. They are passionate and revengeful. It is my duty to warn you that if you drive this boy beyond a certain point you run a great risk."

Cooper gave a contemptuous chuckle.

"What do you think he'll do?"

"I think he'll kill you."

"Why should you mind?"

"Oh, I wouldn't," replied Mr. Warburton, with a faint laugh. "I should bear it with the utmost fortitude. But I feel the official obligation to give you a proper warning."

"Do you think I'm afraid of a damned nigger?"

"It's a matter of entire indifference to me."

"Well, let me tell you this, I know how to take care of myself; that boy Abas is a dirty, thieving rascal, and if he tries any monkey tricks on me, by God, I'll wring his bloody neck."

"That was all I wished to say to you," said Mr. Warburton. "Good evening."

Mr. Warburton gave him a little nod of dismissal. Cooper flushed, did not for a moment know what to say or do, turned on his heel and stumbled out of the room. Mr. Warburton watched him go with an icy smile on his lips. He had done his duty. But what would he have thought had he known that when Cooper got back to his bungalow, so silent and cheerless, he threw himself down on his bed and in his bitter loneliness on a sudden lost all control of himself? Painful sobs tore his chest and heavy tears rolled down his thin cheeks.

After this Mr. Warburton seldom saw Cooper, and never spoke to him. He read his Times every morning, did his work at the office, took his exercise, dressed for dinner, dined and sat by the river smoking his cheroot. If by chance he ran across Cooper he cut him dead. Each, though never for a moment unconscious of the propinquity, acted as though the other did not exist. Time did nothing to assuage their animosity. They watched one another's actions and each knew what the other did. Though Mr. Warburton had been a keen shot in his youth, with age he had acquired a distaste for killing the wild things of the jungle, but on Sundays and holidays Cooper went out with his gun: if he got something it was a triumph over Mr. Warburton; if not, Mr. Warburton shrugged his shoulders and chuckled. These counter-jumpers trying to be sportsmen! Christmas was a bad time for both of them: they ate their dinners alone, each in his own quarters, and they got deliberately drunk. They were the only white men within two hundred miles and they lived within shouting distance of each other. At the beginning of the year Cooper went down with fever, and when Mr. Warburton caught sight of him again he was surprised to see how thin he had grown. He looked ill and worn. The solitude, so much more unnatural because it was due to no necessity, was getting on his nerves. It was getting on Mr. Warburton's too, and often he could not sleep at night. He lay awake brooding. Cooper was drinking heavily and surely the breaking point was near; but in his dealings with the natives he took care to do nothing that might expose him to his chief's rebuke. They fought a grim and silent battle with one another. It was a test of endurance. The months passed, and neither gave sign of weakening. They were like men dwelling in regions of eternal night, and their souls were oppressed with the knowledge that never would the day dawn for them. It looked as though their lives would continue for ever in this dull and hideous monotony of hatred.

And when at last the inevitable happened it came upon Mr. Warburton with all the shock of the unexpected. Cooper accused the boy Abas of stealing some of his clothes, and when the boy denied the theft took him by the scruff of the neck and kicked him down the steps of the bungalow. The boy demanded his wages, and Cooper flung at his head every word of abuse he knew. If he saw him in the compound in an hour he would hand him over to the police. Next morning the boy waylaid him outside the Fort when he was walking over to his office, and again demanded his wages. Cooper struck him in the face with his clenched fist. The boy fell to the ground and got up with blood streaming from his nose.

Cooper walked on and set about his work. But he could not attend to it. The blow had calmed his irritation, and he knew that he had gone too far. He was worried. He felt ill, miserable and discouraged. In the adjoining office sat Mr. Warburton, and his impulse was to go and tell him what he had done; he made a movement in his chair, but he knew with what icy scorn he would listen to the story. He could see his patronizing smile. For a moment he had an uneasy fear of what Abas might do. Warburton had warned him all right. He sighed. What a fool he had been! But he shrugged his shoulders impatiently. He did not care; a fat lot he

had to live for. It was all Warburton's fault; if he hadn't put his back up nothing like this would have happened. Warburton had made life a hell for him from the start. The snob. But they were all like that: it was because he was a Colonial. It was a damned shame that he had never got his commission in the war; he was as good as any one else. They were a lot of dirty snobs. He was damned if he was going to knuckle under now. Of course Warburton would hear of what had happened; the old devil knew everything. He wasn't afraid. He wasn't afraid of any Malay in Borneo, and Warburton could go to blazes.

He was right in thinking that Mr. Warburton would know what had happened. His head-boy told him when he went in to tiffin.

"Where is your nephew now?"

"I do not know, Tuan. He has gone."

Mr. Warburton remained silent. After luncheon as a rule he slept a little, but to-day he found himself very wide awake. His eyes involuntarily sought the bungalow where Cooper was now resting.

The idiot! Hesitation for a little was in Mr. Warburton's mind. Did the man know in what peril he was? He supposed he ought to send for him. But each time he had tried to reason with Cooper, Cooper had insulted him. Anger, furious anger welled up suddenly in Mr. Warburton's heart, so that the veins on his temples stood out and he clenched his fists. The cad had had his warning. Now let him take what was coming to him. It was no business of his and if anything happened it was not his fault. But perhaps they would wish in Kuala Solor that they had taken his advice and transferred Cooper to another station.

He was strangely restless that night. After dinner he walked up and down the verandah. When the boy went away to his own quarters, Mr. Warburton asked him whether anything had been seen of Abas.

"No, Tuan, I think maybe he has gone to the village of his mother's brother."

Mr. Warburton gave him a sharp glance, but the boy was looking down and their eyes did not meet. Mr. Warburton went down to the river and sat in his arbour. But peace was denied him. The river flowed ominously silent. It was like a great serpent gliding with sluggish movement towards the sea. And the trees of the jungle over the water were heavy with a breathless menace. No bird sang. No breeze ruffled the leaves of the cassias. All around him it seemed as though something waited.

He walked across the garden to the road. He had Cooper's bungalow in full view from there. There was a light in his sitting-room and across the road floated the sound of rag-time. Cooper was playing his gramophone. Mr. Warburton shuddered; he had never got over his instinctive dislike of that instrument. But for that he would have gone over and spoken to Cooper. He turned and went back to his own house. He read late into the night, and at last he slept. But he did not sleep very long, he had terrible dreams, and he seemed to be awakened by a cry. Of course that was a dream too, for no cry—from the bungalow for instance—could be heard in his room. He lay awake till dawn. Then he heard hurried steps and the sound of voices, his head-boy burst suddenly into the room without his fez, and Mr. Warburton's heart stood still.

"Tuan, Tuan."

Mr. Warburton jumped out of bed.

"I'll come at once."

He put on his slippers, and in his sarong and pyjama-jacket walked across his compound and into Cooper's. Cooper was lying in bed, with his mouth open, and a kris sticking in his heart. He had been killed in his sleep. Mr. Warburton started, but not because he had not expected to see just such a sight, he started because he felt in himself a sudden glow of exultation. A great burden had been lifted from his shoulders.

Cooper was quite cold. Mr. Warburton took the kris out of the wound, it had been thrust in with such force that he had to use an effort to get it out, and looked at it. He recognized it. It was a kris that a dealer had offered him some weeks before and which he knew Cooper had bought.

"Where is Abas?" he asked sternly.

"Abas is at the village of his mother's brother."

The sergeant of the native police was standing at the foot of the bed.

"Take two men and go to the village and arrest him."

Mr. Warburton did what was immediately necessary. With set face he gave orders. His words were short and peremptory. Then he went back to the Fort. He shaved and had his bath, dressed and went into the dining-room. By the side of his plate The Times in its wrapper lay waiting for him. He helped himself to some fruit. The headboy poured out his tea while the second handed him a dish of eggs. Mr. Warburton ate with a good appetite. The head-boy waited.

"What is it?" asked Mr. Warburton.

"Tuan, Abas, my nephew, was in the house of his mother's brother all night. It can be proved. His uncle will swear that he did not leave the kampong."

Mr. Warburton turned upon him with a frown.

"Tuan Cooper was killed by Abas. You know it as well as I know. Justice must be done."

"Tuan, you would not hang him?"

Mr. Warburton hesitated an instant, and though his voice remained set and stern a change came into his eyes. It was a flicker which the Malay was quick to notice and across his own eyes flashed an answering look of understanding.

"The provocation was very great. Abas will be sentenced to a term of imprisonment." There was a pause while Mr. Warburton helped himself to marmalade. "When he has served a part of his sentence in prison I will take him into this house as a boy. You can train him in his duties. I have no doubt that in the house of Tuan Cooper he got into bad habits."

"Shall Abas give himself up, Tuan?"

"It would be wise of him."

The boy withdrew. Mr. Warburton took his Times and neatly slit the wrapper. He loved to unfold the heavy, rustling pages. The morning, so fresh and cool, was delicious and for a moment his eyes wandered out over his garden with a friendly glance. A great weight had been lifted from his mind. He turned to the columns in which were announced the births, deaths, and marriages. That was what he always looked at first. A name he knew caught his attention. Lady Ormskirk had had a son at last. By George, how pleased the old dowager must be! He would write her a note of congratulation by the next mail.

Abas would make a very good house-boy. That fool Cooper!

HEART OF DARKNESS

Joseph Conrad
(1857–1924)

I

The *Nellie,* a cruising yawl, swung to her anchor without a flutter of the sails, and was at rest. The flood had made, the wind was nearly calm, and being bound down the river, the only thing for it was to come to and wait for the turn of the tide.

The sea-reach of the Thames stretched before us like the beginning of an interminable waterway. In the offing the sea and the sky were welded together without a joint, and in the luminous space the tanned sails of the barges drifting up with the tide seemed to stand still in red clusters of canvas sharply peaked, with gleams of varnished sprits. A haze rested on the low shores that ran out to sea in vanishing flatness. The air was dark above Gravesend, and farther back still seemed condensed into a mournful gloom, brooding motionless over the biggest, and the greatest, town on earth.

The Director of Companies was our captain and our host. We four affectionately watched his back as he stood in the bows looking to seaward. On the whole river there was nothing that looked half so nautical. He resembled a pilot, which to a seaman is trustworthiness personified. It was difficult to realize his work was not out there in the luminous estuary, but behind him, within the brooding gloom.

Between us there was, as I have already said somewhere, the bond of the sea. Besides holding our hearts together through long periods of separation, it had the effect of making us tolerant of each other's yarns—and even convictions. The Lawyer—the best of old fellows—had, because of his many years and many virtues, the only cushion on deck, and was lying on the only rug. The Accountant had brought out already a box of dominoes, and was toying architecturally with the bones. Marlow sat cross-legged right aft, leaning against the mizzen-mast. He had sunken cheeks, a yellow complexion, a straight back, an ascetic aspect, and, with his arms dropped, the palms of hands outwards, resembled an idol. The director, satisfied the anchor had good hold, made his way aft and sat down amongst us. We exchanged a few words lazily. Afterwards there was silence on board the yacht. For some reason or other we did not begin that game of dominoes. We felt meditative, and fit for nothing but placid staring. The day was ending in a serenity of still and exquisite brilliance. The water shone pacifically; the sky, without a speck, was a benign immensity of unstained light; the very mist on the Essex marshes was like a gauzy and radiant fabric, hung from the wooded rises inland, and draping the low shores in diaphanous folds. Only the gloom to the west, brooding over the upper reaches, became more somber every minute, as if angered by the approach of the sun.

And at last, in its curved and imperceptible fall, the sun sank low, and from glowing white changed to a dull red without rays and without heat, as if about to go out suddenly, stricken to death by the touch of that gloom brooding over a crowd of men.

Forthwith a change came over the waters, and the serenity became less brilliant but more profound. The old river in its broad reach rested unruffled at the decline of day, after ages of good service done to the race that peopled its banks, spread out in the tranquil dignity of a waterway leading to the uttermost ends of the earth. We looked at the venerable stream not in the vivid flush of a short day that comes and departs forever, but in the august light of abiding memories. And indeed nothing is easier for a man who has, as the phrase goes, "followed the sea" with reverence and affection, than to evoke the great spirit of the past upon the lower reaches of the Thames. The tidal current runs to and fro in its unceasing service, crowded with memories of men and ships it had borne to the rest of home or to the battles of the sea. It had known and served all the men of whom the nation is proud, from Sir Francis Drake to Sir John Franklin, knights all, tilted and untitled—the knights-errant of the sea. It had borne all the ships whose names are like jewels flashing in the night of time, from the *Golden Hind* returning with her round flanks full of treasure, to be visited by the Queen's Highness and thus pass out of the gigantic tale to the *Erebus* and *Terror,* bound on other conquests—and that never returned. It had known the ships and the men. They had sailed from Deptford, from Greenwich, from Erith—the adventurers and the settlers; kings' ships and the ships of men on 'Change; captains, admirals, the dark "interlopers" of the Eastern trade, and the commissioned "generals" of East India fleets. Hunters for gold or pursuers of fame, they all had gone out on that stream, bearing the sword, and often the torch, messengers of the might within the land, bearers of a spark from the sacred fire. What greatness had not floated on the ebb of that river into the mystery of an unknown earth! . . . The dreams of men, the seed of commonwealths, the germs of empires.

The sun set; the dusk fell on the stream, and lights began to appear along the shore. The Chapman lighthouse, a three-legged thing erect on a mudflat, shone strongly. Lights of ships moved in the fairway—a great stir of lights going up and going down. And farther west on the upper reaches the place of the monstrous town was still marked ominously on the sky, a brooding gloom in sunshine, a lurid glare under the stars.

"And this also," said Marlow suddenly, "has been one of the dark places on the earth."

He was the only man of us who still "followed the sea." The worst that could be said of him was that he did not represent his class. He was a seaman, but he was a wanderer, too, while most seamen lead, if one may so express it, a sedentary life. Their minds are of the stay-at-home order, and their home is always with them—the ship; and so is their country—the sea. One ship is very much like another, and the sea is always the same. In the immutability of their surroundings the foreign shores, the foreign faces, the changing immensity of life, glide past, veiled not by a sense of mystery but by a slightly disdainful ignorance; for there is nothing mysterious to a seaman unless it be the sea itself, which is the mistress of his existence and as inscrutable as Destiny. For the rest, after his hours of work, a casual stroll or a casual spree on shore suffices to unfold for him the secret of a whole continent, and generally he finds the secret not worth knowing. The yarns of seamen have a direct simplicity, the whole meaning of which lies within the shell of a cracked nut. But Marlow was not typical (if his propensity to spin yarns be excepted), and to him the meaning of an episode was not inside like a kernel but outside, enveloping the tale which brought it out only as a glow brings out a haze, in the likeness of one of these misty halos that sometimes are made visible by the spectral illumination of moonshine.

His remark did not seem at all surprising. It was just like Marlow. It was accepted in silence. No one took the trouble to grunt even; and presently he said, very slow—

"I was thinking of very old times, when the Romans first came here, nineteen hundred years ago—the other day. . . . Light came out of this river since—you say Knights? Yes; but it is like a running blaze on a plain, like a flash of lightning in the clouds. We live in the flicker—may it last as long as the old earth keeps rolling! But darkness was here yesterday. Imagine the feelings of a commander of a fine—what d'ye call 'em—trireme in the Mediterranean, ordered suddenly to the north; run overland across the Gauls in a hurry; put in charge of one of these craft the legionaries—a wonderful lot of handy men they must have been, too—used to build, apparently by the hundred, in a month or two, if we may believe what we read. Imagine him here—the very end of the world, a sea the color of lead, a sky the color of smoke, a kind of ship about as rigid as a concertina—and going up this river with stores, or orders, or what you like. Sandbanks, marshes, forests, savages,—precious little to eat fit for a civilized man, nothing but Thames water to drink. No Falernian wine here, no going ashore. Here and there a military camp lost in a wilderness, like a needle in a bundle of hay—cold, fog, tempests, disease, exile, and death,—death skulking the air, in the water, in the bush. They must have been dying like flies here. Oh, yes—he did it. Did it very well, too, no doubt, and without thinking much about it either, except afterwards to brag of what he had gone through in his time, perhaps. They were men enough to face the darkness. And perhaps he was cheered by keeping his eye on a chance of promotion to the fleet at Ravenna by and by, if he had good friends in Rome and survived the awful climate. Or think of a decent young citizen in a toga—perhaps too much dice, you know—coming out here in the train of some prefect, or tax-gatherer, or trader even, to mend his fortunes. Land in a swamp, march through the woods, and in some inland post feel the savagery, the utter savagery, had closed round him,—all that mysterious life of the wilderness that stirs in the forest, in the jungles, in the hearts of wild men. There's no initiation either into such mysteries. He has to live in the midst of the incomprehensible, which is also detestable. And it has a fascination, too, that goes to work upon him. The fascination of the abomination—you know, imagine the growing regrets, the longing to escape, the powerless disgust, the surrender, the hate."

He paused.

"Mind," he began again, lifting one arm from the elbow, the palm of the hand outwards, so that, with his legs folded before him, he had the pose of a Buddha preaching in European clothes and without a lotus-flower—"Mind, none of us would feel exactly like this. What saves us is efficiency—the devotion to efficiency. But these chaps were not much account, really. They were no colonists; their administration was merely a squeeze, and nothing more, I suspect. They were conquerors, and for that you want only brute force—nothing to boast of, when you have it, since your strength is just an accident arising from the weakness of others. They grabbed what they could get for the sake of what was to be got. It was just robbery with violence, aggravated murder on a great scale, and men going at it blind—as is very proper for those who tackle a darkness. The conquest of the earth, which mostly means the taking it away from those who have a different complexion or slightly flatter noses than ourselves, is not a pretty thing when you look into it too much. What redeems it is the idea only. An idea at the back of it; not a sentimental pretense but an idea; and an unselfish belief in the idea—something you can set up, and bow down before, and offer a sacrifice to. . . ."

He broke off. Flames glided in the river, small green flames, red flames, white flames, pursuing, overtaking, joining, crossing each other—then separating slowly or hastily. The traffic of the great city went on in the deepening night upon the sleepless river. We looked on, waiting patiently—there was nothing else to do till the end of the flood; but it was only after a long silence, when he said, in a hesitating voice, "I suppose you fellows remember I did once turn fresh-water sailor for a bit," that we knew we were fated, before the ebb began to run, to hear one of Marlow's inconclusive experiences.

"I don't want to bother you much with what happened to me personally," he began, showing in this remark the weakness of many tellers of tales who seem so often unaware of what their audience would best like to hear; "yet to understand the effect of it on me you ought to know how I got out there, what I saw, how I went up that river to the place where I first met the poor chap. It was the farthest point of navigation and the culminating point of my experience. It seemed somehow to throw a kind of light on everything about me—and into my thoughts. It was somber enough, too—and pitiful— not extraordinary in any way—not very clear either. No, not very clear. And yet it seemed to throw a kind of light.

"I had then, as you remember, just returned to London after a lot of Indian Ocean, Pacific, China Seas—a regular dose of the East—six years or so, and I was loafing about, hindering you fellows in your work and invading your homes, just as though I had got a heavenly mission to civilize you. It was very fine for a time, but after a bit I did get tired of resting. Then I began to look for a ship—I should think the hardest work on earth. But the ships wouldn't even look at me. And I got tired of that game, too.

"Now when I was a little chap I had a passion for maps. I would look for hours at South America, or Africa, or Australia, and lose myself in all the glories of exploration. At that time there were many blank spaces on the earth, and when I saw one that looked particularly inviting on a map (but they all look that) I would put my finger on it and say, When I grow up I will go there. The North Pole was one of these places, I remember. Well, I haven't been there yet, and shall not try now. The glamour's off. Other places were scattered about the Equator, and in every sort of latitude all over the two hemispheres. I have been in some of them, and . . . well, we won't talk about that. But there was one yet—the biggest, the most blank, so to speak—that I had a hankering after.

"True, by this time it was not a blank space any more. It had got filled since my childhood with rivers and lakes and names. It had ceased to be a blank space of delightful mystery—a white patch for a boy to dream gloriously over. It had become a place of darkness. But there was in it one river especially, a mighty big river, that you could see on the map, resembling an immense snake uncoiled, with its head in the sea, its body at rest curving afar over a vast country, and its tail lost in the depths of the land. And as I looked at the map of it in a shop-window, it

fascinated me as a snake would a bird—a silly little bird. Then I remembered there was a big concern, a Company for trade on that river. Dash it all! I thought to myself, they can't trade without using some kind of craft on that lot of fresh water—steamboats! Why shouldn't I try to get charge of one? I went on along Fleet Street, but could not shake off the idea. The snake had charmed me.

"You understand it was a Continental concern, that Trading society; but I have a lot of relations living on the Continent, because it's cheap and not so nasty as it looks, they say.

"I am sorry to own I began to worry them. This was already a fresh departure for me. I was not used to getting things that way, you know. I always went my own road and on my own legs where I had a mind to go. I wouldn't have believed it of myself; but, then—you see—I felt somehow I must get there by hook or by crook. So I worried them. The men said 'My dear fellow,' and did nothing. Then—would you believe it?—I tried the women. I, Charlie Marlow, set the women to work—to get a job. Heavens! Well, you see, the notion drove me. I had an aunt, a dear enthusiastic soul. She wrote: 'It will be delightful. I am ready to do anything, anything for you. It is a glorious idea. I know the wife of a very high personage in the Administration, and also a man who has lots of influence with,' etc., etc. She was determined to make no end of fuss to get me appointed skipper of a river steamboat, if such was my fancy.

"I got my appointment—of course; and I got it very quick. It appears the Company had received news that one of their captains had been killed in a scuffle with the natives. This was my chance, and it made me the more anxious to go. It was only months and months afterwards, when I made the attempt to recover what was left of the body, that I heard the original quarrel arose from a misunderstanding about some hens. Yes, two black hens. Fresleven—that was the fellow's name, a Dane—thought himself wronged somehow in the bargain, so he went ashore and started to hammer the chief of the village with a stick. Oh, it didn't surprise me in the least to hear this, and at the same time to be told that Fresleven was the gentlest, quietest creature that ever walked on two legs. No doubt he was; but he had been a couple of years already out there engaged in the noble cause, you know, and he probably felt the need at last of asserting his self-respect in some way. Therefore he whacked the old nigger mercilessly, while a big crowd of his people watched him, thunderstruck, till some man—I was told the chief's son—in desperation at hearing the old chap yell, made a tentative jab with a spear at the white man—and of course it went quite easy between the shoulder-blades. Then the whole population cleared into the forest, expecting all kinds of calamities to happen, while, on the other hand, the steamer Fresleven commanded left also in a bad panic, in charge of the engineer, I believe. Afterwards nobody seemed to trouble much about Fresleven's remains, till I got out and stepped into his shoes. I couldn't let it rest, though; but when an opportunity offered at last to meet my predecessor, the grass growing through his ribs was tall enough to hide his bones. They were all there. The supernatural being had not been touched after he fell. And the village was deserted, the huts gaped black, rotting, all askew within the fallen enclosures. A calamity had come to it, sure enough. The people had vanished. Mad terror had scattered them, men, women, and children, through the bush, and they had never returned. What became of the hens I don't know either. I should think the cause of progress got them, anyhow. However, through this glorious affair I got my appointment, before I had fairly begun to hope for it.

"I flew around like mad to get ready, and before forty-eight hours I was crossing the Channel to show myself to my employers, and sign the contract. In a very few hours I arrived in a city that always makes me think of a whited sepulcher. Prejudice no doubt. I had no difficulty in finding the Company's offices. It was the biggest thing in the town, and everybody I met was full of it. They were going to run an over-sea empire, and make no end of coin by trade.

"A narrow and deserted street in deep shadow, high houses, innumerable windows with venetian blinds, a dead silence, grass sprouting between the stones, imposing carriage archways right and left, immense double doors standing ponderously ajar. I slipped through one of these cracks, went up a swept and ungarnished staircase, as arid as a desert, and opened the first door I came to. Two women, one fat and the other slim, sat on strawbottomed chairs, knitting black wool. The slim one got up and walked straight at me—still knitting with down-cast eyes—and only just as I began to think of getting out of her way, as you would for a somnambulist, stood still, and looked up. Her dress was as plain as an umbrella-cover, and she turned round without a word and preceded me into a waiting-room. I gave my name, and looked about. Deal table in the middle, plain chairs all around the walls, on one end a large shining map, marked with all the colors of a rainbow. There was a vast amount of red—good to see at any time, because one knows that some real work is done in there, a deuce of a lot of blue, a little green, smears of orange, and, on the East Coast, a purple patch, to show where the jolly pioneers of progress drink the jolly lager-beer. However, I wasn't going into any of these. I was going into the yellow. Dead in the center. And the river was there—fascinating—deadly—like a snake. Ough! A door opened, a white-haired secretarial head, but wearing a compassionate expression, appeared, and a skinny forefinger beckoned me into the sanctuary. Its light was dim, and a heavy writing-desk squatted in the middle. From behind that structure came out an impression of pale plumpness in a frock-coat. The great man himself. He was five feet six, I should judge, and had his grip on the handle-end of ever so many millions. He shook hands, I fancy, murmured vaguely, was satisfied with my French. *Bon voyage.*

"In about forty-five seconds I found myself again in the waiting-room with the compassionate secretary, who, full of desolation and sympathy, made me sign some document. I believe I undertook amongst other things not to disclose any trade secrets. Well, I am not going to.

"I began to feel slightly uneasy. You know I am not used to such ceremonies, and there was something ominous in the atmosphere. It was just as though I had been let into some conspiracy—I don't know—something not quite right; and I was glad to get out. In the outer room the two women knitted black wool feverishly. People were arriving, and the younger one was walking back and forth introducing them. The old one sat on her chair. Her flat cloth slippers were propped up on a foot-warmer, and a cat reposed on her lap. She wore a starched white affair on her head, had a wart on one cheek, and silver-rimmed spectacles hung on the tip of her nose. She glanced at me above the glasses. The swift and indifferent placidity of that look troubled me. Two youths with foolish and cheery countenances were being piloted over, and she threw at them the same quick glance of unconcerned wisdom. She seemed to know all about them and about me, too. An eerie feeling came over me. She seemed uncanny and fateful. Often far away there I thought of these two, guarding the door of Darkness, knitting black wool as for a warm pall, one introducing, introducing continuously to the unknown, the other scrutinizing the cheery and foolish faces with unconcerned old eyes. *Ave!* Old knitter of black wool. *Morituri te salutant.* Not many of those she looked at ever saw her again—not half, by a long way.

"There was yet a visit to the doctor. 'A simple formality,' assured me the secretary, with an air of taking an immense part in all my sorrows. Accordingly a young chap wearing his hat over the left eyebrow, some clerk I suppose,—there must have been clerks in the business, though the house was as still as a house in a city of the dead—came from somewhere upstairs, and led me forth. He was shabby and careless, with inkstains on the sleeves of his jacket, and his cravat was large and billowy, under a chin shaped like the toe of an old boot. It was a little too early

for the doctor, so I proposed a drink, and thereupon he developed a vein of joviality. As we sat over our vermouths he glorified the Company's business, and by and by I expressed casually my surprise at him not going out there. He became very cool and collected all at once. 'I am not such a fool as I look, quoth Plato to his disciples,' he said sententiously, emptied his glass with great resolution, and we rose.

"The old doctor felt my pulse, evidently thinking of something else the while. 'Good, good for there,' he mumbled, and then with a certain eagerness asked me whether I would let him measure my head. Rather surprised, I said Yes, when he produced a thing like calipers and got the dimensions back and front and every way, taking notes carefully. He was an unshaven little man in a threadbare coat like a gaberdine, with his feet in slippers, and I thought him a harmless fool. 'I always ask leave, in the interests of science, to measure the crania of those going out there,' he said. 'And when they come back, too?' I asked. 'Oh, I never see them,' he remarked; and, moreover, the changes take place inside, you know.' He smiled, as if at some quiet joke. 'So you are going out there. Famous. Interesting, too.' He gave me a searching glance, and made another note. 'Ever any madness in your family?' he asked, in a matter-of-fact tone. I felt very annoyed. 'Is that question in the interests of science, too?' 'It would be,' he said, without taking notice of my irritation, 'interesting for science to watch the mental changes of individuals, on the spot, but . . .' 'Are you an alienist?' I interrupted. 'Every doctor should be—a little,' answered that original, imperturbably. 'I have a little theory which you Messieurs who go out there must help me to prove. This is my share in the advantages my country shall reap from the possession of such a magnificent dependency. The mere wealth I leave to others. Pardon my questions, but you are the first Englishman coming under my observation . . .' I hastened to assure him I was not in the least typical. 'If I were,' said I, 'I wouldn't be talking like this with you.' 'What you say is rather profound, and probably erroneous,' he said, with a laugh. 'Avoid irritation more than exposure to the sun. Adieu. How do you English say, eh? Good-by. Ah! Good-by. Adieu. In the tropics one must before everything keep calm.'. . . . He lifted a warning forefinger. . . . *'Du calme, du calme. Adieu.'*

"One thing more remained to do—say good-by to my excellent aunt. I found her triumphant. I had a cup of tea—the last decent cup of tea for many days—and in a room that most soothingly looked just as you would expect a lady's drawing-room to look, we had a long quiet chat by the fireside. In the course of these confidences it became quite plain to me I had been represented to the wife of the high dignitary, and goodness knows to how many more people besides, as an exceptional and gifted creature—a piece of good fortune for the Company—a man you don't get hold of every day. Good heavens! and I was going to take charge of a two-penny-half-penny river-steamboat with a penny whistle attached! It appeared, however, I was also one of the Workers, with a capital—you know. Something like an emissary of light, something like a lower sort of apostle. There had been a lot of such rot let loose in print and talk just about that time, and the excellent woman, living right in the rush of all that humbug, got carried off her feet. She talked about 'weaning those ignorant millions from their horrid ways,' till, upon my word, she made me quite uncomfortable. I ventured to hint that the Company was run for profit.

" 'You forget, dear Charlie, that the laborer is worthy of his hire,' she said, brightly. It's queer how out of touch with truth women are. They live in a world of their own, and there has never been anything like it, and never can be. It is too beautiful altogether, and if they were to set it up it would go to pieces before the first sunset. Some confounded fact we men have been living contentedly with ever since the day of creation would start up and knock the whole thing over.

"After this I got embraced, told to wear flannel, be sure to write often, and so on—and I left. In the street—I don't know why—a queer feeling came to me that I was an impostor. Odd thing that I, who used to clear out for any part of the world at twenty-four hours' notice, with less thought than most men give to the crossing of a street, had a moment—I won't say of hesitation, but of startled pause, before this commonplace affair. The best way I can explain it to you is by saying that, for a second or two, I felt as though, instead of going to the center of a continent, I were about to set off for the center of the earth.

"I left in a French steamer, and she called in every blamed port they have out there, for, as far as I could see, the sole purpose of landing soldiers and custom-house officers. I watched the coast. Watching a coast as it slips by the ship is like thinking about an enigma. There it is before you—smiling, frowning, inviting, grand, mean, insipid, or savage, and always mute with an air of whispering, Come and find out. This one was almost featureless, as if still in the making, with an aspect of monotonous grimness. The edge of a colossal jungle, so dark-green as to be almost black, fringed with white surf, ran straight, like a ruled line, far, far away along a blue sea whose glitter was blurred by a creeping mist. The sun was fierce, the land seemed to glisten and drip with steam. Here and there grayish-whitish specks showed up clustered inside the white surf, with a flag flying above them perhaps. Settlements some centuries old, and still no bigger than pinheads on the untouched expanse of their background. We pounded along, stopped, landed soldiers; went on, landed custom-house clerks to levy toll in what looked like a God-forsaken wilderness, with a tin shed and a flag-pole lost in it; landed more soldiers—to take care of the custom-house clerks, presumably. Some, I heard, got drowned in the surf; but whether they did or not, nobody seemed particularly to care. They were just flung out there, and on we went. Every day the coast looked the same, as though we had not moved; but we passed various places—trading places—with names like Gran' Bas-

sam, Little Popo; names that seemed to belong to some sordid farce acted in front of a
sinister backcloth. The idleness of a passenger, my isolation amongst all these men with
whom I had no point of contact, the oily
and languid sea, the uniform somberness of
the coast, seemed to keep me away from the
truth of things, within the toil of a mournful
and senseless delusion. The voice of the surf
heard now and then was a positive pleasure,
like the speech of a brother. It was something natural, that had its reason, that had
a meaning. Now and then a boat from the
shore gave one a momentary contact with
reality. It was paddled by black fellows. You
could see from afar the white of their eyeballs glistening. They shouted, sang; their
bodies streamed with perspiration; they had
faces like grotesque masks—these chaps; but
they had bone, muscle, a wild vitality, an intense energy of movement, that was as natural and true as the surf along their coast.
They wanted no excuse for being there. They
were a great comfort to look at. For a time I
would feel I belonged still to a world of
straightforward facts; but the feeling would
not last long. Something would turn up to
scare it away. Once, I remember, we came
upon a man-of-war anchored off the coast.
There wasn't even a shed there, and she was
shelling the bush. It appears the French had
one of their wars going on thereabouts. Her
ensign dropped limp like a rag; the muzzles
of the long six-inch guns stuck out all over
the low hull; the greasy, slimy swell swung
her up lazily and let her down, swaying her
thin masts. In the empty immensity of earth,
sky, and water, there she was, incomprehensible, firing into a continent. Pop, would go
one of the six-inch guns; a small flame would
dart and vanish, a little white smoke would
disappear, a tiny projectile would give a feeble screech—and nothing happened. Nothing could happen. There was a touch of
insanity in the proceeding, a sense of lugu-
brious drollery in the sight; and it was not
dissipated by somebody on board assuring
me earnestly there was a camp of natives—
he called them enemies!—hidden out of
sight somewhere.

"We gave her her letters (I heard the men
in that lonely ship were dying of fever at the
rate of three a day) and went on. We called
at some more places with farcical names,
where the merry dance of death and trade
goes on in a still and earthy atmosphere as
of an overheated catacomb; all along the
formless coast bordered by dangerous surf, as
if Nature herself had tried to ward off intruders; in and out of rivers, streams of death
in life, whose banks were rotting into mud,
whose waters, thickened into slime, invaded
the contorted mangroves, that seemed to
writhe at us in the extremity of an impotent
despair. Nowhere did we stop long enough
to get a particularized impression, but the
general sense of vague and oppressive wonder grew upon me. It was like a weary pilgrimage amongst hints for nightmares.

"It was upward of thirty days before I saw
the mouth of the big river. We anchored off
the seat of the government. But my work
would not begin till some two hundred miles
farther on. So as soon as I could I made a
start for a place thirty miles higher up.

"I had my passage on a little sea-going
steamer. Her captain was a Swede, and
knowing me for a seaman, invited me on the
bridge. He was a young man, lean, fair, and
morose, with lanky hair and a shuffling gait.
As we left the miserable little wharf, he
tossed his head contemptuously at the shore.
'Been living there?' he asked. I said, 'Yes.'
'Fine lot these government chaps—are they
not?' he went on, speaking English with
great precision and considerable bitterness.
'It is funny what some people will do for a
few francs a month. I wonder what becomes
of that kind when it goes up-country?' I said
to him I expected to see that soon. 'So-o-o!'
he exclaimed. He shuffled athwart, keeping
one eye ahead vigilantly. 'Don't be too sure,'
he continued. 'The other day I took up a man
who hanged himself on the road. He was a
Swede, too.' 'Hanged himself! Why, in God's
name?' I cried. He kept on looking out
watchfully. 'Who knows? The sun was too
much for him, or the country perhaps.'

"At last we opened a reach. A rocky cliff
appeared, mounds of turned-up earth by the

shore, houses on a hill, others with iron roofs, amongst a waste of excavations, or hanging to the declivity. A continuous noise of the rapids above hovered over this scene of inhabited devastation. A lot of people, mostly black and naked, moved about like ants. A jetty projected into the river. A blinding sunlight drowned all this at times in a sudden recrudescence of glare. 'There's your Company's station,' said the Swede, pointing to three wooden barrack-like structures on the rocky slope. 'I will send your things up. Four boxes did you say? So. Farewell.'

"I came upon a boiler wallowing in the grass, then found a path leading up the hill. It turned aside for the bowlders, and also for an undersized railway-truck lying there on its back with its wheels in the air. One was off. The thing looked as dead as the carcass of some animal. I came upon more pieces of decaying machinery, a stack of rusty rails. To the left a clump of trees made a shady spot, where dark things seemed to stir feebly. I blinked, the path was steep. A horn tooted to the right, and I saw the black people run. A heavy and dull detonation shook the ground, a puff of smoke came out of the cliff, and that was all. No change appeared on the face of the rock. They were building a railway. The cliff was not in the way or anything; but this objectless blasting was all the work going on.

"A slight clinking behind me made me turn my head. Six black men advanced in a file, toiling up the path. They walked erect and slow, balancing small baskets full of earth on their heads, and the clink kept time with their footsteps. Black rags were wound round their loins, and the short ends behind waggled to and fro like tails. I could see every rib, the joints of their limbs were like knots in a rope; each had an iron collar on his neck, and all were connected together with a chain whose bights swung between them, rhythmically clinking. Another report from the cliff made me think suddenly of that ship of war I had seen firing into a continent. It was the same kind of ominous voice; but these men could by no stretch of imagination be called enemies. They were called criminals, and the outraged law, like the bursting shells, had come to them, an insoluble mystery from the sea. All their meager breasts panted together, the violently dilated nostrils quivered, the eyes stared stonily up-hill. They passed me within six inches, without a glance, with that complete, death-like indifference of unhappy savages. Behind this raw matter one of the reclaimed, the product of the new forces at work, strolled despondently, carrying a rifle by its middle. He had a uniform jacket with one button off, and seeing a white man on the path, hoisted his weapon to his shoulder with alacrity. This was simple prudence, white men being so much alike at a distance that he could not tell who I might be. He was speedily reassured, and with a large, white rascally grin, and a glance at his charge, seemed to take me into partnership in his exalted trust. After all, I also was a part of the great cause of these high and just proceedings.

"Instead of going up, I turned and descended to the left. My idea was to let that chain-gang get out of sight before I climbed the hill. You know I am not particularly tender; I've had to strike and to fend off. I've had to resist and to attack sometimes—that's only one way of resisting—without counting the exact cost, according to the demands of such sort of life as I had blundered into. I've seen the devil of violence, and the devil of greed, and the devil of hot desire; but, by all the stars! these were strong, lusty, red-eyed devils, that swayed and drove men— men, I tell you. But as I stood on this hillside, I foresaw that in the blinding sunshine of that land I would become acquainted with a flabby, pretending, weak-eyed devil of a rapacious and pitiless folly. How insidious he could be, too, I was only to find out several months later and a thousand miles farther. For a moment I stood appalled, as though by a warning. Finally I descended the hill, obliquely, towards the trees I had seen.

"I avoided a vast artificial hole somebody had been digging on the slope, the purpose of which I found it impossible to divine. It wasn't a quarry or a sandpit, anyhow. It was just a hole. It might have been connected with the philanthropic desire of giving the criminals something to do. I don't know. Then I nearly fell into a very narrow ravine, almost no more than a scar in the hillside. I discovered that a lot of imported drainage-pipes for the settlement had been tumbled in there. There wasn't one that was not broken. It was a wanton smash-up. At last I got under the trees. My purpose was to stroll into the shade for a moment; but no sooner within than it seemed to me I had stepped into the gloomy circle of some Inferno. The rapids were near, and an uninterrupted, uniform, headlong, rushing noise filled the mournful stillness of the grove, where not a breath stirred, not a leaf moved, with a mysterious sound—as though the tearing pace of the launched earth had suddenly become audible.

"Black shapes crouched, lay, sat between the trees leaning against the trunks, clinging to the earth, half coming out, half effaced within the dim light, in all the attitudes of pain, abandonment, and despair. Another mine on the cliff went off, followed by a slight shudder of the soil under my feet. The work was going on. The work! And this was the place where some of the helpers had withdrawn to die.

"They were dying slowly—it was very clear. They were not enemies, they were not criminals, they were nothing earthly now,—nothing but black shadows of disease and starvation, lying confusedly in the greenish gloom. Brought from all the recesses of the coast in all the legality of time contracts, lost in uncongenial surroundings, fed on unfamiliar food, they sickened, became inefficient, and were then allowed to crawl away and rest. These moribund shapes were free as air—and nearly as thin. I began to distinguish the gleam of the eyes under the trees. Then, glancing down, I saw a face near my hand. The black bones reclined at full length with one shoulder against the tree, and slowly the eyelids rose and the sunken eyes looked up at me, enormous and vacant, a kind of blind, white flicker in the depths of the orbs, which died out slowly. The man seemed young—almost a boy—but you know with them it's

hard to tell. I found nothing else to do but to offer him one of my good Swede's ship's biscuits I had in my pocket. The fingers closed slowly on it and held—there was no other movement and no other glance. He had tied a bit of white worsted round his neck— Why? Where did he get it? Was it a badge—an ornament—a charm—a propitiatory act? Was there any idea at all connected with it? It looked startling round his black neck, this bit of white thread from beyond the seas.

"Near the same tree two more bundles of acute angles sat with their legs drawn up. One, with his chin propped on his knees, stared at nothing, in an intolerable and appalling manner: his brother phantom rested its forehead, as if overcome with a great weariness; and all about others were scattered in every pose of contorted collapse, as in some picture of a massacre or a pestilence. While I stood horror-struck, one of these creatures rose to his hands and knees, and went off on all-fours towards the river to drink. He lapped out of his hand, then sat up in the sunlight, crossing his shins in front of him, and after a time let his woolly head fall on his breastbone.

"I didn't want any more loitering in the shade, and I made haste towards the station. When near the buildings I met a white man, in such an unexpected elegance of get-up that in the first moment I took him for a sort of vision. I saw a high starched collar, white cuffs, a light alpaca jacket, snowy trousers, a clean necktie, and varnished boots. No hat. Hair parted, brushed, oiled, under a green-lined parasol held in a big white hand. He was amazing, and had a penholder behind his ear.

"I shook hands with this miracle, and I learned he was the Company's chief accountant, and that all the book-keeping was done at this station. He had come out for a moment, he said, 'to get a breath of fresh air.' The expression sounded wonderfully odd, with its suggestion of sedentary desk-life. I wouldn't have mentioned the fellow to you at all, only it was from his lips that I first heard the name of the man who is so indissolubly connected with the memories of that time. Moreover, I respected the fellow. Yes; I respected his collars, his vast cuffs, his brushed hair. His appearance was certainly that of a hairdresser's dummy; but in the great demoralization of the land he kept up his appearance. That's backbone. His starched collars and got-up shirt-fronts were achievements of character. He had been out nearly three years; and, later, I could not help asking him how he managed to sport such linen. He had just the faintest blush, and said modestly, 'I've been teaching one of the native women about the station. It was difficult. She had a distaste for the work.' Thus this man had verily accomplished something. And he was devoted to his books, which were in apple-pie order.

"Everything else in the station was in a muddle,—heads, things, buildings. Strings of dusty niggers with splay feet arrived and departed; a stream of manufactured goods, rubbishy cottons, beads, and brass-wire set into the depths of darkness, and in return came a precious trickle of ivory.

"I had to wait in the station for ten days —an eternity. I lived in a hut in the yard, but to be out of the chaos I would sometimes get into the accountant's office. It was built of horizontal planks, and so badly put together that, as he bent over his high desk, he was barred from neck to heels with narrow strips of sunlight. There was no need to open the big shutter to see. It was hot there, too; big flies buzzed fiendishly, and did not sting, but stabbed. I sat generally on the floor, while, of faultless appearance (and even slightly scented), perching on a high stool, he wrote, he wrote. Sometimes he stood up for exercise. When a trucklebed with a sick man (some invalid agent from up-country) was put in there, he exhibited a gentle annoyance. 'The groans of this sick person,' he said, 'distract my attention. And without that it is extremely difficult to guard against clerical errors in this climate.'

"One day he remarked, without lifting his head, 'In the interior you will no doubt meet Mr. Kurtz.' On my asking who Mr. Kurtz was, he said he was a first-class agent; and

seeing my disappointment at this information, he added slowly, laying down his pen, 'He is a very remarkable person.' Further questions elicited from him that Mr. Kurtz was at present in charge of a trading post, a very important one, in the true ivory-country, at 'the very bottom of there. Sends in as much ivory as all the others put together. . . .' He began to write again. The sick man was too ill to groan. The flies buzzed in a great peace.

"Suddenly there was a growing murmur of voices and a great tramping of feet. A caravan had come in. A violent babble of uncouth sounds burst out on the other side of the planks. All the carriers were speaking together, and in the midst of the uproar the lamentable voice of the chief agent was heard 'giving it up' tearfully for the twentieth time that day. . . . He rose slowly. 'What a frightful row,' he said. He crossed the room gently to look at the sick man, and returning, said to me, 'He does not hear.' 'What! Dead?' I asked, startled. 'No, not yet,' he answered, with great composure. Then, alluding with a toss of the head to the tumult in the stationyard, 'When one has got to make correct entries, one comes to hate those savages—hate them to the death.' He remained thoughtful for a moment. 'When you see Mr. Kurtz,' he went on, 'tell him for me that everything here'—he glanced at the desk —'is very satisfactory. I don't like to write to him—with those messengers of ours you never know who may get hold of your letter —at that Central Station.' He stared at me for a moment with his mild, bulging eyes. 'Oh, he will go far, very far,' he began again. 'He will be a somebody in the Administration before long. They, above—the Council in Europe, you know—mean him to be.'

"He turned to his work. The noise outside had ceased, and presently in going out I stopped at the door. In the steady buzz of flies the homeward-bound agent was lying flushed and insensible; the other, bent over his books, was making correct entries of perfectly correct transactions; and fifty feet below the doorstep I could see the still tree-tops of the grove of death.

"Next day I left that station at last, with a caravan of sixty men, for a two-hundred-mile tramp.

"No use telling you much about that. Paths, paths, everywhere; a stamped-in network of paths spreading over the empty land, through long grass, through burnt grass, through thickets, down and up chilly ravines, up and down stony hills ablaze with heat; and a solitude, a solitude, nobody, not a hut. The population had cleared out a long time ago. Well, if a lot of mysterious niggers armed with all kinds of fearful weapons suddenly took to traveling on the road between Deal and Gravesend, catching the yokels right and left to carry heavy loads for them, I fancy every farm and cottage thereabouts would get empty very soon. Only here the dwellings were gone, too. Still I passed through several abandoned villages. There's something pathetically childish in the ruins of grass walls. Day after day, with the stamp and shuffle of sixty pair of bare feet behind me, each pair under a sixty-lb. load. Camp, cook, sleep, strike camp, march. Now and then a carrier dead in harness, at rest in the long grass near the path, with an empty water-gourd and his long staff lying by his side. A great silence around and above. Perhaps on some quiet night the tremor of far-off drums, sinking, swelling, a tremor vast, faint; a sound weird, appealing, suggestive, and wild—and perhaps with as profound a meaning as the sound of bells in a Christian country. Once a white man in an unbuttoned uniform, camping on the path with an armed escort of lank Zanzibars, very hospitable and festive—not to say drunk. Was looking after the upkeep of the road, he declared. Can't say I saw any road or any upkeep, unless the body of a middle-aged Negro, with a bullet-hole in the forehead, upon which I absolutely stumbled three miles farther on, may be considered as a permanent improvement. I had a white companion, too, not a bad chap, but rather too fleshy and with the exasperating habit of fainting on the hot hillsides, miles away from the least bit of shade and water. Annoying, you know, to hold your own coat like a parasol over a man's head while he is coming-to. I couldn't help asking him once what he meant by coming there at all. 'To make money, of course. What do you think?' he said, scornfully. Then he got fever, and had to be carried in a hammock slung under a pole. As he weighed sixteen stone I had no end of rows with the carriers. They jibbed, ran away, sneaked off with their loads in the night—quite a mutiny. So, one evening, I made a speech in English with gestures, not one of which was lost to the sixty pairs of eyes before me, and the next morning I started the hammock off in front all right. An hour afterwards I came upon the whole concern wrecked in a bush—man, hammock, groans, blankets, horrors. The heavy pole had skinned his poor nose. He was very anxious for me to kill somebody, but there wasn't the shadow of a carrier near. I remembered the old doctor—'It would be interesting for science to watch the mental changes of individuals, on the spot.' I felt I was becoming scientifically interesting. However, all that is to no purpose. On the fifteenth day I came in sight of the big river again, and hobbled into the Central Station. It was on a back water surrounded by scrub and forest, with a pretty border of smelly mud on one side, and on the three others enclosed by a crazy fence of rushes. A neglected gap was all the gate it had, and the first glance at the place was enough to let you see the flabby devil was running that show. White men with long staves in their hands appeared languidly from amongst the buildings, strolling up to take a look at me, and then retired out of sight somewhere. One of them, a stout, excitable chap with black mustaches, informed me with great volubility and many digressions, as soon as I told him who I was, that my steamer was at the bottom of the river. I was thunderstruck. What, how, why? Oh, it was 'all right.' The 'manager himself' was there. All quite correct. 'Everybody had behaved splendidly! splendidly!'—'you must,' he said in agitation, 'go and see the general manager at once. He is waiting!'

"I did not see the real significance of that wreck at once. I fancy I see it now, but I am not sure—not at all. Certainly the affair was too stupid—when I think of it—to be altogether natural. Still. . . . But at the moment it presented itself simply as a confounded nuisance. The steamer was sunk. They had started two days before in a sudden hurry up the river with the manager on board, in charge of some volunteer skipper, and before they had been out three hours they tore the bottom out of her on stones, and she sank near the south bank. I asked myself what I was to do there, now my boat was lost. As a matter of fact, I had plenty to do in fishing my command out of the river. I had to set about it the very next day. That, and the repairs when I brought the pieces to the station, took some months.

"My first interview with the manager was curious. He did not ask me to sit down after my twenty-mile walk that morning. He was commonplace in complexion, in feature, in manners, and in voice. He was of middle size and of ordinary build. His eyes, of the usual blue, were perhaps remarkably cold, and he certainly could make his glance fall on one as trenchant and heavy as an ax. But even at these times the rest of his person seemed to disclaim the intention. Otherwise there was only an indefinable, faint expression of his lips, something stealthy—a smile—not a smile—I remember it, but I can't explain. It was unconscious, this smile was, though just after he had said something it got intensified for an instant. It came at the end of his speeches like a seal applied on the words to make the meaning of the commonest phrase appear absolutely inscrutable. He was a common trader, from his youth up employed in these parts—nothing more. He was obeyed, yet he inspired neither love nor fear, nor even respect. He inspired uneasiness. That was it! Uneasiness. Not a definite mistrust —just uneasiness—nothing more. You have no idea how effective such a . . . a . . . faculty can be. He had no genius for organizing, for initiative, or for order even. That was evident in such things as the deplorable state of the station. He had no learning, and no intelligence. His position had come to him —why? Perhaps because he was never ill. . . . He had served three terms of three

years out there. . . . Because triumphant health in the general rout of constitutions is a kind of power in itself. When he went home on leave he rioted on a large scale—pompously. Jack ashore—with a difference —in externals only. This one could gather from his casual talk. He originated nothing, he could keep the routine going—that's all. But he was great. He was great by this little thing that it was impossible to tell what could control such a man. He never gave that secret away. Perhaps there was nothing within him. Such a suspicion made one pause —for out there there were no external checks. Once when various tropical diseases had laid low almost every 'agent' in the station, he was heard to say, 'Men who come out here should have no entrails.' He sealed the utterance with that smile of his, as though it had been a door opening into a darkness he had in his keeping. You fancied you had seen things—but the seal was on. When annoyed at meal-times by the constant quarrels of the white men about precedence, he ordered an immense round table to be made, for which a special house had to be built. This was the station's mess-room. Where he sat was the first place—the rest were nowhere. One felt this to be his unalterable conviction. He was neither civil nor uncivil. He was quiet. He allowed his 'boy' —an over-fed young Negro from the coast— to treat the white men, under his very eyes, with provoking insolence.

"He began to speak as soon as he saw me. I had been very long on the road. He could not wait. Had to start without me. The up-river stations had to be relieved. There had been so many delays already that he did not know who was dead and who was alive, and how they got on—and so on, and so on. He paid no attention to my explanations, and, playing with a stick of sealing-wax, repeated several times that the situation was 'very grave, very grave.' There were rumors that a very important station was in jeopardy, and its chief, Mr. Kurtz, was ill. Hoped it was not true. Mr. Kurtz was . . . I felt weary and irritable. Hang Kurtz, I thought. I interrupted him by saying I had heard of Mr. Kurtz on the coast. 'Ah! So they talk of him down there,' he murmured to himself. Then he began again, assuring me Mr. Kurtz was the best agent he had, an exceptional man, of the greatest importance to the Company; therefore I could understand his anxiety. He was, he said, 'very, very uneasy.' Certainly he fidgeted on his chair a good deal, exclaimed, 'Ah, Mr. Kurtz!' broke the stick of sealing-wax and seemed dumfounded by the accident. Next thing he wanted to know 'how long it would take to.'. . . . I interrupted him again. Being hungry, you know, and kept on my feet too, I was getting savage. 'How can I tell?' I said. 'I haven't even seen the wreck yet—some months, no doubt.' All this talk seemed to me so futile. 'Some months,' he said. 'Well, let us say three months before we can make a start. Yes. That ought to do the affair.' I flung out of his hut (he lived all alone in a clay hut with a sort of veranda) muttering to myself my opinion of him. He was a chattering idiot. Afterwards I took it back when it was borne in upon me startlingly with what extreme nicety he had estimated the time requisite for the 'affair.'

"I went to work the next day, turning, so to speak, my back on that station. In that way only it seemed to me I could keep my hold on the redeeming facts of life. Still, one must look about sometimes; and then I saw this station, these men strolling aimlessly about in the sunshine of the yard. I asked myself sometimes what it all meant. They wandered here and there with their absurd long staves in their hands, like a lot of faithless pilgrims bewitched inside a rotten fence. The word 'ivory' rang in the air, was whispered, was sighed. You would think they were praying to it. A taint of imbecile rapacity blew through it all, like a whiff from some corpse. By Jove! I've never seen anything so unreal in my life. And outside, the silent wilderness surrounding this cleared speck on the earth struck me as something great and invincible, like evil or truth, waiting patiently for the passing away of this fantastic invasion.

"Oh, these months! Well, never mind. Various things happened. One evening a grass shed full of calico, cotton prints, beads, and I don't know what else, burst into a blaze so suddenly that you would have thought the earth had opened to let an avenging fire consume all that trash. I was smoking my pipe quietly by my dismantled steamer, and saw them all cutting capers in the light, with their arms lifted high, when the stout man with mustaches came tearing down to the river, a tin pail in his hand, assured me that everybody was 'behaving splendidly, splendidly,' dipped about a quart of water and tore back again. I noticed there was a hole in the bottom of his pail.

"I strolled up. There was no hurry. You see the thing had gone off like a box of matches. It had been hopeless from the very first. The flame had leaped high, driven everybody back, lighted up everything—and collapsed. The shed was already a heap of embers glowing fiercely. A nigger was being beaten near by. They said he had caused the fire in some way; be that as it may, he was screeching most horribly. I saw him, later, for several days, sitting in a bit of shade looking very sick and trying to recover himself: afterwards he arose and went out—and the wilderness without a sound took him into its bosom again. As I approached the glow from the dark I found myself at the back of two men, talking. I heard the name of Kurtz pronounced, then the words, 'take advantage of this unfortunate accident.' One of the men was the manager. I wished him a good evening. 'Did you ever see anything like it—eh? it is incredible,' he said, and walked off. The other man remained. He was a first-class agent, young, gentlemanly, a bit reserved, with a forked little beard and a hooked nose. He was stand-offish with the other agents, and they on their side said he was the manager's spy upon them. As to me, I had hardly ever spoken to him before. We got into talk, and by and by we strolled away from the hissing ruins. Then he asked me to his room, which was in the main building of the station. He struck a match, and I perceived that this young aristocrat had not only a silver-mounted dressing-case but also a whole candle all to himself. Just at that time the manager was the only man supposed to have any right to candles. Native mats covered the clay walls; a collection of spears, assegais, shields, knives was hung up in trophies. The business intrusted to this fellow was the making of bricks—so I had been informed; but there wasn't a fragment of a brick anywhere in the station, and he had been there more than a year—waiting. It seems he could not make bricks without something, I don't know what —straw, maybe. Anyway, it could not be found there, and as it was not likely to be sent from Europe, it did not appear clear to me what he was waiting for. An act of special creation perhaps. However, they were all waiting—all the sixteen or twenty pilgrims of them—for something; and upon my word it did not seem an uncongenial occupation, from the way they took it, though the only thing that ever came to them was disease— as far as I could see. They beguiled the time by backbiting and intriguing against each other in a foolish kind of way. There was an air of plotting about that station, but nothing came of it, of course. It was as unreal as everything else—as the philanthropic pretense of the whole concern, as their talk, as their government, as their show of work. The only real feeling was a desire to get appointed to a trading-post where ivory was to be had, so that they could earn percentages. They intrigued and slandered and hated each other only on that account,—but as to effectually lifting a little finger—oh, no. By heavens! there is something after all in the world allowing one man to steal a horse while another must not look at a halter. Steal a horse straight out. Very well. He has done it. Perhaps he can ride. But there is a way of looking at a halter that would provoke the most charitable of saints into a kick.

"I had no idea why he wanted to be sociable, but as we chatted in there it suddenly occurred to me the fellow was trying to get at something—in fact, pumping me. He alluded constantly to Europe, to the people I was supposed to know there—putting leading questions as to my acquaintances in the sepulchral city, and so on. His little eyes glittered like mica discs—with curiosity— though he tried to keep up a bit of superciliousness. At first I was astonished, but very soon I became awfully curious to see what he would find out from me. I couldn't possibly imagine what I had in me to make it worth his while. It was very pretty to see how he baffled himself, for in truth my body was full only of chills, and my head had nothing in it but that wretched steamboat business. It was evident he took me for a perfectly shameless prevaricator. At last he got angry, and, to conceal a movement of furious annoyance, he yawned. I rose. Then I noticed a small sketch in oils, on a panel, representing a woman, draped and blindfolded, carrying a lighted torch. The background was somber—almost black. The movement of the woman was stately, and the effect of the torch-light on the face was sinister.

"It arrested me, and he stood by civilly, holding an empty half-pint champagne bottle (medical comforts) with the candle stuck in it. To my question he said Mr. Kurtz had painted this—in this very station more than a year ago—while waiting for means to go to his trading-post. 'Tell me, pray,' said I, 'who is this Mr. Kurtz?'

"'The chief of the Inner Station,' he answered in a short tone, looking away. 'Much obliged,' I said, laughing. 'And you are the brickmaker of the Central Station. Every one knows that.' He was silent for a while. 'He is a prodigy,' he said at last. 'He is an emissary of pity, and science, and progress, and devil knows what else. We want,' he began to declaim suddenly, 'for the guidance of the cause intrusted to us by Europe, so to speak, higher intelligence, wide sympathies, a singleness of purpose.' 'Who says that?' I asked. 'Lots of them,' he replied. 'Some even write that; and so *he* comes here, a special being, as you ought to know.' 'Why ought I to know?' I interrupted, really surprised. He paid no attention. 'Yes. To-day he is chief of the best station, next year he will be assistant-manager, two years more and . . . but I daresay you know what he will be in two years' time. You are of the new gang—the gang of virtue. The same people who sent him specially also recommended you. Oh, don't say no. I've my own eyes to trust.' Light dawned upon me.

My dear aunt's influential acquaintances were producing an unexpected effect upon that young man. I nearly burst into a laugh. 'Do you read the Company's confidential correspondence?' I asked. He hadn't a word to say. It was great fun. 'When Mr. Kurtz,' I continued, severely, 'is General Manager, you won't have the opportunity.'

"He blew the candle out suddenly, and we went outside. The moon had risen. Black figures strolled about listlessly, pouring water on the glow, whence proceeded a sound of hissing; steam ascended in the moonlight, the beaten nigger groaned somewhere. 'What a row the brute makes!' said the indefatigable man with the mustaches, appearing near us. 'Serves him right. Transgression—punishment—bang! Pitiless, pitiless. That's the only way. This will prevent all conflagrations for the future. I was just telling the manager. . . .' He noticed my companion, and became crestfallen all at once. 'Not in bed yet,' he said, with a kind of servile heartiness; 'it's so natural. Ha! Danger—agitation.' He vanished. I went on to the river-side, and the other followed me. I heard a scathing murmur at my ear, 'Heap of muffs—go to.' The pilgrims could be seen in knots gesticulating, discussing. Several had still their staves in their hands. I verily believe they took these sticks to bed with them. Beyond the fence the forest stood up spectrally in the moonlight, and through the dim stir, through the faint sounds of that lamentable courtyard, the silence of the land went home to one's very heart—its mystery, its greatness, the amazing reality of its concealed life. The hurt nigger moaned feebly somewhere near by, and then fetched a deep sigh that made me mend my pace away from there. I felt a hand introducing itself under my arm. 'My dear sir.' said the fellow, 'I don't want to be misunderstood, and especially by you, who will see Mr. Kurtz long before I can have that pleasure. I wouldn't like him to get a false idea of my disposition. . . .'

"I let him run on, this papier-mâché Mephistopheles, and it seemed to me that if I tried I could poke my forefinger through him, and would find nothing inside but a little loose dirt, maybe. He, don't you see, had been planning to be assistant-manager by and by under the present man, and I could see that the coming of that Kurtz had upset them both not a little. He talked precipitately, and I did not try to stop him. I had my shoulders against the wreck of my streamer, hauled up on the slope like a carcass of some big river animal. The smell of mud, of primeval mud, by Jove! was in my nostrils, the high stillness of primeval forest was before my eyes; there were shiny patches on the black creek. The moon had spread over everything a thin layer of silver—over the rank grass, over the mud, upon the wall of matted vegetation standing higher than the wall of a temple, over the great river I could see through a somber gap glittering, glittering, as it flowed broadly by without a murmur. All this was great, expectant, mute, while the man jabbered about himself. I wondered whether the stillness on the face of the immensity looking at us two were meant as an appeal or as a menace. What were we who had strayed in here? Could we handle that dumb thing, or would it handle us? I felt how big, how confoundedly big, was that thing that couldn't talk, and perhaps was deaf as well. What was in there? I could see a little ivory coming out from there, and I had heard Mr. Kurtz was in there. I had heard enough about it, too—God knows! Yet somehow it didn't bring any image with it—no more than if I had been told an angel or a fiend was in there. I believed it in the same way one of you might believe there are inhabitants in the planet Mars. I knew once a Scotch sailmaker who was certain, dead sure, there were people in Mars. If you asked him for some idea how they looked and behaved, he would get shy and mutter something about 'walking on all-fours.' If you as much as smiled, he would—though a man of sixty-four—offer to fight you. I would not have gone so far as to fight for Kurtz, but I went for him near enough to a lie. You know I hate, detest, and can't bear a lie, not because I am straighter than the rest of us, but simply because it appalls me. There is a taint of death, a flavor of mortality in lies—which is exactly what I hate and detest in the world—what I want to forget. It makes me miserable and sick, like biting something rotten would do. Temperament, I suppose. Well, I went near enough to it by letting the young fool there believe anything he liked to imagine as to my influence in Europe. I became in an instant as much of a pretense as the rest of the bewitched pilgrims. This simply because I had a notion it somehow would be of help to that Kurtz whom at the time I did not see—you understand. He was just a word for me. I did not see the man in the name any more than you do. Do you see him? Do you see the story? Do you see anything? It seems to me I am trying to tell you a dream—making a vain attempt, because no relation of a dream can convey the dream-sensation, that commingling of absurdity, surprise, and bewilderment in a tremor of struggling revolt, that notion of being captured by the incredible which is of the very essence of dreams. . . ."

He was silent for a while.

". . . No, it is impossible; it is impossible to convey the life-sensation of any given epoch of one's existence—that which makes its truth, its meaning—its subtle and penetrating essence. It is impossible. We live, as we dream—alone. . . ."

He paused again as if reflecting, then added—

"Of course in this you fellows see more than I could then. You see me, whom you know. . . ."

It had become so pitch dark that we listeners could hardly see one another. For a long time already he, sitting apart, had been no more to us than a voice. There was not a word from anybody. The others might have been asleep, but I was awake. I listened, I listened on the watch for the sentence, for the word, that would give me the clew to the faint uneasiness inspired by this narrative that seemed to shape itself without human lips in the heavy night-air of the river.

". . . Yes—I let him run on," Marlow began again, "and think what he pleased about the powers that were behind me. I did! And there was nothing behind me! There was nothing but that wretched, old, mangled steamboat I was leaning against, while he talked fluently about 'the necessity for every man to get on.' 'And when one comes out here, you conceive, it is not to gaze at the moon.' Mr. Kurtz was a 'universal genius,' but even a genius would find it easier to work with 'adequate tools—intelligent men.' He did not make bricks—why, there was a physical impossibility in the way—as I was well aware; and if he did secretarial work for the manager, it was because 'no sensible man rejects wantonly the confidence of his superiors.' Did I see it? I saw it. What more did I want? What I really wanted was rivets, by heaven! Rivets. To get on with the work—to stop the hole. Rivets I wanted. There were cases of them down at the coast—cases—piled up—burst—split! You kicked a loose rivet at every second step in that station yard on the hillside. Rivets had rolled into the grove of death. You could fill your pockets with rivets for the trouble of stooping down—and there wasn't one rivet to be found where it was wanted. We had plates that would do, but nothing to fasten them with. And every week the messenger, a lone negro, letter-bag on shoulder and staff in hand, left our station for the coast. And several times a week a coast caravan came in with trade goods—ghastly glazed calico that made you shudder only to look at it; glass beads, valued about a penny a quart, confounded spotted cotton handkerchiefs. And no rivets. Three carriers could have brought all that was wanted to set that steamboat afloat.

"He was becoming confidential now, but I fancy my unresponsive attitude must have exasperated him at last, for he judged it necessary to inform me he feared neither God nor devil, let alone any mere man. I said I could see that very well, but what I wanted was a certain quantity of rivets—and rivets were what really Mr. Kurtz wanted, if he had only known it. Now letters went to the coast every week. . . . 'My dear sir,' he cried, 'I write from dictation.' I demanded rivets. There was a way—for an intelligent man. He changed his manner; became very cold, and suddenly began to talk about a hippo-potamus; wondered whether sleeping on board the steamer (I stuck to my salvage night and day) I wasn't distrubed. There was an old hippo that had the bad habit of getting out on the bank and roaming at night over the station grounds. The pilgrims used to turn out in a body and empty every rifle they could lay hands on at him. Some even had sat up o' nights for him. All this energy was wasted, though. 'That animal has a charmed life,' he said; 'but you can say this only of brutes in this country. No man—you apprehend me?—no man here bears a charmed life.' He stood there for a moment in the moonlight with his delicate hooked nose set a little askew, and his mica eyes glittering without a wink, then, with a curt good night, he strode off. I could see he was disturbed and considerably puzzled, which made me feel more hopeful than I had been for days. It was a great comfort to turn from that chap to my influential friend, the battered, twisted, ruined, tin-pot steamboat. I clambered on board. She rang under my feet like an empty Huntley & Palmer biscuit-tin kicked along a gutter; she was nothing so solid in make, and rather less pretty in shape, but I had expended enough hard work on her to make me love her. No influential friend would have served me better. She had given me a chance to come out a bit—to find out what I could do. No. I don't like work. I had rather laze about and think of all the fine things that can be done. I don't like work—no man does—but I like what is in the work,—the chance to find yourself. Your own reality—for yourself, not for others—what no other man can ever know. They can only see the mere show, and never can tell what it really means.

"I was not surprised to see somebody sitting aft, on the deck, with his legs dangling over the mud. You see I rather chummed with the few mechanics there were in that station, whom the other pilgrims naturally despised—on account of their imperfect manners, I suppose. This was the foreman—a boiler-maker by trade—a good worker. He was a lank, bony, yellow-faced man, with big intense eyes. His aspect was worried, and his head was as bald as the palm of my hand; but his hair in falling seemed to have stuck to his chin, and had prospered in the new locality, for his beard hung down to his waist. He was a widower with six young children (he had left them in charge of a sister of his to come out there), and the passion of his life was pigeon-flying. He was an enthusiast and a connoisseur. He would rave about pigeons. After work hours he used sometimes to come over from his hut for a talk about his children and his pigeons; at work, when he had to crawl in the mud under the bottom of the steamboat, he would tie up that beard of his in a kind of white serviette he brought for the purpose. It had loops to go over his ears. In the evening he could be seen squatted on the bank rinsing that wrapper in the creek with great care, then spreading it solemnly on a bush to dry.

"I slapped him on the back and shouted, 'We shall have rivets!' He scrambled to his feet exclaiming, 'No! Rivets!' as though he couldn't believe his ears. Then in a low voice, 'You . . . eh?' I don't know why we behaved like lunatics. I put my finger to the side of my nose and nodded mysteriously. 'Good for you!' he cried, snapped his fingers above his head, lifting one foot. I tried a jig. We capered on the iron deck. A frightful clatter came out of that hulk, and the virgin forest on the other bank of the creek sent it back in a thundering roll upon the sleeping station. It must have made some of the pilgrims sit up in their hovels. A dark figure obscured the lighted doorway of the manager's hut, vanished, then, a second or so after, the doorway itself vanished, too. We stopped, and the silence driven away by the stamping of our feet flowed back again from the recesses of the land. The great wall of vegetation, an exuberant and entangled mass of trunks, branches, leaves, boughs, festoons, motionless in the moonlight, was like a rioting invasion of soundless life, a rolling wave of plants, piled up, crested, ready to topple over the creek, to sweep every little man of us out of his little existence. And it moved not. A deadened burst of mighty splashes and snorts reached us from afar, as though an ichthyosaurus had been taking a bath of glitter in the great river. 'After all,' said the boiler-maker in a reasonable tone, 'why shouldn't we get the rivets?' Why not, indeed? I did not know of any reason why we shouldn't. 'They'll come in three weeks,' I said, confidently.

"But they didn't. Instead of rivets there came an invasion, an infliction, a visitation. It came in sections during the next three weeks, each section headed by a donkey carrying a white man in new clothes and tan shoes, bowing from that elevation right and left to the impressed pilgrims. A quarrelsome band of footsore sulky niggers trod on the heels of the donkeys; a lot of tents, camp-stools, tin boxes, white cases, brown bales would be shot down in the courtyard, and the air of mystery would deepen a little over the muddle of the station. Five such installments came, with their absurd air of disorderly flight with the loot of innumerable outfit shops and provision stores, that, one would think, they were lugging, after a raid, into the wilderness for equitable division. It was an inextricable mess of things decent in themselves but that human folly made look like the spoils of thieving.

"This devoted band called itself the Eldorado Exploring Expedition, and I believe they were sworn to secrecy. Their talk, however, was the talk of sordid buccaneers: it was reckless without hardihood, greedy without audacity, and cruel without courage; there was not an atom of foresight or of serious intention in the whole batch of them, and they did not seem aware these things are wanted for the work of the world. To tear treasure out of the bowels of the land was their desire, with no more moral purpose at the back of it than there is in burglars breaking into a safe. Who paid the expenses of the noble enterprise I don't know; but the uncle of our manager was leader of that lot.

"In exterior he resembled a butcher in a poor neighborhood, and his eyes had a look of sleepy cunning. He carried his fat paunch with ostentation on his short legs, and during the time his gang infested the station spoke to no one but his nephew. You could see these two roaming about all day long with their heads close together in an everlasting confab.

"I had given up worrying myself about the rivets. One's capacity for that kind of folly is more limited than you would suppose. I said Hang!—and let things slide. I had plenty of time for meditation, and now and then I would give some thought to Kurtz. I wasn't very interested in him. No. Still, I was curious to see whether this man, who had come out equipped with moral ideas of some sort, would climb to the top after all and how he would set about his work when there."

2

One evening as I was lying flat on the deck of my steamboat, I heard voices approaching—and there were the nephew and the uncle strolling along the bank. I laid my head on my arm again, and had nearly lost myself in a doze, when somebody said in my ear, as it were: 'I am as harmless as a little child, but I don't like to be dictated to. Am I the manager—or am I not? I was ordered to send him there. It's incredible.' . . . I became aware that the two were standing on the shore alongside the forepart of the steamboat, just below my head. I did not move; it did not occur to me to move: I was sleepy. 'It *is* unpleasant,' grunted the uncle. 'He has asked the Administration to be sent there,' said the other, 'with the idea of showing what he could do; and I was instructed accordingly. Look at the influence that man must have. Is it not frightful?' They both agreed it was frightful, then made several bizarre remarks: 'Make rain and fine weather—one man—the Council—by the nose'—bits of absurd sentences that got the better of my drowsiness, so that I had pretty near the whole of my wits about me when the uncle said, 'The climate may do away with this difficulty for you. Is he alone there?' 'Yes,' answered the manager; 'he sent his assistant down the river with a note to me in these terms: "Clear this poor devil out of the country, and don't bother sending more of that sort. I had rather be alone than have the kind of men you can dispose of with me." It was more than a year ago. Can you imagine such impudence!' 'Anything since then?' asked the other, hoarsely. 'Ivory,' jerked the nephew; 'lots of it—prime sort—lots—most annoying, from him.' 'And with that?' questioned the heavy rumble. 'Invoice,' was the reply fired out, so to speak. Then silence. They had been talking about Kurtz.

"I was broad awake by this time, but, lying perfectly at ease, remained still, having no inducement to change my position. 'How did that ivory come all this way?' growled the elder man, who seemed very vexed. The other explained that it had come with a fleet of canoes in charge of an English half-caste clerk Kurtz had with him; that Kurtz had apparently intended to return himself, the station being by that time bare of goods and stores, but after coming three hundred miles, had suddenly decided to go back, which he started to do alone in a small dugout with four paddlers, leaving the half-caste to continue down the river with the ivory. The two fellows there seemed astounded at anybody attempting such a thing. They were at a loss for an adequate motive. As to me, I seemed to see Kurtz for the first time. It was a distinct glimpse: the dugout, four paddling savages, and the lone white man turning his back suddenly on the headquarters, on relief, on thoughts of home—perhaps; setting his face towards the depths of the wilderness, towards his empty and desolate station. I did not know the motive. Perhaps he was just simply a fine fellow who stuck to his work for its own sake. His name, you understand, had not been pronounced once. He was 'that man.' The half-caste, who, as far as I could see, had conducted a difficult trip with great prudence and pluck, was invariably alluded to as 'that scoundrel.' The 'scoundrel' had reported that the 'man' had been very ill—had recovered imperfectly. . . . The two below me moved away then a few paces, and strolled back and forth at some little distance. I heard: 'Military post—doctor—two hundred miles—quite alone now—unavoidable delays—nine months—no news—strange rumors.' They approached again, just as the

manager was saying, 'No one, as far as I know, unless a species of wandering trader —a pestilential fellow, snapping ivory from the natives.' Who was it they were talking about now? I gathered in snatches that this was some man supposed to be in Kurtz's district, and of whom the manager did not approve. 'We will not be free from unfair competition till one of these fellows is hanged for an example,' he said. 'Certainly,' grunted the other; 'get him hanged! Why not? Anything—anything can be done in this country. That's what I say; nobody here, you understand, *here,* can endanger your position. And why? You stand the climate—you outlast them all. The danger is in Europe; but there before I left I took care to—' They moved off and whispered, then their voices rose again. 'The extraordinary series of delays is not my fault. I did my best.' The fat man sighed. 'Very sad.' 'And the pestiferous absurdity of his talk,' continued the other; 'he bothered me enough when he was here. "Each station should be like a beacon on the road towards better things, a center for trade, of course, but also for humanizing, improving, instructing." Conceive you—that ass! And he wants to be manager! No, it's—' Here he got choked by excessive indignation, and I lifted my head the least bit. I was surprised to see how near they were—right under me. I could have spat upon their hats. They were looking on the ground, absorbed in thought. The manager was switching his leg with a slender twig: his sagacious relative lifted his head. 'You have been well since you came out this time?' he asked. The other gave a start. 'Who? I? Oh! Like a charm—like a charm. But the rest—oh, my goodness! All sick. They die so quick, too, that I haven't the time to send them out of the country—it's incredible!' 'H'm. Just so,' grunted the uncle. 'Ah! my boy, trust to this—I say, trust to this.' I saw him extend his short flipper of an arm for a gesture that took in the forest, the creek, the mud, the river,—seemed to beckon with a dishonoring flourish before the sunlit face of the land a treacherous appeal to the lurking death, to the hidden evil, to the profound darkness of its heart. It was so startling that I leaped to my feet and looked back at the edge of the forest, as though I had expected an answer of some sort to that black display of confidence. You know the foolish notions that come to one sometimes. The high stillness confronted these two figures with its ominous patience, waiting for the passing away of a fantastic invasion.

"They swore aloud together—out of sheer fright, I believe—then pretending not to know anything of my existence, turned back to the station. The sun was low; and leaning forward side by side, they seemed to be tugging painfully uphill their two ridiculous shadows of unequal length, that trailed behind them slowly over the tall grass without bending a single blade.

"In a few days the Eldorado Expedition went into the patient wilderness, that closed upon it as the sea closes over a diver. Long afterwards the news came that all the donkeys were dead. I know nothing as to the fate of the less valuable animals. They, no doubt, like the rest of us, found what they deserved. I did not inquire. I was then rather excited at the prospect of meeting Kurtz very soon. When I say very soon I mean it comparatively. It was just two months from the day we left the creek when we came to the bank below Kurtz's station.

"Going up that river was like traveling back to the earliest beginnings of the world, when vegetation rioted on the earth and the big trees were kings. An empty stream, a great silence, an impenetrable forest. The air was warm, thick, heavy, sluggish. There was no joy in the brilliance of sunshine. The long stretches of the waterway ran on, deserted, into the gloom of overshadowed distances. On silvery sandbanks hippos and alligators sunned themselves side by side. The broadening waters flowed through a mob of wooded islands; you lost your way on that river as you would in a desert, and butted all day long against shoals, trying to find the channel, till you thought yourself bewitched and cut off forever from everything you had known once—somewhere—far away—in another existence perhaps. There were moments when one's past came back to one, as

it will sometimes when you have not a moment to spare to yourself; but it came in the shape of an unrestful and noisy dream, remembered with wonder amongst the overwhelming realities of this strange world of plants, and water, and silence. And this stillness of life did not in the least resemble a peace. It was the stillness of an implacable force brooding over an inscrutable intention. It looked at you with a vengeful aspect. I got used to it afterwards; I did not see it any more; I had no time. I had to keep guessing at the channel; I had to discern, mostly by inspiration, the signs of hidden banks; I watched for sunken stones; I was learning to clap my teeth smartly before my heart flew out, when I shaved by a fluke some infernal sly old snag that would have ripped the life out of the tin-pot steamboat and drowned all the pilgrims; I had to keep a look-out for the signs of dead wood we could cut up in the night for next day's steaming. When you have to attend to things of that sort, to the mere incidents of the surface, the reality—the reality, I tell you—fades. The inner truth is hidden—luckily, luckily. But I felt it all the same; I felt often its mysterious stillness watching me at my monkey tricks, just as it watches you fellows performing on your respective tight-ropes for—what is it? half-a-crown a tumble—"

" 'Try to be civil, Marlow,' growled a voice, and I knew there was at least one listener awake besides myself.

"I beg your pardon. I forgot the heartache which makes up the rest of the price. And indeed what does the price matter, if the trick be well done? You do your tricks very well. And I didn't do badly either, since I managed not to sink that steamboat on my first trip. It's a wonder to me yet. Imagine a blindfolded man set to drive a van over a bad road. I sweated and shivered over that business considerably, I can tell you. After all, for a seaman, to scrape the bottom of the thing that's supposed to float all the time under his care is the unpardonable sin. No one may know of it, but you never forget the thump—eh? A blow on the very heart. You remember it, you dream of it, you wake up at night and think of it—years after—and go hot and cold all over. I don't pretend to say that steamboat floated all the time. More than once she had to wade for a bit, with twenty cannibals splashing around and pushing. We had enlisted some of these chaps on the way for a crew. Fine fellows—cannibals—in their place. They were men one could work with, and I am grateful to them. And, after all, they did not eat each other before my face: they had brought along a provision of hippo-meat which went rotten, and made the mystery of the wilderness stink in my nostrils. Phoo! I can sniff it now. I had the manager on board and three or four pilgrims with their staves—all complete. Sometimes we came upon a station close by the bank, clinging to the skirts of the unknown, and the white men rushing out of a tumble-down hovel, with great gestures of joy and surprise and welcome, seemed very strange—had the appearance of being held there captive by a spell. The word ivory would ring in the air for a while—and on we went again into the silence, along empty reaches, round the still bends, between the high walls of our winding way, reverberating in hollow claps the ponderous beat of the stern-wheel. Trees, trees, millions of trees, massive, immense, running up high; and at their foot, hugging the bank against the stream, crept the little begrimed steamboat, like a sluggish beetle crawling on the floor of a lofty portico. It made you feel very small, very lost, and yet it was not altogether depressing, that feeling. After all, if you were small, the grimy beetle crawled on—which was just what you wanted it to do. Where the pilgrims imagined it crawled to I don't know. To some place where they expected to get something, I bet! For me it crawled towards Kurtz—exclusively; but when the steam-pipes started leaking we crawled very slow. The reaches opened before us and closed behind, as if the forest had stepped leisurely across the water to bar the way for our return. We penetrated deeper and deeper into the heart of darkness. It was very quiet there. At night sometimes the roll of drums behind the curtain of trees would run up the river and remain sustained faintly, as if hovering in the air high over our heads, till the first break of day. Whether it meant war, peace, or prayer we could not tell. The dawns were heralded by the descent of a chill stillness; the wood-cutters slept, their fires burned low; the snapping of a twig would make you start. We were wanderers on a prehistoric earth, on an earth that wore the aspect of an unknown planet. We could have fancied ourselves the first of men taking possession of an accursed inheritance, to be subdued at the cost of profound anguish and of excessive toil. But suddenly, as we struggled round a bend, there would be a glimpse of rush walls, of peaked grass-roofs, a burst of yells, a whirl of black limbs, a mass of hands clapping, of feet stamping, of bodies swaying, of eyes rolling, under the droop of heavy and motionless foliage. The steamer toiled along slowly on the edge of a black and incomprehensible frenzy. The prehistoric man was cursing us, praying to us, welcoming us—who could tell? We were cut off from the comprehension of our surroundings; we glided past like phantoms, wondering and secretly appalled, as sane men would be before an enthusiastic outbreak in a madhouse. We could not understand because we were too far and could not remember, because we were traveling in the night of first ages, of those ages that are gone, leaving hardly a sign—and no memories.

"The earth seemed unearthly. We are accustomed to look upon the shackled form of a conquered monster, but there—there you could look at a thing monstrous and free. It was unearthly, and the men were— No, they were not inhuman. Well, you know, that was the worst of it—this suspicion of their not being inhuman. It would come slowly to one. They howled and leaped, and spun, and made horrid faces; but what thrilled you was just the thought of their humanity—like yours—the thought of your remote kinship with this wild and passionate uproar. Ugly. Yes, it was ugly enough; but if you were man enough you would admit to yourself that there was in you just the faintest trace of a response to the terrible frankness of that

noise, a dim suspicion of there being a meaning in it which you—you so remote from the
night of first ages—could comprehend. And
why not? The mind of man is capable of anything—because everything is in it, all the
past as well as all the future. What was there
after all? Joy, fear, sorrow, devotion, valor,
rage—who can tell?—but truth—truth
stripped of its cloak of time. Let the fool
gape and shudder—the man knows, and can
look on without a wink. But he must at least
be as much of a man as these on the shore.
He must meet that truth with his own true
stuff—with his own inborn strength. Principles won't do. Acquisitions, clothes, pretty
rags—rags that would fly off at the first good
shake. No; you want a deliberate belief. An
appeal to me in this fiendish row—is there?
Very well; I hear; I admit, but I have a voice,
too, and for good or evil mine is the speech
that cannot be silenced. Of course, a fool,
what with sheer fright and fine sentiments,
is always safe. Who's that grunting? You
wonder I didn't go ashore for a howl and a
dance? Well, no—I didn't. Fine sentiments,
you say? Fine sentiments, be hanged! I had
no time. I had to mess about with whitelead
and strips of woolen blanket helping to put
bandages on those leaky steam-pipes—I tell
you. I had to watch the steering, and circum-
vent those snags, and get the tinpot along by
hook or by crook. There was surface-truth
enough in these things to save a wiser man.
And between whiles I had to look after the
savage who was fireman. He was an improved
specimen; he could fire up a vertical boiler.
He was there below me, and, upon my word,
to look at him was as edifying as seeing a
dog in a parody of breeches and a feather
hat, walking on his hind-legs. A few months
of training had done for that really fine chap.
He squinted at the steam-gauge and at the
water-gauge with an evident effort of intre-
pidity—and he had filed teeth, too, the poor
devil, and the wool of his pate shaved into
queer patterns, and three ornamental scars
on each of his cheeks. He ought to have been
clapping his hands and stamping his feet on
the bank, instead of which he was hard at
work, a thrall to strange witchcraft, full of

improving knowledge. He was useful because
he had been instructed; and what he knew
was this—that should the water in that trans-
parent thing disappear, the evil spirit inside
the boiler would get angry through the greatness of his thirst, and take a terrible vengeance. So he sweated and fired up and watched
the glass fearfully (with an impromptu
charm, made of rags, tied to his arm, and a
piece of polished bone, as big as a watch,
stuck flatways through his lower lip), while
the wooden banks slipped past us slowly, the
short noise was left behind, the interminable miles of silence—and we crept on, towards Kurtz. But the snags were thick, the
water was treacherous and shallow, the boiler
seemed indeed to have a sulky devil in it, and
thus neither that fireman nor I had any time
to peer into our creepy thoughts.

"Some fifty miles below the Inner Station
we came upon a hut of reeds, an inclined
and melancholy pole, with the unrecogniza-
ble tatters of what had been a flag of some
sort flying from it, and a neatly stacked wood-
pile. This was unexpected. We came to the
bank, and on the stack of firewood found a
flat piece of board with some faded pencil-
writing on it. When deciphered it said:
'Wood for you. Hurry up. Approach cautiously.' There was a signature, but it was il-
legible—not Kurtz—a much longer word.
'Hurry up.' Where? Up the river? 'Approach
cautiously.' We had not done so. But the
warning could not have been meant for the
place where it could be only found after approach. Something was wrong above. But
what—and how much? That was the question. We commented adversely upon the imbecility of that telegraphic style. The bush
around said nothing, and would not let us
look very far, either. A torn curtain of red
twill hung in the doorway of the hut, and
flapped sadly in our faces. The dwelling was
dismantled; but we could see a white man
had lived there not very long ago. There remained a rude table—a plank on two posts;
a heap of rubbish reposed in a dark corner,
and by the door I picked up a book. It had
lost its covers, and the pages had been
thumbed into a state of extremely dirty soft-

ness; but the back had been lovingly stitched afresh with white cotton thread, which looked clean yet. It was an extraordinary find. Its title was, *An Inquiry into some Points of Seamanship,* by a man Towser, Towson—some such name—Master in his Majesty's Navy. The matter looked dreary reading enough, with illustrative diagrams and repulsive tables of figures, and the copy was sixty years old. I handled this amazing antiquity with the greatest possible tenderness, lest it should dissolve in my hands. Within, Towson or Towser was inquiring earnestly into the breaking strain of ships' chains and tackle, and other such matters. Not a very enthralling book; but at the first glance you could see there a singleness of intention, an honest concern for the right way of going to work, which made these humble pages, thought out so many years ago, luminous with another than a professional light. The simple old sailor, with his talk of chains and purchases, made me forget the jungle and the pilgrims in a delicious sensation of having come upon something unmistakably real. Such a book being there was wonderful enough; but still more astounding were the notes penciled in the margin, and plainly referring to the text. I couldn't believe my eyes! They were in cipher! Yes, it looked like cipher. Fancy a man lugging with him a book of that description into this nowhere and studying it—and making notes—in cipher at that! It was an extravagant mystery.

"I had been dimly aware for some time of a worrying noise, and when I lifted my eyes I saw the wood pile was gone, and the manager, aided by all the pilgrims, was shouting at me from the river-side. I slipped the book into my pocket. I assure you to leave off reading was like tearing myself away from the shelter of an old and solid friendship.

"I started the lame engine ahead. 'It must be this miserable trader—this intruder,' exclaimed the manager, looking back malevolently at the place we had left. 'He must be English,' I said. 'It will not save him from getting into trouble if he is not careful,' muttered the manager darkly. I observed with assumed innocence that no man was safe from trouble in this world.

"The current was more rapid now, the steamer seemed at her last gasp, the stern-wheel flopped languidly, and I caught myself listening on tiptoe for the next beat of the boat, for in sober truth I expected the wretched thing to give up every moment. It was like watching the last flickers of a life. But still we crawled. Sometimes I would pick out a tree a little way ahead to measure our progress towards Kurtz by, but I lost it invariably before we got abreast. To keep the eyes so long on one thing was too much for human patience. The manager displayed a beautiful resignation. I fretted and fumed and took to arguing with myself whether or no I would talk openly with Kurtz; but before I could come to any conclusion it occurred to me that my speech or my silence, indeed any action of mine, would be a mere futility. What did it matter what any one knew or ignored? What did it matter who was manager? One gets sometimes such a flash of insight. The essentials of this affair lay deep under the surface, beyond my reach, and beyond my power of meddling.

"Towards the evening of the second day we judged ourselves about eight miles from Kurtz's station. I wanted to push on; but the manager looked grave, and told me the navigation up there was so dangerous that it would be advisable, the sun being very low already, to wait where we were till next morning. Moreover, he pointed out that if the warning to approach cautiously were to be followed, we must approach in daylight—not at dusk, or in the dark. This was sensible enough. Eight miles meant nearly three hours' steaming for us, and I could also see suspicious ripples at the upper end of the reach. Nevertheless, I was annoyed beyond expression at the delay, and most unreasonably, too, since one night more could not matter much after so many months. As we had plenty of wood, and caution was the word, I brought up in the middle of the stream. The reach was narrow, straight, with high sides like a railway cutting. The dusk came gliding into it long before the sun had set. The current ran smooth and swift, but a dumb immobility sat on the banks. The living trees, lashed together by the creepers and every living bush of the undergrowth, might have been changed into stone, even to the slenderest twig, to the lightest leaf. It was not sleep—it seemed unnatural, like a state of trance. Not the faintest sound of any kind could be heard. You looked on amazed, and began to suspect yourself of being deaf—then the night came suddenly, and struck you blind as well. About three in the morning some large fish leaped, and the loud splash made me jump as though a gun had been fired. When the sun rose there was a white fog, very warm and clammy, and more blinding than the night. It did not shift or drive; it was just there, standing all round you like something solid. At eight or nine, perhaps, it lifted as a shutter lifts. We had a glimpse of the towering multitude of trees, of the immense matted jungle, with the blazing little ball of the sun hanging over it—all perfectly still—and then the white shutter came down again, smoothly, as if sliding in greased grooves. I ordered the chain, which we had begun to heave in, to be paid out again. Before it stopped running with a muffled rattle, a cry, a very loud cry, as of infinite desolation, soared slowly in the opaque air. It ceased. A complaining clamor, modulated in savage discords, filled our ears. The sheer unexpectedness of it made my hair stir under my cap. I don't know how it struck the others: to me it seemed as though the mist itself had screamed, so suddenly, and apparently from all sides at once, did this tumultuous and mournful uproar arise. It culminated in a hurried outbreak of almost intolerably excessive shrieking, which stopped short, leaving us stiffened in a variety of silly attitudes, and obstinately listening to the nearly as appalling and excessive silence. 'Good God! What is the meaning—' stammered at my elbow one of the pilgrims,—a little fat man, with sandy hair and red whiskers, who wore side-spring boots, and pink pajamas tucked into his socks. Two others remained open-mouthed a whole minute, then dashed into the little cabin, to rush out incontinently

and stand darting scared glances, with Winchesters at 'ready' in their hands. What we could see was just the steamer we were on, her outlines blurred as though she had been on the point of dissolving, and a misty strip of water, perhaps two feet broad, around her —and that was all. The rest of the world was nowhere, as far as our eyes and ears were concerned. Just nowhere. Gone, disappeared; swept off without leaving a whisper or a shadow behind.

"I went forward, and ordered the chain to be hauled in short, so as to be ready to trip the anchor and move the steamboat at once if necessary. 'Will they attack?' whispered an awed voice 'We will be all butchered in this fog,' murmured another. The faces twitched with the strain, the hands trembled slightly, the eyes forgot to wink. It was very curious to see the contrast of expressions of the white men and of the black fellows of our crew, who were as much strangers to that part of the river as we, though their homes were only eight hundred miles away. The whites, of course, greatly discomposed, had besides a curious look of being painfully shocked by such an outrageous row. The others had an alert, naturally interested expression; but their faces were essentially quiet, even those of the one or two who grinned as they hauled at the chain. Several exchanged short, grunting phrases, which seemed to settle the matter to their satisfaction. Their headman, a young, broad-chested black, severely draped in dark-blue fringed cloths, with fierce nostrils and his hair all done up artfully in oily ringlets, stood near me. 'Aha!' I said, just for good fellowship's sake. 'Catch 'im,' he snapped, with a bloodshot widening of his eyes and a flash of sharp teeth— 'catch 'im. Give 'im to us.' 'To you, eh?' I asked; 'what would you do with them?' 'Eat 'im!' he said, curtly, and, leaning his elbow on the rail, looked out into the fog in a dignified and profoundly pensive attitude. I would no doubt have been properly horrified, had it not occurred to me that he and his chaps must be very hungry: that they must have been growing increasingly hungry for at least this month past. They had been engaged for six months (I don't think a single one of them had any clear idea of time, as we at the end of countless ages have. They still belonged to the beginnings of time—had no inherited experience to teach them as it were), and of course, as long as there was a piece of paper written over in accordance with some farcical law or other made down the river, it didn't enter anybody's head to trouble how they would live. Certainly they had brought with them some rotten hippo-meat, which couldn't have lasted very long, anyway, even if the pilgrims hadn't, in the midst of a shocking hullabaloo, thrown a considerable quantity of it overboard. It looked like a high-handed proceeding; but it was really a case of legitimate self-defense. You can't breathe dead hippo waking, sleeping, and eating, and at the same time keep your precarious grip on existence. Besides that, they had given them every week three pieces of brass wire, each about nine inches long; and the theory was they were to buy their provisions with that currency in river-side villages. You can see how *that* worked. There were either no villages, or the people were hostile, or the director, who like the rest of us fed out of tins, with an occasional old he-goat thrown in, didn't want to stop the steamer for some more or less recondite reason. So, unless they swallowed the wire itself, or made loops of it to snare the fishes with, I don't see what good their extravagant salary could be to them. I must say it was paid with a regularity worthy of a large and honorable trading company. For the rest, the only thing to eat—though it didn't look eatable in the least—I saw in their possession was a few lumps of some stuff like half-cooked dough, of a dirty lavender color, they kept wrapped in leaves, and now and then swallowed a piece of, but so small that it seemed done more for the looks of the thing than for any serious purpose of sustenance. Why in the name of all the gnawing devils of hunger they didn't go for us—they were thirty to five—and have a good tuck-in for once, amazes me now when I think of it. They were big powerful men, with not much capacity to weigh the conse-

quences, with courage, with strength, even yet, though their skins were no longer glossy and their muscles no longer hard. And I saw that something restraining, one of those human secrets that baffle probability, had come into play there. I looked at them with a swift quickening of interest—not because it occurred to me I might be eaten by them before very long, though I own to you that just then I perceived—in a new light, as it were—how unwholesome the pilgrims looked, and I hoped, yes, I positively hoped, that my aspect was not so—what shall I say? —so—unappetizing: a touch of fantastic vanity which fitted well with the dream-sensation that pervaded all my days at that time. Perhaps I had a little fever, too. One can't live with one's finger everlastingly on one's pulse. I had often 'a little fever,' or a little touch of other things—the playful paw-strokes of the wilderness, the preliminary trifling before the more serious onslaught which came in due course. Yes; I looked at them as you would on any human being, with a curiosity of their impulses, motives, capacities, weaknesses, when brought to the test of an inexorable physical necessity. Restraint! What possible restraint? Was it superstition, disgust, patience, fear— or some kind of primitive honor? No fear can stand up to hunger, no patience can wear it out, disgust simply does not exist where hunger is; and as to superstition, beliefs, and what you may call principles, they are less than chaff in a breeze. Don't you know the devilry of lingering starvation, its exasperating torment, its black thoughts, its somber and brooding ferocity? Well, I do. It takes a man all his inborn strength to fight hunger properly. It's really easier to face bereavement, dishonor, and the perdition of one's soul—than this kind of prolonged hunger. Sad, but true. And these chaps, too, had no earthly reason for any kind of scruple. Restraint! I would just as soon have expected restraint from a hyena prowling amongst the corpses of a battlefield. But there was the fact facing me—the fact dazzling, to be seen, like the foam on the depths of the sea, like a ripple on an unfathomable enigma, a mystery greater—when I thought of it—than the curious, inexplicable note of desperate grief in this savage clamor that had swept by us on the river-bank, behind the blind whiteness of the fog.

"Two pilgrims were quarreling in hurried whispers as to which bank. 'Left.' 'No, no; how can you? Right, right, of course.' 'It is very serious,' said the manager's voice behind me; 'I would be desolated if anything should happen to Mr. Kurtz before we came up.' I looked at him, and had not the slightest doubt he was sincere. He was just the kind of man who would wish to preserve appearances. That was his restraint. But when he muttered something about going on at once, I did not even take the trouble to answer him. I knew, and he knew, that it was impossible. Were we to let go our hold of the bottom, we would be absolutely in the air—in space. We wouldn't be able to tell where we were going to—whether up or down stream, or across—till we fetched against one bank or the other,—and then we wouldn't know at first which it was. Of course I made no move. I had no mind for a smash-up. You couldn't imagine a more deadly place for a shipwreck. Whether drowned at once or not, we were sure to perish speedily in one way or another. 'I authorize you to take all the risks,' he said, after a short silence. 'I refuse to take any,' I said, shortly; which was just the answer he expected, though its tone might have surprised him. 'Well, I must defer to your judgment. You are captain,' he said, with marked civility. I turned my shoulder to him in sign of my appreciation, and looked into the fog. How long would it last? It was the most hopeless look-out. The approach to this Kurtz grubbing for ivory in the wretched bush was beset by as many dangers as though he had been an enchanted princess sleeping in a fabulous castle. 'Will they attack, do you think?' asked the manager, in a confidential tone.

"I did not think they would attack, for several obvious reasons. The thick fog was one. If they left the bank in their canoes they would get lost in it, as we would be if we attempted to move. Still, I had also judged the jungle of both banks quite impenetrable—and yet eyes were in it, eyes that had seen us. The river-side bushes were certainly very thick; but the undergrowth behind was evidently penetrable. However, during the short lift I had seen no canoes anywhere in the reach—certainly not abreast of the steamer. But what made the idea of attack inconceivable to me was the nature of the noise—of the cries we had heard. They had not the fierce character boding immediate hostile intention. Unexpected, wild, and violent as they had been, they had given me an irresistible impression of sorrow. The glimpse of the steamboat had for some reason filled those savages with unrestrained grief. The danger, if any, I expounded, was from our proximity to a great human passion let loose. Even extreme grief may ultimately vent itself in violence—but more generally takes the form of apathy. . . .

"You should have seen the pilgrims stare! They had no heart to grin, or even to revile me: but I believe they thought me gone mad —with fright, maybe. I delivered a regular lecture. My dear boys, it was no good bothering. Keep a look-out? Well, you may guess I watched the fog for the signs of lifting as a cat watches a mouse; but for anything else our eyes were of no more use to us than if we had been buried miles deep in a heap of cotton-wool. It felt like it, too—choking, warm, stifling. Besides, all I said, though it sounded extravagant, was absolutely true to fact. What we afterwards alluded to as an attack was really an attempt at repulse. The action was very far from being aggressive—it was not even defensive, in the usual sense: it was undertaken under the stress of desperation, and in its essence was purely protective.

"It developed itself, I should say, two hours after the fog lifted, and its commencement was at a spot, roughly speaking, about a mile and a half below Kurtz's station. We had just floundered and flopped round a bend, when I saw an islet, a mere grassy hummock of bright green, in the middle of the stream. It was the only thing of the kind; but as we opened the reach more, I perceived it was the head of a long sandbank, or rather of a chain of shallow patches stretching down the middle of the river. They were discolored, just awash, and the whole lot was seen just under the water, exactly as a man's backbone is seen running down the middle of his back under the skin. Now, as far as I did see, I could go to the right or to the left of this. I didn't know either channel, of course. The banks looked pretty well alike, the depth appeared the same; but as I had been informed the station was on the west side, I naturally headed for the western passage.

"No sooner had we fairly entered it than I became aware it was much narrower than I had supposed. To the left of us there was the long uninterrupted shoal, and to the right a high, steep bank heavily overgrown with bushes. Above the bush the trees stood in serried ranks. The twigs overhung the current thickly, and from distance to distance a large limb of some tree projected rigidly over the stream. It was then well on in the afternoon, the face of the forest was gloomy, and a broad strip of shadow had already fallen on the water. In this shadow we steamed up—very slowly, as you may imagine. I sheered her well inshore—the water being deepest near the bank, as the sounding-pole informed me.

"One of my hungry and forbearing friends was sounding in the bows just below me. This steamboat was exactly like a decked scow. On the deck, there were two little teak-wood houses, with doors and windows. The boiler was in the fore-end, and the machinery right astern. Over the whole there was a light roof, supported on stanchions. The funnel projected through that roof, and in front of the funnel a small cabin built of light planks served for a pilot-house. It contained a couch, two camp-stools, a loaded Martini-Henry leaning in one corner, a tiny table, and the steering-wheel. It had a wide door in front and a broad shutter at each side. All these were always thrown open, of course. I spent my days perched up there on the extreme fore-end of that roof, before the door. At night I slept, or tried to, on the couch. An athletic black belonging to some coast tribe, and educated by my poor predecessor, was the helmsman. He sported a pair of brass earrings, wore a blue cloth wrapper from the waist to the ankles, and thought all the world of himself. He was the most unstable kind of fool I had ever seen. He steered with no end of a swagger while you were by; but if he lost sight of you, he became instantly the prey of an abject funk, and would let that cripple of a steamboat get the upper hand of him in a minute.

"I was looking down at the sounding-pole, and feeling much annoyed to see at each try a little more of it stick out of that river, when I saw my poleman give up the business suddenly, and stretch himself flat on the deck, without even taking the trouble to haul his pole in. He kept hold on it though, and it trailed in the water. At the same time the fireman, whom I could also see below me, sat down abruptly before his furnace and ducked his head. I was amazed. Then I had to look at the river mighty quick, because there was a snag in the fairway. Sticks, little sticks, were flying about—thick: they were whizzing before my nose, dropping below me, striking behind me against my pilot-house. All this time the river, the shore, the woods, were very quiet—perfectly quiet. I could only hear the heavy splashing thump of the stern-wheel and the patter of these things. We cleared the snag clumsily. Arrows, by Jove! We were being shot at! I stepped in quickly to close the shutter on the land-side. That fool-helmsman, his hands on the spokes, was lifting his knees high, stamping his feet, champing his mouth, like a reined-in horse. Confound him! And we were staggering within ten feet of the bank. I had to lean right out to swing the heavy shutter, and I saw a face amongst the leaves on the level with my own, looking at me very fierce and steady; and then suddenly, as though a veil had been removed from my eyes, I made out, deep in the tangled gloom, naked breasts, arms, legs, glaring eyes,—the bush was swarming with human limbs in movement, glistening, of bronze color. The twigs shook, swayed, and rustled, the arrows flew out of them, and then the shutter came to. 'Steer her straight,' I said to the helmsman.

He held his head rigid, face forward; but his eyes rolled, he kept on lifting and setting down his feet gently, his mouth foamed a little. 'Keep quiet!' I said in a fury. I might just as well have ordered a tree not to sway in the wind. I darted out. Below me there was a great scuffle of feet on the iron deck; confused exclamations; a voice screamed, 'Can you turn back?' I caught sight of a V-shaped ripple on the water ahead. What? Another snag! A fusillade burst out under my feet. The pilgrims had opened with their Winchesters, and were simply squirting lead into that bush. A deuce of a lot of smoke came up and drove slowly forward. I swore at it. Now I couldn't see the ripple or the snag either. I stood in the doorway, peering, and the arrows came in swarms. They might have been poisoned, but they looked as though they wouldn't kill a cat. The bush began to howl. Our wood-cutters raised a warlike whoop; the report of a rifle just at my back deafened me. I glanced over my shoulder, and the pilot-house was yet full of noise and smoke when I made a dash at the wheel. The fool-nigger had dropped everything, to throw the shutter open and let off that Martini-Henry. He stood before the wide opening, glaring, and I yelled at him to come back, while I straightened the sudden twist out of that steamboat. There was no room to turn even if I had wanted to, the snag was somewhere very near ahead in that confounded smoke, there was no time to lose, so I just crowded her into the bank—right into the bank, where I knew the water was deep.

"We tore slowly along the overhanging bushes in a whirl of broken twigs and flying leaves. The fusillade below stopped short, as I had foreseen it would when the squirts got empty. I threw my head back to a glinting whizz that traversed the pilot-house, in at one shutter-hole and out at the other. Looking past that mad helmsman, who was shaking the empty rifle and yelling at the shore, I saw vague forms of men running bent double, leaping, gliding, distinct, incomplete, evanescent. Something big appeared in the air before the shutter, the rifle went over-board, and the man stepped back swiftly, looked at me over his shoulder in an extraordinary, profound, familiar manner, and fell upon my feet. The side of his head hit the wheel twice, and the end of what appeared a long cane clattered round and knocked over a little camp-stool. It looked as though after wrenching that thing from somebody ashore he had lost his balance in the effort. The thin smoke had blown away, we were clear of the snag, and looking ahead I could see that in another hundred yards or so I would be free to sheer off, away from the bank; but my feet felt so very warm and wet that I had to look down. The man had rolled on his back and stared straight up at me; both his hands clutched that cane. It was the shaft of a spear that, either thrown or lunged through the opening, had caught him in the side just below the ribs; the blade had gone in out of sight, after making a frightful gash; my shoes were full; a pool of blood lay very still, gleaming dark-red under the wheel; his eyes shone with an amazing luster. The fusillade burst out again. He looked at me anxiously, gripping the spear like something precious, with an air of being afraid I would try to take it away from him. I had to make an effort to free my eyes from his gaze and attend to steering. With one hand I felt above my head for the line of the steam whistle, and jerked out screech after screech hurriedly. The tumult of angry and warlike yells was checked instantly, and then from the depths of the woods went out such a tremulous and prolonged wail of mournful fear and utter despair as may be imagined to follow the flight of the last hope from the earth. There was a great commotion in the bush; the shower of arrows stopped, a few dropping shots rang out sharply—then silence, in which the languid beat of the stern-wheel came plainly to my ears. I put the helm hard a-starboard at the moment when the pilgrim in pink pajamas, very hot and agitated, appeared in the doorway. 'The manager sends me—' he began in an official tone, and stopped short. 'Good God!' he said, glaring at the wounded man.

"We two whites stood over him, and his

lustrous and inquiring glance enveloped us both. I declare it looked as though he would presently put to us some question in an understandable language; but he died without uttering a sound, without moving a limb, without twitching a muscle. Only in the very last moment, as though in response to some sign we could not see, to some whisper we could not hear, he frowned heavily, and that frown gave to his black death-mask an inconceivably somber, brooding, and menacing expression. The luster of inquiring glance faded swiftly into vacant glassiness. 'Can you steer?' I asked the agent eagerly. He looked very dubious; but I made a grab at his arm, and he understood at once I meant him to steer whether or no. To tell you the truth, I was morbidly anxious to change my shoes and socks. 'He is dead,' murmured the fellow, immensely impressed. 'No doubt about it,' said I, tugging like mad at the shoe-laces. 'And by the way, I suppose Mr. Kurtz is dead as well by this time.'

"For the moment that was the dominant thought. There was a sense of extreme disappointment, as though I had found out I had been striving after something altogether without a substance. I couldn't have been more disgusted if I had traveled all this way for the sole purpose of talking with Mr. Kurtz. Talking with . . . I flung one shoe overboard, and became aware that that was exactly what I had been looking forward to—a talk with Kurtz. I made the strange discovery that I had never imagined him as doing, you know, but as discoursing. I didn't say to myself, 'Now I will never see him,' or 'Now I will never shake him by the hand,' but, 'Now I will never hear him.' The man presented himself as a voice. Not of course that I did not connect him with some sort of action. Hadn't I been told in all the tones of jealousy and admiration that he had collected, bartered, swindled, or stolen more ivory than all the other agents together? That was not the point. The point was in his being a gifted creature, and that of all his gifts the one that stood out preëminently, that carried with it a sense of real presence, was his ability to talk, his words—the gift of expression,

the bewildering, the illuminating, the most exalted and the most contemptible, the pulsating stream of light, or the deceitful flow from the heart of an impenetrable darkness.

"The other shoe went flying unto the devil-god of that river. I thought, by Jove! it's all over. We are too late; he has vanished—the gift has vanished, by means of some spear, arrow, or club. I will never hear that chap speak after all,—and my sorrow had a startling extravagance of emotion, even such as I had noticed in the howling sorrow of these savages in the bush. I couldn't have felt more lonely desolation somehow, had I been robbed of a belief or had missed my destiny in life. . . . Why do you sigh in this beastly way, somebody? Absurd? Well, absurd. Good Lord! mustn't a man ever—Here, give me some tobacco." . . .

There was a pause of profound stillness, then a match flared, and Marlow's lean face appeared, worn, hollow, with downward folds and drooped eyelids, with an aspect of concentrated attention; and as he took vigorous draws at his pipe, it seemed to retreat and advance out of the night in the regular flicker of the tiny flame. The match went out.

"Absurd!" he cried. "This is the worst of trying to tell. . . . Here you all are, each moored with two good addresses, like a hulk with two anchors, a butcher round one corner, a policeman round another, excellent appetites, and temperature normal—you hear—normal from year's end to year's end. And you say, Absurd! Absurd be—exploded! Absurd! My dear boys, what can you expect from a man who out of sheer nervousness had just flung overboard a pair of new shoes! Now I think of it, it is amazing I did not shed tears. I am, upon the whole, proud of my fortitude. I was cut to the quick at the idea of having lost the inestimable privilege of listening to the gifted Kurtz. Of course I was wrong. The privilege was waiting for me. Oh, yes, I heard more than enough. And I was right, too. A voice. He was very little more than a voice. And I heard—him—it—this voice—other voices—all of them were so little more than voices—and the memory of that time itself lingers around me, impalpable, like a dying vibration of one immense jabber, silly, atrocious, sordid, savage, or simply mean, without any kind of sense. Voices, voices—even the girl herself—now—"

He was silent for a long time.

"I laid the ghost of his gifts at last with a lie," he began, suddenly. "Girl! What? Did I mention a girl? Oh, she is out of it—completely. They—the women I mean—are out of it—should be out of it. We must help them to stay in that beautiful world of their own, lest ours gets worse. Oh, she had to be out of it. You should have heard the disinterred body of Mr. Kurtz saying, 'My Intended.' You would have perceived directly then how completely she was out of it. And the lofty frontal bone of Mr. Kurtz! They say the hair goes on growing sometimes, but this —ah—specimen, was impressively bald. The wilderness had patted him on the head, and, behold, it was like a ball—an ivory ball; it had caressed him, and—lo!—he had withered; it had taken him, loved him, embraced him, got into his veins, consumed his flesh, and sealed his soul to its own by the inconceivable ceremonies of some devilish initiation. He was its spoiled and pampered favorite. Ivory? I should think so. Heaps of it, stacks of it. The old mud shanty was bursting with it. You would think there was not a single tusk left either above or below the ground in the whole country. 'Mostly fossil,' the manager had remarked, disparagingly. It was no more fossil than I am; but they call it fossil when it is dug up. It appears these niggers do bury the tusks sometimes —but evidently they couldn't bury this parcel deep enough to save the gifted Mr. Kurtz from his fate. We filled the steamboat with it, and had to pile a lot on the deck. Thus he could see and enjoy as long as he could see, because the appreciation of this favor had remained with him to the last. You should have heard him say, 'My ivory.' Oh, yes, I heard him. 'My Intended, my ivory, my station, my river, my—' everything belonged to him. It made me hold my breath in expectation of hearing the wilderness burst into a prodigious peal of laughter that would

shake the fixed stars in their places. Everything belonged to him—but that was a trifle. The thing was to know what he belonged to, how many powers of darkness claimed him for their own. That was the reflection that made you creepy all over. It was impossible —it was not good for one either—trying to imagine. He had taken a high seat amongst the devils of the land—I mean literally. You can't understand. How could you?—with solid pavement under your feet, surrounded by kind neighbors ready to cheer you or to fall on you, stepping delicately between the butcher and the policeman, in the holy terror of scandal and gallows and lunatic asylums—how can you imagine what particular region of the first ages a man's untrammeled feet may take him into by the way of solitude—utter solitude without a policeman—by the way of silence—utter silence, where no warning voice of a kind neighbor can be heard whispering of public opinion? These little things make all the great difference. When they are gone you must fall back upon your own innate strength, upon your own capacity for faithfulness. Of course you may be too much of a fool to go wrong—too dull even to know you are being assaulted by the powers of darkness. I take it, no fool ever made a bargain for his soul with the devil: the fool is too much of a fool, or the devil too much of a devil—I don't know which. Or you may be such a thunderingly exalted creature as to be altogether deaf and blind to anything but heavenly sights and sounds. Then the earth for you is only a standing place—and whether to be like this is your loss or your gain I won't pretend to say. But most of us are neither one nor the other. The earth for us is a place to live in, where we must put up with sights, with sounds, with smells, too, by Jove!—breathe dead hippo, so to speak, and not be contaminated. And there, don't you see? your strength comes in, the faith in your ability for the digging of unostentatious holes to bury the stuff in—your power of devotion, not to yourself, but to an obscure, back-breaking business. And that's difficult enough. Mind,

I am not trying to excuse or even explain—I am trying to account to myself for—for—Mr. Kurtz—for the shade of Mr. Kurtz. This initiated wraith from the back of Nowhere honored me with its amazing confidence before it vanished altogether. This was because it could speak English to me. The original Kurtz had been educated partly in England, and—as he was good enough to say himself—his sympathies were in the right place. His mother was half-English, his father was half-French. All Europe contributed to the making of Kurtz; and by and by I learned that, most appropriately, the International Society for the Suppression of Savage Customs had intrusted him with the making of a report, for its future guidance. And he had written it, too. I've seen it. I've read it. It was eloquent, vibrating with eloquence, but too high-strung, I think. Seventeen pages of close writing he had found time for! But this must have been before his—let us say—nerves, went wrong, and caused him to preside at certain midnight dances ending with unspeakable rites, which—as far as I reluctantly gathered from what I heard at various times—were offered up to him—do you understand?—to Mr. Kurtz himself. But it was a beautiful piece of writing. The opening paragraph, however, in the light of later information, strikes me now as ominous. He began with the argument that we whites, from the point of development we had arrived at, 'must necessarily appear to them [savages] in the nature of supernatural beings—we approach them with the might as of a deity,' and so on, and so on. 'By the simple exercise of our will we can exert a power for good practically unbounded,' etc. etc. From that point he soared and took me with him. The peroration was magnificent, though difficult to remember, you know. It gave me the notion of an exotic Immensity ruled by an august Benevolence. It made me tingle with enthusiasm. This was the unbounded power of eloquence—of words—of burning noble words. There were no practical hints to interrupt the magic current of phrases, unless a kind of note at the foot of the last page, scrawled evidently much later, in an unsteady hand, may be regarded as the exposition of a method. It was very simple, and at the end of that moving appeal to every altruistic sentiment it blazed at you, luminous and terrifying, like a flash of lightning in a serene sky: 'Exterminate all the brutes!' The curious part was that he had apparently forgotten all about the valuable postscriptum, because, later on, when he in a sense came to himself, he repeatedly entreated me to take good care of 'my pamphlet' (he called it), as it was sure to have in the future a good influence upon his career. I had full information about all these things, and, besides, as it turned out, I was to have the care of his memory. I've done enough for it to give me the indisputable right to lay it, if I choose, for an everlasting rest in the dustbin of progress, amongst all the sweepings and, figuratively speaking, all the dead cats of civilization. But then, you see, I can't choose. He won't be forgotten. Whatever he was, he was not common. He had the power to charm or frighten rudimentary souls into an aggravated witch-dance in his honor; he could also fill the small souls of the pilgrims with bitter misgivings: he had one devoted friend at least, and he had conquered one soul in the world that was neither rudimentary nor tainted with self-seeking. No; I can't forget him, though I am not prepared to affirm the fellow was exactly worth the life we lost in getting to him. I missed my late helmsman awfully,—I missed him even while his body was still lying in the pilot-house. Perhaps you will think it passing strange this regret for a savage who was no more account than a grain of sand in a black Sahara. Well, don't you see, he had done something, he had steered; for months I had him at my back—a help—an instrument. It was a kind of partnership. He steered for me—I had to look after him, I worried about his deficiencies, and thus a subtle bond had been created, of which I only became aware when it was suddenly broken. And the intimate profundity of that look he gave me when he received his hurt remains to this day in my memory—like a claim of distant kinship affirmed in a supreme moment.

"Poor fool! If he had only left that shutter alone. He had no restraint, no restraint—just like Kurtz—a tree swayed by the wind. As soon as I had put on a dry pair of slippers, I dragged him out, after first jerking the spear out of his side, which operation I confess I performed with my eyes shut tight. His heels leaped together over the little door-step; his shoulders were pressed to my breast; I hugged him from behind desperately. Oh! he was heavy, heavy; heavier than any man on earth, I should imagine. Then without more ado I tipped him overboard. The current snatched him as though he had been a wisp of grass, and I saw the body roll over twice before I lost sight of it forever. All the pilgrims and the manager were then congregated on the awning-deck about the pilot-house, chattering at each other like a flock of excited magpies, and there was a scandalized murmur at my heartless promptitude. What they wanted to keep that body hanging about for I can't guess. Embalm it, maybe. But I had also heard another, and a very ominous, murmur on the deck below. My friends the wood-cutters were likewise scandalized, and with a better show of reason—though I admit that the reason itself was quite inadmissible. Oh, quite! I had made up my mind that if my late helmsman was to be eaten, the fishes alone should have him. He had been a very second-rate helmsman while alive, but now he was dead he might have become a first-class temptation, and possibly cause some startling trouble. Besides, I was anxious to take the wheel, the man in pink pajamas showing himself a hopeless duffer at the business.

"This I did directly the simple funeral was over. We were going half-speed, keeping right in the middle of the stream, and I listened to the talk about me. They had given up Kurtz, they had given up the station; Kurtz was dead, and the station had been burnt—and so on—and so on. The red-haired pilgrim was beside himself with the thought that at least this poor Kurtz had been properly avenged. 'Say! We must have made a glorious slaughter of them in the bush. Eh? What do you think? Say?' He positively danced, the bloodthirsty little gingery beggar. And he had nearly fainted when he saw the wounded man! I could not help saying, 'You made a glorious lot of smoke, anyhow.' I had seen, from the way the tops of the bushes rustled and flew, that almost all the shots had gone too high. You can't hit anything unless you take aim and fire from the shoulder; but these chaps fired from the hip with their eyes shut. The retreat, I maintained—and I was right—was caused by the screeching of the steam-whistle. Upon this they forgot Kurtz, and began to howl at me with indignant protests.

"The manager stood by the wheel murmuring confidentially about the necessity of getting well away down the river before dark at all events, when I saw in the distance a clearing on the river-side and the outlines of some sort of building. 'What's this?' I asked. He clapped his hands in wonder. 'The station!' he cried. I edged in at once, still going half-speed.

"Through my glasses I saw the slope of a hill interspersed with rare trees and perfectly free from undergrowth. A long decaying building on the summit was half buried in the high grass; the large holes in the peaked roof gaped black from afar; the jungle and the woods made a background. There was no enclosure or fence of any kind; but there had been one apparently, for near the house half-a-dozen slim posts remained in a row, roughly trimmed, and with their upper ends ornamented with round carved balls. The rails, or whatever there had been between, had disappeared. Of course the forest surrounded all that. The river-bank was clear, and on the water-side I saw a white man under a hat like a cartwheel beckoning persistently with his whole arm. Examining the edge of the forest above and below, I was almost certain I could see movements—human forms gliding here and there. I steamed past prudently, then stopped the engines and let her drift down. The man on the shore began to shout, urging us to land. 'We have been attacked,' screamed the manager. 'I know—I know. It's all right,' yelled back the other, as cheerful as you please. 'Come along. It's all right. I am glad.'

"His aspect reminded me of something I

had seen—something funny I had seen somewhere. As I maneuvered to get alongside, I was asking myself, 'What does this fellow look like?' Suddenly I got it. He looked like a harlequin. His clothes had been made of some stuff that was brown holland probably, but it was covered with patches all over, with bright patches, blue, red and yellow,—patches on the back, patches on the front, patches on elbows, on knees; colored binding around his jacket, scarlet edging at the bottom of his trousers; and the sunshine made him look extremely gay and wonderfully neat withal, because you could see how beautifully all this patching had been done. A beardless, boyish face, very fair, no features to speak of, nose peeling, little blue eyes, smiles and frowns chasing each other over that open countenance like sunshine and shadow on a windswept plain. 'Look out, captain!' he cried; 'there's a snag lodged in her last night.' 'What! Another snag?' I confess I swore shamefully. I had nearly holed my cripple, to finish off that charming trip. The harlequin on the bank turned his little pug-nose up to me. 'You English?' he asked, all smiles. 'Are you?' I shouted from the wheel. The smiles vanished, and he shook his head as if sorry for my disappointment. Then he brightened up. 'Never mind!' he cried, encouragingly. 'Are we in time?' I asked. 'He is up there,' he replied, with a toss of the head up the hill, and becoming gloomy all of a sudden. His face was like the autumn sky, overcast one moment and bright the next.

"When the manager, escorted by the pilgrims, all of them armed to the teeth, had gone to the house this chap came on board. 'I say, I don't like this. These natives are in the bush,' I said. He assured me earnestly it was all right. 'They are simple people,' he added; 'well, I am glad you came. It took me all my time to keep them off.' 'But you said it was all right,' I cried. 'Oh, they meant no harm,' he said; and as I stared he corrected himself, 'Not exactly.' Then vivaciously, 'My faith, your pilot-house wants a clean-up!' In the next breath he advised me to keep enough steam on the boiler to blow the whistle in case of any trouble. 'One good

screech will do more for you than all your rifles. They are simple people,' he repeated. He rattled away at such a rate he quite overwhelmed me. He seemed to be trying to make up for lots of silence, and actually hinted, laughing, that such was the case. 'Don't you talk with Mr. Kurtz?' I said. 'You don't talk with that man—you listen to him,' he exclaimed with severe exaltation. 'But now—' He waved his arm, and in the twinkling of an eye was in the uttermost depths of despondency. In a moment he came up again with a jump, possessed himself of both my hands, shook them continuously, while he gabbed: 'Brother sailor . . . honor . . . pleasure . . . delight . . . introduce myself . . . Russian . . . son of an arch-priest . . . Government of Tambov. . . . What? Tobacco! English tobacco; the excellent English tobacco! Now, that's brotherly. Smoke? Where's a sailor that does not smoke?'

"The pipe soothed him, and gradually I made out he had run away from school, had gone to sea in a Russian ship; ran away again; served some time in English ships; was now reconciled with the arch-priest. He made a point of that. 'But when one is young one must see things, gather experience, ideas; enlarge the mind.' 'Here!' I interrupted. 'You can never tell! Here I met Mr. Kurtz,' he said, youthfully solemn and reproachful. I held my tongue after that. It appears he had persuaded a Dutch trading house on the coast to fit him out with stores and goods, and had started for the interior with a light heart, and no more idea of what would happen to him than a baby. He had been wandering about that river for nearly two years alone, cut off from everybody and everything. 'I am not so young as I look. I am twenty-five,' he said. 'At first old Van Shuyten would tell me to go to the devil,' he narrated with keen enjoyment; 'but I stuck to him, and talked and talked, till at last he got afraid I would talk the hind-leg off his favorite dog, so he gave me some cheap things and a few guns, and told me he hoped he would never see my face again. Good old Dutchman, Van Shuyten. I've sent him one small lot of ivory a year ago, so that he can't call me a little thief when I get back. I hope he got it. And for the rest I don't care. I had some wood stacked for you. That was my old house. Did you see?'

"I gave him Towson's book. He made as though he would kiss me, but restrained himself. 'The only book I had left, and I thought I had lost it,' he said, looking at it ecstatically. 'So many accidents happen to a man going about alone, you know. Canoes get upset sometimes—and sometimes you've got to clear out so quick when the people get angry.' He thumbed the pages. 'You made notes in Russian?' I asked. He nodded. 'I thought they were written in cipher,' I said. He laughed, then became serious. 'I had lots of trouble to keep these people off,' he said. 'Did they want to kill you?' I asked. 'Oh, no!' he cried, and checked himself. 'Why did they attack us?' I pursued. He hesitated, then said shamefacedly, 'They don't want him to go.' 'Don't they?' I said curiously. He nodded a nod full of mystery and wisdom. 'I tell you,' he cried, 'this man has enlarged my mind.' He opened his arms wide, staring at me with his little blue eyes that were perfectly round."

3

"I looked at him, lost in astonishment. There he was before me, in motley, as though he had absconded from a troupe of mimes, enthusiastic, fabulous. His very existence was improbable, inexplicable, and altogether bewildering. He was an insoluble problem. It was inconceivable how he had existed, how he had succeeded in getting so far, how he had managed to remain—why he did not instantly disappear. 'I went a little farther,' he said, 'then still a little farther—till I had gone so far that I don't know how I'll ever get back. Never mind. Plenty time. I can manage. You take Kurtz away quick—quick—I tell you.' The glamour of youth enveloped his parti-colored rags, his destitution, his loneliness, the essential desolation of his futile wanderings. For months—for years—his life hadn't been worth a day's purchase; and there he was gallantly, thoughtlessly alive, to all appearance indestructible solely by the virtue of his few years and of

his unreflecting audacity. I was seduced into something like admiration—like envy. Glamour urged him on, glamour kept him unscathed. He surely wanted nothing from the wilderness but space to breathe in and to push on through. His need was to exist, and to move onwards at the greatest possible risk, and with a maximum of privation. If the absolutely pure, uncalculating, unpractical spirit of adventure had ever ruled a human being, it ruled this be-patched youth. I almost envied him the possession of this modest and clear flame. It seemed to have consumed all thought of self so completely, that even while he was talking to you, you forgot that it was he—the man before your eyes—who had gone through these things. I did not envy him his devotion to Kurtz, though. He had not meditated over it. It came to him and he accepted it with a sort of eager fatalism. I must say that to me it appeared about the most dangerous thing in every way he had come upon so far.

"They had come together unavoidably, like two ships becalmed near each other, and lay rubbing sides at last. I suppose Kurtz wanted an audience, because on a certain occasion, when encamped in the forest, they had talked all night, or more probably Kurtz had talked. 'We talked of everything,' he said, quite transported at the recollection. 'I forgot there was such a thing as sleep. The night did not seem to last an hour. Everything! Everything! . . . Of love, too.' 'Ah, he talked to you of love!' I said, much amused. 'It isn't what you think,' he cried, almost passionately. 'It was in general. He made me see things—things.'

"He threw his arms up. We were on deck at the time, and the headman of my woodcutters, lounging near by, turned upon him his heavy and glittering eyes. I looked around, and I don't know why, but I assure you that never, never before, did this land, this river, this jungle, the very arch of this blazing sky, appear to me so hopeless and so dark, so impenetrable to human thought, so pitiless to human weakness. 'And, ever since, you have been with him, of course?' I said.

"On the contrary. It appears their intercourse had been very much broken by various causes. He had, as he informed me proudly, managed to nurse Kurtz through two illnesses (he alluded to it as you would to some risky feat), but as a rule Kurtz wandered alone far in the depths of the forest. 'Very often coming to this station, I had to wait days and days before he would turn up,' he said. 'Ah, it was worth waiting for!—sometimes.' 'What was he doing? exploring or what?' I asked. 'Oh, yes, of course'; he had discovered lots of villages, a lake, too—he did not know exactly in what direction; it was dangerous to inquire too much—but mostly his expeditions had been for ivory. 'But he had no goods to trade with by that time,' I objected. 'There's a good lot of cartridges left even yet,' he answered, looking away. 'To speak plainly, he raided the country,' I said. He nodded. 'Not alone, surely!' He muttered something about the villages round that lake. 'Kurtz got the tribe to follow him, did he?' I suggested. He fidgeted a little. 'They adored him,' he said. The tone of these words was so extraordinary that I looked at him searchingly. It was curious to see his mingled eagerness and reluctance to speak of Kurtz. The man filled his life, occupied his thoughts, swayed his emotions. 'What can you expect?' he burst out; 'he came to them with thunder and lightning, you know—and they had never seen anything like it—and very terrible. He could be very terrible. You can't judge Mr. Kurtz as you would an ordinary man. No, no, no! Now—just to give you an idea—I don't mind telling you he wanted to shoot me, too, one day—but I don't judge him.' 'Shoot you!' I cried. 'What for?' 'Well, I had a small lot of ivory the chief of that village near my house gave me. You see I used to shoot game for them. Well, he wanted it, and wouldn't hear reason. He declared he would shoot me unless I gave him the ivory and then cleared out of the country, because he could do so, and had a fancy for it, and there was nothing on earth to prevent him killing whom he jolly well pleased. And it was true, too. I gave him the ivory. What did I care! But I didn't clear out. No, no, I couldn't leave him. I had to be careful, of course, till we got

friendly again for a time. He had his second illness then. Afterwards I had to keep out of the way; but I didn't mind. He was living for the most part in those villages on the lake. When he came down to the river, sometimes he would take to me, and sometimes it was better for me to be careful. This man suffered too much. He hated all this, and somehow he couldn't get away. When I had a chance I begged him to try and leave while there was time; I offered to go back with him. And he would say yes, and then he would remain; go off on another ivory hunt; disappear for weeks; forget himself amongst these people—forget himself—you know.' 'Why! he's mad,' I said. He protested indignantly. Mr. Kurtz couldn't be mad. If I had heard him talk, only two days ago, I wouldn't dare hint at such a thing. . . . I had taken up my binoculars while we talked, and was looking at the shore, sweeping the limit of the forest at each side and at the back of the house. The consciousness of there being people in that bush, so silent, so quiet—as silent and quiet as the ruined house on the hill—made me uneasy. There was no sign on the face of nature of this amazing tale that was not so much told as suggested to me in desolate exclamations, completed by shrugs, in interrupted phrases, in hints ending in deep sighs. The woods were unmoved, like a mask—heavy, like the closed door of a prison—they looked with their air of hidden knowledge, of patient expectation, of unapproachable silence. The Russian was explaining to me that it was only lately that Mr. Kurtz had come down to the river, bringing along with him all the fighting men of that lake tribe. He had been absent for several months—getting himself adored, I suppose—and had come down unexpectedly, with the intention to all appearance of making a raid either across the river or down stream. Evidently the appetite for more ivory had got the better of the—what shall I say?—less material aspirations. However he had got much worse suddenly. 'I heard he was lying helpless, and so I came up—took my chance,' said the Russian. 'Oh, he is bad, very bad.' I directed my glass to the house. There were no signs of life, but there was the ruined roof, the long mud wall peeping above the grass, with three little square window-holes, no two of the same size; all this brought within reach of my hand, as it were. And then I made a brusque movement, and one of the remaining posts of that vanished fence leaped up in the field of my glass. You remember I told you I had been struck at the distance by certain attempts at ornamentation, rather remarkable in the ruinous aspect of the place. Now I had suddenly a nearer view, and its first result was to make me throw my head back as if before a blow. Then I went carefully from post to post with my glass, and I saw my mistake. These round knobs were not ornamental but symbolic; they were expressive and puzzling, striking and disturbing—food for thought and also for vultures if there had been any looking down from the sky; but at all events for such ants as were industrious enough to ascend the pole. They would have been even more impressive, those heads on the stakes, if their faces had not been turned to the house. Only one, the first I had made out, was facing my way. I was not so shocked as you may think. The start back I had given was really nothing but a movement of surprise. I had expected to see a knob of wood there, you know. I returned deliberately to the first I had seen—and there it was, black, dried, sunken, with closed eyelids,—a head that seemed to sleep at the top of that pole, and with the shrunken dry lips showing a narrow white line of the teeth, was smiling, too, smiling continuously at some endless and jocose dream of that eternal slumber.

"I am not disclosing any trade secrets. In fact, the manager said afterwards that Mr. Kurtz's methods had ruined the district. I have no opinion on that point, but I want you clearly to understand that there was nothing exactly profitable in these heads being there. They only showed that Mr. Kurtz lacked restraint in the gratification of his various lusts, that there was something wanting in him—some small matter which, when the pressing need arose, could not be found under his magnificent eloquence. Whether

he knew of this deficiency himself I can't say. I think the knowledge came to him at last—only at the very last. But the wilderness had found him out early, and had taken on him a terrible vengeance for the fantastic invasion. I think it had whispered to him things about himself which he did not know, things of which he had no conception till he took counsel with this great solitude—and the whisper had proved irresistibly fascinating. It echoed loudly within him because he was hollow at the core. . . . I put down the glass, and the head that had appeared near enough to be spoken to seemed at once to have leaped away from me into inaccessible distance.

"The admirer of Mr. Kurtz was a bit crestfallen. In a hurried indistinct voice he began to assure me he had not dared to take these —say, symbols—down. He was not afraid of the natives; they would not stir till Mr. Kurtz gave the word. His ascendancy was extraordinary. The camps of these people surrounded the place, and the chiefs came every day to see him. They would crawl. . . . 'I don't want to know anything of the ceremonies used when approaching Mr. Kurtz,' I shouted. Curious, this feeling that came over me that such details would be more intolerable than those heads drying on the stakes under Mr. Kurtz's windows. After all, that was only a savage sight, while I seemed at one bound to have been transported into some lightless region of subtle horrors, where pure, uncomplicated savagery was a positive relief, being something that had a right to exist—obviously—in the sunshine. The young man looked at me with surprise. I suppose it did not occur to him that Mr. Kurtz was no idol of mine. He forgot I hadn't heard of any of these splendid monologues on, what was it? on love, justice, conduct of life—or what not. If it had come to crawling before Mr. Kurtz, he crawled as much as the veriest savage of them all. I had no idea of the conditions, he said: these heads were the heads of rebels. I shocked him excessively by laughing. Rebels! What would be the next definition I was to hear? There had been enemies, criminals, workers

—and these were rebels. Those rebellious heads looked very subdued to me on their sticks. 'You don't know how such a life tries a man like Kurtz,' cried Kurtz's last disciple. 'Well, and you?' I said. 'I! I! I am a simple man. I have no great thoughts. I want nothing from anybody. How can you compare me to . . . ?' His feelings were too much for speech, and suddenly he broke down. 'I don't understand,' he groaned, 'I've been doing my best to keep him alive and that's enough. I had no hand in all this. I have no abilities. There hasn't been a drop of medicine or a mouthful of invalid food for months here. He was shamefully abandoned. A man like this, with such ideas. Shamefully! Shamefully! I—I—haven't slept for the last ten nights. . . .'

"His voice lost itself in the calm of the evening. The long shadows of the forest had slipped downhill while we talked, had gone far beyond the ruined hovel, beyond the symbolic row of stakes. All this was in the gloom, while we down there were yet in the sunshine, and the stretch of the river abreast of the clearing glittered in a still and dazzling splendor, with a murky and over-shadowed bend above and below. Not a living soul was seen on the shore. The bushes did not rustle.

"Suddenly round the corner of the house a group of men appeared, as though they had come up from the ground. They waded waist-deep in the grass, in a compact body, bearing an improvised stretcher in their midst. Instantly, in the emptiness of the landscape, a cry arose whose shrillness pierced the still air like a sharp arrow flying straight to the very heart of the land; and, as if by enchantment, streams of human beings—of naked human beings—with spears in their hands, with bows, with shields, with wild glances and savage movements, were poured into the clearing by the dark-faced and pensive forest. The bushes shook, the grass swayed for a time, and then everything stood still in attentive immobility.

" 'Now, if he does not say the right thing to them we are all done for,' said the Russian at my elbow. The knot of men with the stretcher had stopped, too, halfway to the steamer, as if petrified. I saw the man on the stretcher sit up, lank and with an uplifted arm, above the shoulders of the bearers. 'Let us hope that the man who can talk so well of love in general will find some particular reason to spare us this time,' I said. I resented bitterly the absurd danger of our situation, as if to be at the mercy of that atrocious phantom had been a dishonoring necessity. I could not hear a sound, but through my glasses I saw the thin arm extended commandingly, the lower jaw moving, the eyes of that apparition shining darkly far in its bony head that nodded with grotesque jerks. Kurtz—Kurtz—that means short in German—don't it? Well, the name was as true as everything else in his life—and death. He looked at least seven feet long. His covering had fallen off, and his body emerged from it pitiful and appalling as from a winding-sheet. I could see the cage of his ribs all astir, the bones of his arm waving. It was as though an animated image of death carved out of old ivory had been shaking its hand with menaces at a motionless crowd of men made of dark and glittering bronze. I saw him open his mouth wide—it gave him a weirdly voracious aspect, as though he had wanted to swallow all the air, all the earth, all the men before him. A deep voice reached me faintly. He must have been shouting. He fell back suddenly. The stretcher shook as the bearers staggered forward again, and almost at the same time I noticed that the crowd of savages was vanishing without any perceptible movement of retreat, as if the forest that had ejected these beings so suddenly had drawn them in again as the breath is drawn in a long aspiration.

"Some of the pilgrims behind the stretcher carried his arms—two shotguns, a heavy rifle, and a light revolver-carbine—the thunderbolts of that pitiful Jupiter. The manager bent over him murmuring as he walked beside his head. They laid him down in one of the little cabins—just a room for a bedplace and a camp-stool or two, you know. We had brought his belated correspondence, and a lot of torn envelopes and open letters littered his bed. His hand roamed feebly amongst these papers. I was struck by the fire of his eyes and the composed languor of his expression. It was not so much the exhaustion of disease. He did not seem in pain. This shadow looked satiated and calm, as though for the moment it had had its fill of all the emotions.

"He rustled one of the letters, and looking straight in my face said, 'I am glad.' Somebody had been writing to him about me. These special recommendations were turning up again. The volume of tone he emitted without effort, almost without the trouble of moving his lips, amazed me. A voice! a voice! It was grave, profound, vibrating, while the man did not seem capable of a whisper. However, he had enough strength in him—factitious no doubt—to very nearly make an end of us, as you shall hear directly.

"The manager appeared silently in the doorway; I stepped out at once and he drew the curtain after me. The Russian, eyed curiously by the pilgrims, was staring at the shore. I followed the direction of his glance.

"Dark human shapes could be made out in the distance, flitting indistinctly against the gloomy border of the forest, and near the river two bronze figures, leaning on tall spears, stood in the sunlight under fantastic head-dresses of spotted skins, warlike and still in statuesque repose. And from right to left along the lighted shore moved a wild and gorgeous apparition of a woman.

"She walked with measured steps, draped in striped and fringed cloths, treading the earth proudly, with a slight jingle and flash of barbarous ornaments. She carried her head high; her hair was done in the shape of a helmet; she had brass leggings to the knee, brass wire gauntlets to the elbow, a crimson spot on her tawny cheek, innumerable necklaces of glass beads on her neck; bizarre things, charms, gifts of witch-men, that hung about her, glittered and trembled at every step. She must have had the value of several elephant tusks upon her. She was savage and superb, wild-eyed and magnificent; there was something ominous and stately in her deliberate progress. And in the hush that had fallen suddenly upon the whole sorrowful land, the immense wilderness, the colossal body of the fecund and mysterious life seemed to look at her, pensive, as though it had been looking at the image of its own tenebrous and passionate soul.

"She came abreast of the steamer, stood still, and faced us. Her long shadow fell to the water's edge. Her face had a tragic and fierce aspect of wild sorrow and of dumb pain mingled with the fear of some struggling, half-shaped resolve. She stood looking at us without a stir, and like the wilderness itself, with an air of brooding over an inscrutable purpose. A whole minute passed, and then she made a step forward. There was a low jingle, a glint of yellow metal, a sway of fringed draperies, and she stopped as if her heart had failed her. The young fellow by my side growled. The pilgrims murmured at my back. She looked at us all as if her life had depended upon the unswerving steadiness of her glance. Suddenly she opened her bared arms and threw them up rigid above her head, as though in an uncontrollable desire to touch the sky, and at the same time the swift shadows darted out on the earth, swept around on the river, gathering the steamer into a shadowy embrace. A formidable silence hung over the scene.

"She turned away slowly, walked on, following the bank, and passed into the bushes to the left. Once only her eyes gleamed back at us in the dusk of the thickets before she disappeared.

"'If she had offered to come aboard I really think I would have tried to shoot her,' said the man of patches, nervously. 'I have been risking my life every day for the last fortnight to keep her out of the house. She got in one day and kicked up a row about those miserable rags I picked up in the storeroom to mend my clothes with. I wasn't decent. At least it must have been that, for she talked like a fury to Kurtz for an hour, pointing at me now and then. I don't understand the dialect of this tribe. Luckily for me, I fancy Kurtz felt too ill that day to care, or there would have been mischief. I don't understand. . . . No—it's too much for me. Ah, well, it's all over now.'

"At this moment I heard Kurtz's deep

voice behind the curtain: 'Save me!—save the ivory, you mean. Don't tell me. Save *me!* Why, I've had to save you. You are interrupting my plans now. Sick! Sick! Not so sick as you would like to believe. Never mind. I'll carry my ideas out yet—I will return. I'll show you what can be done. You with your little peddling notions—you are interfering with me. I will return. I . . .'

"The manager came out. He did me the honor to take me under the arm and lead me aside. 'He is very low, very low,' he said. He considered it necessary to sigh, but neglected to be consistently sorrowful. 'We have done all we could for him—haven't we? But there is no disguising the fact, Mr. Kurtz has done more harm than good to the Company. He did not see the time was not ripe for vigorous action. Cautiously, cautiously—that's my principle. We must be cautious yet. The district is closed to us for a time. Deplorable! Upon the whole, the trade will suffer. I don't deny there is a remarkable quantity of ivory—mostly fossil. We must save it, at all events—but look how precarious the position is—and why? Because the method is unsound.' 'Do you,' said I, looking at the shore, 'call it "unsound method"?' 'Without doubt,' he exclaimed hotly. 'Don't you?' . . . 'No method at all,' I murmured after a while. 'Exactly,' he exulted. 'I anticipated this. Shows a complete want of judgment. It is my duty to point it out in the proper quarter.' 'Oh,' said I, 'that fellow—what's his name?—the brickmaker, will make a readable report for you.' He appeared confounded for a moment. It seemed to me I had never breathed an atmosphere so vile, and I turned mentally to Kurtz for relief—positively for relief. 'Nevertheless I think Mr. Kurtz is a remarkable man,' I said with emphasis. He started, dropped on me a cold heavy glance, said very quietly, 'he *was,*' and turned his back on me. My hour of favor was over; I found myself lumped along with Kurtz as a partisan of methods for which the time was not ripe: I was unsound! Ah! but it was something to have at least a choice of nightmares.

"I had turned to the wilderness really, not to Mr. Kurtz, who, I was ready to admit, was as good as buried. And for a moment it seemed to me as if I also were buried in a vast grave full of unspeakable secrets. I felt an intolerable weight oppressing my breast, the smell of the damp earth, the unseen presence of victorious corruption, the darkness of an impenetrable night. . . . The Russian tapped me on the shoulder. I heard him mumbling and stammering something about 'brother seaman—couldn't conceal—knowledge of matters that would affect Mr. Kurtz's reputation.' I waited. For him evidently Mr. Kurtz was not in his grave; I suspect that for him Mr. Kurtz was one of the immortals. 'Well!' said I at last, 'speak out. As it happens, I am Mr. Kurtz's friend—in a way.'

"He stated with a good deal of formality that had we not been 'of the same profession,' he would have kept the matter to himself without regard to consequences. 'He suspected there was an active ill will towards him on the part of these white men that—' 'You are right,' I said, remembering a certain conversation I had overheard. 'The manager thinks you ought to be hanged.' He showed a concern at this intelligence which amused me at first. 'I had better get out of the way quietly,' he said, earnestly. 'I can do no more for Kurtz now, and they would soon find some excuse. What's to stop them? There's a military post three hundred miles from here.' 'Well, upon my word,' said I, 'perhaps you had better go if you have any friends amongst the savages near by.' 'Plenty,' he said. 'They are simple people—and I want nothing, you know.' He stood biting his lip, then: 'I don't want any harm to happen to these whites here, but of course I was thinking of Mr. Kurtz's reputation—but you are a brother seaman and—' 'All right,' said I, after a time. 'Mr. Kurtz's reputation is safe with me.' I did not know how truly I spoke.

"He informed me, lowering his voice, that it was Kurtz who had ordered the attack to be made on the steamer. 'He hated sometimes the idea of being taken away—and then again. . . . But I don't understand these matters. I am a simple man. He thought it would scare you away—that you would give it up, thinking him dead. I could not stop him. Oh, I had an awful time of it this last month.' 'Very well,' I said. 'He is all right now.' 'Ye-e-es,' he muttered, not very convinced apparently. 'Thanks,' said I; 'I shall keep my eyes open.' 'But quiet—eh?' he urged, anxiously. 'It would be awful for his reputation if anybody here—' I promised a complete discretion with great gravity. 'I have a canoe and three black fellows waiting not very far. I am off. Could you give me a few Martini-Henry cartridges?' I could, and did, with proper secrecy. He helped himself, with a wink at me, to a handful of my tobacco. 'Between sailors—you know—good English tobacco.' At the door of the pilot-house he turned round—'I say, haven't you a pair of shoes you could spare?' He raised one leg. 'Look.' The soles were tied with knotted strings sandal-wise under his bare feet. I rooted out an old pair, at which he looked with admiration before tucking them under his left arm. One of his pockets (bright red) was bulging with cartridges, from the other (dark blue) peeped 'Towson's Inquiry,' etc., etc. He seemed to think himself excellently well equipped for a renewed encounter with the wilderness. 'Ah! I'll never, never meet such a man again. You ought to have heard him recite poetry—his own, too, it was, he told me. Poetry!' He rolled his eyes at the recollection of these delights. 'Oh, he enlarged my mind!' 'Good-by,' said I. He shook hands and vanished in the night. Sometimes I ask myself whether I had ever really seen him—whether it was possible to meet such a phenomenon! . . .

"When I woke up shortly after midnight his warning came to my mind with its hint of danger that seemed, in the starred darkness, real enough to make me get up for the purpose of having a look round. On the hill a big fire burned, illuminating fitfully a crooked corner of the station-house. One of the agents with a picket of a few of our blacks, armed for the purpose, was keeping guard over the ivory; but deep within the forest, red gleams that wavered, that seemed to sink and rise from the ground amongst confused columnar shapes of intense blackness, showed the exact position of the camp where Mr. Kurtz's adorers were keeping their uneasy vigil. The monotonous beating of a big drum filled the air with muffled shocks and a lingering vibration. A steady droning sound of many men chanting each to himself some weird incantation came out from the black, flat wall of the woods as the humming of bees comes out of a hive, and had a strange narcotic effect upon my half-awake senses. I believe I dozed off leaning over the rail, till an abrupt burst of yells, an overwhelming outbreak of a pent-up and mysterious frenzy, woke me up in a bewildered wonder. It was cut short all at once, and the low droning went on with an effect of audible and soothing silence. I glanced casually into the little cabin. A light was burning within, but Mr. Kurtz was not there.

"I think I would have raised an outcry if I had believed my eyes. But I didn't believe them at first—the thing seemed so impossible. The fact is I was completely unnerved by a sheer blank fright, pure abstract terror, unconnected with any distinct shape of physical danger. What made this emotion so overpowering was—how shall I define it?—the moral shock I received, as if something altogether monstrous, intolerable to thought and odious to the soul, had been thrust upon me unexpectedly. This lasted of course the merest fraction of a second, and then the usual sense of commonplace, deadly danger, the possibility of a sudden onslaught and massacre, or something of the kind, which I saw impending, was positively welcome and composing. It pacified me, in fact, so much, that I did not raise an alarm.

"There was an agent buttoned up inside an ulster and sleeping on a chair on deck within three feet of me. The yells had not awakened him; he snored very slightly; I left him to his slumbers and leaped ashore. I did not betray Mr. Kurtz—it was ordered I should never betray him—it was written I should be loyal to the nightmare of my choice. I was anxious to deal with this shadow by myself alone,—and to this day I don't know why I was so jealous of sharing with any one the peculiar blackness of that experience.

"As soon as I got on the bank I saw a trail

—a broad trail through the grass. I remember the exultation with which I said to myself, 'He can't walk—he is crawling on all-fours —I've got him.' The grass was wet with dew. I strode rapidly with clenched fists. I fancy I had some vague notion of falling upon him and giving him a drubbing. I don't know. I had some imbecile thoughts. The knitting old woman with the cat obtruded herself upon my memory as a most improper person to be sitting at the other end of such an affair. I saw a row of pilgrims squirting lead in the air out of Winchesters held to the hip. I thought I would never get back to the steamer, and imagined myself living alone and unarmed in the woods to an advanced age. Such silly things—you know. And I re-member I confounded the beat of the drum with the beating of my heart, and was pleased at its calm regularity.

"I kept to the track though—then stopped to listen. The night was very clear; a dark blue space, sparkling with dew and starlight, in which black things stood very still. I thought I could see a kind of motion ahead of me. I was strangely cocksure of everything that night. I actually left the track and ran in a wide semicircle (I verily believe chuckling to myself) so as to get in front of that stir, of that motion I had seen—if indeed I had seen anything. I was circumventing Kurtz as though it had been a boyish game.

"I came upon him, and, if he had not heard me coming, I would have fallen over him, too, but he got up in time. He rose, unsteady, long, pale, indistinct, like a vapor exhaled by the earth, and swayed slightly, misty and silent before me; while at my back the fires loomed between the trees, and the murmur of many voices issued from the forest. I had cut him off cleverly; but when actually con-fronting him I seemed to come to my senses, I saw the danger in its right proportion. It was by no means over yet. Suppose he began to shout? Though he could hardly stand, there was still plenty of vigor in his voice. 'Go away—hide yourself,' he said, in that profound tone. It was very awful. I glanced back. We were within thirty yards from the nearest fire. A black figure stood up, strode on long black legs, waving long black arms, across the glow. It had horns—antelope horns, I think—on its head. Some sorcerer, some witch-man, no doubt: it looked fiend-like enough. 'Do you know what you are doing?' I whispered. 'Perfectly,' he answered, raising his voice for that single word: it sounded to me far off and yet loud, like a hail through a speaking-trumpet. If he makes a row we are lost, I thought to myself. This clearly was not a case for fisticuffs, even apart from the very natural aversion I had to beat that Shadow—this wandering and tormented thing. 'You will be lost,' I said —'utterly lost.' One gets sometimes such a flash of inspiration, you know. I did say the right thing, though indeed he could not have been more irretrievably lost than he was at this very moment, when the foundations of our intimacy were being laid—to endure—to endure—even to the end—even beyond.

" 'I had immense plans,' he muttered ir-resolutely. 'Yes,' said I; 'but if you try to shout I'll smash your head with—' There was not a stick or a stone near. 'I will throttle you for good,' I corrected myself. 'I was on the threshold of great things,' he pleaded, in a voice of longing, with a wistfulness of tone that made my blood run cold. 'And now for this stupid scoundrel—' 'Your success in Europe is assured in any case,' I affirmed, steadily. I did not want to have the throttling of him, you understand—and indeed it would have been very little use for any practical purpose. I tried to break the spell—the heavy, mute spell of the wilderness—that seemed to draw him to its pitiless breast by the awakening of forgotten and brutal in-stincts, by the memory of gratified and mon-strous passions. This alone, I was convinced, had driven him out to the edge of the forest, to the bush, towards the gleam of fires, the throb of drums, the drone of weird incanta-tions; this alone had beguiled his unlawful soul beyond the bounds of permitted aspira-tions. And, don't you see, the terror of the position was not in being knocked on the head—though I had a very lively sense of that danger, too—but in this, that I had to deal with a being to whom I could not appeal in the name of anything high or low. I had, even like the niggers, to invoke him—him-

self—his own exalted and incredible degradation. There was nothing either above or
below him, and I knew it. He had kicked
himself loose of the earth. Confound the
man! he had kicked the very earth to pieces.
He was alone, and I before him did not
know whether I stood on the ground or
floated in the air. I've been telling you what
we said—repeating the phrases we pronounced—but what's the good? They were
common everyday words—the familiar,
vague sounds exchanged on every waking
day of life. But what of that? They had behind them, to my mind, the terrific suggestiveness of words heard in dreams, of phrases
spoken in nightmares. Soul! If anybody had
ever struggled with a soul, I am the man. And
I wasn't arguing with a lunatic either. Believe me or not, his intelligence was perfectly
clear—concentrated, it is true, upon himself
with horrible intensity, yet clear; and therein
was my only chance—barring, of course, the
killing him there and then, which wasn't so
good, on account of unavoidable noise. But
his soul was mad. Being alone in the wilderness, it had looked within itself, and, by
heavens! I tell you, it had gone mad. I had—
for my sins, I suppose—to go through the
ordeal of looking into it myself. No eloquence could have been so withering to one's
belief in mankind as his final burst of sincerity. He struggled with himself, too. I saw
it,—I heard it. I saw the inconceivable
mystery of a soul that knew no restraint, no
faith, and no fear, yet struggling blindly
with itself. I kept my head pretty well; but
when I had him at last stretched on the
couch, I wiped my forehead, while my legs
shook under me as though I had carried half
a ton on my back down that hill. And yet I
had only supported him, his bony arm clasped
round my neck—and he was not much
heavier than a child.

"When next day we left at noon, the
crowd, of whose presence behind the curtain
of trees I had been acutely conscious all the
time, flowed out of the woods again, filled
the clearing, covered the slope with a mass of
naked, breathing, quivering, bronze bodies. I
steamed up a bit, then swung downstream,
and two thousand eyes followed the evolu-
tions of the splashing, thumping, fierce river-
demon beating the water with its terrible
tail and breathing black smoke into the air.
In front of the first rank, along the river,
three men, plastered with bright red earth
from head to foot, strutted to and fro restlessly. When we came abreast again, they
faced the river, stamped their feet, nodded
their horned heads, swayed their scarlet
bodies; they shook towards the fierce river-
demon a bunch of black feathers, a mangy
skin with a pendent tail—something that
looked like a dried gourd; they shouted
periodically together strings of amazing
words that resembled no sounds of human
language; and the deep murmurs of the
crowd, interrupted suddenly, where like the
responses of some satanic litany.

"We had carried Kurtz into the pilot-
house: there was more air there. Lying on the
couch, he stared through the open shutter.
There was an eddy in the mass of human
bodies, and the woman with helmeted head
and tawny cheeks rushed out to the very
brink of the stream. She put out her hands,
shouted something, and all that wild mob
took up the shout in a roaring chorus of
articulated, rapid, breathless utterance.

" 'Do you understand this?' I asked.

"He kept on looking out past me with
fiery, longing eyes, with a mingled expression of wistfulness and hate. He made no
answer, but I saw a smile, a smile of indefinable meaning, appear on his colorless lips
that a moment after twitched convulsively.
'Do I not?' he said slowly, gasping, as if the
words had been torn out of him by a supernatural power.

"I pulled the string of the whistle, and I
did this because I saw the pilgrims on deck
getting out their rifles with an air of anticipating a jolly lark. At the sudden screech
there was a movement of abject terror
through that wedged mass of bodies. 'Don't!
don't you frighten them away,' cried some
one on deck disconsolately. I pulled the
string time after time. They broke and ran,
they leaped, they crouched, they swerved,
they dodged the flying terror of the sound.

The three red chaps had fallen flat, face down on the shore, as though they had been shot dead. Only the barbarous and superb woman did not so much as flinch, and stretched tragically her bare arms after us over the somber and glittering river.

"And then that imbecile crowd down on the deck started their little fun, and I could see nothing more for smoke.

"The brown current ran swiftly out of the heart of darkness, bearing us down towards the sea with twice the speed of our upward progress; and Kurtz's life was running swiftly, too, ebbing, ebbing out of his heart into the sea of inexorable time. The manager was very placid, he had no vital anxieties now, he took us both in with a comprehensive and satisfied glance: the 'affair' had come off as well as could be wished. I saw the time approaching when I would be left alone of the party of 'unsound method.' The pilgrims looked upon me with disfavor. I was, so to speak, numbered with the dead. It is strange how I accepted this unforeseen partnership, this choice of nightmares forced upon me in the tenebrous land invaded by these mean and greedy phantoms.

"Kurtz discoursed. A voice! a voice! It rang deep to the very last. It survived his strength to hide in the magnificent folds of eloquence the barren darkness of his heart. Oh, he struggled! he struggled! The wastes of his weary brain were haunted by shadowy images now—images of wealth and fame revolving obsequiously round his unextinguishable gift of noble and lofty expression. My Intended, my station, my career, my ideas —these were the subjects for the occasional utterances of elevated sentiments. The shade of the original Kurtz frequented the bedside of the hollow sham, whose fate it was to be buried presently in the mold of primeval earth. But both the diabolic love and the unearthly hate of the mysteries it had penetrated fought for the possession of that soul satiated with primitive emotions, avid of lying fame, of sham distinction, of all the appearances of success and power.

"Sometimes he was contemptibly childish.

He desired to have kings meet him at railway stations on his return from some ghastly Nowhere, where he intended to accomplish great things. 'You show them you have in you something that is really profitable, and then there will be no limits to the recognition of your ability,' he would say. 'Of course you must take care of the motives—right motives —always.' The long reaches that were like one and the same reach, monotonous bends that were exactly alike, slipped past the steamer, with their multitude of secular trees looking patiently after this grimy fragment of another world, the forerunner of change, of conquest, of trade, of massacres, of blessings. I looked ahead—piloting. 'Close the shutter,' said Kurtz suddenly one day; 'I can't bear to look at this.' I did so. There was a silence. 'Oh, but I will wring your heart yet!' he cried at the invisible wilderness.

"We broke down—as I had expected— and had to lie up for repairs at the head of an island. This delay was the first thing that shook Kurtz's confidence. One morning he gave me a packet of papers and a photograph—the lot tied together with a shoestring. 'Keep this for me,' he said. 'This noxious fool' (meaning the manager) 'is capable of prying into my boxes when I am not looking.' In the afternoon I saw him. He was lying on his back with closed eyes, and I withdrew quietly, but I heard him mutter, 'Live rightly, die, die. . . .' I listened. There was nothing more. Was he rehearsing some speech in his sleep, or was it a fragment of a phrase from some newspaper article? He had been writing for the papers and meant to do so again, 'for the furthering of my ideas. It's a duty.'

"His was an impenetrable darkness. I looked at him as you peer down at a man who is lying at the bottom of a precipice where the sun never shines. But I had not much time to give him, because I was helping the engine-driver to take to pieces the leaky cylinders, to straighten a bent connecting-rod, and in other such matters. I lived in an infernal mess of rust, filings, nuts, bolts, spanners, hammers, ratchet-drills—things I abominate, because I don't get on with them.

I tended the little forge we fortunately had aboard; I toiled wearily in a wretched scrap-heap—unless I had the shakes too bad to stand.

"One evening coming in with a candle I was startled to hear him say a little tremulously, 'I am lying here in the dark waiting for death.' The light was within a foot of his eyes. I forced myself to murmur, 'Oh, nonsense!' and stood over him as if transfixed.

"Anything approaching the change that came over his features I have never seen before, and hope never to see again. Oh, I wasn't touched. I was fascinated. It was as though a veil had been rent. I saw on that ivory face the expression of somber pride, of ruthless power, of craven terror—of an intense and hopeless despair. Did he live his life again in every detail of desire, temptation, and surrender during that supreme moment of complete knowledge? He cried in a whisper at some image, at some vision—he cried out twice, a cry that was no more than a breath—

" 'The horror! The horror!'

"I blew the candle out and left the cabin. The pilgrims were dining in the mess-room, and I took my place opposite the manager, who lifted his eyes to give me a questioning glance, which I successfully ignored. He leaned back, serene, with that peculiar smile of his sealing the unexpressed depths of his meanness. A continuous shower of small flies streamed upon the lamp, upon the cloth, upon our hands and faces. Suddenly the manager's boy put his insolent black head in the doorway, and said in a tone of scathing contempt—

" 'Mistah Kurtz—he dead.'

"All the pilgrims rushed out to see. I remained, and went on with my dinner. I believe I was considered brutally callous. However, I did not eat much. There was a lamp in there—light, don't you know—and outside it was so beastly, beastly dark. I went no more near the remarkable man who had pronounced a judgment upon the adventures of his soul on this earth. The voice was gone. What else had been there? But I am of course aware that next day the pilgrims buried something in a muddy hole.

"And then they very nearly buried me.

"However, as you see I did not go to join Kurtz there and then. I did not. I remained to dream the nightmare out to the end, and to show my loyalty to Kurtz once more. Destiny. My destiny! Droll thing life is—that mysterious arrangement of merciless logic for a futile purpose. The most you can hope from it is some knowledge of yourself—that comes too late—a crop of unextinguishable regrets. I have wrestled with death. It is the most unexciting contest you can imagine. It takes place in an impalpable grayness, with nothing underfoot, with nothing around, without spectators, without clamor, without glory, without the great desire of victory, without the great fear of defeat, in a sickly atmosphere of tepid skepticism, without much belief in your own right, and still less in that of your adversary. If such is the form of ultimate wisdom, then life is a greater riddle than some of us think it to be. I was within a hair's breadth of the last opportunity for pronouncement, and I found with humiliation that probably I would have nothing to say. This is the reason why I affirm that Kurtz was a remarkable man. He had something to say. He said it. Since I had peeped over the edge myself, I understand better the meaning of his stare, that could not see the flame of the candle, but was wide enough to embrace the whole universe, piercing enough to penetrate all the hearts that beat in the darkness. He had summed up—he had judged. 'The horror!' He was a remarkable man. After all, this was the expression of some sort of belief; it had candor, it had conviction, it had a vibrating note of revolt in its whisper, it had the appalling face of a glimpsed truth—the strange commingling of desire and hate. And it is not my own extremity I remember best—a vision of grayness without form filled with physical pain, and a careless contempt for the evanescence of all things—even of this pain itself. No! It is his extremity that I seem to have lived through. True, he had made that last stride, he had stepped over the edge, while I had been permitted to draw back my hesitating foot. And perhaps in this is the whole difference; perhaps all the wisdom, and all truth, and all sincerity, are just compressed into the inappreciable moment of time in which we step over the threshold of the invisible. Perhaps! I like to think my summing-up would not have been a word of careless contempt. Better his cry—much better. It was an affirmation, a moral victory paid for by innumerable defeats, by abominable terrors, by abominable satisfactions. But it was a victory! That is why I have remained loyal to Kurtz to the last, and even beyond, when a long time after I heard once more, not his own choice, but the echo of his magnificent eloquence thrown to me from a soul as translucently pure as a cliff of crystal.

"No, they did not bury me, though there is a period of time which I remember mistily, with a shuddering wonder, like a passage through some inconceivable world that had no hope in it and no desire. I found myself back in the sepulchral city resenting the sight of people hurrying through the streets to filch a little money from each other, to devour their infamous cookery, to gulp their unwholesome beer, to dream their insignificant and silly dreams. They trespassed upon my thoughts. They were intruders whose knowledge of life was to me an irritating pretense, because I felt so sure they could not possibly know the things I knew. Their bearing, which was simply the bearing of commonplace individuals going about their business in the assurance of perfect safety, was offensive to me like the outrageous flauntings of folly in the face of a danger it is unable to comprehend. I had no particular desire to enlighten them, but I had some difficulty in restraining myself from laughing in their faces, so full of stupid importance. I daresay I was not very well at that time. I tottered about the streets—there were various affairs to settle—grinning bitterly at perfectly respectable persons. I admit my behavior was inexcusable, but then my temperature was seldom normal in these days. My dear aunt's endeavors to 'nurse up my strength' seemed altogether beside the mark. It was not my strength that wanted nursing, it was my imagination that wanted soothing. I kept the bundle of papers given me by Kurtz, not knowing exactly what to do with it. His mother had died lately, watched over, as I was told, by his Intended. A clean-shaved man, with an official manner and wearing gold-rimmed spectacles, called on me one day and made inquiries, at first circuitous, afterwards suavely pressing, about what he was pleased to denominate certain 'documents.' I was not surprised, because I had had two rows with the manager on the subject out there. I had refused to give up the smallest scrap out of that package, and I took the same attitude with the spectacled man. He became darkly menacing at last, and with much heat argued that the Company had the right to every bit of information about its 'territories.' And said he, 'Mr. Kurtz's knowledge of unexplored regions must have been necessarily extensive and peculiar—owing to his great abilities and to the deplorable circumstances in which he had been placed: therefore—' I assured him Mr. Kurtz's knowledge, however extensive, did not bear upon the problems of commerce or administration. He invoked then the name of science. 'It would be an incalculable loss, if,' etc., etc. I offered him the report on the 'Suppression of Savage Customs,' with the postscriptum torn off. He took it up eagerly, but ended by sniffing at it with an air of contempt. 'This is not what we had a right to expect,' he remarked. 'Expect nothing else,' I said. 'There are only private letters.' He withdrew upon some threat of legal proceedings, and I saw him no more; but another fellow, calling himself Kurtz's cousin, appeared two days later, and was anxious to hear all the details about his dear relative's last moments. Incidentally he gave me to understand that Kurtz had been essentially a great musician. 'There was the making of an immense success,' said the man, who was an organist, I believe, with lank gray hair flowing over a greasy coat-collar. I had no reason to doubt his statement; and to this day I am unable to say what was Kurtz's profession, whether he ever had any—which was the greatest of his talents. I had taken him for a painter who wrote for the papers, or else for a journalist who could paint—but even the cousin (who took snuff during the interview) could not tell me what he had been—exactly. He was a universal genius—

on that point I agreed with the old chap, who thereupon blew his nose noisily into a large cotton handkerchief and withdrew in senile agitation, bearing off some family letters and memoranda without importance. Ultimately a journalist anxious to know something of the fate of his 'dear colleague' turned up. This visitor informed me Kurtz's proper sphere ought to have been politics 'on the popular side.' He had furry straight eyebrows, bristly hair cropped short, an eyeglass on a broad ribbon, and, becoming expansive, confessed his opinion that Kurtz really couldn't write a bit—'but heavens! how that man could talk. He electrified large meetings. He had faith—don't you see?— he had the faith. He could get himself to believe anything—anything. He would have been a splendid leader of an extreme party.' 'What party?' I asked. 'Any party,' answered the other. 'He was an—an—extremist.' Did I not think so? I assented. Did I know, he asked, with a sudden flash of curiosity, 'what it was that had induced him to go out there?' 'Yes,' said I, and forthwith handed him the famous Report for publication, if he thought fit. He glanced through it hurriedly, mumbling all the time, judged 'it would do,' and took himself off with this plunder.

"Thus I was left at last with a slim packet of letters and the girl's portrait. She struck me as beautiful—I mean she had a beautiful expression. I know that the sunlight can be made to lie, too, yet one felt that no manipulation of light and pose could have conveyed the delicate shade of truthfulness upon those features. She seemed ready to listen without mental reservation, without suspicion, without a thought for herself. I concluded I would go and give her back her portrait and those letters myself. Curiosity? Yes; and also some other feeling perhaps. All that had been Kurtz's had passed out of my hands: his soul, his body, his station, his plans, his ivory, his career. There remained only his memory and his Intended—and I wanted to give that up, too, to the past, in a way—to surrender personally all that remained of him with me to that oblivion which is the last word of our common fate.

I don't defend myself. I had no clear perception of what it was I really wanted. Perhaps it was an impulse of unconscious loyalty, or the fulfillment of one of those ironic necessities that lurk in the facts of human existence. I don't know. I can't tell. But I went.

"I thought his memory was like the other memories of the dead that accumulate in every man's life—a vague impress on the brain of shadows that had fallen on it in their swift and final passage; but before the high and ponderous door, between the tall houses of a street as still and decorous as a well-kept alley in a cemetery, I had a vision of him on the stretcher, opening his mouth voraciously, as if to devour all the earth with all its mankind. He lived then before me; he lived as much as he had ever lived—a shadow insatiable of splendid appearances, of frightful realities; a shadow darker than the shadow of the night, and draped nobly in the folds of a gorgeous eloquence. The vision seemed to enter the house with me—the stretcher, the phantom-bearers, the wild crowd of obedient worshipers, the gloom of the forest, the glitter of the reach between the murky bends, the beat of the drum, regular and muffled like the beating of a heart—the heart of a conquering darkness. It was a moment of triumph for the wilderness, an invading and vengeful rush which, it seemed to me, I would have to keep back alone for the salvation of another soul. And the memory of what I had heard him say afar there, with the horned shapes stirring at my back, in the glow of fires, within the patient woods, those broken phrases came back to me, were heard again in their ominous and terrifying simplicity. I remembered his abject pleading, his abject threats, the colossal scale of his vile desires, the meanness, the torment, the tempestuous anguish of his soul. And later on I seemed to see his collected languid manner, when he said one day, 'This lot of ivory now is really mine. The Company did not pay for it. I collected it myself at a very great personal risk. I am afraid they will try to claim it as theirs though. H'm. It is a difficult case. What do you think I ought to do—resist? Eh? I want no more than justice.' . . . He wanted no more than justice —no more than justice. I rang the bell before a mahogany door on the first floor, and while I waited he seemed to stare at me out of the glassy panel—stare with that wide and immense stare embracing, condemning, loathing all the universe. I seemed to hear the whispered cry, 'The horror! The horror!'

"The dusk was falling. I had to wait in a lofty drawing room with three long windows from floor to ceiling that were like three luminous and bedraped columns. The bent gilt legs and backs of the furniture shone in indistinct curves. The tall marble fireplace had a cold and monumental whiteness. A grand piano stood massively in a corner; with dark gleams on the flat surfaces like a somber and polished sarcophagus. A high door opened—closed. I rose.

"She came forward, all in black, with a pale head, floating towards me in the dusk. She was in mourning. It was more than a year since his death, more than a year since the news came; she seemed as though she would remember and mourn forever. She took both my hands in hers and murmured, 'I had heard you were coming.' I noticed she was not very young—I mean not girlish. She had a mature capacity for fidelity, for belief, for suffering. The room seemed to have grown darker, as if all the sad light of the cloudy evening had taken refuge on her forehead. This fair hair, this pale visage, this pure brow, seemed surrounded by an ashy halo from which the dark eyes looked out at me. Their glance was guileless, profound, confident, and trustful. She carried her sorrowful head as though she were proud of that sorrow, as though she would say, I—I alone know how to mourn him as he deserves. But while we were still shaking hands, such a look of awful desolation came upon her face that I perceived she was one of those creatures that are not the playthings of Time. For her he had died only yesterday. And, by Jove! the impression was so powerful that for me, too, he seemed to have died only yesterday—nay, this very minute. I saw her and him in the same instant of time—his death and her sorrow—I saw her sorrow in the very moment of his death.

Do you understand? I saw them together— I heard them together. She had said, with a deep catch of the breath, 'I have survived' while my strained ears seemed to hear distinctly, mingled with her tone of despairing regret, the summing up whisper of his eternal condemnation. I asked myself what I was doing there, with a sensation of panic in my heart as though I had blundered into a place of cruel and absurd mysteries not fit for a human being to behold. She motioned me to a chair. We sat down. I laid the packet gently on the little table, and she put her hand over it. . . . 'You knew him well,' she murmured, after a moment of mourning silence.

" 'Intimacy grows quickly out there,' I said. 'I knew him as well as it is possible for one man to know another.'

" 'And you admired him,' she said. 'It was impossible to know him and not to admire him. Was it?'

" 'He was a remarkable man,' I said, unsteadily. Then before the appealing fixity of her gaze, that seemed to watch for more words on my lips, I went on, 'It was impossible not to—'

" 'Love him,' she finished eagerly, silencing me into an appalled dumbness. 'How true! how true! But when you think that no one knew him so well as I! I had all his noble confidence. I knew him best.'

" 'You knew him best,' I repeated. And perhaps she did. But with every word spoken the room was growing darker, and only her forehead, smooth and white, remained illumined by the unextinguishable light of belief and love.

" 'You were his friend,' she went on. 'His friend,' she repeated, a little louder. 'You must have been, if he had given you this, and sent you to me. I feel I can speak to you— and oh! I must speak. I want you—you have heard his last words—to know I have been worthy of him. . . . It is not pride. . . . Yes! I am proud to know I understood him better than any one on earth—he told me so himself. And since his mother died I have had no one—no one—to—to—'

"I listened. The darkness deepened. I was

not even sure he had given me the right bundle. I rather suspect he wanted me to take care of another batch of his papers which, after his death, I saw the manager examining under the lamp. And the girl talked, easing her pain in the certitude of my sympathy; she talked as thirsty men drink. I had heard that her engagement with Kurtz had been disapproved by her people. He wasn't rich enough or something. And indeed I don't know whether he had not been a pauper all his life. He had given me some reason to infer that it was his impatience of comparative poverty that drove him out there.

" '. . . Who was not his friend who had heard him speak once?' she was saying. 'He drew men towards him by what was best in them.' She looked at me with intensity. 'It is the gift of the great,' she went on, and the sound of her low voice seemed to have the accompaniment of all the other sounds, full of mystery, desolation, and sorrow, I had ever heard—the ripple of the river, the soughing of the trees swayed by the wind, the murmurs of the crowds, the faint ring of incomprehensible words cried from afar, the whisper of a voice speaking from beyond the threshold of an eternal darkness. 'But you have heard him! You know!' she cried.

" 'Yes, I know,' I said with something like despair in my heart, but bowing my head before the faith that was in her, before that great and saving illusion that shone with an unearthly glow in the darkness, in the triumphant darkness from which I could not have defended her—from which I could not even defend myself.

" 'What a loss to me—to us!'—she corrected herself with beautiful generosity; then added in a murmur, 'To the world.' By the last gleams of twilight I could see the glitter of her eyes, full of tears—of tears that would not fall.

" 'I have been very happy—very fortunate—very proud,' she went on. 'Too fortunate. Too happy for a little while. And now I am unhappy for—for life.'

"She stood up; her fair hair seemed to catch all the remaining light in a glimmer of gold. I rose, too.

" 'And of all this,' she went on, mournfully, 'of all his promise, and of all his greatness, of his generous mind, of his noble heart, nothing remains—nothing but a memory. You and I—'

" 'We shall always remember him,' I said, hastily.

" 'No!' she cried. 'It is impossible that all this should be lost—that such a life should be sacrificed to leave nothing—but sorrow. You know what vast plans he had. I knew of them, too—I could not perhaps understand—but others knew of them. Something must remain. His words, at least, have not died.'

" 'His words will remain,' I said.

" 'And his example,' she whispered to herself. 'Men looked up to him—his goodness shone in every act. His example—'

" 'True,' I said; 'his example, too. Yes, his example, I forgot that.'

" 'But I do not. I cannot—I cannot believe—not yet. I cannot believe that I shall never see him again, that nobody will see him again, never, never, never.'

"She put out her arms as if after a retreating figure, stretching them black and with clasped pale hands across the fading and narrow sheen of the window. Never see him! I saw him clearly enough then. I shall see this eloquent phantom as long as I live, and I shall see her, too, a tragic and familiar Shade, resembling in this gesture another one, tragic also, and bedecked with powerless charms, stretching bare brown arms over the glitter of the infernal stream, the stream of darkness. She said suddenly very low, 'He died as he lived.'

" 'His end,' said I, with dull anger stirring in me, 'was in every way worthy of his life.'

" 'And I was not with him,' she murmured. My anger subsided before a feeling of infinite pity.

" 'Everything that could be done—' I mumbled.

" 'Ah, but I believed in him more than any one on earth—more than his own mother, more than—himself. He needed me! Me! I would have treasured every sigh, every word, every sign, every glance.'

"I felt like a chill grip on my chest. 'Don't,' I said, in a muffled voice.

" 'Forgive me. I—I—have mourned so

long in silence—in silence. . . . You were with him—to the last? I think of his loneliness. Nobody near to understand him as I would have understood. Perhaps no one to hear. . . .'

" 'To the very end,' I said, shakily. 'I heard his very last words. . . .' I stopped in a fright.

" 'Repeat them,' she murmured in a heartbroken tone. 'I want—I want—something—something—to—live with.'

"I was on the point of crying at her, 'Don't you hear them?' The dusk was repeating them in a persistent whisper all around us, in a whisper that seemed to swell menacingly like the first whisper of a rising wind. 'The horror! The horror!'

" 'His last word—to live with,' she insisted. 'Don't you understand I loved him—I loved him—I loved him!'

"I pulled myself together and spoke slowly.

" 'The last word he pronounced was—your name.'

"I heard a light sigh and then my heart stood still, stopped dead short by an exulting and terrible cry, by the cry of inconceivable triumph and of unspeakable pain. 'I knew it —I was sure!' . . . She knew. She was sure. I heard her weeping; she had hidden her face in her hands. It seemed to me that the house would collapse before I could escape, that the heavens would fall upon my head. But nothing happened. The heavens do not

fall for such a trifle. Would they have fallen, I wonder, if I had rendered Kurtz that justice which was his due? Hadn't he said he wanted only justice? But I couldn't. I could not tell her. It would have been too dark—too dark altogether. . . ."

Marlow ceased, and sat apart, indistinct and silent, in the pose of a meditating Buddha. Nobody moved for a time. "We have lost the first of the ebb," said the Director, suddenly. I raised my head. The offing was barred by a black bank of clouds, and the tranquil waterway leading to the uttermost ends of the earth flowed somber under an overcast sky—seemed to lead into the heart of an immense darkness.

QUESTIONS

1. What can you learn from "Heart of Darkness" about the world of commerce and colonialism as it existed at the time represented in the story? In answering this question, try to report as many cause-and-effect relations as you feel are represented in the story.

2. Write as complete a report as you can on the functions of Marlow in "Heart of Darkness"—that is, the uses to which the author puts this character as a carrier of meaning and a technical convenience.

GROUP 2: CONTRASTS OF CHARACTER IN TIME AND PLACE

The stories brought together in this group confront the reader with a variety of fictional techniques and revelations of human character in widely separated environments and periods. The settings include American small towns, a back street and a night club in modern Chicago, a village in Russia before the revolution, an apartment in London at the turn of the century, a sheep ranch in the West, a boarding house in Dublin. Perhaps the most inclusive story, in a symbolic sense, is Sherwood Anderson's "The Sad Horn Blowers." Anton Chekhov's story, "The New Villa," portrays a type of social rigidity. The world of hard work, including patience, risk, and self-respect, is shown in "The Homestead Orchard," by H. L. Davis. Among these stories also is the world of the overprotected (Mansfield) and the world of those who believe that the most important thing in life is to know, and be seen with, the "right" people (described caustically by Henry James). Regardless of time or place or social level, each story touches some fundamental aspect of causality or of human character and value.

Stories in this group:

(1) "The Enormous Radio," by John Cheever
(2) "Haircut," by Ring Lardner
(3) "The Blue Hotel," by Stephen Crane
(4) "The Homestead Orchard," by H. L. Davis
(5) "The Boarding House," by James Joyce
(6) "The Sad Horn Blowers," by Sherwood Anderson
(7) "He Don't Plant Cotton," by J. F. Powers
(8) "In Another Country," by Ernest Hemingway
(9) "Stickman's Laughter," by Nelson Algren
(10) "The New Villa," by Anton Chekhov
(11) "The Fight Between Jappe and Do Escobar," by Thomas Mann
(12) "The Daughters of the Late Colonel," by Katherine Mansfield
(13) "Mrs. Medwin," by Henry James
(14) "A Country Doctor," by Franz Kafka

THE ENORMOUS RADIO

John Cheever
(1912–   )

Jim and Irene Westcott were the kind of people who seem to strike that satisfactory average of income, endeavor, and respectability that is reached by the statistical reports in college alumni bulletins. They were the parents of two young children, they had been married nine years, they lived on the twelfth floor of an apartment house in the East Seventies between Fifth and Madison

Avenues, they went to the theatre on an average of 10.3 times a year, and they hoped someday to live in Westchester. Irene Westcott was a pleasant, rather plain girl with soft brown hair and a wide, fine forehead upon which nothing at all had been written, and in the cold weather she wore a coat of fitch skins dyed to resemble mink. You could not say that Jim Westcott, at thirty-seven, looked younger than he was, but you could at least say of him that he seemed to feel younger. He wore his graying hair cut very short, he dressed in the kind of clothes his class had worn at Andover, and his manner was earnest, vehement, and intentionally naïve. The Westcotts differed from their friends, their classmates, and their neighbors only in an interest they shared in serious music. They went to a great many concerts—although they seldom mentioned this to anyone—and they spent a good deal of time listening to music on the radio.

Their radio was an old instrument, sensitive, unpredictable, and beyond repair. Neither of them understood the mechanics of radio—or of any of the other appliances that surrounded them—and when the instrument faltered, Jim would strike the side of the cabinet with his hand. This sometimes helped. One Sunday afternoon, in the middle of a Schubert quartet, the music faded away altogether. Jim struck the cabinet repeatedly, but there was no response; the Schubert was lost to them forever. He promised to buy Irene a new radio, and on Monday when he came home from work he told her that he had got one. He refused to describe it, and said it would be a surprise for her when it came.

The radio was delivered at the kitchen door the following afternoon, and with the assistance of her maid and the handyman Irene uncrated it and brought it into the living room. She was struck at once with the physical ugliness of the large gumwood cabinet. Irene was proud of her living room, she had chosen its furnishings and colors as carefully as she chose her clothes, and now it seemed to her that the new radio stood among her intimate possessions like an aggressive intruder. She was confounded by the number of dials and switches on the instrument panel, and she studied them thoroughly before she put the plug into a wall socket and turned the radio on. The dials flooded with a malevolent green light, and in the distance she heard the music of a piano quintet. The quintet was in the distance for only an instant; it bore down upon her with a speed greater than light and filled the apartment with the noise of music amplified so mightily that it knocked a china ornament from a table to the floor. She rushed to the instrument and reduced the volume. The violent forces that were snared in the ugly gumwood cabinet made her uneasy. Her children came home from school then, and she took them to the Park. It was not until later in the afternoon that she was able to return to the radio.

The maid had given the children their suppers and was supervising their baths when Irene turned on the radio, reduced the volume, and sat down to listen to a Mozart quintet that she knew and enjoyed. The music came through clearly. The new instrument had a much purer tone, she thought, than the old one. She decided that tone was most important and that she could conceal the cabinet behind a sofa. But as soon as she had made her peace with the radio, the interference began. A crackling sound like the noise of a burning powder fuse began to accompany the singing of the strings. Beyond the music, there was a rustling that reminded Irene unpleasantly of the sea, and as the quintet progressed, these noises were joined by many others. She tried all the dials and switches but nothing dimmed the interference, and she sat down, disappointed and bewildered, and tried to trace the flight of the melody. The elevator shaft in her building ran beside the living-room wall, and it was the noise of the elevator that gave her a clue to the character of the static. The rattling of the elevator cables and the opening and closing of the elevator doors were reproduced in her loudspeaker, and, realizing that the radio was sensitive to electrical currents of all sorts, she began to discern through the

Mozart the ringing of telephone bells, the dialing of phones, and the lamentation of a vacuum cleaner. By listening more carefully, she was able to distinguish doorbells, elevator bells, electric razors, and Waring mixers, whose sounds had been picked up from the apartments that surrounded hers and transmitted through her loudspeaker. The powerful and ugly instrument, with its mistaken sensitivity to discord, was more than she could hope to master, so she turned the thing off and went into the nursery to see her children.

When Jim Westcott came home that night, he went to the radio confidently and worked the controls. He had the same sort of experience Irene had had. A man was speaking on the station Jim had chosen, and his voice swung instantly from the distance into a force so powerful that it shook the apartment. Jim turned the volume control and reduced the voice. Then, a minute or two later, the interference began. The ringing of telephones and doorbells set in, joined by the rasp of the elevator doors and the whir of cooking appliances. The character of the noise had changed since Irene had tried the radio earlier; the last of the electric razors was being unplugged, the vacuum cleaners had all been returned to their closets, and the static reflected that change in pace that overtakes the city after the sun goes down. He fiddled with the knobs but couldn't get rid of the noises, so he turned the radio off and told Irene that in the morning he'd call the people who had sold it to him and give them hell.

The following afternoon, when Irene returned to the apartment from a luncheon date, the maid told her that a man had come and fixed the radio. Irene went into the living room before she took off her hat or her furs and tried the instrument. From the loudspeaker came a recording of the "Missouri Waltz." It reminded her of the thin, scratchy music from an old-fashioned phonograph that she sometimes heard across the lake where she spent her summers. She waited until the waltz had finished, expecting an explanation

of the recording, but there was none. The music was followed by silence, and then the plaintive and scratchy record was repeated. She turned the dial and got a satisfactory burst of Caucasian music—the thump of bare feet in the dust and the rattle of coin jewelry —but in the background she could hear the ringing of bells and a confusion of voices. Her children came home from school then, and she turned off the radio and went to the nursery.

When Jim came home that night, he was tired, and he took a bath and changed his clothes. Then he joined Irene in the living room. He had just turned on the radio when the maid announced dinner, so he left it on, and he and Irene went to the table.

Jim was too tired to make even a pretense of sociability, and there was nothing about the dinner to hold Irene's interest, so her attention wandered from the food to the deposits of silver polish on the candlesticks and from there to the music in the other room. She listened for a few moments to a Chopin prelude and then was surprised to hear a man's voice break in. "For Christ's sake, Kathy," he said, "do you always have to play the piano when I get home?" The music stopped abruptly. "It's the only chance I have," a woman said. "I'm at the office all day." "So am I," the man said. He added something obscene about an upright piano, and slammed a door. The passionate and melancholy music began again.

"Did you hear that?" Irene asked.

"What?" Jim was eating his dessert.

"The radio. A man said something while the music was still going on—something dirty."

"It's probably a play."

"I don't think it *is* a play," Irene said.

They left the table and took their coffee into the living room. Irene asked Jim to try another station. He turned the knob. "Have you seen my garters?" a man asked. "Button me up," a woman said. "Have you seen my garters?" the man said again. "Just button me up and I'll find your garters," the woman said. Jim shifted to another station. "I wish you wouldn't leave apple cores in the ash-trays," a man said. "I hate the smell."

"This is strange," Jim said.

"Isn't it?" Irene said.

Jim turned the knob again. " 'On the coast of Coromandel where the early pumpkins blow,' " a woman with a pronounced English accent said, " 'in the middle of the woods lived the Yonghy-Bonghy-Bò. Two old chairs, and half a candle, one old jug with-out a handle . . .' "

"My God!" Irene cried. "That's the Sweeneys' nurse."

" 'These were all his worldly goods,' " the British voice continued.

"Turn that thing off," Irene said. "Maybe they can hear *us*." Jim switched the radio off. "That was Miss Armstrong, the Sweeneys' nurse," Irene said. "She must be reading to the little girl. They live in 17-B. I've talked with Miss Armstrong in the Park. I know her voice very well. We must be getting other people's apartments."

"That's impossible," Jim said.

"Well, that was the Sweeneys' nurse," Irene said hotly. "I know her voice. I know it very well. I'm wondering if they can hear us."

Jim turned the switch. First from a dis-tance and then nearer, nearer, as if borne on the wind, came the pure accents of the Sweeneys' nurse again: " ' "Lady Jingly! Lady Jingly!" ' " she said, " ' "Sitting where the pumpkins blow, will you come and be my wife," said the Yonghy-Bonghy-Bò . . .' "

Jim went over to the radio and said "Hello" loudly into the speaker.

" ' "I am tired of living singly," ' " the nurse went on, " ' "on this coast so wild and shingly, I'm a-weary of my life; if you'll come and be my wife, quite serene would be my life . . ." ' "

"I guess she can't hear us," Irene said. "Try something else."

Jim turned to another station, and the living room was filled with the uproar of a cocktail party that had overshot its mark. Someone was playing the piano and singing the Whiffenpoof Song, and the voices that surrounded the piano were vehement and

happy. "Eat some more sandwiches," a woman shrieked. There were screams of laughter and a dish of some sort crashed to the floor.

"Those must be the Hutchinsons, in 15-B," Irene said. "I knew they were giving a party this afternoon. I saw her in the liquor store. Isn't this too divine? Try something else. See if you can get those people in 18-C."

The Westcotts overheard that evening a monologue on salmon fishing in Canada, a bridge game, running comments on home movies of what had apparently been a fort-night at Sea Island, and a bitter family quar-rel about an overdraft at the bank. They turned off their radio at midnight and went to bed, weak with laughter. Sometime in the night, their son began to call for a glass of water and Irene got one and took it to his room. It was very early. All the lights in the neighborhood were extinguished, and from the boy's window she could see the empty street. She went into the living room and tried the radio. There was some faint cough-ing, a moan, and then a man spoke. "Are you all right, darling?" he asked. "Yes," a woman said wearily. "Yes, I'm all right, I guess," and then she added with great feeling, "But, you know, Charlie, I don't feel like myself any more. Sometimes there are about fifteen or twenty minutes in the week when I feel like myself. I don't like to go to another doctor, because the doctor's bills are so awful al-ready, but I just don't feel like myself, Charlie. I just never feel like myself." They were not young, Irene thought. She guessed from the timbre of their voices that they were middle-aged. The restrained melancholy of the dialogue and the draft from the bedroom window made her shiver, and she went back to bed.

The following morning, Irene cooked breakfast for the family—the maid didn't come up from her room in the basement until ten—braided her daughter's hair, and waited at the door until her children and her husband had been carried away in the eleva-tor. The she went into the living room and tried the radio. "I don't want to go to school," a child screamed. "I hate school. I won't go to school. I hate school." "You will go to school," an enraged woman said. "We paid eight hundred dollars to get you into that school and you'll go if it kills you." The next number on the dial produced the worn record of the "Missouri Waltz." Irene shifted the control and invaded the privacy of several breakfast tables. She overheard demonstrations of indigestion, carnal love, abysmal vanity, faith, and despair. Irene's life was nearly as simple and sheltered as it appeared to be, and the forthright and sometimes brutal language that came from the loudspeaker that morning astonished and troubled her. She continued to listen until her maid came in. Then she turned off the radio quickly, since this insight, she realized, was a furtive one.

Irene had a luncheon date with a friend that day, and she left her apartment at a little after twelve. There were a number of women in the elevator when it stopped at her floor. She stared at their handsome and impassive faces, their furs, and the cloth flowers in their hats. Which one of them had been to Sea Island, she wondered. Which one had overdrawn her bank account? The elevator stopped at the tenth floor and a woman with a pair of Skye terriers joined them. Her hair was rigged high on her head and she wore a mink cape. She was humming the "Missouri Waltz."

Irene had two Martinis at lunch, and she looked searchingly at her friend and wondered what her secrets were. They had intended to go shopping after lunch, but Irene excused herself and went home. She told the maid that she was not to be disturbed; then she went into the living room, closed the doors, and switched on the radio. She heard, in the course of the afternoon, the halting conversation of a woman entertaining her aunt, the hysterical conclusion of a luncheon party, and a hostess briefing her maid about some cocktail guests. "Don't give the best Scotch to anyone who hasn't white hair," the hostess said. "See if you can get rid of that liver paste before you pass those hot things,

and could you lend me five dollars? I want to tip the elevator man."

As the afternoon waned, the conversations increased in intensity. From where Irene sat, she could see the open sky above Central Park. There were hundreds of clouds in the sky, as though the south wind had broken the winter into pieces and were blowing it north, and on her radio she could hear the arrival of cocktail guests and the return of children and businessmen from their schools and offices. "I found a good-sized diamond on the bathroom floor this morning," a woman said. "It must have fallen out of that bracelet Mrs. Dunston was wearing last night." "We'll sell it," a man said. "Take it down to the jeweller on Madison Avenue and sell it. Mrs. Dunston won't know the difference, and we could use a couple of hundred bucks . . ." " 'Oranges and lemons, say the bells of St. Clement's,' " the Sweeneys' nurse sang. " 'Halfpence and farthings, say the bells of St. Martin's. When will you pay me? say the bells at old Bailey . . .' " "It's not a hat," a woman cried, and at her back roared a cocktail party. "It's not a hat, it's a love affair. That's what Walter Florell said. He said it's not a hat, it's a love affair," and then, in a lower voice, the same woman added, "Talk to somebody, for Christ's sake, honey, talk to somebody. If she catches you standing here not talking to anybody, she'll take us off her invitation list, and I love these parties."

The Westcotts were going out for dinner that night, and when Jim came home, Irene was dressing. She seemed sad and vague, and he brought her a drink. They were dining with friends in the neighborhood, and they walked to where they were going. The sky was broad and filled with light. It was one of those splendid spring evenings that excite memory and desire, and the air that touched their hands and faces felt very soft. A Salvation Army band was on the corner playing "Jesus Is Sweeter." Irene drew on her husband's arm and held him there for a minute, to hear the music. "They're really such nice people, aren't they?" she said. "They have such nice faces. Actually, they're so much nicer than a lot of the people we know." She took a bill from her purse and walked over and dropped it into the tambourine. There was in her face, when she returned to her husband, a look of radiant melancholy that he was not familiar with. And her conduct at the dinner party that night seemed strange to him, too. She interrupted her hostess rudely and stared at the people across the table from her with an intensity for which she would have punished her children.

It was still mild when they walked home from the party, and Irene looked up at the spring stars. "'How far that little candle throws its beams,'" she exclaimed. "'So shines a good deed in a naughty world.'" She waited that night until Jim had fallen asleep, and then went into the living room and turned on the radio.

Jim came home at about six the next night. Emma, the maid, let him in, and he had taken off his hat and was taking off his coat when Irene ran into the hall. Her face was shining with tears and her hair was disordered. "Go up to 16-C, Jim!" she screamed. "Don't take off your coat. Go up to 16-C. Mr. Osborn's beating his wife. They've been quarrelling since four o'clock, and now he's hitting her. Go up there and stop him."

From the radio in the living room, Jim heard screams, obscenities, and thuds. "You know you don't have to listen to this sort of thing," he said. He strode into the living room and turned the switch. "It's indecent," he said. "It's like looking in windows. You know you don't have to listen to this sort of thing. You can turn it off."

"Oh, it's so horrible, it's so dreadful," Irene was sobbing. "I've been listening all day, and it's so depressing."

"Well, if it's so depressing, why do you listen to it? I bought this damned radio to give you some pleasure," he said. "I paid a great deal of money for it. I thought it might make you happy. I wanted to make you happy."

"Don't, don't, don't, don't quarrel with me," she moaned, and laid her head on his shoulder. "All the others have been quarrel-ling all day. Everybody's been quarrelling. They're all worried about money. Mrs. Hutchinson's mother is dying of cancer in Florida and they don't have enough money to send her to the Mayo Clinic. At least, Mr. Hutchinson says they don't have enough money. And some woman in this building is having an affair with the superintendent—with that hideous superintendent. It's too disgusting. And Mrs. Melville has heart trouble and Mr. Hendricks is going to lose his job in April and Mrs. Hendricks is horrid about the whole thing and that girl who plays the 'Missouri Waltz' is a whore, a common whore, and the elevator man has tuberculosis and Mr. Osborn has been beating Mrs. Osborn." She wailed, she trembled with grief and checked the stream of tears down her face with the heel of her palm.

"Well, why do you have to listen?" Jim asked again. "Why do you have to listen to this stuff if it makes you so miserable?"

"Oh, don't, don't, don't," she cried. "Life is too terrible, too sordid and awful. But we've never been like that, have we, darling? Have we? I mean we've always been good and decent and loving to one another, haven't we? And we have two children, two beautiful children. Our lives aren't sordid, are they, darling? Are they?" She flung her arms around his neck and drew his face down to hers. "We're happy, aren't we, darling? We are happy, aren't we?"

"Of course we're happy," he said tiredly. He began to surrender his resentment. "Of course we're happy. I'll have that damned radio fixed or taken away tomorrow." He stroked her soft hair. "My poor girl," he said.

"You love me, don't you?" she asked. "And we're not hypercritical or worried about money or dishonest, are we?"

"No, darling," he said.

A man came in the morning and fixed the radio. Irene turned it on cautiously and was happy to hear a California-wine commercial and a recording of Beethoven's Ninth Symphony, including Schiller's "Ode to Joy." She kept the radio on all day and nothing untoward came from the speaker.

A Spanish suite was being played when Jim came home. "Is everything all right?" he asked. His face was pale, she thought. They had some cocktails and went in to dinner to the "Anvil Chorus" from "Il Trovatore." This was followed by Debussy's "La Mer."

"I paid the bill for the radio today," Jim said. "It cost four hundred dollars. I hope you'll get some enjoyment out of it."

"Oh, I'm sure I will," Irene said.

"Four hundred dollars is a good deal more than I can afford," he went on. "I wanted to get something that you'd enjoy. It's the last extravagance we'll be able to indulge in this year. I see that you haven't paid your clothing bills yet. I saw them on your dressing table." He looked directly at her. "Why did you tell me you'd paid them? Why did you lie to me?"

"I just didn't want you to worry, Jim," she said. She drank some water. "I'll be able to pay my bills out of this month's allowance. There were the slipcovers last month, and that party."

"You've got to learn to handle the money I give you a little more intelligently, Irene," he said. "You've got to understand that we won't have as much money this year as we had last. I had a very sobering talk with Mitchell today. No one is buying anything. We're spending all our time promoting new issues, and you know how long that takes. I'm not getting any younger, you know. I'm thirty-seven. My hair will be gray next year. I haven't done as well as I'd hoped to do. And I don't suppose things will get any better."

"Yes, dear," she said.

"We've got to start cutting down," Jim said. "We've got to think of the children. To be perfectly frank with you, I worry about money a great deal. I'm not at all sure of the future. No one is. If anything should happen to me, there's the insurance, but that wouldn't go very far today. I've worked awfully hard to give you and the children a comfortable life," he said bitterly. "I don't like to see all of my energies, all of my youth, wasted in fur coats and radios and slipcovers and—"

"Please, Jim," she said. "Please. They'll hear us."

"Who'll hear us? Emma can't hear us."

"The radio."

"Oh, I'm sick!" he shouted. "I'm sick to death of your apprehensiveness. The radio can't hear us. Nobody can hear us. And what if they can hear us? Who cares?"

Irene got up from the table and went into the living room. Jim went to the door and shouted at her from there. "Why are you so Christly all of a sudden? What's turned you overnight into a convent girl? You stole your mother's jewelry before they probated her will. You never gave your sister a cent of that money that was intended for her—not even when she needed it. You made Grace Howland's life miserable, and where was all your piety and your virtue when you went to that abortionist? I'll never forget how cool you were. You packed your bag and went off to have that child murdered as if you were going to Nassau. If you'd had any reasons, if you'd had any good reasons—"

Irene stood for a minute before the hideous cabinet, disgraced and sickened, but she held her hand on the switch before she extinguished the music and the voices, hoping that the instrument might speak to her kindly, that she might hear the Sweeneys' nurse. Jim continued to shout at her from the door. The voice on the radio was suave and noncommital. "An early-morning railroad disaster in Tokyo," the loudspeaker said, "killed twenty-nine people. A fire in a Catholic hospital near Buffalo for the care of blind children was extinguished early this morning by nuns. The temperature is forty-seven. The humidity is eighty-nine."

HAIRCUT

Ring Lardner
(1885–1933)

I got another barber that comes over from Carterville and helps me out Saturdays, but the rest of the time I can get along all right alone. You can see for yourself that this ain't no New York City and besides that, the most of the boys works all day and don't have no leisure to drop in here and get themselves prettied up.

You're a newcomer, ain't you? I thought I hadn't seen you round before. I hope you like it good enough to stay. As I say, we ain't no New York City or Chicago, but we have pretty good times. Not as good, though, since Jim Kendall got killed. When he was alive, him and Hod Meyers used to keep this town in an uproar. I bet they was more laughin' done here than any town its size in America.

Jim was comical, and Hod was pretty near a match for him. Since Jim's gone, Hod tries to hold his end up just the same as ever, but it's tough goin' when you ain't got nobody to kind of work with.

They used to be plenty fun in here Saturdays. This place is jam-packed Saturdays, from four o'clock on. Jim and Hod would show up right after their supper round six o'clock. Jim would set himself down in that big chair, nearest the blue spittoon. Whoever had been settin' in that chair, why they'd get up when Jim come in and give it to him.

You'd of thought it was a reserved seat like they have sometimes in a theaytre. Hod would generally always stand or walk up and down or some Saturdays, of course, he'd be settin' in this chair part of the time, gettin' a haircut.

Well, Jim would set there a w'ile without openin' his mouth only to spit, and then finally he'd say to me, "Whitey,"—my right name, that is, my right first name, is Dick, but everybody round here calls me Whitey— Jim would say, "Whitey, your nose looks like a rosebud tonight. You must of been drinkin' some of your aw de cologne."

So I'd say, "No, Jim, but you look like you'd been drinkin' somethin' of that kind or somethin' worse."

Jim would have to laugh at that, but then he'd speak up and say, "No, I ain't had nothin' to drink, but that ain't sayin' I wouldn't like somethin'. I wouldn't even mind if it was wood alcohol."

Then Hod Meyers would say, "Neither would your wife." That would set everybody to laughin' because Jim and his wife wasn't

on very good terms. She'd of divorced him only they wasn't no chance to get alimony and she didn't have no way to take care of herself and the kids. She couldn't never understand Jim. He *was* kind of rough, but a good fella at heart.

Him and Hod had all kinds of sport with Milt Sheppard. I don't suppose you've seen Milt. Well, he's got an Adam's apple that looks more like a mush-melon. So I'd be shavin' Milt and when I'd start to shave down here on his neck, Hod would holler, "Hey, Whitey, wait a minute! Before you cut into it, let's make up a pool and see who can guess closest to the number of seeds."

And Jim would say, "If Milt hadn't of been so hoggish, he'd of ordered a half a cantaloupe instead of a whole one and it might not of stuck in his throat."

All the boys would roar at this and Milt himself would force a smile, though the joke was on him. Jim certainly was a card!

There's his shavin' mug, setting on the shelf, right next to Charley Vail's. "Charles M. Vail." That's the druggist. He comes in regular for his shave, three times a week. And Jim's is the cup next to Charley's. "James H. Kendall." Jim won't need no shavin' mug no more, but I'll leave it there just the same for old time's sake. Jim certainly was a character!

Years ago, Jim used to travel for a canned goods concern over in Carterville. They sold canned goods. Jim had the whole northern half of the State and was on the road five days out of every week. He'd drop in here Saturdays and tell his experiences for that week. It was rich.

I guess he paid more attention to playin' jokes than makin' sales. Finally the concern let him out and he come right home here and told everybody he'd been fired instead of sayin' he'd resigned like most fellas would of.

It was a Saturday and the shop was full and Jim got up out of that chair and says, "Gentlemen, I got an important announcement to make. I been fired from my job."

Well, they asked him if he was in earnest and he said he was and nobody could think of nothin' to say till Jim finally broke the ice himself. He says, "I been sellin' canned goods and now I'm canned goods myself."

You see, the concern he'd been workin' for was a factory that made canned goods. Over in Carterville. And now Jim said he was canned himself. He was certainly a card!

Jim had a great trick that he used to play w'ile he was travelin'. For instance, he'd be ridin' on a train and they'd come to some little town like, well, like, well, like, we'll say, like Benton. Jim would look out the train window and read the signs on the stores.

For instance, they'd be a sign, "Henry Smith, Dry Goods." Well, Jim would write down the name and the name of the town and when he got to wherever he was goin' he'd mail back a postal card to Henry Smith at Benton and not sign no name to it, but he'd write on the card, well, somethin' like "Ask your wife about that book agent that spent the afternoon last week," or "Ask your Missus who kept her from gettin' lonesome the last time you was in Carterville." And he'd sign the card, "A Friend."

Of course, he never knew what really come of none of these jokes, but he could picture what *probably* happened and that was enough.

Jim didn't work very steady after he lost his position with the Carterville people. What he did earn, doin' odd jobs round town, why he spent pretty near all of it on gin, and his family might of starved if the stores hadn't of carried them along. Jim's wife tried her hand at dressmakin', but they ain't nobody goin' to get rich makin' dresses in this town.

As I say, she'd of divorced Jim, only she seen that she couldn't support herself and the kids and she was always hopin' that some day Jim would cut out his habits and give her more than two or three dollars a week.

They was a time when she would go to whoever he was workin' for and ask them to give her his wages, but after she done this once or twice, he beat her to it by borrowin' most of his pay in advance. He told it all round town, how he had outfoxed his Missus. He certainly was a caution!

But he wasn't satisfied with just outwittin' her. He was sore the way she had acted, tryin' to grab off his pay. And he made up his mind he'd get even. Well, he waited till Evans's Circus was advertised to come to town. Then he told his wife and two kiddies that he was goin' to take them to the circus. The day of the circus, he told them he would get the tickets and meet them outside the entrance to the tent.

Well, he didn't have no intentions of bein' there or buyin' tickets or nothin'. He got full of gin and laid round Wright's poolroom all day. His wife and the kids waited and waited and of course he didn't show up. His wife didn't have a dime with her, or nowhere else, I guess. So she finally had to tell the kids it was all off and they cried like they wasn't never goin' to stop.

Well, it seems, w'ile they was cryin', Doc Stair come along and he asked what was the matter, but Mrs. Kendall was stubborn and wouldn't tell him, but the kids told him and he insisted on takin' them and their mother in the show. Jim found this out afterwards and it was one reason why he had it in for Doc Stair.

Doc Stair come here about a year and a half ago. He's a mighty handsome young fella and his clothes always look like he has them made to order. He goes to Detroit two or three times a year and w'ile he's there must have a tailor take his measure and then make him a suit to order. They cost pretty near twice as much, but they fit a whole lot better than if you just bought them in a store.

For a w'ile everybody was wonderin' why a young doctor like Doc Stair should come to a town like this where we already got old Doc Gamble and Doc Foote that's both been here for years and all the practice in town was always divided between the two of them.

Then they was a story got round that Doc Stair's gal had throwed him over, a gal up in the Northern Peninsula somewhere, and the reason he come here was to hide himself away and forget it. He said himself that he thought they wasn't nothin' like general practice in a place like ours to fit a man to be a good all round doctor. And that's why he'd came.

Anyways, it wasn't long before he was makin' enough to live on, though they tell me that he never dunned nobody for what they owed him, and the folks here certainly has got the owin' habit, even in my business. If I had all that was comin' to me for just shaves alone, I could go to Carterville and put up at the Mercer for a week and see a different picture every night. For instance, they's old George Purdy—but I guess I shouldn't ought to be gossipin'.

Well, last year, our coroner died, died of the flu. Ken Beatty, that was his name. He was the coroner. So they had to choose another man to be coroner in his place and they picked Doc Stair. He laughed at first and said he didn't want it, but they made him take it. It ain't no job that anybody would fight for and what a man makes out of it in a year would just about buy seeds for their garden. Doc's the kind, though, that can't say no to nothin' if you keep at him long enough.

But I was goin' to tell you about a poor boy we got here in town—Paul Dickson. He fell out of a tree when he was about ten years old. Lit on his head and it done somethin' to him and he ain't never been right. No harm in him, but just silly. Jim Kendall used to call him cuckoo; that's a name Jim had for anybody that was off their head, only he called people's head their bean. That was another of his gags, callin' head bean and callin' crazy people cuckoo. Only poor Paul ain't crazy, but just silly.

You can imagine that Jim used to have all kinds of fun with Paul. He'd send him to the White Front Garage for a left-handed monkey wrench. Of course they ain't no such thing as a left-handed monkey wrench.

And once we had a kind of a fair here and they was a baseball game between the fats and the leans and before the game started Jim called Paul over and sent him way down to Schrader's hardware store to get a key for the pitcher's box.

They wasn't nothin' in the way of gags that Jim couldn't think up, when he put his mind to it.

Poor Paul was always kind of suspicious of people, maybe on account of how Jim had kept foolin' him. Paul wouldn't have much to do with anybody only his own mother and Doc Stair and a girl here in town named Julie Gregg. That is, she ain't a girl no more, but pretty near thirty or over.

When Doc first come to town, Paul seemed to feel like here was a real friend and he hung round Doc's office most of the w'ile; the only time he wasn't there was when he'd go home to eat or sleep or when he seen Julie Gregg doin' her shoppin'.

When he looked out Doc's window and seen her, he'd run downstairs and join her and tag along with her to the different stores. The poor boy was crazy about Julie and she always treated him mighty nice and made him feel like he was welcome, though of course it wasn't nothin' but pity on her side.

Doc done all he could to improve Paul's mind and he told me once that he really thought the boy was getting better, that they was times when he was as bright and sensible as anybody else.

But I was goin' to tell you about Julie Gregg. Old man Gregg was in the lumber business, but got to drinkin' and lost the most of his money and when he died, he didn't leave nothin' but the house and just enough insurance for the girl to skimp along on.

Her mother was a kind of a half invalid and didn't hardly ever leave the house. Julie wanted to sell the place and move somewhere else after the old man died, but the mother said she was born here and would die here. It was tough on Julie as the young people round this town—well, she's too good for them.

She'd been away to school and Chicago and New York and different places and they ain't no subject she can't talk on, where you take the rest of the young folks here and you mention anything to them outside of Gloria Swanson or Tommy Meighan and they think you're delirious. Did you see Gloria in *Wages of Virtue?* You missed somethin'!

Well, Doc Stair hadn't been here more than a week when he come in one day to get shaved and I recognized who he was, as he had been pointed out to me, so I told him about my old lady. She's been ailin' for a couple years and either Doc Gamble or Doc Foote, neither one, seemed to be helpin' her. So he said he would come out and see her, but if she was able to get out herself, it would be better to bring her to his office where he could make a completer examination.

So I took her to his office and w'ile I was waitin' for her in the reception room, in come Julie Gregg. When somebody comes in Doc Stair's office, they's a bell that rings in his inside office so he can tell they's somebody to see him.

So he left my old lady inside and come out to the front office and that's the first time him and Julie met and I guess it was what they call love at first sight. But it wasn't fifty-fifty. This young fella was the slickest lookin' fella she'd ever seen in this town and she went wild over him. To him she was just a young lady that wanted to see the doctor.

She'd came on about the same business I had. Her mother had been doctorin' for years with Doc Gamble and Doc Foote and without no results. So she'd heard they was a new doc in town and decided to give him a try. He promised to call and see her mother that same day.

I said a minute ago that it was love at first sight on her part. I'm not only judgin' by how she acted afterwards but how she looked at him that first day in his office. I ain't no mind reader, but it was wrote all over her face that she was gone.

Now Jim Kendall, besides bein' a joke-smith and a pretty good drinker, well, Jim was quite a lady-killer. I guess he run pretty wild durin' the time he was on the road for them Carterville people, and besides that, he'd had a couple little affairs of the heart right here in town. As I say, his wife would have divorced him, only she couldn't.

But Jim was like the majority of men, and women, too, I guess. He wanted what he couldn't get. He wanted Julie Gregg and worked his head off tryin' to land her. Only he'd of said bean instead of head.

Well, Jim's habits and his jokes didn't ap-peal to Julie and of course he was a married man, so he didn't have no more chance than, well, than a rabbit. That's an expression of Jim's himself. When somebody didn't have no chance to get elected or somethin', Jim would always say they didn't have no more chance than a rabbit.

He didn't make no bones about how he felt. Right in here, more than once, in front of the whole crowd, he said he was stuck on Julie and anybody that could get her for him was welcome to his house and his wife and kids included. But she wouldn't have nothin' to do with him; wouldn't even speak to him on the street. He finally seen he wasn't gettin' nowheres with his usual line so he decided to try the rough stuff. He went right up to her house one evenin' and when she opened the door he forced his way in and grabbed her. But she broke loose and before he could stop her, she run in the next room and locked the door and phoned to Joe Barnes. Joe's the marshal. Jim could hear who she was phonin' to and he beat it before Joe got there.

Joe was an old friend of Julie's pa. Joe went to Jim the next day and told him what would happen if he ever done it again.

I don't know how the news of this little affair leaked out. Chances is that Joe Barnes told his wife and she told somebody else's wife and they told their husband. Anyways, it did leak out and Hod Meyers had the nerve to kid Jim about it, right here in this shop. Jim didn't deny nothin' and kind of laughed it off and said for us all to wait; that lots of people had tried to make a monkey out of him, but he always got even.

Meanw'ile everybody in town was wise to Julie's bein' wild mad over the Doc. I don't suppose she had any idear how her face changed when him and her was together; of course she couldn't of, or she'd of kept away from him. And she didn't know that we was all noticin' how many times she made excuses to go up to his office or pass it on the other side of the street and look up in his window to see if he was there. I felt sorry for her and so did most other people.

Hod Meyers kept rubbin' it into Jim about

how the Doc had cut him out. Jim didn't pay no attention to the kiddin' and you could see he was plannin' one of his jokes.

One trick Jim had was the knack of changin' his voice. He could make you think he was a girl talkin' and he could mimic any man's voice. To show you how good he was along this line, I'll tell you the joke he played on me once.

You know, in most towns of any size, when a man is dead and needs a shave, why the barber that shaves him soaks him five dollars for the job; that is, he don't soak *him,* but whoever ordered the shave. I just charge three dollars because personally I don't mind much shavin' a dead person. They lay a whole lot stiller than live customers. The only thing is that you don't feel like talkin' to them and you get kind of lonesome.

Well, about the coldest day we ever had here, two years ago last winter, the phone rung at the house w'ile I was home to dinner and I answered the phone and it was a woman's voice and she said she was Mrs. John Scott and her husband was dead and would I come out and shave him.

Old John had always been a good customer of mine. But they live seven miles out in the country, on the Streeter road. Still I didn't see how I could say no.

So I said I would be there, but would have to come in a jitney and it might cost three or four dollars besides the price of the shave. So she, or the voice, it said that was all right, so I got Frank Abbott to drive me out to the place and when I got there, who should open the door but old John himself! He wasn't no more dead than, well, than a rabbit.

It didn't take no private detective to figure out who had played me this little joke. Nobody could of thought it up but Jim Kendall. He certainly was a card!

I tell you this incident just to show you how he could disguise his voice and make you believe it was somebody else talkin'. I'd of swore it was Mrs. Scott had called me. Anyways, some woman.

Well, Jim waited till he had Doc Stair's voice down pat; then he went after revenge. He called Julie up on a night when he

knew Doc was over in Carterville. She never questioned but what it was Doc's voice. Jim said he must see her that night; he couldn't wait no longer to tell her somethin'. She was all excited and told him to come to the house. But he said he was expectin' an important long distance call and wouldn't she please forget her manners for once and come to his office. He said they couldn't nothin' hurt her and nobody would see her and he just *must* talk to her a little w'ile. Well, poor Julie fell for it.

Doc always keeps a night light in his office, so it looked to Julie like they was somebody there.

Meanw'ile Jim Kendall had went to Wright's poolroom, where they was a whole gang amusin' themselves. The most of them had drank plenty of gin, and they was a rough bunch even when sober. They was always strong for Jim's jokes and when he told them to come with him and see some fun they give up their card games and pool games and followed along.

Doc's office is on the second floor. Right outside his door they's a flight of stairs leadin' to the floor above. Jim and his gang hid in the dark behind these stairs.

Well, Julie come up to Doc's door and rung the bell and they was nothin' doin'. She rung it again and she rung it seven or eight times. Then she tried the door and found it locked. Then Jim made some kind of a noise and she heard it and waited a minute, and then she says, "Is that you, Ralph?" Ralph is Doc's first name.

They was no answer and it must of came to her all of a sudden that she'd been bunked. She pretty near fell downstairs and the whole gang after her. They chased her all the way home, hollerin', "Is that you, Ralph?" and "Oh, Ralphie, dear, is that you?" Jim says he couldn't holler it himself, as he was laughin' too hard.

Poor Julie! She didn't show up here on Main Street for a long, long time afterward.

And of course Jim and his gang told everybody in town, everybody but Doc Stair. They was scared to tell him, and he might of never knowed only for Paul Dickson. The poor cuckoo, as Jim called him, he was here in the shop one night when Jim was still gloatin' yet over what he'd done to Julie. And Paul took in as much of it as he could understand and he run to Doc with the story.

It's a cinch Doc went up in the air and swore he'd make Jim suffer. But it was a kind of a delicate thing, because if it got out that he had beat Jim up, Julie was bound to hear of it and then she'd know that Doc knew and of course knowin' that he knew would make it worse for her than ever. He was goin' to do somethin', but it took a lot of figurin'.

Well, it was a couple days later when Jim was here in the shop again, and so was the cuckoo. Jim was goin' duck-shootin' the next day and had come in lookin' for Hod Meyers to go with him. I happened to know that Hod had went over to Carterville and wouldn't be home till the end of the week. So Jim said he hated to go alone and he guessed he would call it off. Then poor Paul spoke up and said if Jim would take him he would go along. Jim thought a w'ile and then he said, well, he guessed a half-wit was better than nothin'.

I suppose he was plottin' to get Paul out in the boat and play some joke on him, like pushin' him in the water. Anyways, he said Paul could go. He asked him had he ever shot a duck and Paul said no, he'd never even had a gun in his hands. So Jim said he could set in the boat and watch him and if he behaved himself, he might lend him his gun for a couple of shots. They made a date to meet in the mornin' and that's the last I seen of Jim alive.

Next mornin', I hadn't been open more than ten minutes when Doc Stair come in. He looked kind of nervous. He asked me had I seen Paul Dickson. I said no, but I knew where he was, out duck-shootin' with Jim Kendall. So Doc says that's what he had heard, and he couldn't understand it because Paul had told him he wouldn't never have no more to do with Jim as long as he lived.

He said Paul had told him about the joke Jim had played on Julie. He said Paul had asked him what he thought of the joke and the Doc told him that anybody that would do

a thing like that ought not to be let live. I said it had been a kind of a raw thing, but Jim just couldn't resist no kind of a joke, no matter how raw. I said I thought he was all right at heart, but just bubblin' over with mischief. Doc turned and walked out.

At noon he got a phone call from old John Scott. The lake where Jim and Paul had went shootin' is on John's place. Paul had came runnin' up to the house a few minutes before and said they'd been an accident. Jim had shot a few ducks and then give the gun to Paul and told him to try his luck. Paul hadn't never handled a gun and he was nervous. He was shakin' so hard that he couldn't control the gun. He let fire and Jim sunk back in the boat, dead.

Doc Stair, bein' the coroner, jumped in Frank Abbott's flivver and rushed out to Scott's farm. Paul and old John was down on the shore of the lake. Paul had rowed the boat to shore, but they'd left the body in it, waiting for Doc to come.

Doc examined the body and said they might as well fetch it back to town. They was no use leavin' it there or callin' a jury, as it was a plain case of accidental shootin'.

Personally I wouldn't never leave a person shoot a gun in the same boat I was in unless I was sure they knew somethin' about guns. Jim was a sucker to leave a new beginner have his gun, let alone a half-wit. It probably served Jim right, what he got. But still we miss him round here. He certainly was a card! Comb it wet or dry?

THE BLUE HOTEL

Stephen Crane
(1871–1900)

The Palace Hotel at Fort Romper was painted a light blue, a shade that is on the legs of a kind of heron, causing the bird to declare its position against any background. The Palace Hotel, then, was always screaming and howling in a way that made the dazzling winter landscape of Nebraska seem only a gray swampish hush. It stood alone on the prairie, and when the snow was falling the town two hundred yards away was not visible. But when the traveller alighted at the railway station he was obliged to pass the Palace Hotel before he could come upon the company of low clapboard houses which composed Fort Romper, and it was not to be thought that any traveller could pass the Palace Hotel without looking at it. Pat Scully, the proprietor, had proved himself a master of strategy when he chose his paints. It is true that on clear days, when the great transcontinental expresses, long lines of swaying Pullmans, swept through Fort Romper, passengers were overcome at the sight, and the cult that knows the brown-reds and the subdivisions of the dark greens of the East expressed shame, pity, horror, in a laugh. But to the citizens of this prairie town and to the people who would naturally stop there, Pat Scully had performed a feat. With this opulence and splendor, these creeds, classes, egotisms, that streamed through Romper on the rails day after day, they had no color in common.

As if the display delights of such a blue hotel were not sufficiently enticing, it was Scully's habit to go every morning and evening to meet the leisurely trains that stopped at Romper and work his seductions upon any man that he might see wavering, gripsack in hand.

One morning, when a snow-crusted engine dragged its long string of freight cars and its one passenger coach to the station, Scully performed the marvel of catching three men. One was a shaky and quick-eyed Swede, with a great shining cheap valise; one was a tall bronzed cowboy, who was on his way to a ranch near the Dakota line; one was a little silent man from the East, who didn't look it, and didn't announce it. Scully practically made them prisoners. He was so nimble and merry and kindly that each probably felt it would be the height of brutality to try to escape. They trudged off over the creaking board sidewalks in the wake of the eager little Irishman. He wore a heavy fur cap squeezed tightly down on his head. It caused his two red ears to stick out stiffly, as if they were made of tin.

At last, Scully, elaborately, with boisterous hospitality, conducted them through the portals of the blue hotel. The room which they entered was small. It seemed to be merely a proper temple for an enormous stove, which, in the center, was humming with godlike violence. At various points on its surface the iron had become luminous and glowed yellow from the heat. Beside the stove Scully's son Johnnie was playing High-Five with an old farmer who had whiskers both gray and sandy. They were quarrelling. Frequently the old farmer turned his face toward a box of sawdust—colored brown from tobacco juice —that was behind the stove, and spat with an air of great impatience and irritation. With a loud flourish of words Scully destroyed the game of cards, and bustled his son up-stairs with part of the baggage of the new guests. He himself conducted them to three basins of the coldest water in the world. The cowboy and the Easterner burnished themselves fiery red with this water, until it seemed to be some kind of metal polish. The Swede, however, merely dipped his fingers gingerly and with trepidation. It was notable that throughout this series of small ceremonies the three travellers were made to feel that Scully was very benevolent. He was conferring great favors upon them. He handed the towel from one to another with an air of philanthropic impulse.

Afterward they went to the first room, and, sitting about the stove, listened to Scully's officious clamor at his daughters, who were preparing the midday meal. They reflected in the silence of experienced men who tread carefully amid new people. Nevertheless, the old farmer, stationary, invincible in his chair near the warmest part of the stove, turned his face from the sawdust-box frequently and addressed a glowing commonplace to the strangers. Usually he was answered in short but adequate sentences by either the cowboy or the Easterner. The Swede said nothing. He seemed to be occupied in making furtive estimates of each man in the room. One might have thought that he had the sense of silly suspicion which comes to guilt. He resembled a badly frightened man.

Later, at dinner, he spoke a little, addressing his conversation entirely to Scully. He volunteered that he had come from New York, where for ten years he had worked as a tailor. These facts seemed to strike Scully as fascinating, and afterward he volunteered that he had lived at Romper for fourteen years. The Swede asked about the crops and the price of labor. He seemed barely to listen to Scully's extended replies. His eyes continued to rove from man to man.

Finally, with a laugh and a wink, he said that some of these Western communities were very dangerous; and after his statement he straightened his legs under the table, tilted his head, and laughed again, loudly. It was plain that the demonstration had no meaning to the others. They looked at him wondering and in silence.

2

As the men trooped heavily back into the front room, the two little windows presented views of a turmoiling sea of snow. The huge arms of the wind were making attempts— mighty, circular, futile—to embrace the flakes as they sped. A gate-post like a still man with a blanched face stood aghast amid this profligate fury. In a hearty voice Scully announced the presence of a blizzard. The guests of the blue hotel, lighting their pipes, assented with grunts of lazy masculine contentment. No island of the sea could be exempt in the degree of this little room with its humming stove. Johnnie, son of Scully, in a tone which defined his opinion of his ability as a cardplayer, challenged the old farmer of both gray and sandy whiskers to a game of High-Five. The farmer agreed with a contemptuous and bitter scoff. They sat close to the stove, and squared their knees under a wide board. The cowboy and the Easterner watched the game with interest. The Swede remained near the window, aloof, but with a countenance that showed signs of an inexplicable excitement.

The play of Johnnie and the gray-beard was suddenly ended by another quarrel. The old man arose while casting a look of heated scorn at his adversary. He slowly buttoned his coat, and then stalked with fabulous dignity from the room. In the discreet silence of all the other men the Swede laughed. His laughter rang somehow childish. Men by this time had begun to look at him askance, as if they wished to inquire what ailed him.

A new game was formed jocosely. The cowboy volunteered to become the partner of Johnnie, and they all then turned to ask the Swede to throw in his lot with the little Easterner. He asked some questions about the game, and, learning that it wore many names, and that he had played it when it was under an alias, he accepted the invitation. He strode toward the men nervously, as if he expected to be assaulted. Finally, seated, he gazed from face to face and laughed shrilly. This laugh was so strange that the Easterner looked up quickly, the cowboy sat intent and with his mouth open, and Johnnie paused, holding the cards with still fingers.

Afterward there was a short silence. Then Johnnie said, "Well, let's get at it. Come on now!" They pulled their chairs forward until their knees were bunched under the board. They began to play, and their interest in the game caused the others to forget the manner of the Swede.

The cowboy was a board-whacker. Each time that he held superior cards he whanged them, one by one, with exceeding force, down upon the improvised table, and took the tricks with a glowing air of prowess and pride that sent thrills of indignation into the hearts of his opponents. A game with a board-whacker in it is sure to become intense. The countenances of the Easterner and the Swede were miserable whenever the cowboy thundered down his aces and kings, while Johnnie, his eyes gleaming with joy, chuckled and chuckled.

Because of the absorbing play none considered the strange ways of the Swede. They paid strict heed to the game. Finally, during a lull caused by a new deal, the Swede suddenly addressed Johnnie: "I suppose there have been a good many men killed in this room." The jaws of the others dropped and they looked at him.

"What in hell are you talking about?" said Johnnie.

The Swede laughed again his blatant laugh, full of a kind of false courage and defiance. "Oh, you know what I mean all right," he answered.

"I'm a liar if I do!" Johnnie protested. The card was halted, and the men stared at the Swede. Johnnie evidently felt that as the son of the proprietor he should make a direct inquiry. "Now, what might you be drivin' at, mister?" he asked. The Swede winked at him. It was a wink full of cunning. His fingers shook on the edge of the board. "Oh, maybe you think I have been to nowheres. Maybe you think I'm a tenderfoot?"

"I don't know nothin' about you," answered Johnnie, "and I don't give a damn where you've been. All I got to say is that I don't know what you're driving at. There hain't never been nobody killed in this room."

The cowboy, who had been steadily gazing at the Swede, then spoke: "What's wrong with you, mister?"

Apparently it seemed to the Swede that he was formidably menaced. He shivered and turned white near the corners of his mouth. He sent an appealing glance in the direction of the little Easterner. During these moments he did not forget to wear his air of advanced pot-valor. "They say they don't know what I mean," he remarked mockingly to the Easterner.

The latter answered after prolonged and cautious reflection. "I don't understand you," he said, impassively.

The Swede made a movement then which announced that he thought he had encountered treachery from the only quarter where he had expected sympathy, if not help. "Oh, I see you are all against me. I see—"

The cowboy was in a state of deep stupefaction. "Say," he cried, as he tumbled the deck violently down upon the board, "say, what are you gittin' at, hey?"

The Swede sprang up with the celerity of a man escaping from a snake on the floor. "I don't want to fight!" he shouted. "I don't want to fight!"

The cowboy stretched his long legs indolently and deliberately. His hands were in his pockets. He spat into the sawdust-box. "Well, who the hell thought you did?" he inquired.

The Swede backed rapidly toward a corner of the room. His hands were out protectingly in front of his chest, but he was making an obvious struggle to control his fright. "Gentlemen," he quavered, "I suppose I am going to be killed before I can leave this house! I suppose I am going to be killed before I can leave this house!" In his eyes was the dying-swan look. Through the windows could be seen the snow turning blue in the shadow of dusk. The wind tore at the house, and some loose thing beat regularly against the clapboards like a spirit tapping.

A door opened, and Scully himself entered. He paused in surprise as he noted the tragic attitude of the Swede. Then he said, "What's the matter here?"

The Swede answered him swiftly and eagerly: "These men are going to kill me."

"Kill you!" ejaculated Scully. "Kill you! What are you talkin'?"

The Swede made the gesture of a martyr.

Scully wheeled sternly upon his son. "What is this, Johnnie?"

The lad had grown sullen. "Damned if I know," he answered. "I can't make no sense to it." He began to shuffle the cards, fluttering them together with an angry snap. "He says a good many men have been killed in this room, or something like that. And he says he's goin' to be killed here too. I don't know what ails him. He's crazy, I shouldn't wonder."

Scully then looked for explanation to the cowboy, but the cowboy simply shrugged his shoulders.

"Kill you?" said Scully again to the Swede. "Kill you? Man, you're off your nut."

"Oh, I know," burst out the Swede. "I know what will happen. Yes, I'm crazy—yes. Yes, of course, I'm crazy—yes. But I know one thing—" There was a sort of sweat of misery and terror upon his face. "I know I won't get out of here alive."

The cowboy drew a deep breath, as if his mind was passing into the last stages of dissolution. "Well, I'm doggoned," he whispered to himself.

Scully wheeled suddenly and faced his son. "You've been troublin' this man!"

Johnnie's voice was loud with its burden of grievance. "Why, good Gawd, I ain't done nothin' to 'im."

The Swede broke in. "Gentlemen, do not disturb yourselves. I will leave this house. I will go away, because"—he accused them dramatically with his glance—"because I do not want to be killed."

Scully was furious with his son. "Will you tell me what is the matter, you young divil? What's the matter, anyhow? Speak out!"

"Blame it!" cried Johnnie in despair, "don't I tell you I don't know? He—he says we want to kill him, and that's all I know. I can't tell what ails him."

The Swede continued to repeat: "Never mind, Mr. Scully; never mind. I will leave this house. I will go away, because I do not wish to be killed. Yes, of course, I am crazy—yes. But I know one thing! I will go away. I will leave this house. Never mind, Mr. Scully; never mind. I will go away."

"You will not go 'way," said Scully. "You will not go 'way until I hear the reason of this business. If anybody has troubled you I will take care of him. This is my house. You are under my roof, and I will not allow any peaceable man to be troubled here." He cast a terrible eye upon Johnnie, the cowboy, and the Easterner.

"Never mind, Mr. Scully; never mind. I will go away. I do not wish to be killed." The Swede moved toward the door which opened upon the stairs. It was evidently his intention to go at once for his baggage.

"No, no," shouted Scully peremptorily; but the white-faced man slid by him and disappeared. "Now," said Scully severely, "what does this mane?"

Johnnie and the cowboy cried together: "Why, we didn't do nothin' to 'im!"

Scully's eyes were cold. "No," he said, "you didn't?"

Johnnie swore a deep oath. "Why, this is the wildest loon I ever see. We didn't do nothin' at all. We were jest sittin' here playin' cards, and he—"

The father suddenly spoke to the Easterner. "Mr. Blanc," he asked, "what has these boys been doin'?"

The Easterner reflected again. "I didn't see anything wrong at all," he said at last, slowly.

Scully began to howl. "But what does it mane?" He stared ferociously at his son. "I have a mind to lather you for this, my boy."

Johnnie was frantic. "Well, what have I done?" he bawled at his father.

3

"I think you are tongue-tied," said Scully finally to his son, the cowboy, and the Easterner; and at the end of this scornful sentence he left the room.

Upstairs the Swede was swiftly fastening the straps of his great valise. Once his back happened to be half turned toward the door, and, hearing a noise there, he wheeled and sprang up, uttering a loud cry. Scully's wrinkled visage showed grimly in the light of the small lamp he carried. This yellow effulgence, streaming upward, colored only his prominent features, and left his eyes, for instance, in mysterious shadow. He resembled a murderer.

"Man! man!" he exclaimed, "have you gone daffy?"

"Oh, no! Oh, no!" rejoined the other. "There are people in this world who know pretty nearly as much as you do—understand?"

For a moment they stood gazing at each other. Upon the Swede's deathly pale cheeks were two spots brightly crimson and sharply edged, as if they had been carefully painted. Scully placed the light on the table and sat himself on the edge of the bed. He spoke ruminatively. "By cracky, I never heard of such a thing in my life. It's a complete muddle. I can't, for the soul of me, think how you ever got this idea into your head." Presently he lifted his eyes and asked: "And did you sure think they were going to kill you?"

The Swede scanned the old man as if he wished to see into his mind. "I did," he said at last. He obviously suspected that this answer might precipitate an outbreak. As he pulled on a strap his whole arm shook, the elbow wavering like a bit of paper.

Scully banged his hand impressively on the footboard of the bed. "Why, man, we're goin' to have a line of ilictric street-cars in this town next spring."

"'A line of electric street-cars,'" repeated the Swede, stupidly.

"And," said Scully, "there's a new railroad goin' to be built down from Broken Arm to here. Not to mintion the four churches and the smashin' big brick schoolhouse. Then there's the big factory, too. Why, in two years Romper'll be a met-tro-*pol*-is."

Having finished the preparation of his baggage, the Swede straightened himself. "Mr. Scully," he said, with sudden hardihood, "how much do I owe you?"

"You don't owe me anythin'," said the old man, angrily.

"Yes, I do," retorted the Swede. He took seventy-five cents from his pocket and tendered it to Scully; but the latter snapped his fingers in disdainful refusal. However, it happened that they both stood gazing in a strange fashion at three silver pieces on the Swede's open palm.

"I'll not take your money," said Scully at last. "Not after what's been goin' on here." Then a plan seemed to strike him. "Here," he cried, picking up his lamp and moving toward the door. "Here! Come with me a minute."

"No," said the Swede, in overwhelming alarm.

"Yes," urged the old man. "Come on! I want you to come and see a picter—just across the hall—in my room."

The Swede must have concluded that his hour was come. His jaw dropped and his teeth showed like a dead man's. He ultimately followed Scully across the corridor, but he had the step of one hung in chains.

Scully flashed the light on the wall of his own chamber. There was revealed a ridiculous photograph of a little girl. She was leaning against a balustrade of gorgeous decoration, and the formidable bang to her hair was prominent. The figure was as graceful as an upright sled-stake, and, withal, it was of the hue of lead. "There," said Scully, tenderly, "that's the picter of my little girl that died. Her name was Carrie. She had the purtiest hair you ever saw! I was that fond of her, she—"

Turning then, he saw that the Swede was not contemplating the picture at all, but, instead, was keeping keen watch on the gloom in the rear.

"Look, man!" cried Scully, heartily. "That's the picter of my little gal that died. Her name was Carrie. And then here's the picter of my oldest boy. Michael. He's a lawyer in Lincoln, an' doin' well. I gave that boy a grand eddication, and I'm glad for it now. He's a fine boy. Look at 'im now. Ain't he bold as blazes, him there in Lincoln, an honored an' respicted gintleman! An honored and respicted gintleman," concluded Scully with a flourish. And, so saying, he smote the Swede jovially on the back.

The Swede faintly smiled.

"Now," said the old man, "there's only one more thing." He dropped suddenly to the floor and thrust his head beneath the bed. The Swede could hear his muffled voice. "I'd keep it under me piller if it wasn't for that boy Johnnie. Then there's the old woman— Where is it now? I never put it twice in the same place. Ah, now come out with you!"

Presently he backed clumsily from under the bed, dragging with him an old coat rolled into a bundle. "I've fetched him," he muttered. Kneeling on the floor, he unrolled the coat and extracted from its heart a large yellow-brown whiskey-bottle.

His first maneuver was to hold the bottle up to the light. Reassured, apparently, that nobody had been tampering with it, he thrust it with a generous movement toward the Swede.

The weak-kneed Swede was about to eagerly clutch this element of strength, but he suddenly jerked his hand away and cast a look of horror upon Scully.

"Drink," said the old man affectionately. He had risen to his feet, and now stood facing the Swede.

There was a silence. Then again Scully said: "Drink!"

The Swede laughed wildly. He grabbed the bottle, put it to his mouth; and as his lips curled absurdly around the opening and his throat worked, he kept his glance, burning with hatred, upon the old man's face.

4

After the departure of Scully the three men with the cardboard still upon their knees, preserved for a long time an astounded silence. Then Johnnie said: "That's the doddangedest Swede I ever see."

"He ain't no Swede," said the cowboy, scornfully.

"Well, what is he then?" cried Johnnie. "What is he then?"

"It's my opinion," replied the cowboy deliberately, "he's some kind of a Dutchman." It was a venerable custom of the country to entitle as Swedes all light-haired men who spoke with a heavy tongue. In consequence the idea of the cowboy was not without its daring. "Yes, sir," he repeated. "It's my opinion this feller is some kind of a Dutchman."

"Well, he says he's a Swede, anyhow," muttered Johnnie, sulkily. He turned to the Easterner: "What do you think, Mr. Blanc?"

"Oh, I don't know," replied the Easterner.

"Well, what do you think makes him act that way?" asked the cowboy.

"Why, he's frightened." The Easterner knocked his pipe against a rim of the stove. "He's clear frightened out of his boots."

"What at?" cried Johnnie and the cowboy together.

The Easterner reflected over his answer.

"What at?" cried the others again.

"Oh, I don't know, but it seems to me this man has been reading dime novels, and he

thinks he's right out in the middle of it— the shootin' and stabbin' and all."

"But," said the cowboy, deeply scandalized, "this ain't Wyoming, ner none of them places. This is Nebrasker."

"Yes," added Johnnie, "an' why don't he wait till he gits *out West?*"

The travelled Easterner laughed. "It isn't different there even—not in these days. But he thinks he's right in the middle of hell."

Johnnie and the cowboy mused long.

"It's awful funny," remarked Johnnie at last.

"Yes," said the cowboy. "This is a queer game. I hope we don't git snowed in, because then we'd have to stand this here man bein' around with us all the time. That wouldn't be no good."

"I wish pop would throw him out," said Johnnie.

Presently they heard a loud stamping on the stairs, accompanied by ringing jokes in the voice of old Scully, and laughter, evidently from the Swede. The men around the stove stared vacantly at each other. "Gosh!" said the cowboy. The door flew open, and old Scully, flushed and anecdotal, came into the room. He was jabbering at the Swede, who followed him, laughing bravely. It was the entry of two roisterers from a banquet hall.

"Come now," said Scully sharply to the three seated men, "move up and give us a chance at the stove." The cowboy and the Easterner obediently sidled their chairs to make room for the newcomers. Johnnie, however, simply arranged himself in a more indolent attitude, and then remained motionless.

"Come! Git over, there," said Scully.

"Plenty of room on the other side of the stove," said Johnnie.

"Do you think we want to sit in the draught?" roared the father.

But the Swede here interposed with a grandeur of confidence. "No, no. Let the boy sit where he likes," he cried in a bullying voice to the father.

"All right! All right!" said Scully, deferentially. The cowboy and the Easterner exchanged glances of wonder.

The five chairs were formed in a crescent about one side of the stove. The Swede began to talk; he talked arrogantly, profanely, angrily. Johnnie, the cowboy, and the Easterner maintained a morose silence, while old Scully appeared to be receptive and eager, breaking in constantly with sympathetic ejaculations.

Finally the Swede announced that he was thirsty. He moved in his chair, and said that he would go for a drink of water.

"I'll git it for you," cried Scully at once.

"No," said the Swede, contemptuously. "I'll get it for myself." He arose and stalked with the air of an owner off into the executive parts of the hotel.

As soon as the Swede was out of hearing Scully sprang to his feet and whispered intensely to the others: "Up-stairs he thought I was tryin' to poison 'im."

"Say," said Johnnie, "this makes me sick. Why don't you throw 'im out in the snow?"

"Why, he's all right now," declared Scully. "It was only that he was from the East, and he thought this was a tough place. That's all. He's all right now."

The cowboy looked with admiration upon the Easterner. "You were straight," he said. "You were on to that there Dutchman."

"Well," said Johnnie to his father, "he may be all right now, but I don't see it. Other time he was scared, but now he's too fresh."

Scully's speech was always a combination of Irish brogue and idiom, Western twang and idiom, and scraps of curiously formal diction taken from the story-books and newspapers. He now hurled a strange mass of language at the head of his son. "What do I keep? What do I keep? What do I keep?" he demanded, in a voice of thunder. He slapped his knee impressively, to indicate that he himself was going to make reply, and that all should heed. "I keep a hotel," he shouted. "A hotel, do you mind? A guest under my roof has sacred privileges. He is to be intimidated by none. Not one word shall he hear that would prijudice him in favor of goin' away. I'll not have it. There's no place in this here town where they can say they iver took in a guest of mine because he was

afraid to stay here." He wheeled suddenly upon the cowboy and the Easterner. "Am I right?"

"Yes, Mr. Scully," said the cowboy, "I think you're right."

"Yes, Mr. Scully," said the Easterner, "I think you're right."

5

At six-o'clock supper, the Swede fizzed like a fire-wheel. He sometimes seemed on the point of bursting into riotous song, and in all his madness he was encouraged by old Scully. The Easterner was encased in reserve; the cowboy sat in wide-mouthed amazement, forgetting to eat, while Johnnie wrathily demolished great plates of food. The daughters of the house, when they were obliged to replenish the biscuits, approached as warily as Indians, and, having succeeded in their purpose, fled with ill-concealed trepidation. The Swede domineered the whole feast, and he gave it the appearance of a cruel bacchanal. He seemed to have grown suddenly taller; he gazed, brutally disdainful, into every face. His voice rang through the room. Once when he jabbed out harpoon-fashion with his fork to pinion a biscuit, the weapon nearly impaled the hand of the Easterner, which had been stretched quietly out for the same biscuit.

After supper, as the men filed toward the other room, the Swede smote Scully ruthlessly on the shoulder. "Well, old boy, that was a good, square meal." Johnnie looked hopefully at his father; he knew that shoulder was tender from an old fall; and, indeed, it appeared for a moment as if Scully was going to flame out over the matter, but in the end he smiled a sickly smile and remained silent. The others understood from his manner that he was admitting his responsibility for the Swede's new viewpoint.

Johnnie, however, addressed his parent in an aside. "Why don't you license somebody to kick you downstairs?" Scully scowled darkly by way of reply.

When they were gathered about the stove, the Swede insisted on another game of High-

Five. Scully gently deprecated the plan at first, but the Swede turned a wolfish glare upon him. The old man subsided, and the Swede canvassed the others. In his tone there was always a great threat. The cowboy and the Easterner both remarked indifferently that they would play. Scully said that he would presently have to go to meet the 6.58 train, and so the Swede turned menacingly upon Johnnie. For a moment their glances crossed like blades, and then Johnnie smiled and said, "Yes, I'll play."

They formed a square, with the little board on their knees. The Easterner and the Swede were again partners. As the play went on, it was noticeable that the cowboy was not board-whacking as usual. Meanwhile, Scully, near the lamp, had put on his spectacles and, with an appearance curiously like an old priest, was reading a newspaper. In time he went out to meet the 6.58 train, and, despite his precautions, a gust of polar wind whirled into the room as he opened the door. Besides scattering the cards, it chilled the players to the marrow. The Swede cursed frightfully. When Scully returned, his entrance disturbed a cosy and friendly scene. The Swede again cursed. But presently they were once more intent, their heads bent forward and their hands moving swiftly. The Swede had adopted the fashion of board-whacking.

Scully took up his paper and for a long time remained immersed in matters which were extraordinarily remote from him. The lamp burned badly, and once he stopped to adjust the wick. The newspaper, as he turned from page to page, rustled with a slow and comfortable sound. Then suddenly he heard three terrible words: "You are cheatin'!"

Such scenes often prove that there can be little of dramatic import in environment. Any room can present a tragic front; any room can be comic. This little den was now hideous as a torture-chamber. The new faces of the men themselves had changed it upon the instant. The Swede held a huge fist in front of Johnnie's face, while the latter looked steadily over it into the blazing orbs of his accuser. The Easterner had grown pallid; the cowboy's jaw had dropped in that expression of bovine amazement which was one of his important mannerisms. After the three words, the first sound in the room was made by Scully's paper as it floated forgotten to his feet. His spectacles had also fallen from his nose, but by a clutch he had saved them in air. His hand, grasping the spectacles, now remained poised awkwardly and near his shoulder. He stared at the card-players.

Probably the silence was while a second elapsed. Then, if the floor had been suddenly twitched out from under the men they could not have moved quicker. The five had projected themselves headlong toward a common point. It happened that Johnnie, in rising to hurl himself upon the Swede, had stumbled slightly because of his curiously instinctive care for the cards and the board. The loss of the moment allowed time for the arrival of Scully, and also allowed the cowboy time to give the Swede a great push which sent him staggering back. The men found tongue together, and hoarse shouts of rage, appeal, or fear burst from every throat. The cowboy pushed and jostled feverishly at the Swede, and the Easterner and Scully clung wildly to Johnnie; but through the smoky air, above the swaying bodies of the peace-compellers, the eyes of the two warriors ever sought each other in glances of challenge that were at once hot and steely.

Of course the board had been overturned, and now the whole company of cards was scattered over the floor, where the boots of the men trampled the fat and painted kings and queens as they gazed with their silly eyes at the war that was waging above them.

Scully's voice was dominating the yells. "Stop now! Stop, I say! Stop, now—"

Johnnie, as he struggled to burst through the rank formed by Scully and the Easterner, was crying, "Well, he says I cheated! He says I cheated! I won't allow no man to say I cheated! If he says I cheated, he's a———!"

The cowboy was telling the Swede, "Quit, now! Quit, d'ye hear—"

The screams of the Swede never ceased: "He did cheat! I saw him! I saw him—"

As for the Easterner, he was importuning in a voice that was not heeded: "Wait a moment, can't you? Oh, wait a moment. What's the good of a fight over a game of cards? Wait a moment—"

In this tumult no complete sentences were clear. "Cheat"—"Quit"—"He says"—these fragments pierced the uproar and rang out sharply. It was remarkable that, whereas Scully undoubtedly made the most noise, he was the least heard of any of the riotous band.

Then suddenly there was a great cessation. It was as if each man had paused for breath; and although the room was still lighted with the anger of men, it could be seen that there was no danger of immediate conflict, and at once Johnnie, shouldering his way forward, almost succeeded in confronting the Swede. "What did you say I cheated for? What did you say I cheated for? I don't cheat, and I won't let no man say I do!"

The Swede said, "I saw you! I saw you!"

"Well," cried Johnnie, "I'll fight any man what says I cheat!"

"No, you won't," said the cowboy. "Not here."

"Ah, be still, can't you?" said Scully, coming between them.

The quiet was sufficient to allow the Easterner's voice to be heard. He was repeating, "Oh, wait a moment, can't you? What's the good of a fight over a game of cards? Wait a moment!"

Johnnie, his red face appearing above his father's shoulder, hailed the Swede again. "Did you say I cheated?"

The Swede showed his teeth. "Yes."

"Then," said Johnnie, "we must fight."

"Yes, fight," roared the Swede. He was like a demoniac. "Yes, fight! I'll show you what kind of a man I am! I'll show you who you want to fight! Maybe you think I can't fight! Maybe you think I can't! I'll show you, you skin, you card-sharp! Yes, you cheated! You cheated! You cheated!"

"Well, let's go at it, then, mister," said Johnnie, coolly.

The cowboy's brow was beaded with sweat from his efforts in intercepting all sorts of raids. He turned in despair to Scully. "What are you goin' to do now?"

A change had come over the Celtic visage of the old man. He now seemed all eagerness; his eyes glowed.

"We'll let them fight," he answered, stalwartly. "I can't put up with it any longer. I've stood this damned Swede till I'm sick. We'll let them fight."

6

The men prepared to go out-of-doors. The Easterner was so nervous that he had great difficulty in getting his arms into the sleeves of his new leather coat. As the cowboy drew his fur cap down over his ears his hands trembled. In fact, Johnnie and old Scully were the only ones who displayed no agitation. These preliminaries were conducted without words.

Scully threw open the door. "Well, come on," he said. Instantly a terrific wind caused the flame of the lamp to struggle at its wick, while a puff of black smoke sprang from the chimney-top. The stove was in mid-current of the blast, and its voice swelled to equal the roar of the storm. Some of the scarred and bedabbled cards were caught up from the floor and dashed helplessly against the farther wall. The men lowered their heads and plunged into the tempest as into a sea.

No snow was falling, but great whirls and clouds of flakes, swept up from the ground by the frantic winds, were streaming southward with the speed of bullets. The covered land was blue with the sheen of an unearthly satin, and there was no other hue save where, at the low, black railway station —which seemed incredibly distant—one light gleamed like a tiny jewel. As the men floundered into a thigh-deep drift, it was known that the Swede was bawling out something. Scully went to him, put a hand on his shoulder, and projected an ear. "What's that you say?" he shouted.

"I say," bawled the Swede again, "I won't stand much show against this gang. I know you'll all pitch on me."

Scully smote him reproachfully on the arm. "Tut, man!" he yelled. The wind tore the words from Scully's lips and scattered them far alee.

"You are all a gang of—" boomed the Swede, but the storm also seized the remainder of this sentence.

Immediately turning their backs upon the wind, the men had swung around a corner to the sheltered side of the hotel. It was the function of the little house to preserve here, amid this great devastation of snow, an irregular V-shape of heavily encrusted grass, which crackled beneath the feet. One could imagine the great drifts piled against the windward side. When the party reached the comparative peace of this spot it was found that the Swede was still bellowing.

"Oh, I know what kind of a thing this is! I know you'll all pitch on me. I can't lick you all!"

Scully turned upon him panther-fashion. "You'll not have to whip all of us. You'll have to whip my son Johnnie. An' the man what troubles you durin' that time will have me to dale with."

The arrangements were swiftly made. The two men faced each other, obedient to the harsh commands of Scully, whose face, in the subtly luminous gloom, could be seen set in the austere impersonal lines that are pictured on the countenances of the Roman veterans. The Easterner's teeth were chattering, and he was hopping up and down like a mechanical toy. The cowboy stood rocklike.

The contestants had not stripped off any clothing. Each was in his ordinary attire. Their fists were up, and they eyed each other in a calm that had the elements of leonine cruelty in it.

During this pause, the Easterner's mind, like a film, took lasting impressions of three men—the iron-nerved master of the ceremony; the Swede, pale, motionless, terrible; and Johnnie, serene yet ferocious, brutish yet heroic. The entire prelude had in it a tragedy greater than the tragedy of action, and this aspect was accentuated by the long, mellow cry of the blizzard, as it sped the tumbling and wailing flakes into the black abyss of the south.

"Now!" said Scully.

The two combatants leaped forward and crashed together like bullocks. There was heard the cushioned sound of blows, and of a curse squeezing out from between the tight teeth of one.

As for the spectators, the Easterner's pent-up breath exploded from him with a pop of relief, absolute relief from the tension of the preliminaries. The cowboy bounded into the air with a yowl. Scully was immovable as from supreme amazement and fear at the fury of the fight which he himself had permitted and arranged.

For a time the encounter in the darkness was such a perplexity of flying arms that it presented no more detail than would a swiftly revolving wheel. Occasionally a face, as if illumined by a flash of light, would shine out, ghastly and marked with pink spots. A moment later, the men might have been known as shadows, if it were not for the involuntary utterance of oaths that came from them in whispers.

Suddenly a holocaust of warlike desire caught the cowboy, and he bolted forward with the speed of a broncho. "Go it, Johnnie! Go it! Kill him! Kill him!"

Scully confronted him. "Kape back," he said; and by his glance the cowboy could tell that this man was Johnnie's father.

To the Easterner there was a monotony of unchangeable fighting that was an abomination. This confused mingling was eternal to his sense, which was concentrated in a longing for the end, the priceless end. Once the fighters lurched near him, and as he scrambled hastily backward he heard them breathe like men on the rack.

"Kill him, Johnnie! Kill him! Kill him! Kill him!" the cowboy's face was contorted like one of those agony masks in museums.

"Keep still," said Scully, icily.

Then there was a sudden loud grunt, incomplete, cut short, and Johnnie's body swung away from the Swede and fell with sickening heaviness to the grass. The cowboy was barely in time to prevent the mad Swede from flinging himself upon his prone adversary. "No, you don't," said the cowboy, interposing an arm. "Wait a second."

Scully was at his son's side. "Johnnie! Johnnie, me boy!" His voice had a quality of melancholy tenderness. "Johnnie! Can you go on with it?" He looked anxiously down into the bloody, pulpy face of his son.

There was a moment of silence, and then Johnnie answered in his ordinary voice, "Yes, I—it—yes."

Assisted by his father he struggled to his feet. "Wait a bit now till you git your wind," said the old man.

A few paces away the cowboy was lecturing the Swede. "No, you don't! Wait a second!"

The Easterner was plucking at Scully's sleeve. "Oh, this is enough," he pleaded. "This is enough! Let it go as it stands. This is enough!"

"Bill," said Scully, "git out of the road." The cowboy stepped aside. "Now." The combatants were actuated by a new caution as they advanced toward collision. They glared at each other, and then the Swede aimed a lightning blow that carried with it his entire weight. Johnnie was evidently half stupid from weakness, but he miraculously dodged, and his fist sent the overbalanced Swede sprawling.

The cowboy, Scully, and the Easterner burst into a cheer that was like a chorus of triumphant soldiery, but before its conclusion the Swede had scuffled agilely to his feet and come in berserk abandon at his foe. There was another perplexity of flying arms, and Johnnie's body again swung away and fell, even as a bundle might fall from a roof. The Swede instantly staggered to a little wind-waved tree and leaned upon it, breathing like an engine, while his savage and flame-lit eyes roamed from face to face as the men bent over Johnnie. There was a splendor of isolation in his situation at this time which the Easterner felt once when, lifting his eyes from the man on the ground, he beheld that mysterious and lonely figure, waiting.

"Are you any good yet, Johnnie?" asked Scully in a broken voice.

The son gasped and opened his eyes languidly. After a moment he answered, "No—

I ain't—any good—any—more." Then, from shame and bodily ill, he began to weep, the tears furrowing down through the blood-stains on his face. "He was too—too—too heavy for me."

Scully straightened and addressed the waiting figure. "Stranger," he said, evenly, "it's all up with our side." Then his voice changed into that vibrant huskiness which is commonly the tone of the most simple and deadly announcements. "Johnnie is whipped."

Without replying, the victor moved off on the route to the front door of the hotel.

The cowboy was formulating new and unspellable blasphemies. The Easterner was startled to find that they were out in a wind that seemed to come direct from the shadowed arctic floes. He heard again the wail of the snow as it was flung to its grave in the south. He knew now that all this time the cold had been sinking into him deeper and deeper, and he wondered that he had not perished. He felt indifferent to the condition of the vanquished man.

"Johnnie, can you walk?" asked Scully.

"Did I hurt—hurt him any?" asked the son.

"Can you walk, boy? Can you walk?"

Johnnie's voice was suddenly strong. There was a robust impatience in it. "I asked you whether I hurt him any!"

"Yes, yes, Johnnie," answered the cowboy, consolingly; "he's hurt a good deal."

They raised him from the ground, and as soon as he was on his feet he went tottering off, rebuffing all attempts at assistance. When the party rounded the corner they were fairly blinded by the pelting of the snow. It burned their faces like fire. The cowboy carried Johnnie through the drift to the door. As they entered, some cards again rose from the floor and beat against the wall.

The Easterner rushed to the stove. He was so profoundly chilled that he almost dared to embrace the glowing iron. The Swede was not in the room. Johnnie sank into a chair and, folding his arms on his knees, buried his face in them. Scully, warming one foot and then the other at a rim of the stove, muttered to himself with Celtic mournfulness. The cowboy had removed his fur cap, and with a dazed and rueful air he was running one hand through his tousled locks. From overhead they could hear the creaking of boards, as the Swede tramped here and there in his room.

The sad quiet was broken by the sudden flinging open of a door that led toward the kitchen. It was instantly followed by an inrush of women. They precipitated themselves upon Johnnie amid a chorus of lamentation. Before they carried their prey off to the kitchen, there to be bathed and harangued with that mixture of sympathy and abuse which is a feat of their sex, the mother straightened herself and fixed old Scully with an eye of stern reproach. "Shame be upon you, Patrick Scully!" she cried. "Your own son, too. Shame be upon you!"

"There, now! Be quiet, now!" said the old man, weakly.

"Shame be upon you, Patrick Scully!" The girls, rallying to this slogan, sniffed disdainfully in the direction of those trembling accomplices, the cowboy and the Easterner. Presently they bore Johnnie away, and left the three men to dismal reflection.

7

"I'd like to fight this here Dutchman myself," said the cowboy, breaking a long silence.

Scully wagged his head sadly. "No, that wouldn't do. It wouldn't be right. It wouldn't be right."

"Well, why wouldn't it?" argued the cowboy. "I don't see no harm in it."

"No," answered Scully, with mournful heroism. "It wouldn't be right. It was Johnnie's fight, and now we mustn't whip the man just because he whipped Johnnie."

"Yes, that's true enough," said the cowboy; "but—he better not get fresh with me, because I couldn't stand no more of it."

"You'll not say a word to him," commanded Scully, and even then they heard the tread of the Swede on the stairs. His entrance was made theatric. He swept the door back with a bang and swaggered to the middle of the room. No one looked at

him. "Well," he cried, insolently, at Scully, "I s'pose you'll tell me now how much I owe you?"

The old man remained stolid. "You don't owe me nothin'."

"Huh!" said the Swede, "huh! Don't owe 'im nothin'."

The cowboy addressed the Swede. "Stranger, I don't see how you come to be so gay around here."

Old Scully was instantly alert. "Stop!" he shouted, holding his hand forth, fingers upward. "Bill, you shut up!"

The cowboy spat carelessly into the sawdust-box. "I didn't say a word, did I?" he asked.

"Mr. Scully," called the Swede, "how much do I owe you?" It was seen that he was attired for departure, and that he had his valise in his hand.

"You don't owe me nothin'," repeated Scully in the same imperturbable way.

"Huh!" said the Swede. "I guess you're right. I guess if it was any way at all, you'd owe me somethin'. That's what I guess." He turned to the cowboy. " 'Kill him! Kill him! Kill him!' " he mimicked, and then guffawed victoriously. " 'Kill him!' " He was convulsed with ironical humor.

But he might have been jeering the dead. The three men were immovable and silent, staring with glassy eyes at the stove.

The Swede opened the door and passed into the storm, giving one derisive glance backward at the still group.

As soon as the door was closed, Scully and the cowboy leaped to their feet and began to curse. They trampled to and fro, waving their arms and smashing into the air with their fists. "Oh, but that was a hard minute!" wailed Scully. "That was a hard minute! Him there leerin' and scoffin'! One bang at his nose was worth forty dollars to me that minute! How did you stand it, Bill?"

"How did I stand it?" cried the cowboy in a quivering voice. "How did I stand it? Oh!"

The old man burst into sudden brogue. "I'd loike to take that Swade," he wailed, "and hould 'im down on a shtone flure and bate 'im to a jelly wid a shtick!"

The cowboy groaned in sympathy. "I'd like to git him by the neck and ha-ammer him"—he brought his hand down on a chair with a noise like a pistol-shot—"hammer that there Dutchman until he couldn't tell himself from a dead coyote!"

"I'd bate 'im until he—"

"I'd show *him* some things—"

And then together they raised a yearning, fanatic cry—"Oh-o-oh! if we only could—"

"Yes!"

"Yes!"

"And then I'd—"

"O-o-oh!"

8

The Swede, tightly gripping his valise, tacked across the face of the storm as if he carried sails. He was following a line of little naked, gasping trees which, he knew, must mark the way of the road. His face, fresh from the pounding of Johnnie's fists, felt more pleasure than pain in the wind and the driving snow. A number of square shapes loomed upon him finally, and he knew them as the houses of the main body of the town. He found a street and made travel along it, leaning heavily upon the wind whenever, at a corner, a terrific blast caught him.

He might have been in a deserted village. We picture the world as thick with conquering and elate humanity, but here, with the bugles of the tempest pealing, it was hard to imagine a peopled earth. One viewed the existence of man then as a marvel, and conceded a glamor of wonder to these lice which were caused to cling to a whirling, fire-smitten, ice-locked, disease-stricken, space-lost bulb. The conceit of man was explained by this storm to be the very engine of life. One was a coxcomb not to die in it. However, the Swede found a saloon.

In front of it an indomitable red light was burning, and the snowflakes were made blood-color as they flew through the circumscribed territory of the lamp's shining. The Swede pushed open the door of the saloon and entered. A sanded expanse was before him, and at the end of it four men sat about a table drinking. Down one side of the room extended a radiant bar, and its guardian was leaning upon his elbows listening to the talk of the men at the table. The Swede dropped his valise upon the floor and, smiling fraternally upon the barkeeper, said, "Gimme some whiskey, will you?" The man placed a bottle, a whiskey-glass, and a glass of ice-thick water upon the bar. The Swede poured himself an abnormal portion of whiskey and drank it in three gulps. "Pretty bad night," remarked the bartender, indifferently. He was making the pretension of blindness which is usually a distinction of his class; but it could have been seen that he was furtively studying the half-erased blood-stains on the face of the Swede. "Bad night," he said again.

"Oh, it's good enough for me," replied the Swede, hardily, as he poured himself some more whiskey. The barkeeper took his coin and maneuvered it through its reception by the highly nickelled cash-machine. A bell rang; a card labelled "20 cts." had appeared.

"No," continued the Swede, "this isn't too bad weather. It's good enough for me."

"So?" murmured the barkeeper, languidly.

The copious drams made the Swede's eyes swim, and he breathed a trifle heavier. "Yes, I like this weather. I like it. It suits me." It was apparently his design to impart a deep significance to these words.

"So?" murmured the bartender again. He turned to gaze dreamily at the scroll-like birds and bird-like scrolls which had been drawn with soap upon the mirrors in back of the bar.

"Well, I guess I'll take another drink," said the Swede, presently. "Have something?"

"No, thanks; I'm not drinkin'," answered the bartender. Afterward he asked, "How did you hurt your face?"

The Swede immediately began to boast loudly. "Why, in a fight. I thumped the soul out of a man down here at Scully's hotel."

The interest of the four men at the table was at last aroused.

"Who was it?" said one.

"Johnnie Scully," blustered the Swede. "Son of the man what runs it. He will be pretty near dead for some weeks, I can tell you. I made a nice thing of him, I did. He couldn't get up. They carried him in the house. Have a drink?"

Instantly the men in some subtle way encased themselves in reserve. "No, thanks," said one. The group was of curious formation. Two were prominent local business men; one was the district attorney; and one was a professional gambler of the kind known as "square." But a scrutiny of the group would not have enabled an observer to pick the gambler from the men of more reputable pursuits. He was, in fact, a man so delicate in manner, when among people of fair class, and so judicious in his choice of victims, that in the strictly masculine part of the town's life he had come to be explicitly trusted and admired. People called him a thoroughbred. The fear and contempt with which his craft was regarded were undoubtedly the reason why his quiet dignity shone conspicuous above the quiet dignity of men who might be merely hatters, billiard-markers, or grocery-clerks. Beyond an occasional unwary traveller who came by rail, this gambler was supposed to prey solely upon reckless and senile farmers, who, when flush with good crops, drove into town in all the pride and confidence of an absolutely invulnerable stupidity. Hearing at times in circuitous fashion of the despoilment of such a farmer, the important men of Romper invariably laughed in contempt of the victim, and if they thought of the wolf at all, it was with a kind of pride at the knowledge that he would never dare think of attacking their wisdom and courage. Besides, it was popular that this gambler had a real wife and two real children in a neat cottage in a suburb, where he led an exemplary home life; and when any one even suggested a discrepancy in his character, the crowd immediately vociferated descriptions of this virtuous family circle. Then men who led exemplary home lives, and men who did not lead exemplary home lives, all subsided in a bunch, remarking that there was nothing more to be said.

However, when a restriction was placed upon him—as, for instance, when a strong clique of members of the new Pollywog Club refused to permit him, even as a spectator, to appear in the rooms of the organization—the candor and gentleness with which he accepted the judgment disarmed many of his foes and made his friends more desperately partisan. He invariably distinguished between himself and a respectable Romper man so quickly and frankly that his manner actually appeared to be a continual broadcast compliment.

And one must not forget to declare the fundamental fact of his entire position in Romper. It is irrefutable that in all affairs outside his business, in all matters that occur eternally and commonly between man and man, this thieving card-player was so generous, so just, so moral, that, in a contest, he could have put to flight the consciences of nine-tenths of the citizens of Romper.

And so it happened that he was seated in this saloon with the two prominent local merchants and the district attorney.

The Swede continued to drink raw whiskey, meanwhile babbling at the barkeeper and trying to induce him to indulge in potations. "Come on. Have a drink. Come on. What—no? Well, have a little one, then. By gawd, I've whipped a man to-night, and I want to celebrate. I whipped him good, too. Gentlemen," the Swede cried to the men at the table, "have a drink?"

"Ssh!" said the barkeeper.

The group at the table, although furtively attentive, had been pretending to be deep in talk, but now a man lifted his eyes toward the Swede and said, shortly, "Thanks. We don't want any more."

At this reply the Swede ruffled out his chest like a rooster. "Well," he exploded, "it seems I can't get anybody to drink with me in this town. Seems so, don't it? Well!"

"Ssh!" said the barkeeper.

"Say," snarled the Swede, "don't you try to shut me up. I won't have it. I'm a gentleman, and I want people to drink with me. And I want 'em to drink with me now. *Now*—do you understand?" He rapped the bar with his knuckles.

Years of experience had calloused the bartender. He merely grew sulky. "I hear you," he answered.

"Well," cried the Swede, "listen hard then. See those men over there? Well, they're going to drink with me, and don't you forget it. Now you watch."

"Hi!" yelled the barkeeper, "this won't do!"

"Why won't it?" demanded the Swede. He stalked over to the table, and by chance laid his hand upon the shoulder of the gambler. "How about this?" he asked wrathfully. "I asked you to drink with me."

The gambler simply twisted his head and spoke over his shoulder. "My friend, I don't know you."

"Oh, hell!" answered the Swede, "come and have a drink."

"Now, my boy," advised the gambler, kindly, "take your hand off my shoulder and go 'way and mind your own business." He was a little, slim man, and it seemed strange to hear him use this tone of heroic patronage to the burly Swede. The other men at the table said nothing.

"What! You won't drink with me, you little dude? I'll make you, then! I'll make you!" The Swede had grasped the gambler frenziedly at the throat, and was dragging him from his chair. The other men sprang up. The barkeeper dashed around the corner of his bar. There was a great tumult, and then was seen a long blade in the hand of the gambler. It shot forward, and a human body, this citadel of virtue, wisdom, power, was pierced as easily as if it had been a melon. The Swede fell with a cry of supreme astonishment.

The prominent merchants and the district attorney must have at once tumbled out of the place backward. The bartender found himself hanging limply to the arm of a chair and gazing into the eyes of a murderer.

"Henry," said the latter, as he wiped his knife on one of the towels that hung beneath the bar rail, "you tell 'em where to find me. I'll be home, waiting for 'em." Then he vanished. A moment afterward the barkeeper was in the street dinning through the storm for help and, moreover, companionship.

The corpse of the Swede, alone in the saloon, had its eyes fixed upon a dreadful legend that dwelt atop of the cash-machine: "This registers the amount of your purchase."

9

Months later, the cowboy was frying pork over the stove of a little ranch near the Dakota line, when there was a quick thud of hoofs outside, and presently the Easterner entered with the letters and the papers.

"Well," said the Easterner at once, "the chap that killed the Swede has got three years. Wasn't much, was it?"

"He has? Three years?" The cowboy poised his pan of pork, while he ruminated upon the news. "Three years. That ain't much."

"No. It was a light sentence," replied the Easterner as he unbuckled his spurs. "Seems there was a good deal of sympathy for him in Romper."

"If the bartender had been any good," observed the cowboy, thoughtfully, "he would have gone in and cracked that there Dutchman on the head with a bottle in the beginnin' of it and stopped all this here murderin'."

"Yes, a thousand things might have happened," said the Easterner, tartly.

The cowboy returned his pan of pork to the fire, but his philosophy continued. "It's funny, ain't it? If he hadn't said Johnnie was cheatin' he'd be alive this minute. He was an awful fool. Game played for fun, too. Not for money. I believe he was crazy."

"I feel sorry for that gambler," said the Easterner.

"Oh, so do I," said the cowboy. "He don't deserve none of it for killin' who he did."

"The Swede might not have been killed if everything had been square."

"Might not have been killed?" exclaimed the cowboy. "Everythin' square? Why, when he said that Johnnie was cheatin' and acted like such a jackass? And then in the saloon he fairly walked up to git hurt?" With these arguments the cowboy browbeat the Easterner and reduced him to rage.

"You're a fool!" cried the Easterner, viciously. "You're a bigger jackass than the Swede by a million majority. Now let me tell you one thing. Let me tell you something. Listen! Johnnie *was* cheating!"

"'Johnnie,'" said the cowboy, blankly. There was a minute of silence, and then he said, robustly, "Why, no. The game was only for fun."

"Fun or not," said the Easterner, "Johnnie was cheating. I saw him. I know it. I saw him. And I refused to stand up and be a man. I let the Swede fight it out alone. And you—you were simply puffing around the place and wanting to fight. And then old Scully himself! We are all in it! This poor gambler isn't even a noun. He is kind of an adverb. Every sin is the result of a collaboration. We, five of us, have collaborated in the murder of this Swede. Usually there are from a dozen to forty women really involved in every murder, but in this case it seems to be only five men—you, I, Johnnie, old Scully; and that fool of an unfortunate gambler came merely as a culmination, the apex of a human movement, and gets all the punishment."

The cowboy, injured and rebellious, cried out blindly into this fog of mysterious theory: "Well, I didn't do anythin', did I?"

QUESTIONS

1. There is a surprise in the ending of this story. What is it? What is its significance? What does this knowledge do to your view of the stranger who is supposed to have "started" all the trouble, and to your view of his fate? Has the author established a probability that the stranger would meet much the same fate anyway?

2. The hotelkeeper, the father, acts according to more than one abstract or ideal code of conduct. What are these codes? Do human beings, to your knowledge, adopt codes of behavior and follow them as mechanically as the hotelkeeper does? What is the author's probable intention in portraying the hotelkeeper as a keeper of codes? As a man who changes from one code to another?

3. Does this story seem to convey any generally applicable "truth" about human affairs, or does it seem confined to questions of

what will happen next and to the humorous antics of the stranger?

4. Do you know what the social status of gamblers was in the early West? Is there any way to find the answer to such a question?

THE HOMESTEAD ORCHARD

H. L. Davis
(1896–   )

The patch of sagebrush which young Linus Ollivant's charge of six hundred lambed ewes had selected as a bed ground for themselves and their progeny was an old starved-out homestead halfway down the slope of Boulder River Canyon, with a few broken-down sheds, a naked slope of red conglomerate that had once been plowed, and a slow trickle of water, small, but holding its flow steady in spite of the drying wind that had driven most of the country's water supply off into the unknown, and a considerable proportion of the country along with it.

It lacked a good deal of being an ideal location for a range camp, being altogether too far from pasture. The sheep, in the three days they had been there, had put in most of their waking hours plodding out to feed and trudging back to water, but they refused to omit either end of the circuit; and Linus, trying to handle them alone until an extra herder could be raked loose from a boxcar and sent out from town, shoved his old herding horse along behind them in the hard glare of a windy twilight and pulled up on the slope above the bed ground to count them into camp before going down into the shadows after them.

The intense blackness of the shadows in that clear air made the camp so dark that even the white tent looked ghostly against the gloom. There was one clear patch of light where the sky reflected in the pond of water, and the mass of dark-wooled old ewes and white-fleeced and inquisitive lambs trailed down into it and stood patterned against it clear and distinct as they drank and crossed to their bed ground for the night.

When they had all crossed, Linus strained his eyes back over the naked rock ridges of the canyon, hoping, because he was too inexperienced at sheepherding to know that it contained no pleasant surprises, that some tail-end bunch of late feeders might still come moseying along in time to bring his count up somewhere near where it belonged.

As might have been expected, he saw nothing except the ridges, ranked one behind another, as frail-looking as if they had been shadows in the pale red sky, darkening to gray at the edges where they touched it. The country's lifelessness was a new thing to Linus. His family had homesteaded on the divide back of that river canyon in his childhood, and one of his few pleasant recollections from that time was of standing on high ground at dark and counting the lights of other homesteads where families had settled to grow up with the country. Now there were no signs of life visible anywhere except in the range camp, where the sheep fidgeted themselves into position for the night and where Linus' father, suffering from a case of dust blindness from the alkali flats back in the desert, fumbled matches into a pile of greasewood in an effort to get a fire started for supper.

His fire building didn't make much headway. His eyes were so inflamed that they were not only useless but so agonizingly sensitive that they had to be kept heavily bandaged against the least light or wind or irritation. Most of his matches blew out while he fumbled around for fuel to touch them to, and Linus, seeing that he was about to run a fit of temper over his own helplessness, gave up hopes of the stray sheep and hurried down to help him out. The fire started easily enough, with a little coddling, and old Ollivant settled gloomily back against the tent pole, hauled his bandage down into place as if he were conferring a favor on society by tolerating the thing, and supplied what entertainment he could by offering conversational leads as Linus got their cooking under way.

"It ain't right for you to have all this work put on you," he said. "It looks like them people in town could have raked up some hobo herder to ship out here, if they had any consideration for a man. How did the sheep handle today? It didn't sound to me like there was as many come in as usual. Did you get a count on 'em?"

Linus raked the fire, clattered buckets and said he had counted them in carefully. He didn't mention what his count had come to. He thought of owning up to it, and then reflected that it would be better to hold back until daylight, when he could make sure that the strays were actually lost and not merely yarded up in the brush, waiting to be sent for.

"They pulled in too tired to make much noise, I expect," he said. "They had a long lug in from pasture tonight. Three or four miles, anyhow."

Side-stepping one disturbing circumstance, he ran squarely into another. His father picked on his estimate of the distance to pasture as if it were a dynamiting he had confessed to.

"We can't carry these old pelters where they've got to trail four miles to pasture," he said. "They'll wear themselves to death on it. If I could trust you to stay out of trouble with people, I'd be about in the notion to hold the whole bunch here in camp for a day or two, till you could scout up some better place to bed 'em. You'd probably land up in some fight, though. Blame it, what does a man have to depend on sheep for, anyhow?"

That was something of a dig; it was Linus' fault that he had been reduced to depending on sheep. Ordinarily, he wouldn't have made a point of that, but enforced inaction made him short of patience. Linus knew enough to humor him.

"It wouldn't do any good to scout around here," he said. "There ain't any other place around here where we could camp sheep at all. You'd see that if you could see what this country looked like."

"If I ever get these old buzzard baits sheared and turned off to ship, I'll kill the next man that says 'sheep' to me," old

Ollivant said. "There ain't a jury in the land that would cinch me for it, the provocation I've had." He stopped and lifted one hand for silence for a minute. "I heard horses," he said. "If them people in town have sent out a herder, I'll never complain about my luck again."

It was a handsome offer, and Linus hated to sound as discouraging about it as he felt obliged to.

"It can't be anybody to see us," he said. "We've moved camp five times since you sent for a herder, and the people in town wouldn't know where to send one. You heard some bunch of wild cayuses. Maybe it's Indians out to dig camass."

"It was a shod horse I heard," old Ollivant said.

They both listened, saying nothing and even taking care not to rattle the dishes as they ate supper. Neither of them heard a sound, and Linus fell to thinking over their homesteading days up on the ridge, and of the long string of accidents that had led him back to it against his will. His father had come to that country to homestead a likely quarter-section of sagebrush and find out whether high-altitude soil and climate couldn't be adapted to raising domestic fruits, and he had been obliged to give that up, the orcharding and the homesteading together, through a run of misfortune for which Linus was a good deal to blame.

Afterward he worked around a feed yard in one of the river towns long enough to figure that it led nowhere, and finally he allowed himself to be tempted into taking a half interest in a flock of rickety old ewes, on a chance that, given a decent year and careful handling, they might bring in a crop of lambs worth three times his original investment in them, with the wool figuring at enough extra to cover incidental expenses, taxes, and possibly even day wages for his work.

It had been a tempting project, with little risk showing on its exterior, to begin with. But there had been enough risk about it to make it a gamble, and, like most gambles

undertaken by people who couldn't afford to lose, things had gone wrong with it almost from the outset.

The roster of bad luck began with a feed shortage and a rise in hay prices, proceeded onward into an outlandishly protracted dry spell and a shortening of the country's water supply, and held on into a failure of all the spring pastures at the exact time when the entire country had counted on them as a last hope to keep going on. A vast invasion of cast-off scrub horses used up what little coarse grass the land had managed to hold on to, and old Ollivant's dust blindness had topped off the whole structure of calamities and left, as far as Linus could see, scarcely any possibility of their pulling through to shearing time with any sheep at all.

He had done his best to keep going single-handed, and though he had been forced to several emergency measures that his father would not have approved of, he had kept the herd up better than most professional herders would have bothered to do.

He hadn't wanted to pasture back so near the scene of his father's abandoned experiments with dry-country orcharding. That was one of the emergency measures he had not been able to avoid. The sheep had wandered down from the alkali desert with no notion in their heads except to move where they could find something to eat, and the line of grass had led them, almost as if it had been set out for the purpose, straight down into Boulder River Canyon and through it to the water hole where they were bedded. It wasn't a good place for them, but it was the only water in the neighborhood where sheep could be held without running into opposition from the resident landowners.

One of the few useful things Linus had got out of his homesteading years on the ridge over Boulder River was a knowledge of the country and its limitations and prejudices. He knew the region well, and he knew there were no open camping places in it that had even as many advantages as the one where they were. One of the points about it was that there were thirty head of his father's sheep running loose somewhere around it, and he couldn't leave until he had taken some kind of a stab at finding them. He roused out of his train of reflections and remarked that it was a cold wind to be sitting out in with a case of inflammation of the eyes. Old Ollivant said morosely that he wasn't responsible for the temperature of the wind.

"It's a blamed funny thing we don't hear any coyotes," he remarked. "This is the first night since we've been out here that there ain't been a dozen of 'em on the yip all around us. They couldn't all have left the country in a day."

"You can't tell about coyotes around these blamed rock piles," Linus said vaguely. The coyotes had not left the country, and he knew the reason they weren't making themselves heard from as they usually did. With thirty head of sheep wandering at large, they had something better to while away their time on than hunkering on a cold rock to howl.

He tried to decide whether to own up about the strays, and heard metal grate on rock somewhere up on the ridge. He held up his hand for silence, heard it again, and let the strays slip out of his thoughts with a feeling of relief at not having to make up his mind about them.

"Somebody with horses," he said. "You'd better fetch out the gun. It might be some of these neighborhood busybodies come to drag us out of here in a sack."

"Guns can make more trouble for some people than draggin' in a sack," old Ollivant said, without moving. "I told you I heard shod horses fifteen minutes ago. It's somebody from town come out to see what's happened to us, I expect."

The wind shifted, and for a long time they heard nothing more at all. Then the hoofs clattered on the ridge above them, and they could tell that it was several horses in charge of one man who was humming a loud mixture of three or four different tunes as an indication that he was not trying to sneak up on anybody. Linus stirred the fire into a blaze, and he stopped his humming, shaded his eyes against the glare, and rode down into the full light, so they could look him over before he offered to dismount.

"They told me in town that some people named Ollivant wanted a herder," he said. He was a large-built man with a saddle a couple of sizes too snug for him, and he had three pack ponies strung, head and tail, behind him. He kept yanking their lead rope to keep them from trying to lie down.

"My name is Dee Radford. I'm a herder, and I ain't ever worked this country before, so I come out to see what your layout looked like. They had this order of groceries made up for you, so I brung it along. This place ain't fit to camp sheep on. I'll bet you've lost a couple of dozen head in the last two days, if you'll count."

Linus didn't consider it necessary to mention what the correct statistics on his shortage were. "How did the people in town know where to send you?" he asked.

"They didn't. I had to work out your trail from the scenery," Dee Radford said.

He dismounted so heavily that he almost pulled the weary animal over on top of himself, and proceeded to unsaddle and unpack in the dark, working as confidently as if nobody had ever told him what a lantern was for.

"When you've been in this business as long as I have, you don't need to know where people are to find 'em," he explained, unraveling a complicated four-way hitch from a pack. "A man that can't find what he wants without help ain't entitled to call himself a herder. This ain't any place to camp a band of sheep like these of yours. They walk off their feed gittin' to water, and they dry out thirsty trailin' back to feed, and they're too old to stand it. I picked out a place up on the ridge where they'll handle better. There's an old homestead with a patch of run-down orchard around it, and there's water enough to make out on if we're careful. You can git your camp struck and packed, and we'll move up there the first thing in the morning."

To Linus, it seemed a little high-handed for even a skilled herder to drop into the middle of a strange camp and start issuing orders as if it belonged to him.

Old Ollivant was less touchy and more interested. At mention of a ridge homestead surrounded by an old orchard, he sat up and said he had been agitating to have their camp moved, and that Linus had assured him the thing was impossible.

"It is," Linus said. "That ridge country ain't open land. It belongs to people that use it to feed cattle on. If we move in with sheep, they'll throw us out, and maybe run the sheep to death for good measure. I know the people around here. I know how they act with pasture thieves, and I don't blame 'em for it."

"We won't be pasture thieves, because there ain't any pasture on that ridge to thieve," Dee Radford said. "There's been cattle over every foot of it, and they've cleaned the grass right down to the roots. The only thing about it is that there's a big scatter of grass seed blowed around into horse tracks and under rocks where the cattle couldn't reach it. Sheep can, and there ought to be enough of it to run us for three weeks or more anyhow. We won't be trespassers, because the place don't belong to anybody. I asked some men in the road about that. I told 'em I was a mind to buy it, and they said it hadn't ever been proved up on. We'll move up there in the morning, if it's all right with both of you."

It was not all right with Linus and he said nothing, but his father said there was no use palavering around about a move so plainly commendable and necessary.

"We'll move any time you say, and don't you pay any attention to anything this boy says," he said. "He's always balky at the wrong times, and there ain't much you can do with him. He's done well to handle the sheep by himself without any losses, but he's got to learn to listen to other people sometimes, and he can't start any younger."

Linus still remained silent, so he fumbled his way inside the camp tent and began rattling small articles into his war bag to save having to pack them in the morning. They heard his boots thump and the blankets rustle as he spread down in them, and then the noises subsided as he went to sleep.

Dee Radford remarked that they had better be thinking about rest themselves, if they were to make it up to the ridge homestead in a day's trailing. Linus replied that he didn't plan to make it to any ridge homestead, and that he would rest when he felt like it. He tried to sound chilling, but Dee Radford merely sat back and studied him thoughtfully.

"I've seen young squirts act like this when I've pulled into some camp to help through a bad season," he said. "You're a different cut from that, if looks is anything. You don't look like a squirt, and you ought to know that you'll lose all your sheep if you try to handle 'em down here. You don't think I'd be in this business if I didn't know something about it, do you?"

"You know your business, I guess," Linus conceded, a trifle sullenly. "What you don't know about is this country. You've got it fixed to land us all in trouble with the people in it. That old ridge orchard you've picked for us to move to ain't open land. If any men told you it was, they lied. It used to be our homestead. My old man planted that orchard, and I took care of it, and I could draw you a picture right now of every tree in it. We'd be there yet, but I got into a rumpus, so the old man had to sell out his homestead rights and leave to get away from lawsuits. I shot a man, if you want to know what it was. Maybe that homestead ain't been proved up on, but it ain't ours, because we sold the rights to it. If we take sheep onto it we'll have trouble, and people around here will swear I started it to show off. The old man don't know about that, because he don't know what part of the country we've drifted back to. He'll probably claim I sneaked back here to hunt up some more cussedness, if he ever finds it out."

Dee Radford stirred the fire and said that cleared up two or three points that he hadn't understood at first. He added that old Ollivant's dust blindness had looked serious, and that they might manage to get the sheep sheared and off their hands and get clear away from the Boulder River country before he cured up enough to realize that they had been there.

"It would be playin' underhanded with him, but that ain't any business of mine," he said. "Sheep is all I claim to know anything about, and there ain't but one thing to do with this bunch of yours. We can keep 'em alive on that ridge homestead, and we'll try to handle 'em so people won't find out we're there. If they have to stay here they'll die, and if you'd sooner they done that, say so and I'll leave you to handle 'em. You'll go broke, but that ain't any of my put-in. How many head have you lost since you've been here that you ain't told your old man about?"

That was a sharp surmise, and Linus took no risks in replying to it. He nodded toward the tent, and stated in clear tones that he had lost no sheep at all. Then he opened and closed the fingers of his hands three times, traced the course of one setting sun down the sky, and waited to see if Dee Radford had ever stopped long enough in one place to know what Indian sign talk was.

Dee indicated his comprehension with a nod, and remarked cautiously that he would have expected the shrinkage to have run higher and started sooner. If they had dropped out only that afternoon, they might still be alive. Having turned in that reflection, he got up, got his horse out of the corral, and reached down his saddle.

"I'm goin' to show you that a man don't need to know a country to handle sheep in it," he said. "You show me which direction you pastured today, and I'll find them strays for you. You git packed and line the sheep for the ridge the first thing in the morning, and quit this shiverin' around for fear of trouble. People ain't fools enough to fight us over a place as worthless as that homestead. If they do, I'll tend to 'em, and if we damage the premises, I'll stand good for it. We won't hurt your old man's orchard, if that's what you're uneasy about."

"I don't care what you do to the orchard,"

Linus said. "I put in four years' hard work on it, and all I ever got for it was a pile of trouble, and all I want is to make sure we won't get into any more. Trouble ain't easy to dodge out on in this country."

"Trouble ain't easy to dodge out on in any country that you spend too much of your time in. You ought to learn your trade and travel around with it, like I do, and then you wouldn't have to bother about what people thought of you."

Linus and his father packed camp an hour or so before sunup, Linus getting everybody's personal belongings together into one of the packs, and reflecting that it did look as if Dee Radford's system of short-staking around had paid better than any protracted residence in one place.

Dee's outfit included such show pieces as a leather-faced bed roll, double-lined goatskin chaps, and a hand-carved rifle scabbard, all of which were expensive and none of which either Linus or his father possessed at all. His rifle was a new flat-shooting rig with box magazine, oiled stock, peep sight with micrometer scale, buckhorn tips, and all the trimmings. Linus' father had a common little saddle carbine with iron sights and a squared-off butt, and Linus not only had no gun at all but wasn't even supposed to handle one except under his father's personal supervision.

Except that it showed what he had missed by staying too long in the shadow of his youthful reputation, the contrast in the rifles didn't bother Linus much. The old piece of momentary recklessness that had ended his residence on the ridge homestead had also destroyed most of his interest in guns, and the sight of one was generally enough to bring the whole unlucky episode back to him clearly and painfully.

Its beginning cause had been the old homestead orchard. He had put in an entire spring on it, pruning, cultivating, whitewashing and spraying for insects, and, as he was applying a few final touches against twig borers, a contingent of old Lucas Waymark's cowboys pulled in and camped a herd of starved-out old cows right against a weak place in the fence where they were certain to break through the minute they were left to themselves.

Linus was alone on the place at the time and, not feeling disposed to let a pack of scrub cows grab what he had barely finished rescuing from all the other pests in the country, he forted up behind some baled hay with the family musket and ordered the Waymark minions to begone.

The minions hadn't kept up with their reading sufficiently to realize that they were supposed to slink away in baffled rage, so they offered to spank him if he didn't take the gun straight indoors and put it back where it belonged. One of them straddled the orchard fence to illustrate how they would go at it, and Linus tightened down and cut loose, intending to hit the post under his hand as a final warning. The fore sight of the old gun had got knocked out of line and, instead of jarring the post, he spread the Waymark man across the top wire of the fence with a smashed collarbone.

There was never any general agreement in the country over which of the parties to the incident had been most to blame for it. The homesteaders blamed old Waymark for running his cattle around the neighborhood as if he owned it. The Waymark men blamed their stricken co-worker for trying to walk down a gun in the hands of a frightened youngster. Linus blamed the gun for not shooting straight, Linus' father blamed Linus for pointing it at a man he didn't intend to shoot, and several people blamed Linus' father for keeping a firearm on the premises without making sure the sights were lined up properly.

All the bestowals of blame were probably partly justified, but none of them could clear Linus of the responsibility for injuring a fellow man with a deadly weapon, and old Waymark played that fact for all there was in it. He worked up claims for doctors' bills, wages for the wounded man's lost time, physical suffering and mental anguish, and complaints against Linus for everything from juvenile delinquency to attempted manslaughter. In the end, Linus' father gave up, sold him the homestead relinquishment, and moved away.

The change was no particular misfortune, but Linus' mismanagement in bringing it on was something he never liked to be reminded of. The old gun that had done the shooting was so painful a memento that he stuck it back of a rafter in the homestead cabin, out of sight, and neither he nor Linus thought enough of it to get it down when they moved. They never mentioned the shooting afterward, and there was always a little strained note in their conversation with each other, because they so painstakingly avoided any subject that seemed likely to lead into it.

They both steered around handling the two herding rifles while they were packing up. After Linus had got them wrapped in some bedding and stowed quietly on one of the packs, his father went out and felt carefully over the horses to make sure where they were. It wasn't that he suspected Linus of having stolen them; he merely wanted to see that they hadn't been overlooked, and he preferred to hunt them out rather than open a subject which neither of them took anything but distrust and uneasiness in thinking back over.

Trailing the sheep was slow, but not troublesome. The cold kept them well bunched, and since there was not enough grass to tempt them to loiter, they moved along without needing any encouragement beyond a little rock throwing to keep them pointed right.

Old Ollivant dragged along behind with the pack horses, holding his eye bandage down against the wind with one hand and his reins, trail rope and saddle horn with the other.

Linus pulled into the homestead about an hour past sundown, and found Dee Radford waiting. Dee sat beside a fresh-banked pond, watching it fill up from the spring. He had turned the little quarter-inch trickle of water away from the sink back of the orchard where it disappeared into the ground, and he was storing it for the sheep to drink.

"We may have to ration it out, the way it's runnin'," he said. "We'll know about that after they've watered a couple of times. You notice I collected your strays."

There was probably not another man in the country who could have found those strays in that river canyon in the dark. Linus paid his respectful acknowledgments to the feat, and looked doubtful about the arrangements for conserving the water. The thing that came into his mind, in spite of him, was that the trees must have come to depend on the flow of water into the ground. They looked so wild and worthless, all broken and tangled and killed down by cattle and heavy snows and freezing, that he kept his thoughts to himself, for fear of sounding sentimental. He did remark that the trees belonged to somebody, and Dee took him up hard on that.

"You've got a patch of fruit trees that ain't worth anything, and a band of sheep that'll bring your old man ten thousand dollars if they stay alive," he said. "You've got an old orchard that nobody thinks enough of to prove up on, and you've got sheep that your old man has run himself alkali-blind over, besides the work you've put in on 'em yourself. I don't see how you can even argue about turnin' this water. I'd be ashamed to be that big a fool about any place I'd ever lived."

"I ain't any fool about this place," Linus said. "You may have to answer a claim for damages to these trees before you're through here, that's all. Don't think you'll be able to argue yourself out of it, either. There's harder outfits around here than you might think."

Old Ollivant drew up with the pack horses, and Dee searched his box-magazine rifle out from under the bedding and hung it ceremoniously on a fence post.

"If anybody shows up to be fought, he's mine," he said. "I don't notice any signs of heavy travel around here, so it ain't likely that anybody will. You don't need to look that far ahead for anything to worry about, anyhow. When you've stood a week or two of feedin' sheep on grass seed in these rocks, you'll wish you had a good quiet fight to rest up on. We'll make a herd camp here where we can take turns standin' guard over the

bed ground, and we'll put the tent off yonder in the orchard where your father can be out of the wind."

Old Ollivant didn't think much of that arrangement, insisting, with a stubbornness of conviction that turned out to be almost clairvoyant, that Linus would land in some trouble if he stood guard over the bed ground without somebody to stand guard over him. He gave in only when Dee, having pitched the tent in the cove, helped him down from his horse and led him into it, with instructions to stay there until his eyes felt better.

The ridge was not so abundantly supplied with either grass seed or water as it had looked to begin with. It had barely enough of both to keep the old ewes from bawling loud enough to be heard clear down to the road, and even that frugal measure of sustenance didn't last well.

Trouble started one evening when Linus brought the herd in by himself; Dee having gone down to the road to put up a flag for the shearing crew. Instead of bedding down quietly, the sheep milled, changed ground and collected in little bunches, blatting tunelessly and persistently. Linus was too tired to hear them, and Dee, getting back late, didn't discover till daylight that they had run short of water. Some animal—a skunk or a sage rat, by the signs—had burrowed into the ditch between the spring and the catch pond, and the entire night's supply had seeped out into the ground behind the orchard.

He patched up the break, but that was no immediate help. The ditch and pond basin had dried out so deep that getting them primed and getting the pond filled afterward took the entire day. The sheep waited and continued their blatting, and, to get out of listening to them, Linus went out and cut bundles of willow and wild-cherry sprouts as something for them to practice eating on, even though it couldn't be considered food.

Coming back through the high sagebrush behind the camp with his harvest of shrubbery, he heard men talking and Dee's voice rising in an argument which, to judge by the sound of horses moving restlessly, didn't seem to be commanding much attention. He dropped his brush and crept up behind the old homestead cabin for a look, knowing beforehand who the visitors were and what they had come for.

Old Waymark's bad-news commitee hadn't changed its membership in the years that Linus had been away. There was old Waymark himself, undersized and savage-looking. Behind him was his foreman, a sandy-haired man with red eyes who kept fiddling with his rope; back of him were a couple of ordinary herders, and off to one side was old Slickear Cowan, who would have classed as an ordinary herder, except that he was the man whom Linus had rimmed with the shot heard round as much of the world as old Waymark could command a hearing from.

The injury hadn't damaged Slickear Cowan's vitality much. He carried a long jute woolsack on his saddle fork, and he kept working his horse sideways, getting, as if accidentally, between Dee and the post where he had hung his rifle. Linus' father was asleep in the tent, out of range of the conference, and Dee was so absorbed in handling the case for the defense that he didn't notice the maneuver being organized against his peace and dignity.

He proved that he was not stealing pasture, pointed out that, instead of damaging the homestead, he had kept it from falling apart, and touched on various phases of the land-title question with so much authority that old Waymark acted apologetic about being there at all. His sandy-haired foreman shook out a turn of his rope and looked thoughtful, Slickear Cowan gathered his reins and sat forward in his saddle, and old Waymark studied the tent in the orchard as if half wondering whether there was anybody in it who ought to be invited to see the fun.

It was clear enough what they were up to. Dee Radford was about to be taken through the rural ceremony known as a sheepherder's sleigh ride. Slickear Cowan would make a run and snatch his rifle; when he turned to see what was up, the foreman would hang a rope on him and dump him. The woolsack

would be yanked over him and tied shut, and he would be dragged behind a horse over the rugged countryside, with special attention to those portions of it that would bounce him highest.

That was the standard treatment for men who ran sheep on somebody else's land, and there was only one way to head it off. Linus tiptoed inside the old homestead cabin, noticing, with a little half-homesick feeling, that a worn-out pair of his own shoes were still on the kitchen floor where he had dropped them on leaving, and how woebegone they looked with the strings trailing loose and the dust heavy on them.

He had not been tall enough to reach the rafters the day his father hid the old rifle back of them. Now he put his hand up to it without even having to stretch. The rifle was dusty and the action was rusted shut, so it wouldn't work, but that didn't disturb him. He didn't intend to shoot, and it added something to his confidence to know that he couldn't, even if he felt tempted to. He tiptoed to the back door, kicked it open and stood in it with the rifle trained, in involuntary deference to the past, on the fork of Slickear Cowan's collarbone.

"Pull up that horse and drop them reins," he ordered. "Put your hands under your belt and take your feet out of the stirrups. Now move out of here, the whole bunch of you."

If he had appeared draped in a sheet and clanking a chain, he couldn't have quenched the delegation's high spirits more completely. Everybody stared, and nobody moved. Linus motioned Dee Radford toward the rifle on the post, and Dee roused himself, got it and backed off, still staring.

"Where in creation did you find that gun?" he asked. "You ain't robbed any Indian graves, have you?"

"It didn't come out of any Indian grave," Linus said. His voice, with the empty house backing it up, sounded so spooky that he hardly recognized it himself. "We left this gun here when we moved away, and I remembered where it was." He turned apologetically to old Waymark. "I don't want to shoot any of your men. All I want is for you to let us alone. We'll pay for any damage we've done here."

Old Waymark edged his horse sideways, picking up his spirits a little.

"You're that young Ollivant hoodlum that like to killed one of my men once before," he said, as if he expected Linus to deny it. "You ought to have gone to jail then, and I'll see that you do go now. I bought this place from your father, and I want these men to witness that you've ordered me off of it at the point of a gun. You'll hear from it, you and your father both."

He picked up his reins, and Dee asked him to hold on a minute.

"There's a point or two about this trespass business," he said. "This boy has told me that his father moved out of here before he got this homestead proved up on. What you bought was his relinquishment, wasn't it?"

Old Waymark conceded that it was, and said that had nothing to do with the main issue. "One of my men went down and filed on it. You'll find that out plenty soon, if you've got any doubts about it."

"I've got a few," Dee said. "There's a residence requirement about homesteads, and your man ain't ever lived here. This boy's father left that gun in the house when he moved out, and it ain't been touched till now."

Old Waymark's whiskers pointed slightly astern again. It was not unusual for people in remote districts to be a little neglectful about residence on their homesteads. The fact that his man had followed the general custom was the main reason he had come there. There was nothing on the homestead worth squabbling over, and he wouldn't have cared how many sheep camped on it if his title had held a little closer to legal standards, but a counterentry on the place was worth going to some trouble to head off. He said an old gun being overlooked in some hiding place meant nothing, and picked up his reins again.

His men were all staring down into the orchard. The tent had come open, and Linus' father came slowly up from it, holding his bandage clear of one tortured eye, so he could see his way between the tangle of neglected old trees that he had set out to be a light and a beacon to horticultural expansion in the sagebrush. He drew up and fixed Linus with a glare that was all the more impressive because it was so obviously agonizing to him.

"This is the kind of high-handed thuggery you've sneaked in on me, is it?" he demanded. "You tore loose with a gun once, and got yourself in trouble till I had to sell out and leave here to get you clear of it. A man would think that would have been enough to last you, but here you're back for more. You wait till I get my eyesight crippled, so I can't see what you're up to, and then you gallop straight back to the same place to do the same trick all over again. You promised me never to touch a gun unless I was around to watch you, and you know it. You know we ain't got any right to be here too. You know this old skunk bought this place off of me, and you've got no right to order him to leave it. Put that gun down."

Linus leaned the gun against the wall outside the door. The Waymark men watched thoughtfully as he stood back from it, and Slickear Cowan lifted his hands clear of his belt. Dee Radford advised him to avoid rashness, jiggled the safety catch on his rifle to indicate that he was serious and told Linus' father to cover his eyes from the light and show a little sense.

"You didn't sell anything to this outfit but your homestead rights," he said. "Nobody has ever used 'em, and we can prove it. This homestead is open to anybody that wants to live on it the legal time. This boy of yours has got a right to occupy it and he's got a right to use a gun on anybody that tries to run him off of it. He may intend to file a contest on it himself, how do you know?"

"It was on his account that I sold it to start with," old Ollivant said. He did cover his eyes from the light. "How would it look if he come back and took it away from the man I sold it to? It wouldn't be honest."

"You didn't sell his rights to it, because he was too young to have any," Dee said. "He's old enough now to file on any open land he wants to, and it ain't anybody else's business. It ain't even yours."

Old Waymark started to say something about principles, and Linus put in ahead of him, seeing that the argument was reaching a little too far into metaphysics to be practical.

"I don't want to file on any homestead and I wouldn't file on this one if I did," he said. "I've put in too much time in one neighborhood already, and I don't aim to do any more of it."

That was a sentiment that Dee Radford had done a good deal of arguing in favor of, and yet he seemed disappointed.

"I'll be blamed if I'll see this place go back to this outfit, after the way they've acted," he said. "I'll file on it myself, if I have to. I want you men to take notice that there's a contest to be entered on this claim and you can keep off of it till the law settles it. Now move, before I shoot up a few of your horses for you." He watched them until they were a little distance away, and then turned to Linus. "Pick up that old pacifier of yours and touch it off somewhere over their heads. I'd like to hear what it sounds like, and I'd like to see how they take it."

"It won't touch off," Linus said, feeling a little foolish over having to admit it. "The breech is rusted shut. I didn't bring it out to shoot with. Them men was about to drag you in a sack, and all I wanted was to head 'em off till you could get clear of 'em. It come out all right."

Linus' father pulled his bandage clear of one eye, looked the old gun over and tried unsuccessfully to budge the hammer. He put it down again and looked at Linus. The light and wind must have been agony to him, and yet he didn't appear conscious of any particular pain.

"It did come out all right," he said. "Not but what it took a blamed long time to it. I've distrusted you all these years, and the Lord knows how much longer I'd have kept on at it if you'd got hold of a gun that would

shoot. You've turned out dependable in spite of me, it looks like. If you've got a mind to take this homestead for yourself, I've got no right to forbid you. It used to be a sightly place, when it was kept in shape."

"I don't want it," Linus said. "There never was anything to it except that patch of orchard, and the trees is all killed out. I whittled into some of 'em, and they're as dry as a wagon spoke."

"Not any more," his father said. "That was what I started up here to tell you, and then I heard them men. There's been a funny kind of a noise outside that tent ever since the sheep blat let up. It got so loud I couldn't rest, so I went out to see what it was. It was bees. Them old fruit trees has all come into bloom. You didn't waste all the work you put into 'em, after all."

"I wouldn't call it wasted, even if them trees all dried up and fell down," Dee Radford said. "If you hadn't recognized them men and remembered about that old rifle, we'd have lost them sheep sure. It would have been the first herd of sheep I ever lost in my life, and I wouldn't want that on my record."

The breaking up of that drought was not especially beautiful in itself, but it ended the long monotony of dust and dry wind and cold sun, and its contrasting mildness and silence made it seem one of the most beautiful things imaginable. A night rain laid the dust, the sky clouded over, the air was so still that the sheep shearers didn't even bother to anchor their burlap corral panels down, and the sheep, having come through their pasturing season, turned from a care and a burden into a salable asset that strange workmen labored over and strange buyers bid for and strange feed yards were almost embarrassingly gratified to advance wagonloads of hay on.

Dee Radford knelt outside the old herding tent, packing up to leave the sheep he had half killed himself to save from the buzzards. That was an old ceremony for him, and he took it tranquilly. Linus couldn't feel quite so lighthearted about it. He detested sheep, but there seemed something unnatural about working so hard over something that had to be given up afterward, with nothing left to show where his work had gone. There were wages, but they were the same for bad work as for good.

He walked down into the orchard, thinking about that, and saw, in the scrubby tangle of old trees in bloom, something he had worked hard on that had not disappeared afterward, but had lived and developed courage to bring forth its clumps of perfect flowers, pink apricot and apple, green-white plum and white pear and cherry, through all the tangle of dead and broken and mutilated limbs that showed how hard it had been to live at all. That much of his work had not been wasted, since it had helped to bring into life a courage and patience and doggedness in putting forth such delicate beauty against all the hostility of nature and against even the imminence of death.

Linus' father was sitting under one of the trees with his bandage lifted from one eye, and Linus sat down beside him. "I've decided to try this old homestead for a while," he said. "It's—"

He didn't bother to finish.

His father nodded. "I know how you feel," he said. "I know how it feels to have something you've raised turn out better than you expected."

QUESTIONS

1. In what ways is this a success story? What kinds of success are involved?
2. It is assumed by some readers that an author can write a good story without "knowing" anything. What kinds of knowledge did the author have to have in order to write this story? Compare this story with "The Country Doctor," by Franz Kafka, in respect to the kinds of knowledge needed by the author.
3. The characters in this story are living out their lives in a remote environment; they follow a trade which is little known to the outside world. Do these facts lessen the appeal of the story in any way for you? What percentage of the people in the United States belong in about the same economic class as the characters in this story? Do you feel that a higher social and economic position is almost necessary for the characters if a story is to have maximum force?

THE BOARDING HOUSE

James Joyce
(1882–1941)

Mrs. Mooney was a butcher's daughter. She was a woman who was quite able to keep things to herself: a determined woman. She had married her father's foreman and opened a butcher's shop near Spring Gardens. But as soon as his father-in-law was dead Mr. Mooney began to go to the devil. He drank, plundered the till, ran head-long into debt. It was no use making him take the pledge: he was sure to break out again a few days after. By fighting his wife in the presence of customers and by buying bad meat he ruined his business. One night he went for his wife with the cleaver and she had to sleep in a neighbour's house.

After that they lived apart. She went to the priest and got a separation from him with care of the children. She would give him neither money nor food nor house-room; and so he was obliged to enlist himself as a sheriff's man. He was a shabby stooped little drunkard with a white face and a white moustache and white eyebrows, pencilled above his little eyes, which were pink-veined and raw; and all day long he sat in the bailiff's room, waiting to be put on a job. Mrs. Mooney, who had taken what remained of her money out of the butcher business and set up a boarding house in Hardwicke Street, was a big imposing woman. Her house had a floating population made up of tourists from Liverpool and the Isle of Man and, occasionally, *artistes* from the music halls. Its resident population was made up of clerks from the city. She governed the house cunningly and firmly, knew when to give credit, when to be stern and when to let things pass.

All the resident young men spoke of her as *The Madam.*

Mrs. Mooney's young men paid fifteen shillings a week for board and lodgings (beer or stout at dinner excluded). They shared in common tastes and occupations and for this reason they were very chummy with one another. They discussed with one another the chances of favourites and outsiders. Jack Mooney, the Madam's son, who was clerk to a commission agent in Fleet Street, had the reputation of being a hard case. He was fond of using soldiers' obscenities: usually he came home in the small hours. When he met his friends he had always a good one to tell them and he was always sure to be on to a good thing—that is to say, a likely horse or a likely *artiste.* He was also handy with the mits and sang comic songs. On Sunday nights there would often be a reunion in Mrs. Mooney's front drawing-room. The music-hall *artistes* would oblige; and Sheridan played waltzes and polkas and vamped accompaniments. Polly Mooney, the Madam's daughter, would also sing. She sang:

> *"I'm a . . . naughty girl.*
> *You needn't sham:*
> *You know I am."*

Polly was a slim girl of nineteen; she had light soft hair and a small full mouth. Her eyes, which were grey with a shade of green through them, had a habit of glancing upwards when she spoke with anyone, which made her look like a little perverse madonna. Mrs. Mooney had first sent her daughter to be a typist in a corn-factor's office but, as a disreputable sheriff's man used to come every other day to the office, asking to be allowed to say a word to his daughter, she had taken her daughter home again and set her to do housework. As Polly was very lively the intention was to give her the run of the young men. Besides, young men like to feel that there is a young woman not very far away. Polly, of course, flirted with the young men but Mrs. Mooney, who was a shrewd judge, knew that the young men were only passing the time away: none of them meant business. Things

went on so for a long time and Mrs. Mooney began to think of sending Polly back to type-writing when she noticed that something was going on between Polly and one of the young men. She watched the pair and kept her own counsel.

Polly knew that she was being watched, but still her mother's persistent silence could not be misunderstood. There had been no open complicity between mother and daughter, no open understanding but, though people in the house began to talk of the affair, still Mrs. Mooney did not intervene. Polly began to grow a little strange in her manner and the young man was evidently perturbed. At last, when she judged it to be the right moment, Mrs. Mooney intervened. She dealt with moral problems as a cleaver deals with meat: and in this case she had made up her mind.

It was a bright Sunday morning of early summer, promising heat, but with a fresh breeze blowing. All the windows of the boarding house were open and the lace curtains ballooned gently towards the street beneath the raised sashes. The belfry of George's Church sent out constant peals and worshippers, singly or in groups, traversed the little circus before the church, revealing their purpose by their self-contained demeanour no less than by the little volumes in their gloved hands. Breakfast was over in the boarding house and the table of the breakfast-room was covered with plates on which lay yellow streaks of eggs with morsels of bacon-fat and bacon-rind. Mrs. Mooney sat in the straw arm-chair and watched the servant Mary remove the breakfast things. She made Mary collect the crusts and pieces of broken bread to help to make Tuesday's bread-pudding. When the table was cleared, the broken bread collected, the sugar and butter safe under lock and key, she began to re-construct the interview which she had had the night before with Polly. Things were as she had suspected: she had been frank in her questions and Polly had been frank in her answers. Both had been somewhat awkward, of course. She had been made awkward by her not wishing to receive the news in too cavalier a fashion or to seem to have connived and Polly had been made awkward not merely because allusions of that kind always made her awkward but also because she did not wish it to be thought that in her wise innocence she had divined the intention behind her mother's tolerance.

Mrs. Mooney glanced instinctively at the little gilt clock on the mantelpiece as soon as she had become aware through her revery that the bells of George's Church had stopped ringing. It was seventeen minutes past eleven: she would have lots of time to have the matter out with Mr. Doran and then catch short twelve at Marlborough Street. She was sure she would win. To begin with she had all the weight of social opinion on her side: she was an outraged mother. She had allowed him to live beneath her roof, assuming that he was a man of honour, and he had simply abused her hospitality. He was thirty-four or thirty-five years of age, so that youth could not be pleaded as his excuse; nor could ignorance be his excuse since he was a man who had seen something of the world. He had simply taken advantage of Polly's youth and inexperience: that was evident. The question was: What reparation would he make?

There must be reparation made in such case. It is all very well for the man: he can go his ways as if nothing had happened, having had his moment of pleasure, but the girl has to bear the brunt. Some mothers would be content to patch up such an affair for a sum of money; she had known cases of it. But she would not do so. For her only one reparation could make up for the loss of her daughter's honour: marriage.

She counted all her cards again before sending Mary up to Mr. Doran's room to say that she wished to speak with him. She felt sure she would win. He was a serious young man, not rakish or loud-voiced like the others. If it had been Mr. Sheridan or Mr. Meade or Bantam Lyons her task would have been much harder. She did not think he would face publicity. All the lodgers in the house knew

something of the affair; details had been invented by some. Besides, he had been employed for thirteen years in a great Catholic wine-merchant's office and publicity would mean for him, perhaps, the loss of his job. Whereas if he agreed all might be well. She knew he had a good screw for one thing and she suspected he had a bit of stuff put by.

Nearly the half-hour! She stood up and surveyed herself in the pier-glass. The decisive expression of her great florid face satisfied her and she thought of some mothers she knew who could not get their daughters off their hands.

Mr. Doran was very anxious indeed this Sunday morning. He had made two attempts to shave but his hand had been so unsteady that he had been obliged to desist. Three days' reddish beard fringed his jaws and every two or three minutes a mist gathered on his glasses so that he had to take them off and polish them with his pocket-handkerchief. The recollection of his confession of the night before was a cause of acute pain to him; the priest had drawn out every ridiculous detail of the affair and in the end had so magnified his sin that he was almost thankful at being afforded a loophole of reparation. The harm was done. What could he do now but marry her or run away? He could not brazen it out. The affair would be sure to be talked of and his employer would be certain to hear of it. Dublin is such a small city: everyone knows everyone else's business. He felt his heart leap warmly in his throat as he heard in his excited imagination old Mr. Leonard calling out in his rasping voice: "Send Mr. Doran here, please."

All his long years of service gone for nothing! All his industry and diligence thrown away! As a young man he had sown his wild oats, of course; he had boasted of his freethinking and denied the existence of God to his companions in public-houses. But that was all passed and done with . . . nearly. He still bought a copy of *Reynolds's Newspaper* every week but he attended to his religious duties and for nine-tenths of the year lived a regular life. He had money enough to settle down on; it was not that. But the family would look down on her. First of all there was her disreputable father and then her mother's boarding house was beginning to get a certain fame. He had a notion that he was being had. He could imagine his friends talking of the affair and laughing. She *was* a little vulgar; some times she said "I seen" and "If I had've known." But what would grammar matter if he really loved her? He could not make up his mind whether to like her or despise her for what she had done. Of course he had done it too. His instinct urged him to remain free, not to marry. Once you are married you are done for, it said.

While he was sitting helplessly on the side of the bed in shirt and trousers she tapped lightly at his door and entered. She told him all, that she had made a clean breast of it to her mother and that her mother would speak with him that morning. She cried and threw her arms round his neck, saying:

"O Bob! Bob! What am I to do? What am I to do at all?"

She would put an end to herself, she said.

He comforted her feebly, telling her not to cry, that it would be all right, never fear. He felt against his shirt the agitation of her bosom.

It was not altogether his fault that it had happened. He remembered well, with the curious patient memory of the celibate, the first casual caresses her dress, her breath, her fingers had given him. Then late one night as he was undressing for bed she had tapped at his door, timidly. She wanted to relight her candle at his for hers had been blown out by a gust. It was her bath night. She wore a loose open combing jacket of printed flannel. Her white instep shone in the opening of her furry slippers and the blood glowed warmly behind her perfumed skin. From her hands and wrists too as she lit and steadied her candle a faint perfume arose.

On nights when he came in very late it was she who warmed up his dinner. He scarcely knew what he was eating feeling her beside him alone, at night, in the sleeping house. And her thoughtfulness! If the night was anyway cold or wet or windy there was sure to be a little tumbler of punch ready for him. Perhaps they could be happy together. . . .

They used to go upstairs together on tip-toe, each with a candle, and on the third landing exchange reluctant good-nights. They used to kiss. He remembered well her eyes, the touch of her hand and his delirium. . . .

But delirium passes. He echoed her phrase, applying it to himself: *"What am I to do?"* The instinct of the celibate warned him to hold back. But the sin was there; even his sense of honour told him that reparation must be made for such a sin.

While he was sitting with her on the side of the bed Mary came to the door and said that the missus wanted to see him in the parlour. He stood up to put on his coat and waistcoat, more helpless than ever. When he was dressed he went over to her to comfort her. It would be all right, never fear. He left her crying on the bed and moaning softly: *"O my God!"*

Going down the stairs his glasses became so dimmed with moisture that he had to take them off and polish them. He longed to ascend through the roof and fly away to another country where he would never hear again of his trouble, and yet a force pushed him downstairs step by step. The implacable faces of his employer and of the Madam stared upon his discomfiture. On the last flight of stairs he passed Jack Mooney who was coming up from the pantry nursing two bottles of *Bass*. They saluted coldly; and the lover's eyes rested for a second or two on a thick bulldog face and a pair of thick short arms. When he reached the foot of the staircase he glanced up and saw Jack regarding him from the door of the return-room.

Suddenly he remembered the night when one of the music-hall *artistes*, a little blond Londoner, had made a rather free allusion to Polly. The reunion had been almost broken up on account of Jack's violence. Everyone tried to quiet him. The music-hall *artiste*, a little paler than usual, kept smiling and saying that there was no harm meant: but Jack kept shouting at him that if any fellow tried that sort of a game on with his sister he'd

bloody well put his teeth down his throat, so
he would.

. . . .

Polly sat for a little time on the side of
the bed, crying. Then she dried her eyes and
went over to the looking-glass. She dipped
the end of the towel in the water-jug and refreshed her eyes with the cool water. She
looked at herself in profile and readjusted
a hairpin above her ear. Then she went back
to the bed again and sat at the foot. She regarded the pillows for a long time and the
sight of them awakened in her mind secret,
amiable memories. She rested the nape of her
neck against the cool iron bed-rail and fell
into a revery. There was no longer any
perturbation visible on her face.

She waited on patiently, almost cheerfully,
without alarm, her memories gradually giving place to hopes and visions of the future.
Her hopes and visions were so intricate that
she no longer saw the white pillows on which
her gaze was fixed or remembered that she
was waiting for anything.

At last she heard her mother calling. She
started to her feet and ran to the banisters.

"Polly! Polly!"

"Yes, mamma?"

"Come down, dear. Mr. Doran wants to
speak to you."

Then she remembered what she had been
waiting for.

QUESTIONS

1. Can you detect in this story any sign of the
   author's attitudes toward the mother, the
   daughter, the father, or Mr. Doran? How
   are these attitudes conveyed if they are
   here? What is the difficulty in being sure
   that these attitudes are those of the author?
2. Compare "The Boarding House" with
   "Stickman's Laughter" and with "The
   Homestead Orchard" in respect to the objectivity of the method or technique. Compare all three in respect to the ease or difficulty of discovering the author's probable
   attitudes toward characters and events.

THE SAD HORN-BLOWERS

Sherwood Anderson
(1876–1941)

It had been a disastrous year in Will's
family. The Appletons lived on one of the
outlying streets of Bidwell and Will's father
was a house painter. In early February, when
there was deep snow on the ground, and a
cold bitter wind blew about the houses,
Will's mother suddenly died. He was seventeen years old then, and rather a big fellow
for his age.

The mother's death happened abruptly,
without warning, as a sleepy man kills a fly
with the hand in a warm room on a summer
day. On one February day there she was
coming in at the kitchen door of the Appletons' house, from hanging the wash out on
the line in the back yard, and warming her
long hands, covered with blue veins, by holding them over the kitchen stove—and then,
looking about at the children with that half-
hidden, shy smile of hers—there she was like
that, as the three children had always known
her, and then, but a week later, she was cold
in death and lying in her coffin in the place
vaguely spoken of in the family as "the other
room."

After that, and when summer came and
the family was trying hard to adjust itself to
the new conditions, there came another disaster. Up to the very moment when it happened, it looked as though Tom Appleton,
the house painter, was in for a prosperous
season. The two boys, Fred and Will, were to
be his assistants that year.

To be sure, Fred was only fifteen, but he
was one to lend a quick alert hand at almost
any undertaking. For example, when there
was a job of paperhanging to be done, he was
the fellow to spread on the paste, helped by
an occasional sharp word from his father.

Down off his stepladder Tom Appleton
hopped and ran to the long board where the
paper was spread out. He liked this business

of having two assistants about. Well, you see, one had the feeling of being at the head of something, of managing affairs. He grabbed the pastebrush out of Fred's hand. "Don't spare the paste," he shouted. "Slap her on like this. Spread her out—so. Do be sure to catch all the edges."

It was all very warm, and comfortable, and nice, working at paper-hanging jobs in the houses on the March and April days. When it was cold or rainy outside, stoves were set up in the new houses being built, and in houses already inhabited the folks moved out of the rooms to be papered, spread newspapers on the floors over the carpets and put sheets over the furniture left in the rooms. Outside it rained or snowed, but inside it was warm and cozy.

To the Appletons it seemed, at the time, as though the death of the mother had drawn them closer together. Both Will and Fred felt it, perhaps Will the more consciously. The family was rather in the hole financially —the mother's funeral had cost a good deal of money, and Fred was being allowed to stay out of school. That pleased him. When they worked in a house where there were other children, they came home from school in the late afternoon and looked in through the door to where Fred was spreading paste over the sheets of wallpaper. He made a slapping sound with the brush, but did not look at them. "Ah, go on, you kids," he thought. This was a man's business he was up to. Will and his father were on the stepladders, putting the sheets carefully into place on the ceilings and walls. "Does she match down there?" the father asked sharply. "O-kay, go ahead," Will replied. When the sheet was in place, Fred ran and rolled out the laps with a little wooden roller. How jealous the kids of the house were! It would be a long time before any of them could stay out of school and do a man's work, as Fred was doing.

And then in the evening, walking homeward, it was nice, too. Will and Fred had been provided with suits of white overalls that were now covered with dried paste and spots of paint and looked really professional. They kept them on and drew their overcoats on over them. Their hands were stiff with paste, too. On Main Street the lights were lighted, and other men passing called to Tom Appleton. He was called Tony in the town. "Hello, Tony!" some storekeeper shouted. It was rather too bad, Will thought, that his father hadn't more dignity. He was too boyish. Young boys growing up and merging into manhood do not fancy fathers being too boyish. Tom Appleton played a cornet in the Bidwell Silver Cornet Band and didn't do the job very well—rather made a mess of it, when there was a bit of solo work to be done —but was so well liked by the other members of the band that no one said anything. And then he talked so grandly about music, and about the lip of a cornet player, that everyone thought he must be all right. "He has an education. I tell you what, Tony Appleton knows a lot. He's a smart one," the other members of the band were always saying to each other.

"Well, the devil! A man should grow up after a time, perhaps. When a man's wife had died but a short time before, it was just as well to walk through Main Street with more dignity—for the time being, anyway."

Tom Appleton had a way of winking at men he passed in the street, as though to say, "Well, now I've got my kids with me, and we won't say anything, but didn't you and I have the very hell of a time last Wednesday night, eh? Mum's the word, old pal. Keep everything quiet. There are gay times ahead for you and me. We'll cut loose, you bet, when you and me are out together next time."

Will grew a little angry about something he couldn't exactly understand. His father stopped in front of Jake Mann's meat market. "You kids go along home. Tell Kate I am bringing a steak. I'll be right on your heels," he said.

He would get the steak and then he would go into Alf Geiger's saloon and get a good, stiff drink of whiskey. There would be no one now to bother about smelling it on his breath when he got home later. Not that his wife had ever said anything when he wanted a drink—but you know how a man feels when there's a woman in the house. "Why, hello, Bildad Smith—how's the old game leg? Come on, have a little nip with me. Were you on Main Street last band meeting night and did you hear us do that new gallop? It's a humdinger. Turkey White did that trombone solo simply grand."

Will and Fred had got beyond Main Street now, and Will took a small pipe with a curved stem out of his overcoat pocket and lighted it. "I'll bet I could hang a ceiling without father there at all, if only someone would give me a chance," he said. Now that his father was no longer present to embarrass him with his lack of dignity, he felt comfortable and happy. Also, it was something to be able to smoke a pipe without discomfiture. When mother was alive, she was always kissing a fellow when he came home at night, and then one had to be mighty careful about smoking. Now it was different. One had become a man and one accepted manhood with its responsibilities. "Don't it make you sick at all?" Fred asked. "Huh, naw!" Will answered contemptuously.

The new disaster to the family came late in August, just when the fall work was all ahead, and the prospects good too. A. P. Wrigley, the jeweler, had just built a big, new house and barn on a farm he had bought the year before. It was a mile out of town on the Turner Pike.

That would be a job to set the Appletons up for the winter. The house was to have three coats outside, with all the work inside, and the barn was to have two coats—and the two boys were to work with their father and were to have regular wages.

And just to think of the work to be done inside that house made Tom Appleton's mouth water. He talked of it all the time, and in the evenings liked to sit in a chair in the Appletons' front yard, get some neighbor over, and then go on about it. How he slung house painter's lingo about! The doors and cupboards were to be grained in imitation of weathered oak, the front door was to be curly maple, and there was to be black walnut, too. Well, there wasn't another painter in the town could imitate all the various kinds of wood as Tom could. Just show him the wood, or tell him—you didn't have to show him anything. Name what you wanted—that was enough. To be sure, a man had to have the right tools, but give him the tools and then just go off and leave everything to him. What the devil! When A. P. Wrigley gave him this new house to do, he showed he was a man who knew what he was doing.

As for the practical side of the matter, everyone in the family knew that the Wrigley job meant a safe winter. There wasn't any speculation, as when taking work on the contract plan. All work was to be paid for by the day, and the boys were to have their wages, too. It meant new suits for the boys, a new dress and maybe a hat for Kate, the house rent paid all winter, potatoes in the cellar. It meant safety—that was the truth.

In the evenings, sometimes, Tom got out his tools and looked at them. Brushes and graining tools were spread out on the kitchen table, and Kate and the boys gathered about. It was Fred's job to see that all brushes were kept clean and, one by one, Tom ran his fingers over them, and then worked them back and forth over the palm of his hand. "This is a camel's-hair," he said, picking a soft fine-haired brush up and handing it to Will. "I paid four dollars and eighty cents for that." Will also worked it back and forth over the palm of his hand, just as his father had done, and then Kate picked it up and did the same thing. "It's as soft as the cat's back," she said. Will thought that rather silly. He looked forward to the day when he would have brushes, ladders, and pots of his own, and could show them off before people, and through his mind went words he had picked up from his father's talk. One spoke of the "heel" and "toe" of a brush. The way to put on varnish was to "flow" it on. Will knew all the words of his trade now and didn't have to talk like one of the kind of muts who just does, now and then, a jack job of house-painting.

On the fatal evening a surprise party was held for Mr. and Mrs. Bardshare, who lived just across the road from the Appletons on

Piety Hill. That was a chance for Tom Appleton. In any such affair he liked to have a hand in the arrangements. "Come on now, we'll make her go with a bang. They'll be setting in the house after supper, and Bill Bardshare will be in his stocking feet, and Ma Bardshare washing the dishes. They won't be expecting nothing, and we'll slip up, all dressed in our Sunday clothes, and let out a whoop. I'll bring my cornet and let out a blast on that too. 'What in Sam Hill is that?' Say, I can just see Bill Bardshare jumping up and beginning to swear, thinking we're a gang of kids come to bother him, like Hallowe'en, or something like that. You just get the grub, and I'll make the coffee over to my house and bring it over hot. I'll get ahold of two big pots and make a whooping lot of it."

In the Appleton house all was in a flurry. Tom, Will, and Fred were painting a barn, three miles out of town, but they knocked off work at four and Tom got the farmer's son to drive them to town. He himself had to wash up, take a bath in a tub in the woodshed, shave and everything—just like Sunday. He looked more like a boy than a man when he got all dogged up.

And then the family had to have supper, over and done with, a little after six, and Tom didn't dare go outside the house until dark. It wouldn't do to have the Bardshares see him so fixed up. It was their wedding anniversary, and they might suspect something. He kept trotting about the house, and occasionally looked out of the front window toward the Bardshare house. "You kid, you," Kate said, laughing. Sometimes she talked up to him like that, and after she said it he went upstairs and getting out his cornet blew on it so softly you could hardly hear him downstairs. When he did that, you couldn't tell how badly he played, as when the band was going it on Main Street and he had to carry a passage right through alone. He sat in the room upstairs thinking. When Kate laughed at him, it was like having his wife back, alive. There was the same shy sarcastic gleam in her eyes.

Well, it was the first time he had been out anywhere since his wife had died, and there might be some people think it would be better if he stayed at home now—look better, that is. When he had shaved, he had cut his chin, and the blood had come. After a time he went downstairs and stood before the looking glass, hung above the kitchen sink, and dabbed at the spot with the wet end of a towel.

Will and Fred stood about.

Will's mind was working—perhaps Kate's, too. "Was there—could it be?—well, at such a party—only older people invited—there were always two or three widow women thrown in for good measure, as it were."

Kate didn't want any woman fooling around her kitchen. She was twenty years old.

"And it was just as well not to have any monkey-shine talk about motherless children," such as Tom might indulge in. Even Fred thought that. There was a little wave of resentment against Tom in the house. It was a wave that didn't make much noise, just crept, as it were softly, up a low sandy beach.

"Widow women went to such places, and then, of course, people were always going home in couples." Both Kate and Will had the same picture in mind. It was late at night and in fancy they were both peeking out at front upper windows of the Appleton house. There were all the people coming out at the front door of the Bardshare house, and Bill Bardshare was standing there and holding the door open. He had managed to sneak away during the evening, and got his Sunday clothes on all right.

And the couples were coming out. "There was that woman now, that widow, Mrs. Childers." She had been married twice, both husbands dead now, and she lived away over Maumee Pike way. "What makes a woman of her age want to act silly like that? It is the very devil how a woman can keep looking young and handsome after she has buried two men. There are some who say that, even when her last husband was alive—"

"But whether that's true or not, what makes her want to act and talk silly that way?" Now her face is turned to the light and she is saying to old Bill Bardshare, "Sleep light, sleep tight, sweet dreams to you tonight."

"It's only what one may expect when one's father lacks a sense of dignity. There is that old fool Tom now, hopping out of the Bardshare house like a kid, and running right up to Mrs. Childers. 'May I see you home?' he is saying, while all the others are laughing and smiling knowingly. It makes one's blood run cold to see such a thing."

"Well, fill up the pots. Let's get the old coffee pots started, Kate. The gang'll be creeping along up the street pretty soon now," Tom shouted self-consciously, skipping busily about and breaking the little circle of thoughts in the house.

What happened was that—just as darkness came and when all the people were in the front yard before the Appleton house—Tom went and got it into his head to try to carry his cornet and two big coffee pots at the same time. Why didn't he leave the coffee until later? There the people were in the dusk outside the house, and there was that kind of low whispering and tittering that always goes on at such a time—and then Tom stuck his head out at the door and shouted, "Let her go!"

And then he must have gone quite crazy, for he ran back into the kitchen and grabbed both of the big coffee pots, hanging on to his cornet at the same time. Of course he stumbled in the darkness in the road outside and fell, and of course all of that boiling hot coffee had to spill right over him.

It was terrible. The flood of boiling hot coffee made steam under his thick clothes, and there he lay screaming with the pain of it. What a confusion! He just writhed and screamed, and the people ran round and round in the half darkness like crazy things. Was it some kind of joke the crazy fellow was up to at the last minute? Tom always was such a devil to think up things. "You should see him down at Alf Geigers, sometimes on Saturday nights, imitating the way Joe Douglas got out on a limb, and then sawed it off between

himself and the tree, and the look on Joe's face when the limb began to crack. It would make you laugh until you screamed to see him imitate that."

"But what now? My God!" There was Kate Appleton trying to tear her father's clothes off, and crying and whimpering, and young Will Appleton knocking people aside. "Say, the man's hurt! What's happened? My God! Run for the doctor, someone. He's burnt, something awful!"

Early in October Will Appleton sat in the smoking car of a day train that runs between Cleveland and Buffalo. His destination was Erie, Pennsylvania, and he had got on the passenger train at Ashtabula, Ohio. Just why his destination was Erie he couldn't very easily have explained. He was going there anyway, going to get a job in a factory or on the docks there. Perhaps it was just a quirk of the mind that had made him decide upon Erie. It wasn't as big as Cleveland or Buffalo or Toledo or Chicago, or any one of a lot of other cities to which he might have gone, looking for work.

At Ashtabula he came into the car and slid into a seat beside a little old man. His own clothes were wet and wrinkled, and his hair, eyebrows, and ears were black with coal dust.

At the moment, there was in him a kind of bitter dislike of his native town, Bidwell. "Sakes alive, a man couldn't get any work there—not in the winter." After the accident to his father, and the spoiling of all the family plans, he had managed to find employment during September on the farms. He worked for a time with a threshing crew, and then got work cutting corn. It was all right. "A man made a dollar a day and board, and as he wore overalls all the time, he didn't wear out no clothes. Still and all, the time when a fellow could make any money in Bidwell was past now, and the burns on his father's body had gone pretty deep, and he might be laid up for months."

Will had just made up his mind one day, after he had tramped about all morning from farm to farm without finding work, and then he had gone home and told Kate. "Dang it all," he hadn't intended lighting out right away—had thought he would stay about for a week or two, maybe. Well, he would go uptown in the evening, dressed up in his best clothes, and stand around. "Hello, Harry, what you going to do this winter? I thought I would run over to Erie, Pennsylvania. I got an offer in a factory over there. Well, so long—if I don't see you again."

Kate hadn't seemed to understand, had seemed in an almighty hurry about getting him off. It was a shame she couldn't have a little more heart. Still, Kate was all right—worried a good deal, no doubt. After their talk she had just said, "Yes, I think that's best, you had better go," and had gone to change the bandages on Tom's legs and back. The father was sitting among pillows in a rocking chair in the front room.

Will went upstairs and put his things, overalls and a few shirts, into a bundle. Then he went downstairs and took a walk—went out along a road that led into the country, and stopped on a bridge. It was near a place where he and other kids used to come swimming on summer afternoons. A thought had come into his head. There was a young fellow worked in Pawsey's jewelry store came to see Kate sometimes on Sunday evenings and they went off to walk together. "Did Kate want to get married?" If she did, his going away now might be for good. He hadn't thought about that before. On that afternoon, and quite suddenly, all the world outside of Bidwell seemed huge and terrible to him and a few secret tears came into his eyes, but he managed to choke them back. For just a moment his mouth opened and closed queerly, like the mouth of a fish, when you take it out of the water and hold it in your hand.

When he returned to the house at supper-time, things were better. He had left his bundle on a chair in the kitchen and Kate had wrapped it more carefully, and had put in a number of things he had forgotten. His father called him into the front room. "It's all right, Will. Every young fellow ought to take a whirl out in the world. I did it myself, at about your age," Tom had said, a little pompously.

Then supper was served, and there was apple pie. That was a luxury the Appletons had perhaps better not have indulged in at that time, but Will knew Kate had baked it during the afternoon—it might be as a way of showing him how she felt. Eating two large slices had rather set him up.

And then, before he realized how the time was slipping away, ten o'clock had come, and it was time for him to go. He was going to beat his way out of town on a freight train, and there was a local going toward Cleveland at ten o'clock. Fred had gone off to bed, and his father was asleep in the rocking chair in the front room. He had picked up his bundle, and Kate had put on her hat. "I'm going to see you off," she had said.

Will and Kate had walked in silence along the streets to where he was to wait, in the shadow of Whaley's warehouse, until the freight came along. Later, when he thought back over that evening, he was glad, that although she was three years older, he was taller than Kate.

How vividly everything that happened later stayed in his mind. After the train came, and he had crawled into an empty coal car, he sat hunched up in a corner. Overhead he could see the sky, and when the train stopped at towns, there was always the chance the car in which he was concealed would be shoved into a siding, and left. The brakemen walked along the tracks beside the car shouting to each other and their lanterns made little splashes of light in the darkness.

"How black the sky!" After a time it began to rain. "His suit would be in a pretty mess. After all, a fellow couldn't come right out and ask his sister if she intended to marry. If Kate married, then his father would also marry again. It was all right for a young woman like Kate, but for a man of forty to think of marriage—the devil! Why didn't Tom Appleton have more dignity? After all, Fred was only a kid and a new woman coming in, to be his mother—that might be all right for a kid."

All during that night on the freight train

Will had thought a good deal about marriage —rather vague thoughts—coming and going like birds flying in and out of a bush. It was all a matter—this business of man and woman—that did not touch him very closely —not yet. The matter of having a home— that was something else. A home was something at a fellow's back. When one went off to work all week at some farm, and at night maybe went into a strange room to sleep, there was always the Appleton house—floating, as it were, like a picture at the back of the mind—the Appleton house, and Kate moving about. She had been uptown, and now had come home and was going up the stairs. Tom Appleton was fussing about in the kitchen. He liked a bite before he went off to bed for the night, but presently he would go upstairs and into his own room. He liked to smoke his pipe before he slept and sometimes he got out his cornet and blew two or three soft sad notes.

At Cleveland Will had crawled off the freight train and had gone across the city in a streetcar. Workingmen were just going to the factories and he passed among them unnoticed. If his clothes were crumpled and soiled, their clothes weren't so fine. The workingmen were all silent, looking at the car floor, or out at the car windows. Long rows of factories stood along the streets through which the car moved.

He had been lucky, and had caught another freight out of a place called Collinswood at eight, but at Ashtabula had made up his mind it would be better to drop off the freight and take a passenger train. If he was to live in Erie, it would be just as well to arrive, looking more like a gentleman and having paid his fare.

As he sat in the smoking car of the train, he did not feel much like a gentleman. The coal dust had got into his hair and the rain had washed it in long dirty streaks down over his face. His clothes were badly soiled and wanted cleaning and brushing and the paper package, in which his overalls and shirts were tied, had become torn and dirty.

Outside the train window the sky was gray, and no doubt the night was going to turn cold. Perhaps there would be a cold rain.

It was an odd thing about the towns through which the train kept passing—all of the houses in all the towns looked cold and forbidding. "Dang it all!" In Bidwell—before the night when his father got so badly burned being such a fool about old Bill Bardshare's party—all the houses had always seemed warm cozy places. When one was alone, one walked along the streets whistling. At night warm lights shone through the windows of the houses. "John Wyatt, the drayman, lives in that house. His wife has a wen on her neck. In that barn over there old Doctor Musgrave keeps his bony old white horse. The horse looks like the devil, but you bet he can go."

Will squirmed about on the car seat. The old man who sat beside him was small, almost as small as Fred, and he wore a queer-looking suit. The pants were brown, and the coat checked, gray and black. There was a small leather case on the floor at his feet.

Long before the man spoke, Will knew what would happen. It was bound to turn out that such a fellow played a cornet. He was a man, old in years, but there was no dignity in him. Will remembered his father's marchings through the main street of Bidwell with the band. It was some great day, Fourth of July, perhaps, and all the people were assembled, and there was Tony Appleton, making a show of blowing his cornet at a great rate. Did all the people along the street know how badly he played and was there a kind of conspiracy that kept grown men from laughing at each other? In spite of the seriousness of his own situation, a smile crept over Will's face.

The little man at his side smiled in return.

"Well," he began, not stopping for anything but plunging headlong into a tale concerning some dissatisfaction he felt with life, "well, you see before you a man who is up against it, young fellow." The old man tried to laugh at his own words, but did not make much of a success of it. His lip trembled. "I

FICTION

got to go home like a dog, with my tail 'twixt my legs," he declared abruptly.

The old man balanced back and forth between two impulses. He had met a young man on a train, and hungered for companionship, and one got oneself in with others by being jolly, a little gay, perhaps. When one met a stranger on a train, one told a story—"By the way, Mister, I heard a new one the other day—perhaps you haven't heard it? It's about the miner up in Alaska who hadn't seen a woman for years." One began in that way, and then later, perhaps, spoke of oneself, and one's affairs.

But the old man wanted to plunge at once into his own story. He talked, saying sad discouraged words, while his eyes kept smiling with a peculiar appealing little smile. "If the words uttered by my lips annoy or bore you, do not pay any attention to them. I am really a jolly fellow, although I am an old man, and not of much use any more," the eyes were saying. The eyes were pale blue and watery. How strange to see them set in the head of an old man! They belonged in the head of a lost dog. The smile was not really a smile. "Don't kick me, young fellow. If you can't give me anything to eat, scratch my head. At least show you are a fellow of good intentions. I've been kicked about quite enough." It was so very evident the eyes were speaking a language of their own.

Will found himself smiling sympathetically. It was true there was something doglike in the little old man and Will was pleased with himself for having so quickly caught the sense of him. "One who can see things with his eyes will perhaps get along all right in the world, after all," he thought. His thoughts wandered away from the old man. In Bidwell there was an old woman lived alone and owned a shepherd dog. Every summer she decided to cut away the dog's coat, and then—at the last moment and after she had in fact started the job—she changed her mind. Well, she grasped a long pair of scissors firmly in her hand and started on the dog's flanks. Her hand trembled a little. "Shall I go ahead, or shall I stop?"

After two minutes she gave up the job. "It makes him look too ugly," she thought, justifying her timidity.

Later the hot days came, the dog went about with his tongue hanging out, and again the old woman took the scissors in her hand. The dog stood patiently waiting, but, when she had cut a long wide furrow through the thick hair of his back, she stopped again. In a sense, and to her way of looking at the matter, cutting away his splendid coat was like cutting away a part of himself. She couldn't go on. "Now there—that made him look worse than ever," she declared to herself. With a determined air she put the scissors away, and all summer the dog went about looking a little puzzled and ashamed.

Will kept smiling and thinking of the old woman's dog and then looked again at his companion of the train. The variegated suit the old man wore gave him something of the air of the half-sheared shepherd dog. Both had the same puzzled, ashamed air.

Now Will had begun using the old man for his own ends. There was something inside himself that wanted facing, he didn't want to face—not yet. Ever since he had left home, in fact ever since that day when he had come home from the country and had told Kate of his intention to set out into the world, he had been dodging something. If one thought of the little old man, and of the half-sheared dog, one did not have to think of oneself.

One thought of Bidwell on a summer afternoon. There was the old woman, who owned the dog, standing on the porch of her house, and the dog had run down to the gate. In the winter, when his coat had again fully grown, the dog would bark and make a great fuss about a boy passing in the street, but now he started to bark and growl, and then stopped. "I look like the devil, and I'm attracting unnecessary attention to myself," the dog seemed to have decided suddenly. He ran furiously down to the gate, opened his mouth to bark, and then, quite abruptly, changed his mind and trotted back to the house with his tail between his legs.

Will kept smiling at his own thoughts. For the first time since he had left Bidwell, he felt quite cheerful.

And now the old man was telling a story of himself and his life, but Will wasn't listening. Within the young man a cross-current of impulses had been set up and he was like one standing silently in the hallway of a house, and listening to two voices, talking at a distance. The voices came from two widely separated rooms of the house and one couldn't make up one's mind to which voice to listen.

To be sure, the old man was another cornet player like his father—he was a horn blower. That was his horn in the little worn leather case on the car floor.

And after he had reached middle age, and after his first wife had died, he had married again. He had a little property then and, in a foolish moment, went and made it all over to his second wife, who was fifteen years younger than himself. She took the money and bought a large house in the factory district of Erie, and then began taking in boarders.

There was the old man, feeling lost, of no account in his own house. It just came about. One had to think of the boarders—their wants had to be satisfied. His wife had two sons, almost fully grown now, both of whom worked in a factory.

Well, it was all right—everything on the square—the sons paid board all right. Their wants had to be thought of, too. He liked blowing his cornet awhile in the evenings, before he went to bed, but it might disturb the others in the house. One got rather desperate going about saying nothing, keeping out of the way, and he had tried getting work in a factory himself, but they wouldn't have him. His gray hairs stood in his way, and so one night he had just got out, had gone to Cleveland, where he had hoped to get a job in a band, in a movie theater, perhaps. Anyway, it hadn't turned out and now he was going back to Erie and to his wife. He had written and she had told him to come on home.

"They didn't turn me down back there in Cleveland because I'm old. It's because my lip is no good any more," he explained. His shrunken old lip trembled a little.

Will kept thinking of the old woman's dog. In spite of himself, and when the old man's lip trembled, his lip also trembled.

What was the matter with him?

He stood in the hallway of a house hearing two voices. Was he trying to close his ears to one of them? Did the second voice, the one he had been trying all day, and all the night before, not to hear, did that have something to do with the end of his life in the Appleton house at Bidwell? Was the voice trying to taunt him, trying to tell him that now he was a thing swinging in air, that there was no place to put down his feet? Was he afraid? Of what was he afraid? He had wanted so much to be a man, to stand on his own feet, and now what was the matter with him? Was he afraid of manhood?

He was fighting desperately now. There were tears in the old man's eyes, and Will also began crying silently and that was the one thing he felt he must not do.

The old man talked on and on, telling the tale of his troubles, but Will could not hear his words. The struggle within was becoming more and more definite. His mind clung to the life of his boyhood, to the life in the Appleton house in Bidwell.

There was Fred, standing in the field of his fancy now, with just the triumphant look in his eyes that came when other boys saw him doing a man's work. A whole series of pictures floated up before Will's mind. He and his father and Fred were painting a barn and two farmer boys had come along a road and stood looking at Fred, who was on a ladder, putting on paint. They shouted, but Fred wouldn't answer. There was a certain air Fred had—he slapped on the paint, and then, turning his head, spat on the ground. Tom Appleton's eyes looked into Will's and there was a smile playing about the corners of the father's eyes and the son's eyes too. The father and his oldest son were like two men, two workmen, having a delicious little secret between them. They were both looking lovingly at Fred. "Bless him! He's thinks he's a man already."

And now Tom Appleton was standing in the kitchen of his house, and his brushes were laid out on the kitchen table. Kate was rubbing a brush back and forth over the palm of her hand. "It's as soft as the cat's back," she was saying.

Something gripped at Will's throat. As in a dream, he saw his sister Kate walking off along the street on Sunday evening with that young fellow who clerked in the jewelry store. They were going to church. Her being with him meant—well, it perhaps meant the beginning of a new home—it meant the end of the Appleton home.

Will started to climb out of the seat beside the old man in the smoking car of the train. It had grown almost dark in the car. The old man was still talking, telling his tale over and over. "I might as well not have any home at all," he was saying. Was Will about to begin crying aloud on a train, in a strange place, before many strange men? He tried to speak, to make some commonplace remark, but his mouth only opened and closed like the mouth of a fish taken out of the water.

And now the train had run into a train shed, and it was quite dark. Will's hand clutched convulsively into the darkness and alighted upon the old man's shoulder.

Then suddenly, the train had stopped, and the two stood half-embracing each other. The tears were quite evident in Will's eyes, when a brakeman lighted the overhead lamps in the car, but the luckiest thing in the world had happened. The old man, who had seen Will's tears, thought they were tears of sympathy for his own unfortunate position in life and a look of gratitude came into his blue watery eyes. Well, this was something new in life for him, too. In one of the pauses, when he had first begun telling his tale, Will had said he was going to Erie to try to get work in some factory, and now, as they got off the train, the old man clung to Will's arm. "You might as well come live at our house," he said. A look of hope flared up in

the old man's eyes. If he could bring home with him, to his young wife, a new boarder, the gloom of his own home-coming would be somewhat lightened. "You come on. That's the best thing to do. You just come on with me to our house," he pleaded, clinging to Will.

Two weeks had passed and Will had, outwardly, and to the eyes of the people about him, settled into his new life as a factory hand at Erie, Pennsylvania.

Then suddenly, on a Saturday evening, the thing happened that he had unconsciously been expecting and dreading ever since the moment when he climbed aboard the freight train in the shadow of Whaley's warehouse at Bidwell. A letter, containing great news, had come from Kate.

At the moment of their parting, and before he settled himself down out of sight in a corner of the empty coal car, on that night of his leaving, he had leaned out for a last look at his sister. She had been standing silently in the shadows of the warehouse, but just as the train was about to start, stepped toward him and a light from a distant street lamp fell on her face.

Well, the face did not jump toward Will, but remained dimly outlined in the uncertain light.

Did her lips open and close, as though in an effort to say something to him, or was that an effect produced by the distant, uncertain, and wavering light? In the families of working people the dramatic and vital moments of life are passed over in silence. Even in the moments of death and birth, little is said. A child is born to a laborer's wife and he goes into the room. She is in bed with the little red bundle of new life beside her and her husband stands a moment, fumblingly, beside the bed. "Take care of yourself, Ma. Have a good rest," he says, and hurries out of the room.

In the darkness by the warehouse at Bidwell, Kate had taken two or three steps toward Will, and then had stopped. There was a little strip of grass between the warehouse and the tracks, and she stood upon it. Was there a more final farewell trembling on her lips at the moment? A kind of dread had swept over Will, and no doubt Kate had felt the same thing. At the moment she had become altogether the mother, in the presence of her child, and the thing within that wanted utterance became submerged. There was a word to be said that she could not say. Her form seemed to sway a little in the darkness and, to Will's eyes, she became a slender indistinct thing. "Goodbye," he had whispered into the darkness, and perhaps her lips had formed the same words. Outwardly there had been only the silence, and in the silence she had stood as the train rumbled away.

And now, on the Saturday evening, Will had come home from the factory and had found Kate saying in the letter what she had been unable to say on the night of his departure. The factory closed at five on Saturday and he came home in his overalls and went to his room. He had found the letter on a little broken table under a spluttering oil lamp, by the front door, and had climbed the stairs carrying it in his hand. He read the letter anxiously, waiting as for a hand to come out of the blank wall of the room and strike.

His father was getting better. The deep burns that had taken such a long time to heal were really healing now and the doctor had said the danger of infection had passed. Kate had found a new and soothing remedy. One took slippery elm and let it lie in milk until it became soft. This applied to the burns enabled Tom to sleep better at night.

As for Fred, Kate and her father had decided he might as well go back to school. It was really too bad for a young boy to miss the chance to get an education, and anyway there was no work to be had. Perhaps he could get a job, helping in some store on Saturday afternoons.

A woman from the Woman's Relief Corps had had the nerve to come to the Appleton house and ask Kate if the family needed help. Well, Kate had managed to hold herself

back, and had been polite, but, had the woman known what was in her mind, her ears would have been itching for a month. The idea!

It had been fine of Will to send a post-card, as soon as he had got to Erie and got a job. As for his sending money home—of course the family would be glad to have anything he could spare—but he wasn't to go depriving himself. "We've got good credit at the stores. We'll get along all right," Kate had said stoutly.

And then it was she had added the line, had said the thing she could not say that night when he was leaving. It concerned herself and her future plans. "That night when you were going away I wanted to tell you something, but I thought it was silly, talking too soon." After all, though, Will might as well know she was planning to be married in the spring. What she wanted was for Fred to come and live with her and her husband. He could keep on going to school, and perhaps they could manage so that he could go to college. Someone in the family ought to have a decent education. Now that Will had made his start in life, there was no point in waiting longer before making her own.

Will sat, in his tiny room at the top of the huge frame house, owned now by the wife of the old cornet-player of the train, and held the letter in his hand. The room was on the third floor, under the roof, in a wing of the house, and beside it was another small room, occupied by the old man himself. Will had taken the room because it was to be had at a low price and he could manage the room and his meals, get his washing done, send three dollars a week to Kate, and still have left a dollar a week to spend. One could get a little tobacco, and now and then see a movie.

"Ugh!" Will's lips made a little grunting noise as he read Kate's words. He was sitting in a chair, in his oily overalls, and where his fingers gripped the white sheets of the letter there was a little oily smudge. Also his hand trembled a little. He got up, poured water out of a pitcher into a white bowl, and began washing his face and hands.

When he had partly dressed, a visitor came. There was the shuffling sound of weary feet along a hallway, and the cornet-player put his head timidly in at the door. The dog-like appealing look Will had noted on the train was still in his eyes. Now he was planning something, a kind of gentle revolt against his wife's power in the house, and he wanted Will's moral support.

For a week he had been coming for talk to Will's room almost every evening. There were two things he wanted. In the evening sometimes, as he sat in his room, he wanted to blow upon his cornet, and he wanted a little money to jingle in his pockets.

And there was a sense in which Will, the newcomer in the house, was his property, did not belong to his wife. Often in the evenings he had talked to the weary and sleepy young workman, until Will's eyes had closed and he snored gently. The old man sat on the one chair in the room, and Will sat on the edge of the bed, while old lips told the tale of a lost youth, boasted a little. When Will's body had slumped down upon the bed, the old man got to his feet and moved with catlike steps about the room. One mustn't raise the voice too loudly, after all. Had Will gone to sleep? The cornet-player threw his shoulders back and bold words came, in a half-whisper, from his lips. To tell the truth, he had been a fool about the money he had made over to his wife, and, if his wife had taken advantage of him, it wasn't her fault. For his present position in life he had no one to blame but himself. What from the very beginning he had most lacked was boldness. It was a man's duty to be a man and, for a long time, he had been thinking—well, the boarding house no doubt made a profit and he should have his share. His wife was a good girl all right, but when one came right down to it, all women seemed to lack a sense of a man's position in life.

"I'll have to speak to her—yes-siree, I'm going to speak right up to her. I may have to be a little harsh, but it's my money runs this house, and I want my share of the profits.

No foolishness now. Shell out, I tell you," the old man whispered, peering out of the corners of his blue, watery eyes at the sleeping form of the young man on the bed.

And now again the old man stood at the door of the room, looking anxiously in. A bell called insistently, announcing that the evening meal was ready to be served, and they went below, Will leading the way. At a long table in the dining room several men had already gathered, and there was the sound of more footsteps on the stairs.

Two long rows of young workmen eating silently. Saturday night and two long rows of young workmen eating in silence.

After the eating, and on this particular night, there would be a swift flight of all these young men down into the town, down into the lighted parts of the town.

Will sat at his place gripping the sides of his chair.

There were things men did on Saturday nights. Work was at an end for the week and money jingled in pockets. Young workmen ate in silence and hurried away, one by one, down into the town.

Will's sister Kate was going to be married in the spring. Her walking about with the young clerk from the jewelry store, in the streets of Bidwell, had come to something.

Young workmen employed in factories in Erie, Pennsylvania, dressed themselves in their best clothes and walked about in the lighted streets of Erie on Saturday evenings. They went into parks. Some stood talking to girls while others walked with girls through the streets. And there were still others who went into saloons and had drinks. Men stood talking together at a bar. "Dang that foreman of mine! I'll bust him in the jaw if he gives me any of his lip."

There was a young man from Bidwell, sitting at a table in a boarding house at Erie, Pennsylvania, and before him on a plate was a great pile of meat and potatoes. The room was not very well lighted. It was dark and gloomy, and there were black streaks on the gray wallpaper. Shadows played on the walls. On all sides of the young man sat other young men—eating silently, hurriedly.

Will got abruptly up from the table and started for the door that led into the street, but the others paid no attention to him. If he did not want to eat his meat and potatoes, it made no difference to them. The mistress of the house, the wife of the old cornet-player, waited on table when the men ate, but now she had gone away to the kitchen. She was a silent grim-looking woman, dressed always in a black dress.

To the others in the room—except only the old cornet-player—Will's going or staying meant nothing at all. He was a young workman, and at such places young workmen were always going and coming.

A man with broad shoulders and a black mustache, a little older than most of the others, did glance up from his business of eating. He nudged his neighbor, and then made a jerky movement with his thumb over his shoulder. "The new guy has hooked up quickly, eh?" he said, smiling. "He can't even wait to eat. Lordy, he's got an early date—some skirt waiting for him."

At his place, opposite where Will had been seated, the cornet-player saw Will go, and his eyes followed, filled with alarm. He had counted on an evening of talk, of speaking to Will about his youth, boasting a little in his gentle hesitating way. Now Will had reached the door that led to the street, and in the old man's eyes tears began to gather. Again his lip trembled. Tears were always gathering in the man's eyes, and his lips trembled at the slightest provocation. It was no wonder he could no longer blow a cornet in a band.

And now Will was outside the house in the darkness and, for the cornet-player, the evening was spoiled, the house a deserted empty place. He had intended being very plain in his evening's talk with Will, and wanted particularly to speak of a new attitude he hoped to assume toward his wife in the matter of money. Talking the whole matter out with Will would give him new courage, make him bolder. Well, if his money had bought the house, that was now a boarding house, he should have some share in its profits. There must be profits. Why run a

boarding house without profits? The woman he had married was no fool.

Even though a man were old, he needed a little money in his pockets. Well, an old man, like himself, has a friend, a young fellow, and now and then he wanted to be able to say to his friend, "Come on, friend, let's have a glass of beer. I know a good place. Let's have a glass of beer and go to the movies. This is on me."

The cornet-player could not eat his meat and potatoes. For a time he stared over the heads of the others, and then got up to go to his room. His wife followed into the little hallway at the foot of the stairs. "What's the matter, dearie—are you sick?" she asked.

"No," he answered, "I just didn't want any supper." He did not look at her, but tramped slowly and heavily up the stairs.

Will was walking hurriedly through the streets, but did not go down into the brightly lighted sections of town. The boarding house stood on a factory street, and, turning northward, he crossed several railroad tracks and went toward the docks, along the shore of Lake Erie. There was something to be settled with himself, something to be faced. Could he manage the matter?

He walked along, hurriedly at first, and then more slowly. It was getting into late October now and there was a sharpness like frost in the air. The spaces between street lamps were long, and he plunged in and out of areas of darkness. Why was it that everything about him seemed suddenly strange and unreal? He had forgotten to bring his overcoat from Bidwell and would have to write Kate to send it.

Now he had almost reached the docks. Not only the night, but his own body, the pavements under his feet, and the stars far away in the sky—even the solid factory buildings he was now passing—seemed strange and unreal. It was almost as though one could thrust out an arm and push a hand through the walls, as one might push his hand into a fog or a cloud of smoke. All the people Will passed seemed strange, and acted in a strange way. Dark figures surged toward him out of the darkness. By a factory wall there was a man standing—perfectly still, motionless. There was something almost unbelievable about the actions of such men and the strangeness of such hours as the one through which he was now passing. He walked within a few inches of the motionless man. Was it a man or a shadow on the wall? The life Will was now to lead alone had become a strange, a vast terrifying thing. Perhaps all life was like that, a vastness and emptiness.

He came out into a place where ships were made fast to a dock, and stood for a time, facing the high wall-like side of a vessel. It looked dark and deserted. When he turned his head, he became aware of a man and a woman passing along a roadway. Their feet made no sound in the thick dust of the road-way, and he could not see or hear them, but knew they were there. Some part of a woman's dress—something white—flashed faintly into view and the man's figure was a dark mass against the dark mass of the night. "Oh, come on, don't be afraid," the man whispered, hoarsely. "There won't anything happen to you."

"Do shut up," a woman's voice answered, and there was a quick outburst of laughter. The figures fluttered away. "You don't know what you are talking about," the woman's voice said again.

Now that he had got Kate's letter, Will was no longer a boy. A boy is, quite naturally, and without his having anything to do with the matter, connected with something—and now that connection had been cut. He had been pushed out of the nest, and that fact, the pushing of himself off the nest's rim, was something accomplished. The difficulty was that, while he was no longer a boy, he had not yet become a man. He was a thing swing-ing in space. There was no place to put down his feet.

He stood in the darkness under the shadow of the ship, making queer little wriggling motions with his shoulders that had become now almost the shoulders of a man. No need now to think of evenings at the Appleton house with Kate and Fred standing about, and his father, Tom Appleton, spreading his paint brushes on the kitchen table, no need

of thinking of the sound of Kate's feet going up a stairway of the Appleton house, late at night, when she had been out walking with her clerk. What was the good of trying to amuse oneself by thinking of a shepherd dog in an Ohio town, a dog made ridiculous by the trembling hand of a timid old woman?

One stood face to face with manhood now —one stood alone. If only one could get one's feet down upon something, could get over this feeling of falling through space, through a vast emptiness.

"Manhood"—the word had a queer sound in the head. What did it mean?

Will tried to think of himself as a man, doing a man's work in a factory. There was nothing in the factory, where he was now employed, upon which he could put down his feet. All day he stood at a machine and bored holes in pieces of iron. A boy brought to him the little, short, meaningless pieces of iron in a box-like truck and, one by one, he picked them up and placed them under the point of a drill. He pulled a lever and the drill came down and bit into the piece of iron. A little, smoke-like vapor arose, and then he squirted oil on the spot where the drill was working. Then the lever was thrown up again. The hole was drilled and now the meaningless piece of iron was thrown into another box-like truck. It had nothing to do with him. He had nothing to do with it.

At the noon hour, at the factory, one moved about a bit, stepped outside the factory door to stand for a moment in the sun. In-side, men were sitting along benches eating lunches out of dinner pails, and some had washed their hands while others had not bothered about such a trivial matter. They were eating in silence. A tall man spat on the floor and then drew his foot across the spot. Nights came and one went home from the factory to eat, sitting with other silent men, and later a boastful old man came into one's room to talk. One lay on a bed and tried to listen, but presently fell asleep. Men were like the pieces of iron in which holes had been bored—one pitched them aside into a box-like truck. One had nothing really to do with them. They had nothing to do with oneself. Life became a procession of days and perhaps all life was just like that—just a procession of days.

"Manhood."

Did one go out of one place and into another? Were youth and manhood two houses, in which one lived during different periods in life? It was evident something of importance must be about to happen to his sister Kate. First, she had been a young woman, having two brothers and a father, living with them in a house at Bidwell, Ohio.

And then a day was to come when she became something else. She married and went to live in another house and had a husband. Perhaps children would be born to her. It was evident Kate had got hold of something, that her hands had reached out and had grasped something definite. Kate had swung herself off the rim of the home nest and, right away, her feet had landed on another limb of the tree of life—womanhood.

As he stood in the darkness, something caught at Will's throat. He was fighting again, but what was he fighting? A fellow like himself did not move out of one house and into another. There was a house in which one lived, and then suddenly and unexpectedly, it fell apart. One stood on the rim of the nest and looked about, and a hand reached out from the warmth of the nest and pushed one off into space. There was no place for a fellow to put down his feet. He was one swinging in space.

What—a great fellow, nearly six feet tall now, and crying in the darkness, in the shadow of a ship, like a child! He walked, filled with determination, out of the darkness, along many streets of factories and came into a street of houses. He passed a store where groceries were sold and looking in saw, by a clock on the wall, that it was already ten o'clock. Two drunken men came out at the door of a house and stood on a little porch. One of them clung to a railing about the porch, and the other pulled at his arm. "Let me alone. It's settled. I want you to let me alone," grumbled the man clinging to the railing.

Will went to his boarding house and climbed the stairs wearily. The devil—one might face anything if one but knew what was to be faced!

He turned on a light and sat down in his room on the edge of the bed, and the old cornet-player pounced upon him, pounced like a little animal, lying under a bush along a path in a forest, and waiting for food. He came into Will's room carrying his cornet, and there was an almost bold look in his eyes. Standing firmly on his old legs in the center of the room, he made a declaration. "I'm going to play it. I don't care what she says, I'm going to play it," he said.

He put the cornet to his lips and blew two or three notes—so softly that even Will, sitting so closely, could barely hear. Then his eyes wavered. "My lip's no good," he said. He thrust the cornet at Will. "You blow it," he said.

Will sat on the edge of the bed and smiled. There was a notion floating in his mind now. Was there something, a thought in which one could find comfort? There was now, before him, standing before him in the room, a man who was, after all, not a man. He was a child as Will was too really, had always been such a child, would always be such a child. One need not be too afraid. Children were all about, everywhere. If one were a child and lost in a vast, empty space, one could at least talk to some other child. One could have conversations, understand perhaps something of the eternal childishness of oneself and others.

Will's thoughts were not very definite. He only felt suddenly warm and comfortable in the little room at the top of the boarding house.

And now the man was again explaining himself. He wanted to assert his manhood. "I stay up here," he explained, "and don't go down there, to sleep in the room with my wife because I don't want to. That's the only reason. I could if I wanted to. She has the bronchitis—but don't tell anyone. Women hate to have anyone told. She isn't so bad. I can do what I please."

He kept urging Will to put the cornet

to his lips and blow. There was in him an intense eagerness. "You can't really make any music—you don't know how—but that don't make any difference," he said. "The thing to do is to make a noise, make a deuce of a racket, blow like the devil."

Again Will felt like crying, but the sense of vastness and loneliness, that had been in him since he got aboard the train that night at Bidwell, had gone. "Well, I can't go on forever being a baby. Kate has a right to get married," he thought, putting the cornet to his lips. He blew two or three notes, softly.

"No, I tell you, no! That isn't the way! Blow on it! Don't be afraid! I tell you I want you to do it. Make a deuce of a racket! I tell you what, I own this house. We don't need to be afraid. We can do what we please. Go ahead! Make a deuce of a racket!" the old man kept pleading.

QUESTIONS

1. In what ways are the problems of the young man and the old man in this story similar?
2. The author of this story was attracted by the problems and moods of young people as material for fiction. His seemingly simple stories often have a surprising depth and universality. Does the story strike you as an accurate report of the ways of the young? Do you like the author's attitudes toward his characters? Would you call this, in any sense, a "moral" story? Is there any element of sadness in this story? Does the adjective "sad" in the title mean merely that the old man and the young man are frustrated?

HE DON'T PLANT COTTON

J. F. Powers
(1917–   )

Spring entered the black belt in ashes, dust, and drabness, without benefit of the saving green. The seasons were known only by the thermometer and the clothing of the people. There were only a few nights in the whole year when the air itself told you. Perhaps a night in April or May might escape the plague of smells, achieve a little of the enchantment, be the diminished echo of spring happening ardently in the suburbs, but it was all over in a night and the streets were filled with summer, as a hollow mouth with bad breath, and even the rain could not wash it away. And winter . . .

The beginning snow swirled in from the lake, dusting the streets with white. Baby squinted down the lonesome tracks. The wind twisted snow into his eyes, the flakes as sharp as sand, grinding, and his eyeballs were coated with cold tears. Baby worked his hands in his overcoat pockets to make heat. He saw a woman cross the street to catch the Big Red, which was coming now, but the woman refused stiffly to run for it. The wind went off hooting down the tracks ahead. Baby got on. The conductor held out one hand for the fare and yanked a cord twice with the other, prodding the red monster into motion.

Baby sat down inside. A cold breeze swept the floor, rattling old transfers and gum wrappers. Baby placed his feet uneasily on the heater to make the meager warmth funnel up his pants' legs. The dark flesh beneath the tuxedo was chilled to chalky gray at the joints. He listened to the wheels bump over the breaks in the track, and the warmth from the heater rose higher on his legs. He became warm and forgetful of the weather, except as scenery. The streets were paved evenly with snow twinkling soft and clean and white under the lights, and velvet red and green from the neon signs.

New York may be all right, he hummed to himself, but Beale Street's paved with gold. That's a lie, he thought; I been down on Beale. And Chicago, same way. All my life playing jobs in Chicago, and I still got to ride the Big Red. And that's no lie. Jobs were getting harder and harder to find. What they wanted was Mickey Mouse sound effects, singing strings, electric guitars, neon violins, even organs and accordions and harmonica teams. Hard to find a spot to play in, and when you did it was always a white place with drunken advertising men wanting to hear "a old song"—"My Wild Irish Rose" or "I Love You Truly." So you played it, of course, and plenty of schmaltz. And the college kids who wanted swing—any slick popular song. So you played that, too. And always you wanted to play the music you were born to, blue or fast, music that had no name. You managed somehow to play that, too, when there was a lull or the place was empty and you had to stay until 4 A.M. anyway.

Baby got off the streetcar and walked the same two blocks he saw every night except Tuesday. The wind had died down almost entirely and the snow whirled in big flakes end over end. Padding along, Baby told himself he liked winter better than summer. Then he came to the place, said, "How's it, Chief?" to the doorman, an Indian passing for Negro, went down three steps, and forgot all about winter and summer. It was always the same here. It was not so much a place of temperatures as a place of lights and shades and chromium, pastel mirrors, the smell of beer, rum, whisky, smoke—a stale blend of odors and shadows, darkness and music. It was a place of only one climate and that was it.

Baby's overcoat, hat, and scarf went into a closet and settled familiarly on hooks. His old tuxedo walked over to the traps. Its black hands rubbed together briskly, driving out the chill. One hand fumbled in the dark at the base of the big drum, and a second later a watery blue light winked on dully and flooded the drumhead, staring like a blind blue eye. Immediately the tuxedo sat down and worked its feet with a slight rasping noise into the floor. The fingers thumped testingly on the hide, tightened the snare. They knew, like the ears, when it was right. Gingerly, as always, the right foot sought the big drum's pedal. The tuxedo was not ready yet. It had to fidget and massage its seat around on the chair, stretch out its arms, and hug the whole outfit a fraction of an inch this way and that. Then the eyes glanced at the

piano player, signaling ready. The drumsticks paused a moment tensely, slid into the beat, barely heard, accenting perfectly the shower of piano notes. Everything worked together for two choruses. Then the piano player tapered his solo gently, so that at a certain point Baby knew it was his. He brought the number to a lifeless close, run down. Too early in the evening.

"Dodo," Baby said to the piano player, "Libby come in yet?"

Dodo sent a black hand up, slow as smoke, toward the ceiling. "Upstairs," he said, letting the hand fall to the keyboard with a faint, far-off chord. It stirred there, gently worming music from the battered upright. Notes drew nearer, riding on ships and camels through a world of sand and water, till they came forthright from the piano, taking on patterns, as the other black hand came to life on the bass keys, dear to Dodo. Baby picked up his sticks, recognizing the number. He called it "Dodo's Blues," though he knew Dodo called it nothing. Every night about this time, when there was no crowd and Dodo hadn't yet put on the white coat he wore servicing the bar, they would play it. Baby half closed his eyes. With pleasure he watched Dodo through the clouds of rhythm he felt shimmering up like heat from his drums. Baby's eyes were open only enough to frame Dodo like a picture; everything else was out. It was a picture of many dimensions; music was only one of them.

Here was a man, midgety, hunchbacked, black, and proud—mostly all back and music. A little man who, when he was fixing to play, had to look around for a couple of three-inch telephone directories. Piling them on top of the piano bench, he sat down, with all their names and streets and numbers and exchanges under him. He had very little of thighs and stomach—mostly just back, which threw a round shadow on the wall. When he leaned farther away from the piano, so the light slanted through his hands, his shadow revealed him walking on his hands down the keyboard, dancing on the tips of fingery toes. Sometimes it seemed to Baby through half-closed eyes, when Dodo's body was bobbing on the wall and his hands were feet dancing on the keyboard, as though the dim light shaped him into a gigantic, happy spider. When he became a spider you could forget he was a man, hunchbacked, runtish, black; and he, too, could forget perhaps that he had to be careful and proud. Perhaps he could be happy always if his back and size and color and pride were not always standing in the way. The piano made him whole. The piano taught him to find himself and jump clean over the moon. When he played, his feet never touched the pedals.

People were beginning to fill the place. They finished off the number, Baby smiling his admiration, Dodo scrupulously expressionless.

"For a young man . . ." Baby said.

Dodo got down off the telephone directories and threw them under the piano at the bass end, beyond the blue glow of the big drum. He had seen Libby come down the steps from the dressing room—a red dress, a gardenia. Dodo went behind the bar and put on his white service coat. Libby sat down at the piano.

Helplessly attracted, several men came over from the bar and leaned on the piano. They stared, burdening Libby's body with calculations. Singly at first and then, gathering unity, together. Libby sang a popular song. The men went back to the bar to get their drinks, which they brought over and set on top of the upright. Libby sang the words about lost love, and the men licked their lips vacantly. At the end of the song they clapped fiercely. Libby ignored them with a smile.

"Say, that was just fine," one man said. "Where you from anyhow?"

With a little grin Libby acknowledged Baby. Baby, beaming his veteran admiration of a fine young woman, nodded.

"Where you from? Huh?"

"New Orleans."

"Well, you don't say!" the man blurted out joyfully. "We're from down South, too . . . Mississippi, matter of fact!"

Icily, Libby smiled her appreciation of this coincidence. She looked at Baby, who was also registering appropriately. Just think of that! Small world! And welcome to our city!

"Well, what do you know!" crowed the gentleman from Mississippi. "So you're from down South!" He was greatly pleased and already very drunk. He eyed his friends, four or five of them, distributing his discovery equally among them.

"You never know," he explained. Then he appeared to suffer a pang of doubt. He turned quickly to Libby again, as though to make sure she was still there. His eyes jellied blearily and in them an idea was born.

"I know," he said. "Sing . . . sing—sing 'Ol' Man River' for the boys. They all'd sure like that."

Without responding, Libby looked down at her hands, smiling. She measured chords between her thumbs and little fingers, working her amusement into the keys. Baby stared at the mottled hide of his snare drum, at the big one's rim worn down from playing "Dixieland." The gentleman from Mississippi got worried.

"Aw, sing it," he pleaded. So Libby sang a chorus. The gentlemen from Mississippi were overwhelmed. They loved the song, they loved the South, the dear old Southland. Land of cotton, cinnamon seed, and sandy bottom. Look away! Look away! They loved themselves. Look away! Look away! There was the tiniest touch of satire in Libby's voice, a slightly overripe fervor. Baby caught it and behind the bar Dodo caught it, but the gentlemen did not. Dodo had put down the martini glass he was polishing and look away! look away!—good.

At the bridge of the second chorus, Libby nodded "Take it!" to Baby. He stood up, staggering from the heat of the fields, clenching his black, toilworn fists. In profound anguish, he hollered, giving the white folks his all, really knocking himself out.

"Tote that bar!
Lift that bale!
Git a little drunk—"

Baby grimaced in torment and did his best to look like ol' Uncle Tom out snatchin' cotton.

Behind the bar, unnoticed, Dodo's sad black face had turned beatific. "—And you land in jail!" Dodo could not see the other faces, the big white ones, but he could imagine them, the heads fixed and tilted. It was too dark in the place, and he could make out only blurrily the outlines of the necks. Ordinarily he was capable only of hating them. Now he had risen to great unfamiliar heights and was actually enjoying them. Surprised at this capacity in himself, yet proud he could feel this way, he was confused. He went further and started to pity them. But his memory stood up outraged at his forgetfulness and said, Kill that pity dead. Then he remembered he was really alone in the place. It was different with Libby and Baby, though they were black, too. He did not understand why. Say their skin was thicker—only that was not why. Probably this was not the first time they had jived white folks to death and them none the wiser. Dodo was not like that; he had to wait a long time for his kicks. From his heart no pity went out for the white men. He kept it all to himself, where it was needed. But he had to smile inside of him with Libby and Baby. Only more. Look at that fool Baby! Jam up!

> "Bend your knees!
> Bow your head!
> And pick that cotton!
> Tiiillllll you're dead!"

Baby sat down with a thud, exhausted. The gentlemen from Mississippi brayed their pleasure. My, it was good to see that black boy all sweatin' and perspirin' that way. They clapped furiously, called for drinks, gobbled . . .

"And bring some for the darkies!"

Baby swallowed some of his drink. He looked at the beaten rim of the big drum, then at the sticks. He took out his pocketknife and scraped the rough, splintery places smooth. He glanced at Libby and ventured the kind of smile he felt and knew she did.

He finished his drink. The gentlemen from Mississippi hung around the piano, getting drunker, shouting in one another's faces. Nervously Libby lighted a cigarette. A college boy tried to make conversation with her while his honey-haired girl assumed an attitude of genuine concern.

"Can you play 'Hot Lips'?" He was the real American Boy.

"Don't know it," Libby lied. She wished she didn't.

"Can you play 'Sugar Blues'?" Right back. "Don't know it."

One of the Mississippi gentlemen, who had been hanging back, crowded up to the piano, making his move. He drained his drink and pushed closer to the piano so as to brush Libby's left hand with the front of his trousers. Libby moved her hand, sounding a chord that Baby caught. The gentleman, grinning lewdly, tried to follow her hand up the keyboard.

"That's all right," he snickered. "Play lots of bass, honey."

The first gentleman from Mississippi, drink in hand, stumbled over from the bar. He told Libby to play that "Ol' Man River" song some more. Libby hesitated. Then she lit into it, improvising all around it, and it was a pleasure for Baby, but the first gentleman from Mississippi was not happy. He said if that was the best she could do she had better try singing. Libby sang only one chorus. The gentlemen from Mississippi, though they applauded, were not gratified. There was an air of petulance among them. They remembered another time they heard the song, but it was not clear now what had made it different and better. They saw Baby all right, but they did not remember that he was the one who had sung before, the good one that toted their bars, lifted their bales, and landed drunk in their jails. Something was wrong, but they saw no remedy. Each gentleman suspected the fault was personal, what with him drinking so heavy and all.

Dodo, behind the bar, had not enjoyed the song the last time, hating the coercion the white men worked on Libby and Baby, and feared his advantage was slipping away. In a minute he would be hating them to pieces again.

"Can you play 'Tiger Rag'?" The American Boy was back.

"No." Libby made a face and then managed to turn it into a smile for him. He held his drink up for the world to see on the night before the big game.

The honey-haired girl wrenched her face into a winning smile and hit the jack pot. "Can you play 'St. Louis Blues'?"

"How you want it?" Libby said. She put out her cigarette. "Blues, rhumba . . . what kind a way?"

"Oh, play it low down. The way *you people* play it." So Libby would understand, she executed a ponderous wink, narrowed her eyes, and made them glitter wantonly behind the lashes. *"You* know," she said.

Libby knew. She played "St. Louis," losing herself in it with Baby. She left the college boy and the honey-haired girl behind. She forgot she knew. She gazed at Baby with her eyes dreamy, unseeing, blind with the blue drum, her head nodding in that wonderful, graceful way. Baby saw his old tuxedo in the mirror, its body shimmying on the chair, and he was pleased. The drums, beating figures, rocked with a steady roll. They were playing "Little Rock Getaway" now, the fine, young-woman music.

And Libby was pleased, watching Baby. And then, somehow, he vanished for her into the blue drum. The sticks still danced at an oblique angle on the snare, but there were no hands to them and Libby could not see Baby on the chair. She could only feel him somewhere in the blue glow. Abandoning herself, she lost herself in the piano. Now, still without seeing him, she could feel him with a clarity and warmth beyond vision. Miniature bell notes, mostly blue, blossomed ecstatically, perished *affettuoso,* weaving themselves down into the dark beauty of the lower keys, because it was closer to the drum, and multiplied. They came back to "St. Louis" again.

"Stop." The first gentleman from Mississippi touched Libby on the arm. "When I do

that to you, that means 'Stop,'" he said. Libby chorded easily. "Some of the boys like to hear that 'Ol' Man River' some more." He straightened up, turning to the other gentlemen, his smile assuring them it would not be long now.

"Kick off," Baby sighed.

But Libby broke into "St. Louis" again. Baby, with a little whoop, came clambering after, his sticks slicing into the drum rim, a staccato "Dixieland."

The first gentleman frowned, touching Libby's arm, "Remember what that means? Means 'Ol' Man River,'" he said calmly, as though correcting a slight error. "Toot sweet. Know what that means? That's French. Means right now." No harm done, however. Just that his friends here, a bunch of boys from down South, were dying to hear that song again—up to him to see that they got satisfaction—knew there would be no trouble about it.

"We'll play it for you later on," Libby said quickly. "We got some other requests besides yours. How many you got now, Baby?"

Baby held up eight fingers, very prompt.

"Coming up," he said.

The first gentleman was undecided. "Well . . ." he drawled. Libby began a popular song. The first gentleman faced his friends. His eyes more or less met theirs and found no agreement. The boys looked kind of impatient, like a bunch of boys out for a little fun and not doing so well. He turned to Libby again.

"We just gotta have that 'Ol' Man River' some more. Boys all got their hearts set on it," he said. "Right away! Toot sweet! Toot—away!" There he'd gone and made a joke, and the boys all laughed and repeated it to each other. Libby played on, as though she had not heard. The first gentleman took hold of her arm. She gazed steadily up into his bleary eyes.

"Not now. Later."

"No, you don't. You gotta play it right now. For a bunch of boys from down South. They all got a hankerin' to hear that 'Ol' Man River' some more."

"So you best play it," another gentleman

said, leaning down hard on the old upright piano. "On account of I'm gonna take and give ear. We kinda like how that old song sounds up North. Whatcha all need. The drummer will sing," he said, and looked at Baby. Baby looked back, unsmiling.

Libby chorded lightly, waiting for the gentlemen from Mississippi to get tired. They could not see how it was with her and Baby—never.

"You ain't gonna play?"

Baby's eyes strained hard in their sockets.

"We ain't comin'," Libby said.

Baby's eyes relaxed and he knew the worst part was over. They felt the same way about it. They had made up their minds. The rest was easy. Baby was even a little glad it had happened. A feeling was growing within him that he had wanted to do this for a long time—for years and years, in a hundred different places he had played.

Secretly majestic, Baby sat at his drums, the goal of countless uplifted eyes—beseeching him. For it seemed that hordes of white people were far below him, making their little commotions and noises, asking favors of him, like Lord, please bring the rain, or Lord, please take it away. Lord Baby. Waves of warm exhilaration washed into him, endearing him to himself. No, he smiled, I am sorry, no favors today. Yes, Lord, they all said, if that's the way it is, so be it.

But somebody objected. The manager's voice barked, far below, scarcely audible to Baby in his new eminence. ". . . honoring requests," he heard, and ". . . trouble with the local," and ". . . wanting to get a sweet-swing trio in this place a long time now." And the manager, strangely small, an excited, pale pygmy, explaining to the gentlemen from Mississippi, also small, how it was, "That's all I can do in the circumstances," and them saying, "Well, I guess so; well, I guess so all right; don't pay to pamper 'em, to give 'em an inch."

Baby noticed Libby had got up from the piano and put on her coat, the long dress hanging out at the bottom, red.

"I won't change," she said, and handed Baby the canvas cover for the snare drum.

"Huh?" Baby said foggily. He set about taking his traps apart. Dodo, not wearing his white service coat, came over to help.

"You don't have to," Baby said.

Chief, freezing outside in his long, fancy maroon coat, opened the door for them. "You all through, Baby?"

"Yeah, Chief. You told that right."

They walked down the street toward the car line. Baby, going first, plowed a path for Libby and Dodo in the snow. Window sills, parked cars, and trees were padded with it. The wind was dead and buried. Baby bore the big drum on his shoulder and felt the sticks pressing tight and upright in his vest pockets, two on each side. Libby had her purse and street clothes rolled up under her arm. Dodo carried the snare drum.

Softly as snow, Libby laughed, "That's all I can do in the circumstances," she said.

"I got your old circumstances," Baby said.

Then they were silent, tramping in the snow.

At the corner they waited in a store entrance for a southbound streetcar. Libby raised a foot now and then, shuddering with cold. Dead still, Dodo breathed down inside the collar of his overcoat, retarding his breath, frowning at the little smoke trickling out, as though it were the only thing left in the world to remind him he was alive. Baby talked of taking a cab and finally did go out into the street to hail one approaching. It slowed up, pulled over to the curb, hesitated . . . and lurched away, with Baby's hand reaching for the door. Baby watched the cab speed down the snowy street, following it for a few steps, speechless. There was nothing to do. Without looking, he saw Libby and Dodo shivering in the store entrance. They had seen the cab come and go. They had not moved an inch. They waited unfooled, as before, for the Big Red.

"What's wrong with you, Baby?" Libby called out. A tiny moment of silence, and she was laughing, gradually louder, mellow octaves of it, mounting, pluming . . .

Like her piano, it seemed to Baby—that fine, young-woman laughter.

"Why you laugh so much, woman?" he inquired plaintively from the street. Then he moved to join them, a few steps only, dallying at the curb to temper the abruptness of his retreat. Like her piano on "Little Rock" —that fine, young-woman laughter.

IN ANOTHER COUNTRY

Ernest Hemingway
(1898–   )

In the fall the war was always there, but we did not go to it any more. It was cold in the fall in Milan and the dark came very early. Then the electric lights came on, and it was pleasant along the streets looking in the windows. There was much game hanging outside the shops, and the snow powdered in the fur of the foxes and the wind blew their tails. The deer hung stiff and heavy and empty, and small birds blew in the wind and the wind turned their feathers. It was a cold fall and the wind came down from the mountains.

We were all at the hospital every afternoon, and there were different ways of walking across the town through the dusk to the hospital. Two of the ways were alongside canals, but they were long. Always, though, you crossed a bridge across a canal to enter the hospital. There was a choice of three bridges. On one of them a woman sold roasted chestnuts. It was warm, standing in front of her charcoal fire, and the chestnuts were warm afterward in your pocket. The hospital was very old and very beautiful, and you entered through a gate and walked across a courtyard and out a gate on the other side. There were usually funerals starting from the courtyard. Beyond the old hospital were the new brick pavilions, and there we met every afternoon and were all very polite and interested in what was the matter, and sat in the machines that were to make so much difference.

The doctor came up to the machine where I was sitting and said: "What did you like best to do before the war? Did you practice a sport?"

I said: "Yes, football."

"Good," he said. "You will be able to play football again better than ever."

My knee did not bend and the leg dropped straight from the knee to the ankle without a calf, and the machine was to bend the knee and make it move as in riding a tricycle. But it did not bend yet, and instead the machine lurched when it came to the bending part. The doctor said: "That will all pass. You are a fortunate young man. You will play football again like a champion."

In the next machine was a major who had a little hand like a baby's. He winked at me when the doctor examined his hand, which was between two leather straps that bounced up and down and flapped the stiff fingers, and said: "And will I too play football, captain-doctor?" He had been a very great fencer, and before the war the greatest fencer in Italy.

The doctor went to his office in a back room and brought a photograph which showed a hand that had been withered almost as small as the major's, before it had taken a machine course, and after was a little larger. The major held the photograph with his good hand and looked at it very carefully. "A wound?" he asked.

"An industrial accident," the doctor said.

"Very interesting, very interesting," the major said, and handed it back to the doctor.

"You have confidence?"

"No," said the major.

There were three boys who came each day who were about the same age I was. They were all three from Milan, and one of them was to be a lawyer, and one was to be a painter, and one had intended to be a soldier, and after we were finished with the machines, sometimes we walked back together to the Café Cova, which was next door to the Scala. We walked the short way through the communist quarter because we were four together. The people hated us because we were officers, and from a wineshop someone called out, "A basso gli ufficiali!" as we passed. Another boy who walked with us sometimes and made us five wore a black silk handkerchief across his face because he had no nose then and his face was to be rebuilt. He had gone out to the front from the military academy and been wounded within an hour after he had gone into the front line for the first time. They rebuilt his face, but he came from a very old family and they could never get the nose exactly right. He went to South America and worked in a bank. But this was a long time ago, and then we did not any of us know how it was going to be afterward. We only knew then that there was always the war, but that we were not going to it any more.

We all had the same medals, except the boy with the black silk bandage across his face, and he had not been at the front long enough to get any medals. The tall boy with a very pale face who was to be a lawyer had been a lieutenant of Arditi and had three medals of the sort we each had only one of. He had lived a very long time with death and was a little detached. We were all a little detached, and there was nothing that held us together except that we met every afternoon at the hospital. Although, as we walked to the Cova through the tough part of town, walking in the dark, with light and singing coming out of the wineshops, and sometimes having to walk into the street when the men and women would crowd together on the sidewalk so that we would have had to jostle them to get by, we felt held together by there being something that had happened that they, the people who disliked us, did not understand.

We ourselves all understood the Cova, where it was rich and warm and not too brightly lighted, and noisy and smoky at certain hours, and there were always girls at the tables and the illustrated papers on a rack on the wall. The girls at the Cova were very patriotic, and I found that the most patriotic people in Italy were the café girls—and I believe they are still patriotic.

The boys at first were very polite about my medals and asked me what I had done to get them. I showed them the papers, which were written in very beautiful language and full of *fratellanza* and *abnegazione,* but which really said, with the adjectives removed, that I had been given the medals because I was an American. After that their manner changed a little toward me, although I was their friend against outsiders. I was a friend, but I was never really one of them after they had read the citations, because it had been different with them and they had done very different things to get their medals. I had been wounded, it was true; but we all knew that being wounded, after all, was really an accident. I was never ashamed of the ribbons, though, and sometimes, after the cocktail hour, I would imagine myself having done all the things they had done to get their medals; but walking home at night through the empty streets with the cold wind and all the shops closed, trying to keep near the street lights, I knew that I would never have done such things, and I was very much afraid to die, and often lay in bed at night by myself, afraid to die and wondering how I would be when I went back to the front again.

The three with the medals were like hunting-hawks; and I was not a hawk, although I might seem a hawk to those who had never hunted; they, the three, knew better and so we drifted apart. But I stayed good friends with the boy who had been wounded his first day at the front, because he would never know now how he would have turned out; so he could never be accepted either, and I liked him because I thought perhaps he would not have turned out to be a hawk either.

The major, who had been the great fencer, did not believe in bravery, and spent much time while we sat in the machines correcting my grammar. He had complimented me on how I spoke Italian, and we talked together very easily. One day I had said that Italian seemed such an easy language to me that I could not take a great interest in it; everything was so easy to say. "Ah, yes," the major said. "Why, then, do you not take up the use of grammar?" So we took up the use of grammar, and soon Italian was such a difficult language that I was afraid to talk to him until I had the grammar straight in my mind.

The major came very regularly to the hospital. I do not think he ever missed a day, although I am sure he did not believe in the machines. There was a time when none of us believed in the machines, and one day the major said it was all nonsense. The machines were new then and it was we who were to prove them. It was an idiotic idea, he said, "a theory, like another." I had not learned my grammar, and he said I was a stupid impossible disgrace, and he was a fool to have bothered with me. He was a small man and he sat straight up in his chair with his right hand thrust into the machine and looked straight ahead at the wall while the straps thumped up and down with his fingers in them.

"What will you do when the war is over if it is over?" he asked me. "Speak grammatically!"

"I will go to the States."

"Are you married?"

"No, but I hope to be."

"The more of a fool you are," he said. He seemed very angry. "A man must not marry."

"Why, Signor Maggiore?"

"Don't call me 'Signor Maggiore.' "

"Why must not a man marry?"

"He cannot marry. He cannot marry," he said angrily. "If he is to lose everything, he should not place himself in a position to lose that. He should not place himself in a position to lose. He should find things he cannot lose."

He spoke very angrily and bitterly, and looked straight ahead while he talked.

"But why should he necessarily lose it?"

"He'll lose it," the major said. He was looking at the wall. Then he looked down at the machine and jerked his little hand out from between the straps and slapped it hard against his thigh. "He'll lose it," he almost shouted. "Don't argue with me!" Then he called to the attendant who ran the machines. "Come and turn this damned thing off."

He went back into the other room for the light treatment and the massage. Then I heard him ask the doctor if he might use his telephone and he shut the door. When he came back into the room, I was sitting in another machine. He was wearing his cape and had his cap on, and he came directly toward

my machine and put his arm on my shoulder.

"I am so sorry," he said, and patted me on the shoulder with his good hand. "I would not be rude. My wife has just died. You must forgive me."

"Oh—" I said, feeling sick for him. "I am *so* sorry."

He stood there biting his lower lip. "It is very difficult," he said. "I cannot resign myself."

He looked straight past me and out through the window. Then he began to cry. "I am utterly unable to resign myself," he said and choked. And then crying, his head up looking at nothing, carrying himself straight and soldierly, with tears on both his cheeks and biting his lips, he walked past the machines and out the door.

The doctor told me that the major's wife, who was very young and whom he had not married until he was definitely invalided out of the war, had died of pneumonia. She had been sick only a few days. No one expected her to die. The major did not come to the hospital for three days. Then he came at the usual hour, wearing a black band on the sleeve of his uniform. When he came back, there were large framed photographs around the wall, of all sorts of wounds before and after they had been cured by the machines. In front of the machine the major used were three photographs of hands like his that were completely restored. I do not know where the doctor got them. I always understood we were the first to use the machines. The photographs did not make much difference to the major because he only looked out of the window.

STICKMAN'S LAUGHTER

Nelson Algren
(1909–   )

Banty Longobardi trudged up his own back steps; his cap was in his hand and his pay on his hip. He'd take the old woman to the Little Pulaski—triple horror feature with blue enamel ovenware to the ladies and community singing.

But the door was locked and the woman was out, so he went down the steps again. She ought to know better than to go visiting on a community-singing, free-ovenware night.

He came to the alley beneath the El, where Punchdrunk Murphy so patiently watched, before the gamblers' door. Punchdrunk let him pass by raising one arm, and he stood at the dice table just to watch. The stickman pointed the stick at Banty; but Banty kept his pay in his pocket.

"I'm cold," he explained, when the dice came by again, meaning the dice didn't yet feel right to his hand. He opened his collar, the place was so warm, and unbuttoned the pocket where the week's pay hid. When they came by again he felt a bit warmer. Bought two chips for a dollar and bet them both on the field. Saw the dice turn a five and watched the banker making two chips four. Let the four ride, without betting on a pass, and saw a ten come up. So he pinched his little package and let some spook beside him finish his hand.

"Four soldiers to the good," he assured himself, "that's got it over community singin'. That's eight double features, any night of the week." She could go by herself or take Mrs. Prystalski some evening when he was putting in overtime. He felt them coming his way again as though bringing him money from home.

At half-past eight Banty had forty chips. At a quarter of nine he had ninety and had torn the top button off his shirt. At ten after ten he cashed in for forty dollars, and the stickman pointed jokingly with the stick while Banty tried buttoning a button that wasn't there.

"Tell 'em where you got it, Shorty," he advised Banty Longobardi, "'n how easy it was."

Banty left through Murphy's door. He picked his way down the littered tunnel of the El, seeing the places where the gray cats lived and smelling the tar-wagon smell where someone's roof was being repaired in the summer weather. He heard the rush of city waters, beneath the city streets, and the passionate passing of the day's last express. So came again to his own back steps and trudged up a flight with a way roll clutched in his bumpy, toughened little palm. And the old pay roll still on his hip.

But the door was locked and the woman was out, and Banty stood alone in the yellow kitchen. He stood beneath an unshaded bulb, the yellow light on his broken face, and walked into the tiny bedroom as into a stranger's place. There was nothing to see in there, however, but a disheveled bed with a chemise among the covers. He felt done in for a moment and sat on the bed's very edge, rubbing the nob of his nose. He had had the bridge of it removed ten years before, at a promoter's urging, when he wasn't yet twenty and had won four professional bouts. The promoter's theory had been that Banty would have earned enough, by the time he retired, to buy a wax bridge. The theory hadn't worked out: Banty sat swinging a pavement-colored cap between his knees without any bridge at all and tired enough for any two men. But when his head touched the pillow he felt alone all over again, and rose.

He left the bedroom light burning.

"To show her I been in here too," he considered sulkily, and pulled a half-gallon empty from under the kitchen sink—an empty was good for a sixteen-ouncer by Bruno the bartender any time.

He sat in the abandoned tavern before a schooner of winter beer. Why couldn't she have been home the one time he'd won? Once he'd lost his check at blackjack and had mumbled that he'd been jackrolled. She'd caught him in the lie, and he'd tried to convince her that she'd misunderstood: he hadn't said "jackroll," he'd said "blackjack." That was when she'd started laughing, he'd sounded that silly. But the way she'd laughed—it had let him laugh with her. That was how that one had ended. Some old woman.

Once he'd dropped ten dollars on something called Harp Weaver at Boston and she'd been home then too.

But this time, when he'd put them two

months up on the landlord, she was gone for hours. And he didn't want to gamble any more. Banty felt he didn't want to gamble again the rest of his life. "A man's got to quit it sometime, and when he's thirty and a working stiff, then that's as good a time as any," he assured himself.

It didn't matter to him where his girl was. Wherever she was, she was taking care of herself. But he wanted her by his side, to take care of him now.

" 'What is life without a wife?' " he hummed idly, tapping the sweating glass with his stubby fingers. He had jammed the knuckles of the hand in his last bout, and in moments like this the knuckles ached a little: tapping them relieved the ache.

Then he had three shots, to relieve the ache further, and began wondering how long he'd been gone. He didn't want to drink up too much of the extra pay roll; but he'd give her plenty of time to get home and miss him a spell too.

Knowing that she was at her mother's didn't make the minutes pass any faster. And to her mother's was the only place she ever went that Banty didn't want to come along too. Her people didn't trust wops. They said things in Polish about Dagos that made Banty wish, sometimes, that he was a flannel-mouth Polak too.

The bartender was a flannelmouth. Everyone in the ward was a flannelmouth. Banty threw two slugs down his throat in rapid succession, waited till they hit his stomach, then wandered idly over to the bar.

"C'mere," Banty commanded.

Bruno the bartender bent an ear over the pretzels. Banty leaned over, his pudgy palms gripping the bar's edge, and whispered confidentially:

"Can I say somethin'?"

"Go ahead."

"I wanta say somethin'."

"Okay, okay, go ahead and say something."

"What should I say?"

The bartender turned away, but Banty caught his sleeve.

"God *damn,* what kind of man are you, tellin' me t' say somethin'?"

Bruno the bartender brushed Banty off his sleeve, folded his arms on the bar, and leaned toward his customer with huge patience.

"Look, I not tell *you* what to say. *You* want to say something by me. Okay. Free country. I'm wait. You say."

"Okay," Banty said suddenly, "I'll say it! Chickory-chick-chala-chala—how's *that?*" He was proud of himself.

Bruno the bartender studied him one long moment. "Now I'll tell *you* something," Bruno said. "Your old lady just went by. You go home by her."

"Ler her wait," Banty answered. "Let her wait till I'm good 'n ready."

"You lose your money," Bruno warned him.

Banty put his hand across his eyes because a light was in them. He saw a string attached to the light and stood up to pull it, to make everything dark like everything should be.

Everything got dark all right, and got dark with a roaring; the dark was a roaring in his head and he came to hearing the thunder of the Garfield Park local overheard and seeing the littered places, between the beams, where the gray cats lived. He heard the local slowing toward Damen. Saw Murphy opening a familiar door.

"It don't mean a thing if it don't cross the string," someone intoned warningly. But added hopefully, "Double your money 'n beat the banker."

He edged to the table, as curious as though he'd never seen a dice game in his life. A nice little package for anyone's starter, and he made an effort to remember whether he'd paid for them yet. Banty didn't want to cheat anyone.

"It ain't hard—nobody's barred . . ."

When he looked at the package again it was smaller. But in a moment it was almost as high as before. He wanted to ask them what he was doing and when she'd get home. But if he asked them something like that they could tell he was drunk and would start cheating, he thought cunningly. He fitted the table's edge into his palms to keep from falling backward onto his skull.

"When I'm in a public place," he explained obscurely, "that's where I am."

But no one was listening any more, and Bruno had told him something and now he'd gone and forgotten it.

The pile grew again. And grew a little more. Until, all of a sudden, it was the smallest pile he had ever seen and everyone was smiling, because it wasn't there at all. He felt the dice between his fingers and knew there was something he'd just forgotten to do. He shook absently and remembered at last: he'd forgotten to pinch his package. The stickman touched Banty's hand: the boy was shaking, but nothing was riding.

"What goes?" the stickman asked.

Banty reached uncertainly to his hip, pulled out the pay roll he'd worked for and slapped it down with the flat of his palm on pass. He saw one dice cross the string and turn up an ace while the other rolled endlessly on—bounced against the table's guard and hurried anxiously back toward its resting mate. An inch away from the ace it wavered between a deuce and a six, then rolled wearily over on its back. Double ace. Snake-eyes.

The aces looked up at Banty with such sober reproach that he felt his own head clearing. He returned their stare, pleadingly, and they looked back as though saying, "Sorry, pal, we done our best." And the stickman pointing his mocking stick:

"Tell 'em where you got it, Shorty, 'n how easy it was."

"Where's my pack-age?" Banty demanded, wanting to be drunk again so badly that he pronounced each word distinctly and too politely.

"Where at is my pack-age?"

"You put the pack-age on, friend."

"The whole pack-age?"

"The whole pack-age."

Banty swayed. They'd done it again.

"How do I feel?" he asked hopelessly. And then he began getting mad.

"I don't know," the stickman answered solemnly, "but you look like the wrath of God."

Banty rolled up his left sleeve to the shoulder. The muscle was tattooed with a pair of boxing gloves. He flexed the gloves in front of the stickman.

"What's that for?" the stickman asked.

"That's the Army," Banty explained.

He stood a moment, thinking it all over, rolling up the other sleeve to expose the right muscle. That one was tattooed with a broken heart.

"What's *that* for?" someone that sounded like Punchdrunk Murphy asked on his other side.

"That's the Navy," Banty explained. But his voice sounded intimidated to his own ear when he felt Murphy's fist grip his arm, urging him through the shadowed door, and he went humbly.

When Banty tried his own back door, the knob turned easily. The light he had left in the bedroom was out. He sensed her lying awake in the dark, worrying about where he'd been with the rent. Knowing that she did not speak because she did not want him lying to her, knowing that she could tell where he'd been, by his movements, without making him lie like a schoolboy. Sometimes he almost wished she'd ask foolish questions like other women did. And get fooled by the answers, too.

He undressed in the kitchen, wishing that there were a front room with one of those fancy red plush sofas in it so he could crawl onto it on nights like this and pretend to her, in the morning, that he'd been too drunk to know where he was lying down, he couldn't remember a thing. "I'd like to set on plush anyhow," he thought wonderingly. "I never set on plush in my life. I bet she'd like settin' on plush too."

"Banty!"

As though she'd read his mind. As though they had a plush couch and he'd been planning to evade her for a few hours with it. He did not reply. Maybe she'd ask him something foolish just this once, and he'd give her an answer as mocking as the stickman's laughter.

"You went out of the house 'n left all the lights on and the back door wide open."

"I thought somebody'd come in 'n leave us somethin'— Ha! Ha!"

His laughter broke. It hadn't sounded like the stickman's after all.

He stood in the bedroom doorway in his long workman's underwear, shifting on his naked feet. She sat up and pulled on the light.

"What's the matter with you? Quit disguisin' your eyes. There. Look at me. You look drunk. Come over here."

She certainly had her own way of putting things, the old woman. He took his hands off his eyes, ceasing the pretense of shielding them from the light, and wished humbly again that he were a Polak, feeling somehow that that would fix everything. He tried to think whether Punchdrunk Murphy were a Polak, but couldn't decide. If he just wasn't a wop, things like this wouldn't be happening to him week in and week out.

Every time you saw in the papers that some guy was going to the chair, it was a Dago. Why didn't they fry a Greek or a Swede for a change?

"Are you coming to bed or are you going to stand there on one foot all night?"

When she saw him shuffling toward her she switched off the light and lay back waiting for him in the dark. When he reached the bed he had only to wait for her to take his head on her breast.

That's the kind of old woman Banty had himself.

"My fault," she assured him softly, like a storyteller making up stories to put a child to sleep. "I knew it was payday but I went out just the same. No supper for poor Banty either. Poor Banty. Lost all his money and no supper either. Wanted to go to community singing and got hisself drunked up instead."

She felt his tenseness lessening. Felt his tears between the shadowed valley of her breasts. And knew they were for her.

His body jerked a little, once, as it relaxed toward sleep. She held him so, watching the dim carnations of the wall, till his breath began coming regularly and untroubled. When his hand clutched at hers in sleep she smiled a little: she could feel the place in the hand where the knuckles had jammed.

So nothing important had been lost after all.

THE NEW VILLA

Anton Chekhov
(1860–1904)

Two miles from the village of Obrutcha-novo a huge bridge was being built. From the village, which stood up high on the steep river-bank, its trellis-like skeleton could be seen, and in foggy weather and on still winter days, when its delicate iron girders and all the scaffolding around was covered with hoar frost, it presented a picturesque and even fantastic spectacle. Kutcherov, the engineer who was building the bridge, a stout, broad-shouldered, bearded man in a soft crumpled cap drove through the village in his racing droshky or his open carriage. Now and then on holidays navvies working on the bridge would come to the village; they begged for alms, laughed at the women, and sometimes carried off something. But that was rare; as a rule the days passed quietly and peacefully as though no bridge-building were going on, and only in the evening, when camp fires gleamed near the bridge, the wind faintly wafted the songs of the navvies. And by day there was sometimes the mournful clang of metal, don-don-don.

It happened that the engineer's wife came to see him. She was pleased with the river-banks and the gorgeous view over the green valley with trees, churches, flocks, and she began begging her husband to buy a small piece of ground and to build them a cottage on it. Her husband agreed. They bought sixty acres of land, and on the high bank in a field, where in earlier days the cows of Obrutcha-novo used to wander, they built a pretty house of two storeys with a terrace and a verandah, with a tower and a flagstaff on which a flag fluttered on Sundays—they built it in about three months, and then all the winter they were planting big trees, and when spring came and everything began to be green there were already avenues to the new house, a gardener and two labourers in white aprons were digging near it, there was a little fountain, and a globe of looking-glass flashed so brilliantly that it was painful to look at. The house had already been named the New Villa.

On a bright, warm morning at the end of May two horses were brought to Obrutcha-novo to the village blacksmith, Rodion Pe-trov. They came from the New Villa. The horses were sleek, graceful beasts, as white as snow, and strikingly alike.

"Perfect swans!" said Rodion, gazing at them with reverent admiration.

His wife Stepanida, his children and grandchildren came out into the street to look at them. By degrees a crowd collected. The Lytchkovs, father and son, both men with swollen faces and entirely beardless, came up bareheaded. Kozov, a tall, thin old man with a long, narrow beard, came up lean-ing on a stick with a crook handle: he kept winking with his crafty eyes and smiling ironically as though he knew something.

"It's only that they are white; what is there in them?" he said. "Put mine on oats, and they will be just as sleek. They ought to be in a plough and with a whip, too. . . ."

The coachman simply looked at him with disdain, but did not utter a word. And after-wards, while they were blowing up the fire at the forge, the coachman talked while he smoked cigarettes. The peasants learned from him various details: his employers were wealthy people; his mistress, Elena Ivanovna, had till her marriage lived in Moscow in a poor way as a governess; she was kind-hearted, compassionate, and fond of helping the poor. On the new estate, he told them, they were not going to plough or to sow, but simply to live for their pleasure, live only to breathe the fresh air. When he had finished and led the horses back a crowd of boys fol-lowed him, the dogs barked, and Kozov, look-ing after him, winked sarcastically.

"Landowners, too-oo!" he said. "They have built a house and set up horses, but I bet they are nobodies—landowners, too-oo."

Kozov for some reason took a dislike from the first to the new house, to the white horses, and to the handsome, well-fed coachman. Kozov was a solitary man, a widower; he had a dreary life (he was prevented from work-ing by a disease which he sometimes called a rupture and sometimes worms); he was maintained by his son, who worked at a con-fectioner's in Harkov and sent him money; and from early morning till evening he saun-tered at leisure about the river or about the village; if he saw, for instance, a peasant cart-ing a log, or fishing, he would say: "That log's dry wood—it is rotten," or, "They won't bite in weather like this." In times of drought he would declare that there would not be a drop of rain till the frost came; and when the rains came he would say that everything would rot in the fields, that everything was ruined. And as he said these things he would wink as though he knew something.

At the New Villa they burned Bengal lights and sent up fireworks in the evenings, and a sailing-boat with red lanterns floated by Obrutchanovo. One morning the engi-neer's wife, Elena Ivanovna, and her little daughter drove to the village in a carriage with yellow wheels and a pair of dark bay ponies; both mother and daughter were wearing broadbrimmed straw hats, bent down over their ears.

This was exactly at the time when they were carting manure, and the blacksmith Rodion, a tall, gaunt old man, bareheaded and barefooted, was standing near his dirty and repulsive-looking cart and, flustered, looked at the ponies, and it was evident by his face that he had never seen such little horses before.

"The Kutcherov lady has come!" was whispered around. "Look, the Kutcherov lady has come!"

Elena Ivanovna looked at the huts as though she were selecting one, and then stopped at the very poorest, at the windows of which there were so many children's heads —flaxen, red, and dark. Stepanida, Rodion's wife, a stout woman, came running out of the hut; her kerchief slipped off her grey head; she looked at the carriage facing the sun, and her face smiled and wrinkled up as though she were blind.

"This is for your children," said Elena Ivanovna, and she gave her three roubles.

Stepanida suddenly burst into tears and bowed down to the ground. Rodion, too, flopped to the ground, displaying his brownish bald head, and as he did so he almost caught his wife in the ribs with the fork. Elena Ivanovna was overcome with confusion and drove back.

2

The Lytchkovs, father and son, caught in their meadows two cart-horses, a pony, and a broad-faced Aalhaus bull-calf, and with the help of redheaded Volodka, son of the blacksmith Rodion, drove them to the village. They called the village elder, collected witnesses, and went to look at the damage.

"All right, let 'em!" said Kozov, winking, "le-et 'em! Let them get out of it if they can, the engineers! Do you think there is no such thing as law? All right! Send for the police inspector, draw up a statement! . . ."

"Draw up a statement," repeated Volodka.

"I don't want to let this pass!" shouted the younger Lytchkov. He shouted louder and louder, and his beardless face seemed to be more and more swollen. "They've set up a nice fashion! Leave them free, and they will ruin all the meadows! You've no sort of right to ill-treat people! We are not serfs now!"

"We are not serfs now!" repeated Volodka.

"We got on all right without a bridge," said the elder Lytchkov gloomily; "we did not ask for it. What do we want a bridge for? We don't want it!"

"Brothers, good Christians, we cannot leave it like this!"

"All right, let 'em!" said Kozov, winking. "Let them get out of it if they can! Land-owners, indeed!"

They went back to the village, and as they walked the younger Lytchkov beat himself on the breast with his fist and shouted all the way, and Volodka shouted, too, repeating his words. And meanwhile quite a crowd had gathered in the village round the thorough-bred bull-calf and the horses. The bull-calf was embarrassed and looked up from under

his brows, but suddenly lowered his muzzle to the ground and took to his heels, kicking up his hind legs; Kozov was frightened and waved his stick at him, and they all burst out laughing. Then they locked up the beasts and waited.

In the evening the engineer sent five roubles for the damage, and the two horses, the pony and the bull-calf, without being fed or given water, returned home, their heads hanging with a guilty air as though they were convicted criminals.

On getting the five roubles the Lytchkovs, father and son, the village elder and Volodka, punted over the river in a boat and went to a hamlet on the other side where there was a tavern, and there had a long carousal. Their singing and the shouting of the younger Lytchkov could be heard from the village. Their women were uneasy and did not sleep all night. Rodion did not sleep either.

"It's a bad business," he said, sighing and turning from side to side. "The gentleman will be angry, and then there will be trouble. . . . They have insulted the gentleman. . . . Oh, they've insulted him. It's a bad business. . . ."

It happened that the peasants, Rodion amongst them, went into their forest to divide the clearings for mowing, and as they were returning home they were met by the engineer. He was wearing a red cotton shirt and high boots; a setter dog with its long tongue hanging out, followed behind him.

"Good-day, brothers," he said.

The peasants stopped and took off their hats.

"I have long wanted to have a talk with you, friends," he went on. "This is what it is. Ever since the early spring your cattle have been in my copse and garden every day. Everything is trampled down; the pigs have rooted up the meadow, are ruining everything in the kitchen garden, and all the undergrowth in the copse is destroyed. There is no getting on with your herdsmen; one asks them civilly, and they are rude. Damage is done on my estate every day and I do nothing—I don't fine you or make a complaint; meanwhile you impounded my horses and my bull-calf and exacted five roubles. Was that right? Is that neighbourly?" he went on, and his face was so soft and persuasive, and his expression was not forbidding. "Is that the way decent people behave? A week ago one of your people cut down two oak saplings in my copse. You have dug up the road to Eresnevo, and now I have to go two miles round. Why do you injure me at every step? What harm have I done you? For God's sake, tell me! My wife and I do our utmost to live with you in peace and harmony; we help the peasants as we can. My wife is a kind, warm-hearted woman; she never refuses you help. That is her dream—to be of use to you and your children. You reward us with evil for our good. You are unjust, my friends. Think of that. I ask you earnestly to think it over. We treat you humanely; repay us in the same coin."

He turned and went away. The peasants stood a little longer, put on their caps and walked away. Rodion, who always understood everything that was said to him in some peculiar way of his own, heaved a sigh and said:

"We must pay. 'Repay in coin, my friends' . . . he said."

They walked to the village in silence. On reaching home Rodion said his prayer, took off his boots, and sat down on the bench beside his wife. Stepanida and he always sat side by side when they were at home, and always walked side by side in the street; they ate and they drank and they slept always together, and the older they grew the more they loved one another. It was hot and crowded in their hut, and there were children everywhere—on the floors, in the windows, on the stove. . . . In spite of her advanced years Stepanida was still bearing children, and now, looking at the crowd of children, it was hard to distinguish which were Rodion's and which were Volodka's. Volodka's wife, Lukerya, a plain young woman with prominent eyes and a nose like the beak of a bird, was kneading dough in a tub; Volodka was sitting on the stove with his legs hanging.

"On the road near Nikita's buckwheat . . . the engineer with his dog . . ." Rodion

began, after a rest, scratching his ribs and his elbow. "'You must pay,' says he . . . 'coin,' says he. . . . Coin or no coin, we shall have to collect ten kopecks from every hut. We've offended the gentleman very much. I am sorry for him. . . ."

"We've lived without a bridge," said Volodka, not looking at anyone, "and we don't want one."

"What next; the bridge is a government business."

"We don't want it."

"Your opinion is not asked. What is it to you?"

"'Your opinion is not asked,'" Volodka mimicked him. "We don't want to drive anywhere; what do we want with a bridge? If we have to, we can cross by the boat."

Someone from the yard outside knocked at the window so violently that it seemed to shake the whole hut.

"Is Volodka at home?" he heard the voice of the younger Lytchkov. "Volodka, come out, come along."

Volodka jumped down off the stove and began looking for his cap.

"Don't go, Volodka," said Rodion diffidently. "Don't go with them, son. You are foolish, like a little child; they will teach you no good; don't go!"

"Don't go, son," said Stepanida, and she blinked as though about to shed tears. "I bet they are calling you to the tavern."

"'To the tavern,'" Volodka mimicked.

"You'll come back drunk again, you currish Herod," said Lukerya, looking at him angrily. "Go along, go along, and may you burn up with vodka, you tailless Satan!"

"You hold your tongue," shouted Volodka.

"They've married me to a fool, they've ruined me, a luckless orphan, you redheaded drunkard . . ." wailed Lukerya, wiping her face with a hand covered with dough. "I wish I had never set eyes on you."

Volodka gave her a blow on the ear and went off.

3

Elena Ivanovna and her little daughter visited the village on foot. They were out for a walk. It was a Sunday, and the peasant women and girls were walking up and down the street in their brightly-coloured dresses. Rodion and Stepanida, sitting side by side at their door, bowed and smiled to Elena Ivanovna and her little daughter as to acquaintances. From the windows more than a dozen children stared at them; their faces expressed amazement and curiosity, and they could be heard whispering:

"The Kutcherov lady had come! The Kutcherov lady!"

"Good-morning," said Elena Ivanovna, and she stopped; she paused, and then asked: "Well, how are you getting on?"

"We get along all right, thank God," answered Rodion, speaking rapidly. "To be sure we get along."

"The life we lead!" smiled Stepanida. "You can see our poverty yourself, dear lady! The family is fourteen souls in all, and only two breadwinners. We are supposed to be blacksmiths, but when they bring us a horse to shoe we have no coal, nothing to buy it with. We are worried to death, lady," she went on, and laughed. "Oh, oh, we are worried to death."

Elena Ivanovna sat down at the entrance and, putting her arm round her little girl, pondered something, and judging from the little girl's expression, melancholy thoughts were straying through her mind, too; as she brooded she played with the sumptuous lace on the parasol she had taken out of her mother's hands.

"Poverty," said Rodion, "a great deal of anxiety—you see no end to it. Here, God sends no rain . . . our life is not easy, there is no denying it."

"You have a hard time in this life," said Elena Ivanovna, "but in the other world you will be happy."

Rodion did not understand her, and simply coughed into his clenched hand by way of reply. Stepanida said:

"Dear lady, the rich men will be all right in the next world, too. The rich put up candles, pay for services; the rich give to beggars, but what can the poor man do? He has no time to make the sign of the cross. He is the beggar of beggars himself; how can he think of his soul? And many sins come from poverty; from trouble we snarl at one another like dogs, we haven't a good word to say to one another, and all sorts of things happen, dear lady—God forbid! It seems we have no luck in this world nor the next. All the luck has fallen to the rich."

She spoke gaily; she was evidently used to talking of her hard life. And Rodion smiled, too; he was pleased that his old woman was so clever, so ready of speech.

"It is only on the surface that the rich seem to be happy," said Elena Ivanovna. "Every man has his sorrow. Here my husband and I do not live poorly, we have means, but are we happy? I am young, but I have had four children; my children are always being ill. I am ill, too, and constantly being doctored."

"And what is your illness?" asked Rodion.

"A woman's complaint. I get no sleep; a continual headache gives me no peace. Here I am sitting and talking, but my head is bad, I am weak all over, and I should prefer the hardest labour to such a condition. My soul, too, is troubled; I am in continual fear for my children, my husband. Every family has its own trouble of some sort; we have ours. I am not of noble birth. My grandfather was a simple peasant, my father was a tradesman in Moscow; he was a plain, uneducated man, too, while my husband's parents were wealthy and distinguished. They did not want him to marry me, but he disobeyed them, quarrelled with them, and they have not forgiven us to this day. That worries my husband; it troubles him and keeps him in constant agitation; he loves his mother, loves her dearly. So I am uneasy, too, my soul is in pain."

Peasants, men and women, were by now standing round Rodion's hut and listening. Kozov came up, too, and stood twitching his long, narrow beard. The Lytchkovs, father and son, drew near.

"And say what you like, one cannot be happy and satisfied if one does not feel in one's proper place." Elena Ivanovna went on. "Each of you has his strip of land, each of you works and knows what he is working for; my husband builds bridges—in short, everyone has his place, while I, I simply walk about. I have not my bit to work. I don't work, and feel as though I were an outsider. I am saying all this that you may not judge from outward appearances; if a man is expensively dressed and has means it does not prove that he is satisfied with his life."

She got up to go away and took her daughter by the hand.

"I like your place here very much," she said, and smiled, and from that faint, diffident smile one could tell how unwell she really was, how young and how pretty; she had a pale, thinnish face with dark eyebrows and fair hair. And the little girl was just such another as her mother: thin, fair, and slender. There was a fragrance of scent about them.

"I like the river and the forest and the village," Elena Ivanovna went on; "I could live here all my life, and I feel as though here I should get strong and find my place. I want to help you—I want to dreadfully—to be of use, to be a real friend to you. I know your need, and what I don't know I feel, my heart guesses. I am sick, feeble, and for me perhaps it is not possible to change my life as I would. But I have children. I will try to bring them up that they may be of use to you, may love you. I shall impress upon them continually that their life does not belong to them, but to you. Only I beg you earnestly, I beseech you, trust us, live in friendship with us. My husband is a kind, good man. Don't worry him, don't irritate him. He is sensitive to every trifle, and yesterday, for instance, your cattle were in our vegetable garden, and one of your people broke down the fence to the bee-hives, and such an attitude to us drives my husband to despair. I beg you," she went on in an imploring voice, and she clasped her hands on her bosom—"I beg you to treat us as good neighbours; let us live in peace! There is a saying, you know, that even a bad peace is better than a good quarrel, and, 'Don't buy property, but buy neighbours.' I repeat my husband is a kind man and good; if all goes well we promise to do

everything in our power for you; we will mend the roads, we will build a school for your children. I promise you."

"Of course we thank you humbly, lady," said Lytchkov the father, looking at the ground; "you are educated people; it is for you to know best. Only, you see, Voronov, a rich peasant at Eresnevo, promised to build a school; he, too, said, 'I will do this for you,' 'I will do that for you,' and he only put up the framework and refused to go on. And then they made the peasants put the roof on and finish it; it cost them a thousand roubles. Voronov did not care; he only stroked his beard, but the peasants felt it a bit hard."

"That was a crow, but now there's a rook, too," said Kozov, and he winked.

There was the sound of laughter.

"We don't want a school," said Volodka sullenly. "Our children go to Petrovskoe, and they can go on going there; we don't want it."

Elena Ivanovna seemed suddenly intimidated; her face looked paler and thinner, she shrank into herself as though she had been touched with something coarse, and walked away without uttering another word. And she walked more and more quickly, without looking round.

"Lady," said Rodion, walking after her, "lady, wait a bit; hear what I would say to you."

He followed her without his cap, and spoke softly as though begging.

"Lady, wait and hear what I will say to you."

They had walked out of the village, and Elena Ivanovna stopped beside a cart in the shade of an old mountain ash.

"Don't be offended, lady," said Rodion. "What does it mean? Have patience. Have patience for a couple of years. You will live here, you will have patience, and it will all come round. Our folks are good and peaceable; there's no harm in them; it's God's truth I'm telling you. Don't mind Kozov and the Lytchkovs, and don't mind Volodka. He's a fool; he listens to the first that speaks. The others are quiet folks; they are silent. Some would be glad, you know, to say a word from the heart and to stand up for themselves, but cannot. They have a heart and a conscience, but no tongue. Don't be offended . . . have patience. . . . What does it matter?"

Elena Ivanovna looked at the broad, tranquil river, pondering, and tears flowed down her cheeks. And Rodion was troubled by those tears; he almost cried himself.

"Never mind . . ." he muttered. "Have patience for a couple of years. You can have the school, you can have the roads, only not all at once. If you went, let us say, to sow corn on that mound you would first have to weed it out, to pick out all the stones, and then to plough, and work and work . . . and with the people, you see, it is the same . . . you must work and work until you overcome them."

The crowd had moved away from Rodion's hut, and was coming along the street towards the mountain ash. They began singing songs and playing the concertina, and they kept coming closer and closer. . . .

"Mamma, let us go away from here," said the little girl, huddling up to her mother, pale and shaking all over; "let us go away, mamma!"

"Where?"

"To Moscow. . . . Let us go, mamma."

The child began crying.

Rodion was utterly overcome; his face broke into profuse perspiration; he took out of his pocket a little crooked cucumber, like a half-moon, covered with crumbs of rye bread, and began thrusting it into the little girl's hands.

"Come, come," he muttered, scowling severely; "take the little cucumber, eat it up. . . . You mustn't cry. Mamma will whip you. . . . She'll tell your father of you when you get home. Come, come. . . ."

They walked on, and he still followed behind them, wanting to say something friendly and persuasive to them. And seeing that they were both absorbed in their own thoughts and their own griefs, and not noticing him, he stopped and, shading his eyes from the sun, looked after them for a long time till they disappeared into their copse.

4

The engineer seemed to grow irritable and petty, and in every trivial incident saw an act of robbery or outrage. His gate was kept bolted even by day, and at night two watchmen walked up and down the garden beating a board; and they gave up employing anyone from Obrutchanovo as a labourer. As ill-luck would have it someone (either a peasant or one of the workmen) took the new wheels off the cart and replaced them by old ones, then soon afterwards two bridles and a pair of pincers were carried off, and murmurs arose even in the village. People began to say that a search should be made at the Lytchkovs' and at Volodka's, and then the bridles and the pincers were found under the hedge in the engineer's garden; someone had thrown them down there.

It happened that the peasants were coming in a crowd out of the forest, and again they met the engineer on the road. He stopped, and without wishing them good-day he began, looking angrily first at one, then at another:

"I have begged you not to gather mushrooms in the park and near the yard, but to leave them for my wife and children, but your girls come before daybreak and there is not a mushroom left. . . . Whether one asks you or not it makes no difference. Entreaties, and friendliness, and persuasion I see are all useless."

He fixed his indignant eyes on Rodion and went on:

"My wife and I behaved to you as human beings, as to our equals, and you? But what's the use of talking! It will end by our looking down upon you. There is nothing left!"

And making an effort to restrain his anger, not to say too much, he turned and went on.

On getting home Rodion said his prayer, took off his boots, and sat down beside his wife.

"Yes . . ." he began with a sigh. "We were walking along just now, and Mr. Kutcherov met us. . . . Yes. . . . He saw the girls at daybreak. . . . 'Why don't they bring mushrooms,' he said . . . 'to my wife and children?' he said. . . . And then he looked at me and he said: 'I and my wife will look after you,' he said. I wanted to fall down at his feet, but I hadn't the courage. . . . God give him health. . . . God bless him! . . ."

Stepanida crossed herself and sighed.

"They are kind, simple-hearted people," Rodion went on. " 'We shall look after you.' . . . He promised me that before everyone. In our old age . . . it wouldn't be a bad thing. . . . I should always pray for them. . . . Holy Mother, bless them. . . ."

The Feast of the Exaltation of the Cross, the fourteenth of September, was the festival of the village church. The Lytchkovs, father and son, went across the river early in the morning and returned to dinner drunk; they spent a long time going about the village, alternately singing and swearing; then they had a fight and went to the New Villa to complain. First Lytchkov the father went into the yard with a long ashen stick in his hands. He stopped irresolutely and took off his hat. Just at that moment the engineer and his family were sitting on the verandah, drinking tea.

"What do you want?" shouted the engineer.

"Your honour . . ." Lytchkov began, and burst into tears. "Show the Divine mercy, protect me . . . my son makes my life a misery . . . your honour. . . ."

Lytchkov the son walked up, too; he, too, was bareheaded and had a stick in his hand; he stopped and fixed his drunken senseless eyes on the verandah.

"It is not my business to settle your affairs," said the engineer. "Go to the rural captain or the police officer."

"I have been everywhere. . . . I have lodged a petition . . ." said Lytchkov the father, and he sobbed. "Where can I go now? He can kill me now, it seems. He can do anything. Is that the way to treat a father? A father?"

He raised his stick and hit his son on the head; the son raised his stick and struck his father just on his bald patch such a blow that the stick bounced back. The father did

not even flinch, but hit his son again and again on the head. And so they stood and kept hitting one another on the head, and it looked not so much like a fight as some sort of a game. And peasants, men and women, stood in a crowd at the gate and looked into the garden, and the faces of all were grave. They were the peasants who had come to greet them for the holiday, but seeing the Lytchkovs, they were ashamed and did not go in.

The next morning Elena Ivanovna went with the children to Moscow. And there was a rumour that the engineer was selling his house. . . .

5

The peasants had long ago grown used to the sight of the bridge, and it was difficult to imagine the river at that place without a bridge. The heap of rubble left from the building of it had long been overgrown with grass, the navvies were forgotten, and instead of the strains of the "Dubinushka" that they used to sing, the peasants heard almost every hour the sounds of a passing train.

The New Villa has long ago been sold; now it belongs to a government clerk who comes here from the town for the holidays with his family, drinks tea on the terrace, and then goes back to the town again. He wears a cockade on his cap; he talks and clears his throat as though he were a very important official, though he is only of the rank of a collegiate secretary, and when the peasants bow he makes no response.

In Obrutchanovo everyone has grown older; Kozov is dead. In Rodion's hut there are even more children. Volodka has grown a long red beard. They are still as poor as ever.

In the early spring the Obrutchanovo peasants were sawing wood near the station. And after work they were going home; they walked without haste one after the other. Broad saws curved over their shoulders; the sun was reflected in them. The nightingales were singing in the bushes on the bank, larks were trilling in the heavens. It was quiet at the New Villa; there was not a soul there, and only golden pigeons—golden because the sunlight was streaming upon them —were flying over the house. All of them —Rodion, the two Lytchkovs, and Volodka—thought of the white horses, the little ponies, the fireworks, the boat with the lanterns; they remembered how the engineer's wife, so beautiful and so grandly dressed, had come into the village and talked to them in such a friendly way. And it seemed as though all that had never been; it was like a dream or a fairy-tale.

They trudged along, tired out, and mused as they went. . . . In their village, they mused, the people were good, quiet, sensible, fearing God, and Elena Ivanovna, too, was quiet, kind, and gentle; it made one sad to look at her, but why had they not got on together? Why had they parted like enemies? How was it that some mist had shrouded from their eyes what mattered most, and had let them see nothing but damage done by cattle, bridles, pincers, and all those trivial things which now, as they remembered them, seemed so nonsensical? How was it that with the new owner they lived in peace, and yet had been on bad terms with the engineer?

And not knowing what answer to make to these questions they were all silent except Volodka, who muttered something.

"What is it?" Rodion asked.

"We lived without a bridge . . ." said Volodka gloomily. "We lived without a bridge, and did not ask for one . . . and we don't want it. . . ."

No one answered him and they walked on in silence with drooping heads.

THE FIGHT BETWEEN JAPPE AND DO ESCOBAR

Thomas Mann
(1875–1955)

I was very much taken aback when Johnny Bishop told me that Jappe and Do Escobar were going to fight each other and that we must go and watch them do it.

It was in the summer holidays at Travemünde, on a sultry day with a slight land breeze and a flat sea ever so far away across the sands. We had been some three-quarters of an hour in the water and were lying on the hard sand under the props of the bathing-cabins—we two and Jürgen Brattström the shipowner's son. Johnny and Brattström were lying on their backs entirely naked; I felt more comfortable with my towel wrapped round my hips. Brattström asked me why I did it and I could not think of any sensible answer; so Johnny said with his winning smile that I was probably too big now to lie naked. I really was larger and more developed than Johnny and Brattström; also a little older, about thirteen; so I accepted Johnny's explanation in silence, although with a certain feeling of mortification. For in Johnny Bishop's presence you actually felt rather out of it if you were any less small, fine, and physically childlike than he, who was all these things in such a very high degree. He knew how to look up at you with his pretty, friendly blue eyes, which had a certain mocking smile in them too, with an expression that said: "What a great, gawky thing you are, to be sure!" The ideal of manliness and long trousers had no validity in his presence —and that at a time, not long after the war, when strength, courage, and every hardy virtue stood very high among us youth and all sorts of conduct were banned as effeminate. But Johnny, as a foreigner—or half-foreigner—was exempt from this atmosphere. He was a little like a woman who preserves her youth and looks down on other women who are less successful at the feat. Besides he was far and away the best-dressed boy in town, distinctly aristocratic and elegant in his real English sailor suit with the linen collar, sailor's knot, laces, a silver whistle in his pocket, and an anchor on the sleeves that narrowed round his wrists. Anyone else would have been laughed at for that sort of thing—it would have been jeered at as "girls' clothes." But he wore them with such a disarming and confident air that he never suffered in the least.

He looked rather like a thin little cupid

as he lay there, with his pretty, soft blond curls and his arms up over the narrow English head that rested on the sand. His father had been a German business man who had been naturalized in England and died some years since. His mother was English by blood, a long-featured lady with quiet, gentle ways, who had settled in our town with her two children, Johnny and a mischievous little girl just as pretty as he. She still wore black for her husband, and she was probably honouring his last wishes when she brought the children to grow up in Germany. Obviously they were in easy circumstances. She owned a spacious house outside the city and a villa at the sea and from time to time she travelled with Johnny and Sissie to more distant resorts. She did not move in society, although it would have been open to her. Whether on account of her mourning or perhaps because the horizon of our best families was too narrow for her, she herself led a retired life, but she managed that her children should have social intercourse. She invited other children to play with them and sent them to dancing and deportment lessons, thus quietly arranging that Johnny and Sissie should associate exclusively with the children of well-to-do families—of course not in pursuance of any well-defined principle, but just as a matter of course. Mrs. Bishop contributed, remotely, to my own education: it was from her I learned that to be well thought of by others no more is needed than to think well of yourself. Though deprived of its male head the little family showed none of the marks of neglect or disruption which often in such cases make people fight shy. Without further family connection, without title, tradition, influence, or public office, and living a life apart, Mrs. Bishop by no means lacked social security or pretensions. She was definitely accepted at her own valuation and the friendship of her children was much sought after by their young contemporaries.

As for Jürgen Brattström, I may say in passing that his father had made his own money, achieved public office, and built for himself and his family the red sandstone house on the Burgfeld, next to Mrs. Bishop's. And that lady had quietly accepted his son as Johnny's playmate and let the two go to school together. Jürgen was a decent, phlegmatic, short-legged lad without any prominent characteristics. He had begun to do a little private business in licorice sticks.

As I said, I was extremely shocked when Johnny told me about the impending meeting between Jappe and Do Escobar which was to take place at twelve o'clock that day on the Leuchtenfeld. It was dead earnest— might have a serious outcome, for Jappe and Do Escobar were both stout and reckless fellows and had strong feelings about knightly honour. The issue might well be frightful. In my memory they still seem as tall and manly as they did then, though they could not have been more than fifteen at the time. Jappe came from the middle class of the city; he was not much looked after at home, he was already almost his own master, a combination of loafer and man-about-town. Do Escobar was an exotic and bohemian foreigner, who did not even come regularly to school but only attended lectures now and then—an irregular but paradisial existence! He lived *en pension* with some middle-class people and rejoiced in complete independence. Both were people who went late to bed, visited public-houses, strolled of evenings in the Broad Street, followed girls about, performed crazy "stunts"—in short, were regular blades. Although they did not live in the Kurhotel at Travemünde—where they would scarcely have been acceptable—but somewhere in the village, they frequented the Kurhaus and garden and were at home there as cosmopolitans. In the evening, especially on a Sunday, when I had long since been in my bed in one of the chalets and gone off to sleep to the pleasant sound of the Kurhaus band, they, and other members of the young generation —as I was aware—still sauntered up and down in the stream of tourists and guests, loitered in front of the long awning of the café, and sought and found grown-up entertainment. And here they had come to blows, goodness knows how and why. It is possible that they had only brushed against each other in passing and in the sensitiveness of their knightly honour had made a fighting matter of the encounter. Johnny, who of course had been long since in bed too and was instructed only by hearsay in what happened, expressed himself in his pleasant, slightly husky childish voice, that the quarrel was probably about some "gal"—an easy assumption, considering Jappe's and Do Escobar's precocity and boldness. In short, they had made no scene among the guests, but in few and biting words agreed upon hour and place and witnesses for the satisfaction of their honour. The next day, at twelve, rendezvous at such and such a spot on the Leuchtenfeld. Good evening.— Ballet-master Knaak from Hamburg, master of ceremonies and leader of the Kurhaus cotillions, had been on the scene and promised his presence at the appointed hour and place.

Johnny rejoiced wholeheartedly in the fray —I think that neither he nor Brattström would have shared my apprehensions. Johnny repeatedly assured me, forming the *r* far forward on his palate, with his pretty enunciation, that they were both "in dead eahnest" and certainly meant business. Complacently and with a rather, ironic objectivity he weighed the chances of victory for each. They were both frightfully strong, he grinned; both of them great fighters—it would be fun to have it settled which of them was the greater. Jappe, Johnny thought, had a broad chest and capital arm and leg muscles, he could tell that from seeing him swimming. But Do Escobar was uncommonly wiry and savage—hard to tell beforehand who would get the upper hand. It was strange to hear Johnny discourse so sovereignly upon Jappe's and Do Escobar's qualifications, looking at his childish arms, which could never have given or warded off a blow. As for me, I was indeed far from absenting myself from the spectacle. That would have been absurd and moreover the proceedings had a great fascination for me. Of course I must go, I must see it all, now that I knew about it. I felt a certain sense of duty, along with other and conflicting emotions: a great shyness and shame, all unwarlike as I was, and not at all minded to trust myself upon the scene of manly ex-

ploits. I had a nervous dread of the shock which the sight of a duel *à outrance,* a fight for life and death, as it were, would give me. I was cowardly enough to ask myself whether, once on the field, I might not be caught up in the struggle and have to expose my own person to a proof of valour which I knew in my inmost heart I was far from being able or willing to give. On the other hand I kept putting myself in Jappe's and Do Escobar's place and feeling consuming sensations which I assumed to be what they were feeling. I visualized the scene of the insult and the challenge, summoned my sense of good form and with Jappe and Do Escobar resisted the impulse to fall to there and then. I experienced the agony of an overwrought passion for justice, the flaring, shattering hatred, the attacks of raving impatience for revenge, in which they must have passed the night. Arrived at the last ditch, lost to all sense of fear, I fought myself blind and bloody with an adversary just as inhuman, drove my fist into his hated jaw with all the strength of my being, so that all his teeth were broken, received in exchange a brutal kick in the stomach and went under in a sea of blood. After which I woke in my bed with ice-bags, quieted nerves, and a chorus of mild reproaches from my family. In short, when it was half past twelve and we got up to dress I was half worn out with my apprehensions. In the cabin and afterwards when we were dressed and went outdoors, my heart throbbed exactly as though it was I myself who was to fight with Jappe or Do Escobar, in public and with all the rigours of the game.

I still remember how we took the narrow wooden bridge which ran diagonally up from the beach to the cabins. Of course we jumped, in order to make it sway as much as possible, so that we bounced as though on a spring-board. But once below we did not follow the board walk which led along the beach past the tents and the basket chairs; but held inland in the general direction of the Kurhaus but rather more leftwards. The sun brooded over the dunes and sucked a dry, hot odour from the sparse and withered vegetation, the reeds and thistles that stuck into our legs. There was no sound but the ceaseless humming of the blue-bottle flies which hung apparently motionless in the heavy warmth, suddenly to shift to another spot and begin afresh their sharp, monotonous whine. The cooling effect of the bath was long since spent. Brattström and I kept lifting our hats, he his Swedish sailor cap with the oilcloth visor, I my round Heligoland woollen bonnet—the so-called tam-o'-shanter—to wipe our brows. Johnny suffered little from heat, thanks to his slightness and also because his clothing was more elegantly adapted than ours to the summer day. In his light and comfortable sailor suit of striped washing material which left bare his throat and legs, the blue, short-ribboned cap with English lettering on his pretty little head, the long slender feet in fine, almost heelless white leather shoes, he walked with mounting strides and somewhat bent knees between Brattström and me and sang with his charming accent "Little Fisher Maiden"—a ditty which was then the rage. He sang it with some vulgar variation in the words, such as boys like to invent. Curiously enough, in all his childishness he knew a good deal about various matters and was not at all too prudish to take them in his mouth. But always he would make a sanctimonious little face and say: "Fie! Who would sing such dirty songs?"—as though Brattström and I had been the ones to make indecent advances to the little fisher maiden.

I did not feel at all like singing, we were too near the fatal spot. The prickly grass of the dunes had changed to the sand and sea moss of a barren meadow; this was the Leuchtenfeld, so called after the yellow lighthouse towering up in the far distance. We soon found ourselves at our goal.

It was a warm, peaceful spot, where almost nobody ever came: protected from view by scrubby willow trees. On the free space among the bushes a crowd of youths lay or sat in a circle. They were almost all older than we and from various strata of society. We seemed to be the last spectators to arrive. Everybody was waiting for Knaak the dancing-master, who was needed in the capacity of neutral and umpire. Both Jappe and Do Escobar were there—I saw them at once. They were sitting far apart in the circle and pretending not to see each other. We greeted a few acquaintances with silent nods and squatted in our turn on the sun-warmed ground.

Some of the group were smoking. Both Jappe and Do Escobar held cigarettes in the corners of their mouths. Each kept one eye shut against the smoke and I instantly felt and knew that they were aware how grand it was to sit there and smoke before entering the ring. They were both dressed in grown-up clothes, but Do Escobar's were more gentlemanly than Jappe's. He wore yellow shoes with pointed toes, a light-grey summer suit, a rose-coloured shirt with cuffs, a coloured silk cravat, and a round, narrow-brimmed straw hat sitting far back on his head, so that his mop of shiny black hair showed on one side beneath it, in a big hummock. He kept raising his right hand to shake back the silver bangle he wore under his cuff. Jappe's appearance was distinctly less pretentious. His legs were encased in tight trousers of a lighter colour than his coat and waistcoat and fastened with straps under his waxed black boots. A checked cap covered his curly blond hair; in contrast to Do Escobar's jaunty headgear he wore it pulled down over his forehead. He sat with his arms clasped round one knee; you could see that he had on loose cuffs over his shirt-sleeves, also that his finger-nails were either cut too short or else that he indulged in the vice of biting them. Despite the smoking and the assumed nonchalance, the whole circle was serious and silent, restraint was in the air. The only one to make head against it was Do Escobar, who talked without stopping to his neighbours, in a loud, strained voice, rolling his *r*'s and blowing smoke out of his nose.

I was rather put off by his volubility; it inclined me, despite the bitten finger-nails, to side with Jappe, who at most addressed a word or two over his shoulder to his neighbour and for the rest gazed in apparent composure at the smoke of his cigarette.

Then came Herr Knaak—I can still see him, in his blue striped flannel morning suit, coming with winged tread from the direction of the Kurhaus and lifting his hat as he paused outside the circle. That he wanted to come I do not believe; I am convinced rather that he had made a virtue of necessity when he honoured the fight with his presence. And the necessity, the compulsion, was due to his equivocal position in the eyes of martially- and masculinely-minded youth. Dark-skinned and comely, plump, particularly in the region of the hips, he gave us dancing and deportment lessons in the wintertime—private, family lessons as well as public classes in the Casino; and in the summer he acted as bathing-master and social manager at Travemünde. He rocked on his hips and weaved in his walk, turning out his toes very much and setting them first on the ground as he stepped. His eyes had a vain expression, his speech was pleasant but affected, and his way of entering a room as though it were a stage, his extraordinary and fastidious mannerisms charmed all the female sex, while the masculine world, and especially critical youth, viewed him with suspicion. I have often pondered over the position of François Knaak in life and always I have found it strange and fantastic. He was of humble origins, his parents were poor, and his taste for the social graces left him as it were hanging in the air—not a member of society, yet paid by it as a guardian and instructor of its conventions. Jappe and Do Escobar were his pupils too; not in private lessons, like Johnny, Brattström, and me, but in the public classes in the Casino. It was in these that Herr Knaak's character and position were most sharply criticized. We of the private classes were less austere. A fellow who taught you the proper deportment towards little girls, who was thrillingly reported to wear a corset, who picked up the edge of his frock-coat with his finger-tips, curtsied, cut capers, leaped suddenly into the air, where he twirled his toes before he came down again—what sort of chap was he, after all? These were the suspicions harboured by militant youth on the score of Herr Knaak's

character and mode of life, and his exaggerated airs did nothing to allay them. Of course, he was a grown-up man (he was even, comically enough, said to have a wife and children in Hamburg); and his advantage in years and the fact that he was never seen except officially and in the dance-hall, prevented him from being convicted and unmasked. Could he do gymnastics? Had he ever been able to? Had he courage? Had he parts? In short, could one accept him as an equal? He was never in a position to display the soldier characteristics which might have balanced his salon arts and made him a decent chap. So there were youths who made no bones of calling his straight out a coward and a jackanapes. All this he knew and therefore he was here today to manifest his interest in a good stand-up fight and to put himself on terms with the young, though in his official position he should not have countenanced such goings-on. I am convinced, however, that he was not comfortable—he knew he was treading on thin ice. Some of the audience looked coldly at him and he himself gazed uneasily round to see if anybody was coming.

He politely excused his late arrival, saying that he had been kept by a consultation with the management of the Kurhaus about the next Sunday's ball. "Are the combatants present?" he next inquired in official tones. "Then we can begin." Leaning on his stick with his feet crossed he gnawed his soft brown moustache with his under lip and made owl eyes to look like a connoisseur.

Jappe and Do Escobar stood up, threw away their cigarettes, and began to prepare for the fray. Do Escobar did it in a hurry, with impressive speed. He threw hat, coat, and waistcoat on the ground, unfastened tie, collar, and braces and added them to the pile. He even drew his rose-coloured shirt out of his trousers, pulled his arms briskly out of the sleeves, and stood up in a red and white striped undershirt which exposed the larger part of his yellow arms, already covered with a thick black fell. "At your service, sir," he said, with a rolling *r*, stepping into the middle of the ring, expanding his chest and throwing back his shoulders. He still wore the silver bangle.

Jappe was not ready yet. He turned his head, elevated his brows, and looked at Do Escobar's feet a moment with narrowed eyes —as much as to say: "Wait a bit—I'll get there too, even if I don't swagger so much." He was broader in the shoulder; but as he took his place beside Do Escobar he seemed nowhere near so fit or athletic. His legs in the tight strapped boots inclined to be knock-kneed and his fit-out was not impressive— grey braces over a yellowed white shirt with loose buttoned sleeves. By contrast Do Escobar's striped tricot and the black hair on his arms looked uncommonly grim and business-like. Both were pale but it showed more in Jappe as he was otherwise blond and red-cheeked, with jolly, not-too-refined features including a rather turned-up nose with a saddle of freckles. Do Escobar's nose was short, straight, and drooping and there was a downy black growth on his full upper lip.

They stood with hanging arms almost breast to breast, and looked at one another darkly and haughtily in the region of the stomach. They obviously did not know how to begin—and how well I could understand that! A night and half a day had intervened since the unpleasantness. They had wanted to fly at each other's throats and had only been held in check by the rules of the game. But they had had time to cool off. To do to order, as it were, before an audience, by appointment, in cold blood, what they had wanted to do yesterday when the fit was on them—it was not the same thing at all. After all, they were not gladiators. They were civilized young men. And in possession of one's senses one has a certain reluctance to smash a sound human body with one's fists. So I thought, and so, very likely, it was.

But something had to be done, that honour might be satisfied, so each began to work the other up by hitting him contemptuously with the finger-tips on the breast, as though that would be enough to finish him off. And, indeed, Jappe's face began to be distorted with anger—but just at that moment Do Escobar broke off the skirmish.

"Pardon," said he, taking two steps backwards and turning aside. He had to tighten the buckle at the back of his trousers, for he was narrow-hipped and in the absence of braces they had begun to slip. He took his position again almost at once, throwing out his chest and saying something in guttural and rattling Spanish, probably to the effect that he was again at Jappe's service. It was clear that he was inordinately vain.

The skirmishing with shoulders and buffeting with palms began again. Then unexpectedly there ensued a blind and raging hand-to-hand scuffle with the fists, which lasted three seconds and broke off without notice.

"Now they are warming up," said Johnny, sitting next to me with a dry grass in his mouth. "I'll wager Jappe beats him. Look how he keeps squinting over at us—Jappe keeps his mind on his job. Will you bet he won't give him a good hiding?"

They had now recoiled and stood, fists on hips, their chests heaving. Both had doubtless taken some punishment, for they both looked angry, sticking out their lips furiously as much as to say: "What do you mean by hurting me like that?" Jappe was red-eyed and Do Escobar showed his white teeth as they fell to again.

They were hitting out now with all their strength on shoulders, forearms, and breasts by turns and in quick succession. "That's nothing," Johnny said, with his charming accent. "They won't get anywhere that way, either of them. They must go at it under the chin, with an uppercut to the jaw. That does it." But meanwhile Do Escobar had caught both Jappe's arms with his left arm, pressed them as in a vise against his chest, and with his right went on pummelling Jappe's flanks.

There was great excitement. "No clinching!" several voices cried out, and people jumped up. Herr Knaak hastened between the combatants, in horror. "You are holding him fast, my dear friend. That is against all the rules." He separated them and again instructed Do Escobar in the regulations. Then he withdrew once more outside the ring.

Jappe was obviously in a fury. He was

quite white, rubbing his side and looking at Do Escobar with a slow nod that boded no good. When the next round began, his face looked so grim that everybody expected him to deliver a decisive blow.

And actually as soon as contact had been renewed Jappe carried out a coup—he practised a feint which he had probably planned beforehand. A thrust with his left caused Do Escobar to protect his head; but as he did so Jappe's right hit him so hard in the stomach that he crumpled forwards and his face took on the colour of yellow wax.

"That went home," said Johnny. "That's where it hurts. Maybe now he will pull himself together and take things seriously, so as to pay it back." But the blow to the stomach had been too telling, Do Escobar's nerve was visibly shaken. It was clear he could not even clench his fists properly, and his eyes took on a glazed look. However, finding his muscles thus affected, his vanity counselled him to play the agile southron, dancing round the German bear and rendering him desperate by his own dexterity. He took tiny steps and made all sorts of useless passes, moving round Jappe in little circles and trying to assume an arrogant smile—which in his reduced condition struck me as really heroic. But it did not upset Jappe at all—he simply turned round on his heel and got in many a good blow with his right while with his left he warded off Do Escobar's feeble attack. But what sealed Do Escobar's fate was that his trousers kept slipping. His tricot shirt even came outside and rucked up, showing a little strip of his bare yellow skin—some of the audience sniggered. But why had he taken off his braces? He would have done better to leave aesthetic considerations on one side. For now his trousers bothered him, they had bothered him during the whole fight. He kept wanting to pull them up and stuff in his shirt, for however much he was punished he could bear it better than the thought that he might be cutting a ridiculous figure. In the end he was fighting with one hand while with the other he tried to put himself to rights; and thus Jappe was able to land such a blow on his nose that to this day I do not understand why it was not broken.

But the blood poured out, and Do Escobar turned and went apart from Jappe, trying with his right hand to stop the bleeding and with his left making an eloquent gesture behind him as he went. Jappe stood there with his knock-kneed legs spread out and waited for Do Escobar to come back. But Do Escobar was finished with the business. If I interpret him aright he was the more civilized of the two and felt that it was high time to call a halt. Jappe would beyond doubt have fought on with his nose bleeding; but almost as certainly Do Escobar would equally have refused to go on, and he did so with even more conviction in that it was himself that bled. They had made the claret run out of his nose—in his view things should never have been allowed to go so far, devil take it! The blood ran between his fingers onto his clothes, it soiled his light trousers and dripped on his yellow shoes. It was beastly and nothing but beastly—and under such circumstances he declined to take part in more fighting. It would be inhuman.

And his attitude was accepted by the majority of the spectators. Herr Knaak came into the ring and declared that the fight was over. Both sides had behaved with distinction. You could see how relieved he felt that the affair had gone off so smoothly.

"But neither of them was brought to a fall," said Johnny, surprised and disappointed. However, even Jappe was quite satisfied to consider the affair as settled. Drawing a long breath he went to fetch his clothes. Everybody generally accepted Herr Knaak's delicate fiction that the issue was a draw. Jappe was congratulated, but only surreptitiously; on the other hand some people lent Do Escobar their handkerchiefs, as his own was soon drenched. And now the cry was for more. Let two other fellows fight. That was the sense of the meeting; Jappe's and Do Escobar's business had taken so little time, hardly ten minutes; since they were all there and it was still quite early something more ought to come. Another pair must enter the arena—whoever wanted to show that he deserved being called a lad of parts.

Nobody offered. But why at this summons did my heart begin to beat like a little drum?

What I had feared had come to pass: the challenge had become general. Why did I feel as though I had all the time been awaiting this very moment with shivers of delicious anticipation and now when it had come why was I plunged into a whirl of conflicting emotions? I looked at Johnny. Perfectly calm and detached he sat beside me, turned his straw about in his mouth and looked about the ring with a frankly curious air, to see whether a couple of stout chaps would not be found to let their noses be broken for his amusement. Why was it that I had to feel personally challenged to conquer my nervous timidity, to make an unnatural effort and draw all eyes upon myself by heroically stepping into the ring? In an access of self-consciousness mingled with vanity I was about to raise my hand and offer myself for combat when somewhere in the circle the shout arose:

"Herr Knaak ought to fight!"

All eyes fastened themselves upon Herr Knaak. I have said that he was walking upon slippery ice in exposing himself to the danger of such a test of his kidney. But he simply answered:

"No, thanks, very much—I had enough beatings when I was young."

He was safe. He had slipped like an eel out of the trap. How astute of him, to bring in his superiority in years, to imply that at our age he would not have avoided an honourable fight—and that without boasting at all, even making his words carry irresistible conviction by admitting with a disarming laugh at himself that he too had taken beatings in his time. They let him alone. They perceived that it was hard, if not impossible, to bring him to book.

"Then somebody must wrestle!" was the next cry. This suggestion was not taken up either; but in the midst of the discussion over it (and I shall never forget the painful impression it made) Do Escobar said in his hoarse Spanish voice from behind his gory handkerchief: "Wrestling is for cowards. Only Germans wrestle." It was an unheard-of piece of tactlessness, coming from him, and got its reward at once in the capital retort made by Herr Knaak: "Possibly," said he.

"But it looks as though the Germans know how to give pretty good beatings sometimes too!" He was rewarded by shouts of approving laughter; his whole position was improved, and Do Escobar definitely put down for the day.

But it was the general opinion that wrestling was a good deal of a bore, and so various athletic feats were resorted to instead: leapfrog, standing on one's head, handsprings and so on, to fill in the time.

"Come on, let's go," said Johnny to Brattström and me, and got up. That was Johnny Bishop for you. He had come to see something real, with the possibility of a bloody issue. But the thing had petered out and so he left.

He gave me my first impression of the peculiar superiority of the English character, which later on I came so greatly to admire.

THE DAUGHTERS OF THE LATE COLONEL

Katherine Mansfield
(1888–1923)

I

The week after was one of the busiest weeks of their lives. Even when they went to bed it was only their bodies that lay down and rested; their minds went on, thinking things out, talking things over, wondering, deciding, trying to remember where . . .

Constantia lay like a statue, her hands by her sides, her feet just overlapping each other, the sheet up to her chin. She stared at the ceiling.

"Do you think that father would mind if we gave his top-hat to the porter?"

"The porter?" snapped Josephine. "Why ever the porter? What a very extraordinary idea!"

"Because," said Constantia slowly, "he must often have to go to funerals. And I noticed at —at the cemetery that he only had a bowler." She paused. "I thought then how very much he'd appreciate a top-hat. We ought to give him a present, too. He was always very nice to father."

"But," cried Josephine, flouncing on her pillow and staring across the dark at Constantia, "father's head!" And suddenly, for one awful moment, she nearly giggled. Not, of course, that she felt in the least like giggling. It must have been habit. Years ago, when they had stayed awake at night talking, their beds had simply heaved. And now the porter's head, disappearing, popped out, like a candle, under father's hat. . . . The giggle mounted, mounted; she clenched her hands; she fought it down; she frowned fiercely at the dark and said, "Remember" terribly sternly.

"We can decide tomorrow," she sighed.

Constantia had noticed nothing; she sighed.

"Do you think we ought to have our dressing-gowns dyed as well?"

"Black?" almost shrieked Josephine.

"Well, what else?" said Constantia. "I was thinking—it doesn't seem quite sincere, in a way, to wear black out of doors when we're fully dressed, and then when we're at home—"

"But nobody sees us," said Josephine. She gave the bedclothes such a twitch that both her feet became uncovered, and she had to creep up the pillows to get them well under again.

"Kate does," said Constantia. "And the postman very well might."

Josephine thought of her dark-red slippers, which matched her dressing-gown, and of Constantia's favorite indefinite green ones which went with hers. Black! Two black dressing-gowns and two pairs of black woolly slippers, creeping off to the bathroom like black cats.

"I don't think it's absolutely necessary," said she.

Silence. Then Constantia said, "We shall have to post the papers with the notice in them tomorrow to catch the Ceylon mail. . . . How many letters have we had up till now?"

"Twenty-three."

Josephine had replied to them all, and twenty-three times when she came to "We miss our dear father so much," she had broken down and had to use her handkerchief, and on some of them even to soak up a very light-blue tear with an edge of blotting-paper. Strange! She couldn't have put it on— but twenty-three times. Even now, though, when she said over to herself sadly, "We miss our dear father *so* much" she could have cried if she'd wanted to.

"Have you got enough stamps?" came from Constantia.

"Oh, how could I tell?" said Josephine crossly. "What's the good of asking me that now?"

"I was just wondering," said Constantia mildly.

Silence again. There came a little rustle, a scurry, a hop.

"A mouse," said Constantia.

"It can't be a mouse because there aren't any crumbs," said Josephine.

"But it doesn't know there aren't," said Constantia.

A spasm of pity squeezed her heart. Poor little thing! She wished she'd left a tiny piece of biscuit on the dressing-table. It was awful to think of it not finding anything. What would it do?

"I can't think of how they manage to live at all," she said slowly.

"Who?" demanded Josephine.

And Constantia said more loudly than she meant to, "Mice."

Josephine was furious. "Oh, what nonsense, Con!" she said. "What have mice got to do with it? You're asleep."

"I don't think I am," said Constantia. She shut her eyes to make sure. She was.

Josephine arched her spine, pulled up her knees, folded her arms so that her fists came under her ears, and pressed her cheek hard against the pillow.

2

Another thing that complicated matters was they had Nurse Andrews staying on with them that week. It was their own fault; they had asked her. It was Josephine's idea. On the morning—well, on the last morning, when the doctor had gone, Josephine had said to Constantia, "Don't you think it would be rather nice if we asked Nurse Andrews to stay on for a week as our guest?"

"Very nice," said Constantia.

"I thought," went on Josephine quickly, "I should just say this afternoon, after we've paid her, 'My sister and I would be very pleased, after all you've done for us, Nurse Andrews, if you would stay on for a week as our guest.' I'd have to put that in about being our guest in case—"

"Oh, but she could hardly expect to be paid!" cried Constantia.

"One never knows," said Josephine sagely.

Nurse Andrews had, of course, jumped at the idea. But it was a bother. It meant they had to have regular sit-down meals at the proper times, whereas if they'd been alone they could have just asked Kate if she wouldn't have minded bringing them a tray wherever they were. And meal-times now that the strain was over were rather a trial.

Nurse Andrews was simply fearful about butter. Really they couldn't help feeling that about butter, at least, she took advantage of their kindness. And she had that maddening habit of asking for just an inch more bread to finish what she had on her plate, and then, at the last mouthful, absentmindedly—of course it wasn't absentmindedly—taking another helping. Josephine got very red when this happened, and she fastened her small, bead-like eyes on the table-cloth as if she saw a minute strange insect creeping through the web of it. But Constantia's long, pale face lengthened and set, and she gazed away—away—far over the desert to where that line of camels unwound like a thread of wool.

"When I was with Lady Tukes," said Nurse Andrews, "she had such a daintly little contrayvance for the buttah. It was a silvah Cupid balanced on the—on the bordah of a glass dish, holding a tayny fork. And when you wanted some buttah you simply pressed his foot and he bent down and speared you a piece. It was quite a gayme."

Josephine could hardly bear that. But "I think those things are very extravagant," was all she said.

"But whey?" asked Nurse Andrews, beaming through her eye-glasses. "No one, surely, would take more buttah than one wanted—would one?"

"Ring, Con," cried Josephine. She couldn't trust herself to reply.

And proud young Kate, the enchanted princess, came in to see what the old tabbies wanted now. She snatched away their plates of mock something or other and slapped down a white, terrified blanc-mange.

"Jam, please, Kate," said Josephine kindly.

Kate knelt and burst open the side-board, lifted the lid of the jam-pot, saw it was empty, put it on the table, and stalked off.

"I'm afraid," said Nurse Andrews a moment later, "there isn't any."

"Oh, what a bother!" said Josephine. She bit her lip. "What had we better do?"

Constantia looked dubious. "We can't disturb Kate again," she said softly.

Nurse Andrews waited, smiling at them both. Her eyes wandered, spying at everything behind her eye-glasses. Constantia in despair went back to her camels. Josephine frowned heavily—concentrated. If it hadn't been for this idiotic woman she and Con would, of course, have eaten their blanc-mange without. Suddenly the idea came.

"I know," she said. "Marmalade. There's some marmalade in the sideboard. Get it, Con."

"I hope," laughed Nurse Andrews, and her laugh was like a spoon tinkling against a medicine-glass—"I hope it's not very bittah marmalayde."

3

But, after all, it was not long now, and then she'd be gone for good. And there was no getting away from the fact that she had been very kind to father. She had nursed him day and night at the end. Indeed, both Constantia and Josephine felt privately that she had rather overdone the not leaving him at the very last. For when they had gone in to say good-bye Nurse Andrews had sat beside his bed the whole time, holding his wrist and pretending to look at her watch. It couldn't have been necessary. It was so tactless, too. Supposing father had wanted to say something—something private to them. Not that he had. Oh, far from it! He lay there, purple, a dark, angry purple in the face, and never even looked at them when they came in. Then, as they were standing there, wondering what to do, he had suddenly opened one eye. Oh, what a difference it would have made, what a difference to their memory of him, how much easier to tell people about it, if he had only opened both! But no—one eye only. It glared at them a moment and then . . . went out.

4

It had made it very awkward for them when Mr. Farolles, of St. John's, called the same afternoon.

"The end was quite peaceful, I trust?" were the first words he said as he glided towards them through the dark drawing-room.

"Quite," said Josephine faintly. They both hung their heads. Both of them felt certain that eye wasn't at all a peaceful eye.

"Won't you sit down?" said Josephine.

"Thank you, Miss Pinner," said Mr. Farolles gratefully. He folded his coattails and began to lower himself into father's armchair, but just as he touched it he almost sprang up and slid into the next chair instead.

He coughed. Josephine clasped her hands; Constantia looked vague.

"I want you to feel, Miss Pinner," said Mr. Farolles, "and you, Miss Constantia, that I'm trying to be helpful. I want to be helpful to you both, if you will let me. These are the times," said Mr. Farolles, very simply and earnestly, "when God means us to be helpful to one another."

"Thank you very much, Mr. Farolles," said Josephine and Constantia.

"Not at all," said Mr. Farolles gently. He drew his kid gloves through his fingers and leaned a little forward. "And if either of you would like a little Communion, either or both of you, here *and* now, you have only to

tell me. A little Communion is often very helpful—a great comfort," he added tenderly.

But the idea of a little Communion terrified them. What! In the drawing-room by themselves—with no—no altar or anything! The piano would be much too high, thought Constantia, and Mr. Farolles could not possibly lean over it with the chalice. And Kate would be sure to come bursting in and interrupt them, thought Josephine. And supposing the bell rang in the middle? It might be somebody important—about their mourning. Would they get up reverently and go out, or would they have to wait . . . in torture?

"Perhaps you will send round a note by your good Kate if you would care for it later," said Mr. Farolles.

"Oh, yes, thank you very much!" they both said.

Mr. Farolles got up and took his black straw hat from the round table.

"And about the funeral," he said softly. "I may arrange that—as your dear father's old friend and yours, Miss Pinner—and Miss Constantia?"

Josephine and Constantia got up too.

"I should like it to be quite simple," said Josephine firmly, "and not too expensive. At the same time, I should like—"

"A good one that will last," thought dreamy Constantia, as if Josephine were buying a night-gown. But of course Josephine didn't say that. "One suitable to our father's position." She was very nervous.

"I'll run round to our good friend Mr. Knight," said Mr. Farolles soothingly. "I will ask him to come and see you. I am sure you will find him very helpful indeed."

5

Well, at any rate, all that part of it was over, though neither of them could possibly believe that father was never coming back. Josephine had had a moment of absolute terror at the cemetery, while the coffin was lowered, to think that she and Constantia had done this thing without asking his permission. What would father say when he found out? For he was bound to find out sooner or later. He always did. "Buried. You two girls had me *buried!*" She heard his stick thumping. Oh, what would they say? What possible excuse could they make? It sounded such an appallingly heartless thing to do. Such a wicked advantage to take of a person because he happened to be helpless at the moment. The other people seemed to treat it all as a matter of course. They were strangers; they couldn't be expected to understand that father was the very last person for such a thing to happen to. No, the entire blame for it all would fall on her and Constantia. And the expense, she thought, stepping. into the tight-buttoned cab. When she had to show him the bills. What would he say then?

She heard him absolutely roaring, "And do you expect me to pay for this gimcrack excursion of yours?"

"Oh," groaned poor Josephine aloud, "we shouldn't have done it, Con!"

And Constantia, pale as a lemon in all that blackness, said in a frightened whisper, "Done what, Jug?"

"Let them bu-bury father like that," said Josephine, breaking down and crying into her new, queer-smelling mourning handkerchief.

"But what else could we have done?" asked Constantia wonderingly. "We couldn't have kept him, Jug—we couldn't have kept him unburied. At any rate, not in a flat that size."

Josephine blew her nose; the cab was dreadfully stuffy.

"I don't know," she said forlornly. "It is all so dreadful. I feel we ought to have tried to, just for a time at least. To make perfectly sure. One thing's certain"—and her tears sprang out again—"father will never forgive us for this—never!

6

Father would never forgive them. That was what they felt more than ever when, two mornings later, they went into his room to go through his things. They had discussed it quite calmly. It was even down on Josephine's list of things to be done. *Go through father's things and settle about them.* But that was a very different matter from saying after breakfast:

"Well, are you ready, Con?"

"Yes, Jug—when you are."

"Then I think we'd better get it over."

It was dark in the hall. It had been a rule for years never to disturb father in the morning, whatever happened. And now they were going to open the door without knocking even. . . . Constantia's eyes were enormous at the idea; Josephine felt weak in the knees.

"You—you go first," she gasped, pushing Constantia.

But Constantia said, as she always had said on those occasions. "No, Jug, that's not fair. You're eldest."

Josephine was going to say—what at other times she wouldn't have owned to for the world—what she kept for her very last weapon, "But you're tallest," when they noticed that the kitchen door was open, and there stood Kate. . . .

"Very stiff," said Josephine, grasping the door-handle and doing her best to turn it. As if anything ever deceived Kate.

It couldn't be helped. That girl was . . . Then the door was shut behind them, but—but they weren't in father's room at all. They might have suddenly walked through the wall by mistake into a different flat altogether. Was the door just behind them? They were too frightened to look. Josephine knew that if it was it was holding itself tight shut; Constantia felt that, like the doors in dreams, it hadn't any handle at all. It was the coldness which made it so awful. Or the whiteness—which? Everything was covered. The blinds were down, a cloth hung over the mirror, a sheet hid the bed; a huge fan of white paper filled the fireplace. Constantia timidly put out her hand; she almost expected a snowflake to fall. Josephine felt a queer tingling in her nose, as if her nose was freezing. Then a cab klop-klopped over the cobbles below, and the quiet seemed to shake into little pieces.

"I had better pull up a blind," said Josephine bravely.

"Yes, it might be a good idea," whispered Constantia.

They only gave the blind a touch, but it flew up and the cord flew after, rolling round the blind-stick, and the little tassel tapped as if trying to get free. That was too much for Constantia.

"Don't you think—don't you think we might put it off for another day?" she whispered.

"Why?" snapped Josephine, feeling, as usual, much better now that she knew for certain that Constantia was terrified. "It's got to be done. But I do wish you wouldn't whisper, Con."

"I didn't know I was whispering," whispered Constantia.

"And why do you keep staring at the bed?" said Josephine, raising her voice almost defiantly. "There's nothing on the bed."

"Oh, Jug, don't say so!" said poor Connie. "At any rate, not so loudly."

Josephine felt herself that she had gone too far. She took a wide swerve over to the chest of drawers, put out her hand, but quickly drew it back again.

"Connie!" she gasped, and she wheeled round and leaned with her back against the chest of drawers.

"Oh, Jug—What?"

Josephine could only glare. She had the most extraordinary feeling that she had just escaped something awful. But how could she explain to Constantia that father was in the chest of drawers? He was in the top drawer with his handkerchiefs and neckties, or in the next with his shirts and pajamas, or in the lowest of all with his suits. He was watching there, hidden away—just behind the door-handle—ready to spring.

She pulled a funny old-fashioned face at Constantia, just as she used to in the old days when she was going to cry.

"I can't open," she nearly wailed.

"No, don't, Jug," whispered Constantia, earnestly. "It's much better not to. Don't let's open anything. At any rate, not for a long time."

"But—but it seems so weak," said Josephine, breaking down.

"But why not be weak for once, Jug?" argued Constantia, whispering quite fiercely. "If it is weak." And her pale stare flew from the locked writing-table—so safe—to the huge glittering wardrobe, and she began to breathe in a queer, panting way. "Why shouldn't we be weak for once in our lives, Jug? It's quite excusable. Let's be weak—be weak, Jug. It's much nicer to be weak than to be strong."

And then she did one of those amazingly bold things that she'd done about twice before in their lives; she marched over to the wardrobe, turned the key, and took it out of the lock. Took it out of the lock and held it up to Josephine, showing Josephine by her extraordinary smile that she knew what she'd done, she'd risked deliberately father being in there among his overcoats.

If the huge wardrobe had lurched forward, had crashed down on Constantia, Josephine wouldn't have been surprised. On the contrary, she would have thought it the only suitable thing to happen. But nothing happened. Only the room seemed quieter than ever, and bigger flakes of cold air fell on Josephine's shoulders and knees. She began to shiver.

"Come, Jug," said Constantia, still with that awful callous smile, and Josephine followed just as she had that last time, when Constantia had pushed Benny into the round pond.

7

But the strain told on them when they were back in the dining-room. They sat down, very shaky, and looked at each other.

"I don't feel I can settle to anything," said Josephine, "until I've had something. Do you think we could ask Kate for two cups of hot water?"

"I really don't see why we shouldn't," said Constantia carefully. She was quite normal again. "I won't ring. I'll go to the kitchen door and ask her."

"Yes, do," said Josephine, sinking down

into a chair. "Tell her, just two cups, Con, nothing else—on a tray."

"She needn't even put the jug on, need she?" said Constantia, as though Kate might very well complain if the jug had been there.

"Oh, no, certainly not! The jug's not at all necessary. She can pour it direct out of the kettle," cried Josephine, feeling that would be a labour-saving indeed.

Their cold lips quivered at the greenish brims. Josephine curved her small red hands round the cup; Constantia sat up and blew on the wavy steam, making it flutter from one side to the other.

"Speaking of Benny," said Josephine.

And though Benny hadn't been mentioned Constantia immediately looked as though he had.

"He'll expect us to send him something of father's, of course. But it's so difficult to know what to send to Ceylon."

"You mean things get unstuck so on the voyage," murmured Constantia.

"No, lost," said Josephine sharply. "You know there's no post. Only runners."

Both paused to watch a black man in white linen drawers running through the pale fields for dear life, with a large brown-paper parcel in his hands. Josephine's black man was tiny; he scurried along glistening like an ant. But there was something blind and tireless about Constantia's tall, thin fellow which made him, she decided, a very unpleasant person indeed . . . On the veranda, dressed all in white and wearing a cork helmet, stood Benny. His right hand shook up and down, as father's did when he was impatient. And behind him, not in the least interested, sat Hilda, the unknown sister-in-law. She swung in a cane rocker and flicked over the leaves of the *Tatler*.

"I think his watch would be the most suitable present," said Josephine.

Constantia looked up; she seemed surprised.

"Oh, would you trust a gold watch to a native?"

"But of course I'd disguise it," said Josephine. "No one would know it was a watch." She liked the idea of having to make a parcel such a curious shape that no one could possibly guess what it was. She even thought for a moment of hiding the watch in a narrow cardboard corset-box that she'd kept by her for a long time, waiting for it to come in for something. It was such a beautiful firm cardboard. But, no, it wouldn't be appropriate for this occasion. It had lettering on it: *Medium Women's 28. Extra Firm Busks.* It would be almost too much of a surprise for Benny to open that and find father's watch inside.

"And of course it isn't as though it would be going—ticking, I mean," said Constantia, who was still thinking of the native love of jewellery. "At least," she added, "it would be very strange if after all that time it was."

8

Josephine made no reply. She had flown off on one of her tangents. She had suddenly thought of Cyril. Wasn't it more usual for the only grandson to have the watch? And then dear Cyril was so appreciative, and a gold watch meant so much to a young man. Benny, in all probability, had quite got out of the habit of watches; men so seldom wore waistcoats in those hot climates. Whereas Cyril in London wore them from year's end to year's end. And it would be so nice for her and Constantia, when he came to tea, to know it was there. "I see you've got on grandfather's watch, Cyril." It would be somehow so satisfactory.

Dear boy! What a blow his sweet, sympathetic little note had been. Of course they quite understood; but it was most unfortunate.

"It would have been such a point, having him," said Josephine.

"And he would have enjoyed it so," said Constantia, not thinking what she was saying.

However, as soon as he got back he was coming to tea with his aunties. Cyril to tea was one of their rare treats.

"Now, Cyril, you mustn't be frightened of our cakes. Your Auntie Con and I bought them at Buzzard's this morning. We know what a man's appetite is. So don't be ashamed of making a good tea."

Josephine cut recklessly into the rich dark cake that stood for her winter gloves or the soling and heeling of Constantia's only respectable shoes. But Cyril was most unmanlike in appetite.

"I say, Aunt Josephine, I simply can't. I've only just had lunch, you know."

"Oh, Cyril, that can't be true! It's after four," cried Josephine. Constantia sat with her knife poised over the chocolate-roll.

"It is, all the same," said Cyril, "I had to meet a man at Victoria, and he kept me hanging about till . . . there was only time to get lunch and to come on here. And he gave me—phew"—Cyril put his hand to his forehead—"a terrific blowout," he said.

It was disappointing—today of all days. But still he couldn't be expected to know.

"But you'll have a meringue, won't you, Cyril?" said Aunt Josephine. "These meringues were bought specially for you. Your dear father was so fond of them. We were sure you are, too."

"I *am*, Aunt Josephine," cried Cyril ardently. "Do you mind if I take half to begin with?"

"Not at all, dear boy; but we mustn't let you off with that."

"Is your dear father still so fond of meringues?" asked Auntie Con gently. She winced faintly as she broke through the shell of hers.

"Well, I don't quite know, Auntie Con," said Cyril breezily.

At that they both looked up.

"Don't know?" almost snapped Josephine. "Don't know a thing like that about your own father, Cyril?"

"Surely," said Auntie Con softly.

Cyril tried to laugh it off. "Oh, well," he said, "it's such a long time since—" He faltered. He stopped. Their faces were too much for him.

"Even *so,*" said Josephine.

And Auntie Con looked.

Cyril put down his teacup. "Wait a bit," he cried. "Wait a bit, Aunt Josephine. What am I thinking of?"

He looked up. They were beginning to brighten. Cyril slapped his knee.

"Of course," he said, "it was meringues.

How could I have forgotten? Yes, Aunt Josephine, you're perfectly right. Father's most frightfully keen on meringues."

They didn't only beam. Aunt Josephine went scarlet with pleasure; Auntie Con gave a deep, deep sigh.

"And now, Cyril, you must come and see father," said Josephine. "He knows you were coming today."

"Right," said Cyril, very firmly and heartily. He got up from his chair; suddenly he glanced at the clock.

"I say, Auntie Con, isn't your clock a bit slow? I've got to meet a man at—at Paddington just after five. I'm afraid I shan't be able to stay very long with grandfather."

"Oh he won't expect you to stay *very* long!" said Aunt Josephine.

Constantia was still gazing at the clock. She couldn't make up her mind if it was fast or slow. It was one or the other, she felt almost certain of that. At any rate, it had been.

Cyril still lingered. "Aren't you coming along, Auntie Con?"

"Of course," said Josephine, "we shall all go. Come on, Con."

9

They knocked at the door, and Cyril followed his aunts into grandfather's hot, sweetish room.

"Come on," said Grandfather Pinner. "Don't hang about. What is it? What've you been up to?"

He was sitting in front of a roaring fire, clasping his stick. He had a thick rug over his knees. On his lap there lay a beautiful pale yellow silk handkerchief.

"It's Cyril, father," said Josephine shyly. And she took Cyril's hand and led him forward.

"Good afternoon, grandfather," said Cyril, trying to take his hand out of Aunt Josephine's. Grandfather Pinner shot his eyes at Cyril in the way he was famous for. Where was Auntie Con? She stood on the other side of Aunt Josephine; her long arms hung down in front of her; her hands were clasped. She never took her eyes off grandfather.

"Well," said Grandfather Pinner, beginning to thump, "what have you got to tell me?"

What had he, what had he got to tell him? Cyril felt himself smiling like a perfect imbecile. The room was stifling, too.

But Aunt Josephine came to his rescue. She cried brightly, "Cyril says his father is still very fond of meringues, father dear."

"Eh?" said Grandfather Pinner, curving his hand like a purple meringue-shell over one ear.

Josephine repeated, "Cyril says his father is still very fond of meringues."

"Can't hear," said old Colonel Pinner. And he waved Josephine away with his stick, then pointed to Cyril. "Tell me what she's trying to say," he said.

(My God!) "Must I?" said Cyril, blushing and staring at Aunt Josephine.

"Do, dear," she smiled. "It will please him so much."

"Come on, out with it!" cried Colonel Pinner testily, beginning to thump again.

And Cyril leaned forward and yelled, "Father's still very fond of meringues."

At that Grandfather Pinner jumped as though he had been shot.

"Don't shout!" he cried. "What's the matter with the boy? *Meringues!* What about 'em?"

"Oh, Aunt Josephine, must we go on?" groaned Cyril desperately.

"It's quite all right, dear boy," said Aunt Josephine, as though he and she were at the dentist's together. "He'll understand in a minute." And she whispered to Cyril, "He's getting a bit deaf, you know." Then she leaned forward and really bawled at Grandfather Pinner, "Cyril only wanted to tell you, father dear, that *his* father is still very fond of meringues."

Colonel Pinner heard that time, heard and brooded, looking Cyril up and down.

"What an esstraordinary thing!" said old Grandfather Pinner. "What an esstraordinary thing to come all this way here to tell me!"

And Cyril felt it *was*.

"Yes, I shall send Cyril the watch," said Josephine.

"That would be very nice," said Constantia.

"I seem to remember last time he came here there was some little trouble about the time."

10

They were interrupted by Kate bursting through the door in her usual fashion, as though she had discovered some secret panel in the wall.

"Fried or boiled?" asked the bold voice.

Fried or boiled? Josephine and Constantia were quite bewildered for the moment. They could hardly take it in.

"Fried or boiled what, Kate?" asked Josephine, trying to begin to concentrate.

Kate gave a loud sniff. "Fish."

"Well, why didn't you say so immediately?" Josephine reproached her gently. "How could you expect us to understand? There are a great many things in this world, you know, which are fried or boiled." And after such a display of courage, she said quite brightly to Constantia, "Which do you prefer, Con?"

"I think it might be nice to have it fried," said Constantia. "On the other hand, of course boiled fish is very nice. I think I prefer both equally well. . . . Unless you . . . In that case—"

"I shall fry it," said Kate, and she bounced back, leaving their door open and slamming the door of her kitchen.

Josephine gazed at Constantia; she raised her pale eyebrows until they rippled away into her pale hair. She got up. She said in a very lofty, imposing way, "Do you mind following me into the drawing-room, Constantia? I've something of great importance to discuss with you."

For it was always to the drawing-room they retired when they wanted to talk over Kate.

Josephine closed the door meaningly. "Sit down, Constantia," she said, still very grand. She might have been receiving Constantia for the first time. And Con looked round vaguely for a chair, as though she felt indeed quite a stranger.

"Now, the question is," said Josephine, bending forward, "whether we shall keep her or not."

"That is the question," agreed Constantia.

"And this time," said Josephine firmly, "we must come to a definite decision."

Constantia looked for a moment as though she might begin going over all the other times, but she pulled herself together and said, "Yes, Jug."

"You see, Con," explained Josephine, "everything is so changed now." Constantia looked up quickly. "I mean," went on Josephine, "we're not dependent on Kate as we were." And she blushed faintly. "There's not father to cook for."

"That is perfectly true," agreed Constantia. "Father certainly doesn't want any cooking now, whatever else—"

Josephine broke in sharply, "You're not sleepy, are you, Con?"

"Sleepy, Jug?" Constantia was wide-eyed.

"Well, concentrate more," said Josephine sharply, and she returned to the subject. "What it comes to is, if we did"—and this she barely breathed, glancing at the door—"give Kate notice"—she raised her voice again—"we could manage our own food."

"Why not?" cried Constantia. She couldn't help smiling. The idea was so exciting. She clasped her hands. "What should we live on, Jug?"

"Oh, eggs in various forms!" said Jug, lofty again. "And besides, there are all the cooked foods."

"But I've always heard," said Constantia, "they are considered so very expensive."

"Not if one buys them in moderation," said Josephine. But she tore herself away from the fascinating bypath and dragged Constantia after her.

"What we've got to decide now, however, is whether we really do trust Kate or not."

Constantia leaned back. Her flat little laugh flew from her lips.

"Isn't it curious, Jug," said she, "that just on this one subject I've never been able to quite make up my mind."

11

She never had. The whole difficulty was to prove anything. How did one prove things, how could one? Suppose Kate had stood in front of her and deliberately made a face. Mightn't she very well have been in pain? Wasn't it impossible, at any rate, to ask Kate if she was making a face at her? If Kate answered "No"—and of course she would say "No"—what a position! How undignified! Then again Constantia suspected, she was almost certain that Kate went to her chest of drawers when she and Josephine were out, not to take things but to spy. Many times she had come back to find her amethyst cross in the most unlikely places, under her lace ties or on top of her evening Bertha. More than once she had laid a trap for Kate. She had arranged things in a special order and then called Josephine to witness.

"You see, Jug?"

"Quite, Con."

"Now we shall be able to tell."

But, oh, dear, when she did go to look, she was as far off from proof as ever! If anything was displaced, it might so very well have happened as she closed the drawer; a jolt might have done it so easily.

"You come, Jug, and decide. I really can't. It's too difficult."

But after a long pause and a long glare Josephine would sigh, "Now you've put the doubt into my mind, Con, I'm sure I can't tell myself."

"Well, we can't postpone it again," said Josephine. "If we postpone it this time—"

12

But at that moment in the street below a barrel-organ struck up. Josephine and Constantia sprang to their feet together.

"Run, Con," said Josephine. "Run quickly. There's six-pence on the—"

Then they remembered. It didn't matter. They would never have to stop the organ-grinder again. Never again would she and Constantia be told to make that monkey take his noise somewhere else. Never would sound that loud, strange bellow when father thought they were not hurrying enough. The organ-grinder might play there all day and the stick would not thump.

It never will thump again,
It never will thump again,

played the barrel-organ.

What was Constantia thinking? She had such a strange smile; she looked different. She couldn't be going to cry.

"Jug, Jug," said Constantia softly, pressing her hands together. "Do you know what day it is? It's Saturday. It's a week today, a whole week."

A week since father died,
A week since father died,

cried the barrel-organ. And Josephine, too, forgot to be practical and sensible; she smiled faintly, strangely. On the Indian carpet there fell a square of sunlight, pale red; it came and went and came—and stayed, deepened—until it shone almost golden.

"The sun's out," said Josephine, as though it really mattered.

A perfect fountain of bubbling notes shook from the barrel-organ, round, bright notes, carelessly scattered.

Constantia lifted her big, cold hands as if to catch them, and then her hands fell again. She walked over to the mantel-piece to her favourite Buddha. And the stone and gilt image, whose smile always gave her such a queer feeling, almost a pain and yet a pleasant pain, seemed today to be more than smiling. He knew something; he had a secret. "I know something you don't know," said her Buddha. Oh, what was it, what could it be? And yet she had always felt there was . . . something.

The sunlight pressed through the windows, thieved its way in, flashed its light over the furniture and the photographs. Josephine watched it. When it came to mother's photograph, the enlargement over the piano, it lingered as though puzzled to find so little remained of mother, except the earrings shaped like tiny pagodas and a black feather boa. Why did the photographs of dead people always fade so? wondered Josephine. As soon as a person was dead her photograph died too. But, of course, this one of mother was very old. It was thirty-five years old.

Josephine remembered standing on a chair and pointing out that feather boa to Constantia and telling her that it was a snake that had killed their mother in Ceylon. . . . Would everything have been different if mother hadn't died? She didn't see why. Aunt Florence had lived with them until they had left school, and they had moved three times and had their yearly holiday and . . . and there'd been changes of servants, of course.

Some little sparrows, young sparrows they sounded, chirped on the window-ledge. *Yeep-eyeep-yeep.* But Josephine felt they were not sparrows, not on the window-ledge. It was inside her, that queer little crying noise. *Yeep-eyeep-yeep.* Ah, what was it crying, so weak and forlorn?

If mother had lived, might they have married? But there had been nobody for them to marry. There had been father's Anglo-Indian friends before he quarrelled with them. But after that she and Constantia never met a single man except clergymen. How did one meet men? Or even if they'd met them, how could they have got to know men well enough to be more than strangers? One read of people having adventures, being followed, and so on. But nobody had ever followed Constantia and her. Oh, yes, there had been one year at Eastbourne a mysterious man at their boarding-house who had put a note on the jug of hot water outside their bedroom door! But by the time Connie had found it the steam had made the writing too faint to read; they couldn't even make out to which of them it was addressed. And he had left the next day. And that was all. The rest had been looking after father, and at the same time keeping out of father's way. But now? But now? The thieving sun touched Josephine gently. She lifted her face. She was drawn over to the window by gentle beams . . .

Until the barrel-organ stopped playing Constantia stayed before the Buddha, wondering, but not as usual, not vaguely. This time her wonder was like longing. She remembered the times she had come in here, crept out of bed in her nightgown when the moon was full, and lain on the floor with her arms outstretched, as though she was crucified. Why? The big, pale moon had made her do it. The horrible dancing figures on the carved screen had leered at her and she hadn't minded. She remembered too how, whenever they were at the seaside, she had gone off by herself and got as close to the sea as she could, and sung something, something she had made up, while she gazed all over that restless water. There had been this other life, running out, bringing things home in bags, getting things on approval, discussing them with Jug, taking them back to get more things on approval, and arranging father's trays and trying not to annoy father. But it all seemed to have happened in a kind of tunnel. It wasn't real. It was only when she came out of the tunnel into the moonlight or by the sea or into a thunderstorm that she really felt herself. What did it mean? What did it all lead to? Now? Now?

She turned away from the Buddha with one of her vague gestures. She went over to where Josephine was standing. She wanted to say something to Josephine, something frightfully important, about—about the future and what . . .

"Don't you think perhaps—" she began.

But Josephine interrupted her. "I was wondering if now—" she murmured. They stopped; they waited for each other.

"Go on, Con," said Josephine.

"No, no, Jug; after you," said Constantia.

"No, say what you were going to say. You began," said Josephine.

"I . . . I'd rather hear what you were going to say first," said Constantia.

"Don't be absurd, Con."

"Really, Jug."

"Connie!"

"Oh, *Jug!*"

A pause. Then Constantia said faintly, "I can't say what I was going to say, Jug, because I've forgotten what it was . . . that I was going to say."

Josephine was silent for a moment. She stared at a big cloud where the sun had been. Then she replied shortly, "I've forgotten too."

MRS. MEDWIN

Henry James
(1843–1916)

I

"Well, we *are* a pair!" the poor lady's visitor broke out to her, at the end of her explanation, in a manner disconcerting enough. The poor lady was Miss Cutter, who lived in South Audley Street, where she had an "upper half" so concise that it had to pass, boldly, for convenient; and her visitor was her half-brother, whom she had not seen for three years. She was remarkable for a maturity of which every symptom might have been observed to be admirably controlled, had not a tendency to stoutness just affirmed its independence. Her present, no doubt, insisted too much on her past, but with the excuse, sufficiently valid, that she must certainly once have been prettier. She was clearly not contented with once—she wished to be prettier again. She neglected nothing that could produce that illusion, and, being both fair and fat, dressed almost wholly in black. When she added a little colour it was not, at any rate, to her drapery. Her small rooms had the peculiarity that everything they contained appeared to testify with vividness to her position in society, quite as if they had been furnished by the bounty of admiring friends. They were adorned indeed almost exclusively with objects that nobody buys, as had more than once been remarked by spectators of her own sex, for herself, and would have been luxurious if luxury consisted mainly in photographic portraits slashed across with signatures, in baskets of flowers beribboned with the cards of passing compatriots, and in a neat collection of red volumes, blue volumes, alphabetical volumes, aids to London lucidity, of every sort, devoted to addresses and engagements. To be in Miss Cutter's tiny drawing-room, in short, even with Miss Cutter alone—should you by any chance have found her so—was somehow to be in the world and in a crowd. It was like an agency—it bristled with particulars.

This was what the tall, lean, loose gentleman lounging there before her might have appeared to read in the suggestive scene over which, while she talked to him, his eyes moved without haste and without rest. "Oh, come, Mamie!" he occasionally threw off; and the words were evidently connected with the impression thus absorbed. His comparative youth spoke of waste even as her positive—her too positive—spoke of economy. There was only one thing, that is, to make up in him for everything he had lost, though it was distinct enough indeed that this thing might sometimes serve. It consisted in the perfection of an indifference, an indifference at the present moment directed to the plea—a plea of inability, of pure destitution—with which his sister had met him. Yet it had even now a wider embrace, took in quite sufficiently all consequences of queerness, confessed in advance to the false note that, in such a setting, he almost excruciatingly constituted. He cared as little that he looked at moments all his impudence as that he looked all his shabbiness, all his cleverness, all his history. These different things were written in him—in his premature baldness, his seamed, strained face, the lapse from bravery of his long tawny moustache; above all, in his easy, friendly, universally acquainted eye, so much too sociable for mere conversation. What possible relation with him could be natural enough to meet it? He wore a scant, rough Inverness cape and a pair of black trousers, wanting in substance and marked with the sheen of time, that had presumably once served for evening use. He spoke with the slowness helplessly permitted to Americans—as something too slow to be stopped—and he repeated that he found himself associated with Miss Cutter in a harmony worthy of wonder. She had been telling him not only that she couldn't possibly give him ten pounds, but that his unexpected arrival, should he insist on being much in view,

might seriously interfere with arrangements necessary to her own maintenance; on which he had begun by replying that he of course knew she had long ago spent her money, but that he looked to her now exactly because she had, without the aid of that convenience, mastered the art of life.

"I'd really go away with a fiver, my dear, if you'd only tell me how you do it. It's no use saying only, as you've always said, that 'people are very kind to you.' What the devil are they kind to you *for?*"

"Well, one reason is precisely that no particular inconvenience has hitherto been supposed to attach to me. I'm just what I am," said Mamie Cutter; "nothing less and nothing more. It's awkward to have to explain to you, which, moreover, I really needn't in the least. I'm clever and amusing and charming." She was uneasy and even frightened, but she kept her temper and met him with a grace of her own. "I don't think you ought to ask me more questions than I ask you."

"Ah, my dear," said the odd young man, *"I've* no mysteries. Why in the world, since it was what you came out for and have devoted so much of your time to, haven't you pulled it off? Why haven't you married?"

"Why haven't *you?"* she retorted. "Do you think that if I had it would have been better for you?—that my husband would for a moment have put up with you? Do you mind my asking you if you'll kindly go *now?"* she went on after a glance at the clock. "I'm expecting a friend, whom I must see alone, on a matter of great importance—"

"And my being seen with you may compromise your respectability or undermine your nerve?" He sprawled imperturbably in his place, crossing again, in another sense, his long black legs and showing, above his low shoes, an absurd reach of parti-coloured sock. "I take your point well enough, but mayn't you be after all quite wrong? If you can't do anything for me couldn't you at least do something *with* me? If it comes to that, I'm clever and amusing and charming too! I've been such an ass that you don't appreciate me. But people like me—I assure you they do. They usually don't know what an ass I've been; they only see the surface, which"— and he stretched himself afresh as she looked him up and down—"you *can* imagine them, can't you, rather taken with? *I'm* 'what I am' too; nothing less and nothing more. That's true of us as a family, you see. We *are* a crew!" He delivered himself serenely. His voice was soft and flat, his pleasant eyes, his simple tones tending to the solemn, achieved at moments that effect of quaintness which is, in certain connections, socially so known and enjoyed. "English people have quite a weakness for me—more than any others. I get on with them beautifully. I've always been with them abroad. They think me," the young man explained, "diabolically American."

"You!" Such stupidity drew from her a sigh of compassion.

Her companion apparently quite understood it. "Are you homesick, Mamie?" he asked, with wondering irrelevance.

The manner of the question made her for some reason, in spite of her preoccupations, break into a laugh. A shade of indulgence, a sense of other things, came back to her. "You *are* funny, Scott!"

"Well," remarked Scott, "that's just what I claim. But *are* you so homesick?" he spaciously inquired, not as if to a practical end, but from an easy play of intelligence.

"I'm just dying of it!" said Mamie Cutter.

"Why, so am I!" Her visitor had a sweetness of concurrence.

"We're the only decent people," Miss Cutter declared. "And I know. *You* don't— you can't; and I can't explain. Come in," she continued with a return of her impatience and an increase of her decision, "at seven sharp."

She had quitted her seat some time before, and now, to get him into motion, hovered before him while, still motionless, he looked up at her. Something intimate, in the silence, appeared to pass between them—a community of fatigue and failure and, after all, of intelligence. There was a final, cynical humour in it. It determined him, at any rate, at last, and he slowly rose, taking in again as

he stood there the testimony of the room. He might have been counting the photographs, but he looked at the flowers with detachment. "Who's coming?"

"Mrs. Medwin."

"American?"

"Dear no!"

"Then what are you doing for her?"

"I work for everyone," she promptly returned.

"For everyone who pays? So I suppose. Yet isn't it only we who do pay?"

There was a drollery, not lost on her, in the way his queer presence lent itself to his emphasised plural. "Do you consider that *you* do?"

At this, with his deliberation, he came back to his charming idea. "Only try me, and see if I can't be *made* to. Work me in." On her sharply presenting her back he stared a little at the clock. "If I come at seven may I stay to dinner?"

It brought her round again. "Impossible. I'm dining out."

"With whom?"

She had to think. "With Lord Considine."

"Oh, my eye!" Scott exclaimed.

She looked at him gloomily. "Is *that* sort of tone what makes you pay? I think you might understand," she went on, "that if you're to sponge on me successfully you mustn't ruin me. I must have *some* remote resemblance to a lady."

"Yes? But why must *I*?" Her exasperated silence was full of answers, of which, however, his inimitable manner took no account. "You don't understand my real strength; I doubt if you even understand your own. You're clever, Mamie, but you're not so clever as I supposed. However," he pursued, "it's out of Mrs. Medwin that you'll get it."

"Get what?"

"Why, the cheque that will enable you to assist me."

On this, for a moment, she met his eyes. "If you'll come back at seven sharp—not a minute before, and not a minute after, I'll give you two five-pound notes."

He thought it over. "Whom are you expecting a minute after?"

It sent her to the window with a groan almost of anguish, and she answered nothing till she had looked at the street. "If you injure me, you know, Scott, you'll be sorry."

"I wouldn't injure you for the world. What I want to do in fact is really help you, and I promise you that I won't leave you—by which I mean won't leave London—till I've effected something really pleasant for you. I like you, Mamie, because I like pluck; I like you much more than you like me. I like you very, *very* much." He had at last with this reached the door and opened it, but he remained with his hand on the latch. "What does Mrs. Medwin want of you?" he thus brought out.

She had come round to see him disappear, and in the relief of this prospect she again just indulged him. "The impossible."

He waited another minute. "And you're going to do it?"

"I'm going to do it," said Mamie Cutter.

"Well, then, that ought to be a haul. Call it *three* fivers!" he laughed. "At seven sharp." And at last he left her alone.

2

Miss Cutter waited till she heard the house-door close; after which, in a sightless, mechanical way, she moved about the room, readjusting various objects that he had not touched. It was as if his mere voice and accent had spoiled her form. But she was not left too long to reckon with these things, for Mrs. Medwin was promptly announced. This lady was not, more than her hostess, in the first flush of her youth; her appearance—the scattered remains of beauty manipulated by taste—resembled one of the light repasts in which the fragments of yesterday's dinner figure with a conscious ease that makes up for the want of presence. She was perhaps of an effect still too immediate to be called interesting, but she was candid, gentle and surprised—not fatiguingly surprised, only just in the right degree; and her white face—it was too white—with the fixed eyes, the somewhat touzled hair and the Louis Seize hat, might at the end of the very long neck

have suggested the head of a princess carried, in a revolution, on a pike. She immediately took up the business that had brought her, with the air, however, of drawing from the omens then discernible less confidence than she had hoped. The complication lay in the fact that if it was Mamie's part to present the omens, that lady yet had so to colour them as to make her own service large. She perhaps over-coloured, for her friend gave way to momentary despair.

"What you mean is then that it's simply impossible?"

"Oh no," said Mamie, with a qualified emphasis. "It's *possible*."

"But disgustingly difficult?"

"As difficult as you like."

"Then what can I do that I haven't done?"

"You can only wait a little longer."

"But that's just what I *have* done. I've done nothing else. I'm always waiting a little longer!"

Miss Cutter retained, in spite of this pathos, her grasp of the subject. "*The* thing, as I've told you, is for you first to be seen."

"But if people won't look at me?"

"They will."

"They *will?*" Mrs. Medwin was eager.

"They shall," her hostess went on. "It's their only having heard—without having seen."

"But if they stare straight the other way?" Mrs. Medwin continued to object. "You can't simply go up to them and twist their heads about."

"It's just what I can," said Mamie Cutter.

But her charming visitor, heedless for the moment of this attenuation, had found the way to put it. "It's the old story. You can't go into the water till you swim, and you can't swim till you go into the water. I can't be spoken to till I'm seen, but I can't be seen till I'm spoken to."

She met this lucidity, Miss Cutter, with but an instant's lapse. "You say I can't twist their heads about. But I *have* twisted them."

It had been quietly produced, but it gave her companion a jerk. "They say 'Yes'?"

She summed it up. "All but one. *She* says 'No.'"

Mrs. Medwin thought; then jumped. "Lady Wantridge?"

Miss Cutter, as more delicate, only bowed admission. "I shall see her either this afternoon or late to-morrow. But she has written."

Her visitor wondered again. "May I see her letter?"

"No." She spoke with decision. "But I shall square her."

"Then how?"

"Well"—and Miss Cutter, as if looking upward for inspiration, fixed her eyes awhile on the ceiling—"well, it will come to me."

Mrs. Medwin watched her—it was impressive. "And will *they* come to you—the others?" This question drew out the fact that they would—so far, at least, as they consisted of Lady Edward, Lady Bellhouse and Mrs. Pouncer, who had engaged to muster, at the signal of tea, on the 14th—prepared, as it were, for the worst. There was of course always the chance that Lady Wantridge might take the field in such force as to paralyse them, though that danger, at the same time, seemed inconsistent with her being squared. It didn't perhaps all quite ideally hang together; but what it sufficiently came to was that if she was the one who could do most *for* a person in Mrs. Medwin's position she was also the one who could do most against. It would therefore be distinctly what our friend familiarly spoke of as "collar-work." The effect of these mixed considerations was at any rate that Mamie eventually acquiesced in the idea, handsomely thrown out by her client, that she should have an "advance" to go on with. Miss Cutter confessed that it seemed at times as if one scarce *could* go on; but the advance was, in spite of this delicacy, still more delicately made—made in the form of a banknote, several sovereigns, some loose silver and two coppers, the whole contents of her purse, neatly disposed by Mrs. Medwin on one of the tiny tables. It seemed to clear the air for deeper intimacies, the fruit of which was that Mamie, lonely, after all, in her crowd, and always more helpful than helped, eventually brought out that the way Scott had been going on was what seemed

momentarily to overshadow her own power to do so.

"I've had a descent from him." But she had to explain. "My half-brother—Scott Homer. A wretch."

"What kind of a wretch?"

"Every kind. I lose sight of him at times—he disappears abroad. But he always turns up again, worse then ever."

"Violent?"

"No."

"Maudlin?"

"No."

"Only unpleasant?"

"No. Rather pleasant. Awfully clever—awfully travelled and easy."

"Then what's the matter with him?"

Mamie mused, hesitated—seemed to see a wide past. "I don't know."

"Something in the background?" Then as her friend was silent, "Something queer about cards?" Mrs. Medwin threw off.

"I don't know—and I don't want to!"

"Ah well, I'm sure *I* don't," Mrs. Medwin returned with spirit. The note of sharpness was perhaps also a little in the observation she made as she gathered herself to go. "Do you mind my saying something?"

Mamie took her eyes quickly from the money on the little stand. "You may say what you like."

"I only mean that anything awkward you may have to keep out of the way does seem to make more wonderful, doesn't it, that you should have got just where you are? I allude, you know, to your position."

"I see." Miss Cutter somewhat coldly smile "To my power."

"So awfully remarkable in an American."

"Ah, you like us so."

Mrs. Medwin candidly considered. "But we don't, dearest."

Her companion's smile brightened. "Then why do you come to me?"

"Oh, I like *you!*" Mrs. Medwin made out.

"Then that's it. There are no 'Americans.' It's always 'you.'"

"Me?" Mrs. Medwin looked lovely, but a little muddled.

"*Me!*" Mamie Cutter laughed. "But if you like me, you dear thing, you can judge if I like *you*." She gave her a kiss to dismiss her. "I'll see you again when I've seen her."

"Lady Wantridge? I hope so, indeed. I'll turn up late to-morrow, if you don't catch me first. Has it come to you yet?" the visitor, now at the door, went on.

"No; but it will. There's time."

"Oh, a little less every day!"

Miss Cutter had approached the table and glanced again at the gold and silver and the note, not indeed absolutely overlooked the two coppers. "The balance," she put it, "the day after?"

"That very night, if you like."

"Then count on me."

"Oh, if I didn't—!" But the door closed on the dark idea. Yearningly then, and only when it had done so, Miss Cutter took up the money.

She went out with it ten minutes later, and, the calls on her time being many, remained out so long that at half-past six she had not come back. At that hour, on the other hand, Scott Homer knocked at her door, where her maid, who opened it with a weak pretence of holding it firm, ventured to announce to him, as a lesson well learnt, that he had not been expected till seven. No lesson, none the less, could prevail against his native art. He pleaded fatigue, her, the maid's, dreadful depressing London, and the need to curl up somewhere. If she would just leave him quiet half an hour that old sofa upstairs would do for it, of which he took quickly such effectual possession that when, five minutes later, she peeped, nervous for her broken vow, into the drawing-room, the faithless young woman found him extended at his length and peacefully asleep.

3

The situation before Miss Cutter's return developed in other directions still, and when that event took place, at a few minutes past seven, these circumstances were, by the foot of the stair, between mistress and maid, the subject of some interrogative gasps and scared admissions. Lady Wantridge had arrived shortly after the interloper, and wishing, as she said, to wait, had gone straight up in spite of being told he was lying down.

"She distinctly understood he was there?"

"Oh yes, ma'am; I thought it right to mention."

"And what did you call him?"

"Well, ma'am, I thought it unfair to *you* to call him anything but a gentleman."

Mamie took it all in, though there might well be more of it than one could quickly embrace. "But if she has had time," she flashed, "to find out he isn't one?"

"Oh, ma'am, she had a quarter of an hour."

"Then she isn't with him still?"

"No, ma'am; she came down again at last. She rang, and I saw her here, and she said she wouldn't wait longer."

Miss Cutter darkly mused. "Yet had already waited—?"

"Quite a quarter."

"Mercy on us!" She began to mount. Before reaching the top, however, she had reflected that quite a quarter was long if Lady Wantridge had only been shocked. On the other hand, it was short if she had only been pleased. But how *could* she have been pleased? The very essence of their actual crisis was just that there was no pleasing her. Mamie had but to open the drawing-room door indeed to perceive that this was not true at least of Scott Homer, who was horribly cheerful.

Miss Cutter expressed to her brother without reserve her sense of the constitutional, the brutal selfishness that had determined his mistimed return. It had taken place, in violation of their agreement, exactly at the moment when it was most cruel to her that he should be there, and if she must now completely wash her hands of him he had only himself to thank. She had come in flushed with resentment and for a moment had been voluble; but it would have been striking that, though the way he received her might have seemed but to aggravate, it presently justified him by causing their relation really to take a stride. He had the art of confounding those who would quarrel with him by reducing them to the humiliation of an irritated curiosity.

"What *could* she have made of you?" Mamie demanded.

"My dear girl, she's not a woman who's eager to make too much of anything—anything, I mean, that will prevent her from doing as she likes, what she takes into her head. Of course," he continued to explain, "if it's something she doesn't want to do, she'll make as much as Moses."

Mamie wondered if that was the way he talked to her visitor, but felt obliged to own to his acuteness. It was an exact description of Lady Wantridge, and she was conscious of tucking it away for future use in a corner of her miscellaneous little mind. She withheld, however, all present acknowledgment, only addressing him another question. "Did you really get on with her?"

"Have you still to learn, darling—I can't help again putting it to you—that I get on with everybody? That's just what I don't seem able to drive into you. Only see how I get on with *you*."

She almost stood corrected. "What I mean is, of course, whether—"

"Whether she made love to me? Shyly, yet—or because—shamefully? She would certainly have liked awfully to stay."

"Then why didn't she?"

"Because, on account of some other matter—and I could see it was true—she hadn't time. Twenty minutes—she was here less—were all she came to give you. So don't be afraid I've frightened her away. She'll come back."

Mamie thought it over. "Yet you didn't go with her to the door?"

"She wouldn't let me, and I know when to do what I'm told—quite as much as what I'm not told. She wanted to find out about me. I mean from your little creature; a pearl of fidelity, by the way."

"But what on earth did she come up for?" Mamie again found herself appealing, and, just by that fact, showing her need of help.

"Because she always goes up." Then, as, in the presence of this rapid generalisation, to say nothing of that of such a relative altogether, Miss Cutter could only show as comparatively blank: "I mean she knows when to go up and when to come down. She has instincts; she didn't know whom you might have up here. It's a kind of compliment to you anyway. Why, Mamie," Scott pursued, "you don't know the curiosity we any of us inspire. You wouldn't believe what I've seen. The bigger bugs they are the more they're on the look-out."

Mamie still followed, but at a distance. "The look-out for what?"

"Why, for anything that will help them to live. You've been here all this time without making out then, about them, what I've had to pick out as I can? They're dead, don't you see? And *we're* alive."

"You? Oh!"—Mamie almost laughed about it.

"Well, they're a worn-out old lot, anyhow; they've used up their resources. They do look out; and I'll do them the justice to say they're not afraid—not even of me!" he continued as his sister again showed something of the same irony. "Lady Wantridge, at any rate, wasn't; that's what I mean by her having made love to me. She does what she likes. Mind it, you know." He was by this time fairly teaching her to know one of her best friends, and when, after it, he had come back to the great point of his lesson—that of her failure, through feminine inferiority, practically to grasp the truth that their being just as they were, he and she, was the real card for them to play—when he had renewed that reminder he left her absolutely in a state of dependence. Her impulse to press him on the subject of Lady Wantridge dropped; it was as if she had felt that, whatever had taken place, something would somehow come of it. She was to be, in a manner, disappointed, but the impression helped to keep her over to the next morning, when, as Scott had foretold, his new acquaintance did reappear, explaining to Miss Cutter that she had acted the day before to gain time and that she even now sought to gain it by not waiting longer. What, she promptly intimated she had asked herself, could that friend be thinking of?

She must show where she stood before things had gone too far. If she had brought her answer without more delay she wished to make it sharp. Mrs. Medwin? Never! "No, my dear—not I. *There* I stop."

Mamie had known it would be "collar-work," but somehow now, at the beginning, she felt her heart sink. It was not that she had expected to carry the position with a rush, but that, as always after an interval, her visitor's defences really loomed—and quite, as it were, to the material vision—too large. She was always planted with them, volumi-nous, in the very centre of the passage; was like a person accommodated with a chair in some unlawful place at the theatre. She wouldn't move and you couldn't get round. Mamie's calculation indeed had not been on getting round; she was obliged to recognise that, too foolishly and fondly, she had dreamed of producing a surrender. Her dream had been the fruit of her need; but, conscious that she was even yet unequipped for pres-sure, she felt, almost for the first time in her life, superficial and crude. She was to be paid —but with what was she, to that end, to pay? She had engaged to find an answer to this question, but the answer had not, according to her promise, "come." And Lady Wantridge meanwhile massed herself, and there was no view of her that didn't show her as verily, by some process too obscure to be traced, the hard depository of the social law. She was no younger, no fresher, no stronger, really, than any of them; she was only, with a kind of haggard fineness, a sharpened taste for like, and, with all sorts of things behind and be-neath her, more abysmal and more immoral, more secure and more impertinent. The points she made were two in number. One was that she absolutely declined; the other was that she quite doubted if Mamie herself had measured the job. The thing couldn't be done. But say it *could* be; was Mamie quite the person to do it? To this Miss Cutter, with a sweet smile, replied that she quite under-stood how little she might seem so. "I'm only one of the persons to whom it has appeared that *you* are."

"The who are the others?"

"Well, to begin with, Lady Edward, Lady Bellhouse and Mrs. Pouncer."

"Do you mean that they'll come to meet her?"

"I've seen them, and they've promised."

"To come, of course," Lady Wantridge said, "if *I* come."

Her hostess hesitated. "Oh, of course, you could prevent them. But I should take it as awfully kind of you not to. *Won't* you do this for me?" Mamie pleaded.

Her friend looked about the room very much as Scott had done. "Do they really understand what it's *for?*"

"Perfectly. So that she may call."

"And what good will that do her?"

Miss Cutter faltered, but she presently brought it out. "Of course what one hopes is that you'll ask her."

"Ask her to call?"

"Ask her to dine. Ask her, if you'd be so *truly* sweet, for a Sunday, or something of that sort, and even if only in one of your *most* mixed parties, to Catchmore."

Miss Cutter felt the less hopeful after this effort in that her companion only showed a strange good nature. And it was not the amiability of irony; yet it *was* amusement. "Take Mrs. Medwin into my family?"

"Some day, when you're taking forty others."

"Ah, but what I don't see is what it does for *you.* You're already so welcome among us that you can scarcely improve your posi-tion even by forming for us the most delight-ful relation."

"Well, I know how dear you are," Mamie Cutter replied; "but one has, after all, more than one side, and more than one sympathy. I like her, you know." And even at this Lady Wantridge was not shocked; she showed that ease and blandness which were her way, un-fortunately, of being most impossible. She remarked that *she* might listen to such things, because she was clever enough for them not to matter; only Mamie should take care how she went about saying them at large. When she became definite, however, in a minute, on the subject of the public facts, Miss Cutter soon found herself ready to make her own concession. Of course, she didn't dispute *them:* there they were; they were unfortunately on record, and nothing was to be done about them but to—Mamie found it, in truth, at this point, a little difficult.

"Well, what? Pretend already to have forgotten them?"

"Why not, when you've done it in so many other cases?"

"There *are* no other cases so bad. One meets them, at any rate, as they come. Some you can manage, others you can't. It's no use, you must give them up. They're past patching; there's nothing to be done with them. There's nothing, accordingly, to be done with Mrs. Medwin but to put her off." And Lady Wantridge rose to her height.

"Well, you know, I *do* do things," Mamie quavered with a smile so strained that it partook of exaltation.

"You help people? Oh yes, I've known you to do wonders. But stick," said Lady Wantridge with strong and cheerful emphasis, "to your Americans!"

Miss Cutter, gazing, got up. "You don't do justice, Lady Wantridge, to your own compatriots. Some of them are really charming. Besides," said Mamie, "working for mine often strikes me, so far as the interest—the inspiration and excitement, don't you know? —go, as rather too easy. You all, as I constantly have occasion to say, like us so!"

Her companion frankly weighed it. "Yes; it takes that to account for your position. I've always thought of you, nevertheless, as keeping, for their benefit, a regular working agency. They come to you, and you place them. There remains, I confess," her ladyship went on in the same free spirit, "the great wonder—"

"Of how I first placed my poor little self? Yes," Mamie bravely conceded, "when *I* began there was no agency. I just worked my passage. I didn't even come to *you,* did I? You never noticed me till, as Mrs. Short Stokes says, 'I was 'way, 'way up!' Mrs. Medwin," she threw in, "can't get over it." Then, as her friend looked vague: "Over my social situation."

"Well, it's no great flattery to you to say,"

Lady Wantridge good-humouredly returned, "that she certainly can't hope for one resembling it." Yet it really seemed to spread there before them. "You simply *made* Mrs. Short Stokes."

"In spite of her name!" Mamie smiled.

"Oh, your names—! In spite of everything."

"Ah, I'm something of an artist." With which, and a relapse marked by her wistful eyes into the gravity of the matter, she supremely fixed her friend. She felt how little she minded betraying at last the extremity of her need, and it was out of this extremity that her appeal proceeded. "Have I really had your last word? It means so much to me."

Lady Wantridge came straight to the point. "You mean you depend on it?"

"Awfully!"

"Is it all you have?"

"All. Now."

"But Mrs. Short Stokes and the others— 'rolling,' aren't they? Don't they pay up?"

"Ah," sighed Mamie, "if it wasn't for them—!"

Lady Wantridge perceived. "You've had so much?"

"I couldn't have gone on."

"Then what do you do with it all?"

"Oh, most of it goes back to them. There are all sorts, and it's all help. Some of them have nothing."

"Oh, if you feed the hungry," Lady Wantridge laughed, "you're indeed in a great way of business. Is Mrs. Medwin"—her transition was immediate—"really rich?"

"Really. He left her everything."

"So that if I do say 'yes'—"

"It will quite set me up."

"I see—and how much more responsible it makes one! But I'd rather myself give you the money."

"Oh!" Mamie coldly murmured.

"You mean I mayn't suspect your prices? Well, I daresay I don't! But I'd rather give you ten pounds."

"Oh!" Mamie repeated in a tone that sufficiently coverd her prices. The question was in every way larger. "Do you *never* forgive?" she reproachfully inquired. The door opened, however, at the moment she spoke, and Scott Homer presented himself.

4

Scott Homer wore exactly, to his sister's eyes, the aspect he had worn the day before, and it also formed, to her sense, the great feature of his impartial greeting.

"How d'ye do, Mamie? How d'ye do, Lady Wantridge?"

"How d'ye do again?" Lady Wantridge replied with an equanimity striking to her hostess. It was as if Scott's own had been contagious; it was almost indeed as if she had seen him before. *Had* she ever so seen him—before the previous day? While Miss Cutter put to herself this question her visitor, at all events, met the one she had previously uttered.

"Ever 'forgive'?" this personage echoed in a tone that made as little account as possible of the interruption. "Dear, yes! The people I *have* forgiven!" She laughed—perhaps a little nervously; and she was now looking at Scott. The way she looked at him was precisely what had already had its effect for his sister. "The people I can!"

"Can you forgive *me?*" asked Scott Homer.

She took it so easily. "But—what?"

Mamie interposed; she turned directly to her brother. "Don't try her. Leave it so." She had had an inspiration; it was the most extraordinary thing in the world. "Don't try *him*"—she had turned to their companion. She looked grave, sad, strange. "Leave it so." Yes, it was a distinct inspiration, which she couldn't have explained, but which had come, prompted by something she had caught—the extent of the recognition expressed—in Lady Wantridge's face. It had come absolutely of a sudden, straight out of the opposition of the two figures before her—quite as if a concussion had struck a light. The light was helped by her quickened sense that her friend's silence on the incident of the day before showed some sort of consciousness. She looked surprised. "Do you know my brother?"

"*Do* I know you?" Lady Wantridge asked of him.

"No, Lady Wantridge," Scott pleasantly confessed, "not one little mite!"

"Well, then, if you *must* go—!" and Mamie offered her a hand. "But I'll go down with you. Not *you!*" she launched at her brother, who immediately effaced himself. His way of doing so—and he had already done so, as for Lady Wantridge, in respect to their previous encounter—struck her even at the moment as an instinctive, if slightly blind, tribute to her possession of an idea; and as such, in its celerity, made her so admire him, and their common wit, that, on the spot, she more than forgave him his queerness. He was right. He could be as queer as he liked! The queerer the better! It was at the foot of the stairs, when she had got her guest down, that what she had assured Mrs. Medwin would come did indeed come. "*Did* you meet him here yesterday?"

"Dear, yes. Isn't he too funny?"

"Yes," said Mamie gloomily. "He *is* funny. But had you ever met him before?"

"Dear, no!"

"Oh!"—and Mamie's tone might have meant many things.

Lady Wantridge, however, after all, easily overlooked it. "I only knew he was one of your odd Americans. That's why, when I heard yesterday, here, that he was up there awaiting your return, I didn't let that prevent me. I thought he might be. He certainly," her ladyship laughed, "is."

"Yes, he's very American," Mamie went on in the same way.

"As you say, we *are* fond of you! Good-bye," said Lady Wantridge.

But Mamie had not half done with her. She felt more and more—or she hoped at least—that she looked strange. She *was*, no doubt, if it came to that, strange. "Lady Wantridge," she almost convulsively broke out, "I don't know whether you'll understand me, but I seem to feel that I must act with you—I don't know what to call it!—responsibly. He *is* my brother."

"Surely—and why not?" Lady Wantridge stared. "He's the image of you!"

"Thank you!"—and Mamie was stranger than ever.

"Oh, he's good-looking. He's handsome, my dear. Oddly—but distinctly!" Her ladyship was for treating it much as a joke.

But Mamie, all sombre, would have none of this. She boldly gave him up. "I think he's awful."

"He is indeed—delightfully. And where *do* you get your ways of saying things? It isn't anything—and the things aren't anything. But it's so droll."

"Don't let yourself, all the same," Mamie consistently pursued, "be carried away by it. The thing can't be done—simply."

Lady Wantridge wondered. " 'Done simply'?"

"Done at all."

"But what can't be?"

"Why, what you might think—from his pleasantness. What he spoke of your doing for him."

Lady Wantridge recalled. "Forgive him?"

"He asked you if you couldn't. But you can't. It's too dreadful for me, as so near a relation, to have, loyally—loyally to *you*—to say it. But he's impossible."

It was so portentously produced that her ladyship had somehow to meet it. "What's the matter with him?"

"I don't know."

"Then what's the matter with *you?*" Lady Wantridge inquired.

"It's because I *won't* know," Mamie—not without dignity—explained.

"Then *I* won't either!"

"Precisely. Don't. It's something," Mamie pursued, with some inconsequence, "that—somewhere or other, at some time or other—he appears to have done; something that has made a difference in his life."

" 'Something'?" Lady Wantridge echoed again. "What kind of thing?"

Mamie looked up at the light above the door, through which the London sky was doubly dim. "I haven't the least idea."

"Then what kind of difference?"

Mamie's gaze was still at the light. "The difference you see."

Lady Wantridge, rather obligingly, seemed to ask herself what she saw. "But I don't see

any! It seems, at least," she added, "such an amusing one! And he has such nice eyes."

"Oh, *dear* eyes!" Mamie conceded; but with too much sadness, for the moment, about the connections of the subject, to say more.

It almost forced her companion, after an instant, to proceed. "Do you mean he can't go home?"

She weighed her responsibility. "I only make out—more's the pity!—that he doesn't."

"Is it then something too terrible—?"

She thought again. "I don't know what—for men—*is* too terrible."

"Well then, as you don't know what 'is' for women either—good-bye!" her visitor laughed.

It practically wound up the interview; which, however, terminating thus on a considerable stir of the air, was to give Miss Cutter, the next few days, the sense of being much blown about. The degree to which, to begin with, she had been drawn—or perhaps rather pushed—closer to Scott was marked in the brief colloquy that, of her friend's departure, she had with him. He had immediately said it. "You'll see if she doesn't ask me down!"

"So soon?"

"Oh, I've know them at places—at Cannes, at Pau, at Shanghai—to do it sooner still. I always know when they will. You *can't* make out they don't love me!" He spoke almost plaintively, as if he wished she could.

"Then I don't see why it hasn't done you more good."

"Why, Mamie," he patiently reasoned, "what more good *could* it? As I tell you," he explained, "it has just been my life."

"Then why do you come to me for money?"

"Oh, they don't give me *that!*" Scott returned.

"So that it only means then, after all, that I, at the best, must keep you up?"

He fixed on her the nice eyes that Lady Wantridge admired. "Do you mean to tell me that already—at this very moment—I am not distinctly keeping *you?*"

She gave him back his look. "Wait till she

has asked you, and then," Mamie added, "decline."

Scott, not too grossly, wondered. "As acting for *you?*"

Mamie's next injunction was answer enough. "But *before*—yes—call."

He took it in. "Call—but decline. Good."

"The rest," she said, "I leave to you." And she left it in fact with such confidence that for a couple of days she was not only conscious of no need to give Mrs. Medwin another turn of the screw, but positively evaded, in her fortitude, the reappearance of that lady. It was not till the third day that she waited upon her, finding her, as she had expected, tense.

"Lady Wantridge *will*—?"

"Yes, though she says she won't."

"She says she won't? O—oh!" Mrs. Medwin moaned.

"Sit tight all the same. I *have* her!"

"But how?"

"Through Scott—whom she wants."

"Your bad brother!" Mrs. Medwin stared. "What does she want of him?"

"To amuse them at Catchmore. Anything for that. And he *would*. But he sha'n't!" Mamie declared. "He sha'n't go unless she comes. She must meet you first—you're my condition."

"O—o—oh!" Mrs. Medwin's tone was a wonder of hope and fear. "But doesn't he want to go?"

"He wants what *I* want. She draws the line at *you*. I draw the line at *him*."

"But *she*—doesn't she mind that he's bad?"

It was so artless that Mamie laughed. "No; it doesn't touch her. Besides, perhaps he isn't. It isn't as for *you*—people seem not to know. He has settled everything, at all events, by going to see her. It's before her that he's the thing she will have to have."

"Have to?"

"For Sundays in the country. A feature—*the* feature."

"So she has asked him?"

"Yes; and he has declined."

"For *me?*" Mrs. Medwin panted.

"For me," said Mamie, on the doorstep.

"But I don't leave him for long." Her hansom had waited. "She'll come."

Lady Wantridge did come. She met in South Audley Street, on the fourteenth, at tea, the ladies whom Mamie had named to her, together with three or four others, and it was rather a masterstroke for Miss Cutter that, if Mrs. Medwin was modestly present, Scott Homer was as markedly not. This occasion, however, is a medal that would take rare casting, as would also, for that matter, even the minor light and shade, the lower relief, of the pecuniary transaction that Mrs. Medwin's flushed gratitude scarce awaited the dispersal of the company munificently to complete. A new understanding indeed, on the spot rebounded from it, the conception of which, in Mamie's mind, had promptly bloomed. "He sha'n't go *now* unless he takes you." Then, as her fancy always moved quicker for her client than her client's own—"Down with him to Catchmore! When he goes to amuse them, *you*," she comfortably declared, "shall amuse them too." Mrs. Medwin's response was again rather oddly divided, but she was sufficiently intelligible when it came to meeting the intimation that this latter would be an opportunity involving a separate fee. "Say," Mamie had suggested, "the same."

"Very well; the same."

The knowledge that it was to be the same had perhaps something to do, also, with the obliging spirit in which Scott eventually went. It was all, at the last, rather hurried—a party rapidly got together for the Grand Duke, who was in England but for the hour, who had good-naturedly proposed himself, and who liked his parties small, intimate and funny. This one was of the smallest, and it was finally judged to conform neither too little nor too much to the other conditions—after a brief whirlwind of wires and counter-wires, and an iterated waiting of hansoms at various doors—to include Mrs. Medwin. It was from Catchmore itself that, snatching a moment on the wondrous Sunday afternoon, this lady had the harmonious thought of sending the new cheque. She was in bliss enough, but her scribble none the less intimated that it was Scott who amused them most. He *was* the feature.

QUESTIONS

1. The characters in this story, living at the turn of the century, are much concerned in their own ways with the problem of who meets whom socially. Can you imagine any parallel in our day to this concern, either the desire to meet the "right" people or the willingness actually to pay, or take pay, for desired social arrangements?
2. Who, in your opinion, is presented as the most upright and admirable character in the story? Is there any major character who is without flaw in his ethical behavior?
3. Is there anything wrong, in your opinion, with making a deliberate arrangement to enter a given social group?
4. Is it true that people today would never or seldom make payment for admission to coveted social circles?
5. What is meant by the suggestion in the story that the Americans are more alive than the other characters?

A COUNTRY DOCTOR

Franz Kafka
(1883–1924)

I was in great perplexity; I had to start on an urgent journey; a seriously ill patient was waiting for me in a village ten miles off; a thick blizzard of snow filled all the wide spaces between him and me; I had a gig, a light gig with big wheels, exactly right for our country roads; muffed in furs, my bag of instruments in my hand, I was in the courtyard all ready for the journey; but there was no horse to be had, no horse. My own horse had died in the night, worn out by the fatigues of this icy winter; my servant girl was now running round the village trying to borrow a horse; but it was hopeless, I knew it, and I stood there forlornly, with the snow gathering more and more thickly upon me, more and more unable to move. In the gateway the girl appeared, alone, and waved the lantern; of course, who would lend a horse at this time for such a journey? I strode through the courtway once more; I could see no way out; in my confused distress I kicked at the dilapidated door of the year-long uninhabited pigsty. It flew open and flapped to and fro on its hinges. A steam and smell as of horses came out of it. A dim stable lantern was swinging inside from a rope. A man, crouching on his hams in that low space, showed an open blue-eyed face. "Shall I yoke up?" he asked, crawling out on all fours. I did not know what to say and merely stooped down to see what else was in the sty. The servant girl standing beside me. "You never know what you're going to find in your own house," she said, and we both laughed. "Hey there, Brother, hey there, Sister!" called the groom, and two horses, enormous creatures with powerful flanks, one after the other, their legs tucked close to their bodies, each well-shaped head lowered like a camel's, by sheer strength of buttocking squeezed out through the door hole which they filled entirely. But at once they were standing up, with their long legs and their bodies steaming thickly. "Give him a hand," I said, and the willing girl hurried to help the groom with the harnessing. Yet hardly was she beside him when the groom clipped hold of her and pushed his face against hers. She screamed and fled back to me; on her cheek stood out in red the marks of two rows of teeth. "You brute," I yelled in fury, "do you want a whipping?" but in the same moment reflected that the man was a stranger; that I did not know where he came from, and that of his own free will he was helping me out when everyone else had failed me. As if he knew my thoughts he took no offense at my threat but, still busied with the horses, only turned round once towards me. "Get in," he said then, and indeed: everything was ready. A magnificent pair of horses, I observed, such as I had never sat behind, and I climbed in happily. "But I'll drive, you don't know the way," I said. "Of course," said he, "I'm not coming with you anyway, I'm staying with Rose." "No," shrieked Rose, fleeing into the house with a justified presentiment that her fate was inescapable; I heard the door chain rattle as she put it up; I heard the key turn in the lock; I could see, moreover, how she put out the lights in the entrance hall and in further flight all through the rooms to keep herself from being discovered. "You're coming with me," I said to the groom, "or I won't go, urgent as my journey is. I'm not thinking of paying for it by handing the girl over to you." "Gee up!" he said; clapped his hands; the gig whirled off like a log in a freshet; I could just hear the door of my house splitting and bursting as the groom charged at it and then I was deafened and blinded by a storming rush that steadily buffeted all my senses. But this only for a moment, since, as if my patient's farmyard had opened out just before my courtyard gate, I was already there; the horses had come quietly to a standstill; the blizzard had stopped; the moonlight all around; my patient's parents hurried out of the house, his sister behind them; I was almost lifted out of the gig; from their confused ejaculations I gathered not a word; in the sick room the air was almost unbreathable; the neglected stove was smoking; I wanted to push open a window; but first I had to look at my patient. Gaunt, without any fever, not cold, not warm, with vacant eyes, without a shirt, the youngster heaved himself up from under the feather bedding, threw his arms around my neck, and whispered in my ear: "Doctor, let me die." I glanced round the room; no one had heard it; the parents were leaning forward in silence waiting for my verdict; the sister had set a chair for my handbag; I opened the bag and hunted among my instruments; the boy kept clutching at me from his bed to remind me of his entreaty; I picked up a pair of tweezers, examined them in the candlelight and laid them down again. "Yes," I thought blasphemously, "in cases like this the gods are helpful, send the missing horse, add to it a second because of the urgency, and to crown everything bestow even a groom—" And only now did I remember Rose again;

what was I to do, how could I rescue her, how could I pull her away from under that groom at ten miles' distance, with a team of horses I couldn't control. These horses, now, they had somehow slipped the reins loose, pushed the window open from the outside, I did not know how; each of them had stuck a head in at a window and, quite unmoved by the startled cries of the family, stood eyeing the patient. "Better go back at once," I thought, as if the horses were summoning me to the return journey, yet I permitted the patient's sister, who fancied that I was dazed by the heat, to take my fur coat from me. A glass of rum was poured out for me, the old man clapped me on the shoulder, a familiarity justified by this offer of his treasure. I shook my head; in the narrow confines of the old man's thoughts I felt ill; that was my only reason for refusing the drink. The mother stood by the bedside and cajoled me towards it. I yielded, and, while one of the horses whinnied loudly to the ceiling, laid my head to the boy's breast, which shivered under my wet beard. I confirmed what I already knew; the boy was quite sound, something a little wrong with his circulation, saturated with coffee by his solicitous mother, but sound and best turned out of bed with one shove. I am no world reformer and so I let him lie. I was the district doctor and I did my duty to the uttermost, to the point where it became almost too much. I was badly paid and yet generous and helpful to the poor. I had still to see that Rose was all right, and then the boy might have his way and I wanted to die too. What was I doing there in that endless winter! My horse was dead, and not a single person in the village would lend me another. I had to get my team out of the pigsty; if they hadn't chanced to be horses I should have had to travel with swine. That was how it was. And I nodded to the family. They knew nothing about it, and, had they known, would not have believed it. To write prescriptions is easy, but to come to an understanding with people is hard. Well, this should be the end of my visit, I had once more been called out needlessly, I was used to that, the whole district made my life a torment with my night bell, but that I should have to sacrifice Rose this time as well, the pretty girl who had lived in my house for years almost without my noticing her—that sacrifice was too much to ask, and I had somehow to get it reasoned out in my head with the help of what craft I could muster, in order not to let fly at this family, which with the best will in the world could not restore Rose to me. But as I shut my bag and put an arm out for my fur coat, the family meanwhile standing together, the father sniffing at the glass of rum in his hand, the mother, apparently disappointed in me —why, what do people expect?—biting her lips with tears in her eyes, the sister fluttering a blood-soaked towel, I was somehow ready to admit conditionally that the boy might be ill after all. I went towards him, he welcomed me smiling as if I were bringing him the most nourishing invalid broth—ah, now both horses were whinnying together; the noise, I suppose, was ordained by heaven to assist my examination of the patient—and this time I discovered that the boy was indeed ill. In his right side, near the hip, was an open wound as big as the palm of my hand. Rose-red, in many variations of shade, dark in the hollows, lighter at the edges, softly granulated, with irregular clots of blood, open as a surface mine to the daylight. That was how it looked from a distance. But on a closer inspection there was another complication. I could not help a low whistle of surprise. Worms, as thick and as long as my little finger, themselves rose-red and blood-spotted as well, were wriggling from their fastness in the interior of the wound towards the light, with small white heads and many little legs. Poor boy, you were past helping. I had discovered your great wound; this blossom in your side was destroying you. The family was pleased; they saw me busying myself; the sister told the mother, the mother the father, the father told several guests who were coming in, through the moonlight at the open door, walking on tiptoe, keeping their balance with outstretched arms. "Will you save me?" whispered the boy with a sob, quite blinded by the life within his wound. That is what peo-

ple are like in my district. Always expecting the impossible from the doctor. They have lost their ancient beliefs; the parson sits at home and unravels his vestments, one after another; but the doctor is supposed to be omnipotent with his merciful surgeon's hand. Well, as it pleases them; I have not thrust my services on them; if they misuse me for sacred ends, I let that happen to me too; what better do I want, old country doctor that I am, bereft of my servant girl! And so they came, the family and the village elders, and stripped my clothes off me; a school choir with the teacher at the head of it stood before the house and sang these words to an utterly simple tune:

Strip his clothes off, then he'll heal us,
If he doesn't, kill him dead!
Only a doctor, only a doctor.

Then my clothes were off and I looked at the people quietly, my fingers in my beard and my head cocked to one side. I was altogether composed and equal to the situation and remained so, although it was no help to me, since they now took me by the head and feet and carried me to the bed. They laid me down in it next to the wall, on the side of the wound. Then they all left the room; the door was shut; the singing stopped; clouds covered the moon; the bedding was warm around me; the horses' heads in the opened windows wavered like shadows. "Do you know," said a voice in my ear, "I have very little confidence in you. Why, you were only blown in here, you didn't come on your own feet. Instead of helping me, you're cramping me on my death bed. What I'd like best is to scratch your eyes out." "Right," I said, "it's a shame. And yet I am a doctor. What am I to do? Believe me, it is not too easy for me either." "Am I supposed to be content with this apology? Oh, I must be, I can't help it. I always have to put up with things. A fine wound is all I brought into the world; that was my sole endowment." "My young friend," said I, "your mistake is: you have not a wide enough view. I have been in all the sickrooms, far and wide, and I tell you: your wound is not so bad. Done in a tight corner

with two strokes of the ax. Many a one prof-
fers his side and can hardly hear the ax in
the forest, far less that it is coming nearer to
him." "Is that really so, or are you deluding
me in my fever?" "It is really so, take the
word of honor of an official doctor." And he
took it and lay still. But now it was time for
me to think of escaping. The horses were
still standing faithfully in their places. My
clothes, my fur coat, my bag were quickly collected; I didn't want to waste time dressing;
if the horses raced home as they had come,
I should only be springing, as it were, out of
this bed into my own. Obediently a horse
backed away from the window; I threw my
bundle into the gig; the fur coat missed its
mark and was caught on a hook only by the
sleeve. Good enough. I swung myself on to
the horse. With the reins loosely trailing, one
horse barely fastened to the other, the gig
swaying behind, my fur coat last of all in
the snow. "Geeup!" I said, but there was no
galloping; slowly, like old men, we crawled
through the snowy wastes; a long time
echoed behind us the new but faulty song of
the children:

O be joyful, all you patients,
The doctor's laid in bed beside you!

Never shall I reach home at this rate; my
flourishing practice is done for; my successor
is robbing me, but in vain, for he cannot
take my place; in my house the disgusting
groom is raging; Rose is the victim; I do not
want to think about it any more. Naked, exposed to the frost of this most unhappy of
ages, with an earthly vehicle, unearthly
horses, old man that I am, I wander astray.
My fur coat is hanging from the back of
the gig, but I cannot reach it, and none of my
limber pack of patients lifts a finger. Betrayed! Betrayed! A false alarm on the night
bell once answered—it cannot be made
good, not ever.

QUESTIONS

1. To achieve perspective on this story, which
   is heavily symbolic, work out some preliminary answers to the following question:

  What would you say are the typical problems of a doctor's life? Think of physical
  necessities, problems of time, problems
  of "duty," possible attitudes and expectations of patients and their families.
  Think also of specifically professional
  problems, such as those of diagnosis.
  Think also of possible ways in which any
  person might like to spend his time,
  apart from the demands of a profession.
Reread the story with the ideas in mind
which you have worked out. Can you discover that the doctor in the story faces any
typical problems?

2. What degree of success does the doctor in
   the story experience? What personal and
   professional frustrations seem to be most
   troublesome? What is the nature of the
   patient's illness? of his wound?

3. What symbols can you find in this story
   which seem to be Christian in orgin? How
   are they used?

4. Can you discover any likelihood that doctor
   and patient are in any way to be equated—
   to be regarded, in other words, as having
   either similar problems or a similar fate?

5. The doctor leads a busy mental life, with
   thoughts ranging from the practical "conscious" level to thoughts, feelings, and
   wants which may be half-realized or even
   below the threshold of conscious awareness. What conflicts within the doctor are
   suggested by this material in the story? Particularly, what are the wants and the fears?
   Is all this dreamlike material a fair symbol
   of man's mental life?

6. What of the environment in which the
   doctor lives and works? Include in your
   thought about this the physical environment, the patient and family, the other
   live creatures, and especially the weather.
   Is this environment friendly, unfriendly, or
   just neutrally accidental?

7. Is the doctor a fair symbol of man's life
   and work in the world we know?

8. Is there, possibly, a humorous element in
   the author's attitude? What effect does it
   have?

GROUP 3: TWENTIETH-CENTURY CAUSES
AND LOYALTIES

It has been said more than once that twentieth-century men and women have had to find, anew and for themselves, something outside themselves to live by. The classic choices in the twentieth-century world have been religion, a social cause, national patriotism, some mixture of the three, or personal ethical systems. One prime difficulty among many, in our century, has been the fact that social causes attractive in theory have turned out to be ruinous in reality. Ends have been used to justify the most terrible of means. Doctrines pointing to the emancipation of man have resulted in practical enslavement. No one has defined these issues more clearly than those creators of literature who are themselves inheritors of the humanistic wisdom of the past.

Stories in this group:

(1) "Guests of the Nation," by Frank O'Connor
(2) "Flowering Judas," by Katherine Anne Porter
(3) "Delta Autumn," by William Faulkner

GUESTS OF THE NATION[1]

Frank O'Connor
(1903–   )

At dusk the big Englishman, Belcher, would shift his long legs out of the ashes and say "Well, chums, what about it?" and Noble or me would say "All right, chum" (for we had picked up some of their curious expressions), and the little Englishman, Hawkins, would light the lamp and bring out the cards. Sometimes Jeremiah Donovan would come up and supervise the game and get excited over Hawkins's cards, which he always played badly, and shout at him as if he was one of

[1] Time of action: the Anglo-Irish war of the twentieth century, which ended "officially" with the creation of the Irish Free State in 1921–22. Settlement of "the Irish question" was an issue in England for hundreds of years. From the Irish point of view, it was "the English question."

our own "Ah, you divil, you, why didn't you play the tray?"

But ordinarily Jeremiah was a sober and contented poor devil like the big Englishman, Belcher, and was looked up to only because he was a fair hand at documents, though he was slow enough even with them. He wore a small cloth hat and big gaiters over his long pants, and you seldom saw him with his hands out of his pockets. He reddened when you talked to him, tilting from toe to heel and back, and looking down all the time at his big farmer's feet. Noble and me used to make fun of his broad accent, because we were from the town.

I couldn't at the time see the point of me and Noble guarding Belcher and Hawkins at all, for it was my belief that you could have planted that pair down anywhere from this to Claregalway and they'd have taken root there like a native weed. I never in my short experience seen two men to take to the country as they did.

228

They were handed on to us by the Second Battalion when the search for them became too hot, and Noble and myself, being young, took over with a natural feeling of responsibility, but Hawkins made us look like fools when he showed that he knew the country better than we did.

"You're the bloke they calls Bonaparte," he says to me. "Mary Brigid O'Connell told me to ask you what you done with the pair of her brother's socks you borrowed."

For it seemed, as they explained it, that the Second used to have little evenings, and some of the girls of the neighbourhood turned in, and, seeing they were such decent chaps, our fellows couldn't leave the two Englishmen out of them. Hawkins learned to dance "The Walls of Limerick," "The Siege of Ennis," and "The Waves of Tory" as well as any of them, though, naturally, he couldn't return the compliment, because our lads at that time did not dance foreign dances on principle.

So whatever privileges Belcher and Hawkins had with the Second they just naturally took with us, and after the first day or two we gave up all pretence of keeping a close eye on them. Not that they could have got far, for they had accents you could cut with a knife and wore khaki tunics and overcoats with civilian pants and boots. But it's my belief that they never had any idea of escaping and were quite content to be where they were.

It was a treat to see how Belcher got off with the old woman of the house where we were staying. She was a great warrant to scold, and cranky even with us, but before ever she had a chance of giving our guests, as I may call them, a lick of her tongue, Belcher had made her his friend for life. She was breaking sticks, and Belcher, who hadn't been more than ten minutes in the house, jumped up from his seat and went over to her.

"Allow me, madam," he says, smiling his queer little smile, "please allow me"; and he takes the bloody hatchet. She was struck too paralytic to speak, and after that, Belcher would be at her heels, carrying a bucket, a basket, or a load of turf, as the case might be.

As Noble said, he got into looking before she leapt, and hot water, or any little thing she wanted, Belcher would have it ready for her. For such a huge man (and though I am five foot ten myself I had to look up at him) he had an uncommon shortness—or should I say lack?—of speech. It took us some time to get used to him, walking in and out, like a ghost, without a word. Especially because Hawkins talked enough for a platoon, it was strange to hear big Belcher with his toes in the ashes come out with a solitary "Excuse me, chum," or "That's right, chum." His one and only passion was cards, and I will say for him that he was a good card-player. He could have fleeced myself and Noble, but whatever we lost to him Hawkins lost to us, and Hawkins played with the money Belcher gave him.

Hawkins lost to us because he had too much old gab, and we probably lost to Belcher for the same reason. Hawkins and Noble would spit at one another about religion into the early hours of the morning, and Hawkins worried the soul out of Noble, whose brother was a priest, with a string of questions that would puzzle a cardinal. To make it worse, even in treating of holy subjects, Hawkins had a deplorable tongue. I never in all my career met a man who could mix such a variety of cursing and bad language into an argument. He was a terrible man, and a fright to argue. He never did a stroke of work, and when he had no one else to talk to, he got stuck in the old woman.

He met his match in her, for one day when he tried to get her to complain profanely of the drought, she gave him a great come-down by blaming it entirely on Jupiter Pluvius (a deity neither Hawkins nor I had ever heard of, though Noble said that among the pagans it was believed that he had something to do with the rain). Another day he was swearing at the capitalists for starting the German war when the old lady laid down her iron, puckered up her little crab's mouth, and said: "Mr. Hawkins, you can say what you like about the war, and think you'll deceive me because I'm only a simple poor country-woman, but I know what started the war. It was the Italian Count that stole the heathen divinity out of the temple in Japan. Believe me, Mr. Hawkins, nothing but sorrow and want can follow the people that disturb the hidden powers."

A queer old girl, all right.

2

We had our tea one evening, and Hawkins lit the lamp and we all sat into cards. Jeremiah Donovan came in too, and sat down and watched us for a while, and it suddenly struck me that he had no great love for the two Englishmen. It came as a great surprise to me, because I hadn't noticed anything about him before.

Late in the evening a really terrible argument blew up between Hawkins and Noble, about capitalists and priests and love of your country.

"The capitalists," says Hawkins with an angry gulp, "pays the priests to tell you about the next world so as you won't notice what the bastards are up to in this."

"Nonsense, man!" says Noble, losing his temper. "Before ever a capitalist was thought of, people believed in the next world."

Hawkins stood up as though he was preaching a sermon.

"Oh, they did, did they?" he says with a sneer. "They believed all the things you believe, isn't that what you mean? And you believe that God created Adam, and Adam created Shem, and Shem created Jehoshophat. You believe all that silly old fairytale about Eve and Eden and the apple. Well, listen to me, chum. If you're entitled to hold a silly belief like that, I'm entitled to hold my silly belief—which is that the first thing your God created was a bleeding capitalist, with morality and Rolls-Royce complete. Am I right, chum?" he says to Belcher.

"You're right, chum," says Belcher with his amused smile, and got up from the table to stretch his long legs into the fire and stroke his moustache. So, seeing that Jeremiah Donovan was going, and that there was no knowing when the argument about religion would be over, I went out with him. We strolled down to the village together, and then he stopped and started blushing and mumbling and saying I ought to be behind, keeping guard on the prisoners. I didn't like the tone he took with me, and anyway I was bored with life in the cottage, so I replied by asking him what the hell we wanted guarding them at all for. I told him I'd talked it over with Noble, and that we'd both rather be out with a fighting column.

"What use are those fellows to us?" says I.

He looked at me in surprise and said: "I thought you knew we were keeping them as hostages."

"Hostages?" I said.

"The enemy have prisoners belonging to us," he says, "and now they're talking of shooting them. If they shoot our prisoners, we'll shoot theirs."

"Shoot them?" I said.

"What else did you think we were keeping them for?" he says.

"Wasn't it very unforeseen of you not to warn Noble and myself of that in the beginning?" I said.

"How was it?" says he. "You might have known it."

"We couldn't know it, Jeremiah Donovan," says I. "How could we when they were on our hands so long?"

"The enemy have our prisoners as long and longer," says he.

"That's not the same thing at all," says I.

"What difference is there?" says he.

I couldn't tell him, because I knew he wouldn't understand. If it was only an old dog that was going to the vet's, you'd try and not get too fond of him, but Jeremiah Donovan wasn't a man that would ever be in danger of that.

"And when is this thing going to be decided?" says I.

"We might hear tonight," he says. "Or tomorrow or the next day at latest. So if it's only hanging round here that's a trouble to you, you'll be free soon enough."

It wasn't the hanging round that was a trouble to me at all by this time. I had worse things to worry about. When I got back to the cottage the argument was still on. Hawkins was holding forth in his best style, maintaining that there was no next world, and Noble was maintaining that there was; but I could see that Hawkins had had the best of it.

"Do you know what, chum?" he was saying with a saucy smile. "I think you're just as big a bleeding unbeliever as I am. You say you believe in the next world, and you know just as much about the next world as I do, which is sweet damn-all. What's heaven? You don't know. Where's heaven? You don't know. You know sweet damn-all! I ask you again, do they wear wings?"

"Very well, then," says Noble, "they do. Is that enough for you? They do wear wings."

"Where do they get them, then? Who makes them? Have they a factory for wings? Have they a sort of store where you hands in your chit and takes your bleeding wings?"

"You're an impossible man to argue with," says Noble. "Now, listen to me—" And they were off again.

It was long after midnight when we locked up and went to bed. As I blew out the candle I told Noble what Jeremiah Donovan was after telling me. Noble took it very quietly. When we'd been in bed about an hour he asked me did I think we ought to tell the Englishmen. I didn't think we should, because it was more than likely that the English wouldn't shoot our men, and even if they did, the brigade officers, who were always up and down with the Second Battalion and knew the Englishmen well, wouldn't be likely to want them plugged. "I think so too," says Noble. "It would be great cruelty to put the wind up them now."

"It was very unforeseen of Jeremiah Donovan anyhow," says I.

It was next morning that we found it so hard to face Belcher and Hawkins. We went about the house all day scarcely saying a word. Belcher didn't seem to notice; he was stretched into the ashes as usual, with his usual look of waiting in quietness for something unforeseen to happen, but Hawkins noticed and put it down to Noble's being beaten in the argument of the night before.

"Why can't you take a discussion in the proper spirit?" he says severely. "You and your Adam and Eve! I'm a Communist, that's

what I am. Communist or anarchist, it all comes to much the same thing." And for hours he went round the house, muttering when the fit took him. "Adam and Eve! Adam and Eve! Nothing better to do with their time than picking bleeding apples!"

3

I don't know how we got through that day, but I was very glad when it was over, the tea things were cleared away, and Belcher said in his peaceable way: "Well, chums, what about it?" We sat round the table and Hawkins took out the cards, and just then I heard Jeremiah Donovan's footstep on the path and a dark presentiment crossed my mind. I rose from the table and caught him before he reached the door.

"What do you want?" I asked.

"I want those two soldier friends of yours," he says, getting red.

"Is that the way, Jeremiah Donovan?" I asked.

"That's the way. There were four of our lads shot this morning, one of them a boy of sixteen."

"That's bad," I said.

At that moment Noble followed me out, and the three of us walked down the path together, talking in whispers. Feeney, the local intelligence officer, was standing by the gate.

"What are you going to do about it?" I asked Jeremiah Donovan.

"I want you and Noble to get them out; tell them they're being shifted again; that'll be the quietest way."

"Leave me out of that," says Noble under his breath.

Jeremiah Donovan looks at him hard.

"All right," he says. "You and Feeney get a few tools from the shed and dig a hole by the far end of the bog. Bonaparte and myself will be after you. Don't let anyone see you with the tools. I wouldn't like it to go beyond ourselves."

We saw Feeney and Noble go round to the shed and went in ourselves. I left Jeremiah Donovan to do the explanations. He told them that he had orders to send them back to the Second Battalion. Hawkins let out a mouthful of curses, and you could see that though Belcher didn't say anything, he was a bit upset too. The old woman was for having them stay in spite of us, and she didn't stop advising them until Jeremiah Donovan lost his temper and turned on her. He had a nasty temper, I noticed. It was pitch-dark in the cottage by this time, but no one thought of lighting the lamp, and in the darkness the two Englishmen fetched their topcoats and said good-bye to the old woman.

"Just as a man makes a home of a bleeding place, some bastard at headquarters thinks you're too cushy and shunts you off," says Hawkins, shaking her hand.

"A thousand thanks, madam," says Belcher. "A thousand thanks for everything"—as though he'd made it up.

We went round to the back of the house and down towards the bog. It was only then that Jeremiah Donovan told them. He was shaking with excitement.

"There were four of our fellows shot in Cork this morning and now you're to be shot as a reprisal."

"What are you talking about?" snaps Hawkins. "It's bad enough being mucked about as we are without having to put up with your funny jokes."

"It isn't a joke," says Donovan. "I'm sorry, Hawkins, but it's true," and begins on the usual rigmarole about duty and how unpleasant it is.

I never noticed that people who talk a lot about duty find it much of a trouble to them.

"Oh, cut it out!" says Hawkins.

"Ask Bonaparte," says Donovan, seeing that Hawkins isn't taking him seriously. "Isn't it true, Bonaparte?"

"It is," I say, and Hawkins stops.

"Ah, for Christ's sake, chum!"

"I mean it, chum," I say.

"You don't sound as if you meant it."

"If he doesn't mean it, I do," says Donovan, working himself up.

"What have you against me, Jeremiah Donovan?"

"I never said I had anything against you. But why did your people take out four of our prisoners and shoot them in cold blood?"

He took Hawkins by the arm and dragged him on, but it was impossible to make him understand that we were in earnest. I had the Smith and Wesson in my pocket and I kept fingering it and wondering what I'd do if they put up a fight for it or ran, and wishing to God they'd do one or the other. I knew if they did run for it, that I'd never fire on them. Hawkins wanted to know was Noble in it, and when we said yes, he asked us why Noble wanted to plug him. Why did any of us want to plug him? What had he done to us? Weren't we all chums? Didn't we understand him and didn't he understand us? Did we imagine for an instant that he'd shoot us for all the so-and-so officers in the so-and-so British Army?

By this time we'd reached the bog, and I was so sick I couldn't even answer him. We walked along the edge of it in the darkness, and every now and then Hawkins would call a halt and begin all over again, as if he was wound up, about our being chums, and I knew that nothing but the sight of the grave would convince him that we had to do it. And all the time I was hoping that something would happen; that they'd run for it or that Noble would take over the responsibility from me. I had the feeling that it was worse on Noble than on me.

4

At last we saw the lantern in the distance and made towards it. Noble was carrying it, and Feeney was standing somewhere in the darkness behind him, and the picture of them so still and silent in the bogland brought it home to me that we were in earnest, and banished the last bit of hope I had.

Belcher, on recognizing Noble, said: "Hallo, chum," in his quiet way, but Hawkins flew at him at once, and the argument began all over again, only this time Noble had nothing to say for himself and stood with his head down, holding the lantern between his legs.

It was Jeremiah Donovan who did the answering. For the twentieth time, as though it was haunting his mind, Hawkins asked if anybody thought he'd shoot Noble.

"Yes, you would," says Jeremiah Donovan.

"No, I wouldn't, damn you!"

"You would, because you'd know you'd be shot for not doing it."

"I wouldn't, not if I was to be shot twenty times over. I wouldn't shoot a pal. And Belcher wouldn't—isn't that right, Belcher?"

"That's right, chum," Belcher said, but more by way of answering the question than of joining in the argument. Belcher sounded as though whatever unforeseen thing he'd always been waiting for had come at last.

"Anyway, who says Noble would be shot if I wasn't? What do you think I'd do if I was in his place, out in the middle of a blasted bog?"

"What would you do?" asks Donovan.

"I'd go with him wherever he was going, of course. Share my last bob with him and stick by him through thick and thin. No one can ever say of me that I let down a pal."

"We had enough of this," says Jeremiah Donovan, cocking his revolver. "Is there any message you want to send?"

"No, there isn't."

"Do you want to say your prayers?"

Hawkins came out with a cold-blooded remark that even shocked me and turned on Noble again.

"Listen to me, Noble," he says. "You and me are chums. You can't come over to my side, so I'll come over to your side. That show you I mean what I say? Give me a rifle and I'll go along with you and the other lads."

Nobody answered him. We knew that was no way out.

"Hear what I'm saying?" he says. "I'm through with it. I'm a deserter or anything else you like. I don't believe in your stuff, but it's no worse than mine. That satisfy you?"

Noble raised his head, but Donovan began to speak and he lowered it again without replying.

"For the last time, have you any messages to send?" says Donovan in a cold, excited sort of voice.

"Shut up, Donovan! You don't understand me, but these lads do. They're not the sort to make a pal and kill a pal. They're not the tools of any capitalist."

I alone of the crowd saw Donovan raise his Webley to the back of Hawkins's neck, and as he did so I shut my eyes and tried to pray. Hawkins had begun to say something else when Donovan fired, and as I opened my eyes at the bang, I saw Hawkins stagger at the knees and lie out flat at Noble's feet, slowly and as quiet as a kid falling asleep, with the lantern-light on his lean legs and bright farmer's boots. We all stood very still, watching him settle out in the last agony.

Then Belcher took out a handkerchief and began to tie it about his own eyes (in our excitement we'd forgotten to do the same for Hawkins), and, seeing it wasn't big enough, turned and asked for the loan of mine. I gave it to him and he knotted the two together and pointed with his foot at Hawkins.

"He's not quite dead," he says. "Better give him another."

Sure enough, Hawkins's left knee is beginning to rise. I bend down and put my gun to his head; then, recollecting myself, I get up again. Belcher understands what's in my mind.

"Give him his first," he says. "I don't mind. Poor bastard, we don't know what's happening to him now."

I knelt and fired. By this time I didn't seem to know what I was doing. Belcher, who was fumbling a bit awkwardly with the handkerchiefs, came out with a laugh as he heard the shot. It was the first time I heard him laugh and it sent a shudder down my back; it sounded so unnatural.

"Poor bugger!" he said quietly. "And last night he was so curious about it all. It's very queer, chums, I always think. Now he knows as much about it as they'll ever let him know, and last night he was all in the dark."

Donovan helped him to tie the handkerchiefs about his eyes. "Thanks, chum," he said. Donovan asked if there were any messages he wanted sent.

"No, chum," he says. "Not for me. If any

of you would like to write to Hawkins's mother, you'll find a letter from her in his pocket. He and his mother were great chums. But my missus left me eight years ago. Went away with another fellow and took the kid with her. I like the feeling of a home, as you may have noticed, but I couldn't start again after that."

It was an extraordinary thing, but in those few minutes Belcher said more than in all the weeks before. It was just as if the sound of the shot had started a flood of talk in him and he could go on the whole night like that, quite happily, talking about himself. We stood round like fools now that he couldn't see us any longer. Donovan looked at Noble, and Noble shook his head. Then Donovan raised his Webley, and at that moment Belcher gives his queer laugh again. He may have thought we were talking about him, or perhaps he noticed the same thing I'd noticed and couldn't understand it.

"Excuse me, chums," he says. "I feel I'm talking the hell of a lot, and so silly, about my being so handy about a house and things like that. But this thing came on me suddenly. You'll forgive me, I'm sure."

"You don't want to say a prayer?" asks Donovan.

"No, chum," he says. "I don't think it would help. I'm ready, and you boys want to get it over."

"You understand that we're only doing our duty?" says Donovan.

Belcher's head was raised like a blind man's, so that you could only see his chin and the tip of his nose in the lantern-light.

"I never could make out what duty was myself," he said. "I think you're all good lads, if that's what you mean. I'm not complaining."

Noble, just as if he couldn't bear any more of it, raised his fist at Donovan, and in a flash Donovan raised his gun and fired. The big man went over like a sack of meal, and this time there was no need of a second shot.

I don't remember much about the burying, but that it was worse than all the rest because we had to carry them to the grave. It was all mad lonely with nothing but a patch of lantern-light between ourselves and the dark, and birds hooting and screeching all round, disturbed by the guns. Noble went through Hawkins's belongings to find the letter from his mother, and then joined his hands together. He did the same with Belcher. Then, when we'd filled in the grave, we separated from Jeremiah Donovan and Feeney and took our tools back to the shed. All the way we didn't speak a word. The kitchen was dark and cold as we'd left it, and the old woman was sitting over the hearth, saying her beads. We walked past her into the room, and Noble struck a match to light the lamp. She rose quietly and came to the doorway with all her cantankerousness gone.

"What did ye do with them?" she asked in a whisper, and Noble started so that the match went out in his hand.

"What's that?" he asked without turning round.

"I heard ye," she said.

"What did you hear?" asked Noble.

"I heard ye. Do ye think I didn't hear ye, putting the spade back in the houseen?"

Noble struck another match and this time the lamp lit for him.

"Was that what ye did to them?" she asked.

Then, by God, in the very doorway, she fell on her knees and began praying, and after looking at her for a minute or two Noble did the same by the fireplace. I pushed my way out past her and left them at it. I stood at the door, watching the stars and listening to the shrieking of the birds dying out over the bogs. It is so strange what you feel at times like that that you can't describe it. Noble says he saw everything ten times the size, as though there were nothing in the whole world but that little patch of bog with the two Englishmen stiffening into it, but with me it was as if the patch of bog where the Englishmen were was a million miles away, and even Noble and the old woman, mumbling behind me, and the birds and the bloody stars were all far away, and I was somehow very small and very lost and lonely like a child astray in the snow. And anything that happened to me afterwards, I never felt the same about again.

FLOWERING JUDAS

Katherine Anne Porter
(1894–   )

Braggioni sits heaped upon the edge of a straight-backed chair much too small for him, and sings to Laura in a furry, mournful voice. Laura has begun to find reasons for avoiding her own house until the latest possible moment, for Braggioni is there almost every night. No matter how late she is, he will be sitting there with a surly, waiting expression, pulling at his kinky yellow hair, thumbing the strings of his guitar, snarling a tune under his breath. Lupe the Indian maid meets Laura at the door, and says with a flicker of a glance towards the upper room, "He waits."

Laura wishes to lie down, she is tired of her hairpins and the feel of her long tight sleeves, but she says to him, "Have you a new song for me this evening?" If he says yes, she asks him to sing it. If he says no, she remembers his favorite one, and asks him to sing it again. Lupe brings her a cup of chocolate and a plate of rice, and Laura eats at the small table under the lamp, first inviting Braggioni, whose answer is always the same: "I have eaten, and besides, chocolate thickens the voice."

Laura says, "Sing, then," and Braggioni heaves himself into song. He scratches the guitar familiarly as though it were a pet animal, and sings passionately off key, taking the high notes in a prolonged painful squeal. Laura, who haunts the markets listening to the ballad singers, and stops every day to hear the blind boy playing his reed-flute in Sixteenth of September Street, listens to Braggioni with pitiless courtesy, because she dares not smile at his miserable performance. Nobody dares to smile at him. Braggioni is cruel to everyone, with a kind of specialized insolence, but he is so vain of his talents, and so sensitive to slights, it would require a cruelty and vanity greater than his own to lay a finger on the vast cureless wound of his self-esteem. It would require courage, too, for it is dangerous to offend him, and nobody has this courage.

Braggioni loves himself with such tenderness and amplitude and eternal charity that his followers—for he is a leader of men, a skilled revolutionist, and his skin has been punctured in honorable warfare—warm themselves in the reflected glow, and say to each other: "He has a real nobility, a love of humanity raised above mere personal affections." The excess of this self-love has flowed out, inconveniently for her, over Laura, who, with so many others, owes her comfortable situation and her salary to him. When he is in a very good humor, he tells her, "I am tempted to forgive you for being a *gringa, gringita!*" and Laura, burning, imagines herself leaning forward suddenly, and with a sound back-handed slap wiping the suety smile from his face. If he notices her eyes at these moments he gives no sign.

She knows what Braggioni would offer her, and she must resist tenaciously without appearing to resist, and if she could avoid it she would not admit even to herself the slow drift of his intention. During these long evenings which have spoiled a long month for her, she sits in her deep chair with an open book on her knees, resting her eyes on the consoling rigidity of the printed page when the sight and sound of Braggioni singing threaten to identify themselves with all her remembered afflictions and to add their weight to her uneasy premonitions of the future. The gluttonous bulk of Braggioni has become a symbol of her many disillusions, for a revolutionist should be lean, animated by heroic faith, a vessel of abstract virtues. This is nonsense, she knows it now and is ashamed of it. Revolution must have leaders, and leadership is a career for energetic men. She is, her comrades tell her, full of romantic error, for what she defines as cynicism in them is merely "a developed sense of reality." She is almost too willing to say, "I am wrong, I suppose I don't really understand the principles," and afterward she makes a secret truce with herself, determined not to surrender her will to such expedient logic. But she cannot help feeling that she has been betrayed irreparably by the disunion between her way of living and her feeling of what life should be, and at times she is almost contented to rest in this sense of grievance as a private store of consolation. Sometimes she wishes to run away, but she stays. Now she longs to fly out of this room, down the narrow stairs, and into the street where the houses lean together like conspirators under a single mottled lamp, and leave Braggioni singing to himself.

Instead she looks at Braggioni, frankly and clearly, like a good child who understands the rules of behavior. Her knees cling together under sound blue serge, and her round white collar is not purposely nun-like. She wears the uniform of an idea, and has renounced vanities. She was born Roman Catholic, and in spite of her fear of being seen by someone who might make a scandal of it, she slips now and again into some crumbling little church, kneels on the chilly stone, and says a Hail Mary on the gold rosary she bought in Tehuantepec. It is no good and she ends by examining the altar with its tinsel flowers and ragged brocades, and feels tender about the battered doll-shape of some male saint whose white, lace-trimmed drawers hang limply around his ankles below the hieratic dignity of his velvet robe. She has encased herself in a set of principles derived from her early training, leaving no detail of gesture or of personal taste untouched, and for this reason she will not wear lace made on machines. This is her private heresy, for in her special group the machine is sacred, and will be the salvation of the workers. She loves fine lace, and there is a tiny edge of fluted cobweb on this collar, which is one of twenty precisely alike, folded in blue tissue paper in the upper drawer of her clothes chest.

Braggioni catches her glance solidly as if he had been waiting for it, leans forward, balancing his paunch between his spread knees, and sings with tremendous emphasis, weighing his words. He has, the song relates, no father and no mother, nor even a friend to console him; lonely as a wave of the sea he comes and goes, lonely as a wave. His mouth opens round and yearns sideways, his balloon cheeks grow oily with the labor of song. He bulges marvelously in his expensive garments. Over his lavender collar, crushed upon a purple necktie, held by a diamond hoop: over his ammunition belt of tooled leather worked in silver, buckled cruelly around his gasping middle: over the tops of his glossy yellow shoes Braggioni swells with ominous ripeness, his mauve silk hose stretched taut, his ankles bound with the stout leather thongs of his shoes.

When he stretches his eyelids at Laura she notes again that his eyes are the true tawny yellow cat's eyes. He is rich, not in money, he tells her, but in power, and this power brings with it the blameless ownership of things, and the right to indulge his love of small luxuries. "I have a taste for the elegant refinements," he said once, flourishing a yellow silk handkerchief before her nose. "Smell that? It is Jockey Club, imported from New York." Nonetheless he is wounded by life. He will say so presently. "It is true everything turns to dust in the hand, to gall on the tongue." He sighs and his leather belt creaks like a saddle girth. "I am disappointed in everything as it comes. Everything." He shakes his head. "You, poor thing, you will be disappointed too. You are born for it. We are more alike than you realize in some things. Wait and see. Some day you will remember what I have told you, you will know that Braggioni was your friend."

Laura feels a slow chill, a purely physical sense of danger, a warning in her blood that violence, mutilation, a shocking death, wait for her with lessening patience. She has translated this fear into something homely, immediate, and sometimes hesitates before crossing the street. "My personal fate is nothing, except as the testimony of a mental attitude," she reminds herself, quoting from some forgotten philosophic primer, and is sensible enough to add, "Anyhow, I shall not be killed by an automobile if I can help it."

"It may be true I am as corrupt, in another way, as Braggioni," she thinks in spite of herself, "as callous, as incomplete," and if this is so, any kind of death seems preferable. Still she sits quietly, she does not run. Where could she go? Uninvited she has promised herself to this place; she can no longer imagine herself as living in another country, and there is no pleasure in remembering her life before she came here.

Precisely what is the nature of this devotion, its true motives, and what are its obligations? Laura cannot say. She spends part of her days in Xochimilco, near by, teaching Indian children to say in English, "The cat is on the mat." When she appears in the classroom they crowd about her with smiles on their wise, innocent, clay-colored faces, crying, "Good morning, my titcher!" in immaculate voices, and they make of her desk a fresh garden of flowers every day.

During her leisure she goes to union meetings and listens to busy important voices quarreling over tactics, methods, internal politics. She visits the prisoners of her own political faith in their cells, where they entertain themselves with counting cockroaches, repenting of their indiscretions, composing their memoirs, writing out manifestoes and plans for their comrades who are still walking about free, hands in pockets, sniffing fresh air. Laura brings them food and cigarettes and a little money, and she brings messages disguised in equivocal phrases from the men outside who dare not set foot in the prison for fear of disappearing into the cells kept empty for them. If the prisoners confuse night and day, and complain, "Dear little Laura, time doesn't pass in this infernal hole, and I won't know when it is time to sleep unless I have a reminder," she brings them their favorite narcotics, and says in a tone that does not wound them with pity, "Tonight will really be night for you," and though her Spanish amuses them they find her comforting, useful. If they lose patience and all faith, and curse the slowness of their friends in coming to their rescue with money and influence, they trust her not to repeat everything, and if she inquires, "Where do you think we can find money, or influence?" they are certain to answer, "Well, there is Braggioni, why doesn't he do something?"

She smuggles letters from headquarters to men hiding from firing squads in back streets in mildewed houses, where they sit in tumbled beds and talk bitterly as if all Mexico were at their heels, when Laura knows positively they might appear at the band concert in the Alameda on Sunday morning, and no one would notice them. But Braggioni says, "Let them sweat a little. The next time they may be careful. It is very restful to have them out of the way for a while." She is not afraid to knock on any door in any street after midnight, and enter in the darkness, and say to one of these men who is really in danger: "They will be looking for you—seriously—tomorrow morning after six. Here is some money from Vicente. Go to Vera Cruz and wait."

She borrows money from the Roumanian agitator to give to his bitter enemy the Polish agitator. The favor of Braggioni is their disputed territory, and Braggioni holds the balance nicely, for he can use them both. The Polish agitator talks love to her over café tables, hoping to exploit what he believes is her secret sentimental preference for him, and he gives her misinformation which he begs her to repeat as the solemn truth to certain persons. The Roumanian is more adroit. He is generous with his money in all good causes, and lies to her with an air of ingenuous candor, as if he were her good friend and confidant. She never repeats anything they may say. Braggioni never asks questions. He has other ways to discover all that he wishes to know about them.

Nobody touches her, but all praise her gray eyes, and the soft, round under lip which promises gayety, yet is always grave, nearly always firmly closed: and they cannot understand why she is in Mexico. She walks back and forth on her errands, with puzzled eyebrows, carrying her little folder of drawings and music and school papers. No dancer dances more beautifully than Laura walks, and she inspires some amusing, unexpected ardors, which cause little gossip, because nothing comes of them. A young captain who had been a soldier in Zapata's army attempted, during a horseback ride near Cuernavaca, to express his desire for her with the noble simplicity befitting a rude folk-hero: but gently, because he was gentle. This gentleness was his defeat, for when he alighted, and removed her foot from the stirrup, and essayed to draw her down into his arms, her horse, ordinarily a tame one, shied fiercely, reared and plunged away. The young hero's horse careened blindly after his stable-mate, and the hero did not return to the hotel until rather late that evening. At breakfast he came to her table in full charro dress, gray buckskin jacket and trousers with strings of silver buttons down the leg, and he was in a humorous, careless mood. "May I sit with you?" and "You are a wonderful rider. I was terrified that you might be thrown and dragged. I should never have forgiven myself. But I cannot admire you enough for your riding."

"I learned to ride in Arizona," said Laura.

"If you will ride with me again this morning, I promise you a horse that will not shy with you," he said. But Laura remembered that she must return to Mexico City at noon.

Next morning the children made a celebration and spent their playtime writing on the blackboard, "We lov ar titcher," and with tinted chalks they drew wreaths of flowers around the words. The young hero wrote her a letter: "I am a very foolish, wasteful, impulsive man. I should have first said I love you, and then you would not have run away. But you shall see me again." Laura thought, "I must send him a box of colored crayons," but she was trying to forgive herself for having spurred her horse at the wrong moment.

A brown shock-haired youth came and stood in her patio one night and sang like a lost soul for two hours, but Laura could think of nothing to do about it. The moonlight spread a wash of gauzy silver over the clear spaces of the garden, and the shadows were cobalt blue. The scarlet blossoms of the Judas tree were dull purple, and the names of the colors repeated themselves automatically in her mind, while she watched not the boy, but his shadow, fallen like a dark garment across the fountain rim, trailing in the water. Lupe came silently and whispered expert counsel in her ear: "If you will throw him one little flower, he will sing another song or two and go away." Laura threw the flower, and he sang a last song and went away with the flower tucked in the band of his hat. Lupe said, "He is one of the organizers of the Typographers Union, and before that he sold corridos in the Merced market, and before that, he came from Guanajuato, where I was born. I would not trust any man, but I trust least those from Guanajuato."

She did not tell Laura that he would be back again the next day, and the next, nor that he would follow her at a certain fixed distance around the Merced market, through the Zocolo, up Francesco I. Madero Avenue, and so along the Paseo de la Reforma to Chapultepec Park, and into the Philosopher's Footpath, still with that flower withering in his hat, and an indivisible attention in his eyes.

Now Laura is accustomed to him, it means nothing except that he is nineteen years old and is observing a convention with all propriety, as though it were founded on a law of nature, which in the end it might very well prove to be. He is beginning to write poems which he prints on a wooden press, and he leaves them stuck like handbills in her door. She is pleasantly disturbed by the abstract, unhurried watchfulness of his black eyes which will in time turn easily towards another object. She tells herself that throwing the flower was a mistake, for she is twenty-two years old and knows better; but she refuses to regret it, and persuades herself that her negation of all external events as they occur is a sign that she is gradually perfecting herself in the stoicism she strives to cultivate against that disaster she fears, though she cannot name it.

She is not at home in the world. Every day she teaches children who remain strangers to her, though she loves their tender round hands and their charming opportunistic savagery. She knocks at unfamiliar doors not knowing whether a friend or a stranger shall answer, and even if a known face emerges from the sour gloom of that unknown interior, still it is the face of a stranger. No matter what this stranger says to her, nor what her message to him, the very cells of her flesh reject knowledge and kinship in one monotonous word. No. No. No. She draws her strength from this one holy talismanic word which does not suffer her to be led into evil. Denying everything, she may walk anywhere in safety, she looks at everything without amazement.

No, repeats this firm unchanging voice of her blood; and she looks at Braggioni without amazement. He is a great man, he wishes to impress this simple girl who covers her great round breasts with thick dark cloth, and who hides long, invaluably beautiful legs under a heavy skirt. She is almost thin except for the incomprehensible fullness of her breasts, like a nursing mother's, and Braggioni, who considers himself a judge of women, speculates again on the puzzle of her notorious virginity, and takes the liberty of speech which she permits without a sign of modesty, indeed, without any sort of sign, which is disconcerting.

"You think you are so cold, *gringita!* Wait and see. You will surprise yourself someday! May I be there to advise you!" He stretches his eyelids at her, and his ill-humored cat's eyes waver in a separate glance for the two points of light marking the opposite ends of a smoothly drawn path between the swollen curve of her breasts. He is not put off by that blue serge, nor by her resolutely fixed gaze. There is all the time in the world. His cheeks are bellying with the wind of song. "O girl with the dark eyes," he sings, and reconsiders. "But yours are not dark. I can change all that. O girl with the green eyes, you have stolen my heart away." Then his mind wanders to the song, and Laura feels the weight of his attention being shifted elsewhere. Singing thus, he seems harmless, he is quite harmless, there is nothing to do but sit patiently and say "No," when the moment comes. She draws a full breath, and her mind wanders also, but not far. She dares not wander too far.

Not for nothing has Braggioni taken pains to be a good revolutionist and a professional lover of humanity. He will never die of it.

He has the malice, the cleverness, the wickedness, the sharpness of wit, the hardness of heart, stipulated for loving the world profitably. He *will never die of it.* He will live to see himself kicked out from his feeding trough by other hungry world-saviours. Traditionally he must sing in spite of his life which drives him to bloodshed, he tells Laura, for his father was a Tuscany peasant who drifted to Yucatan and married a Maya woman: a woman of race, an aristocrat. They gave him the love and knowledge of music, thus: and under the rip of his thumbnail, the strings of the instrument complain like exposed nerves.

Once he was called Delgadito by all the girls and married women who ran after him; he was so scrawny all his bones showed under his thin cotton clothing, and he could squeeze his emptiness to the very backbone with his two hands. He was a poet and the revolution was only a dream then; too many women loved him and sapped away his youth, and he could never find enough to eat anywhere, anywhere! Now he is a leader of men, crafty men who whisper in his ear, hungry men who wait for hours outside his office for a word with him, emaciated men with wild faces who waylay him at the street gate with a timid, "Comrade, let me tell you . . ." and they blow the foul breath from their empty stomachs in his face.

He is always sympathetic. He gives them handfuls of small coins from his own pockets, he promises them work, there will be demonstrations, they must join the unions and attend the meetings, above all they must be on the watch for spies. They are closer to him than his own brothers, without them he can do nothing—until tomorrow, comrade!

Until tomorrow. "They are stupid, they are lazy, they are treacherous, they would cut my throat for nothing," he says to Laura. He has good food and abundant drink, he hires an automobile and drives in the Paseo on Sunday morning, and enjoys plenty of sleep in a soft bed beside a wife who dares not disturb him; and he sits pampering his bones in easy billows of fat, singing to Laura, who knows and thinks these things about him. When he was fifteen, he tried to drown himself because he loved a girl, his first love, and she laughed at him. "A thousand women have paid for that," and his tight little mouth turns down at the corners. Now he perfumes his hair with Jockey Club, and confides to Laura: "One woman is really as good as another for me in the dark. I prefer them all."

His wife organizes unions among the girls in the cigarette factories, and walks in picket lines, and even speaks at meetings in the evening. But she cannot be brought to acknowledge the benefits of true liberty. "I tell her I must have my freedom, net. She does not understand my point of view." Laura has heard this many times. Braggioni scratches the guitar and meditates. "She is an instinctively virtuous woman, pure gold, no doubt of that. If she were not, I should lock her up, and she knows it."

His wife, who works so hard for the good of the factory girls, employs part of her leisure lying on the floor weeping because there are so many women in the world, and only one husband for her, and she never knows where nor when to look for him. He told her: "Unless you can learn to cry when I am not here, I must go away for good." That day he went away and took a room at the Hotel Madrid.

It is this month of separation for the sake of higher principles that has been spoiled not only for Mrs. Braggioni, whose sense of reality is beyond criticism, but for Laura, who feels herself bogged in a nightmare. Tonight Laura envies Mrs. Braggioni, who is alone, and free to weep as much as she pleases about a concrete wrong. Laura has just come from a visit to the prison, and she is waiting for tomorrow with a bitter anxiety as if tomorrow may not come, but time may be caught immovably in this hour, with herself transfixed, Braggioni singing on forever, and Eugenio's body not yet discovered by the guard.

Braggioni says: "Are you going to sleep?" Almost before she can shake her head, he begins telling her about the May-day disturbances coming on in Morelia, for the Catholics hold a festival in honor of the Blessed Virgin, and the Socialists celebrate their martyrs on that day. "There will be two independent processions, starting from either end of town, and they will march until they meet, and the rest depends . . ." He asks her to oil and load his pistols. Standing up, he unbuckles his ammunition belt, and spreads it laden across her knees. Laura sits with the shells slipping through the cleaning cloth dipped in oil, and he says again he cannot understand why she works so hard for the revolutionary idea unless she loves some man who is in it. "Are you not in love with someone?" "No," says Laura. "And no one is in love with you?" "No." "Then it is your own fault. No woman need go begging. Why, what is the matter with you? The legless beggar woman in the Alameda has a perfectly faithful lover. Did you know that?"

Laura peers down the pistol barrel and says nothing, but a long, slow faintness rises and subsides in her; Braggioni curves his swollen fingers around the throat of the guitar and softly smothers the music out of it, and when she hears him again he seems to have forgotten her, and is speaking in the hypnotic voice he uses when talking in small rooms to a listening, close-gathered crowd. Some day this world, now seemingly so composed and eternal, to the edges of every sea shall be merely a tangle of gaping trenches, of crashing walls and broken bodies. Everything must be torn from its accustomed place where it has rotted for centuries, hurled skyward and distributed, cast down again clean as rain, without separate identity. Nothing shall survive that the stiffened hands of poverty have created for the rich and no one shall be left alive except the elect spirits destined to procreate a new world cleansed of cruelty and injustice, ruled by benevolent anarchy: "Pistols are good, I love them, cannon are even better, but in the end I pin my faith to good dynamite," he concludes, and strokes the pistol lying in her hands. "Once I dreamed of destroying this city, in case it offered resistance to General Ortiz, but it fell into his hands like an overripe pear."

He is made restless by his own words, rises and stands waiting. Laura holds up the belt to him: "Put that on, and go kill somebody in Morella, and you will be happier," she says softly. The presence of death in the room makes her bold. "Today, I found Eugenio going into a stupor. He refused to allow me to call the prison doctor. He had taken all the tablets I brought him yesterday. He said he took them because he was bored."

"He is a fool, and his death is his own business," says Braggioni, fastening his belt carefully.

"I told him if he had waited only a little while longer, you would have got him set free," says Laura. "He said he did not want to wait."

"He is a fool and we are well rid of him," says Braggioni, reaching for his hat.

He goes away. Laura knows his mood has changed, she will not see him any more for a while. He will send word when he needs her to go on errands into strange streets, to speak to the strange faces that will appear, like clay masks with the power of human speech, to mutter their thanks to Braggioni for his help. Now she is free, and she thinks, I must run while there is time. But she does not go.

Braggioni enters his own house where for a month his wife has spent many hours every night weeping and tangling her hair upon her pillow. She is weeping now, and she weeps more at the sight of him, the cause of all her sorrows. He looks about the room. Nothing is changed, the smells are good and familiar, he is well acquainted with the woman who comes toward him with no reproach except grief on her face. He says to her tenderly: "You are so good, please don't cry any more, you dear good creature." She says, "Are you tired, my angel? Sit here and I will wash your feet." She brings a bowl of water, and kneeling, unlaces his shoes, and when from her knees she raises her sad eyes under her blackened lids, he is sorry for everything, and bursts into tears. "Ah, yes, I am hungry, I am tired, let us eat something together," he says, between sobs. His wife leans her head on his arm and says, "Forgive me!" and this time he is refreshed by the solemn, endless rain of her tears.

Laura takes off her serge dress and puts on a white linen nightgown and goes to bed. She turns her head a little to one side, and lying still, reminds herself that it is time to sleep. Numbers tick in her brain like little clocks, soundless doors close of themselves around her. If you would sleep, you must not remember anything, the children will say tomorrow, good morning, my teacher, the poor prisoners who come every day bringing flowers to their jailor. 1–2–3–4–5—it is monstrous to confuse love with revolution, night with day, life with death—ah Eugenio!

The tolling of the midnight bell is a signal, but what does it mean? Get up, Laura, and follow me: come out of your sleep, out of your bed, out of this strange house. What are you doing in this house? Without a word, without fear she rose and reached for Eugenio's hand, but he eluded her with a sharp, sly smile and drifted away. This is not all, you shall see—Murderer, he said, follow me, I will show you a new country, but it is far away and we must hurry. No, said Laura, not unless you take my hand, no; and she clung first to the stair rail, and then to the topmost branch of the Judas tree that bent down slowly and set her upon the earth, and then to the rocky ledge of a cliff, and then to the jagged wave of a sea that was not water but a desert of crumbling stone. Where are you taking me? she asked in wonder but without fear. To death, and it is a long way off, and we must hurry, said Eugenio. No, said Laura, not unless you take my hand. Then eat these flowers, poor prisoner, said Eugenio in a voice of pity, take and eat: and from the Judas tree he stripped the warm bleeding flowers, and held them to her lips. She saw that his hand was fleshless, a cluster of small white petrified branches, and his eye sockets were without light, but she ate the flowers greedily for they satisfied both hunger and thirst. Murderer! said Eugenio, and Cannibal! This is my body and my blood. Laura cried No! and at the sound of her own voice, she awoke trembling, and was afraid to sleep again.

QUESTIONS

1. Reread the first three paragraphs of this story closely, and notice that detail is reported as follows:

   (a) in the dramatic present: "Braggioni

sits heaped upon the edge of a straight-backed chair . . ."

(b) in summary narrative: "No matter how late she is, he will be sitting there . . ."
"Laura, who haunts the markets listening to the ballad singers, and stops every day . . ."

After identifying these two ways of reporting events, and after noting the frequent shifting from the one to the other, fix also in your mind the fact that the author makes a constant use of the progressive tense: "Braggioni sits, Laura says, Laura wishes to lie down, Laura haunts the marketplace and stops every day," etc.

With these technical features in mind, read into the story again. What effects do you suppose are achieved by the steady use of the present progressive tense and the shifting from dramatic present to summary narrative and back again?

2. In the last paragraph of "Flowering Judas" the tense changes suddenly and sharply from present progressive, which has been used throughout the story, to past: "Without a word, without fear she *rose* and *reached* for Eugenio's hand . . ." What effects are achieved by this sudden use of the *past* tense after the reader's long immersion in the *present* tense? (The best way to answer this question is to read up to and through this transition yourself.)

3. Make a short list of all the ways in which Laura can feel that something or someone has betrayed her or proved undependable. Make another short list of all the ways in which Laura may feel that she herself has betrayed something or someone. Does this combination of hurt and guilt in Laura justify, in your opinion, the condition of near-paralysis in which she finds herself?

4. Is Laura's condition of being partly hurt and partly guilty a just symbol of any kind of individual or group life in our time? Would you say that Laura is mainly a symbol of "fear of life, wish for death," or of "the barrenness of causes"?

5. Is it possible, in your opinion, for a human being to be so preoccupied with either fear or guilt or a cause that he is unaware of his surroundings or of danger?

6. Laura is more aware of some kinds of "danger" than of others. What are these "dangers" and what do they show you about Laura?

7. In what ways are the major sources of security in our times mirrored in "Flowering Judas"? Is the Judas tree a symbol of multiple or single betrayal?

8. What are the attitudes of Braggioni to the "causes" he serves?

DELTA AUTUMN

William Faulkner
(1897–   )

Soon now they would enter the Delta. The sensation was familiar to him. It had been renewed like this each last week in November for more than fifty years—the last hill, at the foot of which the rich unbroken alluvial flatness began as the sea began at the base of its cliffs, dissolving away beneath the unhurried November rain as the sea itself would dissolve away.

At first they had come in wagons: the guns, the bedding, the dogs, the food, the whisky, the keen heart-lifting anticipation of hunting; the young men who could drive all night and all the following day in the cold rain and pitch a camp in the rain and sleep in the wet blankets and rise at daylight the next morning and hunt. There had been bear then. A man shot a doe or a fawn as quickly as he did a buck, and in the afternoons they shot wild turkey with pistols to test their stalking skill and marksmanship, feeding all but the breast to the dogs. But that time was gone now. Now they went in cars, driving faster and faster each year because the roads were better and they had farther and farther to drive, the territory in which game still existed drawing yearly inward as his life was drawing inward, until now he was the last of those who had once made the journey in wagons without feeling it and now those who accompanied him were the sons and even grandsons of the men who had ridden for twenty-four hours in the rain or sleet behind the steaming mules. They called him 'Uncle Ike' now, and he no longer told anyone how near eighty he actually was because he knew as well as they did that he no longer had any business making such expeditions, even by car.

In fact, each time now, on that first night in camp, lying aching and sleepless in the harsh blankets, his blood only faintly warmed by the single thin whisky-and-water which he allowed himself, he would tell himself that this would be his last. But he would stand that trip—he still shot almost as well as he ever had, still killed almost as much of the game he saw as he ever killed; he no longer even knew how many deer had fallen before his gun—and the fierce long heat of the next summer would renew him. Then November would come again, and again in the car with two of the sons of his old companions, whom he had taught not only how to distinguish between the prints left by a buck or a doe but between the sound they made in moving, he would look ahead past the jerking arc of the windshield wiper and see the land flatten suddenly and swoop, dissolving away beneath the rain as the sea itself would dissolve, and he would say, "Well, boys, there it is again."

This time though, he didn't have time to speak. The driver of the car stopped it, slamming it to a skidding halt on the greasy pavement without warning, actually flinging the two passengers forward until they caught themselves with their braced hands against the dash. "What the hell, Roth!" the man in the middle said. "Cant you whistle first when you do that? Hurt you, Uncle Ike?"

"No," the old man said. "What's the matter?" The driver didn't answer. Still leaning forward, the old man looked sharply past the face of the man between them, at the face of his kinsman. It was the youngest face of them all, aquiline, saturnine, a little ruthless, the face of his ancestor too, tempered a little, altered a little, staring sombrely through the streaming windshield across which the twin wipers flicked and flicked.

"I didn't intend to come back in here this time," he said suddenly and harshly.

"You said that back in Jefferson last week," the old man said. "Then you changed your mind. Have you changed it again? This aint a very good time to—"

"Oh, Roth's coming," the man in the middle said. His name was Legate. He seemed to be speaking to no one, as he was looking at neither of them. "If it was just a buck he was coming all this distance for, now. But he's got a doe in here. Of course a old man like Uncle Ike cant be interested in no doe, not one that walks on two legs—when she's standing up, that is. Pretty light-colored, too. The one he was after them nights last fall when he said he was coon-hunting, Uncle Ike. The one I figured maybe he was still running when he was gone all that month last January. But of course a old man like Uncle Ike aint got no interest in nothing like that." He chortled, still looking at no one, not completely jeering.

"What?" the old man said. "What's that?" But he had not even so much as glanced at Legate. He was still watching his kinsman's face. The eyes behind the spectacles were the blurred eyes of an old man, but they were quite sharp too; eyes which could still see a gun-barrel and what ran beyond it as well as any of them could. He was remembering himself now: how last year, during the final stage by motor boat in to where they camped, a box of food had been lost overboard and how on the next day his kinsman had gone back to the nearest town for supplies and had been gone overnight. And when he did return, something had happened to him. He would go into the woods with his rifle each dawn when the others went, but the old man, watching him, knew that he was not hunting. "All right," he said. "Take me and Will on to shelter where we can wait for the truck, and you can go on back."

"I'm going in," the other said harshly. "Don't worry. Because this will be the last of it."

"The last of deer hunting, or of doe hunting?" Legate said. This time the old man paid no attention to him even by speech. He still watched the young man's savage and brooding face.

"Why?" he said.

"After Hitler gets through with it? Or Smith or Jones or Roosevelt or Willkie or whatever he will call himself in this country?"

"We'll stop him in this country," Legate said. "Even if he calls himself George Washington."

"How?" Edmonds said. "By singing God bless America in bars at midnight and wearing dime-store flags in our lapels?"

"So that's what's worrying you," the old man said. "I aint noticed this country being short of defenders yet, when it needed them. You did some of it yourself twenty-odd years ago, before you were a grown man even. This country is a little mite stronger than any one man or group of men, outside of it or even inside of it either. I reckon, when the time comes and some of you have done got tired of hollering we are whipped if we dont go to war and some more are hollering we are whipped if we do, it will cope with one Austrian paper-hanger, no matter what he will be calling himself. My pappy and some other better men than any of them you named tried once to tear it in two with a war, and they failed."

"And what have you got left?" the other said. "Half the people without jobs and half the factories closed by strikes. Half the people on public dole that wont work and half that couldn't work even if they would. Too much cotton and corn and hogs, and not enough for people to eat and wear. The country full of people to tell a man how he cant raise his own cotton whether he will or wont, and Sally Rand with a sergeant's stripes and not even the fan couldn't fill the army rolls. Too much not-butter and not even the guns—"

"We got a deer camp—if we ever get to it," Legate said. "Not to mention does."

"It's a good time to mention does," the old man said. "Does and fawns both. The only fighting anywhere that ever had anything of

God's blessing on it has been when men fought to protect does and fawns. If it's going to come to fighting, that's a good thing to mention and remember too."

"Haven't you discovered in—how many years more than seventy is it?—that women and children are one thing there's never any scarcity of?" Edmonds said.

"Maybe that's why all I am worrying about right now is that ten miles of river we still have got to run before we can make camp," the old man said. "So let's get on."

They went on. Soon they were going fast again, as Edmonds always drove, consulting neither of them about the speed just as he had given neither of them any warning when he slammed the car to stop. The old man relaxed again. He watched, as he did each recurrent November while more than sixty of them passed, the land which he had seen change. At first there had been only the old towns along the River and the old towns along the hills, from each of which the planters with their gangs of slaves and then of hired laborers had wrested from the impenetrable jungle of water-standing cane and cypress, gum and holly and oak and ash, cotton patches which as the years passed became fields and then plantations. The paths made by deer and bear became roads and then highways, with towns in turn springing up along them and along the rivers Tallahatchie and Sunflower which joined and became the Yazoo, the River of the Dead of the Choctaws—the thick, slow, black, unsunned streams almost without current, which once each year ceased to flow at all and then reversed, spreading, drowning the rich land and subsiding again, leaving it still richer.

Most of that was gone now. Now a man drove two hundred miles from Jefferson before he found wilderness to hunt in. Now the land lay open from the cradling hills on the East to the rampart of levee on the West, standing horseman-tall with cotton for the world's looms—the rich black land, imponderable and vast, fecund up to the very doorsteps of the negroes who worked it and of the white men who owned it; which exhausted the hunting life of a dog in one year, the working life of a mule in five and of a man in twenty—the land in which neon flashed past them from the little countless towns and countless shining this-year's automobiles sped past them on the broad plumb-ruled highways, yet in which the only permanent mark of man's occupation seemed to be the tremendous gins, constructed in sections of sheet iron and in a week's time though they were, since no man, millionaire though he be, would build more than a roof and walls to shelter the camping equipment he lived from when he knew that once each ten years or so his house would be flooded to the second storey and all within it ruined;—the land across which there came now no scream of panther but instead the long hooting of locomotives: trains of incredible length and drawn by a single engine, since there was no gradient anywhere and no elevation save those raised by forgotten aboriginal hands as refuges from the yearly water and used by their Indian successors to sepulchre their fathers' bones, and all that remained of that old time were the Indian names on the little towns and usually pertaining to water—Aluschaskuna, Tillatoba, Homochitto, Yazoo.

By early afternoon, they were on water. At the last little Indian-named town at the end of pavement they waited until the other car and the two trucks—the one carrying the bedding and tents and food, the other the horses—overtook them. They left the concrete and, after another mile or so, the gravel too. In caravan they ground on through the ceaselessly dissolving afternoon, with skid-chains on the wheels now, lurching and splashing and sliding among the ruts, until presently it seemed to him that the retrograde of his remembering had gained an inverse velocity from their own slow progress, that the land had retreated not in minutes from the last spread of gravel but in years, decades, back toward what it had been when he first knew it: the road they now followed once more the ancient pathway of bear and deer, the diminishing fields they now passed once more scooped punily and terrifically by

axe and saw and mule-drawn plow from the wilderness' flank, out of the brooding and immemorial tangle, in place of ruthless mile-wide parallelograms wrought by ditching the dyking machinery.

They reached the river landing and unloaded, the horses to go overland down stream to a point opposite the camp and swim the river, themselves and the bedding and food and dogs and guns in the motor launch. It was himself, though no horseman, no farmer, not even a countryman save by his distant birth and boyhood, who coaxed and soothed the two horses, drawing them by his own single frail hand until, backing, filling, trembling a little, they surged, halted, then sprang scrambling down from the truck, possessing no affinity for them as creatures, beasts, but being merely insulated by his years and time from the corruption of steel and oiled moving parts which tainted the others.

Then, his old hammer double gun which was only twelve years younger than he standing between his knees, he watched even the last puny marks of man—cabin, clearing, the small and irregular fields which a year ago were jungle and in which the skeleton stalks of this year's cotton stood almost as tall and rank as the old cane had stood, as if man had had to marry his planting to the wilderness in order to conquer it—fall away and vanish. The twin banks marched with wilderness as he remembered it—the tangle of brier and cane impenetrable even to sight twenty feet away, the tall tremendous soaring of oak and gum and ash and hickory which had rung to no axe save the hunter's, had echoed to no machinery save the beat of old-time steam boats traversing it or to the snarling of launches like their own of people going into it to dwell for a week or two weeks because it was still wilderness. There was some of it left, although now it was two hundred miles from Jefferson when once it had been thirty. He had watched it, not being conquered, destroyed, so much as retreating since its purpose was served now and its time an outmoded time, retreating southward through this inverted-apex, this ∇-shaped section of earth between hills and River until what was left of it seemed now to be gathered and for the time arrested in one tremendous density of brooding and inscrutable impenetrability at the ultimate funnelling tip.

They reached the site of their last-year's camp with still two hours left of light. "You go on over under that driest tree and set down," Legate told him. "—if you can find it. Me and these other young boys will do this." He did neither. He was not tired yet. That would come later. *Maybe it wont come at all this time,* he thought, as he had thought at this point each November for the last five or six of them. *Maybe I will go out on stand in the morning too;* knowing that he would not, not even if he took the advice and sat down under the driest shelter and did nothing until camp was made and supper cooked. Because it would not be the fatigue. It would be because he would not sleep tonight but would lie instead wakeful and peaceful on the cot amid the tent-filling snoring and the rain's whisper as he always did on the first night in camp; peaceful, without regret or fretting, telling himself that was all right too, who didn't have so many of them left as to waste one sleeping.

In his slicker he directed the unloading of the boat—the tents, the stove, the bedding, the food for themselves and the dogs until there should be meat in camp. He sent two of the negroes to cut firewood; he had the cook-tent raised and the stove up and a fire going and supper cooking while the big tent was still being staked down. Then in the beginning of dusk he crossed in the boat to where the horses waited, backing and snorting at the water. He took the lead-ropes and with no more weight than that and his voice, he drew them down into the water and held them beside the boat with only their heads above the surface, as though they actually were suspended from his frail and strengthless old man's hands, while the boat recrossed and each horse in turn lay prone in the shallows, panting and trembling, its eyes rolling in the dusk, until the same weightless hand and unraised voice gathered it surging upward, splashing and thrashing up the bank.

Then the meal was ready. The last of light was gone now save the thin stain of it snared somewhere between the river's surface and the rain. He had the single glass of thin whisky-and-water, then, standing in the churned mud beneath the stretched tarpaulin, he said grace over the fried slabs of pork, the hot soft shapeless bread, the canned beans and molasses and coffee in iron plates and cups,—the town food, brought along with them—then covered himself again, the others following. "Eat," he said. "Eat it all up. I dont want a piece of town mean in camp after breakfast tomorrow. Then you boys will hunt. You'll have to. When I first started hunting in this bottom sixty years ago with old General Compson and Major de Spain and Roth's grandfather and Will Legate's too, Major de Spain wouldn't allow but two pieces of foreign grub in his camp. That was one side of pork and one ham of beef. And not to eat for the first supper and breakfast neither. It was to save until along toward the end of camp when everybody was so sick of bear meat and coon and venison that we couldn't even look at it."

"I thought Uncle Ike was going to say the pork and beef was for the dogs," Legate said, chewing. "But that's right; I remember. You just shot the dogs a mess of wild turkey every evening when they got tired of deer guts."

"Times are different now," another said. "There was game here then."

"Yes," the old man said quietly. "There was game here then."

"Besides, they shot does then too," Legate said. "As it is now, we aint got but one doe-hunter in—"

"And better men hunted it," Edmonds said. He stood at the end of the rough plank table, eating rapidly and steadily as the others ate. But again the old man looked sharply across at the sullen, handsome, brooding face which appeared now darker and more sullen still in the light of the smoky lantern. "Go on. Say it."

"I didn't say that," the old man said. "There are good men everywhere, at all times. Most men are. Some are just unlucky, because most men are a little better than their circumstances give them a chance to be. And I've known some that even the circumstances couldn't stop."

"Well, I wouldn't say—" Legate said.

"So you've lived almost eighty years," Edmonds said. "And that's what you finally learned about the other animals you lived among. I suppose the question to ask you is, where have you been all the time you were dead?"

There was a silence; for the instant even Legate's jaw stopped chewing while he gaped at Edmonds. "Well, by God, Roth—" the third speaker said. But it was the old man who spoke, his voice still peaceful and untroubled and merely grave:

"Maybe so," he said. "But if being what you call alive would have learned me any different, I reckon I'm satisfied, wherever it was I've been."

"Well, I wouldn't say that Roth—" Legate said.

The third speaker was still leaning forward a little over the table, looking at Edmonds. "Meaning that it's only because folks happen to be watching him that a man behaves at all," he said. "Is that it?"

"Yes," Edmonds said. "A man in a blue coat, with a badge on it watching him. Maybe just the badge."

"I deny that," the old man said. "I dont—"

The other two paid no attention to him. Even Legate was listening to them for the moment, his mouth still full of food and still open a little, his knife with another lump of something balanced on the tip of the blade arrested halfway to his mouth. "I'm glad I dont have your opinion of folks," the third speaker said. "I take it you include yourself."

"I see," Edmonds said. "You prefer Uncle Ike's opinion of circumstances. All right. Who makes the circumstances?"

"Luck," the third said. "Chance. Happen-so. I see what you are getting at. But that's just what Uncle Ike said: that now and then, maybe most of the time, man is a little better than the net result of his and his neighbors' doings, when he gets the chance to be."

This time Legate swallowed first. He was not to be stopped this time. "Well, I wouldn't say that Roth Edmonds can hunt one doe every day and night for two weeks and was a poor hunter or a unlucky one neither. A man that still have the same doe left to hunt on again next year—"

"Have some meat," the man next to him said.

"—aint no unlucky— What?" Legate said.

"Have some meat." The other offered the dish.

"I got some," Legate said.

"Have some more," the third speaker said. "You and Roth Edmonds both. Have a heap of it. Clapping your jaws together that way with nothing to break the shock." Someone chortled. Then they all laughed, with relief, the tension broken. But the old man was speaking, even into the laughter, in that peaceful and still untroubled voice:

"I still believe. I see proof everywhere. I grant that man made a heap of his circumstances, him and his living neighbors between them. He even inherited some of them already made, already almost ruined even. A while ago Henry Wyatt there said how there used to be more game here. There was. So much that we even killed does. I seem to remember Will Legate mentioning that too—" Someone laughed, a single guffaw, stillborn. It ceased and they all listened, gravely, looking down at their plates. Edmonds was drinking his coffee, sullen, brooding, inattentive.

"Some folks still kill does," Wyatt said. "There wont be just one buck hanging in this bottom tomorrow night without any head to fit it."

"I didn't say all men," the old man said. "I said most men. And not just because there is a man with a badge to watch us. We probably wont even see him unless maybe he will stop here about noon tomorrow and eat dinner with us and check our licenses—"

"We dont kill does because if we did kill does in a few years there wouldn't even be any bucks left to kill, Uncle Ike," Wyatt said.

"According to Roth yonder, that's one thing we wont never have to worry about," the old man said. "He said on the way here this morning that does and fawns—I believe he said women and children—are two things this world aint ever lacked. But that aint all of it," he said. "That's just the mind's reason a man has to give himself because the heart dont always have time to bother with thinking up words that fit together. God created man and He created the world for him to live in and I reckon He created the kind of world He would have wanted to live in if He had been a man—the ground to walk on, the big woods, the trees and the water, and the game to live in it. And maybe He didn't put the desire to hunt and kill game in man but I reckon He knew it was going to be there, that man was going to teach it to himself, since he wasn't quite God himself yet—"

"When will he be?" Wyatt said.

"I think that every man and woman, at the instant when it dont even matter whether they marry or not, I think that whether they marry then or afterward or dont never, at that instant the two of them together were God."

"Then there are some Gods in this world I wouldn't want to touch, and with a damn long stick," Edmonds said. He set his coffee cup down and looked at Wyatt. "And that includes myself, if that's what you want to know. I'm going to bed." He was gone. There was a general movement among the others. But it ceased and they stood again about the table, not looking at the old man, apparently held there yet by his quiet and peaceful voice as the heads of the swimming horses had been held above the water by his weightless hand. The three negroes—the cook and his helper and old Isham—were sitting quietly in the entrance of the kitchen tent, listening too, the three faces dark and motionless and musing.

"He put them both here: man, and the game he would follow and kill, foreknowing it. I believe He said, 'So be it.' I reckon He even foreknew the end. But He said, 'I will give him his chance. I will give him warning and foreknowledge too, along with the desire to follow and the power to slay. The woods and fields he ravages and the game he devas-

tates will be the consequence and signature of his crime and guilt, and his punishment.' —Bed time," he said. His voice and inflection did not change at all. "Breakfast at four oclock, Isham. We want meat on the ground by sunup time."

There was a good fire in the sheet-iron heater; the tent was warm and was beginning to dry out, except for the mud underfoot. Edmonds was already rolled into his blankets, motionless, his face to the wall. Isham had made up his bed too—the strong, battered iron cot, the stained mattress which was not quite soft enough, the worn, often-washed blankets which as the years passed were less and less warm enough. But the tent was warm; presently, when the kitchen was cleaned up and readied for breakfast, the young negro would come in to lie down before the heater, where he could be roused to put fresh wood into it from time to time. And then, he knew now he would not sleep tonight anyway; he no longer needed to tell himself that perhaps he would. But it was all right now. The day was ended now and night faced him, but alarmless, empty of fret. *Maybe I came for this,* he thought: *Not to hunt, but for this. I would come anyway, even if only to go back home tomorrow.* Wearing only his bagging woolen underwear, his spectacles folded away in the worn case beneath the pillow where he could reach them readily and his lean body fitted easily into the old worn groove of mattress and blankets, he lay on his back, his hands crossed on his breast and his eyes closed while the others undressed and went to bed and the last of the sporadic talking died into snoring. Then he opened his eyes and lay peaceful and quiet as a child, looking up at the motionless belly of rain-murmured canvas upon which the glow of the heater was dying slowly away and would fade still further until the young negro, lying on two planks before it, would sit up and stoke it and lie back down again.

They had a house once. That was sixty years ago, when the Big Bottom was only thirty miles from Jefferson and old Major de Spain, who had been his father's cavalry commander in '61 and '2 and '3 and '4, and his cousin (his older brother; his father too) had taken him into the woods for the first time. Old Sam Fathers was alive then, born in slavery, son of a Negro slave and a Chickasaw chief, who had taught him how to shoot, not only when to shoot but when not to; such a November dawn as tomorrow would be and the old man led him straight to the great cypress and he had known the buck would pass exactly there because there was something running in Sam Fathers' veins which ran in the veins of the buck too, and they stood there against the tremendous trunk, the old man of seventy and the boy of twelve, and there was nothing save the dawn until suddenly the buck was there, smoke-colored out of nothing, magnificent with speed: and Sam Fathers said, 'Now. Shoot quick and shoot slow:' and the gun levelled rapidly without haste and crashed and he walked to the buck lying still intact and still in the shape of that magnificent speed and bled it with Sam's knife and Sam dipped his hands into the hot blood and marked his face forever while he stood trying not to tremble, humbly and with pride too though the boy of twelve had been unable to phrase it then: *I slew you; my bearing must not shame your quitting life. My conduct forever onward must become your death;* marking him for that and for more than that: that day and himself and McCaslin juxtaposed not against the wilderness but against the tamed land, the old wrong and shame itself, in repudiation and denial at least of the land and the wrong and shame even if he couldn't cure the wrong and eradicate the shame, who at fourteen when he learned of it had believed he could do both when he became competent and when at twenty-one he became competent he knew that he could do neither but at least he could repudiate the wrong and shame, at least in principle, and at least the land itself in fact, for his son at least: and did, thought he had: then (married then) in a rented cubicle in a back-street stock-traders' boarding-house, the first and last time he ever saw her naked body, himself and his wife juxtaposed in their turn against that same land, that same wrong and shame from whose regret and grief he would at least save and free his son and, saving and freeing his son, lost him. They had the house then. That roof, the two weeks of each November which they spent under it, had become his home. Although since that time they had lived during the two fall weeks in tents and not always in the same place two years in succession and now his companions were the sons and even the grandsons of them with whom he had lived in the house and for almost fifty years now the house itself had not even existed, the conviction, the sense and feeling of home, had been merely transferred into the canvas. He owned a house in Jefferson, a good house though small, where he had had a wife and lived with her and lost her, ay, lost her even though he had lost her in the rented cubicle before he and his old clever dipsomaniac partner had finished the house for them to move into it: but lost her, because she loved him. But women hope for so much. They never live too long to still believe that anything within the scope of their passionate wanting is likewise within the range of their passionate hope: and it was still kept for him by his dead wife's widowed niece and her children and he was comfortable in it, his wants and needs and even the small trying harmless crochets of an old man looked after by blood at least related to the blood which he had elected out of all the earth to cherish. But he spent the time within those walls waiting for November, because even this tent with its muddy floor and the bed which was not wide enough nor soft enough nor even warm enough, was his home and these men, some of whom he only saw during these two November weeks and not one of whom even bore any name he used to know—De Spain and Compson and Ewell and Hogganbeck—were more his kin than any. Because this was his land—

The shadow of the youngest negro loomed. It soared, blotting the heater's dying glow from the ceiling, the wood billets thumping into the iron maw until the glow, the flame, leaped high and bright across the canvas. But the negro's shadow still remained, by its length and breadth, standing, since it covered most of the ceiling, until after a moment he raised himself on one elbow to look. It was not the negro, it was his kinsman; when he spoke the other turned sharp against the red firelight the sullen and ruthless profile.

"Nothing," Edmonds said. "Go on back to sleep."

"Since Will Legate mentioned it," McCaslin said, "I remember you had some trouble sleeping in here last fall too. Only you called it coon-hunting then. Or was it Will Legate called it that?" The other didn't answer. Then he turned and went back to his bed. McCaslin, still propped on his elbow, watched until the other's shadow sank down the wall and vanished, became one with the mass of sleeping shadows. "That's right," he said. "Try to get some sleep. We must have meat in camp tomorrow. You can do all the setting up you want to after that." He lay down again, his hands crossed again on his breast, watching the glow of the heater on the canvas ceiling. It was steady again now, the fresh wood accepted, being assimilated; soon it would begin to fade again, taking with it the last echo of that sudden upflare of a young man's passion and unrest. Let him lie awake for a little while, he thought; He will lie still some day for a long time without even dissatisfaction to disturb him. And lying awake here, in these surroundings, would soothe him if anything could, if anything could soothe a man just forty years old. Yes, he thought; Forty years old or thirty, or even the trembling and sleepless ardor of a boy; already the tent, the rain-murmured canvas globe, was once more filled with it. He lay on his back, his eyes closed, his breathing quiet and peaceful as a child's, listening to it—that silence which was never silence but was myriad. He could almost see it, tremendous, primeval, looming, musing downward upon this puny evanescent clutter of human sojourn which after a single brief week would vanish and in another week would be completely healed, traceless in the unmarked solitude. Because it was his land, although he had never owned

a foot of it. He had never wanted to, not even after he saw plain its ultimate doom, watching it retreat year by year before the onslaught of axe and saw and log-lines and then dynamite and tractor plows, because it belonged to no man. It belonged to all; they had only to use it well, humbly and with pride. Then suddenly he knew why he had never wanted to own any of it, arrest at least that much of what people called progress, measure his longevity at least against that much of its ultimate fate. It was because there was just exactly enough of it. He seemed to see the two of them—himself and the wilderness—as coevals, his own span as a hunter, a woodsman, not contemporary with his first breath but transmitted to him, assumed by him gladly, humbly, with joy and pride, from that old Major de Spain and that old Sam Fathers who had taught him to hunt, the two spans running out together, not toward oblivion, nothingness, but into a dimension free of both time and space where once more the untreed land warped and wrung to mathematical squares of rank cotton for the frantic old-world people to turn into shells to shoot at one another, would find ample room for both—the names, the faces of the old men he had known and loved and for a little while outlived, moving again among the shades of tall unaxed trees and sightless brakes where the wild strong immortal game ran forever before the tireless belling immortal hounds, falling and rising phoenix-like to the soundless guns.

He had been asleep. The lantern was lighted now. Outside in the darkness the oldest negro, Isham, was beating a spoon against the bottom of a tin pan and crying, "Raise up and get yo foa clock coffy. Raise up and get yo foa clock coffy," and the tent was full of low talk and of men dressing, and Legate's voice, repeating: "Get out of here now and let Uncle Ike sleep. If you wake him up, he'll go out with us. And he aint got any business in the woods this morning."

So he didn't move. He lay with his eyes closed, his breathing gentle and peaceful, and heard them one by one leave the tent. He listened to the breakfast sounds from the table beneath the tarpaulin and heard them depart—the horses, the dogs, the last voice until it died away and there was only the sounds of the negroes clearing breakfast away. After a while he might possibly even hear the first faint cry of the first hound ring through the wet woods from where the buck had bedded, then he would go back to sleep again—The tent-flap swung in and fell. Something jarred sharply against the end of the cot and a hand grasped his knee through the blanket before he could open his eyes. It was Edmonds, carrying a shotgun in place of his rifle. He spoke in a harsh, rapid voice:

"Sorry to wake you. There will be a—"

"I was awake," McCaslin said. "Are you going to shoot that shotgun today?"

"You just told me last night you want meat," Edmonds said. "There will be a—"

"Since when did you start having trouble getting meat with your rifle?"

"All right," the other said, with that harsh, restrained, furious impatience. Then Mc-Caslin saw in his hand a thick oblong: an envelope. "There will be a message here some time this morning, looking for me. Maybe it wont come. If it does, give the messenger this and tell h— say I said No."

"A what?" McCaslin said. "Tell who?" He half rose onto his elbow as Edmonds jerked the envelope onto the blanket, already turning toward the entrance, the envelope striking solid and heavy and without noise and already sliding from the bed until McCaslin caught it, divining by feel through the paper as instantaneously and conclusively as if he had opened the envelope and looked, the thick sheaf of banknotes. "Wait," he said. "Wait:"—more than the blood kinsman, more even than the senior in years, so that the other paused, the canvas lifted, looking back, and McCaslin saw that outside it was already day. "Tell her No," he said. "Tell her." They stared at one another—the old face, wan, sleep-raddled above the tumbled bed, the dark and sullen younger one at once furious and cold. "Will Legate was right. This is what you called coon-hunting. And now this." He didn't raise the envelope. He made no

motion, no gesture to indicate it. "What did you promise her that you haven't the courage to face her and retract?"

"Nothing!" the other said. "Nothing! This is all of it. Tell her I said No." He was gone. The tent flap lifted on an in-waft of faint light and the constant murmur of rain, and fell again, leaving the old man still half-raised onto one elbow, the envelope clutched in the other shaking hand. Afterward it seemed to him that he had begun to hear the approaching boat almost immediately, before the other could have got out of sight even. It seemed to him that there had been no interval whatever: the tent flap falling on the same out-waft of faint and rain-filled light like the suspiration and expiration of the same breath and then in the next second lifted again—the mounting snarl of the outboard engine, increasing, nearer and nearer and louder and louder then cut short off, ceasing with the absolute instantaneity of a blown-out candle, into the lap and plop of water under the bows as the skiff slid in to the bank, the youngest negro, the youth, raising the tent flap beyond which for that instant he saw the boat—a small skiff with a negro man sitting in the stern beside the up-slanted motor—then the woman entering, in a man's hat and a man's slicker and rubber boots, carrying the blanket-swaddled bundle on one arm and holding the edge of the un-buttoned raincoat over it with the other hand: and bringing something else, something intangible, an effluvium which he knew he would recognise in a moment be-cause Isham had already told him, warned him, by sending the young negro to the tent to announce the visitor instead of coming himself, the flap falling at last on the young negro and they were alone—the face indistinct and as yet only young and with dark eyes, queerly colorless but not ill and not that of a country woman despite the garments she wore, looking down at him where he sat upright on the cot now, clutch-ing the envelope, the soiled undergarment bagging about him and the twisted blankets huddled about his hips.

"Is that his?" he cried. "Dont lie to me!"

"Yes," she said. "He's gone."

"Yes. He's gone. You wont jump him here. Not this time. I dont reckon even you expected that. He left you this. Here." He fumbled at the envelope. It was not to pick it up, because it was still in his hand; he had never put it down. It was as if he had to fumble somehow to co-ordinate physically his heretofore obedient hand with what his brain was commanding of it, as if he had never performed such an action before, extending the envelope at last, saying again, "Here. Take it. Take it:" until he became aware of her eyes, or not the eyes so much as the look, the regard fixed now on his face with that immersed contemplation, that bottomless and intent candor, of a child. If she had ever seen either the envelope or his movement to extend it, she did not show it.

"You're Uncle Isaac," she said.

"Yes," he said. "But never mind that. Here. Take it. He said to tell you No." She looked at the envelope, then she took it. It was sealed and bore no superscription. Nevertheless, even after she glanced at the front of it, he watched her hold it in the one free hand and tear the corner off with her teeth and manage to rip it open and tilt the neat sheaf of bound notes onto the blanket without even glancing at them and look into the empty envelope and take the edge between her teeth and tear it completely open before she crumpled and dropped it.

"That's just money," she said.

"What did you expect? What else did you expect? You have known him long enough or at least often enough to have got that child, and you dont know him any better than that?"

"Not very often. Not very long. Just that week here last fall, and in January he sent for me and we went West, to New Mexico. We were there six weeks, where I could at least sleep in the same apartment where I cooked for him and looked after his clothes—"

"But not marriage," he said. "Not marriage. He didn't promise you that. Dont lie to me. He didn't have to."

"No. He didn't have to. I didn't ask him

to. I knew what I was doing. I knew that to begin with, long before honor I imagine he called it told him the time had come to tell me in so many words what his code I suppose he would call it would forbid him forever to do. And we agreed. Then we agreed again before he left New Mexico, to make sure. That that would be all of it. I believed him. No, I dont mean that; I mean I believed myself. I wasn't even listening to him anymore by then because by that time it had been a long time since he had had anything else to tell me for me to have to hear. By then I wasn't even listening enough to ask him to please stop talking. I was listening to myself. And I believed it. I must have believed it. I dont see how I could have helped but believe it, because he was gone then as we had agreed and he didn't write as we had agreed, just the money came to the bank in Vicksburg in my name but coming from nobody as we had agreed. So I must have believed it. I even wrote him last month to make sure again and the letter came back unopened and I was sure. So I left the hospital and rented myself a room to live in until the deer season opened so I could make sure myself and I was waiting beside the road yesterday when your car passed and he saw me and so I was sure."

"Then what do you want?" he said. "What do you want? What do you expect?"

"Yes," she said. And while he glared at her, his white hair awry from the pillow and his eyes, lacking the spectacles to focus them, blurred and irisless and apparently pupilless, he saw again that grave, intent, speculative and detached fixity like a child watching him. "His great great—Wait a minute.—great great *great* grandfather was your grandfather. McCaslin. Only it got to be Edmonds. Only it got to be more than that. Your cousin McCaslin was there that day when your father and Uncle Buddy won Tennie from Mr Beauchamp for the one that had no name but Terrel so you called him Tomey's Terrel, to marry. But after that it got to be Edmonds." She regarded him, almost peacefully, with that unwinking and heatless fixity— the dark wide bottomless eyes in the face's dead and toneless pallor which to the old man looked anything but dead, but young and incredibly and even ineradicably alive—as though she were not only not looking at anything, she was not even speaking to anyone but herself. "I would have made a man of him. He's not a man yet. You spoiled him. You, and Uncle Lucas and Aunt Mollie. But mostly you."

"Me?" he said. "Me?"

"Yes. When you gave to his grandfather that land which didn't belong to him, not even half of it by will or even law."

"And never mind that too," he said. "Never mind that too. You," he said. "You sound like you have been to college even. You sound almost like a Northerner even, not like the draggle-tailed women of these Delta peckerwoods. Yet you meet a man on the street one afternoon just because a box of groceries happened to fall out of a boat. And a month later you go off with him and live with him until he got a child on you: and then, by your own statement, you sat there while he took his hat and said good-bye and walked out. Even a Delta peckerwood would look after even a draggle-tail better than that. Haven't you got any folks at all?"

"Yes," she said. "I was living with one of them. My aunt, in Vicksburg. I came to live with her two years ago when my father died; we lived in Indianapolis then. But I got a job, teaching school here in Aluschaskuna, because my aunt was a widow, with a big family, taking in washing to sup—"

"Took in what?" he said. "Took in washing?" He sprang, still seated even, flinging himself backward onto one arm, awry-haired, glaring. Now he understood what it was she had brought into the tent with her, what old Isham had already told him by sending the youth to bring her in to him—the pale lips, the skin pallid and dead-looking yet not ill, the dark and tragic and foreknowing eyes. *Maybe in a thousand or two thousand years in America,* he thought. *But not now! Not now!* He cried, not loud, in a voice of amazement, pity, and outrage: "You're a nigger!"

"Yes," she said. "James Beauchamp—you called him Tennie's Jim though he had a name—was my grandfather. I said you were Uncle Isaac."

"And he knows?"

"No," she said. "What good would that have done?"

"But you did," he cried. "But you did. Then what do you expect here?"

"Nothing."

"Then why did you come here? You said you were waiting in Aluschaskuna yesterday and he saw you. Why did you come this morning?"

"I'm going back North. Back home. My cousin brought me up the day before yesterday in his boat. He's going to take me on to Leland to get the train."

"Then go," he said. Then he cried again in that thin not loud and grieving voice: "Get out of here! I can do nothing for you! Cant nobody do nothing for you!" She moved; she was not looking at him again, toward the entrance. "Wait," he said. She paused again, obediently still, turning. He took up the sheaf of banknotes and laid it on the blanket at the foot of the cot and drew his hand back beneath the blanket. "There," he said.

Now she looked at the money, for the first time, one brief blank glance, then away again. "I dont need it. He gave me money last winter. Besides the money he sent to Vicksburg. Provided. Honor and code too. That was all arranged."

"Take it," he said. His voice began to rise again, but he stopped it. "Take it out of my tent." She came back to the cot and took up the money; whereupon once more he said, "Wait:" although she had not turned, still stooping, and he put out his hand. But, sitting, he could not complete the reach until she moved her hand, the single hand which held the money, until he touched it. He didn't grasp it, he merely touched it—the gnarled, bloodless, bone-light bone-dry old man's fingers touching for a second the smooth young flesh where the strong old blood ran after its long lost journey back to home. "Tennie's Jim," he said. "Tennie's Jim." He drew the hand back beneath the blanket again: he said harshly now: "It's a boy, I reckon. They usually are, except that one that was its own mother too."

"Yes," she said. "It's a boy." She stood for a moment longer, looking at him. Just for an instant her free hand moved as though she were about to lift the edge of the raincoat away from the child's face. But she did not. She turned again when once more he said Wait and moved beneath the blanket.

"Turn your back," he said. "I am going to get up. I aint got my pants on." Then he could not get up. He sat in the huddled blanket, shaking, while again she turned and looked down at him in dark interrogation. "There," he said harshly, in the thin and shaking old man's voice. "On the nail there. The tent-pole."

"What?" she said.

"The horn!" he said harshly. "The horn." She went and got it, thrust the money into the slicker's side pocket as if it were a rag, a soiled handkerchief, and lifted down the horn, the one which General Compson had left him in his will, covered with the unbroken skin from a buck's shank and bound with silver.

"What?" she said.

"It's his. Take it."

"Oh," she said. "Yes. Thank you."

"Yes," he said, harshly, rapidly, but not so harsh now and soon not harsh at all but just rapid, urgent, until he knew that his voice was running away with him and he had neither intended it nor could stop it: "That's right. Go back North. Marry: a man in your own race. That's the only salvation for you—for a while yet, maybe a long while yet. We will have to wait. Marry a black man. You are young, handsome, almost white; you could find a black man who would see in you what it was you saw in him, who would ask nothing of you and expect less and get even still less than that, if it's revenge you want. Then you will forget all this, forget it ever happened, that he ever existed—" until he could stop it at last and did, sitting there in his huddle of blankets during the instant when, without moving at all, she blazed silently down at him. Then

that was gone too. She stood in the gleaming and still dripping slicker, looking quietly down at him from under the sodden hat.

"Old man," she said, "have you lived so long and forgotten so much that you dont remember anything you ever knew or felt or even heard about love?"

Then she was gone too. The waft of light and the murmur of the constant rain flowed into the tent and then out again as the flap fell. Lying back once more, trembling, panting, the blanket huddled to his chin and his hands crossed on his breast, he listened to the pop and snarl, the mounting then fading whine of the motor until it died away and once again the tent held only silence and the sound of rain. And cold too: he lay shaking faintly and steadily in it, rigid save for the shaking. This Delta, he thought: This Delta. *This land which man has deswamped and denuded and derivered in two generations so that white men can own plantations and commute every night to Memphis and black men own plantations and ride in jim crow cars to Chicago to live in millionaires' mansions on Lakeshore Drive, where white men rent farms and live like niggers and niggers crop on shares and live like animals, where cotton is planted and grows man-tall in the very cracks of the sidewalks, and usury and mortgage and bankruptcy and measureless wealth, Chinese and African and Aryan and Jew, all breed and spawn together until no man has time to say which one is which nor cares. . . .* No wonder the ruined woods I used to know dont cry for retribution! he thought: The people who have destroyed it will accomplish its revenge.

The tent flap jerked rapidly in and fell. He did not move save to turn his head and open his eyes. It was Legate. He went quickly to Edmonds' bed and stooped, rummaging hurriedly among the still-tumbled blankets.

"What is it?" he said.

"Looking for Roth's knife," Legate said. "I come back to get a horse. We got a deer on the ground." He rose, the knife in his hand, and hurried toward the entrance.

"Who killed it?" McCaslin said. "Was it Roth?"

"Yes," Legate said, raising the flap.

"Wait," McCaslin said. He moved, suddenly, onto his elbow. "What was it?" Legate paused for an instant beneath the lifted flap. He did not look back.

"Just a deer, Uncle Ike," he said impatiently. "Nothing extra." He was gone; again the flap fell behind him, wafting out of the tent again the faint light and the constant and grieving rain. McCaslin lay back down, the blanket once more drawn to his chin, his crossed hands once more weightless on his breast in the empty tent.

"It was a doe," he said.

QUESTIONS

1. You may be aided in reading this story if you are informed that Uncle Ike McCaslin and Roth Edmonds and the girl in the story are all distantly related. Uncle Ike's aunt married an Edmonds. Uncle Ike's grandfather is one of the girl's ancestors. (See Faulkner's *Go Down, Moses.*) Uncle Ike has refused an inheritance which therefore passed to the Edmonds branch of the family, the refusal being based on idealistic grounds—that is, unwillingness to accept property developed through slavery. Roth Edmonds and Ike differ in this story on a question involving idealism. What is the question?

2. The wilderness has special symbolic meanings for Uncle Ike McCaslin. What are these meanings?

3. It has been said that Faulkner, as a writer of fiction, is especially interested in presenting the view that the past is implicit in the present. Can you find this point of view in "Delta Autumn"?

4. What views of religion are expressed in this story?

5. Can you find in this story, which carries references to Hitler and World War II, any kind of forecast of the human future in the delta country?

6. Can you think of any reason why Roth Edmonds, in this story, is inclined to argue that man will do the right thing only because someone may be watching? Do you agree with this point of view?

7. From images used, from wording, and from connotations of words, what can you discover about the author's views of modern life, including business and work?

8. Did the girl go to the camp to get money, to let Roth Edmonds see his son, or for what reason?

9. What is the author's apparent attitude toward the girl? What is Ike McCaslin's apparent attitude?

Problems

The reader who will work at a few of the following problems will almost certainly increase his awareness of the nature and uses of fiction, as well as his pleasure in reading. Any one problem, with the reading it demands, should lead to the production of a piece of critical-analytical writing appropriate to a course in literature. These are genuine problems requiring personal investigation and thought, not mere rhetorical questions which suggest their own answers. It is probably more important for the student to gather his materials and reach conclusions than it is for his conclusions to agree with those of the student next to him. The process, including differences of opinion which may arise, will take all concerned deeper into the act, or art, of reading. In writing his report, the student should remember that his own development is greater if he does his own thinking than if he runs to the library searching for "answers."

(1) Choose some fact or principle having to do with the function of focus or point of view, from pages 44–46. Then apply this principle or fact to two stories in order to test its meaning and validity. Report what you discover about the functions of point of view and about the fact or principle you started with.

(2) Review what is said about plot and conflict on page 33. Outline one story by listing all the events, major or minor. Find a second story which has a noticeably different organization. Then try to see, and say, why each story is organized as it is, in the light of effects achieved or the inner necessities of the story. Ask yourself why the author may have summarized some actions and treated other actions more fully. Ask whether any events could have been omitted without loss of effect.

(3) Find two stories, one of which causes a noticeable degree of emotional involvement for you, one of which does not touch your emotion in anything like the same degree. Do not assume, however, that the story which touches you less is therefore "inferior," for this is not that kind of inquiry. After you have found these stories, try to account for the difference in their effects on you. Keep in mind what has been said about the ways in which fiction can touch emotion, pages 24–26. The difference you are seeking to explain may lie in your own nature, in your view of "reality," or in the values you hold, the things you care about or don't care about. Try to reach and state some conclusions about the two stories and their effect on you. It does not matter in the least whether anyone else would agree.

(4) Which story in this book contains, in your opinion, the most complete picture of human motivation, and which the least complete? Support what you say as well as you can. You will be bound to notice differences in depth or completeness.

(5) Test what has been said about dramatic irony on page 45 by applying the concept to two or three stories. Is the effect there? How is it achieved in one story? In which story is it most important as a source of interest and pleasure?

(6) Find a descriptive passage in one story in which the author succeeds, in your opinion, in so using language as to suggest an attitude, a feeling, or

a judgment. Then examine the wording carefully to see what words or details are mainly responsible for the effects you have noted. Compare this descriptive passage, then, with a descriptive passage selected at random from another story. State any conclusions you feel are justified on the basis of this limited comparison between writers.

(7) "Translate" the basic human situation or conflict or problem in one story into as many "real" parallels as you can think of in your own experience or in what you have heard about. As part of this effort to "translate," state the problem in as many ways as you can think of, from the general statement to the particular. This ability to translate means that you can see a story as a symbol, and is related directly to your capacity as a reader.

(8) Compare two stories, carefully chosen for contrast, in respect to the amount of meaning which is conveyed by overt, external action alone (*not* thoughts or feelings inside a character, not comment by the author, not even what the characters *say*). In other words, you are asking how much is achieved by action alone. If one story achieves more meaning by means of this one story element, try to show that it does and to explain why.

(9) Compare and contrast two stories in one of which the characterization seems to be relatively complete and individualized. Would you advise additions to the story in which the characterization is less complete? Why or why not?

(10) If tragedy is defined as the loss or waste of human potentialities, dramatized in such a way as to arouse pity and fear, what story in this book most nearly fits the definition? Form a conclusion about this and explain it and defend it.

(11) What story in this book seems to emphasize the greatest number of *general* ideas? Do not confuse general ideas obviously present in the story with the many situations outside the story to which the ideas might be applied.

(12) What story in this book contains the largest amount of detail of setting or environment? What purposes are served by this detail? Is there, in your opinion, too much detail of this kind?

(13) Explain as well as you can the interdependence of the fictional elements in one story. Remember that element X is interdependent with Y if the absence of X would give Y a different meaning.

(14) Find one story in which the conflict is very definite and clear; find a second story in which the conflict is much less apparent. What seems to be achieved in the second story? Is anything gained by having the conflict less prominent? What is gained? What is lost?

The Art of Reading Poetry

The first section of this book presented the reader with stories of several kinds, dealing with a variety of human concerns and illustrating varieties of writing from the straightforward and literal to the indirect and symbolic. Most of what was said in the introduction to those stories holds true for other forms of literature as well. In this section, however, we approach a different kind of writing, and immediately a fundamental question arises. It may be summed up in two words: Why poetry? Why, that is, from the beginning of history have sane and often sensible persons gone out of their way to produce, usually with a good deal of labor, artificial arrangements of words in verse, when, as far as factual content goes, they could have said the same thing much more easily in plain prose? The question is a practical one, for an answer to it should help a reader learn what to look for in poetry and how to read it.

No complete, incontrovertible answer, however, can be given. A student may naturally enough become irritated if his instructor, having asserted that poetry is a great art, is forced to admit that he cannot define it with precision and cannot formulate a set of standards by which the exact worth of every poem can be measured. The truth is that poetry, like most other human activities, will not be definable through a formula so long as man himself is imperfectly understood. If authorities are still unable to agree on such fundamental questions as how much of an individual's character is formed by environment and how much by heredity, or whether "free will" is a reality or an illusion, or which, if any, religion is "true," no one should be surprised to find incompleteness or inconsistency in the accounts of an art created by this imperfectly known human race. No one imagines he must wait to exercise his "free will" until he knows whether he has it or not; if man had waited for that, civilization would have died at its birth. Like the other major achievements of civilization, including even science, the arts have developed without waiting for final proofs. If men ever come to a perfect mathematical agreement about religion, philosophy, psychology, and all scientific theory, then we shall no doubt be able to devise exact standards of poetry. In the meantime, fortunately, some things can be said with a fair degree of certainty.

By and large, poetry has no subject matter distinct from that of prose. Hence, much that was said in the introduction to fiction is equally applicable to poetry and need not be repeated here. Conceivably, anything of interest to man may be a subject for a poem. A great subject, love, inspires statistics in a Kinsey, fiction in a Hemingway, sonnets in a Shakespeare. But poetry does not rule out even so small and sordid an object as the common house fly; there are poems and at least one well-known short story, as well as scientific treatises, on this little pest. The distinction of poetry lies, not in the subject itself, but in the poet's attitude, in his intention and feeling, and, ultimately, in *what he does with his subject*. These are the important considerations. The first three, however—attitude, intention, feeling—are subjective matters about which there may be endless argument. Something must be said of them later, but it is the end product we are chiefly interested in. We can approach this best by considering first its most obvious and least disputable characteristic.

When we open the pages of a book at random, the first thing we know about it is that it is prose, or that it is verse. The spaced printing tells us this without our having to read a word. Not that the spacing in itself is important; it is a mere convenience. It exists as a sign that we are to expect something different from prose and something that must be read differently. It exists also as a guide to the reading. What it points to is rhythm, the first and most obvious distinction between poetry and prose. However much individual poems differ from each other, they are in general marked by a rhythm more regular and more noticeable than any found in prose. An inquiry into rhythm should therefore throw some light on poetry as a whole.

RHYTHM AND PATTERN

Rhythm is instinctive in man. We walk and breathe rhythmically. Though we can do both unrhythmically for a short time if we try, the moment we relax our attention the rhythm returns. A simple and regular rhythm, however, quickly becomes intolerable if we focus conscious attention upon it. If we sit in a room with a loudly ticking clock, we find ourselves unconsciously varying the sound by thinking we hear *tick-tock*, though the actual sound is *tick-tick*. But *tick-tock* also is too simple, and soon, to avoid unbearable monotony, we have to stop listening or throw out the clock. Rhythm rides us unpleasantly unless we cease to notice it altogether or else succeed in riding it—in manipulating it, that is, to suit our own will. That is why in imagination we tend to hear a tune or words to vary the mechanical rhythms of a clock or a railroad train. Rhythm in good poetry, therefore, cannot be mechanical or simple but must be flexible and varied.

An analogy will illustrate this. Poetry, one might say, is to prose what dancing is to walking. Though sometimes we stroll for pleasure, ordinarily walking is a means to an end: we walk, scarcely aware of the physical sensation of walking, in order to get somewhere, the sooner the better. But we dance to stay where we are, enjoying the repetitive yet varied flowing of one movement into another, and enjoying the harmony between our own movements and that of the music and of our partner. Prose is often read quickly to see how the story comes out or to learn all the facts (though it may also be read more slowly in order to reflect, enjoy, or remember). But just as one cannot properly hurry through a dance, so one cannot read poetry in a hurry, with muscles taut, ready to go somewhere. It should be read with at least a little leisure and either actually aloud or with the imagined sound present to the mind's ear. To a really good dancer, the music—itself full of rhythmic and melodic variety—becomes a basis for further variations of turn, whirl, and syncopation; such a dancer does not go clopping along, woodenly following the *one, two, one, two* of the music. He anticipates, delays, whirls, then returns just in time to pick up the beat again. The conventional rules of versification (see pp. 402–403) provide for poetry the elementary clop-clop or tick-tock. Some writers of third-rate verse and some sing-song readers never get much beyond this. The rhythm and music of good poetry, however, are as far beyond it in gracefulness, expressiveness, and variety as the fine dancer is beyond the crude clodhopper who can barely keep time. Good poetry, in short, like good dancing, is a satisfying expression of perfect freedom within the bounds of a convention or a form.

If anyone doubts the importance of rhythm, as well as other effects of sound, among the fused elements that make up a poem, he may find an illustration in a common nursery rhyme. Few people who have once known it ever forget the old rhyme about "Pease porridge hot,/Pease porridge cold." Yet it seems strange that a grown man should remember these useless verses when he has forgotten a thousand more interesting, more personal, and more important things that he knew as a child. Frequent repetition is only part of the answer, for he has forgotten many things that he has heard or repeated much oftener. The attraction cannot be in the meaning, for that is so slight as to be almost non-existent. Though a man may remember the lines for seventy years, he probably does not even know what pease porridge is (perhaps a near relation of split pea soup); and he certainly does not care whether it is hot or cold, since he does not expect to eat it. This is a surprising phenomenon, the almost universal memory, surviving through a lifetime out of the welter of things once known and forgotten, of a trivial statement about an uninteresting and unidentified food.

The explanation is simply that it is good poetry, of a small sort and on its own level. It satisfies, for one thing, the natural liking for a rhythm that is both strongly marked and varied. Though comparatively simple, the rhythm of "Pease Porridge" has surprising variety: no two lines of the stanza are exactly alike. The sounds, moreover, are appropriate, for they are inextricably interwoven with what little meaning there is. The key words *hot* and *cold* are emphasized by pauses and rhyme. *Hot* is a light quick word, whose sounds cannot be prolonged (try prolonging a *t* sound or even a short *o* sound); it easily coalesces with its meaning: we drop the word as quickly as we would a hot object. *Cold*, on the other hand, is a long slow syllable, and solid—like congealed porridge, one might almost say. A diagram may be unpoetical but will show something of what is meant.

The accents and timing:

The tune: a rising inflection in lines 1 and 3 with staccato endings; a falling in lines 2 and 4 with prolonged endings:

Pease/pórridge/hot
Pease/pórridge/cold
Pease/pórridge/in the/pot
Nine/days/old

In poetry, rhythm is usually, as it is here, reinforced by other effects of sound. The poet may employ rhyme to mark the ends of lines, and he nearly always makes use of other kinds of repetition, such as assonance and alliteration (see *Glossary*). Like rhythm itself, these are a natural development of man's almost instinctive liking for repetitive echoes. Any child would prefer "Ring a round a Rosy" to "Make a circle about Rosie." Such patterns, used more subtly and interwoven with the meaning of a poem, appeal equally to the maturer mind and ear. In the lines

> And malt does more than Milton can
> To justify God's ways to man,

Housman preferred *malt* to *ale* obviously because its alliteration sharpened the absurd contrast between ale and Milton (who announced in *Paradise Lost* that his purpose was "to justify the ways of God to Men"). In these lines, rhyme, meter, and alliteration combine to heighten the writer's cynical statement that only when a man is drunk can he think well of the universe.

In good verse the irregular patterns of alliteration and assonance and the more regular rhythmic beats within the line are bound together in larger rhythmic and structural units. Neither the sense nor the sound pattern of the opening of "Pease porridge" is complete till the fourth line ends, and here again the nursery rhyme illustrates a principle of poetic structure. What goes up, it is said, must come down; and though this may not be strictly true in space, we usually expect it in poetry. Hence the use of stanzas in many poems. The close of the stanza brings to rest a movement of tune, rhythm, and thought which began four, or eight, or however many lines it may be, earlier. Rhyme too, in its usual place at the ends of lines, helps in creating this larger pattern. Endless combinations of verse forms are available to the poet, but they are better observed in individual poems than incompletely enumerated or theorized about here.

INTENSITY AND EMOTION

Poetry, however, is much more than patterns of sound. It is made of language, and language has meaning. Even "Pease porridge" conveys a little sense, and we have not been able to discuss its music without reference to its meaning, for the two are obviously inseparable. Even so-called nonsense verse deals in meanings or hints of meanings. If a poet wished to create pure sound effects without any conceptual thoughts or images, he would write instrumental music, not poetry. So we are brought back to the question we began with, in a slightly different form: Under what circumstances or for what purpose is a writer impelled to convey his meanings through an elaborate musical pattern?

One answer is *intensity*. It is sometimes said, and there is a certain amount of truth in the statement, that one writes poetry rather than prose "to achieve intensity, whether of emotion or of intellect." This is not always true in the most obvious sense. The poet Suckling (see p. 306), who boasts of his faithfulness—he has been in love for three days, he says, and if the lady is accommodating he may remain in love for three more—probably does not feel very intensely about his lady. Furthermore, even a moderately good prose thriller will tie its reader into more "intense" knots than any poem will, even if the reader is one who likes poetry better than thrillers.

T. S. Eliot explained that it is not a matter of "greatness" or "intensity" in the raw material from which the poem is made but of intensity in "the artistic process, the pressure . . . under which the fusion takes place." An earlier critic wrote that the poetic impulse arises when an experience "takes such a hold of the mind as to make us dwell upon it," when the mind "seeks to prolong and repeat the emotion, to bring all other objects into accord with it, and to give the same movement of harmony . . . to the sounds that express it."

Everyone has experienced the pleasure and pride of having something perfectly ship-shape: rows of extra-straight, fine-growing corn in a field; tools all in order, bright and sharp; desk or bureau drawer reorganized so that its former chaos is transformed into perfect and intelligible order. One dwells upon such things a little longer and more intently and warmly than the practical value alone warrants. A man likes to go out and look at such a field, though looking will not increase its yield or bring him in more money. This "dwelling upon" something, this pleasure in its perfect fitness, is an impulse almost like a caress. In a poem, the "caress" is the language itself—the sound, the images, the completeness and intensity bestowed by poetic form. But we dwell on our sorrows as well as our satisfactions, embalming our dead, bringing flowers to their grave, preserving mementos; and we do the same with even a trivial experience when we really sink ourselves into it till we feel it, it seems, through every bone and fingertip. In a poem, the experience relished or dwelt upon may be pleasant or unpleasant, great or small, personal or impersonal, real or imaginary; only it must have been realized to the full. The poet's awareness of it must have been so vivid and intense that the images, sounds, and meaning all become fused in "the same movement of harmony."

This does not mean that the poet is sentimental or even that he is always highly emotional about his subject. It means only that his interest has become so sharply focused that he is able to crystallize his subject—to sharpen and condense it by giving it the point, pith, and emphasis of verse form. Robert Frost saw a colt in a field frightened by its first snowstorm. It was not his colt, and he probably did not care enough about it to go and see it again; yet the moment of interest in its fright and the visual image of it running wildly in the snow were enough to make a poem ("The Runaway"). At the other extreme, Milton condensed into fourteen lines the tremendous events of a religious massacre, his own indignation, and a prayer that the evil might in the end be turned to good (the sonnet "On the Late Massacre in Piedmont").

For most people, the unforgettable moments of life are as incommunicable as they are unforgettable. The very words someone spoke, the tone, the room may be photographed with utmost vividness in one's memory, along with the feeling that made the occasion unforgettable. The moment of pride and excitement of the athlete carrying the ball for his greatest achievement may be relived in his memory, sensation for sensation. But few people can transfer this experience whole and alive into the mind, emotions, and sensations of another person. As the poet Yeats once observed, a man may work the conversation around till he can introduce the name of the woman he loves in order to say it, and to hear others talk of her. But the result disappoints him: his companion merely looks absent-minded, scarcely noticing—"as if another name ran in his head" ("Her Praise"). The poet, however, through his remarkable power over language, succeeds in communicating the otherwise incommunicable. He does more, for he makes the ever-transitory moments of life permanent—at least for the duration of the language. The passing experience that he has "immortalized" becomes an experience shared with others, with men present and future, illuminating their own experience. And it is there on record, to be recaptured, revisited at will.

The Poet's Words

Like most objects that are used a great deal, words are subject to two somewhat contrary processes. They become freighted with innumerable associations of all sorts—which means they become rich in their power of suggestion. Yet they also become defaced and dull, their distinguishing features rubbed flat by careless, half-accurate, everyday use. What the poet does through his fresh awareness of language is to bring to us its inherited load of richness and at the same time to clear away the incrustations of careless use, so that his words have the value both of fresh bright newness and old rich association.

For example, the expression "glamorous eyes" one would think is pretty stale; it has long been a sentimental cliché fit only for the cover of a Hollywood magazine, if that. But the poet de la Mare uses it. He precedes it by "stare," a hard unsentimental word, rather than the conventional soft "gaze"; and he employs it to describe not a woman but a moth hovering about a candle: the moth "stares from her glamorous eyes." The worn-out coin "glamorous" is here new-minted, with its stale, cheap associations dusted off by "stares" and by the reader's memory of bug eyes, yet with its original powerful associations remaining. A second example of real yet scarcely noticeable originality in the use of language occurs in another poet's use of the simple word *pick* (in the sense of picking flowers or leaves). Instead of an elaborate description of late, cold autumn, W. H. Davies wrote a single phrase, "the cold, leaf-picking winds of autumn." His originality consisted of nothing more than making winds instead of human beings the picker; yet by this means he conveys a sense of the season with physical, tactual vividness. These are typical examples—all the more typical because so small and so far from spectacular—of the poet's language. They may help to show how alert the reader must be to catch the full force of what the poet writes. For in poetry the words and phrases are packed, often with layers and layers of meaning. The hurried or half-attentive reader will miss most of the worth of a poem.

When S. T. Coleridge said that good prose consists of "words in the best order," poetry of "the best words in the best order," he was perhaps casting a needless slur upon prose. The point underlying his distinction, however, is this: when words are arranged metrically, the rhythm and the accompanying pauses—which are more frequent and more marked in poetry than in prose—give more than ordinary prominence to each individual word or phrase and send the reader's mind, during the pause, rolling back for an instant over the phrase just past. That means that the words must be worth the prominence they receive; otherwise they will seem excessively dull or foolish. There is nothing wrong in prose with the phrase "When he called me on the telephone. . . ." But if a song writer should write, as one did (approximately, if not exactly),

When hĕ called mé-e-e
On the telephone,

he needs a very good tune to cover up the flatness of the words that have been made conspicuous, syllable for syllable, by rhythm and pause.

IMAGERY AND METAPHOR

What was said earlier about symbolism in prose (pp. 38–43) is equally true in poetry and even more important, partly for the reason just suggested, the prominence that meter gives to the language. Though most of the words in poetry are common words familiar to everyone, the inexperienced reader often has difficulty in making out even the literal meaning of a poem. This is in part because the poet will not weaken the impact of what he writes by inserting routine explanations that have not enough value in themselves to deserve the prominence of rhythm and that would sound unpleasantly flat in verse. He may therefore leave explanatory matter for the reader to figure out. With a little practice the reader becomes mentally agile enough to do this most of the time without much trouble. His reward is in finding the poem a packed piece, with inessentials and dullness left out.

A celebrated and rather extreme modern example of a gap left for the reader to supply occurs in T. S. Eliot's "The Love Song of J. Alfred Prufrock," when Prufrock interrupts his inner soliloquy. Should he, he has been asking himself, propose marriage (or possibly an affair) to a woman? As he wonders what he might say to her, he breaks off abruptly with

I should have been a pair of ragged claws
Scuttling across the floors of silent seas.

The reader is left to understand from this that, brought face to face with the thought of actually proposing to a woman, Prufrock recognizes that his nature is solitary, that he is incapable of *coming out of his shell* (the everyday trite version of the "ragged claws" image). By comparison with the average man, Prufrock might have explained, he is like a lobster which, as every elementary student of biology knows, wears its skeleton on the outside as protective covering and which is a cold-blooded creature living a lonely life at the bottom of the sea (the poem was written before Rachel Carson and other recent writers had removed some of the solitude from the sea-bottom). Instead of explaining all this at length, the poet takes for granted that his reader has a mind sufficiently agile to make the jump. It is the kind of jump everyone's mind makes in musing. By presenting it without explanation, Eliot gains realism and a striking dramatic effect, at the same time avoiding dull exposition.

The concentration and the force of poetry are achieved, as this illustration from "Prufrock" suggests, in great measure through imagery and figurative language. Concrete words that call up images of sight, touch, sound, movement, heat or cold almost always make a stronger impression than abstract or generalized language. The statement "I want to travel and see the world" leaves the mind of the reader unimpressed by comparison with "I want to see London, the pyramids, the South Sea Islands," a sentence that may fill the mind with remembered or imagined images not only of these places but also of others that the listener himself would like to see. The word *motherhood* is likely to pass through the mind without leaving a stir, whereas "my mother in the kitchen" may stir up memories, pictures, and feelings too numerous to list. Part of the poet's power lies in his ability to choose images that will most fully communicate the experience he writes of.

Much of the concrete image-making language of poetry is figurative: it communicates a truth or an idea, that is, without itself being literally true. The image in "Prufrock" is such a figure. We do not suppose Prufrock literally wished to be a lobster; and besides, claws do not scuttle by themselves without the rest of the body. Poets, and many non-poets too, think naturally in such images, as the reader of the preceding stories will already have seen; it is not in the least a forced way of writing.

Even in ordinary conversation we use figures as a kind of emphatic shorthand. One man, we say, is "down to earth"; another "has his head in the clouds." The expressions are stale and overworked, yet even so they tell us more, and tell it more forcefully, than if we said, literally, that the men were "practical" and "impractical." To supplement "impractical" with all the additional implications of "head in the clouds" without using figurative language would require several sentences at least; and the long literal statement would still lack the force and vividness of the figurative one.

LITERARY ALLUSION

Many poetic allusions have this same value of saying much in little, though they are sometimes an obstacle to immediate understanding. In former times, the stories of Greek mythology were as familiar to children as Superman or Spaceman is today, and Greek myth is particularly rich in natural symbolic meaning. Assuming that everyone knows the story of Helen and the Trojan war—a story that has long been, among other things, a classic symbol of the destructive power of feminine beauty—one modern poet, seeing an unknown woman walk by, exclaims: "Now I know what Helen was!" After that, he does not need to describe the passing beauty. Another poet pays a double-edged tribute to the woman he loves: "Was there another Troy for her to burn?" The mere name of Helen and the image of Troy burning (if one knows the story of the daughter of Zeus and Leda and of the nine years' siege of Troy and the tenth year of looting and burning) are explosive capsules in which is concentrated a whole world of experience past and present. That is why, though a reader is often inconvenienced and sometimes irritated by having to look up unfamiliar allusions, in the long run we do not ask the poet to reduce his circle of reference to our smaller or different experience but, instead, find it worthwhile to try to extend our own. If the poet had to give up Helen and Troy, he could not convey with any such richness of suggestion or such force and concentration, the combination of beauty, power, danger, and destruction—along with the living reminder that some problems of man are as old as history—represented by the ancient story.

The name of Ulysses (Odysseus) is still a tremendous piece of shorthand if we know the *Odyssey*. James Joyce took advantage of Homer when he wrote the twentieth century's most celebrated novel, *Ulysses*. So did a less famous novelist who named a book about Iowa, *The Odyssey of a Nice Girl*. When Tennyson wrote of Ulysses (p. 357) as a particular man with an urge to travel, he was also writing about man's eternal desire for knowledge and experience, a desire that is at the very root of civilization. Tennyson could say this and many other things at once because the name from the ancient story telescopes a whole world of meaning. It also keeps us reminded of the long view, reminded that man's search began with pre-history and may not end with the hydrogen bomb or a trip to the moon.

THE READER'S RESPONSIBILITY

Poetry, like music, is meant to be revisited; it is not composed for a single reading or hearing. This follows from the mood in which it originates, the impulse to "dwell upon" something, to experience fully whatever it is the poem represents. A poem therefore may have many layers of significance; in saying one thing it often, as with Tennyson's "Ulysses," indirectly says other more general or more universal things.

From all that has been said here about poetry, it will be obvious that the first reading of a poem may be little more than an aerial tour from which one gets a preliminary rough map of the region. Real exploration may begin only with the second reading. Housman opened his poem "To an Athlete Dying Young" with these stanzas:

> The time you won your town the race
> We chaired you through the market-place;
> Man and boy stood cheering by,
> And home we brought you shoulder-high.
>
> Today, the road all runners come,
> Shoulder-high we bring you home,
> And set you at your threshold down,
> Townsman of a stiller town.

The outline of this poem is simple enough to be grasped immediately. Every reader knows (if only from the title) that the runner has died. But at first he may not notice that the funeral is described in the same images as the triumph, or see how the images that are literally true in the first stanza become metaphorical in the second. *Town, runner, home, being carried on others' shoulders* are all repeated; only, in the second stanza, it is the road "*all* runners" travel, and the town is "stiller," the "cheering" gone. Death has not been mentioned. For the reader, a view of the peak of life and its extinction presented in this way through the same images—images perfectly appropriate to both—breaks down some of the rigid categories in which he ordinarily thinks of triumph, life and death; and though he comes away with no definable new truth, he finds himself seeing all with a wider, if ironical, vision—but only on a second, or third, or fourth reading.

There is no strict, clear-cut line of demarcation between poetry and prose. Sir Walter Raleigh's apostrophe to Death (p. 309) was written and originally printed as prose, yet the reader will have no difficulty in seeing why it is printed here among poems. Sometimes a writer chooses verse form when his mood is only slightly heightened, when—to repeat an analogy used earlier—his walk is only half inclined to turn into a dance. Of the poems that follow here, many in the first group (and some later) belong to this half-heightened realm of poetry. They have more of the elements of prose than most other poetry has. But even in these, the rhythm, with its frequent pauses, holds us back so that each thing that is said reverberates in the mind. In reading any poetry that amounts to anything, the reader must let it reverberate.

Note: In this part of the book, brief explanations of certain proper names, unusual words, and unusual uses of words are given in the text. Longer explanations and all other notes and discussions will be found on pp. 374–401. As a rule, no notes are provided for words and names for which sufficient information is available in standard college dictionaries.

Standard texts have been followed for each poet, making no alterations for the sake of general consistency in spelling and punctuation.

1. CHARACTERS

RICHARD CORY

Edwin Arlington Robinson
(1869–1935)

Whenever Richard Cory went down town,
We people on the pavement looked at him:
He was a gentleman from sole to crown,
Clean favored, and imperially slim.

And he was always quietly arrayed,
And he was always human when he talked;
But still he fluttered pulses when he said,
"Good-morning," and he glittered when he
    walked.

And he was rich—yes, richer than a king—
And admirably schooled in every grace: 10
In fine, we thought that he was everything
To make us wish that we were in his place.

So on we worked, and waited for the light,
And went without the meat, and cursed the
    bread;
And Richard Cory, one calm summer night,
Went home and put a bullet through his
    head.

MR. FLOOD'S PARTY

Edwin Arlington Robinson

Old Eben Flood, climbing alone one night
Over the hill between the town below

And the forsaken upland hermitage
That held as much as he should ever know
On earth again of home, paused warily.
The road was his with not a native near;
And Eben, having leisure, said aloud,
For no man else in Tilbury Town to hear:

"Well, Mr. Flood, we have the harvest moon
Again, and we may not have many more;   10
The bird is on the wing, the poet says,
And you and I have said it here before.
Drink to the bird." He raised up to the light
The jug that he had gone so far to fill,
And answered huskily: "Well, Mr. Flood,
Since you propose it, I believe I will."

Alone, as if enduring to the end
A valiant armor of scarred hopes outworn,
He stood there in the middle of the road
Like Roland's ghost winding a silent horn.
Below him, in the town among the trees,   21
Where friends of other days had honored
    him,
A phantom salutation of the dead
Rang thinly till old Eben's eyes were dim.

Then, as a mother lays her sleeping child
Down tenderly, fearing it may awake,
He set the jug down slowly at his feet
With trembling care, knowing that most
    things break;
And only when assured that on firm earth
It stood, as the uncertain lives of men   30
Assuredly did not, he paced away,
And with his hand extended paused again:

269

"Well, Mr. Flood, we have not met like this
In a long time; and many a change has come
To both of us, I fear, since last it was
We had a drop together. Welcome home!"
Convivially returning with himself,
Again he raised the jug up to the light;
And with an acquiescent quaver said:
"Well, Mr. Flood, if you insist, I might.   40

"Only a very little, Mr. Flood—
For auld lang syne. No more, sir; that will
  do."
So, for the time, apparently it did,
And Eben evidently thought so too;
For soon amid the silver loneliness
Of night he lifted up his voice and sang,
Secure, with only two moons listening,
Until the whole harmonious landscape
  rang—

"For auld lang syne." The weary throat gave
  out,
The last word wavered; and the song being
  done,   50
He raised again the jug regretfully
And shook his head, and was again alone.
There was not much that was ahead of him,
And there was nothing in the town below—
Where strangers would have shut the many
  doors
That many friends had opened long ago.

Miniver sighed for what was not,
  And dreamed, and rested from his la-
    bors;   10
He dreamed of Thebes and Camelot,
  And Priam's neighbors.

Miniver mourned the ripe renown
  That made so many a name so fragrant;
He mourned Romance, now on the town,
  And Art, a vagrant.

Miniver loved the Medici,
  Albeit he had never seen one;
He would have sinned incessantly
  Could he have been one.   20

Miniver cursed the commonplace
  And eyed a khaki suit with loathing;
He missed the mediæval grace
  Of iron clothing.

Miniver scorned the gold he sought,
  But sore annoyed was he without it;
Miniver thought, and thought, and thought,
  And thought about it.

Miniver Cheevy, born too late,
  Scratched his head and kept on think-
    ing;   30
Miniver coughed, and called it fate,
  And kept on drinking.

l. 15. on the town: on relief.

MINIVER CHEEVY

Edwin Arlington Robinson

Miniver Cheevy, child of scorn,
  Grew lean while he assailed the seasons;
He wept that he was ever born,
  And he had reasons.

Miniver loved the days of old
  When swords were bright and steeds were
    prancing;
The vision of a warrior bold
  Would set him dancing.

MUSEUMS

Louis MacNeice
(1907–   )

Museums offer us, running from among the
  buses,
A centrally heated refuge, parquet floors and
  sarcophaguses,
Into whose tall fake porches we hurry without a sound
Like a beetle under a brick that lies, useless,
  on the ground.

Warmed and cajoled by the silence the
 cowed cypher revives,
Mirrors himself in the cases of pots, paces
 himself by marble lives,
Makes believe it was he that was the glory
 that was Rome,
Soft on his cheek the nimbus of other people's martyrdom,
And then returns to the street, his mind an
 arena where sprawls
Any number of consumptive Keatses and
 dying Gauls.   10

nobody loses all the time

e. e. cummings
(1894–   )

nobody loses all the time

i had an uncle named
Sol who was a born failure and
nearly everybody said he should have gone
into vaudeville perhaps because my Uncle
 Sol could
sing McCann He Was A Diver on Xmas Eve
 like Hell Itself which
may or may not account for the fact that my
 Uncle

Sol indulged in that possibly most inexcusable
of all to use a highfalootin phrase
luxuries that is or to   10
wit farming and be
it needlessly
added

my Uncle Sol's farm
failed because the chickens
ate the vegetables so
my Uncle Sol had a
chicken farm till the
skunks ate the chickens when

my Uncle Sol   20
had a skunk farm but
the skunks caught cold and
died and so

my Uncle Sol imitated the
skunks in a subtle manner

or by drowning himself in the watertank
but somebody who'd given my Uncle Sol a
 Victor
Victrola and records while he lived presented
 to
him upon the auspicious occasion of his de-
 cease a
scrumptious not to mention splendiferous
 funeral with   30
tall boys in black gloves and flowers and
 everything and

i remember we all cried like the Missouri
when my Uncle Sol's coffin lurched because
somebody pressed a button
(and down went
my Uncle
Sol

and started a worm farm)

SONNET

TO MY MOTHER

George Barker
(1913–   )

Most near, most dear, most loved and most
 far,
Under the window where I often found her
Sitting as huge as Asia, seismic with laughter,
Gin and chicken helpless in her Irish hand,
Irresistible as Rabelais, but most tender for
The lame dogs and hurt birds that surround
 her,—
She is a procession no one can follow after
But be like a little dog following a brass
 band.

She will not glance up at the bomber, or con-
 descend
To drop her gin and scuttle to a cellar,   10
But lean on the mahogany table like a mountain

Whom only faith can move, and so I send
O all my faith and all my love to tell her
That she will move from mourning into
  morning.

MY LAST DUCHESS

Robert Browning
(1812–1889)

FERRARA

That's my last Duchess painted on the wall,
Looking as if she were alive. I call
That piece a wonder, now: Frà Pandolf's
  hands
Worked busily a day, and there she stands.
Will't please you sit and look at her? I said
"Frà Pandolf" by design, for never read
Strangers like you that pictured countenance,
The depth and passion of its earnest glance,
But to myself they turned (since none
  puts by
The curtain I have drawn for you, but I)   10
And seemed as they would ask me, if they
  durst,
How such a glance came there; so, not the
  first
Are you to turn and ask thus. Sir, 'twas not
Her husband's presence only, called that spot
Of joy into the Duchess' cheek: perhaps
Frà Pandolf chanced to say "Her mantle laps
Over my lady's wrist too much," or "Paint
Must never hope to reproduce the faint
Half-flush that dies along her throat:" such
  stuff
Was courtesy, she thought, and cause enough
For calling up that spot of joy. She had   21
A heart—how shall I say?—too soon made
  glad,
Too easily impressed; she liked whate'er
She looked on, and her looks went every-
  where.
Sir, 'twas all one! My favour at her breast,
The dropping of the daylight in the West,
The bough of cherries some officious fool
Broke in the orchard for her, the white mule

She rode with round the terrace—all and
  each
Would draw from her alike the approving
  speech,   30
Or blush, at least. She thanked men,—good!
  but thanked
Somehow—I know not how—as if she ranked
My gift of a nine-hundred-years-old name
With anybody's gift. Who'd stoop to blame
This sort of trifling? Even had you skill
In speech—(which I have not)—to make
  your will
Quite clear to such an one, and say, "Just this
Or that in you disgusts me; here you miss,
Or there exceed the mark"—and if she let
Herself be lessoned so, nor plainly set   40
Her wits to yours, forsooth, and made excuse,
—E'en then would be some stooping; and I
  choose
Never to stoop. Oh sir, she smiled, no doubt,
Whene'er I passed her; but who passed with-
  out
Much the same smile? This grew; I gave
  commands;
Then all smiles stopped together. There she
  stands
As if alive. Will 't please you rise? We'll
  meet
The company below, then. I repeat,
The Count your master's known munificence
Is ample warrant that no just pretense   50
Of mine for dowry will be disallowed;
Though his fair daughter's self, as I avowed
At starting, is my object. Nay, we'll go
Together down, sir. Notice Neptune, though,
Taming a sea-horse, thought a rarity,
Which Claus of Innsbruck cast in bronze for
  me!

THE BISHOP ORDERS HIS TOMB AT SAINT PRAXED'S CHURCH

Robert Browning

Rome, 15—

Vanity, saith the preacher, vanity!
Draw round my bed: is Anselm keeping
  back?

Nephews—sons mine . . . ah God, I know
  not! Well—
She, men would have to be your mother once,
Old Gandolf envied me, so fair she was!
What's done is done, and she is dead beside,
Dead long ago, and I am Bishop since,
And as she died so must we die ourselves,
And thence ye may perceive the world's a
  dream.
Life, how and what is it? As here I lie   10
In this state-chamber, dying by degrees,
Hours and long hours in the dead night, I ask
"Do I live, am I dead?" Peace, peace seems
  all.
Saint Praxed's ever was the church for peace;
And so, about this tomb of mine. I fought
With tooth and nail to save my niche, ye
  know:
—Old Gandolf cozened me, despite my care;
Shrewd was that snatch from out the corner
  South
He graced his carrion with, God curse the
  same!
Yet still my niche is not so cramped but
  thence   20
One sees the pulpit o' the epistle-side,
And somewhat of the choir, those silent seats,
And up into the aery dome where live
The angels, and a sunbeam's sure to lurk:
And I shall fill my slab of basalt there,
And 'neath my tabernacle take my rest,
With those nine columns round me, two and
  two,
The odd one at my feet where Anselm stands:
Peach-blossom marble all, the rare, the ripe
As fresh-poured red wine of a mighty pulse.
—Old Gandolf with his paltry onion-stone,
Put me where I may look at him! True
  peach,   32
Rosy and flawless: how I earned the prize!
Draw close: that conflagration of my church
—What then? So much was saved if aught
  were missed!
My sons, ye would not be my death? Go dig
The white-grape vineyard where the oil-press
  stood,
Drop water gently till the surface sink,
And if ye find . . . Ah God, I know not,
  I! . . .
Bedded in store of rotten fig-leaves soft,   40

And corded up in a tight olive-frail,
Some lump, ah God, of *lapis lazuli,*
Big as a Jew's head cut off at the nape,
Blue as a vein o'er the Madonna's breast . . .
Sons, all have I bequeathed you, villas, all,
That brave Frascati villa with its bath,
So, let the blue lump poise between my
  knees,
Like God the Father's globe on both his
  hands
Ye worship in the Jesu Church so gay,
For Gandolf shall not choose but see and
  burst!   50
Swift as a weaver's shuttle fleet our years:
Man goeth to the grave, and where is he?
Did I say basalt for my slab, sons? Black—
'Twas ever antique-black I meant! How else
Shall ye contrast my frieze to come beneath?
The bas-relief in bronze ye promised me,
Those Pans and Nymphs ye wot of, and per-
  chance
Some tripod, thyrsus, with a vase or so,
The Saviour at his sermon on the mount,
Saint Praxed in a glory, and one Pan   60
Ready to twitch the Nymph's last garment
  off,
And Moses with the tables . . . but I know
Ye mark me not! What do they whisper thee,
Child of my bowels, Anselm? Ah, ye hope
To revel down my villas while I gasp
Bricked o'er with beggar's mouldy travertine
Which Gandolf from his tomb-top chuckles
  at!
Nay, boys, ye love me—all of jasper, then!
'Tis jasper ye stand pledged to, lest I grieve
My bath must needs be left behind, alas! 70
One block, pure green as a pistachio-nut,
There's plenty jasper somewhere in the
  world—
And have I not Saint Praxed's ear to pray
Horses for ye, and brown Greek manuscripts,
And mistresses with great smooth marbly
  limbs?
—That's if ye carve my epitaph aright,
Choice Latin, picked phrase, Tully's every
  word,
No gaudy ware like Gandolf's second line—
Tully, my masters? Ulpian serves his need!
And then how I shall lie through centuries,
And hear the blessed mutter of the mass, 81

And see God made and eaten all day long,
And feel the steady candle-flame, and taste
Good strong thick stupefying incense-smoke!
For as I lie here, hours of the dead night,
Dying in state and by such slow degrees,
I fold my arms as if they clasped a crook,
And stretch my feet forth straight as stone
    can point,
And let the bedclothes, for a mortcloth, drop
Into great laps and folds of sculptor's-work:
And as yon tapers dwindle, and strange
    thoughts   91
Grow, with a certain humming in my ears,
About the life before I lived this life,
And this life too, popes, cardinals and priests,
Saint Praxed at his sermon on the mount,
Your tall pale mother with her talking eyes,
And new-found agate urns as fresh as day,
And marble's language, Latin pure, discreet,
—Aha, ELUCESCEBAT quoth our friend?
No Tully, said I, Ulpian at the best!   100
Evil and brief hath been my pilgrimage.
All *lapis*, all, sons! Else I give the Pope
My villas! Will ye ever eat my heart?
Ever your eyes were as a lizard's quick,
They glitter like your mother's for my soul,
Or ye would heighten my impoverished
    frieze,
Piece out its starved design, and fill my vase
With grapes, and add a visor and a Term,
And to the tripod ye would tie a lynx
That in his struggle throws the thyrsus down,
To comfort me on my entablature   111
Whereon I am to lie till I must ask
"Do I live, am I dead?" There, leave me,
    there!
For ye have stabbed me with ingratitude
To death—ye wish it—God, ye wish it!
Stone—
Gritstone, a-crumble! Clammy squares which
    sweat
As if the corpse they keep were oozing
    through—
And no more *lapis* to delight the world!
Well go! I bless ye. Fewer tapers there,
But in a row: and, going, turn your backs
—Ay, like departing altar-ministrants,   121
And leave me in my church, the church for
    peace,
That I may watch at leisure if he leers—

Old Gandolf, at me, from his onion-stone,
As still he envied me, so fair she was!

l. 41. frail: a basket
l. 46. Frascati: a resort near Rome.
l. 87. crook: a bishop's staff.
l. 89. mortcloth: death or funeral cloth.
l. 108. Term: end-post decorated with a head.

SONNET

ON MISTRESS NICELY, A PATTERN FOR HOUSEKEEPERS

Thomas Hood
(1799–1845)

She was a woman peerless in her station,
    With household virtues wedded to her
        name;
    Spotless in linen, grass-bleach'd in her
        fame,
And pure and clear-starch'd in her conversa-
        tion;
Thence in my Castle of Imagination
    She dwells for evermore, the dainty dame,
    To keep all airy draperies from shame,
And all dream furnitures in preservation:
    There walketh she with keys quite silver
        bright,
In perfect hose, and shoes of seemly black,
    Apron and stomacher of lily-white,   11
And decent order follows in her track:
    The burnish'd plate grows lustrous in her
        sight,
And polish'd floors and tables shine her back.

l. 12. decent: suitable and pleasing.

LUCINDA MATLOCK

Edgar Lee Masters
(1869–1950)

I went to the dances at Chandlerville,
And played snap-out at Winchester.
One time we changed partners,
Driving home in the moonlight of middle
    June,

And then I found Davis.
We were married and lived together for
seventy years,
Enjoying, working, raising the twelve chil-
dren,
Eight of whom we lost
Ere I had reached the age of sixty.
I spun, I wove, I kept the house, I nursed the
sick,   10
I made the garden, and for holiday
Rambled over the fields where sang the larks,
And by Spoon River gathering many a shell,
And many a flower and medicinal weed—
Shouting to the wooded hills, singing to the
green valleys.
At ninety-six I had lived enough, that is all,
And passed to a sweet repose.
What is this I hear of sorrow and weariness,
Anger, discontent and drooping hopes?
Degenerate sons and daughters,   20
Life is too strong for you—
It takes life to love Life.

HER PRAISE

William Butler Yeats
(1865–1939)

She is foremost of those that I would hear
praised.
I have gone about the house, gone up and
down
As a man does who has published a new book,
Or a young girl dressed out in her new gown,
And though I have turned the talk by hook
or crook
Until her praise should be the uppermost
theme,
A woman spoke of some new tale she had
read,
A man confusedly in a half dream
As though some other name ran in his head.
She is foremost of those that I would hear
praised.   10
I will talk no more of books or the long war
But walk by the dry thorn until I have found
Some beggar sheltering from the wind, and
there

Manage the talk until her name come round.
If there be rags enough he will know her
name
And be well pleased remembering it, for in
the old days,
Though she had young men's praise and old
men's blame,
Among the poor both old and young gave her
praise.

NO SECOND TROY

William Butler Yeats

Why should I blame her that she filled my
days
With misery, or that she would of late
Have taught to ignorant men most violent
ways,
Or hurled the little streets upon the great,
Had they but courage equal to desire?
What could have made her peaceful with a
mind
That nobleness made simple as a fire,
With beauty like a tightened bow, a kind
That is not natural in an age like this,
Being high and solitary and most stern?   10
Why, what could she have done, being what
she is?
Was there another Troy for her to burn?

THAT THE NIGHT COME

William Butler Yeats

She lived in storm and strife,
Her soul had such desire
For what proud death may bring
That it could not endure
The common good of life,
But lived as 'twere a king
That packed his marriage day
With banneret and pennon,
Trumpet and kettledrum,
And the outrageous cannon,   10
To bundle time away
That the night come.

2. TWO MODERN AMERICAN NARRATIVES

THE DEATH OF
THE HIRED MAN

Robert Frost
(1875–   )

Mary sat musing on the lamp-flame at the
    table
Waiting for Warren. When she heard his step,
She ran on tip-toe down the darkened passage
To meet him in the doorway with the news
And put him on his guard. 'Silas is back.'
She pushed him outward with her through
    the door
And shut it after her. 'Be kind,' she said.
She took the market things from Warren's
    arms
And set them on the porch, then drew him
    down
To sit beside her on the wooden steps.   10

'When was I ever anything but kind to him?
But I'll not have the fellow back,' he said.
'I told him so last haying, didn't I?
If he left then, I said, that ended it.
What good is he? Who else will harbor him
At his age for the little he can do?
What help he is there's no depending on.
Off he goes always when I need him most.
He thinks he ought to earn a little pay,
Enough at least to buy tobacco with,   20
So he won't have to beg and be beholden.
"All right," I say, "I can't afford to pay
Any fixed wages, though I wish could."
"Someone else can." "Then someone else will
    have to."
I shouldn't mind his bettering himself
If that was what it was. You can be certain,

When he begins like that, there's someone at
    him
Trying to coax him off with pocket-money,—
In haying time, when any help is scarce.
In winter he comes back to us. I'm done.'   30

'Sh! not so loud: he'll hear you,' Mary said.

'I want him to: he'll have to soon or late.'

'He's worn out. He's asleep beside the stove.
When I came up from Rowe's I found him
    here,
Huddled against the barn-door fast asleep,
A miserable sight, and frightening, too—
You needn't smile—I didn't recognize him—
I wasn't looking for him—and he's changed.
Wait till you see.'

            'Where did you say he'd been?'

'He didn't say. I dragged him to the house,
And gave him tea and tried to make him
    smoke.   41
I tried to make him talk about his travels.
Nothing would do: he just kept nodding off.'

'What did he say? Did he say anything?'

'But little.'

            'Anything? Mary, confess
He said he'd come to ditch the meadow for
    me.'

'Warren!'

            'But did he? I just want to know.'

'Of course he did. What would you have him
    say?

276

Surely you wouldn't grudge the poor old man
Some humble way to save his self-respect.
He added, if you really care to know,   51
He meant to clear the upper pasture, too.
That sounds like something you have heard
   before?
Warren, I wish you could have heard the way
He jumbled everything. I stopped to look
Two or three times—he made me feel so
   queer—
To see if he was talking in his sleep.
He ran on Harold Wilson—you remember—
The boy you had in haying four years since.
He's finished school, and teaching in his
   college.   60
Silas declares you'll have to get him back.
He says they two will make a team for work:
Between them they will lay this farm as
   smooth!
The way he mixed that in with other things.
He thinks young Wilson a likely lad, though
   daft
On education—you know how they fought
All through July under the blazing sun,
Silas up on the cart to build the load,
Harold along beside to pitch it on.'   69

'Yes, I took care to keep well out of earshot.'

'Well, those days trouble Silas like a dream.
You wouldn't think they would. How some
   things linger!
Harold's young college boy's assurance piqued
   him.
After so many years he still keeps finding
Good arguments he sees he might have used.
I sympathize. I know just how it feels
To think of the right thing to say too late.
Harold's associated in his mind with Latin.
He asked me what I thought of Harold's say-
   ing
He studied Latin like the violin   80
Because he liked it—that an argument!
He said he couldn't make the boy believe
He could find water with a hazel prong—
Which showed how much good school had
   ever done him.
He wanted to go over that. But most of all
He thinks if he could have another chance
To teach him how to build a load of hay—'

'I know, that's Silas' one accomplishment.
He bundles every forkful in its place,
And tags and numbers it for future reference,
So he can find and easily dislodge it   91
In the unloading. Silas does that well.
He takes it out in bunches like big birds'
   nests.
You never see him standing on the hay
He's trying to lift, straining to lift himself.'

'He thinks if he could teach him that, he'd be
Some good perhaps to someone in the world.
He hates to see a boy the fool of books.
Poor Silas, so concerned for other folk,
And nothing to look backward to with pride,
And nothing to look forward to with hope,
So now and never any different.'   102

Part of a moon was falling down the west,
Dragging the whole sky with it to the hills.
Its light poured softly in her lap. She saw it
And spread her apron to it. She put out her
   hand
Among the harp-like morning-glory strings,
Taut with the dew from garden bed to eaves,
As if she played unheard some tenderness
That wrought on him beside her in the
   night.   110
'Warren,' she said, 'he has come home to die:
You needn't be afraid he'll leave you this
   time.'

'Home,' he mocked gently.

             'Yes, what else but home?
It all depends on what you mean by home.
Of course he's nothing to us, any more
Than was the hound that came a stranger to
   us
Out of the woods, worn out upon the trail.'

'Home is the place where, when you have to
   go there,
They have to take you in.'

             'I should have called it   119
Something you somehow haven't to deserve.'

Warren leaned out and took a step or two,
Picked up a little stick, and brought it back

And broke it in his hand and tossed it by.
'Silas has better claim on us you think
Than on his brother? Thirteen little miles
As the road winds would bring him to his
    door.
Silas has walked that far no doubt today.
Why didn't he go there? His brother's rich,
A somebody—director in the bank.'

'He never told us that.'

            'We know it though.'   130

'I think his brother ought to help, of course.
I'll see to that if there is need. He ought of
    right
To take him in, and might be willing to—
He may be better than appearances.
But have some pity on Silas. Do you think
If he had any pride in claiming kin
Or anything he looked for from his brother,
He'd keep so still about him all this time?'

'I wonder what's between them.'

            'I can tell you.
Silas is what he is—we wouldn't mind him—
But just the kind that kinsfolk can't abide.
He never did a thing so very bad.   142
He don't know why he isn't quite as good
As anybody. Worthless though he is,
He won't be made ashamed to please his
    brother.'

'I can't think Si ever hurt any one.'

'No, but he hurt my heart the way he lay
And rolled his old head on that sharp-edged
    chair-back.
He wouldn't let me put him on the lounge.
You must go in and see what you can do.
I made the bed up for him there tonight.
You'll be surprised at him—how much he's
    broken.   152
His working days are done; I'm sure of it.'

'I'd not be in a hurry to say that.'

'I haven't been. Go, look, see for yourself.
But, Warren, please remember how it is:

He's come to help you ditch the meadow.
He has a plan. You mustn't laugh at him.
He may not speak of it, and then he may.
I'll sit and see if that small sailing cloud
Will hit or miss the moon.'   161

              It hit the moon.
Then there were three there, making a dim
    row,
The moon, the little silver cloud, and she.

Warren returned—too soon, it seemed to her,
Slipped to her side, caught up her hand and
    waited.

'Warren?' she questioned.

            'Dead,' was all he answered.

from JOHN BROWN'S BODY

Stephen Vincent Benét
(1898–1943)

[Harper's Ferry]

They reached the Maryland bridge of Har-
    per's Ferry
That Sunday night. There were twenty-two in
    all,
Nineteen were under thirty, three not twenty-
    one,
Kagi, the self-taught scholar, quiet and cool,
Stevens, the cashiered soldier, Puritan-fa-
    thered,
A singing giant, gunpowder-tempered and
    rash.
Dauphin Thompson, the pippin-cheeked
    country-boy,
More like a girl than a warrior; Oliver
    Brown,
Married last year when he was barely nine-
    teen;
Dangerfield Newby, colored and born a slave,
Freeman now, but married to one not free

Who, with their seven children, waited him
South, 12
The youngest baby just beginning to crawl;
Watson Brown, the steady lieutenant, who
wrote
Back to his wife,
      "Oh, Bell, I want to see you
And the little fellow very much but must
wait.
There was a slave near here whose wife was
sold South.
They found him hanging in Kennedy's
orchard next morning.
I cannot come home as long as such things
are done here.
I sometimes think that we shall not meet
again." 20

These were some of the band. For better or
worse
They were all strong men.
      The bearded faces look strange
In the old daguerreotypes: they should be
the faces
Of prosperous, small-town people, good sons
and fathers,
Good horse-shoe pitchers, good at plowing a
field,
Good at swapping stories and good at pray-
ing,
American wheat, firm-rooted, good in the ear.
There is only one whose air seems out of the
common,
Oliver Brown. That face has a masculine
beauty
Somewhat like the face of Keats.
      They were all strong men. 30

They tied up the watchmen and took the
rifle-works.
Then John Brown sent a raiding party away
To fetch in Colonel Washington from his
farm.
The Colonel was George Washington's great-
grand-nephew,
Slave-owner, gentleman-farmer, but, more
than these,
Possessor of a certain fabulous sword
Given to Washington by Frederick the Great.

They captured him and his sword and
brought them along
Processionally.
      The act has a touch of drama,
Half costume-romance, half unmerited farce.
On the way, they told the Washington slaves
they were free, 41
Or free to fight for their freedom.
      The slaves heard the news
With the dazed, scared eyes of cattle before
a storm.
A few came back with the band and were
given pikes,
And, when John Brown was watching, pre-
tended to mount
A slipshod guard over the prisoners.
But, when he had walked away, they put down
their pikes
And huddled together, talking in mourning
voices.
It didn't seem right to play at guarding the
Colonel
But they were afraid of the bearded patriarch
With the Old Testament eyes. 51
      A little later
It was Patrick Higgins' turn. He was the
night-watchman
Of the Maryland bridge, a tough little Irish-
man
With a canny, humorous face, and a twist in
his speech.
He came humming his way to his job.
      "Halt!" ordered a voice.
He stopped a minute, perplexed. As he told
men later,
"Now I didn't know what 'Halt!' mint, any
more
Than a hog knows about a holiday."
      There was a scuffle.
He got away with a bullet-crease in his scalp
And warned the incoming train. It was half-
past-one. 60
A moment later, a man named Shepherd
Heyward,
Free negro, baggage-master of the small
station,
Well-known in the town, hardworking,
thrifty and fated,
Came looking for Higgins.

"Halt!" called the voice again,
But he kept on, not hearing or understanding,
Whichever it may have been.
                              A rifle cracked.
He fell by the station-platform, gripping his
    belly,
And lay for twelve hours of torment, asking
    for water
Until he was able to die.
                              There is no stone,
No image of bronze or marble green with
    the rain   70
To Shepherd Heyward, free negro of Har-
    per's Ferry,
And even the books, the careful, ponderous
    histories,
That turn live men into dummies with smiles
    of wax
Thoughtfully posed against a photographer's
    background
In the act of signing a treaty or drawing a
    sword,
Tell little of what he was.
                              And yet his face
Grey with pain and puzzled at sudden death
Stares out at us through the bookworm-dust
    of the years
With an uncomprehending wonder, a blind
    surprise.
"I was getting along," it says, "I was doing
    well.   80
I had six thousand dollars saved in the bank.
It was a good town, a nice town, I liked the
    folks
And they liked me. I had a good job there,
    too.
On Sundays I used to dress myself up slick
    enough
To pass the plate in church, but I wasn't
    proud
Not even when trashy niggers called me
    Mister,
Though I could hear the old grannies over
    their snuff
Mumbling along, 'Look, chile, there goes
    Shepherd Heyward.
Ain't him fine in he Sunday clo'es—ain't him
    sassy and fine?
You grow up decent and don't play ball in
    the street,   90

And maybe you'll get like him, with a gold
    watch and chain.'
And then, suddenly—and what was it all
    about?
Why should anyone want to kill me? Why
    was it done?"

So the grey lips. And so the hurt in the eyes.
A hurt like a child's, at punishment unex-
    plained
That makes the whole child-universe fall to
    pieces.
At the time of death, most men turn back
    toward the child.

Brown did not know at first that the first man
    dead
By the sword he thought of so often as
    Gideon's sword
Was one of the race he had drawn that sword
    to free.   100
It had been dark on the bridge. A man had
    come
And had not halted when ordered. Then the
    shot
And the scrape of the hurt man dragging
    himself away.
That was all. The next man ordered to halt
    would halt.
His mind was too full of the burning judg-
    ments of God
To wonder who it had been. He was cool and
    at peace.
He dreamt of a lamb, lying down by a rush-
    ing stream.

So the night wore away, indecisive and
    strange.
The raiders stuck by the arsenal, waiting
    perhaps
For a great bell of jubilation to toll in the
    sky,   110
And the slaves to rush from the hills with
    pikes in their hands,
A host redeemed, black rescue-armies of God.
It did not happen.
                    Meanwhile, there was casual firing.
A townsman named Boerley was killed.
    Meanwhile, the train
Passed over the bridge to carry its wild news

Of abolition-devils sprung from the ground
A hundred and fifty, three hundred, a thousand strong
To pillage Harper's Ferry, with fire and sword.
Meanwhile the whole countryside was springing to arms.
The alarm-bell in Charlestown clanged "Nat Turner has come!   120
Nat Turner has come again, all smoky from Hell,
Setting the slave to murder and massacre!"
The Jefferson Guards fell in. There were boys and men.
They had no uniforms but they had weapons.
Old squirrel-rifles, taken down from the wall,
Shot guns loaded with spikes and scraps of iron.
A boy dragged a blunderbuss as big as himself.
They started for the Ferry.
                                    In a dozen
A score of other sleepy, neighboring towns
The same bell clanged, the same militia assembled.   130

The Ferry itself was roused and stirring with dawn.
And the firing began again.
                         A queer, harsh sound
In the ordinary streets of that clean, small town,
A desultory, vapid, meaningless sound.

God knows why John Brown lingered! Kagi, the scholar,
Who, with two others, held the rifle-works,
All morning sent him messages urging retreat.
They had the inexorable weight of common sense
Behind them, but John Brown neither replied
Nor heeded, brooding in the patriarch-calm
Of a lean, solitary pine that hangs   141
On the cliff's edge, and sees the world below
A tiny pattern of toy fields and trees,
And only feels its roots gripping the rock
And the almighty wind that shakes its boughs,

Blowing from eagle-heaven to eagle-heaven.

Of course they were cut off. The whole attempt
Was fated from the first.
                         Just about noon
The Jefferson Guards took the Potomac Bridge
And drove away the men Brown posted there.   150

There were three doors of possible escape
Open to Brown. With this the first slammed shut.
The second followed it a little later
With the recapture of the other bridge
That cut Brown off from Kagi and the arsenal
And penned the larger body of the raiders
In the armory.
                  Again the firing rolled,
And now the first of the raiders fell and died,
Dangerfield Newby, the freed Scotch-mulatto
Whose wife and seven children, slaves in Virginia,   160
Waited for him to bring them incredible freedom.
They were sold South instead, after the raid.
His body lay where the townspeople could reach it.
They cut off his ears for trophies.
                         If there are souls,
As many think that there are or wish that there might be,
Crystalline things that rise on light wings exulting
Out of the spoilt and broken cocoon of the body,
Knowing no sorrow or pain but only deliverance,
And yet with the flame of speech, the patterns of memory,
One wonders what the soul of Dangerfield Newby   170
Said, in what terms, to the soul of Shepherd Heyward,
Both born slave, both freed, both dead the same day.
What do the souls that bleed from the corpse of battle
Say to the tattered night?

Perhaps it is better
We have no power to visage what they might
   say.

The firing now was constant, like the heavy
And drumming rains of summer. Twice
   Brown sent
Asking a truce. The second time there went
Stevens and Watson Brown with a white
   flag.
But things had gone beyond the symbol of
   flags.   180
Stevens, shot from a window, fell in the gut-
   ter
Horribly wounded. Watson Brown crawled
   back
To the engine house that was the final fort
Of Brown's last stand, torn through and
   through with slugs.

A Mr. Brua, one of Brown's prisoners,
Strolled out from the unguarded prison-room
Into the bullets, lifted Stevens up,
Carried him over to the old hotel
They called the Wager House, got a doctor
   for him,
And then strolled back to take his prisoner's
   place   190
With Colonel Washington and the scared
   rest.
I know no more than this of Mr. Brua
But he seems curiously American,
And I imagine him a tall, stooped man
A little yellow with the Southern sun,
With slow, brown eyes and a slow way of
   talking,
Shifting the quid of tobacco in his cheek
Mechanically, as he lifted up
The dirty, bloody body of the man
Who stood for everything he most detested
And slowly carrying him through casual
   wasps   201
Of death to the flyspecked but sunny room
In the old hotel, wiping the blood and grime
Mechanically from his Sunday coat,
Settling his black string-tie with big, tanned
   hands,
And, then, incredibly, going back to jail.
He did not think much about what he'd done
But sat himself as comfortably as might be

On the cold bricks of that dejected guard-
   room
And slowly started cutting another quid   210
With a worn knife that had a brown bone-
   handle.

He lived all through the war and died long
   after,
This Mr. Brua I see. His last advice
To numerous nephews was "Keep out of
   trouble,
But if you're in it, chew and don't be hasty,
Just do whatever's likeliest at hand."

I like your way of talking, Mr. Brua,
And if there still are people interested
In cutting literary clothes for heroes
They might do worse than mention your
   string-tie.   220

There were other killings that day. On the
   one side, this,
Leeman, a boy of eighteen and the youngest
   raider,
Trying to flee from the death-trap of the
   engine-house
And caught and killed on an islet in the
   Potomac.
The body lay on a tiny shelf of rock
For hours, a sack of clothes still stung by
   bullets.

On the other side—Fontaine Beckham, mayor
   of the town,
Went to look at Heyward's body with Patrick
   Higgins.
The slow tears crept to his eyes. He was
   getting old.
He had thought a lot of Heyward. He had no
   gun   230
But he had been mayor of the town for a
   dozen years,
A peaceful, orderly place full of decent peo-
   ple,
And now they were killing people, here in
   his town,
He had to do something to stop it, somehow
   or other.
He wandered out on the railroad, half-dis-
   traught

And peeped from behind a water-tank at the raiders.

"Squire, don't go any farther," said Higgins, "It ain't safe."

He hardly heard him, he had to look out again.

Who were these devils with horns who were shooting his people?

They didn't look like devils. One was a boy

Smooth-cheeked, with a bright half-dreamy face, a little   241

Like Sally's eldest.

         Suddenly, the air struck him

A stiff, breath-taking blow. "Oh," he said, astonished.

Took a step and fell on his face, shot through the heart.

Higgins watched him for twenty minutes, wanting to lift him

But not quite daring. Then he turned away

And went back to the town.

         The bars had been open all day,

Never to better business.

When the news of Beckham's death spread from bar to bar,

It was like putting loco-weed in the whiskey,

The mob came together at once, the American mob,   251

They mightn't be able to take Brown's last little fort

But there were two prisoners penned in the Wager House.

One was hurt already, Stevens, no fun killing him.

But the other was William Thompson, whole and unwounded,

Caught when Brown tried to send his first flag of truce.

They stormed the hotel and dragged him out to the bridge,

Where two men shot him, unarmed, then threw the body

Over the trestle. It splashed in the shallow water,

But the slayers kept on firing at the dead face.   260

The carcass was there for days, a riven target, Barbarously misused.

         Meanwhile the armory yard

Was taken by a new band of Beckham's avengers,

The most of Brown's prisoners freed and his last escape cut off.

What need to tell of the killing of Kagi the scholar,

The wounding of Oliver Brown and the other deaths?

Only this remains to be told. When the drunken day

Reeled into night, there were left in the engine-house

Five men, alive and unwounded, of all the raiders.

Watson and Oliver Brown

Both of them hurt to the death, were stretched on the floor

Beside the corpse of Taylor, the young Canadian.

There was no light, there. It was bitterly cold.

A cold chain of lightless hours that slowly fell

In leaden beads between two fingers of stone.

Outside, the fools and the drunkards yelled in the streets,

And, now and then, there were shots. The prisoners talked

And tried to sleep.

         John Brown did not try to sleep,

The live coals of his eyes severed the darkness;

Now and then he heard his young son Oliver calling   280

In the thirsty agony of his wounds, "Oh, kill me!

Kill me and put me out of this suffering!"

John Brown's jaw tightened. "If you must die," he said,

"Die like a man." Toward morning the crying ceased.

John Brown called out to the boy but he did not answer.

"I guess he's dead," said John Brown.

         If his soul wept

They were the incredible tears of the squeezed stone.

He had not slept for two days, but he would not sleep.

The night was a chained, black leopard that
   he stared down,
Erect, on his feet. One wonders what sights
   he saw   290
In the cloudy mirror of his most cloudy heart,
Perhaps God clothed in a glory, perhaps him-
   self
The little boy who had stolen three brass pins
And been well whipped for it.
              When he was six years old
An Indian boy had given him a great wonder,
A yellow marble, the first he had ever seen.
He treasured it for months but lost it at last,
Boylike. The hurt of the loss took years to
   heal.
He never quite forgot.
             He could see it now,
Smooth, hard and lovely, a yellow, glistening
   ball,   300
But it kept rolling away through cracks of
   darkness
Whenever he tried to catch it and hold it
   fast.
If he could only touch it, he would be safe,
But it trickled away and away, just out of
   reach,
There by the wall . . .
            Outside the blackened East
Began to tarnish with a faint, grey stain
That caught on the fixed bayonets of the
   marines.
Lee of Virginia, Light Horse Harry's son,
Observed it broaden, thinking of many
   things,
But chiefly wanting to get his business done,
A curious, wry, distasteful piece of work
For regular soldiers.   312
           Therefore to be finished
As swiftly and summarily as possible
Before this yelling mob of drunk civilians
And green militia once got out of hand.
His mouth set. Once already he had offered
The honor of the attack to the militia,
Such honor as it was.
           Their Colonel had
Declined with a bright nervousness of haste.
"Your men are paid for doing this kind of
   work.   320
Mine have their wives and children." Lee
   smiled briefly,

Remembering that. The smile had a sharp
   edge.
Well, it was time.
          The whooping crowd fell silent
And scattered, as a single man walked out
Toward the engine-house, a letter in his
   hand.
Lee watched him musingly. A good man,
   Stuart.
Now he was by the door and calling out.
The door opened a crack.
           Brown's eyes were there
Over the cold muzzle of a cocked carbine.
The parleying began, went on and on,   330
While the crowd shivered and Lee watched
   it all
With the strict commonsense of a Greek
   sword
And with the same sure readiness.
               Unperceived,
The dawn ran down the valleys of the wind,
Coral-footed dove, tracking the sky with
   coral . . .
Then, sudden as powder flashing in a pan,
The parleying was done.
          The door slammed shut.
The little figure of Stuart jumped aside
Waving its cap.
          And the marines came on.
Brown watched them come. One hand was on
   his carbine.   340
The other felt the pulse of his dying son.
"Sell your lives dear," he said. The rifle-shots
Rattled within the bricked-in engine-room
Like firecrackers set off in a stone jug,
And there was a harsh stink of sweat and
   powder.
There was a moment when the door held
   firm.
Then it was cracked with sun.
          Brown fired and missed.
A shadow with a sword leaped through the
   sun.
"That's Ossawattomie," said the tired voice
Of Colonel Washington.
          The shadow lunged   350
And Brown fell to his knees.
          The sword bent double,
A light sword, better for parades than fight-
   ing,

The shadow had to take it in both hands
And fairly rain his blows with it on Brown
Before he sank.
                    Now two marines were down,
The rest rushed in over their comrades'
  bodies,
Pinning one man of Brown's against the wall

With bayonets, another to the floor.

Lee, on his rise of ground, shut up his watch.
It had been just a quarter of an hour   360
Since Stuart gave the signal for the storm,
And now it was over.
                    All but the long dying.

3. BALLADS AND OTHER NARRATIVES

THE HAYSTACK IN THE FLOODS

William Morris
(1834–1896)

Had she come all the way for this,
To part at last without a kiss?
Yea, had she borne the dirt and rain
That her own eyes might see him slain
Beside the haystack in the floods?

Along the dripping leafless woods,
The stirrup touching either shoe,
She rode astride as troopers do;
With kirtle kilted to her knee,
To which the mud splash'd wretchedly;   10
And the wet dripped from every tree
Upon her head and heavy hair,
And on her eyelids broad and fair;
The tears and rain ran down her face.
By fits and starts they rode apace,
And very often was his place
Far off from her; he had to ride
Ahead to see what might betide
When the roads cross'd; and sometimes when
There rose a murmuring from his men,   20
Had to turn back with promises;
Ah me! she had but little ease;
And often for pure doubt and dread
She sobb'd, made giddy in the head
By the swift riding; while, for cold,
Her slender fingers scarce could hold
The wet reins; yea, and scarcely, too,
She felt the foot within her shoe
Against the stirrup: all for this
To part at last without a kiss   30
Beside the haystack in the floods.

For when they near'd that old soak'd hay,
They saw across the only way

That Judas, Godmar, and the three
Red running lions dismally
Grinn'd from his pennon, under which,
In one straight line along the ditch,
They counted thirty heads.
                          So then,
While Robert turn'd round to his men,
She saw at once the wretched end,   40
And, stooping down, tried hard to rend
Her coif the wrong way from her head,
And hid her eyes; while Robert said:
"Nay, love, 'tis scarcely two to one,
At Poictiers where we made them run
So fast—why, sweet my love, good cheer.
The gascon frontier is so near,
Nought after this."
                          But, "O," she said,
"My God! my God! I have to tread
The long way back without you; then   50
The court at Paris; those six men;
The gratings of the Chatelet;
The swift Seine on some rainy day
Like this, and people standing by,
And laughing, while my weak hands try
To recollect how strong men swim.
All this, or else a life with him,

For which I should be damned at last,
Would God that this next hour were past!"

He answer'd not, but cried his cry,   60
"St. George for Marny!" cheerily;
And laid his hand upon her rein.
Alas! no man of all his train
Gave back that cheery cry again;
And, while for rage his thumb beat fast
Upon his sword-hilts, someone cast
About his neck a kerchief long,
And bound him.
                          Then they went along
To Godmar; who said: "Now, Jehane,
Your lover's life is on the wane   70
So fast, that, if this very hour

286

You yield not as my paramour,
He will not see the rain leave off—
Nay, keep your tongue from gibe and scoff,
Sir Robert, or I slay you now."

She laid her hand upon her brow,
Then gazed upon her palm, as though
She thought her forehead bled, and—"No."
She said, and turn'd her head away,
As there were nothing else to say,   80
And everything were settled: red
Grew Godmar's face from chin to head:
"Jehane, on yonder hill there stands
My castle, guarding well my lands:
What hinders me from taking you,
And doing that I list to do
To your fair willful body, while
Your knight lies dead?"
                        A wicked smile
Wrinkled her face, her lips grew thin,
A long way out she thrust her chin: 90
"You know that I would strangle you
While you were sleeping; or bite through
Your throat, by God's help—ah!" she said,
"Lord Jesus, pity your poor maid!
For in such wise they hem me in,
I cannot choose but sin and sin,
Whatever happens: yet I think
They could not make me eat or drink,
And so should I just reach my rest."
"Nay, if you do not my behest,   100
O Jehane! though I love you well,"
Said Godmar, "would I fail to tell
All that I know?" "Foul lies," she said.
"Eh? lies, my Jehane? by God's head,
At Paris folks would deem them true!
Do you know, Jehane, they cry for you,
'Jehane the brown! Jehane the brown!
Give us Jehane to burn or drown!'—
Eh—gag me, Robert!—sweet my friend,
This were indeed a piteous end   110
For those long fingers, and long feet,
And long neck, and smooth shoulders sweet;
An end that few men would forget
That saw it— So, an hour yet:
Consider, Jehane, which to take
Of life or death!"
                        So, scarce awake,
Dismounting, did she leave that place,
And totter some yards: with her face

Turn'd upward to the sky she lay,
Her head on a wet heap of hay,   120
And fell asleep: and while she slept,
And did not dream, the minutes crept
Round to the twelve again; but she,
Being waked at last, sigh'd quietly,
And strangely childlike came, and said:
"I will not." Straightway Godmar's head,
As though it hung on strong wires, turn'd
Most sharply round, and his face burn'd.
For Robert—both his eyes were dry,
He could not weep, but gloomily   130
He seemed to watch the rain; yea, too,
His lips were firm; he tried once more
To touch her lips; she reach'd out, sore
And vain desire so tortured them,
The poor gray lips, and now the hem
Of his sleeve brush'd them.
                        With a start
Up Godmar rose, thrust them apart;
From Robert's throat he loosed the bands
Of silk and mail; with empty hands
Held out, she stood and gazed, and saw,   140
The long bright blade without a flaw
Glide out from Godmar's sheath, his hand
In Robert's hair; she saw him bend
Back Robert's head; she saw him send
The thin steel down; the blow told well,
Right backward the knight Robert fell,
And moan'd as dogs do, being half dead,
Unwitting, as I deem: so then
Godmar turned grinning to his men,
Who ran, some five or six, and beat   150
His head to pieces at their feet.

Then Godmar turn'd again and said:
"So, Jehane, the first fitte is read!
Take note, my lady, that your way
Lies backward to the Chatelet!"
She shook her head and gazed awhile
At her cold hands with a rueful smile,
As though this thing had made her mad.

This was the parting that they had
Beside the haystack in the floods.   160

l. 45. Poictiers: battle in which English defeated
French forces.
l. 52. Chatelet: a prison in Paris.
l. 153. fitte: canto or division of a long poem.

Since my love died for me to-day,
I'll die for him to-morrow."

[ANON.]

l. 1. Martinmas: November 11.
l. 8. gin: if.
l. 9. hooly: slowly.
l. 31. jow: stroke. geid: gave.

BONNY BARBARA ALLAN

It was in and about the Martinmas time,
    When the green leaves were a falling,
That Sir John Græme, in the West Country,
    Fell in love with Barbara Allan.

He sent his men down through the town,
    To the place where she was dwelling:
"O haste and come to my master dear,
    Gin ye be Barbara Allan."

O hooly, hooly rose she up,
    To the place where he was lying,   10
And when she drew the curtain by,
    "Young man, I think you 're dying."

"O it's I 'm sick, and very, very sick,
    And 't is a' for Barbara Allan:"
"O the better for me ye 's never be,
    Tho your heart's blood were a spilling.

"O dinna ye mind, young man," said she,
    "When ye was in the tavern a drinking,
That ye made the healths gae round and
        round,
    And slighted Barbara Allan?"   20

He turned his face unto the wall,
    And death was with him dealing:
"Adieu, adieu, my dear friends all,
    And be kind to Barbara Allan."

And slowly, slowly raise she up,
    And slowly, slowly left him,
And sighing said, she coud not stay,
    Since death of life had reft him.

She had not gane a mile but twa,
    When she heard the dead-bell ringing,
And every jow that the dead-bell geid,   31
    It cry'd, Woe to Barbara Allan!

"O Mother, mother, make my bed!
    O make it saft and narrow!

MARIE HAMILTON

Word's gane to the kitchen,
    And word's gane to the ha,
That Marie Hamilton gangs wi bairn
    To the hichest Stewart of a'.

He's courted her in the kitchen,
    He's courted her in the ha,
He's courted her in the laigh cellar,
    And that was warst of a'.

She's tyed it in her apron
    And she's thrown it in the sea;   10
Says, "Sink ye, swim ye, bonny wee babe!
    You'l neer get mair o me."

Down then cam the auld queen,
    Goud tassels tying her hair:
"O Marie, where's the bonny wee babe
    That I heard greet sae sair?"

"There was never a babe intill my room,
    As little designs to be;
It was but a touch o my sair side,
    Come oer my fair bodie."   20

"O Marie, put on your robes o black,
    Or else your robes o brown,
For ye maun gang wi me the night,
    To see fair Edinbro town."

"I winna put on my robes o black,
    Nor yet my robes o brown;
But I'll put on my robes o white,
    To shine through Edinbro town."

When she gaed up the Cannogate,
    She laughd loud laughters three;   30

But whan she cam down the Cannogate
    The tear blinded her ee.

When she gaed up the Parliament stair,
    The heel cam aff her shee;
And lang or she cam down again
    She was condemnd to dee.

When she cam down the Cannogate,
    The Cannogate sae free,
Many a ladie lookd oer her window,
    Weeping for this ladie.   40

"Ye need nae weep for me," she says,
    "Ye need nae weep for me;
For had I not slain mine own sweet babe,
    This death I wadna dee.

"Bring me a bottle of wine," she says,
    "The best that eer ye hae,
That I may drink to my weil-wishers,
    And they may drink to me.

"Here's a health to the jolly sailors,
    That sail upon the main;   50
Let them never let on to my father and
    mother
But what I'm coming hame.

"Here's a health to the jolly sailors,
    That sail upon the sea;
Let them never let on to my father and
    mother
That I cam here to dee.

"Oh little did my mother think,
    The day she cradled me,
What lands I was to travel through,
    What death I was to dee.   60

"Oh little did my father think,
    The day he held up me,
What lands I was to travel through,
    What death I was to dee.

"Last night I washd the queens feet,
    And gently laid her down;
And a' the thanks I've gotten the nicht
    To be hangd in Edinbro town!

"Last nicht there was four Maries,
    The nicht there'l be but three;   70
There was Marie Seton, and Marie Beton,
    And Marie Carmichael, and me."

                   [ANON.]

l. 3. gangs wi bairn: is pregnant.
l. 4. The Stewarts were the royal family of Scotland.
l. 7. laigh: low.
l. 14. goud: gold.
l. 16. greet: weep.
l. 29. Cannogate: street leading from the palace to the Parliament House.

JOHNIE ARMSTRONG

There dwelt a man in faire Westmerland,
    Ionnë Armestrong men did him call,
He had nither lands nor rents coming in,
    Yet he kept eight score men in his hall.

He had horse and harness for them all,
    Goodly steeds were all milke-white;
O the golden bands an about their necks,
    And their weapons, they were all alike.

Newes then was brought unto the king
    That there was sicke a won as hee,   10
That livëd lyke a bold out-law,
    And robbëd all the north country.

The king he writt an a letter then,
    A letter which was large and long;
He signëd it with his owne hand,
    And he promised to doe him no wrong.

When this letter came Ionnë untill,
    His heart it was a blythe as birds on the
        tree:
"Never was I sent for before any king,
    My father, my grandfather, nor none but
        mee.   20

"And if wee goe the king before,
    I would we went most orderly;
Every man of you shall have his scarlet cloak,
    Laced with silver laces three.

"Every won of you shall have his velvett coat,
  Laced with sillver lace so white;
O the golden bands an about your necks,
  Black hatts, white feathers, all alyke."

By the morrow morninge at ten of the clock,
  Towards Edenburough gon was hee,   30
And with him all his eight score men;
  Good lord, it was a goodly sight for to see!

When Ionnë came befower the king,
  He fell downe on his knee;
"O pardon, my soveraine leige," he said,
  "O pardon my eight score men and mee!"

"Thou shalt have no pardon, thou traytor strong,
  For thy eight score men nor thee;
For to-morrow morning by ten of the clock,
  Both thou and them shall hang on the gallow-tree."   40

But Ionnë looked over his left shoulder,
  Good Lord, what a grevious look looked hee!
Saying, "Asking grace of a graceles face—
  Why there is none for you nor me."

But Ionnë had a bright sword by his side,
  And it was made of the mettle so free,
That had not the king stept his foot aside,
  He had smitten his head from his faire boddë.

Saying, "Fight on, my merry men all,
  And see that none of you be taine;   50
For rather than men shall say we were hanged,
  Let them report how we were slaine."

Then, God wott, faire Eddenburrough rose,
  And so besett poore Ionnë rounde,
That fowerscore and tenn of Ionnës best men
  Lay gasping all upon the ground.

Then like a mad man Ionnë laide about,
  And like a mad man then fought hee,
Untill a falce Scot came Ionnë behinde,
  And runn him through the faire boddee.

Saying, "Fight on, my merry men all,   61
  And see that none of you be taine;
For I will stand by and bleed but awhile,
  And then will I come and fight againe."

Newes then was brought to young Ionnë Armestrong,
  As he stood by his nurses knee,
Who vowed if ere he lived for to be a man,
  O the treacherous Scots revengd hee 'd be.
                    [ANON.]

_____

l. 10. sicke: such.

SIR PATRICK SPENCE

The king sits in Dumferling toune,
  Drinking the blude-reid wine:
"O whar will I get guid sailor,
  To sail this schip of mine?"

Up and spak an eldern knicht,
  Sat at the kings richt kne:
"Sir Patrick Spence is the best sailor,
  That sails upon the se."

The king has written a braid letter,
  And signd it wi his hand,   10
And sent it to Sir Patrick Spence,
  Was walking on the sand.

The first line that Sir Patrick red,
  A loud lauch lauched he;
The next line that Sir Patrick red,
  The teir blinded his ee.

"O wha is this has don this deid,
  This ill deid don to me,
To send me out this time o' the yeir,
  To sail upon the se!   20

"Mak hast, mak haste, my mirry men all,
  Our guid schip sails the morne:"
"O say na sae, my master deir,
  For I feir a deadlie storme.

"Late late yestreen I saw the new moone,
  Wi the auld moone in hir arme,

And I feir, I feir, my deir master,
  That we will cum to harme."

O our Scots nobles wer richt laith
  To weet their cork-heild schoone;   30
Bot lang owre a' the play wer playd,
  Their hats they swam aboone.

O lang, lang may their ladies sit,
  Wi thair fans into their hand,
Or eir they se Sir Patrick Spence
  Cum sailing to the land.

O lang, lang may the ladies stand,
  Wi thair gold kems in their hair,
Waiting for thar ain deir lords,
  For they 'll se thame na mair.   40

Haf owre, haf owre to Aberdour,
  It 's fiftie fadom deip,
And thair lies guid Sir Patrick Spence,
  Wi the Scots lords at his feit.
                          [ANON.]

---

l. 9. braid: broad.
l. 14. lauch: laugh.
l. 29. laith: loath.
l. 32. aboone: above.

THE TWA CORBIES

As I was walking all alane,
I herd twa corbies making a mane;
The tane unto the t' other say,
"Where sall we gang and dine to-day?"

"In behint yon auld fail dyke,
I wot there lies a new slain knight;
And naebody kens that he lies there,
But his hawk, his hound, and lady fair.

"His hound is to the hunting gane,
His hawk to fetch the wild-fowl hame,   10
His lady's ta'en another mate,
So we may mak our dinner sweet.

"Ye'll sit on his white hause-bane,
And I'll pike out his bonny blue een;
Wi ae lock o his gowden hair
We'll theek our nest when it grows bare.

"Mony a one for him makes mane,
But nane sall ken where he is gane;
Oer his white banes when they are bare,
The wind sall blaw for evermair."   20
                          [ANON.]

---

l. 2. corbies: ravens or crows. mane: moan, lament.
l. 5. fail: turf.
l. 7. kens: knows.
l. 13. hause-bane: neck bone.
l. 16. theek: thatch.

PROUD MAISIE

Sir Walter Scott
(1771–1832)

[From *The Heart of Midlothian*]
Proud Maisie is in the wood,
  Walking so early;
Sweet Robin sits on the bush,
  Singing so rarely.

"Tell me, thou bonny bird,
  When shall I marry me?"—
"When six braw gentlemen
  Kirkward shall carry ye."

"Who makes the bridal bed,
  Birdie, say truly?"—   10
"The grey-headed sexton
  That delves the grave duly.

"The glow-worm o'er grave and stone
  Shall light thee steady.
The owl from the steeple sing,
  'Welcome, proud lady.'"

---

l. 7. braw: fine.

[BACK AND SIDE GO BARE, GO BARE]

[From *Gammer Gurton's Needle*]
Back and side go bare, go bare,
  Both foot and hand go cold;
But, belly, God send thee good ale enough,
  Whether it be new or old.

I cannot eat but little meat,
   My stomach is not good;
But sure I think that I can drink
   With him that wears a hood.
Though I go bare, take ye no care,
   I am nothing a-cold;   10
I stuff my skin so full within
   Of jolly good ale and old.

   Back and side go bare, go bare, etc.

I love no roast but a nutbrown toast,
   And a crab laid in the fire;
A little bread shall do me stead,
   Much bread I not desire.
No frost nor snow, no wind, I trow,
   Can hurt me if I would,
I am so wrapt, and throughly lapt   20
   Of jolly good ale and old.

   Back and side go bare, go bare, etc.

And Tib my wife, that as her life
   Loveth well good ale to seek,
Full oft drinks she, till ye may see
   The tears run down her cheek.
Then doth she troll to me the bowl,
   Even as a maltworm should;
And saith, "Sweetheart, I took my part
   Of this jolly good ale and old."   30

   Back and side go bare, go bare, etc.

Now let them drink, till they nod and wink,
   Even as good fellows should do;
They shall not miss to have the bliss
   Good ale doth bring men to.
And all poor souls that have scouréd bowls,
   Or have them lustily trolled,
God save the lives of them and their wives,
   Whether they be young or old.

   Back and side go bare, go bare, etc.   40

     [ANON. SIXTEENTH CENTURY]

---

l. 8. him that wears a hood: a friar.
l. 14. nutbrown toast: toast soaked in ale.
l. 15. crab: crab apple.
l. 27. troll: pass around.
l. 28. maltworm: toper.
l. 36. scoured: emptied.

FOLLOW ME 'OME

Rudyard Kipling
(1865–1936)

There was no one like 'im, 'Orse or Foot,
   Nor any o' the Guns I knew;
An' because it was so, why, o' course 'e went
       an' died,
   Which is just what the best men do.

   So it 's knock out your pipes an' follow me!
   An' it 's finish up your swipes an' follow
      me!
    Oh, 'ark to the big drum callin',
     Follow me—follow me 'ome!

'Is mare she neighs the 'ole day long,
   She paws the 'ole night through,   10
An' she won't take 'er feed 'cause o' waitin'
      for 'is step,
   Which is just what a beast would do.

'Is girl she goes with a bombardier
   Before 'er month is through;
An' the banns are up in church, for she 's got
      the beggar hooked,
   Which is just what a girl would do.

We fought 'bout a dog—last week it
      were—
   No more than a round or two;
But I strook 'im cruel 'ard, an' I wish I 'ad n't
      now,
   Which is just what a man can't do.   20

'E was all that I 'ad in the way of a friend,
   An' I 've 'ad to find one new;
But I 'd give my pay an' stripe for to get the
      beggar back,
   Which it 's just too late to do.

   So it 's knock out your pipes an' follow me!
   An' it 's finish up your swipes an' follow
      me!
    Oh, 'ark to the fifes a-crawlin'!
     Follow me—follow me 'ome!

Take 'im away! 'E 's gone where the best
    men go.
Take 'im away! An' the gun-wheels turnin'
    slow.   30
Take 'im away! There 's more from the
    place 'e come.
Take 'im away, with the limber an' the
    drum.

For it 's "Three rounds blank" an' follow
    me,
An' it 's "Thirteen rank" an' follow me;
    Oh, passin' the love o' women,
      Follow me—follow me 'ome!

l. 6. swipes: weak beer.

THE CASTAWAY

William Cowper
(1731–1800)

Obscurest night involv'd the sky,
  Th' Atlantic billows roar'd,
When such a destin'd wretch as I,
  Wash'd headlong from on board,
Of friends, of hope, of all bereft,
His floating home for ever left.

No braver chief could Albion boast
  Than he with whom he went,
Nor ever ship left Albion's coast,
  With warmer wishes sent.   10
He lov'd them both, but both in vain,
Nor him beheld, nor her again.

Not long beneath the whelming brine,
  Expert to swim, he lay;
Nor soon he felt his strength decline,
  Or courage die away;
But wag'd with death a lasting strife,
Supported by despair of life.

He shouted: nor his friends had failed
  To check the vessel's course,   20
But so the furious blast prevail'd,
  That, pitiless perforce,
They left their outcast mate behind,
And scudded still before the wind.

Some succour yet they could afford;
  And, such as storms allow,
The cask, the coop, the floated cord,
  Delay'd not to bestow.
But he (they knew) nor ship, nor shore,
Whate'er they gave, should visit more.   30

Nor, cruel as it seem'd, could he
  Their haste himself condemn,
Aware that flight, in such a sea,
  Alone could rescue them;
Yet bitter felt it still to die
Deserted, and his friends so nigh.

He long survives, who lives an hour
  In ocean, self-upheld;
And so long he, with unspent pow'r,
  His destiny repell'd;   40
And ever, as the minutes flew,
Entreated help, or cried—Adieu!

At length, his transient respite past,
  His comrades, who before
Had heard his voice in ev'ry blast,
  Could catch the sound no more.
For then, by toil subdued, he drank
The stifling wave, and then he sank.

No poet wept him: but the page
  Of narrative sincere,   50
That tells his name, his worth, his age,
  Is wet with Anson's tear.
And tears by bards or heroes shed
Alike immortalize the dead.

I therefore purpose not, or dream,
  Descanting on his fate,
To give the melancholy theme
  A more enduring date:
But misery still delights to trace
Its 'semblance in another's case.   60

No voice divine the storm allay'd,
  No light propitious shone;
When, snatch'd from all effectual aid,
  We perish'd, each alone:
But I beneath a rougher sea,
And whelm'd in deeper gulphs than he.

LA BELLE DAME
SANS MERCI

John Keats
(1795–1821)

O what can ail thee, knight-at-arms,
   Alone and palely loitering?
The sedge has wither'd from the lake,
   And no birds sing.

O what can ail thee, knight-at-arms!
   So haggard and so woe-begone?
The squirrel's granary is full,
   And the harvest's done.

I see a lily on thy brow,
   With anguish moist and fever dew,   10
And on thy cheeks a fading rose
   Fast withereth too.

I met a lady in the meads,
   Full beautiful—a faery's child,
Her hair was long, her foot was light,
   And her eyes were wild.

I made a garland for her head,
   And bracelets too, and fragrant zone;
She look'd at me as she did love,
   And made sweet moan.   20

I set her on my pacing steed,
   And nothing else saw all day long,
For sidelong would she bend, and sing
   A faery's song.

She found me roots of relish sweet,
   And honey wild, and manna dew,
And sure in language strange she said—
   "I love thee true."

She took me to her elfin grot,
   And there she wept, and sigh'd full sore,
And there I shut her wild wild eyes   31
   With kisses four.

And there she lulled me asleep,
   And there I dream'd—Ah! woe betide!

The latest dream I ever dream'd
   On the cold hill side.

I saw pale kings and princes too,
   Pale warriors, death-pale were they all;
They cried—"La Belle Dame sans Merci
   Hath thee in thrall!"   40

I saw their starv'd lips in the gloam
   With horrid warning gaped wide,
And I awoke and found me here,
   On the cold hill's side.

And this is why I sojourn here,
   Alone and palely loitering,
Though the sedge has wither'd from the lake,
   And no birds sing.

────────
l. 18. fragrant zone: girdle, presumably of flowers.

THE HOST OF THE AIR

William Butler Yeats

O'Driscoll drove with a song
The wild duck and the drake
From the tall and the tufted reeds
Of the drear Hart Lake.

And he saw how the reeds grew dark
At the coming of night-tide,
And dreamed of the long dim hair
Of Bridget his bride.

He heard while he sang and dreamed
A piper piping away,   10
And never was piping so sad,
And never was piping so gay.

And he saw young men and young girls
Who danced on a level place,
And Bridget his bride among them,
With a sad and a gay face.

The dancers crowded about him,
And many a sweet thing said,
And a young man brought him red wine
And a young girl white bread.   20

But Bridget drew him by the sleeve,
Away from the merry bands,
To old men playing at cards
With a twinkling of ancient hands.

The bread and the wine had a doom,
For these were the host of the air;
He sat and played in a dream
Of her long dim hair.

He played with the merry old men
And thought not of evil chance,   30
Until one bore Bridget his bride
Away from the merry dance.

He bore her away in his arms,
The handsomest young man there,
And his neck and his breast and his arms
Were drowned in her long dim hair.

O'Driscoll scattered the cards
And out of his dream awoke:
Old men and young men and young girls
Were gone like a drifting smoke;   40

But he heard high up in the air
A piper piping away,
And never was piping so sad,
And never was piping so gay.

THE THREE BEGGARS

William Butler Yeats

"Though to my feathers in the wet,
I have stood here from break of day,
I have not found a thing to eat,
For only rubbish comes my way.
Am I to live on lebeen-lone?"
Muttered the old crane of Gort.
"For all my pains on lebeen-lone?"

King Guaire walked amid his court
The palace-yard and river-side
And there to three old beggars said,   10
"You that have wandered far and wide
Can ravel out what's in my head.

Do men who least desire get most,
Or get the most who most desire?"
A beggar said, "They get the most
Whom man or devil cannot tire,
And what could make their muscles taut
Unless desire had made them so?"
But Guaire laughed with secret thought,
"If that be true as it seems true,   20
One of you three is a rich man,
For he shall have a thousand pounds
Who is first asleep, if but he can
Sleep before the third noon sounds."
And thereon, merry as a bird
With his old thoughts, King Guaire went
From river-side and palace-yard
And left them to their argument.
"And if I win," one beggar said,
"Though I am old I shall persuade   30
A pretty girl to share my bed";
The second: "I shall learn a trade";
The third: "I'll hurry to the course
Among the other gentlemen,
And lay it all upon a horse";
The second: "I have thought again:
A farmer has more dignity."
One to another sighed and cried:
The exorbitant dreams of beggary,
That idleness had borne to pride,   40
Sang through their teeth from noon to noon;
And when the second twilight brought
The frenzy of the beggars' moon
None closed his blood-shot eyes but sought
To keep his fellows from their sleep;
All shouted till their anger grew
And they were whirling in a heap.

They mauled and bit the whole night
  through;
They mauled and bit till the day shone;
They mauled and bit through all that day   50
And till another night had gone,
Or if they made a moment's stay
They sat upon their heels to rail,
And when old Guaire came and stood
Before the three to end this tale,
They were commingling lice and blood.
"Time's up," he cried, and all the three
With blood-shot eyes upon him stared.
"Time's up," he cried, and all the three
Fell down upon the dust and snored.   60

"Maybe I shall be lucky yet,
Now they are silent," said the crane.
"Though to my feathers in the wet
I've stood as I were made of stone
And seen the rubbish run about,
It's certain there are trout somewhere
And maybe I shall take a trout
If but I do not seem to care."

---

l. 5. lebeen: minnows.
l. 6. Gort: an Irish place name.

[O WHAT IS THAT SOUND]

W. H. Auden
(1907–   )

O what is that sound which so thrills the ear
    Down in the valley drumming, drum-
        ming?
Only the scarlet soldiers, dear,
    The soldiers coming.

O what is that light I see flashing so clear
    Over the distance brightly, brightly?
Only the sun on their weapons, dear,
    As they step lightly.

O what are they doing with all that gear,
    What are they doing this morning, this
        morning?   10
Only their usual manoeuvres, dear,
    Or perhaps a warning.

O why have they left the road down there,
    Why are they suddenly wheeling,
        wheeling?
Perhaps a change in the orders, dear,
    Why are you kneeling?

O haven't they stopped for the doctor's care,
    Haven't they reined their horses, their
        horses?
Why, they are none of them wounded, dear,
    None of these forces.   20

O is it the parson they want, with white hair,
    Is it the parson, is it, is it?
No, they are passing his gateway, dear,
    Without a visit.

O it must be the farmer who lives so near.
    It must be the farmer so cunning, so
        cunning?
They have passed the farmyard already, dear,
    And now they are running.

O where are you going? Stay with me here!
    Were the vows you swore deceiving, de-
        ceiving?   30
No, I promised to love you, dear,
    But I must be leaving.

O it's broken the lock and splintered the
    door,
    O it's the gate where they're turning, turn-
        ing;
Their boots are heavy on the floor
    And their eyes are burning.

4. TWO MODERN POETS

Robert Frost
THE RUNAWAY

Once when the snow of the year was begin-
   ning to fall,
We stopped by a mountain pasture to say,
   "Whose colt?"
A little Morgan had one forefoot on the wall,
The other curled at his breast. He dipped his
   head
And snorted at us. And then he had to bolt.
We heard the miniature thunder where he
   fled,
And we saw him, or thought we saw him,
   dim and gray,
Like a shadow against the curtain of falling
   flakes.
"I think the little fellow's afraid of the snow.
He isn't winter-broken. It isn't play   10
With the little fellow at all. He's running
   away.
I doubt if even his mother could tell him,
   'Sakes,
It's only weather.' He'd think she didn't
   know!
Where is his mother? He can't be out alone."
And now he comes again with a clatter of
   stone
And mounts the wall again with whited eyes
And all his tail that isn't hair up straight.
He shudders his coat as if to throw off flies.
"Whoever it is that leaves him out so late,
When other creatures have gone to stall and
   bin,   20
Ought to be told to come and take him in."

DUST OF SNOW

The way a crow
Shook down on me
The dust of snow
From a hemlock tree

Has given my heart
A change of mood
And saved some part
Of a day I had rued.

AFTER APPLE-PICKING

My long two-pointed ladder's sticking
   through a tree
Toward heaven still,
And there's a barrel that I didn't fill
Beside it, and there may be two or three
Apples I didn't pick upon some bough.
But I am done with apple-picking now.
Essence of winter sleep is on the night,
The scent of apples: I am drowsing off.
I cannot rub the strangeness from my sight
I got from looking through a pane of glass
I skimmed this morning from the drinking
   trough   11
And held against the world of hoary grass.
It melted, and I let it fall and break.
But I was well
Upon my way to sleep before it fell,
And I could tell
What form my dreaming was about to take.
Magnified apples appear and disappear,
Stem end and blossom end,
And every fleck of russet showing clear.   20
My instep arch not only keeps the ache,
It keeps the pressure of a ladder-round.
I feel the ladder sway as the boughs bend.
And I keep hearing from the cellar bin
The rumbling sound

Of load on load of apples coming in.
For I have had too much
Of apple-picking: I am overtired
Of the great harvest I myself desired.
There were ten thousand thousand fruit to
    touch,   30
Cherish in hand, lift down, and not let fall.
For all
That struck the earth,
No matter if not bruised or spiked with stub-
ble,
Went surely to the cider-apple heap
As of no worth.
One can see what will trouble
This sleep of mine, whatever sleep it is.
Were he not gone,
The woodchuck could say whether it's like
    his   40
Long sleep, as I describe its coming on,
Or just some human sleep.

MENDING WALL

Something there is that doesn't love a wall,
That sends the frozen-ground-swell under it,
And spills the upper boulders in the sun;
And makes gaps even two can pass abreast.
The work of hunters is another thing:
I have come after them and made repair
Where they have left not one stone on a
    stone,
But they would have the rabbit out of hiding,
To please the yelping dogs. The gaps I mean,
No one has seen them made or heard them
    made,   10
But at spring mending-time we find them
    there.
I let my neighbor know beyond the hill;
And on a day we meet to walk the line
And set the wall between us once again.
We keep the wall between us as we go.
To each the boulders that have fallen to each.
And some are loaves and some so nearly balls
We have to use a spell to make them bal-
ance:
"Stay where you are until our backs are
turned!"

We wear our fingers rough with handling
    them.   20
Oh, just another kind of out-door game,
One on a side. It comes to little more:
There where it is we do not need the wall:
He is all pine and I am apple orchard.
My apple trees will never get across
And eat the cones under his pines, I tell him.
He only says, "Good fences make good
    neighbors."
Spring is the mischief in me, and I wonder
If I could put a notion in his head:
"Why do they make good neighbors? Isn't
    it   30
Where there are cows? But here there are
    no cows.
Before I built a wall I'd ask to know
What I was walling in or walling out,
And to whom I was like to give offense.
Something there is that doesn't love a wall,
That wants it down." I could say "Elves" to
    him,
But it's not elves exactly, and I'd rather
He said it for himself. I see him there
Bringing a stone grasped firmly by the top
In each hand, like an old-stone savage
    armed.   40
He moves in darkness as it seems to me,
Not of woods only and the shade of trees.
He will not go behind his father's saying,
And he likes having thought of it so well
He says again, "Good fences make good
    neighbors."

NOTHING GOLD CAN STAY

Nature's first green is gold,
Her hardest hue to hold.
Her early leaf's a flower;
But only so an hour.
Then leaf subsides to leaf.
So Eden sank to grief,
So dawn goes down to day.
Nothing gold can stay.

FIRE AND ICE

Some say the world will end in fire,
Some say in ice.
From what I've tasted of desire
I hold with those who favor fire.
But if it had to perish twice,
I think I know enough of hate
To say that for destruction ice
Is also great
And would suffice.

Walter de la Mare
(1873–1956)

THE LISTENERS

"Is there anybody there?" said the Traveller,
Knocking on the moonlit door;
And his horse in the silence champed the
grasses
Of the forest's ferny floor:
And a bird flew up out of the turret,
Above the Traveller's head:
And he smote upon the door again a second
time;
"Is there anybody there?" he said.
But no one descended to the Traveller;
No head from the leaf-fringed sill   10
Leaned over and looked into his gray eyes,
Where he stood perplexed and still.
But only a host of phantom listeners
That dwelt in the lone house then
Stood listening in the quiet of the moonlight
To that voice from the world of men:
Stood thronging the faint moonbeams on the
dark stair,
That goes down to the empty hall,
Hearkening in an air stirred and shaken
By the lonely Traveller's call.   20
And he felt in his heart their strangeness,
Their stillness answering his cry,
While his horse moved, cropping the dark
turf,
'Neath the starred and leafy sky;
For he suddenly smote on the door, even
Louder, and lifted his head:—

"Tell them I came, and no one answered,
That I kept my word," he said.
Never the least stir made the listeners,
Though every word he spake   30
Fell echoing through the shadowiness of the
still house
From the one man left awake:
Ay, they heard his foot upon the stirrup,
And the sound of iron on stone,
And how the silence surged softly backward,
When the plunging hoofs were gone.

THE GHOST

"Who knocks?" "I, who was beautiful,
Beyond all dreams to restore,
I, from the roots of the dark thorn am hither.
And knock on the door."

"Who speaks?" "I—once was my speech
Sweet as the bird's on the air,
When echo lurks by the waters to heed;
'Tis I speak thee fair."

"Dark is the hour!" "Ay, and cold."
"Lone is my house." "Ah, but mine?"   10
"Sight, touch, lips, eyes yearned in vain."
"Long dead these to thine . . ."

Silence. Still faint on the porch
Brake the flames of the stars.
In gloom groped a hope-wearied hand
Over keys, bolts, and bars.

A face peered. All the grey night
In chaos of vacancy shone;
Nought but vast sorrow was there—
The sweet cheat gone.   20

THE MOCKING FAIRY

"Won't you look out of your window, Mrs.
Gill?"
Quoth the Fairy, nidding, nodding in the
garden;

"*Can't* you look out of your window, Mrs.
    Gill?"
    Quoth the Fairy, laughing softly in the
       garden;
But the air was still, the cherry boughs were
    still,
And the ivy-tod 'neath the empty sill,
And never from her window looked out Mrs.
    Gill
    On the Fairy shrilly mocking in the gar-
      den.

"What have they done with you, you poor
    Mrs. Gill?"
    Quoth the Fairy brightly glancing in the
      garden;   10
"Where have they hidden you, you poor old
    Mrs. Gill?"
    Quoth the Fairy dancing lightly in the gar-
      den;
But night's faint veil now wrapped the hill,
Stark 'neath the stars stood the dead-still
    Mill,
And out of her cold cottage never answered
    Mrs. Gill
    The Fairy mimbling mambling in the gar-
      den.

AT THE KEYHOLE

"Grill me some bones," said the Cobbler,
    "Some bones, my pretty Sue;
I'm tired of my lonesome with heels and
    soles,
Springsides and uppers too;
A mouse in the wainscot is nibbling;
A wind in the keyhole drones;
And a sheet webbed over my candle, Susie,
    Grill me some bones!"

"Grill me some bones," said the Cobbler,
    "I sat at my tic-tac-to;   10
And a footstep came to my door and stopped,
And a hand groped to and fro;
And I peered up over my boot and last;
And my feet went cold as stones:—
I saw an eye at the keyhole, Susie!—
    Grill me some bones!"

---

l. 7. sheet: vapor or mist.

THE OLD MEN

Old and alone, sit we,
    Caged, riddle-rid men;
Lost to Earth's "Listen!" and "See!"
    Thought's "Wherefore?" and "When?"

Only far memories stray
    Of a past once lovely, but now
Wasted and faded away,
    Like green leaves from the bough.

Vast broods the silence of night,
    The ruinous moon   10
Lifts on our faces her light,
    Whence all dreaming is gone.

We speak not; trembles each head;
    In their sockets our eyes are still;
Desire as cold as the dead;
    Without wonder or will.
And One, with a lanthorn, draws near,
    At clash with the moon in our eyes:
"Where art thou?" he asks: "I am here,"
    One by one we arise.   20

And none lifts a hand to withhold
    A friend from the touch of that foe:
Heart cries unto heart, "Thou art old!"
    Yet, reluctant, we go.

5. LOVE POEMS AND POEMS ABOUT WOMEN

[WHO WOULD HAVE THOUGHT]

Thomas Howell
(Sixteenth century)

Who would have thought that face of thine
  Had been so full of doubleness?
Or else within those crystal eyne
  Had rest so much unstableness?
Thy face so fair, thy look so strange,
Who would have thought so full of change?

———
l. 3. eyne: eyes.

[WHY DO WE LOVE]

Sir Benjamin Rudyerd
(1572–1658)

Why do we love these things which we call
    women,
  Which are like feathers blown with every
    wind,
Regarding least those which do most esteem
    them,
  And most deceitful when they seem most
    kind;
    And all the virtue that their beauty
      graces,
    It is but painted like unto their faces?

Their greatest glory is in rich attire,
  Which is extracted from some hopeful
    livers
Whose wits and wealth are bent to their de-
    sire,

When they regard the gift more than the
    givers;   10
And to increase their hopes of future
    bliss,
  They'll sometimes stretch their con-
    science for a kiss.

Some love the winds that bring in golden
    flowers,
  And some are merely won with commen-
    dation;
Some love and hate, and all within two hours,
  And that's a fault amongst them most in
    fashion;
    But put them all within a scale together,
    Their worth in weight will scarce pull
      down a feather.

And yet I would not discommend them all,
  If I did know some worth to be in any;
'Tis strange, that since the time of Adam's
    fall,   21
  That God did make none good, and made
    so many;
    And if he did, for those I truly mourn,
    Because they died before that I was
      born.

[BROWN IS MY LOVE]

Anon.
(1597)

Brown is my Love, but graceful:
And each renownèd whiteness
Matched with thy lovely brown loseth its
    brightness.

301

Fair is my Love, but scornful:
  Yet have I seen despisëd
Dainty white lilies, and sad flowers well
  prizëd.

_____

l. 6. sad: dark, somber.

[THOU SLEEPEST FAST]

Anon.
(c. 1550)

Thou sleepest fast, and I with woeful heart
  Stand here alone sighing and cannot fly:
Thou sleepest fast, when cruel Love his dart
  On me doth cast, alas, so painfully!
Thou sleepest fast, and I, all full of smart,
  To thee, my foe, in vain do call and cry:
And yet, methinkës, though thou sleepest fast
Thou dreamest still which way my life to
  wast.

_____

l. 8. wast: waste.

TO A LADY TO ANSWER DIRECTLY WITH YEA OR NAY

Sir Thomas Wyatt
(1503?–1542)

Madam, withouten many words,
  Once, I am sure, ye will or no:
And if ye will, then leave your bords
  And use your wit and show it so:
And with a beck ye shall me call;
  And if of one, that burneth alway,
Ye have any pity at all,
  Answer him fair with yea, or nay.
If it be yea, I shall be fain;
  If it be nay, friends as before;   10
Ye shall another man obtain,
  And I mine own and yours no more.

_____

l. 3. bords: jests, games.

THE LOVER SHOWETH HOW HE IS FORSAKEN OF SUCH AS HE SOMETIME ENJOYED

Sir Thomas Wyatt

They flee from me that sometime did me
  seek,
With naked foot stalking within my chamber:
Once have I seen them gentle, tame, and
  meek,
That now are wild, and do not once remember
That sometime they have put themselves in
  danger
To take bread at my hand; and now they
  range,
Busily seeking in continual change.

Thankèd be fortune, it hath been otherwise
Twenty times better; but once especïal,
In thin array, after a pleasant guise,   10
When her loose gown did from her shoulders fall,
And she me caught in her arms long and
  small,
And therewithal so sweetly did me kiss,
And softly said, "Dear heart, how like you
  this?"

It was no dream; for I lay broad awaking:
But all is turned now, through my gentleness,
Into a bitter fashion of forsaking;
And I have leave to go, of her goodnèss;
And she also to use new-fangleness.
But since that I unkindly so am servèd, 20
"How like you this?"—what hath she now
  deservèd?

_____

l. 1. sometime: formerly.

SONG

George Peele
(1558?–1597?)

Whenas the rye reach to the chin,
And chopcherry, chopcherry ripe within,
Strawberries swimming in the cream,
And schoolboys playing in the stream;
Then oh, then oh, then oh, my true Love said,
Till that time come again
She could not live a maid.

THE PASSIONATE SHEP-
HERD TO HIS LOVE

Christopher Marlowe
(1564–1593)

Come live with me and be my Love,
And we will all the pleasures prove
That valleys, groves, hills, and fields,
Woods, or steepy mountains yields.

And we will sit upon the rocks
Seeing the shepherds feed their flocks,
By shallow rivers, to whose falls
Melodious birds sing madrigals.

And I will make thee beds of roses,
And a thousand fragrant posies,   10
A cap of flowers, and a kirtle
Embroidered all with leaves of myrtle;

A gown made of the finest wool,
Which from our pretty lambs we pull;
Fair linèd slippers for the cold,
With buckles of the purest gold;

A belt of straw and ivy buds
With coral clasps and amber studs:
And if these pleasures may thee move,
Come live with me, and be my Love.   20

The shepherd swains shall dance and sing
For thy delight each May morning:

If these delights thy mind may move,
Then live with me and be my Love.

l. 11. kirtle: gown.

THE NYMPH'S REPLY
TO THE SHEPHERD

? Sir Walter Raleigh
(1552?–1618)

If all the world and love were young,
And truth in every shepherd's tongue,
These pretty pleasures might me move
To live with thee and be thy Love.

Time drives the flocks from field to fold,
When rivers rage and rocks grow cold;
And Philomel becometh dumb;
The rest complains of cares to come.

The flowers do fade, and wanton fields
To wayward winter reckoning yields: 10
A honey tongue, a heart of gall,
Is fancy's spring, but sorrow's fall.

Thy gowns, thy shoes, thy beds of roses,
Thy cap, thy kirtle, and thy posies
Soon break, soon wither, soon forgotten,
In folly ripe, in reason rotten.

Thy belt of straw and ivy buds,
Thy coral clasps and amber studs,
All these in me no means can move
To come to thee and be thy Love.   20

But could youth last, and love still breed,
Had joys no date, nor age no need,
Then these delights my mind might move
To live with thee and be thy Love.

l. 21. still: always, constantly.
l. 22. date: terminal date, termination.

THE BAIT

John Donne
(1573–1631)

Come live with me, and be my love,
And we will some new pleasures prove

Of golden sands, and crystal brooks,
With silken lines, and silver hooks.

There will the river whispering run
Warm'd by thy eyes, more than the sun;
And there the enamour'd fish will stay,
Begging themselves they may betray.

When thou wilt swim in that live bath,
Each fish, which every channel hath,　　10
Will amorously to thee swim,
Gladder to catch thee, than thou him.

If thou to be so seen be'st loath
By Sun, or Moon, thou dark'nest both,
And if myself have leave to see,
I need not their light, having thee.

Let others freeze with angling reeds,
And cut their legs with shells and weeds,
Or treacherously poor fish beset,
With strangling snare, or windowy net:　　20

Let coarse bold hands, from slimy nest
The bedded fish in banks out-wrest;
Or curious traitors, sleave-silk flies,
Bewitch poor fishes' wand'ring eyes.

For thee, thou need'st no such deceit,
For thou thyself art thine own bait;
That fish that is not catch'd thereby,
Alas, is wiser far than I.

l. 17. reeds: rods.
l. 23. sleave-silk flies: artificial flies made of floss
or raw silk.

SONG

John Donne

Go and catch a falling star,
　Get with child a mandrake root,
Tell me where all past years are,
　Or who cleft the Devil's foot,
Teach me to hear mermaids singing,
Or to keep off envy's stinging,
　　And find
　　What wind
Serves to advance an honest mind.

If thou be'st born to strange sights,　　10
　Things invisible to see,
Ride ten thousand days and nights,
　Till age snow white hairs on thee;
Thou, when thou return'st, wilt tell me
All strange wonders that befell thee,
　　And swear
　　Nowhere
Lives a woman true, and fair.

If thou findst one, let me know,
　Such a pilgrimage were sweet;—　　20
Yet do not, I would not go,
　Though at next door we might meet;
Though she were true, when you met her,
And last, till you write your letter,
　　Yet she
　　Will be
False, ere I come, to two, or three.

THE INDIFFERENT

John Donne

I can love both fair and brown,
Her whom abundance melts, and her whom
　want betrays,
Her who loves loneness best, and her who
　masks and plays,
Her whom the country form'd, and whom
　the town,
Her who believes, and her who tries,
Her who still weeps with spongy eyes,
And her who is dry cork and never cries;
I can love her, and her, and you, and you,
I can love any, so she be not true.

Will no other vice content you?　　10
Will it not serve your turn to do as did your
　mothers?
Or have you all old vices spent, and now
　would find out others?
Or doth a fear, that men are true, torment
　you?
O we are not, be not you so.
Let me, and do you, twenty know.
Rob me, but bind me not, and let me go.

Must I, who came to travel thorough you,
Grow your fix'd subject, because you are
    true?

Venus heard me sigh this song,
And by love's sweetest part, variety, she
    swore   20
She heard not this till now; and that it should
    be so no more.
She went, examin'd, and return'd ere long,
And said, "Alas, some two or three
Poor heretics in love there be,
Which think to stablish dangerous constancy.
But I have told them: 'Since you will be true,
You shall be true to them, who are false to
    you!'"

l. 1. fair and brown: blonde and brunette.

[STILL TO BE NEAT]

Ben Jonson
(1572–1637)

Still to be neat, still to be drest,
As you were going to a feast;
Still to be powder'd, still perfum'd;—
Lady, it is to be presum'd,
Though art's hid causes are not found,
All is not sweet, all is not sound.

Give me a look, give me a face,
That makes simplicity a grace;
Robes loosely flowing, hair as free:
Such sweet neglect more taketh me   10
Than all th' adulteries of art;
They strike mine eyes, but not my heart.

UPON JULIA'S CLOTHES

Robert Herrick
(1591–1674)

When as in silks my *Julia* goes,
Then, then (methinks) how sweetly flowes
That liquefaction of her clothes.

Next, when I cast mine eyes and see
That brave Vibration each way free;
O how that glittering taketh me!

[SHALL I, WASTING IN DESPAIR]

George Wither
(1588–1667)

Shall I, wasting in despair,
Die, because a woman's fair?
Or make pale my cheeks with care,
'Cause another's rosy are?
Be she fairer than the day,
Or the flowery meads in May!
    If she be not so to me,
    What care I how fair she be?

Should my heart be griev'd or pin'd,
'Cause I see a woman kind?   10
Or a well disposed nature
Joined with a lovely feature?
Be she meeker, kinder than
Turtle dove, or pelican!
    If she be not so to me,
    What care I how kind she be?

Shall a woman's virtues move
Me to perish for her love?
Or, her well deserving known,
Make me quite forget mine own?   20
Be she with that goodness blest,
Which may gain her, name of best!
    If she be not such to me,
    What care I how good she be?

'Cause her fortune seems too high,
Shall I play the fool, and die?
Those that bear a noble mind,
Where they want of riches find,
Think "What, with them, they would do,
That, without them, dare to woo!"   30
    And unless that mind I see,
    What care I though great she be?

Great, or good, or kind, or fair,
I will ne'er the more despair!

If she love me (this believe!)
I will die, ere she shall grieve!
If she slight me, when I woo,
I can scorn, and let her go!
    For if she be not for me,
    What care I for whom she be?   40

[WHY SO PALE AND WAN, FOND LOVER?]

Sir John Suckling
(1609–1642)

Why so pale and wan, fond lover?
    Prithee, why so pale?
Will, when looking well can't move her,
    Looking ill prevail?
    Prithee, why so pale?

Why so dull and mute, young sinner?
    Prithee, why so mute?
Will, when speaking well can't win her,
    Saying nothing do 't?
    Prithee, why so mute?   10

Quit, quit, for shame, this will not move:
    This cannot take her.
If of herself she will not love,
    Nothing can make her:
    The devil take her!

[OUT UPON IT! I HAVE LOVED]

Sir John Suckling

Out upon it! I have lov'd
    Three whole days together;
And am like to love three more,
    If it prove fair weather.

Time shall moult away his wings,
    Ere he shall discover
In the whole wide world again
    Such a constant lover.

But the spite on 't is, no praise
    Is due at all to me: 10
Love with me had made no stays,
    Had it any been but she.

Had it any been but she,
    And that very face,
There had been at least ere this
    A dozen dozen in her place.

---

l. 1. Out upon it: exclamation of impatience, often used lightly.

TO LUCASTA, ON GOING TO THE WARS

Richard Lovelace
(1618–1658)

Tell me not, Sweet, I am unkind,
    That from the Nunnery
Of thy chaste breast, and quiet mind,
    To War and Arms I fly.

True; a new Mistress now I chase,
    The first Foe in the Field;
And with a stronger Faith embrace
    A Sword, a Horse, a Shield.

Yet this Inconstancy is such,
    As you too shall adore;   10
I could not love thee, Dear, so much,
    Lov'd I not Honour more.

[O WESTERN WIND, WHEN WILT THOU BLOW]

Anon.
(Sixteenth Century?)

O western wind, when wilt thou blow,
That the small rain down can rain?
Christ, if my love were in my arms
And I in my bed again!

PRECURSORS

Louis MacNeice
(1907–   )

O that the rain would come—the rain in big
    battalions—
Or thunder flush the hedge a more clairvoy-
    ant green
Or wind walk in and whip us and strip us or
    booming
Harvest moon transmute this muted scene.

But all is flat, matt, mute, unlivened, unex-
    pectant,
And none but insects dare to sing or pirou-
    ette;
That Man is a dancer is an anachronism—
Who has forgotten his steps or hardly learnt
    them yet.

Yet one or two we have known who had the
    gusto
Of wind or water-spout, and one or two   10
Who carry an emerald lamp behind their
    faces
And—during thunder-storms—the light
    comes shining through.

———
l. 5. matt: without luster or gloss.

[WHAT SHALL I DO WHEN THE SUMMER TROUBLES]

Emily Dickinson
(1830–1886)

What shall I do when the Summer troubles—
What, when the Rose is ripe—
What when the Eggs fly off in Music
From the Maple Keep?

What shall I do when the Skies a'chirrup
Drop a Tune on me—
When the Bee hangs all Noon in the Butter-
    cup
What will become of me?

Oh, when the Squirrel fills His Pockets
And the Berries stare   10
How can I bear their jocund Faces
Thou from Here, so far?

'Twould'nt afflict a Robin—
All His Goods have Wings—
I—do not fly, so wherefore
My Perennial Things?

[THE SOUL SELECTS]

Emily Dickinson

The Soul selects her own Society—
Then—shuts the Door—
To her divine Majority—
Present no more—

Unmoved—she notes the Chariots—paus-
    ing—
At her low Gate—
Unmoved—an Emperor be kneeling
Upon her Mat—

I've known her—from an ample nation—
Choose One—
Then—close the Valves of her attention—
Like Stone—

THE RIVER-MERCHANT'S WIFE: A LETTER

Ezra Pound
(1885–   )

While my hair was still cut straight across my
    forehead
Played I about the front gate, pulling flowers.
You came by on bamboo stilts, playing horse,
You walked about my seat, playing with blue
    plums.
And we went on living in the village of Cho-
    kan:
Two small people, without dislike or suspi-
    cion.

At fourteen I married My Lord you.
I never laughed, being bashful.
Lowering my head, I looked at the wall.
Called to, a thousand times, I never looked
    back.   10

At fifteen I stopped scowling,
I desired my dust to be mingled with yours
Forever and forever and forever.
Why should I climb the look out?

At sixteen you departed,
You went into far Ku-to-yen, by the river of
    swirling eddies,
And you have been gone five months.

The monkeys make sorrowful noise over-
    head.
You dragged your feet when you went out.
By the gate now, the moss is grown, the dif-
    ferent mosses,   20
Too deep to clear them away!
The leaves fall early this autumn, in wind.
The paired butterflies are already yellow with
    August
Over the grass in the West garden;
They hurt me. I grow older.
If you are coming down through the narrows
    of the river Kiang,
Please let me know beforehand,
And I will come out to meet you
                    As far as Cho-fu-Sa.

6. DEATH

from THE HISTORY OF THE WORLD

Sir Walter Raleigh

[APOSTROPHE TO DEATH]

O eloquent, just, and mighty Death! whom none could advise, thou hast persuaded; what none hath dared, thou hast done; and whom all the world hath flattered, thou only hast cast out of the world and despised; thou hast drawn together all the far-stretched greatness, all the pride, cruelty, and ambition of man, and covered it all over with these two narrow words, *Hic jacet!*   9

l. 9. *Hic jacet:* Here [he] lies.

A LYKE-WAKE DIRGE

Anon.
(? Sixteenth Century)

This ae nighte, this ae nighte,
  —*Every nighte and alle,*
Fire and fleet and candle-lighte,
  And Christe receive thy saule.

When thou from hence away art past,
  —*Every nighte and alle,*
To Whinny-muir thou com'st at last:
  And Christe receive thy saule.

If ever thou gavest hosen and shoon,
  —*Every nighte and alle,*   10
Sit thee down and put them on:
  And Christe receive thy saule.

If hosen and shoon thou ne'er gav'st nane
  —*Every nighte and alle,*
The whinnes sall prick thee to the bare bane;
  And Christe receive thy saule.

From Brig o' Dread when thou may'st pass,
  —*Every nighte and alle,*
To Purgatory fire thou com'st at last;
  And Christe receive thy saule.   20

If ever thou gavest meat or drink,
  —*Every nighte and alle,*
The fire sall never make thee shrink;
  And Christe receive thy saule.

If meat or drink thou ne'er gav'st nane,
  —*Every nighte and alle,*
The fire will burn thee to the bare bane;
  And Christe receive thy saule.

This ae nighte, this ae nighte,
  —*Every nighte and alle,*   30
Fire and fleet and candle-lighte,
  And Christe receive thy saule.

Title. Lyke: body.
l. 1. ae: one.
l. 3. fleet: perhaps a paved floor, but the meaning of the word here is not certainly known.
l. 7. Whinny-muir: a moor covered with whin (gorse, furze), a shrub in which sharp spines take the place of leaves.
l. 9. hosen and shoon: hose and shoes.
l. 13. nane: none.
l. 15. bane: bone.
l. 19. brig: bridge.

[FEAR NO MORE]

William Shakespeare
(1564–1616)

Fear no more the heat o' th' sun,
    Nor the furious winter's rages;
Thou thy worldly task hast done,
    Home art gone, and ta'en thy wages:
Golden lads and girls all must,
As chimney-sweepers, come to dust.

Fear no more the frown o' th' great;
    Thou art past the tyrant's stroke;
Care no more to clothe and eat;
    To thee the reed is as the oak: 10
The sceptre, learning, physic, must
All follow this, and come to dust.

Fear no more the lightning-flash,
    Nor th' all-dreaded thunder-stone;
Fear not slander, censure rash;
    Thou hast finish'd joy and moan:
All lovers young, all lovers must
Consign to thee, and come to dust.

No exorciser harm thee!
    Nor no witchcraft charm thee!   20
Ghost unlaid forbear thee!
    Nothing ill come near thee!
Quiet consummation have;
And renowned be thy grave!

[FULL FATHOM FIVE]

William Shakespeare

Full fathom five thy father lies;
    Of his bones are coral made;
Those are pearls that were his eyes;
    Nothing of him that doth fade
But doth suffer a sea change
Into something rich and strange.
Sea-nymphs hourly ring his knell:
                                    Ding-dong!
Hark! now I hear them,—Ding-dong, bell!

LETHE

H. D. (Hilda Doolittle)
(1886–   )

Nor skin nor hide nor fleece
    Shall cover you,
Nor curtain of crimson nor fine
Shelter of cedar-wood be over you,
    Nor the fir-tree
    Nor the pine.

Nor sight of whin nor gorse
    Nor river-yew,
Nor fragrance of flowering bush,
Nor wailing of reed-bird to waken you,   10
    Nor of linnet,
    Nor of thush.

Nor word nor touch nor sight
    Of lover, you
Shall long through the night but for this:
The roll of the full tide to cover you
    Without question,
    Without kiss.

SQUIRREL

Marsden Hartley
(1877–1943)

Singular how look of death in squirrel's face
can seem so reverent; but this is one of
many little comedies,
claws folded as hands of violinist, as in
peace, with thanks for the lovely party
which now—forbid—is over,
no chance to know again guile
of spring love,
wealth of nut, sweet smell of bayberry
and dry cloves.   10

[A SLUMBER DID MY SPIRIT SEAL]

William Wordsworth
(1770–1850)

A slumber did my spirit seal;
　I had no human fears:
She seemed a thing that could not feel
　The touch of earthly years.

No motion has she now, no force;
　She neither hears nor sees;
Rolled round in earth's diurnal course,
　With rocks, and stones, and trees.

BREDON HILL

A. E. Housman
(1859–1936)

In summertime on Bredon
　The bells they sound so clear;
Round both the shires they ring them
　In steeples far and near,
　A happy noise to hear.

Here of a Sunday morning
　My love and I would lie,
And see the coloured counties,
　And hear the larks so high
　About us in the sky.　　　　10

The bells would ring to call her
　In valleys miles away:
"Come all to church, good people;
　Good people, come and pray."
　But here my love would stay.

And I would turn and answer
　Among the springing thyme,
"Oh, peal upon our wedding,
　And we will hear the chime,
　And come to church in time."　　　20

But when the snows at Christmas
　On Bredon top were strown,

My love rose up so early
　And stole out unbeknown
　And went to church alone.

They tolled the one bell only,
　Groom there was none to see,
The mourners followed after,
　And so to church went she,
　And would not wait for me.　　　30

The bells they sound on Bredon,
　And still the steeples hum.
"Come all to church, good people,"—
　Oh, noisy bells, be dumb;
　I hear you, I will come.

[THE RAIN, IT STREAMS ON STONE AND HILLOCK]

A. E. Housman

The rain, it streams on stone and hillock,
　The boot clings to the clay.
Since all is done that's due and right
Let's home; and now, my lad, good-night,
　For I must turn away.

Good-night, my lad, for nought's eternal;
　No league of ours, for sure.
To-morrow I shall miss you less,
And ache of heart and heaviness
　Are things that time should cure.　　　10

Over the hill the highway marches
　And what's beyond is wide:
Oh soon enough will pine to nought
Remembrance and the faithful thought
　That sits the grave beside.

The skies, they are not always raining
　Nor grey the twelvemonth through;
And I shall meet good days and mirth,
And range the lovely lands of earth
　With friends no worse than you.　　　20

But oh, my man, the house is fallen
　That none can build again;
My man, how full of joy and woe
Your mother bore you years ago
　To-night to lie in the rain.

THE HOUSE

Walter de la Mare

'Mother, it's such a lonely house,'
The child cried; and the wind sighed.
  'A narrow but a lovely house,'
    The mother replied.

'Child, it is such a narrow house,'
The ghost cried; and the wind sighed.
  'A narrow and a lonely house,'
  The withering grass replied.

THE DEATH OF A SOLDIER

Wallace Stevens
(1879–1955)

Life contracts and death is expected,
As in a season of autumn.
The soldier falls.

He does not become a three-days personage,
Imposing his separation,
Calling for pomp.

Death is absolute and without memorial,
As in a season of autumn,
When the wind stops,

When the wind stops and, over the heav-
    ens,   10
The clouds go, nevertheless,
In their direction.

7. SONNETS

[NUNS FRET NOT AT THEIR CONVENT'S NARROW ROOM]

William Wordsworth

Nuns fret not at their convent's narrow
    room;
And hermits are contented with their cells;
And students with their pensive citadels;
Maids at the wheel, the weaver at his loom,
Sit blithe and happy; bees that soar for
    bloom,
High as the highest Peak of Furness-fells,
Will murmur by the hour in foxglove bells:
In truth, the prison, unto which we doom
Ourselves, no prison is: and hence for me,
In sundry moods, 't was pastime to be
    bound   10
Within the Sonnet's scanty plot of ground;
Pleased if some Souls (for such there needs
    must be)
Who have felt the weight of too much lib-
    erty,
Should find brief solace there, as I have
    found.

l. 4. wheel: spinning wheel.
l. 6. Furness-fells: mountains in the English Lake
District.

[IF BY DULL RHYMES OUR ENGLISH MUST BE CHAIN'D]

John Keats

If by dull rhymes our English must be
    chain'd,

And, like Andromeda, the Sonnet sweet
Fetter'd, in spite of pained loveliness;
Let us find out, if we must be constrain'd,
    Sandals more interwoven and complete
To fit the naked foot of poesy:
Let us inspect the lyre, and weigh the stress
Of every chord, and see what may be gain'd
    By ear industrious, and attention meet;
Misers of sound and syllable, no less   10
Than Midas of his coinage, let us be
    Jealous of dead leaves in the bay wreath
      crown;
So, if we may not let the Muse be free,
    She will be bound with garlands of her
    own.

A RENOUNCING OF LOVE

Sir Thomas Wyatt

Farewell, Love, and all thy laws for ever;
Thy baited hooks shall tangle me no more:
Senec and Plato call me from thy lore,
To perfect wealth, my wit for to endeavour;
In blind errour when I did persever,
Thy sharp repulse, that pricketh aye so sore,
Taught me in trifles that I set no store;
But 'scape forth thence, since liberty is lever:
Therefore, farewell, go trouble younger
    hearts,
And in me claim no more authority;   10
With idle youth go use thy property,
And thereon spend thy many brittle darts:
    For hitherto though I have lost my time,
    Me list no longer rotten boughs to climb.

l. 3. Senec: Seneca, a Roman philosopher.
l. 7. Taught me that I should set no store in trifles.
l. 8. lever: more desirable.

313

[SINCE THERE'S NO HELP, COME LET US KISS AND PART]

Michael Drayton
(1563–1631)

Since there's no help, come let us kiss and
    part;
Nay, I have done, you get no more of me,
And I am glad, yea glad with all my heart
That thus so cleanly I myself can free;
Shake hands for ever, cancel all our vows,
And when we meet at any time again,   6
Be it not seen in either of our brows
That we one jot of former love retain.
Now at the last gasp of love's latest breath,
When, his pulse failing, passion speechless
    lies,   10
When faith is kneeling by his bed of death,
And innocence is closing up his eyes,
    Now if thou wouldst, when all have given
      him over,
    From death to life thou mightst him yet
      recover.

SONNETS

William Shakespeare

18

Shall I compare thee to a summer's day?
Thou art more lovely and more temperate:
Rough winds do shake the darling buds of
    May,
And summer's lease hath all too short a date:
Sometime too hot the eye of heaven shines,
And often is his gold complexion dimm'd;
And every fair from fair sometime declines,
By chance, or nature's changing course un-
    trimm'd;
But thy eternal summer shall not fade,
Nor lose possession of that fair thou ow'st,

Nor shall Death brag thou wander'st in his
    shade,   11
When in eternal lines to time thou grow'st;
    So long as men can breathe, or eyes can see,
    So long lives this, and this gives life to
      thee.

l. 10. ow'st: ownest.

29

When in disgrace with fortune and men's
    eyes
I all alone beweep my outcast state,
And trouble deaf heaven with my bootless
    cries,
And look upon myself, and curse my fate,
Wishing me like to one more rich in hope,
Featur'd like him, like him with friends
    possess'd,
Desiring this man's art, and that man's scope,
With what I most enjoy contented least;
Yet in these thoughts myself almost despis-
    ing,
Haply I think on thee,—and then my state,
Like to the lark at break of day arising   11
From sullen earth, sings hymns at heaven's
    gate;
    For thy sweet love remember'd such wealth
      brings
    That then I scorn to change my state with
      kings.

30

When to the sessions of sweet silent thought
I summon up remembrance of things past,
I sigh the lack of many a thing I sought,
And with old woes new wail my dear times'
    waste:
Then can I drown an eye, unus'd to flow,
For precious friends hid in death's dateless
    night,
And weep afresh love's long since cancell'd
    woe,
And moan th' expense of many a vanish'd
    sight:
Then can I grieve at grievances foregone,
And heavily from woe to woe tell o'er   10
The sad account of fore-bemoaned moan,

Which I new pay as if not paid before.
    But if the while I think on thee, dear
        friend,
    All losses are restor'd and sorrows end.

33

Full many a glorious morning have I seen
Flatter the mountain-tops with sovereign eye,
Kissing with golden face the meadows green,
Gilding pale streams with heavenly alchemy;
Anon permit the basest clouds to ride
With ugly rack on his celestial face,
And from the forlorn world his visage hide,
Stealing unseen to west with this disgrace.
Even so my sun one early morn did shine
With all-triumphant splendour on my brow;
But, out! alack! he was but one hour mine,
The region cloud hath mask'd him from me
    now.   12
    Yet him for this my love no whit dis-
        daineth;
    Suns of the world may stain when heaven's
        sun staineth.

_____

l. 6. rack: a wind-driven mass of high clouds.
l. 14. stain: become darkened.

65

Since brass, nor stone, nor earth, nor bound-
    less sea,
But sad mortality o'er-sways their power,
How with this rage shall beauty hold a plea,
Whose action is no stronger than a flower?
O! how shall summer's honey breath hold out
Against the wrackful siege of batt'ring days,
When rocks impregnable are not so stout,
Nor gates of steel so strong, but Time de-
    cays?
O fearful meditation! where, alack,
Shall Time's best jewel from Time's chest lie
    hid?   10
Or what strong hand can hold his swift foot
    back?
Or who his spoil of beauty can forbid?
    O! none, unless this miracle have might,
    That in black ink my love may still shine
        bright.

71

No longer mourn for me when I am dead
Than you shall hear the surly sullen bell
Give warning to the world that I am fled
From this vile world, with vilest worms to
    dwell:
Nay, if you read this line, remember not
The hand that writ it; for I love you so,
That I in your sweet thoughts would be for-
    got,
If thinking on me then should make you woe.
O! if, I say, you look upon this verse,
When I perhaps compounded am with clay,
Do not so much as my poor name rehearse,
But let your love even with my life decay;
    Lest the wise world should look into your
        moan,   13
    And mock you with me after I am gone.

73

That time of year thou mayst in me behold
When yellow leaves, or none, or few, do hang
Upon those boughs which shake against the
    cold,
Bare ruin'd choirs, where late the sweet birds
    sang.
In me thou see'st the twilight of such day
As after sunset fadeth in the west,
Which by and by black night doth take away,
Death's second self, that seals up all in rest.
In me thou see'st the glowing of such fire
That on the ashes of his youth doth lie,   10
As the death-bed whereon it must expire,
Consum'd with that which it was nourish'd
    by.
    This thou perceiv'st, which makes thy love
        more strong,
    To love that well which thou must leave
        ere long.

106

When in the chronicle of wasted time
I see descriptions of the fairest wights,
And beauty making beautiful old rime,
In praise of ladies dead and lovely knights;
Then, in the blazon of sweet beauty's best,

Of hand, of foot, of lip, of eye, of brow,
I see their antique pen would have express'd
Even such a beauty as you master now.
So all their praises are but prophecies
Of this our time, all you prefiguring;   10
And, for they look'd but with divining eyes,
They had not skill enough your worth to
    sing:
    For we, which now behold these present
        days,
    Have eyes to wonder, but lack tongues to
        praise.

116

Let me not to the marriage of true minds
Admit impediments. Love is not love
Which alters when it alteration finds,
Or bends with the remover to remove:
O, no! it is an ever-fixed mark
That looks on tempests and is never shaken;
It is the star to every wand'ring bark,
Whose worth's unknown, although his height
    be taken.
Love's not Time's fool, though rosy lips and
    cheeks   9
Within his bending sickle's compass come;
Love alters not with his brief hours and
    weeks,
But bears it out even to the edge of doom.
    If this be error, and upon me prov'd,
    I never writ, nor no man ever lov'd.

[WHEN I CONSIDER HOW MY LIGHT IS SPENT]

John Milton
(1608–1674)

When I consider how my light is spent,
E're half my days, in this dark world and
    wide,
And that one Talent which is death to hide,
Lodg'd with me useless, though my Soul more
    bent
To serve therewith my Maker, and present
My true account, least he returning chide,
Doth God exact day-labour, light deny'd,
I fondly ask; But patience to prevent

That murmur, soon replies, God doth not
    need
Either man's work or his own gifts, who best
Bear his milde yoak, they serve him best, his
    State   11
Is Kingly. Thousands at his bidding speed
And post o're Land and Ocean without rest:
They also serve who only stand and waite.

l. 6. least: lest.
l. 8. fondly: foolishly.

ON THE LATE MASSACRE IN PIEDMONT

John Milton

Avenge O Lord thy slaughter'd Saints, whose
    bones
Lie scatter'd on the Alpine mountains cold,
Ev'n them who kept thy truth so pure of old
When all our Fathers worship't Stocks and
    Stones,
Forget not: in thy book record their groanes
Who were thy Sheep and in their antient
    Fold
Slayn by the bloody *Piemontese* that roll'd
Mother with Infant down the Rocks. Their
    moans
The Vales redoubl'd to the Hills, and they
To Heav'n. Their martyr'd blood and ashes
    sow   10
O're all th' *Italian* fields where still doth sway
The triple Tyrant: that from these may grow
A hunder'd-fold, who having learnt thy way
Early may fly the *Babylonian* wo.

l. 12. triple Tyrant: the pope, who wears a triple-
crowned tiara.

COMPOSED UPON WESTMINSTER BRIDGE, SEPTEMBER 3, 1802

William Wordsworth

Earth has not anything to show more fair:
Dull would he be of soul who could pass by
A sight so touching in its majesty:
This City now doth, like a garment, wear

The beauty of the morning; silent, bare,
Ships, towers, domes, theatres, and temples lie
Open unto the fields, and to the sky;
All bright and glittering in the smokeless air.
Never did sun more beautifully steep
In his first splendour, valley, rock, or hill;
Ne'er saw I, never felt, a calm so deep!   11
The river glideth at his own sweet will:
Dear God! the very houses seem asleep;
And all that mighty heart is lying still!

[THE WORLD IS TOO MUCH WITH US]

William Wordsworth

The world is too much with us; late and soon,
Getting and spending, we lay waste our powers:
Little we see in Nature that is ours;
We have given our hearts away, a sordid boon!
This Sea that bares her bosom to the moon;
The winds that will be howling at all hours,
And are up-gathered now like sleeping flowers;
For this, for everything, we are out of tune;
It moves us not.—Great God! I'd rather be
A Pagan suckled in a creed outworn;   10
So might I, standing on this pleasant lea,
Have glimpses that would make me less forlorn;
Have sight of Proteus rising from the sea;
Or hear old Triton blow his wreathèd horn.

ll. 13–14. Proteus and Triton: sea gods of classical mythology.

ON FIRST LOOKING INTO CHAPMAN'S HOMER

John Keats

Much have I travell'd in the realms of gold,
    And many goodly states and kingdoms seen;
Round many western islands have I been
Which bards in fealty to Apollo hold.
Oft of one wide expanse had I been told
    That deep-brow'd Homer ruled as his demesne;
    Yet did I never breathe its pure serene
Till I heard Chapman speak out loud and bold:
Then felt I like some watcher of the skies
    When a new planet swims into his ken;
Or like stout Cortez when with eagle eyes
    He star'd at the Pacific—and all his men   12
Look'd at each other with a wild surmise—
    Silent, upon a peak in Darien.

l. 11. Cortez: a mistake for Balboa.

[WHEN I HAVE FEARS THAT I MAY CEASE TO BE]

John Keats

When I have fears that I may cease to be
    Before my pen has glean'd my teeming brain,
Before high-piled books, in charact'ry,
    Hold like rich garners the full-ripen'd grain;
When I behold, upon the night's starr'd face,
    Huge cloudy symbols of a high romance,
And think that I may never live to trace
    Their shadows, with the magic hand of chance;
And when I feel, fair creature of an hour!
    That I shall never look upon thee more,
Never have relish in the faery power   11
    Of unreflecting love!—then on the shore
Of the wide world I stand alone, and think
Till love and fame to nothingness do sink.

SONNET NO. 23

Robert Bridges
(1844–1930)

[from *The Growth of Love*]

O weary pilgrims, chanting of your woe,
That turn your eyes to all the peaks that shine,

Hailing in each the citadel divine
The which ye thought to have enter'd long
   ago;
Until at length your feeble steps and slow
Falter upon the threshold of the shrine,
And your hearts overburden'd doubt in fine
Whether it be Jerusalem or no:

Dishearten'd pilgrims, I am one of you;
For, having worshipp'd many a barren face,
I scarce now greet the goal I journey'd to:
I stand a pagan in the holy place;   12
Beneath the lamp of truth I am found un-
   true,
And question with the God that I embrace.

8. IMAGE, MOVEMENT, AND PATTERN

FOG

Carl Sandburg
(1878–   )

The fog comes
on little cat feet.

It sits looking
over harbor and city
on silent haunches
and then moves on.

AUTUMN

T. E. Hulme
(1886–1917)

A touch of cold in the Autumn night—
I walked abroad,
And saw the ruddy moon lean over a hedge
Like a red-faced farmer.
I did not stop to speak, but nodded,
And round about were the wistful stars
With white faces like town children.

THE EMBANKMENT

*(The fantasia of a fallen gentleman
on a cold, bitter night.)*

T. E. Hulme

Once, in finesse of fiddles found I ecstasy,
In a flash of gold heels on the hard pavement.
Now see I
That warmth's the very stuff of poesy.
Oh, God, make small

The old star-eaten blanket of the sky,
That I may fold it round me and in comfort
lie.

———

Title. The embankment along the River Thames
in London.

THE BALLOON OF THE MIND

William Butler Yeats

Hands, do what you're bid:
Bring the balloon of the mind
That bellies and drags in the wind
Into its narrow shed.

[FRAGMENT]

Gerard Manley Hopkins
(1844–1889)

Strike, churl; hurl, cheerless wind, then;
heltering hail
May's beauty massacre and wispèd wild
clouds grow
Out on the giant air; tell Summer No,
Bid joy back, have at the harvest, keep Hope
pale.

TO AN ATHLETE DYING YOUNG

A. E. Housman

The time you won your town the race
We chaired you through the market-place;

Man and boy stood cheering by,
And home we brought you shoulder-high.

Today, the road all runners come,
Shoulder-high we bring you home,
And set you at your threshold down,
Townsman of a stiller town.

Smart lad, to slip betimes away
From fields where glory does not stay 10
And early though the laurel grows
It withers quicker than the rose.

Eyes the shady night has shut
Cannot see the record cut,
And silence sounds no worse than cheers
After earth has stopped the ears:

Now you will not swell the rout
Of lads that wore their honors out,
Runners whom renown outran
And the name died before the man. 20

So set, before its echoes fade,
The fleet foot on the sill of shade,
And hold to the low lintel up
The still-defended challenge-cup.

And round that early-laureled head
Will flock to gaze the strengthless dead,
And find unwithered on its curls
The garland briefer than a girl's.

a pretty a day

e. e. cummings

a pretty a day
(and every fades)
is here and away
(but born are maids
to flower an hour
in all,all)

o yes to flower
until so blithe
a doer a wooer
some limber and lithe 10

some very fine mower
a tall;tall

some jerry so very
(and nellie and fan)
some handsomest harry
(and sally and nan
they tremble and cower
so pale:pale)

for betty was born
to never say nay 20
but lucy could learn
and lily could pray
and fewer were shyer
than doll. doll

QUESTION

May Swenson
(contemporary)

Body my house
my horse my hound
what will I do
when you are fallen

Where will I sleep
How will I ride
What will I hunt

Where can I go
without my mount
all eager and quick 10
How will I know

in thicket ahead
is danger or treasure
when Body my good
bright dog is dead

How will it be
To lie in the sky
without roof or door
and wind for an eye

With cloud for shift 20
How will I hide?

---

l. 20. shift: chemise.

KUBLA KHAN

Samuel Taylor Coleridge
(1772–1834)

In Xanadu did Kubla Khan
A stately pleasure-dome decree:
Where Alph, the sacred river, ran
Through caverns measureless to man
  Down to a sunless sea.
So twice five miles of fertile ground
With walls and towers were girdled round:
And there were gardens bright with sinuous
  rills,
Where blossomed many an incense-bearing
  tree;
And here were forests ancient as the hills,
Enfolding sunny spots of greenery.   11

But oh! that deep romantic chasm which
  slanted
Down the green hill athwart a cedarn cover!
A savage place! as holy and enchanted
As e'er beneath a waning moon was haunted
By woman wailing for her demon-lover!
And from this chasm, with ceaseless turmoil
  seething,
As if this earth in fast thick pants were
  breathing,
A mighty fountain momently was forced:
Amid whose swift half-intermitted burst 20
Huge fragments vaulted like rebounding
  hail,
Or chaffy grain beneath the thresher's flail:
And 'mid these dancing rocks at once and
  ever
It flung up momently the sacred river.
Five miles meandering with a mazy motion
Through wood and dale the sacred river ran,
Then reached the caverns measureless to man,
And sank in tumult to a lifeless ocean:
And 'mid this tumult Kubla heard from far
Ancestral voices prophesying war! 30
  The shadow of the dome of pleasure
  Floated midway on the waves;
  Where was heard the mingled measure
  From the fountain and the caves.
It was a miracle of rare device,
A sunny pleasure-dome with caves of ice!

A damsel with a dulcimer
In a vision once I saw:
It was an Abyssinian maid,
And on her dulcimer she played, 40
Singing of Mount Abora.
Could I revive within me
Her symphony and song,
To such a deep delight 'twould win me,
That with music loud and long,
I would build that dome in air,
That sunny dome! those caves of ice!
And all who heard should see them there,
And all should cry, Beware! Beware!
His flashing eyes, his floating hair! 50
Weave a circle round him thrice,
And close your eyes with holy dread,
For he on honey-dew hath fed,
And drunk the milk of Paradise.

BIRDS AT WINTER NIGHTFALL
TRIOLET

Thomas Hardy
(1840–1928)

Around the house the flakes fly faster,
And all the berries now are gone
From holly and cotonea-aster
Around the house. The flakes fly!—faster
Shutting indoors that crumb-outcaster
We used to see upon the lawn
Around the house. The flakes fly faster,
And all the berries now are gone!

TRIOLET

Robert Bridges

When first we met we did not guess
That Love would prove so hard a master;
Of more than common friendliness
When first we met we did not guess.
Who could foretell this sore distress,
This irretrievable disaster
When first we met?—We did not guess
That Love would prove so hard a master.

9. REFLECTIONS ON EVERYDAY LIFE, MAN AND SOCIETY

THE CHIMNEY SWEEPER

William Blake
(1757–1827)

[from *Songs of Innocence*]

When my mother died I was very young,
And my father sold me while yet my tongue
Could scarcely cry " 'weep! 'weep! 'weep!
'weep!"
So your chimneys I sweep & in soot I sleep.

There's little Tom Dacre, who cried when his
head,
That curl'd like a lamb's back, was shav'd: so
I said,
"Hush, Tom! never mind it, for when your
head's bare
You know that the soot cannot spoil your
white hair."

And so he was quiet, & that very night,
As Tom was a-sleeping, he had such a sight!
That thousands of sweepers, Dick, Joe, Ned
& Jack,   11
Were all of them lock'd up in coffins of black.

And by came an Angel who had a bright key,
And he open'd the coffins & set them all free;
Then down a green plain leaping, laughing,
they run,
And wash in a river, and shine in the Sun.

Then naked & white, all their bags left behind,
They rise upon clouds, and sport in the wind;

And the Angel told Tom, if he'd be a good
boy,
He'd have God for his father, & never want
joy.   20

And so Tom awoke; and we rose in the dark,
And got with our bags & our brushes to work,
Tho' the morning was cold, Tom was happy
& warm;
So if all do their duty they need not fear
harm.

LONDON

William Blake

I wander thro' each charter'd street,
Near where the charter'd Thames does flow,
And mark in every face I meet
Marks of weakness, marks of woe.

In every cry of every Man,
In every Infant's cry of fear,
In every voice, in every ban,
The mind-forg'd manacles I hear.

How the Chimney-sweeper's cry
Every black'ning church appalls;   10
And the hapless Soldier's sigh
Runs in blood down Palace walls.

But most thro' midnight streets I hear
How the youthful Harlot's curse
Blasts the newborn Infant's tear,
And blights with plagues the Marriage
hearse.

from MILTON

William Blake

And did those feet in ancient time
  Walk upon England's mountains green?
And was the holy Lamb of God
  On England's pleasant pastures seen?

And did the Countenance Divine
  Shine forth upon our clouded hills?
And was Jerusalem builded here
  Among these dark Satanic Mills?

Bring me my Bow of burning gold:
  Bring me my Arrows of desire: 10
Bring me my Spear: O clouds unfold!
  Bring me my chariot of fire.

I will not cease from Mental Fight,
  Nor shall my Sword sleep in my hand
Till we have built Jerusalem
  In England's green & pleasant Land.

[WHAT I EXPECTED]

Stephen Spender
(1909–   )

What I expected, was
Thunder, fighting,
Long struggles with men
And climbing.
After continual straining
I should grow strong;
Then the rocks would shake
And I rest long.

What I had not foreseen
Was the gradual day   10
Weakening the will
Leaking the brightness away,
The lack of good to touch,
The fading of body and soul
—Smoke before wind,
Corrupt, unsubstantial.

The wearing of Time,
And the watching of cripples pass
With limbs shaped like questions
In their odd twist,   20
The pulverous grief
Melting the bones with pity,
The sick falling from earth—
These, I could not foresee.

Expecting always
Some brightness to hold in trust,
Some final innocence
Exempt from dust,
That, hanging solid,
Would dangle through all,   30
Like the created poem,
Or faceted crystal.

THE UNKNOWN CITIZEN
(TO JS/07/M/378
THIS MARBLE MONUMENT
IS ERECTED BY THE STATE)

W. H. Auden

He was found by the Bureau of Statistics to
  be
One against whom there was no official com-
  plaint,
And all the reports on his conduct agree
That, in the modern sense of an old-fashioned
  word, he was a saint,
For in everything he did he served the
  Greater Community.
Except for the War till the day he retired
He worked in a factory and never got fired,
But satisfied his employers, Fudge Motors
  Inc.
Yet he wasn't a scab or odd in his views,
For his Union reports that he paid his dues,
(Our report on his Union shows it was
  sound)   11
And our Social Psychology workers found
That he was popular with his mates and liked
  a drink.
The Press are convinced that he bought a
  paper every day
And that his reactions to advertisements were
  normal in every way.

Policies taken out in his name prove that he
was fully insured,
And his Health-card shows he was once in
hospital but left it cured.
Both Producers Research and High-Grade
Living declare
He was fully sensible to the advantages of
the Instalment Plan
And had everything necessary to the Modern
Man,   20
A phonograph, a radio, a car and a frigidaire.
Our researchers into Public Opinion are con-
tent
That he held the proper opinions for the time
of year;
When there was peace, he was for peace;
when there was war, he went.
He was married and added five children to
the population,
Which our Eugenist says was the right num-
ber for a parent of his generation,
And our teachers report that he never inter-
fered with their education.
Was he free? Was he happy? The question is
absurd:
Had anything been wrong, we should certainly have heard.

POT-LUCK AMONG THE CASUALS

Marsden Hartley

A dog came loping to his side:
"have you any of a speechless bone?"
"no—but I have foul weathers in
my head,
and why should you want another one?
you who are all but wrack of bone
and nearly dead,
why every wind plays tunes upon
your ribs; the birds could build a nest
in the hollow of your spine;   10
who is it fed you on broken stone,
you walking, pallid skeleton?"

He gave him hunk of what he had,
"'tis good enough for me; none," or so he
said,

"when you want to go, is sweeter,
from worse to something better;
bone will maybe sharpen teeth
but makes pain sharper underneath;
a bowl of downright summer blood
would do you heaps of good."   20

The dog looked up to him and said,
"save me, save me from a speedy grave,
give anything of what you have";
he gave two hunks of what he little had
it was as if his jaw would crack
it felt so good;
a smile came out of canine face
and fairly shamed the listless place;
a dog that wants is tragical to see;
we're used to men that get that way.   30

BAGPIPE MUSIC

Louis MacNeice

It's no go the merry-go-round, it's no go the
rickshaw,
All we want is a limousine and ticket for the
peepshow.
Their knickers are made of crêpe-de-chine,
their shoes are made of python,
Their halls are lined with tiger rugs and their
walls with heads of bison.

John MacDonald found a corpse, put it under
the sofa,
Waited till it came to life and hit it with a
poker,
Sold its eyes for souvenirs, sold its blood for
whiskey,
Kept its bones for dumb-bells to use when he
was fifty.

It's no go the Yogi-Man, it's no go Blavatsky,
All we want is a bank balance and a bit of
skirt in a taxi.   10

Annie MacDougall went to milk, caught her
foot in the heather,
Woke to hear a dance record playing of Old
Vienna.
It's no go your maidenheads, it's no go your
culture,

All we want is a Dunlop tyre and the devil
mend the puncture.

The Laird o'Phelps spent Hogmannay de-
claring he was sober;
Counted his feet to prove the fact and found
he had one foot over.
Mrs. Carmichael had her fifth, looked at the
job with repulsion,
Said to the midwife "Take it away; I'm
through with overproduction."

It's no go the gossip column, it's no go the
Ceilidh,
All we want is a mother's help and a sugar-
stick for the baby.   20

Willie Murray cut his thumb, couldn't count
the damage,
Took the hide of an Ayrshire cow and used
it for a bandage.
His brother caught three hundred cran when
the seas were lavish,
Threw the bleeders back in the sea and went
upon the parish.

It's no go the Herring Board, it's no go the
Bible,
All we want is a packet of fags when our
hands are idle.

It's no go the picture palace, it's no go the
stadium,
It's no go the country cot with a pot of pink
geraniums.
It's no go the Government grants, it's no go
the elections,
Sit on your arse for fifty years and hang your
hat on a pension.   30

It's no go my honey love, it's no go my pop-
pet;
Work your hands from day to day, the winds
will blow the profit.
The glass is falling hour by hour, the glass
will fall for ever,
But if you break the bloody glass you won't
hold up the weather.

l. 15. Hogmannay: New Year's Eve in Scotland.
l. 19. Ceilidh (pron. *Kaily*): a social gathering.
l. 23. cran: unit of measure for herring.

SUNDAY MORNING

Louis MacNeice

Down the road some one is practising scales,
The notes like little fishes vanish with a wink
of tails,
Man's heart expands to tinker with his car
For this is Sunday morning, Fate's great
bazaar;
Regard these means as ends, concentrate on
this Now,
And you may grow to music or drive beyond
Hindhead anyhow,
Take corners on two wheels until you go so
fast
That you can clutch a fringe or two of the
windy past,
That you can abstract this day and make it to
the week of time
A small eternity, a sonnet self-contained in
rhyme.   10

But listen, up the road, something gulps, the
church spire
Opens its eight bells out, skulls' mouths
which will not tire
To tell how there is no music or movement
that ensures
Escape from the weekday time. Which dead-
ens and endures.

THE INQUISITORS

Robinson Jeffers
(1887–   )

Coming around a corner of the dark trail
. . . what was wrong with the valley?
Azevedo checked his horse and sat staring: it
was all changed. It was occupied. There
were three hills
Where none had been: and firelight flickered
red on their knees between them: if they
were hills:

They were more like Red Indians around a
    camp-fire, grave and dark, mountain-high,
    hams on heels
Squatting around a little fire of hundred-foot
    logs. Azevedo remembers he felt an ice-
    brook
Glide on his spine; he slipped down from
    the saddle and hid
In the brush by the trail, above the black red-
    wood forest. There was the Little Sur South
    Fork,
Its forest valley; the man had come in at
    nightfall over Bowcher's Gap, and a high
    moon hunted
Through running clouds. He heard the rum-
    ble of a voice, heavy not loud, saying, "I
    gathered some,
You can inspect them." One of the hills
    moved a huge hand   10
And poured its contents on a table-topped
    rock that stood in the firelight; men and
    women fell out;
Some crawled and some lay quiet; the hills
    leaned to eye them. One said: "It seems
    hardly possible
Such fragile creatures could be so noxious."
    Another answered,
"True, but we've seen. But it is only recently
    they have the power." The third answered,
    "That bomb?"
"Oh," he said, "—and the rest." He reached
    across and picked up one of the mites
    from the rock, and held it
Close to his eyes, and very carefully with
    finger and thumbnail peeled it: by chance
    a young female
With long black hair: it was too helpless
    even to scream. He held it by one white
    leg and stared at it:
"I can see nothing strange: only so fragile."

The third hill answered, "We suppose it is
    something
Inside the head." Then the other split the
    skull with his thumbnail, squinting his eyes
    and peering, and said,
"A drop of marrow. How could that spoil the
    earth?" "Nevertheless," he answered,   20
"They have that bomb. The blasts and the
    fires are nothing: freckles on the earth:
    the emanations
Might set the whole planet into a tricky fever
And destroy much." "Themselves," he an-
    swered. "Let them. Why not?" "No," he
    answered, "life."

Azevedo

Still watched in horror, and all three of the
    hills
Picked little animals from the rock, peeled
    them and cracked them, or toasted them
On the red coals, or split their bodies from
    the crotch upward
To stare inside. They said, "It remains a
    mystery. However," they said,
"It is not likely they can destroy all life: the
    planet is capacious. Life would surely grow
    up again
From grubs in the soil, or the newt and toad
    level, and be beautiful again. And again
    perhaps break its legs
On its own cleverness: who can forecast the
    future?" The speaker yawned, and with his
    flat hand   30
Brushed the rock clean; the three slowly
    stood up,
Taller than Pico Blanco into the sky, their
    Indian-beaked heads in the moon-cloud,
And trampled their watchfire out and went
    away southward, stepping across the Ven-
    tana mountains.

10. MODERN POETIC TECHNIQUE

THE LOVE SONG OF J. ALFRED PRUFROCK

T. S. Eliot

(1888–   )

S'io credesse che mia risposta fosse
A persona che mai tornasse al mondo,
Questa fiamma staria senza piu scosse.
Ma perciocche giammai di questo fondo
Non torno vivo alcun, s'i'odo il vero,
Senza tema d'infamia ti rispondo.

Let us go then, you and I,
When the evening is spread out against the
    sky
Like a patient etherised upon a table;
Let us go, through certain half-deserted
    streets,
The muttering retreats
Of restless nights in one-night cheap hotels
And sawdust restaurants with oyster-shells:
Streets that follow like a tedious argument
Of insidious intent
To lead you to an overwhelming ques-
    tion . . .   10
Oh, do not ask, "What is it?"
Let us go and make our visit.

In the room the women come and go
Talking of Michelangelo.

The yellow fog that rubs its back upon the
    window-panes,
The yellow smoke that rubs its muzzle on the
    window-panes
Licked its tongue into the corners of the
    evening,
Lingered upon the pools that stand in drains,
Let fall upon its back the soot that falls from
    chimneys,
Slipped by the terrace, made a sudden leap,
And seeing that it was a soft October night,
Curled once about the house, and fell asleep.

And indeed there will be time   23
For the yellow smoke that slides along the
    street,
Rubbing its back upon the window-panes;
There will be time, there will be time
To prepare a face to meet the faces that you
    meet;
There will be time to murder and create,
And time for all the works and days of hands
That lift and drop a question on your plate;
Time for you and time for me,   31
And time yet for a hundred indecisions,
And for a hundred visions and revisions,
Before the taking of a toast and tea.

In the room the women come and go
Talking of Michelangelo.

And indeed there will be time
To wonder, "Do I dare?" and, "Do I dare?"
Time to turn back and descend the stair,
With a bald spot in the middle of my hair—
[They will say: "How his hair is growing
    thin!"]   41
My morning coat, my collar mounting firmly
    to the chin,
My necktie rich and modest, but asserted by a
    simple pin—
[They will say: "But how his arms and legs
    are thin!"]
Do I dare
Disturb the universe?
In a minute there is time
For decisions and revisions which a minute
    will reverse.

For I have know them all already, known
        them all:—
Have known the evenings, mornings, after-
        noons,   50
I have measured out my life with coffee
        spoons;
I know the voices dying with a dying fall
Beneath the music from a farther room.
        So how should I presume?

And I have known the eyes already, known
        them all—
The eyes that fix you in a formulated phrase,
And when I am formulated, sprawling on a
        pin,
When I am pinned and wriggling on the wall,
Then how should I begin
To spit out all the butt-ends of my days and
        ways?   60
        And how should I presume?

And I have known the arms already,
        known them all—
Arms that are braceleted and white and bare
[But in the lamplight, downed with light
        brown hair!]
Is it perfume from a dress
That makes me so digress?
Arms that lie along a table, or wrap about a
        shawl.
        And should I then presume?
        And how should I begin?

                .   .   .   .   .

Shall I say, I have gone at dusk through nar-
        row streets   70
And watched the smoke that rises from the
        pipes
Of lonely men in shirt-sleeves, leaning out of
        windows? . . .

I should have been a pair of ragged claws
Scuttling across the floors of silent seas.

                .   .   .   .   .

And the afternoon, the evening, sleeps so
        peacefully!
Smoothed by long fingers,
Asleep . . . tired . . . or it malingers,

Stretched on the floor, here beside you and
        me.
Should I, after tea and cakes and ices,
Have the strength to force the moment to its
        crisis?   80
But though I have wept and fasted, wept and
        prayed,
Though I have seen my head [grown slightly
        bald] brought in upon a platter,
I am no prophet—and here's no great matter;
I have seen the moment of my greatness
        flicker,
And I have seen the eternal Footman hold
        my coat, and snicker,
And in short, I was afraid.

        And would it have been worth it, after all,
After the cups, the marmalade, the tea,
Among the porcelain, among some talk of
        you and me,
Would it have been worth while,   90
To have bitten off the matter with a smile,
To have squeezed the universe into a ball
To roll it toward some overwhelming ques-
        tion,
To say: "I am Lazarus, come from the dead,
Come back to tell you all, I shall tell you
        all"—
If one, settling a pillow by her head,
        Should say: "That is not what I meant at
        all.
        That is not it, at all."

        And would it have been worth it, after all,
Would it have been worth while,   100
After the sunsets and the dooryards and the
        sprinkled streets,
After the novels, after the teacups, after the
        skirts that trail along the floor—
And this, and so much more?—
It is impossible to say just what I mean!
But as if a magic lantern threw the nerves in
        patterns on a screen:
Would it have been worth while
If one, settling a pillow or throwing off a
        shawl,
And turning toward the window, should say:
        "That is not it at all,
        That is not what I meant, at all."   110

                .   .   .   .   .

No! I am not Prince Hamlet, nor was meant
    to be;
Am an attendant lord, one that will do
To swell a progress, start a scene or two,
Advise the prince; no doubt, an easy tool,
Deferential, glad to be of use,
Politic, cautious, and meticulous;
Full of high sentence, but a bit obtuse;
At times, indeed, almost ridiculous—
Almost, at times, the Fool.

    I grow old . . . I grow old . . .   120
I shall wear the bottoms of my trousers rolled.

    Shall I part my hair behind? Do I dare to
      eat a peach?
I shall wear white flannel trousers, and walk
    upon the beach.
I have heard the mermaids singing, each to
    each.

    I do not think that they will sing to me.

    I have seen them riding seaward on the
    waves
Combing the white hair of the waves blown
    back
When the wind blows the water white and
    black.

    We have lingered in the chambers of the
    sea
By sea-girls wreathed with seaweed red and
    brown   130
Till human voices wake us, and we drown.

COLONEL FANTOCK
(to Osbert and Sacheverell)

Edith Sitwell
(1887–   )

Thus spoke the lady underneath the trees:
I was a member of a family
Whose legend was of hunting—(all the rare
And unattainable brightness of the air)—
A race whose fabled skill in falconry
Was used on the small songbirds and a
    winged

And blinded Destiny. . . . I think that only
Winged ones know the highest eyrie is so
    lonely.
There in a land, austere and elegant,
The castle seemed an arabesque in music;
We moved in an hallucination born   11
Of silence, which like music gave us lotus
To eat, perfuming lips and our long eyelids
As we trailed over the sad summer grass,
Or sat beneath a smooth and mournful tree.

And Time passed, suavely, imperceptibly.

But Dagobert and Peregrine and I
Were children then; we walked like shy
    gazelles
Among the music of the thin flower-bells.
And life still held some promise—never ask
Of what—but life seemed less a stranger
    then,   21
Than ever after in this cold existence.
I always was a little outside life—
And so the things we touch could comfort
    me;
I loved the shy dreams we could hear and
    see—
For I was like one dead, like a small ghost,
A little cold air wandering and lost.

All day within the straw-roofed arabesque
Of the towered castle and the sleepy gardens
    wandered
We; those delicate paladins, the waves   30
Told us fantastic legends that we pondered.

And the soft leaves were breasted like a dove,
Crooning old mournful tales of untrue love.

When night came, sounding like the growth
    of trees,
My great-grandmother bent to say good
    night,
And the enchanted moonlight seemed trans-
    formed
Into the silvery tinkling of an old
And gentle music-box that played a tune
Of Circean enchantments and far seas;
Her voice was lulling like the splash of
    these.   40
When she had given me her good-night
    kiss,

There, in her lengthened shadow, I saw this
Old military ghost with May-fly whiskers—
Poor harmless creature, blown by the cold
    wind,
Boasting of unseen unreal victories
To a harsh unbelieving world unkind:
For all the battles that this warrior fought
Were with cold poverty and helpless age—
His spoils were shelters from the winter's
    rage.
And so forever through his braggart voice,
Through all that martial trumpet's sound, his
    soul   51
Wept with a little sound so pitiful,
Knowing that he is outside life forever
With no one that will warm or comfort
    him. . . .
He is not even dead, but Death's buffoon
On a bare stage, a shrunken pantaloon.
His military banner never fell,
Nor his account of victories, the stories
Of old apocryphal misfortunes, glories
Which comforted his heart in later life   60
When he was the Napoleon of the school-
    room
And all the victories he gained were over
Little boys who would not learn to spell.

All day within the sweet and ancient gardens
He had my childish self for audience—
Whose body flat and strange, whose pale
    straight hair
Made me appear as though I had been
    drowned—
(We all have the remote air of a legend)—
And Dagobert my brother, whose large
    strength,
Great body, and grave beauty still reflect   70
The Angevin dead kings from whom we
    spring;
And sweet as the young tender winds that
    stir
In thickets when the earliest flower-bells sing
Upon the boughs was his just character;
And Peregrine the youngest with a naïve
Shy grace like a faun's, whose slant eyes
    seemed
The warm green light beneath eternal
    boughs.
His hair was like the fronds of feathers, life

In him was changing ever, springing fresh
As the dark songs of birds . . . the furry
    warmth   80
And purring sound of fires was in his voice,
Which never failed to warm and comfort me.

And there were haunted summers in Troy
    Park
When all the stillness budded into leaves;
We listened, like Ophelia drowned in blond
And fluid hair, beneath stag-antlered trees;
Then in the ancient park the country-pleas-
    ant
Shadows fell as brown as any pheasant,
And Colonel Fantock seemed like one of
    these.
Sometimes for comfort in the castle kitchen
He drowsed, where with a sweet and velvet
    lip   91
The snapdragons within the fire
Of their red summer never tire.
And Colonel Fantock liked our company;
For us he wandered over each old lie,
Changing the flowering hawthorn, full of
    bees,
Into the silver helm of Hercules,
For us defended Troy from the top stair
Outside the nursery, when the calm full
    moon
Was like the sound within the growth of
    trees.   100

But then came one cruel day in deepest June,
When pink flowers seemed a sweet Mozartian
    tune,
And Colonel Fantock pondered o'er a book.
A gay voice like a honeysuckle nook—
So sweet—said, "It is Colonel Fantock's age
Which makes him babble." . . . Blown by
    winter's rage,
The poor old man then knew his creeping
    fate,
The darkening shadow that would take his
    sight
And hearing; and he thought of his saved
    pence
Which scarce would rent a grave . . . That
    youthful voice   110
Was a dark bell which ever clanged "Too
    late"—

A creeping shadow that would steal from him
Even the little boys who would not spell—
His only prisoners. . . . On that June day
Cold Death had taken his first citadel.

AFTER THE FUNERAL
(*In memory of Ann Jones*)

Dylan Thomas
(1914–1953)

After the funeral, mule praises, brays,
Windshake of sailshaped ears, muffle-toed
    tap
Tap happily of one peg in the thick
Grave's foot, blinds down the lids, the teeth
    in black,
The spittled eyes, the salt ponds in the
    sleeves,
Morning smack of the spade that wakes up
    sleep,
Shakes a desolate boy who slits his throat
In the dark of the coffin and sheds dry leaves,
That breaks one bone to light with a judg-
    ment clout,
After the feast of tear-stuffed time and
    thistles   10
In a room with a stuffed fox and a stale fern,
I stand, for this memorial's sake, alone
In the snivelling hours with dead, humped
    Ann
Whose hooded, fountain heart once fell in
    puddles
Round the parched worlds of Wales and
    drowned each sun
(Though this for her is a monstrous image
    blindly
Magnified out of praise; her death was a still
    drop;

She would not have me sinking in the holy
Flood of her heart's fame; she would lie dumb
    and deep
And need no druid of her broken body).   20
But I, Ann's bard on a raised hearth, call all
The seas to service that her wood-tongued
    virtue
Babble like a bellbuoy over the hymning
    heads,
Bow down the walls of the ferned and foxy
    woods
That her love sing and swing through a
    brown chapel,
Bless her bent spirit with four, crossing birds.
Her flesh was meek as milk, but this skyward
    statue
With the wild breast and blessed and giant
    skull
Is carved from her in a room with a wet
    window
In a fiercely mourning house in a crooked
    year.   30
I know her scrubbed and sour humble hands
Lie with religion in their cramp, her thread-
    bare
Whisper in a damp word, her wits drilled
    hollow,
Her fist of a face died clenched on a round
    pain;
And sculptured Ann is seventy years of stone.
These cloud-sopped, marble hands, this mon-
    umental
Argument of the hewn voice, gesture and
    psalm
Storm me forever over her grave until
The stuffed lung of the fox twitch and cry
    Love
And the strutting fern lay seeds on the black
    sill.   40

11. NATURE AND THE MACHINE AGE

[SUMER IS ICUMEN IN]

Anon.

(probably late thirteenth century)

Sumer is icumen in,
  Lhude sing cuccu!
Groweth sed and bloweth med
  And springth the wode nu.
    Sing cuccu!
Awe bleteth after lomb,
  Lhouth after calve cu
Bulluc sterteth, bucke verteth.
  Murie sing cuccu!
    Cuccu, cuccu,   10
  Wel singes thu, cuccu
  Ne swik thu naver nu!
Sing cuccu nu, Sing cuccu!
Sing cuccu, Sing cuccu nu!

l. 2. Lhude: loud.
l. 3. sed: seed. bloweth med: blossoms [the]
meadow.
l. 4. wode: wood. nu: now.
l. 6. Awe: ewe.
l. 7. Lhouth: loweth or lows. cu: cow.
l. 8. sterteth: leaps. verteth: probably veers or
starts.
l. 9. murie: merrily.
l. 12. swik: cease.

ANCIENT MUSIC

Ezra Pound

Winter is icummen in,
Lhude sing Goddamm,
Raineth drop and staineth slop,
And how the wind doth ramm!
    Sing: Goddamm.

Skiddeth bus and sloppeth us,
An ague hath my ham.
Freezeth river, turneth liver,
    Damn you, sing: Goddamm.
Goddamm, Goddamm, 'tis why I am, God-
damm,   10
    So 'gainst the winter's balm.
Sing goddamm, damm, sing Goddamm,
Sing goddamm, sing goddamm, DAMM.

SPRING

William Shakespeare

When daisies pied and violets blue
  And lady-smocks all silver-white
And cuckoo-buds of yellow hue
  Do paint the meadows with delight,
The cuckoo then, on every tree,
Mocks married men; for thus sings he,
            Cuckoo;
Cuckoo, cuckoo: O, word of fear,
Unpleasing to a married ear!

When shepherds pipe on oaten straws,   10
  And merry larks are plowmen's clocks,
When turtles tread, and rooks, and daws,
  And maidens bleach their summer smocks,
The cuckoo then, on every tree,
Mocks married men; for thus sings he,
            Cuckoo;
Cuckoo, cuckoo: O, word of fear,
Unpleasing to a married ear!

l. 2. lady-smocks: a white-flowered plant of the
cress family.
l. 3. The name *cuckoo-flower* was applied to several different species of plant.
l. 12. turtles: turtle-doves. tread: mate.

WINTER

William Shakespeare

When icicles hang by the wall,
   And Dick the shepherd blows his nail,
And Tom bears logs into the hall,
   And milk comes frozen home in pail,
When blood is nipp'd, and ways be foul,
Then nightly sings the staring owl,
            Tu-who;
Tu-whit, tu-who—a merry note,
While greasy Joan doth keel the pot.

When all aloud the wind doth blow,   10
   And coughing drowns the parson's saw,
And birds sit brooding in the snow,
   And Marian's nose looks red and raw,
When roasted crabs hiss in the bowl,
Then nightly sings the staring owl,
            Tu-who;
Tu-whit, tu-who—a merry note,
While greasy Joan doth keel the pot.

l. 8. keel: cool.
l. 13. crabs: crabapples, used to flavor a bowl of
ale.

O sweet spontaneous

e. e. cummings

O sweet spontaneous
earth how often have
the
doting

      fingers of
prurient philosophers pinched
and
poked

thee
, has the naughty thumb   10
of science prodded
thy

beauty   . how
often have religions taken
thee upon their scraggy knees
squeezing and

buffeting thee that thou mightest conceive
gods
      (but
true   20

to the incomparable
couch of death thy
rhythmic
lover

      thou answerest

them only with

         spring)

CHANSONS INNOCENTES

e. e. cummings

I

in Just-
spring   when the world is mud-
luscious the little
lame balloonman

whistles   far   and wee

and eddieandbill come
running from marbles and
piracies and it's
spring

when the world is puddle-wonderful   10

the queer
old balloonman whistles
far   and   wee
and bettyandisbel come dancing

from hop-scotch and jump-rope and
it's

spring
and
  the

     goat-footed   20

balloonMan   whistles
far
and
wee

FERN HILL

Dylan Thomas

Now as I was young and easy under the
    apple boughs
About the lilting house and happy as the
    grass was green,
    The night above the dingle starry,
      Time let me hail and climb
    Golden in the heydays of his eyes,
And honoured among wagons I was prince
    of the apple towns
And once below a time I lordly had the
    trees and leaves
    Trail with daisies and barley
    Down the rivers of the windfall light.

And as I was green and carefree, famous
    among the barns   10
About the happy yard and singing as the
    farm was home,
    In the sun that is young once only,
      Time let me play and be
    Golden in the mercy of his means,
And green and golden I was huntsman and
    herdsman, the calves
Sang to my horn, the foxes on the hills
    barked clear and cold,
    And the sabbath rang slowly
    In the pebbles of the holy streams.

All the sun long it was running, it was
    lovely, the hay
Fields high as the house, the tunes from the
    chimneys, it was air   20

And playing, lovely and watery
    And fire green as grass.
And nightly under the simple stars
As I rode to sleep the owls were bearing the
    farm away,
All the moon long I heard, blessed among
    stables, the nightjars
    Flying with the ricks, and the horses
    Flashing into the dark.

And then to awake, and the farm, like a
    wanderer white
With the dew, come back, the cock on his
    shoulder: it was all
    Shining, it was Adam and maiden,   30
    The sky gathered again
And the sun grew round that very day.
So it must have been after the birth of the
    simple light
In the first, spinning place, the spellbound
    horses walking warm
    Out of the whinnying green stable
    On to the fields of praise.

And honoured among foxes and pheasants
    by the gay house
Under the new made clouds and happy as
    the heart was long,
    In the sun born over and over,
      I ran my heedless ways,   40
    My wishes raced through the house high
    hay
And nothing I cared, at my sky blue trades,
    that time allows
In all his tuneful turning so few and such
    morning songs
    Before the children green and golden
    Follow him out of grace,

Nothing I cared, in the lamb white days,
    that time would take me
Up to the swallow thronged loft by the
    shadow of my hand,
    In the moon that is always rising,
    Nor that riding to sleep
    I should hear him fly with the high fields
And wake to the farm forever fled from the
    childless land.   51
Oh as I was young and easy in the mercy of
    his means,

Time held me green and dying
Though I sang in my chains like the sea.

---

l. 25. nightjars: birds related to the whippoor-
wills.

THE GALLOWS

Edward Thomas
(1878–1917)

There was a weasel lived in the sun
With all his family,
Till a keeper shot him with his gun
And hung him up on a tree,
Where he swings in the wind and rain
In the sun and in the snow,
Without pleasure, without pain,
On the dead oak tree bough.

There was a crow who was no sleeper,
But a thief and a murderer   10
Till a very late hour; and this keeper
Made him one of the things that were,
To hang and flap in rain and wind
In the sun and in the snow.
There are no more sins to be sinned
On the dead oak tree bough.

There was a magpie, too,
Had a long tongue and a long tail;
He could both talk and do—
But what did that avail?   20
He, too, flaps in the wind and rain
Alongside weasel and crow,
Without pleasure, without pain,
On the dead oak tree bough.

And many other beasts
And birds, skin, bone, and feather,
Have been taken from their feasts
And hung up there together.
To swing and have endless leisure
In the sun and in the snow,   30
Without pain, without pleasure,
On the dead oak tree bough.

OUT IN THE DARK

Edward Thomas

Out in the dark over the snow
The fallow fawns invisible go
With the fallow doe;
And the winds blow
Fast as the stars are slow.

Stealthily the dark haunts round
And, when the lamp goes, without sound
At a swifter bound
Than the swiftest hound,
Arrives, and all else is drowned;   10

And I and star and wind and deer,
Are in the dark together,—near,
Yet far,—and fear
Drums on my ear
In that sage company drear.

How weak and little is the light,
All the universe of sight,
Love and delight,
Before the might,
If you love it not, of night.   20

---

l. 2. The fallow deer is a small pale-yellow European deer.

THE HERMIT

William H. Davies
(1870–1940)

What moves that lonely man is not the boom
    Of waves that break against the cliff so
        strong;
Nor roar of thunder, when that traveling
    voice
    Is caught by rocks that carry far along.

'Tis not the groan of oak tree in its prime,
    When lightning strikes its solid heart to
        dust;

Nor frozen pond when, melted by the sun,
  It suddenly doth break its sparkling crust.

What moves that man is when the blind bat
    taps
  His window when he sits alone at night;
Or when the small bird sounds like some
    great beast   11
  Among the dead, dry leaves so frail and
    light.

Or when the moths on his night-pillow beat
  Such heavy blows he fears they'll break
    his bones;
Or when a mouse inside the papered walls,
  Comes like a tiger crunching through the
    stones.

[I HEAR THE CRIES
OF EVENING]

Stephen Spender

I hear the cries of evening, while the paw
Of dark, creeps up the turf:
Sheep bleating, swaying gulls' cry, the rook's
    "Caw,"
The hammering surf.

I am inconstant, yet this constancy
Of natural rest, pulls at my heart;
Town-bred, I feel the roots of each earth-
    cry
Tear me apart.

These are the creakings of the dusty day
When the dog Night bites sharp,   10
These fingers grip my soul and tear away
And pluck me like a harp.

I feel the huge sphere turn, the great wheel
    sing
While beasts move to their ease:
Sheep's love, gulls' peace—I feel my chatter-
    ing
Uncared by these.

DESERT PLACES

Robert Frost

Snow falling and night falling fast, oh, fast
In a field I looked into going past,
And the ground almost covered smooth in
    snow,
But a few weeds and stubble showing last.

The woods around it have it—it is theirs.
All animals are smothered in their lairs.
I am too absent-spirited to count;
The loneliness includes me unawares.

And lonely as it is that loneliness
Will be more lonely ere it will be less—   10
A blanker whiteness of benighted snow
With no expression, nothing to express.

They cannot scare me with their empty
    spaces
Between stars—on stars where no human
    race is.
I have it in me so much nearer home
To scare myself with my own desert places.

UNDER COVER

Abbie Huston Evans

Rain with the old sound, with the country
    sough
From fields and meadows overpast and trees
That strip it into whip-lash, I hear now
Beat on this hill and cut about its knees.
Now while the lithe wind turns and springs
    again
On the spent tree, and rain floods down the
    glass,
I hear the sounds earth knew before we men
Came on, and shall know after we shall pass.
While ancient rumor rising to a shriek
Comes in to tell of matters we forget,   10
I am one more of the beasts of the field in
    bleak

Ecstatic cover, huddled from the wet.
So stands the ox, so crouches now the mole,
So sits the dry woodpecker in his hole.

EUROCLYDON

Abbie Huston Evans
(1881–   )

The east-northeaster pounds the coast to-
night,
Thudding and grinding at the knees of
islands;
It sets the bell-buoys clanging and calls out
The gruff storm-warnings up and down the
coast.
—So this, none else, was Paul's Euroclydon,
That old tempestuous wind that leaped from
Crete
And heaped the seas up till they broke the
ship,
But not the man. —Pull out the Book again:
"When the south wind blew softly—" (O
sweet words,
The spring is in them. Hark!)—"we loosed
from Crete."   10
I sit and listen while Euroclydon,
That old storm-wind that had a name of its
own
Two thousand years before I yet had mine,
Pelts on my pane with blizzard snow like
grit,
Shrieks down my chimney, grips my house
foursquare,
And pants against my door.

Old tiger, hail!

TO A LOCOMOTIVE IN WINTER

Walt Whitman
(1819–1892)

Thee for my recitative,
Thee in the driving storm even as now, the snow, the winter-day declining,
Thee in thy panoply, thy measur'd dual throbbing and thy beat convulsive,
Thy black cylindric body, golden brass and silvery steel,
Thy ponderous side-bars, parallel and connecting rods, gyrating, shuttling at thy sides,
Thy metrical, now swelling pant and roar, now tapering in the distance,
Thy great protruding head-light fix'd in front,
Thy long, pale, floating vapor-pennants, tinged with delicate purple,
The dense and murky clouds out-belching from thy smoke-stack,
Thy knitted frame, thy springs and valves, the tremulous twinkle of thy wheels,   10
Thy train of cars behind, obedient, merrily following,
Through gale or calm, now swift, now slack, yet steadily careering;
Type of the modern—emblem of motion and power—pulse of the continent,
For once come serve the Muse and merge in verse, even as here I see thee,
With storm and buffeting gusts of wind and falling snow,
By day thy warning ringing bell to sound its notes,
By night thy silent signal lamps to swing.

Fierce-throated beauty!
Roll through my chant with all thy lawless music, thy swinging lamps at night,

Thy madly-whistled laughter, echoing, rumbling like an earthquake, rousing all,   20
Law of thyself complete, thine own track firmly holding,
(No sweetness debonair of tearful harp or glib piano thine,)
Thy trills of shrieks by rocks and hills return'd,
Launch'd o'er the prairies wide, across the lakes,
To the free skies unpent and glad and strong.

[I LIKE TO SEE IT LAP THE MILES]

Emily Dickinson

I like to see it lap the Miles—
And lick the Valleys up—
And stop to feed itself at Tanks—
And then—prodigious step

Around a Pile of Mountains—
And supercilious peer
In Shanties—by the sides of Roads—
And then a Quarry pare

To fit it's sides
And crawl between   10
Complaining all the while
In horrid—hooting stanza—
Then chase itself down Hill—

And neigh like Boanerges—
Then—prompter than a Star
Stop—docile and omnipotent
At it's own stable door—

OVERTURE TO A DANCE OF LOCOMOTIVES

William Carlos Williams
(1883–   )

Men with picked voices chant the names
of cities in a huge gallery: promises
that pull through descending stairways
to a deep rumbling.
                    The rubbing feet
of those coming to be carried quicken a

grey pavement into soft light that rocks
to and fro, under the domed ceiling,
across and across from pale
earthcolored walls of bare limestone.

Covertly the hands of a great clock   10
go round and round! Were they to
move quickly and at once the whole
secret would be out and the shuffling
of all ants be done forever.

A leaning pyramid of sunlight, narrowing
out at a high window, moves by the clock;
discordant hands straining out from
a center: inevitable postures infinitely
repeated—

two—twofour—twoeight!   20

Porters in red hats run on narrow platforms.

This way ma'am!
                    —important not to take
the wrong train!
                    Lights from the concrete
ceiling hang crooked but—
                    Poised horizontal
on glittering parallels the dingy cylinders
packed with a warm glow—inviting entry—
pull against the hour. But brakes can
hold a fixed posture till—
                    The whistle!

Not twoeight. Not twofour. Two!

Gliding windows. Colored cooks sweating
in a small kitchen. Taillights—   31

In time: twofour!
In time: twoeight!

—rivers are tunneled: trestles
cross oozy swampland: wheels repeating

the same gesture remain relatively
stationary: rails forever parallel
return on themselves infinitely.
                              The dance is sure.

THE EXPRESS

Stephen Spender

After the first powerful, plain manifesto
The black statement of pistons, without more
    fuss
But gliding like a queen, she leaves the sta-
    tion.
Without bowing and with restrained uncon-
    cern
She passes the houses which humbly crowd
    outside,
The gasworks, and at last the heavy page
Of death, printed by gravestones in the
    cemetery.
Beyond the town, there lies the open country
Where, gathering speed, she acquires mys-
    tery,
The luminous self-possession of ships on
    ocean.   10
It is now she begins to sing—at first quite
    low
Then loud, and at last with a jazzy madness—
The song of her whistle screaming at curves,
Of deafening tunnels, brakes, innumerable
    bolts.
And always light, aerial, underneath,

Retreats the elate metre of her wheels.
Steaming through metal landscape on her
    lines,
She plunges new eras of white happiness,
Where speed throws up strange shapes,
    broad curves
And parallels clean like trajectories from
    guns.   20
At last, further than Edinburgh or Rome,
Beyond the crest of the world, she reaches
    night
Where only a low stream-line brightness
Of phosphorus on the tossing hills is light.
Ah, like a comet through flame, she moves
    entranced,
Wrapt in her music no bird song, no, nor
    bough
Breaking with honey buds, shall ever equal.

LIMITED

Carl Sandburg

I am riding on a limited express, one of the
    crack trains of the nation.
Hurtling across the prairie into blue haze and
    dark air go fifteen all-steel coaches holding
    a thousand people.
(All the coaches shall be scrap and rust and
    all the men and women laughing in the
    diners and sleepers shall pass to ashes.)
I ask a man in the smoker where he is going
    and he answers: "Omaha."

12. ODES, ELEGIES, AND SIMILAR POEMS

ODE TO A NIGHTINGALE

John Keats

1

My heart aches, and a drowsy numbness pains
  My sense, as though of hemlock I had
    drunk,
Or emptied some dull opiate to the drains
  One minute past, and Lethe-wards had
    sunk:
'Tis not through envy of thy happy lot,
  But being too happy in thine happiness,—
    That thou, light-winged Dryad of the
    trees,
      In some melodious plot
Of beechen green, and shadows number-
    less,
  Singest of summer in full-throated ease.

2

O, for a draught of vintage! that hath been
  Cool'd a long age in the deep-delved earth,
Tasting of Flora and the country green,   13
  Dance, and Provençal song, and sunburnt
    mirth!
O for a beaker full of the warm South,
  Full of the true, the blushful Hippocrene,
    With beaded bubbles winking at the
    brim,
      And purple-stained mouth;
    That I might drink, and leave the world
    unseen,
  And with thee fade away into the forest
    dim: 20

3

Fade far away, dissolve, and quite forget
  What thou among the leaves hast never
    known,

The weariness, the fever, and the fret
  Here, where men sit and hear each other
    groan;
Where palsy shakes a few, sad, last gray hairs,
  Where youth grows pale, and spectre-thin,
    and dies;
    Where but to think is to be full of sor-
    row
      And leaden-eyed despairs,
  Where Beauty cannot keep her lustrous
    eyes,
    Or new Love pine at them beyond to-
    morrow.   30

4

Away! away! for I will fly to thee,
  Not charioted by Bacchus and his pards,
But on the viewless wings of Poesy,
  Though the dull brain perplexes and re-
    tards:
Already with thee! tender is the night,
  And haply the Queen-Moon is on her
    throne,
    Cluster'd around by all her starry Fays;
      But here there is no light,
Save what from heaven is with the breezes
    blown
    Through verdurous glooms and winding
    mossy ways.   40

5

I cannot see what flowers are at my feet,
  Nor what soft incense hangs upon the
    boughs,
But, in embalmed darkness, guess each sweet
  Wherewith the seasonable month endows
The grass, the thicket, and the fruit-tree
    wild;
    White hawthorn, and the pastoral eglan-
    tine;

Fast fading violets cover'd up in leaves;
And mid-May's eldest child,
The coming musk-rose, full of dewy wine,
The murmurous haunt of flies on sum-
mer eves. 50

6

Darkling I listen; and, for many a time
I have been half in love with easeful
Death,
Call'd him soft names in many a mused
rhyme,
To take into the air my quiet breath;
Now more than ever seems it rich to die,
To cease upon the mignight with no pain,
While thou art pouring forth thy soul
abroad
In such an ecstasy!
Still wouldst thou sing, and I have ears in
vain—
To thy high requiem become a sod. 60

7

Thou wast not born for death, immortal
Bird!
No hungry generations tread thee down;
The voice I hear this passing night was heard
In ancient days by emperor and clown:
Perhaps the self-same song that found a path
Through the sad heart of Ruth, when, sick
for home,
She stood in tears amid the alien corn;
The same that oft-times hath
Charm'd magic casements, opening on the
foam
Of perilous seas, in faery lands for-
lorn. 70

8

Forlorn! the very word is like a bell
To toll me back from thee to my sole self!
Adieu! the fancy cannot cheat so well
As she is fam'd to do, deceiving elf.
Adieu! adieu! thy plaintive anthem fades
Past the near meadows, over the still
stream,
Up the hill-side; and now 't is buried
deep
In the next valley-glades:

Was it a vision, or a waking dream?
Fled is that music:—Do I wake or
sleep? 80

ODE ON A GRECIAN URN

John Keats

1

Thou still unravish'd bride of quietness,
Thou foster-child of silence and slow time,
Sylvan historian, who canst thus express
A flowery tale more sweetly than our
rhyme:
What leaf-fring'd legend haunts about thy
shape
Of deities or mortals, or of both,
In Tempe or the dales of Arcady?
What men or gods are these? What maidens
loth?
What mad pursuit? What struggle to es-
cape?
What pipes and timbrels? What wild
ecstasy? 10

2

Heard melodies are sweet, but those un-
heard
Are sweeter; therefore, ye soft pipes, play
on;
Not to the sensual ear, but, more endeared,
Pipe to the spirit ditties of no tone:
Fair youth, beneath the trees, thou canst not
leave
Thy song, nor ever can those trees be
bare;
Bold Lover, never, never canst thou kiss,
Though winning near the goal—yet, do not
grieve;
She cannot fade, though thou hast not thy
bliss,
For ever wilt thou love, and she be
fair! 20

3

Ah, happy, happy boughs! that cannot shed
Your leaves, nor ever bid the Spring
adieu;

And, happy melodist, unwearied,
    For ever piping songs for ever new;
More happy love! more happy, happy love!
    For ever warm and still to be enjoyed,
      For ever panting, and for ever young;
All breathing human passion far above,
    That leaves a heart high-sorrowful and
      cloy'd,
      A burning forehead, and a parching
      tongue.   30

4

Who are these coming to the sacrifice?
    To what green altar, O mysterious priest,
Lead'st thou that heifer lowing at the skies,
    And all her silken flanks with garlands
      drest?
What little town by river or sea shore,
    Or mountain-built with peaceful citadel,
      Is emptied of this folk, this pious morn?
And, little town, thy streets for evermore
    Will silent be; and not a soul to tell
      Why thou art desolate, can e'er re-
      turn.   40

5

O Attic shape! Fair attitude! with brede
    Of marble men and maidens overwrought,
With forest branches and the trodden weed;
    Thou, silent form, dost tease us out of
      thought
As doth eternity: Cold Pastoral!
    When old age shall this generation waste,
      Thou shalt remain, in midst of other
      woe
Than ours, a friend to man, to whom thou
    say'st,
    Beauty is truth, truth beauty,—that is all
    Ye know on earth, and all ye need to
    know.   50

l. 13. sensual: senuous.
l. 41. brede: embroidery.

TO AUTUMN

John Keats

1

Season of mists and mellow fruitfulness,
    Close bosom-friend of the maturing sun;

Conspiring with him how to load and bless
    With fruit the vines that round the thatch-
      eaves run;
To bend with apples the moss'd cottage-trees,
    And fill all fruit with ripeness to the core;
      To swell the gourd, and plump the hazel
      shells
With a sweet kernel; to set budding more,
    And still more, later flowers for the bees,
    Until they think warm days will never
    cease,   10
      For Summer has o'er-brimm'd their
      clammy cells.

2

Who hath not seen thee oft amid thy store?
    Sometimes whoever seeks abroad may find
Thee sitting careless on a granary floor,
    Thy hair soft-lifted by the winnowing
      wind;
Or on a half-reap'd furrow sound asleep,
    Drows'd with the fume of poppies, while
      thy hook
      Spares the next swath and all its twined
      flowers:
And sometimes like a gleaner thou dost keep
    Steady thy laden head across a brook; 20
    Or by a cyder-press, with patient look,
      Thou watchest the last oozings hours by
      hours.

3

Where are the songs of Spring? Ay, where
    are they?
    Think not of them, thou hast thy music
    too,—
While barred clouds bloom the soft-dying
    day,
    And touch the stubble-plains with rosy
    hue;
Then in a wailful choir the small gnats
    mourn
    Among the river shallows, borne aloft
      Or sinking as the light wind lives or
      dies;
And full-grown lambs loud bleat from hilly
    bourn;   30
    Hedge-crickets sing; and now with treble
    soft

The redbreast whistles from a garden-
croft;
And gathering swallows twitter in the
skies.

NOVEMBER

Robert Bridges

The lonely season in lonely lands, when fled
Are half the birds, and mists lie low, and the
sun
Is rarely seen, nor strayeth far from his bed;
The short days pass unwelcomed one by one.

Out by the ricks the mantled engine stands
Crestfallen, deserted,—for now all hands
Are told to the plough,—and ere it is dawn
appear
The teams following and crossing far and
near,
As hour by hour they broaden the brown
bands
Of the striped fields; and behind them firk
and prance   10
The heavy rooks, and daws grey-pated dance:
As awhile, surmounting a crest, in sharp out-
line
(A miniature of toil, a gem's design,)
They are pictured, horses and men, or now
near by
Above the lane they shout lifting the share,
By the trim hedgerow bloom'd with purple
air;
Where, under the thorns, dead leaves in hud-
dle lie
Packed by the gales of Autumn, and in and
out
The small wrens glide
With a happy note of cheer,   20
And yellow amorets flutter above and about,
Gay, familiar in fear.

And now, if the night shall be cold, across
the sky
Linnets and twites, in small flocks helter-
skelter,
All the afternoon to the gardens fly,

From thistle-pastures hurrying to gain the
shelter
Of American rhododendron or cherry-laurel:
And here and there, near chilly setting of
sun,
In an isolated tree a congregation
Of starlings chatter and chide,   30
Thickset as summer leaves, in garrulous quar-
rel:
Suddenly they hush as one,—
The tree top springs,—
And off, with a whirr of wings,
They fly by the score
To the holly-thicket, and there with myriads
more
Dispute for the roosts; and from the unseen
nation
A babel of tongues, like running water un-
ceasing,
Makes live the wood, the flocking cries in-
creasing,
Wrangling discordantly, incessantly,   40
While falls the night on them self-occupied;
The long dark night, that lengthens slow,
Deepening with Winter to starve grass and
tree,
And soon to bury in snow
The Earth, that, sleeping 'neath her frozen
stole,
Shall dream a dream crept from the sunless
pole
Of how her end shall be.

---

l. 10. firk: hasten or be frisky.
l. 11. Rooks and daws resemble crows.
l. 15. share: plowshare.
l. 16. bloom'd: silvered over with autumn haze.
l. 24. twite or twite finch: another kind of linnet.

NIGHTINGALES

Robert Bridges

Beautiful must be the mountains whence
ye come,
And bright in the fruitful valleys the
streams, wherefrom
Ye learn your song:

Where are those starry woods? O might I
    wander there,
    Among the flowers, which in that heav-
      enly air
      Bloom the year long!

Nay, barren are those mountains and spent
    the streams:
    Our song is the voice of desire, that haunts
    our dreams,
      A throe of the heart,
Whose pining visions dim, forbidden hopes
    profound,   10
No dying cadence nor long sigh can
    sound,
      For all our art.

Alone, aloud in the raptured ear of men
We pour our dark nocturnal secret; and
    then,
      As night is withdrawn
From these sweet-springing meads and burst-
    ing boughs of May,
    Dream, while the innumerable choir of
    day
      Welcome the dawn.

PHILOMELA

Matthew Arnold
(1822–1888)

Hark! ah, the nightingale—
The tawny-throated!
Hark, from that moonlit cedar what a burst!
What triumph! hark!—what pain!

O wanderer from a Grecian shore,
Still, after many years, in distant lands,
Still nourishing in thy bewilder'd brain
That wild, unquench'd, deep-sunken, old-
    world pain—
Say, will it never heal?
And can this fragrant lawn   10
With its cool trees, and night,
And the sweet, tranquil Thames,
And moonshine, and the dew,
To thy rack'd heart and brain
Afford no balm?

Dost thou to-night behold,
Here, through the moonlight on this English
    grass,
The unfriendly palace in the Thracian wild?
Dost thou again peruse
With hot cheeks and sear'd eyes   20
The too clear web, and thy dumb sister's
    shame?
Dost thou once more assay
Thy flight, and feel come over thee,
Poor fugitive, the feathery change
Once more, and once more seem to make re-
    sound
With love and hate, triumph and agony,
Lone Daulis, and the high Cephissian vale?
Listen, Eugenia—
How thick the bursts come crowding through
    the leaves!
Again—thou hearest?   30
Eternal passion!
Eternal pain!

ODE TO THE WEST WIND

Percy Bysshe Shelley
(1792–1822)

I

O wild West Wind, thou breath of Autumn's
    being,
Thou, from whose unseen presence the leaves
    dead
Are driven, like ghosts from an enchanter
    fleeing,

Yellow, and black, and pale, and hectic red,
Pestilence-stricken multitudes: O thou,
Who chariotest to their dark wintry bed

The wingèd seeds, where they lie cold and
    low,
Each like a corpse within its grave, until
Thine azure sister of the Spring shall blow

Her clarion o'er the dreaming earth, and
    fill   10
(Driving sweet buds like flocks to feed in
    air)
With living hues and odors plain and hill:

Wild Spirit, which art moving everywhere;
Destroyer and preserver; hear! oh, hear!

2

Thou on whose stream, mid the steep sky's
  commotion,
Loose clouds like earth's decaying leaves are
  shed,
Shook from the tangled boughs of Heaven
  and Ocean,

Angels of rain and lightning: there are
  spread
On the blue surface of thine aëry surge,
Like the bright hair uplifted from the
  head   20

Of some fierce Mænad, even from the dim
  verge
Of the horizon to the zenith's height,
The locks of the approaching storm. Thou
  dirge

Of the dying year, to which this closing night
Will be the dome of a vast sepulchre,
Vaulted with all thy congregated might

Of vapours, from whose solid atmosphere
Black rain, and fire, and hail will burst: oh,
  hear!

3

Thou who didst waken from his summer
  dreams
The blue Mediterranean, where he lay,   30
Lulled by the coil of his crystàlline streams,

Beside a pumice isle in Baiæ's bay,
And saw in sleep old palaces and towers
Quivering within the wave's intenser day,

All overgrown with azure moss and flowers
So sweet, the sense faints picturing them!
  Thou
For whose path the Atlantic's level powers

Cleave themselves into chasms, while far below
The sea-blooms and the oozy woods which
  wear
The sapless foliage of the ocean, know   40

Thy voice, and suddenly grow gray with fear,
And tremble and despoil themselves: oh,
  hear!

4

If I were a dead leaf thou mightest bear;
If I were a swift cloud to fly with thee;
A wave to pant beneath thy power, and share

The impulse of thy strength, only less free
Than thou, O uncontrollable! If even
I were as in my boyhood, and could be

The comrade of thy wanderings over Heaven,
As then, when to outstrip thy skiey speed
Scarce seemed a vision; I would ne'er have
  striven   51

As thus with thee in prayer in my sore need.
Oh, lift me as a wave, a leaf, a cloud!
I fall upon the thorns of life! I bleed!

A heavy weight of hours has chained and
  bowed
One too like thee—tameless, and swift, and
  proud.

5

Make me thy lyre, even as the forest is:
What if my leaves are falling like its own!
The tumult of thy mighty harmonies

Will take from both a deep, autumnal
  tone,   60
Sweet though in sadness. Be thou, Spirit
  fierce,
My spirit! Be thou me, impetuous one!

Drive my dead thoughts over the universe
Like withered leaves to quicken a new
  birth!
And, by the incantation of this verse,

Scatter, as from an unextinguished hearth
Ashes and sparks, my words among man-
  kind!
Be through my lips to unawakened earth

The trumpet of a prophecy! O, Wind,
If Winter comes, can Spring be far behind?   70

LYCIDAS

John Milton

In this Monody the Author bewails a
learned Friend, unfortunatly drown'd in
his Passage from Chester on the Irish
Seas, 1637. And by occasion fortels the
ruine of our corrupted clergy then in
their height.

YET once more, O ye Laurels, and once more
Ye Myrtles brown, with Ivy never-sear,
I com to pluck your Berries harsh and crude,
And with forc'd fingers rude,
Shatter your leaves before the mellowing
   year.
Bitter constraint, and sad occasion dear,
Compels me to disturb your season due:
For *Lycidas* is dead, dead ere his prime
Young *Lycidas,* and hath not left his peer:
Who would not sing for *Lycidas?* he knew
Himself to sing, and build the lofty rhyme.
He must not flote upon his watry bear   12
Unwept, and welter to the parching wind,
Without the meed of som melodious tear.
   Begin then, Sisters of the sacred well,
That from beneath the seat of *Jove* doth
   spring,
Begin, and somwhat loudly sweep the string.
Hence with denial vain, and coy excuse,
So may som gentle Muse
With lucky words favour my destin'd
   Urn,   20
And as he passes turn,
And bid fair peace be to my sable shrowd.
For we were nurst upon the self-same hill,
Fed the same flock, by fountain, shade, and
   rill.
   Together both, ere the high Lawns ap-
   pear'd
Under the opening eye-lids of the morn,
We drove a field, and both together heard
What time the Gray-fly winds her sultry
   horn,
Batt'ning our flocks with the fresh dews of
   night,

Oft till the Star that rose, at Ev'ning, bright
Toward Heav'ns descent had slop'd his west-
   ering wheel.   31
Mean while the Rural ditties were not mute,
Temper'd to th'Oaten Flute;
Rough *Satyrs* danc'd, and *Fauns* with clov'n
   heel,
From the glad sound would not be absent
   long,
And old *Damætas* lov'd to hear our song.
   But O the heavy change, now thou art
   gon,
Now thou art gon, and never must return!
Thee Shepherd, thee the Woods, and desert
   Caves,
With wilde Thyme and the gadding Vine
   o'regrown,   40
And all their echoes mourn.
The Willows, and the Hazle Copses green,
Shall now no more be seen,
Fanning their joyous Leaves to thy soft layes.
As killing as the Canker to the Rose,
Or Taint-worm to the weanling Herds that
   graze,
Or Frost to Flowers, that their gay wardrop
   wear,
When first the White thorn blows;
Such, *Lycidas,* thy loss to Shepherds ear.
   Where were ye Nymphs when the re-
   morseless deep   50
Clos'd o're the head of your lov'd *Lycidas?*
For neither were ye playing on the steep,
Where your old *Bards,* the famous *Druids* ly,
Nor on the shaggy top of *Mona* high,
Nor yet where *Deva* spreads her wisard
   stream:
Ay me, I fondly dream!
Had ye bin there—for what could that have
   don?
What could the Muse her self that *Orpheus*
   bore,
The Muse her self, for her inchanting son
Whom Universal nature did lament,   60
When by the rout that made the hideous
   roar,
His goary visage down the stream was sent,
Down the swift *Hebrus* to the *Lesbian* shore.
   Alas! What boots it with uncessant care
To tend the homely slighted Shepherds trade,
And strictly meditate the thankles Muse,

Were it not better don as others use,
To sport with *Amaryllis* in the shade,
Or with the tangles of *Neæra's* hair?
Fame is the spur that the clear spirit doth
    raise   70
(That last infirmity of Noble mind)
To scorn delights, and live laborious dayes;
But the fair Guerdon when we hope to find,
And think to burst out into sudden blaze,
Comes the blind *Fury* with th'abhorred
    shears,
And slits the thin spun life. But not the
    praise,
Phœbus repli'd, and touch'd my trembling
    ears;
Fame is no plant that grows on mortal soil,
Nor in the glistering foil
Set off to th' world, nor in broad rumour
    lies,   80
But lives and spreds aloft by those pure eyes,
And perfet witnes of all judging *Jove;*
As he pronounces lastly on each deed,
Of so much fame in Heav'n expect thy meed.
    O Fountain *Arethuse,* and thou honour'd
    floud,
Smooth-sliding *Mincius,* crown'd with vocall
    reeds,
That strain I heard was of a higher mood:
But now my Oate proceeds,
And listens to the Herald of the Sea
That came in *Neptune's* plea,   90
He ask'd the Waves, and ask'd the Fellon
    winds,
What hard mishap hath doom'd this gentle
    swain?
And question'd every gust of rugged wings
That blows from off each beaked Promon-
    tory,
They knew not of his story,
And sage *Hippotades* their answer brings,
That not a blast was from his dungeon
    stray'd,
The Ayr was calm, and on the level brine,
Sleek *Panope* with all her sisters play'd.
It was that fatall and perfidious Bark   100
Built in th'eclipse, and rigg'd with curses
    dark,
That sunk so low that sacred head of thine.
    Next *Camus,* reverend Sire, went footing
    slow,

His Mantle hairy, and his Bonnet sedge,
Inwrought with figures dim, and on the edge
Like to that sanguine flower inscrib'd with
    woe.
Ah; Who hath reft (quoth he) my dearest
    pledge?
Last came, and last did go,
The Pilot of the *Galilean* lake,
Two massy Keyes he bore of metals
    twain,   110
(The Golden opes, the Iron shuts amain)
He shook his Miter'd locks, and stern be-
    spake,
How well could I have spar'd for thee, young
    swain,
Anow of such as for their bellies sake,
Creep and intrude, and climb into the fold?
Of other care they little reck'ning make,
Then how to scramble at the shearers feast,
And shove away the worthy bidden guest.
Blind mouthes! that scarce themselves know
    how to hold
A Sheep-hook, or have learn'd ought els the
    least   120
That to the faithfull Herdmans art belongs!
What recks it them? What need they? They
    are sped;
And when they list, their lean and flashy
    songs
Grate on their scrannel Pipes of wretched
    straw,
The hungry Sheep look up, and are not
    fed,
But swoln with wind, and the rank mist they
    draw,
Rot inwardly, and foul contagion spread:
Besides what the grim Woolf with privy paw
Daily devours apace, and nothing sed,
But that two-handed engine at the door, 130
Stands ready to smite once, and smite no
    more.
    Return *Alpheus,* the dread voice is past,
That shrunk thy streams; Return *Sicilian*
    Muse,
And call the Vales, and bid them hither cast
Their Bels, and Flourets of a thousand
    hues.
Ye valleys low where the milde whispers use,
Of shades and wanton winds, and gushing
    brooks,

On whose fresh lap the swart Star sparely
    looks,
Throw hither all your quaint enameld eyes,
That on the green terf suck the honied
    showres,   140
And purple all the ground with vernal
    flowres.
Bring the rathe Primrose that forsaken dies.
The tufted Crow-toe, and pale Gessamine,
The white Pink, and the Pansie freakt with
    jeat,
The glowing Violet.
The Musk-rose, and the well attir'd Wood-
    bine.
With Cowslips wan that hang the pensive
    hed,
And every flower that sad embroidery wears:
Bid *Amaranthus* all his beauty shed,   149
And Daffadillies fill their cups with tears,
To strew the Laureat Herse where *Lycid* lies.
For so to interpose a little ease,
Let our frail thoughts dally with false sur-
    mise.
Ay me! Whilst thee the shores, and sounding
    Seas
Wash far away, where ere thy bones are
    hurld,
Whether beyond the stormy *Hebrides,*
Where thou perhaps under the whelming
    tide
Visit'st the bottom of the monstrous world;
Or whether thou to our moist vows deny'd,
Sleep'st by the fable of *Bellerus* old,   160
Where the great vision of the guarded
    Mount
Looks toward *Namancos* and *Bayona's* hold;
Look homeward Angel now, and melt with
    ruth.
And, O ye *Dolphins,* waft the haples youth.
    Weep no more, woful Shepherds weep no
    more,
For *Lycidas* your sorrow is not dead,
Sunk though he be beneath the watry floar,
So sinks the day-star in the Ocean bed,
And yet anon repairs his drooping head,
And tricks his beams, and with new spangled
    Ore,   170
Flames in the forehead of the morning sky:
So *Lycidas* sunk low, but mounted high,

Through the dear might of him that walk'd
    the waves
Where other groves, and other streams along,
With *Nectar* pure his oozy Lock's he laves,
And hears the unexpressive nuptiall Song,
In the blest Kingdoms meek of joy and love.
There entertain him all the Saints above,
In solemn troops, and sweet Societies   179
That sing, and singing in their glory move,
And wipe the tears for ever from his eyes.
Now *Lycidas* the Shepherds weep no more;
Hence forth thou art the Genius of the shore,
In thy large recompense, and shalt be good
To all that wander in that perilous flood.
    Thus sang the uncouth Swain to th'Okes
    and rills,
While the still morn went out with Sandals
    gray,
He touch'd the tender stops of various Quills,
With eager thought warbling his *Dorick* lay:
And now the Sun had stretch'd out all the
    hills,   190
And now was dropt into the Western bay;
At last he rose, and twitch'd his Mantle blew:
To morrow to fresh Woods, and Pastures
    new.

l. 12. bear: bier.
l. 15. Sisters . . . : the Muses.
l. 48. White thorn: hawthorn.
l. 54. Mona: island of Anglesey, near which King
had drowned.
l. 55. Deva: the river Dee.
l. 79. glistering foil: glittering gold foil.
l. 85. Arethuse: fountain in Sicily associated with
the Greek pastoral poet Theocritus.
l. 86. Mincius: river associated with Virgil, who
wrote Latin pastoral poetry.
l. 96. Hippotades: Aeolus, god of the winds.
l. 99. Panope: a sea nymph.
l. 103. Camus: the river Cam, from which Cambridge receives its name.
l. 114. Anow: enough.
l. 124. scrannel: thin and discordant.
l. 128. privy: furtive private.
l. 138. swart Star: Sirius, the Dog Star, whose
name means "scorching."
l. 142. rathe: early.
l. 143. Crow-toe: crowfoot, ranunculus.
l. 144. freakt: streaked.
l. 168. day-star: sun.
l. 183. genius: guardian spirit.
l. 186. uncouth: unknown or rustic.
l. 189. Doric: the dialect of Greek pastoral poetry.

ELEGY WRITTEN IN A COUNTRY CHURCHYARD

Thomas Gray
(1716–1771)

The Curfew tolls the knell of parting day,
The lowing herd wind slowly o'er the lea,
The plowman homeward plods his weary way,
And leaves the world to darkness and to me.

Now fades the glimmering landscape on the sight,
And all the air a solemn stillness holds,
Save where the beetle wheels his droning flight,
And drowsy tinklings lull the distant folds;

Save that from yonder ivy-mantled tower
The moping owl does to the moon complain   10
Of such as, wandering near her secret bower,
Molest her ancient solitary reign.

Beneath those rugged elms, that yew-tree's shade,
Where heaves the turf in many a mouldering heap,
Each in his narrow cell forever laid,
The rude Forefathers of the hamlet sleep.

The breezy call of incense-breathing Morn,
The swallow twittering from the straw-built shed,
The cock's shrill clarion, or the echoing horn,
No more shall rouse them from their lowly bed.   20

For them no more the blazing hearth shall burn,
Or busy housewife ply her evening care:
No children run to lisp their sire's return,
Or climb his knees the envied kiss to share.

Oft did the harvest to their sickle yield,
Their furrow oft the stubborn glebe has broke;
How jocund did they drive their team afield!
How bowed the woods beneath their sturdy stroke!

Let not Ambition mock their useful toil,
Their homely joys, and destiny obscure;   30
Nor Grandeur hear with a disdainful smile
The short and simple annals of the poor.

The boast of heraldry, the pomp of power,
And all that beauty, all that wealth e'er gave,
Awaits alike the inevitable hour.
The paths of glory lead but to the grave.

Nor you, ye Proud, impute to These the fault,
If Memory o'er their Tomb no Trophies raise,
Where through the long-drawn aisle and fretted vault   39
The pealing anthem swells the note of praise.

Can storied urn or animated bust
Back to its mansion call the fleeting breath?
Can Honour's voice provoke the silent dust,
Or Flattery soothe the dull cold ear of Death?

Perhaps in this neglected spot is laid
Some heart once pregnant with celestial fire;
Hands, that the rod of empire might have swayed,
Or waked to extasy the living lyre.

But Knowledge to their eyes her ample page
Rich with the spoils of time did ne'er unroll;   50
Chill Penury repressed their noble rage,
And froze the genial current of the soul.

Full many a gem of purest ray serene,
The dark unfathomed caves of ocean bear:
Full many a flower is born to blush unseen,
And waste its sweetness on the desert air.

Some village-Hampden, that with dauntless breast

The little Tyrant of his fields withstood;
Some mute, inglorious Milton here may rest,
Some Cromwell guiltless of his country's
   blood.   60

The applause of listening senates to com-
   mand,
The threats of pain and ruin to despise,
To scatter plenty o'er a smiling land,
And read their history in a nation's eyes,

Their lot forbad: nor circumscribed alone
Their growing virtues, but their crimes con-
   fined;
Forbad to wade through slaughter to a
   throne,
And shut the gates of mercy on mankind;

The struggling pangs of conscious truth to
   hide,
To quench the blushes of ingenuous shame,
Or heap the shrine of Luxury and Pride   71
With incense kindled at the Muse's flame.

Far from the madding crowd's ignoble strife,
Their sober wishes never learned to stray;
Along the cool sequestered vale of life
They kept the noiseless tenor of their way.

Yet ev'n these bones from insult to protect,
Some frail memorial still erected nigh,
With uncouth rhymes and shapeless sculp-
   ture decked,
Implores the passing tribute of a sigh.   80

Their name, their years, spelt by the unlet-
   tered Muse,
The place of fame and elegy supply;
And many a holy text around she strews,
That teach the rustic moralist to die.

For who, to dumb Forgetfulness a prey,
This pleasing anxious being e'er resigned,
Left the warm precincts of the cheerful day,
Nor cast one longing lingering look behind?

On some fond breast the parting soul relies,
Some pious drops the closing eye requires;
Ev'n from the tomb the voice of Nature cries,
Ev'n in our Ashes live their wonted Fires.

For thee who, mindful of the unhonoured
   Dead,   93
Dost in these lines their artless tale relate;
If chance, by lonely contemplation led,
Some kindred Spirit shall inquire thy fate,

Haply some hoary-headed Swain may say,
"Oft have we seen him at the peep of dawn
Brushing with hasty steps the dews away,
To meet the sun upon the upland lawn.

"There at the foot of yonder nodding beech
That wreathes its old fantastic roots so high,
His listless length at noontide would he
   stretch,   103
And pore upon the brook that babbles by.

"Hard by yon wood, now smiling as in scorn,
Muttering his wayward fancies he would
   rove;
Now drooping, woeful wan, like one forlorn,
Or crazed with care, or crossed in hopeless
   love.

"One morn I missed him on the customed
   hill,
Along the heath, and near his favourite
   tree;   110
Another came; nor yet beside the rill,
Nor up the lawn, nor at the wood was he;

"The next with dirges due in sad array,
Slow through the church-way path we saw
   him borne.
Approach and read (for thou canst read) the
   lay,
Graved on the stone beneath yon agèd
   thorn."

THE EPITAPH

Here rests his head upon the lap of Earth,
A Youth to Fortune and to Fame un-
   known.
Fair Science frowned not on his humble
   birth,
And Melancholy marked him for her
   own.   120

Large was his bounty, and his soul sincere,
Heaven did a recompense as largely send:

He gave to Misery all he had, a tear,
 He gained from Heaven ('twas all he
  wished) a friend.

No farther seek his merits to disclose,
Or draw his frailties from their dread
 abode,
(There they alike in trembling hope re-
 pose,)
The bosom of his Father and his God.

---

l. 43. provoke: call forth.
l. 51. rage: enthusiasm.
l. 57. John Hampden, 17th-century statesman, opponent of Charles I.

IN MEMORY OF
W. B. YEATS
(d. Jan. 1939)

W. H. Auden

1

He disappeared in the dead of winter:
The brooks were frozen, the airports almost
 deserted,
And snow disfigured the public statues;
The mercury sank in the mouth of the dying
 day.
O all the instruments agree
The day of his death was a dark cold day.

Far from his illness
The wolves ran on through the evergreen
 forests,
The peasant river was untempted by the fash-
 ionable quays;
By mourning tongues   10
The death of the poet was kept from his
 poems.

But for him it was his last afternoon as him-
 self,
An afternoon of nurses and rumours;
The provinces of his body revolted,
The squares of his mind were empty,
Silence invaded the suburbs,
The current of his feeling failed: he became
 his admirers.

Now he is scattered among a hundred cities
And wholly given over to unfamiliar affec-
 tions;
To find his happiness in another kind of
 wood   20
And be punished under a foreign code of
 conscience.
The words of a dead man
Are modified in the guts of the living.

But in the importance and noise of tomorrow
When the brokers are roaring like beasts on
 the floor of the Bourse,
And the poor have the sufferings to which
 they are fairly accustomed,
And each in the cell of himself is almost con-
 vinced of his freedom;
A few thousand will think of this day
As one thinks of a day when one did some-
 thing slightly unusual.

O all the instruments agree   30
The day of his death was a dark cold day.

2

You were silly like us: your gift survived it
 all;
The parish of rich women, physical decay,
Yourself; mad Ireland hurt you into poetry.
Now Ireland has her madness and her
 weather still,
For poetry makes nothing happen: it survives
In the valley of its saying where executives
Would never want to tamper; it flows south
From ranches of isolation and the busy griefs,
Raw towns that we believe and die in; it sur-
 vives,   40
A way of happening, a mouth.

3

Earth, receive an honored guest;
William Yeats is laid to rest:
Let the Irish vessel lie
Emptied of its poetry.

Time that is intolerant
Of the brave and innocent,
And indifferent in a week
To a beautiful physique,

Worships language and forgives   50
Everyone by whom it lives;
Pardons cowardice, conceit,
Lays its honours at their feet.

Time that with this strange excuse
Pardoned Kipling and his views,
And will pardon Paul Claudel,
Pardons him for writing well.

In the nightmare of the dark
All the dogs of Europe bark,
And the living nations wait,   60
Each sequestered in its hate;

Intellectual disgrace
Stares from every human face,

And the seas of pity lie
Locked and frozen in each eye.

Follow, poet, follow right
To the bottom of the night,
With your unconstraining voice
Still persuade us to rejoice;

With the farming of a verse   70
Make a vineyard of the curse,
Sing of human unsuccess
In a rapture of distress;

In the deserts of the heart
Let the healing fountain start,
In the prison of his days
Teach the free man how to praise.

---

l. 56. Paul Claudel: modern French poet.

13. TIME, SPACE, AND MUTABILITY

TO THE VIRGINS, TO MAKE MUCH OF TIME

Robert Herrick
(1591–1674)

Gather ye Rose-buds while ye may,
   Old Time is still a flying:
And this same flower that smiles to day,
   To morrow will be dying.

The glorious Lamp of Heaven, the Sun,
   The higher he's a getting;
The sooner will his Race be run,
   And neerer he's to Setting.

That Age is best, which is the first,
   When Youth and Blood are warmer;   10
But being spent, the worse, and worst
   Times, still succeed the former.

Then be not coy, but use your time;
   And while ye may, goe marry:
For having lost but once your prime,
   You may for ever tarry.

BLUE GIRLS

John Crowe Ransom
(1888–   )

Twirling your blue skirts, travelling the
   sward
Under the towers of your seminary,
Go listen to your teachers old and contrary
Without believing a word.

Tie the white fillets then about your hair
And think no more of what will come to pass
Than bluebirds that go walking on the grass
And chattering on the air.

Practise your beauty, blue girls, before it fail;
And I will cry with my loud lips and pub-
   lish   10
Beauty which all our power shall never estab-
   lish,
It is so frail.

For I could tell you a story which is true;
I know a lady with a terrible tongue,
Blear eyes fallen from blue,
All her perfections tarnished—yet it is not
   long
Since she was lovelier than any of you.

TO HIS COY MISTRESS

Andrew Marvell
(1621–1678)

Had we but World enough, and Time,
This coyness Lady were no crime.
We would sit down, and think which way
To walk, and pass our long Loves Day.
Thou by the *Indian Ganges* side
Should'st Rubies find: I by the Tide
Of *Humber* would complain. I would
Love you ten years before the Flood:
And you should if you please refuse
Till the Conversion of the *Jews*.   10
My vegetable Love should grow
Vaster than Empires, and more slow.
An hundred years should go to praise
Thine Eyes, and on thy Forehead Gaze.
Two hundred to adore each Breast:

But thirty thousand to the rest.
An Age at least to every part,
And the last Age should show your Heart.
For Lady you deserve this State;
Nor would I love at lower rate.   20
    But at my back I alwaies hear
Times wingèd Chariot hurrying near:
And yonder all before us lye
Desarts of vast Eternity.
Thy Beauty shall no more be found,
Nor, in thy marble Vault, shall sound
My echoing Song: then Worms shall try
That long preserv'd Virginity:
And your quaint Honour turn to dust;
And into ashes all my Lust.   30
The Grave's a fine and private place,
But none I think do there embrace.
    Now therefore, while the youthful hew
Sits on thy skin like morning dew,
And while they willing Soul transpires
At every pore with instant Fires,
Now let us sport us while we may;
And now, like am'rous birds of prey,
Rather at once our Time devour,
Than languish in his slow-chapt pow'r.   40
Let us roll all our Strength, and all
Our Sweetness, up into one Ball;
And tear our Pleasures with rough strife,
Thorough the Iron gates of Life.
Thus, though we cannot make our Sun
Stand still, yet we will make him run.

l. 35. transpires: breathes forth.
l. 44. thorough: through.

YOU, ANDREW MARVELL

Archibald MacLeish
(1892–   )

And here face down beneath the sun
And here upon earth's noonward height
To feel the always coming on
The always rising of the night

To feel creep up the curving east
The earthy chill of dusk and slow
Upon those under lands the vast
And everclimbing shadow grow

And strange at Ecbatan the trees   10
Take leaf by leaf the evening strange
The flooding dark about their knees
The mountains over Persia change

And now at Kermanshah the gate
Dark empty and the withered grass
And through the twilight now the late
Few travelers in the westward pass

And Baghdad darken and the bridge
Across the silent river gone
And through Arabia the edge
Of evening widen and steal on   20

And deepen on Palmyra's street
The wheel rut in the ruined stone
And Lebanon fade out and Crete
High through the clouds and overblown

And over Sicily the air
Still flashing with the landward gulls
And loom and slowly disappear
The sails above the shadowy hulls

And Spain go under and the shore
Of Africa the gilded sand   30
And evening vanish and no more
The low pale light across that land

Nor now the long light on the sea

And here face downward in the sun
To feel how swift how secretly
The shadow of the night comes on . . .

l. 9. Ecbatan: ancient name of the Persian city of Hamadan.
l. 13. Kermanshah: Persian city west of Hamadan.
l. 16. westward pass: probably the Zagros Gate, a pass west of Kermanshah.
l. 21. Palmyra: ancient caravan center, with ruins of various past epochs.

MUTABILITY

William Wordsworth

From low to high doth dissolution climb,
And sink from high to low, along a scale
Of awful notes, whose concord shall not fail;
A musical but melancholy chime,
Which they can hear who meddle not with
      crime,
Nor avarice, nor over-anxious care.
Truth fails not; but her outward forms that
      bear
The longest date do melt like frosty rime,
That in the morning whitened hill and plain
And is no more; drop like the tower sub-
      lime   10
Of yesterday, which royally did wear
His crown of weeds, but could not even sus-
      tain
Some casual shout that broke the silent air,
Or the unimaginable touch of Time.

THE NEW HOUSE

Edward Thomas

Now first, as I shut the door,
    I was alone
In the new house; and the wind
    Began to moan.

Old at once was the house,
    And I was old;
My ears were teased with the dread
    Of what was foretold,

Nights of storm, days of mist, without end;
    Sad days when the sun   10
Shone in vain: old griefs and griefs
    Not yet begun.

All was foretold me; naught
    Could I foresee;
But I learned how the wind would sound
    After these things should be.

14. POEMS ON THE MEANING AND VALUE OF LIFE

DOVER BEACH

Matthew Arnold

The sea is calm to-night.
The tide is full, the moon lies fair
Upon the straits;—on the French coast the light
Gleams and is gone; the cliffs of England stand,
Glimmering and vast, out in the tranquil bay.
Come to the window, sweet is the night-air!

Only, from the long line of spray
Where the sea meets the moon-blanch'd land,
Listen! you hear the grating roar
Of pebbles which the waves draw back, and fling,   10
At their return, up the high strand,
Begin, and cease, and then again begin,
With tremulous cadence slow, and bring
The eternal note of sadness in.

Sophocles long ago
Heard it on the Ægæan, and it brought
Into his mind the turbid ebb and flow
Of human misery; we
Find also in the sound a thought,
Hearing it by this distant northern sea.   20

The Sea of Faith
Was once, too, at the full, and round earth's shore
Lay like the folds of a bright girdle furl'd.
But now I only hear
Its melancholy, long, withdrawing roar,
Retreating, to the breath
Of the night-wind, down the vast edges drear
And naked shingles of the world.

Ah, love, let us be true
To one another! for the world, which seems
To lie before us like a land of dreams,   31
So various, so beautiful, so new,
Hath really neither joy, nor love, nor light,
Nor certitude, nor peace, nor help for pain;
And we are here as on a darkling plain
Swept with confused alarms of struggle and flight,
Where ignorant armies clash by night.

MUSÉE DES BEAUX ARTS

W. H. Auden

About suffering they were never wrong,
The Old Masters: how well they understood
Its human position; how it takes place
While someone else is eating or opening a window or just walking dully along;
How, when the aged are reverently, passionately waiting
For the miraculous birth, there always must be
Children who did not specially want it to happen, skating
On a pond at the edge of the wood:
They never forgot
That even the dreadful martyrdom must run its course   10
Anyhow in a corner, some untidy spot
Where the dogs go on with their doggy life and the torturer's horse
Scratches its innocent behind on a tree.

In Brueghel's *Icarus*, for instance: how everything turns away

356

Quite leisurely from the disaster; the plough-
    man may
Have heard the splash, the forsaken cry,
But for him it was not an important failure;
    the sun shone
As it had to on the white legs disappearing
    into the green
Water; and the expensive delicate ship that
    must have seen
Something amazing, a boy falling out of the
    sky,   20
Had somewhere to get to and sailed calmly
    on.

ULYSSES

Alfred, Lord Tennyson
(1809–1892)

It little profits that an idle king,
By this still hearth, among these barren crags,
Match'd with an aged wife, I mete and dole
Unequal laws unto a savage race,
That hoard, and sleep, and feed, and know
    not me.
I cannot rest from travel: I will drink
Life to the lees: all times I have enjoy'd
Greatly, have suffer'd greatly, both with those
That loved me, and alone; on shore, and
    when
Thro' scudding drifts the rainy Hyades   10
Vext the dim sea. I am become a name;
For always roaming with a hungry heart
Much have I seen and known; cities of men
And manners, climates, councils, govern-
    ments,
Myself not least, but honour'd of them all;
And drunk delight of battle with my peers,
Far on the ringing plains of windy Troy.
I am a part of all that I have met;
Yet all experience is an arch wherethro'
Gleams that untravel'd world, whose margin
    fades   20
For ever and for ever when I move.
How dull it is to pause, to make an end,
To rust unburnish'd, not to shine in use!
As tho' to breathe were life. Life piled on
    life
Were all too little, and of one to me
Little remains: but every hour is saved
From that eternal silence, something more,
A bringer of new things; and vile it were
For some three suns to store and hoard my-
    self,
And this gray spirit yearning in desire   30
To follow knowledge like a sinking star,
Beyond the utmost bound of human thought.
    This is my son, mine own Telemachus,
To whom I leave the sceptre and the isle—
Well-loved of me, discerning to fulfill
This labour, by slow prudence to make mild
A rugged people, and thro' soft degrees
Subdue them to the useful and the good.
Most blameless is he, centered in the sphere
Of common duties, decent not to fail   40
In offices of tenderness, and pay
Meet adoration to my household gods,
When I am gone. He works his work, I mine.
    There lies the port; the vessel puffs her
    sail:
There gloom the dark broad seas. My mari-
    ners,
Souls that have toil'd, and wrought, and
    thought with me—
That ever with a frolic welcome took
The thunder and the sunshine, and opposed
Free hearts, free foreheads—you and I are
    old;
Old age hath yet his honour and his toil;   50
Death closes all: but something ere the
    end,
Some work of noble note, may yet be done,
Not unbecoming men that strove with Gods.
The lights begin to twinkle from the rocks:
The long day wanes: the slow moon climbs:
    the deep
Moans round with many voices. Come, my
    friends,
'T is not too late to seek a newer world.
Push off, and sitting well in order smite
The sounding furrows; for my purpose holds
To sail beyond the sunset, and the baths   60
Of all the western stars, until I die.
It may be that the gulfs will wash us down:
It may be we shall touch the Happy Isles,
And see the great Achilles, whom we knew.
Tho' much is taken, much abides; and tho'

We are not now that strength which in old
    days
Moved earth and heaven, that which we are,
    we are;
One equal temper of heroic hearts,
Made weak by time and fate, but strong in
    will   69
To strive, to seek, to find, and not to yield.

THE LOTOS-EATERS

Alfred, Lord Tennyson

"Courage!" he said, and pointed toward the
    land,
"This mounting wave will roll us shoreward
    soon."
In the afternoon they came unto a land
In which it seemèd always afternoon.
All round the coast the languid air did swoon,
Breathing like one that hath a weary dream.
Full-faced above the valley stood the moon;
And like a downward smoke, the slender
    stream
Along the cliff to fall and pause and fall did
    seem.

A land of streams! some, like a downward
    smoke,   10
Slow-dropping veils of thinnest lawn, did go;
And some thro' wavering lights and shadows
    broke,
Rolling a slumbrous sheet of foam below.
They saw the gleaming river seaward flow
From the inner land: far off, three mountain-
    tops,
Three silent pinnacles of aged snow,
Stood sunset-flush'd: and, dew'd with show-
    ery drops,
Up-clomb the shadowy pine above the woven
    copse.

The charmèd sunset linger'd low adown
In the red West: thro' mountain clefts the
    dale   20
Was seen far inland, and the yellow down
Border'd with palm, and many a winding vale
And meadow, set with slender galingale;

A land where all things always seem'd the
    same!
And round about the keel with faces pale,
Dark faces pale against that rosy flame,
The mild-eyed melancholy Lotos-eaters came.

Branches they bore of that enchanted stem,
Laden with flower and fruit, whereof they
    gave
To each, but whoso did receive of them   30
And taste, to him the gushing of the wave
Far far away did seem to mourn and rave
On alien shores; and if his fellow spake,
His voice was thin, as voices from the grave;
And deep-asleep he seem'd, yet all awake,
And music in his ears his beating heart did
    make.

They sat them down upon the yellow sand,
Between the sun and moon upon the shore;
And sweet it was to dream of Fatherland,
Of child, and wife, and slave; but ever-
    more   40
Most weary seem'd the sea, weary the oar,
Weary the wandering fields of barren foam.
Then someone said, "We will return no
    more,"
And all at once they sang, "Our island home
Is far beyond the wave; we will no longer
    roam."

CHORIC SONG

I

There is sweet music here that softer falls
Than petals from blown roses on the grass,
Or night-dews on still waters between walls
Of shadowy granite, in a gleaming pass;
Music that gentlier on the spirit lies,   50
Than tir'd eyelids upon tir'd eyes;
Music that brings sweet sleep down from the
    blissful skies.
Here are cool mosses deep,
And thro' the moss the ivies creep,
And in the stream the long-leaved flowers
    weep,
And from the craggy ledge the poppy hangs
    in sleep.

II

Why are we weigh'd upon with heaviness,
And utterly consumed with sharp distress,

While all things else have rest from weari-
ness?
All things have rest: why should we toil
alone, 60
We only toil, who are the first of things,
And make perpetual moan,
Still from one sorrow to another thrown:
Nor ever fold our wings,
And cease from wanderings,
Nor steep our brows in slumber's holy balm;
Nor harken what the inner spirit sings,
"There is no joy but calm!"
Why should we only toil, the roof and crown
of things?

III

Lo! in the middle of the wood, 70
The folded leaf is woo'd from out the bud
With winds upon the branch, and there
Grows green and broad, and takes no care,
Sun-steep'd at noon, and in the moon
Nightly dew-fed; and turning yellow
Falls, and floats adown the air.
Lo! sweeten'd with the summer light,
The full-juiced apple, waxing over-mellow,
Drops in a silent autumn night.
All its allotted length of days, 80
The flower ripens in its place,
Ripens and fades, and falls, and hath no toil,
Fast-rooted in the fruitful soil.

IV

Hateful is the dark-blue sky,
Vaulted o'er the dark-blue sea.
Death is the end of life; ah, why
Should life all labour be?
Let us alone. Time driveth onward fast,
And in a little while our lips are dumb.
Let us alone. What is it that will last? 90
All things are taken from us, and become
Portions and parcels of the dreadful Past.
Let us alone. What pleasure can we have
To war with evil? Is there any peace
In ever climbing up the climbing wave?
All things have rest, and ripen toward the
grave
In silence; ripen, fall, and cease:
Give us long rest or death, dark death, or
dreamful ease.

V

How sweet it were, hearing the downward
stream
With half-shut eyes ever to seem 100
Falling asleep in a half-dream!
To dream and dream, like yonder amber
light,
Which will not leave the myrrh-bush on the
height;
To hear each other's whispered speech;
Eating the Lotos day by day,
To watch the crisping ripples on the beach,
And tender curving lines of creamy spray;
To lend our hearts and spirits wholly
To the influence of mild-minded melan-
choly;
To muse and brood and live again in mem-
ory, 110
With those old faces of our infancy
Heap'd over with a mound of grass,
Two handfuls of white dust, shut in an urn
of brass!

VI

Dear is the memory of our wedded lives,
And dear the last embraces of our wives
And their warm tears; but all hath suffered
change:
For surely now our household hearts are
cold:
Our sons inherit us: our looks are strange:
And we should come like ghosts to trouble
joy.
Or else the island princes over-bold 120
Have eat our substance, and the minstrel
sings
Before them of the ten years' war in Troy,
And our great deeds, as half-forgotten things.
Is there confusion in the little isle?
Let what is broken so remain.
The gods are hard to reconcile:
'Tis hard to settle order once again.
There *is* confusion worse than death,
Trouble on trouble, pain on pain,
Long labour unto aged breath, 130
Sore task to hearts worn out by many wars
And eyes grown dim with gazing on the
pilot-stars.

VII

But, propt on beds of amaranth and moly,
How sweet (while warm airs lull us, blow-
  ing lowly)
With half-dropt eyelid still,
Beneath a heaven dark and holy,
To watch the long bright river drawing
  slowly
His waters from the purple hill—
To hear the dewy echoes calling
From cave to cave thro' the thick-twined
  vine—   140
To watch the emerald-coloured water falling
Thro' many a wov'n acanthus-wreath divine!
Only to hear and see the far-off sparkling
  brine,
Only to hear were sweet, stretch'd out be-
  neath the pine.

VIII

The Lotos blooms below the barren peak:
The Lotos blows by every winding creek:
All day the wind breathes low with mellower
  tone:
Thro' every hollow cave and alley lone
Round and round the spicy downs the yel-
  low Lotos-dust is blown.
We have had enough of action, and of mo-
  tion we,   150
Roll'd to starboard, roll'd to larboard, when
  the surge was seething free,
Where the wallowing monster spouted his
  foam-fountains in the sea.
Let us swear an oath, and keep it with an
  equal mind,
In the hollow Lotos-land to live and lie re-
  clined
On the hills like Gods together, careless of
  mankind.
For they lie beside their nectar, and the bolts
  are hurl'd
Far below them in the valleys, and the clouds
  are lightly curl'd
Round their golden houses, girdled with the
  gleaming world:
Where they smile in secret, looking over
  wasted lands,
Blight and famine, plague and earthquake,
  roaring deeps and fiery sands,   160

Clanging fights, and flaming towns, and sinking ships, and praying hands.
But they smile, they find a music centred in
  a doleful song
Steaming up, a lamentation and an ancient
  tale of wrong,
Like a tale of little meaning tho' the words
  are strong;
Chanted from an ill-used race of men that
  cleave the soil,
Sow the seed, and reap the harvest with enduring toil,
Storing yearly little dues of wheat, and wine
  and oil;
Till they perish and they suffer—some, 'tis
  whisper'd—down in hell
Suffer endless anguish, others in Elysian valleys dwell,
Resting weary limbs at last on beds of
  asphodel.   170
Surely, surely, slumber is more sweet than
  toil, the shore
Than labour in the deep mid-ocean, wind
  and wave and oar;
O rest ye, brother mariners, we will not wander more.

---

l. 21. down: open hilly land.
l. 106. crisping: curling.

[A LOSS OF SOMETHING EVER FELT I]

Emily Dickinson

A loss of something ever felt I—
The first that I could recollect
Bereft I was—of what I knew not
Too young that any should suspect

A Mourner walked among the children
I notwithstanding went about
As one bemoaning a Dominion
Itself the only Prince cast out—

Elder, Today, a session wiser
And fainter, too, as Wiseness is—   10
I find myself still softly searching
For my Delinquent Palaces—

And a Suspicion, like a Finger
Touches my Forehead now and then
That I am looking oppositely
For the site of the Kingdom of Heaven—

[FINDING IS THE FIRST ACT]

Emily Dickinson

Finding is the first Act
The second, loss,
Third, Expedition for
the "Golden Fleece"

Fourth, no Discovery—
Fifth, no Crew—
Finally, no Golden Fleece—
Jason—sham—too.

[THE WAYFARER]

Stephen Crane
(1871–1900)

The wayfarer,
Perceiving the pathway to truth,
Was struck with astonishment.
It was thickly grown with weeds.
"Ha," he said,
"I see that none has passed here
"In a long time."
Later he saw that each weed
Was a singular knife.
"Well," he mumbled at last,   10
"Doubtless there are other roads."

[A MAN SAID TO THE UNIVERSE]

Stephen Crane

A man said to the Universe:
"Sir, I exist!"
"However," replied the universe,
"The fact has not created in me
"A sense of obligation."

THE CONVERGENCE OF THE TWAIN
(*Lines on the loss of the "Titanic"*)

Thomas Hardy

I

In a solitude of the sea
Deep from human vanity,
And the Pride of Life that planned her, stilly
couches she.

II

Steel chambers, late the pyres
Of her salamandrine fires,
Cold currents thrid, and turn to rhythmic
tidal lyres.

III

Over the mirrors meant
To glass the opulent
The sea-worm crawls—grotesque, slimed,
dumb, indifferent.

IV

Jewels in joy designed   10
To ravish the sensuous mind
Lie lightless, all their sparkles bleared and
black and blind.

V

Dim moon-eyed fishes near
Gaze at the gilded gear
And query: "What does this vaingloriousness
down here?" . . .

VI

Well: while was fashioning
This creature of cleaving wing,
The Immanent Will that stirs and urges
everything

VII

Prepared a sinister mate
For her—so gaily great—   20
A Shape of Ice, for the time far and disso-
ciate.

VIII

And as the smart ship grew
In stature, grace, and hue,
In shadowy silent distance grew the Iceberg
    too.

IX

Alien they seemed to be:
No mortal eye could see
The intimate welding of their later history,

X

Or sign that they were bent
By paths coincident
On being anon twin halves of one august
    event,   30

XI

Till the Spinner of the Years
Said "Now!" And each one hears,
And consummation comes, and jars two
    hemispheres.

WAITING BOTH

Thomas Hardy

A star looks down at me,
And says: "Here I and you
Stand, each in our degree.
What do you mean to do,—
    Mean to do?"

I say: "For all I know,
Wait, and let Time go by,
Till my change come,"—"Just so."
The star says: "So mean I:—
    So mean I."   10

BY THE EARTH'S CORPSE

Thomas Hardy

I

"O Lord, why grievest Thou?—
Since Life has ceased to be

Upon this globe, now cold
    As lunar land and sea,
And humankind, and fowl, and fur
    Are gone eternally,
All is the same to Thee as ere
    They knew mortality."

II

"O Time," replied the Lord,
    "Thou readest me ill, I ween;   10
Were all *the same,* I should not grieve
    At that late earthly scene,
Now blestly past—though planned by me
    With interest close and keen!—
Nay, nay: things now are *not* the same
    As they have earlier been.

III

"Written indelibly
    On my eternal mind
Are all the wrongs endured
    By Earth's poor patient kind,   20
Which my too oft unconscious hand
    Let enter undesigned.
No god can cancel deeds foredone,
    Or thy old coils unwind!

"As when, in Noë's days,
    I whelmed the plains with sea,
So at this last, when flesh
    And herb but fossils be,
And, all extinct, their piteous dust
    Revolves obliviously,   30
That I made Earth, and life, and man,
    It still repenteth me!"

THE LIFE OF MAN

Francis Bacon
(1561–1626)

The world's a bubble, and the life of man
    Less than a span:
In his conception wretched, from the womb
    So to the tomb;
Curst from his cradle, and brought up to
    years
        With cares and fears.

Who then to frail mortality shall trust,
But limns the water, or but writes in dust.

Yet since with sorrow here we live oppressed,
      What life is best?   10
Courts are but only superficial schools
      To dandle fools:
The rural parts are turned into a den
      Of savage men:
And where's a city from all vice so free,
But may be termed the worst of all the
    three?

Domestic cares afflict the husband's bed,
      Or pains his head:
Those that live single, take it for a curse,
      Or do things worse: 20
Some would have children; those that have
    them, moan
      Or wish them gone:
What is it, then, to have, or have no wife,
But single thraldom, or a double strife?

Our own affections still at home to please
      Is a disease:
To cross the seas to any foreign soil,
      Perils and toil:
Wars with their noise affright us; when they
    cease,
      We're worse in peace;—   30
What then remains, but that we still should
    cry
Not to be born, or, being born, to die?

---

l. 11. Courts: royal (not legal) courts.

[WHEN SMOKE STOOD UP FROM LUDLOW]

A. E. Housman

When smoke stood up from Ludlow,
    And mist blew off from Teme,
And blithe afield to plowing
    Against the morning beam
    I strode beside my team,

The blackbird in the coppice
    Looked out to see me stride,
And hearkened as I whistled
    The trampling team beside,
    And fluted and replied: 10

"Lie down, lie down, young yeoman;
    What use to rise and rise?
Rise man a thousand mornings
    Yet down at last he lies,
    And then the man is wise."

I heard the tune he sang me,
    And spied his yellow bill;
I picked a stone and aimed it
    And threw it with a will:
    Then the bird was still.   20

Then my soul within me
    Took up the blackbird's strain,
And still beside the horses
    Along the dewy lane
    It sang the song again:

"Lie down, lie down, young yeoman;
    The sun moves always west;
The road one treads to labour
    Will lead one home to rest,
    And that will be the best."   30

15. RELIGION

[AT THE ROUND EARTH'S IMAGINED CORNERS]

John Donne

At the round earth's imagined corners, blow
Your trumpets, angels, and arise, arise
From death, you numberless infinities
Of souls, and to your scattered bodies go;
All whom the flood did, and fire shall
    o'erthrow,
All whom war, dearth, age, agues, tyrannies,
Despair, law, chance, hath slain, and you,
    whose eyes
Shall behold God, and never taste death's
    woe.
But let them sleep, Lord, and me mourn a
    space;
For, if above all these my sins abound,   10
'Tis late to ask abundance of Thy grace,
When we are there. Here on this lowly
    ground,
Teach me how to repent, for that's as good
As if Thou hadst seal'd my pardon with
    Thy blood.

[DEATH, BE NOT PROUD]

John Donne

Death, be not proud, though some have
    called thee
Mighty and dreadful, for thou art not so;
For those, whom thou think'st thou dost
    overthrow,
Die not, poor Death, nor yet canst thou kill
    me.

From rest and sleep, which but thy pictures
    be,
Much pleasure, then from thee much more
    must flow,
And soonest our best men with thee do go,
Rest of their bones, and soul's delivery.
Thou'rt slave to Fate, chance, kings, and
    desperate men,
And dost with poison, war, and sickness
    dwell;   10
And poppy, or charms can make us sleep as
    well,
And better than thy stroke; why swell'st thou
    then?
One short sleep past, we wake eternally,
And Death shall be no more; Death, thou
    shalt die.

THE COLLAR

George Herbert
(1593–1633)

I struck the board, and cry'd, No more.
    I will abroad.
What? shall I ever sigh and pine?
My lines and life are free, free as the road,
    Loose as the winde, as large as store.
        Shall I be still in suit?
    Have I no harvest but a thorn
    To let me bloud, and not restore
    What I have lost with cordiall fruit?
        Sure there was wine   10
Before my sighs did drie it; there was corn
    Before my tears did drown it.
    Is the yeare onely lost to me?
        Have I no bayes to crown it?
    No flowers, no garlands gay? all blasted?
        All wasted?
    Not so, my heart: but there is fruit,
        And thou hast hands.

Recover all thy sigh-blown age
On double pleasures: Leave thy cold dis-
    pute   20
Of what is fit, and not. Forsake thy cage,
    Thy rope of sands,
Which pettie thoughts have made, and made
    to thee
Good cable, to enforce and draw,
    And be thy law,
While thou didst wink and wouldst not
    see.
    Away; take heed:
    I will abroad.
Call in thy death's-head there: tie up thy
    fears.
    He that forbears   30
    To suit and serve his need,
    Deserves his load.
But as I rav'd and grew more fierce and wilde
    At every word,
Methought I heard one calling, *Child!*
And I reply'd *My Lord!*

---

l. 1. board: table.
l. 5. store: abundance.
l. 6. still in suit: always in the position of begging for something.
l. 9. cordiall fruit: fruit having the property of a
cordial; invigorating.

THE PULLEY

George Herbert

When God at first made man,
Having a glass of blessings standing by;
Let us (said he) poure on him all we can:
Let the worlds riches, which dispersed lie,
    Contract into a span.

So strength first made a way;
Then beautie flow'd, then wisdome, honour,
    pleasure:
When almost all was out, God made a stay,
Perceiving that alone of all his treasure
    Rest in the bottome lay.   10

For if I should (said he)
Bestow this jewell also on my creature,

He would adore my gifts instead of me,
And rest in Nature, not the God of Nature:
    So both should losers be.

Yet let him keep the rest,
But keep them with repining restlessnesse:
Let him be rich and wearie, that at least,
If goodnesse leade him not, yet wearinesse
    May tosse him to my breast.   20

JOURNEY OF THE MAGI

T. S. Eliot

"A cold coming we had of it,
Just the worst time of the year
For a journey, and such a long journey:
The ways deep and the weather sharp,
The very dead of winter."
And the camels galled, sore-footed, refrac-
    tory,
Lying down in the melting snow.
There were times we regretted
The summer palaces on slopes, the terraces,
And the silken girls bringing sherbet.   10
Then the camel men cursing and grumbling
And running away, and wanting their liquor
    and women,
And the night-fires going out, and the lack
    of shelters,
And the cities hostile and the towns un-
    friendly
And the villages dirty and charging high
    prices:
A hard time we had of it.
At the end we preferred to travel all night,
Sleeping in snatches,
With the voices singing in our ears, saying
That this was all folly.   20

Then at dawn we came down to a temperate
    valley,
Wet, below the snow line, smelling of vege-
    tation;
With a running stream and a water-mill beat-
    ing the darkness,
And three trees on the low sky,

And an old white horse galloped away in the meadow.
Then we came to a tavern with vine-leaves over the lintel,
Six hands at an open door dicing for pieces of silver,
And feet kicking the empty wine-skins.
But there was no information, and so we continued
And arrived at evening, not a moment too soon   30
Finding the place; it was (you may say) satisfactory.

All this was a long time ago, I remember,
And I would do it again, but set down
This set down
This: were we led all that way for
Birth or Death? There was a Birth, certainly,
We had evidence and no doubt. I had seen birth and death,
But had thought they were different; this Birth was
Hard and bitter agony for us, like Death, our death.
We returned to our places, these Kingdoms,   40

But no longer at ease here, in the old dispensation,
With an alien people clutching their gods.
I should be glad of another death.

EASTER HYMN

A. E. Housman

If in that Syrian garden, ages slain,
You sleep, and know not you are dead in vain,
Nor even in dreams behold how dark and bright
Ascends in smoke and fire by day and night
The hate you died to quench and could but fan,
Sleep well and see no morning, son of man.

But if, the grave rent and the stone rolled by,
At the right hand of majesty on high
You sit, and sitting so remember yet
Your tears, your agony and bloody sweat,   10
Your cross and passion and the life you gave,
Bow hither out of heaven and see and save.

16. FOUR POETS

John Donne

THE FUNERAL

Whoever comes to shroud me, do not harm
    Nor question much
That subtle wreath of hair, which crowns my
    arm;
The mystery, the sign, you must not touch,
    For 'tis my outward Soul,
Viceroy to that, which then to heaven being
    gone,
    Will leave this to control,
And keep these limbs, her provinces, from
    dissolution.

For if the sinewy thread my brain lets fall
    Through every part,   10
Can tie those parts, and make me one of all;
These hairs which upward grew, and strength
    and art
    Have from a better brain,
Can better do it; except she meant that I
    By this should know my pain,
As prisoners then are manacled, when they're
    condemn'd to die.

Whate'er she meant by it, bury it with me,
    For since I am
Love's martyr, it might breed idolatry
If into others' hands these relics came;   20
    As 'twas humility
To afford to it all that a soul can do,
    So, 'tis some bravery,
That since you would save none of me, I
    bury some of you.

l. 9. sinewy thread: the nervous system.
l. 23. bravery: boldness.

THE GOOD-MORROW

I wonder, by my troth, what thou and I
Did, till we loved? Were we not wean'd till
    then?
But suck'd on country pleasures, childishly?
Or snorted we in the Seven Sleepers' den?
'Twas so; but this, all pleasures fancies be:
If ever any beauty I did see,
Which I desir'd, and got, 'twas but a dream
    of thee.

And now good-morrow to our waking souls,
Which watch not one another out of fear;
For love, all love of other sights con-
    trols,   10
And makes one little room, an everywhere.
Let sea-discoverers to new worlds have gone,
Let maps to others, worlds on worlds have
    shown,
Let us possess one world, each hath one, and
    is one.

My face in thine eye, thine in mine appears,
And true plain hearts do in the faces rest;
Where can we find two better hemispheres,
Without sharp North, without declining
    West?
Whatever dies, was not mix'd equally;
If our two loves be one, or, thou and I   20
Love so alike, that none do slacken, none
    can die.

l. 5. but: except for.
l. 21. none: neither.

THE ANNIVERSARY

All Kings, and all their favourites,
  All glory of honours, beauties, wits,
The Sun itself, which makes times, as they
    pass,
Is elder by a year, now, than it was
When thou and I first one another saw:
All other things to their destruction draw,
  Only our love hath no decay;
This, no tomorrow hath, nor yesterday;
Running it never runs from us away,
But truly keeps his first, last, everlasting
    day.   10

  Two graves must hide thine and my corse;
  If one might, death were no divorce:
Alas, as well as other Princes, we
(Who Prince enough in one another be)
Must leave at last in death, these eyes, and
    ears,
Oft fed with true oaths, and with sweet salt
    tears;
  But souls where nothing dwells but love
(All other thoughts being inmates) then
    shall prove
This, or a love increasèd there above,
When bodies to their graves, souls from their
    graves remove.   20

  And then we shall be throughly blest,
  But we no more than all the rest;
Here upon earth, we are Kings, and none
    but we
Can be such kings, nor of such subjects be:
Who is so safe as we, where none can do
Treason to us, except one of us two?
  True and false fears let us refrain,
Let us love nobly, and live, and add again
Years and years unto years, till we attain
To write threescore; this is the second of
    our reign.   30

l. 11. corse: corpse.
l. 18. inmates: lodgers, not permanent dwellers.
prove: test out, or experience.

THE CANONIZATION

For God's sake hold your tongue, and let me
    love,
  Or chide my palsy, or my gout,
My five gray hairs, or ruin'd fortune flout,
With wealth your state, your mind with arts
    improve,
    Take you a course, get you a place,
    Observe his honour, or his grace,
Or the King's real, or his stamped face
    Contemplate; what you will, approve,
    So you will let me love.

Alas, alas, who's injured by my love?   10
  What merchant's ships have my sighs
    drown'd?
Who says my tears have overflow'd his
    ground?
When did my colds a forward spring re-
    move?
    When did the heats which my veins fill
    Add one man to the plaguy bill?
Soldiers find wars, and lawyers find out still
    Litigious men, which quarrels move,
    Though she and I do love.

Call us what you will, we are made such by
    love;
  Call her one, me another fly,   20
We are tapers too, and at our own cost die,
And we in us find the Eagle and the Dove.
    The Phoenix riddle hath more wit
    By us; we two being one, are it.
So to one neutral thing both sexes fit,
    We die and rise the same, and prove
    Mysterious by this love.

We can die by it, if not live by love,
  And if unfit for tombs and hearse
Our legend be, it will be fit for verse;   30
And if no piece of chronicle we prove,
    We'll build in sonnets pretty rooms;
    As well a well-wrought urn becomes
The greatest ashes, as half-acre tombs,

And by these hymns, all shall approve
Us *canoniz'd* for Love;

And thus invoke us: "You, whom reverend
    love
  Made one another's hermitage;
You, to whome love was peace, that now is
    rage;
Who did the whole world's soul contract, and
    drove   40
  Into the glasses of your eyes
  (So made such mirrors, and such spies,
That they did all to you epitomize)
  Countries, towns, courts: beg from above
  A pattern of your love!"

l. 5. course: either a course of study or a career.
place: a job, at court (or elsewhere).
ll. 13–14. colds . . . heats: chills and fevers of
love.
l. 15. plaguy bill: published list of those who
have died of plague.
l. 22. Eagle . . . Dove: strength and gentleness.

William Blake
THE CLOD AND THE PEBBLE

"Love seeketh not Itself to please,
  Nor for itself hath any care,
But for another gives its ease,
  And builds a Heaven in Hell's despair."

So sung a little Clod of Clay
  Trodden with the cattle's feet,
But a Pebble of the brook
  Warbled out these metres meet:

"Love seeketh only Self to please,
  To bind another to Its delight,   10
Joys in another's loss of ease,
  And builds a Hell in Heaven's despite."

THE TYGER

Tyger! Tyger! burning bright
In the forests of the night,

What immortal hand or eye
Could frame thy fearful symmetry?

In what distant deeps or skies
Burnt the fire of thine eyes?
On what wings dare he aspire?
What the hand dare seize the fire?

And what shoulder, & what art,
Could twist the sinews of thy heart?   10
And when thy heart began to beat,
What dread hand? & what dread feet?

What the hammer? what the chain?
In what furnace was thy brain?
What the anvil? what dread grasp
Dare its deadly terrors clasp?

When the stars threw down their spears,
And water'd heaven with their tears,
Did he smile his work to see?
Did he who made the Lamb make thee?   20

Tyger! Tyger! burning bright
In the forests of the night,
What immortal hand or eye,
Dare frame thy fearful symmetry?

MAD SONG

The wild winds weep,
And the night is a-cold;
Come hither, Sleep,
And my griefs unfold:
But lo! the morning peeps
Over the eastern steeps,
And the rustling birds of dawn
The earth do scorn.

Lo! to the vault
Of paved heaven,   10
With sorrow fraught
My notes are driven:
They strike the ear of night,
Make weep the eyes of day;
They make mad the roaring winds,
And with tempests play.

Like a fiend in a cloud,
With howling woe,
After night I do crowd,
And with night will go;   20
I turn my back to the east,
From whence comforts have increas'd;
For light doth seize my brain
With frantic pain.

A POISON TREE

I was angry with my friend:
I told my wrath, my wrath did end.
I was angry with my foe:
I told it not, my wrath did grow.

And I water'd it in fears,
Night & morning with my tears;
And I sunned it with smiles,
And with soft deceitful wiles.

And it grew both day and night,
Till it bore an apple bright;   10
And my foe beheld it shine,
And he knew that it was mine,

And into my garden stole
When the night had veil'd the pole:
In the morning glad I see
My foe outstretch'd beneath the tree.

Gerard Manley Hopkins

[NO WORST, THERE IS NONE]

No worst, there is none. Pitched past pitch of
     grief,
More pangs will, schooled at forepangs,
     wilder wring.
Comforter, where, where is your comforting?
Mary, mother of us, where is your relief?
My cries heave, herds-long; huddle in a main,
     a chief
Woe, world-sorrow; on an age-old anvil
     wince and sing—
Then lull, then leave off. Fury had shrieked
     "No ling-
ering! Let me be fell: force I must be
     brief."

O the mind, mind has mountains; cliffs of
     fall
Frightful, sheer, no-man-fathomed. Hold
     them cheap   10
May who ne'er hung there. Nor does long
     our small
Durance deal with that steep or deep. Here!
     creep,
Wretch, under a comfort serves in a whirl-
     wind: all
Life death does end and each day dies with
     sleep.

HEAVEN-HAVEN

A NUN TAKES THE VEIL

I have desired to go
     Where springs not fail,
To fields where flies no sharp and sided hail,
     And a few lilies blow.

And I have asked to be
     Where no storms come,
Where the green swell is in the havens
     dumb,
     And out of the swing of the sea.

PIED BEAUTY

Glory be to God for dappled things—
     For skies of couple-colour as a brinded
          cow;
     For rose-moles all in stipple upon trout
          that swim;
Fresh-firecoal chestnut-falls; finches' wings;
     Landscape plotted and pieced—fold, fal-
          low, and plough;
     And áll trádes, their gear and tackle and
          trim.

All things counter, original, spare, strange;
     Whatever is fickle, freckled (who knows
          how?)
     With swift, slow; sweet, sour; adazzle,
          dim;
He fathers-forth whose beauty is past
     change: 10
          Praise him.

THE WINDHOVER:

TO CHRIST OUR LORD

I caught this morning morning's minion, king-
    dom of daylight's dauphin, dapple-dawn-drawn Falcon, in
      his riding
    Of the rolling level underneath him steady air, and striding
High there, how he rung upon the rein of a wimpling wing
In his ecstasy! then off, off forth on swing,   5
    As a skate's heel sweeps smooth on a bow-bend: the hurl and
      gliding
    Rebuffed the big wind. My heart in hiding
Stirred for a bird,—the achieve of, the mastery of the thing!

Brute beauty and valour and act, oh, air, pride, plume, here
    Buckle! AND the fire that breaks from thee then, a billion   10
Times told lovelier, more dangerous, O my chevalier!

    No wonder of it: shéer plód makes plough down sillion
Shine, and blue-bleak embers, ah my dear,
    Fall, gall themselves, and gash gold-vermilion.

William Butler Yeats

THE MAGI

Now as at all times I can see in the mind's
eye,
In their stiff, painted clothes, the pale unsatisfied ones
Appear and disappear in the blue depth of
the sky
With all their ancient faces like rain-beaten
stones,
And all their helms of silver hovering side
by side,
And all their eyes still fixed, hoping to find
once more,
Being by Calvary's turbulence unsatisfied,
The uncontrollable mystery on the bestial
floor.

THE SECOND COMING

Turning and turning in the widening gyre
The falcon cannot hear the falconer;
Things fall apart; the centre cannot hold;
Mere anarchy is loosed upon the world,
The blood-dimmed tide is loosed, and every-
where
The ceremony of innocence is drowned;
The best lack all conviction, while the worst
Are full of passionate intensity.

Surely some revelation is at hand;
Surely the Second Coming is at hand.   10
The Second Coming! Hardly are those words
out
When a vast image out of *Spiritus Mundi*
Troubles my sight: somewhere in sands of
the desert
A shape with lion body and the head of a
man,
A gaze blank and pitiless as the sun,
Is moving its slow thighs, while all about it
Reel shadows of the indignant desert birds.
The darkness drops again; but now I know
That twenty centuries of stony sleep
Were vexed to nightmare by a rocking cradle,
And what rough beast, its hour come round
at last,   21
Slouches towards Bethlehem to be born?

THE COLD HEAVEN

Suddenly I saw the cold and rook-delighting
heaven
That seemed as though ice burned and was
but the more ice,
And thereupon imagination and heart were
driven
So wild that every casual thought of that and
this
Vanished, and left but memories, that should
be out of season
With the hot blood of youth, of love crossed
long ago;
And I took all the blame out of all sense and
reason,
Until I cried and trembled and rocked to and
fro,
Riddled with light. Ah! when the ghost be-
gins to quicken,
Confusion of the death-bed over, is it sent
Out naked on the roads, as the books say,
and stricken   11
By the injustice of the skies for punishment?

AMONG SCHOOL CHILDREN

I

I walk through the long schoolroom question-
ing;
A kind old nun in a white hood replies;
The children learn to cipher and to sing,
To study reading-books and histories,
To cut and sew, be neat in everything
In the best modern way—the children's eyes
In momentary wonder stare upon
A sixty-year-old smiling public man.

II

I dream of a Ledaean body, bent
Above a sinking fire, a tale that she   10
Told of a harsh reproof, or trivial event
That changed some childish day to tragedy—
Told, and it seemed that our two natures
blent
Into a sphere from youthful sympathy,
Or else, to alter Plato's parable,
Into the yolk and white of the one shell.

III

And thinking of that fit of grief or rage
I look upon one child or t'other there
And wonder if she stood so at that age—
For even daughters of the swan can share
Something of every paddler's heritage—   21
And had that color upon cheek or hair,
And thereupon my heart is driven wild:
She stands before me as a living child.

IV

Her present image floats into the mind—
Did Quattrocento finger fashion it
Hollow of cheek as though it drank the wind
And took a mess of shadows for its meat?
And I though never of Ledaean kind
Had pretty plumage once—enough of that,
Better to smile on all that smile, and show
There is a comfortable kind of scarecrow.

V

What youthful mother, a shape upon her lap
Honey of generation had betrayed,   34
And that must sleep, shriek, struggle to
escape
As recollection or the drug decide,
Would think her son, did she but see that
shape
With sixty or more winters on its head,
A compensation for the pang of his birth,
Or the uncertainty of his setting forth?   40

VI

Plato thought nature but a spume that plays
Upon a ghostly paradigm of things;
Solider Aristotle played the taws
Upon the bottom of a king of kings;
World-famous golden-thighed Pythagoras
Fingered upon a fiddle-stick or strings
What a star sang and careless Muses heard:
Old clothes upon old sticks to scare a bird.

VII

Both nuns and mothers worship images,
But those the candles light are not as those
That animate a mother's reveries,   51
But keep a marble or a bronze repose.
And yet they too break hearts—O Presences
That passion, piety or affection knows,
And that all heavenly glory symbolise—
O self-born mockers of man's enterprise;

VIII

Labour is blossoming or dancing where
The body is not bruised to pleasure soul,
Nor beauty born out of its own despair,
Nor blear-eyed wisdom out of midnight oil.
O chestnut tree, great-rooted blossomer,   61
Are you the leaf, the blossom or the bole?

O body swayed to music, O brightening glance,
How can we know the dancer from the dance?

---

l. 9. Ledaean: referring to Helen, daughter of Leda.

l. 43. taws: whips.

POETRY: NOTES AND COMMENTS

I

The poems in this first group are for the most part character sketches, a type of writing that commonly employs prose. The selections are not "poetical" in a superficial or old-fashioned sense. They do not use elaborate language, and they are not outpourings of emotion, though several have a strong emotional undercurrent. In some the writing is cool and objective; the writer may use verse form only to give what he says a neat, crisp outline, or to point up a few key words or thoughts, or to make each thing said stand out with emphasis. The reader might pause to consider whether he thinks he would like the poems better if they were written in prose. He should also look out for passages in which the verse form contributes to the effectiveness of the whole.

Some of the poems are focused on a particular individual, some on a type. Several sum up a lifetime's knowledge of a person in a few lines. All were written by poets who saw and judged for themselves; hence they are free from the "stock response." Barker writes affectionately about his mother, Yeats about the woman he loved for many years. But there is no ideal, standard, or ready-made mother or lover in the group.

Robinson, "Richard Cory"

Is characterization the main purpose, or is this subordinate to the theme?

What natural question does the poet fail to answer? Has his omission anything to do with the theme? Might one say that the lack of answer is part of the point of the poem?

Robinson, "Mr. Flood's Party"

line 20. Roland's ghost. When treacherously attacked, Roland, a hero of French medieval legend, refused to blow his horn to summon aid till he lay dying.

Is the tone of the poem ironic or sympathetic or both? Point out some of the details that influence your opinion.

Robinson, "Miniver Cheevy"

lines 11–12. Thebes, Camelot, and Priam's neighbors refer to the legends of Oedipus, King Arthur, and the Trojan war.

lines 23–24. How graceful is armor? What is the value here of calling it "iron clothing"?

Does Robinson mean that Miniver would actually have been happy in some past age? What point is made by the reference to numerous past times rather than one?

Is the tone sympathetic? ironic? Compare it with that of the preceding poem.

MacNeice, "Museums"

line 3. tall fake porches: modern imitations of Greek or Roman architecture. Has the word *fake* any broader reference to the theme of the poem?

What is the significance of the figurative expressions "beetle under a brick," "the cowed cypher," "paces himself by marble lives"?

cummings, "nobody loses all the time"

Is there any similarity of theme between this poem, "Miniver Cheevy," and "Museums"? Compare the writers' tone and their attitude toward failure in the three poems.

Is this really a poem or is it just fun? or both?

Barker, "Sonnet: To My Mother"

line 5. Rabelais: the sixteenth-century French author of racy, often coarse satiric tales of the giant Gargantua.

What is the meaning of the last two lines of the first stanza?

Is the use of the homonyms at the end effective, or does it seem inappropriate?

Discuss the suitability of this poem as a tribute to one's mother.

What is the effect of "O" in line 13?

Browning, "My Last Duchess"

This and the following selection from Browning are dramatic monologues, poems in which the author speaks through the mouth of someone not himself. Browning constructs a situation in which the character reveals himself merely by talking.

Many students, reading this poem in secondary school, find it an interesting puzzle to unravel. On later readings does it seem less convincing, or more contrived?

Browning, "The Bishop Orders His Tomb at St. Praxed's Church"

The Bishop is meant to typify some incongruous aspects of the Renaissance: love of beauty, genuine Christian belief mingling with pagan attitudes, worldliness, cynical immorality.

lines 77–79. Tully's . . . Ulpian. The choice Latin of Cicero contrasted with the inferior Latin of a later writer.

line 99. *elucescebat:* he shone. The Bishop is still contemptuous of Gandolf's unclassical epitaph. The classical form is *elucebat.*

Hood, "Sonnet"

line 3. grass-bleach'd. Good housewives used to bleach their white linens by spreading them on sunny grass to dry.

Masters, "Lucinda Matlock"

In *Spoon River Anthology,* Masters undertook to represent the people of a Middle Western town by a series of imaginary epitaphs spoken by persons buried in the local cemetery. The free verse form and more particularly the frankness of some of the confessions created a furor when the work appeared in 1915. Now that the novelty has worn off, many critics consider the plan of the book more interesting than the execution.

If this were printed as prose, would it differ much from other prose?

In real life, almost anyone would prefer a Lucinda Matlock, who lived her life fully, to a Mistress Nicely, who is described merely as a meticulous housekeeper and laundress. Does the same preference hold for the poems about them? If not, why not?

Yeats, "Her Praise"

The subject of this and the two following poems is Maud Gonne, a well-known and beautiful Irishwoman who devoted her life to the Irish revolutionary struggle against England. Yeats loved her for many years but did not always like her activities and opinions. This biographical fact is not essential for the understanding of the poems. But the three poems together, treating one person in three such different ways, illustrate the fresh and varied perceptions of a poet who is awake to what happens both inside and outside himself if he has not prefurnished his mind with stereotypes instead of actual experience.

Yeats, "No Second Troy"

lines 3–5. Maud Gonne had been urging violent rebellion in Ireland.

Comment on the meaning and effectiveness of the image relating to Helen.

Yeats, "That the Night Come"

What statement is made about the woman through the image of the king's marriage day?

Comment on Yeats' use of the word *outrageous* in line 10.

What different aspects of a single individual are brought out in the three poems? What is accomplished by the variety of metaphors and comparisons?

2

Apart from their verse form, do these narratives differ in any respect from prose narratives? The story of one might have been made into a short story; that of the other has often been told in prose histories.

Frost, "The Death of the Hired Man"

What is the effect of our seeing the hired man only indirectly, through the conversation of husband and wife?

Benét, [Harper's Ferry Episode]

The selection reprinted here is one of many self-contained episodes that form a part of

Benét's book-length poem on the Civil War. The historical background is well known and does not require explanation.

3

Ballads were originally "songs that tell a story," composed orally, it is thought, and handed down through the centuries without any poet's name. These folk or "popular" ballads are simple in style and language. Frequently they employ repetition in the form of a refrain, a question-and-answer formula through which the story is told, or stock descriptive phrases. The story is usually presented in a single dramatic scene or in a series of detached scenes rather than by consecutive narrative. The ballads seldom explain motives and seldom express emotion directly. The listener's imagination and, when they are sung, the music must supply what the words leave unsaid.

A ballad hero, as a rule, was permitted to die in bed only if he died of a broken heart: the stories, in other words, are most often violent and tragic. Today, purveyors of popular entertainment in television, movies, or fiction usually consider a happy ending prerequisite to success. Yet the ballads too were the entertainment of the common man, not of the intellectual or the highly educated. This raises interesting questions. Has the common man changed so radically in modern times? Or can we account otherwise for the difference in taste?

During the last two centuries poets have found much to admire in these old ballads and have written "literary" ballads, not meant for actual song, in which some of the old simplicity and immediacy are revived. Both kinds of ballads are represented here, along with a few other poems that bear some resemblance to them.

Morris, "The Haystack in the Floods"

Morris sets the scene of this story in the Middle Ages. Sir Robert de Marny, an Englishman, is attempting to rescue Jehane from a trial for witchcraft in Paris. They are making for the border of Gascony, which was then held by the English.

lines 53–56. These lines refer to the "trial by water," in which guilt or innocence was determined by whether the accused witch floated or sank.

"Bonny Barbara Allan"

This ballad combines stock ballad materials ("She had not gane a mile but twa" and "make my bed," the latter as a token of approaching death) with unusually individual and complex motivation. Is the situation that of a girl who "bites off her nose to spite her face"? Though people do not die overnight of a broken heart —at least not nowadays—the poem is essentially true to human nature. In what way?

"Marie Hamilton"

The last stanza makes the objective statement that tomorrow there will be one Mary fewer (in her circle) and then simply names the others. Does this conclusion have an emotional impact? Why?

"Sir Patrick Spence"

lines 33–40. Note how the waiting is stretched out through two stanzas. What is the effect of this and of the only two descriptive details given about the wives: the fans in their hands and gold combs in their hair?

"The Twa Corbies"

What is the spirit or tone of this ballad— pathetic, tragic, gruesome, ironic, or something else?

Scott, "Proud Maisie"

Scott was fond of the old folk ballads and helped to collect and preserve them.

This poem uses the same device as "The Twa Corbies" of having birds speak. Compare the two poems.

Kipling, "Follow Me 'ome"

This is one of those borderline poems on which opinions are likely to vary. It is so close to being good and so close to being bad that the same reader may feel differently at different times. The best men do not always die young and horses are not always more devoted than women. For this and other reasons we may feel that Kipling is giving us cheap cynicism dressed, to look original, in Cockney dialect. But the poem may also be felt as a moving and eloquent one, saved from sentimentality by hard and commonplace language. The truth is that both elements are present. Sometimes one, sometimes the other will strike the reader more forcibly.

Cowper, "The Castaway"

The incident upon which the poem is based was reported in Admiral George Anson's *A Voyage Round the World* (see line 52). In the story of the dead seaman, Cowper saw an emblem of his own spiritual despair. A deeply religious, conscientious, and gentle man, Cowper several times sank into a state of horror in which he believed himself abandoned by God, his soul doomed to eternal Hell. Long struggles against despair won him some years of cheerful friendliness and sanity, but the dream in which a voice had once announced his doom continued to haunt him. "The Castaway" was written not long before his final descent into insanity. In line 3 and the conclusion he makes specific the parallel between his state and that of Anson's seaman. What effect does this have on the "story" part of the poem?

Keats, "La Belle Dame sans Merci" ("The beautiful lady without mercy")

This poem has been variously interpreted. Is it just a supernatural story written to produce an eerie atmosphere? Does it symbolize the evil of purely sensual love? Is it a way of saying that human beings must live in the real world of responsibilities, that to escape from this is not happiness but death? In short, what gives the poem reality for modern readers who may have little interest in knights and who are skeptical about the existence of witches, vampires, and other supernatural ladies?

What is the value of the frame within which Keats tells his story—that is, of the scene and circumstances of the opening and closing stanzas? Lines 3–4, 47–48 are a celebrated example of poetic economy: a scene and a mood created by means of only two positive concrete things (a lake and withered sedge) and one negative (the absence of birds' song). Can you explain (altogether or in part) what makes this combination effective?

Yeats, "The Host of the Air"

Yeats said this poem was founded on an old Irish folk ballad. The title refers to the "trooping fairies" of Irish legend, described by Yeats in *Irish Fairy and Folk Tales*. The name "Sidhe" (pronounced "shee"), he explained, in Gaelic means wind as well as fairies. The Sidhe ride the wind; and country people, seeing in the road a whirlwind of straws and leaves, say it is the fairies passing. The Sidhe are not always little but take what size and shape they choose. They like to feast, fight, dance, and make love; and they play the most beautiful music. They are inconstant and irresponsible.

When Yeats first wrote this poem he made the conclusion explicit in an additional stanza: O'Driscoll recognized his companions as "the folk of the air"; filled with dread, he ran home, where he found old women keening his dead wife. Yeats thought the meaning was evident without this stanza and discarded it because it had no "rhythmical charm" and broke the unity of mood.

Can the mood or tone of the poem be described? Does it owe anything to contradictory words and images?

Yeats, "The Three Beggars"

What contrast is intended between the crane and the beggars? What is meant by the last line? Does the poet seem to be expressing a general view of life?

Comment on the language in which the poem is written.

Auden, "O what is that sound"

In what respects does this resemble the old folk ballads? In what is it different?

The poem was published in England in the volume *Look, Stranger* in 1935, the year in which Neville Chamberlain became prime minister. Auden and others felt that England was not sufficiently awake to the danger of Hitler. To appreciate the poem is it necessary to understand this connection?

4
ROBERT FROST

Frost is one of the most "native" of American writers. His scene is almost always the country and farm life in New England. Though appreciation of individual poems, regardless of author, is the prime concern, a poem often gains by being read together with others by the same author. This small sampling of conversational, descriptive, and lyric poems, together with "The Death of the Hired Man" and "Desert Places," will give some idea of Frost's range and quality.

"The Runaway"

See the comment on this poem on page 263.

"After Apple-Picking"

lines 39–41. The woodchuck is an animal that hibernates.

Notice that the subject of the poem is not apple-picking but the half-dreaming memory and the after-images that follow a day of apple-picking. How does this fact affect the choice of details throughout the poem?

"Mending Wall"

The physical situation is that of rocky New England country, where the original farmers used stones cleared from their fields for boundary walls. These were built roughly without mortar, merely by piling up the uncut stones, and the frost in winter often dislodges them.

What other kind of wall is the poet talking about? Does he say anything to make it certain that this is a poem with more than one level of meaning? What about lines 41–42? Do any other lines clearly imply a symbolic meaning?

Is there any similar indication of double meaning in "After Apple-Picking," or is that a different and simpler kind of poem? If the latter is true, what appeal has the poem for people who do not pick apples?

"Nothing Gold Can Stay"

This poem is made from the simplest possible material. The words are all of one or two syllables, and all, except perhaps *hue* and *Eden,* are everyday words. Yet Frost's use of this language is original and imaginative.

What statements does he make that are not literally true?

Comment on the verbs used in the latter half of the poem.

"Fire and Ice"

Why are the rhyme sounds so conspicuous in this poem? Do they serve to emphasize the meaning? How?

What is the effect of the monosyllabic opening lines and the high proportion of monosyllables throughout? What is the effect of the short second line?

Is the conclusion weak, or does the colorless understatement of "would suffice" produce a strong effect?

WALTER DE LA MARE

On the surface, de la Mare's subjects frequently seem conventional and out of date: horsemen, ghosts, the fairies and elves of old-fashioned children's stories. Beneath this surface, however, there is often the sadness of universal themes of death and separation, primitive fears of the mysterious, often also a chilly hint of evil or malice at work behind the visible world.

"The Listeners"

De la Mare is reported to have said that the Traveller is the ghost. Does this reading make everything in the poem clear? or the reverse? Compare the theme with that of "The Ghost."

Point out some of the means by which the poet creates the feeling of silence.

"The Ghost"

Even supposing a ghost could actually revisit the living man she loved, this is scarcely the conversation that would take place between them. In the dialogue, does the living person seem to hear what the dead says, or is it only the dead who seems to hear the living?

Is the poet really imagining a reunion, or is he emphasizing the opposite, the loneliness and separation?

"The Mocking Fairy"

line 2. *Nidding* is not an actual word, but *niddle-noddle* means to nod the head unsteadily to and fro.

line 16. *Mimbling* is not a word either. *Mamble* is a dialect word for stammer, mutter, or mumble.

What the Fairy says might be paraphrased as a taunt, "Yah! you're dead, aren't you!" Almost everything mentioned is beautiful or dainty. How do the nastiness and horror creep in? Do the words *mimbling mambling* (line 16) suggest a witless, subhuman mumbling?

"At the Keyhole"

Grilled or broiled bones are a meat dish for which recipes may be found in English cookbooks. Do they seem to have been selected as a refrain here, in preference to other dishes, for any poetic reason? The slight metrical irregularity of the first line places particular stress on *grill* and *bones*. What is the psychological effect of this?

Is there any natural connection between irrational night fears and the request for food?

Do you regard this as a children's poem, or a grown-ups' poem, or both?

"The Old Men"

For the theme, see R. L. Stevenson's "Aes Triplex": "By the time a man gets well into the seventies, his continued existence is a mere miracle; and when he lays his old bones in bed for the night, there is an overwhelming probability that he will never see the day. Do the old men mind it, as a matter of fact? Why, no. . . . they hear of the death of people about their own age, or even younger, not as if it was a grisly warning, but with a simple childlike pleasure at having outlived someone else."

line 2. What is meant by "caged" and "riddle-rid"? The answer will be found in lines 3 and 4.

line 10. Comment on the epithet *ruinous*.

line 14. The phrase *in their sockets* is a good example of poetic economy of language. In one sense, the phrase is altogether unnecessary, since all human eyes are in sockets. But on the other hand, the mere fact that the word *socket* is not needed for literal truth makes it particularly emphatic and vivid as a descriptive word. It is thus both more vivid and more economical than a longer phrase describing deep-sunken eyes might be.

5

Cynical verses about women enjoyed a vogue during the sixteenth and seventeenth centuries (the poets, of course, were men). Consider the varieties of cynicism expressed in the poems of this group. What do we mean by "sincerity" in connection with such poems?

Which of the poems here are serious? Other serious love poems will be found in Sections 7, 16, and elsewhere.

Rudyerd, "Why do we love"
line 13. golden flowers: wealth, money.

Anon., "Brown is my Love'
Officially, a girl had to be blonde to be beautiful. Unofficially, of course, poets as well as other men often found brunettes beautiful also.

Wyatt, "To a Lady to Answer Directly with Yea or Nay"
Try to describe the mood of this poem. Is it possible to tell what the speaker's real feeling is toward the lady?

Notice the style: there are no descriptive adjectives or adverbs. Relate this fact to the theme.

Wyatt, "The Lover Showeth How He Is Forsaken"
The image underlying the first stanza has been shown by Mr. A. K. Moore to be probably that of a falcon: *flee* often meant *fly, gentle* was a common epithet for a female falcon, and falcons were often kept in their master's chamber. The women, then, who once came to the poet "gentle, tame, and meek" now have flown off like falcons reverting to the wild.

Some writers have chosen to believe that the lady of the second and third stanzas is Fortune personified, instead of a flesh-and-blood woman. Considering both the title and the poem as a whole, does this seem likely to you?

This poem is notable for its grace and its musical expressiveness. Observe, for instance, the effect of the occasional inversion of the accent. *Stalking,* in line 2, is a good example of an inverted accent that serves to emphasize the meaning of the word. Notice also how the run-on lines and imperfect but harmonious rhymes help to carry the movement forward through the first stanza.

Peele, "Song"

line 2. Chop-cherry was a game in which the players tried to catch a hanging cherry with their teeth. Here it merely means the season for the game, when cherries are ripe.

Marlowe, "The Passionate Shepherd to His Love"

This is an example of the fashion for "pastoral" poetry in which artificial shepherds are presented in an artificial country setting. In such poetry the fields are never muddy, the shepherds never work, and life consists largely of love and conversation.

(?) Raleigh, "The Nymph's Reply to the Shepherd"

line 7. Philomel is a name for the nightingale, derived from the Greek story of Philomela, Procne, and Tereus.

Is the poet mocking pastoral poetry in general, or is he merely inventing a girl's answer to Marlowe's shepherd?

Donne, "The Bait"

line 8. What is the syntax of *themselves?*

What is the meaning of lines 13–16?

Observe that the whole poem is the elaboration of a *conceit* (a striking, often far-fetched figure of speech or comparison). The poet has found a new, exaggerated way of telling the girl that she is pretty and captivating. Not a single adjective directly describes her beauty or her captivating qualities. But he is "caught," and the play on that word furnishes the basis for the poem.

Trace the working out of the conceit through each stanza.

Donne, "Song"

line 2. mandrake (mandragora): a plant that has been the subject of many superstitions. It has a forked root which is said to resemble the human form.

About what else besides women is Donne passingly cynical in the first stanza?

Donne, "The Indifferent"

What light does this poem throw on the preceding one?

A recent editor, Theodore Redpath, suggests the following interpretations:

line 2. The woman "made amorous by living in luxury, and the woman who gives herself because she needs money."

line 5. believes [him] . . . tries (i.e., tests) [him].

line 17. travel. The older form of the same word is *travail.* A double meaning may be intended.

Herrick, "Upon Julia's Clothes"

line 1. *goes.* In Herrick's time the meaning of *go* was more specific than it is now. It meant to *walk.*

line 5. vibration. Bentham in the eighteenth century described his *walking* for exercise as "vibrating."

The opening of the second tercet clearly marks some change. Is it a change from clothes to no clothes?

Wither, "Shall I, wasting in despair"

line 14. The female pelican was once believed to feed her young with her own blood.

Anon., "O western wind, when wilt thou blow"

For so short a poem, this one has caused a good deal of discussion, chiefly because of the difficulty of finding a logical link between the first two lines and the last two. Does a logical connection matter in this case, so long as the poem creates the feeling of longing, which is the essence of its meaning?

MacNeice, "Precursors"

This is not a love poem but is placed here because it seems to have been partly suggested by "O western wind." Is the reason for the longing for rain more apparent here? What is it? Is this a better poem? Who or what do you take to be the "precursors" of the title?

Does the strange image in line 11 produce the effect that is evidently intended by the poet?

Dickinson, "What shall I do when the Summer troubles"

Is the imagery in this poem original? In what sense?

Which lines give the key to the meaning?

Dickinson, "The soul selects"
What is implied concerning the soul by the images of chariot, gate, emperor, kneeling, and nation?

Pound, "The River-Merchant's Wife: A Letter"
According to Pound, this is from the Chinese of Rihaku (eighth century A.D.).

6

A group of poems such as this on a single universal subject serves to illustrate within a limited compass the great variety of resources open to the poet—variety of thought, emotion, imagery, music—variety, indeed, in the whole character of the poems produced. Longer elegies will be found in Sections 10 (by Thomas) and 12 (by Milton, Gray, Auden).

Raleigh, [Apostrophe to Death]
This is the celebrated conclusion of *The History of the World,* written while Raleigh was in prison (he was later executed). It was written and printed as prose. What poetic characteristics does it exhibit? If it were divided into lines and printed as verse, would it differ from other poetry?

Anon., "A Lyke-Wake Dirge"
The refrain of the fourth line suggests, obviously, a prayer for the dead, but that in the second line does not. What purpose does it serve?

By what means is the feeling of solemnity conveyed?

Shakespeare, "Fear no more"
lines 5–6. Comment on the use of *golden* and *chimney-sweepers.*

Sum up the attitude toward death implied in this poem. Does it mean that death is preferable to life?

Shakespeare, "Full fathom five"
In this song, *ding-dong* is a "burden" or undersong, probably to be sung softly as an accompaniment while the other words are sung more distinctly.

Is this poem simply a decorative fantasy on the subject of death by water? If not, can you account for the fantastic images of human bones turning into coral and eyes into pearls?

H. D., "Lethe"
In Greek mythology, Lethe is the river of forgetfulness in the world of the dead.

Whin and gorse (line 7) are the same. Though harsh and spiny, the bush in bloom is bright with golden flowers.

Notice that all the language is purely objective except for the one word *long.* Does the poem itself seem objective? What is its mood? What is the effect of the negative formula "nor . . . nor . . . nor," and of the repeated and almost-repeated groups of images: skin, hide, fleece; cedar, fir, pine; whin, gorse, flowering bush; reed-bird, linnet, thrush?

Does the poem make any statement at all that is not negative?

Hartley, "Squirrel"
During his lifetime, Hartley was famous as a painter but almost unknown as a poet, though he himself valued his poetry as highly as his painting. His imagery often has a sharpness of visual outline and a vividness that suggest the painter's eye, though he did not write what is ordinarily thought of as "descriptive" poetry.

Consider the resemblances and the differences between this and "Lethe."

Wordsworth, "A slumber did my spirit seal"
Why does the poet make a point of associating the girl with the earth's rotation, when in literal fact the living as well as the dead rotate with the earth?

Study the meter of this poem. It is founded on the common ballad stanza but is full of subtle variations. Notice particularly the many degrees of lightness and of accent. Try to mark the scansion, keeping the meaning in mind as well as the standard meter and indicating intermediate or half-accents as well as the full accents. These variations help the poet avoid the sing-song into which ballad measure easily falls. Do they also help to point up the meaning? Where and how? How does the poem change in pace and in its pauses as it proceeds?

Housman, "Bredon Hill"

A successful poem seldom arises from the poet's attacking an important subject directly and squarely as a whole. More often it develops when an image, a line or two, or an oblique slant upon the subject occurs to the writer. "Bredon Hill" is a good poem in which to observe this fact. Its real subject, obviously, is the death of a girl and the grief of the lover who had hoped to marry her and who would now like to die too. But the poet says almost nothing directly about this. Instead, he writes about church bells, about going or not going to church, and about sitting on a hill. The whole seems very simple. Is it? There is no direct statement of emotion in the poem. Is emotion communicated? If so, how?

Housman often employs a stanza of five lines in which the fifth rhymes with the fourth. Does the extra line produce any noticeable effect here in every stanza? or in some particularly?

Housman, "The rain, it streams on stone and hillock"

In three of the five stanzas the speaker is telling himself that he will miss his friend less once he has got over the shock of his death. This is the kind of condolence often uselessly given to a bereaved person by friends. Does it make the poem more or less sad? Can you tell why?

Does the image in line 2 suggest more than the physical surroundings of rain and a freshly dug grave? Notice the inversion of the accent in the second foot and the prominence this gives to the word *cling*.

Stevens, "The Death of a Soldier"

What is meant by "three-days personage" (line 14), and what does the second stanza as a whole describe?

Notice how continuous the movement of the verse is, both in cadence and in grammatical structure, through the last two stanzas. The imagery in these stanzas presents an opposition between stillness and motion: the wind stops (this is repeated), yet the clouds move on "in their direction." What has all this to do with the death of a soldier?

This poem lacks rhyme, and its meter is somewhat irregular. Do you find any patterns of rhythm or other elements of sound to take the place of conventional form?

Discuss the effect of repetition with its relation to meaning in this and the preceding poem ("The House").

7

The sonnet was introduced into England in the sixteenth century, mainly as a result of the popularity of the Italian love sonnets of Petrarch. Though there have been many variations, the two chief sonnet forms in English poetry are known as the Italian and the English or Shakespearean.

Both consist of fourteen lines of iambic pentameter. For the Italian form, the poet chooses a two-part subject, involving perhaps a question and answer or some other shift of thought or mood that will fit a two-part form. The first eight lines, or octave, are held together in a fixed rhyme scheme (*a b b a, a b b a*). With the "turn" of subject comes a change of rhyme in the sestet (the last six lines), where the poet has a freer choice. The rhyme may be *c d e c d e* or any of several other arrangements.

The "English" form has been used most notably by Shakespeare. It consists of three quatrains of alternate rhyme (*a b a b, c d c d, e f e f*), followed by a couplet. Sometimes the Shakespearean sonnet follows a two-part scheme of thought like the Italian; sometimes it does not.

In the Elizabethan Age, many poets wrote "sonnet sequences," series of independent sonnets dealing with one subject or carrying a thread of story, usually about the poet's real or imagined love. Those of Shakespeare belong to such a sequence.

The sonnet form, particularly the Italian, is rather strict and artificial. Something of its attraction for poets is described in the first two sonnets printed here.

Other sonnets will be found scattered through other sections. See, for example, Hood's on "Mistress Nicely," Wordsworth's "Mutability," Abbie Evans's "Under Cover," several by G. M. Hopkins and Donne.

Keats, "If by dull rhymes"
Try to work out a prose equivalent of what Keats says.

Drayton, "Since there's no help"
This sonnet is remarkable for its modern tone. Notice the exceptionally high proportion of everyday, one-syllable words, and the change in style that accompanies the turn of thought in the third quatrain.

Does the latter part of the sonnet cast an ironic light upon the statement made in the first two quatrains? Is the change in style appropriate to the content?

Shakespeare, Sonnets
Shakespeare's sonnets were composed in two sequences, but the order in which some belong is uncertain. Readers who are curious about the story behind them should read the whole series.

Sonnet 18
Trace the unity of the imagery in this sonnet and note the main divisions of thought.

Sonnet 29
This and the next sonnet present moods of depression. But note how different they are and how accurately each state is portrayed: one an almost paranoid mood in which the poet feels as if everything in the world is against him, the other a mood of sadness and loss.

Do you find any connection in this sonnet between the unity, the suspense, and the grammatical construction?

Sonnet 30
How many commercial and legal terms do you find in this sonnet? For example, in line 1, "sessions," used with "summon," in Shakespeare's day would have brought to mind the session or sitting of a court of law. And "dateless" (line 6), meaning "without fixed due date or date of termination," again suggests business or law. What is the effect of such terms, in view of the theme of love?

Consider the assonance and alliteration in this sonnet. Do these sound effects contribute to the difference in tone between this and sonnet 29?

Sonnet 33
Observe how a single analogy controls the language throughout.

Sonnet 65
line 6. batt'ring. The association is with battering-rams, used in besieging a walled city.
What contrast is maintained in the imagery of the first two quatrains?

Milton, "When I consider how my light is spent" (often referred to under the title "On his Blindness")
lines 3–7. The reference here is to the parable of the "talents" (an ancient unit of money) in Matt. 25.

Milton, "On the Late Massacre in Piedmont"
The occasion of this sonnet was the Catholic persecution, in 1655, of an ancient Protestant sect in northern Italy.

Notice the high proportion of long and sonorous vowel sounds, particularly the long *o's.* Is there anything unusual about the rhymes? What is the relation here between sound and sense?

Where does the "turn" of thought occur, and what is the thought of the concluding lines?

Wordsworth, "Composed upon Westminster Bridge"
Wordsworth disliked and disapproved of the city and idealized nature and country life. Consider this sonnet about London in the light of that fact.

Compare the sound of this and the preceding poem.

Keats, "On First Looking into Chapman's Homer"
George Chapman's translation of Homer appeared in 1598–1616.
What key idea unifies the thought and imagery of this sonnet?

Bridges, Sonnet No. 23
The real subject, of course, is love, though the entire octave deals with pilgrims to the Holy Land.
Explain the "doubt" in line 7. What is its equivalent in the sestet?

8

In this section are grouped for study a few poems notable for their imagery, movement, or pattern. Obviously, since poetry is full of all three, many examples just as good will be found in the other sections.

A reminder may not be out of place that these and all poems are to be read aloud or heard with the mind's ear.

Occasionally the force of a poem may depend almost entirely on the effect of a single image (or two or three related or contrasted images) presented in clear and concentrated language. The first five poems in the group should be considered from this standpoint.

Hopkins, [Fragment]

What is the effect of all the imperative verbs? of the epithet *giant* used to describe the air?

Housman, "To an Athlete Dying Young"

line 11. laurel. The European laurel or bay tree, whose evergreen leaves were used for the crown of victory. Why does Housman deliberately reverse nature here (obviously, the real laurel long outlasts the rose)? The last two lines of the poem should clear up any uncertainty.

lines 21–28. The scene here derives from the Greek conception of the world—or, as it was often thought to be, the house—of the dead, where the souls were "shades."

Consider how the poem is unified by the use of recurring imagery (see the comments in the introduction to poetry, p. 267, on Housman's redoubled use of the images connected with the race).

What two key words transform the celebration of victory in Stanza I into a funeral in Stanza II? What other images and words in the poem are reminders of racing?

cummings, "a pretty a day"

This and the following poem illustrate swift movement secured by means of short lines and repeated sounds tumbling fast over each other.

Study the rhymes and the punctuation.

Does the poem sound as if it were written to a tune? How should the extra-short last line of each stanza be read?

Is the poem about death? or the fragility of young girls' virtue? or the fragility of youthful beauty? Or does it seem deliberately ambiguous, suggesting all three? Or is it a half-meaningless jingle, a sophisticated nursery rhyme?

Swenson, "Question"

There are only a few rhymes here. What takes their place in making recurrent patterns? Compare the technique used here with that of "Lethe" (p. 310).

Coleridge, "Kubla Khan"

Coleridge had been reading from an old account of eastern travel (Purchas's *Pilgrimage*): "In Xamdu did Cublai Can build a stately Palace, encompassing sixteene miles of plaine ground with a wall, wherein are fertile meddowes, pleasant Springs, delightful Streames, . . . and in the middest thereof a sumptuous house of pleasure." Lines 1–36 describe the pleasure-grounds.

The latter part is Coleridge's poetic explanation of why he had not completed the poem: he had lost his inspiration. In a vision, he says, he once heard music (that of the Abyssinian maid) which, if he could only revive it, would inspire him to create the scene of Kubla's paradise in such poetry as the world would listen to in awe. The magic circle, flashing eyes, and floating hair of the last lines are ancient conventional properties of divinely inspired poet-prophets.

Notice the extremely elaborate patterns of alliteration and assonance: X*an* . . . Kubla Kh*an* (pronounced like Can), *d*ome *d*ecree, river *r*an, *m*easure—*m*an; X*an* . . . Kh*an*, *A*lph . . . *r*an, *c*averns . . . *m*an; *pleasure* . . . *measureless*, etc.

The poem is celebrated for its incantatory poetic music.

Hardy, "Birds at Winter Nightfall"

The triolet is one of the most rigid and artificial of all verse forms. Excellence consists in creating the illusion of freedom: of seeming, that is, to say what one wishes to say in the way one wishes to say it, without breaking the boundaries of the form. A triolet consists of eight lines with only two rhymes. The whole first line is repeated as the fourth and again as the seventh line, the second is repeated as the eighth. Once the poet has composed his first two lines, he has very little leeway; yet he must not seem encumbered by the obligation to repeat and to rhyme so rigidly.

line 3. cotonea-aster (usually written "cotoneaster" but pronounced as Hardy's spelling and the rhyme suggest). It is a flowering shrub of which some varieties bear bright berries.

line 5. crumb-outcaster. Undoubtedly one of the most ingenious rhymes in English poetry. Is it so forced as to seem a defect in the poem?

Does the poem otherwise successfully avoid monotony and stiffness? How?

Bridges, "Triolet"

Notice the extreme plainness, the absence of imagery, the monosyllabic opening, and the way in which the *ess* rhyme is reinforced by other short *e*'s throughout.

What is the effect of the five-syllable word *irretrievable* in line 6?

What things contribute to make the poem rise to a climax and then subside?

How does it avoid giving the effect of repetitive flatness?

9

Many selections in this group are examples of social criticism made vivid without preaching. They also illustrate the poet's ability to convey much in little space.

Blake, "The Chimney Sweeper" (*from Songs of Innocence*)

line 3. 'weep: a pun made from the lisped cry of the small "sweep" as he went through the streets calling out his occupation.

The enforced employment of youngsters as "climbing boys" was widely condemned but still practiced in Blake's time.

Is it possible to tell whether the conclusion is intended to be ironical or straight?

Spender, "What I expected"

This poem has been said to epitomize what happens when the idealist feels the impact of reality.

Is the poet describing an individual experience or a fairly universal one?

Auden, "The Unknown Citizen"

Can you find anything that distinguishes this poem from prose?

What is the theme? Can you relate Auden's apparent purpose to his technique?

Hartley, "Pot-Luck among the Casuals"

Title. Casuals are drifters, those subject to chance. In British usage the word refers to poor persons, vagrants, and migrant laborers.

In this dialogue between hungry man and hungry dog, the technical ambiguity of reference in the pronoun *he* and *his* is obviously intentional. The ambiguity is only apparent, however, for the reader is never in doubt.

Consider the images of bone that dominate the poem. Consider also the choice of language throughout. How would you characterize the language and the tone?

Does the generalization at the end weaken the poem?

MacNeice, "Bagpipe Music"

The scene is Scotland (hence the Scottish words); the time, the depression of the 1930's. The title suggests not only the place but the tone—shrill, plaintive, and, like the cockeyed rhymes in the poem, sounding off key.

line 9. Mme. Blavatsky was a Theosophist leader. This cult and Yoga attracted a good many persons who were searching for salvation or truth through mystical religions.

MacNeice, "Sunday Morning"

How does this poem differ from most other sonnets?

What is the theme, and how are the images of the first four lines brought to bear upon it?

Jeffers, "The Inquisitors"

This poem suggests a gigantic nightmare in which mountains come alive to wonder briefly about, and then dismiss, the insignificant evil insect, man.

Does Jeffers make the reader "see" the extraordinary scene?

Point out words and images that produce the effect of violence and that contribute to the extreme effects of magnitude and smallness.

10

Section 1 presented a number of character sketches or portraits of people, most of them brief thumbnail sketches. The present section contains three celebrated modern poems, each centered more or less upon an individual character. They are notable not only as portraits but also as examples of modern poetic styles and technique. The first one, "Prufrock," since its publication in 1915 has become one of the most famous poems of the century.

Eliot, "The Love Song of J. Alfred Prufrock"
Although interpretations of "Prufrock" vary in emphasis, the main outlines are familiar enough to be fairly well agreed upon. There will continue to be differences of opinion about details because, to a greater degree than most earlier poets, Eliot excludes mere explanation, and omits transitions, just as the mind itself, in associating ideas, often seems to do.

The epigraph comes from Dante's *Inferno,* Canto 27. Guido da Montefeltro, one of the damned, has been asked about himself and speaks from out of a flame: "If I believed that my answer were to one who ever could return to the world, this flame should shake no more. But since, if what I hear is true, no one ever returned alive from this depth, without fear of infamy I answer you." The poet perhaps implies that what Prufrock (or the poem) says will be understood only by those who share his hell. What that hell is, appears gradually in the poem.

In outline, the poem resembles a dramatic monologue of Browning in which the speaker, placed in a specific situation, talks about the situation and in so doing reveals his own character. Prufrock, however, does not speak to another character in the poem. He speaks as if to himself—his other or split self—but also possibly to the other Prufrocks of the world, who will understand him. The "you and I" of the opening and the "we," who share the same fate at the close, are appropriate to either or both of these interpretations.

The moment chosen for Prufrock's self-revelation is that of a decision. Shall he, can he, dare he propose to a woman (marriage probably, possibly an affair)? The answer is no, and so the "love song" of the title is ironic, for Prufrock is incapable of breaking through the barrier of his reserve, incapable of any genuine relationships with other human beings. The rise and fall of the merest possibility of action provides the structure or "plot" of his soliloquy. At the beginning he is irresolute: "Let us go (line 1) . . . and make our visit (line 12) . . . there will be time (line 23) . . . And indeed there will be time . . . to turn back (lines 37–40) . . . Do I dare disturb the universe? (lines 45–46) . . . should I then presume? And how should I begin?" (lines 68–69).

This teetering of the will leads Prufrock to the point—almost—of thinking he really will make his proposal. The turning point of decision is not explicitly stated. It is reflected as if unconsciously in the imagery and even in the grammar, particularly the shifting between indicative and subjunctive moods of the verbs. At his most hopeful moment, thinking in the regular future tense, he asks himself how he "shall" do it. Shall he say he does not want to be lonely all his life (lines 70–72)? He thinks of those streets of "one-night cheap hotels" (lines 4–6), where "lonely men in shirt-sleeves," with no home and nothing to do but look on at other people's lives, lean out of windows smoking pipes. Shall he say he does not wish to be one of these?

This moment is the peak of his will, when he comes closest to reaching an affirmative decision; but the very contemplation of action as something he may in real life carry out brings an extreme revulsion. Retreating, he flees in spirit to the bottom of the sea; his real self is a subhuman "pair of ragged claws," a lobster that avoids impingement of the external world by wearing its skeleton on the outside. It is an image of the essentially cold solitary spirit. Prufrock's decision is crystallized in this instant. After his flight to the bottom of the sea he ceases to think of his choice in affirmative or future indicative verbs. He thinks in subjunctive and then in "contrary to fact" constructions: "Should I . . . have the strength (lines 79–80) . . . in short, I was afraid. And *would it have been worth it,* after all?" (lines 89–90). So the reader knows by the tenses and moods of verbs that the possible moment has gone by. The several-times-repeated question "Would it have been worth while?" is the dying fall of Prufrock's subsided will. It leads presently to his clear recognition: "No! I am not Prince Hamlet, nor was meant to be." Even Hamlet, without much will to act, acted finally. But not Prufrock. And he is not even the center of the piece, he reminds himself. He is no hero, no prophet, but "an attendant lord"— cautious, well-intentioned, at best an adviser, at worst almost a buffoon, but in either case a man on the fringe of life. So he will accept his fate and continue as he was, keeping up appearances and taking care of himself. But love is not for him. He knows its lure, at a distance only and with its back turned: the mermaids are "riding seaward" (lines 124–125).

At the end (as occasionally earlier) Prufrock speaks again in the plural. He has been talking of himself as "I." Now he returns to the "you and I" of the opening, since his plight is not unique. He has spoken as an individual, but the world contains others like him, and most people have a touch of Prufrock. His conclusion is therefore appropriately inclusive, though still framed in terms of his own experience. In our solitude "in the chambers of the sea," he says, "we" are capable of love ("by sea-girls wreathed"), but it is only a dream love. The approach of reality wakes us from the dream ("*human* voices wake us"), and at the touch of the real "we drown."

This is the outline of Prufrock's monologue, and through it his hell is defined. The imagery that runs through his mind completes the picture and makes vivid for the reader both his outer and his inner life. Possibly *hell* is too strong a word. Certainly it is strong for the elements of Prufrock's outer life: the social boredom, the women who chatter about art, the current novels, the innumerable teas, the measuring of one's life by that least of units the after-dinner coffee spoon. The word *hell* is appropriate, however, for the more significant internal imagery that presents him as a man paralyzed by self-distrust and agonizing self-consciousness.

These last terms are not those in which a psychologist would explain Prufrock's malaise.

Eliot, however, is not psychoanalyzing Prufrock. What he presents is *what it feels like* to be Prufrock, not what is wrong with him or why it is wrong. Much of the excellence of the poem derives from the vividness with which the imagery conveys this.

Most of what might be called the "subjective" images are concerned with stagnation or inaction, varying degrees of ill health, and the feeling of being split in two. The tone is set immediately by the apparently outrageous image of the evening sky as "a patient etherized upon a table"—pale, stagnant, and scarcely alive. The pools in drains, the cat-like fog, and the smoke are stagnant; the evening itself "malingers," psychological malaise disguising itself as physical.

Images revealing his selfconsciousness (*selfconsciousness,* of course, is a surface term for deeper things) range from petty anxieties of everyday life—thin hair, thin arms, thin legs that "they" will notice—to the greater, when the petty fear of servants who may snicker behind his back is magnified to the universal, the "eternal Footman" (line 88). More violent images express the extremes of his self-shattering consciousness. "The eyes that fix you," pin you to the wall like an insect specimen to be stared at as it dies, ejecting its insides at both ends in its death agony: this is rather a horrible image (lines 55–60). And scarcely less so is Prufrock's feeling as if his whole nervous system were exposed, projected "in patterns on a screen" to be examined (line 105). There is the split-self in the image of John the Baptist: Prufrock has *seen his own head* brought in upon a platter (lines 82–83). Finally, there is the image that brings back the initial quotation from Dante. Supposing he did try to make a human contact, did tell her he was "Lazarus, come from the dead" to tell her "all" (lines 94–98). She would not understand. What have those in hell to say that others could understand?

Eliot has presented a dramatic picture of a man who from the outside is correct, well dressed, over-selfconscious, perhaps a trifle pathetic and a trifle absurd. But Prufrock knows he is all this, and the acceptance of this knowledge dignifies him. Moreover, his sufferings are real and in some degree universal. Eliot presents him, sufferings and all, in a dry tone; the man himself is a dry man.

The poem is a complex one and therefore many other meanings can be extracted from it or read into it. More could be said of the superficial society in which Prufrock lives. What we have given here, however, is the main thread that holds it all together.

lines 29 and 33. works and days, visions and revisions: phrases borrowed from titles, the first an ancient Greek poem by Hesiod, the second a book by John Cowper Powys, published in 1915.

lines 94–95. There are Biblical accounts of two different men named Lazarus who died. One was raised from the dead. The other was not, but Abraham was asked to let him return from the dead to testify. See Luke 16 and John 11–12.

lines 97–98. In Kipling's "The Vampire," the woman ("a rag and a bone and a hank of hair") did not understand, "and it wasn't the least what the lady meant."

line 117. high sentence: high thoughts. The phrase is borrowed from Chaucer's description of a scholar who was as thin as Prufrock.

line 121. trousers rolled. Robert H. Llewellyn furnished the undoubted key to this often misunderstood detail; he noted that trousers with cuffs had recently come into fashion. The word rolled was sometimes used for this. Here (as in lines 42–43, 123) Prufrock is concerned with wearing precisely the right clothes.

line 122. Peaches used to be considered indigestible.

Is it possible to tell what makes Prufrock poetry rather than prose, in view of the apparently prosaic character of much of its content?

Sitwell, "Colonel Fantock"

Dame Edith Sitwell is descended from an ancient aristocratic English family, and her poetry often reflects this background. Much of her earlier poetry consists of experiments in elaborate patterns of rhythm, rhyme, assonance, and movement. She calls them "abstract" poems, though their titles are concrete enough: "Clowns' Houses" ("Beneath the flat and paper sky") and "Trio for Two Cats and a Trombone," for example. Since World War II, she has dealt constantly with serious themes: "Still Falls the Rain" was inspired by the air raids on England.

"Colonel Fantock" is one of the more serious of her earlier poems. In it she recalls her early life at "Troy Park" with her brothers Osbert and Sacheverell ("Dagobert and Peregrine," line 17) and sketches the character of the boys' tutor, "Colonel Fantock." The unity of the poem is one of mood rather than of subject or theme. The imagery should be closely studied for its effect on the mood.

lines 10–15. What effect or mood is produced by the author's deliberate confusion of senses and facts: a castle that is like music; music and silence that are like the lotus flower "to eat," perfumed; grass and trees that are "sad" and "mournful"; and, later, the child who was like "a little cold air wandering" (line 27)? Does this use of mixed imagery persist throughout the poem? The poet is obviously using nonlogical language to convey experience that is real and vivid but for which factual and logical language is inadequate.

line 43. A picture of a May-fly in an encyclopedia will show perfectly the shape of the Colonel's whiskers. But why does the poet bring in the image of an airy, delicate flying creature when her subject is a retired army officer who has taken a position as a tutor?

lines 44–56. What resemblances are suggested between the old man and the poet herself as a child?

What is the effect on the whole poem of the concluding stanza?

Does the irregular off-and-on rhyme seem to be suitable for this particular poem? Why or why not?

Thomas, "After the funeral"

Dylan Thomas writes in what may be a new language to some readers, for though he usually preserves the form of regular grammatical statements, the statements themselves are often nonlogical. The language is addressed directly to the imagination and the emotions, often by-passing the logical mind altogether. With Thomas more conspicuously than with most poets, the patterns of sound and imagery dominate the poem.

"After the funeral" honors Ann Jones, a poor, bent, hard-working old woman for whom the poet feels an affection that goes back to his boyhood. Its general outline is clear enough, but individual phrases sometimes telescope two or three images into one and therefore may puzzle the reader. In "Blinds down the lids" (line 4), for example, are telescoped the window blinds drawn down as a sign of mourning, the closed eyelids of the dead, which are "blinds" of another sort, and the coffin lid. The phrase just before this, "muffle-toed . . . one peg in the thick grave's foot" seems to fit both the perfunctory mourners, indifferent old people who themselves have one foot in the grave, and the nailing of the coffin lid.

Thomas first describes the funeral with its "mule praises," the stupid, perfunctory praise of those who do not recognize Ann's worth. But the sound of the spade "wakes" him back into his boyhood, so that he feels her death as he would have felt it then (lines 6–9). Afterwards, in her room with its stuffed fox and stale fern he holds his own funeral service for her. The hearth of her room is now the "raised hearth" (line 21)—that is, the altar. He praises her in images magnified beyond what she would have expected or thought suitable (lines 15–20). He calls upon the seas to make her inarticulate virtue "babble," and upon the "ferned and foxy woods" to make her love "sing and swing through a brown chapel" (which may be the woods or her room or both). And he blesses her with the sign of the cross made by flying birds. Then he describes her as she truly was—in contrast to the "mule praises" of the actual funeral. His praises are a monument ("this skyward statue"), and the monument is this poem that he is writing, which "storms" at him over her grave until by writing it he can bring to life again her love: "the stuffed fox cries Love and the stale fern is fertile."

II

The twentieth century has seen a good deal of discussion of a modern literary question: why poets should continue to write so much more about nature than about towns and machinery, when so many people now live in an urban and industrial environment. Are poets, it is sometimes asked, simply refusing to face modern life as it is, or is there a sound and natural reason in human nature for their choice of subjects and imagery? We raise the question here but will not attempt to answer it categorically. Some have said, however, that the mechanical things which man himself can make, he can understand and deal with in equations or by strict reasoning, and that he does not need much imagination to deal with them once they are invented. His factories, however, cannot manufacture human beings, nature, or the powers and laws behind the world. These all-important and familiar, yet half-unknown things he must deal with partly by imagination. Whether or not this is the reason, the fact is that even in modern poetry we see a great deal more of nature than we do of machines. It is not easy to find first-rate poems on urban or industrial themes.

In this section are grouped a few that are primarily about nature (many more and many of the best are included in other sections; see particularly Section 12) and a small sampling of attempts to deal poetically with machinery.

Shakespeare, "Spring"

This and the next poem form a slightly mocking conclusion to the comedy *Love's Labor's Lost*. They are introduced as a "dialog" that two "learned men have compiled in praise of the owl and the cuckoo." The singers are the two seasons.

This apparently simple poem is double-edged, for its pretty, cheerful picture of Spring is given a cynical twist. The song of the cuckoo is loved by the English as a sign of Spring. But it is a bird that lays its eggs in other birds' nests, and from this circumstance is derived the word *cuckold,* a mocking term for a man whose wife is unfaithful.

cummings, "O sweet spontaneous"

What character is ascribed to philosophy, science, and religion? How serious does this attitude seem to be: is it a settled disapproval or a springtime mood?

What is meant by "the couch of death thy rhythmic lover"?

cummings, "Chansons Innocentes: I"

Is the attitude of the poet that of a child, or is it that of a grownup imagining a child's world? How does the language of the poem bear out your view?

Can you find reasons for the unconventional spacing of words?

Who, besides a seller of balloons, is the balloonman? The epithet *goat-footed* is the key.

D. Thomas, "Fern Hill"

The theme is an obvious one, the loss of childhood's carefree joy. The poet re-creates the joy even while he takes it away. Crudely expressed in prose, the thought runs somewhat like this:

As a boy, he and the farm were almost as one. Each day was fresh and full of delight. At night the farm vanished while he slept, only to appear again next morning as fresh and new as Eden. He had not thought that this would end, or that all the while time held him prisoner until a night should come when time would fly away with the farm—that is, with his childhood.

The poem is sprinkled with variations on set phrases from children's stories—"happy as the day is long," "once upon a time," "all the day long"—and with an extension of an ancient poetic device called the "transferred epithet," by which, for special effects, a descriptive word is attached, not to the object to which it logically applies, but to some other. Thomas carries this device to an extreme here and elsewhere, using it constantly instead of only occasionally: the house sings, the yard is happy, the boy is green, the stable is green and whinnies. How does this contribute to the mood of the poem?

Point out other original and expressive phrases and images.

What passages particularly convey the bursting egotism of childhood, the distinctive feeling of the child that the universe is his apple?

E. Thomas, "Gallows"

The animals referred to here, as country-bred readers will know, are destructive and so may be shot by farmers, who sometimes hang them up afterwards to keep others away.

Is this an S.P.C.A. poem? If not, what is the author's evident attitude toward his subject?

Comment on the effect of the imagery and of the repetitive structure of the refrain.

E. Thomas, "Out in the Dark"

This and the three following poems record similar or comparable experiences. What is each one? What images contribute most to the mood of each? What else besides the imagery contributes to the effect?

Spender, "I hear the cries of evening"

What is the effect of the images (lines 1–2, 10) that treat the darkness as an animal?

Evans, "Euroclydon"

The title is the Greek name for a tempestuous northeast wind in the Mediterranean.

lines 8–10. The New Testament (Acts 27) describes the shipwreck of the Apostle Paul.

Evans, "Under Cover"

What is the effect of the couplet rhyme and the parallel construction in the last two lines of this sonnet?

POEMS ON MACHINERY

See the general note that precedes the poems about nature in this section. For more than a century poets have been trying to produce a great poem about machinery. Whether the cause of failure lies in them or in the subject remains debatable. None of the poems printed here are first rate, yet they are about as good as can be found. Study them, trying to see what they lack as well as what they have to offer.

Whitman, "To a Locomotive in Winter"

This and the following locomotives are all a trifle old-fashioned. The diesel engine apparently has not yet grown rich enough in associative values to have inspired a good, or even a fairly good, poem.

Dickinson, "I like to see it lap the Miles"

From what point of view is this train seen?

line 13. In the New Testament account, Jesus called James and his brother John to be disciples, "and he surnamed them Boanerges, which is, The sons of thunder" (Mark 3:17).

Williams, "Overture to a Dance of Locomotives"

The scene is a large railroad station, first in the waiting room, then moving to the train platform.

Is the description purely objective, or does the emphasis on the clock, taken together with the conclusion, suggest a further meaning?

Sandburg, "Limited"

Is the last line an anticlimax? If not, what do you consider its function?

Is the title a pun?

12

Odes and elegies are serious poems, dignified and rather slow in movement. As a rule, they are longer and more reflective than most lyric poems.

The subject of an ode may be anything that has sufficient magnitude to warrant its lofty tone and its frequently formal treatment. The form varies. Some English odes follow more or less closely the structure of the Greek odes of Pindar, others have irregular rhyme and stanza, and still others employ regular stanzas of various kinds.

An elegy is a commemoration of the dead. It may be written in any verse form that is capable of the requisite dignity.

Keats, "Ode to a Nightingale"

Keats had an unusually keen feeling for sensuous experience and an exceptional power of communicating it. His short life, however, was not one of easy pleasure but was heavily burdened with responsibility, sickness, and death. His father died early, and he watched first his mother and then his younger brother die of tuberculosis with, perhaps, toward the end a guess that he himself might follow. The desire to escape sorrow and responsibility is a frequent theme in his poetry. It is always balanced by the recognition that there is no escape, that one must, after all, live in the real world and meet whatever comes (cf. "La Belle Dame sans Merci"). More than commonly susceptible to pleasure, and more than commonly experienced in pain, he often brings the two extremes together in his poetry.

Trace the theme of escape through its transformations in this ode.

Study the language of the poem carefully.

line 14. Provençal song. From Provence came much of the lyric poetry of the Middle Ages.

line 26. Keats's brother Tom had died a few months before this was written.

lines 66–67. alien corn: a poetic epitome of part of the Old Testament book of Ruth. Note how this foreshadows the later "forlorn."

Stanza 7 introduces the distant past. It also makes the obviously false statement that the nightingale does not die. What is the meaning of this stanza, and what is its function in relation to the rest of the poem?

Keats, "Ode on a Grecian Urn"

This is one of the most discussed, and perhaps over-discussed, of English poems, chiefly because of the closing statement about truth and beauty. As a universal principle, it seems to many people false, absurd, or immoral. By various ingenious explanations, critics have tried to rescue Keats from what appears to be a weak position. The question cannot be argued out here, but readers should keep in mind that Keats was using a commonplace as old as Plato, whose triad of values—the good, the true, and the beautiful—were regarded as approximately three aspects of the same thing. In a letter, Keats once wrote of the "truth" of creative imagination, "What the imagination seizes as Beauty must be truth—whether it existed before or not." This may throw some light on the poem. And Hazlitt, whom Keats admired, had said that "to the genuine artist, truth, nature, beauty are almost different names for the same thing." Though these statements do not fully explain the poem or necessarily validate its concluding lines, they suggest something of what people were thinking when they so often spoke of "truth and beauty" in connection with painting, sculpture, and poetry.

line 2. foster-child. "Time" and "silence," though not the original creators (parents), were the foster-parents who had preserved the urn through the ages.

lines 11–12. What do these lines mean?

Stanzas 2–3. Art makes permanent and hence re-experienceable the experiences and emotions which in life are transitory.

line 44–45. dost tease: taxes our thought or imagination beyond its capacity, as does the attempt to imagine eternity.

Keats, "To Autumn"

line 25. bloom. Keats may have two different senses of this word in mind: the common one, having to do with blossoming; and the other, not quite as common but not at all unusual, meaning to cover with a soft, powdery silver, such as often appears on plums and other fruit.

line 28. Some texts of the poem have *sallows* (willows) for *shallows*.

What time of autumn is described here? What images contribute most to the feeling of ripeness and fulfillment?

What change in tone or mood accompanies the change in time of day between the beginning and end? What images bring this about?

Bridges, "November"

line 21. amorets: probably a local name for some kind of bird. This meaning of the word does not appear in standard reference works, but *amore* in Anglo-Saxon was a name for a kind of bird. Bridges' word is probably a local survival of this.

What is the effect of all the birds in this poem? With what are they contrasted?

Point out some words and images that help to set the tone of the poem.

What deepened significance does the conclusion give to the scene or the poem? Is the conclusion prepared for in advance?

Bridges, "Nightingales"

It has long been disputed whether the song of the nightingale (from the standpoint of the human listener) is sad or joyous. The old Greek legend of Philomela, which the reader should look up if he does not already know it, suggests tragic memories and associations, and Milton called the bird "most musicall, most melancholy." Others have called it "merry" or

happy. This is the background of Bridges' double view.

Bridges is known for the beauty and expressiveness of his music, particularly the subtly varied rhythms and the subtly interlaced echoes of alliteration and assonance. These are rarely used for their own sake alone; they are almost always closely bound up with the mood and meaning. A good example occurs in the first two lines of this poem, where every sound of the key word "beautiful" is heard again in "*bright in the fruitful*." The abstract thought of "beautiful" thus becomes concrete in the two echoing words; and the sound of the word also continues to be heard underlying the second line, where the tone color, however, is brightened by the meaning of the word "bright" and by the addition of the *r* sounds throughout the line. Subtle musical effects such as this are often felt without being analyzed, but an occasional analysis of this sort can help sharpen the reader's perception.

Arnold, "Philomela"

This poem refers directly to the Greek legend of Philomela, mentioned in the preceding note.

Shelley, "Ode to the West Wind"

This is the most famous example in English verse of *terza rima* (see Glossary), though the scheme is interrupted by a couplet marking the end of each division of the poem.

The ode is famous also for its almost mathematical organization of thought and imagery. What is the presiding image in each of the first three divisions? What images do you find in each of Sections 2–5 that reflect or repeat the presiding images of other sections? Trace particularly the links by which Section 5 circles back to Section 1.

What thought about himself is Shelley expressing when he writes of the wind? Does this thought of self seem to you to weaken the effect of the poem, or does it deepen and enrich it? Opinions differ on this question.

Milton, "Lycidas"

Usually an elegy both laments and praises the dead. Some English elegies adopt the conventions of pastoral poetry, using as a background nature and the life of shepherds, with idealized and conventionalized scenes and classical names. Though pastoral elegies are artificial in their borrowing of these elements from classical poetry, they nevertheless tend to follow the natural course of human experience. When someone dies young or in his prime, the first feeling of the mourner is one of irreparable loss and irreconcilable grief. Why should death, he feels, have taken this one particular person? Why was the loss not prevented? Then, if he is not overwhelmed by a shattering grief (if he is a friend, perhaps, and not a lover) his next thought may be of himself: "There but for the grace of God I lie." This leads him to an examination of his own goals and way of life. Finally, his thought returns to the dead, but with the passing of time he has become more reconciled and perhaps turns to faith or some sort of hope: the friend, after all, is not really dead, or has not died in vain.

The conventional pattern of the elegy, then, like the normal course of any sorrow that is less than overwhelming, runs through the three stages: (1) the irreconcilable cry: "Weep, he is gone forever. Why could he not have been saved?"; (2) taking stock of oneself, and sometimes more broadly of the world of the living; (3) the reconciliation: "Do not weep; he is not really dead"; something of value survives.

In "Lycidas" Milton mourns the death by shipwreck of Edward King, a young man whom he had known, probably not intimately, when both were students at Cambridge. He follows the tradition of the pastoral elegy, writing of himself and King as shepherds whose poems are songs sung to the accompaniment of "oaten flute" (a simple flute made from a hollow stem). But King had intended to become a clergyman, and so the other sense of *pastor* and *pastoral* enters into the poem too: King was to have been not only a poet but also a spiritual shepherd of a flock.

To what extent does Milton follow the progression of thought usual in elegies?

lines 1–7. He is called upon to write this poem before his powers have matured.

lines 23–36. Milton translates the fact ("We went to college together") into its elaborate pastoral equivalent.

line 36. Damætas. Like "Lycidas," this name is common in pastoral poetry. The person meant by Milton is not known.

line 58. Muse. Calliope, the Muse of epic poetry, was the mother of Orpheus, legendary singer, inspirer of song, and leader of a Greek religious cult. According to one tradition, Maenads killed and dismembered him, and threw him into the stream. His head floated singing to Lesbos.

lines 64–84. What argument does the poet carry on with himself in this paragraph?

line 75. blind Fury. The Furies and the three Fates in mythology are not actually the same, though Milton identifies them here. Two Fates prepare and spin the thread of life; the third, Atropos the "inflexible" one, who is blindfold, cuts it.

lines 89–90. Herald of the Sea. Triton, a sea god, defends his father Neptune against the accusation of having drowned Lycidas.

line 106. sanguine flower . . . The youth Hyacinthus was loved but accidentally killed by Apollo. From his blood Apollo caused to spring up the hyacinth flower, whose petals were said to bear markings resembling the letters of the Greek word for "woe."

line 109. The Pilot: St. Peter, customarily represented in old paintings as carrying the keys of Heaven. He had been a fisherman on the Sea of Galilee and was with Jesus during a storm at sea. As the founder of the Church he may be called its first "pastor." As the first bishop of Rome, he is represented with a bishop's headdress ("Miter'd," line 112).

lines 113–31. Milton attacks the English clergy. Comment on the language and images used in this passage.

line 119. What does Milton mean by "blind mouthes"?

line 128. grim Woolf: the Roman Catholic Church, endeavoring to win converts among Protestants.

lines 130–31. The "two-handed engine" has never been satisfactorily identified.

line 132. Alpheus: god of the river Alpheus and lover of Arethusa. He is associated here with pastoral poetry. In addressing him at this point, Milton returns to the theme with which the poem opened.

lines 152–53. The poet has imagined a suitable flowery funeral but now reminds himself that the body of Lycidas was never found.

lines 160–61. Bellerus, guarded mount, Namancos and Bayona. Land's End, the southwestern promontory of England; and St. Michael's Mount, near Land's End, which looks toward Spain (Namancos and Bayona). The Mount is supposed to be guarded by the Archangel Michael. Milton urges him to turn and look homeward, for the dangers are now domestic rather than foreign.

line 164. Dolphins. The Greek poet Arion was thrown overboard, according to Herodotus, and was carried to land by a dolphin. Milton may also have known of a Roman belief that spirits of the dead were borne by dolphins to the next world.

line 173. Matt. 14:25–33.

To what extent is *Lycidas* unified by recurring or related themes and images, such as those of shepherds (in both senses) and of water and shipwreck? Trace these through the poem to show the variety as well as the unity in Milton's use of them.

Study the sound patterns and the sonority of the verse.

13

Herrick, "To the Virgins, to Make Much of Time"

The theme here and in the next selection is that of *carpe diem,* "seize the day"—enjoy today, for it will not last.

Marvell, "To His Coy Mistress"

lines 5–7. Ganges . . . Humber. The lovers would begin their leisurely approach to each other from the opposite ends of the earth. The Humber is an English river.

line 11. Why would their loves be "vegetable"?

lines 21–22. These are among the most celebrated lines on the urgency of time.

lines 39–40. -chapt: from *chap,* meaning *jaw.* Let us devour time before he slowly devours us.

Try to describe the tone or the attitude of the poet toward his subject. What words and images particularly help to set the tone?

MacLeish, "You, Andrew Marvell"

As the title implies, this poem was inspired by the preceding one. MacLeish drops the love theme, however, and makes his poem entirely out of time and space.

Perhaps the most notable feature of the poem is its grammatical structure: there is not one sentence. There is not even a subordinate clause or a finite verb until the very last line, where a single dependent clause is hung upon an infinitive. Everywhere else, instead of verbs there are only infinitives depending on other infinitives, and participles and gerunds depending on infinitives: "To feel . . . chill . . . creep up . . . and . . . shadow grow . . . and . . . trees take leaf by leaf the evening . . . [to feel] . . . the mountains . . . change . . . and Baghdad darken . . . and Spain go under. . . ." This linked structure is continuous and never reaches completion because there is no sentence, no end, no cessation of the movement of time. Thus the grammar itself is expressive of the theme.

MacLeish traces only half a revolution of the earth, and even that only in imagination, as he lies beneath the noonday sun somewhere in America, thinking of the edge of night approaching from the other side of the earth. Within this still moment in time and space, which frames the poem, he opens out the vastness and remoteness of past ages and distance. The place names, which mark the advance of the westward-moving shadow, are all rich in associations that go back through the Middle Ages to antiquity, and along with these names go many images suggesting evening and time past, such as the "earthly chill of dusk," the "ever-climbing shadow," and the "wheel rut in the ruined stone."

Wordsworth, "Mutability"

lines 10–13. A tower so old that weeds have grown on its roof, and so fragile that sound waves could destroy it.

What effect has the last line, with its abstract language and six-syllable word, on the sonnet as a whole?

14

Auden, "Musée des Beaux Arts"

Religious paintings of the Renaissance often contained figures of people and animals from everyday life that had little or nothing to do with the theme of the picture. These were painted with realistic and sometimes humorous detail. The same combination of the lofty and the commonplace occasionally appears in paintings of mythological subjects.

line 14. Icarus. According to Greek legend, Daedalus built wings by means of which he and his son Icarus escaped from the labyrinth in Crete. Icarus flew too close to the sun and was drowned when the wax of his wings melted.

Tennyson, "Ulysses"

In this dramatic monologue Tennyson writes of Ulysses (Odysseus) after the end of Homer's *Odyssey.* What broader theme is involved besides the situation of one man?

In the *Odyssey* the time of day that comes most often to mind is dawn, the most natural time for setting out on a journey in the ancient world. What is the time of day here? Why is it appropriate and what is its effect on the tone of the poem as a whole?

Line 18, simple as it appears, is considered a very fine line. Can you see why?

line 4. savage race. Ulysses' island kingdom of Ithaca was on the fringes rather than at the center of Greek culture.

line 63. Happy Isles: the Isles of the Blest in the western ocean, where heroes especially favored by the gods might live exempt from death.

Tennyson, "The Lotos-Eaters"

The subject is from the *Odyssey.* In the land of the Lotos-Eaters, those who ate the lotos flower or fruit became languid and lost all desire for action.

What is the relation in theme between this and the preceding poem? In *Ulysses,* Tennyson seemed to share the attitude of the speaker. Does he do so here? Does this raise questions of the poet's consistency or sincerity?

Why is the land described as a place "in which it seemed always afternoon"? What other images contribute most to the lotos-eating mood?

How do the sound and movement of the verse contribute to the mood? The first part is written in the Spenserian stanza. Look this up, and notice the effect of the complicated rhyming and the extended last line.

Choric Song. Who are the "we" of the second stanza?

Hardy, "The Convergence of the Twain"

In 1912 the Titanic, then the world's largest ship, struck an iceberg on her maiden voyage and sank, though she had been supposed unsinkable.

Stanza VI. The Immanent Will. Hardy expressed a fatalistic view of the world in various terms at different times. The primary power was "fate"; or "chance"; or the "Immanent Will," which was unconscious and nonhuman; or some other form of blind and irresponsible power.

Housman, "When smoke stood up from Ludlow"

What is the significance of the bird—at what, that is, did the speaker really throw his stone?

Here, as in *Bredon Hill* (p. 311), Housman employs an unusual five-line stanza that resembles an ordinary quatrain with an extra rhyming line added. To what uses does he put the extra line?

15

Other religious poems will be found scattered through other sections. See particularly those of Hopkins in Section 16.

Donne, "At the round earth's imagined corners . . ."

How suitable, for the purpose of making vivid the Judgment Day, is this expressly contradictory image, with its suggestion of the normally impossible squaring of the circle, as well as its combining of the old and the modern belief about the earth?

lines 5–8. Observe the inclusiveness and concreteness of this list.

lines 7–8. In Luke 9:27 it is prophesied that

some living men would see heaven without going through death.

What shift in thought is marked by the "turn" of the sonnet?

Herbert, "The Collar"

What is the collar?

Note that the mood of rebellion does not end, as a hasty reading may lead one to suppose, with the end of the question in line 16, but only with line 32.

Herbert, "The Pulley"

What is the "pulley" of the title? Does the image seem inconsistent with the seriousness of the subject?

lines 16–17. rest . . . restlessness. Does the pun on these words detract from the seriousness of the poem, or does it add a desirable edge or spice?

How does the five-line stanza here differ from that used by Housman (pp. 311, 363) in rhyme scheme? in poetic effect?

Eliot, "The Journey of the Magi"

The quotation marks at the beginning have no significance except as an acknowledgment that Eliot is using almost word for word the language of a sermon on the Nativity by the seventeenth-century bishop Lancelot Andrewes. Eliot quoted the passage elsewhere in an essay on Andrewes, commenting on the older writer's remarkable "sentences in which, before extracting all the spiritual meaning of a text, Andrewes forces a concrete presence upon us." Perhaps this is what Eliot too does in the apparently irrelevant concrete details he gives.

The specific subject is the journey of the Magi, and the ostensible theme is Birth. Yet the poem says at least as much about Death. Perhaps the underlying theme is the painful difficulty of bringing about in oneself a deep inner change, a difficulty so great as to make the birth of a new self seem more like a death.

line 31. The climax of the difficult journey, the seeing and worshiping of the Christ-child, is recorded in this colorless understatement. Why do you suppose this was done? Does it seem to you good or bad poetically?

Housman, "Easter Hymn"

Housman was an atheist but retained a love of the Bible and a reverence for the goodness of Jesus, as well as some sympathy for the Church of England. Here he writes rather as an agnostic, as one who does not know whether Christ rose from the dead or not.

What is the effect of the single periodic sentence in each stanza and the parallel construction of the two? Do these grammatical and rhetorical elements contribute to the emotional intensity of the poem?

The date of the poem is not known, but Housman is clearly thinking of the modern war-ridden world, perhaps specifically the First World War.

16

The four poets of whose writing a small sample is given here have been particularly admired by poets and critics of the last two generations. In time, they range from Donne, a younger contemporary of Shakespeare, to Yeats, who is remembered by many persons still alive. Though they are all highly individual writers, they have in common a more than ordinary complexity of temperament and style. The writing of all four is particularly characterized by its intense fusion of thought and feeling.

JOHN DONNE

See also the five other poems of Donne in Sections 5 and 15.

"The Funeral"

line 3. wreath of hair. Bracelets used to be made from a lock of a person's hair, woven or braided with strands of gold thread.

lines 12–13. The superior power of the bracelet is fancifully reasoned. Hair grows up from the brain, the nerves down; and the lady's brain that bore the hair was better than his. So surely this bracelet, after his death, will hold him together as a whole unified being better than the network of his nerves ever did—unless, he adds, she gave it to him only to remind him that he is still her manacled prisoner.

line 22. The meaning is uncertain. It may be: "to confer on it all that a Soul can confer" (the suggestion is that of a recent editor of Donne, Theodore Redpath).

What is meant by the image involving "Viceroy" and "provinces" (lines 5–8)?

What is the tone of the poem? Does it seem too intellectually ingenious for serious feeling?

"The Good-Morrow"

line 4. According to tradition, the Seven Sleepers of Ephesus were seven Christians, in flight from persecution, who hid in a cave, were walled in, and slept till they were rescued two hundred years later.

lines 10–18. What variation does Donne play on the hackneyed expressions, "think the world of each other," "live in a world of their own"?

line 19. not mixed equally. An old scientific belief held that compound substances whose elements are equally mixed are stable and cannot be dissolved.

How should the first stanza be read aloud, with what inflections and in what spirit?

"The Anniversary"

line 3. The "times" are hours, days, seasons, etc. It is not certain whether Donne meant "they" to refer to "Kings," etc., or to "times." If the latter, he probably meant that though the sun is the cause of "times," the very passing of these times makes the sun itself older.

lines 18–20. The general meaning is that their loving souls will be even happier after death.

lines 25–26. What is meant here?

"The Canonization"

line 7. stamped: on coins. The meaning is: pursue the King's favor, or go and get rich.

line 15. man. Some texts of the poem have *more*.

line 23. Phoenix: a bird in Egyptian mythology, of which only one exists. It lives 500 years, then consumes itself by fire, and from the ashes another rises. Since it reproduces itself, it may be considered as a union of both sexes.

lines 29–34. An almost identical thought is repeated three times in these lines: if we are not important enough in a worldly way for a big funeral, a "half-acre tomb," or a place in history ("chronicle"), we shall at any rate be a fit subject for poems.

lines 36–45. The subject of "invoke" is "all" (line 35). "Beg" (line 44) is imperative. Since the lovers are now canonized (have become saints), they are asked to intercede with heaven to send down a pattern by which others may have as perfect a love.

After studying this small selection, try to describe or characterize Donne's poetry as a whole.

WILLIAM BLAKE

See also the poems by Blake in Section 9.

"The Clod and the Pebble"

What do the symbols of clod and pebble represent? What physical properties make each an appropriate symbol?

"The Tyger"

Ordinarily, lamb and tiger, used as symbols, are likely to represent good and evil or gentleness and ferocity. This is not quite what Blake meant. His tiger is fearful but beautiful. He had never seen a real tiger, and his beast is rather a vision than a live animal. The meaning of the poem has been much disputed. The tiger is sometimes thought to represent divine Wrath, in contrast with Forgiveness of the lamb; or Experience in contrast with Innocence. In Blake's *Songs of Innocence,* the poem "The Lamb" asks much the same question ("Little Lamb, who made thee?"). The answer partly identifies the lamb with Jesus. "The Tyger" is the corresponding poem in *Songs of Experience.*

What is the effect of the poem's being written entirely in the form of questions? Is the over-all feeling one of questioning? of exclamation? or neither?

"Mad Song"

"Tom-o'-Bedlam," or "mad" songs, were once fairly common, but Blake's is perhaps the only one that seems to penetrate convincingly into a deranged spirit.

What feeling is conveyed by the poem?

Does it make any kind of sense?

Can you understand the flight toward night and the horror of day expressed in the last stanza?

What words do the most to make this an extreme and intense poem?

"A Poison Tree"

An earlier title for this poem, "Christian Forbearance," should make the meaning clear if it is not already so. What is Blake's opinion of Christian forbearance? The answer must take account of everything in the poem.

Notice the contrast between the complex statement and the apparently simple, crisp verse in which it is made.

GERARD MANLEY HOPKINS
See also the fragment in Section 8.

Nearly all Hopkins's poetry is religious. He was converted to Roman Catholicism while a student at Oxford and became a Jesuit priest.

"No worst, there is none"

In form and style, this sonnet is less strange than "The Windhover." It is one of what have been called "the terrible sonnets," in which Hopkins reaches the depths of spiritual despair. The cause of this despair is not fully known.

How do lines 5-6 characterize the suffering?

lines 12-13. What is the one "comfort" under which he can "creep"?

"Heaven-Haven"

line 3. sided. "Hailstones are shaped like the cut of diamonds called brilliants [i.e., with numerous flat sides or facets]," Hopkins recorded in a notebook. This was a mistaken scientific observation made in the nineteenth century.

Does the sound of the verse reflect the theme? How does the changed meter of the last line reflect the meaning?

"Pied Beauty"

Title: pied: piebald, of different colors, as spotted black and white. Here the poet means variegated. The theme might be summed up: Praise God, himself changeless yet the source of all change.

line 4. In his journal one autumn, Hopkins noted that the chestnuts that year were "as bright as coals or spots of vermilion."

line 10. fathers-forth is a verb, He (God) is its subject, and the preceding all things, etc., its object.

Trace the progression of the imagery from multitudinous variety in nature to duality (pairs of contrasts), and finally to unity.

"The Windhover"

Title. The windhover is a small falcon, said to be named for its habit of hovering almost motionless, staying itself in the air with its head against the wind.

The meaning of this sonnet has been much in dispute, but the interpretation given here is, in the editors' opinion, the only one that draws all the parts of the poem together into a coherent whole.

In the octave, the poet describes the bird of which he caught sight this morning. It is the favorite (minion), the crown prince (dauphin) of the morning because of the beauty of its movement and its mastery over its element, the air. The poet's heart, which before had been stagnant and unwilling to feel anything (in hiding), was stirred by the bird's power and mastery.

When the sestet opens, the individual bird has been enlarged to stand for the whole of material creation or nature: "brute [i.e., animal] beauty . . . air, pride, plume." But as he contemplates it, this material world of nature, with all its beauty and power, seems to buckle, break open, collapse—like a structure that is burning from within. AND (the capitalization makes the word equivalent to "and behold!") through and beyond the material reality "breaks" the infinitely more beautiful, and more daring or dangerous, fire of the spirit of Christ (my chevalier), whom the poet is now addressing directly. No wonder this happens, he says, for the most commonplace things break open to show inward beauty. The ordinary labor of ploughing breaks dull-colored earth into a shining furrow (sillion) of fresh soil (Hopkins's journal describes a recently ploughed hill "glistening with very bright newly turned sods"). And the coals of a fire (the English use very large chunks of coal in fireplaces) that seem dead on the outside (blue-bleak embers) fall open and show the still-bright fire (gold-vermilion) inside.

This train of thought was common in Hopkins: the beauty of the material world stirred him for its own sake, then led him on to think of the spiritual beauty dwelling in or beyond the material.

line 4. rung upon the rein: a term used in the training of a horse: at the end of a long rein the horse describes a circle. Here the falcon, using one wing as pivot, swings the circle.

line 6. skate's heel . . . bow-bend: another image of smooth circling, drawn from the art of skating.

line 11. chevalier: a term of honor: a chivalrous man, a knight. Here it is Christ, to whom the poem is addressed. Hopkins did not follow the modern custom of capitalizing nouns and pronouns referring to God or Christ (in another poem he addressed God as "sir").

What are some elements of strangeness in the style of this poem?

Is there an unusual amount of alliteration and assonance? Is this distracting, or does it help to bind the material of the poem into greater unity?

The meter is very complicated, but without elaborate analysis the poem can be read by keeping in mind a rhythm of five major accents to the line.

WILLIAM BUTLER YEATS

See also the other poems by Yeats in Sections 1, 3, and 8. By many critics Yeats is regarded as the greatest of all modern poets. Some of his most famous poems have been omitted from this selection because a full appreciation of them is almost impossible without a considerable knowledge of his other work. The reader who is interested in the little he finds here will find a great deal more in Yeats's collected poems and plays.

"The Magi"

Early in life Yeats had rejected most of the traditional beliefs of Christianity. Though the nominal subjects are the same, there is little basis for comparison between this and Eliot's poem in Section 15.

The construction of Yeats's poem as a single sentence should be noticed. Further tension or suspense is produced by the slightly interrupted order of words. In the first line, for example, the verb see waits for its object till the end of the next line. In line 6, to find is sus-

pended till its object, mystery, is reached two lines later; and, in the interval, even the phrase being unsatisfied (line 7) is interrupted by an inserted phrase. These scarcely noticeable grammatical tensions help to create the feeling that something important is being said and perhaps that something important is impending. The imagery and language contribute to the same effect, and these should be well studied. The most striking word in the poem is bestial, which on the surface means only belonging to beasts—referring, that is, to the stable and manger where the Magi saw Jesus—but which nevertheless also conveys a strong suggestion of subhuman brutishness and violence.

The individual parts of this poem are clear enough, but the whole seems somewhat mysterious. Compare it with the poem that follows.

"The Second Coming"

The title refers, of course, to the prophecy of Christ's second coming, but here the words are partly ironical. Yeats had a theory about historical cycles, each of about 2,000 years' duration, each an antithesis of the preceding, and each ushered in by a supernatural birth. The Greek era, by this theory, began with the birth of Helen of Troy, whose mother, Leda, was a mortal but whose father was Zeus. He had visited Leda in the form of a swan. Next came the Christian era with the birth of Christ. A third, Yeats said, is now approaching. Sometimes he imagined it as better, sometimes as worse than our era. The Greek gods might return again; or, as he expressed it in his autobiography, there might come "after us the Savage God."

The first stanza describes the state of the world as Yeats viewed it shortly after the close of World War I. A century earlier, in Prometheus Unbound, Shelley had expressed the same thought in very similar terms:

"The good want power, but to weep
   barren tears.
The powerful goodness want; worse
   need for them.
The wise want love; and those who
   love want wisdom;
And all best things are thus confused
   to ill."

line 12. *Spiritus Mundi:* a "general store house of images which have ceased to be a property of any personality or spirit" (Yeats), much like the unconscious racial memory described by the philosophical psychologist Jung.

line 14. The image here suggests a sphinx and a "brazen winged beast," as well as other combinations of man and beast such as the centaur, all of which Yeats wrote about elsewhere.

lines 19–20. Comment on the images and the meaning of these lines describing the Christian era.

"The Cold Heaven"

Like so many others of Yeats' poems, "The Cold Heaven" refers to his love (see the poems in Section 1). But its essential subject is something broader, for it represents any moment when the cold light of truth suddenly breaks into one's consciousness to shatter a long illusion on which one's past life has been built.

The poem, it will be noticed, is extremely subjective: all that happens is purely internal. Comment on the imagery with this in mind, and consider how the effect of violence is produced in a poem in which nothing external can be said to happen.

What is conveyed by the phrase "riddled with light"? Is it the climax of the poem?

"Among School Children"

While he was writing this poem, Yeats referred to it in a letter as his "curse upon old age." In the end, it became much more than that.

The shape of the poem might be described in terms of Yeats's own image of a "gyre." It begins with a small commonplace event and spirals out in theme until at the end it raises questions almost too vast to be expressed clearly in language: What is reality or what is value? The emotional energy that starts the widening spiral movement is sparked, once more, by the thought of Maud Gonne. Because of this, an experience that begins as a cursory visit of inspection by Yeats, in his official capacity as an Irish senator, to a convent school, comes to engage all his power of feeling and thought, makes him wonder what he has given his life to, what others give their lives to—

ultimately, what is worth giving one's life to.

Stanza II. Seeing the little girls in school, the poet is reminded of an occasion when "she" had once sat by the fire telling him a story of her childhood. He remembers it as a rare moment when he and she had felt united.

lines 15–16. The story of the origin of love in Plato's *Symposium*. Man, originally whole, attacked the gods and for this was punished by Zeus, who split him in two "as you might divide an egg with a hair." Since then, the halves forever try to unite: "the pursuit of the whole is called love."

line 26. Quattrocento. Usually this would mean the fifteenth century. Yeats, however, may have meant the fourteenth and may have been thinking of pictures of Dante, whose "hollow face," he said, was "more plain to the mind's eye than any face but that of Christ." Maud Gonne's portraits show exaggeratedly hollow cheeks and eyes in her later years.

line 28. *Mess* here has nothing to do with untidiness; it means a quantity of food for a meal.

lines 33–35. honey of generation. Yeats explained this as a legendary drug that destroys the recollection of prenatal freedom. It therefore makes life tolerable while its effect lasts.

The connection of Stanza VI with the preceding is made clear by Yeats's explanation of its meaning, "that even the greatest men are old scarecrows by the time their fame has come."

Lines 41–42 refer to Plato's theory of reality.

lines 43–44. Aristotle was the tutor of Alexander the Great.

lines 45–47. Pythagoras (who was believed by his followers to have golden thighs) discovered the mathematical relation between the harmony of the octave and the length of strings. He therefore reasoned that the order of the whole universe consists of number. Applying the theory to the heavenly bodies produced the famous notion of the "music of the spheres" ("what a star sang," line 47).

Stanza VII. The images worshiped by nuns are unchanging, those worshiped by mothers (their children) change; but both break the hearts of worshipers, Yeats says. Here he breaks off and addresses the images themselves as "Presences," bringing together the three devotions from the earlier stanzas: "passion" (Yeats' for his love), "piety" (the nuns to religion), "affection" (mothers for children). To the worshiper, these Presences symbolize "all heavenly glory." But in the end they only mock him, for in a sense they are not real but are "self-born," self-created: the value that man worships in them—supposing it to be an objective value, outside of himself—is only the value that he has subjectively created.

In the last stanza, the specific materials of the earlier part of the poem are still recognizable: the nun's asceticism (line 58), Maud Gonne's hollow beauty (line 59), his own wisdom that is not worth what it cost him (line 60); but these have grown far beyond their individual meaning and have become part of the universal question of values. The thought of the final stanza can be paraphrased only very crudely. It may be expressed in terms of ends and means: that the end cannot be separated from the means, that labor *brings* reward (blossoming, dancing) only when it *is* in itself reward. Or of the chestnut tree, the question asked is: Which is means—leaf, blossom, or bole—and which end? Which is the real, the essence? Does the dancer exist except through the dance? The implied answer may be phrased even more abstractly: that there is no *being* except *becoming*.

A paraphrase is never more than an aid in approaching a poem, and here it is especially weak. In fact, here it is almost ruinous to the

poem, because, quite apart from the feeling, the *idea* Yeats is getting at is something almost beyond the reach of logical thought. He could have described it in terms of his own very elaborate system of philosophical or semiphilosophical thought, but that required an entire book for him to explain, and we should need no less. Here he takes the poetic short cut, by which he suggests it to the imagination and emotions.

We shall not attempt to explain or describe the final poetic character and quality of "Among School Children" further than to call attention once more to the gyre-like structure of the poem and to the extraordinary style of Yeats, who can combine the most colloquial language and undignified imagery with the most dignified and remote in such a way as to create something quite different from either alone. Consider the homely and undignified "comfortable kind of scarecrow," for example, and the "old clothes upon old sticks," in which the mere repetition of *old* before *sticks* helps transform the phrase from commonplace into poetry. The pattern of contrast between such phrases as these and very different ones like "a marble or a bronze repose" or the abstract apostrophe "O Presences," a contrast that runs through the poem almost to the end, contributes to produce the combined feeling of reality and importance in the poem. The dropping away of commonplace material toward the end is part of the gyre-like movement of the whole.

VERSIFICATION

I

English versification is an extremely complicated as well as a controversial subject. The definitions given here consist merely of those most commonly applied. It should always be remembered that the poet's ear is his final guide and that the established verse forms in English are full of variations.

The unit of traditional English verse is the foot, which ordinarily consists of either two or three syllables. The iambic foot, the most common of all, has two syllables with stress on the second (bĕtráy; hĕ laughĕd); the trochaic, two syllables with stress on the first (wíckĕt; beát ĭt). The anapest consists of three syllables with stress on the last (ĭntĕrfére; ĭn ă stéw), and the dactyl of three with stress on the first (Flóridă). Ordinarily, one or another of these feet will predominate in a poem and the meter of the poem will be named accordingly: iambic pentameter, for example, if the standard foot is iambic and there are five feet to a line; or iambic hexameter if six to a line; tetrameter if four; trimeter, three; and so on.

Two other feet are common: the spondee, a foot made up of two stressed syllables; and the pyrrhic, a foot of two unstressed syllables. These are used, not as the meter for a whole poem, but as frequent variations from one of the standard meters. The standard ones themselves are to some extent interchangeable: a poem whose basic meter, for example, is iambic will usually contain some feet in which the stress is inverted and which are therefore trochaic; or it may contain an occasional anapestic foot, as well as spondees and pyrrhics.

The distinction between stressed and unstressed syllables is not a hard-and-fast one. In actual speech, syllables run the whole gamut from the syllabically almost nonexistent *-tle* in *little* to a strong and long one such as *prowled*. Poetry should be read with these varied shadings in mind and not in rigid categories of stressed and unstressed. A mechanical reading of the following lines of Wordsworth would give:

> Ă slúm/bĕr dĭd / mў spír/ĭt seál;
> Ĭ hăd / nŏ hú/măn feárs.

But such a reading kills the meaning. The lines should rather be read (with ᷉ representing an intermediate degree of stress):

> Ă slúm/bĕr dĭd / mў spír/ĭt seál;
> Ĭ hăd / nó hú/măn feárs.
>
> or perhaps
>
> Ĭ hăd / nó hú/măn feárs.

402

Even this grossly oversimplifies what should be the real reading. For in the first line, *my*, though unaccented, has a great deal more weight than the opening syllable *A* or the *-it* of *spirit*. Every syllable in the line, in fact, has a slightly different degree of stress and pitch (varying as the voice is louder or softer, higher or lower) and a different timing. Some modern writers of what is called *free verse* have succeeded in producing poetic rhythms without employing any of the traditional metrical schemes. In reading, it is far more important to be able to avoid a deadly metrical sing-song than it is to be able to scan lines by rule; nevertheless, it is convenient to know something of the traditional rules.

2

GLOSSARY OF TERMS COMMONLY EMPLOYED IN VERSIFICATION

alliteration. Correspondence of sounds at the beginning of syllables (usually accented syllables) that are close together: "The *p*lowman homeward *p*lods his *w*eary *w*ay." Some writers confine the use of the term to consonant sounds and include initial repetition of vowels under *assonance, q.v.*

anapest (noun), *anapestic* (adj.). See 1.

assonance. Repetition of a vowel sound in consecutive or nearby words: "The *a*ngels keep their *a*ncient pl*a*ces."

ballad meter or *ballad stanza.* These terms commonly designate a quatrain of alternating four- and three-stress lines, with the second and fourth rhyming (*abcb*). This is sometimes printed as a couplet of seven-foot lines. The term is also used for the same quatrain with alternate rhyme (*abab*).

blank verse. Unrhymed iambic pentameter. See the special discussion of Shakespeare's blank verse, p. 451.

caesura. An internal pause in a line of verse, usually a pause required by the meaning.

consonance. Repetition of consonant sounds elsewhere than at the beginning of syllables: "Pa*rch*ed, he lu*rch*ed to the bar."

couplet. A unit of two lines rhyming with each other; they are usually of the same length.

dactyl (noun), *dactylic* (adj.). See 1.

dimeter. A line consisting of two feet.

elegy. A poem of lamentation for the dead (formerly the term had a broader meaning).

enjambment. See *run-on line.*

feminine ending. An extra unstressed syllable at the end of an iambic or anapestic line.

feminine rhyme. See *rhyme.*

foot. See 1.

free verse. Verse which follows no regular metrical scheme.

heroic couplet. Iambic pentameter rhyming in couplets. Some writers confine the use of the term to the "closed" couplet, in which the two rhyming lines form an independent unit of thought or a complete sentence.

hexameter. A line consisting of six feet.

iamb (noun), *iambic* (adj.). See 1.

lyric. Originally, a poem to be sung to the accompaniment of the lyre. The term has come to include, besides poems suitable for singing, a wide variety of forms: sonnets, odes, elegies, and poems in many different stanza arrangements. The lyric is usually short or of moderate length and is never primarily narrative or didactic. Directly or indirectly, it is subjective: that is, it is meant to convey emotions, attitudes, or states of mind.

masculine rhyme. See *rhyme*.

metaphor. A metaphor is an implied (not expressed) comparison between unlike things. "A shower of leaves" is a metaphor: leaves are essentially unlike rain, but one resemblance is seized upon. A metaphor may imply the comparison by taking for granted the identity of two things, as in this example where, by the mere use of the word *shower*, the identity of leaves and rain is implied. Or the identity of unlike things may be stated outright as if it were a fact, as in saying, "Joe is a pig," in order to express vividly his greed. See *simile*.

In recent years the term *metaphor* has come to be used in a much broader sense for almost all nonliteral statement. It is even applied to language itself because, unlike such things as pictures, which can represent objects by imitating them, language is by nature symbolic. The word *hat*, for example, does not resemble a hat; it is an arbitrary sign, quite unlike the object, yet representing it.

ode. One of the longer forms of lyric, an ode is a lofty and dignified treatment of some theme. As originally developed in ancient Greece, its form was complex and somewhat rigid. An English ode may follow the classical pattern, or it may be written in either irregular or regular rhymed stanzas.

onomatopoeia. The use of sounds that by imitation suggest the meaning, as in the words *buzz, hiss, bubble*. This is a device more commonly discussed in the classroom than actually used by poets, for there are very few genuinely onomatopoetic words.

ottava rima. An eight-line stanza of iambic pentameter, rhyming *abababcc*.

pentameter. A line consisting of five feet.

pyrrhic. See 1.

quatrain. Any four-line stanza.

rhyme (or *rime*). In its broadest sense (rarely used) the term may refer to any repetition of the sounds of words. Commonly it means *end-rhyme*, repetition at the ends of lines. It consists usually in the matching of sounds beginning with an accented vowel and continuing to the end of the word: *blow, go; haul, maul; dart, apart; destroy, joy*. These are masculine, or one-syllable rhymes, by far the most common in English verse. *Feminine* or *double* rhyme occurs in lines with feminine endings, when the last two syllables rhyme (*reeling, peeling*). Triple, or three-syllable rhyme (*bearable, wearable*) is uncommon except in comic verse. *Internal rhyme* occurs when one or both rhymes are within the line instead of at the end:

> We were the *first* that ever *burst*
> Into that silent sea.

run-on line (enjambment). A line in which the sense runs on to the following line without a noticeable pause, as in

> Dust to the dust! but the pure spirit shall flow
> Back to the burning fountain whence it came.

simile. An expressed comparison between unlike things. A simile differs from a metaphor in being introduced by "like" or "as." For one of the most famous similes in modern poetry, see the opening lines of Eliot's "Prufrock."

sonnet. See pp. 382–383.

Spenserian stanza. A stanza of nine lines. The first eight are iambic pentameter, the ninth is hexameter. The rhyme is *ababbcbcc*.

spondee (noun), *spondaic* (adj.). See 1.

terza rima. A three-line stanza or group of lines in which the middle one is linked by rhyme to the following group. *aba/bcb/cdc*, and so on. For an example, see Shelley's "Ode to the West Wind."

tetrameter. A line consisting of four feet.

trimeter. A line consisting of three feet.

trochee (noun), *trochaic* (adj.). See 1.

The Art of Reading Drama

PLAYS AS FICTION

It seems obvious that stories and novels are fiction, not fact. But when we are thinking about literature, the terms *fact* and *fiction* cause more difficulty than might at first appear. Let us say that stories and novels describe human thoughts and actions that never existed or occurred. But if they had existed or occurred, these thoughts and actions would have taken a form closely similar to the form they receive in the story or novel that happens to be before the reader. In short, history, fact, what actually happened, is a record of particular events. Fiction, story, is an account of events that might have happened. Fiction may also consider the implications of these things that might have happened. By leaving the realm of fact with (1) possible or probable events (2) presented in their meaningful implications, we have moved from the category known in philosophy as "particulars" to the category called "universals." Thus fiction, we may say, deals with actions of universal significance. It is a generalized account of human deeds and human thoughts.[1]

This distinction between fiction and actuality was formulated by the philosopher Aristotle more than two thousand years ago. It has been a fruitful source of meditation for literary critics ever since. [We have discussed the point, using our own terms, in the introduction to fiction. There, among other things, we indicated how (partly because of Aristotle's principle of universality) the reader of a story may become involved in it, at least to the extent of wanting to know what will happen next, and how the story can yield him information or inspire him to certain ideas and beliefs.]

A play is also a work of fiction, and for the same reasons. However real it may seem on stage or screen, it did not "happen" in the sense that the death of Caesar or stubbing your toe yesterday happened; but it might have happened in pretty much the way the author has shown it on the stage or screen, and you, the viewer or reader of the play, may become emotionally or intellectually involved in it.

Further, the artistry of a play—how the author gets his effects—is in many ways the same as the artistry of a story. Like a short story, a play is written about a theme or idea as well as about a series of events, and this theme or idea can usually be stated in universal terms. A play, even a light comedy, generally shows conflict of some sort: man against himself, against another person, or against the whole of his environment. Like a story, a play has to show a progressive development from a starting point to a point of conclusion, and somewhere along the way there must be a place of climax or crisis, a

---

[1] So is history but, insofar as a historian interprets facts, perhaps he too is writing a kind of fiction. For more on this point, see the introduction to biography in this volume.

point at which the forces in conflict are at their most intense opposition. In all these ways a play resembles other forms of fiction.

A play differs from short stories and novels primarily in that it is written to be seen and heard, not read. This means that its words and ideas are here at one moment and gone the next; the listener has no chance to go back and think about what has just been said, as he can when he is reading. This fleeting quality of dialogue means that a playwright has to deal in somewhat broader effects than the writer of a complex story. If the audience is to understand what is happening on the stage, most of the speeches of the play must be brief and give the illusion of being conversation. Generally the members of an audience will not follow a dialogue that is greatly involved. Consequently the playwright, at least in the twentieth century, commonly makes the speeches short, uses repetition, artfully builds up minor climaxes in order to emphasize certain ideas, and dares to employ long speeches only occasionally, probably late in the action, when he wants to state his main ideas and feels that now, if ever, he may for a moment or two have the full attention of his audience.

Yet he may not speak directly to his audience. In the written version of the play he may speak to the reader by describing the stage set and the characters and by giving stage directions, but in performance these things reach the audience only as visible results, not as words to be heard.

We ought, therefore, to be able to say that drama works an unusual spell over us because it is more objective and impersonal than stories and novels are, that in a play we may see life without interference from an author. But this is not true. Much modern fiction that is serious in artistic purpose is objective and impersonal in that the author almost never speaks to the reader directly. Direct comment has been diminishing since the nineteenth century. But a novelist may select and manipulate his material, without comment, so that his readers will receive the impressions he wants them to receive.

The dramatist has precisely the same resources and the same methods. He selects and emphasizes. In the sense that it consists of dramatized speeches, his play is objective and impersonal. In the sense that it was written by an author who decided what material would go into it, it is subjective and personal, just as a story or a novel is.

Why Write Plays?

Why, then, do plays exist? When a story is to be told, why not simply write it down? Why go to the trouble of hiring a hall, paying actors to speak certain rigidly prescribed speeches, and persuading the public to pay money to look and listen?

The reason is buried deep in the history of humanity. Plays existed long before prose narrative. The first recorded plays are in verse, and they grew out of ritualistic processions with songs and dances. Probably these themselves originated in the common human desire to ape, to mime, to re-enact. We see it in primitive people and children, to whom re-enacting a battle or an encounter with an animal is more vivid and more understandable than a "prosy" narrative told at third hand.

One clue to the reason for plays is, therefore, their vividness and apparent directness. It seems to us that we are not merely talking or reading about life but are seeing life unfold itself before us. This is a false impression, to be sure, for a play is by definition an imitation of life. Nevertheless the play seems to be real and direct.

Further, its very vividness makes it easy to understand. The actors speak in familiar words. If they philosophize, it is only in brief speeches. As we shall discuss later, the ideas and implications of some plays, like those reprinted in this volume, can attract the most sophisticated and highly educated playgoers. But—let us be honest about it—the basic appeal of the drama is to spectators who want vivid, direct action in understandable language. In the first play in this volume you would see, if it were performed for you, a man coming on stage with eyes streaming blood because he has just blinded himself. In the second play you would watch a Moorish general strangle his young, beautiful wife. These episodes sound lurid when isolated in this way, but the two plays in which these events occur are also a source of intense intellectual discussion.

Plays also attract audiences because the stories in them are compressed. It would be possible to write long novels about the people and the events portrayed in the five plays of this text. Instead, for reasons to be discussed presently, each drama takes only about two hours of actual playing time.

A play is vivid, direct, brief, and, on one level, immediately understandable. It is therefore attractive to the person who thinks he would have neither the time to read a novel nor the patience to puzzle out a complex human problem.

How the Playwright Works

There are limitations on the performance time of any play. The human body is not designed to sit motionless for an indefinite period; consequently, a play cannot last much longer than two hours and it has to be interrupted with intermissions for the relief of cramped muscles and tired minds. In the theater of our own age a play begins after dinner, fairly late in the evening (usually 8:30), and must end in time for playgoers to use some of the night for sleeping. The ancient Greek theater and Shakespeare's theater had other customs, but the plays of former ages were also limited in length of performance.

Space is just as basic a physical limitation as is time. Everything in a play must be performed on a platform no larger than thirty by forty feet, and often smaller. Many of the problems of the playwright arise from that simple fact.

Authors and stage managers have devised wonderfully ingenious methods for transcending the limitations of space. One method, now generally considered ineffective, has been the attempt to imitate life with painstaking realism in scenery and stage properties. It is ineffective because the audience cannot be fooled: this on the stage is not a real interior but an imitation three-sided room. Therefore the other methods try to make the most of the fact that the stage is by definition an imitation of life. Perhaps all the events of the play are crowded into one setting, and the audience accepts the assumption that all these things could happen in one living room. Or scenes more or less realistic in appearance may follow each other rapidly, the rapid sequence being helped by the modern invention of the revolving stage. Sometimes simple furniture is set up in a space surrounded by the audience on all four sides, as in the arena technique. Electric lighting— a recent innovation when we consider the long history of the drama—adds greatly to the variety and flexibility of stage settings, changes in light patterns being sometimes the only method of indicating new scenes. But the simplest and perhaps the best device is merely to pretend that the scene is before the audience.

> What country, friends, is this?
> This is Illyria, lady.

And the magic of the words that follow is so great that the audience needs no scenery to help it imagine that the bare stage is the seacoast of Illyria. This, with a few modifications, is the method used by Sophocles and by Shakespeare.

Probably nowadays most people get their introduction to drama through television. But during the period of transition from radio to television there must have been many habitual listeners to radio who had a vague feeling of disappointment when they first saw a play on television. A little reflection told them that what they were seeing was someone else's idea of scene and setting and even character, whereas on radio they had always been able to construct an ideal scene through that most accurate of stage managers, the mind's eye, the imagination. Similarly, a member of a theater audience can always use his own power of creative imagination to help the playwright overcome those limitations of time and space that are part of the defined conditions of the theater.

The stage method of presenting a story may even possess real advantages over all other forms—radio, television, motion pictures, and narratives experienced through reading. It has immediate life, for the actors are not shadows on a screen but people breathing and talking in the same room with us. Even radio drama, television plays, and motion pictures can, in a sense, seem more real than a novel or a short story. This is because they are plays, and their words are the words of human speech, which is a medium of immense power and variety. When in a "live" theater the pleasures of costume, lighting, music, a few properties, and a judicious use of scenery have been added to the power of human speech, the playgoer can often experience the genuine thrill of the theater. It is a unique feeling, one never to be forgotten.

WHY READ PLAYS?

We should therefore never forego an opportunity to see a good play well performed; but we should also acquire a taste for reading plays. Sometimes, as with *Oedipus Rex* and *Othello*, we cannot well understand what we are seeing on the stage without previous study. Further, a play makes enjoyable reading because it presents a direct and economical version of its story. Finally, as was said before, with a few hints from the playwright the reader can set the scene himself, clothe the characters in such costumes as he will, and read the speeches with all the emphasis of which he is capable. He can see the play in his mind's eye, hear it in his mind's ear.

All this is true but it does not constitute the whole case for reading plays—or for seeing them in the theater. We said a few moments ago that people watch plays because plays are short, vivid, and apparently easy to understand. Actually, the last quality is both true and not true.

If a play is memorable, it demands study. In this respect it is precisely like other forms of literature. In previous parts of this volume the student has discovered that stories and poems can be difficult, but he has also learned how rewarding it is to work out some of their meanings and implications. He will find the same difficulty and the same reward in plays. Their subject is also the endless complexity of human life.

Even in the westerns and the detective stories of television, which is a medium hampered by the vagaries of commercial sponsors and the whims of a heterogeneous mass audience, the viewer will occasionally detect the touch of an artistic playwright. The western sheriff shoots the bandit more in sorrow than in anger; like the rest of us he wishes this were a world in which bandits would behave like good citizens. Or showing through the formula of the murder story there is a glimpse of complicated human motives. The television writer might write on a higher level more often if he were allowed to.

For depth we turn to the full-dress play of the traditional theater. Here we see our own problems enacted before us in vivid spectacle and recited for us in words of especial poignancy. We must reflect on the meaning of the play as we must reflect about stories and poems, but the meaning is also discovered in the immediacy of the experience.

"O Iago, the pity of it, Iago!" exclaims Othello as it seems to him that his illusions of happiness have faded around him. And similarly,

> Let every man in mankind's frailty
> Consider his last day; and let none
> Presume on his good fortune until he find
> Life, at his death, a memory without pain.

These are the final words of *Oedipus Rex*. When such passages are spoken on the stage or when we read them in an armchair, we are directly and forcibly moved to meditate about what it means to be a human being. That, in the final analysis, is why we read plays, and that is why we go to see them performed.

The Types of Drama

There is no scientifically accurate nomenclature for classifying plays. We are likely to think of two general classifications, tragedy and comedy. These depend upon our attitude toward life. We tend to designate as comedies any plays that stress life's goodness and as tragedies those plays which demonstrate that life is an avenue to disappointment, frustration, overthrow, and death. But obviously most manifestations of human life are comprised of both good and bad. We do not even believe that death is always and inevitably a calamity. For these and other reasons, we must find more accurate meanings for the terms *tragedy* and *comedy*, and we must supplement them with other technical terms.

For the limited degree of classification needed in this volume we may be content with thinking of the vast body of plays in all the European languages as ranging in tone from dark to light.

1. The dark ones we may call tragedy. Such plays may stress the imminence or inevitability of death and assume that death is something to be avoided as long as possible. Or a tragedy may show that death comes at the end of a wasted or frustrated life: man, made in the image of God, seldom lives up to his godlike potentiality. Or, assuming just the opposite, that the directing hand of a supernatural agency is but outworn superstition, a tragedy may depict a central figure who is doomed by circumstance to failure in life

and oblivion in death. A tragedy always appears to end unhappily, but the unhappiness is not merely death; it is a combination of death plus disappointment or disillusion or the revelation of a defect in character or a sudden reversal of fortune or the realization that life is at best an inescapable trap. Which of these it is depends on the philosophy of the playwright. According to a tradition that goes back to Aristotle, there is a means of mitigating the effect of tragedy on us. Except for the type of tragedy that treats life as a trap, the final effect of tragedy on a playgoer is supposed to be an uplifting one. The older types of tragedy, at least, are said to reassure the playgoer that justice and essential sanity finally prevail in the world. We are supposed to be better people for having watched this tragic story.

2. After tragedy we may consider the broad central area in which life appears to the playwright as a thing of mixed sorrow and pleasure, or as alternating between pleasure and pain. In the plays in this area not all seems lost: out of death arises new life, or perhaps the central figure is enabled to work out his problems in some kind of hopeful way. There are various names but no single designation for these essentially serious plays of mixed joy and sorrow. We sometimes call them "tragicomedies." One type, which discusses any one of a number of specific problems or preoccupations or ideas, as for instance some aspect of marriage, we call a "problem play." Most often a playwright who has written a play in this middle range simply avoids the problem of nomenclature and calls his work a "drama" or a "play." By whatever name, these plays that are neither tragedy nor comedy are serious in intent, discuss some phase of the complex human problems spoken of in the preceding section of this introduction, and use humor as a means of conveying ideas, lightening the gloom, and generally making the discussion of ideas or problems palatable to the audience.

3. Comedies are at the lighter end of our tonal range. The essence of comedy is humor. Humor, which may range from quiet understatement to uproarious noise, may be derived from all sorts of sources. There is wit, which is primarily verbal humor, often of an intellectual type. One important division of comedy is thus the "comedy of manners," in which the playwright wittily depicts and mildly ridicules the peculiarities of a few individuals more or less typical of the upper classes in a stratified society. Another kind of comedy is "satire," in which the wit acquires barbs and the ridicule becomes savage thrusts. There is "situation comedy," which often depends on the bringing together of incongruous characters in unlikely situations. Finally, at the extreme right end of this range from dark to light is the kind of comedy called "farce." This depends on bodily humor, sometimes gross and ribald, sometimes harmless, as when a pompous character slips and falls.

Most drama is mixed. Its sources of serious reflection are varied; the kinds of humor possible in plays are infinite; and all elements, serious or humorous, can be mingled in one play.

Probably the student will find most reward in examining the plays reprinted in this volume singly and empirically, considering the various elements of tragedy, neither-tragedy-nor-comedy, and comedy, not in the abstract but as they become visible in each play.

Two Kinds of Tragedy

From the earliest times critics and readers have considered tragedy the most important form of drama, probably because life itself is a serious matter and potentially tragic. Bertrand Russell has well stated this attitude toward tragedy as an art in "A Free Man's Worship."

> . . . Of all the arts, Tragedy is the proudest, the most triumphant; for it builds its shining citadel in the very centre of the enemy's country, on the very summit of his highest mountain; from its impregnable watchtowers, his camps and arsenals, his columns and forts, are all revealed; within its walls the free life continues, while the legions of Death and Pain and Despair, and all the servile captains of tyrant Fate, afford the burghers of that dauntless city new spectacles of beauty.

The subject of tragedy is thus the conduct of man in the face of death and pain and despair. In that sentence perhaps the most important word is *man*. All species face death and pain; only man has learned how to philosophize about them, and perhaps only man has learned how to despair. Until the last part of the nineteenth century nearly everyone assumed that this fact—that man knows enough about his fate to write tragedies about it—demonstrated clearly man's importance in the universe. Man, it was believed, is a special creation. He is a child of God. In *Oedipus Rex* and *Othello*, the two older tragedies in this volume, the authors assume that it is important for us to be concerned with what happens to Oedipus and Othello, not only because they are men of high estate, but first of all because they are human beings, not animals, and possess the divine gift of reason.

But Oedipus is a king, and Othello is a general who ranks with the nobility. Thus a second assumption is involved in these plays: that only men of high degree are suitable subjects for tragedy. It would not have occurred to Sophocles that he could write a tragedy about the shepherd who rescued the infant Oedipus, or to Shakspeare that there was material for tragedy in one of the servants of the Duke at the court of Venice. A great man, such as a ruler or a general, seemed more important than the rest of us, and because he was in a high position, he had farther to fall. Greatness on this earth was somehow equated with greatness in some larger scheme of things.

During the nineteenth century people began to doubt both of these assumptions: that mankind is important and that a great man is especially important. In the twentieth century the doubts became widespread. Much of our thinking is now colored by the impersonality, the mechanistic philosophy, and the determinism of natural science. If man is "a flea on the epidermis of the universe," as someone has said, how can he be the subject of tragedy, at least of tragedy of the older type? Millions of people in our century are also convinced that royalty and nobility no longer serve any useful purpose. A king or a general should receive no better treatment in the cosmic scheme of things than a common person. Although, according to this opinion, what a king or a general does may affect us all, he is intrinsically important only to himself, just as the rest of us are. If tragedies are to be written, they must be of some other sort.

A playwright who has abandoned the earlier assumptions is likely to find what may be called tragedy in the very denial of the assumptions. He pictures man as a victim of circumstances over which he has no control. A single person is only one of two or three billion people who happen, through no wish of their own, to inhabit this planet at the same time. Like the others, he is doomed to death, and there is nothing for him to look forward to after death. He can count himself lucky if his life is not nasty and furtive and his death is not painful.

This is only one point of view, to be sure, but it is clearly a source of despair to those who hold it. Whether it constitutes tragedy is a matter of definition. At any rate, it is a theme that pervades much of twentieth-century literature, and plays that stress this theme are often called tragedies. One of the most interesting of this kind is the third play in this volume, Elmer Rice's *The Adding Machine*, which is an explicit statement of the denials discussed above: that man has any importance beyond his own desire to survive, or that there are individual great men who are more important than other people. The protagonist of this play is called, not King Oedipus or General Othello, but Mr. Zero. In the universal equations he is only a cipher.

The fact that in this play and in other literature of the twentieth century some of our authors are still concerned with the place of man in the universe would seem to indicate that as yet the mechanistic philosophy has not become fully accepted, and, to be sure, only a minority of the people in the Western world accept the mechanistic assumptions. Even if one accepts such a hypothesis, he finds that it includes a possible contradiction. If man is of no over-all importance, he still enjoys the importance he always possessed, his importance to himself, and so why write tragedies about the belief that he is of no worth to the rest of the universe? In short, according to the mechanistic hypothesis, man still has precisely the same importance that he had when he believed in the supposed illusions. To an observer who for the time being makes no attempt to decide between hypotheses, overstressing the mechanistic assumptions may seem to be a form of naïveté reserved for certain types of people in the twentieth century.

Whatever our beliefs at any particular time in the world's history, we are always faced with the problem of how to live and how to die. The first three plays in this section demonstrate Bertrand Russell's point that tragedy is the proudest, the most triumphant of the arts because it attacks the problem directly and without evasion.

OEDIPUS REX

Sophocles

(496?–406 B.C.)

The theater in which *Oedipus Rex* was first performed differed markedly from the modern theater. The reader should picture to himself rows of stone seats arranged in a semicircle on a hillside, the whole not unlike the closed end of a huge football stadium. At about the spot where the goal posts would stand there is a large circular paved area with an altar in the center. Behind the area stands a building with doors for entrance and exit. At each end of the semicircle (the rest of the modern stadium, of course, is missing) is a passageway so that actors and chorus may come and go. Since an arena of this size, such as the theater at Athens, sometimes seated about 15,000 people, there could be none of the intimate effects of the modern stage. The actors wore footgear that increased their height and masks that projected their voices.

The ancient Greek drama was religious in origin and spirit. The plays of Sophocles and his fellow-dramatists, which were presented during one or two weeks of the year only, were an outgrowth and a continuation of the ancient choral procession and dance that annually honored the God Dionysos. Hence the part of the Chorus in such plays. Some of the lines assigned to the Chorus in *Oedipus Rex* were sung or chanted; some of them were accompanied by ritual dance. Some of the lines were spoken by all the Chorus in unison, some by part of the Chorus, and some by the Leader of the Chorus (Choragos). Few scenes of violence occurred in view of the audience; the death of one of the characters was commonly described by a Messenger.

The basic material of the plays was known to the audience. It was drawn from the stories of the Greek past: incidents connected with the Trojan War, for example, or King Agamemnon's return to his home after the war. One aim of the playwright was to retell the incident in a new way without changing the essential story. Since religion and the state were but two aspects of the same thing, the citizen of Athens went to the plays not merely for excitement and intellectual diversion, but also in a spirit of pious patriotism or patriotic piety. It was as though nowadays Americans would go to the theater early in the morning of an annual civic Play Week to see, that day, three tragedies on the landing of the Pilgrims at Plymouth, Washington at Valley Forge, and the assassination of Lincoln, plus one comedy on Rip Van Winkle.

The writers of the Greek tragedies discussed in these plays the profoundest questions of ethics and morality. Their subject was the relation of man to the gods, or, as we might say nowadays, the place of man in the universe.

Of all the Greek plays perhaps the most famous is *Oedipus Rex*. In the century after it was written the philosopher Aristotle formulated a definition of tragedy, based partly on his observation of this play in performance, that ever since has deeply affected the thinking of playwrights and critics. (Excerpts from Aristotle's *Poetics* are printed elsewhere in this volume.) Tragedy, said Aristotle, must show the misfortune of a personage of great reputation and prosperity, "a man not pre-eminently virtuous and just, whose misfortune . . . is brought upon him not by vice and depravity but by some error of judgement."[1] This misfortune is shown by means of a "reversal of Intention"—that is, an action intended to produce one effect actually produces just the opposite effect. Thus the situation in which the central figure of the tragedy finds himself at the beginning of the play is completely reversed at the end.

[1] As translated by Ingram Bywater. The Clarendon Press, Oxford.

An important incident in this reversal is likely to be a "recognition," in which a character is recognized by his true name, or in his true self or personality. Through these devices and others the audience is brought to feel the emotions of pity and fear.

In most respects *Oedipus Rex* exactly fulfills this definition of tragedy. In the popular philosophy of the Greeks one of the worst of sins was the sin of excessive pride, known as "hubris." If a man felt that life was going so well for him that he could safely risk breaking the laws of the gods, or if he even unknowingly broke a moral law because he was too proud of his status in the world, the gods would surely punish him for his presumption.

Therefore, after familiarizing himself with the story, the reader should try to find the tragic flaw, if any, in the character of Oedipus. Is it hubris? Note that he refers to himself as "I, Oedipus, who bear the famous name." Is his treatment of Creon and Teiresias an example of the humility before the gods that should be present even in a great king?

The reader will also want to note the superb dramatic irony with which Oedipus is made the instrument of the reversal of his situation and thus the immediate cause of his own downfall. And the reader will trace the successive recognitions of the true identity of Oedipus.

Was Oedipus the ultimate as well as the immediate cause of his own fall? After all, the oracle had made a certain prophecy about him. Could he have avoided it? Consideration of this matter will lead the student into one of the most baffling of all philosophical questions, the problem of whether or not the will is free.

But mostly the student reading this play for the first time is likely to be impressed by its dramatic quality. As he reads it (or sees it in the theater), he should have the same feeling he would have if he were to watch a friend heedlessly walking into certain destruction and, as in a bad dream, find himself powerless to interfere. This play must have been the talk of Athens for many days after the morning of its first performance.

There is always a question as to how closely we can enter into the meaning and spirit of a piece written in an ancient language. Some translators attempt to modernize *Oedipus* so that it may seem like a play written for our own stage. Dudley Fitts and Robert Fitzgerald have made a translation in flexible modern English verse but have kept some of the evidence that the play is 2,500 years old.[1]

As they took their seats, the Athenian audience knew what they were about to see, but we need at least a brief introduction. Oedipus was King of Thebes, a city-state founded long ago by Kadmos. The last King of Thebes, Laïos, had been slain in a highway brawl. At about that same time Oedipus had left his former home, Corinth, in order to avoid fulfilling a prophecy he had heard, that he was fated to kill his father, King Polybus of Corinth, and marry his mother, Queen Merope. But everyone in the audience knows something that Oedipus does not: that these were only his foster-father and foster-mother.

Coming to Thebes, Oedipus overthrew the Sphinx, a monster which had been oppressing the city. The monster required all on pain of death to answer her riddle: what is it that walks on four legs in the morning, two at noon, and three at night? Oedipus correctly answered "man." This enabled him to marry the widowed Queen of Thebes, Iocaste, and become King. Oedipus and Iocaste had four children.

Now Thebes is in trouble again.

---

[1] The traditional Latin form of the title, *Oedipus Rex*, means "Oedipus the King" or "King Oedipus." The translators have retained some of the technical terms used in the Greek theater. The *prologue* is the speech of a single actor or the dialogue between actors that begins a play. The *parodos* is the part that contains the first entrance of the Chorus. A *scene* consists of further dialogue between actors. An *ode* is an utterance of the Chorus, divided into *strophe* and *antistrophe*. Sometimes half the Chorus delivered the strophe and the other half the antistrophe; sometimes the whole Chorus delivered both but changed position on the stage to indicate the difference between the two parts. The *exodos* is the final part of the play containing the departure of the Chorus from the stage.

OEDIPUS REX

AN ENGLISH VERSION BY DUDLEY FITTS AND ROBERT FITZGERALD

—

PERSONS REPRESENTED:

OEDIPUS
A PRIEST
CREON
TEIRESIAS
IOCASTE
MESSENGER
SHEPHERD OF LAÏOS
SECOND MESSENGER
CHORUS OF THEBAN ELDERS

THE SCENE. *Before the palace of Oedipus, King of Thebes. A central door and two lateral doors open onto a platform which runs the length of the façade. On the platform, right and left, are altars; and three steps lead down into the "orchestra," or chorus-ground. At the beginning of the action these steps are crowded by suppliants who have brought branches and chaplets of olive leaves and who lie in various attitudes of despair.* OEDIPUS *enters.*

PROLOGUE

OEDIPUS:

My children, generations of the living
In the line of Kadmos, nursed at his ancient hearth:
Why have you strewn yourselves before these altars
In supplication, with your boughs and garlands?
The breath of incense rises from the city
With a sound of prayer and lamentation. Children,
I would not have you speak through messengers,
And therefore I have come myself to hear you—
I, Oedipus, who bear the famous name.
                                    [To a PRIEST:
You, there, since you are eldest in the company,
Speak for them all, tell me what preys upon you,
Whether you come in dread, or crave some blessing:
Tell me, and never doubt that I will help you
In every way I can; I should be heartless
Were I not moved to find you suppliant here.

PRIEST:

Great Oedipus, O powerful King of Thebes!
You see how all the ages of our people
Cling to your altar steps: here are boys
Who can barely stand alone, and here are priests
By weight of age, as I am a priest of God,

416

And young men chosen from those yet
    unmarried;
As for the others, all that multitude,
They wait with olive chaplets in the
    squares,
At the two shrines of Pallas, and where
    Apollo
Speaks in the glowing embers.
                  Your own eyes
Must tell you: Thebes is in her extremity
And can not lift her head from the surge
    of death.
A rust consumes the buds and fruits of
    the earth;
The herds are sick; children die unborn,
And labor is vain. The god of plague and
    pyre
Raids like detestable lightning through the
    city,
And all the house of Kadmos is laid waste,
All emptied, and all darkened: Death
    alone
Battens upon the misery of Thebes.

You are not one of the immortal gods, we
    know;
Yet we have come to you to make our
    prayer
As to the man of all men best in adversity
And wisest in the ways of God. You saved
    us
From the Sphinx, that flinty singer, and
    the tribute
We paid to her so long; yet you were
    never
Better informed than we, nor could we
    teach you:
It was some god breathed in you to set
    us free.

Therefore, O mighty King, we turn to
    you:
Find us our safety, find us a remedy,
Whether by counsel of the gods or men.
A king of wisdom tested in the past
Can act in a time of troubles, and act well.
Noblest of men, restore
Life to your city! Think how all men call
    you
Liberator for your triumph long ago;

Ah, when your years of kingship are re-
    membered,
Let them not say *We rose, but later fell*—
Keep the State from going down in the
    storm!
Once, years ago, with happy augury,
You brought us fortune; be the same
    again!
No man questions your power to rule the
    land:
But rule over men, not over a dead city!
Ships are only hulls, citadels are nothing,
When no life moves in the empty passage-
    ways.

OEDIPUS:

Poor children! You may be sure I know
All that you longed for in your coming
    here.
I know that you are deathly sick; and yet,
Sick as you are, not one is as sick as I.
Each of you suffers in himself alone
His anguish, not another's; but my spirit
Groans for the city, for myself, for you.

I was not sleeping, you are not waking me.
No, I have been in tears for a long while
And in my restless thought walked many
    ways.
In all my search, I found one helpful
    course,
And that I have taken: I have sent Creon,
Son of Menoikeus, brother of the Queen,
To Delphi, Apollo's place of revelation,
To learn there, if he can,
What act or pledge of mine may save the
    city.
I have counted the days, and now, this
    very day,
I am troubled, for he has overstayed his
    time.
What is he doing? He has been gone too
    long.
Yet whenever he comes back, I should
    do ill
To scant whatever hint the god may give.

PRIEST:

It is a timely promise. At this instant
They tell me Creon is here.

OEDIPUS:

          O Lord Apollo!
May his news be fair as his face is radiant!

PRIEST:

  It could not be otherwise: he is crowned
     with bay,
  The chaplet is thick with berries.

OEDIPUS:

          We shall soon know;
He is near enough to hear us now.
              [*Enter* CREON
            O Prince:
Brother: son of Menoikeus:
What answer do you bring us from the
    god?

CREON:

  It is favorable. I can tell you, great afflic-
    tions
  Will turn out well, if they are taken well.

OEDIPUS:

  What was the oracle? These vague words
  Leave me still hanging between hope and
    fear.

CREON:

  Is it your pleasure to hear me with all
    these
  Gathered around us? I am prepared to
    speak,
  But should we not go in?

OEDIPUS:

          Let them all hear it.
  It is for them I suffer, more than for
    myself.

CREON:

  Then I will tell you what I heard at
    Delphi.

  In plain words
  The god commands us to expel from the
    land of Thebes
  An old defilement that it seems we shelter.
  It is a deathly thing, beyond expiation.
  We must not let it feed upon us longer.

OEDIPUS:

  What defilement? How shall we rid our-
    selves of it?

CREON:

  By exile or death, blood for blood. It was
  Murder that brought the plague-wind on
    the city.

OEDIPUS:

  Murder of whom? Surely the god has
    named him?

CREON:

  My lord: long ago Laïos was our king,
  Before you came to govern us.

OEDIPUS:

                I know;
  I learned of him from others; I never saw
    him.

CREON:

  He was murdered; and Apollo commands
    us now
  To take revenge upon whoever killed him.

OEDIPUS:

  Upon whom? Where are they? Where
    shall we find a clue
  To solve that crime, after so many years?

CREON:

  Here in this land, he said.
               If we make enquiry,
  We may touch things that otherwise es-
    cape us.

OEDIPUS:

  Tell me: Was Laïos murdered in his
    house,
  Or in the fields, or in some foreign coun-
    try?

CREON:

  He said he planned to make a pilgrimage.
  He did not come home again.

OEDIPUS:

             And was there no one,
  No witness, no companion, to tell what
    happened?

CREON:

  They were all killed but one, and he got
    away
  So frightened that he could remember one
    thing only.

OEDIPUS:

What was that one thing? One may be the key
To everything, if we resolve to use it.

CREON:

He said that a band of highwaymen attacked them,
Outnumbered them, and overwhelmed the King.

OEDIPUS:

Strange, that a highwayman should be so daring—
Unless some faction here bribed him to do it.

CREON:

We thought of that. But after Laïos' death
New troubles arose and we had no avenger.

OEDIPUS:

What troubles could prevent your hunting down the killers?

CREON:

The riddling Sphinx's song
Made us deaf to all mysteries but her own.

OEDIPUS:

Then once more I must bring what is dark to light.
It is most fitting that Apollo shows,
As you do, this compunction for the dead.
You shall see how I stand by you, as I should,
To avenge the city and the city's god,
And not as though it were for some distant friend,
But for my own sake, to be rid of evil.
Whoever killed King Laïos might—who knows?—
Decide at any moment to kill me as well.
By avenging the murdered king I protect myself.

Come, then, my children: leave the altar steps,
Lift up your olive boughs!
                                        One of you go
And summon the people of Kadmos to gather here.

I will do all that I can; you may tell them that.

                                        [Exit a PAGE
So, with the help of God,
We shall be saved—or else indeed we are lost.

PRIEST:

Let us rise, children. It was for this we came,
And now the King has promised it himself.
Phoibos has sent us an oracle; may he descend
Himself to save us and drive out the plague.

                    [Exeunt OEDIPUS and CREON into
                    the palace by the central door. The
                    PRIEST and the SUPPLIANTS dis-
                    perse R and L. After a short pause
                    the CHORUS enters the orchestra.

PÁRODOS

CHORUS:

                                        [STROPHE 1
What is the god singing in his profound
Delphi of gold and shadow?
What oracle for Thebes, the sunwhipped city?

Fear unjoints me, the roots of my heart tremble.

Now I remember, O Healer, your power, and wonder:
Will you send doom like a sudden cloud, or weave it
Like nightfall of the past?

Ah no: be merciful, issue of holy sound:
Dearest to our expectancy: be tender!

                                        [ANTISTROPHE 1
Let me pray to Athenê, the immortal daughter of Zeus,
And to Artemis her sister
Who keeps her famous throne in the market ring,
And to Apollo, bowman at the far butts of heaven—

O gods, descend! Like three streams leap
    against
The fires of our grief, the fires of darkness;
Be swift to bring us rest!

As in the old time from the brilliant house
Of air you stepped to save us, come again!

[STROPHE 2
Now our afflictions have no end,
Now all our stricken host lies down
And no man fights off death with his
    mind;

The noble plowland bears no grain,
And groaning mothers can not bear—

See, how our lives like birds take wing,
Like sparks that fly when a fire soars,
To the shore of the god of evening.

[ANTISTROPHE 2
The plague burns on, it is pitiless,
Though pallid children laden with death
Lie unwept in the stony ways,

And old gray women by every path
Flock to the strand about the altars

There to strike their breasts and cry
Worship of Zeus in wailing prayers:
Be kind, God's golden child!

[STROPHE 3
There are no swords in this attack by fire,
No shields, but we are ringed with cries.

Send the besieger plunging from our
    homes
Into the vast sea-room of the Atlantic
Or into the waves that foam eastward of
    Thrace—

For the day ravages what the night
    spares—

Destroy our enemy, lord of the thunder!
Let him be riven by lightning from
    heaven!

[ANTISTROPHE 3
Phoibos Apollo, stretch the sun's bow-
    string,

That golden cord, until it sing for us,
Flashing arrows in heaven!

                    Artemis, Huntress,
Race with flaring lights upon our moun-
    tains!

O scarlet god, O golden-banded brow,
O Theban Bacchos in a storm of Maenads,
               [*Enter* OEDIPUS, *C.*
Whirl upon Death, that all the Undying
    hate!
Come with blinding cressets, come in joy!

SCENE I

OEDIPUS:
    Is this your prayer? It may be answered.
        Come,
    Listen to me, act as the crisis demands,
    And you shall have relief from all these
        evils.

    Until now I was a stranger to this tale,
    As I had been a stranger to the crime.
    Could I track down the murderer without
        a clue?
    But now, friends,
    As one who became a citizen after the
        murder,
    I make this proclamation to all Thebans:
    If any man knows by whose hand Laïos,
        son of Labdakos,
    Met his death, I direct that man to tell me
        everything,
    No matter what he fears for having so
        long withheld it.
    Let it stand as promised that no further
        trouble
    Will come to him, but he may leave the
        land in safety.

    Moreover: If anyone knows the murderer
        to be foreign,
    Let him not keep silent: he shall have his
        reward from me.
    However, if he does conceal it; if any man
    Fearing for his friend or for himself dis-
        obeys this edict,
    Hear what I propose to do:

I solemnly forbid the people of this country,
Where power and throne are mine, ever to receive that man
Or speak to him, no matter who he is, or let him
Join in sacrifice, lustration, or in prayer.
I decree that he be driven from every house,
Being, as he is, corruption itself to us: the Delphic
Voice of Zeus has pronounced this revelation.
Thus I associate myself with the oracle
And take the side of the murdered king.

As for the criminal, I pray to God—
Whether it be a lurking thief, or one of a number—
I pray that that man's life be consumed in evil and wretchedness.
And as for me, this curse applies no less
If it should turn out that the culprit is my guest here,
Sharing my hearth.
                    You have heard the penalty.
I lay it on you now to attend to this
For my sake, for Apollo's, for the sick
Sterile city that heaven has abandoned.
Suppose the oracle had given you no command:
Should this defilement go uncleansed for ever?
You should have found the murderer: your king,
A noble king, had been destroyed!
                             Now I,
Having the power that he held before me,
Having his bed, begetting children there
Upon his wife, as he would have, had he lived—
Their son would have been my children's brother,
If Laïos had had luck in fatherhood!
(But surely ill luck rushed upon his reign)—
I say I take the son's part, just as though
I were his son, to press the fight for him
And see it won! I'll find the hand that brought

Death to Labdakos' and Polydoros' child,
Heir of Kadmos' and Agenor's line.
And as for those who fail me,
May the gods deny them the fruit of the earth,
Fruit of the womb, and may they rot utterly!
Let them be wretched as we are wretched, and worse!

For you, for loyal Thebans, and for all
Who find my actions right, I pray the favor
Of justice, and of all the immortal gods.

CHORAGOS:
Since I am under oath, my lord, I swear
I did not do the murder, I can not name
The murderer. Might not the oracle
That has ordained the search tell where to find him?

OEDIPUS:
An honest question. But no man in the world
Can make the gods do more than the gods will.

CHORAGOS:
There is one last expedient—

OEDIPUS:
                              Tell me what it is.
Though it seem slight, you must not hold it back.

CHORAGOS:
A lord clairvoyant to the lord Apollo,
As we all know, is the skilled Teiresias.
One might learn much about this from him, Oedipus.

OEDIPUS:
I am not wasting time:
Creon spoke of this, and I have sent for him—
Twice, in fact; it is strange that he is not here.

CHORAGOS:
The other matter—that old report—seems useless.

OEDIPUS:
Tell me. I am interested in all reports.

CHORAGOS:
   The King was said to have been killed by
      highwaymen.

OEDIPUS:
   I know. But we have no witnesses to that.

CHORAGOS:
   If the killer can feel a particle of dread,
   Your curse will bring him out of hiding!

OEDIPUS:
                              No.
   The man who dared that act will fear no
      curse.
                     [*Enter the blind seer* TEIRESIAS,
                              led by a PAGE

CHORAGOS:
   But there is one man who may detect the
      criminal.
   This is Teiresias, this is the holy prophet
   In whom, alone of all men, truth was born.

OEDIPUS:
   Teiresias: seer: student of mysteries,
   Of all that's taught and all that no man
      tells,
   Secrets of Heaven and secrets of the earth:
   Blind though you are, you know the city
      lies
   Sick with plague; and from this plague,
      my lord,
   We find that you alone can guard or save
      us.

   Possibly you did not hear the messengers?
   Apollo, when we sent to him,
   Sent us back word that this great pesti-
      lence
   Would lift, but only if we established
      clearly
   The identity of those who murdered Laïos.
   They must be killed or exiled.
                              Can you use
   Birdflight or any art of divination
   To purify yourself, and Thebes, and me
   From this contagion? We are in your
      hands.
   There is no fairer duty
   Than that of helping others in distress.

TEIRESIAS:
   How dreadful knowledge of the truth can
      be
   When there's no help in truth! I knew
      this well,
   But did not act on it: else I should not
      have come.

OEDIPUS:
   What is troubling you? Why are your eyes
      so cold?

TEIRESIAS:
   Let me go home. Bear your own fate, and
      I'll
   Bear mine. It is better so: trust what I say.

OEDIPUS:
   What you say is ungracious and unhelpful
   To your native country. Do not refuse to
      speak.

TEIRESIAS:
   When it comes to speech, your own is
      neither temperate
   Nor opportune. I wish to be more prudent.

OEDIPUS:
   In God's name, we all beg you—

TEIRESIAS:
                     You are all ignorant.
   No; I will never tell you what I know.
   Now it is my misery; then, it would be
      yours.

OEDIPUS:
   What! You do know something and will
      not tell us?
   You would betray us all and wreck the
      State?

TEIRESIAS:
   I do not intend to torture myself, or you.
   Why persist in asking? You will not per-
      suade me.

OEDIPUS:
   What a wicked old man you are! You'd
      try a stone's
   Patience! Out with it! Have you no
      feeling at all?

TEIRESIAS:

You call me unfeeling. If you could only
see
The nature of your own feelings . . .

OEDIPUS:

Why,
Who would not feel as I do? Who could
endure
Your arrogance toward the city?

TEIRESIAS:

What does it matter!
Whether I speak or not, it is bound to
come.

OEDIPUS:

Then, if "it" is bound to come, you are
bound to tell me.

TEIRESIAS:

No, I will not go on. Rage as you please.

OEDIPUS:

Rage? Why not!
And I'll tell you what I think:
You planned it, you had it done, you all
but
Killed him with your own hands: if you
had eyes,
I'd say the crime was yours, and yours
alone.

TEIRESIAS:

So? I charge you, then,
Abide by the proclamation you have made:
From this day forth
Never speak again to these men or to me;
You yourself are the pollution of this
country.

OEDIPUS:

You dare say that! Can you possibly think
you have
Some way of going free, after such insolence?

TEIRESIAS:

I have gone free. It is the truth sustains
me.

OEDIPUS:

Who taught you shamelessness? It was not
your craft.

TEIRESIAS:

You did. You made me speak. I did not
want to.

OEDIPUS:

Speak what? Let me hear it again more
clearly.

TEIRESIAS:

Was it not clear before? Are you tempting me?

OEDIPUS:

I did not understand it. Say it again.

TEIRESIAS:

I say that you are the murderer whom you
seek.

OEDIPUS:

Now twice you have spat out infamy.
You'll pay for it!

TEIRESIAS:

Would you care for more? Do you wish
to be really angry?

OEDIPUS:

Say what you will. Whatever you say is
worthless.

TEIRESIAS:

I say that you live in hideous love with her
Who is nearest you in blood. You are
blind to the evil.

OEDIPUS:

It seems you can go on mouthing like this
for ever.

TEIRESIAS:

I can, if there is power in truth.

OEDIPUS:

There is:
But not for you, not for you,
You sightless, witless, senseless, mad old
man!

TEIRESIAS:

You are the madman. There is no one here
Who will not curse you soon, as you
curse me.

OEDIPUS:

You child of endless night! You can not
hurt me
Or any other man who sees the sun.

TEIRESIAS:

True: it is not from me your fate will
come.
That lies within Apollo's competence,
As it is his concern.

OEDIPUS:

Tell me:
Are you speaking for Creon, or for yourself?

TEIRESIAS:

Creon is no threat. You weave your own
doom.

OEDIPUS:

Wealth, power, craft of statesmanship!
Kingly position, everywhere admired!
What savage envy is stored up against
these,
If Creon, whom I trusted, Creon my
friend,
For this great office which the city once
Put in my hands unsought—if for this
power
Creon desires in secret to destroy me!

He has brought this decrepit fortune-
teller, this
Collector of dirty pennies, this prophet
fraud—
Why, he is no more clairoyant than I am!
Tell us:
Has your mystic mummery ever ap-
proached the truth?
When that hellcat the Sphinx was per-
forming here,
What help were you to these people?
Her magic was not for the first man who
came along:
It demanded a real exorcist. Your birds—
What good were they? or the gods, for the
matter of that?
But I came by,
Oedipus, the simple man, who knows
nothing—
I thought it out for myself, no birds
helped me!
And this is the man you think you can
destroy,
That you may be close to Creon when he's
king!

Well, you and your friend Creon, it seems
to me,
Will suffer most. If you were not an old
man,
You would have paid already for your
plot.

CHORAGOS:

We can not see that his words or yours
Have been spoken except in anger,
Oedipus,
And of anger we have no need. How can
God's will
Be accomplished best? That is what most
concerns us.

TEIRESIAS:

You are a king. But where argument's
concerned
I am your man, as much a king as you.
I am not your servant, but Apollo's.
I have no need of Creon to speak for me.

Listen to me. You mock my blindness,
do you?
But I say that you, with both your eyes,
are blind:
You can not see the wretchedness of your
life,
Nor in whose house you live, no, nor
with whom.
Who are your father and mother? Can you
tell me?
You do not even know the blind wrongs
That you have done them, on earth and
in the world below.
But the double lash of your parents' curse
will whip you
Out of this land some day, with only night
Upon your precious eyes.
Your cries then—where will they not be
heard?
What fastness of Kithairon will not echo
them?
And that bridal-descant of yours—you'll
know it then,
The song they sang when you came here
to Thebes
And found your misguided berthing.
All this, and more, that you can not guess
at now,

Will bring you to yourself among your
children.

Be angry, then. Curse Creon. Curse my
words.
I tell you, no man that walks upon the
earth
Shall be rooted out more horribly than you.

OEDIPUS:

Am I to bear this from him?—Damnation
Take you! Out of this place! Out of my
sight!

TEIRESIAS:

I would not have come at all if you had
not asked me.

OEDIPUS:

Could I have told that you'd talk nonsense,
that
You'd come here to make a fool of yourself, and of me?

TEIRESIAS:

A fool? Your parents thought me sane
enough.

OEDIPUS:

My parents again!—Wait: who were my
parents?

TEIRESIAS:

This day will give you a father, and break
your heart.

OEDIPUS:

Your infantile riddles! Your damned abra-
cadabra!

TEIRESIAS:

You were a great man once at solving
riddles.

OEDIPUS:

Mock me with that if you like; you will
find it true.

TEIRESIAS:

It was true enough. It brought about your
ruin.

OEDIPUS:

But if it saved this town?

TEIRESIAS:

[*To the* PAGE:
Boy, give me your hand.

OEDIPUS:

Yes, boy; lead him away.
                              —While you are here
We can do nothing. Go; leave us in
peace.

TEIRESIAS:

I will go when I have said what I have
to say.
How can you hurt me? And I tell you
again:
The man you have been looking for all
this time,
The damned man, the murderer of Laïos,
That man is in Thebes. To your mind he
is foreign-born,
But it will soon be shown that he is a
Theban,
A revelation that will fail to please.
                              A blind man,
Who has his eyes now; a penniless man,
who is rich now;
And he will go tapping the strange earth
with his staff.
To the children with whom he lives now
he will be
Brother and father—the very same; to her
Who bore him, son and husband—the
very same
Who came to his father's bed, wet with
his father's blood.

Enough. Go think that over.
If later you find error in what I have
said,
You may say that I have no skill in
prophecy.
                    [*Exit* TEIRESIAS, *led by his* PAGE.
                    OEDIPUS *goes into the palace.*

ODE I

CHORUS:

[STROPHE I
The Delphic stone of prophecies
Remembers ancient regicide
And a still bloody hand.

That killer's hour of flight has come.
He must be stronger than riderless
Coursers of untiring wind,
For the son of Zeus armed with his
    father's thunder
Leaps in lightning after him;
And the Furies follow him, the sad Furies.

[ANTISTROPHE 1

Holy Parnassos' peak of snow
Flashes and blinds that secret man,
That all shall hunt him down:
Though he may roam the forest shade
Like a bull gone wild from pasture
To rage through glooms of stone.
Doom comes down on him; flight will not
    avail him;
For the world's heart calls him desolate,
And the immortal Furies follow, for ever
    follow.

[STROPHE 2

But now a wilder thing is heard
From the old man skilled at hearing Fate
    in the wingbeat of a bird.
Bewildered as a blown bird, my soul hov-
    ers and can not find
Foothold in this debate, or any reason or
    rest of mind.
But no man ever brought—none can bring
Proof of strife between Thebes' royal
    house,
Labdakos' line, and the son of Polybos;
And never until now has any man brought
    word
Of Laïos' dark death staining Oedipus the
    King.

[ANTISTROPHE 2

Divine Zeus and Apollo hold
Perfect intelligence alone of all tales ever
    told;
And well though this diviner works, he
    works in his own night;
No man can judge that rough unknown or
    trust in second sight,
For wisdom changes hands among the
    wise.
Shall I believe my great lord criminal
At a raging word that a blind old man let
    fall?

I saw him, when the carrion woman
    faced him of old,
Prove his heroic mind! These evil words
    are lies.

SCENE II

CREON:

Men of Thebes:
I am told that heavy accusations
Have been brought against me by King
    Oedipus.

I am not the kind of man to bear this
    tamely.

If in these present difficulties
He holds me accountable for any harm to
    him
Through anything I have said or done—
    why, then,
I do not value life in this dishonor.
It is not as though this rumor touched
    upon
Some private indiscretion. The matter is
    grave.
The fact is that I am being called disloyal
To the State, to my fellow citizens, to my
    friends.

CHORAGOS:

He may have spoken in anger, not from
    his mind.

CREON:

But did you not hear him say I was the
    one
Who seduced the old prophet into lying?

CHORAGOS:

The thing was said; I do not know how
    seriously.

CREON:

But you were watching him! Were his
    eyes steady?
Did he look like a man in his right mind?

CHORAGOS:

                    I do not know.
I can not judge the behavior of great men.
But here is the King himself.

[Enter OEDIPUS

OEDIPUS:

      So you dared come back.
Why? How brazen of you to come to my
  house,
You murderer!
      Do you think I do not know
That you plotted to kill me, plotted to
  steal my throne?
Tell me, in God's name: am I coward, a
  fool,
That you should dream you could accom-
  plish this?
A fool who could not see your slippery
  game?
A coward, not to fight back when I saw it?
You are the fool, Creon, are you not?
  hoping
Without support or friends to get a
  throne?
Thrones may be won or bought: you could
  do neither.

CREON:

  Now listen to me. You have talked; let
    me talk, too.
  You can not judge unless you know the
    facts.

OEDIPUS:

  You speak well: there is one fact; but I
    find it hard
  To learn from the deadliest enemy I have.

CREON:

  That above all I must dispute with you.

OEDIPUS:

  That above all I will not hear you deny.

CREON:

  If you think there is anything good in
    being stubborn
  Against all reason, then I say you are
    wrong.

OEDIPUS:

  If you think a man can sin against his own
    kind
  And not be punished for it, I say you are
    mad.

CREON:

  I agree. But tell me: what have I done to
    you?

OEDIPUS:

  You advised me to send for that wizard,
    did you not?

CREON:

  I did. I should do it again.

OEDIPUS:

      Very well. Now tell me:
  How long has it been since Laïos—

CREON:

        What of Laïos?

OEDIPUS:

  Since he vanished in that onset by the
    road?

CREON:

  It was long ago, a long time.

OEDIPUS:

       And this prophet,
  Was he practicing here then?

CREON:

      He was, and with honor, as now.

OEDIPUS:

  Did he speak of me at that time?

CREON:

         He never did;
  At least, not when I was present.

OEDIPUS:

      But . . . the enquiry?
  I suppose you held one?

CREON:

      We did, but we learned nothing.

OEDIPUS:

  Why did the prophet not speak against me
    then?

CREON:

  I do not know; and I am the kind of man
  Who holds his tongue when he has no
    facts to go on.

OEDIPUS:

  There's one fact that you know, and you
    could tell it.

CREON:

  What fact is that? If I know it, you shall
    have it.

OEDIPUS:

If he were not involved with you, he could not say

That it was I who murdered Laïos.

CREON:

If he says that, you are the one that knows it!—

But now it is my turn to question you.

OEDIPUS:

Put your questions. I am no murderer.

CREON:

First, then: You married my sister?

OEDIPUS:

                   I married your sister.

CREON:

And you rule the kingdom equally with her?

OEDIPUS:

Everything that she wants she has from me.

CREON:

And I am the third, equal to both of you?

OEDIPUS:

That is why I call you a bad friend.

CREON:

No. Reason it out, as I have done.

Think of this first: Would any sane man prefer

Power, with all a king's anxieties,

To that same power and the grace of sleep?

Certainly not I.

I have never longed for the king's power

    —only his rights.

Would any wise man differ from me in this?

As matters stand, I have my way in everything

With your consent, and no responsibilities.

If I were king, I should be a slave to policy.

How could I desire a scepter more

Than what is now mine—untroubled influence?

No, I have not gone mad; I need no honors,

Except those with the perquisites I have now.

I am welcome everywhere; every man salutes me,

And those who want your favor seek my ear,

Since I know how to manage what they ask.

Should I exchange this ease for that anxiety?

Besides, no sober mind is treasonable.

I hate anarchy

And never would deal with any man who likes it.

Test what I have said. Go to the priestess

At Delphi, ask if I quoted her correctly.

And as for this other thing: if I am found

Guilty of treason with Teiresias,

Then sentence me to death! You have my word

It is a sentence I should cast my vote for—

But not without evidence!

                   You do wrong

When you take good men for bad, bad men for good.

A true friend thrown aside—why, life itself

Is not more precious!

               In time you will know this well:

For time, and time alone, will show the just man,

Though scoundrels are discovered in a day.

CHORAGOS:

This is well said, and a prudent man would ponder it.

Judgments too quickly formed are dangerous.

OEDIPUS:

But is he not quick in his duplicity?

And shall I not be quick to parry him?

Would you have me stand still, hold my peace, and let

This man win everything, through my inaction?

CREON:
  And you want—what is it, then? To ban-
    ish me?

OEDIPUS:
  No, not exile. It is your death I want,
  So that all the world may see what treason
    means.

CREON:
  You will persist, then? You will not be-
    lieve me?

OEDIPUS:
  How can I believe you?

CREON:
                  Then you are a fool.

OEDIPUS:
  To save myself?

CREON:
              In justice, think of me.

OEDIPUS:
  You are evil incarnate.

CREON:
              But suppose that you are wrong?

OEDIPUS:
  Still I must rule.

CREON:
              But not if you rule badly.

OEDIPUS:
  O city, city!

CREON:
              It is my city, too!

CHORAGOS:
  Now, my lords, be still. I see the Queen,
  Iocastê, coming from her palace chambers;
  And it is time she came, for the sake of
    you both.
  This dreadful quarrel can be resolved
    through her.

                              [Enter IOCASTE

IOCASTE:
  Poor foolish men, what wicked din is this?
  With Thebes sick to death, is it not
    shameful

That you should rake some private quarrel
  up?
                              [To OEDIPUS:
  Come into the house.

                —And you, Creon, go now:
  Let us have no more of this tumult over
    nothing.

CREON:
  Nothing? No, sister: what your husband
    plans for me
  Is one of two great evils: exile or death.

OEDIPUS:
  He is right.
    Why, woman I have caught him squarely
  Plotting against my life.

CREON:
                  No! Let me die
  Accurst if ever I have wished you harm!

IOCASTE:
  Ah, believe it, Oedipus!
  In the name of the gods, respect this oath
    of his
  For my sake, for the sake of these people
    here!

CHORAGOS: [STROPHE 1
  Open your mind to her, my lord. Be ruled
    by her, I beg you!

OEDIPUS:
  What would you have me do?

CHORAGOS:
  Respect Creon's word. He has never spo-
    ken like a fool,
  And now he has sworn an oath.

OEDIPUS:
              You know what you ask?

CHORAGOS:
                              I do.

OEDIPUS:
                      Speak on, then.

CHORAGOS:
  A friend so sworn should not be baited so,
  In blind malice, and without final proof.

OEDIPUS:
  You are aware, I hope, that what you say
  Means death for me, or exile at the least.

CHORAGOS: [STROPHE 2
  No, I swear by Helios, first in Heaven!
  May I die friendless and accurst,
  The worst of deaths, if ever I meant that!
      It is the withering fields
      That hurt my sick heart:
    Must we bear all these ills,
      And now your bad blood as well?

OEDIPUS:
  Then let him go. And let me die, if I must,
  Or be driven by him in shame from the
      land of Thebes.
  It is your unhappiness, and not his talk,
  That touches me.
            As for him—
  Wherever he is, I will hate him as long as
      I live.

CREON:
  Ugly in yielding, as you were ugly in rage!
  Natures like yours chiefly torment them-
      selves.

OEDIPUS:
  Can you not go? Can you not leave me?

CREON:
                  I can.
  You do not know me; but the city knows
      me,
  And in its eyes I am just, if not in yours.
            [Exit CREON

CHORAGOS: [ANTISTROPHE I
  Lady Iocastê, did you not ask the King to
      go to his chambers?

IOCASTE:
  First tell me what has happened.

CHORAGOS:
  There was supicion without evidence; yet
      it rankled
  As even false charges will.

IOCASTE:
                  On both sides?

CHORAGOS:
                  On both

IOCASTE:
                  But what was said?

CHORAGOS:
  Oh let it rest, let it be done with!
  Have we not suffered enough?

OEDIPUS:
  You see to what your decency has brought
      you:
  You have made difficulties where my heart
      saw none.

CHORAGOS: [ANTISTROPHE 2
  Oedipus, it is not once only I have told
      you—
      You must know I should count myself
          unwise
  To the point of madness, should I now
      forsake you—
      You, under whose hand,
        In the storm of another time,
      Our dear land sailed out free.
        But now stand fast at the helm!

IOCASTE:
  In God's name, Oedipus, inform your wife
      as well:
  Why are you so set in this hard anger?

OEDIPUS:
  I will tell you, for none of these men de-
      serves
  My confidence as you do. It is Creon's
      work,
  His treachery, his plotting against me.

IOCASTE:
  Go on, if you can make this clear to me.

OEDIPUS:
  He charges me with the murder of Laïos.

IOCASTE:
  Has he some knowledge? Or does he speak
      from hearsay?

OEDIPUS:
  He would not commit himself to such a
      charge,
  But he has brought in that damnable
      soothsayer
  To tell his story.

IOCASTE:

                Set your mind at rest.
If it is a question of soothsayers, I tell you
That you will find no man whose craft
    gives knowledge
Of the unknowable.

              Here is my proof:

An oracle was reported to Laïos once
(I will not say from Phoibos himself, but
    from
His appointed ministers, at any rate)
That his doom would be death at the
    hands of his own son—
His son, born of his flesh and of mine!

Now, you remember the story: Laïos was
    killed
By marauding strangers where three high-
    ways meet;
But his child had not been three days in
    this world
Before the King had pierced the baby's
    ankles
And had him left to die on a lonely moun-
    tain.

Thus, Apollo never caused that child
To kill his father, and it was not Laïos'
    fate
To die at the hands of his son, as he had
    feared.
This is what prophets and prophecies are
    worth!
Have no dread of them.
              It is God himself
Who can show us what he wills, in his
    own way.

OEDIPUS:

How strange a shadowy memory crossed
    my mind,
Just now while you were speaking; it
    chilled my heart.

IOCASTE:

What do you mean? What memory do you
    speak of?

OEDIPUS:

If I understand you, Laïos was killed
At a place where three roads meet.

IOCASTE:

                So it was said;
We have no later story.

OEDIPUS:

             Where did it happen?

IOCASTE:

Phokis, it is called: at a place where the
    Theban Way
Divides into the roads toward Delphi and
    Daulia.

OEDIPUS:

When?

IOCASTE:

          We had the news not long be-
          fore you came
And proved the right to your succession
    here.

OEDIPUS:

Ah, what net has God been weaving for
    me?

IOCASTE:

Oedipus! Why does this trouble you?

OEDIPUS:

             Do not ask me yet.
First, tell me how Laïos looked, and tell
    me
How old he was.

IOCASTE:

         He was tall, his hair just touched
With white; his form was not unlike your
    own.

OEDIPUS:

I think that I myself may be accurst
By my own ignorant edict.

IOCASTE:

            You speak strangely.
It makes me tremble to look at you, my
    King.

OEDIPUS:

I am not sure that the blind man can not
    see.
But I should know better if you were to
    tell me—

IOCASTE:

Anything—though I dread to hear you ask it.

OEDIPUS:

Was the King lightly escorted, or did he ride
With a large company, as a ruler should?

IOCASTE:

There were five men with him in all: one was a herald;
And a single chariot, which he was driving.

OEDIPUS:

Alas, that makes it plain enough!
But who—
Who told you how it happened?

IOCASTE:

A household servant,
The only one to escape.

OEDIPUS:

And is he still
A servant of ours?

IOCASTE:

No; for when he came back at last
And found you enthroned in the place of the dead king,
He came to me, touched my hand with his, and begged
That I would send him away to the frontier district
Where only the shepherds go—
As far away from the city as I could send him.
I granted his prayer; for although the man was a slave,
He had earned more than this favor at my hands.

OEDIPUS:

Can he be called back quickly?

IOCASTE:

Easily.
But why?

OEDIPUS:

I have taken too much upon myself
Without enquiry; therefore I wish to consult him.

IOCASTE:

Then he shall come.
But am I not one also
To whom you might confide these fears of yours?

OEDIPUS:

That is your right; it will not be denied you,
Now least of all; for I have reached a pitch
Of wild foreboding. Is there anyone
To whom I should sooner speak?

Polybos of Corinth is my father.
My mother is a Dorian: Meropê.
I grew up chief among the men of Corinth
Until a strange thing happened—
Not worth my passion, it may be, but strange.

At a feast, a drunken man maundering in his cups
Cries out that I am not my father's son!

I contained myself that night, though I felt anger
And a sinking heart. The next day I visited
My father and mother, and questioned them. They stormed,
Calling it all the slanderous rant of a fool;
And this relieved me. Yet the suspicion
Remained always aching in my mind;
I knew there was talk; I could not rest;
And finally, saying nothing to my parents,
I went to the shrine at Delphi.
The god dismissed my question without reply;
He spoke of other things.
Some were clear,
Full of wretchedness, dreadful, unbearable:
As, that I should lie with my own mother, breed
Children from whom all men would turn their eyes;
And that I should be my father's murderer.

I heard all this, and fled. And from that day
Corinth to me was only in the stars
Descending in that quarter of the sky,

As I wandered farther and farther on my
way
To a land where I should never see the
evil
Sung by the oracle. And I came to this
country
Where, so you say, King Laïos was killed.

I will tell you all that happened there, my
lady.

There were three highways
Coming together at a place I passed;
And there a herald came towards me, and
a chariot
Drawn by horses, with a man such as you
describe
Seated in it. The groom leading the horses
Forced me off the road at his lord's com-
mand;
But as this charioteer lurched over towards
me
I struck him in my rage. The old man saw
me
And brought his double goad down upon
my head
As I came abreast.
      He was paid back, and more!
Swinging my club in this right hand I
knocked him
Out of his car, and he rolled on the
ground.
          I killed him.

I killed them all.
Now if that stranger and Laïos were—kin,
Where is a man more miserable than I?
More hated by the gods? Citizen and alien
alike
Must never shelter me or speak to me—
I must be shunned by all.
          And I myself
Pronounced this malediction upon myself!

Think of it: I have touched you with these
hands,
These hands that killed your husband.
What defilement!

Am I all evil, then? It must be so,
Since I must flee from Thebes, yet never
again

See my own countrymen, my own country,
For fear of joining my mother in marriage
And killing Polybos, my father.
               Ah,
If I was created so, born to this fate,
Who could deny the savagery of God?

O holy majesty of heavenly powers!
May I never see that day! Never!
Rather let me vanish from the race of men
Than know the abomination destined me!

CHORAGOS:
We too, my lord, have felt dismay at this.
But there is hope: you have yet to hear
the shepherd.

OEDIPUS:
Indeed, I fear no other hope is left me.

IOCASTE:
What do you hope from him when he
comes?

OEDIPUS:
               This much:
If his account of the murder tallies with
yours,
Then I am cleared.

IOCASTE:
            What was it that I said
Of such importance?

OEDIPUS:
           Why, "marauders," you said,
Killed the King, according to this man's
story.
If he maintains that still, if there were sev-
eral,
Clearly the guilt is not mine: I was alone.
But if he says one man, singlehanded, did
it,
Then the evidence all points to me.

IOCASTE:
You may be sure that he said there were
several;
And can he call back that story now? He
cán not.
The whole city heard it as plainly as I.
But suppose he alters some detail of it:
He can not ever show that Laïos' death
Fulfilled the oracle: for Apollo said

My child was doomed to kill him; and my
    child—
Poor baby!—it was my child that died
    first.

No. From now on, where oracles are con-
    cerned,
I would not waste a second thought on
    any.

OEDIPUS:
You may be right.
                    But come: let someone go
For the shepherd at once. This matter
    must be settled.

IOCASTE:
I will send for him.
I would not wish to cross you in anything,
And surely not in this.—Let us go in.
                    [*Exeunt into the palace*

ODE II

CHORUS: [STROPHE I
Let me be reverent in the ways of right,
Lowly the paths I journey on;
Let all my words and actions keep
The laws of the pure universe
From highest Heaven handed down.
For Heaven is their bright nurse,
Those generations of the realms of light;
Ah, never of mortal kind were they begot,
Nor are they slaves of memory, lost in
    sleep:
Their Father is greater than Time, and
    ages not.

                    [ANTISTROPHE I
The tyrant is a child of Pride
Who drinks from his great sickening cup
Recklessness and vanity,
Until from his high crest headlong
He plummets to the dust of hope.
That strong man is not strong.
But let no fair ambition be denied;
May God protect the wrestler for the State
In government, in comely policy,
Who will fear God, and on His ordinance
    wait.

                    [STROPHE 2

Haughtiness and the high hand of disdain
Tempt and outrage God's holy law;
And any mortal who dares hold
No immortal Power in awe
Will be caught up in a net of pain:
The price for which his levity is sold.
Let each man take due earnings, then,
And keep his hands from holy things,
And from blasphemy stand apart—
Else the crackling blast of heaven
Blows on his head, and on his desperate
    heart;
Though fools will honor impious men,
In their cities no tragic poet sings.

                    [ANTISTROPHE 2
Shall we lose faith in Delphi's obscurities,
We who have heard the world's core
Discredited, and the sacred wood
Of Zeus at Elis praised no more?
The deeds and the strange prophecies
Must make a pattern yet to be understood.
Zeus, if indeed you are lord of all,
Throned in light over night and day,
Mirror this in your endless mind:
Our masters call the oracle
Words on the wind, and the Delphic vi-
    sion blind!
Their hearts no longer know Apollo,
And reverence for the gods has died away.

SCENE III

                    [*Enter* IOCASTE
IOCASTE:
Princes of Thebes, it has occurred to me
To visit the altars of the gods, bearing
These branches as a suppliant, and this in-
    cense.
Our King is not himself: his noble soul
Is overwrought with fantasies of dread,
Else he would consider
The new prophecies in the light of the
    old.
He will listen to any voice that speaks dis-
    aster,
And my advice goes for nothing.
                    [*She approaches the altar, R.*
                    To you, then, Apollo,
Lycean lord, since you are nearest, I turn
    in prayer.

Receive these offerings, and grant us deliverance
From defilement. Our hearts are heavy
with fear
When we see our leader distracted, as
helpless sailors
Are terrified by the confusion of their
helmsman.

[*Enter* MESSENGER

MESSENGER:
Friends, no doubt you can direct me:
Where shall I find the house of Oedipus,
Or, better still, where is the King himself?

CHORAGOS:
It is this very place, stranger; he is inside.
This is his wife and mother of his chil-
dren.

MESSENGER:
I wish her happiness in a happy house,
Blest in all the fulfillment of her marriage.

IOCASTE:
I wish as much for you: your courtesy
Deserves a like good fortune. But now,
tell me:
Why have you come? What have you to
say to us?

MESSENGER:
Good news, my lady, for your house and
your husband.

IOCASTE:
What news? Who sent you here?

MESSENGER:
I am from Corinth.
The news I bring ought to mean joy for
you,
Though it may be you will find some grief
in it.

IOCASTE:
What is it? How can it touch us in both
ways?

MESSENGER:
The people of Corinth, they say,
Intend to call Oedipus to be their king.

IOCASTE:
But old Polybos—is he not reigning still?

MESSENGER:
No. Death holds him in his sepulchre.

IOCASTE:
What are you saying? Polybos is dead?

MESSENGER:
If I am not telling the truth, may I die
myself.

IOCASTE: [*To a* MAIDSERVANT:
Go in, go quickly; tell this to your master.

O riddlers of God's will, where are you
now!
This was the man whom Oedipus, long
ago,
Feared so, fled so, in dread of destroying
him—
But it was another fate by which he died.

[*Enter* OEPIDUS, C.

OEDIPUS:
Dearest Iocastê, why have you sent for
me?

IOCASTE:
Listen to what this man says, and then tell
me
What has become of the solemn prophecies.

OEDIPUS:
Who is this man? What is his news for
me?

IOCASTE:
He has come from Corinth to announce
your father's death!

OEDIPUS:
Is it true, stranger? Tell me in your own
words.

MESSENGER:
I can not say it more clearly: the King is
dead.

OEDIPUS:
Was it by treason? Or by an attack of illness?

MESSENGER:
A little thing brings old men to their rest.

OEDIPUS:
It was sickness, then?

MESSENGER:

        Yes, and his many years.

OEDIPUS:

Ah!

Why should a man respect the Pythian
    hearth, or

Give heed to the birds that jangle above
    his head?

They prophesied that I should kill Polybos,

Kill my own father; but he is dead and
    buried,

And I am here—I never touched him,
    never,

Unless he died of grief for my departure,

And thus, in a sense, through me. No.
    Polybos

Has packed the oracles off with him under-
    ground.

They are empty words.

IOCASTE:

        Had I not told you so?

OEDIPUS:

You had; it was my faint heart that be-
    trayed me.

IOCASTE:

From now on never think of those things
    again.

OEDIPUS:

And yet—must I not fear my mother's
    bed?

IOCASTE:

Why should anyone in this world be
    afraid,

Since Fate rules us and nothing can be
    foreseen?

A man should live only for the present
    day.

Have no more fear of sleeping with your
    mother:

How many men, in dreams, have lain with
    their mothers!

No reasonable man is troubled by such
    things.

OEDIPUS:

That is true; only—

If only my mother were not still alive!

But she is alive. I can not help my dread.

IOCASTE:

Yet this news of your father's death is
    wonderful.

OEDIPUS:

Wonderful. But I fear the living woman.

MESSENGER:

Tell me, who is this woman that you fear?

OEDIPUS:

It is Meropê, man; the wife of King Poly-
    bos.

MESSENGER:

Meropê? Why should you be afraid of
    her?

OEDIPUS:

An oracle of the gods, a dreadful saying.

MESSENGER:

Can you tell me about it or are you sworn
    to silence?

OEDIPUS:

I can tell you, and I will.

Apollo said through his prophet that I
    was the man

Who should marry his own mother, shed
    his father's blood

With his own hands. And so, for all these
    years

I have kept clear of Corinth, and no harm
    has come—

Though it would have been sweet to see
    my parents again.

MESSENGER:

And is this the fear that drove you out of
    Corinth?

OEDIPUS:

Would you have me kill my father?

MESSENGER:

        As for that

You must be reassured by the news I gave
    you.

OEDIPUS:

If you could reassure me, I would reward
    you.

MESSENGER:

I had that in mind, I will confess: I thought
I could count on you when you returned to Corinth.

OEDIPUS:

No: I will never go near my parents again.

MESSENGER:

Ah, son, you still do not know what you are doing—

OEDIPUS:

What do you mean? In the name of God tell me!

MESSENGER:

—If these are your reasons for not going home.

OEDIPUS:

I tell you, I fear the oracle may come true.

MESSENGER:

And guilt may come upon you through your parents?

OEDIPUS:

That is the dread that is always in my heart.

MESSENGER:

Can you not see that all your fears are groundless?

OEDIPUS:

How can you say that? They are my parents, surely?

MESSENGER:

Polybos was not your father.

OEDIPUS:

Not my father?

MESSENGER:

No more your father than the man speaking to you.

OEDIPUS:

But you are nothing to me!

MESSENGER:

Neither was he.

OEDIPUS:

Then why did he call me son?

MESSENGER:

I will tell you:
Long ago he had you from my hands, as a gift.

OEDIPUS:

Then how could he love me so, if I was not his?

MESSENGER:

He had no children, and his heart turned to you.

OEDIPUS:

What of you? Did you buy me? Did you find me by chance?

MESSENGER:

I came upon you in the crooked pass of Kithairon.

OEDIPUS:

And what were you doing there?

MESSENGER:

Tending my flocks.

OEDIPUS:

A wandering shepherd?

MESSENGER:

But your savior, son, that day.

OEDIPUS:

From what did you save me?

MESSENGER:

Your ankles should tell you that.

OEDIPUS:

Ah, stranger, why do you speak of that childhood pain?

MESSENGER:

I cut the bonds that tied your ankles together.

OEDIPUS:

I have had the mark as long as I can remember.

MESSENGER:

That was why you were given the name you bear.

OEDIPUS:

God! Was it my father or my mother who did it?
Tell me!

MESSENGER:
                    I do not know. The man who
                gave you to me
Can tell you better than I.

OEDIPUS:
    It was not you that found me, but an-
        other?

MESSENGER:
    It was another shepherd gave you to me.

OEDIPUS:
    Who was he? Can you tell me who he
        was?

MESSENGER:
    I think he was said to be one of Laïos'
        people.

OEDIPUS:
    You mean the Laïos who was king here
        years ago?

MESSENGER:
    Yes; King Laïos; and the man was one of
        his herdsmen.

OEDIPUS:
    Is he still alive? Can I see him?

MESSENGER:
                        These men here
Know best about such things.

OEDIPUS:
                    Does anyone here
    Know this shepherd that he is talking
        about?
    Have you seen him in the fields, or in the
        town?
    If you have, tell me. It is time things were
        made plain.

CHORAGOS:
    I think the man he means is that same
        shepherd
    You have already asked to see. Iocastê per-
        haps
    Could tell you something.

OEDIPUS:
                    Do you know anything
    About him, Lady? Is he the man we have
        summoned?
    Is that the man this shepherd means?

IOCASTE:
                        Why think of him?
    Forget this herdsman. Forget it all.
    This talk is a waste of time.

OEDIPUS:
                        How can you say that,
    When the clues to my true birth are in my
        hands?

IOCASTE:
    For God's love, let us have no more ques-
        tioning!
    Is your life nothing to you?
    My own is pain enough for me to bear.

OEDIPUS:
    You need not worry. Suppose my mother
        a slave,
    And born of slaves: no baseness can touch
        you.

IOCASTE:
    Listen to me, I beg you: do not do this
        thing!

OEDIPUS:
    I will not listen; the truth must be made
        known.

IOCASTE:
    Everything that I say is for your own
        good!

OEDIPUS:
                        My own good
    Snaps my patience, then; I want none of it.

IOCASTE:
    You are fatally wrong! May you never
        learn who you are!

OEDIPUS:
    Go, one of you, and bring the shepherd
        here.
    Let us leave this woman to brag of her
        royal name.

IOCASTE:
    Ah, miserable!
    That is the only word I have for you now.
    That is the only word I can ever have.

                            [Exit into the palace

CHORAGOS:

Why has she left us, Oedipus? Why has
    she gone
In such a passion of sorrow? I fear this
    silence:
Something dreadful may come of it.

OEDIPUS:
                   Let it come!
However base my birth, I must know
    about it.
The Queen, like a woman, is perhaps
    ashamed
To think of my low origin. But I
Am a child of Luck; I can not be dis-
    honored.
Luck is my mother; the passing months,
    my brothers,
Have seen me rich and poor.
                  If this is so,
How could I wish that I were someone
    else?
How could I not be glad to know my
    birth?

ODE III

CHORUS:
                     [STROPHE
If ever the coming time were known
To my heart's pondering,
Kithairon, now by Heaven I see the torches
At the festival of the next full moon,
And see the dance, and hear the choir sing
A grace to your gentle shade:
Mountain where Oedipus was found,
O mountain guard of a noble race!
May the god who heals us lend his aid,
And let that glory come to pass
For our king's cradling-ground.

                    [ANTISTROPHE
Of the nymphs that flower beyond the
    years,
Who bore you, royal child,
To Pan of the hills or the timberline
    Apollo,
Cold in delight where the upland clears,
Or Hermês for whom Kyllenê's heights
    are piled?
Or flushed as evening cloud,

Great Dionysos, roamer of mountains,
He—was it he who found you there,
And caught you up in his own proud
Arms from the sweet god-ravisher
Who laughed by the Muses' fountains?

SCENE IV

OEDIPUS:
Sirs: though I do not know the man,
I think I see him coming, this shepherd
    we want:
He is old, like our friend here, and the
    men
Bringing him seem to be servants of my
    house.
But you can tell, if you have ever seen
    him.
    [*Enter* SHEPHERD *escorted by servants*

CHORAGOS:
I know him, he was Laïos' man. You can
    trust him.

OEDIPUS:
Tell me first, you from Corinth: is this the
    shepherd
We were discussing?

MESSENGER:
              This is the very man.

OEDIPUS: [*To* SHEPHERD:
Come here. No, look at me. You must an-
    swer
Everything I ask.—You belonged to Laïos?

SHEPHERD:
Yes: born his slave, brought up in his
    house.

OEDIPUS:
Tell me: what kind of work did you do
    for him?

SHEPHERD:
I was a shepherd of his, most of my life.

OEDIPUS:
Where mainly did you go for pasturage?

SHEPHERD:
Sometimes Kithairon, sometimes the hills
    near-by.

OEDIPUS:

Do you remember ever seeing this man out there?

SHEPHERD:

What would he be doing there? This man?

OEDIPUS:

This man standing here. Have you ever seen him before?

SHEPHERD:

No. At least, not to my recollection.

MESSENGER:

And that is not strange, my lord. But I'll refresh
His memory: he must remember when we two
Spent three whole seasons together, March to September,
On Kithairon or thereabouts. He had two flocks;
I had one. Each autumn I'd drive mine home
And he would go back with his to Laïos' sheepfold.—
Is this not true, just as I have described it?

SHEPHERD:

True, yes; but it was all so long ago.

MESSENGER:

Well, then: do you remember, back in those days,
That you gave me a baby boy to bring up as my own?

SHEPHERD:

What if I did? What are you trying to say?

MESSENGER:

King Oedipus was once that little child.

SHEPHERD:

Damn you, hold your tongue!

OEDIPUS:

                 No more of that!
It is your tongue needs watching, not this man's.

SHEPHERD:

My King, my Master, what is it I have done wrong?

OEDIPUS:

You have not answered his question about the boy.

SHEPHERD:

He does not know . . . He is only making trouble . . .

OEDIPUS:

Come, speak plainly, or it will go hard with you.

SHEPHERD:

In God's name, do not torture an old man!

OEDIPUS:

Come here, one of you; bind his arms behind him.

SHEPHERD:

Unhappy king! What more do you wish to learn?

OEDIPUS:

Did you give this man the child he speaks of?

SHEPHERD:

                     I did.
And I would to God I had died that very day.

OEDIPUS:

You will die now unless you speak the truth.

SHEPHERD:

Yet if I speak the truth, I am worse than dead.

OEDIPUS:

Very well; since you insist upon delaying—

SHEPHERD:

No! I have told you already that I gave him the boy.

OEDIPUS:

Where did you get him? From your house? From somewhere else?

SHEPHERD:

Not from mine, no. A man gave him to me.

OEDIPUS:

Is that man here? Do you know whose slave he was?

SHEPHERD:

For God's love, my King, do not ask me any more!

OEDIPUS:

You are a dead man if I have to ask you again.

SHEPHERD:

Then . . . Then the child was from the palace of Laïos.

OEDIPUS:

A slave child? or a child of his own line?

SHEPHERD:

Ah, I am on the brink of dreadful speech!

OEDIPUS:

And I of dreadful hearing. Yet I must hear.

SHEPHERD:

If you must be told, then . . .
                    They said it was Laïos' child;
But it is your wife who can tell you about that.

OEDIPUS:

My wife!—Did she give it to you?

SHEPHERD:

                    My lord, she did.

OEDIPUS:

Do you know why?

SHEPHERD:

                    I was told to get rid of it.

OEDIPUS:

An unspeakable mother!

SHEPHERD:

                    There had been prophecies . . .

OEDIPUS:

Tell me.

SHEPHERD:

It was said that the boy would kill his own father.

OEDIPUS:

Then why did you give him over to this old man?

SHEPHERD:

I pitied the baby, my King,
And I thought that this man would take him far away
To his own country.
            He saved him—but for what a fate!
For if you are what this man says you are,
No man living is more wretched than Oedipus.

OEDIPUS:

Ah God!
It was true!
            All the prophecies!
                                —Now,
O Light, may I look on you for the last time!
I, Oedipus,
Oedipus, damned in his birth, in his marriage damned,
Damned in the blood he shed with his own hand!

            [He rushes into the palace

ODE IV

CHORUS:

Alas for the seed of men.   [STROPHE 1

What measure shall I give these generations
That breathe on the void and are void
And exist and do not exist?

Who bears more weight of joy
Than mass of sunlight shifting in images,
Or who shall make his thoughts stay on
That down time drifts away?

Your splendor is all fallen.

O naked brow of wrath and tears,
O change of Oedipus!

I who saw your days call no man blest—
Your great days like ghósts góne.

[ANTISTROPHE 1
That mind was a strong bow.

Deep, how deep you drew it then, hard
    archer,
At a dim fearful range,
And brought dear glory down!

You overcame the stranger—
The virgin with her hooking lion claws—
And though death sang, stood like a tower
To make pale Thebes take heart.

Fortress against our sorrow!

Divine king, giver of laws,
Majestic Oedipus!
No prince in Thebes had ever such re-
    nown,
No prince won such grace of power.

[STROPHE 2
And now of all men ever known
Most pitiful is this man's story:
His fortunes are most changed, his state
Fallen to a low slave's
Ground under bitter fate.

O Oedipus, most royal one!
The great door that expelled you to the
    light
Gave at night—ah, gave night to your
    glory:
As to the father, to the fathering son.

All understood too late.

How could that queen whom Laïos won,
The garden that he harrowed at his height,
Be silent when that act was done?

[ANTISTROPHE 2
But all eyes fail before time's eye,
All actions come to justice there.
Though never willed, though far down the
    deep past,
Your bed, your dread sirings,
Are brought to book at last.

Child by Laïos doomed to die,
Then doomed to lose that fortunate little
    death,
Would God you never took breath in this
    air
That with my wailing lips I take to cry:

For I weep the world's outcast.

Blind I was, and can not tell why;
Asleep, for you had given ease of breath;
A fool, while the false years went by.

ÉXODOS

[Enter, from the palace, SECOND MESSENGER

SECOND MESSENGER:
    Elders of Thebes, most honored in this
        land,
    What horrors are yours to see and hear,
        what weight
    Of sorrow to be endured, if, true to your
        birth,
    You venerate the line of Labdakos!
    I think neither Istros nor Phasis, those
        great rivers,
    Could purify this place of the corruption
    It shelters now, or soon must bring to
        light—
    Evil not done unconsciously, but willed.

    The greatest griefs are those we cause our-
        selves.

CHORAGOS:
    Surely, friend, we have grief enough al-
        ready;
    What new sorrow do you mean?

SECOND MESSENGER:
                                The Queen is dead.
CHORAGOS:
    Iocastê? Dead? But at whose hand?

SECOND MESSENGER:
                                Her own.
    The full horror of what happened you can
        not know,
    For you did not see it; but I, who did, will
        tell you
    As clearly as I can how she met her death.

When she had left us,
In passionate silence, passing through the court,
She ran to her apartment in the house,
Her hair clutched by the fingers of both hands.
She closed the doors behind her; then, by that bed
Where long ago the fatal son was conceived—
That son who should bring about his father's death—
We heard her call upon Laïos, dead so many years,
And heard her wail for the double fruit of her marriage,
A husband by her husband, children by her child.

Exactly how she died I do not know:
For Oedipus burst in moaning and would not let us
Keep vigil to the end: it was by him
As he stormed about the room that our eyes were caught.
From one to another of us he went, begging a sword,
Cursing the wife who was not his wife, the mother
Whose womb had carried his own children and himself.
I do not know: it was none of us aided him,
But surely one of the gods was in control!
For with a dreadful cry
He hurled his weight, as though wrenched out of himself,
At the twin doors: the bolts gave, and he rushed in.
And there we saw her hanging, her body swaying
From the cruel cord she had noosed about her neck.
A great sob broke from him, heartbreaking to hear,
As he loosed the rope and lowered her to the ground.

I would blot out from my mind what happened next!

For the King ripped from her gown the golden brooches
That were her ornament, and raised them, and plunged them down
Straight into his own eyeballs, crying, "No more,
No more shall you look on the misery about me,
The horrors of my own doing! Too long you have known
The faces of those whom I should never have seen,
Too long been blind to those for whom I was searching!
From this hour, go in darkness!" And as he spoke,
He struck at his eyes—not once, but many times;
And the blood spattered his beard,
Bursting from his ruined sockets like red hail.

So from the unhappiness of two this evil has sprung,
A curse on the man and woman alike. The old
Happiness of the house of Labdakos
Was happiness enough: where is it today?
It is all wailing and ruin, disgrace, death—all
The misery of mankind that has a name—
And it is wholly and for ever theirs.

CHORAGOS:
Is he in agony still? Is there no rest for him?

SECOND MESSENGER:
He is calling for someone to lead him to the gates
So that all the children of Kadmos may look upon
His father's murderer, his mother's—no,
I can not say it!
          And then he will leave Thebes,
Self-exiled, in order that the curse
Which he himself pronounced may depart from the house.
He is weak, and there is none to lead him,
So terrible is his suffering.
          But you will see:

Look, the doors are opening; in a moment
You will see a thing that would crush a
    heart of stone.
    [*The central door is opened;* OEDIPUS,
    blinded, is led in

CHORAGOS:
    Dreadful indeed for men to see.
    Never have my own eyes
    Looked on a sight so full of fear.

    Oedipus!
    What madness came upon you, what dae-
        mon
    Leaped on your life with heavier
    Punishment than a mortal man can bear?
    No: I can not even
    Look at you, poor ruined one.
    And I would speak, question, ponder,
    If I were able. No.
    You make me shudder.

OEDIPUS:
    God. God.
    Is there a sorrow greater?
    Where shall I find harbor in this world?
    My voice is hurled far on a dark wind.
    What has God done to me?

CHORAGOS:
    Too terrible to think of, or to see.

OEDIPUS:
    O cloud of night,   [STROPHE 1
    Never to be turned away: night coming
        on,
    I can not tell how: night like a shroud!

    My fair winds brought me here.
                            O God. Again
    The pain of the spikes where I had sight,
        the flooding pain
    Of memory, never to be gouged out.

CHORAGOS:
    This is not strange.
    You suffer it all twice over, remorse in
        pain,
    Pain in remorse.

OEDIPUS:
    Ah dear friend   [ANTISTROPHE 1
    Are you faithful even yet, you alone?

Are you still standing near me, will you
    stay here,
Patient, to care for the blind?
                        The blind man!
Yet even blind I know who it is attends
    me,
By the voice's tone—
Though my new darkness hide the com-
    forter.

CHORAGOS:
    Oh fearful act!
    What god was it drove you to rake black
    Night across your eyes?

OEDIPUS:
    Apollo. Apollo. Dear   [STROPHE 2
    Children, the god was Apollo.
    He brought my sick, sick fate upon me.
    But the blinding hand was my own!
    How could I bear to see
    When all my sight was horror every-
        where?

CHORAGOS:
    Everywhere; that is true.

OEDIPUS:
    And now what is left?
    Images? Love? A greeting even,
    Sweet to the senses? Is there anything?
    Ah, no, friends: lead me away.
    Lead me away from Thebes.
                        Lead the great wreck
    And hell of Oedipus, whom the gods hate.

CHORAGOS:
    Your fate is clear, you are not blind to
        that.
    Would God you had never found it out!

OEDIPUS: [ANTISTROPHE 2
    Death take the man who unbound
    My feet on that hillside
    And delivered me from death to life!
        What life?
    If only I had died,
    This weight of monstrous doom
    Could not have dragged me and my dar-
        lings down.

CHORAGOS:
    I would have wished the same.

OEDIPUS:

Oh never to have come here
With my father's blood upon me! Never
To have been the man they call his mother's husband!
Oh accurst! Oh child of evil,
To have entered that wretched bed—
                the selfsame one!
More primal than sin itself, this fell to me.

CHORAGOS:

I do not know how I can answer you.
You were better dead than alive and blind.

OEDIPUS:

Do not counsel me any more. This punishment
That I have laid upon myself is just.
If I had eyes,
I do not know how I could bear the sight
Of my father, when I came to the house of Death,
Or my mother: for I have sinned against them both
So vilely that I could not make my peace
By strangling my own life.
            Or do you think my children,
Born as they were born, would be sweet to my eyes?
Ah never, never! Nor this town with its high walls,
Nor the holy images of the gods.
                For I,
Thrice miserable!—Oedipus, noblest of all the line
Of Kadmos, have condemned myself to enjoy
These things no more, by my own malediction
Expelling that man whom the gods declared
To be a defilement in the house of Laïos.
After exposing the rankness of my own guilt,
How could I look men frankly in the eyes?
No, I swear it,
If I could have stifled my hearing at its source,
I would have done it and made all this body

A tight cell of misery, blank to light and sound:
So I should have been safe in a dark agony
Beyond all recollection.
                Ah Kithairon!
Why did you shelter me? When I was cast upon you,
Why did I not die? Then I should never
Have shown the world my execrable birth.

Ah Polybos! Corinth, city that I believed
The ancient seat of my ancestors: how fair
I seemed, your child! And all the while this evil
Was cancerous within me!
                For I am sick
In my daily life, sick in my origin.

O three roads, dark ravine, woodland and way
Where three roads met: you, drinking my father's blood,
My own blood, spilled by my own hand: can you remember
The unspeakable things I did there, and the things
I went on from there to do?
           O marriage, marriage!
The act that engendered me, and again the act
Performed by the son in the same bed—
              Ah, the net
Of incest, mingling fathers, brothers, sons,
With brides, wives, mothers: the last evil
That can be known by men: no tongue can say
How evil!
       No. For the love of God, conceal me
Somewhere far from Thebes; or kill me; or hurl me
Into the sea, away from men's eyes for ever.

Come, lead me. You need not fear to touch me.
Of all men, I alone can bear this guilt.
           [*Enter* CREON

CHORAGOS:

We are not the ones to decide; but Creon here

May fitly judge of what you ask. He only
Is left to protect the city in your place.

OEDIPUS:
Alas, how can I speak to him? What right
    have I
To beg his courtesy whom I have deeply
    wronged?

CREON:
I have not come to mock you, Oedipus,
Or to reproach you, either.
                        [To ATTENDANTS:
                —You, standing there:
If you have lost all respect for man's dig-
    nity,
At least respect the flame of Lord Helios:
Do not allow this pollution to show itself
Openly here, an affront to the earth
And Heaven's rain and the light of day.
    No, take him
Into the house as quickly as you can.
For it is proper
That only the close kindred see his grief.

OEDIPUS:
I pray you in God's name, since your
    courtesy
Ignores my dark expectation, visiting
With mercy this man of all men most
    execrable:
Give me what I ask—for your good, not
    for mine.

CREON:
And what is it that you would have me
    do?

OEDIPUS:
Drive me out of this country as quickly as
    may be
To a place where no human voice can
    ever greet me.

CREON:
I should have done that before now—
    only,
God's will had not been wholly revealed
    to me.

OEDIPUS:
But his command is plain: the parricide
Must be destroyed. I am that evil man.

CREON:
That is the sense of it, yes; but as things
    are,
We had best discover clearly what is to be
    done.

OEDIPUS:
You would learn more about a man like
    me?

CREON:
You are ready now to listen to the god.

OEDIPUS:
I will listen. But it is to you
That I must turn for help. I beg you, hear
    me.

The woman in there—
Give her whatever funeral you think
    proper:
She is your sister.
                —But let me go, Creon!
Let me purge my father's Thebes of the
    pollution
Of my living here, and go out to the wild
    hills,
To Kithairon, that has won such fame
    with me,
The tomb my mother and father ap-
    pointed for me,
And let me die there, as they willed I
    should.
And yet I know
Death will not ever come to me through
    sickness
Or in any natural way: I have been pre-
    served
For some unthinkable fate. But let that
    be.

As for my sons, you need not care for
    them.
They are men, they will find some way to
    live.
But my poor daughters, who have shared
    my table,
Who never before have been parted from
    their father—
Take care of them, Creon; do this for me.
And will you let me touch them with my
    hands

A last time, and let us weep together?
Be kind, my lord,
Great prince, be kind!
                    Could I but touch them,
They would be mine again, as when I had
     my eyes.
     [*Enter* ANTIGONE *and* ISMENE, *attended*
Ah, God!
Is it my dearest children I hear weeping?
Has Creon pitied me and sent my daugh-
     ters?

CREON:
Yes, Oedipus: I knew that they were dear
     to you
In the old days, and know you must love
     them still.

OEDIPUS:
May God bless you for this—and be a
     friendlier
Guardian to you than he has been to me!

Children, where are you?
Come quickly to my hands: they are your
     brother's—
Hands that have brought your father's
     once clear eyes
To this way of seeing—
                    Ah dearest ones,
I had neither sight nor knowledge then,
     your father
By the woman who was the source of his
     own life!
And I weep for you—having no strength
     to see you—,
I weep for you when I think of the bitter-
     ness
That men will visit upon you all your
     lives.
What homes, what festivals can you at-
     tend
Without being forced to depart again in
     tears?
And when you come to marriageable age,
Where is the man, my daughters, who
     would dare
Risk the bane that lies on all my children?
Is there any evil wanting? Your father
     killed
His father; sowed the womb of her who
     bore him;

Engendered you at the fount of his own
     existence!
That is what they will say of you.

                              Then, whom
Can you ever marry? There are no bride-
     grooms for you,
And your lives must wither away in sterile
     dreaming.

O Creon, son of Menoikeus!
You are the only father my daughters
     have,
Since we, their parents, are both of us
     gone for ever.
They are your own blood: you will not let
     them
Fall into beggary and loneliness;
You will keep them from the miseries that
     are mine!
Take pity on them; see, they are only chil-
     dren,
Friendless except for you. Promise me
     this,
Great Prince, and give me your hand in
     token of it.
               [CREON *clasps his right hand*
Children:
I could say much, if you could understand
     me,
But as it is, I have only this prayer for
     you:
Live where you can, be as happy as you
     can—
Happier, please God, than God has made
     your father!

CREON:
Enough. You have wept enough. Now go
     within.

OEDIPUS:
I must; but it is hard.

CREON:
                    Time eases all things.

OEDIPUS:
But you must promise—

CREON:
                    Say what you desire.

OEDIPUS:
Send me from Thebes!

CREON:

God grant that I may!

OEDIPUS:

But since God hates me . . .

CREON:

No, he will grant your wish.

OEDIPUS:

You promise?

CREON:

I can not speak beyond my knowledge.

OEDIPUS:

Then lead me in.

CREON:

Come now, and leave your children.

OEDIPUS:

No! Do not take them from me!

CREON:

Think no longer
That you are in command here, but rather
think
How, when you were, you served your
own destruction.

[*Exeunt into the house all but the* CHORUS;
the CHORAGOS *chants directly to the audience:*

CHORAGOS:

Men of Thebes: look upon Oedipus.

This is the king who solved the famous
riddle
And towered up, most powerful of men.
No mortal eyes but looked on him with
envy,
Yet in the end ruin swept over him.

Let every man in mankind's frailty
Consider his last day; and let none
Presume on his good fortune until he find
Life, at his death, a memory without pain.

SUGGESTIONS FOR STUDY

1. In a modern court Oedipus would obviously be considered guilty of murder and incest, and even of hubris, if that were a crime. Nevertheless, since everyone is entitled to the services of a lawyer, how would you as his attorney try to defend him and perhaps obtain a less severe sentence?

2. Trace the successive steps by which Oedipus is forced to recognize his true parentage and the fulfillment of the prophecy.

3. Why is it ironically right that it is the blind prophet who teaches Oedipus to "see"? Why does Oedipus blind himself? What are some of the examples of the ironic use of the terms "sight" and "blindness" throughout the play?

4. When does Iocastê learn the horror of the situation? If you were directing the play in a modern theater, how would you have the actress play this scene?

5. To what extent is Iocastê guilty of hubris? Note her words

   From now on, when oracles are concerned,
   I would not waste a second thought on any.

6. Why are the daughters of Oedipus brought in at the end of the play? Would this in the modern theater be considered an unnecessary additional harrowing of the emotions?

OTHELLO

William Shakespeare
(1564–1616)

Othello was first produced in 1604, by which time Shakespeare, who some years before had come up to London from his home town in the provinces, was an actor in and part owner of the most successful theatrical company in London. He also wrote some of its plays. His tragedy of *Hamlet* had lately proved to be one of the most popular of the plays performed at his company's theater, called the Globe, located just south of the Thames River in Southwark.

It was an outdoor theater. This means that some of the stage and some of the audience were under a roof, some were not. The stage consisted of three parts: a large platform which extended into the central arena of the theater and could not be curtained off, an inner stage with a curtain, and a balcony or upper stage. One result of this arrangement was a greater sense of reciprocal relationship between actors and audience than is possible in the modern theater, for the audience was closer to the actors and surrounded them on three sides. Another result was fluidity. Scenes followed each other rapidly on the large platform or outer stage or swiftly alternated between inner stage and balcony.

Since Shakespeare's audience was a mixture of all types and classes of Londoners, his plays had to provide a mixture of excitement and pleasure of many kinds, ranging from the representation of violent death to subtle disquisitions in philosophy. Sometimes, to be sure, Shakespeare's company performed *Othello* and other plays at the Blackfriars Theater in London proper. We know less about the conditions of performance there; probably the audience was less heterogeneous and had a higher degree of appreciation of the finer points of acting and poetic language. Since the Blackfriars was an enclosed theater, the physical arrangements may have approximated those of the modern stage. But whichever the theater, the playwright was expected to entertain the audience, as he is today.

No one expected a playwright to make up new stories. Shakespeare took the story of *Othello* from a collection written by an Italian named Cinthio. Cinthio's tale is a sordid account of the murder of a Venetian lady by her husband, a Venetian general of Moorish descent, and his ensign, or subordinate officer. As usual, Shakespeare transmuted the story into the highest type of dramatic poetry while retaining what to many modern tastes are essentially squalid details of murder and suggested sexual intrigue. How did he do it?

One aspect of his method was to convert the central figures he found in his source into characters whose motives and actions are, for the two hours of the play's performance, entirely believable, no matter how preposterous the same acts and motives might seem in real life. Though Shakespeare was not a psychologist in the modern sense, he had the faculty of creating for the stage characters who pass as real people with credible reasons for their remarkable acts. To understand how Shakespeare performed the feat in this particular play requires an analysis of two characters, Othello and Iago.

Though Othello, the Moor, is black, this play is not a study in race relations. Othello is an experienced and successful commander, a man of assured authority and even lofty personal dominance. "Keep up your bright swords, for the dew will rust them," he says when confronted with enemies in the street. When he is accused of winning Desdemona by witchcraft, his reply is so dignified and so manfully convincing that the Duke comments dryly, "I think this tale would win my daughter too." How can so wise and so experienced a man be deceived into believing that his bride has been guilty of misconduct with one of his own officers?

For one thing, his enemy, Iago, says of him that he

> is of a free and open nature
> That thinks men honest that but seem
>   to be so;
> And will as tenderly be led by the nose
> As asses are. (I, 3, 405–408.)

But the most important clue to the deception is to be found in the nature of Iago, the villain.

Commentators have written hundreds of pages about Iago. For a preliminary understanding of the play it will be sufficient to search out the words Shakespeare has Iago say about himself and to mention one or two facts about the technique of writing plays for the theater of Shakespeare's time. *Othello* is, after all, a play, not a true account of something that really happened. However Iago's motivation may resemble or diverge from that of real villains, it must be judged primarily as a problem in dramatic composition.

At the beginning of any play the playwright must tell the audience who his characters are and what has recently happened to them. One convention accepted in most plays is that the audience is supposed to believe whatever one character tells another in the opening scene. Accordingly, Shakespeare has Iago tell Roderigo that he, Iago, is angry because Othello has passed him over for promotion and promoted instead a Florentine, Michael Cassio, whom Iago considers incompetent because he knows only the theory of war. Hence Iago, though pretending loyalty to Othello, plots with Roderigo a scheme by which he may revenge himself on Othello. We must therefore accept the idea that one reason for Iago's villainy is a desire for revenge that arises out of a wounded ego.

Another convention, invariably followed in Shakespeare, is that the audience must believe whatever a character says directly to the audience in a soliloquy or an aside. Iago speaks three soliloquies in the first two acts: I, 3, 389–410 (Act I, scene 3, lines 389–410); II, 1, 295–321; and II, 3, 342–368. In them Iago tells us bluntly, "I hate the Moor." This statement must be accepted as true. Shakespeare would not even be required to state the reasons for this hatred if he did not want to, but, as we have seen, he has already given desire for revenge as one reason. Second, Iago mentions in the first soliloquy a rumor that Othello and Iago's wife, Emilia, are guilty of adultery. Third (and much the least important of the three), Iago hints in the second soliloquy that Cassio may also be guilty of adultery with Emilia, and therefore he will try to destroy Cassio too. These are the reasons given in the play—the internal evidence—for Iago's villainy.

We must also call on our knowledge of other plays written in Shakespeare's time. His audiences were familiar with the concept of a villain who delights in villainy for its own sake, taking perverse pleasure in hypocritical dealings in lust and murder and lunges for power. Richard III, whom Shakespeare portrayed in an earlier play, is such a character. Whether we in the twentieth century think such a figure is psychologically possible is beside the point. Basically, Iago represented on Shakespeare's stage a well-known type. He comes, as is said in theater parlance, "out of stock."

The fact that Iago is this kind of villain, motivated as described above, would not be sufficient if Shakespeare had not put into this play one of the most effective pieces of dialogue in all his works. This is the famous "temptation" scene, III, 3, 35–end. Here Iago, by means that are a close enough imitation of life to be convincing in the theater, so employs hints and innuendo, feigned reluctance to speak, and false evidence, and so effectively trades on his own lifelong reputation for honesty, that Othello is persuaded. Those who have watched this scene on the stage do not wonder why Othello, as a character in a play, has been thoroughly duped.

Therefore, to return to the question of how Othello could be so easily fooled, any objections we may have as to the "realism" of the process are irrelevant. Othello is sufficiently fooled for the purposes of the play. Shakespeare's audiences were familiar with Iago's type of villainy. Later audiences and most readers do not question it. Only scholars question the motivation of the drama, but Shakespeare wrote the play for playgoers, not for scholars.

Nevertheless, the fact that *Othello* has caused argument among scholars and others is a tribute to its power. We should briefly note some of the other sources of that power.

The secondary characters are masterfully drawn. Desdemona, who is secondary because she is for the most part essentially passive, touches our emotions at every appearance. Roderigo is so completely a "snipe" (Iago's word for him) that we almost begin to feel for him the reluctant affection we reserve for someone else's bedraggled cur. Emilia, the realist, provides a deft contrast to the more ethereal Desdemona.

Another reason we admire the play is the economy with which it is presented. As Shakespeare's plays go, it is short. The plot—there are no subplots—runs single-mindedly and intensely from beginning to end. The action is confined to a few locations. There is dispute as to how much time is supposed to elapse during the last four acts, but all agree that the general impression is one of swiftness. It is in the mastery of these techniques that Shakespeare, like all other great artists, makes the practice of his art seem easy.

But one of the greatest sources of the power of Othello is its poetry. All readers of the play have their favorite passages—perhaps the "round, unvarnish'd tale" Othello delivers as he describes his courtship, or Othello's calling to memory the malignant and turbaned Turk, or the passage beginning "It is the cause, it is the cause, my soul." To enjoy such passages, the student needs only to learn how to read them.

Most of Shakespeare's lines are in "blank verse," a technical term meaning an un-

rhymed line composed of five each of alternately stressed and unstressed syllables, generally beginning with an unstressed syllable. For example:

> What wound / did e/ver heal / but
> by / degrees? (II, 3, 376.)

Success in using this type of line means knowing how to vary the caesura, or natural pause in the line, and how to vary the stresses for intricate rhythmical effects. Few blank verse lines are regular. Even the one given above can be scanned

> What wound did ever heal but by de-
> grees?

In addition, Shakespeare weaves a kind of counterpoint between his sentences and his lines, not all lines ending with a full stop. That is, a sentence may begin and end anywhere within a line. The result of these two devices of rhythmic and rhetorical variety is a supple medium that sounds like poetry and like speech at the same time. Thus:

> Let husbands know
> Their wives have sense like them: they
> see and smell
> And have their palates both for sweet
> and sour,
> As husbands have. What is it that they
> do
> When they change us for others? Is it
> sport?
> I think it is: and doth affection breed it?
> I think it doth: is't frailty that thus errs?
> It is so too: and have not we affections,
> Desires for sport, and frailty, as men
> have?
> Then let them use us well: else let them
> know
> The ills we do, their ills instruct us so.
> (IV, 3, 94–104.)

For certain purposes Shakespeare at times changes from blank verse to prose (II, 3, 259–341), or to a rhymed couplet—for example, the last two lines above.

Shakespeare's verse is rich in figures of speech, of which the chief and basic figure is metaphor. (See also pp. 265–266). This, a device of prose as well as poetry, consists of saying one thing and meaning something else. When Othello says "Put out the light, and then put out the light," one of the lights is a simple metaphor for Desdemona's life. Here is a more complex metaphor taken from the old sport of falconry:

> If I do prove her haggard,
> Though that her jesses were my dear heart-strings,
> I'ld whistle her off and let her down the wind
> To play at fortune. (III, 3, 260–263.)

Metaphor, once thought to be a mere embellishment, is now generally recognized to be part of the essence of language. When the student has learned how to discover Shakespeare's metaphors and to work out their implications, he will have entered into one of the greatest sources of fascination of Shakespeare's verse.

Othello is a tragedy, but of what kind? It is possible to argue that the play fulfills some of the classical requirements. The central figure, a great man, comes to grief because of a flaw in his character, and we feel the emotions of pity and fear as we watch his fall. According to this formula the flaw in the character of Othello is a combination of jealousy and gullibility.

There are positive reasons, however, for doubting that Shakespeare deliberately created a tragedy on classic lines. If he did, it would be unique among his tragedies. The other great ones, *Hamlet, Macbeth, King Lear,* do not so obviously seem to illustrate the great-man-with-flaw formula of Aristotle. And nothing we know about Shakespeare's training and workmanship and the customs of the theater of his age would make us think that he tried to make *Othello* a play of the Greek type.

Moreover, there is an inherent difficulty in accepting either sexual jealousy or gullibility as a fatal flaw. They probably would have seemed trivial issues to Sophocles. A closer approximation to a Sophoclean flaw would be Iago's comment on Othello, that he is a man of a free and open nature who accepts people at their face value. This can be a serious flaw in great national leaders but it is intangible and seems to be Othello's flaw only secondarily.

Another difficulty, so subtle that it is hard to describe, is the treatment of ethical questions in *Othello.* There is no model for the figure of Iago in any of the Greek plays that have survived. Certainly the ancient Greeks had a fully developed sense of what is right and wrong in human actions, but with Iago we discern a new element: the belief that every man is in an immediate and personal sense morally responsible for his own acts, especially because of the effect of these acts on his status in the next world. So intelligent a character as Iago is fully aware that if his villainy is discovered, his body will suffer dire punishment. More important, he also knows that, whether he is caught or not, his villainous acts place his immortal soul in danger for all eternity. This particular belief, of course, entered the Western world with Christianity, and *Othello* is a product of its own century in that it is pervaded by the long tradition of Christian ethics.

Another element in *Othello* is the presence of comedy. Here as in all of Shakespeare's tragedies the playwright used humor of various sorts to set off by contrast the horror and pathos of the serious scenes and to provide relief from them. The humor is inextricably mixed with the serious parts. It is an overtone to grimness, as it is in much of the literature of the Western world.

To sum up, in certain subtle psychological ways *Othello* is on our side of the divide that separates us from the modes of thinking of the ancients. Though in form it is the most "classic" of Shakespeare's tragedies, *Othello* manifests what scholars call "the Elizabethan world-picture," particularly the ideas of the nature of man that prevailed in England during the reign of Elizabeth I. It is modern in that it reflects the changes that the Christian tradition has wrought in our thinking. It is not modern in that now, in the days of

Elizabeth II, we have perhaps become more sensitive to such enormities of conduct as sordid intrigue and murder. Further, though the Christian tradition is still the strongest tradition in Western civilization, great minorities are now not quite so certain of the certainties as people were during the reign of the first Elizabeth, and we believe that a human being is a far more complex creature than our ancestors supposed.

Therefore, from our study of *Othello* and from our knowledge of other tragedies of the period, including Shakespeare's own plays, we must conclude that Shakespeare was a realist and an empiricist. He wrote what people expected would be performed on his own stage and in his own time. Failure and death are the subject matter of tragedy. Shakespeare showed how Othello failed to understand the circumstances of his own life, destroyed his own richest treasure, and thus condemned himself to death. Shakespeare has so clothed the process in realistic action and poetic language that we accept it as a tragedy of its own sort. In *Othello* the playwright followed no one else's rules. It is unique, but it is tragedy.

At the end of the play the student will find suggestions for further study of the various topics mentioned in this brief introduction to *Othello.* Perhaps at this point a few additional words about how to read Shakespeare will be helpful.

The text used in this volume is the standard Globe text. It gets us about as close to the words written by Shakespeare as is possible. The stage directions are not necessarily Shakespeare's own; some of them were added by eighteenth-century editors. The language of Shakespeare is much the same as that of the King James version of the Bible, published in 1611; thus the language of *Othello* is English of 350 years ago. As Shakepeare recedes into the past, his language becomes increasingly difficult for nonspecialists to understand. Some of his words are no longer used at all; some have changed their meaning. It would be possible to provide a gloss for a great number of the words of *Othello;*

instead the editors have tried to explain at the bottom of the page only those expressions for whose meaning the beginning student might be expected to have very little clue. As for the rest, the student should at first try to read *Othello* as he would read a piece of prose that is not unreasonably difficult. He will not know all the words, but he can get the sense of the passage. For example, in the following passage only *antres* (which means caverns) and *Anthropophagi* (which means cannibals) should be totally unfamiliar to a twentieth-century reader who is beginning the study of Shakespeare:

> Her father loved me; oft invited me;
> Still question'd me the story of my life,
> From year to year, the battles, sieges, fortunes,
> That I have passed.
> I ran it through, even from my boyish days,
> To the very moment that he bade me tell it;
> Wherein it spake of most disastrous chances,
> Of moving accidents by flood and field,
> Of hair-breadth scapes i' the imminent deadly breach,
> Of being taken by the insolent foe
> And sold to slavery, of my redemption thence
> And portance in my travels' history:
> Wherein of antres vast and deserts idle,
> Rough quarries, rocks and hills whose heads touch heaven,
> It was my hint to speak,—such was the process:
> And of the Cannibals that each other eat,
> The Anthropophagi and men whose heads
> Do grow beneath their shoulders. (I, 3, 128–145.)

A little thought will tell the student the meaning in this passage of *breach, portance,* and *idle,* and thus he will have a good preliminary understanding of the lines. Thence he can proceed to further study. He will find his increasing mastery of the plays of Shakespeare to be perhaps the most rewarding task in all literature.

OTHELLO

THE MOOR OF VENICE

~

DRAMATIS PERSONÆ

DUKE OF VENICE.
BRABANTIO, a Senator.
Other Senators.
GRATIANO, brother to Brabantio.
LODOVICO, kinsman to Brabantio.
OTHELLO, a noble Moor in the service of
the Venetian State.
CASSIO, his lieutenant.
IAGO, his ancient.
RODERIGO, a Venetian gentleman.

MONTANO, Othello's predecessor in the government of Cyprus.
Clown, servant to Othello.

DESDEMONA, daughter to Brabantio and
wife to Othello.
EMILIA, wife to Iago.
BIANCA, mistress to Cassio.

Sailor, Messenger, Herald, Officers, Gentlemen, Musicians and Attendants.

SCENE: Venice: a sea-port in Cyprus.

ACT I

SCENE I. *Venice. A street.*

Enter RODERIGO *and* IAGO.

Rod. Tush! never tell me; I take it much
   unkindly
That thou, Iago, who hast had my purse
As if the strings were thine, shouldst know
   of this.
Iago. 'Sblood, but you will not hear me:
If ever I did dream of such a matter
Abhor me.
   Rod. Thou told'st me thou didst hold
   him in thy hate.
Iago. Despise me, if I do not. Three great
   ones of the city,
In personal suit to make me his lieutenant,
Off-capp'd to him: and, by the faith of man,
I know my price, I am worth no worse a
   place: 11
But he, as loving his own pride and purposes,
Evades them, with a bombast circumstance
Horribly stuff'd with epithets of war;
And, in conclusion,
Nonsuits my mediators: for, "Certes," says
   he,
"I have already chose my officer."
And what was he?
Forsooth, a great arithmetician,
One Michael Cassio, a Florentine,   20

A fellow almost damn'd in a fair wife;
That never set a squadron in the field,
Nor the division of a battle knows
More than a spinster; unless the bookish
   theoric,
Wherein the toged consuls can propose
As masterly as he: mere prattle, without
   practice,
In all his soldiership. But he, sir, had the
   election:
And I, of whom his eyes had seen the proof
At Rhodes, at Cyprus and on other grounds
Christian and heathen, must be-lee'd and
   calm'd   30
By debitor and creditor: this counter-caster,
He, in good time, must his lieutenant be,
And I—God bless the mark!—his Moorship's ancient.
   Rod. By heaven, I rather would have
   been his hangman.
Iago. Why, there 's no remedy; 't is the
   curse of service,
Preferment goes by letter and affection,
And not by old gradation, where each second
Stood heir to the first. Now, sir, be judge
   yourself,
Whether I in any just term am affined
To love the Moor.

---

31 *counter-caster,* bookkeeper, petty accountant.
33 *ancient,* ensign.

Rod.   I would not follow him then.
Iago.   O, sir, content you;   41
I follow him to serve my turn upon him:
We cannot all be masters, nor all masters
Cannot be truly follow'd. You shall mark
Many a duteous and knee-crooking knave,
That, doting on his own obsequious bond-
     age,
Wears out his time, much like his master's
     ass,
For nought but provender, and when he 's
     old, cashier'd:
Whip me such honest knaves. Others there
     are
Who, trimm'd in forms and visages of duty,
Keep yet their hearts attending on them-
     selves,   51
And, throwing but shows of service on their
     lords,
Do well thrive by them and when they have
     lined their coats
Do themselves homage: these fellows have
     some soul;
And such a one do I profess myself. For, sir,
It is as sure as you are Roderigo,
Were I the Moor, I would not be Iago:
In following him, I follow but myself;
Heaven is my judge, not I for love and duty,
But seeming so, for my peculiar end: 60
For when my outward action doth demon-
     strate
The native act and figure of my heart
In compliment extern, 't is not long after
But I will wear my heart upon my sleeve
For daws to peck at: I am not what I am.
   Rod.   What a full fortune does the thick-
     lips owe,
If he can carry 't thus!
   Iago.   Call up her father,
Rouse him: make after him, poison his de-
     light,
Proclaim him in the streets; incense her
     kinsmen,
And, though he in a fertile climate dwell,
Plague him with flies: though that his joy be
     joy,   71
Yet throw such changes of vexation on 't,
As it may lose some colour.
   Rod.   Here is her father's house; I'll call
     aloud.

Iago.   Do; with like timorous accent and
     dire yell
As when, by night and negligence, the fire
Is spied in populous cities.
   Rod.   What, ho, Brabantio! Signior Bra-
     bantio, ho!
   Iago.   Awake! what, ho, Brabantio!
     thieves! thieves! thieves!
Look to your house, your daughter and your
     bags   80
Thieves! thieves!

Brabantio appears above, at a window.

   Bra.   What is the reason of this terrible
     summons?
What is the matter there?
   Rod.   Signior, is all your family within?
   Iago.   Are your doors lock'd?
   Bra.   Why, wherefore ask you this?
   Iago.   'Zounds, sir, you're robb'd; for
     shame, put on your gown;
Your heart is burst, you have lost half your
     soul;
Even now, very now, an old black ram
Is tupping your white ewe. Arise, arise;
Awake the snorting citizens with the bell,
Or else the devil will make a grandsire of
     you: 91
Arise, I say.
   Bra.   What, have you lost your wits?
   Rod.   Most reverend signior, do you know
     my voice?
   Bra.   Not I: what are you?
   Rod.   My name is Roderigo.
   Bra.   The worser welcome:
I have charged thee not to haunt about my
     doors:
In honest plainness thou hast heard me say
My daughter is not for thee; and now, in
     madness,
Being full of supper and distempering
     draughts,
Upon malicious bravery, dost thou come 100
To start my quiet.
   Rod.   Sir, sir, sir,—
   Bra.   But thou must needs be sure
My spirit and my place have in them power
To make this bitter to thee.
   Rod.   Patience, good sir.

Bra. What tell'st thou me of robbing?
this is Venice;
My house is not a grange.
Rod. Most grave Brabantio,
In simple and pure soul I come to you. 108
Iago. 'Zounds, sir, you are one of those
that will not serve God, if the devil bid you.
Because we come to do you service and you
think we are ruffians, you'll have your
daughter covered with a Barbary horse;
you'll have your nephews neigh to you;
you'll have coursers for cousins and gennets
for germans.
Bra. What profane wretch art thou?
Iago. I am one, sir, that comes to tell you
your daughter and the Moor are now mak-
ing the beast with two backs.
Bra. Thou art a villain.
Iago. You are—a senator.
Bra. This thou shalt answer; I know thee,
Roderigo. 120
Rod. Sir, I will answer any thing. But, I
beseech you,
If't be your pleasure and most wise consent,
As partly I find it is, that your fair daughter,
At this odd-even and dull watch o' the night,
Transported, with no worse nor better guard
But with a knave of common hire, a gondo-
lier,
To the gross clasps of a lascivious Moor,—
If this be known to you and your allowance,
We then have done you bold and saucy
wrongs;
But if you know not this, my manners tell
me 130
We have your wrong rebuke. Do not believe
That, from the sense of all civility,
I thus would play and trifle with your rever-
ence:
Your daughter, if you have not given her
leave,
I say again, hath made a gross revolt;
Tying her duty, beauty, wit and fortunes
In an extravagant and wheeling stranger
Of here and every where. Straight satisfy
yourself:
If she be in her chamber or your house,

Let loose on me the justice of the state
For thus deluding you. 141
Bra. Strike on the tinder, ho!
Give me a taper! call up all my people!
This accident is not unlike my dream:
Belief of it oppresses me already.
Light, I say! light! [*Exit above.*
Iago. Farewell; for I must leave you:
It seems not meet, nor wholesome to my
place,
To be produced—as, if I stay, I shall—
Against the Moor: for, I do know, the state,
However this may gall him with some check,
Cannot with safety cast him, for he 's em-
bark'd 150
With such loud reason to the Cyprus wars,
Which even now stand in act, that, for their
souls,
Another of his fathom they have none,
To lead their business: in which regard,
Though I do hate him as I do hell-pains,
Yet for necessity of present life,
I must show out a flag and sign of love,
Which is indeed but sign. That you shall
surely find him, 158
Lead to the Sagittary the raised search;
And there will I be with him. So farewell.
[*Exit.*

Enter, below, BRABANTIO, *and*
Servants *with torches.*

Bra. It is too true an evil: gone she is;
And what 's to come of my despised time
Is nought but bitterness. Now, Roderigo,
Where didst thou see her? O unhappy girl!
With the Moor, say'st thou? Who would be
a father!
How didst thou know 't was she? O, she de-
ceives me
Past thought! What said she to you? Get
more tapers;
Raise all my kindred. Are they married,
think you?
Rod. Truly, I think they are.
Bra. O heaven! How got she out? O trea-
son of the blood! 170
Fathers, from hence trust not your daugh-
ters' minds

---

107 *grange,* farmhouse. 113 *gennets,* horses of a
Spanish breed. 114 *germans,* relatives.

159 *Sagittary,* an inn.

By what you see them act. Is there not charms
By which the property of youth and maid-
hood
May be abused? Have you not read, Rode-
rigo,
Of some such thing?
 Rod.   Yes, sir, I have indeed.
 Bra. Call up my brother. O, would you
   had had her!
Some one way, some another. Do you know
Where we may apprehend her and the
  Moor?
 Rod. I think I can discover him, if you
   please   179
To get good guard and go along with me.
 Bra. Pray you, lead on. At every house
   I'll call;
I may command at most. Get weapons, ho!
And raise some special officers of night.
On, good Roderigo: I'll deserve your pains.
            [*Exeunt.*

  SCENE II. *Another street.*

 Enter OTHELLO, IAGO, *and* Attendants
     with torches.

 Iago. Though in the trade of war I have
   slain men,
Yet do I hold it very stuff o' the conscience
To do no cóntrived murder: I lack iniquity
Sometimes to do me service: nine or ten
  times
I had thought to have yerk'd him here under
  the ribs.
 Oth. 'T is better as it is.
 Iago.   Nay, but he prated,
And spoke such scurvy and provoking terms
Against your honour
That, with the little godliness I have,
I did full hard forbear him. But, I pray you,
  sir,   10
Are you fast married? Be assured of this,
That the magnifico is much beloved,
And hath in his effect a voice potential
As double as the duke's: he will divorce you,
Or put upon you what restraint and griev-
ance
The law, with all his might to enforce it on,

Will give him cable.
 Oth.   Let him do his spite;
My services which I have done the signiory
Shall out-tongue his complaints. 'T is yet to
  know,—
Which, when I know that boasting is an
  honour,   20
I shall promulgate—I fetch my life and be-
  ing
From men of royal siege, and my demerits
May speak unbonneted to as proud a for-
tune
As this that I have reach'd: for know, Iago,
But that I love the gentle Desdemona,
I would not my unhoused free condition
Put into circumscription and confine
For the sea's worth. But, look! what lights
  come yond?
 Iago. Those are the raised father and his
   friends:
You were best go in.
 Oth.   Not I: I must be found:
My parts, my title and my perfect soul   31
Shall manifest me rightly. Is it they?
 Iago. By Janus, I think no.

 Enter CASSIO, *and certain* Officers *with*
      torches.

 Oth. The servants of the duke, and my
   lieutenant.
The goodness of the night upon you, friends!
What is the news?
 Cas.   The duke does greet you, general,
And he requires your haste-post-haste ap-
  pearance,
Even on the instant.
 Oth.   What is the matter, think you?
 Cas. Something from Cyprus, as I may
   divine: 39
It is a business of some heat: the galleys
Have sent a dozen sequent messengers
This very night at one another's heels,
And many of the consuls, raised and met,
Are at the duke's already: you have been
  hotly call'd for;
When, being not at your lodging to be
  found,
The senate hath sent about three several
  quests
To search you out.

---

5 *yerk'd,* stabbed. 22 *siege,* position, birth.

Oth.   'T is well I am found by you.
I will but spend a word here in the house,
And go with you.   [*Exit.*
Cas.   Ancient, what makes he here?
Iago. 'Faith, he to-night hath boarded a
          land carack: 50
If it prove lawful prize, he 's made for ever.
Cas. I do not understand.
Iago.   He's married.
Cas.   To who?

Re-enter OTHELLO.

Iago. Marry, to—Come, captain, will you
          go?
Oth.   Have with you.
Cas.   Here comes another troop to seek
          for you.
Iago.   It is Brabantio. General, be ad-
          vised;
He comes to bad intent.

Enter BRABANTIO, RODERIGO, *and* Officers
          with torches and weapons.

Oth.   Holla! stand there!
Rod. Signior, it is the Moor.
Bra.   Down with him, thief!
          [*They draw on both sides.*
Iago. You, Roderigo! come, sir, I am for
          you.
Oth. Keep up your bright swords, for the
          dew will rust them.
Good signior, you shall more command with
          years   60
Than with your weapons.
Bra. O thou foul thief, where hast thou
          stow'd my daughter?
Damn'd as thou art, thou hast enchanted her;
For I'll refer me to all things of sense,
If she in chains of magic were not bound,
Whether a maid so tender, fair and happy,
So opposite to marriage that she shunn'd
The wealthy curled darlings of our nation,
Would ever have, to incur a general mock,
Run from her guardage to the sooty bosom
Of such a thing as thou, to fear, not to de-
          light.   71
Judge me the world, if 't is not gross in sense

That thou hast practised on her with foul
          charms,
Abused her delicate youth with drugs or
          minerals
That weaken motion: I 'll have 't disputed
          on;
'T is probable and palpable to thinking.
I therefore apprehend and do attach thee
For an abuser of the world, a practiser
Of arts inhibited and out of warrant.
Lay hold upon him: if he do resist,   80
Subdue him at his peril.
Oth.   Hold your hands,
Both you of my inclining, and the rest:
Were it my cue to fight, I should have
          known it
Without a prompter. Where will you that I
          go
To answer this your charge?
Bra.   To prison, till fit time
Of law and course of direct session
Call thee to answer.
Oth.   What if I do obey?
How may the duke be therewith satisfied,
Whose messengers are here about my side,
Upon some present business of the state
To bring me to him?   91
First Off. 'T is true, most worthy signior;
The duke 's in council, and your noble self,
I am sure, is sent for.
Bra.   How! the duke in council!
In this time of the night! Bring him away:
Mine 's not an idle cause: the duke himself,
Or any of my brothers of the state,
Cannot but feel this wrong as 't were their
          own;
For if such actions may have passage free,
Bond-slaves and pagans shall our statesmen
          be.
          [*Exeunt.*

SCENE III. *A council-chamber.*

The DUKE *and* Senators *sitting at a table;*
          Officers *attending.*

Duke. There is no composition in these
          news
That gives them credit.

---

50 *carack,* merchant ship. 52 *Marry,* by the Virgin
Mary.

1 *composition,* consistency.

First. Sen. Indeed, they are disproportion'd;
My letters say a hundred and seven galleys.
Duke. And mine, a hundred and forty.
Sec. Sen.   And mine, two hundred:
But though they jump not on a just account,—
As in these cases, where the aim reports,
'T is oft with difference—yet do they all confirm
A Turkish fleet, and bearing up to Cyprus.
Duke. Nay, it is possible enough to judgment:
I do not so secure me in the error,   10
But the main article I do approve
In fearful sense.
Sailor. [*Within*] What, ho! what, ho! what, ho!
First Off. A messenger from the galleys.

Enter a Sailor.

Duke.   Now, what 's the business?
Sail. The Turkish preparation makes for Rhodes;
So was I bid report here to the state
By Signior Angelo.
Duke. How say you by this change?
First Sen.   This cannot be,
By no assay of reason; 't is a pageant,   18
To keep us in false gaze. When we consider
The importancy of Cyprus to the Turk,
And let ourselves again but understand,
That as it more concerns the Turk than Rhodes,
So may he with more facile question bear it,
For that it stands not in such warlike brace,
But altogether lacks the abilities
That Rhodes is dress'd in: if we make thought of this,
We must not think the Turk is so unskilful
To leave that latest which concerns him first,
Neglecting an attempt of ease and gain,
To wake and wage a danger profitless.   31
Duke. Nay, in all confidence, he 's not for Rhodes.
First Off. Here is more news.

Enter a Messenger.

Mess. The Ottomites, reverend and gracious,
Steering with due course towards the isle of Rhodes,
Have there injointed them with an after fleet.
First Sen. Ay, so I thought. How many, as you guess?
Mess. Of thirty sail: and now they do re-stem
Their backward course, bearing with frank appearance
Their purposes toward Cyprus. Signior Montano,
Your trusty and most valiant servitor,   40
With his free duty recommends you thus,
And prays you to believe him.
Duke. 'T is certain, then, for Cyprus.
Marcus Luccicos, is not he in town?
First Sen. He 's now in Florence.
Duke. Write from us to him; post-post-haste dispatch.
First Sen. Here comes Brabantio and the valiant Moor.

Enter BRABANTIO, OTHELLO, IAGO, RODERIGO, *and* Officers.

Duke. Valiant Othello, we must straight employ you
Against the general enemy Ottoman.
[*To Brabantio*] I did not see you; welcome, gentle signior;   50
We lack'd your counsel and your help to-night.
Bra. So did I yours. Good your grace, pardon me;
Neither my place nor aught I heard of business
Hath raised me from my bed, nor doth the general care
Take hold on me, for my particular grief
Is of so flood-gate and o'erbearing nature
That it engluts and swallows other sorrows
And it is still itself.
Duke.   Why, what 's the matter?
Bra. My daughter! O, my daughter!
Duke and Sen.   Dead?
Bra.   Ay, to me;

---

5 *jump,* agree. 6 *aim,* guess.
24 *So . . . it,* so may he (the Turk) capture it with less trouble. 25 *brace,* state of defense. 31 *wake and wage,* arouse and risk.

35 *injointed,* combined. *after,* second. 37 *re-stem,* retrace.

She is abused, stol'n from me, and corrupted
By spells and medicines bought of mounte-
    banks;   61
For nature so preposterously to err,
Being not deficient, blind, or lame of sense,
Sans witchcraft could not.
    Duke. Whoe'er he be that in this foul
    proceeding
Hath thus beguiled your daughter of herself
And you of her, the bloody book of law
You shall yourself read in the bitter letter
After your own sense, yea, though our
    proper son
Stood in your action.   70
    Bra.   Humbly I thank your grace.
Here is the man, this Moor, whom now, it
    seems,
Your special mandate for the state-affairs
Hath hither brought.
    Duke and Sen.   We are very sorry for 't.
    Duke. [*To Othello*] What, in your own
    part, can you say to this?
    Bra. Nothing, but this is so.
    Oth. Most potent, grave, and reverend
    signiors,
My very noble and approved good masters,
That I have ta'en away this old man's daugh-
    ter,
It is most true; true, I have married her: 79
The very head and front of my offending
Hath this extent, no more. Rude am I in my
    speech,
And little bless'd with the soft phrase of
    peace;
For since these arms of mine had seven
    years' pith,
Till now some nine moons wasted, they have
    used
Their dearest action in the tented field,
And little of this great world can I speak,
More than pertains to feats of broil and bat-
    tle,
And therefore little shall I grace my cause
In speaking for myself. Yet, by your gra-
    cious patience,
I will a round unvarnish'd tale deliver   90
Of my whole course of love; what drugs,
    what charms,

---

64 *Sans,* without. 69 *proper,* own.

What conjuration and what mighty magic,
For such proceeding I am charged withal,
I won his daughter.
    Bra.   A maiden never bold;
Of spirit so still and quiet, that her motion
Blush'd at herself; and she, in spite of nature,
Of years, of country, credit, every thing,
To fall in love with what she fear'd to look
    on!
It is a judgement maim'd and most imper-
    fect   99
That will confess perfection so could err
Against all rules of nature and must be
    driven
To find out practices of cunning hell,
Why this should be. I therefore vouch again
That with some mixtures powerful o'er the
    blood,
Or with some dram conjured to this effect,
He wrought upon her.
    Duke.   To vouch this, is no proof,
Without more wider and more overt test
Than these thin habits and poor likelihoods
Of modern seeming do prefer against him.
    First Sen. But, Othello, speak: 110
Did you by indirect and forced courses
Subdue and poison this young maid's affec-
    tions?
Or came it by request and such fair question
As soul to soul affordeth!
    Oth.   I do beseech you,
Send for the lady to the Sagittary,
And let her speak of me before her father:
If you do find me foul in her report,
The trust, the office I do hold of you,
Not only take away, but let your sentence
Even fall upon my life.
    Duke.   Fetch Desdemona hither.
    Oth. Ancient, conduct them; you best
    know the place.   121
        [*Exeunt Iago and Attendants.*
And, till she come, as truly as to heaven
I do confess the vices of my blood,
So justly to your grave ears I 'll present
How I did thrive in this fair lady's love,
And she in mine.
    Duke. Say it, Othello.
    Oth. Her father loved me; oft invited
    me;
Still question'd me the story of my life,

From year to year, the battles, sieges, for-
    tunes,   130
That I have pass'd.
I ran it through, even from my boyish days,
To the very moment that he bade me tell it;
Wherein I spake of most disastrous chances,
Of moving accidents by flood and field,
Of hair-breadth scapes i' the imminent
    deadly breach,
Of being taken by the insolent foe
And sold to slavery, of my redemption
    thence
And portance in my travels' history: 139
Wherein of antres vast and deserts idle,
Rough quarries, rocks and hills whose heads
    touch heaven,
It was my hint to speak,—such was the proc-
    ess;
And of the Cannibals that each other eat,
The Anthropophagi and men whose heads
Do grow beneath their shoulders. This to
    hear
Would Desdemona seriously incline:
But still the house-affairs would draw her
    thence:
Which ever as she could with haste dispatch,
She 'ld come again, and with a greedy ear
Devour up my discourse: which I observing,
Took once a pliant hour, and found good
    means   151
To draw from her a prayer of earnest heart
That I would all my pilgrimage dilate,
Whereof by parcels she had something heard,
But not intentively: I did consent,
And often did beguile her of her tears,
When I did speak of some distressful stroke
That my youth suffer'd. My story being done,
She gave me for my pains a world of sighs:
She swore, in faith, 't was strange, 't was
    passing strange,   160
'T was pitiful, 't was wondrous pitiful:
She wish'd she had not heard it, yet she
    wish'd
That heaven had made her such a man: she
    thank'd me,

And bade me, if I had a friend that loved
    her,
I should but teach him how to tell my story,
And that would woo her. Upon this hint I
    spake:
She loved me for the dangers I had pass'd,
And I loved her that she did pity them.
This only is the witchcraft I have used: 169
Here comes the lady; let her witness it.

Enter DESDEMONA, IAGO, *and* attendants.

  Duke.   I think this tale would win my
    daughter too.
Good Brabantio,
Take up this mangled matter at the best:
Men do their broken weapons rather use
Than their bare hands.
  Bra.   I pray you, hear her speak:
If she confess that she was half the wooer,
Destruction on my head, if my bad blame
Light on the man! Come hither, gentle mis-
    tress:
Do you perceive in all this noble company
Where most you owe obedience?
  Des.   My noble father,
I do perceive here a divided duty: 181
To you I am bound for life and education;
My life and education both do learn me
How to respect you; you are the lord of duty;
I am hitherto your daughter: but here's my
    husband,
And so much duty as my mother show'd
To you, preferring you before her father,
So much I challenge that I may profess
Due to the Moor my lord.
  Bra.   God be wi' you! I have done.
Please it your grace, on to the state-affairs:
I had rather to adopt a child than get it.
Come hither, Moor: 192
I here do give thee that with all my heart
Which, but thou hast already, with all my
    heart
I would keep from thee. For your sake,
    jewel,
I am glad at soul I have no other child;
For thy escape would teach me tyranny,
To hang clogs on them. I have done, my lord.

---

140 *antres,* caverns. 144 *Anthropophagi,* cannibals.
163 *That . . . man,* that she had been a man like
this.

198 *clogs,* chains, hindrances.

Duke. Let me speak like yourself, and lay a sentence,   199
Which, as a grise or step, may help these lovers
Into your favour.
When remedies are past, the griefs are ended
By seeing the worst, which late on hopes depended.
To mourn a mischief that is past and gone
Is the next way to draw new mischief on.
What cannot be preserved when fortune takes,
Patience her injury a mockery makes.
The robb'd that smiles steals something from the thief;
He robs himself that spends a bootless grief.
   Bra. So let the Turk of Cyprus us beguile;   210
We lose it not, so long as we can smile.
He bears the sentence well that nothing bears
But the free comfort which from thence he hears,
But he bears both the sentence and the sorrow
That, to pay grief, must of patience borrow.
These sentences, to sugar, or to gall,
Being strong on both sides, are equivocal:
But words are words; I never yet did hear
That the bruised heart was pierced through the ear.
I humbly beseech you, proceed to the affairs of state.   220
   Duke. The Turk with a most mighty preparation makes for Cyprus. Othello, the fortitude of the place is best known to you; and though we have there a substitute of most allowed sufficiency, yet opinion, a sovereign mistress of effects, throws a more safer voice on you: you must therefore be content to slubber the gloss of your new fortunes with this more stubborn and boisterous expedition.
   Oth. The tyrant custom, most grave senators,   230
Hath made the flinty and steel couch of war

My thrice-driven bed of down: I do agnize
A natural and prompt alacrity
I find in hardness, and do undertake
These present wars against the Ottomites.
Most humbly therefore bending to your state,
I crave fit disposition for my wife,
Due reference of place and exhibition,
With such accommodation and besort
As levels with her breeding.   240
   Duke.   If you please,
Be 't at her father's.
   Bra.   I 'll not have it so.
   Oth. Nor I.
   Des.   Nor I; I would not there reside,
To put my father in impatient thoughts
By being in his eye. Most gracious duke,
To my unfolding lend your prosperous ear;
And let me find a charter in your voice,
To assist my simpleness.
   Duke. What would you, Desdemona?
   Des. That I did love the Moor to live with him,
My downright violence and storm of fortunes
May trumpet to the world: my heart's subdued
Even to the very quality of my lord:
I saw Othello's visage in his mind,
And to his honours and his valiant parts
Did I my soul and fortunes consecrate.
So that, dear lords, if I be left behind,
A moth of peace, and he go to the war,
The rites for which I love him are bereft me,
And I a heavy interim shall support
By his dear absence. Let me go with him.
   Oth. Let her have your voices.   261
Vouch with me, heaven, I therefore beg it not,
To please the palate of my appetite,
Nor to comply with heat—the young affects
In me defunct—and proper satisfaction,
But to be free and bounteous to her mind:
And heaven defend your good souls, that you think
I will your serious and great business scant

---

200 *grise,* step. 222 *fortitude,* strength. 228 *slubber,* soil.

232 *agnize,* acknowledge. 238 *reference,* assignment. *exhibition,* allowance of money. 239 *besort,* fitness. 264 *affects,* desires.

For she is with me: no, when light-wing'd
    toys
Of feather'd Cupid seel with wanton dull-
    ness   270
My speculative and officed instruments,
That my disports corrupt and taint my busi-
    ness,
Let housewives make a skillet of my helm,
And all indign and base adversities
Make head against my estimation!
    Duke. Be it as you shall privately deter-
        mine,
Either for her stay or going: the affair cries
        haste,
And speed must answer it.
    First Sen. You must away to-night.
    Oth.   With all my heart.
    Duke. At nine i' the morning here we 'll
        meet again.   280
Othello, leave some officer behind,
And he shall our commission bring to you;
With such things else of quality and respect
As doth import you.
    Oth.   So please your grace, my ancient;
A man he is of honesty and trust:
To his conveyance I assign my wife,
With what else needful your good grace shall
        think
To be sent after me.
    Duke.   Let it be so.
Good night to every one. [*To Brab.*] And,
        noble signior,
If virtue no delighted beauty lack,   290
Your son-in-law is far more fair than black.
    First Sen. Adieu, brave Moor; use Des-
        demona well.
    Bra. Look to her, Moor, if thou hast eyes
        to see:
She has deceived her father, and may thee.
    [*Exeunt Duke, Senators, Officers, &c.*
    Oth. My life upon her faith! Honest Iago,
My Desdemona must I leave to thee:
I prithee, let thy wife attend on her;
And bring them after in the best advantage.
Come, Desdemona: I have but an hour   299
Of love, of worldly matters and direction,

To spend with thee: we must obey the time.
    [*Exeunt Othello and Desdemona.*
    Rod. Iago,—
    Iago. What say'st thou, noble heart?
    Rod. What will I do, thinkest thou?
    Iago. Why, go to bed, and sleep.
    Rod. I will incontinently drown myself.
    Iago. If thou dost, I shall never love thee
after. Why, thou silly gentleman!
    Rod. It is silliness to live when to live is
torment; and then have we a prescription to
die when death is our physician.   311
    Iago. O villanous! I have looked upon the
world for four times seven years; and since
I could distinguish betwixt a benefit and an
injury, I never found man that knew how to
love himself. Ere I would say I would drown
myself for the love of a guinea-hen, I would
change my humanity with a baboon.
    Rod. What should I do? I confess it is
my shame to be so fond; but it is not in my
virtue to amend it.   321
    Iago. Virtue! a fig! 't is in ourselves that
we are thus or thus. Our bodies are our gardens, to the which our wills are gardeners;
so that if we will plant nettles or sow lettuce,
set hyssop and weed up thyme, supply it with
one gender of herbs or distract it with many,
either to have it sterile with idleness or
manured with industry, why, the power and
corrigible authority of this lies in our wills.
If the balance of our lives had not one scale
of reason to poise another of sensuality, the
blood and baseness of our natures would
conduct us to most preposterous conclusions:
but we have reason to cool our raging motions, our carnal stings, our unbitted lusts,
whereof I take this that you call love to be
a sect or scion.   337
    Rod. It cannot be.
    Iago. It is merely a lust of the blood and
a permission of the will. Come, be a man.
Drown thyself! drown cats and blind pup-
pies. I have professed me thy friend, and I

---

270 *seel,* close. 271 *My . . . instruments,* my
eyes. 274 *indign,* disgraceful. 275 *estimation,* reputation.

321 *fond,* foolish. 333 *poise,* balance. 336 *stings,*
desires. *unbitted,* unbridled. 337 *sect or scion,* cutting or graft.

confess me knit to thy deserving with cables of perdurable toughness; I could never better stead thee than now. Put money in thy purse; follow thou the wars; defeat thy favour with an usurped beard; I say, put money in thy purse. It cannot be that Desdemona should long continue her love to the Moor,—put money in thy purse,—nor he his to her; it was a violent commencement, and thou shalt see an answerable sequestration—put but money in thy purse. These Moors are changeable in their wills:—fill thy purse with money:—the food that to him now is as luscious as locusts, shall be to him shortly as bitter as coloquintida. She must change for youth: when she is sated with his body, she will find the error of her choice: she must have change, she must: therefore put money in thy purse. If thou wilt needs damn thyself, do it a more delicate way than drowning. Make all the money thou canst: if sanctimony and a frail vow betwixt an erring barbarian and a super-subtle Venetian be not too hard for my wits and all the tribe of hell, thou shalt enjoy her; therefore make money. A pox of drowning thyself! it is clean out of the way: seek thou rather to be hanged in compassing thy joy than to be drowned and go without her.

Rod. Wilt thou be fast to my hopes, if I depend on the issue?   370

Iago. Thou art sure of me:—go, make money:—I have told thee often, and I re-tell thee again and again, I hate the Moor: my cause is hearted; thine hath no less reason. Let us be conjunctive in our revenge against him; if thou canst cuckold him, thou dost thyself a pleasure, me a sport. There are many events in the womb of time which will be delivered. Traverse! go, provide thy money. We will have more of this to-morrow. Adieu.   380

Rod. Where shall we meet i' the morning?

Iago. At my lodging.

Rod. I 'll be with thee betimes.

Iago. Go to; farewell. Do you hear, Roderigo?

Rod. What say you?

Iago. No more of drowning, do you hear?

Rod. I am changed: I 'll go sell all my land.   [*Exit.*

Iago. Thus do I ever make my fool my purse;
For I mine own gain'd knowledge should profane,   390
If I would time expend with such a snipe,
But for my sport and profit. I hate the Moor;
And it is thought abroad, that 'twixt my sheets
He has done my office: I know not if 't be true;
But I, for mere suspicion in that kind,
Will do as if for surety. He holds me well;
The better shall my purpose work on him.
Cassio 's a proper man: let me see now:
To get his place and to plume up my will
In   double   knavery—How,   how?—Let's see:—   400
After some time, to abuse Othello's ear
That he is too familiar with his wife.
He hath a person and a smooth dispose
To be suspected, framed to make women false.
The Moor is of a free and open nature,
That thinks men honest that but seem to be so,
And will as tenderly be led by the nose
As asses are.   408
I have 't. It is engender'd. Hell and night
Must bring this monstrous birth to the world's light.   [*Exit.*

ACT II

Scene I. *A Sea-port in Cyprus. An open place near the quay.*

Enter Montano *and two* Gentlemen.

Mon. What from the cape can you discern at sea?

First Gent. Nothing at all: it is a high-wrought flood;

---

344 *stead,* assist. 345 *defeat thy favour,* spoil thy looks. 350 *sequestration,* estrangement. 355 *coloquintida,* a medicine.

391 *snipe,* fool. 399 *plume up,* gratify (by decorating).

I cannot, 'twixt the heaven and the main,
Descry a sail.
    Mon.   Methinks the wind hath spoke
    aloud at land;
A fuller blast ne'er shook our battlements:
If it hath ruffian'd so upon the sea,
What ribs of oak, when mountains melt on
    them,
Can hold the mortise? What shall we hear of
    this?
    Sec. Gent.   A segregation of the Turkish
    fleet: 10
For do but stand upon the foaming shore,
The chidden billow seems to pelt the clouds;
The wind-shaked surge, with high and mon-
    strous mane,
Seems to cast water on the burning bear,
And quench the guards of the ever-fixed
    pole:
I never did like molestation view
On the enchafed flood.
    Mon.   If that the Turkish fleet
Be not enshelter'd and embay'd, they are
    drown'd;
It is impossible they bear it out.

Enter a third Gentleman.

    Third Gent.   News, lads! our wars are
    done.   20
The desperate tempest hath so bang'd the
    Turks,
That their designment halts: a noble ship of
    Venice
Hath seen a grievous wreck and sufferance
On most part of their fleet.
    Mon.   How! is this true?
    Third Gent.   The ship is here put in,
A Veronesa; Michael Cassio,
Lieutenant to the warlike Moor Othello,
Is come on shore: the Moor himself at sea,
And is in full commission here for Cyprus.
    Mon.   I am glad on 't: 't is a worthy
    governor.   30
    Third Gent. But this same Cassio, though
    he speak of comfort
Touching the Turkish loss, yet he looks sadly,

And prays the Moor be safe; for they were
    parted
With foul and violent tempest.
    Mon.   Pray heavens he be;
For I have served him, and the man com-
    mands
Like a full soldier. Let 's to the seaside, ho!
As well to see the vessel that 's come in
As to throw out our eyes for brave Othello,
Even till we make the main and the aerial
    blue
An indistinct regard.
    Third Gent.   Come, let 's do so; 40
For every minute is expectancy
Of more arrivance.

Enter CASSIO.

    Cas.   Thanks, you the valiant of this war-
    like isle,
That so approve the Moor! O, let the
    heavens
Give him defence against the elements,
For I have lost him on a dangerous sea.
    Mon.   Is he well shipp'd?
    Cas.   His bark is stoutly timber'd, and his
    pilot
Of very expert and approved allowance;
Therefore my hopes, not surfeited to death,
Stand in bold cure.   51
    [*A cry within* "A sail, a sail, a sail!"

Enter a fourth Gentleman.

    Cas.   What noise?
    Fourth Gent.   The town is empty; on the
    brow o' the sea
Stand ranks of people, and they cry "A sail!"
    Cas.   My hopes do shape him for the gov-
    ernor.   [*Guns heard.*
    Sec. Gent.   They do discharge their shot
    of courtesy:
Our friends at least.
    Cas.   I pray you, sir, go forth,
And give us truth who 't is that is arrived.
    Sec. Gent. I shall.   [*Exit.*
    Mon.   But, good lieutenant, is your gen-
    eral wived?   60

---

10 *segregation,* scattering. 16 *molestation,* disturbance.

40 *An indistinct regard,* indistinguishable.
49 *allowance,* reputation. 51 *Stand in bold cure,*
may be fulfilled.

Cas. Most fortunately: he hath achieved
   a maid
That paragons description and wild fame;
One that excels the quirks of blazoning pens,
And in the essential vesture of creation
Does tire the ingener.

   Re-enter second Gentleman.

                        How now! who has put in?
Sec. Gent. 'T is one Iago, ancient to the
   general.
Cas. Has had most favourable and happy
   speed:
Tempests themselves, high seas and howling
   winds,
The gutter'd rocks and congregated sands,—
Traitors ensteep'd to clog the guiltless keel,—
As having sense of beauty, do omit   71
Their mortal natures, letting go safely by
The divine Desdemona.
   Mon.   What is she?
Cas. She that I spake of, our great cap-
   tain's captain,
Left in the conduct of the bold Iago,
Whose footing here anticipates our thoughts
A se'nnight's speed. Great Jove, Othello
   guard,
And swell his sail with thine own powerful
   breath,
That he may bless this bay with his tall ship,
Make love's quick pants in Desdemona's
   arms,   80
Give renew'd fire to our extincted spirits,
And bring all Cyprus comfort!

   Enter DESDEMONA, EMILIA, IAGO,
   RODERIGO, *and* Attendants.

                        O, behold,
The riches of the ship is come on shore!
Ye men of Cyprus, let her have your knees.
Hail to thee, lady! and the grace of heaven,
Before, behind thee, and on every hand,
Enwheel thee round!

---

62 *paragons*, surpasses. *fame*, rumor. 63 *quirks*,
extravagant phrases. *blazoning*, praising. 64-5
And . . . ingener, the genuine qualities with
which she is endowed surpass the ability of an inventor of phrases to praise her. 69 *gutter'd*, fur-
rowed. 70 *ensteep'd*, submerged. 71 *omit*, give up.

Des.   I thank you, valiant Cassio.
What tidings can you tell me of my lord?
   Cas. He is not yet arrived: nor know I
   aught   89
But that he 's well and will be shortly here.
   Des. O, but I fear—How lost you com-
   pany?
   Cas. The great contention of the sea and
   skies
Parted our fellowship—But, hark! a sail.
      [*Within* "A sail, a sail!" *Guns heard.*
   Sec. Gent. They give their greeting to the
   citadel:
This likewise is a friend.
   Cas.   See for the news. [*Exit Gentleman.*
Good ancient, you are welcome. [*To Emilia*]
   Welcome, mistress:
Let it not gall your patience, good Iago,
That I extend my manners; 't is my breeding
That gives me this bold show of courtesy.
                              [*Kissing her.*
   Iago. Sir, would she give you so much of
   her lips   101
As of her tongue she oft bestows on me,
You 'ld have enough.
   Des.   Alas, she has no speech.
   Iago. In faith, too much;
I find it still, when I have list to sleep:
Marry, before your ladyship, I grant,
She puts her tongue a little in her heart,
And chides with thinking.
   Emil. You have little cause to say so.
   Iago. Come on, come on; you are pictures
   out of doors,   110
Bells in your parlours, wild-cats in your
   kitchens,
Saints in your injuries, devils being offended,
Players in your housewifery, and housewives
   in your beds.
   Des. O, fie upon thee, slanderer!
   Iago. Nay, it is true, or else I am a Turk:
You rise to play and go to bed to work.
   Emil. You shall not write my praise.
   Iago.   No, let me not.
   Des. What wouldst thou write of me,
   if thou shouldst praise me?
   Iago. O gentle lady, do not put me to 't;

---

106 *Marry*, by the Virgin Mary. 113 *Players*, tri-
flers. *housewives*, hussies.

For I am nothing, if not critical.   120
   Des. Come on, assay. There's one gone
     to the harbour?
   Iago. Ay, madam.
   Des. I am not merry; but I do beguile
The thing I am by seeming otherwise.
Come, how wouldst thou praise me?
   Iago. I am about it; but indeed my inven-
     tion
Comes from my pate as birdlime does from
     frize;
It plucks out brains and all: but my Muse
     labours,
And thus she is deliver'd.
If she be fair and wise, fairness and wit,
The one's for use, the other useth it.   131
   Des. Well praised! How if she be black
     and witty?
   Iago. If she be black, and thereto have a
     wit,
She 'll find a white that shall her blackness
     fit.
   Des. Worse and worse.
   Emil. How if fair and foolish?
   Iago. She never yet was foolish that was
     fair;
For even her folly help'd her to an heir.
   Des. These are old fond paradoxes to
make fools laugh i' the alehouse. What mis-
erable praise hast thou for her that 's foul
and foolish?   141
   Iago. There 's none so foul and foolish
     thereunto,
But does foul pranks which fair and wise
     ones do.
   Des. O heavy ignorance! thou praisest
the worst best. But what praise couldst thou
bestow on a deserving woman indeed, one
that, in the authority of her merit, did justly
put on the vouch of very malice itself?
   Iago. She that was ever fair and never
     proud,   149
Had tongue at will and yet was never loud,
Never lack'd gold and yet went never gay,
Fled from her wish and yet said "Now I
     may,"

She that being anger'd, her revenge being
     nigh,
Bade her wrong stay and her displeasure fly,
She that in wisdom never was so frail
To change the cod's head for the salmon's
     tail,
She that could think and ne'er disclose her
     mind,
See suitors following and not look behind,
She was a wight, if ever such wight were,—
   Des. To do what?   161
   Iago. To suckle fools and chronicle small
     beer.
   Des. O most lame and impotent conclu-
sion! Do not learn of him, Emilia, though
he be thy husband. How say you, Cassio? is
he not a most profane and liberal counsellor?
   Cas. He speaks home, madam: you may
relish him more in the soldier than in the
scholar.
   Iago. [*Aside*] He takes her by the palm:
ay, well said, whisper: with as little a web
as this will I ensnare as great a fly as Cassio.
Ay, smile upon her, do; I will gyve thee in
thine own courtship. You say true; 't is so,
indeed: if such tricks as these strip you out
of your lieutenantry, it had been better you
had not kissed your three fingers so oft,
which now again you are most apt to play
the sir in. Very good; well kissed! an excellent courtesy! 't is so, indeed. Yet again your
fingers to your lips? would they were clyster-
pipes for your sake! [*Trumpet within.*] The
Moor! I know his trumpet.   180
   Cas. 'T is truly so.
   Des. Let 's meet him and receive him.
   Cas. Lo, where he comes!

       Enter OTHELLO *and* Attendants.

   Oth. O my fair warrior!
   Des.   My dear Othello!
   Oth. It gives me wonder great as my
     content
To see you here before me. O my soul's joy!

---

127 *birdlime*, sticky substance to catch birds. *frize,*
woolen cloth. 139 *fond*, foolish. 149 *vouch*, approval.

157 *To . . . tail*, prefer the worst part of a good
thing to the best part of a bad thing. 159 *wight,*
person. 161 *chronicle small beer*, keep petty accounts. 165 *liberal*, licentious. 177 *sir*, gentleman.
179 *clyster-pipes*, syringes.

If after every tempest come such calms,
May the winds blow till they have waken'd
      death!
And let the labouring bark climb hills of
      seas
Olympus-high and duck again as low   190
As hell 's from heaven! If it were now to die,
'T were now to be most happy; for, I fear,
My soul hath her content so absolute
That not another comfort like to this
Succeeds in unknown fate.

Des.   The heavens forbid
But that our loves and comforts should in-
      crease,
Even as our days do grow!

Oth.   Amen to that, sweet powers!
I cannot speak enough of this content;   198
It stops me here; it is too much of joy:
And this, and this, the greatest discords be
                              [*Kissing her.*
That e'er our hearts shall make!

Iago. [*Aside*] O, you are well tuned now!
But I 'll set down the pegs that make this
      music,
As honest as I am.

Oth.   Come, let us to the castle.
News, friends; our wars are done, the Turks
      are drown'd.
How does my old acquaintance of this isle?
Honey, you shall be well desired in Cyprus;
I have found great love amongst them. O my
      sweet,
I prattle out of fashion, and I dote
In mine own comforts. I prithee, good Iago,
Go to the bay and disembark my coffers:
Bring thou the master to the citadel;   211
He is a good one, and his worthiness
Does challenge much respect. Come, Desde-
      mona,
Once more, well met at Cyprus.
            [*Exeunt Othello, Desdemona, and
                                  Attendants.*

Iago. Do thou meet me presently at the
harbour. Come hither. If thou be'st valiant,
—as, they say, base men being in love have
then a nobility in their natures more than is
native to them,—list me. The lieutenant to-
night watches on the court of guard:—
First, I must tell thee this—Desdemona is
directly in love with him.   221

Rod. With him! why, 't is not possible.

Iago. Lay thy finger thus, and let thy soul
be instructed. Mark me with what violence
she first loved the Moor, but for bragging
and telling her fantastical lies: and will she
love him still for prating? let not thy discreet
heart think it. Her eye must be fed; and
what delight shall she have to look on the
devil? When the blood is made dull with
the act of sport, there should be, again to in-
flame it and to give satiety a fresh appetite,
loveliness in favour, sympathy in years, manners and beauties; all which the Moor is defective in: now, for want of these required
conveniences, her delicate tenderness will
find itself abused, begin to heave the gorge,
disrelish and abhor the Moor; very nature
will instruct her in it and compel her to some
second choice. Now, sir, this granted,—as it
is a most pregnant and unforced position—
who stands so eminent in the degree of this
fortune as Cassio does? a knave very voluble;
no further conscionable than in putting on
the mere form of civil and humane seeming,
for the better compassing of his salt and
most hidden loose affection? why, none; why,
none: a slipper and subtle knave, a finder of
occasions, that has an eye can stamp and
counterfeit advantages, though true advantage never present itself; a devilish knave.
Besides, the knave is handsome, young, and
hath all those requisites in him that folly and
green minds look after: a pestilent complete
knave; and the woman hath found him already.   253

Rod. I cannot believe that in her; she 's
full of most blessed condition.

Iago. Blessed fig's-end! the wine she
drinks is made of grapes: if she had been
blessed, she would never have loved the
Moor. Blessed pudding! Didst thou not see
her paddle with the palm of his hand? didst
not mark that?

Rod. Yes, that I did; but that was but
courtesy.   262

Iago. Lechery, by this hand; an index and
obscure prologue to the history of lust and

---

244 *conscionable,* conscientious. 246 *salt,* licentious.

foul thoughts. They met so near with their lips that their breaths embraced together. Villanous thoughts, Roderigo! when these mutualities so marshal the way, hard at hand comes the master and main exercise, the incorporate conclusion. Pish! But, sir, be you ruled by me: I have brought you from Venice. Watch you to-night; for the command, I 'll lay 't upon you. Cassio knows you not. I 'll not be far from you: do you find some occasion to anger Cassio, either by speaking too loud, or tainting his discipline; or from what other course you please, which the time shall more favourably minister. 277

Rod. Well.

Iago. Sir, he is rash and very sudden in choler, and haply may strike at you: provoke him, that he may; for even out of that will I cause these of Cyprus to mutiny; whose qualification shall come into no true taste again but by the displanting of Cassio. So shall you have a shorter journey to your desires by the means I shall then have to prefer them; and the impediment most profitably removed, without the which there were no expectation of our prosperity.

Rod. I will do this, if I can bring it to any opportunity.   290

Iago. I warrant thee. Meet me by and by at the citadel: I must fetch his necessaries ashore. Farewell.

Rod. Adieu.   [*Exit.*

Iago. That Cassio loves her, I do well believe it;

That she loves him, 't is apt and of great credit:

The Moor, howbeit that I endure him not,

Is of a constant, loving, noble nature,

And I dare think he 'll prove to Desdemona

A most dear husband. Now, I do love her too;   300

Not out of absolute lust, though peradventure

I stand accountant for as great a sin,

But partly led to diet my revenge,

For that I do suspect the lusty Moor

Hath leap'd into my seat; the thought whereof

Doth, like a poisonous mineral, gnaw my inwards;

And nothing can or shall content my soul

Till I am even'd with him, wife for wife,

Or failing so, yet that I put the Moor

At least into a jealousy so strong   310

That judgement cannot cure. Which thing to do,

If this poor trash of Venice, whom I trash

For his quick hunting, stand the putting on,

I 'll have our Michael Cassio on the hip,

Abuse him to the Moor in the rank garb—

For I fear Cassio with my night-cap too—

Make the Moor thank me, love me and reward me,

For making him egregiously an ass   318

And practising upon his peace and quiet

Even to madness. 'T is here, but yet confused.

Knavery's plain face is never seen till used.

[*Exit.*

SCENE II. *A street.*

Enter a HERALD *with a proclamation; People following.*

Her. It is Othello's pleasure, our noble and valiant general, that, upon certain tidings now arrived, importing the mere perdition of the Turkish fleet, every man put himself into triumph; some to dance, some to make bonfires, each man to what sport and revels his addiction leads him: for, besides these beneficial news, it is the celebration of his nuptial. So much was his pleasure should be proclaimed. All offices are open, and there is full liberty of feasting from this present hour of five till the bell have told eleven. Heaven bless the isle of Cyprus and our noble general Othello!   [*Exeunt.*

SCENE III. *A hall in the castle.*

Enter OTHELLO, DESDEMONA, CASSIO, *and* Attendants.

Oth. Good Michael, look you to the guard to-night:

Let 's teach ourselves that honourable stop,

Not to outsport discretion.

Cas. Iago hath direction what to do;

But, notwithstanding, with my personal eye Will I look to 't.

312–13 *whom . . . hunting,* whom I keep from acting too fast. 314 *on the hip,* in my power.

Oth.　　　　　　Iago is most honest.
Michael, good night: to-morrow with your earliest
Let me have speech with you.

[To Desdemona]
Come, my dear love,
The purchase made, the fruits are to ensue;
That profit 's yet to come 'tween me and you.
Good night.　　　　　　　　　　11

[Exeunt Othello, Desdemona, and
Attendants.

Enter IAGO.

Cas.　Welcome, Iago; we must to the watch.

Iago.　Not this hour, lieutenant; 't is not yet ten o' the clock. Our general cast us thus early for the love of his Desdemona; who let us not therefore blame: he hath not yet made wanton the night with her; and she is sport for Jove.

Cas.　She 's a most exquisite lady.

Iago.　And, I 'll warrant her, full of game.

Cas.　Indeed, she 's a most fresh and delicate creature.　　　　　　　　　　21

Iago.　What an eye she has! methinks it sounds a parley of provocation.

Cas.　An inviting eye; and yet methinks right modest.

Iago.　And when she speaks, is it not an alarum to love?

Cas.　She is indeed perfection.

Iago.　Well, happiness to their sheets! Come, lieutenant, I have a stoup of wine; and here without are a brace of Cyprus gallants that would fain have a measure to the health of black Othello.

Cas.　Not to-night, good Iago: I have very poor and unhappy brains for drinking: I could well wish courtesy would invent some other custom of entertainment.

Iago.　O, they are our friends; but one cup: I 'll drink for you.　　　　　　39

Cas.　I have drunk but one cup to-night, and that was craftily qualified too, and, behold, what innovation it makes here: I am unfortunate in the infirmity, and dare not task my weakness with any more.

Iago.　What, man! 't is a night of revels: the gallants desire it.

Cas.　Where are they?

Iago.　Here at the door; I pray you, call them in.

Cas.　I 'll do 't; but it dislikes me.

[Exit.

Iago.　If I can fasten but one cup upon him,　　　　　　　　　　50
With that which he hath drunk to-night already,
He 'll be as full of quarrel and offence
As my young mistress' dog. Now, my sick fool Roderigo,
Whom love hath turn'd almost the wrong side out,
To Desdemona hath to-night caroused
Potations pottle-deep; and he 's to watch:
Three lads of Cyprus, noble swelling spirits,
That hold their honours in a wary distance,
The very elements of this warlike isle,　　59
Have I to-night fluster'd with flowing cups,
And they watch too. Now, 'mongst this flock of drunkards,
Am I to put our Cassio in some action
That may offend the isle.—But here they come:
If consequence do but approve my dream,
My boat sails freely, both with wind and stream.

Re-enter CASSIO; *with him* MONTANO
and Gentlemen;
Servants *following with wine.*

Cas.　'Fore God, they have given me a rouse already.

Mon.　Good faith, a little one; not past a pint, as I am a soldier.

Iago.　Some wine, ho!　　　　　　70
[Sings]
　　And let me the canakin clink, clink;
　　And let me the canakin clink:
　　　A soldier's a man;
　　　A life's but a span;
　　Why, then, let a soldier drink.
Some wine, boys!

Cas.　'Fore God, an excellent song.

Iago.　I learned it in England, where, indeed, they are most potent in potting: your Dane, your German, and your swag-bellied Hollander—Drink, ho!—are nothing to your English.　　　　　　　　　　81

Cas. Is your Englishman so expert in his drinking?

Iago. Why, he drinks you, with facility, your Dane dead drunk; he sweats not to overthrow your Almain; he gives your Hollander a vomit, ere the next pottle can be filled.

Cas. To the health of our general!

Mon. I am for it, lieutenant; and I 'll do you justice.

Iago. O sweet England!   91
King Stephen was a worthy peer,
    His breeches cost him but a crown;
He held them sixpence all too dear,
    With that he call'd the tailor lown.

He was a wight of high renown,
    And thou art but of low degree:
'T is pride that pulls the country down;
    Then take thine auld cloak about thee.
Some wine, ho!   100

Cas. Why, this is a more exquisite song than the other.

Iago. Will you hear 't again?

Cas. No; for I hold him to be unworthy of his place that does those things. Well, God's above all; and there be souls must be saved, and there be souls must not be saved.

Iago. It 's true, good lieutenant.

Cas. For mine own part,—no offence to the general, nor any man of quality,—I hope to be saved.   111

Iago. And so do I too, lieutenant.

Cas. Ay, but, by your leave, not before me; the lieutenant is to be saved before the ancient. Let 's have no more of this; let 's to our affairs. God forgive us our sins! Gentlemen, let 's look to our business. Do not think, gentlemen, I am drunk: this is my ancient; this is my right hand, and this is my left: I am not drunk now; I can stand well enough, and speak well enough.   120

All. Excellent well.

Cas. Why, very well then; you must not think then that I am drunk.   [*Exit.*

Mon. To the platform, masters; come, let 's set the watch.

Iago. You see this fellow that is gone before;
He is a soldier fit to stand by Cæsar
And give direction: and do but see his vice;
'T is to his virtue a just equinox,
The one as long as the other: 't is pity of
    him.   130
I fear the trust Othello puts him in,
On some odd time of his infirmity,
Will shake this island.

Mon.   But is he often thus?

Iago. 'T is evermore the prologue to his
    sleep:
He 'll watch the horologe a double set,
If drink rock not his cradle.

Mon.   It were well
The general were put in mind of it.
Perhaps he sees it not, or his good nature
Prizes the virtue that appears in Cassio,
And looks not on his evils: is not this true?

Enter RODERIGO.

Iago. [*Aside to him*] How now, Rod-
    erigo!   141
I pray you, after the lieutenant; go.
                                  [*Exit Roderigo.*

Mon. And 't is great pity that the noble
    Moor
Should hazard such a place as his own second
With one of an ingraft infirmity:
It were an honest action to say
So to the Moor.

Iago.   Not I, for this fair island:
I do love Cassio well; and would do much
To cure him of this evil—But, hark! what
    noise?
                     [*Cry within:* "Help! help!"

Re-enter CASSIO, *driving in* RODERIGO.

Cas. You rogue! you rascal!

Mon.   What 's the matter, lieutenant?

Cas. A knave teach me my duty!   151
I 'll beat the knave into a twiggen bottle.

Rod. Beat me!

Cas. Dost thou prate, rogue?
                           [*Striking Roderigo.*

---

95 *lown,* lout, rascal.

129 *a just equinox,* exactly equal. 135 *horologe,* clock. *double set,* twenty-four hours.
152 *twiggen,* covered with wicker.

Mon. Nay, good lieutenant; I pray you, sir, hold your hand.   [*Staying him.*

Cas. Let me go, sir, or I 'll knock you o'er the mazzard.

Mon. Come, come, you 're drunk.

Cas. Drunk!   [*They fight.*

Iago. [*Aside to Roderigo*] Away, I say; go out, and cry a mutiny.
                          [*Exit Roderigo.*

Nay, good lieutenant!—alas, gentlemen;—
Help, ho!—Lieutenant,—sir,—Montano,—
sir;—   159
Help, masters!—Here 's a goodly watch indeed!   [*Bell rings.*
Who 's that which rings the bell?—Diablo, ho!
The town will rise: God 's will, lieutenant, hold!
You will be shamed for ever.

Re-enter OTHELLO *and* Attendants.

Oth.   What is the matter here?

Mon. 'Zounds, I bleed still; I am hurt to the death.   [*Faints.*

Oth. Hold, for your lives!

Iago. Hold, ho! Lieutenant,—sir,—Montano,—gentlemen,—
Have you forgot all sense of place and duty?
Hold! the general speaks to you; hold, hold, for shame!

Oth. Why, how now, ho! from whence ariseth this?   169
Are we turn'd Turks, and to ourselves do that
Which heaven hath forbid the Ottomites?
For Christian shame, put by this barbarous brawl:
He that stirs next to carve for his own rage
Holds his soul light; he dies upon his motion.
Silence that dreadful bell: it frights the isle
From her propriety. What is the matter, masters?
Honest Iago, that look'st dead with grieving,
Speak, who began this? on thy love, I charge thee.

Iago. I do not know: friends all but now, even now,
In quarter, and in terms like bride and groom   180

Devesting them for bed; and then, but now,
As if some planet had unwitted men,
Swords out, and tilting one at other's breast,
In opposition bloody. I cannot speak
Any beginning to this peevish odds;
And would in action glorious I had lost
Those legs that brought me to a part of it!

Oth. How comes it, Michael, you are thus forgot?

Cas. I pray you, pardon me; I cannot speak.

Oth. Worthy Montano, you were wont be civil;   190
The gravity and stillness of your youth
The world hath noted, and your name is great
In mouths of wisest censure: what 's the matter,
That you unlace your reputation thus
And spend your rich opinion for the name
Of a night-brawler? give me answer to it.

Mon. Worthy Othello, I am hurt to danger:
Your officer, Iago, can inform you,—
While I spare speech, which something now offends me,—   199
Of all that I do know: nor know I aught
By me that 's said or done amiss this night;
Unless self-charity be sometimes a vice,
And to defend ourselves it be a sin
When violence assails us.

Oth.   Now, by heaven,
My blood begins my safer guides to rule;
And passion, having my best judgement collied,
Assays to lead the way: if I once stir,
Or do but lift this arm, the best of you
Shall sink in my rebuke. Give me to know
How this foul rout began, who set it on;
And he that is approved in this offence,
Though he had twinn'd with me, both at a birth,   212
Shall lose me. What! in a town of war,
Yet wild, the people's hearts brimful of fear,
To manage private and domestic quarrel,
In night, and on the court and guard of safety!
'T is monstrous. Iago, who began 't?

---

155 *mazzard,* head. 180 *quarter,* friendship.   206 *collied,* darkened.

Mon. If partially affined, or leagued in office,
Thou dost deliver more or less than truth,
Thou art no soldier.
  Iago.   Touch me not so near:
I had rather have this tongue cut from my mouth   221
Than it should do offence to Michael Cassio;
Yet, I persuade myself, to speak the truth
Shall nothing wrong him. Thus it is, general.
Montano and myself being in speech,
There comes a fellow crying out for help;
And Cassio following him with determined sword,
To execute upon him. Sir, this gentleman
Steps in to Cassio and entreats his pause: 230
Myself the crying fellow did pursue,
Lest by his clamour—as it so fell out—
The town might fall in fright: he, swift of foot,
Outran my purpose; and I return'd the rather
For that I heard the clink and fall of swords,
And Cassio high in oath; which till to-night
I ne'er might say before. When I came back—
For this was brief—I found them close together,
At blow and thrust; even as again they were
When you yourself did part them.
More of this matter cannot I report: 240
But men are men; the best sometimes forget:
Though Cassio did some little wrong to him,
As men in rage strike those that wish them best,
Yet surely Cassio, I believe, received
From him that fled some strange indignity,
Which patience could not pass.
  Oth.   I know, Iago,
Thy honesty and love doth mince this matter,
Making it light to Cassio. Cassio, I love thee;
But never more be officer of mine.   249

Re-enter DESDEMONA, *attended.*

Look, if my gentle love be not raised up!
I 'll make thee an example.
  Des.   What 's the matter?
  Oth. All 's well now, sweeting; come away to bed.

Sir, for your hurts, myself will be your surgeon:
Lead him off.   [*To Montano, who is led off.*
Iago, look with care about the town,
And silence those whom this vile brawl distracted.
Come, Desdemona: 't is the soldiers' life
To have their balmy slumbers waked with strife.
        [*Exeunt all but Iago and Cassio.*
  Iago. What, are you hurt lieutenant?
  Cas. Ay, past all surgery.   260
  Iago. Marry, heaven forbid!
  Cas. Reputation, reputation, reputation! O, I have lost my reputation! I have lost the immortal part of myself, and what remains is bestial. My reputation, Iago, my reputation!
  Iago. As I am an honest man, I thought you had received some bodily wound; there is more sense in that than in reputation. Reputation is an idle and most false imposition: oft got without merit, and lost without deserving: you have lost no reputation at all, unless you repute yourself such a loser. What, man! there are ways to recover the general again: you are but now cast in his mood, a punishment more in policy than in malice; even so as one would beat his offenceless dog to affright an imperious lion: sue to him again, and he 's yours.   277
  Cas. I will rather sue to be despised than to deceive so good a commander with so slight, so drunken, and so indiscreet an officer. Drunk? and speak parrot? and squabble? swagger? swear? and discourse fustian with one's own shadow? O thou invisible spirit of wine, if thou hast no name to be known by, let us call thee devil!
  Iago. What was he that you followed with your sword? What had he done to you?
  Cas. I know not.
  Iago. Is 't possible?   288
  Cas. I remember a mass of things, but nothing distinctly; a quarrel, but nothing wherefore. O God, that men should put an enemy in their mouths to steal away their brains! that we should, with joy, pleasance,

---

218 *If . . . office,* if prejudiced by friendship.

274 *cast in his mood,* dismissed in his anger.
282 *fustian,* nonsense.

revel and applause, transform ourselves into beasts!

Iago. Why, but you are now well enough: how came you thus recovered?

Cas. It hath pleased the devil drunkenness to give place to the devil wrath: one unperfectness shows me another, to make me frankly despise myself.   300

Iago. Come, you are too severe a moraler: as the time, the place, and the condition of this country stands, I could heartily wish this had not befallen; but, since it is at it is, mend it for your own good.

Cas. I will ask him for my place again; he shall tell me I am a drunkard! Had I as many mouths as Hydra, such an answer would stop them all. To be now a sensible man, by and by a fool, and presently a beast! O strange! Every inordinate cup is unblessed and the ingredient is a devil.   312

Iago. Come, come, good wine is a good familiar creature, if it be well used: exclaim no more against it. And, good lieutenant, I think you think I love you.

Cas. I have well approved it, sir. I drunk!

Iago. You or any man living may be drunk at some time, man. I 'll tell you what you shall do. Our general's wife is now the general: I may say so in this respect, for that he hath devoted and given up himself to the contemplation, mark, and denotement of her parts and graces: confess yourself freely to her; importune her help to put you in your place again: she is of so free, so kind, so apt, so blessed a disposition, she hold it a vice in her goodness not to do more than she is requested: this broken joint between you and her husband entreat her to splinter; and, my fortunes against any lay worth naming, this crack of your love shall grow stronger than it was before.   331

Cas. You advise me well.

Iago. I protest, in the sincerity of love and honest kindness.

Cas. I think it freely; and betimes in the morning I will beseech the virtuous Desdemona to undertake for me: I am desperate of my fortunes if they check me here.

Iago. You are in the right. Good night,

lieutenant; I must to the watch.   340

Cas. Good night, honest Iago.   [*Exit.*

Iago. And what 's he then that says I play the villain?

When this advice is free I give and honest,
Probal to thinking and indeed the course
To win the Moor again? For 't is most easy
The inclining Desdemona to subdue
In any honest suit: she 's framed as fruitful
As the free elements. And then for her
To win the Moor—were 't to renounce his baptism,
All seals and symbols of redeemed sin,   350
His soul is so enfetter'd to her love,
That she may make, unmake, do what she list,
Even as her appetite shall play the god
With his weak function. How am I then a villain
To counsel Cassio to this parallel course,
Directly to his good? Divinity of hell!
When devils will the blackest sins put on,
They do suggest at first with heavenly shows,
As I do now: for whiles this honest fool
Plies Desdemona to repair his fortunes
And she for him pleads strongly to the Moor,
I 'll pour this pestilence into his ear,
That she repeals him for her body's lust;
And by how much she strives to do him good,   364
She shall undo her credit with the Moor.
So will I turn her virtue into pitch,
And out of her own goodness make the net
That shall enmesh them all.

Re-enter RODERIGO.

                              How now, Roderigo!

Rod. I do follow here in the chase, not like a hound that hunts, but one that fills up the cry. My money is almost spent; I have been to-night exceedingly well cudgelled; and I think the issue will be, I shall have so much experience for my pains, and so, with no money at all and a little more wit, return again to Venice.

Iago. How poor are they that have not patience!
What wound did ever heal but by degrees?
Thou know'st we work by wit, and not by witchcraft;

---

308 *Hydra,* mythical monster with many heads.

363 *repeals,* recalls; here, sues for his recall.

And wit depends on dilatory time.   379
Does 't not go well? Cassio hath beaten thee,
And thou by that small hurt hast cashier'd
    Cassio:
Though other things grow fair against the
    sun,
Yet fruits that blossom first will first be ripe:
Content thyself awhile. By the mass, 't is
    morning;
Pleasure and action make the hours seem
    short.
Retire thee; go where thou art billeted:
Away, I say; thou shalt know more here-
    after:
Nay, get thee gone. [*Exit Roderigo.*] Two
    things are to be done:
My wife must move for Cassio to her mis-
    tress;
I 'll set her on;   390
Myself the while to draw the Moor apart,
And bring him jump when he may Cassio
    find
Soliciting his wife: ay, that 's the way:
Dull not device by coldness and delay.
                             [*Exit.*

ACT III

SCENE I. *Before the castle.*

Enter CASSIO *and some* Musicians.

Cas. Masters, play here; I will content
    your pains;
Something that 's brief; and bid "Good mor-
    row, general."   [*Music.*

Enter Clown.

Clo. Why, masters, have your instruments
been in Naples, that they speak i' the nose
thus?
First Mus. How, sir, how!
Clo. Are these, I pray you, wind-instru-
ments?
First Mus. Ay, marry, are they, sir.
Clo. O, thereby hangs a tail.   9
First Mus. Whereby hangs a tale, sir?
Clo. Marry, sir, by many a wind-instru-
ment that I know. But, masters, here 's
money for you: and the general so likes
your music, that he desires you, for love's
sake, to make no more noise with it.

First Mus. Well, sir, we will not.
Clo. If you have any music that may not
be heard, to 't again: but, as they say, to hear
music the general does not greatly care.
First Mus. We have none such, sir.   19
Clo. Then put up your pipes in your bag,
for I 'll away: go; vanish into air; away!
                         [*Exeunt Musicians.*
Cas. Dost thou hear, my honest friend?
Clo. No, I hear not your honest friend; I
hear you.
Cas. Prithee, keep up thy quillets. There's
a poor piece of gold for thee: if the gentlewoman that attends the general's wife be
stirring, tell her there's one Cassio entreats
her a little favour of speech: wilt thou do
this?
Clo. She is stirring, sir: if she will stir
hither, I shall seem to notify unto her.
Cas. Do, good my friend.   31
                         [*Exit Clown.*

Enter IAGO.

               In happy time, Iago.
Iago. You have not been a-bed, then?
Cas. Why, no; the day had broke
Before we parted. I have made bold, Iago,
To send in to your wife: my suit to her
Is, that she will to virtuous Desdemona
Procure me some access.
Iago.   I 'll send her to you presently;
And I 'll devise a mean to draw the Moor
Out of the way, that your converse and busi-
    ness
May be more free.
Cas. I humbly thank you for 't.
                         [*Exit Iago.*
        I never knew
A Florentine more kind and honest.

Enter EMILIA.

Emil. Good morrow, good lieutenant: I
    am sorry
For your displeasure; but all will sure be
    well.
The general and his wife are talking of it;
And she speaks for you stoutly: the Moor
    replies,

---

24 *quillets,* plays on words.

That he you hurt is of great fame in Cyprus
And great affinity, and that in wholesome
 wisdom
He might not but refuse you; but he protests
 he loves you   50
And needs no other suitor but his likings
To take the safest occasion by the front
To bring you in again.
  Cas.   Yet, I beseech you,
If you think fit, or that it may be done,
Give me advantage of some brief discourse
With Desdemona alone.
  Emil.   Pray you, come in:
I will bestow you where you shall have time
To speak your bosom freely.
  Cas. I am much bound to you. [*Exeunt.*

SCENE II. *A room in the castle.*

Enter OTHELLO, IAGO, *and* Gentlemen.

 Oth. These letters give, Iago, to the
 pilot;
And by him do my duties to the senate:
That done, I will be walking on the works;
Repair there to me.
 Iago. Well, my good lord, I 'll do 't.
 Oth. This fortification, gentlemen, shall
 we see 't?
 Gent. We 'll wait upon your lordship.
          [*Exeunt.*

SCENE III. *The garden of the castle.*

Enter DESDEMONA, CASSIO, *and* EMILIA.

 Des. Be thou assured, good Cassio, I will
 do
All my abilities in thy behalf.
 Emil. Good madam, do: I warrant it
 grieves my husband,
As if the case were his.
 Des. O, that 's an honest fellow. Do not
 doubt, Cassio,
But I will have my lord and you again
As friendly as you were.
 Cas.   Bounteous madam,
Whatever shall become of Michael Cassio,
He 's never any thing but your true servant.
 Des. I know 't; I thank you. You do love
 my lord: 10

You have known him long; and be you well
 assured
He shall in strangeness stand no further off
Than in a politic distance.
 Cas.   Ay, but, lady,
That policy may either last so long,
Or feed upon such nice and waterish diet,
Or breed itself so out of circumstance,
That, I being absent and my place supplied,
My general will forget my love and service.
 Des. Do not doubt that; before Emilia
 here   19
I give thee warrant of thy place: assure thee,
If I do vow a friendship, I 'll perform it
To the last article: my lord shall never rest;
I 'll watch him tame and talk him out of
 patience;
His bed shall seem a school, his board a
 shrift;
I 'll intermingle every thing he does
With Cassio's suit: therefore be merry,
 Cassio;
For thy solicitor shall rather die
Than give thy cause away.
 Emil. Madam, here comes my lord.
 Cas. Madam, I 'll take my leave. 30
 Des. Nay, stay, and hear me speak.
 Cas. Madam, not now: I am very ill at
 ease,
Unfit for mine own purposes.
 Des. Well, do your discretion.
         [*Exit Cassio.*

Enter OTHELLO *and* IAGO.

 Iago. Ha! I like not that.
 Oth.   What dost thou say?
 Iago. Nothing, my lord: or if—I know
 not what.
 Oth. Was not that Cassio parted from my
 wife?
 Iago. Cassio, my lord! No, sure, I cannot
 think it,
That he would steal away so guilty-like,
Seeing you coming.
 Oth.   I do believe 't was he.
 Des. How now, my lord!   41
I have been talking with a suitor here,
A man that languishes in your displeasure.

---

49 *affinity,* kindred.
52 *front,* forelock.

23 *watch him tame,* keep him awake.

Oth. Who is 't you mean?

Des. Why, your lieutenant, Cassio. Good my lord,
If I have any grace or power to move you,
His present reconciliation take;
For if he be not one that truly loves you,
That errs in ignorance and not in cunning,
I have no judgement in an honest face;
I prithee, call him back.

Oth. Went he hence now?

Des. Ay, sooth; so humbled 52
That he hath left part of his grief with me,
To suffer with him. Good love, call him back.

Oth. Not now, sweet Desdemona; some other time.

Des. But shall 't be shortly?

Oth. The sooner, sweet, for you.

Des. Shall 't be to-night at supper?

Oth. No, not to-night.

Des. To-morrow dinner, then?

Oth. I shall not dine at home;
I meet the captains at the citadel.

Des. Why then to-morrow night; or Tuesday morn; 60
On Tuesday noon, or night; on Wednesday morn:
I prithee, name the time; but let it not
Exceed three days: in faith he's penitent;
And yet his trespass, in our common reason—
Save that, they say, the wars must make examples
Out of their best—is not almost a fault
To incur a private check. When shall he come?
Tell me, Othello: I wonder in my soul,
What you would ask me, that I should deny,
Or stand so mammering on. What! Michael Cassio, 70
That came a-wooing with you, and so many a time,
When I have spoke of you dispraisingly,
Hath ta'en your part; to have so much to do
To bring him in! Trust me, I could do much,—

Oth. Prithee, no more: let him come when he will;
I will deny thee nothing.

Des. Why, this is not a boon;
'T is as I should entreat you wear your gloves,
Or feed on nourishing dishes, or keep you warm,
Or sue to you to do a peculiar profit 79
To your own person: nay, when I have a suit
Wherein I mean to touch your love indeed,
It shall be full of poise and difficult weight,
And fearful to be granted.

Oth. I will deny thee nothing:
Whereon, I do beseech thee, grant me this,
To leave me but a little to myself.

Des. Shall I deny you? no: farewell, my lord.

Oth. Farewell, my Desdemona: I 'll come to thee straight.

Des. Emilia, come. Be as your fancies teach you;
Whate'er you be, I am obedient.
[*Exeunt Desdemona and Emilia.*

Oth. Excellent wretch! Perdition catch my soul, 90
But I do love thee! and when I love thee not,
Chaos is come again

Iago. My noble lord,—

Oth. What dost thou say, Iago?

Iago. Did Michael Cassio, when you woo'd my lady,
Know of your love?

Oth. He did, from first to last: why dost thou ask?

Iago. But for a satisfaction of my thought;
No further harm.

Oth. Why of thy thought, Iago?

Iago. I did not think he had been acquainted with her.

Oth. O, yes; and went between us very oft. 100

Iago. Indeed!

Oth. Indeed! ay, indeed: discern'st thou aught in that?
Is he not honest?

Iago. Honest, my lord!

Oth. Honest! ay, honest.

Iago. My lord, for aught I know.

Oth. What dost thou think?

Iago. Think, my lord!

Oth. Think, my lord!

---

70 *mammering,* hesitating.

82 *poise,* weight.

By heaven, he echoes me,
As if there were some monster in his
　　thought
Too hideous to be shown. Thou dost mean
　　something:
I heard thee say even now, thou likedst not
　　that,
When Cassio left my wife: what didst not
　　like?　　　　　　　　　　　　110
And when I told thee he was of my counsel
In my whole course of wooing, thou criedst
　　"Indeed!"
And didst contract and purse thy brow to-
　　gether,
As if thou then hadst shut up in thy brain
Some horrible conceit: if thou dost love me,
Show me thy thought.
　　Iago.　My lord, you know I love you.
　　Oth.　　　　　　　I think thou dost;
And, for I know thou 'rt full of love and
　　honesty,
And weigh'st thy words before thou givest
　　them breath,
Therefore these stops of thine fright me the
　　more:　　　　　　　　　　120
For such things in a false disloyal knave
Are tricks of custom, but in a man that's just
They are close delations, working from the
　　heart
That passion cannot rule.
　　Iago.　　　　　　　For Michael Cassio,
I dare be sworn I think that he is honest.
　　Oth.　I think so too.
　　Iago.　　Men should be what they seem;
Or those that be not, would they might
　　seem none!
　　Oth.　Certain, men should be what they
　　seem.
　　Iago.　Why, then, I think Cassio's an
　　honest man.
　　Oth.　Nay, yet there's more in this:　130
I prithee, speak to me as to thy thinkings,
As thou dost ruminate, and give thy worst of
　　thoughts
The worst of words.
　　Iago.　　　　　Good my lord, pardon me:
Though I am bound to every act of duty,

I am not bound to that all slaves are free to.
Utter my thoughts? Why, say they are vile
　　and false;
As where 's that palace whereinto foul things
Sometimes intrude not? who has a breast so
　　pure,
But some uncleanly apprehensions　　139
Keep leets and law-days and in session sit
With meditations lawful?
　　Oth.　Thou dost conspire against thy
　　friend, Iago,
If thou but think'st him wrong'd and makest
　　his ear
A stranger to thy thoughts.
　　Iago.　　　　　　I do beseech you—
Though I perchance am vicious in my guess,
As, I confess, it is my nature's plague
To spy into abuses, and oft my jealousy
Shapes faults that are not—that your wisdom
　　yet,
From one that so imperfectly conceits,
Would take no notice, nor build yourself a
　　trouble　　　　　　　　　　150
Out of his scattering and unsure observance.
It were not for your quiet nor your good,
Nor for my manhood, honesty, or wisdom,
To let you know my thoughts.
　　Oth.　　　　　　What dost thou mean?
　　Iago.　Good name in man and woman,
　　dear my lord,
Is the immediate jewel of their souls:
Who steals my purse steals trash; 't is some-
　　thing, nothing;
'T was mine, 't is his, and has been slave to
　　thousands;
But he that filches from me my good name
Robs me of that which not enriches him,
And makes me poor indeed.　　　　161
　　Oth.　By heaven, I 'll know thy thoughts.
　　Iago.　You cannot, if my heart were in
　　your hand;
Nor shall not, whilst 't is in my custody.
　　Oth.　Ha!
　　Iago.　O, beware, my lord, of jealousy;
It is the green-eyed monster which doth
　　mock
The meat it feeds on: that cuckold lives in
　　bliss

---

115 *conceit,* notion. 123 *close delations,* secret
accusations.

140 *Keep leets,* hold court.

Who, certain of his fate, loves not his
    wronger;
But, O, what damned minutes tells he o'er
Who dotes, yet doubts, suspects, yet strongly
    loves!   170
  Oth. O misery!
  Iago. Poor and content is rich and rich
    enough,
But riches fineless is as poor as winter
To him that ever fears he shall be poor.
Good heaven, the souls of all my tribe de-
    fend
From jealousy!
  Oth.   Why, why is this?
Think'st thou I 'ld make a life of jealousy,
To follow still the changes of the moon
With fresh suspicions? No; to be once in
    doubt
Is once to be resolved: exchange me for a
    goat,   180
When I shall turn the business of my soul
To such exsufflicate and blown surmises,
Matching thy inference. 'T is not to make me
    jealous
To say my wife is fair, feeds well, loves com-
    pany,
Is free of speech, sings, plays and dances
    well;
Where virtue is, these are more virtuous:
Nor from mine own weak merits will I draw
The smallest fear or doubt of her revolt;
For she had eyes, and chose me. No, Iago;
I 'll see before I doubt; when I doubt, prove;
And on the proof, there is no more but this,
Away at once with love or jealousy!   192
  Iago. I am glad of it; for now I shall have
    reason
To show the love and duty that I bear you
With franker spirit: therefore, as I am
    bound,
Receive it from me. I speak not yet of proof.
Look to your wife; observe her well with
    Cassio;
Wear you eye thus, not jealous nor secure:
I would not have your free and noble nature,
Out of self-bounty, be abused; look to 't:

I know our country disposition well;   201
In Venice they do let heaven see the pranks
They dare not show their husbands; their
    best conscience
Is not to leave 't undone, but keep 't un-
    known.
  Oth. Dost thou say so?
  Iago.   She did deceive her father, marry-
    ing you;
And when she seem'd to shake and fear your
    looks,
She loved them most.
  Oth.   And so she did.
  Iago.   Why, go to, then;
She that, so young, could give out such a
    seeming,
To seel her father's eyes up close as oak—
He thought 't was witchcraft—but I am
    much to blame;   211
I humbly do beseech you of your pardon
For too much loving you.
  Oth.   I am bound to thee for ever.
  Iago. I see this hath a little dash'd your
    spirits.
  Oth. Not a jot, not a jot.
  Iago.   I' faith, I fear it has.
I hope you will consider what is spoke
Comes from my love. But I do see you 're
    moved:
I am to pray you not to strain my speech
To grosser issues nor to larger reach
Than to suspicion.   220
  Oth. I will not.
  Iago.   Should you do so, my lord,
My speech should fall into such vile success
As my thoughts aim not at. Cassio 's my
    worthy friend—
My lord, I see you 're moved.
  Oth.   No, not much moved:
I do not think but Desdemona's honest.
  Iago. Long live she so! and long live you
    to think so!
  Oth. And yet, how nature erring from
    itself,—
  Iago. Ay, there 's the point: as—to be
    bold with you—
Not to affect many proposed matches   229
Of her own clime, complexion, and degree,

---

173 *fineless,* boundless. 182 *exsufflicate and blown,*
exaggerated.
187 *revolt,* misconduct.

210 *seel,* close. 229 *affect,* favor.

Whereto we see in all things nature tends—
Foh! one may smell in such a will most rank,
Foul disproportion, thoughts unnatural.
But pardon me; I do not in position
Distinctly speak of her; though I may fear
Her will, recoiling to her better judgment,
May fall to match you with her country
 forms
And happily repent.
  Oth.   Farewell, farewell:
If more thou dost perceive, let me know
 more;   239
Set on thy wife to observe: leave me, Iago.
 Iago. [*Going*] My lord, I take my leave.
 Oth. Why did I marry? This honest crea-
 ture doubtless
Sees and knows more, much more, than he
 unfolds.
 Iago. [*Returning*] My lord, I would I
 might entreat your honour
To scan this thing no further; leave it to
 time:
Though it be fit that Cassio have his place
For, sure, he fills it up with great ability,
Yet, if you please to hold him off awhile,
You shall by that perceive him and his
 means: 249
Note, if your lady strain his entertain-
 ment
With any strong or vehement importunity;
Much will be seen in that. In the mean time,
Let me be thought too busy in my fears—
As worthy cause I have to fear I am—
And hold her free, I do beseech your honour.
 Oth. Fear not my government.
 Iago. I once more take my leave. [*Exit.*
 Oth. This fellow 's of exceeding honesty,
And knows all qualities, with a learned
 spirit,
Of human dealings. If I do prove her hag-
 gard,   260
Though that her jesses were my dear heart-
 strings,
I 'ld whistle her off and let her down the
 wind,

To prey at fortune. Haply, for I am black
And have not those soft parts of conversa-
 tion
That chamberers have, or for I am declined
Into the vale of years,—yet that 's not
 much—
She 's gone. I am abused; and my relief
Must be to loathe her. O curse of marriage,
That we can call these delicate creatures
 ours,
And not their appetites! I had rather be a
 toad,   270
And live upon the vapour of a dungeon,
Than keep a corner in the thing I love
For others' uses. Yet, 't is the plague of great
 ones;
Prerogatived are they less than the base;
'T is destiny unshunnable, like death:
Even then this forked plague is fated to us
When we do quicken. Desdemona comes:

Re-enter DESDEMONA *and* EMILIA.

If she be false, O, then heaven mocks itself!
I'll not believe 't.
 Des.   How now, my dear Othello!
Your dinner, and the generous islanders 280
By you invited, do attend your presence.
 Oth. I am to blame.
 Des.   Why do you speak so faintly?
Are you not well?
 Oth. I have a pain upon my forehead
 here.
 Des. 'Faith, that 's with watching; 't will
 away again:
Let me but bind it hard, within this hour
It will be well.
 Oth.   Your napkin is too little:
 [*He puts the handkerchief from him;
        and it drops.*
Let it alone. Come, I 'll go in with you.
 Des. I am very sorry that you are not
 well.
    [*Exeunt Othello and Desdemona.*
 Emil. I am glad I have found this nap-
 kin: 290

---

250 *strain his entertainment,* urge his reinstate-
ment. 255 *hold her free,* consider her innocent.
256 *government,* self-control. 260 *haggard,* unfaithful (a wild hawk). 261 *jesses,* leg-straps.

262–3 *I 'ld . . . fortune,* I would release her and
let her shift for herself. 263 *Haply,* perhaps. 265
chamberers, gallants. 276 *forked plague,* cuckoldry
(a cuckold is said to wear horns in his forehead).

This was her first remembrance from the
    Moor:
My wayward husband hath a hundred times
Woo'd me to steal it; but she so loves the
    token,
For he conjured her she should ever keep it,
That she reserves it evermore about her
To kiss and talk to. I 'll have the work ta'en
    out,
And give 't Iago: what he will do with it
Heaven knows, not I;
I nothing but to please his fantasy.

Re-enter IAGO.

Iago. How now! what do you here alone?
Emil. Do not you chide; I have a thing
    for you.   301
Iago. A thing for me? it is a common
    thing—
Emil. Ha!
Iago. To have a foolish wife.
Emil. O, it that all? What will you give
    me now
For that same handkerchief?
Iago.   What handkerchief?
Emil. What handkerchief!
Why, that the Moor first gave to Desdemona;
That which so often you did bid me steal.
Iago. Hast stol'n it from her?   310
Emil. No, 'faith; she let it drop by negli-
    gence,
And, to the advantage, I, being here, took 't
    up.
Look, here it is.
Iago.   A good wench; give it me.
Emil. What will you do with 't, that you
    have been so earnest
To have me filch it?
Iago. [*Snatching it*] Why, what 's that to
    you?
Emil. If 't be not for some purpose of im-
    port
Give 't me again: poor lady, she 'll run mad
When she shall lack it.
Iago. Be not acknown on 't; I have use
    for it.
Go, leave me.   [*Exit Emilia.* 320
I will in Cassio's lodging lose this napkin,

And let him find it. Trifles light as air
Are to the jealous confirmations strong
As proofs of holy writ: this may do some-
    thing.
The Moor already changes with my poison,
Dangerous conceits are in their natures poi-
    sons,
Which at the first are scarce found to dis-
    taste,
But with a little act upon the blood,
Burn like the mines of sulphur. I did say so:
Look, where he comes!

Re-enter OTHELLO.

       Not poppy, nor mandragora,   330
Nor all the drowsy syrups of the world,
Shall ever medicine thee to that sweet sleep
Which thou owedst yesterday.
Oth.   Ha! ha! false to me?
Iago. Why, how now, general! no more
    of that.
Oth. Avaunt! be gone! thou hast set me
    on the rack:
I swear 't is better to be much abused
Than but to know 't a little.
Iago.   How now, my lord!
Oth. What sense had I of her stol'n hours
    of lust?
I saw 't not, thought it not, it harm'd not me:
I slept the next night well, was free and
    merry;   340
I found not Cassio's kisses on her lips:
He that is robb'd, not wanting what is stol'n,
Let him not know 't, and he 's not robb'd
    at all.
Iago. I am sorry to hear this.
Oth. I had been happy, if the general
    camp,
Pioners and all, had tasted her sweet body,
So I had nothing known. O, now for ever
Farewell the tranquil mind! farewell content!
Farewell the plumed troop and the big wars
That make ambition virtue! O, farewell! 350
Farewell the neighing steed and the shrill
    trump,
The spirit-stirring drum, the ear-piercing fife,
The royal banner, and all quality,

---

296 *the work ta'en out,* the embroidery copied.

330 *mandragora,* a soporific drug.
346 *Pioners,* sappers and miners, soldiers of a low
type.

Pride, pomp and circumstance of glorious
war!
And, O you mortal engines whose rude
throats
The immortal Jove's dread clamours counter-
feit,
Farewell! Othello's occupation 's gone!
   Iago. Is 't possible, my lord?
   Oth. Villain, be sure thou prove my love
a whore,
Be sure of it; give me the ocular proof; 360
Or, by the worth of man's eternal soul,
Thou hadst been better have been born a dog
Than answer my waked wrath!
   Iago.   Is 't come to this?
   Oth. Make me to see 't; at the least, so
prove it,
That the probation bear no hinge nor loop
To hang a doubt on; or woe upon thy life!
   Iago. My noble lord,—
   Oth. If thou dost slander her and torture
me,
Never pray more; abandon all remorse;
On horror's head horrors accumulate; 370
Do deeds to make heaven weep, all earth
amazed;
For nothing canst thou to damnation add
Greater than that.
   Iago.   O grace! O heaven forgive me!
Are you a man? have you a soul or sense?
God be wi' you; take mine office. O wretched
fool,
That livest to make thine honesty a vice!
O monstrous world! Take note, take note, O
world
To be direct and honest is not safe.
I thank you for this profit, and from hence
I 'll love no friend, sith love breeds such of-
fence.   380
   Oth. Nay, stay: thou shouldst be honest.
   Iago. I should be wise, for honesty 's a
fool
And loses that it works for.
   Oth.   By the world,
I think my wife be honest and think she is
not;
I think that thou art just and think thou art
not.

I 'll have some proof. Her name, that was as
fresh
As Dian's visage, is now begrimed and black
As mine own face. If there be cords, or
knives,
Poison, or fire, or suffocating streams, 389
I 'll not endure it. Would I were satisfied!
   Iago. I see, sir, you are eaten up with
passion:
I do repent me that I put it to you.
You would be satisfied?
   Oth.   Would! nay, I will.
   Iago. And may: but, how? how satisfied,
my lord?
Would you, the supervisor, grossly gape
on—
Behold her topp'd?
   Oth.   Death and damnation! O!
   Iago. It were a tedious difficulty I think,
To bring them to that prospect: damn them
then,
If ever mortal eyes do see them bolster
More than their own! What then? how then?
What shall I say? Where 's satisfaction?
It is impossible you should see this,   402
Were they as prime as goats, as hot as mon-
keys,
As salt as wolves in pride, and fools as gross
As ignorance made drunk. But yet, I say,
If imputation and strong circumstances,
Which lead directly to the door of truth,
Will give you satisfaction, you may have 't.
   Oth. Give me a living reason she's dis-
loyal.
   Iago. I do not like the office: 410
But, sith I am enter'd in this cause so far,
Prick'd to 't by foolish honesty and love,
I will go on. I lay with Cassio lately;
And, being troubled with a raging tooth,
I could not sleep.
There are a kind of men so loose of soul,
That in their sleeps will mutter their affairs:
One of this kind is Cassio:
In sleep I heard him say "Sweet Desdemona,
Let us be wary, let us hide our loves";   420
And then, sir, would he gripe and wring my
hand,

---

355 *mortal engines,* deadly cannon.

399 *bolster,* lie together.
403 *prime,* lustful. 404 *salt,* wanton.

Cry "O sweet creature!" and then kiss me
    hard,
As if he pluck'd up kisses by the roots
That grew upon my lips: then laid his leg
Over my thigh, and sigh'd, and kiss'd; and
    then
Cried "Cursed fate that gave thee to the
    Moor!"
    Oth. O monstrous! monstrous!
    Iago.   Nay, this was but his dream.
    Oth. But this denoted a foregone conclu-
    sion:
'T is a shrewd doubt, though it be but a
    dream.
    Iago. And this may help to thicken other
    proofs   430
That do demonstrate thinly.
    Oth.   I'll tear her all to pieces.
    Iago. Nay, but be wise: yet we see
    nothing done;
She may be honest yet. Tell me but this,
Have you not sometimes seen a handker-
    chief
Spotted with strawberries in your wife's
    hand?
    Oth. I gave her such a one; 't was my first
    gift.
    Iago. I know not that: but such a hand-
    kerchief—
I am sure it was your wife's—did I to-day
See Cassio wipe his beard with.
    Oth.   If it be that,—
    Iago. If it be that, or any that was hers,
It speaks against her with the other proofs.
    Oth. O, that the slave had forty thousand
    lives!   442
One is too poor, too weak for my revenge.
Now do I see 't is true. Look here, Iago;
All my fond love thus do I blow to heaven.
'T is gone.
Arise, black vengeance, from thy hollow cell!
Yield up, O love, thy crown and hearted
    throne
To tyrannous hate! Swell, bosom, with thy
    fraught,
For 't is of aspics' tongues!
    Iago.   Yet be content.   450
    Oth. O, blood, blood, blood!

    Iago. Patience, I say; your mind perhaps
    may change.
    Oth. Never, Iago. Like to the Pontic sea,
Whose icy current and compulsive course
Ne'er feels retiring ebb, but keeps due on
To the Propontic and the Hellespont,
Even so my bloody thoughts, with violent
    pace,
Shall ne'er look back, ne'er ebb to humble
    love,
Till that a capable and wide revenge
Swallow them up. Now, by yond marble
    heaven,   460
[*Kneels*] In the due reverence of a sacred
    vow
I here engage my words.
    Iago.   Do not rise yet.
[*Kneels*] Witness, you ever-burning lights
    above,
You elements that clip us round about,
Witness that here Iago doth give up
The execution of his wit, hands, heart,
To wrong'd Othello's service! Let him com-
    mand,
And to obey shall be in me remorse,
What bloody business ever.   [*They rise.*
    Oth.   I greet thy love,
Not with vain thanks, but with acceptance
    bounteous,   470
And will upon the instant put thee to 't:
Within these three days let me hear thee say
That Cassio 's not alive.
    Iago. My friend is dead; 't is done at your
    request:
But let her live.
    Oth.   Damn her, lewd minx! O,
    damn her!
Come, go with me apart; I will withdraw,
To furnish me with some swift means of
    death
For the fair devil. Now art thou my lieuten-
    ant.   479
    Iago. I am your own for ever.   [*Exeunt.*
    SCENE IV. *Before the castle.*
    Enter DESDEMONA, EMILIA, *and* Clown.
    Des. Do you know, sirrah, where Lieuten-
ant Cassio lies?

---

449 *fraught,* freight, burden. 450 *aspics',* asps'.

459 *capable and wide,* sufficient. 464 *clip,* embrace, 468 *remorse,* pity.

Clo. I dare not say he lies any where.

Des. Why, man?

Clo. He is a soldier, and for one to say a soldier lies, is stabbing.

Des. Go to: where lodges he?

Clo. To tell you where he lodges, is to tell you where I lie.

Des. Can any thing be made of this? 10

Clo. I know not where he lodges, and for me to devise a lodging and say he lies here or he lies there, were to lie in mine own throat.

Des. Can you inquire him out, and be edified by report?

Clo. I will catechize the world for him; that is, make questions, and by them answer.

Des. Seek him, bid him come hither: tell him I have moved my lord on his behalf, and hope all will be well. 20

Clo. To do this is within the compass of man's wit; and therefore I will attempt the doing it. [*Exit.*

Des. Where should I lose that handker-chief, Emilia?

Emil. I know not, madam.

Des. Believe me, I had rather have lost my purse
Full of crusadoes: and, but my noble Moor
Is true of mind and made of no such base-ness
As jealous creatures are, it were enough
To put him to ill thinking.

Emil. Is he not jealous?

Des. Who, he? I think the sun where he was born 30
Drew all such humours from him.

Emil. Look, where he comes.

Des. I will not leave him now till Cassio
Be call'd to him.

Enter OTHELLO.

How is 't with you, my lord?

Oth. Well, my good lady. [*Aside*] O, hardness to dissemble!—
How do you, Desdemona?

Des. Well, my good lord.

Oth. Give me your hand: this hand is moist, my lady.

Des. It yet hath felt no age nor known no sorrow.

Oth. This argues fruitfulness and liberal heart:
Hot, hot, and moist: this hand of yours re-quires 39
A sequester from liberty, fasting and prayer,
Much castigation, exercise devout;
For here 's a young and sweating devil here,
That commonly rebels. 'T is a good hand,
A frank one.

Des. You may, indeed, say so;
For 't was that hand that gave away my heart.

Oth. A liberal hand: the hearts of old gave hands;
But our new heraldry is hands, not hearts.

Des. I cannot speak of this. Come now, your promise.

Oth. What promise, chuck?

Des. I have sent to bid Cassio come speak with you. 50

Oth. I have a salt and sorry rheum of-fends me;
Lend me thy handkerchief.

Des. Here, my lord.

Oth. That which I gave you.

Des. I have it not about me.

Oth. Not?

Des. No, indeed, my lord.

Oth. That is a fault. That handkerchief
Did an Egyptian to my mother give;
She was a charmer, and could almost read
The thoughts of people: she told her, while she kept it,
'T would make her amiable and subdue my father
Entirely to her love, but if she lost it 60
Or made a gift of it, my father's eye
Should hold her loathed and his spirits should hunt
After new fancies: she, dying, gave it me;
And bid me, when my fate would have me wive,
To give it her. I did so: and take heed on 't;

---

14 *edified,* instructed. 26 *crusadoes,* Portuguese gold coins. 31 *humours,* notions.

40 *sequester,* separation. 46–7 *the . . . hearts,* unlike the past, we now join hands but not hearts in marriage. 51 *salt and sorry rheum,* wretched cold.

Make it a darling like your precious eye;
To lose 't or give 't away were such perdition
As nothing else could match.

Des.   Is 't possible?

Oth. 'T is true: there 's magic in the web
   of it:
A sibyl, that had number'd in the world   70
The sun to course two hundred compasses,
In her prophetic fury sew'd the work;
The worms were hallow'd that did breed the
   silk;
And it was dyed in mummy which the skil-
   ful
Conserved of maidens' hearts.

Des.   Indeed! is 't true?

Oth. Most veritable; therefore look to 't
   well.

Des. Then would to God that I had never
   seen 't!

Oth. Ha! wherefore?

Des. Why do you speak so startingly and
   rash?

Oth. Is 't lost? is 't gone? speak, is it out
   o' the way?   80

Des. Heaven bless us!

Oth. Say you?

Des. It is not lost; but what an if it were?

Oth. How!

Des. I say, it is not lost.

Oth.   Fetch 't, let me see 't.

Des. Why, so I can, sir, but I will not
   now.
This is a trick to put me from my suit:
Pray you let Cassio be received again.

Oth. Fetch me the handkerchief: my
   mind misgives.

Des. Come, come;   90
You 'll never meet a more sufficient man.

Oth. The handkerchief!

Des.   I pray, talk me of Cassio.

Oth. The handkerchief!

Des.   A man that all his time
Hath founded his good fortunes on your
   love,
Shared dangers with you,—

Oth. The handkerchief!

Des. In sooth, you are to blame.

Oth. Away!   [*Exit.*

Emil. Is not this man jealous?

Des. I ne'er saw this before.   100

Sure, there's some wonder in this handkerchief:
I am most unhappy in the loss of it.

Emil. 'T is not a year or two shows us a
   man:
They are all but stomachs, and we all but
   food;
They eat us hungerly, and when they are full,
They belch us. Look you, Cassio and my
   husband!

Enter CASSIO *and* IAGO.

Iago. There is no other way; 't is she
   must do 't:
And, lo, the happiness! go, and importune
   her.

Des. How now, good Cassio! what 's the
   news with you?

Cas. Madam, my former suit: I do be-
   seech you   110
That by your virtuous means I may again
Exist, and be a member of his love
Whom I with all the office of my heart
Entirely honour: I would not be delay'd.
If my offence be of such mortal kind
That nor my service past, nor present sor-
   rows,
Nor purposed merit in futurity,
Can ransom me into his love again,
But to know so must be my benefit;   119
So shall I clothe me in a forced content,
And shut myself up in some other course,
To fortune's alms.

Des.   Alas, thrice-gentle Cassio!
My advocation is not now in tune;
My lord is not my lord; nor should I know
   him
Were he in favour as in humour alter'd.
So help me every spirit sanctified,
As I have spoken for you all my best
And stood within the blank of his displeas-
   ure
For my free speech! you must awhile be pa-
   tient:
What I can do I will; and more I will   130
Than for myself I dare: let that suffice you.

Iago. Is my lord angry?

---

125 *favour,* features. *humour,* mood. 128 *blank,*
center of the target.

Emil.   He went hence but now,
And certainly in strange unquietness.
  Iago. Can he be angry? I have seen the
      cannon,
When it hath blown his ranks into the air,
And, like the devil, from his very arm
Puff'd his own brother:—and can he be an-
      gry?
Something of moment then: I will go meet
      him:
There's matter in 't indeed, if he be angry.
  Des. I prithee, do so.   [*Exit Iago.*
                    Something, sure, of state,
Either from Venice or some unhatch'd prac-
      tice   141
Made demonstrable here in Cyprus to him,
Hath puddled his clear spirit; and in such
      cases
Men's natures wrangle with inferior things,
Though great ones are their object. 'T is even
      so;
For let our finger ache, and it indues
Our other healthful members even to that
      sense
Of pain: nay, we must think men are not
      gods,
Nor of them look for such observances
As fit the bridal. Beshrew me much, Emilia,
I was, unhandsome warrior as I am,   151
Arraigning his unkindness with my soul;
But now I find I had suborn'd the witness,
And he's indicted falsely.
  Emil. Pray heaven it be state-matters, as
      you think,
And no conception nor no jealous toy
Concerning you.
  Des. Alas the day, I never gave him
      cause!
  Emil. But jealous souls will not be an-
      swer'd so;
They are not ever jealous for the cause,   160
But jealous for they are jealous: 't is a mon-
      ster
Begot upon itself, born on itself.
  Des. Heaven keep that monster from
      Othello's mind!
  Emil. Lady, amen.

  Des. I will go seek him. Cassio, walk
      hereabout:
If I do find him fit, I 'll move your suit,
And seek to effect it to my uttermost.
  Cas. I humbly thank your ladyship.
            [*Exeunt Desdemona and Emilia.*

                Enter BIANCA.

  Bian. Save you, friend Cassio!
  Cas.   What make you from home?
How is it with you, my most fair Bianca?
I' faith, sweet love, I was coming to your
      house.   171
  Bian. And I was going to your lodging,
      Cassio.
What, keep a week away? seven days and
      nights?
Eight score eight hours? and lovers' absent
      hours,
More tedious than the dial eight score times?
O weary reckoning!
  Cas.   Pardon me, Bianca:
I have this while with leaden thoughts been
      press'd;
But I shall, in a more continuate time,
Strike off this score of absence. Sweet Bianca,
      [*Giving her Desdemona's handkerchief.*
Take me this work out.   180
  Bian.   O Cassio, whence came this?
This is some token from a newer friend:
To the felt absence now I feel a cause:
      now
Is 't come to this? Well, well.
  Cas.   Go to, woman!
Throw your vile guesses in the devil's teeth,
From whence you have them. You are jeal-
      ous
That this is from some mistress, some re-
      membrance:
No, in good troth, Bianca.
  Bian.   Why, whose is it?
  Cas. I know not, sweet: I found it in my
      chamber.
I like the work well: ere it be demanded—
As like enough it will—I 'ld have it copied:
Take it, and do 't; and leave me for this time.

---

141 *unhatch'd practice,* unmatured plot. 153 *suborn'd,* induced to swear falsely.

178 *more continuate,* less interrupted. 179 *strike
off this score,* erase this tally. 180 *Take . . . out,*
copy this embroidery for me.

Bian. Leave you! wherefore?   192

Cas. I do attend here on the general;
And think it no addition, nor my wish,
To have him see me woman'd.

Bian.   Why, I pray you?

Cas. Not that I love you not.

Bian.   But that you do not love me.
I pray you, bring me on the way a little,
And say if I shall see you soon at night.

Cas. 'Tis but a little way that I can bring
          you;
For I attend here: but I 'll see you soon.

Bian. 'T is very good; I must be circum-
          stanced.   201

                              [*Exeunt.*

ACT IV

SCENE I. *Cyprus. Before the castle.*

Enter OTHELLO *and* IAGO.

Iago. Will you think so?

Oth.   Think so, Iago!

Iago.   What,
To kiss in private?

Oth.   An unauthorized kiss,

Iago. Or to be naked with her friend in
          bed
An hour or more, not meaning any harm?

Oth. Naked in bed, Iago, and not mean
          harm!
It is hypocrisy against the devil:
They that mean virtuously, and yet do so,
The devil their virtue tempts, and they tempt
          heaven.

Iago. So they do nothing, 't is a venial
          slip;
But if I give my wife a handkerchief,—   10

Oth. What then?

Iago. Why, then, 't is hers, my lord; and,
          being hers,
She may, I think, bestow 't on any man.

Oth. She is protectress of her honour too:
May she give that?

Iago. Her honour is an essence that 's
          not seen;
They have it very oft that have it not:
But, for the handkerchief,—

Oth. By heaven, I would most gladly
          have forgot it.   19
Thou said'st—O, it comes o'er my memory
As doth the raven o'er the infected house,
Boding to all—he had my handkerchief.

Iago. Ay, what of that?

Oth.   That 's not so good now.

Iago.   What,
If I had said I had seen him do you wrong?
Or heard him say,—as knaves be such abroad,
Who having, by their own importunate suit,
Or voluntary dotage of some mistress,
Convinced or supplied them, cannot choose
But they must blab—

Oth.   Hath he said any thing?

Iago. He hath, my lord; but be you well
          assured,   30
No more than he 'll unswear.

Oth.   What hath he said?

Iago. 'Faith, that he did—I know not
          what he did.

Oth. What? what?

Iago. Lie—

Oth.   With her?

Iago.   With her, on her; what you will.

Oth. Lie with her! lie on her! We say lie
on her, when they belie her. Lie with her!
that 's fulsome.—Handkerchief—confessions
—handkerchief!—To confess, and be hanged
for his labour;—first to be hanged, and then
to confess.—I tremble at it. Nature would
not invest herself in such shadowing passion
without some instruction. It is not words
that shake me thus. Pish! Noses, ears, and
lips.—Is 't possible?—Confess—handkerchief!—O devil!

                              [*Falls in a trance.*

Iago. Work on,
My medicine, work! Thus credulous fools
          are caught;
And many worthy and chaste dames even
          thus,
All guiltless, meet reproach. What, ho! my
          lord!
My lord, I say! Othello!

                    Enter CASSIO.

                    How now, Cassio!

---

194 *addition,* credit. 201 *be circumstanced,* yield
to necessity.

22 *Boding,* ominous.
36 *fulsome,* disgusting.

Cas. What 's the matter?   50
Iago. My lord is fall'n into an epilepsy:
This is his second fit; he had one yesterday.
Cas. Rub him about the temples.
Iago.   No, forbear;
The lethargy must have his quiet course:
If not, he foams at mouth and by and by
Breaks out to savage madness. Look, he stirs:
Do you withdraw yourself a little while,
He will recover straight: when he is gone,
I would on great occasion speak with you.
                              [*Exit Cassio.*
How is it, general? have you not hurt your
        head?   60
Oth. Dost thou mock me?
Iago.   I mock you! no, by heaven.
Would you would bear your fortune like a
        man!
Oth. A horned man 's a monster and a
        beast.
Iago. There 's many a beast then in a
        populous city,
And many a civil monster.
Oth. Did he confess it?
Iago.   Good sir, be a man;
Think every bearded fellow that 's but yoked
May draw with you: there's millions now
        alive
That nightly lie in those unproper beds
Which they dare swear peculiar: your case
        is better.   70
O, 't is the spite of hell, the fiend's arch-
        mock,
To lip a wanton in a secure couch,
And to suppose her chaste! No, let me know;
And knowing what I am, I know what she
        shall be.
Oth. O, thou art wise; 't is certain.
Iago.   Stand you awhile apart;
Confine yourself but in a patient list.
Whilst you were here o'erwhelmed with your
        grief—
A passion most unsuiting such a man—
Cassio came hither: I shifted him away,
And laid good 'scuse upon your ecstasy,   80

Bade him anon return and here speak with
        me;
The which he promised. Do but encave your-
        self,
And mark the fleers, the gibes, and notable
        scorns,
That dwell in every region of his face;
For I will make him tell the tale anew,
Where, how, how oft, how long ago, and
        when
He hath, and is again to cope your wife:
I say, but mark his gesture. Marry, patience;
Or I shall say you are all in all in spleen,
And nothing of a man.
Oth.   Dost thou hear, Iago?
I will be found most cunning in my patience;
But—dost thou hear?—most bloody.   92
Iago.   That 's not amiss;
But yet keep time in all. Will you withdraw?
                              [*Othello retires.*
Now will I question Cassio of Bianca,
A housewife that by selling her desires
Buys herself bread and clothes: it is a crea-
        ture
That dotes on Cassio; as 't is the strumpet's
        plague
To beguile many and be beguiled by one:
He, when he hears of her, cannot refrain   99
From the excess of laughter. Here he comes:

Re-enter CASSIO.

As he shall smile, Othello shall go mad;
And his unbookish jealousy must construe
Poor Cassio's smiles, gestures and light be-
        haviour,
Quite in the wrong. How do you now, lieu-
        tenant?
Cas. The worser that you give me the ad-
        dition
Whose want even kills me.
Iago. Ply Desdemona well, and you are
        sure on 't.
[*Speaking lower*] Now, if this suit lay in
        Bianca's power,
How quickly should you speed!
Cas.   Alas, poor caitiff!

---

68 *draw with you,* share your fate. 69 *unproper,*
not their own. 70 *peculiar,* their own. 76 *a patient list,* within bounds. 80 *ecstasy,* trance.

86 *cope,* meet illicitly. 93 *keep time,* act prudently.
102 *unbookish,* ignorant. 105 *addition,* title.
109 *caitiff,* wretch.

Oth. Look, how he laughs already!   110
Iago. I never knew woman love man so.
Cas. Alas, poor rogue! I think, i' faith, she loves me.
Oth. Now he denies it faintly, and laughs it out.
Iago. Do you hear, Cassio?
Oth.   Now he importunes him
To tell it o'er: go to; well said, well said.
Iago. She gives it out that you shall marry her:
Do you intend it?
Cas. Ha, ha, ha!   120
Oth. Do you triumph, Roman? do you triumph?
Cas. I marry her! what? a customer! Prithee, bear some charity to my wit; do not think it so unwholesome. Ha, ha, ha!
Oth. So, so, so, so: they laugh that win.
Iago. 'Faith the cry goes that you shall marry her.
Cas. Prithee, say true.
Iago. I am a very villain else.
Oth. Have you scored me? Well.   130
Cas. This is the monkey's own giving out: she is persuaded I will marry her, out of her own love and flattery, not out of my promise.
Oth. Iago beckons me; now he begins the story.
Cas. She was here even now; she haunts me in every place. I was the other day talking on the sea-bank with certain Venetians; and thither comes the bauble, and, by this hand, she falls me thus about my neck—   140
Oth. Crying "O dear Cassio!" as it were: his gesture imports it.
Cas. So hangs, and lolls, and weeps upon me; so hales, and pulls me: ha, ha, ha!
Oth. Now he tells how she plucked him to my chamber. O, I see that nose of yours, but not that dog I shall throw it to.
Cas. Well, I must leave her company.
Iago. Before me! look, where she comes.
Cas. 'T is such another fitchew! marry, a perfumed one.   151

Enter BIANCA.

What do you mean by this haunting of me?
Bian. Let the devil and his dam haunt you! What did you mean by that same hand-kerchief you gave me even now? I was a fine fool to take it. I must take out the work?—A likely piece of work, that you should find it in your chamber, and not know who left it there! This is some minx's token, and I must take out the work? There; give it your hobby-horse: wheresoever you had it, I 'll take out no work on 't.   161
Cas. How now, my sweet Bianca! how now! how now!
Oth. By heaven, that should be my hand-kerchief!
Bian. An you 'll come to supper to-night, you may; an you will not, come when you are next prepared for.   [*Exit.*
Iago. After her, after her.   170
Cas. 'Faith, I must; she 'll rail in the street else.
Iago. Will you sup there?
Cas. 'Faith, I intend so.
Iago. Well, I may chance to see you: for I would very fain speak with you.
Cas. Prithee, come; will you?
Iago. Go to; say no more.   [*Exit Cassio.*
Oth. [*Advancing*] How shall I murder him, Iago?   180
Iago. Did you perceive how he laughed at his vice?
Oth. O Iago!
Iago. And did you see the handkerchief?
Oth. Was that mine?
Iago. Yours, by this hand: and to see how he prizes the foolish woman your wife! she gave it him, and he hath given it his whore.
Oth. I would have him nine years a-kill-ing. A fine woman! a fair woman! a sweet woman!
Iago. Nay, you must forget that.   190
Oth. Ay, let her rot, and perish, and be damned to-night; for she shall not live: no, my heart is turned to stone; I strike it, and it hurts my hand. O, the world hath not a sweeter creature: she might lie by an em-peror's side and command him tasks.

---

122 *customer,* prostitute. 151 *such another fitchew,* such a polecat.

160 *hobby-horse,* harlot.

Iago. Nay, that 's not your way.

Oth. Hang her! I do but say what she is: so delicate with her needle: an admirable musician: O! she will sing the savageness out of a bear: of so high and plenteous wit and invention:— 201

Iago. She 's the worse for all this.

Oth. O, a thousand thousand times: and then, of so gentle a condition!

Iago. Ay, too gentle.

Oth. Nay, that 's certain: but yet the pity of it, Iago! O Iago, the pity of it, Iago!

Iago. If you are so fond over her iniquity, give her patent to offend; for, if it touch not you, it comes near nobody. 210

Oth. I will chop her into messes: cuckold me!

Iago. O, 't is foul in her.

Oth. With mine officer!

Iago. That 's fouler.

Oth. Get me some poison, Iago; this night: I 'll not expostulate with her, lest her body and beauty unprovide my mind again: this night, Iago. 219

Iago. Do it not with poison, strangle her in her bed, even the bed she hath contaminated.

Oth. Good, good: the justice of it pleases: very good.

Iago. And for Cassio, let me be his undertaker: you shall hear more by midnight.

Oth. Excellent good. [*A trumpet within.*] What trumpet is that same?

Iago. Something from Venice, sure. 'T is Lodovico
Come from the duke: and, see, your wife is with him.

Enter LODOVICO, DESDEMONA, *and* Attendants.

Lod. Save you, worthy general!

Oth. With all my heart, sir.

Lod. The duke and senators of Venice greet you. [*Gives him a letter.*

Oth. I kiss the instrument of their pleasures. [*Opens the letter, and reads.*

Des. And what's the news, good cousin Lodovico? 231

Iago. I am very glad to see you, signior; Welcome to Cyprus.

Lod. I thank you. How does Lieutenant Cassio?

Iago. Lives, sir.

Des. Cousin, there 's fall'n between him and my lord
An unkind breach: but you shall make all well.

Oth. Are you sure of that?

Des. My lord?

Oth. [*Reads*] "This fail you not to do, as you will—" 240

Lod. He did not call; he 's busy in the paper.
Is there division 'twixt my lord and Cassio?

Des. A most unhappy one: I would do much
To atone them, for the love I bear to Cassio.

Oth. Fire and brimstone!

Des. My lord?

Oth. Are you wise?

Des. What, is he angry?

Lod. May be the letter moved him;
For, as I think, they do command him home,
Deputing Cassio in his government.

Des. Trust me, I am glad on 't.

Oth. Indeed!

Des. My lord?

Oth. I am glad to see you mad.

Des. Why, sweet Othello,—

Oth. [*Striking her*] Devil! 251

Des. I have not deserved this.

Lod. My lord, this would not be believed in Venice,
Though I should swear I saw 't: 't is very much:
Make her amends; she weeps.

Oth. O devil, devil!
If that the earth could teem with woman's tears,
Each drop she falls would prove a crocodile.
Out of my sight!

Des. I will not stay to offend you.
[*Going.*

Lod. Truly, an obedient lady: 259
I do beseech your lordship, call her back.

Oth. Mistress!

---

222 *let . . . undertaker*, leave him to me.

257 *crocodile*, hypocrite.

Des. My lord?

Oth. What would you with her, sir?

Lod. Who, I, my lord?

Oth. Ay; you did wish that I would make her turn:

Sir, she can turn, and turn, and yet go on,

And turn again; and she can weep, sir, weep;

And she 's obedient, as you say, obedient,

Very obedient. Proceed you in your tears,

Concerning this, sir,—O well-painted passion!—

I am commanded home. Get you away;

I 'll send for you anon. Sir, I obey the mandate,   270

And will return to Venice. Hence, avaunt!
                              [*Exit Desdemona.*

Cassio shall have my place. And, sir, to-night,

I do entreat that we may sup together:

You are welcome, sir, to Cyprus.—Goats and monkeys!   [*Exit.*

Lod. Is this the noble Moor whom our full senate

Call all in all sufficient? Is this the nature

Whom passion could not shake? whose solid virtue

The shot of accident, nor dart of chance,

Could neither graze nor pierce?

Iago.   He is much changed.

Lod. Are his wits safe? is he not light of brain?   280

Iago. He 's that he is: I may not breathe my censure

What he might be: if what he might he is not,

I would to heaven he were!

Lod.   What, strike his wife!

Iago. 'Faith, that was not so well; yet would I knew

That stroke would prove the worst!

Lod.   Is it his use?

Or did the letters work upon his blood,

And new-create his fault?

Iago.   Alas, alas!

It is not honesty in me to speak

What I have seen and known. You shall observe him,

And his own courses will denote him so

That I may save my speech: do but go after,

---

285 *use,* custom.

And mark how he continues.

Lod. I am sorry that I am deceived in him.   [*Exeunt.*

SCENE II. *A room in the castle.*

Enter OTHELLO *and* EMILIA.

Oth. You have seen nothing then?

Emil. Nor ever heard, nor ever did suspect.

Oth. Yes, you have seen Cassio and she together.

Emil. But then I saw no harm, and then I heard

Each syllable that breath made up between them.

Oth. What, did they never whisper?

Emil.   Never, my lord.

Oth. Nor send you out o' the way?

Emil. Never.

Oth. To fetch her fan, her gloves, her mask, nor nothing?

Emil. Never, my lord.   10

Oth. That 's strange.

Emil. I durst, my lord, to wager she is honest,

Lay down my soul at stake: if you think other,

Remove your thought; it doth abuse your bosom.

If any wretch have put this in your head,

Let heaven requite it with the serpent's curse!

For, if she be not honest, chaste, and true,

There 's no man happy; the purest of their wives

Is foul as slander.

Oth.   Bid her come hither: go.
                              [*Exit Emilia.*

She says enough; yet she 's a simple bawd

That cannot say as much. This is a subtle whore,   21

A closet lock and key of villanous secrets:

And yet she 'll kneel and pray; I have seen her do 't.

Enter DESDEMONA *with* EMILIA.

Des. My lord, what is your will?

Oth.   Pray, chuck, come hither.

Des. What is your pleasure?

Oth.   Let me see your eyes;

Look in my face.

 Des.   What horrible fancy 's this?

 Oth. [*To Emilia*] Some of your function, mistress;

Leave procreants alone and shut the door;

Cough, or cry "hem," if any body come:

Your mystery, your mystery: nay, dispatch.

          [*Exit Emilia.*

 Des. Upon my knees, what doth your speech import?   31

I understand a fury in your words,

But not the words.

 Oth. Why, what art thou?

 Des.   Your wife, my lord; your true

And loyal wife.

 Oth.   Come, swear it, damn thyself;

Lest, being like one of heaven, the devils themselves

Should fear to seize thee: therefore be double damn'd;

Swear thou art honest.

 Des.   Heaven doth truly know it.

 Oth. Heaven truly knows that thou art false as hell.

 Des. To whom, my lord? with whom? how am I false?   40

 Oth. O Desdemona! Away! away! away!

 Des. Alas the heavy day! Why do you weep?

Am I the motive of these tears, my lord?

If haply you my father do suspect

An instrument of this your calling back,

Lay not your blame on me: if you have lost him,

Why, I have lost him too.

 Oth.   Had it pleased heaven

To try me with affliction; had they rain'd

All kinds of sores and shames on my bare head,

Steep'd me in poverty to the very lips, 50

Given to captivity me and my utmost hopes,

I should have found in some place of my soul

A drop of patience: but, alas, to make me

A fixed figure for the time of scorn

To point his slow unmoving finger at!

Yet could I bear that too; well, very well:

But there, where I have garner'd up my heart,

Where either I must live, or bear no life;

The fountain from the which my current runs,

Or else dries up; to be discarded thence! 60

Or keep it as a cistern for foul toads

To knot and gender in! Turn thy complexion there,

Patience, thou young and rose-lipp'd cherubin,—

Ay, there, look grim as hell!

 Des. I hope my noble lord esteems me honest.

 Oth. O, ay; as summer flies are in the shambles,

That quicken even with blowing. O thou weed,

Who art so lovely fair and smell'st so sweet

That the sense aches at thee, would thou hadst ne'er been born!

 Des. Alas, what ignorant sin have I committed?

 Oth. Was this fair paper, this most goodly book,

Made to write "whore" upon? What committed!   70

Committed! O thou public commoner!

I should make very forges of my cheeks,

That would to cinders burn up modesty,

Did I but speak they deeds. What committed!

Heaven stops the nose at it and the moon winks,

The bawdy wind that kisses all it meets

Is hush'd within the hollow mine of earth,

And will not hear it. What committed! 80

Impudent strumpet!

 Des.   By heaven, you do me wrong.

 Oth. Are you not a strumpet?

 Des.   No, as I am a Christian:

If to preserve this vessel for my lord

From any other foul unlawful touch

Be not to be a strumpet, I am none.

 Oth. What, not a whore?

 Des.   No, as I shall be saved.

 Oth. Is 't possible?

 Des. O, heaven forgive us!

---

30 *mystery,* trade, business.

61 *cistern,* cesspool. 62 *Turn . . . there,* blush at that. 66 *shambles,* slaughterhouse. 71 *commoner,* prostitute.

Oth.   I cry you mercy, then:
I took you for that cunning whore of Venice
That married with Othello.

                                    [*Raising his voice.*
         You mistress,   90
That have the office opposite to Saint Peter,
And keep the gate of hell!

                    Re-enter EMILIA.

                         You, you, ay, you!
We have done our course; there 's money
         for your pains:
I pray you, turn the key and keep our coun-
         sel.   [*Exit.*
    Emil. Alas, what does this gentleman
         conceive?
How do you, madam? how do you, my good
         lady?
    Des. 'Faith, half asleep.
    Emil. Good madam, what 's the matter
         with my lord?
    Des. With who?
    Emil. Why, with my lord, madam.   100
    Des. Who is thy lord?
    Emil.   He that is yours, sweet lady.
    Des. I have none: do not talk to me,
         Emilia;
I cannot weep; nor answer have I none,
But what should go by water. Prithee, to-
         night
Lay on my bed my wedding sheets: remem-
         ber;
And call thy husband hither.
    Emil. Here 's a change indeed!   [*Exit.*
    Des. 'T is meet I should be used so, very
         meet.
How have I been behaved, that he might
         stick
The small'st opinion on my least misuse?

              Re-enter EMILIA *with* IAGO.

    Iago. What is your pleasure, madam?
         How is 't with you!   110
    Des. I cannot tell. Those that do teach
         young babes
Do it with gentle means and easy tasks:

He might have chid me so; for, in good
         faith,
I am a child to chiding.
    Iago.   What 's the matter lady?
    Emil. Alas, Iago, my lord hath so be-
         whored her,
Thrown such despite and heavy terms upon
         her,
As true hearts cannot bear.
    Des. Am I that name, Iago?
    Iago.   What name, fair lady?
    Des. Such as she says my lord did say I
         was.
    Emil. He call'd her whore: a beggar in
         his drink   120
Could not have laid such terms upon his
         callet.
    Iago. Why did he so?
    Des. I do not know; I am sure I am none
         such.
    Iago. Do not weep, do not weep. Alas the
         day!
    Emil. Hath she forsook so many noble
         matches,
Her father and her country and her friends,
To be call'd whore? would it not make one
         weep?
    Des. It is my wretched fortune.
    Iago.   Beshrew him for 't!
How comes this trick upon him?
    Des.   Nay, heaven doth know.
    Emil. I will be hang'd, if some eternal
         villain,   130
Some busy and insinuating rogue,
Some cogging, cozening slave, to get some
         office,
Have not devised this slander; I 'll be hang'd
         else.
    Iago. Fie, there is no such man; it is im-
         possible.
    Des. If any such there be, heaven pardon
         him!
    Emil. A halter pardon him! and hell
         gnaw his bones!
Why should he call her whore? who keeps
         her company?
What place? what time? what form? what
         likelihood?

---

104 *go by water,* be expressed in tears. 108–9 *that
. . . . misuse,* that he might consider me guilty of
the slightest fault.

121 *callet,* prostitute. 129 *trick,* delusion. 132 *cogging,* tricking. *cozening,* cheating.

The Moor abused by some most villanous
    knave,
Some base notorious knave, some scurvy
    fellow.   140
O heaven, that such companions thou'ldst
    unfold,
And put in every honest hand a whip
To lash the rascals naked through the world
Even from the east to the west!
   Iago.   Speak within door.
   Emil. O, fie upon them! Some such squire
    he was
That turn'd your wit the seamy side without,
And made you to suspect me with the Moor.
   Iago. You are a fool; go to.
   Des.   O good Iago,
What shall I do to win my lord again?
Good friend, go to him; for, by this light
    of heaven,   150
I know not how I lost him. Here I kneel:
If e'er my will did trespass 'gainst his love,
Either in discourse of thought or actual deed,
Or that mine eyes, mine ears, or any sense,
Delighted them in any other form;
Or that I do not yet, and ever did,
And ever will—though he do shake me off
To beggarly divorcement—love him dearly,
Comfort forswear me! Unkindness may do
    much;
And his unkindness may defeat my life,
But never taint my love. I cannot say
    "whore":   161
It doth abhor me now I speak the word;
To do the act that might the addition earn
Not the world's mass of vanity could make
    me.
   Iago. I pray you, be content; 't is but his
    humour:
The business of the state does him offence,
And he does chide with you.
   Des. If 't were not other,—
   Iago.   'T is but so, I warrant.
                          [*Trumpets within.*
Hark, how those instruments summon to
    supper!   169

The messengers of Venice stay the meat:
Go in, and weep not; all things shall be well.
           [*Exeunt Desdemona and Emilia.*

         Enter RODERIGO.
How now, Roderigo!
   Rod. I do not find that thou dealest justly
    with me.
   Iago. What in the contrary?
   Rod. Every day thou daffest me with
some device, Iago; and rather, as it seems to
me now, keepest from me all conveniency
than suppliest me with the least advantage of
hope. I will indeed no longer endure it, nor
am I yet persuaded to put up in peace what
already I have foolishly suffered.   182
   Iago. Will you hear me, Roderigo?
   Rod. 'Faith, I have heard too much, for
your words and performances are no kin
together.
   Iago. You charge me most unjustly.
   Rod. With nought but truth. I have
wasted myself out of my means. The jewels
you have had from me to deliver to Desdemona would half have corrupted a votarist:
you have told me she hath received them and
returned me expectations and comforts of
sudden respect and acquaintance, but I find
none.   193
   Iago. Well; go to; very well.
   Rod. Very well! go to! I cannot go to,
man; nor 't is not very well: nay, I think it
is scurvy, and begin to find myself fopped
in it.
   Iago. Very well.
   Rod. I tell you 't is not very well. I will
make myself known to Desdemona: if she
will return me my jewels, I will give over
my suit and repent my unlawful solicitation;
if not, assure yourself I will seek satisfaction
of you.   203
   Iago. You have said now.
   Rod. Ay, and said nothing but what I
protest intendment of doing.   209
   Iago. Why, now I see there 's mettle in
thee, and even from this instant do build on
thee a better opinion than ever before. Give

---

141 *companions,* knaves. *unfold,* reveal. 144 *within
door,* quietly. 145 *squire,* fellow. 159 *Comfort forswear me,* may happiness abandon me. 163 *addition,* title. 165 *humour,* whim.

---

191 *votarist,* a person who has sworn a religious
vow; *e.g.,* a nun. 197 *fopped,* made a fool of.

me thy hand, Roderigo: thou hast taken against me a most just exception; but yet, I protest, I have dealt most directly in thy affair.

Rod. It hath not appeared. 212

Iago. I grant indeed it hath not appeared, and your suspicion is not without wit and judgement. But, Roderigo, if thou hast that in thee indeed, which I have greater reason to believe now than ever, I mean purpose, courage and valour, this night show it: if thou the next night following enjoy not Desdemona, take me from this world with treachery and devise engines for my life.

Rod. Well, what is it? is it within reason and compass? 223

Iago. Sir, there is especial commission come from Venice to depute Cassio in Othello's place.

Rod. Is that true? why, then Othello and Desdemona return again to Venice.

Iago. O, no; he goes into Mauritania and takes away with him the fair Desdemona, unless his abode be lingered here by some accident: wherein none can be so determinate as the removing of Cassio. 233

Rod. How do you mean, removing of him?

Iago. Why, by making him uncapable of Othello's place; knocking out his brains.

Rod. And that you would have me do?

Iago. Ay, if you dare do yourself a profit and a right. He sups to-night with a harlotry, and thither will I go to him: he knows not yet of his honourable fortune. If you will watch his going thence, which I will fashion to fall out between twelve and one, you may take him at your pleasure: I will be near to second your attempt, and he shall fall between us. Come, stand not amazed at it, but go along with me; I will show you such a necessity in his death that you shall think yourself bound to put it on him. It is now high supper-time, and the night grows to waste: about it. 250

Rod. I will hear further reason for this.

Iago. And you shall be satisfied. [*Exeunt.*

SCENE III. *Another room in the castle.*

Enter OTHELLO, LODOVICO, DESDEMONA, EMILIA, *and* Attendants.

Lod. I do beseech you, sir, trouble yourself no further.

Oth. O, pardon me; 't will do me good to walk.

Lod. Madam, good night; I humbly thank your ladyship.

Des. Your honour is most welcome.

Oth. Will you walk, sir?

O,—Desdemona,—

Des. My lord?

Oth. Get you to bed on the instant; I will be returned forthwith: dismiss your attendant there: look it be done.

Des. I will, my lord. 10

[*Exeunt Othello, Lodovico, and Attendants.*

Emil. How goes it now? he looks gentler than he did.

Des. He says he will return incontinent: He hath commanded me to go to bed, And bade me to dismiss you.

Emil. Dismiss me!

Des. It was his bidding; therefore, good Emilia,
Give me my nightly wearing, and adieu:
We must not now displease him.

Emil. I would you had never seen him!

Des. So would not I: my love doth so approve him,
That even his stubbornness, his checks, his frowns,— 20
Prithee, unpin me,—have grace and favour in them.

Emil. I have laid those sheets you bade me on the bed.

Des. All 's one. Good faith, how foolish are our minds!
If I do die before thee, prithee, shroud me
In one of those same sheets.

Emil. Come, come, you talk.

Des. My mother had a maid call'd Barbara:
She was in love, and he she loved proved mad

---

222 *engines*, instruments of torture. 223 *compass*, possibility.

12 *incontinent*, immediately.
23 *All's one*, no matter.

And did forsake her: she had a song of
   "willow";
An old thing 't was, but it express'd her
   fortune,
And she died singing it: that song to-night
Will not go from my mind; I have much to
   do   31
But to go hang my head all at one side,
And sing it like poor Barbara. Prithee, dis-
   patch.
   Emil. Shall I go fetch your night-gown?
   Des.   No, unpin me here.
This Lodovico is a proper man.
   Emil. A very handsome man.
   Des. He speaks well.
   Emil. I know a lady in Venice would
have walked barefoot to Palestine for a touch
of his nether lip.   40
   Des. [*Singing*] The poor soul sat sighing
      by a sycamore tree,
Sing all a green willow.
Her hand on her bosom, her head on her
   knee,
Sing willow, willow, willow:
The fresh streams ran by her, and murmur'd
   her moans;
Sing willow, willow, willow;
Her salt tears fell from her, and soften'd
   the stones;—
Lay by these:—
[*Singing*] Sing willow, willow, willow;
Prithee, hie thee; he 'll come anon:—   50
[*Singing*] Sing all a green willow must be
   my garland.
Let nobody blame him; his scorn I ap-
   prove,—
Nay, that 's not next—Hark! who is 't that
   knocks?
   Emil. It 's the wind.
   Des. [*Singing*] I call'd my love false love;
      but what said he then?
Sing willow, willow, willow:
If I court moe women, you 'll couch with
   moe men.—
So, get thee gone; good night. Mine eyes do
   itch;
Doth that bode weeping?
   Emil.   'T is neither here nor there.
   Des. I have heard it said so. O, these men,
these men!   60

Dost thou in conscience think,—tell me,
   Emilia,—
That there be women do abuse their hus-
   bands
In such gross kind?
   Emil.   There be some such, no question.
   Des. Wouldst thou do such a deed for all
   the world?
   Emil. Why, would not you?
   Des.   No, by this heavenly light!
   Emil. Nor I neither by this heavenly
   light;
I might do 't as well i' the dark.
   Des. Wouldst thou do such a deed for
   all the world?
   Emil. The world 's a huge thing: it is a
   great price   69
For a small vice.
   Des.   In troth, I think thou wouldst not.
   Emil. In troth, I think I should; and undo
't when I had done. Marry, I would not do
such a thing for a joint-ring, nor for measures of lawn, nor for gowns, petticoats, nor
caps, nor any petty exhibition; but, for the
whole world,—why, who would not make
her husband a cuckold to make him a mon-
arch? I should venture purgatory for 't.
   Des. Beshrew me, if I would do such a
   wrong
For the whole world.   79
   Emil. Why, the wrong is but a wrong i'
the world; and having the world for your
labour, 't is a wrong in your own world, and
you might quickly make it right.
   Des. I do not think there is any such
woman.
   Emil. Yes, a dozen; and as many to the
vantage as would store the world they played
for.
But I do think it is their husbands' faults
If wives do fall: say that they slack their
   duties,
And pour our treasures into foreign laps,
Or else break out in peevish jealousies,   90
Throwing restraint upon us; or say they
   strike us,
Or scant our former having in despite;

---

74 *exhibition,* present. 92 *scant . . . despite*
spitefully deprive us of our customary allowance.

Why, we have galls, and though we have
    some grace,
Yet have we some revenge. Let husbands
    know
Their wives have sense like them: they see
    and smell
And have their palates both for sweet and
    sour,
As husbands have. What is it that they do
When they change us for others? Is it sport?
I think it is: and doth affection breed it?
I think it doth: is 't frailty that thus errs?
It is so too: and have not we affections,
Desires for sport, and frailty, as men have?
Then let them use us well: else let them
    know,   103
The ills we do, their ills instruct us so.
    Des. Good night, good night: heaven me
    such uses send,
    Not to pick bad from bad, but by bad
    mend!   [*Exeunt.*

ACT V

Scene I. *Cyprus. A street.*

Enter IAGO *and* RODERIGO.

Iago. Here, stand behind this bulk;
    straight will he come:
Wear thy good rapier bare, and put it home:
Quick, quick; fear nothing; I 'll be at thy
    elbow:
It makes us, or it mars us; think on that,
And fix most firm thy resolution.
    Rod. Be near at hand; I may miscarry
    in 't.
    Iago. Here, at thy hand: be bold, and take
    thy stand.   [*Retires.*
    Rod. I have no great devotion to the
    deed;
And yet he hath given me satisfying reasons:
'T is but a man gone. Forth, my sword: he
    dies.   10
    Iago. I have rubb'd this young quat al-
    most to the sense,
And he grows angry. Now, whether he kill
    Cassio,

Or Cassio him, or each do kill the other,
Every way makes my gain: live Roderigo,
He calls me to a restitution large
Of gold and jewels that I bobb'd from him,
As gifts to Desdemona;
It must not be: if Cassio do remain,
He hath a daily beauty in his life   19
That makes me ugly; and, besides, the Moor
May unfold me to him; there stand I in
    much peril:
No, he must die. But so: I hear him coming.

Enter CASSIO.

    Rod. I know his gait, 't is he.—Villain,
    thou diest!
        [*Makes a pass at Cassio.*
    Cas. That thrust had been mine enemy
    indeed,
But that my coat is better than thou know'st:
I will make proof of thine.
        [*Draws, and wounds Roderigo.*
    Rod.   O, I am slain!
        [*Iago from behind wounds Cassio
        in the leg, and exit.*
    Cas. I am maim'd for ever. Help, ho!
    murder! murder!   [*Falls.*

Enter OTHELLO.

    Oth. The voice of Cassio: Iago keeps his
    word.
    Rod. O, villain that I am!
    Oth.   It is even so.
    Cas. O, help, ho! light! a surgeon!   30
    Oth. 'T is he:—O brave Iago, honest and
    just,
That hast such noble sense of thy friend's
    wrong!
Thou teachest me. Minion, your dear lies
    dead,
And your unblest fate hies: strumpet, I come.
Forth of my heart those charms, thine eyes,
    are blotted;
Thy bed, lust-stain'd, shall with lust's blood
    be spotted.   [*Exit.*

Enter LODOVICO *and* GRATIANO.

    Cas. What ho! no watch? no passage?
    murder! murder!

---

93 *galls*, capacity to resent. 105 *uses*, practices.
1 *bulk*, projection, wall. 11 *quat*, pimple. *sense*,
quick.

---

16 *bobb'd*, cheated.
33 *Minion*, hussy. 37 *no passage*, no one passing.

Gra. 'T is some mischance; the cry is very direful.

Cas. O help!

Lod. Hark!   40

Rod. O wretched villain!

Lod. Two or three groan: it is a heavy night:

These may be counterfeits: let 's think 't unsafe

To come in to the cry without more help.

Rod. Nobody come? then shall I bleed to death.

Lod. Hark!

Re-enter IAGO, *with a light.*

Gra. Here 's one comes in his shirt, with light and weapons.

Iago. Who 's there? whose noise is this that cries on murder?

Lod. We do not know.

Iago.   Did not you hear a cry?

Cas. Here, here! for heaven's sake, help me!

Iago.   What 's the matter?

Gra. This is Othello's ancient, as I take it.

Lod. The same indeed; a very valiant fellow.   52

Iago. What are you here that cry so grievously?

Cas. Iago? O, I am spoil'd, undone by villains!

Give me some help.

Iago. O me, lieutenant! what villains have done this?

Cas. I think that one of them is here-about,

And cannot make away.

Iago.   O treacherous villains!

What are you there? come in, and give some help.

                         [*To Lodovico and Gratiano.*

Rod. O, help me here!   60

Cas. That 's one of them.

Iago.   O murdeous slave! O villain!

                              [*Stabs Roderigo.*

Rod. O damn'd Iago! O inhuman dog!

Iago. Kill men i' the dark!—Where be these bloody thieves?—

How silent is this town!—Ho! murder! murder!—

What may you be? are you of good or evil?

Lod. As you shall prove us, praise us.

Iago. Signior Lodovico?

Lod. He, sir.

Iago. I cry you mercy. Here 's Cassio hurt by villains!

Gra. Cassio!   70

Iago. How is 't, brother!

Cas. My leg is cut in two.

Iago.   Marry, heaven forbid!

Light, gentlemen: I'll bind it with my shirt.

Enter BIANCA.

Bian. What is the matter, ho? who is 't that cried?

Iago. Who is 't that cried!

Bian. O my dear Cassio! my sweet Cassio!

O Cassio, Cassio, Cassio!

Iago. O notable strumpet! Cassio, may you suspect

Who they should be that have thus mangled you?

Cas. No.   80

Gra. I am sorry to find you thus: I have been to seek you.

Iago. Lend me a garter. So. O, for a chair,

To bear him easily hence!

Bian. Alas, he faints! O Cassio, Cassio, Cassio!

Iago. Gentlemen all, I do suspect this trash

To be a party in this injury.

Patience awhile, good Cassio. Come, come;

Lend me a light. Know we this face or no?

Alas, my friend and my dear countryman

Roderigo! no:—yes, sure:—O heaven! Roderigo.   90

Gra. What, of Venice?

Iago. Even he, sir: did you know him?

Gra.   Know him! ay.

Iago. Signior Gratiano? I cry you gentle pardon;

These bloody accidents must excuse my manners,

That so neglected you.

Gra.   I am glad to see you.

Iago. How do you, Cassio? O, a chair, a chair!

Gra. Roderigo!

Iago. He, he, 't is he. [*A chair brought
     in.*] O, that 's well said; the chair.
Some good man bear him carefully from
     hence;
I 'll fetch the general's surgeon. [*To Bianca*]
     For you, mistress,   100
Save you your labour. He that lies slain here,
     Cassio,
Was my dear friend: what malice was be-
     tween you?

Cas. None in the world; nor do I know
     the man.

Iago. [*To Bian.*] What, look you pale?
O, bear him out o' the air.

     [*Cassio and Roderigo are borne off.*
Stay you, good gentlemen. Look you pale,
     mistress?
Do you perceive the gastness of her eye?
Nay, if you stare, we shall hear more anon.
Behold her well; I pray you, look upon her:
Do you see, gentlemen? nay, guiltiness will
     speak,
Though tongues were out of use.   110

Enter EMILIA.

Emil. 'Las, what 's the matter? what 's
     the matter, husband?

Iago. Cassio hath here been set on in the
     dark
By Roderigo and fellows that are scaped:
He 's almost slain, and Roderigo dead.

Emil. Alas, good gentleman! alas, good
     Cassio!

Iago. This is the fruit of whoring.
     Prithee, Emilia,
Go know of Cassio where he supp'd to-night.
[*To Bianca*] What, do you shake at that?

Bian. He supp'd at my house; but I
     therefore shake not.

Iago. O, did he so? I charge you, go with
     me.   120

Emil. Fie, fie upon thee, strumpet!

Bian. I am no strumpet; but of life as
     honest
As you that thus abuse me.

Emil.   As I! foh! fie upon thee!

---

106 *gastness of,* terror in.

Iago. Kind gentlemen, let 's go see poor
     Cassio dress'd.
Come, mistress, you must tell 's another tale.
Emilia, run you to the citadel,
And tell my lord and lady what hath happ'd.
Will you go on? I pray. [*Aside*] This is the
     night
That either makes me or fordoes me quite.
                                   [*Exeunt.*

SCENE II. *A bedchamber in the castle:*
DESDEMONA *in bed asleep; a light burning.*

Enter OTHELLO.

Oth. It is the cause, it is the cause, my
     soul,—
Let me not name it to you, you chaste
     stars!—
It is the cause. Yet I 'll not shed her blood;
Nor scar that whiter skin of hers than snow,
And smooth as monumental alabaster.
Yet she must die, else she 'll betray more
     men.
Put out the light, and then put out the light:
If I quench thee, thou flaming minister,
I can again thy former light restore,
Should I repent me: but once put out thy
     light,   10
Thou cunning'st pattern of excelling nature,
I know not where is that Promethean heat
That can thy light relume. When I have
     pluck'd the rose,
I cannot give it vital growth again,
It must needs wither: I 'll smell it on the
     tree.   [*Kissing her.*
Ah, balmy breath, that dost almost persuade
Justice to break her sword! One more, one
     more,
Be thus when thou art dead, and I will kill
     thee,
And love thee after. One more, and this the
     last: 19
So sweet was ne'er so fatal. I must weep,
But they are cruel tears: this sorrow's heav-
     enly;
It strikes where it doth love. She wakes.

Des. Who 's there? Othello?

Oth.   Ay, Desdemona.

Des. Will you come to bed, my lord?

Oth. Have you pray'd to-night, Desde-
     mona?

Des.   Ay, my lord.

Oth. If you bethink yourself of any crime
Unreconciled as yet to heaven and grace,
Solicit for it straight.

Des. Alas, my lord, what do you mean by
that?

Oth. Well, do it, and be brief; I will walk
by: 30
I would not kill thy unprepared spirit;
No; heaven forfend! I would not kill thy
soul.

Des. Talk you of killing?

Oth.   Ay, I do.

Des.   Then heaven
Have mercy on me!

Oth.   Amen, with all my heart!

Des. If you say so, I hope you will not
kill me.

Oth. Hum!

Des. And yet I fear you; for you are
fatal then
When your eyes roll so: why I should fear
I know not,
Since guiltiness I know not; but yet I feel
I fear.

Oth. Think on thy sins.

Des.   They are loves I bear to you.

Oth. Ay, and for that thou diest.   41

Des. That death 's unnatural that kills for
loving.
Alas, why gnaw you so your nether lip?
Some bloody passion shakes your very frame:
These are portents; but yet I hope, I hope,
They do not point on me.

Oth.   Peace, and be still!

Des. I will so. What 's the matter?

Oth. That handkerchief which I so love
and gave thee
Thou gavest to Cassio.

Des.   No, by my life and soul!
Send for the man, and ask him.

Oth.   Sweet soul, take heed,
Take heed of perjury; thou art on thy death-
bed.   51

Des. Ay, but not yet to die.

Oth.   Yes, presently:
Therefore confess thee freely of thy sin;
For to deny each article with oath
Cannot remove nor choke the strong con-
ception

That I do groan withal. Thou art to die.

Des. Then Lord have mercy on me!

Oth.   I say, amen.

Des. And have you mercy too! I never
did
Offend you in my life; never loved Cassio
But with such general warranty of heaven
As I might love; I never gave him token.

Oth. By heaven, I saw my handkerchief
in 's hand.   62
O perjured woman! thou dost stone my heart,
And makest me call what I intend to do
A murder, which I thought a sacrifice:
I saw the handkerchief.

Des.   He found it then;
I never gave it him: send for him hither;
Let him confess a truth.

Oth.   He hath confess'd.

Des. What, my lord?   69

Oth. That he hath used thee.

Des.   How? unlawfully?

Oth.   Ay.

Des. He will not say so.

Oth.   No, his mouth is stopp'd;
Honest Iago hath ta'en order for 't.

Des. O! my fear interprets: what, is he
dead?

Oth. Had all his hairs been lives, my
great revenge
Had stomach for them all.

Des. Alas! he is betray'd and I undone.

Oth. Out, strumpet! weep'st thou for him
to my face?

Des. O, banish me, my lord but kill me
not!

Oth. Down, strumpet!

Des. Kill me to-morrow: let me live to-
night!   80

Oth. Nay, if you strive,—

Des. But half an hour!

Oth.   Being done, there is no pause.

Des. But while I say one prayer!

Oth.   It is too late.
                                        [*He stifles her.*

Emil. [*Within*] My lord, my lord! what,
ho! my lord, my lord!

Oth. What noise is this? Not dead? not
yet quite dead?
I that am cruel am yet merciful;
I would not have thee linger in thy pain:

So, so.

Emil. [*Within*] What, ho! my lord, my lord!

Oth.   Who 's there?

Emil. [*Within*] O, good my lord, I would speak a word with you!   90

Oth. Yes: 't is Emilia. By and by. She 's dead.

'T is like she comes to speak of Cassio's death.—

The noise was here. Ha! no more moving?

Still as the grave. Shall she come in? were 't good?—

I think she stirs again:—no. What 's best to do?

If she come in, she 'll sure speak to my wife:

My wife! my wife! what wife? I have no wife.

O, insupportable! O heavy hour!

Methinks it should be now a huge eclipse

Of sun and moon, and that the affrighted globe   100

Should yawn at alteration.

Emil.   [*Within*] I do beseech you

That I may speak with you, O, good my lord!

Oth. I had forgot thee: O, come in, Emilia:

Soft; by and by. Let me the curtains draw.

Where art thou?   [*Unlocks the door.*

Enter EMILIA.

What 's the matter with thee now?

Emil. O, my good lord, yonder 's foul murders done!

Oth. What, now?

Emil. But now, my lord.

Oth. It is the very error of the moon;

She comes more nearer earth than she was wont,   110

And makes men mad.

Emil. Cassio, my lord, hath kill'd a young Venetian

Call'd Roderigo.

Oth.   Roderigo kill'd

And Cassio kill'd!

Emil.   No, Cassio is not kill'd.

100–1 *affrighted . . . alteration,* that the terrified earth should open at the catastrophe (of the eclipse). 109 *error,* aberration.

Oth. Not Cassio kill'd! then murder 's out of tune,

And sweet revenge grows harsh.

Des. O, falsely, falsely murder'd!

Emil.   Alas, what cry is that?

Oth. That! what?

Emil. Out, and alas! that was my lady's voice.   119

Help! help, ho! help! O lady, speak again!

Sweet Desdemona! O sweet mistress, speak!

Des. A guiltless death I die.

Emil. O, who hath done this deed?

Des. Nobody; I myself. Farewell:

Commend me to my kind lord: O farewell!

[*Dies.*

Oth. Why, how should she be murder'd?

Emil.   Alas, who knows?

Oth. You heard her say herself, it was not I.

Emil. She said so: I must needs report the truth.

Oth. She 's like a liar gone to burning hell:

'T was I that kill'd her.

Emil.   O, the more angel she,

And you the blacker devil!   131

Oth. She turn'd to folly, and she was a whore.

Emil. Thou dost belie her, and thou art a devil.

Oth. She was false as water.

Emil.   Thou art rash as fire, to say

That she was false: O, she was heavenly true!

Oth. Cassio did top her; ask thy husband else.

O, I were damn'd beneath all depth in hell,

But that I did proceed upon just grounds

To this extremity. Thy husband knew it all.

Emil. My husband!   140

Oth. Thy husband.

Emil. That she was false to wedlock?

Oth. Ay, with Cassio. Nay, had she been true,

If heaven would make me such another world

Of one entire and perfect chrysolite,

I 'ld not have sold her for it.

Emil. My husband!

---

145 *chrysolite,* a precious stone.

Oth.   Ay, 't was he that told me first:
An honest man he is, and hates the slime
That sticks on filthy deeds.

  Emil.   My husband!

  Oth. What needs this iteration, woman?
    I say thy husband.   150

  Emil. O mistress, villany hath made
    mocks with love!
My husband say that she was false!

  Oth.   He, woman;
I say thy husband: dost understand the
    word?
My friend, thy husband, honest, honest Iago.

  Emil. If he say so, may his pernicious soul
Rot half a grain a day! he lies to the heart:
She was too fond of her most filthy bargain.

  Oth. Ha!

  Emil. Do thy worst: 159
This deed of thine is no more worthy heaven
Than thou wast worthy her.

  Oth.   Peace, you were best.

  Emil. Thou hast not half that power to
    do me harm
As I have to be hurt. O gull! O dolt!
As ignorant as dirt! thou hast done a deed—
I care not for thy sword; I 'll make thee
    known,
Though I lost twenty lives.—Help! help, ho!
    help!
The Moor hath kill'd my mistress! Murder!
    murder!

        Enter MONTANO, GRATIANO, IAGO,
           and others.

  Mon. What is the matter? How now,
    general!

  Emil. O, are you come, Iago? you have
    done well,
That men must lay their murders on your
    neck.   170

  Gra. What is the matter?

  Emil. Disprove this villain, if thou be'st
    a man:
He says thou told'st him that his wife was
    false:
I know thou didst not, thou 'rt not such a
    villain:
Speak, for my heart is full.

  Iago. I told him what I thought, and told
    no more
Than what he found himself was apt and
    true.

  Emil. But did you ever tell him she was
    false?

  Iago. I did.

  Emil. You told a lie; an odious, damned
    lie;   180
Upon my soul, a lie, a wicked lie.
She false with Cassio!—did you say with
    Cassio?

  Iago. With Cassio, mistress. Go to, charm
    your tongue.

  Emil. I will not charm my tongue; I am
    bound to speak:
My mistress here lies murder'd in her bed,—

  All. O heavens forfend!

  Emil. And your reports have set the mur-
    der on.

  Oth. Nay, stare not, masters: it is true,
    indeed.

  Gra. 'T is a strange truth.

  Mon. O monstrous act!

  Emil.   Villany, villany, villany!
I think upon 't: I think: I smell 't: O vil-
    lany!—   191
I thought so then:—I 'll kill myself for
    grief:—
O villany, villany!

  Iago. What, are you mad? I charge you,
    get you home.

  Emil. Good gentlemen, let me have leave
    to speak:
'T is proper I obey him, but not now.
Perchance, Iago, I will ne'er go home.

  Oth. O! O! O!   [*He falls on the bed.*

  Emil.   Nay, lay thee down and roar;
For thou hast kill'd the sweetest innocent
That e'er did lift up eye.

  Oth.   [*Rising*] O, she was foul!
I scarce did know you, uncle: there lies your
    niece,   201
Whose breath, indeed, these hands have
    newly stopp'd:
I know this act shows horrible and grim.

  Gra. Poor Desdemona! I am glad thy
    father 's dead:
Thy match was mortal to him, and pure grief

Shore his old thread in twain: did he live
  now,
This sight would make him do a desperate
  turn,
Yea, curse his better angel from his side,
And fall to reprobation   209
  Oth. 'T is pitiful; but yet Iago knows
That she with Cassio hath the act of shame
A thousand times committed; Cassio con-
  fess'd it:
And she did gratify his amorous works
With that recognizance and pledge of love
Which I first gave her; I saw it in his hand:
It was a handkerchief, an antique token
My father gave my mother.
  Emil. O heaven! O heavenly powers!
  Iago. Come, hold your peace.
  Emil.   'T will out, 't will out: I peace!
No, I will speak as liberal as the north: 220
Let heaven and men and devils, let them all,
All, all, cry shame against me, yet I 'll speak.
  Iago. Be wise and get you home.
  Emil.   I will not.
          [*Iago offers to stab Emilia.*
  Gra.   Fie!
Your sword upon a woman?
  Emil. O thou dull Moor! that handker-
    chief thou speak'st of
I found by fortune and did give my husband;
For often with a solemn earnestness,
More than indeed belong'd to such a trifle,
He begg'd of me to steal it.
  Iago.   Villanous whore!
  Emil. She give it Cassio! no, alas! I found
    it,   230
And I did give 't my husband.
  Iago.   Filth, thou liest!
  Emil. By heaven, I do not, I do not,
    gentlemen.
O murderous coxcomb! what should such a
  fool
Do with so good a wife?
  Oth.   Are there no stones in heaven
But what serve for the thunder?—Precious
  villain!

[*He runs at Iago; Iago, from behind, stabs
                     Emilia, and exit.*
  Gra. The woman falls; sure, he hath kill'd
    his wife.
  Emil. Ay, ay: O, lay me by my mistress'
    side.
  Gra. He 's gone, but his wife 's kill'd.
  Mon. 'T is a notorious villain. Take you
    this weapon,   239
Which I have here recover'd from the Moor:
Come, guard the door without; let him not
  pass,
But kill him rather. I 'll after that same vil-
  lain,
For 't is a damned slave.
          [*Exeunt Montano and Gratiano.*
  Oth.   I am not valiant neither,
But every puny whipster gets my sword:
But why should honour outlive honesty?
Let it go all.
  Emil.   What did thy song bode, lady?
Hark, canst thou hear me? I will play the
  swan,
And die in music. [*Singing*] Willow, willow,
  willow.—
Moor, she was chaste; she loved thee, cruel
  Moor;   249
So come my soul to bliss, as I speak true;
So speaking as I think, I die, I die.   [*Dies.*
  Oth. I have another weapon in this cham-
    ber;
It is a sword of Spain, the ice-brook's tem-
  per:—
O, here it is. Uncle, I must come forth.
  Gra. [*Within*] If thou attempt it, it will
    cost thee dear:
Thou hast no weapon, and perforce must
  suffer.
  Oth. Look in upon me then and speak
    with me,
Or, naked as I am, I will assault thee.

          Re-enter GRATIANO.
  Gra. What is the matter?
  Oth.   Behold, I have a weapon;
A better never did itself sustain   260

---

207 *turn,* act. 209 *reprobation,* damnation.
220 *liberal as the north,* freely as the north wind.
233 *coxcomb,* fool. 234 *stones,* bolts of lightning.

253 *the ice-brook's temper,* tempered in an ice-
cold brook. 258 *naked,* unarmed.

Upon a soldier's thigh: I have seen the day,
That, with this little arm and this good sword,
I have made my way through more impediments
Than twenty times your stop: but, O vain boast!
Who can control his fate? 't is not so now.
Be not afraid, though you do see me weapon'd;
Here is my journey's end, here is my butt,
And very sea-mark of my utmost sail.
Do you go back dismay'd? 't is a lost fear;
Man but a rush against Othello's breast,
And he retires. Where should Othello go?
Now, how dost thou look now? O ill-starr'd
   wench!   272
Pale as thy smock! when we shall meet at
   compt,
This look of thine will hurl my soul from
   heaven,
And fiends will snatch at it. Cold, cold, my
   girl!
Even like thy chastity. O cursed slave!
Whip me, ye devils,
From the possession of this heavenly sight!
Blow me about in winds! roast me in sul-
   phur!   279
Wash me in steep-down gulfs of liquid fire!
O Desdemona! Desdemona! dead!
Oh! Oh! Oh!

Enter LODOVICO, MONTANO, CASSIO *carried
in a chair, and* Officers *with* IAGO, *prisoner.*

  Lod. Where is this rash and most un-
   fortunate man?
  Oth. That 's he that was Othello: here
   I am.
  Lod. Where is that viper? bring the vil-
   lain forth.
  Oth. I look down towards his feet; but
   that 's a fable.
If that thou be'st a devil, I cannot kill thee.
                [*Wounds Iago.*
  Lod. Wrench his sword from him.
  Iago.   I bleed, sir; but not kill'd.

267-8 *here . . . sail,* here is the end of my voyage. 270 *man but a rush,* take up only a reed. 273 *compt,* judgment day. 286 *I . . . feet,* I examine his feet to see whether they are cloven.

  Oth. I am not sorry neither: I 'ld have
   thee live;
For, in my sense, 't is happiness to die.
  Lod. O thou Othello, that wert once so
   good,   291
Fall'n in the practice of a damned slave,
What shall be said to thee?
  Oth.   Why, any thing:
An honourable murderer, if you will;
For nought I did in hate, but all in honour.
  Lod. This wretch hath part confess'd his
   villany:
Did you and he consent in Cassio's death?
  Oth. Ay.
  Cas. Dear general, I never gave you cause.
  Oth. I do believe it, and I ask your par-
   don.   300
Will you, I pray, demand that demi-devil
Why he hath thus ensnared my soul and
   body?
  Iago. Demand me nothing: what you
   know, you know:
From this time forth I never will speak word.
  Lod. What, not to pray?
  Gra.   Torments will ope your lips.
  Oth. Well, thou dost best.
  Lod. Sir, you shall understand what hath
   befall'n,
Which, as I think, you know not. Here is a
   letter
Found in the pocket of the slain Roderigo;
And here another: the one of them imports
The death of Cassio to be undertook   311
By Roderigo.
  Oth. O villain!
  Cas.   Most heathenish and most gross!
  Lod. Now here 's another discontented
   paper,
Found in his pocket too; and this, it seems,
Roderigo meant to have sent this damned
   villain;
But that belike Iago in the interim
Came in and satisfied him.
  Oth.   O the pernicious caitiff!
How came you, Cassio, by that handkerchief
That was my wife's?
  Cas.   I found it in my chamber:
And he himself confess'd but even now
That there he dropp'd it for a special pur-
   pose   322

Which wrought to his desire.

   Oth.   O fool! fool! fool!

   Cas.   There is besides in Roderigo's letter,
How he upbraids Iago, that he made him
Brave me upon the watch; whereon it came
That I was cast: and even but now he spake,
After long seeming dead, Iago hurt him,
Iago set him on.

   Lod.   You must forsake this room, and go
      with us: 330
Your power and your command is taken off,
And Cassio rules in Cyprus. For this slave,
If there be any cunning cruelty
That can torment him much and hold him
      long,
It shall be his. You shall close prisoner rest,
Till that the nature of your fault be known
To the Venetian state. Come, bring him
      away.

   Oth.   Soft you; a word or two before you
      go.
I have done the state some service, and they
      know 't.
No more of that. I pray you, in your letters,
When you shall these unlucky deeds relate,
Speak of me as I am; nothing extenuate,
Nor set down aught in malice: then must
      you speak   343
Of one that loved not wisely but too well;
Of one not easily jealous, but, being wrought,
Perplex'd in the extreme; of one whose hand,
Like the base Indian, threw a pearl away
Richer than all his tribe; of one whose sub-
      dued eyes,
Albeit unused to the melting mood,
Drop tears as fast as the Arabian trees
Their medicinal gum. Set you down this;
And say besides, that in Aleppo once,   352
Where a malignant and a turban'd Turk
Beat a Venetian and traduced the state,
I took by the throat the circumcised dog,
And smote him, thus.   *[Stabs himself.*

   Lod.   O bloody period!

   Gra.   All that 's spoke is marr'd.

   Oth.   I kiss'd thee ere I kill'd thee: no way
      but this;
Killing myself, to die upon a kiss.

              [Falls on the bed, and dies.

   Cas.   This did I fear, but thought he had
      no weapon;   360

For he was great of heart.

   Lod.   *[To Iago]*   O Spartan dog,
More fell than anguish, hunger, or the sea!
Look on the tragic loading of this bed;
This is thy work: the object poisons sight;
Let it be hid. Gratiano, keep the house,
And seize upon the fortunes of the Moor,
For they succeed on you. To you, lord gover-
      nor,
Remains the censure of this hellish villain;
The time, the place, the torture: O, enforce
      it!   369
Myself will straight aboard; and to the state
This heavy act with heavy heart relate.

                           [Exeunt.

SUGGESTIONS FOR STUDY

1. The introduction to *Othello* stated the reasons for Iago's villainy that are insisted on in the play itself. As further study of Iago's character, consider his speech, I, 3, 322–337, in which he states a philosophical attitude toward life. What is the attitude? (Where necessary, translate his words into modern English.) Iago apparently believes that the human will is free and that we can make ourselves into any sort of person we wish. Does this belief necessarily lead to evil, as in Iago? Consider the teachings on this point of any religion with which you may be familiar.

2. In Shakespeare's *Romeo and Juliet* the tragic ending is at least partly caused by an accident, the delay of a messenger. To what extent does the tragedy in the play *Othello* derive from merely trivial circumstances and details and to what extent from the basic qualities of the character Othello? To answer this you must investigate the importance of the handkerchief.

3. The character Emilia is interesting. She is a realist; is she also a cynic? Consider in this connection her behavior and her fate in the final scene. Study carefully her speeches, III, 4, 103–6, and IV, 3.

4. The introduction to this play mentioned the passages of superlative poetry for which the

---

362 *fell,* cruel. 365 *keep,* guard.

play is famous. Another example is IV, 2, 47–64, especially the basic metaphor and sound of

A fixed figure for the time of scorn
To point his slow unmoving finger at.

Choose a passage in the play that attracted you and analyze its technical poetic devices.

5. Though it is subordinate in importance, there is comedy in at least three scenes in *Othello,* perhaps in more. Which scenes? What sort of comedy is in each of them? Does any of it affect the action of the play?

6. This is a play to be acted in the theater. A study of *Othello* would be incomplete without an attempt to visualize the play on the stage and to hear it spoken by actors. Assuming that you are the director, work out your method of directing the final scene, V, 2, as it would be performed in the modern theater. For example, where would you place your actors as they group and regroup themselves on the stage? Prepare to help your actors read certain of the difficult speeches —for instance, Othello's in lines 91–101. Careful study of the scene will reveal numerous other decisions that would be forced on the director.

THE ADDING MACHINE

Elmer Rice

(1892–   )

The Adding Machine is in content an example of the type of writing known as naturalism. In technique it is an example of expressionism. In both content and technique it is one of the most interesting plays of the modern theater.

To define naturalism we must first define realism. Realism is the attempt to describe life as it is, without bias or color. Naturalism is realism plus a philosophy of determinism. It is pessimistic realism. (Neither of these definitions is accurate in the sense that a scientific definition is accurate, for they depend on the unlikely assumption that an observer-artist is without bias.)

Naturalism is the end product in art of that mode of thinking mentioned in the introduction to drama (p. 412) whereby the philosophy of science has caused many persons in the twentieth century to believe that man, though highly complex, is an animal whose life is governed by the same inexorable and mechanical laws of physics and chemistry that rule the rest of the universe. According to this theory, man is an electro-neural machine. Man has no "mind," for mind is simply a shorthand term for certain phases of the behavior of the total organism. This theory must therefore also hold that "soul" is a meaningless word, since no organ of that name can be identified in the laboratory.

Since man has no mind or soul, he has no "will." (We are still paraphrasing the mechanists.) He cannot choose between good and evil except as, like any other machine, he makes machinelike responses to the successive stimuli of his environment. His behavior is controlled by his environment (determinism) and, since a machine can expect only to be thrown on the scrap heap eventually or melted down to be made into other machines, man is devoid of hope (pessimism). Realism plus a philosophy of determinism equals pessimistic realism, which is naturalism.

Christians and others find gaps and contradictions in this chain of reasoning. One of the most important is the old problem of free will. It is difficult to prove that the will is free (or even that man has a "will"); but to decide that we have no will seems in itself to be an act of the will. To put it another way: if man is a mindless mechanism with no hope of bettering himself, why does such a machine write plays in which he worries about the theory that he is a machine? We do not need to resolve such contradictions in order to understand a piece of naturalistic writing. We must merely entertain the mechanistic philosophy as a temporary hypothesis.

Similarly, as was stated in the introduction to drama, we must temporarily entertain the hypothesis that no single person is worth more than another. This is not the same as the old Christian belief that all men, kings and commoners, are equal in the sight of God. Instead it is a kind of share-the-squalor feeling. It is in no sense an elevating hypothesis. It brings us all down to a level near that of the (other) animals.

In few works of literature are these two hypotheses so apparent as in Elmer Rice's *The Adding Machine*. First produced in New York in 1923, the play is a highly original elaboration of the pessimism it is possible to feel as we contemplate the effect on us of increasing industrialism. Mr. Zero stands for all of us. He is a zero, a cipher. His friends are numbers, not people, and they are interchangeable. His revolt against his grim situation is not an act of will but a blind response to a stimulus. He accepts his punishment as, on the whole, a just fate, and he cannot undertand that any pleasure is possible in the next world. His acquaintance, Shrdlu, who is in a similar predicament, expresses the attitude of both toward their fate in stately, well-rounded clichés. At the end, though the implications of increasing industrialism are pointed out to the witless Zero, he is duped by an illusion of Hope into participating in one more round of his hopeless treadmill.

In the prison scene the Fixer (from the Claim Department) points out to Zero that Zero's replacement by the adding machine is fair from any nonsentimental point of view. And he compares Zero (man) to the dinosaurs. Both species became too expensive to maintain. Of course, at the moment of his death, Zero (man) takes an undeniably sentimental view of his predicament, but the cosmic Fixer is unperturbed.[1]

Perhaps the reader may feel that, although all this may apply to Zero, it cannot possibly be true about a more deserving person, such as the reader himself. Zero is an unusually stupid being who deserves his fate; but the reader, who is intelligent, can expect for himself love, happiness, success, and all the other good things that life can bring. But are these not the same illusions that fool Zero? And has the reader's life none of the characteristics of the treadmill? That is the chilling thought about the naturalistic approach to life: there is always a lingering doubt that we are masters of our fate. At any rate, such plays as *The Adding Machine* vividly picture for us some of the philosophical implications of the complex social and historical phenomena of our time.

The vividness of *The Adding Machine* comes from Elmer Rice's method, which has been given the academic name "expressionism." Expressionism is the attempt to render a truthful picture of life by the use of exaggeration and distortion, generally by means of symbols. We do not perceive accurately.

(Again, the idea that accuracy is possible depends on the assumption, difficult to prove, that there is a reality external to us and independent of our observation.) The pillars of the Parthenon at Athens are said to be not straight but convex. If they were straight we would see them as concave. A candid photograph of a person may catch him with an embarrassing expression. But since we assume that a camera cannot lie, we prefer a posed photograph that exaggerates our good points. What we take for truth is often merely what we see, or prefer to see, not what "is." In a sense, therefore, we are all expressionists. Hence it is possible to contend that an expressionistic play, like *The Adding Machine,* presents an accurate picture of reality, not a distorted caricature.

Expressionism uses symbols. In the introduction to fiction we learned that a symbol is generally a concrete or specific object or action that stands for something else, usually for an abstract idea. Symbolism has always been a device of literature and the other arts; Oedipus' blinding himself is a symbol, and so is Desdemona's handkerchief. Not all symbolism is expressionism, but expressionism could hardly get along without symbolism.

The Adding Machine is rich in these devices. Among them are the whole numerical system of names; the flash of red and the exaggerated noise at the end of Scene Two; other names, including Daisy Diana Dorothea Devore, Etaoin Shrdlu, and Judy O'Grady (a literary allusion); the music in Scene Six; Hope at the end of the play; in fact, the basic concept from which the play gets its title, the adding machine, is a symbol used in an exaggerated or distorted manner.

Certain later American playwrights have combined, like Elmer Rice in this play, a naturalistic approach toward their material with the expressionistic method of treatment. But since pessimism deliberately distorted is likely to create unrelieved gloom, these authors add to the mixture a modicum of "poetic" romanticism—for instance, looking on all events of the play through "the veil of remembrance." Rice's method of relieving

---

[1] The editors are indebted to the author for allowing them to be the first to publish the prison scene. This scene was written at the same time as the rest of the play.

the gloom of *The Adding Machine* is the addition of humor of a grim, sardonic type. The whole of Scene Five is an example. In treating death as an object of humor, the author follows a precedent that goes back to the earliest literature, but he shocks some readers who believe that tragedy is a serious business and that the plight of man is never a subject for laughter.

The introduction to drama described two possible types of tragedy and pointed out that whether we consider the second as tragedy or not is a matter of definition. Let us now consider whether or not *The Adding Machine* is a tragedy. Can there be tragedy when we make the basic assumption that man is a worthless creature—like Zero, only a mindless link in the vast chain of existence? Is it tragedy when such a stupid being as Zero is crushed by outside forces over which he has no control? Remember that Zero is Man—he stands for all of us.

The answer is still a matter of definition. Many critics consider *The Adding Machine* an example of a new kind of tragedy. Others think of it as only a sordid though grimly humorous spectacle with moments of pathos, though not of tragedy. The reader's answer must depend partly on his own philosophy. He must first decide whether he accepts or rejects, wholly or in part, the attitude toward life both assumed and presented in *The Adding Machine*.

THE ADDING MACHINE[1]

CHARACTERS

MR. ZERO	JOE
MRS. ZERO	THE GUIDE
MESSRS. ONE, TWO, THREE, FOUR, FIVE, SIX, *and their respective wives*	A TALL LADY
	A STOUT LADY
DAISY DIANA DOROTHEA DEVORE	CHARLEY
THE BOSS	A SMALL BOY
POLICEMAN	A MOTHER
TWO ATTENDANTS	A YOUTH
JUDY O'GRADY	A BOY OF FOURTEEN
A YOUNG MAN	A FATHER
SHRDLU	THE FIXER
A HEAD	TWO GUARDS
LIEUTENANT CHARLES	

SCENE ONE

A bedroom.

A small room containing an "installment plan" bed, dresser, and chairs. An ugly electric light fixture over the bed with a single glaring naked lamp. One small window with the shade drawn. The walls are papered with sheets of foolscap covered with columns of figures.

MR. ZERO *is lying in the bed, facing the audience, his head and shoulders visible. He is thin, sallow, undersized, and partially bald.* MRS. ZERO *is standing before the dresser ar-*

[1] This play is here reprinted by permission of Elmer Rice, author and copyright owner, and Samuel French, agents and publishers. All rights are fully protected by copyright and are strictly reserved. Permission to give amateur performances may be obtained upon application to Samuel French, 25 West 45th Street, New York. Inquiries about other rights should be addressed to Elmer Rice, % Playwright's Company, 1545 Broadway, New York.

ranging her hair for the night. She is forty-five, sharp-featured, gray streaks in her hair. She is shapeless in her long-sleeved cotton nightgown. She is wearing her shoes, over which sag her ungartered stockings.

MRS. ZERO (*as she takes down her hair*). I'm gettin' sick o' them Westerns. All them cowboys ridin' around an' foolin' with them ropes. I don't care nothin' about that. I'm sick of 'em. I don't see why they don't have more of them stories like *For Love's Sweet Sake*. I like them sweet little love stories. They're nice an' wholesome. Mrs. Twelve was sayin' to me only yesterday, "Mrs. Zero," says she, "what I like is one of them wholesome stories, with just a sweet, simple little love story." "You're right, Mrs. Twelve," I says. "That's what I like, too." They're showin' too many Westerns at the Rosebud. I'm gettin' sick of them. I think we'll start goin' to the Peter Stuyvesant. They got a good bill there Wednesday night. There's a Chubby Delano comedy called *Sea-Sick*. Mrs. Twelve was tellin' me about it. She says it's a scream. They're havin' a picnic in the country and they sit Chubby next to an old maid with a great big mouth. So he gets sore an' when she ain't lookin' he goes and catches a frog and drops it in her clam chowder. An' when she goes to eat the chowder the frog jumps out of it an' right into her mouth. Talk about laugh! Mrs. Twelve was tellin' me she laughed so she nearly passed out. He sure can pull some funny ones. An' they got that big Grace Darling feature, *A Mother's Tears*. She's sweet. But I don't like her clothes. There's no style to them. Mrs. Nine was tellin' me she read in *Pictureland* that she ain't livin' with her husband. He's her second, too. I don't know whether they're divorced or just separated. You wouldn't think it to see her on the screen. She looks so sweet and innocent. Maybe it ain't true. You can't believe all you read. They say some Pittsburgh millionaire is crazy about her and that's why she ain't livin' with her husband. Mrs. Seven was tellin' me her brother-in-law has a friend that used to go to school with Grace Darling. He says her name ain't Grace Darling at all. Her right name is Elizabeth Dugan, he says, an' all them stories about her gettin' five thousand a week is the bunk, he says. She's sweet, though. Mrs. Eight was tellin' me that *A Mother's Tears* is the best picture she ever made. "Don't miss it, Mrs. Zero," she says. "It's sweet," she says. "Just sweet and wholesome. Cry!" she says, "I nearly cried my eyes out." There's one part in it where this big bum of an Englishman— he's a married man, too—an' she's this little simple country girl. An' she nearly falls for him, too. But she's sittin' out in the garden, one day, and she looks up and there's her mother lookin' at her, right out of the clouds. So that night she locks the door of her room. An' sure enough, when everybody's in bed, along comes this big bum of an Englishman an' when she won't let him in what does he do but go an' kick open the door. "Don't miss it, Mrs. Zero," Mrs. Eight was tellin' me. It's at the Peter Stuyvesant Wednesday night, so don't be tellin' me you want to go to the Rosebud. The Eights seen it downtown at the Strand. They go downtown all the time. Just like us—nit! I guess by the time it gets to the Peter Stuyvesant all that part about kickin' in the door will be cut out. Just like they cut out that big cabaret scene in *The Price of Virtue*. They sure are pullin' some rough stuff in the pictures nowadays. "It's no place for a young girl," I was tellin' Mrs. Eleven, only the other day. An' by the time they get uptown half of it is cut out. But you wouldn't go downtown—not if wild horses was to drag you. You can wait till they come uptown! Well, I don't want to wait, see? I want to see 'em when everybody else is seein' them an' not a month later. Now don't go tellin' me you ain't got the price. You could dig up the price all right, all right, if you wanted to. I notice you always got the price to go to the ball game. But when it comes to me havin' a good time then it's always: "I ain't got the price, I gotta start savin'." A fat lot you'll ever save! I got all I can do now makin' both ends meet an' you talkin' about savin'. (*She seats herself on a chair and begins removing her shoes and stockings.*) An' don't go pullin' that stuff about bein' tired. "I been workin' hard all day. Twice a day in the subway's enough for me." Tired! Where do you get that tired stuff, anyhow? What about me? Where do I come in? Scrubbin' floors an' cookin' your meals an' washin' your dirty clothes. An' you sittin' on a chair all day, just addin' figgers an' waitin' for five-thirty. There's no five-thirty for me. I don't wait for no whistle. I don't get no vacations neither. And what's more I don't get no pay envelope every Saturday night neither. I'd like to know where you'd be without me. An' what have I got to show for it?—slavin' my life away to give you a home. What's in it for me, I'd like to know? But it's my own fault, I guess. I was a fool for marryin' you. If I'd 'a' had any sense, I'd 'a' known what you were from the start. I wish I had it to do over again, I hope to tell you. You was goin' to do wonders, you was! You wasn't goin' to be a bookkeeper long—oh, no, not you. Wait till you got started—you was goin' to show 'em. There wasn't no job in the store that was too big for you. Well, I've been waitin'—waitin' for you to get started—see? It's been a good long wait, too. Twenty-five years! An' I ain't seen nothin' happen. Twenty-five years in the same job. Twenty-five years to-morrow! You're proud of it, ain't you? Twenty-five years in the same job an' never missed a day! That's somethin' to be proud of, ain't it? Sittin' for twenty-five years on the same chair, addin' up figures. What about bein' store-manager? I guess you forgot about that, didn't you? An' me at home here lookin' at the same four walls an' workin' my fingers to the bone to make both ends meet. Seven years since you got a raise! An' if you don't get one to-morrow, I'll bet a nickel you won't have the guts to go an' ask for one. I didn't pick much when I picked you, I'll tell the world.

You ain't much to be proud of. (*She rises, goes to the window, and raises the shade. A few lighted windows are visible on the other side of the closed court. Looking out for a moment.*) She ain't walkin' around to-night, you can bet your sweet life on that. An' she won't be walkin' around any more nights, neither. Not in this house, anyhow. (*She turns away from the window.*) The dirty bum! The idea of her comin' to live in a house with respectable people. They should 'a' gave her six years, not six months. If I was the judge I'd of gave her life. A bum like that. (*She approaches the bed and stands there a moment.*) I guess you're sorry she's gone. I guess you'd like to sit home every night an' watch her goin's-on. You're somethin' to be proud of, you are! (*She stands on the bed and turns out the light. . . . A thin stream of moonlight filters in from the court. The two figures are dimly visible.* MRS. ZERO *gets into bed.*) You'd better not start nothin' with women, if you know what's good for you. I've put up with a lot, but I won't put up with that. I've been slavin' away for twenty-five years, makin' a home for you an' nothin' to show for it. If you was any kind of a man you'd have a decent job by now an' I'd be gettin' some comfort out of life—instead of bein' just a slave, washin' pots an' standin' over the hot stove. I've stood it for twenty-five years an' I guess I'll have to stand it twenty-five more. But don't you go startin' nothin' with women—(*She goes on talking as the curtain falls.*)

SCENE TWO

An office in a department store. Wood and glass partitions. In the middle of the room, two tall desks back to back. At one desk on a high stool is ZERO. *Opposite him at the other desk, also on a high stool, is* DAISY DIANA DOROTHEA DEVORE, *a plain, middle-aged woman. Both wear green eye-shades and paper sleeve protectors. A pendent electric lamp throws light upon both desks.* DAISY *reads aloud figures from a pile of slips which lie before her. As she reads the figures,* ZERO *enters them upon a large square sheet of ruled paper which lies before him.*

DAISY (*reading aloud*). Three ninety-eight. Forty-two cents. A dollar fifty. A dollar fifty. A dollar twenty-five. Two dollars. Thirty-nine cents. Twenty-seven fifty.

ZERO (*petulantly*). Speed it up a little, cancha?

DAISY. What's the rush? To-morrer's another day.

ZERO. Aw, you make me sick.

DAISY. An' you make me sicker.

ZERO. Go on. Go on. We're losin' time.

DAISY. Then quit bein' so bossy. (*She reads.*) Three dollars. Two sixty-nine. Eighty-one fifty. Forty dollars. Eight seventy-five. Who do you think you are, anyhow?

ZERO. Never mind who I think I am. You tend to your work.

DAISY. Aw, don't be givin' me so many orders. Sixty cents. Twenty-four cents. Seventy-five cents. A dollar fifty. Two fifty. One fifty. One fifty. Two fifty. I don't have to take it from you and what's more I won't.

ZERO. Aw, quit talkin'.

DAISY. I'll talk all I want. Three dollars. Fifty cents. Fifty cents. Seven dollars. Fifty cents. Two fifty. Three fifty. Fifty cents. One fifty. Fifty cents.

[*She goes bending over the slips and transferring them from one pile to another.* ZERO *bends over his desk, busily entering the figures.*]

ZERO (*without looking up*). You make me sick. Always shootin' off your face about somethin'. Talk, talk, talk. Just like all the other women. Women make me sick.

DAISY (*busily fingering the slips*). Who do you think you are, anyhow? Bossin' me around. I don't have to take it from you, and what's more I won't.

[*They both attend closely to their work, neither looking up.*]

ZERO. Women make me sick. They're all alike. The judge gave her six months. I wonder what they do in the work-house.

Peel potatoes. I'll bet she's sore at me. Maybe she'll try to kill me when she gets out. I better be careful. Hello Girl Slays Betrayer. Jealous Wife Slays Rival. You can't tell what a woman's liable to do. I better be careful.

DAISY. I'm gettin' sick of it. Always pickin' on me about somethin'. Never a decent word out of you. Not even the time o'day.

ZERO. I guess she wouldn't have the nerve at that. Maybe she don't even know it's me. They didn't even put my name in the paper, the big bums. Maybe she's been in the work-house before. A bum like that. She didn't have nothin' on that one time—nothin' but a shirt. (*He glances up quickly, then bends over again.*) You make me sick. I'm sick of lookin' at your face.

DAISY. Gee, ain't that whistle ever goin' to blow? You didn't used to be like that. Not even good mornin' or good evenin'. I ain't done nothin' to you. It's the young girls. Goin' around without corsets.

ZERO. Your face is gettin' all yeller. Why don't you put some paint on it? She was puttin' on paint that time. On her cheeks and on her lips. And that blue stuff on her eyes. Just sittin' there in a shimmy puttin' on the paint. An' walkin' around the room with her legs all bare.

DAISY. I wish I was dead.

ZERO. I was a goddam fool to let the wife get on to me. She oughta get six months at that. The dirty bum. Livin' in a house with respectable people. She'd be livin' there yet, if the wife hadn't o' got on to me. Damn her!

DAISY. I wish I was dead.

ZERO. Maybe another one'll move in. Gee, that would be great. But the wife's got her eye on me now.

DAISY. I'm scared to do it, though.

ZERO. You oughta move into that room. It's cheaper than where you're livin' now. I better tell you about it. I don't mean to be always pickin' on you.

DAISY. Gas. The smell of it makes me sick.

[ZERO *looks up and clears his throat.*]

DAISY (*looking up, startled*). Whadja say?

ZERO. I didn't say nothin'.

DAISY. I thought you did.

ZERO. You thought wrong.

[*They bend over their work again.*]

DAISY. A dollar sixty. A dollar fifty. Two ninety. One sixty-two.

ZERO. Why the hell should I tell you? Fat chance of you forgettin' to pull down the shade!

DAISY. If I asked for carbolic they might get on to me.

ZERO. Your hair's gettin' gray. You don't wear them shirt-waists any more with the low collars. When you'd bend down to pick somethin' up—

DAISY. I wish I knew what to ask for. Girl Takes Mercury After All-Night Party. Woman In Ten-Story Death Leap.

ZERO. I wonder where'll she go when she gets out. Gee, I'd like to make a date with her. Why didn't I go over there the night my wife went to Brooklyn? She never woulda found out.

DAISY. I seen Pauline Frederick do it once. Where could I get a pistol though?

ZERO. I guess I didn't have the nerve.

DAISY. I'll bet you'd be sorry then that you been so mean to me. How do I know, though? Maybe you wouldn't.

ZERO. Nerve! I got as much nerve as anybody. I'm on the level, that's all. I'm a married man and I'm on the level.

DAISY. Anyhow, why ain't I got a right to live? I'm as good as anybody else. I'm too refined, I guess. That's the whole trouble.

ZERO. The time the wife had pneumonia I thought she was goin' to pass out. But she didn't. The doctor's bill was eighty-seven dollars. (*Looking up.*) Hey, wait a minute! Didn't you say eighty-seven dollars?

DAISY (*looking up*). What?

ZERO. Was the last you said eighty-seven dollars?

DAISY (*consulting the slip*). Forty-two fifty.

ZERO. Well, I made a mistake. Wait a minute. (*He busies himself with an eraser.*) All right. Shoot.

DAISY. Six dollars. Three fifteen. Two twenty-five. Sixty-five cents. A dollar twenty. You talk to me as if I was dirt.

ZERO. I wonder if I could kill the wife without anybody findin' out. In bed some night. With a pillow.

DAISY. I used to think you was stuck on me.

ZERO. I'd get found out, though. They always have ways.

DAISY. We used to be so nice and friendly together when I first came here. You used to talk to me then.

ZERO. Maybe she'll die soon. I noticed she was coughin' this mornin'.

DAISY. You used to tell me all kinds o' things. You were goin' to show them all. Just the same, you're still sittin' here.

ZERO. Then I could do what I damn please. Oh, boy!

DAISY. Maybe it ain't all your fault neither. Maybe if you'd had the right kind o' wife —somebody with a lot of common-sense, somebody refined—me!

ZERO. At that, I guess I'd get tired of bummin' around. A feller wants some place to hang his hat.

DAISY. I wish she would die.

ZERO. And when you start goin' with women you're liable to get into trouble. And lose your job maybe.

DAISY. Maybe you'd marry me.

ZERO. Gee, I wish I'd gone over there that night.

DAISY. Then I could quit workin'.

ZERO. Lots o' women would be glad to get me.

DAISY. You could look a long time before you'd find a sensible, refined girl like me.

ZERO. Yes, sir, they could look a long time before they'd find a steady meal-ticket like me.

DAISY. I guess I'd be too old to have any kids. They say it ain't safe after thirty-five.

ZERO. Maybe I'd marry you. You might be all right, at that.

DAISY. I wonder—if you don't want kids—whether—if there's any way—

ZERO (*looking up*). Hey! Hey! Can't you slow up? What do you think I am—a machine?

DAISY (*looking up*). Say, what do you want, anyhow? First it's too slow an' then it's too fast. I guess you don't know what you want.

ZERO. Well, never mind about that. Just you slow up.

DAISY. I'm gettin' sick o' this. I'm goin' to ask to be transferred.

ZERO. Go ahead. You can't make me mad.

DAISY. Aw, keep quite. (*She reads.*) Two forty-five. A dollar twenty. A dollar fifty. Ninety cents. Sixty-three cents.

ZERO. Marry you! I guess not! You'd be as bad as the one I got.

DAISY. You wouldn't care if I did ask. I got a good mind to ask.

ZERO. I was a fool to get married.

DAISY. Then I'd never see you at all.

ZERO. What chance has a guy got with a woman tied around his neck?

DAISY. That time at the store picnic—the year your wife couldn't come—you were nice to me then.

ZERO. Twenty-five years holdin' down the same job!

DAISY. We were together all day—just sittin' around under the trees.

ZERO. I wonder if the boss remembers about it bein' twenty-five years.

DAISY. And comin' home that night—you sat next to me in the big delivery wagon.

ZERO. I got a hunch there's a big raise comin' to me.

DAISY. I wonder what it feels like to be really kissed. Men—dirty pigs! They want the bold ones.

ZERO. If he don't come across I'm goin' right up to the front office and tell him where he gets off.

DAISY. I wish I was dead.

ZERO. "Boss," I'll say, "I want to have a talk with you." "Sure," he'll say, "sit down. Have a Corona Corona." "No," I'll say, "I don't smoke." "How's that?" he'll say. "Well, boss," I'll say, "it's this way. Every time I feel like smokin' I just take a nickel and put it in the old sock. A penny saved is a penny earned, that's the way I look at it." "Damn sensible," he'll say. "You got a wise head on you, Zero."

DAISY. I can't stand the smell of gas. It makes me sick. You coulda kissed me if you wanted to.

ZERO. "Boss," I'll say, "I ain't quite satisfied.

I been on the job twenty-five years now and if I'm gonna stay I gotta see a future ahead of me." "Zero," he'll say, "I'm glad you came in. I've had my eye on you, Zero. Nothin' gets by me." "Oh, I know that, boss," I'll say. That'll hand him a good laugh, that will. "You're a valuable man, Zero," he'll say, "and I want you right up here with me in the front office. You're done addin' figures. Monday mornin' you move up here."

DAISY. Them kisses in the movies—them long ones—right on the mouth—

ZERO. I'll keep a-goin' right on up after that. I'll show some of them birds where they get off.

DAISY. That one the other night—*The Devil's Alibi*—he put his arms around her —and her head fell back and her eyes closed—like she was in a daze.

ZERO. Just give me about two years and I'll show them birds where they get off.

DAISY. I guess that's what it's like—a kinda daze—when I see them like that, I just seem to forget everything.

ZERO. Then me for a place in Jersey. And maybe a little Buick. No tin Lizzie for mine. Wait till I get started—I'll show 'em.

DAISY. I can see it now when I kinda half-close my eyes. The way her head fell back. And his mouth pressed right up against hers. Oh, Gawd! it must be grand!

[*There is a sudden shrill blast from a steam whistle.*]

DAISY *and* ZERO (*together*). The whistle!

[*With great agility they get off their stools, remove their eye-shades and sleeve protectors and put them on the desks. Then each produces from behind the desk a hat —*ZERO, *a dusty derby,* DAISY, *a frowsy straw. . . .* DAISY *puts on her hat and turns toward* ZERO *as though she were about to speak to him. But he is busy cleaning his pen and pays no attention to her. She sighs and goes toward the door at the left.*]

ZERO (*looking up*). G'night, Miss Devore.

[*But she does not hear him and exits.* ZERO *takes up his hat and goes left. The door at the right opens and the* BOSS *enters—middle-aged, stoutish, bald, well-dressed.*]

THE BOSS (*calling*). Oh—er—Mister—er—

[ZERO *turns in surprise, sees who it is and trembles nervously.*]

ZERO (*obsequiously*). Yes, sir. Do you want me, sir?

BOSS. Yes. Just come here a moment, will you?

ZERO. Yes, sir. Right away, sir. (*He fumbles his hat, picks it up, stumbles recovers himself, and approaches the* BOSS, *every fibre quivering.*)

BOSS. Mister—er—er—

ZERO. Zero.

BOSS. Yes, Mr. Zero. I wanted to have a little talk with you.

ZERO (*with a nervous grin*). Yes, sir, I been kinda expectin' it.

BOSS (*staring at him*). Oh, have you?

ZERO. Yes, sir.

BOSS. How long have you been with us, Mister—er—Mister—

ZERO. Zero.

BOSS. Yes, Mister Zero.

ZERO. Twenty-five years to-day.

BOSS. Twenty-five years! That's a long time.

ZERO. Never missed a day.

BOSS. And you've been doing the same work all the time?

ZERO. Yes, sir. Right here at this desk.

BOSS. Then, in that case, a change probably won't be unwelcome to you.

ZERO. No, sir, it won't. And that's the truth.

BOSS. We've been planning a change in this department for some time.

ZERO. I kinda thought you had your eye on me.

BOSS. You were right. The fact is that my efficiency experts have recommended the installation of adding machines.

ZERO (*staring at him*). Addin' machines?

BOSS. Yes, you've probably seen them. A mechanical device that adds automatically.

ZERO. Sure. I've seen them. Keys—and a handle that you pull. (*He goes through the motions in the air.*)

BOSS. That's it. They do the work in half the time and a high-school girl can operate them. Now, of course, I'm sorry to lose an old and faithful employee—

ZERO. Excuse me, but would you mind sayin' that again?

BOSS. I say I'm sorry to lose an employee who's been with me for so many years—

[*Soft music is heard—the sound of the mechanical player of a distant merry-go-round. The part of the floor upon which the desk and stools are standing begins to revolve very slowly.*]

BOSS. But, of course, in an organization like this, efficiency must be the first consideration—

[*The music becomes gradually louder and the revolutions more rapid.*]

BOSS. You will draw your salary for the full month. And I'll direct my secretary to give you a letter of recommendation—

ZERO. Wait a minute, Boss. Let me get this right. You mean I'm canned?

BOSS (*barely making himself heard above the increasing volume of sound.*) I'm sorry—no other alternative—greatly regret —old employee—efficiency—economy— business—*business*—BUSINESS—

[*His voice is drowned by the music. The platform is revolving rapidly now.* ZERO *and the* BOSS *face each other. They are entirely motionless save for the* BOSS'S *jaws, which open and close incessantly. But the words are inaudible. The muic swells and swells. To it is added every off-stage effect of the theatre: the wind, the waves, the galloping horses, the locomotive whistle, the sleigh-bells, the automobile siren, the glass-crash. New Year's Eve, Election Night, Armistice Day, and the Mardi-Gras. The noise deafening, maddening, unendurable. Suddenly it culminates in a terrific peal of thunder. For an instant there is a flash of red and then everything is plunged into blackness.*]

CURTAIN

SCENE THREE

The ZERO *dining-room. Entrance door at right. Doors to kitchen and bedroom at left. The walls, as in the first scene, are papered with foolscap sheets covered with columns of figures. In the middle of the room, up-stage, a table set for two. Along each side wall, seven chairs are ranged in symmetrical rows. [At the rise of the curtain MRS. ZERO is seen seated at the table looking alternately at the entrance door and a clock on the wall. She wears a bungalow apron over her best dress.*

After a few moments, the entrance door opens and ZERO enters. He hangs his hat on a rack behind the door and coming over to the table seats himself at the vacant place. His movements throughout are quiet and abstracted.]

MRS. ZERO (*breaking the silence*). Well, it was nice of you to come home. You're only an hour late and that ain't very much. The supper don't get very cold in an hour. An' of course the part about our havin' a lot of company to-night don't matter. (*They begin to eat.*) Ain't you even got sense enough to come home on time? Didn't I tell you we're goin' to have a lot o' company to-night? Didn't you know the Ones are comin'? An' the Twos? An' the Threes? An' the Fours? An' the Fives? And the Sixes? Didn't I tell you to be home on time? I might as well talk to a stone wall. (*They eat for a few moments in silence.*) I guess you musta had some important business to attend to. Like watchin' the score-board. Or was two kids havin' a fight an' you was the referee? You sure do have a lot of business to attend to. It's a wonder you have time to come home at all. You gotta tough life, you have. Walk in, hang up your hat, an' put on the nose-bag. An' me in the hot kitchen all day, cookin' your supper an' waitin' for you to get good an' ready to come home! (*Again they eat in silence.*) Maybe the boss kept you late to-night. Tellin' you what a big noise you are and how the store couldn't 'a' got along if you hadn't been pushin' a pen for twenty-five years. Where's the gold medal he pinned on you? Did some blind old lady take it away from you or did you leave it on the

seat of the boss's limousine when he brought you home? (*Again a few moments of silence.*) I'll bet he gave you a big raise, didn't he? Promoted you from the third floor to the fourth, maybe. Raise? A fat chance you got o' gettin' a raise. All they gotta do is put an ad in the paper. There's ten thousand like you layin' around the streets. You'll be holdin' down the same job at the end of another twenty-five years—if you ain't forgot how to add by that time.

[*A noise is heard off-stage, a sharp clicking such as is made by the operation of the keys and levers of an adding machine. ZERO raises his head for a moment, but lowers it almost instantly.*]

MRS. ZERO. There's the door-bell. The company's here already. And we ain't hardly finished supper. (*She rises.*) But I'm goin' to clear off the table whether you're finished or not. If you want your supper, you got a right to be home on time. Not standin' around lookin' at score-boards. (*As she piles up the dishes, ZERO rises and goes toward the entrance door.*) Wait a minute! Don't open the door yet. Do you want the company to see all the mess? An' go an' put on a clean collar. You got red ink all over it. (*ZERO goes toward bedroom door.*) I should think after pushin' a pen for twenty-five years, you'd learn how to do it without gettin' ink on your collar. (*ZERO exits to bedroom. MRS. ZERO takes dishes to kitchen talking as she goes.*) I guess I can stay up all night now washin' dishes. You should worry! That's what a man' got a wife for, ain't it? Don't he buy her her clothes an' let her eat with him at the same table? An' all she's gotta do is cook the meals an' do the washin' an' scrub the floor, an' wash the dishes, when the company goes. But, believe me, you're goin' to sling a mean dish-towel when the company goes to-night!

[*While she is talking ZERO enters from bedroom. He wears a clean collar and is cramming the soiled one furtively into his pocket. MRS. ZERO enters from kitchen. She has removed her apron and carries a* table cover which she spreads hastily over the table. The clicking noise is heard again.]

MRS. ZERO. There's the bell again. Open the door, cancha?

[ZERO goes to the entrance door and opens it. Six men and six women file into the room in a double column. The men are all shapes and sizes, but their dress is identical with that of ZERO in every detail. Each, however, wears a wig of a different color. The women are all dressed alike, too, except that the dress of each is of a different color.]

MRS. ZERO (taking the first woman's hand). How de do, Mrs. One.

MRS. ONE. How de do, Mrs. Zero.

[MRS. ZERO repeats this formula with each woman in turn. ZERO does the same with the men except that he is silent throughout. The files now separate, each man taking a chair from the right wall and each woman one from the left wall. Each sex forms a circle with the chairs very close together. The men—all except ZERO—smoke cigars. The women munch chocolates.]

SIX. Some rain we're havin'.

FIVE. Never saw the like of it.

FOUR. Worst in fourteen years, paper says.

THREE. Y' can't always go by the papers.

TWO. No, that's right, too.

ONE. We're liable to forget from year to year.

SIX. Yeh, come t' think, last year was pretty bad, too.

FIVE. An' how about two years ago?

FOUR. Still this year's pretty bad.

THREE. Yeh, no gettin' away from that.

TWO. Might be a whole lot worse.

ONE. Yeh, it's all the way you look at it. Some rain, though.

MRS. SIX. I like them little organdie dresses.

MRS. FIVE. Yeh, with a little lace trimmin' on the sleeves.

MRS. FOUR. Well, I like 'em plain myself.

MRS. THREE. Yeh, what I always say is the plainer the more refined.

MRS. TWO. Well, I don't think a little lace does any harm.

MRS. ONE. No, it kinda dresses it up.

MRS. ZERO. Well, I always say it's all a matter of taste.

MRS. SIX. I saw you at the Rosebud Movie Thursday night, Mr. One.

ONE. Pretty punk show, I'll say.

TWO. They're gettin' worse all the time.

MRS. SIX. But who was the charming lady, Mr. One?

ONE. Now don't you go makin' trouble for me. That was my sister.

MRS. FIVE. Oho! That's what they all say.

MRS. FOUR. Never mind! I'll bet Mrs. One knows what's what, all right.

MRS. ONE. Oh, well, he can do what he likes —'slong as he behaves himself.

THREE. You're in luck at that, One. Fat chance I got of gettin' away from the frau even with my sister.

MRS. THREE. You oughta be glad you got a good wife to look after you.

THE OTHER WOMEN (in unison). That's right, Mrs. Three.

FIVE. I guess I know who wears the pants in your house, Three.

MRS. ZERO. Never mind. I saw them holdin' hands at the movie the other night.

THREE. She musta been tryin' to get some money away from me.

MRS. THREE. Swell chance anybody'd have of gettin' any money away from you.

[General laughter.]

FOUR. They sure are a loving couple.

MRS. TWO. Well, I think we oughta change the subject.

MRS. ONE. Yes, let's change the subject.

SIX (sotto voce). Did you hear the one about the travellin' saleman?

FIVE. It seems this guy was in a sleeper.

FOUR. Goin' from Albany to San Diego.

THREE. And in the next berth was an old maid.

TWO. With a wooden leg.

ONE. Well, along about midnight—

[They all put their heads together and whisper.]

MRS. SIX (sotto voce). Did you hear about the Sevens?

MRS. FIVE. They're gettin' a divorce.

MRS. FOUR. It's the second time for him.

MRS. THREE. They're two of a kind, if you ask me.

MRS. TWO. One's as bad as the other.

MRS. ONE. Worse.

MRS. ZERO. They say that she—

[*They all put their heads together and whisper.*]

SIX. I think this woman suffrage is the bunk.

FIVE. It sure is! Politics is a man's business.

FOUR. Woman's place is in the home.

THREE. That's it! Lookin' after the kids, 'stead of hangin' around the streets.

TWO. You hit the nail on the head that time.

ONE. The trouble is they don't know what they want.

MRS. SIX. Men sure get me tired.

MRS. FIVE. They sure are a lazy lot.

MRS. FOUR. And dirty.

MRS. THREE. Always grumblin' about somethin'.

MRS. TWO. When they're not lyin'!

MRS. ONE. Or messin' up the house.

MRS. ZERO. Well, believe me, I tell mine where he gets off.

SIX. Business conditions are sure bad.

FIVE. Never been worse.

FOUR. I don't know what we're comin' to.

THREE. I look for a big smash-up in about three months.

TWO. Wouldn't surprise me a bit.

ONE. We're sure headin' for trouble.

MRS. SIX. My aunt has gall-stones.

MRS. FIVE. My husband has bunions.

MRS. FOUR. My sister expects next month.

MRS. THREE. My cousin's husband has erysipelas.

MRS. TWO. My niece has St. Vitus's dance.

MRS. ONE. My boy has fits.

MRS. ZERO. I never felt better in my life. Knock wood!

SIX. Too damn much agitation, that's at the bottom of it.

FIVE. That's it!—too damn many strikes.

FOUR. Foreign agitators, that's what it is.

THREE. They oughta be run outa the country.

TWO. What the hell do they want, anyhow?

ONE. They don't know what they want, if you ask me.

SIX. America for the Americans is what I say!

ALL (*in unison*). That's it! Damn foreigners! Damn dagoes! Damn Catholics! Damn sheenies! Damn niggers! Jail 'em! shoot 'em! hang 'em! lynch 'em! burn 'em! (*They all rise.*)

ALL (*sing in unison*).
"My country 'tis of thee,
    Sweet land of liberty!"

MRS. FOUR. Why so pensive, Mr. Zero?

ZERO (*speaking for the first time*). I'm thinkin'.

MRS. FOUR. Well, be careful not to sprain your mind.

[*Laughter.*]

MRS. ZERO. Look at the poor men all by themselves. We ain't very sociable.

ONE. Looks like we're neglectin' the ladies.

[*The women cross the room and join the men, all chattering loudly. The door-bell rings.*]

MRS. ZERO. Sh! The door-bell!

[*The volume of sound slowly diminishes. Again the door-bell.*]

ZERO (*quietly*). I'll go. It's for me.

[*They watch curiously as* ZERO *goes to the door and opens it, admitting a policeman. There is a murmur of surprise and excitement.*]

POLICEMAN. I'm lookin' for Mr. Zero.

[*They all point to* ZERO.]

ZERO. I've been expectin' you.

POLICEMAN. Come along!

ZERO. Just a minute. (*He puts his hand in his pocket.*)

POLICEMAN. What's he tryin' to pull? (*He draws a revolver.*) I got you covered.

ZERO. Sure, that's all right. I just want to give you somethin'. (*He takes the collar from his pocket and gives it to the* POLICEMAN.)

POLICEMAN (*suspiciously*). What's that?

ZERO. The collar I wore.

POLICEMAN. What do I want it for?

ZERO. It's got blood-stains on it.

POLICEMAN (*pocketing it*). All right, come along!

ZERO (*turning to* MRS. ZERO). I gotta go with him. You'll have to dry the dishes yourself.

MRS. ZERO (*rushing forward*). What are they takin' you for?

ZERO (*calmly*). I killed the boss this afternoon.

[*Quick curtain as the* POLICEMAN *takes him off.*]

SCENE FOUR

A court of justice. Three bare white walls without door or windows except for a single door in the right wall. At the right is a jury-box in which are seated MESSRS. ONE, TWO, THREE, FOUR, FIVE, *and* SIX *and their respective wives. On either side of the jury-box stands a uniformed officer. Opposite the jury-box is a long, bare oak table piled high with law books. Behind the books* ZERO *is seated, his face buried in his hands. There is no other furniture in the room.*

[*A moment after the rise of the curtain, one of the officers rises and, going around the table, taps* ZERO *on the shoulder.* ZERO *rises and accompanies the* OFFICER. *The* OFFICER *escorts him to the great empty space in the middle of the courtroom, facing the jury. He motions to* ZERO *to stop, then points to the jury and resumes his place beside the jury-box.* ZERO *stands there looking at the jury, bewildered and half afraid. The* JURORS *give no sign of having seen him. Throughout they sit with folded arms, staring stolidly before them.*]

ZERO (*beginning to speak; haltingly*). Sure I killed him. I ain't sayin' I didn't, am I? Sure I killed him. Them lawyers! They give me a good stiff pain, that's what they give me. Half the time I don't know what the hell they're talkin' about. Objection sustained. Objection overruled. What's the big idea, anyhow? You ain't heard me do any objectin', have you? Sure not! What's the idea of objectin'? You got a right to know. What I say is if one bird kills another bird, why, you got a right to call him for it. That's what I say. I know all about that. I been on the jury, too. Them lawyers! Don't let 'em fill you full of bunk. All that bull about it bein' red ink on the bill-file. Red ink nothin'! It was blood, see? I want you to get that right. I killed him, see? Right through the heart with the bill-file, see? I want you to get that right—all of you. One, two, three, four, five, six, seven, eight, nine, ten, eleven, twelve. Twelve of you. Six and six. That makes twelve. I figured it up often enough. Six and six makes twelve. And five is seventeen. And eight is twenty-five. And three is twenty-eight. Eight and carry two. Aw, cut it out! Them damn figgers! I can't forget 'em. Twenty-five years, see? Eight hours a day, exceptin' Sundays. And July and August half-day Saturday. One week's vacation with pay. And another week without pay if you want it. Who the hell wants it? Layin' around the house listenin' to the wife tellin' you where you get off. Nix! An' legal holidays. I nearly forgot them. New Year's, Washington's Birthday, Decoration Day, Fourth o' July, Labor Day, Election Day, Thanksgivin', Christmas. Good Friday if you want it. An' if you're a Jew, Young Kipper an' the other one—I forget what they call it. The dirty sheenies—always gettin' two to the other bird's one. An' when a holiday comes on Sunday, you get Monday off. So that's fair enough. But when the Fourth o' July comes on Saturday, why, you're out o' luck on account of Saturday bein' a half-day anyhow. Get me? Twenty-five years—I'll tell you somethin' funny. Decoration Day an' the Fourth o' July are always on the same day o' the week. Twenty-five years. Never missed a day, and never more'n five minutes late. Look at my time card if you don't believe me. Eight twenty-seven, eight thirty, eight twenty-nine, eight twenty-seven, eight thirty-two. Eight an' thirty-two's forty an'—Goddam them figgers! I can't forget 'em. They're funny things, them figgers. They look like people sometimes. The eights, see? Two dots for the eyes and a dot for the nose. An' a line. That's the mouth, see? An' there's others remind you of other things—but I can't talk about them, on account of there bein' ladies here. Sure I killed him. Why didn't he shut up? If he'd only shut up! Instead o' talkin' an' talkin' about how sorry he was an' what a good guy I was an' this an' that. I felt like sayin' to him: "For Christ's sake, shut up!" But I didn't have the nerve, see? I didn't have the nerve to say that to the boss. An' he went on talkin', sayin' how sorry he was, see? He was standin' right close to me. An' his coat only had two buttons on it. Two an' two makes four an'—aw, can it! An' there was the bill-file on the desk. Right where I could touch it. It ain't right to kill a guy. I know that. When I read all about him in the paper an' about his three kids I felt like a cheap skate, I tell you. They had the kids' pictures in the paper, right next to mine. An' his wife, too. Gee, it must be swell to have a wife like that. Some guys sure is lucky. An' he left fifty thousand dollars just for a rest-room for the girls in the store. He was a good guy, at that. Fifty thousand. That's more'n twice as much as I'd have if I saved every nickel I ever made. Let's see. Twenty-five an' twenty-five an' twenty-five an'—aw, cut it out! An' the ads had a big, black border around 'em; an' all it said was that the store would be closed for three days on account of the boss bein' dead. That nearly handed me a laugh, that did. All them floorwalkers an' buyers an' high-muck-a-mucks havin' me to thank for gettin' three days off. I hadn't oughta killed him. I ain't sayin' nothin' about that. But I thought he was goin' to give me a raise, see? On account of bein' there twenty-five years. He never talked to me before, see? Except one mornin' we happened to come in the store together and I held the door open for him and he said "Thanks." Just like that, see? "Thanks!" That was the only time he ever talked to me. An' when I seen him comin' up to my desk, I didn't know where I got off. A big guy like that comin' up to my desk. I felt like I was chokin' like, and all of a sudden I got a kind o' bad taste in my mouth like when you get up in the mornin'. I didn't have no right to kill him. The district attorney

is right about that. He read the law to you, right out o' the book. Killin' a bird—that's wrong. But there was that girl, see? Six months they gave her. It was a dirty trick tellin' the cops on her like that. I shouldn't 'a' done that. But what was I gonna do? The wife wouldn't let up on me. I hadda do it. She used to walk around the room, just in her undershirt, see? Nothin' else on. Just her undershirt. An' they gave her six months. That's the last I'll ever see of her. Them birds—how do they get away with it? Just grabbin' women, the way you see 'em do in the pictures. I've seen lots I'd like to grab like that, but I ain't got the nerve—in the subway an' on the street an' in the store buyin' things. Pretty soft for them shoe-salesmen, I'll say, lookin' at women' legs all day. Them lawyers! They give me a pain, I tell you—a pain! Sayin' the same thing over an' over again. I never said I didn't kill him. But that ain't the same as bein' a regular murderer. What good did it do me to kill him? I didn't make nothin' out of it. Answer yes or no! Yes or no, me elbow! There's some things you can't answer yes or no. Give me the once-over, you guys. Do I look like a murderer? Do I? I never did no harm to nobody. Ask the wife. She'll tell you. Ask anybody. I never got into trouble. You wouldn't count that one time at the Polo Grounds. That was just fun like. Everybody was yellin', "kill the empire! Kill the empire!" An' before I knew what I was doin' I fired the pop bottle. It was on account of everybody yellin' like that. Just in fun like, see? The yeller dog! Callin' that one a strike—a mile away from the plate. Anyhow, the bottle didn't hit him. An' when I seen the cop comin' up the aisle, I beat it. That didn't hurt anybody. It was just in fun like, see? An' that time in the subway. I was readin' about a lynchin', see? Down in Georgia. They took the nigger an' they tied him to a tree. An' they poured kerosene on him and lit a big fire under him. The dirty nigger! Boy, I'd of liked to been there, with a gat in each hand, pumpin' him full of lead. I was readin' about it in the sub-way, see? Right at Times Square where the big crowd gets on. An' all of a sudden this big nigger steps right on my foot. It was lucky for him I didn't have a gun on me. I'd of killed him sure, I guess. I guess he couldn't help it all right on account of the crowd, but a nigger's got no right to step on a white man's foot. I told him where he got off all right. The dirty nigger. But that didn't hurt nobody, either. I'm a pretty steady guy, you gotta admit that. Twenty-five years in one job an' I never missed a day. Fifty-two weeks in a year. Fifty-two an' fifty-two an' fifty-two an'—They didn't have t' look for me, did they? I didn't try to run away, did I? Where was I goin' to run to! I wasn't thinkin' about it at all, see? I'll tell you what I was thinkin' about—how I was goin' to break it to the wife about bein' canned. He canned me after twenty-five years, see? Did the lawyers tell you about that? I forget. All that talk gives me a headache. Objection sustained. Objection overruled. Answer yes or no. It gives me a headache. And I can't get the figgers outta my head, neither. But that's what I was thinkin' about—how I was goin' t' break it to the wife about bein' canned. An' what Miss Devore would think when she heard about me killin' him. I bet she never thought I had the nerve to do it. I'd of married her if the wife had passed out. I'd be holdin' down my job yet, if he hadn't o' canned me. But he kept talkin' an' talkin'. An' there was the bill-file right where I could reach it. Do you get me? I'm just a regular guy like anybody else. Like you birds now. (*For the first time the* JURORS *relax, looking indignantly at each other and whispering.*) Suppose you was me, now. Maybe you'd 'a' done the same thing. That's the way you oughta look at it, see? Suppose you was me—

THE JURORS (*rising as one and shouting in unison*). GUILTY!

[ZERO *falls back, stunned for a moment by their vociferousness. The* JURORS *right-face in their places and file quickly out of the jury-box and toward the door in a double column.*]

ZERO (*recovering speech as the* JURORS *pass out at the door*). Wait a minute. Jest a minute. You don't get me right. Jest give me a chance an' I'll tell you how it was. I'm all mixed up, see? On account of them lawyers. And the figgers in my head. But I'm goin' to tell you how it was. I was there twenty-five years, see? An' they gave her six months, see? (*He goes on haranguing the empty jury-box as the curtain falls.*)

PRISON SCENE[1]

In the middle of the stage is a large cage with bars on all four sides. The bars are very far apart and the interior of the cage is clearly visible. The floor of the cage is about six feet above the level of the stage. A flight of wooden steps lead up to it on the side facing the audience. ZERO *is discovered in the middle of the cage seated at a table above which is suspended a single naked electric light. Before him is an enormous platter of ham and eggs which he eats voraciously with a large wooden spoon. He wears a uniform of very broad black and white horizontal stripes.*
[*A few moments after the rise of the curtain a man enters at left, wearing the blue uniform and peaked cap of a* GUIDE. *He is followed by a miscellaneous crowd of* MEN, WOMEN *and* CHILDREN—*about a dozen in all.*]

THE GUIDE (*stopping in front of the cage*). Now ladies and gentlemen, if you'll kindly step right this way! (THE CROWD *straggles up and forms a loose semi-circle around him.*) Step right up, please. A little closer so's everybody can hear. (THEY *move up closer.* ZERO *pays no attention whatever to them.*) This, ladies and gentlemen, is a

[1] This scene, which was part of the original script, was performed for the first time (in its present revised form) when the play was revived at the Phoenix Theatre in New York in February, 1956. It is here published for the first time by special permission of the author.

very in-ter-est-in' specimen; The North American murderer, Genus homo sapiens, Habitat North America. (*A titter of excitement.* THEY *all crowd up around the cage.*) Don't push. There's room enough for everybody.

A TALL LADY. Oh, how interesting!

A STOUT LADY (*excitedly*). Look, Charley, he's eating!

CHARLEY (*bored*). Yeh, I see him.

THE GUIDE (*repeating by rote*). This specimen, ladies and gentlemen, exhibits the characteristics which are typical of his kind—

A SMALL BOY (*in a little Lord Fauntleroy suit, whiningly*). Mama!

HIS MOTHER. Be quiet, Eustace, or I'll take you right home.

THE GUIDE. He has the opposable thumbs, the large cranial capacity and the highly developed pre-frontal areas which distinguish him from all other species.

A YOUTH (*who has been taking notes*). What areas did you say?

THE GUIDE (*grumpily*). Pre-front-al areas. He learns by imitation and has a language which is said by some eminent philiologists to bear many striking resemblances to English.

A BOY OF FOURTEEN. Pop, what's a philiologist?

HIS FATHER. Keep quiet, can't you, and listen to what he's sayin'.

THE GUIDE. He thrives and breeds freely in captivity. This specimen was taken alive in his native haunts shortly after murdering his boss.

[*Murmurs of great interest.*]

THE TALL LADY. Oh, how charming!

THE NOTE-TAKING YOUTH. What was that last? I didn't get it.

SEVERAL (*helpfully*). Murdering his boss.

THE YOUTH. Oh—thanks.

THE GUIDE. He was tried, convicted, and sentenced in one hour, thirteen minutes and twenty-four seconds which sets a new record for the territory east of the Rockies and north of the Mason and Dixon line.

LITTLE LORD FAUNTLEROY (*whiningly*). Ma-ma!

HIS MOTHER. Be quiet, Eustace, or Mama won't let you ride in the choo-choo.

THE GUIDE. Now take a good look at him, ladies and gents. It's his last day here. He's goin' to be executed at noon.

[*Murmurs of interest.*]

THE TALL LADY. Oh, how lovely!

A MAN. What's he eating?

THE STOUT LADY. He's quite a big eater, ain't he?

THE GUIDE. Oh, he don't always eat that much. You see we always try to make 'em feel good on their last day. So about a week in advance we let them order what they want to eat on their last day. They can have eight courses and they can order anything they want—don't make no difference what it costs or how hard it is to get. Well, he couldn't make up his mind till last night and then he ordered eight courses of ham and eggs.

[THEY *all push and stare.*]

THE BOY OF FOURTEEN. Look, pop! He's eatin' with a spoon. Don't he know how to use a knife and fork?

THE GUIDE (*overhearing him*). We don't dare trust him with a knife and fork, sonny. He might try to kill himself.

THE TALL LADY. Oh, how fascinating!

THE GUIDE (*resuming his official tone*). And now friends if you'll kindly give me your kind attention for just a moment. (*He takes a bundle of folders from his pocket.*) I have a little souvenir folder, which I'm sure you'll want to have. It contains twelve beautiful colored views, relating to the North American Murderer you have just been looking at. These include a picture of the murderer, a picture of the murderer's wife, the blood-stained weapon, the murderer at the age of six, the spot where the body was found, the little red school house where he went to school, and his vine-covered boyhood home in Southern Illinois, with his sweet-faced white-haired old mother plainly visible in the foreground. And many other interesting views. I'm now going to distribute these little folders for your examination. (*Sotto voce.*) Just pass them back, will you. (*In louder tones.*) Don't be afraid to look at them. You don't have to buy them if you don't want to. It don't cost anything to look at them. (*To the* NOTE-TAKING YOUTH *who is fumbling with a camera.*) Hey, there, young feller, no snapshots allowed. All right now friends, if you'll just step this way. Keep close together and follow me. A lady lost her little boy here one time and by the time we found him, he was smoking cigarettes and hollering for a razor.

[*Much laughter as* THEY *all follow him off left.* ZERO *finishes eating and pushes away his plate.*]

[*As the* CROWD *goes at left,* MRS. ZERO *enters at right. She is dressed in mourning garments. She carries a large parcel. She goes up the steps to the cage, opens the door and enters.* ZERO *looks up and sees her.*]

MRS. ZERO. Hello.

ZERO. Hello, I didn't think you were comin' again.

MRS. ZERO. Well, I thought I'd come again. Are you glad to see me?

ZERO. Sure. Sit down. (*She complies.*) You're all dolled up, ain't you?

MRS. ZERO. Yeh, don't you like it? (*She gets up and turns about like a mannequin.*)

ZERO. Gee. Some class.

MRS. ZERO. I always look good in black. There's some weight to this veil though; I'll tell the world. I got a fierce headache.

ZERO. How much did all that set you back?

MRS. ZERO. Sixty-four dollars and twenty cents. And I gotta get a pin yet and some writin' paper—you know with black around the edges.

ZERO. You'll be scrubbin' floors in about a year, if you go blowin' your coin like that.

MRS. ZERO. Well, I gotta do it right. It don't happen every day. (*She rises and takes up the parcel.*) I brought you somethin'.

ZERO (*interested*). Yeh, what?

MRS. ZERO (*opening the parcel*). You gotta guess.

ZERO. Er—er—gee, search me.

MRS. ZERO. Somethin' you like. (*She takes out a covered plate.*)

ZERO (*with increasing interest*). Looks like somethin' to eat.

MRS. ZERO. (*nodding*). Yeh. (*She takes off the top plate.*) Ham an' eggs!

ZERO (*joyfully*). Oh, boy! Just what I feel like eatin'. (*He takes up the wooden spoon and begins to eat avidly.*)

MRS. ZERO (*pleased*). Are they good?

ZERO (*his mouth full*). Swell.

MRS. ZERO (*a little sadly*). They're the last ones I'll ever make for you.

ZERO (*busily eating*). Uh-huh.

MRS. ZERO. I'll tell you somethin'—shall I?

ZERO. Sure.

MRS. ZERO (*hesitantly*). Well, all the while they were cookin' I was cryin'.

ZERO. Yeh? (*he leans over and pats her hand*).

MRS. ZERO. I jest couldn't help it. The thought of it just made me cry.

ZERO. Well—no use cryin' about it.

MRS. ZERO. I jest couldn't help it.

ZERO. Maybe this time next year you'll be fryin' eggs for some other bird.

MRS. ZERO. Not on your life.

ZERO. You never can tell.

MRS. ZERO. Not me. Once is enough for me.

ZERO. I guess you're right at that. Still, I dunno. You might jest happen to meet some guy—

MRS. ZERO. Well, if I do, there'll be time enough to think about it. No use borrowin' trouble.

ZERO. How do you like bein' alone in the house?

MRS. ZERO. Oh, it's all right.

ZERO. You got plenty room in the bed now, ain't you?

MRS. ZERO. Oh yeh. (*A brief pause.*) It's kinda lonesome though—you know, wakin' up in the mornin' and nobody around to talk to.

ZERO. Yeh, I know. It's the same with me.

MRS. ZERO. Not that we ever did much talkin'.

ZERO. Well, that ain't it. It's just the idea of havin' somebody there in case you want to talk.

MRS. ZERO. Yeh, that's it. (*Another brief*

pause.) I guess maybe I use t' bawl you out quite a lot, didn't I?

ZERO. Oh well—no use talkin' about it now.

MRS. ZERO. We were always at it, weren't we?

ZERO. No more than any other married folks, I guess.

MRS. ZERO (*dubiously*). I dunno—

ZERO. I guess I gave you cause, all right.

MRS. ZERO. Well—I got my faults too.

ZERO. None of us are perfect.

MRS. ZERO. We got along all right, at that, didn't we?

ZERO. Sure! Better'n most.

MRS. ZERO. Remember them Sundays at the beach, in the old days?

ZERO. You bet. (*With a laugh.*) Remember that time I ducked you. Gee, you was mad!

MRS. ZERO (*with a laugh*). I didn't talk to you for a whole week.

ZERO (*chuckling*). Yeh, I remember.

MRS. ZERO. And the time I had pneumonia and you brought me them roses. Remember?

ZERO. Yeh, I remember. And when the doctor told me maybe you'd pass out. I nearly sat down and cried.

MRS. ZERO. Did you?

ZERO. I sure did.

MRS. ZERO. We had some pretty good times at that, didn't we?

ZERO. I'll say we did!

MRS. ZERO (*with a sudden soberness*). It's all over now.

ZERO. All over is right. I ain't got much longer.

MRS. ZERO (*rising and going over to him*). Maybe—maybe—if we had to do it over again, it would be different.

ZERO (*taking her hand*). Yeh. We live and learn.

MRS. ZERO (*crying*). If we only had another chance.

ZERO. It's too late now.

MRS. ZERO. It don't seem right, does it?

ZERO. It ain't right. But what can you do about it?

MRS. ZERO. Ain't there somethin'—somethin' I can do for you—before—

ZERO. No. Nothin'. Not a thing.

MRS. ZERO. Nothin' at all?

ZERO. No. I can't think of anything. (*Suddenly.*) You're takin' good care of that scrap-book, ain't you? With all the clippings in it?

MRS. ZERO. Oh, sure. I got it right on the parlor table. Right where everybody can see it.

ZERO (*pleased*). It must be pretty near full, ain't it?

MRS. ZERO. All but about three pages.

ZERO. Well, there'll be more tomorrow. Enough to fill it, maybe. Be sure to get them all, will you?

MRS. ZERO. I will. I ordered the papers already.

ZERO. Gee, I never thought I'd have a whole book full of clippings all about myself. (*Suddenly.*) Say, that's somethin' I'd like to ask you.

MRS. ZERO. What?

ZERO. Suppose you should get sick or be run over or somethin', what would happen to the book?

MRS. ZERO. Well, I kinda thought I'd leave it to little Beatrice Elizabeth.

ZERO. Who? Your sister's kid?

MRS. ZERO. Yeh.

ZERO. What would she want with it?

MRS. ZERO. Well, it's nice to have, ain't it? And I wouldn't know who else to give it to.

ZERO. Well, I don't want her to have it. That fresh little kid puttin' her dirty fingers all over it.

MRS. ZERO. She ain't fresh and she ain't dirty. She's a sweet little thing.

ZERO. I don't want her to have it.

MRS. ZERO. Who do you want to have it then?

ZERO. Well, I kinda thought I'd like Miss Devore to have it.

MRS. ZERO. Miss Devore?

ZERO. Yeh. You know. Down at the store.

MRS. ZERO. Why should she have it?

ZERO. She'd take good care of it. And anyhow, I'd like her to have it.

MRS. ZERO. Oh you would, would you?

ZERO. Yes.

MRS. ZERO. Well, she ain't goin' to have it. Miss Devore! Where does she come in, I'd like to know, when I got two sisters and a niece.

ZERO. I don't care nothin' about your sisters and your niece.

MRS. ZERO. Well, I do! And Miss Devore ain't goin' to get it. Now put that in your pipe and smoke it.

ZERO. What have you got to say about it? It's my book, ain't it?

MRS. ZERO. No, it ain't. It's mine now—or it will be tomorrow. And I'm goin' to do what I like with it.

ZERO. I should have given it to her in the first place—that's what I should have done.

MRS. ZERO. Oh, should you? And what about me? Am I your wife or ain't I?

ZERO. Why remind me of my troubles?

MRS. ZERO. So it's Miss Devore all of a sudden, is it? What's been goin' on, I'd like to know, between you and Miss Devore?

ZERO. Aw, tie a can to that!

MRS. ZERO. Why didn't you marry Miss Devore, if you think so much of her!

ZERO. I would if I'd of met her first.

MRS. ZERO (*shrieking*). Ooh! A fine way to talk to me. After all I've done for you. You bum! You dirty bum! I won't stand for it! I won't stand for it!

[*In a great rage she takes up the dishes and smashes them on the floor. Then crying hysterically she opens the cage door, bangs it behind her, comes down the steps and goes off towards left.*]

[ZERO *stands gazing ruefully after her for a moment and then with a shrug and a sigh begins picking up the pieces of broken crockery.*]

[*As* MRS. ZERO *exits at left a door in the back of the cage opens and* A MAN *appears. He is dressed in a sky-blue padded silk dressing-gown which is fitted with innumerable pockets. Under this he wears a pink silk union-suit. His bare feet are in sandals. He wears a jaunty Panama hat with a red feather stuck in the brim. Wings are fastened to his sandals and to the shoulders of his dressing-gown.* ZERO *who is busy picking up the broken crockery does not notice him at first.* THE MAN *takes a gold toothpick and begins carefully picking his teeth, waiting for* ZERO *to notice him.* ZERO *happens to look up and suddenly sees the man. He utters a cry of terror and shrinks into the corner of the cage, trembling with fear.*]

ZERO (*hoarsely*). Who are you?

THE MAN (*calmly, as he pockets his toothpick*). I'm the Fixer—from the Claim Department.

ZERO. Whaddya want?

THE FIXER. It's no use, Zero. There are no miracles.

ZERO. I don't know what you're talkin' about.

THE FIXER. Don't lie, Zero. (*Holding up his hand.*) And now that your course is run —now that the end is already in sight, you still believe that some thunderbolt, some fiery bush, some celestial apparition will intervene between you and extinction. But it's no use, Zero. You're done for.

ZERO (*vehemently*). It ain't right! It ain't fair! I ain't gettin' a square deal!

THE FIXER (*wearily*). They all say that, Zero. (*Mildly.*) Now just tell me why you're not getting a square deal.

ZERO. Well, that addin'-machine. Was that a square deal—after twenty-five years?

THE FIXER. Certainly—from any point of view, except a sentimental one. (*Looking at his wrist watch.*) The machine is quicker, it never makes a mistake, it's always on time. It presents no problem of housing, traffic congestion, water supply, sanitation.

ZERO. It costs somethin' to buy them machines, I'll tell you that!

THE FIXER. Yes, you're right there. In one respect you have the advantage over the machine—the cost of manufacture. But we've learned from many years' experience, Zero, that the original cost is an inconsequential item compared to upkeep. Take the Dinosaurs, for example. They literally ate themselves out of existence. I held out for them to the last. They were damned picturesque—but when it came to a question of the nitrate supply, I simply had to yield. (*He begins to empty and clean his pipe.*) And so with you, Zero. It costs a lot to keep up all that delicate mechanism of eye and ear and hand and brain which you've never put to any use. We can't afford to maintain it in idleness —and so you've got to go. (*He puts the pipe in one of his pockets.*)

ZERO (*falling to his knees, supplicatingly*). Gimme a chance, gimme another chance!

THE FIXER. What would you do if I gave you another chance?

ZERO. Well—first thing I'd go out and look for a job.

THE FIXER. Adding figures?

ZERO. Well—I ain't young enough to take up somethin' new. (THE FIXER *takes out a police whistle and blows shrilly. Instantly two guards enter.*)

THE FIXER. Put the skids under him, boys, and make it snappy. (*He strolls away to the other side of the cage, and taking a nail clipper from a pocket, begins to clip his nails as the* GUARDS *seize* ZERO.)

ZERO (*Struggling and shrieking*). Don't kill me! Gimme a chance! Gimme another chance!

GUARD (*soothingly*). Ah come on! Be a good fellow! It'll all be over in a minute!

ZERO. I don't want to die! I don't want to die! I want to live. (THE GUARDS *look at each other dubiously. Then one of them walks rather timidly over to* THE FIXER *who is busy with his nails.*)

GUARD (*clearing his throat*). H'm!

THE FIXER (*looking up*). Well?

GUARD (*timidly*). He says he wants to live.

THE FIXER. No. He's no good.

GUARD (*touching his cap, deferentially*). Yes sir!

[*He goes back to his companion and the two of them drag* ZERO *out at the back of the cage, still struggling and screaming.*]

[THE FIXER *puts away his nailclippers, yawns, then goes to the table and sits on the edge of it. From a pocket he takes an enormous pair of horn-rimmed spectacles. Then from another pocket he takes a folded newspaper, which he unfolds carefully. It is a colored comic supplement. He*

holds it up in front of him and becomes absorbed in it.*]

[*A moment later the door at the back of the cage opens and a tall, brawny, bearded* MAN *enters. He wears a red flannel undershirt and carries a huge, blood-stained axe.* THE FIXER *absorbed in the comic supplement does not look up.*]

MAN (*hoarsely*). O. K.

THE FIXER (*looking up*). What?

MAN. O. K.

THE FIXER (*nodding*). Oh, all right.

[THE MAN *bows deferentially and goes out at the back.* THE FIXER *puts away his spectacles and folds the comic supplement carefully.*]

THE FIXER (*as he folds the paper*). That makes a total of 2137 black eyes for Jeff.

[*He puts away the paper, turns out the electric light over his head and leaves the cage by the front door. Then he takes a padlock from a pocket, attaches it to the door and saunters off as the curtain falls.*]

SCENE FIVE

A graveyard in full moonlight. It is a second-rate graveyard—no elaborate tombstones or monuments—just simple headstones and here and there a cross. At the back is an iron fence with a gate in the middle. At first no one is visible, but there are occasional sounds throughout: the hooting of an owl, the whistle of a distant whippoorwill, the croaking of a bull-frog, and the yowling of a serenading cat.

[*After a few moments two figures appear outside the gate—a man and a woman. She pushes the gate and it opens with a rusty creak. The couple enter. They are now fully visible in the moonlight—*JUDY O'GRADY *and a* YOUNG MAN.]

JUDY (*advancing*). Come on, this is the place.

YOUNG MAN (*hanging back*). This! Why, this here is a cemetery.

JUDY. Aw, quit yer kiddin'!

YOUNG MAN. You don't mean to say—

JUDY. What's the matter with this place?

YOUNG MAN. A cemetery!

JUDY. Sure. What of it?

YOUNG MAN. You must be crazy.

JUDY. This place is all right, I tell you. I been here lots o' times.

YOUNG MAN. Nix on this place for me!

JUDY. Ain't this place as good as another? Whaddya afraid of? They're all dead ones here! They don't bother you. (*With sudden interest.*) Oh, look, here's a new one.

YOUNG MAN. Come on out of here.

JUDY. Wait a minute. Let's see what it says. (*She kneels on a grave in the foreground and putting her face close to headstone spells out the inscription.*) Z-E-R-O. Z-e-r-o. Zero! Say, that's the guy—

YOUNG MAN. Zero? He's the guy killed his boss, ain't he?

JUDY. Yeh, that's him, all right. But what I'm thinkin' of is that I went to the hoosegow on account of him.

YOUNG MAN. What for?

JUDY. You know, same old stuff. Tenement House Law. (*Mincingly.*) Section blaablaa of the Penal Code. Third offense. Six months.

YOUNG MAN. And this bird—

JUDY (*contemptuously*). Him? He was mamma's white-haired boy. We lived in the same house. Across the air-shaft, see? I used to see him lookin' in my window. I guess his wife musta seen him, too. Anyhow, they went and turned the bulls on me. And now I'm out and he's in. (*Suddenly.*) Say—say—(*She bursts into a peal of laughter.*)

YOUNG MAN (*nervously*). What's so funny?

JUDY (*rocking with laughter*). Say, wouldn't it be funny—if—if—(*She explodes again.*) That would be a good joke on him, all right. He can't do nothin' about it now, can he?

YOUNG MAN. Come on out of here. I don't like this place.

JUDY. Aw, you're a bum sport. What do you want to spoil my joke for?

[*A cat yammers mellifluously.*]

YOUNG MAN (*half hysterically*). What's that?

JUDY. It's only the cats. They seem to like it here all right. But come on if you're afraid. (*They go toward the gate. As they go out.*) You nervous men sure are the limit.

[*They go out through the gate. As they disappear,* ZERO'S *grave opens suddenly and his head appears.*]

ZERO (*looking about*). That's funny! I thought I heard her talkin' and laughin'. But I don't see nobody. Anyhow, what would she be doin' here? I guess I must 'a' been dreamin'. But how could I be dreamin' when I ain't been asleep? (*He looks about again.*) Well, no use goin' back. I can't sleep, anyhow. I might as well walk around a little.

[*He rises out of the ground, very rigidly. He wears a full-dress suit of very antiquated cut and his hands are folded stiffly across his breast.*]

ZERO (*walking woodenly*). Gee! I'm stiff! (*He slowly walks a few steps, then stops.*) Gee, it's lonesome here! (*He shivers and walks on aimlessly.*) I should 'a' stayed where I was. But I thought I heard her laughin'.

[*A loud sneeze is heard.* ZERO *stands motionless, quaking with terror. The sneeze is repeated.*]

ZERO (*hoarsely*). What's that?

A MILD VOICE. It's all right. Nothing to be afraid of.

[*From behind a headstone* SHRDLU *appears. He is dressed in a shabby and ill-fitting cutaway. He wears silver-rimmed spectacles and is smoking a cigarette.*]

SHRDLU. I hope I didn't frighten you.

ZERO (*still badly shaken*). No-o. It's all right. You see, I wasn't expectin' to see anybody.

SHRDLU. You're a newcomer, aren't you?

ZERO. Yeh, this is my first night. I couldn't seem to get to sleep.

SHRDLU. I can't sleep, either. Suppose we keep each other company, shall we?

ZERO (*eagerly*). Yeh, that would be great. I been feelin' awful lonesome.

SHRDLU (*nodding*). I know. Let's make ourselves comfortable.

[*He seats himself easily on a grave.* ZERO

tries to follow his example, but he is stiff in every joint and groans with pain.]

ZERO. I'm kinda stiff.

SHRDLU. You mustn't mind the stiffness. It wears off in a few days. (*He seats himself on the grave beside* ZERO *and produces a package of cigarettes.*) Will you have a Camel?

ZERO. No, I don't smoke.

SHRDLU. I find it helps keep the mosquitoes away. (*He lights a cigarette.*)

SHRDLU (*suddenly taking the cigarette out of his mouth*). Do you mind if I smoke, Mr.—Mr.—?

ZERO. No, go right ahead.

SHRDLU (*replacing the cigarette*). Thank you. I didn't catch your name.

[ZERO *does not reply.*]

SHRDLU (*mildly*). I say I didn't catch your name.

ZERO. I heard you the first time. (*Hesitantly.*) I'm scared if I tell you who I am and what I done, you'll be off me.

SHRDLU (*sadly*). No matter what your sins may be, they are as snow compared to mine.

ZERO. You got another guess comin'. (*He pauses dramatically.*) My name's Zero. I'm a murderer.

SHRDLU (*nodding calmly*). Oh, yes, I remember reading about you, Mr. Zero.

ZERO (*a little piqued*). And you still think you're worse than me?

SHRDLU (*throwing away his cigarette*). Oh, a thousand times worse, Mr. Zero—a million times worse.

ZERO. What did you do?

SHRDLU. I, too, am a murderer.

ZERO (*looking at him in amazement*). Go on! You're kiddin' me!

SHRDLU. Every word I speak is the truth, Mr. Zero. I am the foulest, the most sinful of murderers! You only murdered your employer, Mr. Zero. But I—I murdered my mother. (*He covers his face with his hands and sobs.*)

ZERO (*horrified*). The hell yer say!

SHRDLU (*sobbing*). Yes, my mother!—my beloved mother!

ZERO (*suddenly*). Say, you don't mean to say you're Mr.—

SHRDLU (*nodding*). Yes. (*He wipes his eyes, still quivering with emotion.*)

ZERO. I remember readin' about you in the papers.

SHRDLU. Yes, my guilt has been proclaimed to all the world. But that would be a trifle if only I could wash the stain of sin from my soul.

ZERO. I never heard of a guy killin' his mother before. What did you do it for?

SHRDLU. Because I have a sinful heart—there is no other reason.

ZERO. Did she always treat you square and all like that?

SHRDLU. She was a saint—a saint, I tell you. She cared for me and watched over me as only a mother can.

ZERO. You mean to say you didn't have a scrap or nothin'?

SHRDLU. Never a harsh or an unkind word. Nothing except loving care and good advice. From my infancy she devoted herself to guiding me on the right path. She taught me to be thrifty, to be devout, to be unselfish, to shun evil companions and to shut my ears to all the temptations of the flesh—in short, to become a virtuous, respectable, and God-fearing man. (*He groans.*) But it was a hopeless task. At fourteen I began to show evidence of my sinful nature.

ZERO (*breathlessly*). You didn't kill anybody else, did you?

SHRDLU. No, thank God, there is only one murder on my soul. But I ran away from home.

ZERO. You did!

SHRDLU. Yes. A companion lent me a profane book—the only profane book I have ever read, I'm thankful to say. It was called *Treasure Island*. Have you ever read it?

ZERO. No, I never was much on readin' books.

SHRDLU. It is a wicked book—a lurid tale of adventure. But it kindled in my sinful heart a desire to go to sea. And so I ran away from home.

ZERO. What did you do—get a job as a sailor?

SHRDLU. I never saw the sea—not to the day of my death. Luckily, my mother's loving intuition warned her of my intention and I was sent back home. She welcomed me with open arms. Not an angry word, not a look of reproach. But I could read the mute suffering in her eyes as we prayed together all through the night.

ZERO (*sympathetically*). Gee, that must 'a' been tough. Gee, the mosquitoes are bad, ain't they? (*He tries awkwardly to slap at them with his stiff hands.*)

SHRDLU (*absorbed in his narrative*). I thought that experience had cured me of evil and I began to think about a career. I wanted to go in foreign missions at first, but we couldn't bear the thought of the separation. So we finally decided that I should become a proof-reader.

ZERO. Say, slip me one o' them Camels, will you? I'm gettin' all bit up.

SHRDLU. Certainly (*He hands* ZERO *cigarettes and matches.*)

ZERO (*lighting up*). Go ahead. I'm listenin'.

SHRDLU. By the time I was twenty I had a good job reading proof for a firm that printed catalogues. After a year they promoted me and let me specialize in shoe catalogues.

ZERO. Yeh? That must 'a' been a good job.

SHRDLU. It was a very good job. I was on the shoe catalogues for thirteen years. I'd been on them yet, if I hadn't—(*He chokes back a sob.*)

ZERO. They oughta put a shot o' citronella in that embalmin'-fluid.

SHRDLU (*he sighs*). We were so happy together. I had my steady job. And Sundays we would go to morning, afternoon, and evening service. It was an honest and moral mode of life.

ZERO. It sure was.

SHRDLU. Then came that fatal Sunday. Dr. Amaranth, our minister, was having dinner with us—one of the few pure spirits on earth. When he had finished saying grace, we had our soup. Everything was going along as usual—we were eating our soup and discussing the sermon, just like every other Sunday I could remember. Then came the leg of lamb—(*He breaks off, then resumes in a choking voice.*) I see the whole scene before me so plainly —it never leaves me—Dr. Amaranth at my right, my mother at my left, the leg of lamb on the table in front of me, and the cuckoo clock on the little shelf between the windows. (*He stops and wipes his eyes.*)

ZERO. Yeh, but what happened?

SHRDLU. Well, as I started to carve the lamb —Did you ever carve a leg of lamb?

ZERO. No, corned beef was our speed.

SHRDLU. It's very difficult on account of the bone. And when there's gravy in the dish there's danger of spilling it. So Mother always used to hold the dish for me. She leaned forward, just as she always did, and I could see the gold locket around her neck. It had my picture in it and one of my baby curls. Well, I raised my knife to carve the leg of lamb—and instead I cut my mother's throat! (*He sobs.*)

ZERO. You must 'a' been crazy!

SHRDLU (*raising his head, vehemently*). No! Don't try to justify me. I wasn't crazy. They tried to prove at the trial that I was crazy. But Dr. Amaranth saw the truth! He saw it from the first! He knew that it was my sinful nature—and he told me what was in store for me.

ZERO (*trying to be comforting*). Well, your troubles are over now.

SHRDLU (*his voice rising*). Over! Do you think this is the end?

ZERO. Sure. What more can they do to us?

SHRDLU (*his tones growing shriller and shriller*). Do you think there can ever be any peace for such as we are—murderers, sinners? Don't you know what awaits us —flames, eternal flames!

ZERO (*nervously*). Keep your shirt on, Buddy—they wouldn't do that to us.

SHRDLU. There's no escape—no escape for us, I tell you. We're doomed! We're doomed to suffer unspeakable torments through all eternity. (*His voice rises higher and higher.*)

[*A grave opens suddenly and a head appears.*]

THE HEAD. Hey, you birds! Can't you shut up and let a guy sleep?

[ZERO *scrambles painfully to his feet.*]

ZERO (*to* SHRDLU). Hey, put on the soft pedal.

SHRDLU (*too wrought up to attend*). It won't be long now! We'll receive our summons soon.

THE HEAD. Are you goin' to beat it or not? He calls into the grave.) Hey, Bill, lend me your head a minute. (*A moment later his arm appears holding a skull.*)

ZERO (*warningly*). Look out! (*He seizes* SHRDLU *and drags him away just as* THE HEAD *throws the skull.*)

THE HEAD (*disgustedly*). Missed 'em. Damn old tabby cats! I'll get 'em next time. (*A prodigious yawn.*) Ho-hum! Me for the worms!

[THE HEAD *disappears as the curtain falls.*]

SCENE SIX

A pleasant place. A scene of pastoral loveliness. A meadow dotted with fine old trees and carpeted with rich grass and field flowers. In the background are seen a number of tents fashioned of gay-striped silks and beyond gleams a meandering river. Clear air and a fleckless sky. Sweet distant music throughout.

[*At the rise of the curtain,* SHRDLU *is seen seated under a tree in the foreground in an attitude of deep dejection. His knees are drawn up and his head is buried in his arms. He is dressed as in the preceding scene.*

[*A few minutes later,* ZERO *enters at right. He walks slowly and looks about him with an air of half-suspicious curiosity. He, too, is dressed as in the preceding scene. Suddenly he sees* SHRDLU *seated under the tree. He stands still and looks at him half fearfully. Then, seeing something familiar in him, goes closer.* SHRDLU *is unaware of his presence. At last* ZERO *recognizes him and grins in pleased surprise.*]

ZERO. Well, if it ain't—! (*He claps* SHRDLU *on the shoulder.*) Hello, Buddy!

[SHRDLU *looks up slowly, then, recognizing* ZERO, *he rises gravely and extends his hand courteously.*]

SHRDLU. How do you do, Mr. Zero? I'm very glad to see you again.

ZERO. Same here. I wasn't expectin' to see you, either. (*Looking about.*) This is a kinda nice place. I wouldn't mind restin' here a while.

SHRDLU. You may if you wish.

ZERO. I'm kinda tired. I ain't used to bein' outdoors. I ain't walked so much in years.

SHRDLU. Sit down here, under the tree.

ZERO. Do they let you sit on the grass?

SHRDLU. Oh, yes.

ZERO (*seating himself*). Boy, this feels good. I'll tell the world my feet are sore. I ain't used to so much walkin'. Say, I wonder would it be all right if I took my shoes off; my feet are tired.

SHRDLU. Yes. Some of the people here go barefoot.

ZERO. Yeh? They sure must be nuts. But I'm goin' t' leave 'em off for a while. So long as it's all right. The grass feels nice and cool. (*He stretches out comfortably.*) Say, this is the life of Riley all right, all right. This sure is a nice place. What do they call this place, anyhow?

SHRDLU. The Elysian Fields.

ZERO. The which?

SHRDLU. The Elysian Fields.

ZERO (*dubiously*). Oh! Well, it's a nice place, all right.

SHRDLU. They say that this is the most desirable of all places. Only the most favored remain here.

ZERO. Yeh? Well, that lets me out, I guess. (*Suddenly.*) But what are you doin' here? I thought you'd be burned by now.

SHRDLU (*sadly*). Mr. Zero, I am the most unhappy of men.

ZERO (*in mild astonishment*). Why, because you ain't bein' roasted alive?

SHRDLU (*nodding*). Nothing is turning out as I expected. I saw everything so clearly —the flames, the tortures, an eternity of suffering as the just punishment for my unspeakable crime. And it has all turned out so differently.

ZERO. Well, that's pretty soft for you, ain't it?

SHRDLU (*wailingly*). No, no, no! It's right and just that I should be punished. I could have endured it stoically. All through those endless ages of indescribable torment I should have exulted in the magnificence of divine justice. But this—this is maddening! What becomes of justice? What becomes of morality? What becomes of right and wrong? It's maddening—simply maddening! Oh, if Dr. Amaranth were only here to advise me! (*He buries his face and groans.*)

ZERO (*trying to puzzle it out*). You mean to say they ain't called you for cuttin' your mother's throat?

SHRDLU. No! It's terrible—terrible! I was prepared for anything—anything but this.

ZERO. Well, what did they say to you?

SHRDLU (*looking up*). Only that I was to come here and remain until I understood.

ZERO. I don't get it. What do they want you to understand?

SHRDLU (*despairingly*). I don't know—I don't know! If I only had an inkling of what they meant—(*Interrupting him.*) Just listen quietly for a moment; do you hear anything?

[*They are both silent, straining their ears.*]

ZERO (*at length*). Nope.

SHRDLU. You don't hear any music? Do you?

ZERO. Music? No, I don't hear nothin'.

SHRDLU. The people here say that the music never stops.

ZERO. They're kiddin' you.

SHRDLU. Do you think so?

ZERO. Sure thing. There ain't a sound.

SHRDLU. Perhaps. They're capable of anything. But I haven't told you of the bitterest of my disappointments.

ZERO. Well, spill it. I'm gettin' used to hearin' bad news.

SHRDLU. When I came to this place, my first thought was to find my dear mother. I wanted to ask her forgiveness. And I wanted her to help me to understand.

ZERO. An' she couldn't do it?

SHRDLU (*with a deep groan*). She's not here! Mr. Zero! Here where only the most favoured dwell, that wisest and purest of spirits is nowhere to be found. I don't understand it.

A WOMAN'S VOICE (*in the distance*). Mr. Zero! Oh, Mr. Zero!

[ZERO *raises his head and listens attentively.*]

SHRDLU (*going on, unheedingly*). If you were to see some of the people here—the things they do—

ZERO (*interrupting*). Wait a minute, will you? I think somebody's callin' me.

THE VOICE (*somewhat nearer*). Mr. Ze-ro! Oh! Mr. Ze-ro!

ZERO. Who the hell's that now? I wonder if the wife's on my trail already. That would be swell, wouldn't it? An' I figured on her bein' good for another twenty years, anyhow.

THE VOICE (*nearer*). Mr. Ze-ro! Yoo-hoo!

ZERO. No. That ain't her voice. (*Calling, savagely.*) Yoo-hoo. (*To* SHRDLU.) Ain't that always the way? Just when a guy is takin' life easy an' havin' a good time! (*He rises and looks off left.*) Here she comes, whoever she is. (*In sudden amazement.*) Well, I'll be—! Well, what do you know about that!

[*He stands looking in wonderment, as* DAISY DIANA DOROTHEA DEVORE *enters. She wears a much-beruffled white muslin dress which is a size too small and fifteen years too youthful for her. She is red-faced and breathless.*]

DAISY (*panting*). Oh! I thought I'd never catch up to you. I've been followin' you for days—callin' an' callin'. Didn't you hear me?

ZERO. Not till just now. You look kinda winded.

DAISY. I sure am. I can't hardly catch my breath.

ZERO. Well, sit down an' take a load off your feet.

[*He leads her to the tree.* DAISY *sees* SHRDLU *for the first time and shrinks back a little.*]

ZERO. It's all right, he's a friend of mine. (*To* SHRDLU.) Buddy, I want you to meet my friend, Miss Devore.

SHRDLU (*rising and extending his hand courteously*). How do you do, Miss Devore?

DAISY (*self-consciously*). How do!

ZERO (*to* DAISY). He's a friend of mine. (*To* SHRDLU.) I guess you don't mind if she sits here a while an' cools off, do you?

SHRDLU. No, no, certainly not.

[*They all seat themselves under the tree. ZERO and DAISY are a little self-conscious. SHRDLU gradually becomes absorbed in his own thoughts.*]

ZERO. I was just takin' a rest myself. I took my shoes off on account of my feet bein' so sore.

DAISY. Yeh, I'm kinda tired, too. (*Looking about.*) Say, ain't it pretty here, though?

ZERO. Yeh, it is at that.

DAISY. What do they call this place?

ZERO. Why—er—let's see. He was tellin' me just a minute ago. The—er—I don't know. Some kind o' fields. I forget now. (*To* SHRDLU.) Say, Buddy, what do they call this place again? (SHRDLU, *absorbed in his thoughts, does not hear him. To* DAISY.) He don't hear me. He's thinkin' again.

DAISY (*sotto voce*). What's the matter with him?

ZERO. Why, he's the guy that murdered his mother—remember?

DAISY (*interested*). Oh, yeh! Is that him?

ZERO. Yeh. An' he had it all figgered out how they was goin' t' roast him or somethin'. And now they ain't goin' to do nothin' to him an' it's kinda got his goat.

DAISY (*sympathetically*). Poor feller!

ZERO. Yeh. He takes it kinda hard.

DAISY. He looks like a nice young feller.

ZERO. Well, you sure are good for sore eyes. I never expected to see you here.

DAISY. I thought maybe you'd be kinda surprised.

ZERO. Surprised is right. I thought you was alive an' kickin'. When did you pass out?

DAISY. Oh, right after you did—a coupla days.

ZERO (*interested*). Yeh? What happened? Get hit by a truck or somethin'?

DAISY. No. (*Hesitantly.*) You see—it's this way. I blew out the gas.

ZERO (*astonished*). Go on! What was the big idea?

DAISY (*falteringly*). Oh, I don't know. You see, I lost my job.

ZERO. I'll bet you're sorry you did it now, ain't you?

DAISY (*with conviction*). No, I ain't sorry. Not a bit. (*Then hesitantly.*) Say, Mr. Zero, I been thinkin'—(*She stops.*)

ZERO. What?

DAISY (*plucking up courage*). I been thinkin' it would be kinda nice—if you an' me—if we could kinda talk things over.

ZERO. Yeh. Sure. What do you want to talk about?

DAISY. Well—I don't know—but you and me—we ain't really ever talked things over, have we?

ZERO. No, that's right, we ain't. Well, let's go to it.

DAISY. I was thinkin' if we could be alone— just the two of us, see?

ZERO. Oh, yeh! Yeh, I get you. (*He turns to* SHRDLU *and coughs loudly.* SHRDLU *does not stir.*)

ZERO (*to* DAISY). He's dead to the world. (*He turns to* SHRDLU.) Say, Buddy! (*No answer.*) Say, Buddy!

SHRDLU (*looking up with a start*). Were you speaking to me?

ZERO. Yeh. How'd you guess it? I was thinkin' that maybe you'd like to walk around a little and look for your mother.

SHRDLU (*shaking his head*). It's no use. I've looked everywhere. (*He relapses into thought again.*)

ZERO. Maybe over there they might know.

SHRDLU. No, no! I've searched everywhere. She's not here.

[ZERO *and* DAISY *look at each other in despair.*]

ZERO. Listen, old shirt, my friend here and me—see?—we used to work in the same store. An' we got some things to talk over

—business, see?—kinda confidential. So if it ain't askin' too much—

SHRDLU (*springing to his feet*). Why, certainly! Excuse me! (*He bows politely to* DAISY *and walks off.* DAISY *and* ZERO *watch him until he has disappeared.*)

ZERO (*with a forced laugh*). He's a good guy at that.

[*Now that they are alone, both are very self-conscious, and for a time they sit in silence.*]

DAISY (*breaking the silence*). It sure is pretty here, ain't it?

ZERO. Sure is.

DAISY. Look at the flowers! Ain't they just perfect! Why, you'd think they was artificial, wouldn't you?

ZERO. Yeh, you would.

DAISY. And the smell of them. Like perfume.

ZERO. Yeh.

DAISY. I'm crazy about the country, ain't you?

ZERO. Yeh. It's nice for a change.

DAISY. Them store picnics—remember?

ZERO. You bet. They sure was fun.

DAISY. One time—I guess you don't remember—the two of us—me and you—we sat down on the grass together under a tree—just like we're doin' now.

ZERO. Sure I remember.

DAISY. Go on! I'll bet you don't.

ZERO. I'll bet I do. It was the year the wife didn't go.

DAISY (*her face brightening*). That's right! I didn't think you'd remember.

ZERO. An' comin' home we sat together in the truck.

DAISY (*eagerly, rather shamefacedly*). Yeh! There's somethin' I've always wanted to ask you.

ZERO. Well, why didn't you?

DAISY. I don't know. It didn't seem refined. But I'm goin' to ask you now, anyhow.

ZERO. Go ahead. Shoot.

DAISY (*falteringly*). Well—while we was comin' home—you put your arm up on the bench behind me—and I could feel your knee kinda pressin' against mine. (*She stops.*)

ZERO (*becoming more and more interested*). Yea—well—what about it?

DAISY. What I wanted to ask you was—was it just kinda accidental?

ZERO (*with a laugh*). Sure it was accidental. Accidental on purpose.

DAISY (*eagerly*). Do you mean it?

ZERO. Sure I mean it. You mean to say you didn't know it?

DAISY. No. I've been wantin' to ask you—

ZERO. Then why did you get sore at me?

DAISY. Sore? I wasn't sore! When was I sore?

ZERO. That night. Sure you was sore. If you wasn't sore, why did you move away?

DAISY. Just to see if you meant it. I thought if you meant it, you'd move up closer. An' then when you took your arm away, I was sure you didn't mean it.

ZERO. An' I thought all the time you was sore. That's why I took my arm away. I thought if I moved up you'd holler and then I'd be in a jam, like you read in the paper all the time about guys gettin' pulled in for annoyin' women.

DAISY. An' I was wishin' you'd put your arm around me—just sittin' there wishin' all the way home.

ZERO. What do you know about that? That sure is hard luck, that is. If I'd 'a' only knew! You know what I felt like doin'—only I didn't have the nerve?

DAISY. What?

ZERO. I felt like kissin' you.

DAISY (*fervently*). I wanted you to.

ZERO (*astonished*). You would 'a' let me?

DAISY. I wanted you to! I wanted you to! Oh, why didn't you—why didn't you?

ZERO. I didn't have the nerve. I sure was a dumb-bell.

DAISY. I would 'a' let you all you wanted to. I wouldn't 'a' cared. I know it would 'a' been wrong, but I wouldn't 'a' cared. I wasn't thinkin' about right an' wrong at all. I didn't care—see? I just wanted you to kiss me.

ZERO (*feelingly*). If I'd only knew. I wanted to do it, I swear I did. But I didn't think you cared nothin' about me.

DAISY (*passionately*). I never cared nothin' about nobody else.

ZERO. Do you mean it—on the level? You ain't kiddin' me, are you?

DAISY. No, I ain't kiddin'. I mean it. I'm tellin' you the truth. I ain't never had the nerve to tell you before—but now I don't care. It don't make no difference now. I mean it—every word of it.

ZERO (*dejectedly*). If I'd only knew it.

DAISY. Listen to me. There's somethin' else I want to tell you. I may as well tell you everything now. It don't make no difference now. About my blowin' out the gas —see? Do you know why I done it?

ZERO. Yeh, you told me—on account o' bein' canned.

DAISY. I just told you that. That ain't the real reason. The real reason is on account o' you.

ZERO. You mean to say on account o' me passin' out—?

DAISY. Yeh. That's it. I didn't want to go on livin'. What for? What did I want to go on livin' for? I didn't have nothin' to live for with you gone. I often thought of doin' it before. But I never had the nerve. An' anyhow I didn't want to leave you.

ZERO. An' me bawlin' you out, about readin' too fast an' readin' too slow.

DAISY (*reproachfully*). Why did you do it?

ZERO. I don't know, I swear I don't. I was always stuck on you. An' while I'd be addin' them figgers, I'd be thinkin' how, if the wife died, you an' me could get married.

DAISY. I used to think o' that, too.

ZERO. An' then, before I knew it, I was bawlin' you out.

DAISY. Them was the times I'd think o' blowin' out the gas. But I never did till you was gone. There wasn't nothin' to live for then. But it wasn't so easy to do, anyhow. I never could stand the smell o' gas. An' all the while I was gettin' ready, you know, stuffin' up all the cracks, the way you read about in the paper—I was thinkin' of you and hopin' that maybe I'd meet you again. An' I made up my mind if I ever did see you, I'd tell you.

ZERO (*taking her hand*). I'm sure glad you did. I'm sure glad. (*Ruefully.*) But it don't do much good now, does it?

DAISY. No, I guess it don't. (*Summoning courage.*) But there's one thing I'm goin' to ask you.

ZERO. What's that?

DAISY (*in a low voice*). I want you to kiss me.

ZERO. You bet I will! (*He leans over and kisses her cheek.*)

DAISY. Not like that. I don't mean like that. I mean really kiss me. On the mouth. I ain't never been kissed like that.

[ZERO *puts his arms about her and presses his lips to hers. A long embrace. At last they separate and sit side by side in silence.*]

DAISY (*putting her hands to her cheeks*). So that's what it's like. I didn't know it could be like that. I didn't know anythin' could be like that.

ZERO (*fondling her hand*). Your cheeks are red. They're all red. And your eyes are shinin'. I never seen your eyes shinin' like that before.

DAISY (*holding up her hand*). Listen—do you hear it? Do you hear the music?

ZERO. No I don't hear nothin'!

DAISY. Yeh—music. Listen an' you'll hear it. (*They are both silent for a moment.*)

ZERO (*excitedly*). Yeh! I hear it! He said there was music, but I didn't hear it till just now.

DAISY. Ain't it grand?

ZERO. Swell! Say, do you know what?

DAISY. What?

ZERO. It makes me feel like dancin'.

DAISY. Yeh? Me, too.

ZERO (*springing to his feet*). Come on! Let's dance! (*He seizes her hands and tries to pull her up.*)

DAISY (*resisting laughingly*). I can't dance. I ain't danced in twenty years.

ZERO. That's nothin'. I ain't, neither. Come on! I feel just like a kid! (*He pulls her to her feet and seizes her about the waist.*)

DAISY. Wait a minute! Wait till I fix my skirt.

[*She turns back her skirts and pins them above the ankles.* ZERO *seizes her about the waist. They dance clumsily, but with gay abandon.* DAISY'S *hair becomes loosened and tumbles over her shoulders. She lends herself more and more to the spirit of the dance. But* ZERO *soon begins to tire and dances with less and less zest.*]

ZERO (*stopping at last, panting for breath*). Wait a minute! I'm all winded.

[*He releases* DAISY, *but before he can turn away, she throws her arms about him and presses her lips to his.*]

ZERO (*freeing himself*). Wait a minute! Let me get my wind!

[*He limps to the tree and seats himself under it, gasping for breath.* DAISY *looks after him, her spirits rather dampened.*]

ZERO. Whew! I sure am winded! I ain't used to dancin'. (*He takes off his collar and tie and opens the neckband of his shirt.* DAISY *sits under the tree near him, looking at him longingly. But he is busy catching his breath.*) Gee, my heart's goin' a mile a minute.

DAISY. Why don't you lay down an' rest? You could put your head on my lap.

ZERO. That ain't a bad idea. (*He stretches out, his head in* DAISY'S *lap.*)

DAISY (*fondling his hair*). It was swell, wasn't it?

ZERO. Yeh. But you gotta be used to it.

DAISY. Just imagine if we could stay here all the time—you an' me together—wouldn't it be swell?

ZERO. Yeh. But there ain't a chance.

DAISY. Won't they let us stay?

ZERO. No. This place is only for the good ones.

DAISY. Well, we ain't so bad, are we?

ZERO. Go on! Me a murderer an' you committin' suicide. Anyway, they wouldn't stand for this—the way we been goin' on.

DAISY. I don't see why.

ZERO. You don't! You know it ain't right. Ain't I got a wife?

DAISY. Not any more you ain't. When you're dead, that ends it. Don't they always say "until death do us part?"

ZERO. Well, maybe you're right about that, but they wouldn't stand for us here.

DAISY. It would be swell—the two of us together—we could make up for all them years.

ZERO. Yeh, I wish we could.

DAISY. We sure were fools. But I don't care. I've got you now. (*She kisses his forehead and cheeks and mouth.*)

ZERO. I'm sure crazy about you. I never saw you lookin' so pretty before, with your cheeks all red. An' your hair hangin' down. You got swell hair. (*He fondles and kisses her hair.*)

DAISY (*ecstatically*). We got each other now, ain't we?

ZERO. Yeh. I'm crazy about you. Daisy! That's a pretty name. It's a flower, ain't it? Well—that's what you are—just a flower.

DAISY (*happily*). We can always be together now, can't we?

ZERO. As long as they'll let us. I sure am crazy about you. (*Suddenly he sits upright.*) Watch your step!

DAISY (*alarmed*). What's the matter?

ZERO (*nervously*). He's comin' back.

DAISY. Oh, is that all? Well, what about it?

ZERO. You don't want him to see us layin' around like this, do you?

DAISY. I don't care if he does.

ZERO. Well, you oughta care. You don't want him to think you ain't a refined girl, do you? He's an awful moral bird, he is.

DAISY. I don't care nothin' about him. I don't care nothin' about anybody but you.

ZERO. Sure, I know. But we don't want people talkin' about us. You better fix your hair an' pull down your skirts.

[DAISY *complies rather sadly. They are both silent as* SHRDLU *enters.*]

ZERO (*with feigned nonchalance*). Well, you got back all right, didn't you?

SHRDLU. I hope I haven't returned too soon.

ZERO. No, that's all right. We were just havin' a little talk. You know—about business an' things.

DAISY (*boldly*). We were wishin' we could stay here all the time.

SHRDLU. You may if you like.

ZERO *and* DAISY (*in astonishment*). What!

SHRDLU. Yes. Any one who likes may remain—

ZERO. But I thought you were tellin' me—

SHRDLU. Just as I told you, only the most favored do remain. But any one may.

ZERO. I don't get it. There's a catch in it somewheres.

DAISY. It don't matter as long as we can stay.

ZERO (*to* SHRDLU). We were thinkin' about gettin' married, see?

SHRDLU. You may or not, just as you like.

ZERO. You don't mean to say we could stay if we didn't, do you?

SHRDLU. Yes. They don't care.

ZERO. An' there's some here that ain't married?

SHRDLU. Yes.

ZERO (*to* DAISY). I don't know about this place, at that. They must be kind of a mixed crowd.

DAISY. It don't matter, so long as we got each other.

ZERO. Yeh, I know, but you don't want to mix with people that ain't respectable.

DAISY (*to* SHRDLU). Can we get married right away? I guess there must be a lot of ministers here, ain't there?

SHRDLU. Not as many as I had hoped to find. The two who seem most beloved are Dean Swift and the Abbé Rabelais. They are both much admired for some indecent tales which they have written.

ZERO (*shocked*). What! Ministers writin' smutty stories! Say, what kind of a dump is this, anyway?

SHRDLU (*despairingly*). I don't know, Mr. Zero. All these people here are so strange, so unlike the good people I've known. They seem to think of nothing but enjoyment or of wasting their time in profitless occupations. Some paint pictures from morning until night, or carve blocks of stone. Others write songs or put words together, day in and day out. Still others do nothing but lie under the trees and look at the sky. There are men who spend all their time reading books and women who think only of adorning themselves. And

forever they are telling stories and laughing and singing and drinking and dancing. There are drunkards, thieves, vagabonds, blasphemers, adulterers. There is one—

ZERO. That's enough. I heard enough. (*He seats himself and begins putting on his shoes.*)

DAISY (*anxiously*). What are you goin' to do?

ZERO. I'm goin' to beat it, that's what I'm goin' to do.

DAISY. You said you liked it here.

ZERO (*looking at her in amazement*). Liked it! Say, you don't mean to say you want to stay here, do you, with a lot of rummies an' loafers an' bums?

DAISY. We don't have to bother with them. We can just sit here together an' look at the flowers an' listen to the music.

SHRDLU (*eagerly*). Music! Did you hear music?

DAISY. Sure. Don't you hear it?

SHRDLU. No, they say it never stops. But I've never heard it.

ZERO (*listening*). I thought I heard it before, but I don't hear nothin' now. I guess I must 'a' been dreamin'. (*Looking about.*) What's the quickest way out of this place?

DAISY (*pleadingly*). Won't you stay just a little longer?

ZERO. Didn't yer hear me say I'm goin'? Good-bye, Miss Devore. I'm goin' to beat it. (*He limps off at the right.* DAISY *follows him slowly.*)

DAISY (*to* SHRDLU). I won't ever see him again.

SHRDLU. Are you goin' to stay here?

DAISY. It don't make no difference now. Without him I might as well be alive.

[*She goes off right.* SHRDLU *watches her a moment, then sighs, and, seating himself under the tree, buries his head on his arm. Curtain falls.*]

SCENE SEVEN

Before the curtain rises the clicking of an adding machine is heard. The curtain rises upon an office similar in appearance to that in Scene Two, except that there is a door in the back wall through which can be seen a glimpse of the corridor outside. In the middle of the room ZERO *is seated completely absorbed in the operation of an adding machine. He presses the keys and pulls the lever with mechanical precision. He still wears his full-dress suit, but he has added to it sleeve protectors and a green eye-shade. A strip of white paper-tape flows steadily from the machine as* ZERO *operates. The room is filled with this tape—streamers, festoons, billows of it everywhere. It covers the floor and the furniture, it climbs the walls and chokes the doorways. A few moments later,* LIEUTENANT CHARLES *and* JOE *enter at the left.* LIEUTENANT CHARLES *is middle-aged and inclined to corpulence. He has an air of world-weariness. He is barefooted, wears a Panama hat, and is dressed in bright-red tights which are a very bad fit—too tight in some places, badly wrinkled in others.* JOE *is a youth with a smutty face dressed in dirty blue overalls.*

CHARLES (*after contemplating* ZERO *for a few moments*). All right, Zero, cease firing.

ZERO (*looking up, surprised*). Whaddja say?

CHARLES. I said stop punching that machine.

ZERO (*bewildered*). Stop? (*He goes on working mechanically.*)

CHARLES (*impatiently*). Yes. Can't you stop? Here, Joe, give me a hand. He can't stop.

[JOE *and* CHARLES *each take one of* ZERO'S *arms and with enormous effort detach him from the machine. He resists passively— mere inertia. Finally they succeed and swing him around on his stool.* CHARLES *and* JOE *mop their foreheads.*]

ZERO (*querulously*). What's the idea? Can't you lemme alone?

CHARLES (*ignoring the question*). How long have you been here?

ZERO. Jes' twenty-five years. Three hundred months, ninety-one hundred and thirty-one days, one hundred thirty-six thousand—

CHARLES (*impatiently*). That'll do! That'll do!

ZERO (*proudly*). I ain't missed a day, not an hour, not a minute. Look at all I got done. (*He points to the maze of paper.*)

CHARLES. It's time to quit.

ZERO. Quit? Whaddye mean quit? I ain't goin' to quit!

CHARLES. You've got to.

ZERO. What for? What do I have to quit for?

CHARLES. It's time for you to go back.

ZERO. Go back where? Whaddya talkin' about?

CHARLES. Back to earth, you dub. Where do you think?

ZERO. Aw, go on, Cap, who are you kiddin'?

CHARLES. I'm not kidding anybody. And don't call me Cap. I'm a lieutenant.

ZERO. All right, Lieutenant, all right. But what's this you're tryin' to tell me about goin' back?

CHARLES. Your time's up, I'm telling you. You must be pretty thick. How many times do you want to be told a thing?

ZERO. This is the first time I heard about goin' back. Nobody ever said nothin' to me about it before.

CHARLES. You didn't think you were going to stay here forever, did you?

ZERO. Sure. Why not? I did my bit, didn't I? Forty-five years of it. Twenty-five years in the store. Then the boss canned me and I knocked him cold. I guess you ain't heard about that—

CHARLES (*interrupting*). I know all about that. But what's that got to do with it?

ZERO. Well, I done my bit, didn't I? That oughta let me out.

CHARLES (*jeeringly*). So you think you're all through, do you?

ZERO. Sure, I do. I did the best I could while I was there, and then I passed out. And now I'm sittin' pretty here.

CHARLES. You've got a fine idea of the way they run things, you have. Do you think they're going to all of the trouble of making a soul just to use it once?

ZERO. Once is often enough, it seems to me.

CHARLES. It seems to you, does it? Well,

who are you? And what do you know about it? Why, man, they use a soul over and over again—over and over until it's worn out.

ZERO. Nobody ever told me.

CHARLES. So you thought you were all through, did you? Well, that's a hot one, that is.

ZERO (*sullenly*). How was I to know?

CHARLES. Use your brains! Where would we put them all? We're crowded enough as it is. Why, this place is nothing but a kind of repair and service station—a sort of cosmic laundry, you might say. We get the souls in here by the bushelful. Then we get busy and clean them up. And you ought to see some of them. The muck and the slime. Phoo! And as full of holes as a flour-sifter. But we fix them up. We disinfect them and give them a kerosene rub and mend the holes, and back they go— practically as good as new.

ZERO. You mean to say I've been here before—before the last time, I mean?

CHARLES. Been here before! Why, you poor boob—you've been here thousands of times—fifty thousand, at least.

ZERO (*suspiciously*). How is it I don't remember nothin' about it?

CHARLES. Well—that's partly because you're stupid. But it's mostly because that's the way they fix it. (*Musingly.*) They're funny that way—every now and then they'll do something white like that— when you'd least expect it. I guess economy's at the bottom of it, though. They figure that the souls would get worn out quicker if they remembered.

ZERO. And don't any of 'em remember?

CHARLES. Oh, some do. You see there's different types: there's the type that gets a little better each time it goes back—we just give them a wash and send them right through. Then there's another type —the type that gets a little worse each time. That's were you belong!

ZERO (*offended*). Me? You mean to say I'm gettin' worse all the time?

CHARLES (*nodding*). Yes. A little worse each time.

ZERO. Well—what was I when I started? Somethin' big?—A king or somethin'?

CHARLES (*laughing derisively*). A king! that's a good one! I'll tell you what you were the first time—if you want to know so much—a monkey.

ZERO (*shocked and offended*). A monkey!

CHARLES (*nodding*). Yes, sir—just a hairy, chattering, long-tailed monkey.

ZERO. That musta been a long time ago.

CHARLES. Oh, not so long. A million years or so. Seems like yesterday to me.

ZERO. Then look here, whaddya mean by sayin' I'm gettin' worse all the time?

CHARLES. Just what I said. You weren't so bad as a monkey. Of course, you did just what all the other monkeys did, but still it kept you out in the open air. And you weren't women-shy—there was one little red-headed monkey—Well, never mind. Yes, sir, you weren't so bad then. But even in those days there must have been some bigger and brainier monkey that you kowtowed to. The mark of the slave was on you from the start.

ZERO (*sullenly*). You ain't very particular about what you call people, are you?

CHARLES. You wanted the truth, didn't you? If there ever was a soul in the world that was labelled slave, it's yours. Why, all the bosses and kings that there ever were have left their trademarks on your backside.

ZERO. It ain't fair, if you ask me.

CHARLES (*shrugging his shoulders*). Don't tell me about it. I don't make the rules. All I know is you've been getting worse— worse each time. Why, even six thousand years ago you weren't so bad. That was the time you were hauling stones for one of those big pyramids in a place they call Africa. Ever hear of the pyramids?

ZERO. Them big pointy things?

CHARLES (*nodding*). That's it.

ZERO. I seen a picture of them in the movies.

CHARLES. Well, you helped build them. It was a long step down from the happy days in the jungle, but it was a good job —even though you didn't know what you were doing and your back was striped by the foreman's whip. But you've been going down, down. Two thousand years ago you were a Roman galley-slave. You were on one of the triremes that knocked the Carthaginian fleet for a goal. Again the whip. But you had muscles then—chest muscles, back muscles, biceps. (*He feels* ZERO'S *arm gingerly and turns away in disgust.*) Phoo! A bunch of mush!

[*He notices that* JOE *has fallen asleep. Walking over, he kicks him in the shin.*]

CHARLES. Wake up, you mutt! Where do you think you are! (*He turns to* ZERO *again.*) And then another thousand years and you were a serf—a lump of clay digging up other lumps of clay. You wore an iron collar then—white ones hadn't been invented yet. Another long step down. But where you dug, potatoes grew and that helped fatten the pigs. Which was something. And now—well, I don't want to rub it in—

ZERO. Rub it in is right! Seems to me I got a pretty healthy kick comin'. I ain't had a square deal! Hard work! That's all I've ever had!

CHARLES (*callously*). What else were you ever good for?

ZERO. Well, that ain't the point. The point is I'm through! I had enough! Let 'em find somebody else to do the dirty work. I'm sick of bein' the goat! I quit right here and now!

[*He glares about defiantly. There is a thunderclap and a bright flash of lightning.*]

ZERO (*screaming*). Ooh! What's that? (*He clings to* CHARLES.)

CHARLES. It's all right. Nobody's going to hurt you. It's just their way of telling you that they don't like you to talk that way. Pull yourself together and calm down. You can't change the rules—nobody can —they've got it all fixed. It's a rotten system—but what are you going to do about it?

ZERO. Why can't they stop pickin' on me? I'm satisfied here—doin' my day's work. I don't want to go back.

CHARLES. You've got to, I tell you. There's no way out of it.

ZERO. What chance have I got—at my age? Who'll give me a job?

CHARLES. You big boob, you don't think you're going back the way you are, do you?

ZERO. Sure; how then?

CHARLES. Why, you've got to start all over.

ZERO. All over?

CHARLES (*nodding*). You'll be a baby again —a bald, red-faced little animal, and then you'll go through it all again. There'll be millions of others like you—all with their mouths open, squalling for food. And then when you get a little older you'll begin to learn things—and you'll learn all the wrong things and learn them all in the wrong way. You'll eat the wrong food and wear the wrong clothes and you'll live in swarming dens where there's no light and no air! You'll learn to be a liar and a bully and a braggart and a coward and a sneak. You'll learn to fear the sunlight and to hate beauty. By that time you'll be ready for school. There they'll tell you the truth about a great many things that you don't give a damn about and they'll tell you lies about all the things you ought to know—and about all the things you want to know they'll tell you nothing at all. When you get through you'll be equipped for your life-work. You'll be ready to take a job.

ZERO (*eagerly*). What'll my job be? Another adding machine?

CHARLES. Yes. But not one of these antiquated adding machines. It will be a superb, super-hyper-adding machine, as far from this old piece of junk as you are from God. It will be something to make you sit up and take notice, that adding machine. It will be an adding machine which will be installed in a coal mine and which will record the individual output of each miner. As each miner down in the lower galleries takes up a shovelful of coal, the impact of his shovel will automatically set in motion a graphite pencil in your gallery. The pencil will make a mark in white upon a blackened, sensitized drum. Then your work comes in.

With the great toe of your right foot you release a lever which focuses a violet ray on the drum. The ray, playing upon and through the white mark, falls upon a selenium cell which in turn sets the keys of the adding apparatus in motion. In this way the individual output of each minor is recorded without any human effort except the slight pressure of the great toe of your right foot.

ZERO (*in breathless, round-eyed wonder*). Say, that'll be some machine, won't it?

CHARLES. Some machine is right. It will be the clumination of human effort—the final triumph of the evolutionary process. For millions of years the nebulous gases swirled in space. For more millions of years the gases cooled and then through inconceivable ages they hardened into rocks. And then came life. Floating green things on the waters that covered the earth. More millions of years and a step upward—an animate organism in the ancient slime. And so on—step by step, down through the ages—a gain here, a gain there—the mollusc, the fish, the reptile, the mammal, man! And all so that you might sit in the gallery of a coal mine and operate the super-hyper-adding machine with the great toe of your right foot!

ZERO. Well then—I ain't so bad, after all.

CHARLES. You're a failure, Zero, a failure. A waste product. A slave to a contraption of steel and iron. The animal's instinct's but not his strength and skill. The animal's appetites, but not his unashamed indulgence of them. True, you move and eat and digest and excrete and reproduce. But any microscopic organism can do as much. Well—time's up! Back you go—back to your sunless groove—the raw material of slums and wars—the ready prey of the first jingo or demagogue or political adventurer who takes the trouble to play upon your ignorance and credulity and provincialism. You poor, spineless, brainless boob—I'm sorry for you!

ZERO (*falling to his knees*). Then keep me here! Don't send me back! Let me stay!

CHARLES. Get up. Didn't I tell you I can't do anything for you? Come on, time's up!

ZERO. I can't! I can't! I'm afraid to go through it all again.

CHARLES. You've got to, I tell you. Come on, now!

ZERO. What did you tell me so much for? Couldn't you just let me go, thinkin' everythin' was goin' to be all right?

CHARLES. You wanted to know, didn't you?

ZERO. How did I know what you were goin' to tell me? Now I can't stop thinkin' about it! I can't stop thinkin'! I'll be thinkin' about it all the time.

CHARLES. All right! I'll do the best I can for you. I'll send a girl with you to keep you company.

ZERO. A girl? What for? What good will a girl do me?

CHARLES. She'll help make you forget.

ZERO (*eagerly*). She will? Where is she?

CHARLES. Wait a minute, I'll call her. (*He calls in a loud voice.*) Oh! Hope! Yoo-hoo! (*He turns his head aside and says in the manner of a ventriloquist imitating a distant feminine voice.*) Ye-es. (*Then in his own voice.*) Come here, will you? There's a fellow who wants you to take him back. (*Ventriloquously again.*) All right. I'll be right over, Charlie dear. (*He turns to* ZERO.) Kind of familiar, isn't she? Charlie dear!

ZERO. What did you say her name is?

CHARLES. Hope. H-o-p-e.

ZERO. Is she good-lookin'?

CHARLES. Is she good-looking! Oh, boy, wait until you see her! She's a blonde with big blue eyes and red lips and little white teeth and—

ZERO. Say, that listens good to me. Will she be long?

CHARLES. She'll be here right away. There she is now! Do you see her?

ZERO. No. Where?

CHARLES. Out in the corridor. No, not there. Over farther. To the right. Don't you see her blue dress? And the sunlight on her hair?

ZERO. Oh, sure! Now I see her! What's the

matter with me, anyhow? Say, she's some jane! Oh, you baby vamp!

CHARLES. She'll make you forget your troubles.

ZERO. What troubles are you talkin' about?

CHARLES. Nothing. Go on. Don't keep her waiting.

ZERO. You bet I won't. Oh, Hope! Wait for me! I'll be right with you! I'm on my way!

[*He stumbles out eagerly.* JOE *bursts into uproarious laughter.*]

CHARLES (*eyeing him in surprise and anger*). What in hell's the matter with you?

JOE (*shaking with laughter*). Did you get that? He thinks he saw somebody and he's following her! (*He rocks with laughter.*)

CHARLES (*punching him in the jaw*). Shut your face!

JOE (*nursing his jaw*). What's the idea? Can't I even laugh when I see something funny?

CHARLES. Funny! You keep your mouth shut or I'll show you something funny. Go on, hustle out of here and get something to clean up this mess with. There's another fellow moving in. Hurry now.

[*He makes a threatening gesture.* JOE *exits hastily.* CHARLES *goes to a chair and seats himself. He looks weary and dispirited.*]

CHARLES (*shaking his head*). Hell, I'll tell the world this is a lousy job! (*He takes a flask from his pocket, uncorks it, and slowly drains it.*)

CURTAIN

SUGGESTIONS FOR STUDY

1. One feature of most naturalistic writing is an analysis of the causes of the predicament in which the central figure finds himself. How does Rice analyze Mr. Zero? Consider especially Scene One and the places in other scenes in which we are shown the circumstances of Zero's employment, his marriage, his attitude toward sex. Does this play illustrate the familiar axiom of the naturalists that life is a trap?

2. Scene Two contains both monologue and dialogue. How could the difference between the two be indicated on the stage?

3. In Scenes Three and Four what are the various implications of the fact that the characters have numbers for names? One implication: are there any original thinkers among them?

4. This play presents three beliefs about life after death. What are they?

5. What are "the Elysian Fields"? Why cannot Zero and Shrdlu hear the music at the end of the scene?

6. What kind of man is Shrdlu? How does he speak? What is the origin of his name, and how does this symbolize his essential qualities?

7. What would be some of the technical difficulties in producing this play? How would these difficulties, if overcome, make this an interesting and spectacular production?

THE CHERRY ORCHARD

Anton Chekhov
(1860–1904)

When read for the first time, *The Cherry Orchard* may seem to contain difficulties of a sort not found in most plays. When read again, and perhaps again, or when read for the second time and then seen in a good performance, *The Cherry Orchard* is likely to become one of the most realistic and sensible plays in the reader's experience.

Perhaps we can account for this paradox in two ways. First, the play is Russian and therefore foreign in a particular and peculiar sense. Second, and more important, in *The Cherry Orchard,* his last play, Chekhov brought to perfection his realistic technique.

First produced in 1904, *The Cherry Orchard* represents one phase of life in pre-revolutionary Russia. As a country and as a civilization, Russia has always borne its Christianity and its culture with a difference. If this were a Chinese or a Japanese play the reader would expect characters and manners from the exotic East. Instead, he becomes acquainted with characters who at first look and sound like Americans or West Europeans, but who are subtly different. They drink quantities of tea instead of quantities of coffee. They kiss each other's hands. They sit about and talk in a tone of melancholy reminiscence.

Further, these characters supposedly lived some time ago. We are partially familiar with the ways of life of the people of the modern Soviet Union, who are so like us and yet so different. The characters in *The Cherry Orchard* are drawn from the Russia of 1903, a year which, considering what has happened since that time, now seems like at least a couple of centuries ago. The Russians had abolished serfdom just forty-two years before. The Industrial Revolution had lately affected the lives of many Russians. There were railroads and factories and large cities,

but not on the scale known to Western Europe. There was a middle class but it had not taken over the country, as it had in Western Europe. The government was an imperial despotism and bureaucracy. (For example, certain lines from Trofimoff's speeches in Act II of *The Cherry Orchard* were cut out by the Czarist censor.) In short, if any historical period was ever more an "age of transition" than any other, Chekhov's Russia, from the freeing of the slaves in 1861 to the Communist Revolution of 1917, was such an age. The passing of the estate containing the once profitable cherry orchard is a symbol of the disappearance of the old Russia, and Trofimoff's speeches (for he may be taken as Chekhov's spokesman) contain both Chekhov's realization of the change and his prescription for health in the Russia to come. (Chekhov was by profession a physician.)

Finally, language difficulties make this seem like a foreign play. No translation can quite do justice to the tone and spirit of the original; this is particularly true of Russian, which is further removed from English than are French and German. In *The Cherry Orchard,* for instance, we seem to be confronted with Russian proper names of bewildering complexity. They are, however, fairly simple to understand.

First, Russian names are masculine or feminine in form. Thus, the central character in *The Cherry Orchard,* Liuboff Andreievna, was born into a family whose name in the masculine form was Gaieff. Since her name has to be feminine, she was Liuboff Andreievna Gaieva. When she married a man named Ranevsky, her name was thus Ranevskaya. Second, Russians use the device of the patronymic, masculine and feminine, for a middle name. Liuboff Andreievna means Liuboff the daughter of Andrei, Charlotta

Ivanovna means Charlotte the daughter of Ivan, and so on. In the masculine, Leonid Andreievitch is Leonid the son of Andrei (the same Andrei as in Andreievna), Boris Borisovitch is Boris the son of Boris, and so on. This combination of first names plus patronymic solves the problem of how to address a person with whom one is only moderately well acquainted. You would have used the playwright's first name alone only if you were on intimate terms with him: Anton. You would have used his title if you were formally acquainted and if you wished to show him especial respect: Dr. Chekhov. Most people of his acquaintance would have addressed him as Anton Pavlovitch: Anton the son of Paul.

Third, Russian names admit a variety of nicknames. Liuboff, which means "Love" (the same sort of name as Constance, Patience, and Faith in English), sometimes becomes Liuba. Leonid becomes Leo or Leon. Varya is a variant of Varvara, or Barbara. Anya, Dunyasha (for Avdotya Fyodorovna), and Yasha are nicknames, or intimate names.

All these—Russian manners, the differences caused by the erosion of time, and the strange Russian names—are, after all, only superficialities which will be sufficiently comprehensible on the second reading of the play. Much more important is an understanding of the reasons why this is a play of complete and delightful realism.

Chekhov boasted that there is not a single pistol shot in *The Cherry Orchard*. He meant that too often a playwright depends on the violent action of melodrama to hold his audience (as Chekhov himself did in his early plays). Chekhov's aim in his later plays was to make his art imitate life as closely as possible. There ought to be no more violence in a play than there is, on the average, in life, and that is very little.

But in imitating life and in foregoing the dramatic situations that violence provides, Chekhov deprived himself of action, the one element generally considered indispensable to a play. Most of life is dull. The imitation of dullness makes for even greater dullness on the stage. Thus Chekhov's method would

seem to mean that he was unnecessarily handicapping himself by trying to write something self-contradictory: drama that is undramatic.

But the most important part of life is what happens inside us—and that always seems dramatic to ourselves. External events, our jobs, our adventures, our love-affairs—all are determined by the internal realities, by what we essentially are. A practiced observer such as a playwright knows how to judge our actions so as to decide what is going on within. Everything we say or do is an indication of what we are. Therefore, according to Chekhov's theory, the highest aim of a playwright is to show character revealing itself subtly rather than "dramatically."

Obviously Chekhov's attitude toward his material differs from that of the three authors of the tragedies reprinted in this volume. This is not to say that murder, incest, sexual intrigue, or man's attitude toward death and toward the gods are not proper subjects of plays. It does say that Chekhov has shown us that plays need not be about the startling, the lurid. What happens to people like Liuboff Andreievna and Lopakhin may or may not be tragic—that, as we have seen, depends on one's definition of tragedy. But Chekhov has developed for us a theory of realism. Most of life is neither high tragedy nor comedy. It is simply life, and the function of the artist is to picture its most significant aspects—the evidence of internal action and feeling—without bias or undue color.

Thus Chekhov has pictured the inhabitants of a particular imaginary Russian estate that contains a cherry orchard during one summer when, without their fully realizing it, all Russia is changing around them. But he has insisted that what is important for us is not simply the sociological situation. Instead he has drawn our attention to subtle indications of character. All the important figures except Lopakhin are feckless individuals unable to face what the changing times will inevitably bring them. They are, as Firce calls them, "bunglers." Liuboff is an impractical spendthrift who escapes a second time to an unsatisfactory hole-and-corner sort of life in France. She reveals these details about herself as she talks and as she gives gold to an undeserving beggar. Gaieff is going to work in a bank, but we know he will be lucky to last a week there. His essential qualities come out when he makes speeches, eats candy, and plays imaginary billiards. Trofimoff, "the eternal student," knows how to save others, but he cannot save himself from a life of ludicrous futility. When he rushes off in anger after an interview with Liuboff, he falls down the stairs. When he leaves in order to return to the university one more time, he cannot find his rubbers.

These are only part of the subtleties of the drama. What are we to think of a play in which, as two characters come on stage, one says to the other, apropos of nothing: "My dog eats nuts, too"? Or of a situation in which an important character, for no reason we can see, sticks his head in a door and moos?

We are to think two things. First, this play has the kind of realism that is an exact imitation of the externalities as well as the internalities of life. If the reader will listen to these characters in the same way he listens to members of his own family talking in another room with no suspicion that they are overheard, he will realize that Chekhov has caught the precise mood and tone of conversations full of inconsequential and incoherent remarks.

Second, we are to realize that the play was intended to be comedy as well as realism. The experts on Chekhov tell us that he thought of *The Cherry Orchard* as a comic play, a hilarious affair tending to farce in some places. Although he wrote it for production by the pre-Revolutionary Moscow Art Theater, an eminently successful group of actors capable of subtle discernment in the interpretation of lines, Chekhov could not get the actors to play for comedy. They persisted in seeing pathos and tragedy in these figures, and so also have actors ever since.

Probably the actors are right, for there is evidence that Chekhov thought of his play not merely as a comedy but also as a means of discussing serious ideas. One serious element is his message spoken by Trofimoff— "all Russia is our orchard." Here Chekhov was criticizing the irresponsibility and laziness of certain types of people in contemporary Russian society.

Another serious element is Chekhov's use of symbols. The cherry orchard itself is one. Other interesting symbols are the sound effects in the play: the singing in Act II, the band in Act III, the sound of chopping offstage as the last curtain and the first cherry tree fall. Each sound underscores in a particular way the significance of what is happening on the stage. The three symbols named are all realistic sounds; we know what produced them. A more baffling sound is the twang of a breaking string in Act II and at the very end of the play. We are not told in the play itself what this sound comes from. The biographers of Chekhov say he heard it in his youth as the sound of the fall of a bucket in a distant coal mine. It is thus here a private, nonrealistic symbol, a note of romanticism. Its "public" meaning—its meaning for readers and playgoers—can be for the student a fruitful source of study.

From all this we must conclude that *The Cherry Orchard* is in its substance a play of intellectual sophistication and philosophical wisdom, in its technique an example of dramatic art of a high order. This play does not discuss the really big questions, as do the tragedies in this volume, but on its own level it also enters into the essential complexities of life. It assumes that art must be a compendium and compost of tragedy, pathos, comedy, farce, and everyday living, just as life is.

THE CHERRY ORCHARD

Translated by Jennie Covan

CHARACTERS

LIUBOFF ANDREIEVNA RANEVSKAYA, *a landowner*

ANYA, *her daughter, aged seventeen*

VARYA, *her adopted daughter, aged twenty-seven*

LEONID ANDREIEVITCH GAIEFF, *Liuboff Andreievna's brother*

YERMOLAI ALEXEIEVITCH LOPAKHIN, *a merchant*

PETER SERGEIEVITCH TROFIMOFF, *a student*

BORIS BORISOVITCH SEMYONOFF-PISHCHIK, *a landowner*

CHARLOTTA IVANOVNA, *a governess*

SEMYON PANTELEIEVITCH YEPIKHODOFF, *a clerk*

DUNYASHA (AVDOTYA FYODOROVNA), *a maidservant*

FIRCE, *an old footman, aged eighty-seven*

YASHA, *a young footman*

A TRAMP

A STATION-MASTER

POST OFFICE CLERK

GUESTS

A SERVANT

SCENE. *Mme. Ranevskaya's estate.*

ACT I

A room still called the nursery. One of the doors leads into Anya's room. It is almost sunrise of a day in May. The cherry-trees are in bloom, but the chill of early morning is in the garden. The windows are shut.

(DUNYASHA *enters with a candle, and* LOPAKHIN *with a book in his hand.*)

LOP. The train has arrived, thank God. What's the time?

DUN. It will soon be two. (*Blows out candle.*) It is already light.

LOP. How late was the train? At least two hours. (*Yawns and stretches himself.*) I certainly made a fool of myself! I came here on purpose to meet them at the station, and then overslept myself . . . in my chair. It's a pity. I wish you'd called me.

DUN. I thought you'd gone. (*Listening.*) I think I hear them coming.

LOP. (*listens*). No . . . They have to collect their baggage and so on. . . . (*Pause.*) Liuboff Andreievna has been living abroad for five years; I don't know what she'll be like now . . . She's a good sort—an easy, simple person. I remember when I was a boy of fifteen, my father, who is dead—he used to keep a shop in the village here—hit me with his fist, and my nose bled . . . We had gone into the yard for something or other, and he was a little drunk. Liuboff Andreievna, as I remember her now, was still young, and very slight, and she took me to the wash-stand here in this very room, the nursery. She said, "Don't cry, my small peasant, all wounds heal at last." (*Pause.*) . . . Small peasant! My father was a peasant, true, but here I am in a white vest and brown shoes . . . like a pearl in an oyster shell. I'm rich now, with lots of money, but just think about it and examine me, and you'll find I'm still a peasant to the core. (*Turns over the pages of his book.*) Here I've been reading this book, but I understand nothing. I read and fell asleep. (*Pause.*)

DUN. The dogs didn't sleep all night; they feel that their masters are coming.

LOP. What's the matter with you, Dunyasha. . . .

DUN. My hands are shaking. I am going to faint.

LOP. You're too sensitive, Dunyasha. You dress just like a lady, and you do your hair like one, too. You shouldn't. You must remember your place in life.

YEP. (*enters with a bouquet. He wears a short jacket and brilliantly polished boots which squeak audibly. He drops the bouquet as he enters, then picks it up*). The gardener sent these; says they're to go into the dining-room. (*Gives the bouquet to* DUNYASHA.)

LOP. And you'll bring me some kvass.

DUN. Yes, sir. (*Exit.*)

YEP. There's a frost this morning—three degrees, and the cherry-trees are all in flower. I can't approve of our climate. (*Sighs.*) I can't. Our climate refuses to favor us even this once. And, Yermolai Alexeievitch, allow me to say to you, in addition, that I bought myself a pair of boots two days ago, and I beg to assure you that they squeak in a perfectly intolerable manner. What shall I put on them?

LOP. Go away. You bore me.

YEP. Some misfortune happens to me every day. But I don't complain; I'm used to it, and I even smile at it. (DUNYASHA *comes in and brings* LOPAKHIN *a glass of kvass.*) I am going. (*Knocks over a chair.*) There. . . . (*Triumphantly.*) There, you see, if I may use the word, what circumstances I am in, so to speak. It is simply extraordinary. (*Exit.*)

DUN. Let me confess to you, Yermolai Alexeievitch, that Yepikhodoff has proposed to me.

LOP. Ah!

DUN. I don't know what to do about it. He's a nice young man, but every now and then, when he begins talking, you can't understand a word he says. It sounds sincere enough, only I can't understand it. I think I like him. He's madly in love with me. He's an unlucky man; every day something happens to him. We tease him about it. They call him "Two-and-twenty troubles."

LOP. (*listens*). There they come, I think.

DUN. They're coming! What's the matter with me? I'm cold all over.

LOP. There they are, really. Let's go and meet them. Will she know me? We haven't seen each other for five years.

DUN. (*excited*). I shall faint in a minute. . . . Oh, I'm fainting!

(*Two carriages are heard driving up to the house.* LOPAKHIN *and* DUNYASHA *quickly go out. The stage is empty. There are noises in the adjoining rooms.* FIRCE, *leaning on a stick, walks quickly across the stage; he has just been to meet* LIUBOFF ANDREIEVNA. *He wears an old-fashioned livery and a tall hat. He is saying something to himself, but not a word can be made out. The noise back stage grows louder and louder. A voice is heard: "Let's go in there." Enter* LIUBOFF ANDREIEVNA, ANYA, *and* CHARLOTTA IVANOVNA *leading a little dog on a chain, all dressed in traveling clothes,* VARYA *in a long coat and with a kerchief on her head.* GAIEFF, SEMYONOFF-PISHCHIK, LOPAKHIN, DUNYASHA *with a parcel and an umbrella, and a servant with suitcases—all cross the room.*)

ANYA. Let's go through here. Do you remember this room, mother?

LIUB. (*joyfully, through her tears*). The nursery!

VARYA. How cold it is! My hands are quite numb. (*To* LIUBOFF ANDREIEVNA.) Your rooms, the white one and the violet one, are just as they used to be, mother.

LIUB. My dear, beautiful nursery . . . I used to sleep here when I as a baby. (*Kisses her brother, then* VARYA, *then her brother again.*) And Varya is just as she used to be, exactly like a nun. And I recognized Dunyasha. (*Kisses her.*)

GAI. The train was two hours late. There now; how's that for punctuality?

CHAR. (*to* PISHCHIK). My dog eats nuts, too.

PISH. (*astonished*). Just imagine!

(*All leave except* ANYA *and* DUNYASHA.)

DUN. We did have to wait for you! (*Takes off* ANYA'S *cloak and hat.*)

ANYA. For four nights on the journey I didn't sleep . . . I'm awfully cold.

DUN. You left during Lent, when it was snowing and frosty, but now? Darling! (*Laughs and kisses her.*) We did have to wait for you, my darling pet! . . . I must tell you at once, I can't wait a minute.

ANYA (*listlessly*). Something else now . . . ?

DUN. The clerk, Yepikhodoff, proposed to me after Easter.

ANYA. Always the same . . . (*Puts her hair straight.*) I've lost all my hairpins . . . (*She is very tired, and even staggers as she walks.*)

DUN. I don't know what to think about it. He loves me, he loves me so much!

ANYA (*looks into her room; in a gentle voice*). My room, my windows, as if I'd never left! I'm at home! Tomorrow morning I'll get up and run out into the garden. . . . Oh, if I could only sleep! I didn't sleep the whole journey, I was so restless.

DUN. Peter Sergeievitch came two days ago.

ANYA (*joyfully*). Peter!

DUN. He sleeps in the bath-house, he lives there. He said he was afraid he'd be in the way. (*Looks at her watch.*) I should call him, but Varvara Mihkailovna told me not to. "Don't wake him," she said.

(*Enter* VARYA, *a bunch of keys hanging from her belt.*)

VARYA. Dunyasha, coffee, quick. Mother wishes some.

DUN. In a moment. (*Exit.*)

VARYA. Well, you've come, thank God. Home again. (*Caressing her.*) My darling is home again! My pretty one is back at last!

ANYA. I had an awful time, I tell you.

VARYA. I can just imagine it!

ANYA. I went away in Holy Week; it was very cold then. Charlotta talked the whole way and would go on performing her tricks. Why did you force her on me?

VARYA. You couldn't go alone, darling, at seventeen!

ANYA. We went to Paris; it's cold there and snowing. I talk French perfectly dreadfully. My mother lives on the fifth floor. I go to her, and find her there with several Frenchmen, women, an old abbé with a book, and everything wreathed in tobacco smoke and the whole place so uninviting. I suddenly became very sorry for mother—so sorry that I took her head in my arms and hugged her and wouldn't let her go. Then mother started hugging me and crying. . . .

VARYA (*weeping*). Don't say any more, don't say any more . . .

ANYA. She's already sold her villa near Mentone; she has nothing left, nothing. And I haven't a kopeck either; we only just managed to get here. And mother won't understand! We had dinner at a station; she asked for all the expensive things, and tipped the waiters one ruble each. And Charlotta too. Yasha demands a share, too— It is simply awful. Mother has a footman now, Yasha; we've brought him along.

VARYA. I saw the fellow.

ANYA. How's business? Has the interest been paid?

VARYA. Not much chance of that.

ANYA. Oh God, oh God . . .

VARYA. The place will be sold in August.

ANYA. Oh God . . .

LOP. (*looks in at the door and moos*). Moo! (*Exit.*)

VARYA (*through her tears*). I'd like to . . . (*Shakes her fist.*)

ANYA (*embraces* VARYA, *softly*). Varya, has he proposed to you? (VARYA *shakes her head.*) But he loves you. . . . Why don't you decide? Why do you keep on waiting?

VARYA. I'm afraid it will all come to nothing. He's a busy man. I'm not his sort . . . he pays no attention to me. Bless the man, I don't wish to see him. . . . But everybody talks about our marriage, everybody congratulates me, and there's nothing in it at all, it's all like a dream. (*A different voice.*) You have a brooch that looks like a bee.

ANYA (*wistfully*). Mother bought it. (*Goes into her room, and talks lightly, like a child.*) In Paris I went up in a balloon!

VARYA. My darling has come back, my pretty one is home again! (DUNYASHA *has already returned with the coffee-pot and is making coffee.*) I go about all day, looking after the house, and I think all the time, if only you could marry a rich man, I'd be happy and would go away somewhere by myself, perhaps to Kieff . . . or to Moscow, and so on, from one holy place to another. I'd tramp and tramp. That would be splendid!

ANYA. The birds are singing in the garden. What time is it now?

VARYA. It must be getting on towards three. It's time you went to sleep, darling. (*Goes into* ANYA'S *room.*) Splendid!

(*Enter* YASHA *with a plaid shawl and a traveling bag.*)

YASHA (*crossing the stage; politely*). May I go this way?

DUN. I hardly recognized you, Yasha. You have changed abroad.

YASHA. Hm . . . and who are you?

DUN. When you went away I was only so high. (*Showing with her hand.*) I'm Dunyasha, the daughter of Fyodor Kozoyedoff. You don't remember?

YASHA. Oh, you small cucumber! (*Looks round and embraces her. She screams and drops a saucer.* YASHA *goes out quickly.*)

VARYA (*in the doorway in an angry voice*). What's that?

DUN. (*through her tears*). I've broken a saucer.

VARYA. It may bring luck.

ANYA. (*coming out of her room*). We must tell mother that Peter's here.

VARYA. I told them not to call him.

ANYA (*thoughtfully*). Father died six years ago, and a month later my brother Grisha was drowned in the river—such a dear little boy of seven! Mother couldn't bear it; she went away, away, without looking round. . . . (*Shudders.*) Now I understand her; if only she knew! (*Pause.*) And Peter Trofimoff was Grisha's tutor, he might remind her. . . .

(*Enter* FIRCE *in a short jacket and white vest. Goes to the coffee-pot.*)

FIRCE. Madame is going to have a bite here. (*He is preoccupied, putting on white gloves.*) Is the coffee ready? (*To* DUNYASHA, *severely.*) You!

DUN. Oh, dear me . . . ! (*Leaving hurriedly.*)

FIRCE (*fussing round the coffee-pot*). Oh, you bungler . . . (*Murmurs to himself.*) Back from Paris . . . the master went to

Paris once . . . in a carriage . . . (*Laughs.*)

VARYA. What are you mumbling, Firce?

FIRCE. I beg your pardon? (*Joyfully.*) The mistress is home again. I've lived to see her! I don't care if I die now . . . (*Weeps with joy.*)

(*Enter* LIUBOFF ANDREIEVNA, GAIEFF, LOPAKHIN, *and* SEMYONOFF-PISHCHIK, *the latter in a long jacket of thin cloth and loose trousers.* GAIEFF, *coming in, moves his arms and body about as if he were playing billiards.*)

LIUB. Let me remember now. Red into the corner! Twice into the center!

GAI. Right into the pocket! Once upon a time you and I, sister, both slept in this room, and now I'm fifty-one; it does seem strange.

LOP. Yes, time does fly!

GAI. What?

LOP. I said that time does fly.

GAI. It smells of patchouli here.

ANYA. I'm going to bed. Good-night, mother. (*Kisses her.*)

LIUB. My dear little child. (*Kisses her hand.*) Glad to be at home? I can't get over it.

ANYA. Good-night, uncle.

GAI. (*kisses her face and hands*). God be with you. How you do resemble your mother! (*To his sister.*) You were just like her at her age, Liuba.

(ANYA *gives her hand to* LOPAKHIN *and* PISHCHIK *and goes out shutting the door behind her.*)

LIUB. She's awfully tired.

PISH. It's a very long journey.

VARYA (*to* LOPAKHIN *and* PISHCHIK). Well, gentlemen, it's getting on toward three. High time to retire.

LIUB. (*laughs*). You're just the same as ever, Varya. (*Draws her close and kisses her.*) I'll have some coffee now; then we'll all go. (FIRCE *lays a cushion under her feet.*) Thank you, dear. I'm used to coffee. I drink it day and night. Thank you, dear old man. (*Kisses* FIRCE.)

VARYA. I'll go and see whether they've brought in all the luggage. (*Exit.*)

LIUB. Is it really I who am sitting here?

(*Laughs.*) I feel like jumping about and waving my arms. (*Covers her face with her hands.*) But suppose I'm dreaming! God knows I love my own country, I love it dearly; I couldn't look out of the railway carriage, I cried so much. (*Through her tears.*) Still, I must have my coffee. Thank you, Firce. Thank you, dear old man. I'm so glad you're still with us.

FIRCE. The day before yesterday.

GAI. He doesn't hear well.

LOP. I have to go to Kharkoff by the five o'clock train. I'm awfully sorry! I should like to have a look at you, to gossip a little. You're as fine-looking as ever.

PISH. (*breathes heavily*). Even finer-looking . . . dressed in Paris fashion . . . confound it all.

LOP. Your brother, Leonid Andreievitch, says I'm a snob, a usurer, but that is absolutely nothing to me. Let him talk. Only I do wish you would believe in me as you once did, that your wonderful, touching eyes would look at me as they used to. Merciful God! My father was the serf of your grandfather and your own father, but you—more than anybody else—did so much for me once upon a time that I've forgotten everything and love you as if you were one of my own family . . . and even more.

LIUB. I can't sit still, I can't! (*Jumps up and walks about in great excitement.*) I'll never survive this happiness. . . . You can laugh at me; I'm a silly woman . . . My dear little cupboard. (*Kisses cupboard.*) My little table.

GAI. Nurse died during your absence.

LIUB. (*sits and drinks coffee*). Yes, God rest her soul. I heard by letter.

GAI. And Anastasia died, too. Peter Kosoy has left me and now lives in town with the Commissioner of Police. (*Takes a box of candy out of his pocket and sucks a piece.*)

PISH. My daughter, Dashenka, sends her love.

LOP. I wish to say something very pleasant, very delightful, to you. (*Looks at his watch.*) I'm going away at once, I haven't much time . . . but I'll tell you all about it in two or three words. As you already know,

your cherry orchard is to be sold to pay your debts, and the sale is arranged for August 22; but you needn't be alarmed, dear madam, you may sleep in peace; there's a way out. Here's my plan. Please listen carefully! Your estate is only thirteen miles from town, the railway runs past it and if the cherry orchard and the land by the river are broken up into building parcels and are then leased as villa sites, you'll have at least twenty-five thousand rubles a year income.

GAI. How utterly absurd!

LIUB. I don't understand you at all, Yermolai Alexeievitch.

LOP. You will get twenty-five rubles a year for each dessiatine from the leaseholders at the very least, and if you advertise now, I'm willing to bet that you won't have a vacant parcel left by the autumn; they'll all go. In a word, you're saved. I congratulate you. Only, of course, you'll have to straighten things out carefully . . . For instance, you'll have to pull down all the old buildings, this house, which is of no use to anybody now, and cut down the old cherry orchard. . . .

LIUB. Cut it down? My dear man, you must forgive me, but you don't understand anything at all. If there's anything interesting or remarkable in the whole province, it's this cherry orchard of ours.

LOP. The only remarkable thing about the orchard is its great size. It bears fruit only every other year, and even then you don't know what to do with the cherries; nobody buys any.

GAI. This orchard is mentioned in the "Encyclopaedia."

LOP. (*looks at his watch*). If we can't think of anything and don't make up our minds, then on August 22 both the cherry orchard and the whole estate will be sold at auction. Make up your mind! I swear there's no other way out. You may believe me!

FIRCE. In the old days, forty or fifty years ago, they dried the cherries, soaked them and pickled them, and made jam, and it used to happen that . . .

GAI. Be quiet, Firce.

FIRCE. And then we'd send the dried cherries in carts to Moscow and Kharkoff. And money! And the dried cherries were soft, juicy, sweet, and fragrant. They knew the way. . . .

LIUB. How was it done?

FIRCE. They've forgotten. Nobody remembers.

PISH. (*to* LIUBOFF ANDREIEVNA). What about Paris? Eh? Did you eat frogs?

LIUB. I ate crocodiles.

PISH. Just imagine!

LOP. Formerly there were only the gentry and the laborers, in the villages, and now the people who live in villas have arrived. All towns now, even small ones, are surrounded by villas. And it's safe to say that in twenty years' time the villa residents will have increased tremendously. At present they sit on their balconies, and drink tea, but it may well happen that they'll commence to cultivate their patches of land, and then your cherry orchard will be happy, rich, glorious.

GAI. (*angry*). What nonsense!

(*Enter* VARYA *and* YASHA.)

VARYA. There are two telegrams for you, mother dear. (*Picks out a key and noisily unlocks an antique cupboard.*) Here they are.

LIUB. They're from Paris . . . (*Tears them up without reading them.*) I'm through with Paris.

GAI. And do you know, Liuba, how old this cupboard is? A week ago I pulled out the bottom drawer; I looked and saw numbers carved in it. That cupboard was made exactly a hundred years ago. What do you think of that? What? We could celebrate its jubilee. It hasn't a soul of its own, but still, say what you will, it's a fine piece of furniture.

PISH. (*astonished*). A hundred years . . . Just imagine!

GAI. Yes . . . it's a genuine thing. (*Examining it.*) My dear and honored cupboard! I congratulate you on your career, which has for more than a hundred years been devoted to the noble ideals of good and justice; your silent call to productive labor has not decreased in the hundred years (*Weeping.*) during which you have inspired in our generation virtue and courage and faith for a better future, holding before our eyes lofty ideals and the knowledge of a common consciousness. (*Pause.*)

LOP. Yes.

LIUB. You're just the same as ever, Leon.

GAI. (*a little confused*). Off the white on the right, into the corner pocket. Red ball goes into the center pocket!

LOP. (*looks at his watch*). It's time I went.

YASHA (*giving* LIUBOFF ANDREIEVNA *her medicine*). Will you take your pills now?

PISH. You shouldn't take medicines, dearest; they do you neither harm nor good . . . Give them to me, dearest. (*Takes the pills, turns them out into the palm of his hand, blows on them, puts them into his mouth, and drinks some kvass.*) There!

LIUB. (*frightened*). You're mad!

PISH. I've swallowed all the pills.

LOP. You greedy man! (*All laugh.*)

FIRCE. They were here in Easter week and ate half a pailful of cucumbers . . . (*Mumbles.*)

LIUB. What does he mean?

VARYA. He's been mumbling away for three years. We're used to that.

YASHA. Senile decay.

(CHARLOTTA IVANOVNA *crosses the stage, dressed in white; she is very thin and tightly laced; she has a lorgnette at her waist.*)

LOP. Excuse me, Charlotta Ivanovna, I haven't bidden you welcome yet. *Tries to kiss her hand.*)

CHAR. (*takes her hand away*). If you let people kiss your hand, then they'll want your elbow, then your shoulder, and then . . .

LOP. I'm out of luck today! (*All laugh.*) Show us a trick, Charlotta Ivanovna!

LIUB. Charlotta, do a trick for us!

CHAR. It's not necessary. I must go to bed. (*Exit.*)

LOP. We shall see each other in three weeks. (*Kisses* LIUBOFF ANDREIEVNA'S *hand.*) Now, good-bye. It's time I went. (*To* GAIEFF.) See you again. (*Kisses* PISHCHIK.) Au revoir. (*Gives his hand to* VARYA, *then to* FIRCE *and to* YASHA.) I don't want to go away. (*To* LIUBOFF ANDREIEVNA.) If you think about the villas and come to a decision, just let me know, and I'll raise a loan of 50,000 rubles at once. Think about it seriously.

VARYA (*angrily*). Do go, now!

LOP. I'm going, I'm going. . . . (*Exit.*)

GAI. Snob. Still, I beg pardon . . . Varya's going to marry him, he's Varya's young man.

VARYA. Don't talk too much, uncle.

LIUB. Why not, Varya? I should be glad of it. He's a good man.

PISH. To speak the honest truth . . . he's a worthy man . . . And my Dashenka . . . also says that . . . she says lots of things. (*Snores, but wakes up again at once.*) But still, dear madam, if you could lend me . . . 240 rubles . . . to pay the interest on my mortgage tomorrow . . .

VARYA (*frightened*). We haven't it, we haven't it!

LIUB. It's quite true. I've nothing at all.

PISH. You'll manage somehow. (*Laughs.*) I never lose hope. I used to think, "Everything's lost now. I'm a dead man," when, lo and behold, a railway was built across my land . . . and they paid me for it. And something else will happen today or tomorrow. Dashenka may win 20,000 rubles . . . she's got a lottery ticket.

LIUB. The coffee's all gone, we can go to bed.

FIRCE (*brushing* GAIEFF'S *trousers; in an insistent tone*). You are wearing the wrong trousers again. What am I to do with you?

VARYA (*quietly*). Anya's asleep. (*Opens window quietly.*) The sun has risen already; it isn't cold. Look, mother, dear; what lovely trees! And the air! The starlings are singing!

GAI. (*opens the other window*). The whole garden is white. You haven't forgotten, Liuba? There's that long avenue going straight, straight, like an arrow; it shines on moonlight nights. Do you remember? You haven't forgotten?

LIUB. (*looks into the garden*). Oh, my childhood, days of my innocence! In this nursery I used to sleep; I used to look out from here into the orchard. Happiness used to wake with me every morning, and then it was just as it is now; nothing has changed. (*Laughs with joy.*) It's all, all white! Oh, my orchard! After the dreary autumns and the cold winters, you're young again, full of happiness, the angels of heaven haven't left you . . . If only I could take this strong burden from my breast and shoulders, if I could forget my past!

GAI. Yes, and they'll sell this orchard to pay off the debts. How strange it seems!

LIUB. Look, there's my dead mother walking in the orchard . . . dressed in white! (*Laughs with joy.*) That's she.

GAI. Where?

VARYA. God be with you, mother dear!

LIUB. Nobody is there; I thought I saw somebody. On the right, at the turning by the summer-house, a little white tree bent down, resembling a woman.

(*Enter* TROFIMOFF *in a worn student uniform and spectacles.*) What a marvelous garden! White masses of flowers, the blue sky. . . .

TROF. Liuboff Andreievna! (*She looks round at him.*) I only wish to pay my respects to you, and I'll go away. (*Kisses her hand warmly.*) I was told to wait till the morning, but I didn't have the patience. (LIUBOFF ANDREIEVNA *looks surprised.*)

VARYA (*crying*). It's Peter Trofimoff.

TROF. Peter Trofimoff, once the tutor of your Grisha . . . Have I changed so much? (LIUBOFF ANDREIEVNA *embraces him and cries softly.*)

GAI. (*confused*). That's enough, that's enough, Liuba.

VARYA (*weeps*). But I told you, Peter, to wait till tomorrow.

LIUB. My Grisha . . . my boy . . . Grisha . . . my son.

VARYA. What are we to do, dear mother? It's the will of God.

TROF. (*softly, through his tears*). It's all right, it's all right.

LIUB. (*still weeping*). My boy's dead; he was drowned. Why? Why, my friend? (*Softly*). Anya's asleep in there. I am speaking so loudly, making so much noise . . . Well, Peter? What's made you look so bad? Why have you grown so old?

TROF. In the train an old woman called me a decayed gentleman.

LIUB. You were quite a boy then, a jolly little student, and now your hair has grown thin and you wear spectacles. Are you really still a student? (*Goes to the door.*)

TROF. I suppose I shall always be a student.

LIUB. (*kisses her brother, then* VARYA). Well, let's go to bed . . . And you've grown older, Leonid.

PISH. (*follows her*). Yes, we must go to bed . . . Oh, my gout! I'll stay the night here. If only, Liuboff Andreievna, my dear, you could get me 240 rubles tomorrow morning—

GAI. Still the same story.

PISH. Two hundred and forty rubles . . . to pay the interest on the mortgage.

LIUB. I haven't any money, dear man.

PISH. I'll give it back . . . it's a small sum . . .

LIUB. Well then, Leonid will give it to you . . . Let him have it, Leonid.

GAI. By all means; hold out your hand.

LIUB. Why not? He wants it; he'll give it back.

(LIUBOFF ANDREIEVNA, TROFIMOFF, PISHCHIK *and* FIRCE *go out.* GAIEFF, VARYA, *and* YASHA *remain.*)

GAI. My sister hasn't lost the habit of throwing money away. (*To* YASHA.) Don't come near me: you smell like a chicken-coop!

YASHA (*grins*). You are just the same as ever, Leonid Andreievitch.

GAI. Really? (*To* VARYA.) What's he saying?

VARYA (*to* YASHA). Your mother has come from the village; she's been sitting in the servants' room since yesterday, and wishes to see you . . .

YASHA. Bless the woman!

VARYA. Shameless man.

YASHA. A lot of use there is in her coming. She might just as well have come tomorrow. (*Exit.*)

VARYA. Mother hasn't altered a bit, she's just as she always was. She'd give away everything, if the idea only entered her head.

GAI. Yes . . . (*Pause.*) If there's any illness for which people have a remedy of remedies, you may be sure that particular illness is incurable. I work my brains as hard as I can. I've several remedies, very many, and that really means I've none at all. It would be nice to inherit a fortune from somebody, it would be nice to marry off our Anya to a rich man, it would be nice to go to Yaroslavl and try my luck with my aunt the Countess. My aunt is very, very rich.

VARYA (*weeps*). If only God would help us.

GAI. Don't cry. My aunt's very rich, but she doesn't like us. My sister, in the first place, married a lawyer, not an aristocrat . . . (ANYA *appears in the doorway.*) She not only married a man who was not an aristocrat, but she behaved in a way which cannot be described as proper. She's nice and kind and charming and I'm very fond of her, but say what you will in her favor and you still have to admit that she's bad; you can feel it in her slightest movements.

VARYA (*whispers*). Anya's in the doorway.

GAI. Really? (*Pause.*) It's curious, something's blown into my right eye . . . I can't see out of it properly. And on Thursday, when I was at the District Court . . .

(*Enter* ANYA.)

VARYA. Why aren't you in bed, Anya?

ANYA. I can't sleep. It's no use.

GAI. My darling. (*Kisses* ANYA'S *face and hands.*) My child. (*Crying.*) You're not my niece, you're my angel, you're my all . . . Believe in me, believe . . .

ANYA. I do believe you, uncle. Everybody loves and respects you . . . but, uncle dear, you should say nothing, no more than that. What were you saying just now about my mother, about your own sister! Why did you say such things?

GAI. Yes, yes. (*Covers his face with her hand.*) Yes, really, it was terrible. Save me, my God! And only just now I made a speech before a cupboard . . . it's so silly! And only when I'd finished I knew how silly it was.

VARYA. Yes, uncle dear, you really should say less. Keep quiet, that's all.

ANYA. You'd be so much happier if you only kept quiet.

GAI. All right, I'll be quiet. (*Kisses their hands.*) I'll be quiet. But let's talk business. On Thursday I was in the District Court, and a lot of us met there and we began to talk of this, that, and the other, and now I think I can arrange a loan to pay the interest to the bank.

VARYA. If only God would help us!

GAI. I'll go on Tuesday. I'll talk to you about it again. (*To* VARYA.) Don't cry. (*To* ANYA.) Your mother will have a talk with Lopakhin; he, of course, won't refuse . . . And when you've rested you'll go to Yaroslavl to the Countess, your grandmother. So you see, we shall have three irons in the fire, and we shall be safe. We'll pay the interest. I'm certain. (*Puts some candy in his mouth.*) I swear on my honor, on anything you wish, that the estate will not be sold! (*Excitedly.*) I swear on my happiness! Here's my hand on it! You may call me a dishonorable sinner if I let it be sold at auction! I swear by all I am!

ANYA (*calm again and happy*). How good and clever you are, uncle. (*Embraces him.*) I'm happy now! I'm happy! All's well!

(*Enter* FIRCE.)

FIRCE (*reproachfully*). Leonid Andreievitch, don't you fear God? When are you going to bed?

GAI. Soon, soon. You go away, Firce! I'll undress myself. Well, children, au revoir . . . ! I'll tell you the details tomorrow, but let's go to bed now. (*Kisses* ANYA *and* VARYA.) I'm a man of the eighties . . . People don't praise those years much, but I can still say that I've suffered for my beliefs. The peasants don't love me for nothing, I assure you. We have to learn how to understand the peasants! We should learn how . . .

ANYA. You're doing it again, uncle!

VARYA. Be quiet, uncle!

FIRCE (*angrily*). Leonid Andreievitch!

GAI. I'm coming, I'm coming . . . Go to bed now. Off two cushions into the center! I turn over a new leaf . . . (*Exit.* FIRCE *goes out after him.*)

ANYA. I'm more quiet now. I don't wish to go to Yaroslavl, I don't like grandmother; but I'm calm now, thanks to uncle. (*Sits down.*)

VARYA. It's time to go to sleep. I'll go. There have been amazing things happening here during your absence. In the old servants' quarter of the house, as you know, only the old people live—little old Yefim and Polya and Yevstigny, and Karp as well. They commenced letting tramps or the like spend the night there—I said nothing. Then I heard that they were saying I had ordered them to be fed on peas and nothing else; from meanness, you see . . . And it was all Yevstigny's doing. Very well, I thought, if that's what the matter is, just you wait. So I call Yevstigny . . . (*Yawns.*) He comes. "What's this," I say. "Yevstigny, you old fool" . . . (*Looks at* ANYA.) Anya dear! (*Pause.*) She's dozed off . . . (*Takes* ANYA'S *arm.*) Let's go to bed . . . Come along! . . . (*Leads her.*) My darling's gone to sleep! Come on . . . (*They go. In the distance, the other side of the orchard, a shepherd plays his pipe.* TROFIMOFF *crosses the stage and stops when he sees* VARYA *and* ANYA.) Sh! She's asleep, asleep. Come on, dear.

ANYA (*quietly, half-asleep*). I'm so tired . . . I hear bells . . . uncle, dear! Mother and uncle!

VARYA. Come on, dear, come on! (*They go into* ANYA'S *room.*)

TROF. (*deeply moved*). Sunshine! Springtime of my life!

ACT II

A field. An old, tumble-down shrine, which has been long abandoned; near it a well and large stones, which apparently are old tombstones, and an old garden seat. The road to Gaieff's estate is seen. On one side dark poplars rise, behind them the cherry orchard begins. In the distance is a row of telegraph poles, and on the far horizon are the indistinct signs of a large town, which can be seen only on the finest and clearest days. It is near sunset.

(CHARLOTTA, YASHA, *and* DUNYASHA *are sitting on a bench.* YEPIKHODOFF *stands nearby playing on a guitar; all seem thoughtful.* CHARLOTTA *wears a man's old peaked cap; she has unslung a rifle from her shoulders and is straightening the strap-buckle.*)

CHAR. (*thoughtfully*). I haven't a real passport. I don't know how old I am, but I think I'm young. When I was a little girl my father and mother used to travel from fair to fair and give very good performances, and I used to do the somersault and various little things. And when papa and mamma died, a German lady took me to her home and brought me up. I liked it. I grew up and became a governess. And where I came from and who I am, I don't know. . . . Who my parents were—perhaps they weren't married—I don't know. (*Takes a cucumber from her pocket and eats.*) I don't know anything. (*Pause.*) I do wish to talk, but I haven't anybody to talk to. . . . I haven't anybody at all.

YEP. (*plays on the guitar and sings*).

"What do I care for this noisy earth?
What do I care for friend and foe?"

I like playing on the mandolin!

DUN. That's a guitar, not a mandolin. (*Looks at herself in a little pocket mirror and powders herself.*)

YEP. For a lovelorn lunatic, this constitutes a mandolin. (*Sings.*)

"Oh would the fire of love
Warm my pitiful heart!"

(YASHA *sings, too.*)

CHAR. These people sing so badly. . . . Bah! like jackals.

DUN. (*to* YASHA). Still it must be nice to live abroad.

YASHA. Yes, it is. I can't differ from you there. (*Yawns and lights a cigar.*)

YEP. That is perfectly natural. Abroad everything is in such complete harmony.

YASHA. That goes without saying.

YEP. I'm an educated man, I read various remarkable books, but I cannot understand where I want to go, myself—whether to keep on living or to shoot myself, as it were. So at any rate, I always carry a revolver about with me. Here it is. (*Shows a revolver.*)

CHAR. I've finished. Now I'll go. (*Slings the rifle over her shoulder.*) You, Yepikhod-off, are a very clever man and very frightful; women must be madly in love with you. Brrr! (*Going.*) These wise people are all so stupid. I've nobody to talk to. I'm always alone, alone; I've nobody at all . . . and I don't know who I am or why I live. (*Exit slowly.*)

YEP. As a matter of fact, independently of everything else, I must express my conviction, among other things, that fate has been as merciless in her dealings with me as a storm is to a small ship. Suppose, let us grant, I am wrong; then why did I wake up this morning, for example, and behold an enormous spider on my chest as big as this? (*Shows with both hands.*) And if I do drink kvass, why must I always find in the glass such an unsociable animal as a cockroach! (*Pause.*) Have you read Buckle? (*Pause.*) May I have a few words with you, Avdotya Fyodorovna?

DUN. Go on!

YEP. I should prefer to be alone with you. (*Sighs.*)

DUN. (*shy*). Very well, only please bring me my cloak first. . . . It's by the cupboard. It's a little damp here.

YEP. Very well. . . . I'll bring it. . . . Now I know what to do with my revolver. (*Takes guitar and exit, strumming.*)

YASHA. Two-and-twenty troubles! A foolish man, between you and me and the gatepost. (*Yawns.*)

DUN. (*pause*). I hope to goodness he won't shoot himself. (*Pause.*) I'm so nervous, so worried. I entered service when I was quite a little girl, and now I'm not used to common life, and my hands are as white as a lady's. I'm so tender and so delicate now, respectable and afraid of everything. . . . I'm so frightened. And I don't know what will happen to my nerves if you deceive me, Yasha.

YASHA (*kisses her*). Tiny cucumber! Of course, every girl must respect herself; there's nothing I dislike more than a badly behaved girl.

DUN. I'm so much in love with you; you're educated, you can talk about everything. (*Pause.*)

YASHA (*yawns*). Yes, I think that if a girl loves anybody, it means she's immoral. (*Pause.*) It's nice to smoke a cigar out in the open air. . . . (*Listens.*) Somebody's coming. It's the mistress, and people with her. (DUNYASHA *embraces him suddenly.*) Go to the house, as if you'd been bathing in the river; go by this path, or they'll run across you and will think I've been meeting you. I can't stand that sort of thing.

DUN. (*coughs quietly*). Your cigar has given me a headache.

Exit. YASHA *remains, sitting by the shrine. Enter* LIUBOFF ANDREIEVNA, GAIEFF, *and* LOPAKHIN.)

LOP. You must make up your mind definitely—there's no time to waste. The question is perfectly simple. Are you willing to let the land for villas or no? Just one word, yes or no? Just one word!

LIUB. Who's smoking bad cigars here? (*Sits.*)

GAI. They built that railway; that's made this place very convenient. (*Sits.*) Went to town and had lunch . . . red in the center! I'd like to go to the house now and have just one game.

LIUB. You'll have time.

LOP. Just one word! (*Imploringly.*) Give me an answer!

GAI. (*yawns*). Really!

LIUB. (*looks in her purse*). I had a lot of money yesterday, but there's very little left today. My poor Varya feeds everybody on milk soup to save money; in the kitchen the old people get peas only; and I spend recklessly. (*Drops the purse, scattering gold coins.*) There, money all over the place.

YASHA. Permit me to pick them up. (*Collects the coins.*)

LIUB. Please do, Yasha. And why did I go and lunch there? . . . A terrible restaurant with a band and tablecloths smelling of soap. . . . Why do you drink so much, Leon? Why do you eat so much? Why do you talk so much? You talked too much again today in the restaurant, and it wasn't at all to the point—about the seventies and about decadents. And to whom? Talking to the waiters about decadents! Imagine!

LOP. Yes.

GAI. (*waves his hand*). I can't be cured, that's obvious. . . . (*Irritably to* YASHA.) What's the matter? Why do you always manage to keep in front of me?

YASHA (*laughs*). I can't listen to your voice without laughing.

GAI. (*to his sister*). Either he or I . . .

LIUB. Go away, Yasha! Go!

YASHA (*gives purse to* LIUBOFF ANDREIEVNA). I'll go at once. (*Hardly able to keep from laughing.*) This minute. . . . (*Exit.*)

LOP. That rich man Deriganoff is preparing to buy your estate. They say he'll attend the sale in person.

LIUB. Where did you hear that?

LOP. They say so in town.

GAI. Our aunt in Yaroslavl promised to send something, but I don't know when or how much.

LOP. How much will she send? A hundred thousand rubles? Or two, perhaps?

LIUB. I'd be glad if we get ten or fifteen thousand.

LOP. You must excuse my saying so, but I've never met such frivolous people as you before, or anybody so unbusinesslike and peculiar. Here I am telling you in plain language that your estate will be sold, and you don't seem to understand.

LIUB. What are we to do? Tell us, what?

LOP. I tell you every day. Every day I say the same thing. Both the cherry orchard and the land must be leased for villas and at once,—the auction is staring you in the face: Understand! Once you definitely make up your minds to the villas, you'll have as much money as you wish and you'll be saved.

LIUB. Villas and villa residents—it's so vulgar, pardon me.

GAI. I agree with you entirely.

LOP. I must cry or yell or faint. I can't! You're too much for me! (*To* GAIEFF.) You old woman!

GAI. Really!

LOP. Old woman! (*Going out.*)

LIUB. (*frightened*). No, don't go away, stop; be a dear. Please. Perhaps we'll find some way out!

LOP. There is nothing to think about.

LIUB. Please don't go. It's nicer when you're here. . . . (*Pause.*) I keep on waiting for something to happen, as if the house were going to collapse over our heads.

GAI. (*thinking deeply*). Double in the corner . . . across the center.

LIUB. We have been too sinful. . . .

LOP. What sins have you been guilty of?

GAI. (*puts candy in his mouth*). They say that I've wasted all my money in buying candy. (*Laughs.*)

LIUB. Oh, my sins . . . I've always scattered money about without being able to control myself, like a madwoman, and I married a man who made nothing but debts. My husband died of champagne—he drank terribly—and to my misfortune, I fell in love with another man and went off with him, and just at that time—it was my first punishment, a blow that struck me squarely on the head—here, in the river . . . my boy was drowned, and I went away, abroad, never to return, never to see this river again. . . . I closed my eyes and ran without thinking, but he ran after me . . . without mercy, without respect. I bought a villa near Mentone because he fell ill there, and for three years I knew no rest, day or night; the sick man wore me out, and my soul dried up. And last year, when they had sold the villa to pay my debts, I went to Paris, and there he robbed me of all I had and threw me over and went off with another woman. I tried to poison myself. . . . It was so silly, so shameful . . . And suddenly I longed to go back to Russia, my own country, with my little daughter . . . (*Wipes her tears.*) Lord, Lord be merciful to me, forgive my sins! Punish me no more! (*Takes a telegram from her pocket.*) I had this today from Paris. . . . He begs my forgiveness, he implores me to return . . . (*Tears it up.*) Don't I hear music? (*Listens.*)

GAI. That is our famous Jewish band. You remember—four violins, a flute, and a double-bass.

LIUB. So it still exists? It would be nice if they came some evening.

LOP. (*listens*). I can't hear. . . . (*Sings quietly.*) "For money will the Germans make a Frenchman of a Russian." (*Laughs.*) I saw such an awfully funny thing at the theatre last night.

LIUB. I'm quite sure there wasn't anything funny at all. You shouldn't go and see plays, you ought to go and look at yourself. What a drab life you lead! What a lot of unnecessary things you say!

LOP. It's true. To speak the honest truth, we live a silly life. (*Pause.*) My father was a peasant, an idiot, he understood nothing, he didn't teach me, he was always drunk, and always beat me. As a matter of fact, I'm a fool and an. idiot, too. I've never learned anything, my handwriting is bad, I write so that I'm quite ashamed before people, like a pig!

LIUB. You should marry, my friend.

LOP. Yes . . . that's true.

LIUB. Why not our Varya? She's a nice girl.

LOP. Yes.

LIUB. She's a simple, unaffected girl, works all day, and, what matters most, she's in love with you. And you've liked her for a long time.

LOP. Well? I don't mind . . . She's a nice girl. (*Pause.*)

GAI. I'm offered a place in a bank. Six thousand rubles a year . . . Did you hear?

LIUB. What's the matter with you! Stay where you are . . .

(*Enter* FIRCE *with an overcoat.*)

FIRCE (*to* GAIEFF). Please sir, put this on, it's damp.

GAI. (*putting it on*). You're a nuisance, old man.

FIRCE. It's all very well. . . . You went away this morning without telling me. (*Examining* GAIEFF.)

LIUB. How old you've grown, Firce!

FIRCE. I beg your pardon?

LOP. She says you've grown very old!

FIRCE. I've lived a long time. They were getting ready to marry me before your father was born . . . (*Laughs.*) And when the Emancipation came I was already first valet. Only I didn't agree with the Emancipation and remained with my masters . . . (*Pause.*)

I remember everybody was happy, but they didn't know why.

LOP. It was very good for them in the old days. At any rate, they beat them formerly.

FIRCE (*not hearing*). Rather. The peasants kept their distance from the masters and the masters kept their distance from the peasants, but now everything is in a muddle, and you can't make head or tail of anything.

GAI. Be quiet, Firce. I have to go to town tomorrow. I have the promise of an introduction to a General who may lend me money on a note.

LOP. Nothing will come of it. And you won't pay your interest, don't you worry.

LIUB. He's out of his head. There's no General at all.

(*Enter* TROFIMOFF, ANYA, *and* VARYA.)

GAI. Here, come on, folks!

ANYA. Mother's sitting down here.

LIUB. (*tenderly*). Come, come, my dears . . . (*Embracing* ANYA *and* VARYA.) If you two only knew how much I love you. Sit down next to me, like that. (*All sit down.*)

LOP. Our eternal student is always with the ladies.

TROF. That's none of your business.

LOP. He'll soon be fifty, and he's still a student.

TROF. Stop your silly jokes!

LOP. Getting angry, eh, silly?

TROF. Shut up, can't you?

LOP. (*laughs*). I wonder what you think of me?

TROF. I think, Yermolai Alexeievitch, that you're rich, and you'll soon be a millionaire. Just as the wild beast which eats everything it finds is needed to make certain changes in cosmic matter, so you are needed too. (*All laugh.*)

VARYA. Better tell us something about the planets, Peter.

LIUB. No, let's continue yesterday's discussion.

TROF. What was it about?

GAI. About the proud man.

TROF. Yesterday we talked for a long time, but we arrived at no conclusion. In your opinion there's something mystic in pride. Perhaps you are right from your point of view, but if you look at the matter sanely, without complicating it, then what pride can there be, what logic in a man who is imperfectly made, physiologically speaking, and who in the vast majority of cases is coarse and stupid and profoundly unhappy? We must stop admiring one another. We must work, nothing more.

GAI. You'll die, all the same.

TROF. Who knows? And what does it mean—you'll die? Perhaps a man has a hundred senses, and when he dies only the five known to us are destroyed and the remaining ninety-five are left alive.

LIUB. How clever of you Peter!

LOP. (*ironically*). Oh, awfully!

TROF. The human race progresses, perfecting its powers. Everything that is unattainable now will some day be near and intelligible, but we must work, we must help with all our energy, those who seek to know the truth. Meanwhile in Russia only a very few of us work. The vast majority of those intellectuals whom I know seek for nothing, do nothing, and are at present incapable of hard work. They call themselves intellectuals, but they use "thou" and "thee" to their servants, they treat the peasants like animals, they learn slowly, they read nothing with discernment, they do absolutely nothing, they gabble on about science, about art they understand little. They are all serious, they all have severe faces. They all talk about important things. They philosophize, and at the same time, the vast majority of us, ninety-nine out of a hundred, live like savages, fighting and cursing on the slightest excuse, have filthy table manners, sleep in the dirt, in stuffiness among fleas, stinks, smells, moral stench, and so on. . . . And it's obvious that all our nice talk is only carried on to delude ourselves and others. Tell me, where are those crèches we hear so much of? And where are those reading-rooms? People only write novels about them; they don't really exist. Only dirt, coarseness, and Asiatic barbarism really exist. . . . I'm afraid; and I don't like serious faces at all. I don't like serious conversation. Let's say no more about it.

LOP. You know, I get up at five every morning, I work till evening, I am always dealing with money—my own and other people's—and I see what others are like. You have only to start doing anything at all, and you'll find out how few honest, honorable people there are. Sometimes, when I can't sleep, I think: "Oh Lord, you've given us huge forests, infinite fields, and endless horizons, and we, living here, ought really to be giants."

LIUB. You want giants, do you? . . . They're only good in stories, and even there they frighten one. (YEPIKHODOFF *enters at the back of the stage playing his guitar.* LIUBOFF ANDREIEVNA *speaks thoughtfully.*) Yepikhodoff has come.

ANYA (*thoughtfully*). Yepikhodoff has come.

GAI. The sun's set.

TROF. Yes.

GAI. (*not loudly, as if declaiming*). Oh, Nature, thou art wonderful, thou shinest with eternal radiance! Oh, beautiful and lofty one, thou whom we call mother, thou containest in thyself life and death, thou livest and destroyest. . . .

VARYA (*entreatingly*). Uncle, dear!

ANYA. Uncle, you're doing it again!

TROF. You'd better double the yellow into the center.

GAI. I'll be quiet, I'll be quiet.

(*They all sit thoughtfully. It is quiet. Only the mumbling of* FIRCE *is heard. Suddenly a distant sound comes as if from the sky, the sound of a breaking string, which dies away sadly.*)

LIUB. What's that?

LOP. I don't know. Perhaps a bucket fell, down a well somewhere. But it's a long way off.

GAI. Or perhaps it's some bird . . . like a heron.

TROF. Or an owl.

LIUB. (*shudders*). It's unpleasant, somehow. (*A pause.*)

FIRCE. Before the catastrophe the same thing happened. An owl screamed and the samovar hummed without stopping.

GAI. Before what catastrophe?

FIRCE. Before the Emancipation. (*A pause.*)

LIUB. You know, my friends, let's go in; it's evening now. (*To* ANYA.) You've tears in your eyes. . . . What is it, little girl? (*Embraces her.*)

ANYA. It's nothing, mother.

TROF. Some one's coming.

(*Enter a* TRAMP *in an old white peaked cap and overcoat. He is slightly drunk.*)

TRAMP. Excuse me, may I go this way straight through to the station?

GAI. You may. Go along this path. . . .

TRAMP. I thank you with all my heart. (*Hiccoughs.*) Lovely weather. . . . (*Declaims.*) My brother, my suffering brother. . . . Come out on the Volga, you whose groans . . . (*To* VARYA.) Mademoiselle, please give a hungry Russian thirty kopecks. . . .

(VARYA *screams, frightened.*)

LOP. (*angrily*). Everybody should have some sort of manners!

LIUB. (*with a start*). Take this . . . here you are . . . (*Feels in her purse.*) There's no silver . . . It doesn't matter, here's gold.

TRAMP. I am very grateful to you! (*Exit. Laughter.*)

VARYA (*frightened*). I'm going, I'm going. . . . Oh, mother dear, at home there's nothing for the servants to eat, and yet you gave him gold.

LIUB. What is to be done with such a fool as I am! At home, I'll give you everything I have. Yermolai Alexeievitch, lend me some more! . . .

LOP. Very well.

LIUB. Let's go, it's time. And Varya, we've settled your affairs; I congratulate you.

VARYA (*crying*). You shouldn't joke about this, mother.

LOP. Ophelia! Get thee to a nunnery.

GAI. My hands are trembling; I haven't played billiards for a long time.

LOP. Ophelia! Nymph! Remember me in thine orisons!

LIUB. Come along; it'll soon be supper-time.

VARYA. He frightened me. My heart is beating fast.

LOP. Let me remind you, ladies and gentlemen, on August 22nd, the cherry orchard will be sold. Think of that! . . . Think of that! . . . (*All go out except* TROFIMOFF *and* ANYA.)

ANYA (*laughs*). Thanks to the tramp who frightened Varya, we're alone now.

TROF. Varya's afraid that we may fall in love with each other and won't leave us alone for days on end. Her narrow mind won't permit her to understand that we are above love. To escape all the petty and deceptive things which prevent our being happy and free, such is the aim and object of our lives. Forward! We go irresistibly on to that bright star which burns there, in the distance! Don't lag behind, friends!

ANYA (*clapping her hands*). How beautifully you talk! (*Pause.*) It is glorious here today!

TROF. Yes, the weather is wonderful.

ANYA. What have you done to me, Peter? I don't love the cherry orchard as I used to. I loved it so tenderly, I thought there was no better place in the world than our orchard.

TROF. All Russia is our orchard. The land is great and beautiful, there are many glorious places in it. (*Pause.*) Think, Anya, your grandfather, your great-grandfather, and all your ancestors were serf-owners, they owned human beings; and now, doesn't something human look at you from every cherry in the orchard, every leaf and every branch? Don't you hear voices . . . ? Oh, it's awful, your orchard is frightful; and when in the evening or at night you walk through the orchard, then the old bark on the trees sheds a dim light and the old cherry-trees seem to dream of all that happened a hundred, two hundred years ago, and are burdened with their heavy visions. Still, we've left those two hundred years behind us. So far we've gained nothing at all—we don't yet know what the past will bring us—we only philosophize, we complain that we are dull, or we drink vodka. For it's so clear that to begin to live in the present we must first redeem the past, and that can be done only by suffering, by strenuous, uninterrupted work. Understand that, Anya.

ANYA. The house in which we live has long ceased to be our house; I shall go away, I give you my word.

TROF. If you have the keys of the household, throw them down the well and go away. Be as free as the wind.

ANYA (*enthusiastically*). How beautifully you said that!

TROF. Believe me, Anya, believe me! I'm not thirty yet, I'm young, I'm still a student, but I have gone through so much already! I'm as hungry as the winter, I'm ill, I'm shaken. I'm as poor as a beggar, and where haven't I been—fate has tossed me everywhere! But my soul is always my own; every minute of the day and the night it is filled with glorious and dim visions. I feel that happiness is coming, Anya, I see it already. . . .

ANYA (*thoughtful*). The moon is rising.

(YEPIKHODOFF *is heard playing the same sad song on his guitar. The moon rises. Somewhere near the poplars* VARYA *is looking for* ANYA *and calling, "*ANYA, *where are you?*")

TROF. Yes, the moon has risen. (*Pause.*) There is happiness, there it comes; it comes nearer and nearer; I hear its footsteps already. And if we do not see it, we shall not know it, but what does that matter? Others will see it!

VARYA'S VOICE. Anya! Where are you?

TROF. That's Varya again! (*Angry.*) Disgraceful!

ANYA. Never mind. Let's go to the river. It's nice there.

TROF. Let's go. (*They leave.*)

VARYA'S VOICE. Anya! Anya!

ACT III

A reception-room, separated by an arch from a drawing-room. Lighted chandelier. A

Jewish band, the one referred to in Act II, is heard playing in another room. Evening. In the drawing-room the cotillion is being danced.

(*Voice of* SEMYONOFF PISHCHIK, *"Promenade à une paire!" Dancers come into the reception-room; the first pair are* PISHCHIK *and* CHARLOTTA IVANOVNA; *the second* TROFIMOFF *and* LIUBOFF ANDREIEVNA; *the third* ANYA *and the* POST OFFICE CLERK; *the fourth* VARYA *and the* STATION-MASTER, *and so on.* VARYA *is crying gently and dries her eyes as she dances.* DUNYASHA *is in the last pair. They go off into the drawing-room, shouting, "Grand rond, balancez:" and "Les cavaliers à genoux et remerciez vos dames!"* FIRCE, *in a dress-coat, carries a tray with seltzer-water across the stage. Enter* PISHCHIK *and* TROFIMOFF *from the drawing-room.*)

PISH. I'm full-blooded and already I've had two strokes; it's hard for me to dance, but, as they say, if you're in Rome, you must do as the Romans do. I've the constitution of a horse. My late father, who liked a joke, peace to his ashes, used to say, talking of our ancestors, that the ancient stock of the Semyonoff Pishchiks was descended from the identical horse that Caligula appointed senator. . . . (*Sits.*) But the trouble is, I've no money! A hungry dog believes only in meat. (*Drops off to sleep and wakes up again immediately.*) So I . . . believe only in money. . . .

TROF. Yes. There is something horsy about your figure.

PISH. Well . . . a horse is a valuable animal . . . you can sell a horse.

(*The sound of billiard playing comes from the next room,* VARYA *appears under the arch.*)

TROF. (*teasing*). Madame Lopakhin! Madame Lopakhin!

VARYA (*angry*). Decayed gentleman!

TROF. Yes, I am a decayed gentleman, and I'm proud of it!

VARYA (*bitterly*). We've hired the musicians, but how are they to be paid? (*Exit.*)

TROF. (*to* PISHCHIK). If you would put

to better use the energy which you are wasting day by day, in looking for money to pay interest, I believe you'd finally succeed in moving heaven and earth.

PISH. Nietzsche . . . a philosopher . . . a very great and famous man . . . a man of enormous brain, says in his books that you can forge bank-notes.

TROF. And have you read Nietzsche?

PISH. Well . . . Dashenka told me. Now I'm in such a position, I wouldn't mind making counterfeit money . . . I have to pay 310 rubles day after tomorrow . . . I've obtained 130 already . . . (*Feels his pockets, nervously.*) I've lost the money! The money's gone! (*Crying.*) Where's the money? (*Joyfully.*) Here it is in the lining. . . . Why I was in a cold sweat!

(*Enter* LIUBOFF ANDREIEVNA *and* CHARLOTTA IVANOVNA.)

LIUB. (*humming a Caucasian dance song*). What is keeping Leonid so long? What's he doing in town? (*To* DUNYASHA.) Dunyasha, give the musicians some tea.

TROF. The business is off, I suppose.

LIUB. And the musicians needn't have come, and we needn't have arranged this ball. . . . Well, never mind. . . . (*Sits and sings softly.*)

CHAR. (*gives a pack of cards to* PISHCHIK). Here's a deck of cards, think of any card you like.

PISH. I've thought of one.

CHAR. Now shuffle. All right, now. Pass them over, my dear Mr. Pishchik. Eins, zwei, drei! Now look and you'll find it in your hind pocket.

PISH. (*takes a card out of his hind pocket*). Eight of spades, quite right! (*Surprised.*) Just imagine!

CHAR. (*holds the deck of cards in the palm of her hand. To* TROFIMOFF). Now tell me quickly. What's the top card?

TROF. Well, the queen of spades.

CHAR. Right! (*To* PISHCHIK.) And now? What card's on top?

PISH. Ace of hearts.

CHAR. Right! (*Clasps her hands, the deck of cards vanishes.*) How lovely the weather is today. (*A mysterious woman's voice an-*

swers her, as if from under the floor, "Oh yes, it's lovely weather, Madam.") You are so beautiful, you are my ideal. (*Voice, "You, Madam, please me very much too."*)

STATION-MASTER (*applauds*). Madame the ventriloquist, bravo!

PISH. (*surprised*). Just imagine! Delightful, Charlotta Ivanovna . . . I'm simply in love. . . .

CHAR. In love? (*Shrugging her shoulders.*) Can you love? Guter Mensch aber schlechter Musikant.

TROF. (*slaps* PISHCHIK *on the shoulder*). Oh, you horse!

CHAR. Attention, please, here's another trick. (*Takes a shawl from a chair.*) Here's a very nice plaid shawl. I'm going to sell it. . . . (*Shakes it.*) Won't somebody buy it?

PISH. (*astonished*). Just imagine!

CHAR. Eins, zwei, drei. (*She quickly lifts up the shawl, which is hanging down.* ANYA *appears behind it; she bows and runs to her mother, hugs her and runs back to the drawing-room amid general applause.*)

LIUB. (*applauds*). Bravo, bravo!

CHAR. Once again! Eins, zwei, drei! (*Lifts the shawl.* VARYA *appears behind it and bows.*)

PISH. (*astonished*). Just imagine!

CHAR. The end! (*Throws the shawl at* PISHCHIK, *curtseys and runs into the drawing-room.*)

PISH. (*runs after her*). Little witch! . . . What? Would you? (*Exit.*)

LIUB. Leonid hasn't come yet. I don't understand what is keeping him so long in town! Everything must be over by now. The estate must be sold; or, if the sale never came off, then why does he stay away so long?

VARYA (*tries to soothe her*). Uncle has bought it. I'm certain of it.

TROF. (*sarcastically*). Oh, yes!

VARYA. Grandmother sent him her authority to buy it in her name and transfer the debt to her. She's doing it for Anya. And I'm certain that God will help us and that Uncle will buy it.

LIUB. Grandmother sent fifteen thousand rubles from Yaroslavl to buy the property in her name—she won't trust us—and that wasn't even enough to pay the interest. (*Covers her face with her hands.*) My fate will be settled today, my fate. . . .

TROF. (*teasing* VARYA). Madame Lopakhin!

VARYA (*angry*). Eternal student? He's been expelled from the university, twice already.

LIUB. Why are you growing angry, Varya? He's teasing you about Lopakhin. Well, what of it? You can marry Lopakhin if you wish. He's a good, interesting man. . . . You needn't if you don't wish to; nobody is going to force you against your will, my darling.

VARYA. I look at the matter seriously, mother dear, to be quite frank. He's a good man, and I like him.

LIUB. Then marry him. I don't understand what you're waiting for.

VARYA. I can't propose to him myself, mother dear. People have been talking about him to me for two years now, but he either says nothing, or jokes about it. I understand. He's getting rich, he's busy, he can't bother about me. If I had some money, even a little, even only a hundred rubles, I'd throw up everything and go away. I'd go into a convent.

TROF. What bliss!

VARYA (*to* TROFIMOFF). A student should have common sense! (*Gently, in tears.*) How ugly you are now, Peter, how old you've grown! (*To* LIUBOFF ANDREIEVNA, *no longer crying.*) But I can't go on without working, mother dear. I'm eager to be doing something every minute.

(*Enter* YASHA.)

YASHA (*nearly laughing*). Yepikhodoff's broken a billiard cue! (*Exit.*)

VARYA. Why is Yepikhodoff here? Who said he could play billiards? I don't understand these people. (*Exit.*)

LIUB. Don't tease her, Peter, you see that she's unhappy enough without it.

TROF. She undertakes too much herself; she is continually interfering in other people's business. The whole summer she gave

Anya and me not a moment's peace. She's afraid we'll have a romance all to ourselves. What concern of hers is it? As if I'd ever given her grounds to believe I'd stoop to such vulgarity! We are above love.

LIUB. Then I suppose I must be beneath love. (*In agitation.*) Why isn't Leonid here? If I only knew whether the estate is sold or not! The catastrophe seems to me so unbelievable that I don't know what to think, I'm all at sea . . . I may scream . . . or do something foolish. Save me, Peter. Say something, say something.

TROF. Isn't it all the same whether the estate is sold today or not? For a long time it's been a foregone conclusion that it would be sold. There's no turning back, the path is obliterated. Be calm, dear, you shouldn't deceive yourself; for once in your life, at any rate, you must look the truth straight in the eyes.

LIUB. What truth? You see where truth is, and where falsehood is, but I seem to have lost my sight and see nothing. You settle all important questions boldly, but tell me, dear, isn't it because you're young, because you have not as yet had time to suffer in settling any one of these questions? You look forward boldly, but isn't it because you neither feel nor expect anything terrible, because so far life has been hidden from your young eyes? You are bolder, more honest, deeper than we are, but only think, be just a little magnanimous, and have pity on me. I was born here, my father and mother lived here, my grandfather, too. I love this house. I couldn't understand my life without that cherry orchard, and if it really must be sold, sell me with it! (*Embraces* TROFIMOFF, *kisses his forehead.*) My son was drowned here . . . (*Weeps.*) Have pity on me, good, kind man.

TROF. You know that I sympathize with all my heart.

LIUB. Yes, but it should be said differently. . . . (*Takes another handkerchief, a telegram falls on the floor.*) I'm so sick at heart today, you can't imagine. Here it's so noisy, my soul trembles at every sound. I shake all over, and I can't go away by myself, I'm afraid of the silence. Don't judge me harshly, Peter. . . . I love you, as if you belonged to the family. I'd gladly let Anya marry you, I swear it, only dear, you ought to work to finish your studies. You don't do anything, only fate tosses you about from place to place, it's so strange. . . . Isn't it true? Yes? And you ought to do something to your beard to make it grow better. (*Laughs.*) You are funny!

TROF. (*picking up telegram*). I don't wish to be a Beau Brummell.

LIUB. This telegram's from Paris. I receive one every day. Yesterday and today. That wild man is ill again, he's bad again. . . . He begs for forgiveness, and implores me to come, and I really should go to Paris to be near him. You look severe, Peter, but what can I do, my dear, what can I do? He's ill, he's alone, unhappy, and who's to look after him, who's to keep him out of harm's way, to give him his medicine punctually? And why should I conceal it and say nothing about it? I love him, that's plain, I love him, I love him. . . . That love is a stone round my neck; I shall sink with it to the bottom, but I love that stone and can't live without it. (*Squeezes* TROFIMOFF'S *hand.*) Don't think harshly of me, Peter, don't say anything to me, don't say . . .

TROF. (*weeping*). For God's sake forgive my speaking candidly, but that man has robbed you!

LIUB. No, no, you should not say that! (*Stops her ears.*)

TROF. But he's a scoundrel, you alone don't know it! He's a petty thief, a nobody. . . .

LIUB. (*angry, but restrained*). You're twenty-six or twenty-seven, and still a school-boy of the second grade!

TROF. Why not?

LIUB. You should be a man, at your age you should be able to understand those who love. And you should be in love yourself, you must fall in love! (*Angry.*) Yes, yes! You aren't pure, you're just a freak, a queer fellow, a funny fungus.

TROF. (*in horror*). What is she saying?

LIUB. "I'm above love!" You're not above

love, you're just what our Firce calls a bungler. Not to have a mistress at your age!

TROF. (*in horror*). This is terrible! What is she saying? (*Goes quickly into the drawing-room, seizing his head with both his hands.*) It's awful . . . I can't stand it, I'll go away. (*Exit, but returns at once.*) All is over between us! (*Exit.*)

LIUB. (*shouts after him*). Peter, wait! Silly boy, I was joking! Peter! (*Somebody is heard going out and falling downstairs noisily. ANYA and VARYA scream; laughter is heard immediately.*) What's that? (*ANYA comes running in, laughing.*)

ANYA. Peter's fallen downstairs. (*Runs out again.*)

LIUB. This Peter's a funny creature!

(*The STATION-MASTER stands in the middle of the drawing-room and recites "The Magdalen" by Tolstoy. They listen to him, but he has delivered only a few lines when a waltz is heard from the front room, and the recitation is stopped. Everybody dances. TROFIMOFF, ANYA, VARYA, and LIUBOFF ANDREIEVNA come in from the front room.*)

LIUB. Well, Peter . . . you pure soul . . . I beg your pardon. . . . Let's dance.

(*She dances with PETER. ANYA and VARYA dance. FIRCE enters and leans his stick against a side door. YASHA has also come in and watches the dance.*)

YASHA. Well, grandfather?

FIRCE. I'm not well. At our balls some time ago, generals and barons and admirals used to dance, and now we send for post office clerks and the station-master, and even they come reluctantly. I'm very weak. The dead master, the grandfather, used to give everybody sealing-wax when anything was wrong. I've taken sealing-wax every day for twenty years, and more; possibly that's why I am still alive.

YASHA. I'm tired of you, grandfather. (*Yawns.*) If you'd only hurry up and kick the bucket.

FIRCE (*muttering*). Oh, you . . . bungler!

(*TROFIMOFF and LIUBOFF ANDREIEVNA dance in the reception-room, then into the sitting-room.*)

LIUB. Merci. I'll sit down. (*Sits.*) I'm tired.

(*Enter ANYA.*)

ANYA (*excited*). Somebody in the kitchen was saying just now that the cherry orchard was sold today.

LIUB. Sold to whom?

ANYA. He didn't say to whom. He went away. (*Dances out into the reception-room with TROFIMOFF.*)

YASHA. Some old man was chattering about it a long time ago. A stranger!

FIRCE. And Leonid Andreievitch isn't here yet, he hasn't come. He's wearing a light autumn overcoat. He'll catch cold. Oh, these young fellows.

LIUB. I'll die of this. Go and find out, Yasha, to whom it's sold.

YASHA. Oh, but he's been gone a long time, the old man. (*Laughs.*)

LIUB. (*slightly vexed*). Why do you laugh? What are you so happy about?

YASHA. Yepikhodoff's too funny. He's a foolish man. Two-and-twenty troubles.

LIUB. Firce, if the estate is sold, where will you go?

FIRCE. I'll go wherever you command me to go.

LIUB. Why do you look like that? Are you ill? I think you should go to bed. . . .

FIRCE. Yes . . . (*With a smile.*) I'll go to bed, and who'll hand things round and give orders without me? I've the whole house on my shoulders.

YASHA (*to LIUBOFF ANDREIEVNA*). Liuboff Andreievna! I wish to ask a favor of you, if you'll be so kind! If you go to Paris again, take me along. I beg of you! It's absolutely impossible for me to remain here. (*Looking round; in an undertone.*) What's the good of talking about it? You see for yourself that this is an uncivilized country, with an immoral population, and it's so dull. The food in the kitchen is wretched, and here's this Firce walking about mumbling all kinds of inappropriate things. Take me with you. Please!

(*Enter PISHCHIK.*)

PISH. May I have the pleasure of a little waltz, dear lady . . . ? (LIUBOFF ANDREI-

EVNA *goes to him*.) But all the same, you wonderful woman, I must have 180 little rubles from you. . . . I must. . . . (*They dance.*) 180 little rubles. . . . (*They go through into the drawing-room.*)

YASHA (*sings softly*),

"Oh, will you understand
My soul's deep restlessness?"

(*In the drawing-room a figure in a gray top-hat and in baggy check trousers is waving its hands; and there are cries of "Bravo, CHARLOTTA IVANOVNA!"*)

DUN. (*stops to powder her face*). The young mistress tells me to dance—there are lots of gentlemen, but few ladies—and my head whirls when I dance, and my heart beats, Firce Nikolaievitch; the post office clerk told me something just now that almost took my breath away. (*The music grows faint.*)

FIRCE. What did he tell you?

DUN. He says, "You're like a little flower."

YASHA (*yawns*). Impolite. . . . (*Exit.*)

DUN. Like a little flower. I'm such a delicate girl; I simply love tender words.

FIRCE. You'll lose your head.

(*Enter* YEPIKHODOFF.)

YEP. You, Avdotya Fyodorovna, are about as anxious to see me as if I were some insect. (*Sighs.*) Oh, life!

DUN. What do you wish?

YEP. Perhaps, doubtless, you may be right. (*Sighs.*) But, certainly, if I consider the matter in that light, then you, if I may say so, and you must excuse my candidness, have absolutely reduced me to the state of mind in which I find myself. I know my fate. Every day something unfortunate happens to me, and I've grown used to it a long time ago. I never look at my fate with a smile. You gave me your word, and though I. . . .

DUN. Please, we'll talk later on, but leave me alone now. I'm thinking now. (*Fans herself.*)

YEP. Every day something unfortunate happens to me, and I, if I may so express myself, only smile, and even laugh.

(*VARYA enters from the drawing-room.*)

VARYA. Haven't you gone yet, Semyon? You really have no respect for anybody. (*To* DUNYASHA.) Go away, Dunyasha. (*To* YEPIKHODOFF.) You play billiards and break a cue, and stroll about the drawing-room as if you were a visitor!

YEP. You cannot, if I may say so, call me to order.

VARYA. I'm not calling you to order, I'm only telling you. You just walk about from place to place and never do your work. Goodness only knows why we keep a clerk.

YEP. (*offended*). Whether I work, or walk about, or eat, or play billiards, is only a matter to be settled by people of understanding and my elders.

VARYA. You dare talk to me like that! (*Furious.*) You dare? You mean to insinuate that I know nothing? Go away! This minute!

YEP. (*nervous*). I must ask you to express yourself more delicately.

VARYA (*beside herself*). Get out this minute. Get out! (*He goes to the door, she follows.*) Two-and-twenty troubles! Not another sign of you here! I don't wish to set eyes on you again! (YEPIKHODOFF *has gone out; his voice can be heard outside: "I'll make a complaint against you."*) What, coming back? (*Snatches up the stick left by* FIRCE *near the door.*) Go . . . go . . . go. I'll show you . . . Are you going? Are you going? Well, then take that. (*She lashes out with the stick as* LOPAKHIN *enters.*)

LOP. Much obliged.

VARYA (*angry but amused*). I'm sorry.

LOP. Never mind. I thank you for the pleasant reception you gave me!

VARYA. It isn't worthy of thanks. (*Walks away, then looks back and asks gently.*) I didn't hurt you, did I?

LOP. No, not at all. There'll be a huge bump, no more.

VOICES FROM THE DRAWING-ROOM. Lopakhin's returned! Yermolai Alexeievitch!

PISH. Now we'll see what there is to see and hear what there is to hear. . . . (*Kisses* LOPAKHIN.) You smell of brandy, my dashing soul. And we're all enjoying ourselves.

(*Enter* LIUBOFF ANDREIEVNA.)

LIUB. Is that you, Yermolai Alexeievitch? Why were you so long? Where's Leonid?

LOP. Leonid Andreievitch returned with me, he's coming. . . .

LIUB. (*excited*). Well, what? Is it sold? Tell me?

LOP. (*confused, afraid to show his pleasure*). The sale was over at four o'clock. . . . We missed the train, and had to wait till half-past nine. (*Sighs heavily*). Ooh! My head's swimming a little.

(*Enter* GAIEFF; *in his right hand he carries things that he has bought, with his left he dries his eyes.*)

LIUB. Leon, what's happened? Leon, well? (*Impatiently, in tears.*) Quick, for the love of God. . . .

GAI. (*says nothing to her, only waves his hand; to* FIRCE, *weeping*). Here, take this . . . Here are anchovies, herrings from Kertch. . . . I've had no food today. . . . I have had a time! (*The door from the billiard-room is open; the clicking of the balls is heard, and* YASHA'S *voice, "Seven, eighteen!"* GAIEFF'S *expression changes, he no longer cries.*) I'm awfully tired. Let me change my clothes, Firce. (*Goes out through the drawing-room;* FIRCE *following him.*)

PISH. What happened? Come on, tell us!

LIUB. Is the cherry orchard sold?

LOP. It is sold.

LIUB. Who bought it?

LOP. I bought it. (*Pause.* LIUBOFF ANDREIEVNA *is overwhelmed; she would fall if she were not leaning against an armchair and a table.* VARYA *takes her keys off her belt, throws them on the floor into the middle of the room and goes out.*) I bought it! Wait, ladies and gentlemen, please, my head's going round, I can't talk. . . . (*Laughing.*) When we reached the sale, Deriganoff was there already. Leonid Andreievitch had only fifteen thousand rubles, and Deriganoff offered thirty thousand on top of the mortgage to begin with. I saw how matters stood, so I went right after him and bid forty. He raised his bid to forty-five, I offered fifty-five. That means he went up by fives and I went up by tens. . . . Well, it came to an end at last, I bid ninety more than the mortgage;

and it stayed with me. The cherry orchard is mine now, mine! (*Roars with laughter.*) My God, my God, the cherry orchard's mine! Tell me I'm drunk, or crazy, or dreaming. . . . (*Stamps his feet.*) Don't laugh at me! If my father and grandfather rose from their graves and looked at the whole affair, and saw how their Yermolai, their whipped and illiterate Yermolai, who used to run barefoot in the winter, how that very Yermolai has bought an estate, the most beautiful spot in the world! I've bought the estate where my grandfather and my father were slaves, where they weren't even allowed to enter the kitchen. I'm asleep, it's only a dream, an illusion. . . . It's the fruit of imagination, wrapped in the fog of the unknown. . . . (*Picks up the keys, gaily smiling.*) She threw down the keys, she wished to show that she was no longer mistress here. . . . (*Jingles keys.*) Well, it's all one! (*Hears the band tuning up.*) Eh, musicians, play, I wish to hear you! Come and look at Yermolai Lopakhin swinging his ax against the cherry orchard, come and look at the trees falling! We'll build villas here, and our grandsons and great-grandsons will see a new life here. . . . Play on, music. (*The band plays.* LIUBOFF ANDREIEVNA *sinks into a chair and weeps bitterly.* LOPAKHIN *continues reproachfully.*) Why then, why didn't you take my advice? My poor, dear woman, you can't go back now. (*Weeps.*) Oh, if only the whole thing were finished, if only our uneven, unhappy lives were changed!

PISH. (*takes his arm; in an undertone*). She's crying. Let's go into the drawing-room and leave her by herself . . . come on . . . (*Takes his arm and leads him out.*)

LOP. What's that? Bandsmen, play up! Go on, do just as I wish you to! (*Ironically.*) The new owner, the owner of the cherry orchard is coming! (*He accidentally knocks up against a little table and nearly upsets the candelabra.*) I can pay for everything now! (*Exit with* PISHCHIK.)

(*In the reception-room and the drawing-room nobody remains except* LIUBOFF ANDREIEVNA, *who sits huddled up and weeping bitterly. The band plays softly.* ANYA *and*

TROFIMOFF *come in quickly.* ANYA *goes up to her mother and kneels in front of her.* TROFIMOFF *stands at the drawing-room entrance.*)

ANYA. Mother! Mother, are you crying? My dear, kind, good mother, my beautiful mother, I love you! Bless you! The cherry orchard is sold. We own it no longer, it's true. But don't cry, mother, you still have your life before you, you've still your beautiful pure soul. . . . Come with me, come, dear, away from here, come! We'll plant a new orchard more beautiful than this, and you'll see it, and you'll understand, and deep soothing joy will enfold your soul, like the evening sun, and you'll smile, mother! Come, dear, let's go!

ACT IV

Same as Act I. There are no curtains on the windows, no pictures; only a few pieces of furniture are left piled up in a corner as if for sale. The emptiness is apparent. There are bags and suitcases by the door that leads out of the house and at the back of the stage.

(*The door at the left is open; the voices of* VARYA *and* ANYA *can be heard through it.* LOPAKHIN *stands and waits.* YASHA *holds a tray with little glasses of champagne. Outside,* YEPIKHODOFF *is tying up a box. Voices are heard behind the stage. The peasants have come to say good-bye. The voice of* GAIEFF *is heard: "Thank you, brothers, thank you."*)

YASHA. The peasants have come to say good-bye. I am of the opinion, Yermolai Alexeievitch, that they're good people, but they don't understand very much.

(*The voices die away.* LIUBOFF ANDREIEVNA *and* GAIEFF *enter. She is not crying but is pale, and her face twitches; she can hardly speak.*)

GAI. You gave them your purse, Liuba. You can't go on like that, you can't!

LIUB. I couldn't help myself, I couldn't! (*They go out.*)

LOP. (*in the doorway, looking after them*). Please, I ask you most humbly! Just

a little glass for farewell. I didn't remember to bring any from town and I found only one bottle at the station. Please, do! (*Pause.*) Won't you really have any? (*Goes away from the door.*) If I only knew—I wouldn't have bought any. Well, I shan't drink any, either. (YASHA *carefully puts the tray on a chair.*) You have a drink, Yasha, at any rate.

YASHA. To those departing! And good luck to those who stay behind! (*Drinks.*) I can assure you that this isn't real champagne.

LOP. Eight rubles a bottle. (*Pause.*) It's frightfully cold here.

YASHA. We made no fire today, since we're going away. (*Laughs.*)

LOP. What's the matter with you?

YASHA. I'm happy—that's all!

LOP. It's October, but it's as sunny and quiet as if it were summer. Good for building. (*Looking at his watch and speaking through the door.*) Ladies and gentlemen, please remember that it's only forty-seven minutes till train time! You must leave for the station in twenty minutes. Hurry up.

(TROFIMOFF, *in an overcoat, enters from the outside.*)

TROF. I think it's time we went. The carriages are waiting. Where the devil are my rubbers? They're lost. (*Through the door.*) Anya, I can't find my rubbers! I can't!

LOP. I have to go to Kharkoff. I'm going on the same train as you. I'm going to spend the whole winter in Kharkoff. I've been hanging around with you people. I am tired of doing nothing. I must have something to do with my hands; they seem to belong to a different person if I don't use them.

TROF. We'll go away now and then you'll start again on your useful occupations!

LOP. Have a glass?

TROF. No—thanks!

LOP. So you're off to Moscow now?

TROF. Yes. I'll see them into town and tomorrow I'm going to Moscow.

LOP. Yes . . . I suppose the professors aren't lecturing yet; they're waiting till you turn up!

TROF. That does not concern you.

LOP. How many years have you been going to the university?

TROF. Think of something new! This is old and trite! (*Looking for his rubbers.*) You know, we may not meet again, so just let me give you a parting bit of advice: Don't wave your hands about! Get rid of that habit of waving them about. And then, building villas and reckoning on their residents becoming freeholders in time—that's the same thing; it's all a matter of waving your hands . . . I like you in spite of everything . . . You've slender, delicate fingers, like those of an artist, and you've a gentle, refined soul. . . .

LOP. (*embraces him*). Good-bye, dear fellow. Thanks for all you've said. If you need money for the journey, let me give you some.

TROF. What for? I don't need any.

LOP. But you've nothing!

TROF. Yes, I have, thank you; I received some for a translation. Here it is in my pocket. (*Nervously.*) But I can't find my rubbers!

VARYA (*from the other room*). Take your rubbish away! (*Throws a pair of rubbers on stage.*)

TROF. Why are you angry, Varya? H'm! These aren't my rubbers!

LOP. In the spring I sowed three thousand acres of poppies, and now I've netted forty thousand rubles profit. Why turn up your nose at it? I'm just a simple peasant. . . . And when my poppies were in bloom, what a picture it was! So, as I was saying, I made forty thousand rubles, and I mean I'd like to lend you some, because I can afford it.

TROF. Your father was a peasant, mine was a druggist, and that means nothing at all. (LOPAKHIN *takes out his pocketbook.*) No, no . . . Even if you gave me twenty thousand I should refuse. I'm a free man. And everything that rich and poor alike value so highly carries no more weight with me than thistledown in a wind. I can do without you, I can pass you by. I'm strong and proud. Mankind goes on to the highest possible truths and happiness on earth, and I march in the front ranks!

LOP. Will you reach there?

TROF. I shall! (*Pause.*) I'll reach there and show the way to others. (*Axes cutting the trees are heard in the distance.*)

LOP. Well, good-bye, old man. It's time to go. Here we stand pulling one another's noses, but life goes its own way all the while. When I work for a long stretch tirelessly, my thoughts become clearer and it seems to me that I understand the reasons for existence. But think, brother, how many people live in Russia without knowing why—? But all this is beside the point. Leonid Andreievitch, they say, has accepted a post in a bank; he will get six thousand rubles a year . . . But he won't stand it; he's very lazy.

ANYA (*at the door*). Mother asks if you will stop them cutting down the orchard until she has gone away.

TROF. Yes, really, you ought to have enough tact not to do that. (*Exit.*)

LOP. All right, all right . . . What funny people! (*Exit.*)

ANYA. Has Firce been sent to the hospital?

YASHA. I gave the order this morning. I suppose they've sent him.

ANYA (*to* YEPIKHODOFF, *who crosses the room*). Semyon Panteleievitch, please make inquiries if Firce has been sent to the hospital.

YASHA (*offended*). I told Yegor this morning. What's the use of asking ten times?

YEP. That old Firce, in my conclusive opinion, isn't worth mending; he had better join his ancestors. I only envy him. (*Puts a trunk on a hat-box and squashes it.*) Well, of course. I thought so! (*Exit.*)

YASHA (*grinning.*) Two-and-twenty troubles.

VARYA (*behind the door*). Has Firce been taken away to the hospital?

ANYA. Yes.

VARYA. Why didn't they take the letter to the doctor?

ANYA. It'll have to be sent after him. (*Exit.*)

VARYA (*in the next room*). Where's Yasha? Tell him his mother has come and wishes to say good-bye to him.

YASHA (*waving his hand*). She'll make me lose all patience!

(DUNYASHA *meanwhile has been busying herself with the bags; now that* YASHA *is left alone, she goes to him.*)

DUN. If you would only look at me once, Yasha. You're going away, leaving me behind . . . (*Weeps and hugs him.*)

YASHA. What's the use of crying? (*Drinks champagne.*) In six days I'll be back again in Paris. Tomorrow we get into the express and off we go. I can hardly believe it. Vive la France! It doesn't suit me here, I can't live here . . . it's no good. Well, I've seen the uncivilized world; I have had enough of it. (*Drinks champagne.*) What are you crying for? Behave decently and then you'll have no cause for tears!

DUN. (*powders herself, looking in the mirror*). Write me from Paris! I loved you so much, Yasha, so much! I am a delicate girl, Yasha.

YASHA. Somebody's coming.

(*He bustles around the baggage, singing softly. Enter* LIUBOFF ANDREIEVNA, GAIEFF, ANYA, *and* CHARLOTTA IVANOVNA.)

GAI. We'd better be off. There's no time to lose. (*Looks at* YASHA.) Somebody smells of herring!

LIUB. We needn't get into our carriages for ten minutes. (*Looks round the room.*) Good-bye, dear house, old grandfather. The winter will pass, the spring will come, and then you'll be here no more. You'll be pulled down. How much these walls have seen! (*Passionately kisses her daughter.*) My treasure, you're radiant, your eyes flash like two jewels! Are you happy? Very?

ANYA. Very! A new life is beginning, mother!

GAI. (*gaily*). Yes, really, everything's all right now. Before the cherry orchard was sold we all were excited and worried, and then, when the question was solved once and for all, we all calmed down, and even became cheerful. I'm a bank official now, and a financier . . . red in the center; and you, Liuba, look better for some reason or other, there's no doubt about it.

LIUB. Yes. My nerves are better, it's true.

(*She puts on her coat and hat.*) I sleep well. Take my baggage out, Yasha. It's time. (*To* ANYA.) My little girl, we'll soon see each other again . . . I'm off to Paris. I'll live there on the money your grandmother from Yaroslavl sent to buy the estate—bless her! —though it won't last long.

ANYA. You'll come back soon, soon, mother, won't you? I'll get ready, and pass the examination at the High School, and then I'll work and help you. We'll read all sorts of books together, won't we? (*Kisses her mother's hands.*) We'll read in the autumn evenings; we'll read many books, and a beautiful new world will open up before us . . . (*Thoughtfully.*) You'll come, mother. . . .

LIUB. I'll come, my darling. (*Embraces her.*)

(*Enter* LOPAKHIN. CHARLOTTA *is singing to herself.*)

GAI. Charlotta is happy; she's singing!

CHAR. (*takes a bundle, looking like a wrapped-up baby*). My little baby, bye-bye. (*The baby seems to answer, "Oua, oua!"*) Hush, my nice little boy. (*"Oua! Oua!"*) I'm so sorry for you! (*Throws the bundle back.*) So please find me a new place. I can't go on like this.

LOP. We'll find one, Charlotta Ivanovna, don't you be afraid.

GAI. Everybody's leaving us. Varya's going away . . . we've suddenly become unnecessary.

CHAR. I've nowhere to live in town. I must go away. (*Hums.*) Never mind.

(*Enter* PISHCHIK.)

LOP. The miracle of nature!

PISH. (*puffing*). Oh, let me get my breath again. I'm fagged . . . My honorable friends, give me some water . . .

GAI. Come for money did you? I'm your humble servant, and I'm going out of the way of temptation. (*Exit.*)

PISH. I haven't been here for ever so long . . . dear madam. (*To* LOPAKHIN.) You here? Glad to see you . . . man of tremendous brain . . . take this . . . take it . . . (*Gives* LOPAKHIN *money.*) Four hundred rubles . . . that leaves 841—

LOP. (*shrugs his shoulders in surprise*). It's like a dream. Where did you get this?

PISH. Stop . . . it's hot . . . A most unexpected thing happened. A group of Englishmen came along and found some white clay on my land. . . . (*To* LIUBOFF ANDREIEVNA.) And here's four hundred for you . . . beautiful lady . . . (*Gives her money.*) Give you the rest later . . . (*Drinks water.*) Just now a young man in the train was saying that some great philosopher advises us all to jump from the roofs. "Jump!" he says, and that's all. (*Astonished.*) Just imagine! More water!

LOP. Who were these Englishmen?

PISH. I've leased the land with the clay to them for twenty-four years . . . Now, excuse me, I've no time. I must hurry or—I'll go to Gnoikoff—to Kardamanoff—I owe everybody—(*Drinks.*) Good-bye—I'll drop in Thursday.

LIUB. We're just starting off to town, and tomorrow I go abroad.

PISH. (*agitated*). What? Why to town? I see furniture . . . trunks . . . Well, never mind. (*Crying.*) Never mind. These Englishmen are men of tremendous intellect . . . Never mind . . . Be happy . . . God will help you . . . Never mind . . . Everything in this world comes to an end . . . (*Kisses* LIUBOFF ANDREIEVNA'S *hand.*) And if you should happen to hear that my end has come, just remember this old . . . horse and say: "There used to be a certain fellow called Semyonoff-Pishchik, God bless his soul. . . ." Wonderful weather . . . yes . . . (*Exit deeply moved, but returns at once and says in the door.*) Dashenka sent her love! (*Exit.*)

LIUB. Now we can go. I've two worries, though. The first is poor Firce. (*Looks at her watch.*) We've still five minutes . . .

ANYA. Mother, Firce has already been sent to the hospital. Yasha sent him off this morning.

LIUB. The second is Varya. She's used to getting up early and to work, and now she has no work to do, she's like a fish out of water. She's grown thin and pale, and she cries, poor thing. . . . (*Pause.*) You know

very well, Yermolai Alexeievitch, that I hoped formerly to marry her to you, and I suppose you are going to marry somebody? (*Whispers to* ANYA, *who nods to* CHARLOTTA, *and they both go out.*) She loves you, she's your sort, and I don't understand, I really don't, why you seem to be keeping away from each other. I don't understand!

LOP. To tell the truth, I don't understand it myself. It's all so strange. . . . If there's still time, I'll be ready at once. Let's get it over, once and for all; I don't feel as if I could ever propose to her without you.

LIUB. Excellent. It'll take only a minute. I'll call her.

LOP. The champagne comes in very handy. (*Looking at the glass.*) They're empty, somebody's drunk them already. (YASHA *coughs.*) I call that licking it up. . . .

LIUB. (*animated*). Excellent. We'll go out. Yasha, *allez*. I'll call her . . . (*At the door.*) Varya, leave that and come here. Come! (*Exit with* YASHA.)

LOP. (*looks at his watch*). Yes . . . (*Pause.*)

(*There is a restrained laugh behind the door, a whisper, then* VARYA *comes in. She examines the luggage at length.*)

VARYA. I can't seem to find it . . .

LOP. What are you looking for?

VARYA. I packed it myself and I don't remember. (*Pause.*)

LOP. Where are you going now, Varvara Mikhailovna?

VARYA. I? To the Ragulins . . . I've accepted a position, to look after their household . . . housekeeper or something.

LOP. Is that at Yashnevo? It's about fifty miles. (*Pause.*) So life in this house is finished now. . . .

VARYA (*looking at the baggage*). Where it it? . . . perhaps I've put it away in the trunk . . . Yes, there'll be no more life in this house . . .

LOP. And I'm off to Kharkoff at once . . . by this train. I've a lot of business on hand. I'm leaving Yepikhodoff here . . . I've hired him.

VARYA. Well, well!

LOP. Last year at this time the snow was already falling, if you remember, and now it's nice and sunny. Only it's rather cold . . . There's three degrees of frost.

VARYA. I didn't look. (*Pause.*) And our thermometer's broken. . . . (*Pause.*)

VOICE AT THE DOOR. Yermolai Alexei-evitch!

LOP. (*as if he has long been waiting to be called*). Just a minute. (*Exit quickly.* VARYA, *sitting on the floor, puts her face against a bundle of clothes and weeps gently. The door opens.* LIUBOFF ANDREIEVNA *enters carefully.*)

LIUB. Well? (*Pause.*) We must go.

VARYA (*not crying now, wipes her eyes*). Yes, it's quite time, dear mother. I'll get to the Ragulins today, if I don't miss the train. . . .

LIUB. (*at the door*). Anya, put on your things. (*Enter* ANYA, *then* GAIEFF, *and* CHARLOTTA IVANOVNA. GAIEFF *wears a warm overcoat with a cape. A servant and drivers come in.* YEPIKHODOFF *bustles around the baggage.*) Now we can go away.

ANYA (*joyfully*). Away!

GAI. My friends, my dear friends! Can I be silent, in leaving this house forever?— can I restrain myself, in saying farewell, from expressing those feelings which now fill all my soul?

ANYA (*imploringly*). Uncle!

VARYA. Uncle, you shouldn't!

GAI. (*stupidly*). Double the red into the center . . . I'll be quiet.

(*Enter* TROFIMOFF, *then* LOPAKHIN.)

TROF. Well, it's time to go!

LOP. Yepikhodoff, my coat!

LIUB. I'll sit here one minute more. It's as if I'd never really noticed what the walls and ceilings of this house were like, and now I look at them greedily, with such tender love. . . .

GAI. I remember, when I was six years old, on Trinity Sunday, I sat at this window and looked and watched my father go to church. . . .

LIUB. Have all the things been taken away?

LOP. Yes, all, I think. (*To* YEPIKHODOFF, *putting on his coat.*) You see that everything's quite straight, Yepikhodoff.

YEP. (*hoarsely*). You may depend upon me, Yermolai Alexeievitch!

LOP. What's the matter with your voice?

YEP. I swallowed something just now; I was taking a drink of water.

YASHA (*suspiciously*). What manners . . .

LIUB. We go away, and not a soul remains behind.

LOP. Till the spring.

VARYA (*drags an umbrella out of a bundle, and seems to be waving it about.* LOPAKHIN *appears to be frightened*). What are you doing? . . . I never thought . . .

TROF. Come along, let's take our seats . . . it's time! The train will be in presently.

VARYA. Peter, here they are, your rubbers, by that trunk. (*In tears.*) And how old and dirty they are . . .

TROF. (*putting them on*). Come on!

GAI. (*deeply moved, nearly crying*). The train . . . the station . . . Cross in the center, a white double in the corner. . . .

LIUB. Let's go!

LOP. Are you all here? There's nobody else? (*Locks the side-door on the left.*) There's a lot of things in there. I must lock them up. Come!

ANYA. Good-bye, home! Good-bye, old life!

TROF. Welcome, new life. (*Exit with* ANYA. VARYA *looks round the room and goes out slowly.* YASHA *and* CHARLOTTA, *with her little dog, go out.*)

LOP. Till the spring then! Come on . . . till we meet again!

LIUBOFF ANDREIEVNA *and* GAIEFF *are left alone. They seem to have been waiting for this moment. They fall into each other's arms and sob restrainedly and quietly, fearing that somebody might hear them.*)

GAI. (*in despair*). My sister, my sister . . .

LIUB. My dear, my gentle, beautiful orchard! My life, my youth, my happiness, good-bye! Good-bye!

ANYA'S VOICE (*gaily*). Mother!

TROF'S VOICE (*gaily, excited*). Coo-ee!

LIUB. To look at the walls and the windows for the last time . . . My late mother used to like to walk about this room . . .

GAI. My sister, my sister!

ANYA'S VOICE. Mother!

TROF'S VOICE (*gaily, excited*). Coo-ee!

LIUB. We're coming! (*They go out. The stage is empty. The sound of keys turned in the locks is heard, and then the noise of the carriages driving off. It is quiet. Then the sound of an ax against the trees is heard in the silence sadly and staccato. Footsteps are heard.* FIRCE *comes in from the door on the right. He is dressed as usual, in a short jacket and white vest, with slippers on his feet. He is ill. He goes to the door and tries the handle.*)

FIRCE. It's locked. They've left. (*Sits on sofa.*) They've forgotten me. . . . Never mind, I'll sit here . . . And Leonid Andrei-evitch has probably gone in a light overcoat instead of putting on his fur coat . . . (*Sighs anxiously.*) I didn't see. . . . Oh, these young people! (*Mumbles something unintelligible.*) Life's gone on as if I'd never lived. (*Lying down.*) I'll lie down. . . . You've no strength left in you, nothing left at all. . . . Oh, you . . . bungler! (*He lies motionless. The distant sound is heard, as if from the sky, of a string breaking, dying away morosely. Silence follows it, and only the sound somewhere in the distance, of the ax falling on the trees, is audible.*)

SUGGESTIONS FOR STUDY

1. By what details does Chekhov indicate that the cherry orchard is a symbol of the passing of the old Russia?

2. Although this play is not primarily a document in sociology and economics, Chekhov, as so often happens in literature, has perhaps made a more vivid sociological study than the sociologists could give us. What details about Lopakhin's life could be used in a study of the rise of the Russian middle class in about 1900?

3. Why did Lopakhin and Varya not marry? What is the real attitude of each toward the other?

4. Semyonoff-Pishchik's essential qualities are shown in his name, which is deliberately comic. What details show him to be a kind of comic parody or parallel of Liuboff and Gaieff?

5. Each of the other minor characters is a fully described individual. What are the particular characteristics of Charlotta, Dunyasha, Yasha, Yepikhodoff?

6. Study the sound effects mentioned in the introduction to this play. What, perhaps, does each one symbolize?

7. We are not to believe that Firce is left in the house to die; he is merely left. How is this final incident symbolic of all that has gone on in the previous parts of the play?

ARMS AND THE MAN

George Bernard Shaw
(1856–1950)

Oedipus Rex and *Othello* are, in a sense, impersonal plays. Not only do we know relatively little about their authors (though we know more about Shakespeare than some people suppose), but we also have no knowledge whatever about whether the opinions of Sophocles and Shakespeare are reflected in *Oedipus Rex* and *Othello*. In contrast, we know a great deal about Shaw and about the extent to which his ideas appear in *Arms and the Man,* and we know what those ideas are. Since there is a direct relationship between Shaw's plays and his personality, it is necessary to know something about Shaw himself in order to understand his plays.

Arms and the Man is vintage Shaw, though of an early year. First performed in 1894, it is nevertheless a modern play. It seems archaic only in superficialities, such as costume and the details of warfare. Its author, George Bernard Shaw (also known as Bernard Shaw and as GBS) died, it would seem, just the other day, so vivid was his personality, so urgently controversial his ideas, and so successful his dramaturgy. *Arms and the Man* is therefore a more personal play than *Oedipus* or *Othello* partly because Shaw is still with us in a way that Sophocles and Shakespeare are not. The play contains many of Shaw's characteristic ideas and most of his technical tricks.

In politics and economics Shaw was a Fabian Socialist. He wished to bring about Socialism, but gradually. In philosophic matters perhaps the best word for him is antiscientist. He vehemently opposed vivisection. He accepted the idea of creative evolution instead of the more common Darwinian belief that evolution is purposeless. In addition to these philosophical attitudes, Shaw took a contrary stand on more personal topics. He was a vegetarian, a teetotaller, and a non-user of tobacco. In short, throughout the latter half of his long life Shaw seemed to conventional folk to be a perverse and crotchety opponent of most of the ideas that ordinary people take for granted.

Nevertheless Shaw said some things with which most people can agree. One such idea is the chief point of *Arms and the Man.* The play teaches us that war, "the dream of patriots and heroes," is a fraud. Shaw stated the idea explicitly in the preface to the volume in which this play appeared.

> I am quite aware that the much criticized Swiss officer in *Arms and the Man* is not a conventional stage soldier. He suffers from want of food and sleep; his nerves go to pieces after three days under fire, ending in the horrors of rout and pursuit; he has found by experience that it is more important to have a few bits of chocolate to eat in the field than cartridges for his revolver. When many of my critics rejected these circumstances as fantastically improbable and cynically unnatural, it was not necessary to argue them into common sense: all I had to do was to brain them, so to speak, with the first half dozen military authorities at hand, beginning with the present Commander in Chief.

And Shaw spoke about ". . . the general assault on idealism which is implicit and, indeed, explicit, in *Arms and the Man* and the realistic plays of the modern school."

> . . . for idealism, which is only a flattering name for romance in politics and morals, is as obnoxious to me as romance in ethics or religion.

In spite of a Liberal Revolution or two, I can no longer be satisfied with fictitious morals and fictitious good conduct, shedding fictitious glory on overcrowding, disease, crime, drink, war, cruelty, infant mortality, and all the other commonplaces of civilization which drive men to the theatre to make foolish pretences that these things are progress, science, morals, religion, patriotism, imperial supremacy, national greatness and all the other names the newspapers call them.

All this and the play too were written in 1894, twenty years before the beginning of World War I. Few would now disagree with Shaw as to the fictitious glory of war. Our agreement comes not merely from the distressing events of the twentieth century that we have experienced but also from the fact that, partly under Shaw's leadership, much of our literature has become realistic in that it denies the false and naïve idealism or romanticism enjoyed by the Rainas and Saranoffs of the world. Here, then, is one of the primary functions of literature: in the hands of a Shaw it can not only state for us but also sometimes anticipate one of the attitudes toward life most characteristic of its time. Of course we hope that Shaw's and Bluntschli's derision of false romanticism is an attitude of permanent validity as well, and that it will not have to be reanticipated and restated by some future Shaw.

This is the chief message of the play, but we would not be drawn to it if the play's form were not also attractive. Even this early in his career Shaw perfected the technique of making us laugh at the same time that we take in his ideas. He was a comedian as well as a proponent of serious beliefs. As he himself stated, or might have stated, he would have stood on his head if he thought that standing on his head would have directed our attention to his ideas. One of the methods by which Shaw's comedy brings out meaning is his use of ironic reversal or paradox. An idea that seems not

to be true is made to become true in the course of discussion. There are at least three examples of paradox in *Arms and the Man*. First, Bluntschli is by definition an unheroic soldier, a "chocolate cream soldier," as already noted. Second, Louka and Nicola are servants who have ideas above their station. Louka marries a nobleman. Nicola, charged with having the soul of a servant, replies, "Yes: thats the secret of success in service," and approves of Louka's entrance into the aristocracy so that she and her husband will be able to patronize the shop he is about to open. Students who wish to read later Shaw plays (*Man and Superman, Pygmalion*) will find that Louka and Nicola are the first of a line of servants who are realists rather than romantic idealists.

The last example of paradox is also typical of Shaw's plays. Both Louka and Raina get their men. Already Shaw was foreshadowing one of his characteristic ideas: the female of the species is the chief instrument of the Life Force that drives all of us on. (This is derived from the non-Darwinian idea of evolution mentioned above.) A woman knows that her function is to bear children who, being better than their parents, will advance the race toward the distant goal of perfection. This idea exists only in germ in *Arms and the Man,* but both Louka and Raina are among the first typically Shavian women.

In addition to paradox, Shaw used in this play certain older devices of comedy, even elements of farce. *Arms and the Man* is, in comic structure, an example of the boy-meets-girl formula. Boy (Bluntschli) meets girl (Raina) under unconventional circumstances in her bedroom. Boy loses girl for a time because she is already engaged and because he is an enemy of her country. Boy gets girl because he is able to persuade her that in her true self she is a realist like him, because he admits that he is at least partially romantic like her, because of her own seductive attractiveness (part of Shaw's idea of a Life Force), because he proves that he is not merely a mercenary soldier but a wealthy Swiss hotel man (the revelation of wealth at the end of the play is in itself a hoary device of comedy), and so on. It would be possible to study the last act as an example of the recognition scene. All, except perhaps Major and Catherine Petkoff, recognize themselves or are recognized for what they really are.

The extreme of comedy is farce. All parts of the play, particularly the last act, contain farcical elements. One is the cumulative gag: Saranoff repeats phrases like "I never apologize" until Bluntschli says, in effect, "Yes, we know. You never apologize." Another is the threat of mild physical pain: Nicola almost drops the bag on his master's toes. Another is the use of props (stage properties): the coat, the hidden portrait. Perhaps because his previous three plays had

been too serious and too shocking to be performed on the London stage of the 1890's, Shaw was determined to dress up *Arms and the Man* in whatever cloak of comedy would attract and retain the attention of an audience in the commercial theater.

In short, Bernard Shaw rejuvenated English drama. He used the old tricks, but he used them to make palatable the taste of his new ideas. Some of his ideas, new at the beginning of our century, are still as alive as the old tricks. *Arms and the Man,* which is still being performed, is among the first modern plays to prove that one of the functions of the drama (as of all other literature) is that of calling attention to ideas, old and new.

ARMS AND THE MAN
A PLEASANT PLAY

CHARACTERS

in the order of their appearance

RAINA PETKOFF, *a young Bulgarian lady*
CATHERINE PETKOFF, *her mother*
LOUKA, *Raina's maid*
CAPTAIN BLUNTSCHLI, *a Swiss in the Serbian army*

A RUSSIAN OFFICER, *in the Bulgarian army*
NICOLA, *the Petkoff's manservant*
MAJOR PETKOFF, *Raina's father*
MAJOR SERGIUS SARANOFF, *Raina's fiancé*

The action takes place at the home of Major Petkoff, in a small town in Bulgaria, in the years 1885 and 1886.

ACT I

Night: *A lady's bedchamber in Bulgaria, in a small town near the Dragoman Pass, late in November in the year 1885. Through an open window with a little balcony a peak of the Balkans, wonderfully white and beautiful in the starlit snow, seems quite close at hand, though it is really miles away. The interior of the room is not like anything to be seen in the west of Europe. It is half rich Bulgarian, half cheap Viennese. Above the head of the bed, which stands against a little wall*

cutting off the left hand corner of the room, is a painted wooden shrine, blue and gold, with an ivory image of Christ, and a light hanging before it in a pierced metal ball suspended by three chains. The principal seat, placed towards the other side of the room and opposite the window, is a Turkish ottoman. The counterpane and hangings of the bed, the window curtains, the little carpet, and all the ornamental textile fabrics in the room are oriental and gorgeous; the paper on the walls is occidental and paltry. The washstand, against the wall on the side nearest the ottoman and window, consists of an enamelled iron basin with a pail beneath it in a painted metal frame, and a single towel on the rail at the side. The dressing table, between the bed and the window, is a common pine table, covered with a cloth of many colours, with an expensive toilet mirror on it. The door is on the side nearest the bed; and there is a chest of drawers between. This chest of drawers is also covered by a variegated native cloth; and on it there is a pile of paper backed novels, a box of chocolate creams, and a miniature easel with a large photograph of an extremely handsome officer, whose lofty bearing and magnetic glance can be felt even from the portrait. The room is lighted by a candle on the chest of drawers, and another on the dressing table with a box of matches beside it.

The window is hinged doorwise and stands wide open. Outside, a pair of wooden shutters, opening outwards, also stand open. On the balcony a young lady, intensely conscious of the romantic beauty of the night, and of the fact that her own youth and beauty are part of it, is gazing at the snowy Balkans. She is in her nightgown, well covered by a long mantle of furs, worth, on a moderate estimate, about three times the furniture of the room.

Her reverie is interrupted by her mother, Catherine Petkoff, a woman over forty, imperiously energetic, with magnificent black hair and eyes, who might be a very splendid specimen of the wife of a mountain farmer, but is determined to be a Viennese lady, and to that end wears a fashionable tea gown on all occasions.

CATHERINE [*entering hastily, full of good news*] Raina! [*She pronounces it Rah-eena, with the stress on the ee*]. Raina! [*She goes to the bed, expecting to find Raina there*]. Why, where—? [*Raina looks into the room*]. Heavens, child! are you out in the night air instead of in your bed? Youll catch your death. Louka told me you were asleep.

RAINA [*dreamily*] I sent her away. I wanted to be alone. The stars are so beautiful! What is the matter?

CATHERINE. Such news! There has been a battle.

RAINA [*her eyes dilating*] Ah! [*She comes eagerly to Catherine*].

CATHERINE. A great battle at Slivnitza! A victory! And it was won by Sergius.

RAINA [*with a cry of delight*] Ah! [*They embrace rapturously*] Oh, mother! [*Then, with sudden anxiety*] is father safe?

CATHERINE. Of course! he sends me the news. Sergius is the hero of the hour, the idol of the regiment.

RAINA. Tell me, tell me. How was it? [*Ecstatically*] Oh, mother! mother! mother! [*She pulls her mother down on the ottoman; and they kiss one another frantically*].

CATHERINE [*with surging enthusiasm*] You cant guess how splendid it is. A cavalry charge! think of that! He defied our Russian commanders—acted without orders—led a charge on his own responsibility—headed it himself—was the first man to sweep through their guns. Cant you see it, Raina: our gallant splendid Bulgarians with their swords and eyes flashing, thundering down like an avalanche and scattering the wretched Serbs and their dandified Austrian officers like chaff. And you! you kept Sergius waiting a year before you would be betrothed to him. Oh, if you have a drop of Bulgarian blood in your veins, you will worship him when he comes back.

RAINA. What will he care for my poor little worship after the acclamations of a whole army of heroes? But no matter: I am so happy! so proud! [*She rises and walks about excitedly*]. It proves that all our ideas were real after all.

CATHERINE [*indignantly*] Our ideas real! What do you mean?

RAINA. Our ideas of what Sergius would do. Our patriotism. Our heroic ideals. I sometimes used to doubt whether they were anything but dreams. Oh, what faithless little creatures girls are! When I buckled on Sergius's sword he looked so noble: it was treason to think of disillusion or humiliation or failure. And yet—and yet—[*She sits down again suddenly*] Promise me youll never tell him.

CATHERINE. Dont ask me for promises until I know what I'm promising.

RAINA. Well, it came into my head just as he was holding me in his arms and looking into my eyes, that perhaps we only had our heroic ideas because we are so fond of reading Byron and Pushkin, and because we were so delighted with the opera that season at Bucharest. Real life is so seldom like that! indeed never, as far as I knew it then. [*Remorsefully*] Only think, mother: I doubted him: I wondered whether all his heroic qualities and his soldiership might not prove mere imagination when he went into a real battle. I had an uneasy fear that he might cut a poor figure there beside all those clever officers from the Tsar's court.

CATHERINE. A poor figure! Shame on you! The Serbs have Austrian officers who are just as clever as the Russians; but we have beaten them in every battle for all that.

RAINA [*laughing and snuggling against her mother*] Yes: I was only a prosaic little coward. Oh, to think that it was all true! that Sergius is just as splendid and noble as he looks! that the world is really a glorious world for women who can see its glory and men who can act its romance! What happiness! what unspeakable fulfilment!

They are interrupted by the entry of Louka, a handsome proud girl in a pretty Bulgarian peasant's dress with double apron, so defiant that her servility to Raina is almost insolent. She is afraid of Catherine, but even with her goes as far as she dares.

LOUKA. If you please, madam, all the windows are to be closed and the shutters made fast. They say there may be shooting in the streets. [*Raina and Catherine rise together, alarmed*]. The Serbs are being chased right back through the pass; and they say they may run into the town. Our cavalry will be after them; and our people will be ready for them, you may be sure, now theyre running away. [*She goes out on the balcony, and pulls the outside shutters to; then steps back into the room*].

CATHERINE [*businesslike, housekeeping instincts aroused*] I must see that everything is made safe downstairs.

RAINA. I wish our people were not so cruel. What glory is there in killing wretched fugitives?

CATHERINE. Cruel! Do you suppose they would hesitate to kill you—or worse?

RAINA [*to Louka*] Leave the shutters so that I can just close them if I hear any noise.

CATHERINE [*authoritatively, turning on her way to the door*] Oh no, dear: you must keep them fastened. You would be sure to drop off to sleep and leave them open. Make them fast, Louka.

LOUKA. Yes, madam. [*She fastens them*].

RAINA. Dont be anxious about me. The moment I hear a shot, I shall blow out the candles and roll myself up in bed with my ears well covered.

CATHERINE. Quite the wisest thing you can do, my love. Good night.

RAINA. Goodnight. [*Her emotion comes back for a moment*]. Wish me joy [*They kiss*]. This is the happiest night of my life—if only there are no fugitives.

CATHERINE. Go to bed, dear; and dont think of them. [*She goes out*].

LOUKA [*secretly to Raina*] If you would like the shutters open, just give them a push like this [*she pushes them: they open: she pulls them to again*]. One of them ought to be bolted at the bottom; but the bolt's gone.

RAINA [*with dignity, reproving her*] Thanks, Louka; but we must do what we are told. [*Louka makes a grimace*]. Goodnight.

LOUKA [*carelessly*] Goodnight. [*She goes out, swaggering*].

Raina, left alone, takes off her fur cloak and throws it on the ottoman. Then she goes to the chest of drawers, and adores the portrait there with feelings that are beyond all expression. She does not kiss it or press it to her breast, or shew it any mark of bodily affection; but she takes it in her hands and elevates it, like a priestess.

RAINA [*looking up at the picture*] Oh, I shall never be unworthy of you any more, my soul's hero: never, never, never. [*She replaces it reverently. Then she selects a novel from the little pile of books. She turns over the leaves dreamily; finds her page; turns the book inside out at it; and, with a happy sigh, gets into bed and prepares to read herself to sleep. But before abandoning herself to fiction, she raises her eyes once more, thinking of the blessed reality, and murmurs]* My hero! my hero!

A distant shot breaks the quiet of the night. She starts, listening; and two more shots, much nearer, follow, startling her so that she scrambles out of bed, and hastily blows out the candle on the chest of drawers. Then, putting her fingers in her ears, she runs to the dressing table, blows out the light there, and hurries back to bed in the dark, nothing being visible but the glimmer of the light in the pierced ball before the image, and the starlight seen through the slits at the top of the shutters. The firing breaks out again: there is a startling fusillade quite close at hand. Whilst it is still echoing, the shutters disappear, pulled open from without; and for an instant the rectangle of snowy starlight flashes out with the figure of a man silhouetted in black upon it. The shutters close immediately; and the room is dark again. But the silence is now broken by the sound of panting. Then there is a scratch; and the flame of a match is seen in the middle of the room.

RAINA *[crouching on the bed]* Who's there? *[The match is out instantly].* Who's there? Who is that?

A MAN'S VOICE *[in the darkness, subduedly, but threateningly]* Sh—sh! Dont call out; or youll be shot. Be good; and no harm will happen to you. *[She is heard leaving her bed, and making for the door].* Take care: it's no use trying to run away.

RAINA. But who—

THE VOICE *[warning]* Remember: if you raise your voice my revolver will go off. *[Commandingly].* Strike a light and let me see you. Do you hear. *[Another moment of silence and darkness as she retreats to the chest of drawers. Then she lights a candle; and the mystery is at an end. He is a man of about 35, in a deplorable plight, bespattered with mud and blood and snow, his belt and the strap of his revolver case keeping together the torn ruins of the blue tunic of a Serbian artillery officer. All that the candlelight and his unwashed unkempt condition make it possible to discern is that he is of middling stature and undistinguished appearance, with strong neck and shoulders, roundish obstinate looking head covered with short crisp bronze curls, clear quick eyes and good brows and mouth, hopelessly prosaic nose like that of a strong minded baby, trim soldierlike carriage and energetic manner, and with all his wits about him in spite of his desperate predicament: even with a sense of the humor of it, without, however, the least intention of trifling with it or throwing away a chance. Reckoning up what he can guess about Raina: her age, her social position, her character, and the extent to which she is frightened, he continues, more politely but still most determinedly]* Excuse my disturbing you; but you recognize my uniform? Serb! If I'm caught I shall be killed. *[Menacingly]* Do you understand that?

RAINA. Yes.

THE MAN. Well, I don't intend to get killed if I can help it. *[Still more formidably]* Do you understand that? *[He locks the door quickly but quietly].*

RAINA. *[disdainfully]* I suppose not. *[She draws herself up superbly, and looks him straight in the face, adding, with cutting emphasis]* Some soldiers, I know, are afraid to die.

THE MAN *[with grim goodhumor]* All of them, dear lady, all of them, believe me. It is our duty to live as long as we can. Now, if you raise an alarm—

RAINA *[cutting him short]* You will shoot me. How do you know that *I* am afraid to die?

THE MAN *[cunningly]* Ah; but suppose I dont shoot you, what will happen then? A lot of your cavalry will burst into this pretty room of yours and slaughter me here like a pig; for I'll fight like a demon: they shant get me into the street to amuse themselves with: I know what they are. Are you prepared to receive that sort of company in your present undress? [*Raina, suddenly conscious of her nightgown, instinctively shrinks and gathers it more closely about her neck. He watches her and adds pitilessly*] Hardly presentable, eh? [*She turns to the ottoman. He raises his pistol instantly, and cries*] Stop! [*She stops*]. Where are you going?

RAINA [*with dignified patience*] Only to get my cloak.

THE MAN [*passing swiftly to the ottoman and snatching the cloak*] A good idea! I'll keep the cloak; and you'll take care that nobody comes in and sees you without it. This is a better weapon than the revolver: eh? [*He throws the pistol down on the ottoman*].

RAINA [*revolted*] It is not the weapon of a gentleman!

THE MAN. It's good enough for a man with only you to stand between him and death. [*As they look at one another for a moment, Raina hardly able to believe that even a Serbian officer can be so cynically and selfishly unchivalrous, they are startled by a sharp fusillade in the street. The chill of imminent death hushes the man's voice as he adds*] Do you hear? If you are going to bring those blackguards in on me you shall receive them as you are.

Clamor and disturbance. The pursuers in the street batter at the house door, shouting Open the door! Open the door! Wake up, will you! *A man servant's voice calls to them angrily from within* This is Major Petkoff's house: you cant come in here; *but a renewal of the clamor, and a torrent of blows on the door, end with his letting a chain down with a clank, followed by a rush of heavy footsteps and a din of triumphant yells, dominated at last by the voice of Catherine, indignantly addressing an officer with* What does this mean, sir? Do you know where you are? *The noise subsides suddenly.*

LOUKA [*outside, knocking at the bedroom door*] My lady! my lady! get up quick and open the door. If you dont they will break it down.

The fugitive throws up his head with the gesture of a man who sees that it is all over with him, and drops the manner he has been assuming to intimidate Raina.

THE MAN [*sincerely and kindly*] No use, dear: I'm done for. [*Flinging the cloak to her*] Quick! wrap yourself up: they're coming.

RAINA. Oh, thank you. [*She wraps herself up with intense relief*].

THE MAN [*between his teeth*] Dont mention it.

RAINA [*anxiously*] What will you do?

THE MAN [*grimly*] The first man in will find out. Keep out of the way; and dont look. It wont last long; but it will not be nice. [*He draws his sabre and faces the door, waiting*].

RAINA [*impulsively*] I'll help you. I'll save you.

THE MAN. You cant.

RAINA. I can. I'll hide you. [*She drags him towards the window*]. Here! behind the curtains.

THE MAN [*yielding to her*] Theres just half a chance, if you keep your head.

RAINA [*drawing the curtain before him*] S-sh! [*she makes for the ottoman*].

THE MAN [*putting out his head*] Remember—

RAINA [*running back to him*] Yes?

THE MAN.—nine soldiers out of ten are born fools.

RAINA. Oh! [*She draws the curtain angrily before him*].

THE MAN [*looking out at the other side*] If they find me, I promise you a fight: a devil of a fight.

She stamps at him. He disappears hastily. She takes off her cloak, and throws it across the foot of the bed. Then, with a sleepy, disturbed air, she opens the door. Louka enters excitedly.

LOUKA. One of those beasts of Serbs has been seen climbing up the waterpipe to your balcony. Our men want to search for him; and they are so wild and drunk and furious. [*She makes for the other side of the room to get as far from the door as possible*]. My lady says you are to dress at once and to—

[*She sees the revolver lying on the ottoman, and stops, petrified*].

RAINA [*as if annoyed at being disturbed*] They shall not search here. Why have they been let in?

CATHERINE [*coming in hastily*] Raina, darling, are you safe? Have you seen anyone or heard anything?

RAINA. I heard the shooting. Surely the soldiers will not dare come in here?

CATHERINE. I have found a Russian officer, thank Heaven: he knows Sergius. [*Speaking through the door to someone outside*] Sir: will you come in now. My daughter will receive you.

A young Russian officer, in Bulgarian uniform, enters, sword in hand.

OFFICER [*with soft feline politeness and stiff military carriage*] Good evening, gracious lady. I am sorry to intrude; but there is a Serb hiding on the balcony. Will you and the gracious lady your mother please to withdraw whilst we search?

RAINA [*petulantly*] Nonsense, sir: you can see that there is no one on the balcony. [*She throws the shutters wide open and stands with her back to the curtain where the man is hidden, pointing to the moonlit balcony. A couple of shots are fired right under the window; and a bullet shatters the glass opposite Raina, who winks and gasps, but stands her ground; whilst Catherine screams, and the officer, with a cry of* Take care! *rushes to the balcony*].

THE OFFICER [*on the balcony, shouting savagely down to the street*] Cease firing there, you fools: do you hear? Cease firing, damn you! [*He glares down for a moment; then turns to Raina, trying to resume his polite manner*]. Could anyone have got in without your knowledge? Were you asleep?

RAINA. No: I have not been to bed.

THE OFFICER [*impatiently, coming back into the room*] Your neighbors have their heads so full of runaway Serbs that they see them everywhere. [*Politely*] Gracious lady: a thousand pardons. Goodnight. [*Military bow, which Raina returns coldly. Another to Catherine, who follows him out*].

Raina closes the shutters. She turns and sees Louka, who has been watching the scene curiously.

RAINA. Dont leave my mother, Louka, until the soldiers go away.

Louka glances at Raina, at the ottoman, at the curtain; then purses her lips secretively, laughs insolently, and goes out. Raina, highly offended by this demonstration, follows her to the door, and shuts it behind her with a slam, locking it violently. The man immediately steps out from behind the curtain, sheathing his sabre. Then, dismissing the danger from his mind in a businesslike way, he comes affably to Raina.

THE MAN. A narrow shave; but a miss is as good as a mile. Dear young lady: your servant to the death. I wish for your sake I had joined the Bulgarian army instead of the other one. I am not a native Serb.

RAINA [*haughtily*] No: you are one of the Austrians who set the Serbs on to rob us of our national liberty, and who officer their army for them. We hate them!

THE MAN. Austrian! not I. Dont hate me, dear young lady. I am a Swiss, fighting merely as a professional soldier. I joined the Serbs because they came first on the road from Switzerland. Be generous: youve beaten us hollow.

RAINA. Have I not been generous?

THE MAN. Noble! Heroic! But I'm not saved yet. This particular rush will soon pass through; but the pursuit will go on all night by fits and starts. I must take my chance to get off in a quiet interval. [*Pleasantly*] You dont mind my waiting just a minute or two, do you?

RAINA [*putting on her most genteel society manner*] Oh, not at all. Wont you sit down?

THE MAN. Thanks [*He sits on the foot of the bed*].

Raina walks with studied elegance to the ottoman and sits down. Unfortunately she sits on the pistol, and jumps up with a shriek. The man, all nerves, shies like a frightened horse to the other side of the room.

THE MAN [*irritably*] Dont frighten me like that. What is it?

RAINA. Your revolver! It was staring that officer in the face all the time. What an escape!

THE MAN [*vexed at being unnecessarily terrified*] Oh, is that all?

RAINA [*staring at him rather superciliously as she conceives a poorer and poorer opinion of him, and feels proportionately more and more at her ease*] I am sorry I frightened you. [*She takes up the pistol and hands it to him*]. Pray take it to protect yourself against me.

THE MAN [*grinning wearily at the sarcasm as he takes the pistol*] No use, dear young lady: there's nothing in it. It's not loaded. [*He makes a grimace at it, and drops it disparagingly into his revolver case*].

RAINA. Load it by all means.

THE MAN. Ive no ammunition. What use are cartridges in battle? I always carry chocolate instead; and I finished the last cake of that hours ago.

RAINA [*outraged in her most cherished ideals of manhood*] Chocolate! Do you stuff your pockets with sweets—like a schoolboy —even in the field?

THE MAN [*grinning*] Yes: isnt it contemptible? [*Hungrily*] I wish I had some now.

RAINA. Allow me. [*She sails away scornfully to the chest of drawers, and returns with the box of confectionery in her hand*]. I am sorry I have eaten them all except these. [*She offers him the box*].

THE MAN [*ravenously*] Youre an angel! [*He gobbles the contents*]. Creams! Delicious! [*He looks anxiously to see whether there are any more. There are none: he can only scrape the box with his fingers and suck them. When that nourishment is exhausted he accepts the inevitable with pathetic goodhumor, and says, with grateful emotion*] Bless you, dear lady! You can always tell an old soldier by the inside of his holsters and cartridge boxes. The young ones carry pistols and cartridges: the old ones, grub. Thank you. [*He hands back the box. She snatches it contemptuously from him and*

throws it away. He shies again, as if she had meant to strike him]. Ugh! Dont do things so suddenly, gracious lady. It's mean to revenge yourself because I frightened you just now.

RAINA [*loftily*] Frighten me! Do you know, sir, that though I am only a woman, I think I am at heart as brave as you.

THE MAN. I should think so. You havnt been under fire for three days as I have. I can stand two days without shewing it much; but no man can stand three days: I'm as nervous as a mouse. [*He sits down on the ottoman, and takes his head in his hands*]. Would you like to see me cry?

RAINA [*Alarmed*] No.

THE MAN. If you would, all you have to do is to scold me just as if I were a little boy and you my nurse. If I were in camp now, theyd play all sorts of tricks on me.

RAINA [*a little moved*] I'm sorry. I wont scold you. [*Touched by the sympathy in her tone, he raises his head and looks gratefully at her: she immediately draws back and says stiffly*] You must excuse me: our soldiers are not like that. [*She moves away from the ottoman*].

THE MAN. Oh yes they are. There are only two sorts of soldiers: old ones and young ones. I've served fourteen years: half of your fellows never smelt powder before. Why, how is it that youve just beaten us? Sheer ignorance of the art of war, nothing else. [*Indignantly*] I never saw anything so unprofessional.

RAINA [*ironically*] Oh! was it unprofessional to beat you?

THE MAN. Well, come! is it professional to throw a regiment of cavalry on a battery of machine guns, with the dead certainty that if the guns go off not a horse or man will ever get within fifty yards of the fire? I couldnt believe my eyes when I saw it.

RAINA [*eagerly turning to him, as all her enthusiasm and her dreams of glory rush back on her*] Did you see the great cavalry charge? Oh, tell me about it. Describe it to me.

THE MAN. You never saw a cavalry charge, did you?

RAINA. How could I?

THE MAN. Ah, perhaps not. No: of course not! Well, it's a funny sight. It's like slinging a handful of peas against a window pane: first one comes; then two or three close behind him; and then all the rest in a lump.

RAINA [*her eyes dilating as she raises her clasped hands ecstatically*] Yes, first One! the bravest of the brave!

THE MAN [*prosaically*] Hm! you should see the poor devil pulling at his horse.

RAINA. Why should he pull at his horse?

THE MAN [*impatient of so stupid a question*] It's running away with him, of course: do you suppose the fellow wants to get there before the others and be killed? Then they all come. You can tell the young ones by their wildness and their slashing. The old ones come bunched up under the number one guard: they know that theyre mere projectiles, and that it's no use trying to fight. The wounds are mostly broken knees, from the horses cannoning together.

RAINA. Ugh! But I dont believe the first man is a coward. I know he is a hero!

THE MAN [*goodhumoredly*] Thats what youd have said if youd seen the first man in the charge today.

RAINA [*breathless, forgiving him everything*] Ah, I knew it! Tell me. Tell me about him.

THE MAN. He did it like an operatic tenor. A regular handsome fellow, with flashing eyes and lovely moustache, shouting his warcry and charging like Don Quixote at the windmills. We did laugh.

RAINA. You dared to laugh!

THE MAN. Yes; but when the sergeant ran up as white as a sheet, and told us theyd sent us the wrong ammunition, and that we couldnt fire a round for the next ten minutes, we laughed at the other side of our mouths. I never felt so sick in my life; though Ive been in one or two very tight places. And I hadnt even a revolver cartridge: only chocolate. We'd no bayonets: nothing. Of course, they just cut us to bits. And there was Don Quixote flourishing like a drum major, thinking he'd done the cleverest thing ever known, whereas he ought to be courtmartialled for

it. Of all the fools ever let loose on a field of battle, that man must be the very maddest. He and his regiment simply committed suicide; only the pistol missed fire: thats all.

RAINA [*deeply wounded, but steadfastly loyal to her ideals*] Indeed! Would you know him again if you saw him?

THE MAN. Shall I ever forget him!

She goes to the chest of drawers. He watches her with a vague hope that she may have something more for him to eat. She takes the portrait from its stand and brings it to him.

RAINA. That is a photograph of the gentleman—the patriot and hero—to whom I am betrothed.

THE MAN [*recognizing it with a shock*] I'm really very sorry. [*Looking at her*] Was it fair to lead me on? [*He looks at the portrait again*] Yes: thats Don Quixote: not a doubt of it. [*He stifles a laugh*].

RAINA [*quickly*] Why do you laugh?

THE MAN [*apologetic, but still greatly tickled*] I didnt laugh, I assure you. At least I didnt mean to. But when I think of him charging the windmills and imagining he was doing the finest thing—[*He chokes with suppressed laughter*].

RAINA [*sternly*] Give me back the portrait, sir.

THE MAN [*with sincere remorse*] Of course. Certainly. I'm really very sorry. [*He hands her the picture. She deliberately kisses it and looks him staight in the face before returning to the chest of drawers to replace it. He follows her, apologizing*]. Perhaps I'm quite wrong, you know: no doubt I am. Most likely he had got wind of the cartridge business somehow, and knew it was a safe job.

RAINA. That is to say, he was a pretender and a coward! You did not dare say that before.

THE MAN [*with a comic gesture of despair*] It's no use, dear lady: I cant make you see it from the professional point of view. [*As he turns away to get back to the ottoman, a couple of distant shots threaten renewed trouble*].

RAINA [*sternly, as she sees him listening*

to the shots] So much the better for you!

THE MAN [*turning*] How?

RAINA. You are my enemy; and you are at my mercy. What would I do if I were a professional soldier?

THE MAN. Ah, true, dear young lady: youre always right. I know how good youve been to me: to my last hour I shall remember those three chocolate creams. It was unsoldierly; but it was angelic.

RAINA [*coldly*] Thank you. And now I will do a soldierly thing. You cannot stay here after what you have just said about my future husband; but I will go out on the balcony and see whether it is safe for you to climb down into the street. [*She turns to the window*].

THE MAN [*changing countenance*] Down that waterpipe! Stop! Wait! I cant! I darent! The very thought of it makes me giddy. I came up it fast enough with death behind me. But to face it now in cold blood—! [*He sinks on the ottoman*]. It's no use: I give up: I'm beaten. Give the alarm. [*He drops his head on his hands in the deepest dejection*].

RAINA [*disarmed by pity*] Come: dont be disheartened. [*She stoops over him almost maternally: he shakes his head*]. Oh, you are a very poor soldier: a chocolate cream soldier! Come, cheer up! it takes less courage to climb down than to face capture: remember that.

THE MAN [*dreamily, lulled by her voice*] No: capture only means death; and death is sleep: oh, sleep, sleep, sleep, undisturbed sleep! Climbing down the pipe means doing something—exerting myself—thinking! Death ten times over first.

RAINA [*softly and wonderingly, catching the rhythm of his weariness*] Are you as sleepy as that?

THE MAN. Ive not had two hours undisturbed sleep since I joined. I havnt closed my eyes for forty-eight hours.

RAINA [*at her wit's end*] But what am I to do with you?

THE MAN [*staggering up, roused by her desperation*] Of course. I must do something. [*He shakes himself; pulls himself together; and speaks with rallied vigor and courage*].

You see, sleep or no sleep, hunger or no hunger, tired or not tired, you can always do a thing when you know it must be done. Well, that pipe must be got down: [*he hits himself on the chest*] do you hear that, you chocolate cream soldier? [*He turns to the window*].

RAINA [*anxiously*] But if you fall?

THE MAN. I shall sleep as if the stones were a feather bed. Goodbye. [*He makes boldly for the window; and his hand is on the shutter when there is a terrible burst of firing in the street beneath*].

RAINA [*rushing to him*] Stop! [*She seizes him recklessly, and pulls him quite round*]. Theyll kill you.

THE MAN [*coolly, but attentively*] Never mind: this sort of thing is all in my day's work. I'm bound to take my chance. [*Decisively*] Now do what I tell you. Put out the candle; so that they shant see the light when I open the shutters. And keep away from the window, whatever you do. If they see me theyre sure to have a shot at me.

RAINA [*clinging to him*] Theyre sure to see you: it's bright moonlight. I'll save you. Oh, how can you be so indifferent! You want me to save you, dont you?

THE MAN. I really dont want to be troublesome. [*She shakes him in her impatience*]. I am not indifferent, dear young lady, I assure you. But how is it to be done?

RAINA. Come away from the window. [*She takes him firmly back to the middle of the room. The moment she releases him he turns mechanically towards the window again. She seizes him and turns him back, exclaiming*] Please! [*He becomes motionless, like a hypnotized rabbit, his fatigue gaining fast on him. She releases him, and addresses him patronizingly*]. Now listen. You must trust to our hospitality. You do not yet know in whose house you are. I am a Petkoff.

THE MAN. A pet what?

RAINA [*rather indignantly*] I mean that I belong to the family of the Petkoffs, the richest and best known in our country.

THE MAN. Oh yes, of course. I beg your pardon. The Petkoffs, to be sure. How stupid of me!

RAINA. You know you never heard of them until this moment. How can you stoop to pretend!

THE MAN. Forgive me: I'm too tired to think; and the change of subject was too much for me. Dont scold me.

RAINA. I forgot. It might make you cry. [*He nods, quite seriously. She pouts and then resumes her patronizing tone*]. I must tell you that my father holds the highest command of any Bulgarian in our army. He is [*proudly*] a Major.

THE MAN [*pretending to be deeply impressed*] A Major! Bless me! Think of that!

RAINA. You shewed great ignorance in thinking that it was necessary to climb up to the balcony because ours is the only private house that has two rows of windows. There is a flight of stairs inside to get up and down by.

THE MAN. Stairs! How grand! You live in great luxury indeed, dear young lady.

RAINA. Do you know what a library is?

THE MAN. A library? A roomful of books?

RAINA. Yes. We have one, the only one in Bulgaria.

THE MAN. Actually a real library! I should like to see that.

RAINA [*affectedly*] I tell you these things to shew you that you are not in the house of ignorant country folk who would kill you the moment they saw your Serbian uniform, but among civilized people. We go to Bucharest every year for the opera season; and I have spent a whole month in Vienna.

THE MAN. I saw that, dear young lady. I saw at once that you knew the world.

RAINA. Have you ever seen the opera of Ernani?

THE MAN. Is that the one with the devil in it in red velvet, and a soldiers' chorus?

RAINA [*Contemptuously*] No!

THE MAN [*stifling a heavy sigh of weariness*] Then I dont know it.

RAINA. I thought you might have remembered the great scene where Ernani, flying from his foes just as you are tonight, takes refuge in the castle of his bitterest enemy, an old Castilian noble. The noble refuses to give him up. His guest is sacred to him.

THE MAN [*quickly, waking up a little*] Have your people got that notion?

RAINA [*with dignity*] My mother and I can understand that notion, as you call it. And if instead of threatening me with your pistol as you did you had simply thrown yourself as a fugitive on our hospitality, you would have been as safe as in your father's house.

THE MAN. Quite sure?

RAINA [*turning her back on him in disgust*] Oh, it is useless to try to make you understand.

THE MAN. Dont be angry: you see how awkward it would be for me if there was any mistake. My father is a very hospitable man: he keeps six hotels; but I couldnt trust him as far as that. What about your father?

RAINA. He is away at Slivnitza fighting for his country. I answer for your safety. There is my hand in pledge of it. Will that reassure you? [*She offers him her hand*].

THE MAN [*looking dubiously at his own hand*] Better not touch my hand, dear young lady. I must have a wash first.

RAINA [*touched*] That is very nice of you. I see that you are a gentleman.

THE MAN [*puzzled*] Eh?

RAINA. You must not think I am surprised. Bulgarians of really good standing—people in our position—wash their hands nearly every day. So you see I can appreciate your delicacy. You may take my hand. [*She offers it again*].

THE MAN [*kissing it with his hands behind his back*] Thanks, gracious young lady: I feel safe at last. And now would you mind breaking the news to your mother? I had better not stay here secretly longer than is necessary.

RAINA. If you will be so good as to keep perfectly still whilst I am away.

THE MAN. Certainly. [*He sits down on the ottoman*].

Raina goes to the bed and wraps herself in the fur cloak. His eyes close. She goes to the door. Turning for a last look at him, she sees that he is dropping off to sleep.

RAINA [*at the door*] You are not going asleep, are you? [*He murmurs inarticulately:*

she runs to him and shakes him]. Do you hear? Wake up: you are falling asleep.

THE MAN. Eh? Falling aslee—? Oh no: not the least in the world: I was only thinking. It's all right: I'm wide awake.

RAINA [*severely*] Will you please stand up while I am away. [*He rises reluctantly*]. All the time, mind.

THE MAN [*standing unsteadily*] Certainly. Certainly: you may depend on me.

Raina looks doubtfully at him. He smiles weakly. She goes reluctantly, turning again at the door, and almost catching him in the act of yawning. She goes out.

THE MAN [*drowsily*] Sleep, sleep, sleep, sleep, slee—[*The words trail off into a murmur. He wakes again with a shock on the point of falling*]. Where am I? Thats what I want to know: where am I? Must keep awake. Nothing keeps me awake except danger: remember that: [*intently*] danger, danger, danger, dan—[*trailing off again: another shock*] Wheres danger? Mus' find it. [*He starts off vaguely round the room in search of it*]. What am I looking for? Sleep—danger—dont know. [*He stumbles against the bed*]. Ah yes: now I know. All right now. I'm to go to bed, but not to sleep. Be sure not to sleep, because of danger. Not to lie down either, only sit down. [*He sits on the bed. A blissful expression comes into his face*]. Ah! [*With a happy sigh he sinks back at full length; lifts his boots into the bed with a final effort; and falls fast asleep instantly*].

Catherine comes in, followed by Raina.

RAINA [*looking at the ottoman*] He's gone! I left him here.

CATHERINE. Here! Then he must have climbed down from the—

RAINA [*seeing him*] Oh! [*She points*].

CATHERINE [*scandalized*] Well! [*She strides to the bed, Raina following until she is opposite her on the other side*]. He's fast asleep. The brute!

RAINA [*anxiously*] Sh!

CATHERINE [*shaking him*] Sir! [*Shaking him again, harder*] Sir!! [*Vehemently, shaking very hard*] Sir!!!

RAINA [*catching her arm*] Dont, mamma;

the poor darling is worn out. Let him sleep.

CATHERINE [*letting him go, and turning amazed to Raina*] The poor darling! Raina!!! [*She looks sternly at her daughter*].

The man sleeps profoundly.

ACT II

The sixth of March, 1886. In the garden of Major Petkoff's house. It is a fine spring morning: the garden looks fresh and pretty. Beyond the paling the tops of a couple of minarets can be seen, shewing that there is a valley there, with the little town in it. A few miles further the Balkan mountains rise and shut in the landscape. Looking towards them from within the garden, the side of the house is seen on the left, with a garden door reached by a little flight of steps. On the right the stable yard, with its gateway, encroaches on the garden. There are fruit bushes along the paling and house, covered with washing spread out to dry. A path runs by the house, and rises by two steps at the corner, where it turns out of sight. In the middle, a small table, with two bent wood chairs at it, is laid for breakfast with Turkish coffee pot, cups, rolls, etc.; but the cups have been used and the bread broken. There is a wooden garden seat against the wall on the right.

Louka, smoking a cigaret, is standing between the table and the house, turning her back with angry disdain on a man servant who is lecturing her. He is a middle-aged man of cool temperament and low but clear and keen intelligence, with the complacency of the servant who values himself on his rank in servitude, and the imperturbability of the accurate calculator who has no illusions. He wears a white Bulgarian costume: jacket with embroidered border, sash, wide knickerbockers, and decorated gaiters. His head is shaved up to the crown, giving him a high Japanese forehead. His name is Nicola.

NICOLA. Be warned in time, Louka: mend your manners. I know the mistress. She is so grand that she never dreams that any servant could dare be disrespectful to her; but if she once suspects that you are defying her, out you go.

LOUKA. I do defy her. I will defy her. What do I care for her?

NICOLA. If you quarrel with the family, I never can marry you. It's the same as if you quarrelled with me!

LOUKA. You take her part against me, do you?

NICOLA [sedately] I shall always be dependent on the good will of the family. When I leave their service and start a shop in Sofia, their custom will be half my capital: their bad word would ruin me.

LOUKA. You have no spirit. I should like to catch them saying a word against me!

NICOLA [pityingly] I should have expected more sense from you, Louka. But youre young: youre young!

LOUKA. Yes; and you like me the better for it, dont you? But I know some family secrets they wouldnt care to have told, young as I am. Let them quarrel with me if they dare!

NICOLA [with compassionate superiority] Do you know what they would do if they heard you talk like that?

LOUKA. What could they do?

NICOLA. Discharge you for untruthfulness. Who would believe any stories you told after that? Who would give you another situation? Who in this house would dare be seen speaking to you ever again? How long would your father be left on his little farm? [She impatiently throws away the end of her cigaret, and stamps on it]. Child: you dont know the power such high people have over the like of you and me when we try to rise out of our poverty against them. [He goes close to her and lowers his voice]. Look at me, ten years in their service. Do you think I know no secrets? I know things about the mistress that she wouldnt have the master know for a thousand levas. I know things about him that she wouldnt let him hear the last of for six months if I blabbed them to her. I know things about Raina that would break off her match with Sergius if—

LOUKA [turning on him quickly] How do you know? I never told you!

NICOLA [opening his eyes cunningly] So thats your little secret, is it? I thought it might be something like that. Well, you take my advice and be respectful; and make the mistress feel that no matter what you know or dont know, she can depend on you to hold your tongue and serve the family faithfully. Thats what they like; and thats how youll make most out of them.

LOUKA [with searching scorn] You have the soul of a servant, Nicola.

NICOLA [complacently] Yes: thats the secret of success in service.

A loud knocking with a whip handle on a wooden door is heard from the stable yard.

MALE VOICE OUTSIDE. Hollo! Hollo there! Nicola!

LOUKA. Master! back from the war!

NICOLA [quickly] My word for it, Louka, the war's over. Off with you and get some fresh coffee. [He runs out into the stable yard].

LOUKA [as she collects the coffee pot and cups on the tray, and carries it into the house] Youll never put the soul of a servant into me.

Major Petkoff comes from the stable yard, followed by Nicola. He is a cheerful, excitable, insignificant, unpolished man of about 50, naturally unambitious except as to his income and his importance in local society, but just now greatly pleased with the military rank which the war has thrust on him as a man of consequence in his town. The fever of plucky patriotism which the Serbian attack roused in all the Bulgarians has pulled him through the war; but he is obviously glad to be home again.

PETKOFF [pointing to the table with his whip] Breakfast out here, eh?

NICOLA. Yes, sir. The mistress and Miss Raina have just gone in.

PETKOFF [sitting down and taking a roll] Go in and say Ive come; and get me some fresh coffee.

NICOLA. It's coming, sir. [He goes to the house door. Louka, with fresh coffee, a clean cup, and a brandy bottle on her tray, meets him]. Have you told the mistress?

LOUKA. Yes: she's coming.

Nicola goes into the house. Louka brings the coffee to the table.

PETKOFF. Well: the Serbs havnt run away with you, have they?

LOUKA. No, sir.

PETKOFF. Thats right. Have you brought me some cognac?

LOUKA [*putting the bottle on the table*] Here, sir.

PETKOFF. Thats right. [*He pours some into his coffee*].

Catherine, who, having at this early hour made only a very perfunctory toilet, wears a Bulgarian apron over a once brilliant but now half worn-out dressing gown, and a colored handkerchief tied over her thick black hair, comes from the house with Turkish slippers on her bare feet, looking astonishingly handsome and stately under all the circumstances. Louka goes into the house.

CATHERINE. My dear Paul: what a surprise for us! [*She stoops over the back of his chair to kiss him*]. Have they brought you fresh coffee?

PETKOFF. Yes: Louka's been looking after me. The war's over. The treaty was signed three days ago at Bucharest; and the decree for our army to demobilize was issued yesterday.

CATHERINE [*springing erect, with flashing eyes*] Paul: have you let the Austrians force you to make peace?

PETKOFF [*submissively*] My dear: they didnt consult me. What could *I* do? [*She sits down and turns away from him*] But of course we saw to it that the treaty was an honorable one. It declares peace—

CATHERINE [*outraged*] Peace!

PETKOFF [*appeasing her*]—but not friendly relations: remember that. They wanted to put that in; but I insisted on its being struck out. What more could I do?

CATHERINE. You could have annexed Serbia and made Prince Alexander Emperor of the Balkans. Thats what I would have done.

PETKOFF. I don't doubt it in the least, my dear. But I should have had to subdue the whole Austrian Empire first; and that would

have kept me too long away from you. I missed you greatly.

CATHERINE [*relenting*] Ah! [*She stretches her hand affectionately across the table to squeeze his*].

PETKOFF. And how have you been, my dear?

CATHERINE. Oh, my usual sore throats: thats all.

PETKOFF [*with conviction*] That comes from washing your neck every day. Ive often told you so.

CATHERINE. Nonsense, Paul!

PETKOFF [*over his coffee and cigaret*] I dont believe in going too far with these modern customs. All this washing cant be good for the health: it's not natural. There was an Englishman at Philippopolis who used to wet himself all over with cold water every morning when he got up. Disgusting! It all comes from the English: their climate makes them so dirty that they have to be perpetually washing themselves. Look at my father! he never had a bath in his life; and he lived to be ninety-eight, the healthiest man in Bulgaria. I dont mind a good wash once a week to keep up my position; but once a day is carrying the thing to a ridiculous extreme.

CATHERINE. You are a barbarian at heart still, Paul. I hope you behaved yourself before all those Russian officers.

PETKOFF. I did my best. I took care to let them know that we have a library.

CATHERINE. Ah; but you didnt tell them that we have an electric bell in it? I have had one put up.

PETKOFF. Whats an electric bell?

CATHERINE. You touch a button; something tinkles in the kitchen; and then Nicola comes up.

PETKOFF. Why not shout for him?

CATHERINE. Civilized people never shout for their servants. Ive learnt that while you were away.

PETKOFF. Well I'll tell you something Ive learnt too. Civilized people dont hang out their washing to dry where visitors can see it; so youd better have all that [*indicating the clothes on the bushes*] put somewhere else.

CATHERINE. Oh, thats absurd, Paul: I dont believe really refined people notice such things.

SERGIUS [*knocking at the stable gates*] Gate, Nicola!

PETKOFF. Theres Sergius. [*Shouting*] Hollo, Nicola!

CATHERINE. Oh, dont shout, Paul: it really isnt nice.

PETKOFF. Bosh! [*He shouts louder than before*] Nicola!

NICOLA [*appearing at the house door*] Yes, sir.

PETKOFF. Are you deaf? Dont you hear Major Saranoff knocking? Bring him round this way. [*He pronounces the name with the stress on the second syllable: Sarahnoff*].

NICOLA. Yes, Major. [*He goes into the stable yard*].

PETKOFF. You must talk to him, my dear, until Raina takes him off our hands. He bores my life out about our not promoting him. Over my head, if you please.

CATHERINE. He certainly ought to be promoted when he marries Raina. Besides, the country should insist on having at least one native general.

PETKOFF. Yes; so that he could throw away whole brigades instead of regiments. It's no use, my dear: he hasnt the slightest chance of promotion until we're quite sure that the peace will be a lasting one.

NICOLA [*at the gate, announcing*] Major Sergius Saranoff! [*He goes into the house and returns presently with a third chair, which he places at the table. He then withdraws*].

*Major Sergius Saranoff, the original of the portrait in Raina's room, is a tall romantically handsome man, with the physical hardihood, the high spirit, and the susceptible imagination of an untamed mountaineer chieftain. But his remarkable personal distinction is of a characteristically civilized type. The ridges of his eyebrows, curving with an interrogative twist round the projections at the outer corners; his jealously ob-*servant eye; his nose, thin, keen, and apprehensive in spite of the pugnacious high bridge and large nostril; his assertive chin would not be out of place in a Parisian salon, shewing that the clever imaginative barbarian has an acute critical faculty which has been thrown into intense activity by the arrival of western civilization in the Balkans. The result is precisely what the advent of nineteenth century thought first produced in England: to wit, Byronism. By his brooding on the perpetual failure, not only of others, but of himself, to live up to his ideals; by his consequent cynical scorn for humanity; by his jejune credulity as to the absolute validity of his concepts and the unworthiness of the world in disregarding them; by his wincings and mockeries under the sting of the petty disillusions which every hour spent among men brings to his sensitive observation, he has acquired the half tragic, half ironic air, the mysterious moodiness, the suggestion of a strange and terrible history that has left nothing but undying remorse, by which Childe Harold fascinated the grandmothers of his English contemporaries. It is clear that here or nowhere is Raina's ideal hero. Catherine is hardly less enthusiastic about him than her daughter, and much less reserved in shewing her enthusiasm. As he enters from the stable gate, she rises effusively to greet him. Petkoff is distinctly less disposed to make a fuss about him.*

PETKOFF. Here already, Sergius! Glad to see you.

CATHERINE. My dear Sergius! [*She holds out both her hands*].

SERGIUS [*kissing them with scrupulous gallantry*] My dear mother, if I may call you so.

PETKOFF [*drily*] Mother-in-law, Sergius: mother-in-law! Sit down; and have some coffee.

SERGIUS. Thank you: none for me. [*He gets away from the table with a certain distaste for Petkoff's enjoyment of it, and posts himself with conscious dignity against the rail of the steps leading to the house*].

CATHERINE. You look superb. The campaign has improved you, Sergius. Everybody here is mad about you. We were all wild with enthusiasm about that magnificent cavalry charge.

SERGIUS [with grave irony] Madam: it was the cradle and the grave of my military reputation.

CATHERINE. How so?

SERGIUS. I won the battle the wrong way when our worthy Russian generals were losing it the right way. In short, I upset their plans, and wounded their self-esteem. Two Cossack colonels had their regiments routed on the most correct principles of scientific warfare. Two major-generals got killed strictly according to military etiquette. The two colonels are now major-generals; and I am still a simple major.

CATHERINE. You shall not remain so, Sergius. The women are on your side; and they will see that justice is done you.

SERGIUS. It is too late. I have only waited for the peace to send in my resignation.

PETKOFF [dropping his cup in his amazement] Your resignation!

CATHERINE. Oh, you must withdraw it!

SERGIUS [with resolute measured emphasis, folding his arms] I never withdraw.

PETKOFF [vexed] Now who could have supposed you were going to do such a thing?

SERGIUS [with fire] Everyone that knew me. But enough of myself and my affairs. How is Raina; and where is Raina?

RAINA [suddenly coming round the corner of the house and standing at the top of the steps in the path] Raina is here.

She makes a charming picture as they turn to look at her. She wears an underdress of pale green silk, draped with an overdress of thin ecru canvas embroidered with gold. She is crowned with a dainty eastern cap of gold tinsel. Sergius goes impulsively to meet her. Posing regally, she presents her hand: he drops chivalrously on one knee and kisses it.

PETKOFF [aside to Catherine, beaming with parental pride] Pretty, isnt it? She always appears at the right moment.

CATHERINE [impatiently] Yes; she listens for it. It is an abominable habit.

Sergius leads Raina forward with splendid gallantry. When they arrive at the table, she turns to him with a bend of the head: he bows; and thus they separate, he coming to his place and she going behind her father's chair.

RAINA [stooping and kissing her father] Dear father! Welcome home!

PETKOFF [patting her cheek] My little pet girl. [He kisses her. She goes to the chair left by Nicola for Sergius, and sits down].

CATHERINE. And so youre no longer a soldier, Sergius.

SERGIUS. I am no longer a soldier. Soldiering, my dear madam, is the coward's art of attacking mercilessly when you are strong, and keeping out of harm's way when you are weak. That is the whole secret of successful fighting. Get your enemy at a disadvantage; and never, on any account, fight him on equal terms.

PETKOFF. They wouldnt let us make a fair stand-up fight of it. However, I suppose soldiering has to be a trade like any other trade.

SERGIUS. Precisely. But I have no ambition to shine as a tradesman; so I have taken the advice of that bagman of a captain that settled the exchange of prisoners with us at Pirot, and given it up.

PETKOFF. What! that Swiss fellow? Sergius: I've often thought of that exchange since. He over-reached us about those horses.

SERGIUS. Of course he over-reached us. His father was a hotel and livery stable keeper; and he owed his first step to his knowledge of horse-dealing. [With mock enthusiasm] Ah, he was a soldier: every inch a soldier! If only I had bought the horses for my regiment instead of foolishly leading it into danger, I should have been a field-marshal now!

CATHERINE. A Swiss? What was he doing in the Serbian army?

PETKOFF. A volunteer, of course: keen on picking up his profession. [Chuckling] We shouldnt have been able to begin fighting if these foreigners hadnt shewn us how to do it: we knew nothing about it; and neither did the Serbs. Egad, there'd have been no war without them!

RAINA. Are there many Swiss officers in the Serbian Army?

PETKOFF. No. All Austrians, just as our officers were all Russians. This was the only Swiss I came across. I'll never trust a Swiss again. He humbugged us into giving him fifty ablebodied men for two hundred worn out chargers. They werent even eatable!

SERGIUS. We were two children in the hands of that consummate soldier, Major: simply two innocent little children.

RAINA. What was he like?

CATHERINE. Oh, Raina, what a silly question!

SERGIUS. He was like a commercial traveller in uniform. Bourgeois to his boots!

PETKOFF [grinning] Sergius: tell Catherine that queer story his friend told us about how he escaped after Slivnitza. You remember. About his being hid by two women.

SERGIUS [with bitter irony] Oh yes: quite a romance! He was serving in the very battery I so unprofessionally charged. Being a thorough soldier, he ran away like the rest of them, with our cavalry at his heels. To escape their sabres he climbed a waterpipe and made his way into the bedroom of a young Bulgarian lady. The young lady was enchanted by his persuasive commercial traveller's manners. She very modestly entertained him for an hour or so, and then called in her mother lest her conduct should appear unmaidenly. The old lady was equally fascinated; and the fugitive was sent on his way in the morning, disguised in an old coat belonging to the master of the house, who was away at the war.

RAINA [rising with marked stateliness] Your life in the camp has made you coarse, Sergius. I did not think you would have repeated such a story before me. [She turns away coldly].

CATHERINE [also rising] She is right, Sergius. If such women exist, we should be spared the knowledge of them.

PETKOFF. Pooh! nonsense! what does it matter?

SERGIUS [ashamed] No, Petkoff: I was wrong. [To Raina, with earnest humility] I beg your pardon. I have behaved abominably. Forgive me, Raina. [She bows reservedly]. And you too, madam. [Catherine bows graciously and sits down. He proceeds solemnly, again addressing Raina] The glimpses I have had of the seamy side of life during the last few months have made me cynical; but I should not have brought my cynicism here: least of all into your presence, Raina. I—[Here, turning to the others, he is evidently going to begin a long speech when the Major interrupts him].

PETKOFF. Stuff and nonsense, Sergius! Thats quite enough fuss about nothing: a soldier's daughter should be able to stand up without flinching to a little strong conversation. [He rises]. Come: it's time for us to get to business. We have to make up our minds how those three regiments are to get back to Philippopolis: theres no forage for them on the Sofia route. [He goes towards the house]. Come along. [Sergius is about to follow him when Catherine rises and intervenes].

CATHERINE. Oh, Paul, cant you spare Sergius for a few moments? Raina has hardly seen him yet. Perhaps I can help you to settle about the regiments.

SERGIUS [protesting] My dear madam, impossible: you—

CATHERINE [stopping him playfully] You stay here, my dear Sergius: theres no hurry. I have a word or two to say to Paul. [Sergius instantly bows and steps back]. Now, dear [taking Petkoff's arm]: come and see the electric bell.

PETKOFF. Oh, very well, very well.

They go into the house together affectionately. Sergius, left alone with Raina, looks anxiously at her, fearing that she is still offended. She smiles, and stretches out her arms to him.

SERGIUS [hastening to her] Am I forgiven?

RAINA [placing her hands on his shoulders as she looks up at him with admiration and worship] My hero! My king!

SERGIUS. My queen! [He kisses her on the forehead].

RAINA. How I have envied you, Sergius! You have been out in the world, on the field of battle, able to prove yourself there worthy of any woman in the world; whilst I have had to sit at home inactive—dreaming—useless—doing nothing that could give me the right to call myself worthy of any man.

SERGIUS. Dearest: all my deeds have been yours. You inspired me. I have gone through the war like a knight in a tournament with his lady looking down at him!

RAINA. And you have never been absent from my thoughts for a moment. [*Very solemnly*] Sergius: I think we two have found the higher love. When I think of you, I feel that I could never do a base deed, or think an ignoble thought.

SERGIUS. My lady and my saint! [*He clasps her reverently*].

RAINA [*returning his embrace*] My lord and my—

SERGIUS. Sh—sh! Let me be the worshipper, dear. You little know how unworthy even the best man is of a girl's pure passion!

RAINA. I trust you. I love you. You will never disappoint me, Sergius. [*Louka is heard singing within the house. They quickly release each other*]. I cant pretend to talk indifferently before her: my heart is too full. [*Louka comes from the house with her tray. She goes to the table, and begins to clear it, with her back turned to them*]. I will get my hat; and then we can go out until lunch time. Wouldnt you like that?

SERGIUS. Be quick. If you are away five minutes, it will seem five hours. [*Raina runs to the top of the steps, and turns there to exchange looks with him and wave him a kiss with both hands. He looks after her with emotion for a moment; then turns slowly away, his face radiant with the loftiest exaltation. The movement shifts his field of vision, into the corner of which there now comes the tail of Louka's double apron. His attention is arrested at once. He takes a stealthy look at her, and begins to twirl his moustache mischievously, with his left hand akimbo on his hip. Finally, striking the ground with his heels in something of a cavalry swagger, he strolls over to the other side of the table, opposite her, and says*] Louka: do you know what the higher love is?

LOUKA [*astonished*] No, sir.

SERGIUS. Very fatiguing thing to keep up for any length of time, Louka. One feels the need of some relief after it.

LOUKA [*innocently*] Perhaps you would like some coffee, sir? [*She stretches her hand across the table for the coffee pot*].

SERGIUS [*taking her hand*] Thank you, Louka.

LOUKA [*pretending to pull*] Oh, sir, you know I didnt mean that. I'm surprised at you!

SERGIUS [*coming clear of the table and drawing her with him*] I am surprised at myself, Louka. What would Sergius, the hero of Slivnitza, say if he saw me now? What would Sergius, the apostle of the higher love, say if he saw me now? What would the half dozen Sergiuses who keep popping in and out of this handsome figure of mine say if they caught us here? [*Letting go her hand and slipping his arm dexterously round her waist*] Do you consider my figure handsome, Louka?

LOUKA. Let me go, sir. I shall be disgraced. [*She struggles: he holds her inexorably*]. Oh, will you let go?

SERGIUS [*looking straight into her eyes*] No.

LOUKA. Then stand back where we cant be seen. Have you no common sense?

SERGIUS. Ah! thats reasonable. [*He takes her into the stable yard gateway, where they are hidden from the house*].

LOUKA [*plaintively*] I may have been seen from the windows: Miss Raina is sure to be spying about after you.

SERGIUS [*stung: letting her go*] Take care, Louka. I may be worthless enough to betray the higher love; but do not you insult it.

LOUKA [*demurely*] Not for the world, sir, I'm sure. May I go on with my work, please, now?

SERGIUS [*again putting his arm round her*] You are a provoking little witch, Louka. If you were in love with me, would you spy out of windows on me?

LOUKA. Well, you see, sir, since you say you are half a dozen different gentlemen all at once, I should have a great deal to look after.

SERGIUS [*charmed*] Witty as well as pretty. [*He tries to kiss her.*]

LOUKA [*avoiding him*] No: I dont want your kisses. Gentlefolk are all alike: you making love to me behind Miss Raina's back; and she doing the same behind yours.

SERGIUS [*recoiling a step*] Louka!

LOUKA. It shews how little you really care.

SERGIUS [*dropping his familiarity, and speaking with freezing politeness*] If our conversation is to continue, Louka, you will please remember that a gentleman does not discuss the conduct of the lady he is engaged to with her maid.

LOUKA. It's so hard to know what a gentleman considers right. I thought from your trying to kiss me that you had given up being so particular.

SERGIUS [*turning from her and striking his forehead as he comes back into the garden from the gateway*] Devil! devil!

LOUKA. Ha! ha! I expect one of the six of you is very like me, sir; though I am only Miss Raina's maid. [*She goes back to her work at the table, taking no further notice of him*].

SERGIUS [*speaking to himself*] Which of the six is the real man? thats the question that torments me. One of them is a hero, another a buffoon, another a humbug, another perhaps a bit of a blackguard. [*He pauses, and looks furtively at Louka as he adds, with deep bitterness*] And one, at least, is a coward: jealous, like all cowards. [*He goes to the table*]. Louka.

LOUKA. Yes?

SERGIUS. Who is my rival?

LOUKA. You shall never get that out of me, for love or money.

SERGIUS. Why?

LOUKA. Never mind why. Besides, you would tell that I told you; and I should lose my place.

SERGIUS [*holding out his right hand in affirmation*] No! on the honor of a—[*He checks himself; and his hand drops, nerveless, as he concludes sardonically*]—of a man capable of behaving as I have been behaving for the last five minutes. Who is he?

LOUKA. I dont know. I never saw him. I only heard his voice through the door of her room.

SERGIUS. Damnation! How dare you?

LOUKA [*retreating*] Oh, I mean no harm: youve no right to take up my words like that. The mistress knows all about it. And I tell you that if that gentleman ever comes here again, Miss Raina will marry him, whether he likes it or not. I know the difference between the sort of manner you and she put on before one another and the real manner.

Sergius shivers as if she had stabbed him. Then, setting his face like iron, he strides grimly to her, and grips her above the elbows with both hands.

SERGIUS. Now listen you to me.

LOUKA [*wincing*] Not so tight: youre hurting me.

SERGIUS. That doesnt matter. You have stained my honor by making me a party to your eavesdropping. And you have betrayed your mistress.

LOUKA [*writhing*] Please—

SERGIUS. That shews that you are an abominable little clod of common clay, with the soul of a servant. [*He lets her go as if she were an unclean thing, and turns away, dusting his hands of her, to the bench by the wall, where he sits down with averted head, meditating gloomily*].

LOUKA [*whimpering angrily with her hands up her sleeves, feeling her bruised arms*] You know how to hurt with your tongue as well as with your hands. But I dont care, now Ive found out that whatever clay I'm made of, youre made of the same. As for her, she's a liar; and her fine airs are a cheat; and I'm worth six of her. [*She shakes the pain off hardily; tosses her head; and sets to work to put the things on the tray*].

He looks doubtfully at her. She finishes packing the tray, and laps the cloth over the edges, so as to carry all out together. As she stoops to lift it, he rises.

SERGIUS. Louka! [*She stops and looks defiantly at him*]. A gentleman has no right to hurt a woman under any circumstances.

[*With profound humility, uncovering his head*] I beg your pardon.

LOUKA. That sort of apology may satisfy a lady. Of what use is it to a servant?

SERGIUS [*rudely crossed in his chivalry, throws it off with a bitter laugh, and says slightingly*] Oh! you wish to be paid for the hurt! [*He puts on his shako, and takes some money from his pocket*].

LOUKA [*her eyes filling with tears in spite of herself*] No: I want my hurt made well.

SERGIUS [*sobered by her tone*] How?

She rolls up her left sleeve; clasps her arm with the thumb and fingers of her right hand; and looks down at the bruise. Then she raises her head and looks straight at him. Finally, with a superb gesture, she presents her arm to be kissed. Amazed, he looks at her; at the arm; at her again; hesitates; and then, with shuddering intensity, exclaims Never! *and gets away as far as possible from her.*

Her arm drops. Without a word, and with unaffected dignity, she takes her tray, and is approaching the house when Raina returns, wearing a hat and jacket in the height of the Vienna fashion of the previous year, 1885. Louka makes way proudly for her, and then goes into the house.

RAINA. I'm ready. Whats the matter? [*Gaily*] Have you been flirting with Louka?

SERGIUS [*hastily*] No, no. How can you think such a thing?

RAINA [*ashamed of herself*] Forgive me, dear: it was only a jest. I am so happy today.

He goes quickly to her, and kisses her hand remorsefully. Catherine comes out and calls to them from the top of the steps.

CATHERINE [*coming down to them*] I am sorry to disturb you, children; but Paul is distracted over those three regiments. He doesnt know how to send them to Philippopolis; and he objects to every suggestion of mine. You must go and help him, Sergius. He is in the library.

RAINA [*disappointed*] But we are just going out for a walk.

SERGIUS. I shall not be long. Wait for me just five minutes. [*He runs up the steps to the door*].

RAINA [*following him to the foot of the steps and looking up at him with timid coquetry*] I shall go round and wait in full view of the library windows. Be sure you draw father's attention to me. If you are a moment longer than five minutes, I shall go in and fetch you, regiments or no regiments.

SERGIUS [*laughing*] Very well. [*He goes in*].

Raina watches him until he is out of her sight. Then, with a perceptible relaxation of manner, she begins to pace up and down the garden in a brown study.

CATHERINE. Imagine their meeting that Swiss and hearing the whole story! The very first thing your father asked for was the old coat we sent him off in. A nice mess you have got us into!

RAINA [*gazing thoughtfully at the gravel as she walks*] The little beast!

CATHERINE. Little beast! What little beast?

RAINA. To go and tell! Oh, if I had him here, I'd cram him with chocolate creams til he couldnt ever speak again!

CATHERINE. Dont talk such stuff. Tell me the truth, Raina. How long was he in your room before you came to me?

RAINA. [*whisking round and recommencing her march in the opposite direction*] Oh, I forget.

CATHERINE. You cannot forget! Did he really climb up after the soldiers were gone; or was he there when that officer searched the room?

RAINA. No. Yes: I think he must have been there then.

CATHERINE. You think! Oh, Raina! Raina! Will anything ever make you straightforward? If Sergius finds out, it will be all over between you.

RAINA [*with cool impertinence*] Oh, I know Sergius is your pet. I sometimes wish you could marry him instead of me. You would just suit him. You would pet him, and spoil him, and mother him to perfection.

CATHERINE [*opening her eyes very widely indeed*] Well, upon my word!

RAINA [*capriciously: half to herself*] I always feel a longing to do or say something dreadful to him—to shock his propriety—to scandalize the five senses out of him. [*To Catherine, perversely*] I dont care whether he finds out about the chocolate cream soldier or not. I half hope he may. [*She again turns and strolls flippantly away up the path to the corner of the house*].

CATHERINE. And what should I be able to say to your father, pray?

RAINA [*over her shoulder, from the top of the two steps*] Oh, poor father! As if he could help himself! [*She turns the corner and passes out of sight*].

CATHERINE [*looking after her, her fingers itching*] Oh, if you were only ten years younger! [*Louka comes from the house with a salver, which she carries hanging down by her side*]. Well?

LOUKA. Theres a gentleman just called, madam. A Serbian officer.

CATHERINE [*flaming*] A Serb! And how dare he—[*checking herself bitterly*] Oh, I forgot. We are at peace now. I suppose we shall have them calling every day to pay their compliments. Well: if he is an officer why dont you tell your master? He is in the library with Major Saranoff. Why do you come to me?

LOUKA. But he asks for you, madam. And I dont think he knows who you are: he said the lady of the house. He gave me this little ticket for you. [*She takes a card out of her bosom; puts it on the salver; and offers it to Catherine*].

CATHERINE [*reading*] "Captain Bluntschli"? Thats a German name.

LOUKA. Swiss, madam, I think.

CATHERINE [*with a bound that makes Louka jump back*] Swiss! What is he like?

LOUKA [*timidly*] He has a big carpet bag, madam.

CATHERINE. Oh Heavens! he's come to return the coat. Send him away: say we're not at home: ask him to leave his address and I'll write to him. Oh stop: that will never do. Wait! [*She throws herself into a chair to think it out. Louka waits*]. The master and Major Saranoff are busy in the library, arnt they?

LOUKA. Yes, madam.

CATHERINE [*decisively*] Bring the gentleman out here at once. [*Peremptorily*] And be very polite to him. Dont delay. Here [*impatiently snatching the salver from her*]: leave that here; and go straight back to him.

LOUKA. Yes, madam [*going*].

CATHERINE. Louka!

LOUKA [*stopping*] Yes, madam.

CATHERINE. Is the library door shut?

LOUKA. I think so, madam.

CATHERINE. If not, shut it as you pass through.

LOUKA. Yes, madam [*going*].

CATHERINE. Stop [*Louka stops*]. He will have to go that way [*indicating the gate of the stable yard*]. Tell Nicola to bring his bag here after him. Dont forget.

LOUKA [*surprised*] His bag?

CATHERINE. Yes: here: as soon as possible. [*vehemently*] Be quick! [*Louka runs into the house. Catherine snatches her apron off and throws it behind a bush. She then takes up the salver and uses it as a mirror, with the result that the handkerchief tied round her head follows the apron. A touch to her hair and a shake to her dressing gown make her presentable*]. Oh, how? how? how can a man be such a fool! Such a moment to select! [*Louka appears at the door of the house, announcing* Captain Bluntschli. *She stands aside at the top of the steps to let him pass before she goes in again. He is the man of the midnight adventure in Raina's room, clean, well brushed, smartly uniformed, and out of trouble, but still unmistakably the same man. The moment Louka's back is turned, Catherine swoops on him with impetuous, urgent, coaxing appeal*]. Captain Bluntschli: I am very glad to see you; but you must leave this house at once. [*He raises his eyebrows*]. My husband has just returned with my future son-in-law; and they know nothing. If they did, the consequences would be terrible. You are a foreigner: you do not feel our national animosities as we do. We still hate the Serbs: the effect of the peace on my husband has been to make him feel like a lion baulked of his prey. If he discovers our secret, he will never forgive me; and my daughter's life will hardly be safe. Will you, like the chivalrous gentleman and soldier you are, leave at once before he finds you here?

BLUNTSCHLI [*disappointed, but philosophical*] At once, gracious lady. I only came to thank you and return the coat you lent me. If you will allow me to take it out of my bag and leave it with your servant as I pass out, I need detain you no further. [*He turns to go into the house*].

CATHERINE [*catching him by the sleeve*] Oh, you must not think of going back that way. [*Coaxing him across to the stable gates*] This is the shortest way out. Many thanks. So glad to have been of service to you. Goodbye.

BLUNTSCHLI. But my bag?

CATHERINE. It shall be sent on. You will leave me your address.

BLUNTSCHLI. True. Allow me. [*He takes out his cardcase, and stops to write his address, keeping Catherine in an agony of impatience. As he hands her the card, Petkoff, hatless, rushes from the house in a fluster of hospitality, followed by Sergius*].

PETKOFF [*as he hurries down the steps*] My dear Captain Bluntschli—

CATHERINE. Oh Heavens! [*She sinks on the seat against the wall*].

PETKOFF [*too preoccupied to notice her as he shakes Bluntschli's hand heartily*] Those stupid people of mine thought I was out here, instead of in the—haw!—library [*he cannot mention the library without betraying how proud he is of it*]. I saw you through the window. I was wondering why you didnt come in. Saranoff is with me: you remember him, dont you?

SERGIUS [*saluting humorously, and then offering his hand with great charm of manner*] Welcome, our friend the enemy!

PETKOFF. No longer the enemy, happily. [*Rather anxiously*] I hope youve called as a friend, and not about horses or prisoners.

CATHERINE. Oh, quite as a friend, Paul. I was just asking Captain Bluntschli to stay to lunch; but he declares he must go at once.

SERGIUS [*sardonically*] Impossible, Bluntschli. We want you here badly. We have to send on three cavalry regiments to Philippopolis; and we dont in the least know how to do it.

BLUNTSCHLI [*suddenly attentive and businesslike*] Philippopolis? The forage is the trouble, I suppose.

PETKOFF [*eagerly*] Yes: thats it. [*To Sergius*] He sees the whole thing at once.

BLUNTSCHLI. I think I can shew you how to manage that.

SERGIUS. Invaluable man! Come along! [*Towering over Bluntschli, he puts his hand on his shoulder and takes him to the steps, Petkoff following*].

Raina comes from the house as Bluntschli puts his foot on the first step.

RAINA. Oh! The chocolate cream soldier!

Bluntschli stands rigid. Sergius, amazed, looks at Raina, then at Petkoff, who looks back at him and then at his wife.

CATHERINE [*with commanding presence of mind*] My dear Raina, dont you see that we have a guest here? Captain Bluntschli: one of our new Serbian friends.

Raina bows: Bluntschli bows.

RAINA. How silly of me! [*She comes down into the centre of the group, between Bluntschli and Petkoff*]. I made a beautiful ornament this morning for the ice pudding; and that stupid Nicola has just put down a pile of plates on it and spoilt it. [*To Bluntschli, winningly*] I hope you didnt think that you were the chocolate cream soldier, Captain Bluntschli.

BLUNTSCHLI [*laughing*] I assure you I did. [*Stealing a whimsical glance at her*] Your explanation was a relief.

PETKOFF [*Suspiciously, to Raina*] And since when, pray, have you taken to cooking?

CATHERINE. Oh, whilst you were away. It is her latest fancy.

PETKOFF [*testily*] And has Nicola taken to drinking? He used to be careful enough. First he shews Captain Bluntschli out here when he knew quite well I was in the library; and then he goes downstairs and breaks Raina's chocolate soldier. He must— [*Nicola appears at the top of the steps with the bag. He descends; places it respectfully before Bluntschli; and waits for further orders. General amazement. Nicola, unconscious of the effect he is producing, looks perfectly satisfied with himself. When Petkoff recovers his power of speech, he breaks out at him with] Are you mad, Nicola?

NICOLA [taken aback] Sir?

PETKOFF. What have you brought that for?

NICOLA. My lady's orders, major. Louka told me that—

CATHERINE [interrupting him] My orders! Why should I order you to bring Captain Bluntschli's luggage out here? What are you thinking of, Nicola?

NICOLA [after a moment's bewilderment, picking up the bag as he addresses Bluntschli with the very perfection of servile discretion] I beg your pardon, captain, I am sure. [To Catherine] My fault, madame: I hope youll overlook it. [He bows, and is going to the steps with the bag, when Petkoff addresses him angrily].

PETKOFF. Youd better go and slam that bag, too, down on Miss Raina's ice pudding! [This is too much for Nicola. The bag drops from his hand almost on his master's toes, eliciting a roar of] Begone, you butter-fingered donkey.

NICOLA [snatching up the bag, and escaping into the house] Yes, Major.

CATHERINE. Oh, never mind. Paul: dont be angry.

PETKOFF [blustering] Scoundrel! He's got out of hand while I was away. I'll teach him. Infernal blackguard! The sack next Saturday! I'll clear out the whole establishment—[He is stifled by the caresses of his wife and daughter, who hang round his neck, petting him].

CATHERINE }
RAINA } [together] {
Now, now, now, it
Wow, wow, wow:
mustnt be angry. He meant no
not on your first day at home.
harm. Be good to please me,
I'll make another ice pudding.
dear. Sh-sh-sh-sh!
Tch-ch-ch!

PETKOFF [yielding] Oh well, never mind.

Come, Bluntschli: lets have no more nonsense about going away. You know very well youre not going back to Switzerland yet. Until you do go back youll stay with us.

RAINA. Oh, do, Captain Bluntschli.

PETKOFF [to Catherine] Now, Catherine: it's of you he's afraid. Press him: and he'll stay.

CATHERINE. Of course I shall be only too delighted if [appealingly] Captain Bluntschli really wishes to stay. He knows my wishes.

BLUNTSCHLI [in his driest military manner] I am at madam's orders.

SERGIUS [cordially] That settles it!

PETKOFF [heartily] Of course!

RAINA. You see you must stay.

BLUNTSCHLI [smiling] Well, if I must, I must.

Gesture of despair from Catherine.

ACT III

In the library after lunch. It is not much of a library. Its literary equipment consists of a single fixed shelf stocked with old paper covered novels, broken backed, coffee stained, torn and thumbed; and a couple of little hanging shelves with a few gift books on them: the rest of the wall space being occupied by trophies of war and the chase. But it is a most comfortable sitting room. A row of three large windows shews a mountain panorama, just now seen in one of its friendliest aspects in the mellowing afternoon light. In the corner next the right hand window a square earthenware stove, a perfect tower of glistening pottery, rises nearly to the ceiling and guarantees plenty of warmth. The ottoman is like that in Raina's room, and similarly placed; and the window seats are luxurious with decorated cushions. There is one object, however, hopelessly out of keeping with its surroundings. This is a small kitchen table, much the worse for wear, fitted as a writing table with an old canister full of pens, an eggcup filled with ink, and a deplorable scrap of heavily used pink blotting paper.

At the side of this table, which stands to the left of anyone facing the window, Blunt-

schli is hard at work with a couple of maps before him, writing orders. At the head of it sits Sergius, who is supposed to be also at work, but is actually gnawing the feather of a pen, and contemplating Bluntschli's quick, sure, businesslike progress with a mixture of envious irritation at his own incapacity and awestruck wonder at an ability which seems to him almost miraculous, though its prosaic character forbids him to esteem it. The Major is comfortably established on the ottoman, with a newspaper in his hand and the tube of his hookah within easy reach. Catherine sits at the stove, with her back to them, embroidering. Raina, reclining on the divan, is gazing in a daydream out at the Balkan landscape, with a neglected novel in her lap.

The door is on the same side as the stove, farther from the window. The button of the electric bell is at the opposite side, behind Bluntschli.

PETKOFF [*looking up from his paper to watch how they are getting on at the table*] Are you sure I cant help in any way, Bluntschli?

BLUNTSCHLI [*without interrupting his writing or looking up*] Quite sure, thank you. Saranoff and I will manage it.

SERGIUS [*grimly*] Yes: we'll manage it. He finds out what to do; draws up the orders; and I sign em. Division of labor! [*Bluntschli passes him a paper*]. Another one? Thank you. [*He plants the paper squarely before him; sets his chair carefully parallel to it; and signs with his cheek on his elbow and his protruded tongue following the movements of his pen*]. This hand is more accustomed to the sword than to the pen.

PETKOFF. It's very good of you, Bluntschli: it is indeed, to let yourself be put upon in this way. Now are you quite sure I can do nothing?

CATHERINE [*in a low warning tone*] You can stop interrupting, Paul.

PETKOFF [*starting and looking round at her*] Eh? Oh! Quite right. [*He takes his newspaper up again, but presently lets it drop*]. Ah, you havnt been campaigning, Catherine: you dont know how pleasant it is for us to sit here, after a good lunch, with nothing to do but enjoy ourselves. Theres only one thing I want to make me thoroughly comfortable.

CATHERINE. What is that?

PETKOFF. My old coat. I'm not at home in this one: I feel as if I were on parade.

CATHERINE. My dear Paul, how absurd you are about that old coat! It must be hanging in the blue closet where you left it.

PETKOFF. My dear Catherine, I tell you Ive looked there. Am I to believe my own eyes or not? [*Catherine rises and crosses the room to press the button of the electric bell*]. What are you shewing off that bell for? [*She looks at him majestically, and silently resumes her chair and her needlework*]. My dear: if you think the obstinacy of your sex can make a coat out of two old dressing gowns of Raina's, your waterproof, and my mackintosh, youre mistaken. Thats exactly what the blue closet contains at present.

Nicola presents himself.

CATHERINE. Nicola: go to the blue closet and bring your master's old coat here: the braided one he wears in the house.

NICOLA. Yes, madame. [*He goes out*].

PETKOFF. Catherine.

CATHERINE. Yes, Paul.

PETKOFF. I bet you any piece of jewellery you like to order from Sofia against a week's housekeeping money that the coat isnt there.

CATHERINE. Done, Paul!

PETKOFF [*excited by the prospect of a gamble*] Come: heres an opportunity for some sport. Wholl bet on it? Bluntschli: I'll give you six to one.

BLUNTSCHLI [*imperturbably*] It would be robbing you, Major. Madame is sure to be right. [*Without looking up, he passes another batch of papers to Sergius*].

SERGIUS [*also excited*] Bravo, Switzerland! Major: I bet my best charger against an Arab mare for Raina that Nicola finds the coat in the blue closet.

PETKOFF [*eagerly*] Your best char—

CATHERINE [*hastily interrupting him*] Dont be foolish, Paul. An Arabian mare will cost you 50,000 levas.

RAINA [*suddenly coming out of her pic-*

turesque revery] Really, mother, if you are going to take the jewellery, I don't see why you should grudge me my Arab.

Nicola comes back with the coat, and brings it to Petkoff, who can hardly believe his eyes.

CATHERINE. Where was it, Nicola?

NICOLA. Hanging in the blue closet, madame.

PETKOFF. Well, I am d—

CATHERINE [*stopping him*] Paul!

PETKOFF. I could have sworn it wasnt there. Age is beginning to tell on me. I'm getting hallucinations. [*To Nicola*] Here: help me to change. Excuse me, Bluntschli. [*He begins changing coats, Nicola acting as valet*]. Remember: I didnt take that bet of yours, Sergius. Youd better give Raina that Arab steed yourself, since youve roused her expectations. Eh, Raina? [*He looks round at her; but she is again rapt in the landscape. With a little gush of parental affection and pride, he points her out to them, and says*] She's dreaming, as usual.

SERGIUS. Assuredly she shall not be the loser.

PETKOFF. So much the better for her. *I* shant come off so cheaply, I expect. [*The change is now complete. Nicola goes out with the discarded coat*]. Ah, now I feel at home at last. [*He sits down and takes his newspaper with a grunt of relief*].

BLUNTSCHLI [*to Sergius, handing a paper*] Thats the last order.

PETKOFF [*jumping up*] What! Finished?

BLUNTSCHLI. Finished.

PETKOFF [*with childlike envy*] Havnt you anything for me to sign?

BLUNTSCHLI. Not necessary. His signature will do.

PETKOFF [*inflating his chest and thumping it*] Ah well, I think weve done a thundering good day's work. Can I do anything more?

BLUNTSCHLI. You had better both see the fellows that are to take these. [*Sergius rises*] Pack them off at once; and shew them that Ive marked on the orders the time they should hand them in by. Tell them that if they stop to drink or tell stories—if theyre

five minutes late, theyll have the skin taken off their backs.

SERGIUS [*stiffening indignantly*] I'll say so. [*He strides to the door*]. And if one of them is man enough to spit in my face for insulting him, I'll buy his discharge and give him a pension. [*He goes out*].

BLUNTSCHLI [*confidentially*] Just see that he talks to them properly, Major, will you?

PETKOFF [*officiously*] Quite right, Bluntschli, quite right. I'll see to it. [*He goes to the door importantly, but hesitates on the threshold*]. By the bye, Catherine, you may as well come too. Theyll be far more frightened of you than of me.

CATHERINE [*putting down her embroidery*] I daresay I had better. You would only splutter at them. [*She goes out, Petkoff holding the door for her and following her*].

BLUNTSCHLI. What an army! They make cannons out of cherry trees; and the officers send for their wives to keep discipline! [*He begins to fold and docket the papers*].

Raina, who has risen from the divan, marches slowly down the room with her hands clasped behind her, and looks mischievously at him.

RAINA. You look ever so much nicer than when we last met. [*He looks up, surprised*]. What have you done to yourself?

BLUNTSCHLI. Washed; brushed; good night's sleep and breakfast. Thats all.

RAINA. Did you get back safely that morning?

BLUNTSCHLI. Quite, thanks.

RAINA. Were they angry with you for running away from Sergius's charge?

BLUNTSCHLI [*grinning*] No: they were glad; because theyd all just run away themselves.

RAINA [*going to the table, and leaning over it towards him*] It must have made a lovely story for all them: all that about me and my room.

BLUNTSCHLI. Capital story. But I only told it to one of them: a particular friend.

RAINA. On whose discretion you could absolutely rely?

BLUNTSCHLI. Absolutely.

RAINA. Hm! He told it all to my father and Sergius the day you exchanged the prisoners. [*She turns away and strolls carelessly across to the other side of the room*].

BLUNTSCHLI [*deeply concerned, and half incredulous*] No! You dont mean that, do you?

RAINA [*turning, with sudden earnestness*] I do indeed. But they dont know that it was in this house you took refuge. If Sergius knew, he would challenge you and kill you in a duel.

BLUNTSCHLI. Bless me! then dont tell him.

RAINA. Please be serious, Captain Bluntschli. Can you not realize what it is to me to deceive him? I want to be quite perfect with Sergius: no meanness, no smallness, no deceit. My relation to him is the one really beautiful and noble part of my life. I hope you can understand that.

BLUNTSCHLI [*sceptically*] You mean that you wouldnt like him to find out that the story about the ice pudding was a—a—a— You know.

RAINA [*wincing*] Ah, dont talk of it in that flippant way. I lied: I know it. But I did it to save your life. He would have killed you. That was the second time I ever uttered a falsehood. [*Bluntschli rises quickly and looks doubtfully and somewhat severely at her*]. Do you remember the first time?

BLUNTSCHLI. I! No. Was I present?

RAINA. Yes; and I told the officer who was searching for you that you were not present.

BLUNTSCHLI. True. I should have remembered it.

RAINA [*greatly encouraged*] Ah, it is natural that you should forget it first. It cost you nothing: it cost me a lie! A lie!

She sits down on the ottoman, looking straight before her with her hands clasped around her knee. Bluntschli, quite touched, goes to the ottoman with a particularly reassuring and considerate air, and sits down beside her.

BLUNTSCHLI. My dear young lady, dont let this worry you. Remember: I'm a soldier. Now what are the two things that happen to a soldier so often that he comes to think nothing of them? One is hearing people tell lies [*Raina recoils*]: the other is getting his life saved in all sorts of ways by all sorts of people.

RAINA [*rising in indignant protest*] And so he becomes a creature incapable of faith and of gratitude.

BLUNTSCHLI [*making a wry face*] Do you like gratitude? I dont. If pity is akin to love, gratitude is akin to the other thing.

RAINA. Gratitude! [*Turning on him*] If you are incapable of gratitude you are incapable of any noble sentiment. Even animals are grateful. Oh, I see now exactly what you think of me! You were not surprised to hear me lie. To you it was something I probably did every day! every hour! That is how men think of women. [*She paces the room tragically*].

BLUNTSCHLI [*dubiously*] Theres reason in everything. You said youd told only two lies in your whole life. Dear young lady: isnt that rather a short allowance? I'm quite a straightforward man myself; but it wouldnt last me a whole morning.

RAINA [*staring haughtily at him*] Do you know, sir, that you are insulting me?

BLUNTSCHLI. I cant help it. When you strike that noble attitude and speak in that thrilling voice, I admire you; but I find it impossible to believe a single word you say.

RAINA [*superbly*] Captain Bluntschli!

BLUNTSCHLI [*unmoved*] Yes?

RAINA [*standing over him, as if she could not believe her senses*] Do you mean what you said just now? Do you know what you said just now?

BLUNTSCHLI. I do.

RAINA [*gasping*] I! I!!!! [*She points to herself incredulously, meaning "I, Raina Petkoff tell lies!" He meets her gaze unflinchingly. She suddenly sits down beside him, and adds, with a complete change of manner from the heroic to a babyish familiarity*] How did you find me out?

BLUNTSCHLI [*promptly*] Instinct, dear young lady. Instinct, and experience of the world.

RAINA [*wonderingly*] Do you know, you are the first man I ever met who did not take me seriously?

BLUNTSCHLI. You mean, dont you, that I am the first man that has ever taken you quite seriously?

RAINA. Yes: I suppose I do mean that. [*Cosily, quite at her ease with him*] How strange it is to be talked to in such a way! You know, Ive always gone on like that.

BLUNTSCHLI. You mean the—?

RAINA. I mean the noble attitude and the thrilling voice. [*They laugh together*]. I did it when I was a tiny child to my nurse. She believed in it. I do it before my parents. They believe in it. I do it before Sergius. He believes in it.

BLUNTSCHLI. Yes: he's a little in that line himself, isnt he?

RAINA [*startled*] Oh! Do you think so?

BLUNTSCHLI. You know him better than I do.

RAINA. I wonder—I wonder is he? If I thought that—! [*Discouraged*] Ah, well; what does it matter? I suppose, now youve found me out, you despise me.

BLUNTSCHLI [*warmly, rising*] No, my dear young lady, no, no, no a thousand times. It's part of your youth: part of your charm. I'm like all the rest of them: the nurse, your parents, Sergius: I'm your infatuated admirer.

RAINA [*pleased*] Really?

BLUNTSCHLI [*slapping his breast smartly with his hand, German fashion*] Hand aufs Herz! Really and truly.

RAINA [*very happy*] But what did you think of me for giving you my portrait?

BLUNTSCHLI [*astonished*] Your portrait! You never gave me your portrait.

RAINA [*quickly*] Do you mean to say you never got it?

BLUNTSCHLI. No. [*He sits down beside her, with renewed interest, and says, with some complacency*] When did you send it to me?

RAINA [*indignantly*] I did not send it to you. [*She turns her head away, and adds, reluctantly*] It was in the pocket of that coat.

BLUNTSCHLI [*pursing his lips and rounding his eyes*] Oh-o-oh! I never found it. It must be there still.

RAINA [*springing up*] There still! for my father to find the first time he puts his hand in his pocket! Oh, how could you be so stupid?

BLUNTSCHLI [*rising also*] It doesnt matter: I suppose it's only a photograph: how can he tell who it was intended for? Tell him he put it there himself.

RAINA [*bitterly*] Yes: that is so clever! isnt it? [*Distractedly*] Oh! what shall I do?

BLUNTSCHLI. Ah, I see. You wrote something on it. That was rash.

RAINA [*vexed almost to tears*] Oh, to have done such a thing for you, who care no more—except to laugh at me—oh! Are you sure nobody has touched it?

BLUNTSCHLI. Well, I cant be quite sure. You see, I couldnt carry it about with me all the time: one cant take much luggage on active service.

RAINA. What did you do with it?

BLUNTSCHLI. When I got through to Pirot I had to put it in safe keeping somehow. I thought of the railway cloak room; but thats the surest place to get looted in modern warfare. So I pawned it.

RAINA. Pawned it!!!

BLUNTSCHLI. I know it doesnt sound nice: but it was much the safest plan. I redeemed it the day before yesterday. Heaven only knows whether the pawnbroker cleared out the pockets or not.

RAINA [*furious: throwing the words right into his face*] You have a low shopkeeping mind. You think of things that would never come into a gentleman's head.

BLUNTSCHLI [*phlegmatically*] Thats the Swiss national character, dear lady. [*He returns to the table*].

RAINA. Oh, I wish I had never met you. [*She flounces away, and sits at the window fuming*].

Louka comes in with a heap of letters and telegrams on her salver, and crosses, with her bold free gait, to the table. Her left sleeve is looped up to the shoulder with a brooch, shewing her naked arm, with a broad gilt bracelet covering the bruise.

LOUKA [*to Bluntschli*] For you. [*She empties the salver with a fling on to the table*]. The messenger is waiting. [*She is determined not to be civil to an enemy, even if she must bring him his letters*].

BLUNTSCHLI [*to Raina*] Will you excuse me: the last postal delivery that reached me was three weeks ago. These are the subsequent accumulations. Four telegrams: a week old. [*He opens one*]. Oho! Bad news!

RAINA [*rising and advancing a little remorsefully*] Bad news?

BLUNTSCHLI. My father's dead. [*He looks at the telegram with his lips pursed, musing on the unexpected change in his arrangements. Louka crosses herself hastily*].

RAINA. Oh, how very sad!

BLUNTSCHLI. Yes: I shall have to start for home in an hour. He has left a lot of big hotels behind him to be looked after. [*He takes up a fat letter in a long blue envelope*]. Here's a whacking letter from the family solicitor. [*He puts out the enclosures and glances over them*]. Great Heavens! Seventy! Two hundred! [*In a crescendo of dismay*] Four hundred! Four thousand!! Nine thousand six hundred!!! What on earth am I to do with them all?

RAINA [*timidly*] Nine thousand hotels?

BLUNTSCHLI. Hotels! nonsense. If you only knew! Oh, it's too ridiculous! Excuse me: I must give my fellow orders about starting. [*He leaves the room hastily, with the documents in his hand*].

LOUKA [*knowing instinctively that she can annoy Raina by disparaging Bluntschli*] He has not much heart, that Swiss. He has not a word of grief for his poor father.

RAINA [*bitterly*] Grief! A man who has been doing nothing but killing people for years! What does he care? What does any soldier care? [*She goes to the door, restraining her tears with difficulty*].

LOUKA. Major Saranoff has been fighting too; and he has plenty of heart left. [*Raina, at the door, draws herself up haughtily and goes out*]. Aha! I thought you wouldnt get much feeling out of your soldier. [*She is following Raina when Nicola enters with an armful of logs for the stove*].

NICOLA [*grinning amorously at her*] Ive been trying all the afternoon to get a minute alone with you, my girl. [*His countenance changes as he notices her arm*]. Why, what fashion is that of wearing your sleeve, child?

LOUKA [*proudly*] My own fashion.

NICOLA. Indeed! If the mistress catches you, she'll talk to you. [*He puts the logs down, and seats himself comfortably on the ottoman*].

LOUKA. Is that any reason why you should take it on yourself to talk to me?

NICOLA. Come! dont be so contrary with me. Ive some good news for you. [*She sits down beside him. He takes out some paper money. Louka, with an eager gleam in her eyes, tries to snatch it; but he shifts it quickly to his left hand, out of her reach*]. See! a twenty leva bill. Sergius gave me that, out of pure swagger. A fool and his money are soon parted. Theres ten levas more. The Swiss gave me that for backing up the mistress' and Raina's lies about him. He's no fool, he isnt. You should have heard old Catherine downstairs as polite as you please to me, telling me not to mind the Major being a little impatient; for they knew what a good servant I was—after making a fool and a liar of me before them all! The twenty will go to our savings; and you shall have the ten to spend if youll only talk to me so as to remind me I'm a human being. I get tired of being a servant occasionally.

LOUKA. Yes: sell your manhood for 30 levas, and buy me for 10! [*Rising scornfully*] Keep your money. You were born to be a servant. I was not. When you set up your shop you will only be everybody's servant instead of somebody's servant. [*She goes moodily to the table and seats herself regally in Sergius's chair*].

NICOLA [*picking up his logs, and going to the stove*] Ah, wait til you see. We shall have our evenings to ourselves; and I shall be master in my own house, I promise you. [*He throws the logs down and kneels at the stove*].

LOUKA. You shall never be master in mine.

NICOLA [*turning, still on his knees, and squatting down rather forlornly on his calves, daunted by her implacable disdain*] You have a great ambition in you, Louka.

Remember: if any luck comes to you, it was I that made a woman of you.

LOUKA. You!

NICOLA [*scrambling up and going to her*] Yes, me. Who was it made you give up wearing a couple of pounds of false black hair on your head and reddening your lips and cheeks like any other Bulgarian girl! I did. Who taught you to trim your nails, and keep your hands clean, and be dainty about yourself, like a fine Russian lady! Me: do you hear that? me! [*She tosses her head defiantly; and he turns away, adding more coolly*] Ive often thought that if Raina were out of the way, and you just a little less of a fool and Sergius just a little more of one, you might come to be one of my grandest customers, instead of only being my wife and costing me money.

LOUKA. I believe you would rather be my servant than my husband. You would make more out of me. Oh, I know that soul of yours.

NICOLA [*going closer to her for greater emphasis*] Never you mind my soul; but just listen to my advice. If you want to be a lady, your present behaviour to me wont do at all, unless when we're alone. It's too sharp and impudent; and impudence is a sort of familiarity: it shews affection for me. And dont you try being high and mighty with me, either. Youre like all country girls: you think it's genteel to treat a servant the way I treat a stableboy. Thats only your ignorance; and dont you forget it. And dont be so ready to defy everybody. Act as if you expected to have your own way, not as if you expected to be ordered about. The way to get on as a lady is the same as the way to get on as a servant: youve got to know your place: thats the secret of it. And you may depend on me to know my place if you get promoted. Think over it, my girl. I'll stand by you: one servant should always stand by another.

LOUKA [*rising impatiently*] Oh, I must behave in my own way. You take all the courage out of me with your cold-blooded wisdom. Go and put those logs in the fire: thats the sort of thing you understand.

Before Nicola can retort, Sergius comes in. He checks himself a moment on seeing Louka; then goes to the stove.

SERGIUS [*to Nicola*] I am not in the way of your work, I hope.

NICOLA [*in a smooth, elderly manner*] Oh no, sir: thank you kindly. I was only speaking to this foolish girl about her habit of running up here to the library whenever she gets a chance, to look at the books. Thats the worst of her education, sir: it gives her habits above her station. [*To Louka*] Make that table tidy, Louka, for the Major. [*He goes out sedately*].

Louka, without looking at Sergius, pretends to arrange the papers on the table. He crosses slowly to her, and studies the arrangement of her sleeve reflectively.

SERGIUS. Let me see: is there a mark there? [*He turns up the bracelet and sees the bruise made by his grasp. She stands motionless, not looking at him: fascinated, but on her guard*] Ffff! Does it hurt?

LOUKA. Yes.

SERGIUS. Shall I cure it?

LOUKA [*instantly withdrawing herself proudly, but still not looking at him*] No. You cannot cure it now.

SERGIUS [*masterfully*] Quite sure? [*He makes a movement as if to take her in his arms*].

LOUKA. Dont trifle with me, please. An officer should not trifle with a servant.

SERGIUS [*indicating the bruise with a merciless stroke of his forefinger*] That was no trifle, Louka.

LOUKA [*flinching; then looking at him for the first time*] Are you sorry?

SERGIUS [*with measured emphasis, folding his arms*] I am never sorry.

LOUKA [*wistfully*] I wish I could believe a man could be as unlike a woman as that. I wonder are you really a brave man?

SERGIUS [*unaffectedly, relaxing his attitude*] Yes: I am a brave man. My heart jumped like a woman's at the first shot; but in the charge I found that I was brave. Yes: that at least is real about me.

LOUKA. Did you find in the charge that the men whose fathers are poor like mine were any less brave than the men who are rich like you?

SERGIUS [*with bitter levity*] Not a bit. They all slashed and cursed and yelled like heroes. Psha! the courage to rage and kill is cheap. I have an English bull terrier who has as much of that sort of courage as the whole Bulgarian nation, and the whole Russian nation at its back. But he lets my groom thrash him, all the same. Thats your soldier all over! No, Louka: your poor men can cut throats; but they are afraid of their officers; they put up with insults and blows; they stand by and see one another punished like children: aye, and help to do it when they are ordered. And the officers!!! Well [*with a short harsh laugh*] I am an officer. Oh, [*fervently*] give me the man who will defy to the death any power on earth or in heaven that sets itself up against his own will and conscience: he alone is the brave man.

LOUKA. How easy it is to talk! Men never seem to me to grow up: they all have schoolboy's ideas. You dont know what true courage is.

SERGIUS [*ironically*] Indeed! I am willing to be instructed. [*He sits on the ottoman, sprawling magnificently*].

LOUKA. Look at me! How much am I allowed to have my own will? I have to get your room ready for you: to sweep and dust, to fetch and carry. How could that degrade me if it did not degrade you to have it done for you? But [*with subdued passion*] if I were Empress of Russia, above everyone in the world, then!! Ah then, though according to you I could shew no courage at all, you should see, you should see.

SERGIUS. What would you do, most noble Empress?

LOUKA. I would marry the man I loved, which no other queen in Europe has the courage to do. If I loved you, though you would be as far beneath me as I am beneath you, I would dare to be the equal of my inferior. Would you dare as much if you loved me? No: if you felt the beginnings of love for me you would not let it grow. You would not dare: you would marry a rich man's daughter because you would be afraid of what other people would say of you.

SERGIUS [*bounding up*] You lie: it is not so, by all the stars! If I loved you, and I were the Czar himself, I would set you on the throne by my side. You know that I love another woman, a woman as high above you as heaven is above earth. And you are jealous of her.

LOUKA. I have no reason to be. She will never marry you now. The man I told you of has come back. She will marry the Swiss.

SERGIUS [*recoiling*] The Swiss!

LOUKA. A man worth ten of you. Then you can come to me; and I will refuse you. You are not good enough for me. [*She turns to the door*].

SERGIUS [*springing after her and catching her fiercely in his arms*] I will kill the Swiss; and afterwards I will do as I please with you.

LOUKA [*in his arms, passive and steadfast*] The Swiss will kill you, perhaps. He has beaten you in love. He may beat you in war.

SERGIUS [*tormentedly*] Do you think I believe that she—she! whose worst thoughts are higher than your best ones, is capable of trifling with another man behind my back?

LOUKA. Do you think she would believe the Swiss if he told her now that I am in your arms?

SERGIUS [*releasing her in despair*] Damnation! Oh, damnation! Mockery! mockery everywhere! everything I think is mocked by everything I do. [*He strikes himself frantically on the breast*]. Coward! liar! fool! Shall I kill myself like a man, or live and pretend to laugh at myself? [*She again turns to go*]. Louka! [*She stops near the door*]. Remember: you belong to me.

LOUKA [*turning*] What does that mean? An insult?

SERGIUS [*commandingly*] It means that you love me, and that I have had you here in my arms, and will perhaps have you there again. Whether that is an insult I neither know nor care: take it as you please. But [*vehemently*] I will not be a coward and a trifler. If I choose to love you, I dare marry you, in spite of all Bulgaria. If these hands ever touch you again, they shall touch my affianced bride.

LOUKA. We shall see whether you dare keep your word. And take care. I will not wait long.

SERGIUS [*again folding his arms and standing motionless in the middle of the room*] Yes: we shall see. And you shall wait my pleasure.

Bluntschli, much preoccupied, with his papers still in his hand, enters, leaving the door open for Louka to go out. He goes across to the table, glancing at her as he passes. Sergius, without altering his resolute attitude, watches him steadily. Louka goes out, leaving the door open.

BLUNTSCHLI [*absently, sitting at the table as before, and putting down his papers*] Thats a remarkable looking young woman.

SERGIUS [*gravely, without moving*] Captain Bluntschli.

BLUNTSCHLI. Eh?

SERGIUS. You have deceived me. You are my rival. I brook no rivals. At six o'clock I shall be in the drilling-ground on the Klissoura road, alone, on horseback, with my sabre. Do you understand?

BLUNTSCHLI [*staring, but sitting quite at his ease*] Oh, thank you: thats a cavalry man's proposal. I'm in the artillery; and I have the choice of weapons. If I go, I shall take a machine gun. And there shall be no mistake about the cartridges this time.

SERGIUS [*flushing, but with deadly coldness*] Take care, sir. It is not our custom in Bulgaria to allow invitations of that kind to be trifled with.

BLUNTSCHLI [*warmly*] Pooh! dont talk to me about Bulgaria. You dont know what fighting is. But have it your own way. Bring your sabre along. I'll meet you.

SERGIUS [*fiercely delighted to find his opponent a man of spirit*] Well said, Switzer. Shall I lend you my best horse?

BLUNTSCHLI. No: damn your horse! thank you all the same, my dear fellow. [*Raina comes in, and hears the next sentence*]. I shall fight you on foot. Horseback's too dangerous; I dont want to kill you if I can help it.

RAINA [*hurrying forward anxiously*] I have heard what Captain Bluntschli said, Sergius. You are going to fight. Why? [*Sergius turns away in silence, and goes to the stove, where he stands watching her as she continues, to Bluntschli*] What about?

BLUNTSCHLI. I dont know: he hasnt told me. Better not interfere, dear young lady. No harm will be done: Ive often acted as sword instructor. He wont be able to touch me; and I'll not hurt him. It will save explanations. In the morning I shall be off home; and youll never see me or hear of me again. You and he will then make it up and live happily ever after.

RAINA [*turning away deeply hurt, almost with a sob in her voice*] I never said I wanted to see you again.

SERGIUS [*striding forward*] Ha! That is a confession.

RAINA [*haughtily*] What do you mean?

SERGIUS. You love that man!

RAINA [*scandalized*] Sergius!

SERGIUS. You allow him to make love to you behind my back, just as you treat me as your affianced husband behind his. Bluntschli: you knew our relations; and you deceived me. It is for that that I call you to account, not for having received favors *I* never enjoyed.

BLUNTSCHLI [*jumping up indignantly*] Stuff! Rubbish! I have received no favors. Why, the young lady doesnt even know whether I'm married or not.

RAINA [*forgetting herself*] Oh! [*Collapsing on the ottoman*] Are you?

SERGIUS. You see the young lady's concern, Captain Bluntschli. Denial is useless. You have enjoyed the privilege of being received in her own room, late at night—

BLUNTSCHLI [*interrupting him pepperily*] Yes, you blockhead! she received me with a pistol at her head. Your cavalry were at my heels. I'd have blown out her brains if she'd uttered a cry.

SERGIUS [*taken aback*] Bluntschli! Raina: is this true?

RAINA [*rising in wrathful majesty*] Oh, how dare you, how dare you?

BLUNTSCHLI. Apologize, man: apologize. [*He resumes his seat at the table*].

SERGIUS [*with the old measured emphasis, folding his arms*] I never apologize!

RAINA [*passionately*] This is the doing of that friend of yours, Captain Bluntschli. It is he who is spreading this horrible story about me. [*She walks about excitedly*].

BLUNTSCHLI. No: he's dead. Burnt alive.

RAINA [*stopping, shocked*] Burnt alive!

BLUNTSCHLI. Shot in the hip in a wood-yard. Couldnt drag himself out. Your fellows' shells set the timber on fire and burnt him, with half a dozen other poor devils in the same predicament.

RAINA. How horrible!

SERGIUS. And how ridiculous! Oh, war! war! the dream of patriots and heroes! A fraud, Bluntschli. A hollow sham, like love.

RAINA. [*outraged*] Like love! You say that before me!

BLUNTSCHLI. Come, Saranoff: that matter is explained.

SERGIUS. A hollow sham, I say. Would you have come back here if nothing had passed between you except at the muzzle of your pistol? Raina is mistaken about your friend who was burnt. He was not my informant.

RAINA. Who then? [*Suddenly guessing the truth*] Ah, Louka! my maid! my servant! You were with her this morning all that time after—after—Oh, what sort of god is this I have been worshipping! [*He meets her gaze with sardonic enjoyment of her disenchantment. Angered all the more, she goes closer to him, and says, in a lower, intenser tone*] Do you know that I looked out of the window as I went upstairs, to have another sight of my hero; and I saw something I did not understand then. I know now that you were making love to her.

SERGIUS [*with grim humor*] You saw that?

RAINA. Only too well. [*She turns away, and throws herself on the divan under the centre window, quite overcome*].

SERGIUS [*cynically*] Raina: our romance is shattered. Life's a farce.

BLUNTSCHLI [*to Raina, whimsically*] You see: he's found himself out now.

SERGIUS [*going to him*] Bluntschli: I have allowed you to call me a blockhead. You may now call me a coward as well. I refuse to fight you. Do you know why?

BLUNTSCHLI. No; but it doesnt matter. I didnt ask the reason when you cried on; and I dont ask the reason now that you cry off. I'm a professional soldier! I fight when I have to, and am very glad to get out of it when I havnt to. Youre only an amateur: you think fighting's an amusement.

SERGIUS [*sitting down at the table, nose to nose with him*] You shall hear the reason all the same, my professional. The reason is that it takes two men—real men—men of heart, blood and honor—to make a genuine combat. I could no more fight with you than I could make love to an ugly woman. Youve no magnetism: youre not a man: youre a machine.

BLUNTSCHLI [*apologetically*] Quite true, quite true. I always was that sort of chap. I'm very sorry.

SERGIUS. Psha!

BLUNTSCHLI. But now that youve found that life isnt a farce, but something quite sensible and serious, what further obstacle is there to your happiness?

RAINA [*rising*] You are very solicitous about my happiness and his. Do you forget his new love—Louka? It is not you that he must fight now, but his rival, Nicola.

SERGIUS. Rival!! [*bounding half across the room*].

RAINA. Dont you know that theyre engaged?

SERGIUS. Nicola! Are fresh abysses opening? Nicola!

RAINA [*sarcastically*] A shocking sacrifice, isnt it? Such beauty! such intellect! such modesty! wasted on a middle-aged servant man. Really, Sergius, you cannot stand by and allow such a thing. It would be unworthy of your chivalry.

SERGIUS [*losing all self-control*] Viper! Viper! [*He rushes to and fro, raging*].

BLUNTSCHLI. Look here, Saranoff: youre getting the worst of this.

RAINA [*getting angrier*] Do you realize what he has done, Captain Bluntschli? He has set this girl as a spy on us; and her reward is that he makes love to her.

SERGIUS. False! Monstrous!

RAINA. Monstrous! [*Confronting him*] Do you deny that she told you about Captain Bluntschli being in my room?

SERGIUS. No; but—

RAINA [*interrupting*] Do you deny that you were making love to her when she told you?

SERGIUS. No; but I tell you—

RAINA [*cutting him short contemptuously*] It is unnecessary to tell us anything more. That is quite enough for us. [*She turns away from him and sweeps majestically back to the window*].

BLUNTSCHLI [*quietly, as Sergius, in an agony of mortification, sinks on the ottoman, clutching his averted head between his fists*] I told you you were getting the worst of it, Saranoff.

SERGIUS. Tiger cat!

RAINA [*running excitedly to Bluntschli*] You hear this man calling me names, Captain Bluntschli?

BLUNTSCHLI. What else can he do, dear lady? He must defend himself somehow. Come [*very persuasively*]: dont quarrel. What good does it do?

Raina, with a gasp, sits down on the ottoman, and after a vain effort to look vexedly at Bluntschli, falls a victim to her sense of humor, and actually leans back babyishly against the writhing shoulder of Sergius.

SERGIUS. Engaged to Nicola! Ha! ha! Ah well, Bluntschli, you are right to take this huge imposture of a world coolly.

RAINA [*quaintly to Bluntschli, with an intuitive guess at his state of mind*] I daresay you think us a couple of grown-up babies, don't you?

SERGIUS [*grinning savagely*] He does: he does. Swiss civilization nursetending Bulgarian barbarism, eh?

BLUNTSCHLI [*blushing*] Not at all, I assure you. I'm only very glad to get you two quieted. There! there! let's be pleasant and talk it over in a friendly way. Where is this other young lady?

RAINA. Listening at the door, probably.

SERGIUS [*shivering as if a bullet had struck him, and speaking with quiet but deep indignation*] I will prove that that, at least, is a calumny. [*He goes with dignity to the door and opens it. A yell of fury bursts from him as he looks out. He darts into the passage, and returns dragging in Louka, whom he flings violently against the table, exclaiming*] Judge her, Bluntschli. You, the cool impartial man: judge the eavesdropper.

Louka stands her ground, proud and silent.

BLUNTSCHLI [*shaking his head*] I mustnt judge her. I once listened myself outside a tent when there was a mutiny brewing. It's all a question of the degree of provocation. My life was at stake.

LOUKA. My love was at stake. I am not ashamed.

RAINA [*contemptuously*] Your love! Your curiosity, you mean.

LOUKA [*facing her and returning her contempt with interest*] My love, stronger than anything you can feel, even for your chocolate cream soldier.

SERGIUS [*with quick suspicion, to Louka*] What does that mean?

LOUKA [*fiercely*] I mean—

SERGIUS [*interrupting her slightly*] Oh, I remember: the ice pudding. A paltry taunt, girl!

Major Petkoff enters, in his shirtsleeves.

PETKOFF. Excuse my shirtsleeves, gentlemen. Raina: somebody has been wearing that coat of mine: I'll swear it. Somebody with a differently shaped back. It's all burst open at the sleeve. Your mother is mending it. I wish she'd make haste: I shall catch cold. [*He looks more attentively at them*]. Is anything the matter?

RAINA. No. [*She sits down at the stove, with a tranquil air*].

SERGIUS. Oh no. [*He sits down at the end of the table, as at first*].

BLUNTSCHLI [*who is already seated*] Nothing. Nothing.

PETKOFF [*sitting down on the ottoman in his old place*] Thats all right. [*He notices Louka*]. Anything the matter, Louka?

LOUKA. No, sir.

PETKOFF [*genially*] Thats all right. [*He*

sneezes] Go and ask your mistress for my coat, like a good girl, will you?

Nicola enters with the coat. Louka makes a pretence of having business in the room by taking the little table with the hookah away to the wall near the windows.

RAINA [*rising quickly as she sees the coat on Nicola's arm*] Here it is papa. Give it to me Nicola; and do you put some more wood on the fire. [*She takes the coat, and brings it to the Major, who stands up to put it on. Nicola attends to the fire*].

PETKOFF [*to Raina, teasing her affectionately*] Aha! Going to be very good to poor old papa just for one day after his return from the wars, eh?

RAINA [*with solemn reproach*] Ah, how can you say that to me, father?

PETKOFF. Well, well, only a joke, little one. Come: give me a kiss. [*She kisses him*]. Now give me the coat.

RAINA. No: I am going to put it on for you. Turn your back. [*He turns his back and feels behind him with his arms for the sleeves. She dexterously takes the photograph from the pocket and throws it on the table before Bluntschli, who covers it with a sheet of paper under the very nose of Sergius, who looks on amazed, with his suspicions roused in the highest degree. She then helps Petkoff on with his coat*]. There, dear! Now are you comfortable?

PETKOFF. Quite, little love. Thanks [*He sits down; and Raina returns to her seat near the stove*]. Oh, by the bye, Ive found something funny. Whats the meaning of this? [*He puts his hand into the picked pocket*]. Eh? Hallo! [*He tries the other pocket*]. Well, I could have sworn—! [*Much puzzled, he tries the breast pocket*]. I wonder—[*trying the original pocket*]. Where can it—? [*He rises, exclaiming*] Your mother's taken it!

RAINA [*very red*] Taken what?

PETKOFF. Your photograph, with the inscription: "Raina, to her Chocolate Cream Soldier: a Souvenir." Now you know theres something more in this than meets the eye; and I'm going to find it out. [*Shouting*] Nicola!

NICOLA. [*coming to him*] Sir!

PETKOFF. Did you spoil any pastry of Miss Raina's this morning?

NICOLA. You heard Miss Raina say that I did, sir.

PETKOFF. I know that, you idiot. Was it true?

NICOLA. I am sure Miss Raina is incapable of saying anything that is not true, sir.

PETKOFF. Are you? Then I'm not. [*Turning to the others*] Come: do you think I dont see it all? [*He goes to Sergius, and slaps him on the shoulder*]. Sergius: youre the chocolate cream soldier, arnt you?

SERGIUS [*starting up*] I! A chocolate cream soldier! Certainly not.

PETKOFF. Not! [*He looks at them. They are all very serious and very conscious*]. Do you mean to tell me that Raina sends things like that to other men?

SERGIUS [*enigmatically*] The world is not such an innocent place as we used to think, Petkoff.

BLUNTSCHLI [*rising*] It's all right, Major. I'm the chocolate cream soldier. [*Petkoff and Sergius are equally astonished*]. The gracious young lady saved my life by giving me chocolate creams when I was starving: shall I ever forget their flavour! My late friend Stolz told you the story of Pirot. I was the fugitive.

PETKOFF. You! [*He gasps*]. Sergius: do you remember how those two women went on this morning when we mentioned it? [*Sergius smiles cynically. Petkoff confronts Raina severely*]. Youre a nice young woman, arnt you?

RAINA [*bitterly*] Major Saranoff has changed his mind. And when I wrote that on the photograph, I did not know that Captain Bluntschli was married.

BLUNTSCHLI [*startled into vehement protest*] I'm not married.

RAINA [*with deep reproach*] You said you were.

BLUNTSCHLI. I did not. I positively did not. I never was married in my life.

PETKOFF [*exasperated*] Raina: will you kindly inform me, if I am not asking too much, which of these gentlemen you are engaged to?

RAINA. To neither of them. This young

lady [*introducing Louka, who faces them all proudly*] is the object of Major Saranoff's affections at present.

PETKOFF. Louka! Are you mad, Sergius? Why, this girl's engaged to Nicola.

NICOLA. I beg your pardon, sir. There is a mistake. Louka is not engaged to me.

PETKOFF. Not engaged to you, you scoundrel! Why, you had twenty-five levas from me on the day of your betrothal; and she had that gilt bracelet from Miss Raina.

NICOLA [*with cool unction*] We gave it out so, sir. But it was only to give Louka protection. She had a soul above her station; and I have been no more than her confidential servant. I intend, as you know, sir, to set up a shop later on in Sofia; and I look forward to her custom and recommendation should she marry into the nobility. [*He goes out with impressive discretion, leaving them all staring after him*].

PETKOFF [*breaking the silence*] Well, I am—hm!

SERGIUS. This is either the finest heroism or the most crawling baseness. Which is it, Bluntschli?

BLUNTSCHLI. Never mind whether it's heroism or baseness. Nicola's the ablest man Ive met in Bulgaria. I'll make him manager of a hotel if he can speak French and German.

LOUKA [*suddenly breaking out at Sergius*] I have been insulted by everyone here. You set them the example. You owe me an apology.

Sergius, like a repeating clock of which the spring has been touched, immediately begins to fold his arms.

BLUNTSCHLI [*before he can speak*] It's no use. He never apologizes.

LOUKA. Not to you, his equal and his enemy. To me, his poor servant, he will not refuse to apologize.

SERGIUS [*approvingly*] You are right. [*He bends his knee in his grandest manner*] Forgive me.

LOUKA. I forgive you. [*She timidly gives him her hand, which he kisses*]. That touch makes me your affianced wife.

SERGIUS [*springing up*] Ah! I forgot that.

LOUKA [*coldly*] You can withdraw if you like.

SERGIUS. Withdraw! Never! You belong to me. [*He puts his arm about her*].

Catherine comes in and finds Louka in Sergius' arms, with all the rest gazing at them in bewildered astonishment.

CATHERINE. What does this mean?

Sergius releases Louka.

PETKOFF. Well, my dear, it appears that Sergius is going to marry Louka instead of Raina. [*She is about to break out indignantly at him: he stops her by exclaiming testily*] Dont blame me: Ive nothing to do with it. [*He retreats to the stove*].

CATHERINE. Marry Louka! Sergius: you are bound by your word to us!

SERGIUS [*folding his arms*] Nothing binds me.

BLUNTSCHLI [*much pleased by this piece of common sense*] Saranoff: your hand. My congratulations. These heroics of yours have their practical side after all. [*To Louka*] Gracious young lady: the best wishes of a good Republican! [*He kisses her hand, to Raina's great disgust, and returns to his seat*].

CATHERINE. Louka: you have been telling stories.

LOUKA. I have done Raina no harm.

CATHERINE. [*haughtily*] Raina!

Raina, equally indignant, almost snorts at the liberty.

LOUKA. I have a right to call her Raina: she calls me Louka. I told Major Saranoff she would never marry him if the Swiss gentleman came back.

BLUNTSCHLI [*rising, much surprised*] Hallo!

LOUKA [*turning to Raina*] I thought you were fonder of him than of Sergius. You know best whether I was right.

BLUNTSCHLI. What nonsense! I assure you, my dear Major, my dear Madame, the gracious young lady simply saved my life. nothing else. She never cared two straws for me. Why, bless my heart and soul, look at the young lady and look at me. She, rich, young, beautiful, with her imagination full of fairy princes and noble natures and cavalry charges and goodness knows what! And I, a commonplace Swiss soldier who hardly knows what a decent life is after fifteen years of barracks and battles: a vagabond, a man who has spoiled all his chances in life through an incurably romantic disposition, a man—

SERGIUS [*starting as if a needle had pricked him and interrupting Bluntschli in incredulous amazement*] Excuse me, Bluntschli: what did you say had spoiled your chances in life?

BLUNTSCHLI [*promptly*] An incurably romantic disposition. I ran away from home twice when I was a boy. I went into the army instead of into my father's business. I climbed the balcony of this house when a man of sense would have dived into the nearest cellar. I came sneaking back here to have another look at the young lady when any other man of my age would have sent the coat back—

PETKOFF. My coat!

BLUNTSCHLI.—yes: thats the coat I mean —would have sent it back and gone quietly home. Do you suppose I am the sort of fellow a young girl falls in love with? Why, look at our ages! I'm thirty-four: I dont suppose the young lady is much over seventeen. [*This estimate produces a marked sensation, all the rest turning and staring at one another. He proceeds innocently*] All that adventure which was life or death to me, was only a schoolgirl's game to her—chocolate creams and hide and seek. Heres the proof! [*He takes the photograph from the table*]. Now, I ask you, would a woman who took the affair seriously have sent me this and written on it "Raina, to her Chocolate Cream Soldier: a Souvenir"? [*He exhibits the photograph triumphantly, as if it settled the matter beyond all possibility of refutation*].

PETKOFF. Thats what I was looking for. How the deuce did it get there? [*He comes from the stove to look at it, and sits down on the ottoman*].

BLUNTSCHLI [*to Raina, complacently*] I have put everything right, I hope, gracious young lady.

RAINA [*going to the table to face him*] I quite agree with your account of yourself. You are a romantic idiot. [*Bluntschli is unspeakably taken aback*]. Next time, I hope you will know the difference between a schoolgirl of seventeen and a woman of twenty-three.

BLUNTSCHLI [*stupefied*] Twenty-three!

Raina snaps the photograph contemptuously from his hand; tears it up; throws the pieces in his face; and sweeps back to her former place.

SERGIUS [*with grim enjoyment of his rival's discomfiture*] Bluntschli: my one last belief is gone. Your sagacity is a fraud, like everything else. You have less sense than even I!

BLUNTSCHLI [*overwhelmed*] Twenty-three! Twenty-three!! [*He considers*]. Hm! [*Swiftly making up his mind and coming to his host*] In that case, Major Petkoff, I beg to propose formally to become a suitor for your daughter's hand, in place of Major Saranoff retired.

RAINA. You dare!

BLUNTSCHLI. If you were twenty-three when you said those things to me this afternoon, I shall take them seriously.

CATHERINE [*loftily polite*] I doubt, sir, whether you quite realize either my daughter's position or that of Major Sergius Saranoff, whose place you propose to take. The Petkoffs and the Saranoffs are known as the richest and most important families in the country. Our position is almost historical: we can go back for twenty years.

PETKOFF. Oh, never mind that. Catherine. [*To Bluntschli*] We should be most happy, Bluntschli, if it were only a question of your position; but hang it, you know, Raina is accustomed to a very comfortable establishment. Sergius keeps twenty horses.

BLUNTSCHLI. But who wants twenty horses? We're not going to keep a circus.

CATHERINE [*severely*] My daughter, sir, is accustomed to a first-rate stable.

RAINA. Hush, mother: youre making me ridiculous.

BLUNTSCHLI. Oh well, if it comes to a question of an establishment, here goes! (*He darts impetuously to the table; seizes the pa-*

pers in the blue envelope; and turns to Sergius]. How many horses did you say?

SERGIUS. Twenty, noble Switzer.

BLUNTSCHLI. I have two hundred horses. [*They are amazed*]. How many carriages?

SERGIUS. Three.

BLUNTSCHLI. I have seventy. Twenty-four of them will hold twelve inside, besides two on the box, without counting the driver and conductor. How many tablecloths have you?

SERGIUS. How the deuce do I know?

BLUNTSCHLI. Have you four thousand?

SERGIUS. No.

BLUNTSCHLI. I have. I have nine thousand six hundred pairs of sheets and blankets, with two thousand four hundred eider-down quilts. I have ten thousand knives and forks, and the same quantity of dessert spoons. I have three hundred servants. I have six palatial establishments, besides two livery stables, a tea garden, and a private house. I have four medals for distinguished services; I have the rank of an officer and the standing of a gentleman; and I have three native languages. Shew me any man in Bulgaria that can offer as much!

PETKOFF [*with childish awe*] Are you Emperor of Switzerland?

BLUNTSCHLI. My rank is the highest known in Switzerland: I am a free citizen.

CATHERINE. Then, Captain Bluntschli, since you are my daughter's choice—

RAINA [*mutinously*] He's not.

CATHERINE [*ignoring her*]—I shall not stand in the way of her happiness. [*Petkoff is about to speak*] That is Major Petkoff's feeling also.

PETKOFF. Oh, I shall be only too glad. Two hundred horses! Whew!

SERGIUS. What says the lady?

RAINA [*pretending to sulk*] The lady says that he can keep his tablecloths and his omnibuses. I am not here to be sold to the highest bidder. [*She turns her back on him*].

BLUNTSCHLI. I wont take that answer. I appealed to you as a fugitive, a beggar, and a starving man. You accepted me. You gave me your hand to kiss, your bed to sleep in, and your roof to shelter me.

RAINA. I did not give them to the Emperor of Switzerland.

BLUNTSCHLI. Thats just what I say. [*He catches her by the shoulders and turns her face-to-face with him*]. Now tell us whom you did give them to.

RAINA [*succumbing with a shy smile*] To my chocolate cream soldier.

BLUNTSCHLI [*with a boyish laugh of delight*] Thatll do. Thank you. [*He looks at his watch and suddenly becomes business-like*]. Time's up, Major. Youve managed those regiments so well that youre sure to be asked to get rid of some of the infantry of the Timok division. Send them home by way of Lom Palanka. Saranoff: dont get married until I come back: I shall be here punctually at five in the evening on Tuesday fortnight. Gracious ladies [*his heels click*] good evening. [*He makes them a military bow, and goes*].

SERGIUS. What a man! Is he a man!

SUGGESTIONS FOR STUDY

1. Most older plays, such as *Oedipus Rex* and *Othello,* have come down to us without the stage directions of their authors. Shaw believed that he should fully inform the reader as to the appearance of the stage and the characters and as to the successive emotions the actors are to portray. Examine the first pages of the play up to the entrance of Louka. Just what sorts of details are included in the directions? What would we know if these were not given? Do these directions run contrary to the modern custom of keeping a work of literature impersonal, as was described in the introduction to drama?

2. To what extent do you suppose Shaw relied on an element not visible in print: the physical attractiveness of the actresses who play Raina and Louka?

3. What details about the way of life of upper-class Bulgarians of the 1880's does Shaw use and exaggerate for comic effect?

4. Good comedy moves rapidly. Seeing it on the stage is like watching the score while a Mozart opera is being performed: the

singers traverse the page in an unbelievably short time. Although it is probably impossible for anyone but a practicing playwright to grasp fully the smoothness and rapidity of Shaw's dialogue, the student should try to read some of it aloud, or at least hear it in his mind's ear and note that it is dialogue cut and patterned for the stage. It illustrates the statement which one frequently hears that a great artist makes his art seem easy to the amateur—until the amateur tries it.

The Further Range of Prose

The fictional use of prose (story, novel, play) accounts for only a part of the vast amount of prose daily turned out in newspapers, magazines, and books. Although there have been times in human history when poetry was the accepted medium for transmitting information or instruction, the work of the world has for many centuries been conducted in prose. We think in prose and we normally write in prose.

Most prose may be classified, for want of a better term, as exposition. Exposition is explanation. Though at least some exposition is literature even according to the strictest definition of literature, purely explanatory prose in its many uses does not come within the scope of this volume.

The primary purpose of exposition, whatever its form, is that of giving information. Other types of nonfictional prose, while they may include information, are written to do other things than merely inform the reader—to entertain him, to make him feel anger or happiness, to persuade him, and so on. It is this characteristic which allies these types of prose with the other belletristic forms we have studied—fiction, poetry, and drama.

In this section are presented nine kinds of such nonfictional prose. Benjamin Franklin and Ambrose Bierce show us how an aphorism can state an idea pointedly and concisely in one or a few sentences. The fable is traditionally a brief story in which animals talk and act like human beings and from which a moral, either expressed or implied, is drawn. The uses of the fable are illustrated here by Aesop, who may have lived about 600 B.C., and by James Thurber.

One by-product of the life of a great man, or of a great writer, or of a man who, like Abraham Lincoln, was both, is likely to be a collection of memorable letters. They usually reflect all aspects of the writer's career. In these examples drawn from Lincoln's letters, we observe Lincoln correcting the misapprehension of a critic, admonishing a general, sending a bit of family news to his wife, reprimanding a captain, and comforting a mother on the loss of her sons. Historians tell us that the letter to Mrs. Bixby may have been written by one of Lincoln's secretaries and that the writer was misinformed as to the facts. Nevertheless, it is a justly famous letter.

Religious literature is of many types: prayers, meditations, hymns, devotions, sermons. A famous piece of devotional prose is John Donne's Devotion XVII, from which Ernest Hemingway drew the title for his novel *For Whom the Bell Tolls*.

The purpose of satire is to deride a person, a group, an idea, an attitude through the use of scorn or contempt. Often the satirist pretends to be serious, and the reader must discover for himself that the purpose is derision. The eighteenth-century writer Jonathan

Swift was so incensed at the treatment of the people of Ireland that he wrote one of the best-known satires in all literature. Mark Twain's sarcastic attack on the hypocrisy of his wife's uncle, Andrew Langdon, was not published until 1946, many years after the death of both author and uncle.

Charles Lamb, Stephen Leacock, and E. B. White show us a few of the innumerable modes of humor. Nonfictional prose is frequently used to persuade; Edmund Burke's attempt to persuade others to share his respect for the idea of a chivalric obligation has become a classic statement of this mode of belief.

Some would say that the most important of all uses of nonfictional prose is to discuss man's place in the universe, his relation to "the eternities," as Henry Thoreau called it. In the heart of his book *Walden* Thoreau explains why he lived for a time alone in a simple house he had built for himself on the shore of Walden Pond. Bertrand Russell's early-twentieth-century essay states the essential beliefs of the modern man who is intellectually free. Even the many who disagree with his ideas will admit that they have never been more eloquently expressed.

In the final selections in this section, Sir Winston Churchill and Bruce Catton demonstrate how exciting history can be when it is skillfully written.

THE WAY TO WEALTH

Benjamin Franklin
(1706–1790)

COURTEOUS READER,

I have heard that nothing gives an Author so great Pleasure, as to find his Works respectfully quoted by other learned Authors. This Pleasure I have seldom enjoyed; for tho' I have been, if I may say it without Vanity, an *eminent Author* of Almanacks annually now a full Quarter of a Century, my Brother Authors in the same Way, for what Reason I know not, have ever been very sparing in their Applauses, and no other Author has taken the least Notice of me, so that did not my Writings produce me some solid *Pudding*, the great Deficiency of *Praise* would have quite discouraged me.

I concluded at length, that the People were the best Judges of my merit; for they buy my Works; and besides, in my Rambles, where I am not personally known, I have frequently heard one or other of my Adages repeated, with, *as Poor Richard says,* at the End on 't; this gave me some Satisfaction,

as it showed not only that my Instructions were regarded, but discovered likewise some Respect for my Authority; and I own, that to encourage the Practice of remembering and repeating those wise Sentences, I have sometimes *quoted myself* with great Gravity.

Judge, then how much I must have been gratified by an Incident I am going to relate to you. I stopt my Horse lately where a great Number of People were collected at a Vendue of Merchant Goods. The Hour of Sale not being come, they were conversing on the Badness of the Times and one of the Company call'd to a plain clean old Man, with white Locks, "Pray, Father Abraham, what think you of the Times? Won't these heavy Taxes quite ruin the Country? How shall we be ever able to pay them? What would you advise us to?" Father *Abraham* stood up, and reply'd, "If you'd have my Advice, I'll give it you in short, for *A Word to the Wise is enough,* and *many Words won't fill a Bushel,* as *Poor Richard* says." They join'd in desiring him to speak his Mind, and gathering round him, he proceeded as follows;

"Friends," says he, "and Neighbours, the

Taxes are indeed very heavy, and if those laid on by the Government were the only Ones we had to pay, we might more easily discharge them; but we have many others, and much more grievous to some of us. We are taxed twice as much by our *Idleness,* three times as much by our *Pride,* and four times as much by our *Folly;* and from these Taxes the Commissioners cannot ease or deliver us by allowing an Abatement. However let us hearken to good Advice, and something may be done for us; *God helps them that help themselves,* as Poor Richard says, in his Almanack of 1733.

It would be thought a hard Government that should tax its People one-tenth Part of their *Time,* to be employed in its Service. But *Idleness* taxes many of us much more, if we reckon all that is spent in absolute *Sloth,* or doing of nothing, with that which is spent in idle Employments or Amusements, that amount to nothing. *Sloth,* by bringing on Diseases, absolutely shortens Life. *Sloth, like Rust, consumes faster than Labour wears; while the used Key is always bright,* as Poor Richard says. *But dost thou love Life, then do not squander Time; for that's the stuff Life is made of,* as Poor Richard says. How much more than is necessary do we spend in sleep, forgetting that *The Sleeping Fox catches no Poultry,* and that *There will be sleeping enough in the Grave,* as Poor Richard says.

If Time be of all Things the most precious, wasting Time must be, as Poor Richard says, *the greatest Prodigality;* since, as he elsewhere tells us, *Lost Time is never found again; and what we call Time enough, always proves little enough:* Let us then up and be doing, and doing to the Purpose; so by Diligence shall we do more with less Perplexity. *Sloth makes all Things difficult, but Industry all easy,* as Poor Richard says; and *He that riseth late must trot all Day, and shall scarce overtake his Business at Night; while Laziness travels so slowly, that Poverty soon overtakes him,* as we read in Poor Richard, who adds, *Drive thy Business, let not that drive thee;* and *Early to Bed, and early to rise, makes a Man healthy, wealthy, and wise.*

So what signifies *wishing* and *hoping* for better Times. We may make these Times better, if we bestir ourselves. *Industry need not wish,* as Poor Richard says, *and he that lives upon Hope will die fasting. There are no Gains without Pains; then Help Hands, for I have no Lands,* or if I have, they are smartly taxed. And, as *Poor Richard* likewise observes, *He that hath a Trade hath an Estate; and he that hath a Calling, hath an Office of Profit and Honour;* but then the *Trade* must be worked at, and the *Calling* well followed, or neither the *Estate* nor the *Office* will enable us to pay our Taxes. If we are industrious we shall never starve; for, as *Poor Richard* says, *At the working Man's House Hunger looks in, but dares not enter.* Nor will the Bailiff or the Constable enter, for *Industry pays Debts, while Despair encreaseth them,* says Poor Richard. What though you have found no Treasure, nor has any rich Relation left you a Legacy, *Diligence is the Mother of Goodluck* as Poor Richard says *and God gives all Things to Industry. Then plough deep, while Sluggards sleep, and you shall have Corn to sell and to keep,* says Poor Dick. Work while it is called To-day, for you know not how much you may be hindered To-morrow, which makes *Poor Richard* say, *One to-day is worth two To-morrows,* and farther, *Have you somewhat to do To-morrow, do it To-day.* If you were a Servant, would you not be ashamed that a good Master should catch you idle? Are you then your own Master, *be ashamed to catch yourself idle,* as Poor Dick says. When there is so much to be done for yourself, your Family, your Country, and your gracious King, be up by Peep of Day; *Let not the Sun look down and say, Inglorious here he lies.* Handle your tools without Mittens; remember that *The Cat in Gloves catches no Mice,* as Poor Richard says. 'Tis true there is much to be done, and perhaps you are weak-handed, but stick to it steadily; and you will see great Effects, for *Constant Dropping wears away Stones,* and by *Diligence and Patience the Mouse ate in two the Cable;* and *Little Strokes fell great Oaks,* as Poor Richard says in his Almanack, the Year I cannot just now remember.

Methinks I hear some of you say, *Must a Man afford himself no Leisure?* I will tell thee, my friend, what *Poor Richard* says, *Employ thy Time well, if thou meanest to gain Leisure; and, since thou art not sure of a Minute, throw not away an Hour.* Leisure, is Time for doing something useful; this Leisure the diligent Man will obtain, but the lazy Man never; so that, as *Poor Richard* says, *A Life of Leisure and a Life of Laziness are two Things.* Do you imagine that Sloth will afford you more Comfort than Labour? No, for as *Poor Richard* says, *Trouble springs from Idleness, and grievous Toil from needless Ease. Many without Labour, would live by their Wits only, but they break for want of Stock.* Whereas Industry gives Comfort, and Plenty, and Respect: *Fly Pleasures, and they'll follow you. The diligent Spinner has a large Shift; and now I have a Sheep and a Cow, everybody bids me good Morrow;* all which is well said by *Poor Richard.*

.   .   .   .

And now to conclude, *Experience keeps a dear School, but Fools will learn in no other, and scarce in that;* for it is true, *we may give Advice, but we cannot give Conduct,* as *Poor Richard* says: However, remember this, *They that won't be counselled, can't be helped,* as *Poor Richard* says: and farther, That, *if you will not hear Reason, she'll surely rap your Knuckles."*

Thus the old Gentleman ended his Harangue. The People heard it, and approved the Doctrine, and immediately practised the contrary, just as if it had been a common Sermon; for the Vendue opened, and they began to buy extravagantly, notwithstanding his Cautions and their own Fear of Taxes. I found the good Man had thoroughly studied my Almanacks, and digested all I had dropt on these Topicks during the Course of Five and twenty Years. The frequent Mention he made of me must have tired any one else, but my Vanity was wonderfully delighted with it, though I was conscious that not a tenth Part of the Wisdom was my own, which he ascribed to me, but rather the *Gleanings* I had made of the Sense of all

Ages and Nations. However, I resolved to be the better for the Echo of it; and though I had at first determined to buy Stuff for a new Coat, I went away resolved to wear my old One a little longer. *Reader,* if thou wilt do the same, thy Profit will be as great as mine. I *am, as ever, thine to serve thee.*

RICHARD SAUNDERS.

July 7, 1757

THE DEVIL'S DICTIONARY

Ambrose Bierce
(1842–?1914)

[Certain Entries under the Letter A]

Abasement, n. A decent and customary mental attitude in the presence of wealth or power. Peculiarly appropriate in an employee when addressing an employer.

Abdomen, n. The temple of the god Stomach, in whose worship, with sacrificial rights, all true men engage. From women this ancient faith commands but a stammering assent. They sometimes minister at the altar in a half-hearted and ineffective way, but true reverence for the one deity that men really adore they know not. If women had a free hand in the world's marketing the race would become graminivorous.

Ability, n. The natural equipment to accomplish some small part of the meaner ambitions distinguishing able men from dead ones. In the last analysis ability is commonly found to consist mainly in a high degree of solemnity. Perhaps, however, this impressive quality is rightly appraised; it is no easy task to be solemn.

Abnormal, adj. Not conforming to standard. In matters of thought and conduct, to be independent is to be abnormal, to be abnormal is to be detested. Wherefore the lexicographer adviseth a striving toward a straiter resemblance to the Average Man than he hath to himself. Whoso attaineth thereto shall have peace, the prospect of death and the hope of Hell.

Aborigines, n. Persons of little worth found cumbering the soil of a newly discovered country. They soon cease to cumber; they fertilize.

Abridge, v.t. To shorten.

When in the course of human events it becomes necessary for a people to abridge their king, a decent respect for the opinions of mankind requires that they should declare the causes which impel them to the separation.

Oliver Cromwell.

Abrupt, adj. Sudden, without ceremony, like the arrival of a cannon-shot and the departure of the soldier whose interests are most affected by it. Dr. Samuel Johnson beautifully said of another author's ideas that they were "concatenated without abruption."

Abscond, v.i. To "move in a mysterious way," commonly with the property of another.

> Spring beckons! All things to the call respond;
> The trees are leaving and cashiers abscond.
>
> *Phela Orm.*

Absolute, adj. Independent, irresponsible. An absolute monarchy is one in which the sovereign does as he pleases so long as he pleases the assassins. Not many absolute monarchies are left, most of them having been replaced by limited monarchies, where the sovereign's power for evil (and for good) is greatly curtailed, and by republics, which are governed by chance.

Abstainer, n. A weak person who yields to the temptation of denying himself a pleasure. A total abstainer is one who abstains from everything but abstention, and especially from inactivity in the affairs of others.

Absurdity, n. A statement or belief manifestly inconsistent with one's own opinion.

Academe, n. An ancient school where morality and philosophy were taught.

Academy, n. (from academe). A modern school where football is taught.

Accident, n. An inevitable occurrence due to the action of immutable natural laws.

[TWO FABLES]

Aesop
(c. 620–c. 560 B.C.)
translated by Joseph Jacobs

ANDROCLES

A slave named Androcles once escaped from his master and fled to the forest. As he was wandering about there he came upon a Lion lying down moaning and groaning. At first he turned to flee, but finding that the Lion did not pursue him, he turned back and went up to him. As he came near, the Lion put out his paw, which was all swollen and bleeding, and Androcles found that a huge thorn had got into it, and was causing all the pain. He pulled out the thorn and bound up the paw of the Lion, who was soon able to rise and lick the hand of Androcles like a dog. Then the Lion took Androcles to his cave, and every day used to bring him meat from which to live. But shortly afterwards both Androcles and the Lion were captured, and the slave was sentenced to be thrown to the Lion, after the latter had been kept without food for several days. The Emperor and all his Court came to see the spectacle, and Androcles was led out into the middle of the arena. Soon the Lion was let loose from his den, and rushed bounding and roaring towards his victim. But as soon as he came near to Androcles he recognised his friend, and fawned upon him, and licked his hands like a friendly dog. The Emperor, surprised at this, summoned Androcles to him, who told him the whole story. Whereupon the slave was pardoned and freed, and the Lion let loose to his native forest.

Gratitude is the sign of noble souls.

THE DOG AND THE WOLF

A gaunt wolf was almost dead with hunger when he happened to meet a House-dog who was passing by. "Ah, Cousin," said the

Dog, "I knew how it would be; your irregular life will soon be the ruin of you. Why do you not work steadily as I do, and get your food regularly given to you?"

"I would have no objection," said the Wolf, "if I could only get a place."

"I will easily arrange that for you," said the Dog; "come with me to my master and you shall share my work."

So the Wolf and the Dog went towards the town together. On the way there the Wolf noticed that the hair on a certain part of the Dog's neck was very much worn away, so he asked him how that had come about.

"Oh, it is nothing," said the Dog. "That is only the place where the collar is put on at night to keep me chained up; it chafes a bit, but one soon gets used to it."

"Is that all?" said the Wolf. "Then good-bye to you, Master Dog."

Better starve free than be a fat slave.

[TWO FABLES]*

James Thurber
(1894–   )

DEATH IN THE ZOO

Naturalists, who are easily baffled by the behavior of animals, are still wondering why Big Bill, a polar bear at the Fleishhacker Zoo in San Francisco, killed his mate, Min, so unexpectedly. Bill was lying down, strumming at the headboard with his fingers, dreaming of the ice floes or trying to remember where he had put something, when Min tiptoed into the room. "Tiptoeing again," thought Bill, "like a gahdarn poodle dog."

What she said and did in the next few minutes we shall reconstruct later. At the end of it, Bill rolled out of bed and killed her, after which he dragged her thirty feet to a pool of water and held her under for several minutes, to make sure.

I saw the male polar bear at the Central

Park Zoo duck his mate one Sunday last April. He grabbed her ear, pulled her head under, kept her there ten seconds or so, and then let her go, growling, half-playfully, "That's for nothing." The Central Park polar bears seem to like each other, which is a break for the zoo attendants, the homicide squad, and the female bear.

Perhaps the principal trouble with American zoos, as regards bears, is that the men in charge of them think that all female bears look alike to a male bear. This conclusion, arrived at from the premise that all female bears look alike to the men in the zoo, is unfortunate to the point of being deadly. To a male polar bear, female polar bears are as different as thumbprints to a G-man. A male polar bear likes only about one female in every fifty he comes across in a day's courting swim. Some bears swim seventy-five miles along a bear-infested coast before they find a female cute enough to bother with.

Not knowing this, the Fleishhacker Zoo men brought Bill a mate one spring that he couldn't abide. She put starch into everything she washed and cheese into everything she cooked; what is more, she kept scratching constantly. Bill swatted her out of existence one day as nonchalantly as if she had been a fly.

He was still grumbling about mating conditions in California when the Fleishhacker people brought him still another mate, rousing him from dreams of the Arctic, where a man can have his pick of a thousand gals. "Lookit, Bill," they said, "the lady of our choice!" Bill noted that she smelled faintly like a Los Angeles roadateria, and that she tacked slightly to the left in lumbering, which was going to be bad since he tacked to the right. Furthermore, she giggled. When the Zoo men left, Bill told the newcomer to stay out of his way, and he went back to the cave and lay down.

When Bill did not come out for several days, Min took to tiptoeing in to see if he wanted a glass of water. She would fiddle with doilies, empty ash trays, wash out his briar pipe with soap and water, open the window if it was shut and shut it if it was open.

* From *My World and Welcome To It.*

Once she felt his forehead to see if he had a fever and Bill took a cut at her, but missed. She fled, screaming.

When Bill didn't come out for several more days (he felt fine, but he didn't want to come out), she decided that he was sick, and she determined to take his temperature. She tiptoed in and stuck a thermometer in his mouth before he knew what was happening. Bill watched her tidy up his bureau, putting his socks, handkerchiefs and shirts, which had all been in one drawer, neatly into separate drawers. When she started hanging his ties on a patented nickel-plated cedarwood tie-rack which clasped them in such a way that you couldn't get them off unless you knew how to work the automatic clip-shift tie-release, Bill leaped out of bed and roared into action. He finished off her, the thermometer, and the tie-rack before anybody could stop him. "They turned hoses on me," he said later, "and that helped. I was getting pretty hot."

The Fleishhacker people are probably looking for another mate for Big Bill right now. Well, I have done all *I* can.

INTERVIEW WITH A LEMMING

The weary scientist, tramping through the mountains of northern Europe in the winter weather, dropped his knapsack and prepared to sit on a rock.

"Careful, brother," said a voice.

"Sorry," murmured the scientist, noting with some surprise that a lemming which he had been about to sit on had addressed him. "It is a source of considerable astonishment to me," said the scientist, sitting down beside the lemming, "that you are capable of speech."

"You human beings are always astonished," said the lemming, "when any other animal can do anything you can. Yet there are many things animals can do that you cannot, such as stridulate, or chirr, to name just one. To stridulate, or chirr, one of the minor achievements of the cricket, your species is de-

pendent on the intestines of the sheep and the hair of the horse."

"We are a dependent animal," admitted the scientist.

"You are an amazing animal," said the lemming.

"We have always considered you rather amazing, too," said the scientist. "You are perhaps the most mysterious of creatures."

"If we are going to indulge in adjectives beginning with 'm,'" said the lemming, sharply, "let me apply a few to your species—murderous, maladjusted, maleficent, malicious and muffle-headed."

"You find our behavior as difficult to understand as we do yours?"

"You, as you would say, said it," said the lemming. "You kill, you mangle, you torture, you imprison, you starve each other. You cover the nurturing earth with cement, you cut down elm trees to put up institutions for people driven insane by the cutting down of elm trees, you—"

"You could go on all night like that," said the scientist, "listing our sins and our shames."

"I could go on all night and up to four o'clock tomorrow afternoon," said the lemming. "It just happens that I have made a lifelong study of the self-styled higher animal. Except for one thing, I know all there is to know about you, and a singularly dreary, dolorous and distasteful store of information it is, too, to use only adjectives beginning with 'd.'"

"You say you have made a lifelong study of my species—" began the scientist.

"Indeed I have," broke in the lemming. "I know that you are cruel, cunning and carnivorous, sly, sensual and selfish, greedy, gullible and guileful—"

"Pray don't wear yourself out," said the scientist, quietly. "It may interest you to know that I have made a lifelong study of lemmings, just as you have made a lifelong study of people. Like you, I have found but one thing about my subject which I do not understand."

"And what is that?" asked the lemming.

"I don't understand," said the scientist,

"why you lemmings all rush down to the sea and drown yourselves."

"How curious," said the lemming. "The one thing I don't understand is why you human beings don't."

[FIVE LETTERS]

Abraham Lincoln
(1809–1865)

[TO HORACE GREELEY]

EXECUTIVE MANSION, WASHINGTON,
August 22, 1862

HON. HORACE GREELEY.

Dear Sir: I have just read yours of the 19th, addressed to myself through the New York *Tribune*. If there be in it any statements or assumptions of fact which I may know to be erroneous, I do not, now and here, controvert them. If there be in it any inferences which I may believe to be falsely drawn, I do not, now and here, argue against them. If there be perceptible in it an impatient and dictatorial tone, I waive it in deference to an old friend whose heart I have always supposed to be right.

As to the policy I "seem to be pursuing," as you say, I have not meant to leave any one in doubt.

I would save the Union. I would save it the shortest way under the Constitution. The sooner the national authority can be restored, the nearer the Union will be "the Union as it was." If there be those who would not save the Union unless they could at the same time save slavery, I do not agree with them. If there be those who would not save the Union unless they could at the same time destroy slavery, I do not agree with them. My paramount object in this struggle is to save the Union, and is not either to save or to destroy slavery. If I could save the Union without freeing any slave, I would do it; and if I could save it by freeing all the slaves, I would do it; and if I could save it by freeing

some and leaving others alone, I would also do that. What I do about slavery and the coloured race, I do because I believe it helps to save the Union; and what I forbear, I forbear because I do not believe it would help to save the Union. I shall do less whenever I shall believe what I am doing hurts the cause, and I shall do more whenever I shall believe doing more will help the cause. I shall try to correct errors when shown to be errors, and I shall adopt new views so fast as they shall appear to be true views.

I have here stated my purpose according to my view of official duty; and I intend no modification of my oft-expressed personal wish that all men everywhere could be free.

Yours,

A. LINCOLN

[TO JOSEPH HOOKER]

EXECUTIVE MANSION,
Washington, January 26, 1863.

Major General Hooker:

General

I have placed you at the head of the Army of the Potomac. Of course I have done this upon what appear to me to be sufficient reasons. And yet I think it best for you to know that there are some things in regard to which, I am not quite satisfied with you. I believe you to be a brave and a skillful soldier, which, of course, I like. I also believe you do not mix politics with your profession, in which you are right. You have confidence in yourself, which is a valuable, if not an indispensable quality. You are ambitious, which, within reasonable bounds, does good rather than harm. But I think that during Gen. Burnside's command of the Army, you have taken counsel of your ambition, and thwarted him as much as you could, in which you did a great wrong to the country, and to a most meritorious and honorable brother officer. I have heard, in such way as to believe it, of your recently saying that both the Army and the Government needed a Dictator. Of course it was not *for* this, but in spite of it, that I have given you the command. Only those generals who gain successes, can set up dictators. What I now ask of you is military success, and I will risk the dictatorship. The government will support you to the utmost of its ability, which is neither more nor less than it has done and will do for all commanders. I much fear that the spirit which you have aided to infuse into the Army, of criticising their Commander, and withholding confidence from him, will now turn upon you. I shall assist you as far as I can, to put it down. Neither you, nor Napoleon, if he were alive again, could get any good out of an army, while such a spirit prevails in it.

And now, beware of rashness. Beware of rashness, but with energy, and sleepless vigilance, go forward, and give us victories.

Yours very truly

A. LINCOLN

[TO MRS. LINCOLN]

Washington, August 8, 1863

My dear Wife, All as well as usual, and no particular trouble anyway. I put the money into the Treasury at five per cent., with the privilege of withdrawing it any time upon thirty days' notice. I suppose you are glad to learn this. Tell dear Tad poor "Nanny Goat" is lost, and Mrs. Cuthbert and I are in distress about it. The day you left Nanny was found resting herself and chewing her little cud on the middle of Tad's bed; but now she's gone! The gardener kept complaining that she destroyed the flowers, till it was concluded to bring her down to the White House. This was done, and the second day she had disappeared and has not been heard of since. This is the last we know of poor "Nanny."

[TO JAMES M. CUTTS, JR.]

EXECUTIVE MANSION,
Washington, Oct 26, 1863.

Capt. James M. Cutts.

Although what I am now to say is to be,

in form, a reprimand,[1] it is not intended to add a pang to what you have already suffered upon the subject to which it relates. You have too much of life yet before you, and have shown too much of promise as an officer, for your future to be lightly surrendered. You were convicted of two offences. One of them, not of great enormity, and yet greatly to be avoided, I feel sure you are in no danger of repeating. The other you are not so well assured against. The advice of a father to his son "Beware of entrance to a quarrel, but being in, bear it that the opposed may beware of thee," is good, and yet not the best. Quarrel not at all. No man resolved to make the most of himself, can spare time for personal contention. Still less can he afford to take all the consequences, including the vitiating of his temper, and the loss of self-control. Yield larger things to which you can show no more than equal right; and yield lesser ones, though clearly your own. Better give your path to a dog, than be bitten by him in contesting for the right. Even killing the dog would not cure the bite.

In the mood indicated deal henceforth with your fellow men, and especially with your brother officers; and even the unpleasant events you are passing from will not have been profitless to you.

[TO MRS. BIXBY]

EXECUTIVE MANSION, WASHINGTON
November 21, 1864

MRS. BIXBY, Boston, Massachusetts.

DEAR MADAM: I have been shown in the files of the War Department a statement of the Adjutant-General of Massachusetts that you are the mother of five sons who have died gloriously on the field of battle. I feel how weak and fruitless must be any words of mine which should attempt to beguile you from the grief of a loss so overwhelming. But I cannot refrain from tendering to you the consolation that may be found in the

[1] Captain Cutts had been convicted in court martial of peeping at a woman and quarreling with fellow officers.

thanks of the Republic they died to save. I pray that our heavenly Father may assuage the anguish of your bereavement, and leave you only the cherished memory of the loved and lost, and the solemn pride that must be yours to have laid so costly a sacrifice upon the altar of freedom.

Yours very sincerely and respectfully,

ABRAHAM LINCOLN

[NO MAN IS AN ILAND]*

John Donne

(1572–1631)

Perchance hee for whom this Bell tolls, may be so ill, as that he knowes not it tolls for him; And perchance I may thinke my selfe so much better than I am, as that they who are about mee, and see my state, may have caused it to toll for mee, and I know not that. The Church is Catholike, universall, so are all her Actions; All that she does, belongs to all. When she baptizes a child, that action concernes mee; for that child is thereby connected to that Head which is my Head too, and engraffed into that body, whereof I am a member. And when she buries a Man, that action concernes me: All mankinde is of one Author, and is one volume; when one Man dies, one Chapter is not torne out of the booke, but translated into a better language; and every Chapter must be so translated; God emploies several translators; some peeces are translated by age, some by sicknesse, some by warre, some by justice; but Gods hand is in every translation; and his hand shall binde up all our scattered leaves againe, for that Librarie where every booke shall lie open to one another: As therefore the Bell that rings to a Sermon, calls not upon the Preacher onely, but upon the Congregation to come; so this Bell calls us all: but how much more mee, who am brought so neere the doore by this sicknesse. There was a contention as farre as a suite, (in which both pietie and dignitie, religion,

* No. XVII from *Devotions upon Emergent Occasions*.

and estimation, were mingled) which of the religious Orders should ring to praiers first in the Morning; and it was determined, that they should ring first that rose earliest. If we understand aright the dignitie of this Bell that tolls for our evening prayer, wee would bee glad to make it ours, by rising early, in that application, that it might bee ours, as wel as his, whose indeed it is. The Bell doth toll for him that thinkes it doth; and though it intermit againe, yet from that minute, that that occasion wrought upon him, hee is united to God. Who casts not up his Eye to the Sunne when it rises? but who takes off his Eye from a Comet when that breakes out? Who bends not his eare to any bell, which upon any occasion rings? but who can remove it from that bell, which is passing a peece of himselfe out of this world? No man is an Iland, intire of it selfe; every man is a peece of the Continent, a part of the maine; if a Clod bee washed away by the Sea, Europe is the lesse, as well as if a Promontorie were, as well as if a Mannor of thy friends or of thine owne were; any mans death diminishes mee, because I am involved in Mankinde; And therefore never send to know for whom the bell tolls; It tolls for thee. Neither can we call this a begging of Miserie or a borrowing of Miserie, as though we were not miserable enough of our selves, but must fetch it more from the next house, in taking upon us the Miserie of our Neighbours. Truly it were an excusable covetousnesse if wee did; for affliction is a treasure, and scarce any man hath enough of it. No man hath affliction enough that is not matured, and ripened by it, and made fit for God by that affliction. If a man carry treasure in bullion, or in a wedge of gold, and have none coined into currant Monies, his treasure will not defray him as he travells. Tribulation is Treasure in the nature of it, but it is not currant money in the use of it, except wee get nearer and nearer our home, Heaven, by it. Another man may be sicke too, and sick to death, and this affliction may lie in his bowels, as gold in a Mine, and be of no use to him; but this bell, that tells me of his affliction, digs out, and applies that gold to mee: if by this consideration of anothers danger, I take mine owne into contemplation, and so secure my selfe, by making my recourse to my God, who is our onely securitie.

A MODEST PROPOSAL

FOR PREVENTING THE CHILDREN OF IRELAND FROM BEING A BURDEN TO THEIR PARENTS OR COUNTRY

Jonathan Swift
(1667–1745)

It is a melancholy object to those who walk through this great town or travel in the country, when they see the streets, the roads, and cabin-doors crowded with beggars of the female sex, followed by three, four, or six children, all in rags, and importuning every passenger for an alms. These mothers instead of being able to work for their honest livelihood, are forced to employ all their time in strolling to beg sustenance for their helpless infants, who, as they grow up, either turn thieves for want of work, or leave their dear native country, to fight for the Pretender in Spain, or sell themselves to the Barbadoes.

I think it is agreed by all parties, that this prodigious number of children in the arms, or on the backs, or at the heels of their mothers, and frequently of their fathers, is in the present deplorable state of the kingdom a very great additional grievance; and therefore whoever could find out a fair, cheap, and easy method of making these children sound and useful members of the common-wealth, would deserve so well of the public as to have his statue set up for a preserver of the nation.

But my intention is very far from being confined to provide only for the children of professed beggars; it is of a much greater extent, and shall take in the whole number of infants at a certain age, who are born of parents in effect as little able to support them, as those who demand our charity in the streets.

As to my own part, having turned my thoughts, for many years, upon this important subject, and maturely weighed the several schemes of other projectors, I have always found them grossly mistaken in their computation. It is true, a child just dropt from its dam, may be supported by her milk for a solar year with little other nourishment, at most not above the value of two shillings, which the mother may certainly get, or the value in scraps, by her lawful occupation of begging; and it is exactly at one year old that I propose to provide for them in such a manner, as, instead of being a charge upon their parents, or the parish, or wanting food and raiment for the rest of their lives, they shall, on the contrary, contribute to the feeding and partly to the clothing of many thousands.

There is likewise another great advantage in my scheme, that it will prevent those voluntary abortions, and that horrid practice of women murdering their bastard children, alas! too frequent among us—sacrificing the poor innocent babes, I doubt, more to avoid the expense than the shame—which would move tears and pity in the most savage and inhuman breast.

The number of souls in this kingdom being usually reckoned one million and a half, of these I calculate there may be about two hundred thousand couple whose wives are breeders; from which number I subtract thirty thousand couples, who are able to maintain their own children, although I apprehend there cannot be so many, under the present distresses of the kingdom; but this being granted, there will remain an hundred and seventy thousand breeders. I again subtract fifty thousand, for those women who miscarry, or whose children die by accident or disease within the year. There only remain an hundred and twenty thousand children of poor parents annually born: The question therefore is, How this number shall be reared, and provided for? which, as I have already said, under the present situation of affairs, is utterly impossible by all the methods hitherto proposed; for we can neither employ them in handicraft or agriculture;

we neither build houses, (I mean in the country) nor cultivate land: They can very seldom pick up a livelihood by stealing till they arrive at six years old, except where they are of towardly parts, although, I confess, they learn the rudiments much earlier; during which time they can however be properly looked upon only as probationers; as I have been informed by a principal gentleman in the county of Cavan, who protested to me, that he never knew above one or two instances under the age of six, even in a part of the kingdom so renowned for the quickest proficiency in that art.

I am assured by our merchants, that a boy or a girl before twelve years old, is no saleable commodity, and even when they come to this age, they will not yield above three pounds, or three pounds and half a crown at most, on the exchange; which cannot turn to account either to the parents or kingdom, the charge of nutriment and rags having been at least four times that value.

I shall now therefore humbly propose my own thoughts, which I hope will not be liable to the least objection.

I have been assured by a very knowing American of my acquaintance in London, that a young healthy child well nursed is at a year old a most delicious nourishing and wholesome food, whether stewed, roasted, baked, or boiled; and I make no doubt that it will equally serve in a fricassee, or a ragout.

I do therefore humbly offer it to publick consideration, that of the hundred and twenty thousand children, already computed, twenty thousand may be reserved for breed, whereof only one fourth part to be males; which is more than we allow to sheep, black cattle, or swine, and my reason is, that these children are seldom the fruits of marriage, a circumstance not much regarded by our savages; therefore, one male will be sufficient to serve four females. That the remaining hundred thousand may at a year old be offered in sale to the persons of quality and fortune, through the kingdom, always advising the mother to let them suck plentifully in the last month, so as to render them plump, and fat for a good table. A child will make two dishes at an entertainment for friends, and when the family dines alone, the fore or hind quarter will make a reasonable dish, and seasoned with a little pepper or salt will be very good boiled on the fourth day, especially in winter.

I have reckoned upon a medium, that a child just born will weigh 12 pounds, and in a solar year, if tolerably nursed, encreaseth to 28 pounds.

I grant this food will be somewhat dear, and therefore very proper for landlords, who, as they have already devoured most of the parents seem to have the best title to the children.

Infant's flesh will be in season throughout the year, but more plentiful in March, and a little before and after; for we are told by a grave author, an eminent French physician, that fish being a prolifick dyet, there are more children born in Roman Catholick countries about nine months after Lent, than at any other season; therefore reckoning a year after Lent, the markets will be more glutted than usual, because the number of popish infants, is at least three to one in this kingdom, and therefore it will have one other collateral advantage, by lessening the number of papists among us.

I have already computed the charge of nursing a beggar's child (in which list I reckon all cottagers, labourers, and four fifths of the farmers) to be about two shillings per annum, rags included; and I believe no gentleman would repine to give ten shillings for the carcass of a good fat child, which, as I have said will make four dishes of excellent nutritive meat, when he hath only some particular friend, or his own family to dine with him. Thus the squire will learn to be a good landlord, and grow popular among his tenants; the mother will have eight shillings neat profit, and be fit for work till she produces another child.

Those who are more thrifty (as I must confess the times require) may flay the carcass; the skin of which, artificially dressed, will make admirable gloves for ladies, and summer boots for fine gentlemen.

As to our city of Dublin, shambles may be

appointed for this purpose, in the most convenient parts of it, and butchers we may be assured will not be wanting; although I rather recommend buying the children alive, and dressing them hot from the knife, as we do roasting pigs.

A very worthy person, a true lover of his country, and whose virtues I highly esteem, was lately pleased, in discoursing on this matter, to offer a refinement upon my scheme. He said, that many gentlemen of this kingdom, having of late destroyed their deer, he conceived that the want of venison might be well supplied by the bodies of young lads and maidens, not exceeding fourteen years of age, nor under twelve; so great a number of both sexes in every country being now ready to starve, for want of work and service: And these to be disposed of by their parents if alive, or otherwise by their nearest relations. But with due deference to so excellent a friend, and so deserving a patriot, I cannot be altogether in his sentiments; for as to the males, my American acquaintance assured me from frequent experience, that their flesh was generally tough and lean, like that of our schoolboys, by continual exercise, and their taste disagreeable, and to fatten them would not answer the charge. Then as to the females, it would, I think with humble submission, be a loss to the publick, because they soon would become breeders themselves: And besides it is not improbable that some scrupulous people might be apt to censure such a practice (although indeed very unjustly) as a little bordering upon cruelty, which, I confess, hath always been with me the strongest objection against any project, how well soever intended.

But in order to justify my friend, he confessed, that this expedient was put into his head by the famous Psalmanazar, a native of the island Formosa, who came from thence to London, above twenty years ago, and in conversation told my friend, that in his country when any young person happened to be put to death, the executioner sold the carcass to persons of quality, as a prime dainty, and that, in his time, the body of a plump girl of fifteen, who was crucified for an attempt to poison the Emperor, was sold to his Imperial Majesty's prime minister of state, and other great mandarins of the court, in joints from the gibbet, at four hundred crowns. Neither indeed can I deny, that if the same use were made of several plump young girls in this town, who, without one single groat to their fortunes, cannot stir abroad without a chair, and appear at a play-house and assemblies in foreign fineries which they never will pay for; the kingdom would not be the worse.

Some persons of a desponding spirit are in great concern about that vast number of poor people, who are aged, diseased, or maimed, and I have been desired to employ my thoughts what course may be taken, to ease the nation of so grievous an encumbrance. But I am not in the least pain upon that matter, because it is very well known, that they are every day dying, and rotting, by cold, and famine, and filth, and vermin, as fast as can be reasonably expected. And as to the younger labourers, they are now in almost as hopeful a condition. They cannot get work, and consequently pine away for want of nourishment, to a degree, that if at any time they are accidentally hired to common labour, they have not strength to perform it, and thus the country and themselves are happily delivered from the evils to come.

I have too long digressed, and therefore shall return to my subject. I think the advantages by the proposal which I have made are obvious and many, as well as of the highest importance.

For *first,* as I have already observed, it would greatly lessen the number of papists, with whom we are yearly over-run, being the principal breeders of the nation, as well as our most dangerous enemies, and who stay at home on purpose with a design to deliver the kingdom to the Pretender, hoping to take their advantage by the absence of so many good Protestants, who have chosen rather to leave their country, than stay at home, and pay tithes against their conscience to an episcopal curate.

Secondly, the poorer tenants will have something valuable of their own which by law may be made liable to distress, and help to pay their landlord's rent, their corn and cattle being already seized, and money a thing unknown.

Thirdly, whereas the maintenance of an hundred thousand children, from two years old, and upwards, cannot be computed at less than ten shillings a piece per annum, the nation's stock will be thereby increased fifty thousand pounds per annum, besides the profit of a new dish, introduced to the tables of all gentlemen of fortune in the kingdom who have any refinement in taste, and the money will circulate among our selves, the goods being entirely of our own growth and manufacture.

Fourthly, the constant breeders, besides the gain of eight shillings sterling per annum, by the sale of their children, will be rid of the charge of maintaining them after the first year.

Fifthly, this food would likewise bring great custom to taverns, where the vintners will certainly be so prudent as to procure the best receipts for dressing it to perfection; and consequently have their houses frequented by all the fine gentlemen, who justly value themselves upon their knowledge in good eating; and a skilful cook, who understands how to oblige his guests, will contrive to make it as expensive as they please.

Sixthly, this would be a great inducement to marriage, which all wise nations have either encouraged by rewards, or enforced by laws and penalties. It would encrease the care and tenderness of mothers towards their children, when they were sure of a settlement for life to the poor babes, provided in some sort by the publick, to their annual profit instead of expence; we should soon see an honest emulation among the married women, which of them could bring the fattest child to the market. Men would become as fond of their wives during the time of their pregnancy, as they are now of their mares in foal, their cows in calf, or sows when they are ready to farrow, nor offer to beat or kick them (as is too frequent a practice) for fear of a miscarriage.

Many other advantages might be enumerated. For instance, the addition of some thousand carcasses in our exportation of barreled beef: the propagation of swine's flesh, and improvement in the art of making good bacon, so much wanted among us by the great destruction of pigs, too frequent at our tables, which are no way comparable in taste or magnificence to a well grown, fat yearling child, which roasted whole will make a considerable figure at a Lord Mayor's feast, or any other publick entertainment. But this, and many others, I omit, being studious of brevity.

Supposing that one thousand families in this city, would be constant customers for infant's flesh, besides others who might have it at merry meetings, particularly at weddings and christenings, I compute that Dublin would take off annually about twenty thousand carcasses, and the rest of the kingdom (where probably they will be sold somewhat cheaper) the remaining eighty thousand.

I can think of no one objection, that will possibly be raised against this proposal, unless it should be urged, that the number of people will be thereby much lessened in the kingdom. This I freely own, and 'twas indeed one principal design in offering it to the world. I desire the reader will observe, that I calculate my remedy for this one individual kingdom of Ireland, and for no other that ever was, is, or, I think, ever can be upon earth. Therefore let no man talk to me of other expedients: of taxing our absentees at five shilling a pound: of using neither cloths, nor household furniture, except what is of our own growth and manufacture: of utterly rejecting the materials and instruments that promote foreign luxury: of curing the expensiveness of pride, vanity, idleness, and gaming in our women: of introducing a vein of parsimony, prudence and temperance: of learning to love our country, wherein we differ even from Laplanders, and the inhabitants of Topinamboo: of quitting our animosities, and factions, nor act any longer like the Jews, who were murdering one another at the very moment their city was taken: of being a little cautious not to sell our country and consciences for nothing: of teaching landlords to have at least one degree of mercy towards their tenants. Lastly, of putting a spirit of honesty, industry, and skill into our shop-keepers, who, if a resolution could now be taken to buy only our native goods, would immediately unite to cheat and exact upon us in the price, the measure, and the goodness, nor could ever yet be brought to make one fair proposal of just dealing, though often and earnestly invited to it.

Therefore I repeat, let no man talk to me of these and the like expedients, till he hath at least some glimpse of hope, that there will ever be some hearty and sincere attempt to put them in practice.

But as to my self, having been wearied out for many years with offering vain, idle, visionary thoughts, and at length utterly despairing of success, I fortunately fell upon this proposal, which as it is wholly new, so it hath something solid and real, of no expense and little trouble, full in our own power, and whereby we can incur no danger in disobliging England. For this kind of commodity will not bear exportation, the flesh being of too tender a consistence, to admit a long continuance in salt, although perhaps I could name a country, which would be glad to eat up our whole nation without it.

After all, I am not so violently bent upon my own opinion, as to reject any offer, proposed by wise men, which shall be found equally innocent, cheap, easy, and effectual. But before something of that kind shall be advanced in contradiction to my scheme, and offering a better, I desire the author or authors, will be pleased maturely to consider two points. *First,* as things now stand, how they will be able to find food and raiment for a hundred thousand useless mouths and backs. And *Secondly,* there being a round million of creatures in human figure throughout this kingdom, whose whole subsistence put into a common stock would leave them in debt two millions of pounds sterling, adding those—who are beggars by profession, to the bulk of farmers, cottagers and labourers, with their wives and children, who are beggars in effect; I desire those politicians, who dislike my overture, and may perhaps be so bold to attempt an answer, that they will first ask the parents of these mortals, whether they would not at this day think it a great happiness to have been sold for food at a year old, in the manner I prescribe, and thereby have avoided such a perpetual scene of misfortunes as they have since gone through, by the oppression of landlords, the impossibility of paying rent without money or trade, the want of common sustenance, with neither house nor clothes to cover them from the inclemencies of the weather, and the most inevitable prospect of entailing the like, or greater miseries, upon their breed for ever.

I profess in the sincerity of my heart, that I have not the least personal interest in endeavouring to promote this necessary work, having no other motive than the publick good of my country, by advancing our trade, providing for infants, relieving the poor, and giving some pleasure to the rich. I have no children by which I can propose to get a single penny; the youngest being nine years old and my wife past child-bearing.

LETTER FROM THE RECORDING ANGEL*

Samuel Langhorne Clemens (Mark Twain)
(1835–1910)

Office of the Recording Angel
Department of Petitions, Jan. 20
Andrew Langdon
Coal Dealer
Buffalo, N.Y.

I have the honor, as per command, to inform you that your recent act of benevolence and self-sacrifice has been recorded upon a page by itself of the Book called *Golden Deeds of Men:* a distinction, I am permitted to remark, which is not merely extraordinary, it is unique.

As regards your prayers, for the week end-

* From *Captain Stormfield's Visit to Heaven*

ing the 19th, I have the honor to report as follows:

1. For weather to advance hard coal 15 cents per ton. Granted.

2. For influx of laborers to reduce wages 10 per cent. Granted.

3. For a break in rival soft-coal prices. Granted.

4. For a visitation upon the man, or upon the family of the man, who has set up a competing retail coal-yard in Rochester. Granted, as follows: diphtheria, 2, 1 fatal; scarlet fever, 1, to result in deafness and imbecility. *Note.* This prayer should have been directed against this subordinate's principals, the N. Y. Central R. R. Co.

5. For deportation to Sheol of annoying swarms of persons who apply daily for work, or for favors of one sort or another. Taken under advisement for later decision and compromise, this petition appearing to conflict with another one of same date, which will be cited further along.

6. For application of some form of violent death to neighbor who threw brick at family cat, whilst the same was serenading. Reserved for consideration and compromise, because of conflict with a prayer of even date to be cited further along.

7. To "damn the missionary cause." Reserved also—as above.

8. To increase December profits of $22,230 to $45,000 for January, and perpetuate a proportionate monthly increase thereafter —"which will satisfy you." The prayer granted; the added remark accepted with reservations.

9. For cyclone, to destroy the works and fill up the mine of the North Pennsylvania Co. *Note.* Cyclones are not kept in stock in the winter season. A reliable article of firedamp can be furnished upon application.

Especial note is made of the above list, they being of particular moment. The 298 remaining supplications classifiable under the head of Special Providences, Schedule A, for week ending 19th, are granted in a body, except that 3 of the 32 cases requiring immediate death have been modified to incurable disease.

This completes the week's invoice of petitions known to this office under the technical designation of Secret Supplications of the Heart, and which for a reason which may suggest itself, always receive our first and especial attention.

The remainder of the week's invoice falls under the head of what we term Public Prayers, in which classification we place prayers uttered in Prayer Meeting, Sunday School Class Meeting, Family Worship, etc. These kinds of prayers have value according to classification of Christian uttering them. By rule of this office, Christians are divided into two grand classes, to wit: 1, Professing Christians; 2, Professional Christians. These, in turn, are minutely subdivided and classified by size, species, and family; and finally, standing is determined by carats, the minimum being 1, the maximum 1,000.

As per balance-sheet for quarter ending Dec. 31, 1847, you stood classified as follows: *Grand Classification,* Professing Christian. *Size,* one-fourth of maximum. *Species,* Human-Spiritual. *Family,* A of the Elect, Division 16. *Standing,* 322 carats fine.

As per balance-sheet for quarter just ended —that is to say, forty years later—you stand classified as follows: *Grand Classification,* Professional Christian. *Size,* six one-hundredths of maximum. *Species,* Human-Animal. *Family,* W of the Elect, Division 1547. *Standing,* 3 carats fine.

I have the honor to call your attention to the fact that you seem to have deteriorated.

To resume report upon your Public Prayers—with the side remark that in order to encourage Christians of your grade and of approximate grades, it is the custom of this office to grant many things to them which would not be granted to Christians of a higher grade—partly because they would not be asked for:

Prayer for weather mercifully tempered to the needs of the poor and the naked. Denied. This was a Prayer-Meeting Prayer. It conflicts with Item 1 of this report, which was a Secret Supplication of the Heart. By a rigid rule of this office, certain sorts of Public Prayers of Professional Christians are forbidden to take precedence of Secret Supplications of the Heart.

Prayer for better times and plentier food "for the hard-handed son of toil whose patient and exhausting labors make comfortable the homes, and pleasant the ways, of the more fortunate, and entitle him to our vigilant and effective protection from the wrongs and injustices which grasping avarice would do him, and to the tenderest offices of our grateful hearts." Prayer-Meeting Prayer. Refused. Conflicts with Secret Supplication of the Heart No. 2.

Prayer "that such as in any way obstruct our preferences may be generously blessed, both themselves and their families, we here calling our hearts to witness that in their worldly prosperity we are spiritually blessed, and our joys made perfect." Prayer-Meeting Prayer. Refused. Conflicts with Secret Supplications of the Heart Nos. 3 and 4.

"Oh, let none fall heir to the pains of perdition through words or acts of ours." Family Worship. Received fifteen minutes in advance of Secret Supplication of the Heart No. 5, with which it distinctly conflicts. It is suggested that one or the other of these prayers be withdrawn, or both of them modified.

"Be mercifully inclined toward all who would do us offense in our persons or our property." Includes man who threw brick at cat. Family Prayer. Received some minutes in advance of No. 6, Secret Supplications of the Heart. Modification suggested, to reconcile discrepancy.

"Grant that the noble missionary cause, the most precious labor entrusted to the hands of men, may spread and prosper without let or limit in all heathen lands that do as yet reproach us with their spiritual darkness." Uninvited prayer shoved in at meeting of American Board. Received nearly half a day in advance of No. 7, Secret Supplications of the Heart. This office takes no stock in missionaries, and is not connected in any way with the American Board. We should like to grant one of these prayers but cannot

grant both. It is suggested that the American Board one be withdrawn.

This office desires for the twentieth time to call urgent attention to your remark appended to No. 8. It is a chestnut.

Of the 464 specifications contained in your Public Prayers for the week, and not previously noted in this report, we grant 2, and deny the rest. To-wit: Granted, (1) "that the clouds may continue to perform their office; (2), and the sun his." It was the divine purpose anyhow; it will gratify you to know that you have not disturbed it. Of the 462 details refused, 61 were uttered in Sunday School. In this connection I must once more remind you that we grant no Sunday School Prayers of Professional Christians of the classification technically known in this office as the John Wanamaker grade. We merely enter them as "words," and they count to his credit according to number uttered within certain limits of time; 3,000 per quarter-minute required, or no score; 4,200 in a possible 5,000 is a quite common Sunday School score among experts, and counts the same as two hymns and a bouquet furnished by young ladies in the assassin's cell, execution-morning. Your remaining 401 details count for wind only. We bunch them and use them for head-winds in retarding the ships of improper people, but it takes so many of them to make an impression that we cannot allow anything for their use.

I desire to add a word of my own to this report. When certain sorts of people do a sizable good deed, we credit them up a thousand-fold more for it than we would in the case of a better man—on account of the strain. You stand far away above your classification-record here, because of certain self-sacrifices of yours which greatly exceed what could have been expected of you. Years ago, when you were worth only $100,000, and sent $2 to your impoverished cousin the widow when she appealed to you for help, there were many in heaven who were not able to believe it, and many more who believed that the money was counterfeit. Your character went up many degrees when it was shown that these suspicions were unfounded.

A year or two later, when you sent the poor girl $4 in answer to another appeal, everybody believed it, and you were all the talk here for days together. Two years later you sent $6, upon supplication, when the widow's youngest child died, and that act made perfect your good fame. Everybody in heaven said, "Have you heard about Andrew?"—for you are now affectionately called Andrew here. Your increasing donation, every two or three years, has kept your name on all lips, and warm in all hearts. All heaven watches you Sundays, as you drive to church in your handsome carriage; and when your hand retires from the contribution plate, the glad shout is heard even to the ruddy walls of remote Sheol, "Another nickel from Andrew!"

But the climax came a few days ago, when the widow wrote and said she could get a school in a far village to teach if she had $50 to get herself and her two surviving children over the long journey; and you counted up last month's clear profit from your three coal mines—$22,230—and added to it the certain profit for the current month—$45,000 and a possible fifty—and then got down your pen and your check-book and mailed her *fifteen whole dollars!* Ah, Heaven bless and keep you forever and ever, generous heart! There was not a dry eye in the realms of bliss; and amidst the hand-shakings, and embracings, and praisings, the decree was thundered forth from the shining mount, that this deed should out-honor all the historic self-sacrifices of men and angels, and be recorded by itself upon a page of its own, for that the strain of it upon you had been heavier and bitterer than the strain it costs ten thousand martyrs to yield up their lives at the fiery stake; and all said, "What is the giving up of life, to a noble soul, or to ten thousand noble souls, compared with the giving up of fifteen dollars out of the greedy grip of the meanest white man that ever lived on the face of the earth?"

And it was a true word. And Abraham, weeping, shook out the contents of his bosom and pasted the eloquent label there, *"Reserved";* and Peter, weeping, said, "He shall be received with a torchlight procession when he comes"; and then all heaven boomed, and was glad you were going there. And so was hell.

[Signed]
THE RECORDING ANGEL [Seal.]
By command.

A DISSERTATION UPON ROAST PIG

Charles Lamb
(1775-1834)

Mankind, says a Chinese manuscript, which my friend M. was obliging enough to read and explain to me, for the first seventy thousand ages ate their meat raw, clawing or biting it from the living animal, just as they do in Abyssinia to this day. This period is not obscurely hinted at by their great Confucius in the second chapter of his Mundane Mutations, where he designates a kind of golden age by the term Cho-fang, literally the Cooks' holiday. The manuscript goes on to say, that the art of roasting, or rather broiling (which I take to be the elder brother) was accidentally discovered in the manner following. The swine-herd, Ho-ti, having gone out into the woods one morning, as his manner was, to collect mast for his hogs, left his cottage in the care of his eldest son Bo-bo, a great lubberly boy, who being fond of playing with fire, as younkers of his age commonly are, let some sparks escape into a bundle of straw, which kindling quickly, spread the conflagration over every part of their poor mansion till it was reduced to ashes. Together with the cottage (a sorry antediluvian make-shift of a building, you may think it), what was of much more importance, a fine litter of new-farrowed pigs, no less than nine in number, perished. China pigs have been esteemed a luxury all over the East from the remotest periods that we read of. Bo-bo was in the utmost consternation, as you may think, not so much for the sake of the tenement, which his father and he could easily build up again with a few dry branches, and the labour of an hour or two, at any time, as for the loss of the pigs. While he was thinking what he should say to his father, and wringing his hands over the smoking remnants of one of those untimely sufferers, an odour assailed his nostrils, unlike any scent which he had before experienced. What could it proceed from?—not from the burnt cottage—he had smelt that smell before—indeed, this was by no means the first accident of the kind which had occurred through the negligence of this unlucky young firebrand. Much less did it resemble that of any known herb, weed, or flower. A premonitory moistening at the same time overflowed his nether lip. He knew not what to think. He next stooped down to feel the pig, if there were any signs of life in it. He burnt his fingers, and to cool them he applied them in his booby fashion to his mouth. Some of the crumbs of the scorched skin had come away with his fingers, and for the first time in his life (in the world's life indeed, for before him no man had known it) he tasted—*crackling!* Again he felt and fumbled at the pig. It did not burn him so much now, still he licked his fingers from a sort of habit. The truth at length broke into his slow understanding, that it was the pig that smelt so, and the pig that tasted so delicious; and surrendering himself up to the newborn pleasure, he fell to tearing up whole handfuls of the scorched skin with the flesh next it, and was cramming it down his throat in his beastly fashion, when his sire entered amid the smoking rafters, armed with retributory cudgel, and finding how affairs stood, began to rain blows upon the young rogue's shoulders, as thick as hail-stones, which Bo-bo heeded not any more than if they had been flies. The tickling pleasure, which he experienced in his lower regions, had rendered him quite callous to any inconveniences he might feel in those remote quarters. His father might lay on, but he could not beat him from his pig, till he had fairly made an end of it, when, becoming a little more sensible of his situation, something like the following dialogue ensued.

'You graceless whelp, what have you got there devouring? Is it not enough that you have burnt me down three houses with your dog's tricks, and be hanged to you, but you must be eating fire, and I know not what—what have you got there, I say?'

'O father, the pig, the pig, do come and taste how nice the burnt pig eats.'

The ears of Ho-ti tingled with horror. He cursed his son, and he cursed himself that ever he should beget a son that should eat burnt pig.

Bo-bo, whose scent was wonderfully sharpened since morning, soon raked out another pig, and fairly rending it asunder, thrust the lesser half by main force into the fists of Ho-ti, still shouting out, 'Eat, eat, eat the burnt pig, father, only taste—O Lord!'—with such-like barbarous ejaculations, cramming all the while as if he would choke.

Ho-ti trembled every joint while he grasped the abominable thing, wavering whether he should not put his son to death for an unnatural young monster, when the crackling scorching his fingers, as it had done his son's, and applying the same remedy to them, he in his turn tasted some of its flavour, which, make what sour mouths he would for a pretence, proved not altogether displeasing to him. In conclusion (for the manuscript here is a little tedious), both father and son fairly set down to the mess, and never left off till they had despatched all that remained of the litter.

Bo-bo was strictly enjoined not to let the secret escape, for the neighbours would certainly have stoned them for a couple of abominable wretches, who could think of improving upon the good meat which God had sent them. Nevertheless, strange stories got about. It was observed that Ho-ti's cottage was burnt down now more frequently than ever. Nothing but fires from this time forward. Some would break out in broad day, others in the night-time. As often as the sow farrowed, so sure was the house of Ho-ti to be in a blaze; and Ho-ti himself, which was the more remarkable, instead of chastising his son, seemed to grow more indulgent to him than ever. At length they were watched, the terrible mystery discovered, and father

and son summoned to take their trial at Pe-
kin, then an inconsiderable assize town. Evidence was given, the obnoxious food itself
produced in court, and verdict about to be
pronounced, when the foreman of the jury
begged that some of the burnt pig, of which
the culprits stood accused, might be handed
into the box. He handled it, and they all handled it, and burning their fingers, as Bo-bo
and his father had done before them, and nature prompting to each of them the same
remedy, against the face of all the facts, and
the clearest charge which judge had ever
given—to the surprise of the whole court,
townsfolk, strangers, reporters, and all present—without leaving the box, or any manner
of consultation whatever, they brought in a
simultaneous verdict of Not Guilty.

The judge, who was a shrewd fellow,
winked at the manifest iniquity of the decision: and, when the court was dismissed,
went privily, and bought up all the pigs that
could be had for love or money. In a few
days his Lordship's town house was observed
to be on fire. The thing took wing, and now
there was nothing to be seen but fires in
every direction. Fuel and pigs grew enor-
mously dear all over the district. The insurance offices one and all shut up shop. People
built slighter and slighter every day, until it
was feared that the very science of architecture would in no long time be lost to the
world. Thus this custom of firing houses continued, till in process of time, says my manuscript, a sage arose, like our Locke, who
made a discovery, that the flesh of swine, or
indeed of any other animal, might be cooked
(*burnt,* as they called it) without the necessity of consuming a whole house to dress it.
Then first began the rude form of a gridiron.
Roasting by the string, or spit, came in a
century or two later, I forget in whose dy-
nasty. By such slow degrees, concludes the
manuscript, do the most useful, and seemingly the most obvious arts, make their way
among mankind.——

Without placing too implicit faith in the
account above given, it must be agreed that
if a worthy pretext for so dangerous an ex-
periment as setting houses on fire (especially

in these days) could be assigned in favour
of any culinary object, that pretext and excuse might be found in ROAST PIG.

Of all the delicacies in the whole *mundus
edibilis,** I will maintain it to be the most
delicate—*princeps obsoniorum.**

I speak not of your grown porkers—things
between pig and pork—those hobbledehoys
—but a young and tender suckling—under a
moon old—guiltless as yet of the sty—with
no original speck of the *amor immunditiæ,**
the hereditary failing of the first parent, yet
manifest—his voice as yet not broken, but
something between a childish treble and a
grumble—the mild forerunner or *præludium*
of a grunt.*

He must be roasted. I am not ignorant that
our ancestors ate them seethed, or boiled—
but what a sacrifice of the exterior tegument!

There is no flavour comparable, I will contend, to that of the crisp, tawny, well-
watched, not over-roasted, *crackling,* as it is
well called—the very teeth are invited to
their share of the pleasure at this banquet in
overcoming the coy, brittle resistance—
with the adhesive oleaginous—O call it not
fat! but an indefinable sweetness growing up
to it—the tender blossoming of fat—fat
cropped in the bud—taken in the shoot—in
the first innocence—the cream and quintes-
sence of the child-pig's yet pure food—the
lean, no lean, but a kind of animal manna
—or, rather, fat and lean (if it must be so)
so blended and running into each other, that
both together make but one ambrosian result
or common substance.

Behold him while he is 'doing'—it seemeth
rather a refreshing warmth, than a scorching
heat, that he is so passive to. How equably
he twirleth round the string! Now he is just
done. To see the extreme sensibility of that
tender age! he hath wept out his pretty eyes
—radiant jellies—shooting stars.—

See him in the dish, his second cradle, how
meek he lieth!—wouldst thou have had this
innocent grow up to the grossness and in-
docility which too often accompany maturer

* *Mundus edibilis,* world of edible things; *princeps obsoniorum,* chief of relishes; *amor immundi-
tiae,* love of uncleanliness; *praeludium,* prelude.

swinehood? Ten to one he would have proved a glutton, a sloven, an obstinate, disagreeable animal—wallowing in all manner of filthy conversation—from these sins he is happily snatched away—

Ere sin could blight, or sorrow fade,

Death came with timely care—

his memory is odoriferous—no clown curseth, while his stomach half rejecteth, the rank bacon—no coalheaver bolteth him in reeking sausages—he hath a fair sepulchre in the grateful stomach of the judicious epicure—and for such a tomb might be content to die.

He is the best of Sapors. Pine-apple is great. She is indeed almost too transcendent —a delight, if not sinful, yet so like to sinning, that really a tender-conscienced person would do well to pause—too ravishing for mortal taste, she woundeth and excoriateth the lips that approach her—like lovers kisses, she biteth—she is a pleasure bordering on pain from the fierceness and insanity of her relish—but she stoppeth at the palate —she meddleth not with the appetite—and the coarsest hunger might barter her consistently for a mutton chop.

Pig—let me speak his praise—is no less provocative of the appetite, than he is satisfactory to the criticalness of the censorious palate. The strong man may batten on him, and the weakling refuseth not his mild juices.

Unlike to mankind's mixed characters, a bundle of virtues and vices, inexplicably intertwisted, and not to be unravelled without hazard, he is—good throughout. No part of him is better or worse than another. He helpeth, as far as his little means extend, all around. He is the least envious of banquets. He is all neighbours' fare.

I am one of those who freely and ungrudgingly impart a share of the good things of this life which fall to their lot (few as mine are in this kind) to a friend. I protest I take as great an interest in my friend's pleasures, his relishes, and proper satisfactions, as in mine own. 'Presents,' I often say, 'endear Absents.' Hares, pheasants, partridges, snipes, barn-door chickens (those 'tame villatic fowl'), capons, plovers, brawn, barrels of oysters, I dispense as freely as I receive them.

I love to taste them, as it were, upon the tongue of my friend. But a stop must be put somewhere. One would not, like Lear, 'give everything.' I make my stand upon pig. Methinks it is an ingratitude to the Giver of all good flavours to extra-domiciliate, or send out of the house slightingly (under pretext of friendship, or I know not what) a blessing so particularly adapted, predestined, I may say, to my individual palate.—It argues an insensibility.

I remember a touch of conscience in this kind at school. My good old aunt, who never parted from me at the end of a holiday without stuffing a sweetmeat, or some nice thing, into my pocket, had dismissed me one evening with a smoking plum-cake, fresh from the oven. In my way to school (it was over London Bridge) a grey-headed old beggar saluted me (I have no doubt, at this time of day, that he was a counterfeit). I had no pence to console him with, and in the vanity of self-denial, and the very coxcombry of charity, schoolboy like, I made him a present of—the whole cake! I walked on a little, buoyed up, as one is on such occasions, with a sweet soothing of self-satisfaction; but, before I had got to the end of the bridge, my better feelings returned, and I burst into tears, thinking how ungrateful I had been to my good aunt, to go and give her good gift away to a stranger, that I had never seen before, and who might be a bad man for aught I knew; and then I thought of the pleasure my aunt would be taking in thinking that I—I myself, and not another—would eat her nice cake—and what should I say to her the next time I saw her—how naughty I was to part with her pretty present—and the odour of that spicy cake came back upon my recollection, and the pleasure and the curiosity I had taken in seeing her make it, and her joy when she sent it to the oven, and how disappointed she would feel that I had never had a bit of it in my mouth at last—and I blamed my impertinent spirit of alms-giving, and out-of-place hypocrisy of goodness, and above all I wished never to see the face again of that insidious, good-for-nothing, old grey impostor.

Our ancestors were nice in their methods of sacrificing these tender victims. We read of pigs whipt to death with something of a shock, as we hear of any other obsolete custom. The age of discipline is gone by, or it would be curious to inquire (in a philosophical light merely) what effect this process might have towards intenerating and dulcifying a substance, naturally so mild and dulcet as the flesh of young pigs. It looks like refining a violet. Yet we should be cautious, while we condemn the inhumanity, how we censure the wisdom of the practice. It might impart a gusto—

I remember an hypothesis, argued upon by the young students, when I was at St. Omer's, and maintained with much learning and pleasantry on both sides, "Whether, supposing that the flavor of a pig who obtained his death by whipping (*per flagellationem extremam*),* superadded a pleasure upon the palate of a man more intense than any possible suffering we can conceive in the animal, is man justified in using that method of putting the animal to death?" I forget the decision.

His sauce should be considered. Decidedly, a few bread-crumbs, done up with his liver and brains, and a dash of mild sage. But banish, dear Mrs. Cook, I beseech you, the whole onion tribe. Barbecue your whole hogs to your palate, steep them in shalots, stuff them out with plantations of the rank and guilty garlic; you cannot poison them, or make them stronger than they are,—but consider, he is a weakling—a flower.

* By severe whipping.

ON THE NEED FOR A QUIET COLLEGE*

Stephen Leacock
(1869–1944)

If somebody would give me about two dozen very old elm trees and about fifty acres

* From *Stephen Leacock's Laugh Parade*.

of wooded ground and lawn—not too near anywhere and not too far from everywhere —I think I could set up a college that would put all the big universities of today in the shade. I am not saying that it would be better. But it would be different.

I would need a few buildings, but it doesn't take many—stone, if possible—and a belfry and a clock. The clock wouldn't need to go; it might be better if it didn't. I would want some books—a few thousand would do —and some apparatus. But it is amazing how little apparatus is needed for scientific work of the highest quality: in fact "the higher the fewer."

Most of all, I should need a set of professors. I would need only a dozen of them— but they'd have to be real ones—disinterested men of learning, who didn't even know they were disinterested. And, mind you, these professors of mine wouldn't sit in "offices" dictating letters on "cases" to stenographers, and only leaving their offices to go to "committees" and "conferences." There would be no "offices" in my college and no "committees," and my professors would have no time for conferences, because the job they would be on would need all eternity and would never be finished.

My professors would never be findable at any fixed place except when they were actually giving lectures. Men of thought have no business in an office. Learning runs away from "committee." There would be no "check up" on the time of the professors: there would be no "hire and fire" or "judge by results" or "standards" or "norms" or work for them: or any fixed number of hours.

But, on the other hand, they would, if I got the ones I want, be well worth their apparent irresponsibility: and when they lectured each one would be, though he wouldn't know it, a magician—with such an interest and absorption that those who listened would catch the infection of it, and hurry from the lecture to the library, still warm with thought.

It must be understood that the work of professors is peculiar. Few professors, real ones, ever complete their work: what they give to the world is fragments. The rest remains. Their contributions must be added up, not measured singly. Every professor has his "life work" and sometimes does it, and sometimes dies first.

I can recall—I say it by way of digression—one such who was working on Machiavelli. When I first met him he had worked fourteen years. He worked in a large room covered a foot deep with Machiavelli—notes, pamphlets, remains. I asked him—it seemed a simple question—what he thought of Machiavelli. He shook his head. He said it was too soon to form an opinion. Later, ten years later, he published his book, *Machiavelli*. One of the great continental reviews—one of the really great ones (you and I never hear of them: they have a circulation of about 300) said his work was based on premature judgments. He was hurt, but he felt it was true. He had rushed into print too soon.

Another such devoted himself—he began years ago—to the history of the tariff. He began in a quiet lull of tariff changes when for three or four years public attention was elsewhere. He brought his work up to within a year or so of actual up-to-date completeness. Then the tariff began to move: two years later he was three years behind it. Presently, though he had worked hard, he was five years behind it.

He has never caught it. His only hope now is that the tariff will move back towards free trade, and meet him.

Not that I mean to imply that my professors would be a pack of nuts or freaks. Not at all: their manners might be dreamy and their clothes untidy but they'd be—they'd have to be—the most eminent men in their subjects. To get them would be the main effort of the college: to coax them, buy them, if need be, to kidnap them. Nothing counts beside that. A college is made of men, not by the size of buildings, number of students and footballs records. But trustees don't know this, or, at best, catch only a glimmer of it and lose it. Within a generation all the greatest books on the humanities would come from my college.

The professors bring the students. The students bring, unsought, the benefactions. The thing feeds itself like a flame in straw. But it's the men that count. A college doesn't need students: it's the students who need the college. After twenty years my college would stand all alone. There are little colleges now but they ape bigness. There are quiet colleges but they try to be noisy. There are colleges without big games but they boom little ones. Mine would seem the only one, because the chance is there, wide open, and no one takes it. After twenty years people would drive in motor cars to see my college: and wouldn't be let in.

Round such a college there must be no thought of money. Money ruins life: I mean, to have to think of it, to take account of it, to know that it is there. Men apart from money, men in an army, men on an expedition of exploration, emerge to a new life. Money is gone. At times and places whole classes thus lift up, or partly: as in older countries like England the class called "gentry" that once was. These people lived on land and money from the past—stolen, perhaps, five hundred years ago—and so thought no more of it. They couldn't earn more; they didn't know how. They kept what they had, or dropped out, fell through a trestle bridge of social structure and were gone in the stream. This class, in America, we never had. They grow rare everywhere. Perhaps we don't want them. But they had the good luck that, in their lives, money in the sense here meant, didn't enter. Certain money limits circumscribed their life, but from day to day they never thought of it. A cow in a pasture, a fairly generous pasture, doesn't know it's in. It thinks it's outside. So did they.

So I would have it in my college. Students not rich and not poor—or not using their wealth and not feeling their poverty—an equality as unconscious as that where Evangeline lived.

Nor would their studies lead to, or aim at, or connect with wealth. The so-called practical studies are all astray. Real study, real learning must, for the individual, be quite valueless or it loses its value. The proper studies for my college are history and literature and philosophy and thought and poetry and speculation, in the pursuit of which each shall repeat the eager search, the unending quest, of the past. Looking for one thing he shall find another. Looking for ultimate truth, which is unfindable, they will learn at least to repudiate all that is false.

I leave out at one sweep great masses of stuff usually taught: all that goes under such a name as a university faculty of Commerce. There is no such thing. The faculty of Commerce is down at the docks, at Wall Street, in the steel mills. A "degree" in Commerce is a salary of ten thousand a year. Those who fail to pass go to Atlanta—and stay there. Certain things in Commerce are teachable: accountancy, corporate organization and the principles of embezzlement. But that's not a university.

Out goes economics, except as speculation: not a thing to teach in instalments and propositions like geometry. You *can't* teach it. No one knows it. It's the riddle of the Sphinx. My graduates will be just nicely fitted to think about it when they come out. A first-year girl studying economics is as wide of the mark as an old man studying cosmetics. The philosophical speculative analysis of our economic life is the highest study of all, next to the riddle of our existence, but to cut it into classes and credits is a parody. Out it goes.

Out—but to come back again—goes medicine. Medicine is a great reality: it belongs in a *school,* not a college. My college fits people to study medicine, study it in crowded cities among gas-lights and ambulances and hospitals and human suffering, and keep their souls alive while they do it. Then later, as trained men in the noblest profession in the world, the atmosphere of the college, which they imbibed among my elm trees, grows about them again. The last word in cultivation is, and always has been, the cultivated "medicine man."

The engineers?—that's different. Theirs is the most "manly" of all the professions—among water power and gold mines and throwing bridges half a mile at a throw. But it's a *school* that trains them, not a college. They go to my college but they don't like it. They say it's too damn dreamy. So they kick out of it into engineering. For a time they remember the Latin third declension. Presently they forget it. Doctors grow cultivated as they grow older. Engineers get rougher and rougher.

What I mean is that our studies have drifted away, away from the single-minded absorption of learning. Our students of to-day live in a whirl and clatter of "student activities." They have, in any large college, at least a hundred organizations and societies. They are "all up!" for this today and "all out!" for that tomorrow. Life is a continuous rally! a rah, rah! a parade! They play no games: they use teams for that. But exercise, and air, is their life. They *root,* in an organized hysteria, a code of signals telling them what to feel. They root, they rush, they organize, they play politics, run newspapers—and when they step from college into life, they fit it absolutely, having lived already.

No one is denying here what fine men and women college makes, physically fine and mentally alert. Any one of them could run an elevator the day he steps out of college. But there's something wanting: do they *think?* Or is there anything after all to think about? And yet, surely, in the long run the world has lived on its speculative minds. Or hasn't it?

Some who think of course there must be. You can't submerge humanity in two generations. But mostly, I believe, the little poets fade out on their first-year benches, and the wistful intelligence learns to say *"Rah! Rah!"* and is lost.

Not so in my college. There will be no newspaper, except a last week's paper from the back counties of New England. There will be no politics because there will be no offices to run for. My students will control nothing. The whole movement of student control is a mistake. They're so busy controlling that they're not students.

They shall play games all they want to, but as games, not as a profession, not as college advertising—and no gate receipts. Till only a few years ago the country that taught the world its games, played them as apart from money—as far apart as sheer necessity allowed. If Waterloo was won on the playing fields of Eton (it wasn't, really: it was won in Belgium), there was at least no stadium at two dollars a seat.

One asks, perhaps, about the endowments, about the benefactors of my ideal college. The benefactors are all dead: or at least they must act as if they were. Years ago on the prairies many authorities claimed that the only good Indian was a dead Indian. It may not have been true. But it is certainly true that the best college benefactor is a dead one. After all, the reward in the long run is his, those sculptured letters graven in the stone, "To the greater glory of God and in memory of Johannes Smith." That, in a college among elm trees—that's worth a lifetime of gifts, given and given gladly. Such things should best be graven in Latin. In my college they will be; Latin and lots of it, all over the place, with the mystic conspiracy of pretence, the wholesome humbug, that those who see it know what it means. Latin lasts. English seems to alter every thousand years or so. It's like the tariff that I named above—too mobile for academic use.

As with the benefactors, so with the managing trustees who look after the money and never lose it. Not dead, these, but very silent: solid men who don't need to talk and don't, but who can invest a million dollars over three depressions, and there it still is, like gold in a pot in the Pyramids. You find them chiefly in New England, at least I seem to have seen them there, more than anywhere else. They are at the head of huge investment businesses, so big that you never hear of them. Mostly, if they don't talk, it means that they are thinking where to place fifty million dollars. You see, they hate to break it.

And women? The arrangements in my college for the women students, and the women's dormitories? Oh, no—no, thank you. There aren't any women. Coeducation is a wonderful thing for women: college girls under coeducation leave college more fit to leave college than any others. College girls are better companions, better wives (as your own or as someone else's) than any others. It's the women who have made our college life the bright, happy thing it is—too bright, too happy.

But men can't study when women are around. And it's not only the students. If I let the women in, they'd get round some of my dusty old professors, and marry them—and good-bye to Machiavelli, and the higher thought.

THE DOOR*

E. B. White
(1899–   )

Everything (he kept saying) is something it isn't. And everybody is always somewhere else. Maybe it was the city, being in the city, that made him feel how queer everything was and that it was something else. Maybe (he kept thinking) it was the names of the things. The names were tex and frequently koid. Or they were flex and oid or they were duroid (sani) or flexsan (duro), but everything was glass (but not quite glass) and the thing that you touched (the surface, washable, crease-resistant) was rubber, only it wasn't quite rubber and you didn't quite touch it but almost. The wall, which was glass but thrutex, turned out on being approached not to be a wall, it was something else, it was an opening or doorway—and the doorway (through which he saw himself approaching) turned out to be something else, it was a wall. And what he had eaten not having agreed with him.

He was in a washable house, but he wasn't sure. Now about those rats, he kept saying to himself. He meant the rats that the Professor had driven crazy by forcing them to deal with problems which were beyond the scope of rats, the insoluble problems. He meant the rats that had been trained to jump at the

* From *The Second Tree from the Corner.*

square card with the circle in the middle, and the card (because it was something it wasn't) would give way and let the rat into a place where the food was, but then one day it would be a trick played on the rat, and the card would be changed, and the rat would jump but the card wouldn't give way, and it was an impossible situation (for a rat) and the rat would go insane and into its eyes would come the unspeakably bright imploring look of the frustrated, and after the convulsions were over and the frantic racing around, then the passive stage would set in and the willingness to let anything be done to it, even if it was something else.

He didn't know which door (or wall) or opening in the house to jump at, to get through, because one was an opening that wasn't a door (it was a void, or koid) and the other was a wall that wasn't an opening, it was a sanitary cupboard of the same color. He caught a glimpse of his eyes staring into his eyes, in the thrutex, and in them was the expression he had seen in the picture of the rats—weary after convulsions and the frantic racing around, when they were willing and did not mind having anything done to them. More and more (he kept saying) I am confronted by a problem which is incapable of solution (for this time even if he chose the right door, there would be no food behind it) and that is what madness is, and things seeming different from what they are. He heard, in the house where he was, in the city to which he had gone (as toward a door which might, or might not, give way), a noise—not a loud noise but more of a low prefabricated humming. It came from a place in the base of the wall (or stat) where the flue carrying the filterable air was, and not far from the Minipiano, which was made of the same material nailbrushes are made of, and which was under the stairs. "This, too, has been tested," she said, pointing, but not at it, "and found viable." It wasn't a loud noise, he kept thinking, sorry that he had seen his eyes, even though it was through his own eyes that he had seen them.

First will come the convulsions (he said), then the exhaustion, then the willingness to

let anything be done. "And you better believe it *will* be."

All his life he had been confronted by situations which were incapable of being solved, and there was a deliberateness behind all this, behind this changing of the card (or door), because they would always wait till you had learned to jump at the certain card (or door)—the one with the circle —and then they would change it on you. There have been so many doors changed on me, he said, in the last twenty years, but it is now becoming clear that it is an impossible situation, and the question is whether to jump again, even though they ruffle you in the rump with a blast of air—to make you jump. He wished he wasn't standing by the Minipiano. First they would teach you the prayers and the Psalms, and that would be the right door (the one with the circle), and the long sweet words with the holy sound, and that would be the one to jump at to get where the food was. Then one day you jumped and it didn't give way, so that all you got was the bump on the nose, and the first bewilderment, the first young bewilderment.

I don't know whether to tell her about the door they substituted or not, he said, the one with the equation on it and the picture of the amoeba reproducing itself by division. Or the one with the photostatic copy of the check for thirty-two dollars and fifty cents. But the jumping was so long ago, although the bump is . . . how those old wounds hurt! Being crazy this way wouldn't be so bad if only, if only. If only when you put your foot forward to take a step, the ground wouldn't come up to meet your foot the way it does. And the same way in the street (only I may never get back to the street unless I jump at the right door), the curb coming up to meet your foot, anticipating ever so delicately the weight of the body, which is somewhere else. "We could take your name," she said, "and send it to you." And it wouldn't be so bad if only you could read a sentence all the way through without jumping (your eye) to something else on the same page; and then (he kept thinking) there was that man out in Jersey, the one who started to chop his trees down, one by one, the man who began talking about how he would take his house to pieces, brick by brick, because he faced a problem incapable of solution, probably, so he began to hack at the trees in the yard, began to pluck with trembling fingers at the bricks in the house. Even if a house is not washable, it is worth taking down. It is not till later that the exhaustion sets in.

But it is inevitable that they will keep changing the doors on you, he said, because that is what they are for; and the thing is to get used to it and not let it unsettle the mind. But that would mean not jumping, and you can't. Nobody cannot jump. There will be no not-jumping. Among rats, perhaps, but among people never. Everybody has to keep jumping at a door (the one with the circle on it) because that is the way everybody is, specially some people. You wouldn't want me, standing here, to tell you, would you, about my friend the poet (deceased) who said, "My heart has followed all my days something I cannot name"? (It had the circle on it.) And like many poets, although few so beloved, he is gone. It killed him, the jumping. First, of course, there were the preliminary bouts, the convulsions, and the calm and the willingness.

I remember the door with the picture of the girl on it (only it was spring), her arms outstretched in loveliness, her dress (it was the one with the circle on it) uncaught, beginning the slow, clear, blinding cascade— and I guess we would all like to try that door again, for it seemed like the way and for a while it was the way, the door would open and you would go through winged and exalted (like any rat) and the food would be there, the way the Professor had it arranged, everything O.K., and you had chosen the right door for the world was young. The time they changed that door on me, my nose bled for a hundred hours—how do you like that, Madam? Or would you prefer to show me further through this so strange house, or you could take my name and send it to me, for although my heart has followed all my days something I cannot name, I am

tired of the jumping and I do not know which way to go, Madam, and I am not even sure that I am not tried beyond the endurance of man (rat, if you will) and have taken leave of sanity. What are you following these days, old friend, after your recovery from the last bump? What is the name, or is it something you cannot name? The rats have a name for it by this time, perhaps, but I don't know what they call it. I call it plexikoid and it comes in sheets, something like insulating board, unattainable and ugli-proof.

And there was the man out in Jersey, because I keep thinking about his terrible necessity and the passion and trouble he had gone to all those years in the indescribable abundance of a householder's detail, building the estate and the planting of the trees and in spring the lawn-dressing and in fall the bulbs for the spring burgeoning, and the watering of the grass on the long light evenings in summer and the gravel for the driveway (all had to be thought out, planned) and the decorative borders, probably, the perennials and the bug spray, and the building of the house from plans of the architect, first the sills, then the studs, then the full corn in the ear, the floors laid on the floor timbers, smoothed, and then the carpets upon the smooth floors and the curtains and the rods therefor. And then, almost without warning, he would be jumping at the same old door and it wouldn't give: they had changed it on him, making life no longer supportable under the elms in the elm shade, under the maples in the maple shade.

"Here you have the maximum of openness in a small room."

It was impossible to say (maybe it was the city) what made him feel the way he did, and I am not the only one either, he kept thinking—ask any doctor if I am. The doctors, they know how many there are, they even know where the trouble is only they don't like to tell you about the prefrontal lobe because that means making a hole in your skull and removing the work of centuries. It took so long coming, this lobe, so many, many years. (Is it something you read in the paper, perhaps?) And now, the strain being so great, the door having been changed by the Professor once too often . . . but it only means a whiff of ether, a few deft strokes, and the higher animal becomes a little easier in his mind and more like the lower one. From now on, you see, that's the way it will be, the ones with the small prefrontal lobes will win because the other ones are hurt too much by this incessant bumping. They can stand just so much, eh, Doctor? (And what is that, pray, that you have in your hand?) Still, you never can tell, eh, Madam?

He crossed (carefully) the room, the thick carpet under him softly, and went toward the door carefully, which was glass and he could see himself in it, and which, at his approach, opened to allow him to pass through; and beyond he half expected to find one of the old doors that he had known, perhaps the one with the circle, the one with the girl her arms outstretched in loveliness and beauty before him. But he saw instead a moving stairway, and descended in light (he kept thinking) to the street below and to the other people. As he stepped off, the ground came up slightly, to meet his foot.

[THE AGE OF CHIVALRY IS GONE]*

Edmund Burke
(1729–1797)

It is now sixteen or seventeen years since I saw the Queen of France, then the dauphiness, at Versailles; and surely never lighted on this orb, which she hardly seemed to touch, a more delightful vision. I saw her just above the horizon, decorating and cheering the elevated sphere she just began to move in; glittering like the morning star, full of life, and splendour, and joy. Oh! what a revolution! and what an heart must I have, to contemplate without emotion that elevation and that fall! Little did I dream when she added titles of veneration to those of enthusiastic, distant, respectful love, that she

* From *Reflections on the Revolution in France.*

should ever be obliged to carry the sharp antidote against disgrace concealed in that bosom; little did I dream that I should have lived to see such disasters fallen upon her in a nation of gallant men, in a nation of men of honour and of cavaliers. I thought ten thousand swords must have leaped from their scabbards to avenge even a look that threatened her with insult.—But the age of chivalry is gone. That of sophisters, economists, and calculators, has succeeded; and the glory of Europe is extinguished for ever. Never, never more, shall we behold that generous loyalty to rank and sex, that proud submission, that dignified obedience, that subordination of the heart, which kept alive, even in servitude itself, the spirit of an exalted freedom. The unbought grace of life, the cheap defence of nations, the nurse of manly sentiment and heroic enterprise, is gone! It *is* gone, that sensibility of principle, that chastity of honour, which felt a stain like a wound, which inspired courage whilst it mitigated ferocity, which ennobled whatever it touched, and under which vice itself lost half its evil, by losing all its grossness.

This mixed system of opinion and sentiment had its origin in the ancient chivalry; and the principle, though varied in its appearance by the varying state of human affairs, subsisted and influenced through a long succession of generations, even to the time we live in. If it should ever be totally extinguished, the loss I fear will be great. It is this which has given its character to modern Europe. It is this which has distinguished it under all its forms of government, and distinguished it to its advantage, from the states of Asia, and possibly from those states which flourished in the most brilliant periods of the antique world. It was this which, without confounding ranks, had produced a noble equality, and handed it down through all the gradations of social life. It was this opinion which mitigated kings into companions, and raised private men to be fellows with kings. Without force, or opposition, it subdued the fierceness of pride and power; it obliged sovereigns to submit to the soft collar of social esteem, compelled stern authority to submit to elegance, and gave a dominating vanquisher of laws to be subdued by manners.

But now all is to be changed. All the pleasing illusions, which made power gentle, and obedience liberal, which harmonized the different shades of life, and which, by a bland assimilation, incorporated into politics the sentiments which beautify and soften private society, are to be dissolved by this new conquering empire of light and reason. All the decent drapery of life is to be rudely torn off. All the superadded ideas, furnished from the wardrobe of a moral imagination, which the heart owns, and the understanding ratifies, as necessary to cover the defects of our naked shivering nature, and to raise it to dignity in our own estimation, are to be exploded as a ridiculous, absurd, and antiquated fashion.

On this scheme of things, a king is but a man; a queen is but a woman; a woman is but an animal; and an animal not of the highest order. All homage paid to the sex in general as such, and without distinct views, is to be regarded as romance and folly. Regicide, and parricide, and sacrilege, are but fictions of superstition, corrupting jurisprudence by destroying its simplicity. The murder of a king, or a queen, or a bishop, or a father, are only common homicide; and if the people are by any chance, or in any way, gainers by it, a sort of homicide much the most pardonable, and into which we ought not to make too severe a scrutiny.

On the scheme of this barbarous philosophy, which is the offspring of cold hearts and muddy understandings, and which is as void of solid wisdom as it is destitute of all taste and elegance, laws are to be supported only by their own terrors, and by the concern which each individual may find in them from his own private speculations, or can spare to them from his own private interests. In the groves of *their* academy, at the end of every vista, you see nothing but the gallows. Nothing is left which engages the affections on the part of the commonwealth. On the principles of this mechanic philosophy, our institutions can never be embodied, if I may use the expression, in persons; so as to create in us love, veneration, admiration, or attachment. But that sort of reason which banishes the affections is incapable of filling their place. These public affections, combined with manners, are required sometimes as supplements, sometimes as correctives, always as aids to law. The precept given by a wise man, as well as a great critic, for the construction of poems is equally true as to states. *Non satis est pulchra esse poemata, dulcia sunto.* There ought to be a system of manners in every nation which a well-formed mind would be disposed to relish. To make us love our country, our country ought to be lovely.

But power, of some kind or other, will survive the shock in which manners and opinions perish; and it will find other and worse means for its support. The usurpation which, in order to subvert ancient institutions, has destroyed ancient principles, will hold power by arts similar to those by which it has acquired it. When the old feudal and chivalrous spirit of fealty, which, by freeing kings from fear, freed both kings and subjects from the precautions of tyranny, shall be extinct in the minds of men, plots and assassinations will be anticipated by preventive murder and preventive confiscation, and that long roll of grim and bloody maxims, which form the political code of all power, not standing on its own code of honour, and the honour of those who are to obey it. Kings will be tyrants from policy when subjects are rebels from principle.

WHERE I LIVED, AND WHAT I LIVED FOR*

Henry David Thoreau
(1817–1862)

I went to the woods because I wished to live deliberately, to front only the essential facts of life, and see if I could not learn what it had to teach, and not, when I came to die, discover that I had not lived. I did not wish to live what was not life, living is so dear; nor

* From *Walden.*

did I wish to practice resignation, unless it was quite necessary. I wanted to live deep and suck out all the marrow of life, to live so sturdily and Spartan-like as to put to rout all that was not life, to cut a broad swath and shave close, to drive life into a corner, and reduce it to its lowest terms, and, if it proved to be mean, why then to get the whole and genuine meanness of it, and publish its meanness to the world; or if it were sublime, to know it by experience, and be able to give a true account of it in my next excursion. For most men, it appears to me, are in a strange uncertainty about it, whether it is of the devil or of God, and have *somewhat hastily* concluded that it is the chief end of man here to "glorify God and enjoy him forever."

Still we live meanly, like ants; though the fable tells us that we were long ago changed into men; like pygmies we fight with cranes; it is error upon error, and clout upon clout, and our best virtue has for its occasion a superfluous and evitable wretchedness. Our life is frittered away by detail. An honest man has hardly need to count more than his ten fingers, or in extreme cases he may add his ten toes, and lump the rest. Simplicity, simplicity, simplicity! I say, let your affairs be as two or three, and not a hundred or a thousand; instead of a million count half a dozen, and keep your accounts on your thumb-nail. In the midst of this chopping sea of civilized life, such are the clouds and storms and quicksands and thousand-and-one items to be allowed for, that a man has to live, if he would not founder and go to the bottom and not make his port at all, by dead reckoning, and he must be a great calculator indeed who succeeds. Simplify, simplify. Instead of three meals a day, if it be necessary eat but one; instead of a hundred dishes, five; and reduce other things in proportion. Our life is like a German Confederacy, made up of petty states, with its boundary forever fluctuating, so that even a German cannot tell you how it is bounded at any moment. The nation itself, with all its so-called internal improvements, which, by the way are all external and superficial, is just such an unwieldy and overgrown establishment, clut-

tered with furniture and tripped up by its own traps, ruined by luxury and heedless expense, by want of calculation and a worthy aim, as the million households in the land; and the only cure for it, as for them, is in a rigid economy, a stern and more than Spartan simplicity of life and elevation of purpose. It lives too fast. Men think that it is essential that the *Nation* have commerce, and export ice, and talk through a telegraph, and ride thirty miles an hour, without a doubt, whether *they* do or not; but whether we should live like baboons or like men, is a little uncertain. If we do not get out sleepers, and forge rails, and devote days and nights to the work, but go to tinkering upon our *lives* to improve *them,* who will build railroads? And if railroads are not built, how shall we get to heaven in season? But if we stay at home and mind our business, who will want railroads? We do not ride on the railroad; it rides upon us. Did you ever think what those sleepers are that underlie the railroad? Each one is a man, an Irishman, or a Yankee man. The rails are laid on them, and they are covered with sand, and the cars run smoothly over them. They are sound sleepers, I assure you. And every few years a new lot is laid down and run over; so that, if some have the pleasure of riding on a rail, others have the misfortune to be ridden upon. And when they run over a man that is walking in his sleep, a supernumerary sleeper in the wrong position, and wake him up, they suddenly stop the cars, and make a hue and cry about it, as if this were an exception. I am glad to know that it takes a gang of men for every five miles to keep the sleepers down and level in their beds as it is, for this is a sign that they may sometime get up again.

Why should we live with such hurry and waste of life? We are determined to be starved before we are hungry. Men say that a stitch in time saves nine, and so they take a thousand stitches to-day to save nine tomorrow. As for *work,* we haven't any of any consequence. We have the Saint Vitus's dance, and cannot possibly keep our heads still. If I should only give a few pulls at the parish bell-rope, as for a fire, that is, without setting the bell, there is hardly a man on his farm in the outskirts of Concord, notwithstanding that press of engagements which was his excuse so many times this morning, nor a boy, nor a woman, I might almost say, but would forsake all and follow that sound, not mainly to save property from the flames, but, if we will confess the truth, much more to see it burn, since burn it must, and we, be it known, did not set it on fire,—or to see it put out, and have a hand in it, if that is done as handsomely; yes, even if it were the parish church itself. Hardly a man takes a half-hour's nap after dinner, but when he wakes he holds up his head and asks, "What's the news?" as if the rest of mankind had stood his sentinels. Some give directions to be waked every half-hour, doubtless for no other purpose; and then, to pay for it, they tell what they have dreamed. After a night's sleep the news is as indispensable as the breakfast. "Pray tell me anything new that has happened to a man anywhere on this globe,"—and he reads it over his coffee and rolls, that a man has had his eyes gouged out this morning on the Wachito River; never dreaming the while that he lives in the dark unfathomed mammoth cave of this world, and has but the rudiment of an eye himself.

For my part, I could easily do without the post-office. I think that there are very few important communications made through it. To speak critically, I never received more than one or two letters in my life—I wrote this some years ago—that were worth the postage. The penny-post is, commonly, an institution through which you seriously offer a man that penny for his thoughts which is so often safely offered in jest. And I am sure that I never read any memorable news in a newspaper. If we read of one man robbed, or murdered, or killed by accident, or one house burned, or one vessel wrecked, or one steamboat blown up, or one cow run over on the Western Railroad, or one mad dog killed, or one lot of grasshoppers in the winter,—we never need read of another. One is enough. If you are acquainted with the principle, what do you care for a myriad instances and applications? To a philosopher all *news*, as it is called, is gossip, and they who edit and read it are old women over their tea. Yet not a few are greedy after this gossip. There was such a rush, as I hear, the other day at one of the offices to learn the foreign news by the last arrival, that several large squares of plate glass belonging to the establishment were broken by the pressure,—news which I seriously think a ready wit might write a twelvemonth, or twelve years, beforehand with sufficient accuracy. As for Spain, for instance, if you know how to throw in Don Carlos and the Infanta, and Don Pedro and Seville and Granada, from time to time in the right proportions,—they may have changed the names a little since I saw the papers,—and serve up a bull-fight when other entertainments fail, it will be true to the letter, and give us as good an idea of the exact state or ruin of things in Spain as the most succinct and lucid reports under this head in the newspapers: and as for England, almost the last significant scrap of news from that quarter was the revolution of 1649; and if you have learned the history of her crops for an average year, you never need attend to that thing again, unless your speculations are of a merely pecuniary character. If one may judge who rarely looks into the newspapers, nothing new does ever happen in foreign parts, a French revolution not excepted.

What news! how much more important to know what that is which was never old! "Kieou-he-yu (great dignitary of the state of Wei) sent a man to Khoung-tseu to know his news. Khoung-tseu caused the messenger to be seated near him, and questioned him in these terms: What is your master doing? The messenger answered with respect: My master desires to diminish the number of his faults, but he cannot come to the end of them. The messenger being gone, the philosopher remarked: What a worthy messenger! What a worthy messenger!" The preacher, instead of vexing the ears of drowsy farmers on their day of rest at the end of the week,—for Sunday is the fit conclusion of an ill-spent week, and not the fresh and brave beginning of a new one,—with this one other draggle-tail of a sermon, should shout with thundering voice, "Pause! Avast! Why so seeming fast, but deadly slow?"

Shams and delusions are esteemed for soundest truths, while reality is fabulous. If men would steadily observe realities only, and not allow themselves to be deluded, life, to compare it with such things as we know, would be like a fairy tale and the Arabian Nights' Entertainments. If we respected only what is inevitable and has a right to be, music and poetry would resound along the streets. When we are unhurried and wise, we perceive that only great and worthy things have any permanent and absolute existence, that petty fears and petty pleasures are but the shadow of the reality. This is always exhilarating and sublime. By closing the eyes and slumbering, and consenting to be deceived by shows, men establish and confirm their daily life of routine and habit everywhere, which still is built on purely illusory foundations. Children, who play life, discern its true law and relations more clearly than men, who fail to live it worthily, but who think that they are wiser by experience, that is, by failure. I have read in a Hindoo book, that "there was a king's son, who, being expelled in infancy from his native city, was brought up by a forester, and, growing up to maturity in that state, imagined himself to belong to the barbarous race with which he lived. One of his father's ministers having discovered him, revealed to him what he was, and the misconception of his character was removed, and he knew himself to be a prince. So soul," continues the Hindoo philosopher, "from the circumstances in which it is placed, mistakes its own character, until the truth is revealed to it by some holy teacher, and then it knows itself to be *Brahme*." I perceive that we inhabitants of New England live this mean life that we do because our vision does not penetrate the surface of things. We think that that *is* which *appears* to be. If a man should walk through this town and see only the reality, where, think you, would the "Mill-dam" go to? If he should give us an account of the realities he beheld there, we should not recognize the place in his description. Look at a meeting-house, or a court-house, or a jail, or a shop, or a dwelling-house, and say what that thing really is before a true gaze, and they would all go to pieces in your account of them. Men esteem truth remote, in the outskirts of the system, behind the farthest star, before Adam and after the last man. In eternity there is indeed something true and sublime. But all these times and places and occasions are now and here. God himself culminates in the present moment, and will never be more divine in the lapse of all the ages. And we are enabled to apprehend at all what is sublime and noble only by the perpetual instilling and drenching of the reality that surrounds us. The universe constantly and obediently answers to our conceptions; whether we travel fast or slow, the track is laid for us. Let us spend our lives in conceiving then. The poet or the artist never yet had so fair and noble a design but some of his posterity at least could accomplish it.

Let us spend one day as deliberately as Nature, and not be thrown off the track by every nutshell and mosquito's wing that falls on the rails. Let us rise early and fast, or break fast, gently and without perturbation; let company come and let company go, let the bells ring and the children cry,—determined to make a day of it. Why should we knock under and go with the stream? Let us not be upset and overwhelmed in that terrible rapid and whirlpool called a dinner, situated in the meridian shallows. Weather this danger and you are safe, for the rest of the way is down hill. With unrelaxed nerves, with morning vigor, sail by it, looking another way, tied to the mast like Ulysses. If the engine whistles, let it whistle till it is hoarse for its pains. If the bell rings, why should we run? We will consider what kind of music they are like. Let us settle ourselves, and work and wedge our feet downward through the mud and slush of opinion, and prejudice, and tradition, and delusion, and appearance, that alluvion which covers the globe, through Paris and London, through New York and Boston and Concord, through Church and State, through poetry and philosophy and religion, till we come to a hard bottom and rocks in place, which we can call *reality,* and say, This is, and no mistake; and then begin, having a *point d'appui,* below freshet and frost and fire, a place where you might found a wall or a state, or set a lamppost safely, or perhaps a gauge, not a Nilometer, but a Realometer, that future ages might know how deep a freshet of shams and appearances had gathered from time to time. If you stand right fronting and face to face to a fact, you will see the sun glimmer on both its surfaces, as if it were a cimeter, and feel its sweet edge dividing you through the heart and marrow, and so you will happily conclude your mortal career. Be it life or death, we crave only reality. If we are really dying, let us hear the rattle in our throats and feel cold in the extremities; if we are alive, let us go about our business.

Time is but the stream I go a-fishing in. I drink at it; but while I drink I see the sandy bottom and detect how shallow it is. Its thin current slides away, but eternity remains. I would drink deeper; fish in the sky, whose bottom is pebbly with stars. I cannot count one. I know not the first letter of the alphabet. I have always been regretting that I was not as wise as the day I was born. The intellect is a cleaver; it discerns and rifts its way into the secret of things. I do not wish to be any more busy with my hands than is necessary. My head is hands and feet. I feel all my best faculties concentrated in it. My instinct tells me that my head is an organ for burrowing, as some creatures use their snout and fore paws, and with it I would mine and burrow my way through these hills. I think that the richest vein is somewhere hereabouts; so by the divining-rod and thin rising vapors I judge; and here I will begin to mine.

A FREE MAN'S WORSHIP*

Bertrand Russell
(1872–   )

To Dr. Faustus in his study Mephistopheles told the history of the Creation, saying:

* From *Mysticism and Logic.*

"The endless praises of the choirs of angels had begun to grow wearisome; for, after all, did he not deserve their praise? Had he not given them endless joy? Would it not be more amusing to obtain undeserved praise, to be worshipped by beings whom he tortured? He smiled inwardly, and resolved that the great drama should be performed.

"For countless ages the hot nebula whirled aimlessly through space. At length it began to take shape, the central mass threw off planets, the planets cooled, boiling seas and burning mountains heaved and tossed, from black masses of cloud hot sheets of rain deluged the barely solid crust. And now the first germ of life grew in the depths of the ocean, and developed rapidly in the fructifying warmth into vast forest trees, huge ferns springing from the damp mould, sea monsters breeding, fighting, devouring, and passing away. And from the monsters, as the play unfolded itself, Man was born, with the power of thought, the knowledge of good and evil, and the cruel thirst for worship. And Man saw that all is passing in this mad, monstrous world, that all is struggling to snatch, at any cost, a few brief moments of life before Death's inexorable decree. And Man said: 'There is a hidden purpose, could we but fathom it, and the purpose is good; for we must reverence something, and in the visible world there is nothing worthy of reverence.' And Man stood aside from the struggle, resolving that God intended harmony to come out of chaos by human efforts. And when he followed the instincts which God had transmitted to him from his ancestry of beasts of prey, he called it Sin, and asked God to forgive him. But he doubted whether he could be justly forgiven, until he invented a divine Plan by which God's wrath was to have been appeased. And seeing the present was bad, he made it yet worse, that thereby the future might be better. And he gave God thanks for the strength that enabled him to forgo even the joys that were possible. And God smiled; and when he saw that Man had become perfect in renunciation and worship, he sent another sun through the sky, which crashed into Man's sun; and all returned again to nebula.

" 'Yes,' he murmured, 'it was a good play; I will have it performed again.' "

Such, in outline, but even more purposeless, more void of meaning, is the world which Science presents for our belief. Amid such a world, if anywhere, our ideals henceforward must find a home. That Man is the product of causes which had no prevision of the end they were achieving; that his origin, his growth, his hopes and fears, his loves and his beliefs, are but the outcome of accidental collocations of atoms; that no fire, no heroism, no intensity of thought and feeling, can preserve an individual life beyond the grave; that all the labours of the ages, all the devotion, all the inspiration, all the noonday brightness of human genius, are destined to extinction in the vast death of the solar system, and that the whole temple of Man's achievement must inevitably be buried beneath the débris of a universe in ruins—all these things, if not quite beyond dispute, are yet so nearly certain, that no philosophy which rejects them can hope to stand. Only within the scaffolding of these truths, only on the firm foundation of unyielding despair, can the soul's habitation henceforth be safely built.

How, in such an alien and inhuman world, can so powerless a creature as Man preserve his aspirations untarnished? A strange mystery it is that Nature, omnipotent but blind, in the revolutions of her secular hurryings through the abysses of space, has brought forth at last a child, subject still to her power, but gifted with sight, with knowledge of good and evil, with the capacity of judging all the works of his unthinking Mother. In spite of Death, the mark and seal of the parental control, Man is yet free, during his brief years, to examine, to criticise, to know, and in imagination to create. To him alone, in the world with which he is acquainted, this freedom belongs; and in this lies his superiority to the resistless forces that control his outward life.

The savage, like ourselves, feels the oppression of his impotence before the powers of Nature; but having in himself nothing that he respects more than Power, he is willing to prostrate himself before his gods, with-

out inquiring whether they are worthy of his worship. Pathetic and very terrible is the long history of cruelty and torture, of degradation and human sacrifice, endured in the hope of placating the jealous gods: surely, the trembling believer thinks, when what is most precious has been freely given, their lust for blood must be appeased, and more will not be required. The religion of Moloch—as such creeds may be generically called—is in essence the cringing submission of the slave, who dare not, even in his heart, allow the thought that his master deserves no adulation. Since the independence of ideas is not yet acknowledged, Power may be freely worshipped, and receive an unlimited respect, despite its wanton infliction of pain.

But gradually, as morality grows bolder, the claim of the ideal world begins to be felt; and worship, if it is not to cease, must be given to gods of another kind than those created by the savage. Some, though they feel the demands of the ideal, will still consciously reject them, still urging that naked Power is worthy of worship. Such is the attitude inculcated in God's answer to Job out of the whirlwind: the divine power and knowledge are paraded, but of the divine goodness there is no hint. Such also is the attitude of those who, in our own day, base their morality upon the struggle for survival, maintaining that the survivors are necessarily the fittest. But others, not content with an answer so repugnant to the moral sense, will adopt the position which we have become accustomed to regard as specially religious, maintaining that, in some hidden manner, the world of fact is really harmonious with the world of ideals. Thus Man creates God, all-powerful and all-good, the mystic unity of what is and what should be.

But the world of fact, after all, is not good; and, in submitting our judgment to it, there is an element of slavishness from which our thoughts must be purged. For in all things it is well to exalt the dignity of Man, by freeing him as far as possible from the tyranny of non-human Power. When we have realised that Power is largely bad, that man, with his knowledge of good and evil, is but a helpless atom in a world which has no such knowledge, the choice is again presented to us: Shall we worship Force, or shall we worship Goodness? Shall our God exist and be evil, or shall he be recognised as the creation of our own conscience?

The answer to this question is very momentous, and affects profoundly our whole morality. The worship of Force, to which Carlyle and Nietzsche and the creed of Militarism have accustomed us, is the result of failure to maintain our own ideals against a hostile universe: it is itself a prostrate submission to evil, a sacrifice of our best to Moloch. If strength indeed is to be respected, let us respect rather the strength of those who refuse that false "recognition of facts" which fails to recognise that facts are often bad. Let us admit that, in the world we know, there are many things that would be better otherwise, and that the ideals to which we do and must adhere are not realised in the realm of matter. Let us preserve our respect for truth, for beauty, for the ideal of perfection which life does not permit us to attain, though none of these things meet with the approval of the unconscious universe. If Power is bad, as it seems to be, let us reject it from our hearts. In this lies Man's true freedom: in determination to worship only the God created by our own love of the good, to respect only the heaven which inspires the insight of our best moments. In action, in desire, we must submit perpetually to the tyranny of outside forces; but in thought, in aspiration, we are free, free from our fellowmen, free from the petty planet on which our bodies impotently crawl, free even, while we live, from the tyranny of death. Let us learn, then, that energy of faith which enables us to live constantly in the vision of the good; and let us descend, in action, into the world of fact, with that vision always before us.

When first the opposition of fact and ideal grows fully visible, a spirit of fiery revolt, of fierce hatred of the gods, seems necessary to the assertion of freedom. To defy with Promethean constancy a hostile universe, to keep its evil always in view, always actively hated, to refuse no pain that the malice of Power can invent, appears to be the duty of all who will not bow before the inevitable. But indignation is still a bondage, for it compels our thoughts to be occupied with an evil world; and in the fierceness of desire from which rebellion springs there is a kind of self-assertion which it is necessary for the wise to overcome. Indignation is a submission of our thoughts, but not of our desires; the Stoic freedom in which wisdom consists is found in the submission of our desires, but not of our thoughts. From the submission of our desires springs the virtue of resignation; from the freedom of our thoughts springs the whole world of art and philosophy, and the vision of beauty by which, at last, we half reconquer the reluctant world. But the vision of beauty is possible only to unfettered contemplation, to thoughts not weighted by the load of eager wishes; and thus Freedom comes only to those who no longer ask of life that it shall yield them any of those personal goods that are subject to the mutations of Time.

Although the necessity of renunciation is evidence of the existence of evil, yet Christianity, in preaching it, has shown a wisdom exceeding that of the Promethean philosophy of rebellion. It must be admitted that, of the things we desire, some, though they prove impossible, are yet real goods; others, however, as ardently longed for, do not form part of a fully purified ideal. The belief that what must be renounced is bad, though sometimes false, is far less often false than untamed passion supposes; and the creed of religion, by providing a reason for proving that it is never false, has been the means of purifying our hopes by the discovery of many austere truths.

But there is in resignation a further good element: even real goods, when they are unattainable, ought not to be fretfully desired. To every man comes, sooner or later, the great renunciation. For the young, there is nothing unattainable; a good thing desired with the whole force of a passionate will, and yet impossible, is to them not credible. Yet, by death, by illness, by poverty, or by the voice of duty, we must learn, each one of us, that the world was not made for us, and that, however beautiful may be the things we crave, Fate may nevertheless forbid them. It is the part of courage, when misfortune comes, to bear without repining the ruin of our hopes, to turn away our thoughts from vain regrets. This degree of submission to Power is not only just and right: it is the very gate of wisdom.

But passive renunciation is not the whole of wisdom; for not by renunciation alone can we build a temple for the worship of our own ideals. Haunting foreshadowings of the temple appear in the realm of imagination, in music, in architecture, in the untroubled kingdom of reason, and in the golden sunset magic of lyrics, where beauty shines and glows, remote from the touch of sorrow, remote from the fear of change, remote from the failures and disenchantments of the world of fact. In the contemplation of these things the vision of heaven will shape itself in our hearts, giving at once a touchstone to judge the world about us, and an inspiration by which to fashion to our needs whatever is not incapable of serving as a stone in the sacred temple.

Except for those rare spirits that are born without sin, there is a cavern of darkness to be traversed before that temple can be entered. The gate of the cavern is despair, and its floor is paved with the gravestones of abandoned hopes. There Self must die; there the eagerness, the greed of untamed desire must be slain, for only so can the soul be freed from the empire of Fate. But out of the cavern the Gate of Renunciation leads again to the daylight of wisdom, by whose radiance a new insight, a new joy, a new tenderness, shine forth to gladden the pilgrim's heart.

When, without the bitterness of impotent rebellion, we have learnt both to resign ourselves to the outward rule of Fate and to recognise that the non-human world is unworthy of our worship, it becomes possible at last so to transform and refashion the unconscious universe, so to transmute it in the crucible of imagination, that a new image of shining gold replaces the old idol of clay. In all the multiform facts of the world—in the visual shapes of trees and mountains and clouds, in the events of the life of man, even in the very omnipotence of Death—the insight of creative idealism can find the reflection of a beauty which its own thoughts first made. In this way mind asserts its subtle mastery over the thoughtless forces of Nature. The more evil the material with which it deals, the more thwarting to untrained desire, the greater is its achievement in inducing the reluctant rock to yield up its hidden treasures, the prouder its victory in compelling the opposing forces to swell the pageant of its triumph. Of all the arts, Tragedy is the proudest, the most triumphant; for it builds its shining citadel in the very centre of the enemy's country, on the very summit of his highest mountain; from its impregnable watchtowers, his camps and arsenals, his columns and forts, are all revealed; within its walls the free life continues, while the legions of Death and Pain and Despair, and all the servile captains of tyrant Fate, afford the burghers of that dauntless city new spectacles of beauty. Happy those sacred ramparts, thrice happy the dwellers on that all-seeing eminence. Honour to those brave warriors who, through countless ages of warfare, have preserved for us the priceless heritage of liberty, and have kept undefiled by sacrilegious invaders the home of the unsubdued.

But the beauty of Tragedy does but make visible a quality which, in more or less obvious shapes, is present always and everywhere in life. In the spectacle of Death, in the endurance of intolerable pain, and in the irrevocableness of a vanished past, there is a sacredness, an overpowering awe, a feeling of the vastness, the depth, the inexhaustible mystery of existence, in which, as by some strange marriage of pain, the sufferer is bound to the world by bonds of sorrow. In these moments of insight, we lose all eagerness of temporary desire, all struggling and striving for petty ends, all care for the little trivial things that, to a superficial view, make up the common life of day by day; we see, surrounding the narrow raft illumined by the flickering light of human comradeship, the dark ocean on whose rolling waves we toss for a brief hour; from the great night without, a chill blast breaks in upon our refuge; all the loneliness of humanity amid hostile forces is concentrated upon the individual soul, which must struggle alone, with what of courage it can command, against the whole weight of a universe that cares nothing for its hopes and fears. Victory, in this struggle with the powers of darkness, is the true baptism into the glorious company of heroes, the true initiation into the overmastering beauty of human existence. From that awful encounter of the soul with the outer world, enunciation, wisdom, and charity are born; and with their birth a new life begins. To take into the inmost shrine of the soul the irresistible forces whose puppets we seem to be—Death and change, the irrevocableness of the past, and the powerlessness of man before the blind hurry of the universe from vanity to vanity—to feel these things and know them is to conquer them.

This is the reason why the Past has such magical power. The beauty of its motionless and silent pictures is like the enchanted purity of late autumn, when the leaves, though one breath would make them fall, still glow against the sky in golden glory. The Past does not change or strive; like Duncan, after life's fitful fever it sleeps well; what was eager and grasping, what was petty and transitory, has faded away, the things that were beautiful and eternal shine out of it like stars in the night. Its beauty, to a soul not worthy of it, is unendurable; but to a soul which has conquered Fate it is the key of religion.

The life of Man, viewed outwardly, is but a small thing in comparison with the forces of Nature. The slave is doomed to worship Time and Fate and Death, because they are greater than anything he finds in himself, and because all his thoughts are of things which they devour. But, great as they are, to think of them greatly, to feel their passionless splendour, is greater still. And such thought makes us free men; we no longer bow before the inevitable in Oriental subjection, but we absorb it, and make it a part of ourselves. To abandon the struggle for private happiness, to expel all eagerness of temporary desire, to burn with passion for eternal things—this is emancipation, and this is the free man's worship. And this liberation is effected by a contemplation of Fate; for Fate itself is subdued by the mind which leaves nothing to be purged by the purifying fire of Time.

United with his fellow-men by the strongest of all ties, the tie of a common doom, the free man finds that a new vision is with him always, shedding over every daily task the light of love. The life of Man is a long march through the night, surrounded by invisible foes, tortured by weariness and pain, towards a goal that few can hope to reach, and where none may tarry long. One by one, as they march, our comrades vanish from our sight, seized by the silent orders of omnipotent Death. Very brief is the time in which we can help them, in which their happiness or misery is decided. Be it ours to shed sunshine on their path, to lighten their sorrows by the balm of sympathy, to give them the pure joy of a never-tiring affection, to strengthen failing courage, to instil faith in hours of despair. Let us not weigh in grudging scales their merits and demerits, but let us think only of their need—of the sorrows, the difficulties, perhaps the blindnesses, that make the misery of their lives; let us remember that they are fellow-sufferers in the same darkness, actors in the same tragedy with ourselves. And so, when their day is over, when their good and their evil have become eternal by the immortality of the past, be it ours to feel that, where they suffered, where they failed, no deed of ours was the cause; but wherever a spark of the divine fire kindled in their hearts, we were ready with encouragement, with sympathy, with brave words in which high courage glowed.

Brief and powerless is Man's life; on him and all his race the slow, sure doom falls pitiless and dark. Blind to good and evil, reckless of destruction, omnipotent matter rolls on its relentless way; for Man, condemned to-day to lose his dearest, to-morrow himself to pass through the gate of darkness, it remains only to cherish, ere yet the blow falls, the lofty thoughts that ennoble his little day; disdaining the coward terrors of the slave of Fate, to worship at the shrine that his own hands have built; undismayed by the empire of chance, to preserve a mind free from the wanton tyranny that rules his outward life; proudly defiant of the irresistible forces that tolerate, for a moment, his knowledge and his condemnation, to sustain alone, a weary but unyielding Atlas, the world that his own ideals have fashioned despite the trampling march of unconscious power.

THE FALL OF THE GOVERNMENT*

Sir Winston Churchill
(1874–   )

The many disappointments and disasters of the brief campaign in Norway caused profound perturbation at home, and the currents of passion mounted even in the breasts of some of those who had been most slothful and purblind in the years before the war. The Opposition asked for a debate on the war situation, and this was arranged for May 7. The House was filled with Members in a high state of irritation and distress. Mr. Chamberlain's opening statement did not stem the hostile tide. He was mockingly interrupted and reminded of his speech of April 5, when in quite another connection he had incautiously said, "Hitler missed the bus." He defined my new position and my relationship with the Chiefs of Staff, and in reply to Mr. Herbert Morrison made it clear that I had not held those powers during the Norwegian operations. One speaker after another from both sides of the House attacked the Government and especially its chief with unusual bitterness and vehemence, and found themselves sustained by growing applause from all quarters. Sir Roger Keyes, burning for distinction in the new war, sharply criticised the Naval Staff for their failure to attempt the

* From *The Gathering Storm.*

capture of Trondheim. "When I saw," he said, "how badly things were going, I never ceased importuning the Admiralty and War Cabinet to let me take all responsibility and lead the attack." Wearing his uniform as Admiral of the Fleet, he supported the complaints of the Opposition with technical details and his own professional authority in a manner very agreeable to the mood of the House. From the benches behind the Government, Mr. Amery quoted amid ringing cheers Cromwell's imperious words to the Long Parliament: "You have sat too long here for any good you have been doing. Depart, I say, and let us have done with you. In the name of God, go!" These were terrible words coming from a friend and colleague of many years, a fellow Birmingham Member, and a Privy Councillor of distinction and experience.

On the second day, May 8, the debate, although continuing upon an adjournment motion, assumed the character of a vote of censure, and Mr. Herbert Morrison, in the name of the Opposition, declared their intention to have a vote. The Prime Minister rose again, accepted the challenge, and in an unfortunate passage appealed to his friends to stand by him. He had a right to do this, as these friends had sustained his action, or inaction, and thus shared his responsibility in "the years which the locusts had eaten" before the war. But today they sat abashed and silenced, and some of them had joined the hostile demonstrations. This day saw the last decisive intervention of Mr. Lloyd George in the House of Commons. In a speech of not more than twenty minutes he struck a deeply wounding blow at the head of the Government. He endeavoured to exculpate me: "I do not think that the First Lord was entirely responsible for all the things which happened in Norway." I immediately interposed: "I take complete responsibility for everything that has been done by the Admiralty, and I take my full share of the burden." After warning me not to allow myself to be converted into an air-raid shelter to keep the splinters from hitting my colleagues, Mr. Lloyd George turned upon Mr. Chamberlain:

"It is not a question of who are the Prime Minister's friends. It is a far bigger issue. He has appealed for sacrifice. The nation is prepared for every sacrifice so long as it has leadership, so long as the Government show clearly what they are aiming at, and so long as the nation is confident that those who are leading it are doing their best." He ended: "I say solemnly that the Prime Minister should give an example of sacrifice, because there is nothing which can contribute more to victory in this war than that he should sacrifice the seals of office."

As Ministers we all stood together. The Secretaries of State for War and Air had already spoken. I had volunteered to wind up the debate, which was no more than my duty, not only in loyalty to the chief under whom I served, but also because of the exceptionally prominent part I had played in the use of our inadequate forces during our forlorn attempt to succour Norway. I did my very best to regain control of the House for the Government in the teeth of continuous interruption, coming chiefly from the Labour Opposition benches. I did this with good heart when I thought of their mistaken and dangerous pacifism in former years, and how, only four months before the outbreak of the war, they had voted solidly against conscription. I felt that I, and a few friends who had acted with me, had the right to inflict these censures, but they had not. When they broke in upon me, I retorted upon them and defied them, and several times the clamour was such that I could not make myself heard. Yet all the time it was clear that their anger was not directed against me, but at the Prime Minister, whom I was defending to the utmost of my ability and without regard for any other considerations. When I sat down at eleven o'clock, the House divided. The Government had a majority of eighty-one, but over fifty Conservatives voted with the Labour and Liberal Oppositions, and there was no doubt that in effect, though not in form, both the debate and the division were a violent manifestation of want of confidence in Mr. Chamberlain and his Administration.

After the debate was over, he asked me to go to his room, and I saw at once that he took the most serious view of the sentiment of the House towards himself. He felt he could not go on. There ought to be a National Government. One party alone could not carry the burden. Someone must form a Government in which all parties would serve, or we could not get through. Aroused by the antagonisms of the debate, and being sure of my own past record on the issues at stake, I was strongly disposed to fight on. "This has been a damaging debate, but you have a good majority. Do not take the matter grievously to heart. We have a better case about Norway than it has been possible to convey to the House. Strengthen your Government from every quarter, and let us go on until our majority deserts us." To this effect I spoke. But Chamberlain was neither convinced nor comforted, and I left him about midnight with the feeling that he would persist in his resolve to sacrifice himself, if there was no other way, rather than attempt to carry the war further with a one-party Government.

I do not remember exactly how things happened during the morning of May 9, but the following occurred. Sir Kingsley Wood, Secretary of State for Air, was very close to the Prime Minister as a colleague and a friend. They had long worked together in complete confidence. From him I learned that Mr. Chamberlain was resolved upon the formation of a National Government and, if he could not be the head, he would give way to anyone commanding his confidence who could. Thus, by the afternoon, I became aware that I might be called upon to take the lead. The prospect neither excited nor alarmed me. I thought it would be by far the best plan. I was content to let events unfold. In the afternoon, the Prime Minister summoned me to Downing Street, where I found Lord Halifax, and after a talk about the situation in general, we were told that Mr. Attlee and Mr. Greenwood would visit us in a few minutes for a consultation.

When they arrived, we three Ministers sat on one side of the table and the Opposition leaders on the other. Mr. Chamberlain declared the paramount need of a National Government, and sought to ascertain whether the Labour Party would serve under him. The conference of their party was in session at Bournemouth. The conversation was most polite, but it was clear that the Labour leaders would not commit themselves without consulting their people, and they hinted, not obscurely, that they thought the response would be unfavourable. They then withdrew. It was a bright, sunny afternoon, and Lord Halifax and I sat for a while on a seat in the garden of Number 10 and talked about nothing in particular. I then returned to the Admiralty and was occupied during the evening and a large part of the night in heavy business.

.   .   .   .

The morning of the tenth of May dawned, and with it came tremendous news. Boxes with telegrams poured in from the Admiralty, the War Office, and the Foreign Office. The Germans had struck their long-awaited blow. Holland and Belgium were both invaded. Their frontiers had been crossed at numerous points. The whole movement of the German Army upon the invasion of the Low Countries and of France had begun.

At about ten o'clock, Sir Kingsley Wood came to see me, having just been with the Prime Minister. He told me that Mr. Chamberlain was inclined to feel that the great battle which had broken upon us made it necessary for him to remain at his post. Kingsley Wood had told him that, on the contrary, the new crisis made it all the more necessary to have a National Government, which alone could confront it, and he added that Mr. Chamberlain had accepted this view. At eleven o'clock, I was again summoned to Downing Street by the Prime Minister. There once more I found Lord Halifax. We took our seats at the table opposite Mr. Chamberlain. He told us that he was satisfied that it was beyond his power to form a National Government. The response he had received from the Labour leaders left him in

no doubt of this. The question, therefore, was whom he should advise the King to send for after his own resignation had been accepted. His demeanour was cool, unruffled, and seemingly quite detached from the personal aspect of the affair. He looked at us both across the table.

I have had many important interviews in my public life, and this was certainly the most important. Usually I talk a great deal, but on this occasion I was silent. Mr. Chamberlain evidently had in his mind the stormy scene in the House of Commons two nights before, when I had seemed to be in such heated controversy with the Labour Party. Although this had been in his support and defence, he nevertheless felt that it might be an obstacle to my obtaining their adherence at this juncture. I do not recall the actual words he used, but this was the implication. His biographer, Mr. Feiling, states definitely that he preferred Lord Halifax. As I remained silent, a very long pause ensued. It certainly seemed longer than the two minutes which one observes in the commemorations of Armistice Day. Then at length Halifax spoke. He said that he felt that his position as a peer, out of the House of Commons, would make it very difficult for him to discharge the duties of Prime Minister in a war like this. He would be held responsible for everything, but would not have the power to guide the assembly upon whose confidence the life of every Government depended. He spoke for some minutes in this sense, and by the time he had finished, it was clear that the duty would fall upon me—had in fact fallen upon me. Then, for the first time, I spoke. I said I would have no communication with either of the Opposition Parties until I had the King's commission to form a Government. On this the momentous conversation came to an end, and we reverted to our ordinary easy and familiar manners of men who had worked for years together and whose lives in and out of office had been spent in all the friendliness of British politics. I then went back to the Admiralty, where, as may well be imagined, much awaited me.

The Dutch Ministers were in my room. Haggard and worn, with horror in their eyes, they had just flown over from Amsterdam. Their country had been attacked without the slightest pretext or warning. The avalanche of fire and steel had rolled across the frontiers, and when resistance broke out and the Dutch frontier guards fired, an overwhelming onslaught was made from the air. The whole country was in a state of wild confusion; the long-prepared defence scheme had been put into operation; the dykes were opened; the waters spread far and wide. But the Germans had already crossed the outer lines, and were now streaming across the causeway which enclosed the Zuyder Zee. Could we do anything to prevent this? Luckily, we had a flotilla not far away, and this was immediately ordered to sweep the causeway with fire, and take the heaviest toll possible of the swarming invaders. The Queen was still in Holland, but it did not seem she could remain there long.

As a consequence of these discussions, a large number of orders were dispatched by the Admiralty to all our ships in the neighborhood, and close relations were established with the Royal Dutch Navy. Even with the recent overrunning of Norway and Denmark in their minds, the Dutch Ministers seemed unable to understand how the great German nation, which, up to the night before, had professed nothing but friendship, and was bound by treaty to respect the neutrality of Holland, so strictly maintained, should suddenly have made this frightful and brutal onslaught. Upon these proceedings and other affairs, an hour or two passed. A spate of telegrams pressed in from all the frontiers affected by the forward heave of the German armies. It seemed that the old Schlieffen Plan, brought up to date with its Dutch extension, was already in full operation. In 1914, the swinging right arm of the German invasion had swept through Belgium, but had stopped short of Holland. It was well known then that had that war been delayed for three or four years, the extra army group would have been ready, and the railway terminals and communications adapted, for a movement through Holland. Now the famous movement had been launched with all these facilities and with every circumstance of surprise and treachery. But other developments lay ahead. The decisive stroke of the enemy was not to be a turning movement on the flank, but a break through the main front. This none of us or the French, who were in responsible command, foresaw. Earlier in the year I had, in a published interview, warned these neutral countries of the fate which was impending upon them and which was evident from the troop dispositions and road and rail development, as well as from the captured German plans. My words had been resented.

In the splintering crash of this vast battle, the quiet conversations we had had in Downing Street faded or fell back in one's mind. However, I remember being told that Mr. Chamberlain had gone, or was going, to see the King, and this was naturally to be expected. Presently a message arrived summoning me to the Palace at six o'clock. It only takes two minutes to drive there from the Admiralty along the Mall. Although I suppose the evening newspapers must have been full of the terrific news from the Continent, nothing had been mentioned about the Cabinet crisis. The public had not had time to take in what was happening either abroad or at home, and there was no crowd about the Palace gates.

I was taken immediately to the King. His Majesty received me most graciously and bade me sit down. He looked at me searchingly and quizzically for some moments, and then said: "I suppose you don't know why I have sent for you?" Adopting his mood, I replied: "Sir, I simply couldn't imagine why." He laughed and said: "I want to ask you to form a Government." I said I would certainly do so.

The King had made no stipulation about the Government being national in character, and I felt that my commission was in no formal way dependent upon this point. But in view of what had happened, and the conditions which had led to Mr. Chamberlain's resignation, a Government of national character was obviously inherent in the situation. If I had found it impossible to come to terms with the Opposition Parties, I should not have been constitutionally debarred from trying to form the strongest Government possible of all who would stand by the country in the hour of peril, provided that such a Government could command a majority in the House of Commons. I told the King that I would immediately send for the leaders of the Labour and Liberal Parties, that I proposed to form a War Cabinet of five or six Ministers, and that I hoped to let him have at least five names before midnight. On this I took my leave and returned to the Admiralty.

Between seven and eight, at my request, Mr. Attlee called upon me. He brought with him Mr. Greenwood. I told him of the authority I had to form a Government and asked if the Labour Party would join. He said they would. I proposed that they should take rather more than a third of the places, having two seats in the War Cabinet of five, or it might be six, and I asked Mr. Attlee to let me have a list of men so that we could discuss particular offices. I mentioned Mr. Bevin, Mr. Alexander, Mr. Morrison, and Mr. Dalton as men whose services in high office were immediately required. I had, of course, known both Attlee and Greenwood for a long time in the House of Commons. During the eleven years before the outbreak of war, I had in my more or less independent position come far more often into collision with the Conservative and National Governments than with the Labour and Liberal Oppositions. We had a pleasant talk for a little while, and they went off to report by telephone to their friends and followers at Bournemouth, with whom, of course, they had been in the closest contact during the previous forty-eight hours.

I invited Mr. Chamberlain to lead the House of Commons as Lord President of the Council, and he replied by telephone that he accepted and had arranged to broadcast at nine that night, stating that he had resigned, and urging everyone to support and aid his successor. This he did in magnanimous terms. I asked Lord Halifax to join the War Cabinet while remaining Foreign Secretary. At about ten, I sent the King a list of five names, as I had promised. The appointment of the three Service Ministers was vitally urgent. I had already made up my mind who they should be. Mr. Eden should go to the War Office; Mr. Alexander should come to the Admiralty; and Sir Archibald Sinclair, leader of the Liberal Party, should take the Air Ministry. At the same time I assumed the office of Minister of Defence, without, however, attempting to define its scope and powers.

Thus, then, on the night of the tenth of May, at the outset of this mighty battle, I acquired the chief power in the State, which henceforth I wielded in ever-growing measure for five years and three months of world war, at the end of which time, all our enemies having surrendered unconditionally or being about to do so, I was immediately dismissed by the British electorate from all further conduct of their affairs.

During these last crowded days of the political crisis, my pulse had not quickened at any moment. I took it all as it came. But I cannot conceal from the reader of this truthful account that as I went to bed at about 3 A.M., I was conscious of a profound sense of relief. At last I had the authority to give directions over the whole scene. I felt as if I were walking with Destiny, and that all my past life had been but a preparation for this hour and for this trial. Eleven years in the political wilderness had freed me from ordinary party antagonisms. My warnings over the last six years had been so numerous, so detailed, and were now so terribly vindicated, that no one could gainsay me. I could not be reproached either for making the war or with want of preparation for it. I thought I knew a good deal about it all, and I was sure I should not fail. Therefore, although impatient for the morning, I slept soundly and had no need for cheering dreams. Facts are better than dreams.

LIKE THE NOISE OF GREAT THUNDERS*

Bruce Catton
(1899–   )

The ridge behind the Confederate trenches was not very high, and its slope was gentle and grassy, with dips and hollows here and there, and occasional clumps of trees. It lay naked under the July sun, and no one had ever climbed it (except for a few Confederate artillerists, who had parked some guns in the Jerusalem Plank Road), and it was like a mocking challenge to the Federal soldiers. If they could once reach the crest of that ridge, the war was over, for if they stood there they would be in rear of the entire Confederate line, and they would control Petersburg and everything that was in it, which meant that they could certainly capture Richmond and could probably destroy Lee's army. The crest was less than half a mile from the Union line, and between the crest and the Army of the Potomac there was nothing in particular except the Confederate trench which was about to be blown sky-high.

The Pennsylvania miners had brought the end of the war within whispering distance. Never before had there been a chance like this. A trench properly built and manned by a sufficiency of Southern riflemen and gunners could never be stormed, and by now everybody knew it; but if the trench and everyone in it could suddenly be obliterated the case would be very different, and if this business were handled right men could walk through and take the crest.

Grant finally saw it, and while he had certain doubts about this stunt of Burnside's, he was determined that it must at least be given a fair chance. He was commander of all the armies of the United States and he was not directly responsible for the tactics involved in an assault along half a mile of one front, but if strategy could insure success

of this attack he proposed to use it, and so he laid a plan.

North of the James River, squarely in front of Richmond, there were miles of Confederate trenches held by a thin string of cavalry pickets. Potentially, this was the most sensitive part of Lee's entire line, and a Union attack there was certain to pull Confederate strength into the area just as fast as Lee could get it there. When Grant thought about ways to help Burnside's assault his mind naturally turned to those empty fortifications north of the river.

His plan was simple. He would send Hancock and the II Corps north of the James, accompanied by Sheridan and the cavalry. They would cross the Appomattox below Petersburg, march north back of Butler's lines, and cross the James by a new pontoon bridge at a place called Deep Bottom, and it would not hurt in the least if Lee saw them going. Presumably, Lee would take troops from the Petersburg lines to meet this threat. If Hancock and Sheridan could actually break the lines in front of Richmond, that of course would be all to the good. If they could not it would probably be because Lee had reduced strength in front of Petersburg in order to hold in front of Richmond. In that case Burnside's chance of success would be just so much better.

So Grant planned and so it was ordered, and on the evening of July 26 the II Corps took the road north. The column got to the Appomattox bridge around midnight, and a newspaper correspondent on the north side of the river watched, fascinated, as the line of march wound past a huge bonfire which had been lit to show the way. The men came up out of the dark, passed through the pool of wavering light, and moved on into more darkness, marching steadily for the James River crossing, silent enough except when some brigade staff rode by with a jingling of scabbards and other equipment. Batteries rolled by now and then, firelight gleaming off the polished guns, and the reporter sat and watched for two hours, bemused by "that flow of men, like a river, passing, still passing, but never passed."

* From *A Stillness at Appomattox*.

Early on the morning of July 27 the corps crossed the James. Butler had laid two pontoon bridges at Deep Bottom somewhat earlier, and he had a detachment on the north bank to hold the bridgehead, and Sheridan took his cavalry over to strike the Charles City Road to Richmond, while the infantry fanned out along the banks of a little stream called Bailey's Creek. There was skirmishing all day long in the underbrush and forsaken fields by this brook, the Rebels apparently present in some strength with more coming up.

Back in front of Petersburg, Pleasants's men were carrying the kegs of powder down the long tunnel, each man stooping low under the ceiling and hugging the 25-pound keg against his belly. Over their heads the Confederates had stopped hunting for the rumored Yankee mine—partly, it seems, because Lee's engineers felt just the way Meade's felt: no soldiers could burrow 500 feet under a hill. A correspondent for the London *Times* who was visiting Confederate headquarters at the time helped to confirm this delusion. British army experience, he said, showed that 400 feet was the absolute limit for a tunnel of this kind.

In any case, Grant's feint worked perfectly. Hancock's infantry and the dismounted cavalry gestured and skirmished and fought along a ridge back of Bailey's Creek and made threatening motions on the Charles City Road, and it looked as if a big attack was coming. One after another, Lee called veteran divisions out of the Petersburg lines, and by the morning of July 29 he had more than half of his army north of the James, leaving only 18,000 infantry to hold the five miles of line in front of Petersburg. More than a third of Hancock's people, meanwhile, had already gone back to Petersburg, and everybody else would go back as soon as the darkness came; and Meade was sitting down with Burnside to draw up formal orders for the big attack, which was to begin at 3:30 o'clock the next morning, July 30.

By now, Meade was ready to support Burnside with everything he had. Burnside was to use his entire corps, and two army corps would be on hand to help him—Warren's corps, on the left, and Baldy Smith's old corps, now led by General E. O. C. Ord, on the right. A powerful mass of artillery had been quietly moved up into position during recent nights—eighty field pieces, eighteen huge 10-in mortars, twenty-eight of the lighter coehorn mortars, and eighteen 4½-inch siege guns, all dug in where they could sweep the Confederate position.

Battle orders were precise. Burnside was to attack the moment the mine was sprung and he was to go straight for the crest of the ridge, pausing for no consideration whatever. The objective was a decisive breakthrough and final victory, and the only thing that counted was to get the troops up on the heights. They could get there only if they moved fast. Therefore they must be formed in columns of assault before the mine was exploded, and during the night Burnside's parapets and abatis must be leveled so that those columns could advance in line of battle. There must also be engineer parties at the heads of the columns, to remove Confederate obstructions and prepare a way for Yankee artillery to follow.

The plan was good, and it was about as Burnside had figured it. But Meade made one change in Burnside's original plan. He told Burnside that Ferrero's colored division must not be used as the first wave of the attack. The fight must be spearheaded by the white troops. If the colored troops were to be used at all they must go in later, as support.

Burnside objected, with heat, pointing out that Ferrero's was his biggest, freshest division and that it had been getting special training for weeks in the movements which would be involved in this assault. Meade refused to yield, and after a while Grant came in and Burnside appealed to him. Grant listened, and upheld Meade: the colored troops must not go in first. Profoundly disturbed, Burnside went back to his own headquarters to rearrange his plans and prepare new orders. The moment set for the explosion of the mine was now about twelve hours in the future.

The Army of the Potomac was led to disaster many times, and there is a rather horrible fascination about tracing the steps by which, in each case, it reached that destination. Usually those steps seemed quite reasonable at the time, and they were generally taken with the best intentions in the world, and almost invariably they form a chain of events which might have been broken almost anywhere. So now.

It began with the decision not to put the colored division first. A little later Grant was to admit that this decision was a mistake, but it was made for what seemed excellent reasons. The battle that was coming up was a gamble at best. Nobody could be sure that the mine would actually have the effect Pleasants and Burnside believed it would have. If it did not, the troops that led in the assault would be butchered. If those troops happened to be colored men without combat experience it would immediately be argued that they had been sacrificed callously because no one cared what happened to them. (The argument would be made, incidentally, by some of the most vocal and determined arguers that ever lived, the abolitionists and the radical Republicans.) Neither Grant nor Meade felt that that was a proper risk to take.

But this decision started all the trouble, because its effect was to deflate Burnside completely. Until now, Burnside had done what a good corps commander ought to do. He had seen merit in an unorthodox plan proposed by a subordinate, he had fought to get the idea approved, and he had supported it when higher authority failed to support it. But from this moment on he was as poor a general as a grown man can be, and both the army and the Union cause as a whole would have been much better off if he had taken to his bed, pulled the covers over his handsome face, and let someone else take charge.

First of all he had to pick another division to lead the attack, and he called in the commanding officers of his three white divisions. These were General Potter, to whom Colonel Pleasants had first suggested the mine, a capable man with a good record; General Orlando B. Willcox, a veteran who had been commanding a division ever since Antietam; and Brigadier General James H. Ledlie, a civil engineer without military training or experience when the war began, who had come into the army as major in a New York heavy artillery regiment and who had only recently risen to division command.

Burnside seems to have been pretty numb when he talked with these three generals. He explained that plans had been changed and one of their divisions would have to lead the attack. He confessed that he could not for the life of him see any reason to prefer one division or one general over the other two. Therefore, said Burnside, why should they not simply draw lots to see which division should go in first?

Down under the fabulous whiskers and the kindly dignity, Burnside was a gambler. In the Mexican War he had almost been cashiered because of his weakness for risking everything on the turn of a card. This time he was gambling far beyond his means, and chance played him false. The luck of the draw, when they finally got down to pulling for the short straw, decreed that Ledlie's division must take the lead.

Why Burnside did not immediately call for a new deal is past understanding. Of all of his divisions Ledlie's was the weakest, and of all of his generals Ledlie was the most unfit. The whole division had grown notoriously gun-shy during the past month, and one of its two brigades was made up largely of heavy artillery regiments and dismounted cavalry. Although the heavies had turned into first-rate soldiers for the rest of the army, they were not highly regarded in the IX Corps. A few weeks earlier Burnside himself had said of them: "They are worthless. They didn't enlist to fight and it is unreasonable to expect it of them. In the attack last night I couldn't find thirty of them." But chance had put Ledlie's division in the lead and Burnside let it ride; and chance further decreed that when Ledlie formed his men for the charge it was the weak brigade that was put in front.

The real trouble, however, was in Ledlie himself.

The army contained a good many poor generals, but it had very few who were ever accused of personal cowardice. Ledlie was one who was so accused. His subordinates knew him as a weakling. In the June 18 attack, while his men fought to carry a Rebel entrenchment, Ledlie had taken to the bottle, and at a climactic moment of the fight, he had been stretched out on the ground in a safe place, the world forgetting and by the world forgot. His soldiers knew it and his junior officers knew it, but the IX Corps somehow was the kind of corps in which a thing like that could escape the notice of the commanding general, so Burnside did not know it. Burnside combined the great virtue of being loyal to his underlings with the terrible weakness of being quite unable to tell a good operator from a bad one, and now he was entrusting the supreme assault of the army's career to a soldier who was taken with palsy whenever it came time to go out where enemy bullets were flying.

For good or for ill, the day ended and there was a stir all along the line. The secret of the mine had not been too well kept, and there had been gossip about it for days, but most Federals had at last begun to treat it as the Confederates did—as a rumor which someone had probably dreamed up over a jug of commissary whisky—and few people had taken it very seriously. Still, as June 29 drew to a close, there were omens for all to see. Sick men in the field hospitals were sent back to City Point. There was a great riding to and fro of staff officers and couriers, and practically every unit in the corps was being moved from one place to another. Ferrero's colored troops were brought forward, after dark, and lined up in the bottom of the ravine. They were full of enthusiasm, because in all of the excitement no one had thought to tell them that assignments had been changed, and they still supposed that they were going to lead in the attack. Indeed, they were the only division in the corps which believed that it knew what was going to happen.

During the night Hancock's men came back from the north side of the James, and Meade and Grant got up early and went to Burnside's headquarters, half a mile behind the front—a convenient place, connected with other commands by telegraph, which Meade had designated as temporary headquarters for the army.

Burnside, meanwhile, went forward to a fourteen-gun battery that had been built on a hill a few hundred yards back of the entrance to the mine. The night wore away, silent except for the shuffling of thousands of men moving to their places, and a little after three o'clock in the morning Pleasants sent a man into the mine and shaft to set fire to the fuse.

Back on the hills behind the line the artillerists were ready. They had previously trained their pieces on their targets, and the guns and mortars were all loaded, and from three o'clock on the gunners were standing by, lanyards in hand, ready to fire at the word of command. In the trenches, Ledlie's men were standing up, not knowing what was coming except that they realized they were about to be pushed into a big fight. On the slope behind them, Potter's and Willcox's divisions were waiting, similarly tense and ignorant. Back of all of them were Ferrero's colored men, massed at the bottom of the ravine, expecting at any moment to get the word to go in and capture Petersburg. General Burnside stood in the battery, serene in his ineffable rectitude, conscious that his baggage was packed and that he could take up headquarters in the Rebel city on a moment's notice.

Half-past three came, with the high command fingering watches and staring off into the dark, and nothing happened. Another half hour went by, and half an hour more on top of that, and the silence was unbroken, except for the occasional discharge of some wakeful picket's musket. Grant got impatient, and at last he told Meade to have Burnside make his charge regardless: something had gone wrong with the mine, and there was no use waiting any longer. In the east the sky was turning gray—and five eighths of Lee's army was north of the James River, with the full strength of the Army of the Potomac massed to smash through the fraction that was left.

Grant was impatient, and Meade was impatient, and probably even Burnside was getting a little restless; but the man who was really excited was Colonel Pleasants. About the time Grant was saying that the charge had better go ahead without the explosion, Pleasants called Sergeant Harry Reese, the mine boss, and told him to go into the tunnel and see what was the matter.

In went Reese, on as nerve-racking an assignment as the war could produce, groping forward all bent over along 400 feet of a dark tunnel, never sure that the solid earth ahead was not going to quake and heave and tumble to bury him forever. He got to the fuse, traced it, and found that the spark had died at a place where one fuse had been spliced to another. He started back to get a new fuse, found Lieutenant Jacob Douty coming in, at Pleasants's direction, with the material he needed, and he and Douty went back to the splice and made a new connection. Then he lit the spark again, and he and Lieutenant Douty came out of the tunnel as fast as they could travel—and the sky grew lighter in the east, so that ridges and trees and hillocks became dark shadows outlined against the dying night, and the whole Army of the Potomac stood by gripping its muskets, waiting for nobody knew just what.

Four forty-five: and at last it happened.

To the men who were waiting in the front line it seemed to occur in slow motion: first a long, deep rumble, like summer thunder rolling along a faraway horizon, then a swaying and swelling of the ground up ahead, with the solid earth rising to form a rounded hill, everything seeming very gradual and leisurely. Then the rounded hill broke apart, and a prodigious spout of flame and black smoke went up toward the sky, and the air was full of enormous clods of earth as big as houses, of brass cannon and detached artillery wheels, of wrecked caissons and fluttering tents and weirdly tumbling human bodies; and there was a crash "like the noise of great thunders," followed by other, lesser explosions, and all of the landscape along the firing line had turned into dust and smoke and flying debris, choking and blinding men

and threatening to engulf Burnside's whole army corps.

Different men saw it and felt it in different ways. A soldier in the 36th Massachusetts wrote that "we witnessed a volcano and experienced an earthquake," yet an officer in Ferrero's division, standing not a third of a mile away from the explosion, recalled it as "a dull, heavy thud, not at all startling . . . a heavy, smothered sound, not nearly so distinct as a musket shot." A man in Pleasants's own 48th Pennsylvania remembered it as a "magnificent spectacle," and another soldier recalled that a bronze cannon was tossed nearly over to the Union line. To one man the whole thing looked like "a waterspout as seen at sea," another felt it as "a heavy shaking of the earth, with a rumbling, muffled sound," and to men in Hancock's corps, waiting behind the artillery, it seemed that the solid earth went up "like an enormous whirlwind."

The gunners had been waiting a long time, and some of them had their eyes fixed on the Confederate redoubt, and they jerked their lanyards as soon as they saw the grounds begin to rise, so that the crash of their own guns rocked the air before the sound of the explosion reached them. There was a tremendous concussion from the artillery, with more guns being fired than the Union army had fired in the great artillery duel at Gettysburg. An overwhelming cloud of white smoke from the guns went tumbling down into the ravine and overflowed the farther crest to mix with the hanging black dust and smoke from the mine, so that all along the Yankee line the air was dark as midnight, lit by brief stabbing flames as the shell began to go off.

The troops which had been waiting to make the charge saw a hillside fly up in their faces, and it looked as if the mass of earth was going to fall on them, so that many men turned and ran, and it was five or ten minutes before the officers could get them reformed. Then the order for the charge was sounded and Ledlie's division started to make its attack—at which crucial moment the soldiers realized that nobody had prepared the way for them, so that the kind of charge which everybody had counted on was completely impossible.

In Meade's orders there had been a provision for leveling the parapet so that a line of battle could swing up out of the trench and go forward in fighting formation, but this assignment had dropped out of sight somewhere between "I ordered it done" and "Nobody told me to do it." Nothing whatever had been done. The leading brigade was standing in the bottom of an eight-foot ditch, and men who were loaded down with muskets and cartridge boxes and haversacks just could not scale the wall.

One officer, aware that time was a-wasting, had a squad improvise a ladder by jabbing bayonets into the log wall and holding the outer ends while their comrades climbed up and over. In another place, men tore down sandbags and piled them into a clumsy sort of stairway. Finally, with an additional ten minutes lost, a straggling line of men got up out of the trench and began to run forward by twos and threes—a thin trickle of wholly disorganized men, rather than the connected wave of a line of battle.

Stumbling up the slope through dust and smoke, these men got to the place where the Confederate redoubt had been and found themselves peering down into a great smoking crater.

One hundred and seventy feet of the Confederate line had been blown up. In its place there was a huge chasm, 60 feet across and 30 feet deep. All around this crater, balanced on its rim and tumbled over the ground on every side, were big hunks of solid clay, broken timbers, dismounted guns, and lesser wreckage of every kind. Down at the bottom there was more of the same, including many human bodies. Some Southerners, still living, had been buried to their waists, some had only their heads above the earth. Others had been buried head downward, their legs protruding into the air. As the men of Ledlie's leading brigade came up they paused, stupefied by the sight; then they slid and scrambled down into the crater and began to uproot the buried Confederates. An officer got one squad together to dig out a couple of half-buried cannon.

Nothing could be seen very clearly, for smoke and dust still filled the air. To the rear the Federal guns kept up a furious bombardment, and there was no return fire. For 200 yards on each side of the crater the Confederate trenches were empty, the men who had inhabited them having taken to their heels when the mine blew up. Here and there a few stout souls began to fire their muskets into the haze about the crater, but half an hour would pass before their fire would have any appreciable effect.

Colonel Pleasants's little plan could not possibly have been more successful. Right in the middle of the impregnable Confederate chain of defenses it had created a gap of 500 yards wide, and all the IX Corps had to do was march through and take the ridge. It would need to move briskly, because the gap was not going to stay open very long, but at five o'clock on this morning of July 30 decisive victory was less than half an undefended mile away.

But the one thing which Burnside's corps could not do that morning was to move briskly.

While one of Ledlie's brigades was getting down into the crater and acting partly like a rescue squad, partly like a salvage party, and partly like a group of sight-seers, his other brigade came dribbling out of the Federal trenches to support it. Those engineer parties which were to have cleared the way for the attacking columns had not materialized, and so the only gap in the abatis and *chevaux-de-frise* was right in front of the crater, where the earth thrown out by the explosion had buried the entanglements. This second brigade thus came forward through a funnel which led it straight toward the crater, and since the men were not coming up in regular formation—getting over the parapet was still a matter of every man for himself—and since nobody in particular was shooting at them, the men trotted up to the rim to have a look. While stray officers were urging everyone to continue the advance, most of the men slid down to the bottom of the crater, and presently almost all of Ledlie's division was jammed in there, a confused and aimless mob wholly out of control.

Not a vestige of military organization remained. Officers could not find their men and men could not find their officers, and there was a good deal of rather aimless activity. Along the farther rim of the crater, some industrious souls were trying to prepare a defensive line. The officer who had been digging up the buried cannon was putting men to work to horse them up to the rim where they could be fired—a difficult job, since the final feet of the crater wall were practically vertical—and he had other details hunting about to find the Rebel gunners' magazine. Half-entombed Confederates were still being dug up, and a few files of dazed prisoners were being sent to the rear. A few officers were yelling themselves hoarse, trying to get the men to climb up out of the crater and go on with the attack, but hardly anyone was paying any attention to them.

This, of course, was the kind of situation which generals in charge of infantry divisions had been created to unscramble. Now was the moment for the division commander to take charge, restore order, pull the men out of the pit, form a coherent line of battle, and make his attack. But General Ledlie, who commanded this division, was snugly tucked away in a bombproof 400 yards behind the line, plying himself with rum borrowed from a brigade surgeon. From first to last he never saw the explosion, the soldiers, the crater, or the charge. Now and then reports would come back to him, and he would dispatch a runner with the order that everyone must move forward to the crest of the ridge. Beyond that he did nothing and was capable of doing nothing. And General Burnside, back in the fourteen-gun battery, serenely unaware that anything was wrong, was busily ordering fresh troops forward.

The fresh troops were Potter's and Willcox's divisions. Time would have been saved if these troops had been lined up in brigade front just behind the front-line trench, but it was held that troops moving forward to the front ought to go up through the covered way

—after all, that was what the thing had been built for—and so two infantry divisions were sent up a winding ditch that was wide enough for no more than two or three men abreast, colliding with stragglers, walking wounded, couriers, and other persons, and in due time they got into the front-line trench and scrambled up sandbag stairways, bayonet ladders, and what-not and went forward through the gap toward the crater. Their officers steered them off to the right and left, so that the empty Confederate trenches adjoining the crater could be possessed, and very slowly and with much confusion a trickle of Federal troops began to come up into line on each side of Ledlie's disorganized division.

Meanwhile, the Confederates were rapidly coming to. On the right and left, regiments were being formed so that they could fire on the flanks of the attacking column. Between the crater and the ridge there was a shallow ravine—luckily, from the Southern viewpoint, it was out of reach of the Federal cannon—and an alert Confederate general put troops in it, and the fire from these men was beginning to be very heavy. The golden half hour in which the ridge could have been taken effortlessly was gone forever, and any advance that was made now would be made only after a hard fight.

After Potter's and Willcox's men had moved out into the empty trenches they began to go forward. The going was very bad. The ground beyond the trenches was a labyrinth of bombproofs, rifle pits, covered ways, and support trenches, and in many places the advance was a hoptoad business of jumping into a hole in the ground, scrambling out on the other side, jumping into another hole, and then repeating the scramble. The rising tempo of Confederate musketry did not make this kind of progress any easier.

Worse yet, Rebel artillery was coming into action, with power. A quarter of a mile north of the crater there was a four-gun battery, and the Southern gunners who had decamped when the mine was blown up came back to these guns and trained them on the Yankees who were trying to advance from the captured trenches. Federal artillery pounded this battery mercilessly, but it was well protected by solid earthen traverses and, although the shell dug up the ground all about until it looked as if the whole area had been plowed, the guns remained in action, putting canister right down the flank of the Federal battle line. On the other side of the crater the story was somewhat the same, with a battery posted so as to enfilade the Federal line from the left. This battery also drew a storm of fire, but there was one gun that could not be silenced and it kept firing canister at deadly close range.

Up on the ridge west of the crater the Rebels put sixteen guns in line. The Federal gunners swept the ridge with overwhelming fire, but the Jerusalem Plank Road was sunken and offered a natural gun pit, and although ten of the sixteen guns were wrecked, the six that remained could not be subdued. In addition, the Confederates had mortars tucked away in hollow ground beyond the crater, and these began to toss shell into the dense jam of Federal soldiers.

Minute by minute the situation grew worse. Potter's men gained ground on the right of the crater, but they were under a killing fire and their battle line was slowly pressed back. Mixed elements from half a dozen different commands crawled forward a few dozen yards from the crater itself in a valiant attempt to reach and silence the guns on the ridge, but the Rebels had a good second line in operation now and there were not enough men in this attack to break it. On the left of the crater Willcox's men could do nothing but cower in the captured trench and keep up an ineffective musketry fire.

Meade had been right: if the attack was to succeed at all it would succeed in the first rush. The first rush had failed, and the failure was both incredible and irretrievable. What could have been done easily at five o'clock had become a matter of great difficulty by six o'clock and by seven it had become virtually impossible. The fight now was just one more dreary repetition of the old attempt to capture entrenched positions. Most of the men in the attacking forces knew it perfectly well,

and they hugged the ground. To all intents and purposes the battle was already lost.

But the high command did not know it. Both corps and army headquarters were helpless. Burnside's command post was a quarter of a mile behind the front and Meade's was half a mile behind that, and the fight was out of their hands. An officer might be sent forward to get news. He would spend five or ten minutes jostling forward along the covered way, and take his look around, and then spend another five or ten minutes getting back. By the time his report had been assimilated and orders had been started forward the situation would have changed completely—above all other battles, this one was fluid and every minute counted—and the new orders would be worse than useless.

Burnside might well have been up at the crater himself—Grant said later that if he had commanded a corps in a fight like this, that was where he would have been—but Burnside was a headquarters operator, and this was Fredericksburg all over again: reports coming in out of a blinding fog, orders going forward into the fog, nothing that was ordered having any relation to reality, the men who wrote the orders never once seeing the place where the orders were to be executed or the people who were to execute them; and all Burnside could do was to tell all and sundry to attack and keep on attacking. Meade might have gone forward, but he had announced beforehand that he could be reached at IX Corps headquarters and it seemed to him now that it would only cause more confusion if he left that spot. So he communicated with Burnside by telegraph, and he told Warren and Ord to get their own troops moving to help the attack; and nothing that happened up around the tangle of crater and captured trenches and broken earth was in the least as the officers in the rear thought it was.

Warren went to talk to Burnside about where the V Corps ought to go in, and Burnside suggested that he go forward and take a look, and Warren did so, and when he got back he and Burnside discussed the situation in some detail, after which Warren went over to his own headquarters and ordered Ayres's division forward.

Ord tried to advance, but the way was jammed with IX Corps troops and hardly more than a handful of his men were able to move. At 7:20 Burnside sent a wire to Meade saying that he was doing everything possible to push his men forward to the crest but that it was very hard work, and Meade lost his temper and sent an angry wire asking him what on earth was going on and snapping: "I wish to know the truth and desire an immediate answer." Then Burnside lost his temper and wired Meade that Meade had been "unofficer-like and ungentlemanly"; and up in front the Confederates stitched together a semicircle of fire around the attacking troops and the advance came to a hopeless standstill.

At precisely which moment orders went down to the bottom of the ravine from corps headquarters telling Ferrero's division of colored troops to advance and seize the crest.

The colored boys had been under arms since dawn, and as far as they knew their original assignment was unchanged: charge straight across the place where the mine had exploded and take the high ground that overlooked Petersburg. Top authorities had said that they must not lead the charge lest they be sacrificed; now, with the battle lost beyond recall, they were being sent in for a job that was not even as good as a forlorn hope. They got into the covered way, struggled up to the front line, scrambled over the parapet and ran forward with a cheer. By now the Confederate defense was able to lay heavy fire on the ground between the Union trench and the crater, so that getting forward was costly. As the men advanced General Ferrero dropped off in the same bombproof that housed General Ledlie and borrowed a swig of his jug of rum, leaving his brigadiers to direct the fight.

It was impossible to go through the crater, because it was full of white troops. The colonel of the leading regiment saw this difficulty and led the command off to the right. By this time most of Potter's men had been shoved out of the trenches they had seized, and the colored regiment found itself running along between the Rebel abatis and a trenchful of Southern infantry—so close to the trench that some of the men were bayoneted as they ran, and those who were shot bore powder burns from the flash of Rebel muskets. As soon as the tail of the regiment had cleared the crater the colonel gave the order: "By the left flank—march!" followed by "Charge!" and the men sprang into the trench, using bayonet and clubbed musket, taking prisoners and a stand of colors. A regimental officer had to intervene to keep the men from killing their prisoners.

In the captured trench the colored troops re-formed for a further advance. It was not easy, because the trench was full of dead and wounded men of both armies, and from in front and from the right the Confederates were laying down a blistering fire. A colonel tried to organize a charge, but when he went over the parapet he could not get more than fifty men to follow him, and the hostile fire quickly knocked them back. Then, while officers were trying to figure out what to do next, a runner came up with a message from General Ferrero: "If you have not already done so, you will immediately proceed to take the crest in your front"—which may have sounded like a reasonable order to a man safely tucked away in a dugout far behind the front.

Well, they tried. First the officers leaped up on the parapet, waving their swords and shouting, and most of these were shot before they took another step. Then a scattering of soldiers followed them—200 men, perhaps, from three regiments—and a thin little cheer went up, and the ragged line ran forward. They got almost to the hidden ravine where the Confederates were waiting, and the Rebels came out with a countercharge, and for a moment there was vicious combat rocking back and forth in the open. Then the charge broke, and the colored men came running back, most of their officers gone, regimental and company organizations wholly mixed up, furious Southern infantry on their heels. Such white troops as were on the ground were caught up in this retreat, and in another moment a disorganized mass of black and white soldiers in blue uniforms was running desperately for cover, diving into the trenches and rifle pits or streaming for the deep haven of the crater.

In the captured trenches there was a dreadful crush of men. An officer wrote afterward that people were packed so tightly that he literally could not raise his arms from his side. The Confederates had followed close, and they poked rifles over the edge of the trench and fired into the huddle at three-foot range. Some of them jumped down in with bayonets, and men began to surrender, and the soldiers remembered hearing the Confederates crying: "Take the white man—kill the nigger!" There was a blind flurry of bitter fighting in the maze of trenches and rifle pits and dugouts, and eventually the whole section of captured trench was lost and the Union survivors got into the crater and prepared to hang on as long as they could.

It was all over now, except for the killing. Grant had recognized failure and had told Meade to get the men back and call the whole operation off, and Meade had passed the word on to Burnside, but Burnside still thought that the attack somehow could be reorganized and made successful, and no recall was sounded. Hundreds of Union soldiers were jammed into the crater, most of them down at the bottom where they could do no fighting whatever. Men up along the rim were standing on a slope so steep that after a man fired his rifle he had to turn around, dig in with his heels, and brace his shoulders against the dirt in order to reload.

Confederate mortars had the range and they were dropping shell into the crater on a helpless target that they could not miss; men who got out alive remembered a horrible debris of severed limbs and heads flying through the air after each shell exploded. The sun was high in the sky now and it beat down with unrelenting heat, terribly magnified in this steaming pit, and thirst seemed to be a worse foe than Confederate infantry. A

Rebel countercharge came to the very edge of the crater, and Negroes lined the rim and fired and drove the attackers back, and the noise and the heat and the exploding shell beat on men's brains and dazed them so that nothing was remembered very clearly afterward.

Here and there, officers were able to organize details to search among the dead and wounded for cartridges. Some men were ordered to run back to the Union line with a cluster of canteens to get water, and a few of them managed to make the round trip without being killed. More than 200 men dropped unconscious from sheer heat and exhaustion, and a captain in the 45th Pennsylvania wrote: "The loss of life was terrible. There was death below as well as above ground in the crater. It seemed impossible to maintain life from the intense heat of the sun." He noted that his regiment lost 67 of the 110 men who had gone in.

Somehow, finally—long after noon—it ended. The men who could do so went back to the Union lines; the others stayed where they were and either died or went off to Confederate prison camps. Burnside continued to insist to Meade that the attack could still succeed, but Ord bluntly told Meade that it was nonsense, and defeat at last was accepted. Through it all, Colonel Pleasants had been standing on the parapet of the fourteen-gun battery where he could watch the proceedings, and he stormed and swore in unregimented fury, telling Burnside that he had "nothing but a damned set of cowards in his brigade commanders"; and one of the men in the 48th Pennsylvania recorded that "Pleasants was awful mad when he saw how things were going on."

Mad Colonel Pleasants might well have been. Never before had the army met so completely ignominious a defeat. Grant summed it up by telling Halleck that it was "the saddest affair I have witnessed in the war," and he added: "Such an opportunity for carrying fortifications I have never seen and do not expect again to have." A man in the 36th Massachusetts wrote that this day had been "the saddest in the history of the IX

Corps," and a boy in the 48th Pennsylvania wrote to his sister:

"I expected to write to you of one of the most glorious victories that was ever won by this army, but instead of a victory I have to write about the greatest shame and disgrace that ever happened to us. The people at home may look at it as nothing but a mere defeat, but I look at it as a disgrace to our corps."

In the 115th New York, a sergeant blew his top from heat and fatigue, sprang up and cried, "We'll fight 'em till we die, won't we, boys?" and then dropped unconscious. And in Ferrero's division it was observed that the colored troops never again sang their song:

> *We looks like men a'marching on;*
> *We looks like men o' war.*

As such things went, the great battle of the crater was not, perhaps, unduly expensive. When the butcher's bill was added up it recorded a loss of 3,798 men, more than a third of them in the colored division. Measured by the standards of the Wilderness and Spotsylvania, this was comparatively mild. Most of the casualties occurred after Grant and Meade had ordered the attack given up, when the men were trying to do nothing more than get back to their own trenches.

Yet the casualty lists did not tell the whole story, which indeed was a good deal more complex than most of the participants were able to understand.

Since May 4 everything that had happened had been part of one continuous battle, a battle three months long, with advance and retreat and triumph and disaster all taking place together, so that words like victory and defeat had lost their meaning. All that had gone before was no more than prelude. The nation itself had been heated to an unimaginable pitch by three years of war and now it had been put on the anvil and the hammer was remorselessly coming down, stroke after clanging stroke, beating a glowing metal into a different shape.

There would be change and the war was bringing it, even though it might be that the war could not bring victory. The war had taken on a new magnitude, and perhaps it was no longer the kind of struggle anybody could win. But it was moving inexorably toward its end, and when it ended many things would end with it, in the South and in the North as well. Some of these were things that ought to end because they shackled men to the past, and some of them were fit to be laid away in the shadowland of dreams that are remembered forever, but in any case they were being brought to an end. After that there could be a new beginning.

THE FURTHER RANGE OF PROSE: BIOGRAPHY

Many people feel that biography tells a true story about something that really happened, whereas fiction tells an untrue story about events that did not occur. But, as we have seen, good fiction possesses a truth of its own, the truth of universality, which is, some say, even truer than facts are; and conversely we are not sure that the facts in biography are what they seem to be.

The facts of biography are both elusive and difficult to deal with. First, we do not always have them, or we do not have enough of them—as, for instance, in the life of William Shakespeare. Second, and paradoxically, we sometimes have what seems to be too many facts, as in the life of Franklin Roosevelt, where the very voluminousness of the records makes selection difficult. Third, we may sometimes have the facts but no idea as to their meaning, as with the language of the ancient Etruscans, which no one has ever been able to translate.

A biographer is therefore one who selects and interprets facts. His product often attains a degree and kind of truth that is similar to that of the story writer: the truth of universality. Both the biographer and the writer of fiction deal with the basic stuff of life, human nature; both manipulate it and interpret it in order to paint a "truthful" picture.

The range of biography is vast—as varied as life itself. We print in the following pages some of the shorter forms of biography and autobiography and excerpts from longer biographies. Each excerpt is, however, a self-contained and unified whole.

THE BOOK OF RUTH*

Now it came to pass in the days when the judges ruled, that there was a famine in the land. And a certain man of Bethlehem Judah went to sojourn in the country of Moab, he and his wife, and his two sons. And the name of the man was Elimelech, and the name of his wife Naomi, and the name of his two sons Mahlon and Chilion, Ephrathites of Bethlehem Judah. And they came into the country of Moab, and continued there. And Elimelech Naomi's husband died; and she was left, and her two sons. And they took them wives of the women of Moab; the name of the one was Orpah, and the name of the other Ruth. And they dwelled there about ten years. And Mahlon and Chilion died also both of them; and the woman was left of her two sons and her husband.

Then she arose with her daughters-in-law, that she might return from the country of Moab; for she had heard in the country of Moab how that the Lord had visited his people in giving them bread. Wherefore she went forth out of the place where she was, and her two daughters-in-law with her; and they went on the way to return unto the land of Judah. And Naomi said unto her two daughters-in-law, Go, return each to her

* From the *Old Testament*, King James Version.

mother's house: the Lord deal kindly with you, as ye have dealt with the dead, and with me. The Lord grant you that ye may find rest, each of you in the house of her husband. Then she kissed them; and they lifted up their voice, and wept. And they said unto her, Surely we will return with thee unto thy people.

And Naomi said, Turn again, my daughters: why will ye go with me? are there yet any more sons in my womb, that they may be your husbands? Turn again, my daughters, go your way; for I am too old to have a husband. If I should say, I have hope, if I should have a husband also tonight, and should also bear sons, would ye tarry for them till they were grown? would ye stay for them from having husbands? Nay, my daughters; for it grieveth me much for your sakes that the hand of the Lord is gone out against me.

And they lifted up their voice, and wept again: and Orpah kissed her mother-in-law; but Ruth clave unto her. And she said, Behold, thy sister-in-law is gone back unto her people, and unto her gods: return thou after thy sister-in-law.

And Ruth said, Entreat me not to leave thee, or to return from following after thee: for whither thou goest, I will go; and where thou lodgest, I will lodge: thy people shall be my people, and thy God my God. Where thou diest, will I die, and there will I be buried. The Lord do so to me, and more also, if ought but death part thee and me.

When she saw that she was steadfastly minded to go with her, then she left speaking unto her. So they two went until they came to Bethlehem.

And it came to pass, when they were come to Bethlehem, that all the city was moved about them, and they said, Is this Naomi? And she said unto them, Call me not Naomi, call me Mara: for the Almighty hath dealt very bitterly with me. I went out full, and the Lord hath brought me home again empty: why then call ye me Naomi, seeing the Lord hath testified against me, and the Almighty hath afflicted me?

So Naomi returned, and Ruth the Moab-itess, her daughter-in-law, with her, which returned out of the country of Moab; and they came to Bethlehem in the beginning of barley harvest.

And Naomi had a kinsman of her husband's, a mighty man of wealth, of the family of Elimelech; and his name was Boaz. And Ruth the Moabitess said unto Naomi, Let me now go to the field, and glean ears of corn after him in whose sight I shall find grace. And she said unto her, Go, my daughter. And she went, and came, and gleaned in the field after the reapers: and her hap was to light on a part of the field belonging unto Boaz, who was of the kindred of Elimelech.

And, behold, Boaz came from Bethlehem, and said unto the reapers, The Lord be with you. And they answered him, The Lord bless thee. Then said Boaz unto his servant that was set over the reapers, Whose damsel is this? And the servant that was set over the reapers answered and said, It is the Moabitish damsel that came back with Naomi out of the country of Moab. And she said, I pray you, let me glean and gather after the reapers among the sheaves. So she came, and hath continued even from the morning until now, that she tarried a little in the house.

Then said Boaz unto Ruth, Hearest thou not, my daughter? Go not to glean in another field, neither go from hence, but abide here fast by my maidens. Let thine eyes be on the field that they do reap, and go thou after them; have I not charged the young men that they shall not touch thee? and when thou art athirst, go unto the vessels, and drink of that which the young men have drawn.

Then she fell on her face, and bowed herself to the ground, and said unto him, Why have I found grace in thine eyes, that thou shouldest take knowledge of me, seeing I am a stranger? And Boaz answered and said unto her, It hath fully been showed me, all that thou hast done unto thy mother-in-law since the death of thine husband: and how thou hast left thy father and thy mother, and the land of thy nativity, and art come unto a people which thou knewest not heretofore. The Lord recompense thy work, and a full reward be given thee of the Lord God of

Israel, under whose wings thou art come to trust.

Then she said, Let me find favor in thy sight, my lord; for that thou hast comforted me, and for that thou hast spoken friendly unto thine handmaid, though I be not like unto one of thine handmaidens. And Boaz said unto her, At mealtime come thou hither, and eat of the bread, and dip thy morsel in the vinegar. And she sat beside the reapers: and he reached her parched corn, and she did eat, and was sufficed, and left.

And when she was risen up to glean, Boaz commanded his young men, saying, Let her glean even among the sheaves, and reproach her not. And let fall also some of the handfuls of purpose for her, and leave them, that she may glean them, and rebuke her not. So she gleaned in the field until even, and beat out that she had gleaned; and it was about an ephah of barley.

And she took it up, and went into the city. And her mother-in-law saw what she had gleaned; and she brought forth, and gave to her that she had reserved after she was sufficed. And her mother-in-law said unto her, Where hast thou gleaned today? and where wroughtest thou? blessed be he that did take knowledge of thee. And she showed her mother-in-law with whom she had wrought, and said, The man's name with whom I wrought today is Boaz. And Naomi said unto her daughter-in-law, Blessed be he of the Lord, who hath not left off his kindness to the living and to the dead. And Naomi said unto her, The man is near of kin unto us, one of our next kinsmen. And Ruth the Moabitess said, He said unto me also, Thou shalt keep fast by my young men, until they have ended all my harvest. And Naomi said unto Ruth her daughter-in-law, It is good, my daughter, that thou go out with his maidens, that they meet thee not in any other field. So she kept fast by the maidens of Boaz to glean unto the end of barley harvest and of wheat harvest, and dwelt with her mother-in-law.

Then Naomi her mother-in-law said unto her, My daughter, shall I not seek rest for thee, that it may be well with thee? And now is not Boaz of our kindred, with whose maidens thou wast? Behold, he winnoweth barley tonight in the threshing-floor. Wash thyself therefore, and anoint thee, and put thy raiment upon thee, and get thee down to the floor; but make not thyself known unto the man, until he shall have done eating and drinking. And it shall be, when he lieth down, that thou shalt mark the place where he shall lie, and thou shalt go in, and uncover his feet, and lay thee down; and he will tell thee what thou shalt do. And she said unto her, All that thou sayest unto me I will do.

And she went down unto the floor, and did according to all that her mother-in-law bade her. And when Boaz had eaten and drunk, and his heart was merry, he went to lie down at the end of the heap of corn; and she came softly, and uncovered his feet, and laid her down.

And it came to pass at midnight, that the man was afraid, and turned himself; and, behold, a woman lay at his feet. And he said, Who art thou? And she answered, I am Ruth thine handmaid; spread therefore thy skirt over thine handmaid; for thou art a near kinsman. And he said, Blessed be thou of the LORD, my daughter; for thou hast showed more kindness in the latter end than at the beginning, inasmuch as thou followedst not young men, whether poor or rich. And now, my daughter, fear not; I will do to thee all that thou requirest; for all the city of my people doth know that thou art a virtuous woman. And now it is true that I am thy near kinsman: howbeit there is a kinsman nearer than I. Tarry this night, and it shall be in the morning, that if he will perform unto thee the part of a kinsman, well; let him do the kinsman's part. But if he will not do the part of a kinsman to thee, then will I do the part of a kinsman to thee, as the Lord liveth. Lie down until the morning.

And she lay at his feet until the morning; and she rose up before one could know another. And he said, Let it not be known that a woman came into the floor. Also he said, Bring the veil that thou hast upon thee, and hold it. And when she held it, he measured six measures of barley, and laid it on her;

and she went into the city. And when she came to her mother-in-law, she said, Who art thou, my daughter? And she told her all that the man had done to her. And she said, These six measures of barley gave he me; for he said to me, Go not empty unto thy mother-in-law. Then said she, Sit still, my daughter, until thou know how the matter will fall; for the man will not be in rest, until he have finished the thing this day.

Then went Boaz up to the gate, and sat him down there. And, behold, the kinsman of whom Boaz spake came by; unto whom he said, Ho, such a one! turn aside, sit down here. And he turned aside, and sat down. And he took ten men of the elders of the city, and said, Sit ye down here. And they sat down. And he said unto the kinsman, Naomi, that is come again out of the country of Moab, selleth a parcel of land, which was our brother Elimelech's. And I thought to advertise thee, saying, Buy it before the inhabitants, and before the elders of my people. If thou wilt redeem it, redeem it: but if thou wilt not redeem it, then tell me, that I may know; for there is none to redeem it beside thee; and I am after thee. And he said, I will redeem it.

Then said Boaz, What day thou buyest the field of the hand of Naomi, thou must buy it also of Ruth the Moabitess, the wife of the dead, to raise up the name of the dead upon his inheritance. And the kinsman said, I cannot redeem it for myself, lest I mar mine own inheritance; redeem thou my right to thyself; for I cannot redeem it.

Now this was the manner in former time in Israel concerning redeeming and concerning changing, for to confirm all things: a man plucked off his shoe, and gave it to his neighbor; and this was a testimony in Israel. Therefore the kinsman said unto Boaz, Buy it for thee. So he drew off his shoe.

And Boaz said unto the elders, and unto all the people, Ye are witnesses this day, that I have bought all that was Elimelech's, and all that was Chilion's and Mahlon's, of the hand of Naomi. Moreover Ruth the Moabitess, the wife of Mahlon, have I purchased to be my wife, to raise up the name of the dead upon

his inheritance, that the name of the dead be not cut off from among his brethren, and from the gate of his place. Ye are witnesses this day. And all the people that were in the gate, and the elders, said, We are witnesses. The Lord make the woman that is come unto thine house like Rachel and like Leah, which two did build the house of Israel; and do thou worthily in Ephratah, and be famous in Bethlehem; and let thy house be like the house of Pharez, whom Tamar bare unto Judah, of the seed which the Lord shall give thee of this young woman.

So Boaz took Ruth, and she was his wife; and when he went in unto her, the Lord gave her conception, and she bare a son. And the women said unto Naomi, Blessed be the Lord, which hath not left thee this day without a kinsman, that his name may be famous in Israel. And he shall be unto thee a restorer of thy life, and a nourisher of thine old age; for thy daughter-in-law, which loveth thee, which is better to thee than seven sons, hath borne him. And Naomi took the child, and laid it in her bosom, and became nurse unto it. And the women her neighbors gave it a name, saying, There is a son born to Naomi; and they called his name Obed. He is the father of Jesse, the father of David.

[THE DEATH OF CAESAR]*

Plutarch

(46?-120)

This was the last war that Caesar made. But the triumph he made into Rome for the same did as much offend the Romans, and more, than anything that ever he had done before: because he had not overcome captains that were strangers, nor barbarous kings, but had destroyed the sons of the noblest man in Rome, whom fortune had over-

* From *The Life of Julius Caesar*, one of *The Lives of the Noble Grecians and Romans*. Translated by Sir Thomas North from the French of James Amyot, who translated from the Greek of Plutarch.

thrown. And because he had plucked up his race by the roots, men did not think it meet for him to triumph so for the calamities of his country, rejoicing at a thing for the which he had but one excuse to allege in his defence unto the gods and men, that he was compelled to do that he did. And the rather they thought it not meet, because he had never before sent letters nor messengers unto the commonwealth at Rome for any victory that he had ever won in all the civil wars but did always for shame refuse the glory of it.

This notwithstanding, the Romans inclining to Caesar's prosperity and taking the bit in the mouth, supposing that, to be ruled by one man alone, it would be a good mean for them to take breath a little, after so many troubles and miseries as they had abidden in these civil wars: they chose him perpetual Dictator. This was a plain tyranny: for to this absolute power of Dictator they added this, never to be afraid to be deposed. Cicero propounded before the Senate that they should give him such honours as were meet for a man; howbeit others afterwards added-to honours beyond all reason. For, men striving who should most honour him, they made him hateful and troublesome to themselves that most favoured him by reason of the unmeasurable greatness and honours which they gave him. Thereupon, it is reported that even they that most hated him were no less favourers and furtherers of his honours than they that most flattered him: because they might have greater occasions to rise, and that it might appear they had just cause and colour to attempt that they did against him.

And now for himself, after he had ended his civil wars, he did so honourably behave himself that there was no fault to be found in him; and therefore methinks, amongst other honours they gave him, he rightly deserved this, that they should build him a temple of clemency, to thank him for his courtesy he had used unto them in his victory. For he pardoned many of them that had borne arms against him, and furthermore, did prefer some of them to honour and office in the commonwealth: as, amongst others, Cassius and Brutus, both the which were made Praetors. And where Pompey's images had been thrown down, he caused them to be set up again; whereupon Cicero said then, that Caesar setting up Pompey's images again, he made his own stand the surer. And when some of his friends did counsel him to have a guard for the safety of his person, and some also did offer themselves to serve him, he would never consent to it, but said, it was better to die once than always to be afraid of death.

But to win himself the love and good will of the people, as the honourablest guard and best safety he could have, he made common feasts again and general distributions of corn. Furthermore, to gratify the soldiers also, he replenished many cities again with inhabitants, which before had been destroyed, and placed them there that had no place to repair unto: of the which the noblest and chiefest cities were these two, Carthage and Corinth, and it chanced also that, like as aforetime they had been both taken and destroyed together, even so were they both set afoot again and replenished with people at one self time.

And as for great personages, he wan them also, promising some of them to make them Praetors and Consuls in time to come, and unto others honours and preferments, but to all men generally good hope, seeking all the ways he could to make every man contented with his reign. Insomuch as one of the Consuls called Maximus chancing to die a day before his Consulship ended, he declared Cananius Rebilius Consul only for the day that remained. So, divers going to his house (as the manner was) to salute him, and to congratulate with him of his calling and preferment, being newly chosen officer, Cicero pleasantly said, "Come, let us make haste, and be gone thither before his Consulship come out."

Furthermore, Caesar being born to attempt all great enterprises, and having an ambitious desire to covet great honours, the prosperous good success he had of his former conquests bred no desire in him quietly to enjoy the fruits of his labours, but rather gave him hope of things to come, still kindling more and more in him thoughts of greater enterprises, and desire of new glory, as if that which he had present were stale and nothing worth. This humour of his was no other but an emulation with himself as with another man, and a certain contention to overcome the things he prepared to attempt. For he was determined and made preparation also to make war with the Persians. Then, when he had overcome them, to pass through Hyrcania (compassing in the sea Caspium and Mount Caucasus) into the realm of Pontus, and so to invade Scythia: and over-running all the countries and people adjoining unto high Germany, and Germany itself, at length to return by Gaul into Italy, and so to enlarge the Roman Empire round that it might be every way compassed in with the great sea Oceanus. But whilst he was preparing for this voyage, he attempted to cut the bar of the strait of Peloponnesus, in the place where the city of Corinth standeth.

Then he was minded to bring the rivers of Anien and Tiber straight from Rome into the city of Circeii with a deep channel and high banks cast up on either side, and so to fall into the sea at Terracina, for the better safety and commodity of the merchants that came to Rome to traffic there. Furthermore, he determined to drain and seaw all the water of the marishes betwixt the cities of Nomentum and Setium, to make it firm land for the benefit of many thousands of people: and on the seacoast next unto Rome to cast great high banks, and to cleanse all the haven about Ostia of rocks and stones hidden under the water, and to take away all other impediments that made the harbourough dangerous for ships, and to make new havens and arsenals meet to harbour such ships as did continually traffic thither. All these things were purposed to be done, but took no effect.

But the ordinance of the calendar and reformation of the year, to take away all confusion of time, being exactly calculated by the mathematicians and brought to perfection, was a great commodity unto all men. For the Romans, using then the ancient computation of the year, had not only such incertainty and alteration of the month and times that the sacrifices and yearly feasts came by little and little to seasons contrary for the purpose they were ordained but also in the revolution of the sun (which is called *Annus Solaris*) no other nation agreed with them in account and, of the Romans themselves, only the priests understood it. And therefore, when they listed, they suddenly (no man being able to control them) did thrust in a month above their ordinary number, which they called in old time *Mercedonius*. Some say that Numa Pompilius was the first that devised this way, to put a month between, but it was a weak remedy, and did little help the correction of the errors that were made in the account of the year, to frame them to perfection.

But Caesar, committing this matter unto the philosophers and best expert mathematicians at that time, did set forth an excellent and perfect calendar, more exactly calculated than any other that was before, the which the Romans do use until this present day, and do nothing err as others in the difference of time. But his enemies notwithstanding that envied his greatness did not stick to find fault withal. As Cicero the orator, when one said, "To-morrow the star Lyra will rise": "Yea," said he, "at the commandment of Caesar," as if men were compelled so to say and think by Caesar's edict.

But the chiefest cause that made him mortally hated was the covetous desire he had to be called king: which first gave the people just cause, and next his secret enemies honest colour, to bear him ill will. This notwithstanding, they that procured him this honour and dignity gave it out among the people that it was written in the Sibylline prophecies how the Romans might overcome the Parthians, if they made war with them and were led by a king, but otherwise that they were unconquerable. And furthermore they were so bold besides, that, Caesar returning to Rome from the city of Alba, when they came to salute him, they called him king. But the people being offended and Caesar also angry, he said he was not called king, but

Caesar. Then, every man keeping silence, he went his way heavy and sorrowful.

When they had decreed divers honours for him in the Senate, the Consuls and Praetors accompanied with the whole assembly of the Senate went unto him in the market-place, where he was set by the pulpit for orations, to tell him what honours they had decreed for him in his absence. But he, sitting still in his majesty, disdaining to rise up unto them when they came in, as if they had been private men, answered them that his honours had more need to be cut off than enlarged. This did not only offend the Senate, but the common people also, to see that he should so lightly esteem of the Magistrates of the commonwealth, insomuch as every man that might lawfully go his way departed thence very sorrowfully. Thereupon also Caesar rising departed home to his house, and tearing open his doublet collar, making his neck bare, he cried out aloud to his friends that his throat was ready to offer to any man that would come and cut it.

Notwithstanding, it is reported that afterwards, to excuse this folly, he imputed it to his disease, saying that their wits are not perfect which have his disease of the falling evil, when standing of the feet they speak to the common people, but are soon troubled with a trembling of their body and a sudden dimness and giddiness. But that was not true. For he would have risen up to the Senate, but Cornelius Balbus, one of his friends but rather a flatterer, would not let him, saying: "What, do you not remember that you are Caesar, and will you not let them reverence you, and do their duties?"

Besides these occasions and offences, there followed also his shame and reproach, abusing the Tribunes of the people in this sort. At that time the feast Lupercalia was celebrated, the which in old time men say was the feast of shepherds, or herdmen, and is much like unto the feast of the Lycaeans in Arcadia. But howsoever it is, that day there are divers noblemen's sons, young men, (and some of them Magistrates themselves that govern then) which run naked through the city, striking in sport them they meet in their way with leather thongs, hair and all on, to make them give place. And many noblewomen and gentlewomen also go of purpose to stand in their way, and do put forth their hands to be stricken, as scholars hold them out to their schoolmaster to be stricken with the ferula: persuading themselves that, being with child, they shall have good delivery, and also, being barren, that it will make them to conceive with child. Caesar sat to behold that sport upon the pulpit for orations, in a chair of gold, apparelled in triumphing manner.

Antonius, who was Consul at that time, was one of them that ran this holy course. So, when he came into the marketplace, the people made a lane for him to run at liberty, and he came to Caesar, and presented him a diadem wreathed about with laurel. Whereupon there rose a certain cry of rejoicing, not very great, done only by a few appointed for the purpose. But when Caesar refused the diadem, then all the people together made an outcry of joy. Then, Antonius offering it him again, there was a second shout of joy, but yet of a few. But when Caesar refused it again the second time, then all the whole people shouted. Caesar having made this proof found that the people did not like of it, and thereupon rose out of his chair, and commanded the crown to be carried unto Jupiter in the Capitol.

After that, there were set up images of Caesar in the city with diadems upon their heads, like kings. Those the two Tribunes, Flavius and Marullus, went and pulled down: and furthermore, meeting with them that first saluted Caesar as king, they committed them to prison. The people followed them rejoicing at it, and called them Brutes, because of Brutus, who had in old time driven the kings out of Rome, and that brought the kingdom of one person unto the government of the Senate and people. Caesar was so offended withal that he deprived Marullus and Flavius of their Tribuneships, and, accusing them, he spake also against the people, and called them *Bruti* and *Cumani*, to wit, beasts and fools.

Hereupon the people went straight unto

Marcus Brutus, who from his father came of the first Brutus and by his mother of the house of the Servilians, a noble house as any was in Rome, and was also nephew and son-in-law of Marcus Cato. Notwithstanding, the great honours and favour Caesar shewed unto him kept him back, that of himself alone he did not conspire nor consent to depose him of his kingdom. For Caesar did not only save his life after the battle of Pharsalia when Pompey fled, and did at his request also save many more of his friends besides; but, furthermore, he put a marvellous confidence in him. For he had already preferred him to the Praetorship for that year, and furthermore was appointed to be Consul the fourth year after that, having through Caesar's friendship obtained it before Cassius, who likewise made suit for the same; and Caesar also, as it is reported, said in this contention, "Indeed Cassius hath alleged best reason, but yet shall he not be chosen before Brutus." Some one day accusing Brutus while he practised this conspiracy, Caesar would not hear of it, but clapping his hand on his body told them, "Brutus will look for this skin," meaning thereby that Brutus for his virtue deserved to rule after him, but yet that for ambition's sake he would not shew himself unthankful nor dishonourable.

Now they that desired change and wished Brutus only their prince and governor above all other, they durst not come to him themselves to tell him what they would have him to do, but in the night did cast sundry papers into the Praetor's seat where he gave audience, and the most of them to this effect: "Thou sleepest, Brutus, and art not Brutus indeed." Cassius, finding Brutus' ambition stirred up the more by these seditious bills, did prick him forward and egg him on the more for a private quarrel he had conceived against Caesar, the circumstance whereof we have set down more at large in Brutus' life. Caesar also had Cassius in great jealousy and suspected him much; whereupon he said on a time to his friends, "What will Cassius do, think ye? I like not his pale looks." Another time, when Caesar's friends complained unto him of Antonius and Dolabella that they pretended some mischief towards him, he answered them again, "As for those fat men and smooth-combed heads," quoth he, "I never reckon of them, but these pale-visaged and carrion lean people, I fear them most," meaning Brutus and Cassius.

Certainly, destiny may easier be foreseen than avoided, considering the strange and wonderful signs that were said to be seen before Caesar's death. For, touching the fires in the element and spirits running up and down in the night, and also the solitary birds to be seen at noon-days sitting in the great market-place: are not all these signs perhaps worth the noting in such a wonderful chance as happened? But Strabo the philosopher writeth that divers men were seen going up and down in fire; and furthermore, that there was a slave of the soldiers, that did cast a marvellous burning flame out of his hand, insomuch as they that saw it thought he had been burnt, but when the fire was out, it was found he had no hurt. Caesar self also, doing sacrifice unto the gods, found that one of the beasts which was sacrificed had no heart; and that was a strange thing in nature, how a beast could live without a heart.

Furthermore, there was a certain Soothsayer that had given Caesar warning long time afore, to take heed of the day of the Ides of March (which is the fifteenth of the month), for on that day he should be in great danger. That day being come, Caesar going unto the Senate-house, and speaking merrily to the Soothsayer, told him, "The Ides of March be come." "So be they," softly answered the Soothsayer, "but yet are they not past." And the very day before, Caesar, supping with Marcus Lepidus, sealed certain letters, as he was wont to do, at the board; so, talk falling out amongst them, reasoning what death was best, he preventing their opinions cried out aloud, "Death unlooked for."

Then going to bed the same night as his manner was, and lying with his wife Calpurnia, all the windows and doors of his chamber flying open, the noise awoke him, and made him afraid when he saw such light, but more, when he heard his wife Calpurnia, being fast asleep, weep and sigh, and put forth many fumbling lamentable speeches. For she dreamed that Caesar was slain, and that she had him in her arms. Others also do deny that she had any such dream, as amongst other Titus Livius writeth that it was in this sort. The Senate having set upon the top of Caesar's house, for an ornament and setting forth of the same, a certain pinnacle, Calpurnia dreamed that she saw it broken down, and that she thought she lamented and wept for it.

Insomuch that, Caesar rising in the morning, she prayed him if it were possible not to go out of the doors that day, but to adjourn the session of the Senate until another day. And if that he made no reckoning of her dream, yet that he would search further of the Soothsayers by their sacrifices, to know what should happen him that day. Thereby it seemed that Caesar likewise did fear and suspect somewhat, because his wife Calpurnia until that time was never given to any fear or superstition and then, for that he saw her so troubled in mind with this dream she had. But much more afterwards, when the Soothsayers, having sacrificed many beasts one after another, told him that none did like them; then he determined to send Antonius to adjourn the session of the Senate.

But in the meantime came Decius Brutus, surnamed Albinus, in whom Caesar put such confidence that in his last will and testament he had appointed him to be his next heir, and yet was of the conspiracy with Cassius and Brutus; he, fearing that if Caesar did adjourn the session that day the conspiracy would out, laughed the Soothsayers to scorn, and reproved Caesar, saying that he gave the Senate occasion to mislike with him, and that they might think he mocked them, considering that by his commandment they were assembled, and that they were ready willingly to grant him all things, and to proclaim him king of all the provinces of the Empire of Rome out of Italy, and that he should wear his diadem in all other places both by sea and land. And furthermore, that if any man should tell them from him they should depart for that present time, and return again when Calpurnia should have better dreams, what would his enemies and ill-wishers say and how could they like of his friends' words? And who could persuade them otherwise, but that they would think his dominion a slavery unto them, and tyrannical in himself?

"And yet, if it be so," said he, "that you utterly mislike of this day, it is better that you go yourself in person, and saluting the Senate to dismiss them till another time." Therewithal he took Caesar by the hand, and brought him out of his house. Caesar was not gone far from his house, but a bondman, a stranger, did what he could to speak with him; and, when he saw he was put back by the great press and multitude of people that followed him, he went straight unto his house, and put himself into Calpurnia's hands to be kept till Caesar came back again, telling her that he had great matters to impart unto him.

And one Artemidorus also, born in the Isle of Gnidos, a Doctor of Rhetoric in the Greek tongue, who by means of his profession was very familiar with certain of Brutus' confederates, and therefore knew the most part of all their practices against Caesar, came and brought him a little bill written with his own hand, of all that he meant to tell him. He, marking how Caesar received all the supplications that were offered him, and that he gave them straight to his men that were about him, pressed nearer to him, and said: "Caesar, read this memorial to yourself, and that quickly, for they be matters of great weight, and touch you nearly." Caesar took it of him, but could never read it, though he many times attempted it, for the number of people that did salute him; but holding it still in his hand, keeping it to himself, went on withal into the Senate-house. Howbeit other are of opinion that it was some man else that gave him that memorial, and not Artemidorus, who did what he could all the way as he went to give it Caesar, but he was always repulsed by the people.

For these things they may seem to come by chance; but the place where the murder was prepared, and where the Senate were assembled, and where also there stood up an image of Pompey dedicated by himself amongst other ornaments which he gave unto the Theatre: all these were manifest proofs that it was the ordinance of some god that made this treason to be executed specially in that very place.

It is also reported that Cassius (though otherwise he did favour the doctrine of Epicurus) beholding the image of Pompey, before they entered into the action of their traitorous enterprise, he did softly call upon it to aid him. But the instant danger of the present time, taking away his former reason, did suddenly put him into a furious passion, and made him like a man half beside himself.

Now Antonius, that was a faithful friend to Caesar, and a valiant man besides of his hands, him Decius Brutus Albinus entertained out of the Senate-house, having begun a long tale of set purpose. So, Caesar coming into the house, all the Senate stood up on their feet to do him honour. Then part of Brutus' company and confederates stood round about Caesar's chair, and part of them also came towards him, as though they made suit with Metellus Cimber, to call home his brother again from banishment; and thus, prosecuting still their suit, they followed Caesar till he was set in his chair. Who denying their petitions, and being offended with them one after another, because the more they were denied, the more they pressed upon him, and were the earnester with him, Metellus at length, taking his gown with both his hands, pulled it over his neck, which was the sign given the confederates to set upon him.

Then Casca behind him strake him in the neck with his sword; howbeit the wound was not great nor mortal, because, it seemed, the fear of such a devilish attempt did amaze him, and take his strength from him, that he killed him not at the first blow. But Caesar, turning straight unto him, caught hold of his sword, and held it hard: and they both cried out, Caesar in Latin: "O vile traitor Casca, what doest thou?" And Casca in Greek to his brother, "Brother, help me."

At the beginning of this stir, they that were present, not knowing of the conspiracy, were so amazed with the horrible sight they saw that they had no power to fly, neither to help him, not so much as once to make any outcry. They on the other side that had conspired his death compassed him in on every side with their swords drawn in their hands, that Caesar turned him nowhere but he was stricken at by some, and still had naked swords in his face, and was hacked and mangled among them, as a wild beast taken of hunters. For it was agreed among them that every man should give him a wound, because all their parts should be in this murder; and then Brutus himself gave him one wound about his privities.

Men report also that Caesar did still defend himself against the rest, running every way with his body: but when he saw Brutus with his sword drawn in his hand, then he pulled his gown over his head, and made no more resistance, and was driven either casually or purposely by the counsel of the conspirators against the base whereupon Pompey's image stood, which ran all of a gore-blood till he was slain. Thus it seemed that the image took just revenge of Pompey's enemy, being thrown down on the ground at his feet, and yielding up his ghost there for the number of wounds he had upon him. For it is reported that he had three-and-twenty wounds upon his body; and divers of the conspirators did hurt themselves, striking one body with so many blows.

[THE GREAT FIRE OF LONDON]*

Samuel Pepys
(1633–1703)

2nd (Lord's day). Some of our mayds sitting up late last night to get things ready against our feast to-day, Jane called us up about three in the morning, to tell us of a

* From the *Diary* of Samuel Pepys, September 2 to September 6, 1666.

great fire they saw in the City. So I rose and slipped on my night-gowne, and went to her window, and thought it to be on the back-side of Marke-lane at the farthest; but, being unused to such fires as followed, I thought it far enough off; and so went to bed again and to sleep. About seven rose again to dress my-self, and there looked out at the window, and saw the fire not so much as it was and further off. So to my closett to set things to rights after yesterday's cleaning. By and by Jane comes and tells me that she hears that above 300 houses have been burned down to-night by the fire we saw, and that it is now burning down all Fish-street, by London Bridge. So I made myself ready presently, and walked to the Tower, and there got up upon one of the high places, Sir J. Robin-son's little son going up with me; and there I did see the houses at that end of the bridge all on fire, and an infinite great fire on this and the other side the end of the bridge; which, among other people, did trouble me for poor little Michell and our Sarah on the bridge. So down, with my heart full of trou-ble, to the Lieutenant of the Tower, who tells me that it begun this morning in the King's baker's house in Pudding-lane, and that it hath burned St. Magnus's Church and most part of Fish-street already. So I down to the water-side, and there got a boat and through bridge, and there saw a lamentable fire. Poor Michell's house, as far as the Old Swan, already burned that way, and the fire running further, that in a very little time it got as far as the Steele-yard, while I was there. Everybody endeavouring to remove their goods, and flinging into the river or bringing them into lighters that lay off; poor people staying in their houses as long as till the very fire touched them, and then running into boats, or clambering from one pair of stairs by the water-side to another. And among other things, the poor pigeons, I perceive, were loth to leave their houses, but hovered about the windows and balconys till they were, some of them burned, their wings, and fell down. Having staid, and in an hour's time seen the fire rage every way, and nobody, to my sight, endeavouring to quench it, but to remove their goods, and leave all to the fire, and having seen it get as far as the Steele-yard, and the wind mighty high and driving it into the City; and every thing, after so long a drought, proving com-bustible, even the very stones of churches, and among other things the poor steeple by which pretty Mrs. —— lives, and whereof my old schoolfellow Elborough is parson, taken fire in the very top, and there burned till it fell down: I to White Hall (with a gentleman with me who desired to go off from the Tower, to see the fire, in my boat); to White Hall, and there up to the King's closett in the Chappell, where people come about me, and I did give them an account dismayed them all, and word was carried in to the King. So I was called for, and did tell the King and Duke of Yorke what I saw, and that unless his Majesty did command houses to be pulled down nothing could stop the fire. They seemed much troubled, and the King commanded me to go to my Lord Mayor from him, and command him to spare no houses, but to pull down before the fire every way. The Duke of York bid me tell him that if he would have any more soldiers he shall; and so did my Lord Arlington after-wards, as a great secret. Here meeting with Captain Cocke, I in his coach, which he lent me, and Creed with me to Paul's, and there walked along Watling Street, as well as I could, every creature coming away laden with goods to save, and here and there sick people carried away in beds. Extraordinary good goods carried in carts and on backs. At last met my Lord Mayor in Canning Street, like a man spent, with a handkerchief about his neck. To the King's message he cried, like a fainting woman: "Lord! what can I do? I am spent: people will not obey me. I have been pulling down houses; but the fire overtakes us faster than we can do it." That he needed no more soldiers; and that, for himself, he must go and refresh himself, hav-ing been up all night. So he left me, and I him, and walked home, seeing people all al-most distracted, and no manner of means used to quench the fire. The houses, too, so very thick thereabouts, and full of matter for burning, as pitch and tar, in Thames Street; and warehouses of oil, and wines, and brandy, and other things. Here I saw Mr. Isaac Houblon, the handsome man, prettily dressed and dirty, at his door at Dowgate, receiving some of his brother's things, whose houses were on fire; and, as he says, have been removed twice already; and he doubts (as it soon proved) that they must be in a little time removed from his house also, which was a sad consideration. And to see the churches all filling with goods by people who themselves should have been quietly there at this time. By this time it was about twelve o'clock; and so home, and there find my guests, which was Mr. Wood and his wife Barbara Sheldon, and also Mr. Moone: she mighty fine, and her husband, for aught I see, a likely man. But Mr. Moone's design and mine, which was to look over my closet and please him with the sight thereof, which he hath long desired, was wholly disappointed; for we were in great trouble and disturbance at this fire, not knowing what to think of it. However, we had an extraordinary good dinner, and as merry as at this time we could be. While at dinner Mrs. Batelier come to enquire after Mr. Wolfe and Stanes (who, it seems, are related to them), whose houses in Fish Street are all burned, and they in a sad condition. She would not stay in the fright. Soon as I dined, I and Moone away, and walked through the City, the streets full of nothing but people and horses and carts loaden with goods, ready to run over one another, and removing goods from one burned house to another. They now removing out of Canning Street (which received goods in the morning) into Lombard Street, and further; and among others I now saw my little goldsmith, Stokes, receiving some friend's goods, whose house itself was burned the day after. We parted at Paul's; he home, and I to Paul's Wharf, where I had appointed a boat to attend me, and took in Mr. Carcasse and his brother, whom I met in the street, and carried them below and above bridge to and again to see the fire, which was now got further, both below and above, and no likelihood of stopping it. Met with the King and Duke of York in their barge, and with them to Queenhithe, and there called Sir Richard Browne to them. Their order was only to pull down houses apace, and so below bridge at the waterside; but little was or could be done, the fire coming upon them so fast. Good hopes there was of stopping it at the Three Cranes above, and at Buttolph's wharf below bridge, if care be used; but the wind carries it into the City, so as we know not by the waterside what it do there. River full of lighters and boats taking in goods, and good goods swimming in the water, and only I observed that hardly one lighter or boat in three that had the goods of a house in, but there was a pair of virginals in it. Having seen as much as I could now, I away to Whitehall by appointment, and there walked to St. James Park, and there met my wife and Creed and Wood and his wife, and walked to my boat; and there upon the water again, and to the fire up and down, it still increasing, and the wind great. So near the fire as we could for smoke; and all over the Thames, with one's face in the wind, you were almost burned with a shower of firedrops. This is very true; so as houses were burned by these drops and flakes of fire, three or four, nay, five or six houses, one from another. When we could endure no more upon the water, we to a little ale-house on the Bankside, over against the Three Cranes, and there staid till it was dark almost, and saw the fire grow; and, as it grew darker, churches and houses, as far as we could see up the hill of the City, in a most horrid malicious bloody flame, not like the fine flame of an ordinary fire. Barbary and her husband away before us. We staid till, it being darkish, we saw the fire as only one entire arch of fire from this to the other side the bridge, and in a bow up the hill for an arch of above a mile long: it made me weep to see it. The churches, houses, and all on fire and flaming at once; and a horrid noise and flames made, and the cracking of houses at their ruine. So home with a sad heart, and there find every body discoursing and lamenting the fire; and poor Tom Hater come with some few of his goods saved out of his house, which is burned upon Fish-streete Hill. I invited him to lie at my house, and did receive his goods, but was deceived in his lying there, the newes coming every moment of the growth of the fire; so as we were forced to begin to pack up our owne goods, and prepare for their removal; and did by moonshine (it being brave dry, and moonshine, and warm weather) carry much of my goods into the garden, and Mr. Hater and I did remove my money and iron chests into my cellar, as thinking that the safest place. And got my bags of gold into my office, ready to carry away, and my chief papers of accounts also there, and my tallys into a box by themselves. So great was our fear, as Sir W. Batten hath carts come out of the country to fetch away his goods this night. We did put Mr. Hater, poor man, to bed a little; but he got but very little rest, so much noise being in my house, taking down of goods.

3rd. About four o'clock in the morning, my Lady Batten sent me a cart to carry away all my money, and plate, and best things, to Sir W. Rider's at Bednall-greene. Which I did, riding myself in my night-gowne in the cart; and, Lord! to see how the streets and the highways are crowded with people running and riding, and getting of carts at any rate to fetch away things. I find Sir W. Rider tired with being called up all night, and receiving things from several friends. His house full of goods, and much of Sir W. Batten's and Sir W. Pen's. I am eased at my heart to have my treasure so well secured. Then home, with much ado to find a way, nor any sleep all this night to me nor my poor wife. But then and all this day she and I, and all my people labouring to get away the rest of our things, and did get Mr. Tooker to get me a lighter to take them in, and we did carry them (myself some) over Tower Hill, which was by this time full of people's goods, bringing their goods thither; and down to the lighter, which lay at the next quay, above the Tower Docke. And here was my neighbour's wife, Mrs. ——, with her pretty child, and some few of her things, which I did willingly give way to be saved with mine; but there was no passing with any thing through the postern, the crowd was so great. The Duke of Yorke come this day by the office, and spoke to us, and did ride with his guard up and down the City to keep all quiet (he being now Generall, and having the care of all). This day, Mercer being not at home, but against her mistress's order gone to her mother's, and my wife going thither to speak with W. Hewer, met her there, and was angry; and her mother saying that she was not a 'prentice girl, to ask leave every time she goes abroad, my wife with good reason was angry, and, when she came home, bid her be gone again. And so she went away, which troubled me, but yet less than it would, because of the condition we are in, fear of coming into in a little time of being less able to keepe one in her quality. At night lay down a little upon a quilt of W. Hewer's in the office, all my owne things being packed up or gone; and after me my poor wife did the like, we having fed upon the remains of yesterday's dinner, having no fire nor dishes, nor any opportunity of dressing any thing.

4th. Up by break of day to get away the remainder of my things; which I did by a lighter at the Iron gate: and my hands so few, that it was the afternoon before we could get them all away. Sir W. Pen and I to Tower-streete, and there met the fire burning three or four doors beyond Mr. Howell's, whose goods, poor man, his trayes, and dishes, shovells, &c., were flung all along Tower-street in the kennels, and people working therewith from one end to the other; the fire coming on in that narrow streete, on both sides, with infinite fury. Sir W. Batten not knowing how to remove his wine, did dig a pit in the garden, and laid it in there; and I took the opportunity of laying all the papers of my office that I could not otherwise dispose of. And in the evening Sir W. Pen and I did dig another, and put our wine in it; and I my Parmezan cheese, as well as my wine and some other things. The Duke of York was at the office this day, at Sir W. Pen's; but I happened not to be within. This afternoon, sitting melancholy with Sir W. Pen in our garden, and thinking of the certain burning of this office, without extraordinary means, I did propose for the sending up of all our workmen from Woolwich and Deptford yards (none whereof yet appeared), and to write to Sir W. Coventry to have the Duke of York's permission to pull down houses, rather than lose this office, which would much hinder the King's business. So Sir W. Pen he went down this night, in order to the sending them up tomorrow morning; and I wrote to Sir W. Coventry about the business, but received no answer. This night Mrs. Turner (who, poor woman, was removing her goods all this day, good goods into the garden, and knows not how to dispose of them), and her husband supped with my wife and I at night, in the office, upon a shoulder of mutton from the cook's, without any napkin or any thing, in a sad manner, but were merry. Only now and then walking into the garden, and saw how horridly the sky looks, all on a fire in the night, was enough to put us out of our wits; and, indeed, it was extremely dreadful, for it looks just as if it was at us, and the whole heaven on fire. I after supper walked in the dark down to Tower Street, and there saw it all on fire, at the Trinity House on that side, and the Dolphin Tavern on this side, which was very near us; and the fire with extraordinary vehemence. Now begins the practice of blowing up of houses in Tower Street, those next the Tower, which at first did frighten people more than anything; but it stopped the fire where it was done, it bringing down the houses to the ground in the same places they stood, and then it was easy to quench what little fire was in it, though it kindled nothing almost. W. Hewer this day went to see how his mother did, and comes late home, telling us how he hath been forced to remove her to Islington, her house in Pye Corner being burned; so that the fire is got so far that way, and all the Old Bayly, and was running down to Fleet Street; and Paul's is burned, and all Cheapside. I wrote to my father this night, but the posthouse being burned, the letter could not go.

5th. I lay down in the office again upon W. Hewer's quilt, being mighty weary, and wore in my feet with going till I was hardly able to stand. About two in the morning my wife calls me up and tells me of new cries of fire, it being come to Barking Church, which is the bottom of our lane. I up, and finding it so, resolved presently to take her away, and did, and took my gold, which was about £2,350, W. Hewer, and Jane, down by Proundy's boat to Woolwich; but, Lord! what a sad sight it was by moonlight to see the whole City almost on fire, that you might see it plain at Woolwich, as if you were by it. There, when I come, I find the gates shut, but no guard kept at all, which troubled me, because of discourse now begun, that there is plot in it, and that the French had done it. I got the gates open, and to Mr. Shelden's, where I locked up my gold, and charged my wife and W. Hewer never to leave the room without one of them in it, night or day. So back again, by the way seeing my goods well in the lighters at Deptford, and watched well by people. Home, and whereas I expected to have seen our house on fire, it being now about seven o'clock, it was not. But to the fire, and there find greater hopes than I expected; for my confidence of finding our Office was such, that I durst not ask any body how it was with us, till I come and saw it not burned. But going to the fire, I find by the blowing up of houses, and the great help given by the workmen out of the King's yards, sent up by Sir W. Pen, there is a good stop given to it, as well as at Mark Lane end as ours; it having only burned the dial of Barking Church, and part of the porch, and was there quenched. I up to the top of Barking steeple, and there saw the saddest sight of desolation that I ever saw; every where great fires, oil-cellars, and brimstone, and other things burning. I became afeard to stay there long, and therefore down again as fast as I could, the fire being spread as far as I could see it; and to Sir W. Pen's, and there eat a piece of cold meat, having eaten nothing since Sunday, but the remains of Sunday's dinner. Here I met with Mr. Young and Whistler; and having removed all my things, and received good hopes that the fire at our end is stopped, they and I walked into the town, and find Fan-church-streete, Gracious-streete, and Lumbard-streete all in dust. The Exchange a sad sight, nothing standing there, of all the statues or pillars, but Sir Thomas Gresham's picture in the corner. Walked into Moorefields (our feet ready to burn, walking through the towne among the hot coles), and find that full of people, and poor wretches carrying their goods there, and every body keeping his goods together by themselves (and a great blessing it is to them that it is fair weather for them to keep abroad night and day); drank there, and paid twopence for a plain penny loaf. Thence homeward, having passed through Cheapside and Newgate Market, all burned, and seen Anthony Joyce's house in fire. And took up (which I keep by me) a piece of glasse of Mercers' Chappell in the streete, where much more was, so melted and buckled with the heat of the fire like parchment. I also did see a poor cat taken out of a hole in the chimney, joyning to the wall of the Exchange, with the hair all burned off the body, and yet alive. So home at night, and find there good hopes of saving our office; but great endeavours of watching all night, and having men ready; and so we lodged them in the office, and had drink and bread and cheese for them. And I lay down and slept a good night about midnight, though when I rose I heard that there had been a great alarme of French and Dutch being risen, which proved nothing. But it is a strange thing to see how long this time did look since Sunday, having been always full of variety of actions, and little sleep, that it looked like a week or more, and I had forgot almost the day of the week.

6th. Up about five o'clock, and there met Mr. Gawden at the gate of the office (I intending to go out, as I used, every now and then to-day, to see how the fire is) to call our men to Bishop's-gate, where no fire had yet been near, and there is now one broke out: which did give great grounds to people, and to me too, to think that there is some kind of plot in this (on which many by this time have been taken, and it hath been dangerous for any stranger to walk in the streets), but I went with the men, and we did put it out in a little time; so that that was well again. It was pretty to see how hard the women did work in the cannells, sweeping of water; but then they would scold for drink, and be as drunk as devils. I saw good butts of sugar broke open in the street, and people go and take handsfull out, and put into beer, and drink it. And now all being pretty well, I took boat, and over to Southwarke, and took boat on the other side the bridge, and so to Westminster, thinking to shift myself, being all in dirt from top to bottom; but could not there find any place to buy a shirt or pair of gloves, Westminster Hall being full of people's goods, those in Westminster having removed all their goods, and the Exchequer money put into vessels to carry to Nonsuch; but to the Swan, and there was trimmed; and then to White Hall, but saw nobody; and so home. A sad sight to see how the River looks: no houses nor church near it, to the Temple, where it stopped. At home, did go with Sir W. Batten, and our neighbour, Knightly (who, with one more, was the only man of any fashion left in all the neighbourhood thereabouts, they all removing their goods and leaving their houses to the mercy of the fire), to Sir R. Ford's, and there dined in an earthen platter—a fried breast of mutton; a great many of us, but very merry, and indeed as good a meal, though as ugly a one, as ever I had in my life. Thence down to Deptford, and there with great satisfaction landed all my goods at Sir G. Carteret's safe, and nothing missed I could see, or hurt. This being done to my great content, I home, and to Sir W. Batten's, and there with Sir R. Ford, Mr. Knightly, and one Withers, a professed lying rogue, supped well, and mighty merry, and our fears over.

[DR. JOHNSON AND HIS LITERARY FRIENDS]*

James Boswell
(1740–1795)

On Monday, April 19, he called on me with Mrs. Williams, in Mr. Strahan's coach,

* From *The Life of Samuel Johnson L.L.D.* The passage is taken from the year 1773.

and carried me out to dine with Mr. Elphinston, at his academy at Kensington. A printer having acquired a fortune sufficient to keep his coach, was a good topick for the credit of literature. Mrs. Williams said, that another printer, Mr. Hamilton, had not waited so long as Mr. Strahan, but had kept his coach several years sooner. JOHNSON. 'He was in the right. Life is short. The sooner that a man begins to enjoy his wealth the better.'

Mr. Elphinston talked of a new book that was much admired, and asked Dr. Johnson if he had read it. JOHNSON. 'I have looked into it.' 'What, (said Elphinston,) have you not read it through?' Johnson, offended at being thus pressed, and so obliged to own his cursory mode of reading, answered tartly, 'No, Sir, do *you* read books *through?*'

He this day again defended duelling, and put his argument upon what I have ever thought the most solid basis; that if publick war be allowed to be consistent with morality, private war must be equally so. Indeed we may observe what strained arguments are used to reconcile war with the Christian religion. But, in my opinion, it is exceedingly clear that duelling having better reasons for its barbarous violence, is more justifiable than war in which thousands go forth without any cause of personal quarrel, and massacre each other.

On Wednesday, April 21, I dined with him at Mr. Thrale's. A gentleman attacked Garrick for being vain. JOHNSON. 'No wonder, Sir, that he is vain; a man who is perpetually flattered in every mode that can be conceived. So many bellows have blown the fire, that one wonders he is not by this time become a cinder.' BOSWELL. 'And such bellows too. Lord Mansfield with his cheeks like to burst: Lord Chatham like an Æolus. I have read such notes from them to him, as were enough to turn his head.' JOHNSON. 'True. When he whom every body else flatters, flatters me, I then am truly happy.' MRS. THRALE. 'The sentiment is in Congreve, I think.' JOHNSON. 'Yes, Madam, in *The Way of the World:*

"If there's delight in love, 'tis when I see
     That heart which others bleed for, bleed
     for me."

No, Sir, I should not be surprised though Garrick chained the ocean and lashed the winds.' BOSWELL. 'Should it not be, Sir, lashed the ocean and chained the winds?' JOHNSON. 'No, Sir, recollect the original:

"In corum atque Eurum solitus sævire
     flagellis
     Barbarus, Æolio nunquam hoc in car-
     cere passos,
     Ipsum compedibus qui vinxerat En-
     nosigœum." '

This does very well, when both the winds and the sea are personified, and mentioned by their mythological names, as in Juvenal; but when they are mentioned in plain language, the application of the epithets suggested by me is the most obvious; and accordingly my friend himself, in his imitation of the passage which describes Xerxes, has

'The waves he lashes, and enchains the
     wind.'

The modes of living in different countries, and the various views with which men travel in quest of new scenes, having been talked of, a learned gentleman who holds a considerable office in the law, expatiated on the happiness of a savage life; and mentioned an instance of an officer who had actually lived for some time in the wilds of America, of whom, when in that state, he quoted this reflection with an air of admiration, as if it had been deeply philosophical: 'Here am I, free and unrestrained, amidst the rude magnificence of Nature, with this Indian woman by my side, and this gun with which I can procure food when I want it; what more can be desired for human happiness?' It did not require much sagacity to foresee that such a sentiment would not be permitted to pass without due animadversion. JOHNSON. 'Do not allow yourself, Sir, to be imposed upon by such gross absurdity. It is sad stuff; it is brutish. If a bull could speak, he might as well exclaim,—Here am I with this cow and this grass; what being can enjoy greater felicity?'

We talked of the melancholy end of a gentleman who had destroyed himself. JOHNSON. 'It was owing to imaginary difficulties in his affairs, which, had he talked

with any friend, would soon have vanished.'
BOSWELL. 'Do you think, Sir, that all who
commit suicide are mad?' JOHNSON. 'Sir,
they are often not universally disordered in
their intellects, but one passion presses so
upon them, that they yield to it, and commit suicide, as a passionate man will stab
another.' He added, 'I have often thought,
that after a man has taken the resolution to
kill himself, it is not courage in him to do
any thing, however desperate, because he has
nothing to fear.' GOLDSMITH. 'I don't see
that.' JOHNSON. 'Nay, but my dear Sir, why
should not you see what every one else sees?'
GOLDSMITH. 'It is for fear of something that
he has resolved to kill himself; and will not
that timid disposition restrain him?' JOHN-
SON. 'It does not signify that the fear of
something made him resolve; it is upon the
state of his mind, after the resolution is taken,
that I argue. Suppose a man, either from
fear, or pride, or conscience, or whatever
motive, has resolved to kill himself; when
once the resolution is taken, he has nothing
to fear. He may then go and take the King
of Prussia by the nose, at the head of his
army. He cannot fear the rack, who is resolved to kill himself. When Eustace Budgel
was walking down to the Thames, determined to drown himself, he might, if he
pleased, without any apprehension of danger,
have turned aside, and first set fire to St.
James's palace.'

On Tuesday, April 27, Mr. Beauclerk and
I called on him in the morning. As we
walked up Johnson's-court, I said, 'I have a
veneration for this court;' and was glad to
find that Beauclerk had the same reverential
enthusiasm. We found him alone. We talked
of Mr. Andrew Stuart's elegant and plausible
Letters to Lord Mansfield: a copy of which
had been sent by the author to Dr. Johnson.
JOHNSON. 'They have not answered the end.
They have not been talked of; I have never
heard of them. This is owing to their not
being sold. People seldom read a book which
is given to them; and few are given. The way
to spread a work is to sell it at a low price.
No man will send to buy a thing that costs
even sixpence, without an intention to read

it.' BOSWELL. 'May it not be doubted, Sir,
whether it be proper to publish letters, arraigning the ultimate decision of an important cause by the supreme judicature of the
nation?' JOHNSON. 'No, Sir, I do not think
it was wrong to publish these letters. If they
are thought to do harm, why not answer
them? But they will do no harm. If Mr.
Douglas be indeed the son of Lady Jane, he
cannot be hurt: if he be not her son, and yet
has the great estate of the family of Douglas,
he may well submit to have a pamphlet
against him by Andrew Stuart. Sir, I think
such a publication does good, as it does good
to shew us the possibilities of human life.
And, Sir, you will not say that the Douglas
cause was a cause of easy decision, when it
divided your Court as much as it could do, to
be determined at all. When your Judges are
seven and seven, the casting vote of the
President must be given on one side or other;
no matter, for my argument, on which; one
or the other *must* be taken; as when I am to
move, there is no matter which leg I move
first. And then, Sir, it was otherwise determined here. No, Sir, a more dubious determination of any question cannot be imagined.'[1]

He said, 'Goldsmith should not be for
ever attempting to shine in conversation: he
has not temper for it, he is so much mortified
when he fails. Sir, a game of jokes is composed partly of skill, partly of chance, a man
may be beat at times by one who has not the
tenth part of his wit. Now Goldsmith's putting himself against another, is like a man
laying a hundred to one who cannot spare
the hundred. It is not worth a man's while.
A man should not lay a hundred to one, un-

[1] I regretted that Dr. Johnson never took the
trouble to study a question which interested nations. He would not even read a pamphlet that
I wrote upon it, entitled 'The essence of the
Douglas Cause;' which I have reason to flatter
myself, had considerable effect in favour of Mr.
Douglas; of whose legitimate filiation I was then,
and am still, firmly convinced. Let me add, that
no fact can be more respectably ascertained, than
by the judgment of the most august tribunal in
the world; a judgement in which Lord Mansfield
and Lord Camden united in 1769, and from
which only five of a numerous body entered a
protest.

less he can easily spare it, though he has a hundred chances for him: he can get but a guinea, and he may lose a hundred. Goldsmith is in this state. When he contends, if he gets the better, it is a very little addition to a man of his literary reputation: if he does not get the better, he is miserably vexed.'

Johnson's own superlative powers of wit set him above any risk of such uneasiness. Garrick had remarked to me of him, a few days before, 'Rabelais and all other wits are nothing compared with him. You may be diverted by them; but Johnson gives you a forcible hug, and shakes laughter out of you, whether you will or no.'

Goldsmith, however, was often very fortunate in his witty contests, even when he entered the lists with Johnson himself. Sir Joshua Reynolds was in company with them one day, when Goldsmith said, that he thought he could write a good fable, mentioned the simplicity which that kind of composition requires, and observed, that in most fables the animals introduced seldom talk in character. 'For instance, (said he,) the fable of the little fishes, who saw birds fly over their heads, and envying them, petitioned Jupiter to be changed into birds. The skill (continued he,) consists in making them talk like little fishes.' While he indulged himself in this fanciful reverie, he observed Johnson shaking his sides, and laughing. Upon which he smartly proceeded, 'Why, Dr. Johnson, this is not so easy as you seem to think; for if you were to make little fishes talk, they would talk like WHALES.'

Johnson, though remarkable for his great variety of composition, never exercised his talents in fable, except we allow his beautiful tale published in Mrs. Williams's Miscellanies to be of that species. I have, however, found among his manuscript collections the following sketch of one:

'Glow worm lying in the garden saw a candle in a neighbouring palace,—and complained of the littleness of his own light; another observed—wait a little; soon dark,— have outlasted πολλ [many] of these glaring lights which are only brighter as they haste to nothing.'

On Thursday, April 29, I dined with him at General Oglethorpe's, where were Sir Joshua Reynolds, Mr. Langton, Dr. Goldsmith, and Mr. Thrale. I was very desirous to get Dr. Johnson absolutely fixed in his resolution to go with me to the Hebrides this year; and I told him that I had received a letter from Dr. Robertson the historian, upon the subject, with which he was much pleased; and now talked in such a manner of his long-intended tour, that I was satisfied he meant to fulfil his engagement.

The character of Mallet having been introduced, and spoken of slightingly by Goldsmith; JOHNSON. 'Why, Sir, Mallet had talents enough to keep his literary reputation alive as long as he himself lived; and that, let me tell you, is a good deal.' GOLDSMITH. 'But I cannot agree that it was so. His literary reputation was dead long before his natural death. I consider an authour's literary reputation to be alive only while his name will ensure a good price for his copy from the booksellers. I will get you (to Johnson,) a hundred guineas for any thing whatever that you shall write, if you put your name to it.'

Dr. Goldsmith's new play, *She Stoops to Conquer,* being mentioned; JOHNSON. 'I know of no comedy for many years that has so much exhilarated an audience, that has answered so much the great end of comedy —making an audience merry.'

Goldsmith having said, that Garrick's compliment to the Queen, which he introduced into the play of *The Chances,* which he had altered and revised this year, was mean and gross flattery; JOHNSON. 'Why, Sir, I would not *write,* I would not give solemnly under my hand, a character beyond what I thought really true; but a speech on the stage, let it flatter ever so extravagantly, is formular. It has always been formular to flatter Kings and Queens; so much so, that even in our church-service we have "our most religious King," used indiscriminately, whoever is King. Nay, they even flatter themselves;—"we have been graciously pleased to grant." No modern flattery, however, is so gross as that of the Augustan age, where the Emperour was

deified. *"Præsens Divus habebitur Augustus."*
And as to meanness, (rising into warmth,)
how is it mean in a player,—a showman,—a
fellow who exhibits himself for a shilling,
to flatter his Queen? The attempt, indeed,
was dangerous; for if it had missed, what
became of Garrick, and what became of the
Queen? As Sir William Temple says of a
great General, it is necessary not only that
his designs be formed in a masterly manner,
but that they should be attended with success.
Sir, it is right, at a time when the Royal
Family is not generally liked, to let it be seen
that the people like at least one of them.' SIR
JOSHUA REYNOLDS. 'I do not perceive why
the profession of a player should be despised;
for the great and ultimate end of all the
employments of mankind is to produce
amusement. Garrick produces more amusement than any body.' BOSWELL. 'You say,
Dr. Johnson, that Garrick exhibits himself
for a shilling. In this respect he is only on a
footing with a lawyer who exhibits himself
for his fee, and even will maintain any nonsense or absurdity, if the case requires it.
Garrick refuses a play or a part which he does
not like; a lawyer never refuses.' JOHNSON.
'Why, Sir, what does this prove? only that a
lawyer is worse. Boswell is now like Jack in
The Tale of a Tub, who, when he is puzzled
by an argument, hangs himself. He thinks I
shall cut him down, but I'll let him hang.'
(laughing vociferously.) SIR JOSHUA REYN-
OLDS. 'Mr. Boswell thinks that the profession
of a lawyer being unquestionably honourable,
if he can show the profession of a player to be
more honourable, he proves his argument.'

On Friday, April 30, I dined with him at
Mr. Beauclerk's, where were Lord Charle-
mont, Sir Joshua Reynolds, and some more
members of the LITERARY CLUB, whom he
had obligingly invited to meet me, as I was
this evening to be balloted for as candidate
for admission into that distinguished society.
Johnson had done me the honour to propose
me, and Beauclerk was very zealous for me.

Goldsmith being mentioned; JOHNSON.
'It is amazing how little Goldsmith knows.
He seldom comes where he is not more
ignorant than any one else.' SIR JOSHUA

REYNOLDS. 'Yet there is no man whose company is more liked.' JOHNSON. 'To be sure,
Sir. When people find a man of the most
distinguished abilities as a writer, their in-
feriour while he is with them, it must be
highly gratifying to them. What Goldsmith
comically says of himself is very true,—he
always gets the better when he argues alone;
meaning, that he is master of a subject in his
study, and can write well upon it; but when
he comes into company, grows confused,
and unable to talk. Take him as a poet, his
Traveller is a very fine performance; ay, and
so is his *Deserted Village,* were it not sometimes too much the echo of his *Traveller.*
Whether, indeed, we take him as a poet,—
as a comick writer,—or as an historian, he
stands in the first class.' BOSWELL. 'An historian! My dear Sir, you surely will not rank
his compilation of the Roman History with
the works of other historians of this age?'
JOHNSON. 'Why, who are before him?' BOS-
WELL. 'Hume,—Robertson,—Lord Lyttelton.'
JOHNSON (his antipathy to the Scotch beginning to rise). 'I have not read Hume;
but, doubtless, Goldsmith's *History* is better
than the *verbiage* of Robertson, or the fop-
pery of Dalrymple.' BOSWELL. 'Will you not
admit the superiority of Robertson, in whose
History we find such penetration—such
painting?' JOHNSON. 'Sir, you must consider
how that penetration and that painting are
employed. It is not history, it is imagination.
He who describes what he never saw, draws
from fancy. Robertson paints minds as Sir
Joshua paints faces in a history-piece: he
imagines an heroic countenance. You must
look upon Robertson's work as romance, and
try it by that standard. History it is not. Besides, Sir, it is the great excellence of a
writer to put into his book as much as his
book will hold. Goldsmith has done this in
his *History.* Now Robertson might have put
twice as much into his book. Robertson is
like a man who has packed gold in wool: the
wool takes up more room than the gold. No,
Sir; I always thought Robertson would be
crushed by his own weight,—would be buried
under his own ornaments. Goldsmith tells
you shortly all you want to know: Robertson

detains you a great deal too long. No man will read Robertson's cumbrous detail a second time; but Goldsmith's plain narrative will please again and again. I would say to Robertson what an old tutor of a college said to one of his pupils: "Read over your compositions, and where ever you meet with a passage which you think is particularly fine, strike it out." Goldsmith's abridgement is better than that of Lucius Florus or Eutropius; and I will venture to say, that if you compare him with Vertot, in the same places of the Roman History, you will find that he excels Vertot. Sir, he has the art of compiling, and of saying every thing he has to say in a pleasing manner. He is now writing a Natural History and will make it as entertaining as a Persian Tale.'

I cannot dismiss the present topick without observing, that it is probable that Dr. Johnson, who owned that he often 'talked for victory,' rather urged plausible objections to Dr. Robertson's excellent historical works, in the ardour of contest, than expressed his real and decided opinion; for it is not easy to suppose, that he should so widely differ from the rest of the literary world.

JOHNSON. 'I remember once being with Goldsmith in Westminster-abbey. While we surveyed the Poets' Corner, I said to him,

"Forsitan et nostrum nomen miscebitur istis."[1]

when we got to Temple-bar he stopped me, pointed to the heads upon it, and slily whispered me,

"Forsitan et nostrum nomen miscebitur ISTIS." '

Johnson praised John Bunyan highly. 'His Pilgrim's Progress has great merit, both for invention, imagination, and the conduct of the story; and it has had the best evidence of its merit, the general and continued approbation of mankind. Few books, I believe, have had a more extensive sale. It is remarkable, that it begins very much like the poem of Dante; yet there was no translation of Dante when Bunyan wrote. There is reason to think that he had read Spenser.'

A proposition which had been agitated, that monuments to eminent persons should, for the time to come, be erected in St. Paul's church as well as in Westminster-abbey, was mentioned; and it was asked, who should be honoured by having his monument first erected there. Somebody suggested Pope. JOHNSON. 'Why, Sir, as Pope was a Roman Catholick, I would not have his to be first. I think Milton's rather should have the precedence.[2] I think more highly of him now than I did at twenty. There is more thinking in him and in Butler, than in any of our poets.'

Some of the company expressed a wonder why the authour of so excellent a book as 'The Whole Duty of Man' should conceal himself. JOHNSON. 'There may be different reasons assigned for this, any one of which would be very sufficient. He may have been a clergyman, and may have thought that his religious counsels would have less weight when known to come from a man whose profession was Theology. He may have been a man whose practice was not suitable to his principles, so that his character might injure the effect of his book, which he had written in a season of penitence. Or he may have been a man of rigid self-denial, so that he would have no reward for his pious labours while in this world, but refer it all to a future state.'

The gentlemen went away to their club, and I was left at Beauclerk's till the fate of my election should be announced to me. I sat in a state of anxiety which even the charming conversation of Lady Di Beauclerk could not entirely dissipate. In a short time I received the agreeable intelligence that I was chosen. I hastened to the place of meeting, and was introduced to such a society as

---

[1] Ovid. de Art. Amand. i. iii. v. 13. [Translation: Perhaps even our name will be mingled with those.]

[2] Here is another instance of his high admiration of Milton as a Poet, notwithstanding his just abhorrence of that sour Republican's political principles. His candour and discrimination are equally conspicuous. Let us hear no more of his 'injustice to Milton.'

can seldom be found. Mr. Edmund Burke, whom I then saw for the first time, and whose splendid talents had long made me ardently wish for his acquaintance; Dr. Nugent, Mr. Garrick, Dr. Goldsmith, Mr. (afterwards Sir William) Jones, and the company with whom I had dined. Upon my entrance, Johnson placed himself behind a chair, on which he leaned as on a desk or pulpit, and with humorous formality gave me a *Charge,* pointing out the conduct expected from me as a good member of this club.

Goldsmith produced some very absurd verses which had been publickly recited to an audience for money. JOHNSON. 'I can match this nonsense. There was a poem called *Eugenio,* which came out some years ago, and concludes thus:

> "And now, ye trifling, self-assuming elves,
> Brimful of pride, of nothing, of yourselves,
> Survey Eugenio, view him o'er and o'er,
> Then sink into yourselves, and be no more."

Nay, Dryden in his poem on the Royal Society, has these lines:

> "Then we upon our globe's last verge shall go,
> And see the ocean leaning on the sky;
> From thence our rolling neighbours we shall know,
> And on the lunar world securely pry." '

Much pleasant conversation passed, which Johnson relished with great good humour. But his conversation alone, or what led to it, or was interwoven with it, is the business of this work.

JAMES BOSWELL*

Thomas Seccombe

Boswell, James (1740–1795), Scottish man of letters, the biographer of Samuel

* From *The Encyclopædia Britannica,* 11th edition.

Johnson, was born at Edinburgh on the 29th of October 1740. His grandfather was in good practice at the Scottish bar, and his father, Alexander Boswell of Auchinleck, was also a noted advocate, who, on his elevation to the supreme court in 1754, took the name of his Ayrshire property as Lord Auchinleck. A Thomas Boswell (said upon doubtful evidence to have been a minstrel in the household of James IV.) was killed at Flodden, and since 1513 the family had greatly improved its position in the world by intermarriage with the first Scots nobility. In contradiction to his father, a rigid Presbyterian Whig, James was "a fine boy, wore a white cockade, and prayed for King James until his uncle Cochrane gave him a shilling to pray for King George, which he accordingly did" ("Whigs of all ages are made in the same way" was Johnson's comment). He met one or two English boys, and acquired a "tincture of polite letters" at the high school in Edinburgh. Like R. L. Stevenson, he early frequented society such as that of the actors at the Edinburgh theatre, sternly disapproved of by his father. At the university, where he was constrained for a season to study civil law, he met William Johnson Temple, his future friend and correspondent. The letters of Boswell to his "Atticus" were first published by Bentley in 1857. One winter he spent at Glasgow, where he sat under Adam Smith, who was then lecturing on moral philosophy and rhetoric.

In 1760 he was first brought into contact with "the elegance, the refinement and the liberality" of London society, for which he had long sighed. The young earl of Eglintoun took him to Newmarket and introduced him into the society of "the great, the gay and the ingenious." He wrote a poem called "The Cub at Newmarket," published by Dodsley in 1762, and had visions of entering the Guards. Reclaimed with some difficulty by his father from his rakish companions in the metropolis, he contrived to alleviate the irksomeness of law study in Edinburgh by forcing his acquaintance upon the celebrities then assembled in the northern capital, among them Kames, Blair, Robertson, Hume and Sir

David Dalrymple (Lord Hailes), of whose sayings on the Northern Circuit he kept a brief journal. Boswell had already realized his vocation, the exercise of which was to give a new word to the language. He had begun to Boswellize. He was already on the track of bigger game—the biggest available in the Britain of that day. In the spring of 1763 Boswell came to a composition with his father. He consented to give up his pursuit of a guidon in the Guards and three and sixpence a day on condition that his father would allow him to study civil law on the continent. He set out in April 1763 by "the best road in Scotland" with a servant, on horseback like himself, in "a cocked hat, a brown wig, brown coat made in the court fashion, red vest, corduroy small clothes and long military boots." On Monday, the 16th of May 1763, in the back shop of Tom Davies the bookseller, No. 8 Russell Street, Covent Garden, James Boswell first met "Dictionary Johnson," the great man of his dreams, and was severely buffeted by him. Eight days later, on Tuesday, the 24th of May, Boswell boldly called on Mr. Johnson at his chambers on the first floor of No. 1 Inner Temple Lane. On this occasion Johnson pressed him to stay; on the 13th of June he said, "Come to me as often as you can"; on the 25th of June Boswell gave the great man a little sketch of his own life, and Johnson exclaimed with warmth, "Give me your hand; I have taken a liking to you." Boswell experienced a variety of sensations, among which exultation was predominant. Someone asked, "Who is this Scotch cur at Johnson's heels?" "He is not a cur," replied Goldsmith, "he is only a bur. Tom Davies flung him at Johnson in sport, and he has the faculty of sticking." Johnson was fifty-four at this time and Boswell twenty-three. After June 1763 they met on something like 270 subsequent days. These meetings formed the memorable part of Boswell's life, and they are told inimitably in his famous biography of his friend.

The friendship, consecrated by the most delightful of biographies, and one of the most gorgeous feasts in the banquet of letters, was not so ill-assorted as has been inconsiderately maintained. Boswell's freshness at the table of conversation gave a new zest to every maxim that Johnson enunciated, while Boswell developed a perfect genius for interpreting the kind of worldly philosophy at which Johnson was so unapproachable. Both men welcomed an excuse for avoiding the task-work of life. Johnson's favourite indulgence was to talk; Boswell's great idea of success to elicit memorable conversation. Boswell is almost equally admirable as a reporter and as an interviewer, as a collector and as a researcher. He prepared meetings for Johnson, he prepared topics for him, he drew him out on questions of the day, he secured a copy of his famous letter to Lord Chesterfield, he obtained an almost verbatim report of Johnson's interview with the king, he frequented the tea-table of Miss Williams, he attended the testy old scholar on lengthy peregrinations in the Highlands and in the midlands. "Sir," said Johnson to his follower, "you appear to have only two subjects, yourself and me, and I am sick of both." Yet thorough as the scheme was from the outset, and admirable as was the devotedness of the biographer, Boswell was far too volatile a man to confine himself to any one ambition in life that was not consistent with a large amount of present fame and notoriety. He would have liked to Boswellize the popular idol Wilkes, or Chatham, or Voltaire, or even the great Frederick himself. As it was, during his continental tour he managed in the autumn of 1765 to get on terms with Pasquale di Paoli, the leader of the Corsican insurgents in their unwise struggle against Genoa. After a few weeks in Corsica he returned to London in February 1766, and was received by Johnson with the utmost cordiality. In accordance with the family compact referred to he was now admitted advocate at Edinburgh, and signalized his return to the law by an enthusiastic pamphlet entitled *The Essence of the Douglas Cause* (November 1767), in which he vigorously repelled the charge of imposture from the youthful claimant. In the same year he issued a little book called *Dorando,* containing a history of the Douglas cause in the guise of a Spanish tale, and bringing the story to a conclusion by the triumph of Archibald Douglas in the law courts. Editors who published extracts while the case was still *sub judice* were censured severely by the court of session; but though his identity was notorious the author himself escaped censure. In the spring of 1768 Boswell published through the Foulis brothers of Glasgow his *Account of Corsica, Journal of a Tour to that Island, and Memoirs of Pascal Paoli*. The liveliness of personal impression which he managed to communicate to all his books gained for this one a deserved success, and the *Tour* was promptly translated into French, German, Italian and Dutch. Walpole and others, jeered, but Boswell was talked about everywhere, as Paoli Boswell or Paoli's Englishman, and to aid the mob in the task of identifying him at the Shakespeare jubilee of 1769 he took the trouble to insert a placard in his hat bearing the legend "Corsica Boswell." The amazing costume of "a Corsican chief" which he wore on this occasion was described at length in the magazines.

On the 25th of November 1769, after a short tour in Ireland undertaken to empty his head of Corsica (Johnson's emphatic direction), Boswell married his cousin Margaret Montgomery at Lainshaw in Ayrshire. For some years henceforth his visits to London were brief, but on the 30th of April 1773 he was present at his admission to the Literary Club, for which honour he had been proposed by Johnson himself, and in the autumn of this year in the course of his tour to the Hebrides Johnson visited the Boswells in Ayrshire. Neither Boswell's father nor his wife shared his enthusiasm for the lexicographer. Lord Auchinleck remarked that Jamie was "gane clean gyte . . . And whose tail do ye think he has pinned himself to now, man? A dominie, an auld dominie, that keepit a schule and ca'd it an academy!" Housewives less prim than Mrs. Boswell might have objected to Johnson's habit of turning lighted candles upside down when in the parlour to make them burn better. She called the great man a bear. Boswell's *Journal of a Tour in the Hebrides* was written

for the most part during the journey, but was not published until the spring of 1786. The diary of Pepys was not then known to the public, and Boswell's indiscretions as to the emotions aroused in him by the neat ladies' maids at Inveraray, and the extremity of drunkenness which he exhibited at Corrichatachin, created literary sensation and sent the *Tour* through three editions in one year. In the meantime his pecuniary and other difficulties at home were great; he made hardly more than £100 a year by his profession, and his relations with his father were chronically strained. In 1775 he began to keep terms at the Inner Temple and managed to see a good deal of Johnson, between whom and John Wilkes he succeeded in bringing about a meeting at the famous dinner at Dilly's on the 15th of May 1776. On the 30th of August 1782 his father died, leaving him an estate worth £1600 a year. On the 30th of June 1784, Boswell met Johnson for the last time at a dinner at Sir Joshua Reynolds's. He accompanied him back in the coach from Leicester Square to Bolt Court. "We bade adieu to each other affectionately in the carriage. When he had got down upon the foot pavement he called out 'Fare you well'; and without looking back, sprung away with a kind of pathetic briskness, if I may use that expression, which seemed to indicate a struggle to conceal uneasiness, and impressed me with a foreboding of our long, long separation." Johnson died that year, and two years later the Boswells moved to London. In 1789 Mrs. Boswell died, leaving five children. She had been an excellent mother and a good wife, despite the infidelities and drunkenness of her husband, and from her death Boswell relapsed into worse excesses, grievously aggravated by hypochondria. He died of a complication of disorders at his house in Great Poland Street on the 19th of May 1795, and was buried a fortnight later at Auchinleck.

Up to the eve of his last illness Boswell had been busy upon his magnum opus, *The Life of Samuel Johnson*, which was in process of crystallization to the last. The first edition was published in two quarto volumes in an edition of 1700 copies on the 16th of May

1791. He was preparing a third edition when he died; this was completed by his friend Edmund Malone, who brought out a fifth edition in 1807. That of James Boswell junior (the editor of Malone's *Variorum Shakespeare,* 1821) appeared in 1811.

The *Life of Johnson* was written on a scale practically unknown to biographers before Boswell. It is a full-length with all the blotches and pimples revealed ("I will not make my tiger a cat to please anybody," wrote "Bozzy"). It may be overmuch an exhibition of oddities, but it is also, be it remembered, a pioneer application of the experimental method to the determination of human character. Its size and lack of divisions (to divide it into chapters was an original device of Croker's) are a drawback, and have prevented Boswell's *Life* from that assured triumph abroad which has fallen to the lot of various English classics such as *Robinson Crusoe* or *Gulliver's Travels.* But wherever English is spoken, it has become a veritable sacred book and has pervaded English life and thought in the same way, that the Bible, Shakespeare and Bunyan have done. Boswell has successfully (to use his own phrase) "Johnsonized" Britain, but he has not yet Johnsonized the planet. The model originally proposed to himself by Boswell was Mason's *Life of Gray,* but he far surpassed that, or indeed any other, model. The fashion that Boswell adopted of giving the conversations not in the neutral tints of *oratio obliqua* but in full *oratio recta** was a stroke of genius. But he is far from being the mere mechanical transmitter of good things. He is a dramatic and descriptive artist of the first order. The extraordinary vitality of his figures postulates a certain admixture of fiction, and it is certain that Boswell exaggerates the sympathy expressed in word or deed by Johnson for some of his own tenderer foibles. But, on the whole, the best judges are of opinion that Boswell's accuracy is exceptional, as it is undoubtedly seconded by a power of observation of a singular retentiveness and intensity. The difficulty of dramatic description can only be realized, as Jowett well pointed out, by those who have attempted it, and it is not until we compare Boswell's reports with those of less skilful hearers that we can appreciate the skill with which the essence of a conversation is extracted, and the whole scene indicated by a few telling touches. The result is that Johnson, not, it is true, in the early days of his poverty, total idleness and the pride of literature, but in the fulness of fame and competence of fortune from 1763 to 1784, is better known to us than any other man in history. The old theory to explain such a marvel (originally propounded by Gray when the *Tour in Corsica* appeared) that "any fool may write a valuable book by chance" is now regarded as untenable. If fool is a word to describe Boswell (and his folly was at times transcendent) he wrote his great book because and not in despite of the fact that he was one. There can be no doubt, in fact, that he was a biographical genius, and that he arranged his opportunities just as he prepared his transitions and introduced those inimitable glosses by which Johnson's motives are explained, his state of mind upon particular occasions indicated, and the general feeling of his company conveyed. This remarkable literary faculty, however, was but a fraction of the total make-up requisite to produce such a masterpiece as the *Life.* There is a touch of genius, too, in the naïf and imperturbable good nature and persistency ("Sir, I will not be baited with 'what' and 'why.' 'Why is a cow's tail long?' 'Why is a fox's tail bushy?' "), and even in the abnegation of all personal dignity, with which Boswell pursued his hero. As he himself said of Goldsmith, "He had sagacity enough to cultivate assiduously the acquaintance of Johnson, and his faculties were gradually enlarged." Character, the vital principle of the individual, is the *ignis fatuus** of the mechanical biographer. Its attainment may be secured by a variety of means—witness Xenophon, Cellini, Aubrey, Lockhart and Froude—but it has never been attained with such complete in-

---

* Not in indirect but in direct discourse.

* Misleading influence.

tensity as by Boswell in his *Life of Johnson*. The more we study Boswell, the more we compare him with other biographers, the greater his work appears.

[MY UNCLE'S FARM]*

Samuel Langhorne Clemens
(Mark Twain)
(1835–1910)

It was a heavenly place for a boy, that farm of my uncle John's. The house was a double log one, with a spacious floor (roofed in) connecting it with the kitchen. In the summer the table was set in the middle of that shady and breezy floor, and the sumptuous meals—well, it makes me cry to think of them. Fried chicken, roast pig; wild and tame turkeys, ducks, and geese; venison just killed; squirrels, rabbits, pheasants, partridges, prairie-chickens; biscuits, hot batter cakes, hot buckwheat cakes, hot "wheat bread," hot rolls, hot corn pone; fresh corn boiled on the ear, succotash, butter-beans, string beans, tomatoes, peas, Irish potatoes, sweet potatoes; buttermilk, sweet milk, "clabber"; watermelons, muskmelons, cantaloupes—all fresh from the garden; apple pie, peach pie, pumpkin pie, apple dumplings, peach cobbler—I can't remember the rest. The way that the things were cooked was perhaps the main splendor—particularly a certain few of the dishes. For instance, the corn bread, the hot biscuits and wheat bread, and the fried chicken. These things have never been properly cooked in the North—in fact, no one there is able to learn the art, so far as my experience goes. The North thinks it knows how to make corn bread, but this is mere superstition. Perhaps no bread in the world is quite so good as Southern corn bread, and perhaps no bread in the world is quite so bad as the Northern imitation of it. The North seldom tries to fry chicken, and this is well; the art cannot be learned north of the line of Mason and Dixon, nor anywhere in Europe.

* From *Mark Twain's Autobiography*.

This is not hearsay; it is experience that is speaking. In Europe it is imagined that the custom of serving various kinds of bread blazing hot is "American," but that is too broad a spread; it is custom in the South, but is much less than that in the North. In the North and in Europe hot bread is considered unhealthy. This is probably another fussy superstition, like the European superstition that ice-water is unhealthy. Europe does not need ice-water and does not drink it; and yet, notwithstanding this, its word for it is better than ours, because it describes it, whereas ours doesn't. Europe calls it "iced" water. Our word describes water made from melted ice—a drink which has a characterless taste and which we have but little acquaintance with.

It seems a pity that the world should throw away so many good things merely because they are unwholesome. I doubt if God has given us any refreshment which, taken in moderation, is unwholesome, except microbes. Yet there are people who strictly deprive themselves of each and every eatable, drinkable, and smokable which has in any way acquired a shady reputation. They pay this price for health. And health is all they get for it. How strange it is! It is like paying out your whole fortune for a cow that has gone dry.

The farmhouse stood in the middle of a very large yard, and the yard was fenced on three sides with rails and on the rear side with high palings; against these stood the smoke-house; beyond the palings was the orchard; beyond the orchard were the negro quarters and the tobacco fields. The front yard was entered over a stile made of sawed-off logs of graduated heights; I do not remember any gate. In a corner of the front yard were a dozen lofty hickory trees and a dozen black walnuts, and in the nutting season riches were to be gathered there.

Down a piece, abreast the house, stood a little log cabin against the rail fence; and there the woody hill fell sharply away, past the barns, the corn-crib, the stables, and the tobacco-curing house, to a limpid brook which sang along over its gravelly bed and curved and frisked in and out and here and there and yonder in the deep shade of over-hanging foliage and vines—a divine place for wading, and it had swimming pools, too, which were forbidden to us and therefore much frequented by us. For we were little Christian children and had early been taught the value of forbidden fruit. . . .

As I have said, I spent some part of every year at the farm until I was twelve or thirteen years old. The life which I led there with my cousins was full of charm, and so is the memory of it yet. I can call back the solemn twilight and mystery of the deep woods, the earthy smells, the faint odors of the wild flowers, the sheen of rain-washed foliage, the rattling clatter of drops when the wind shook the trees, the far-off hammering of woodpeckers and the muffled drumming of wood pheasants in the remoteness of the forest, the snapshot glimpses of disturbed wild creatures scurrying through the grass —I can call it all back and make it as real as it ever was, and as blessed. I can call back the prairie, and its loneliness and peace, and a vast hawk hanging motionless in the sky, with his wings spread wide and the blue of the vault showing through the fringe of their end feathers. I can see the woods in their autumn dress, the oaks purple, the hickories washed with gold, the maples and the su-machs luminous with crimson fires, and I can hear the rustle made by the fallen leaves as we plowed through them. I can see the blue clusters of wild grapes hanging among the foliage of the saplings, and I remember the taste of them and the smell. I know how the wild blackberries looked, and how they tasted, and the same with the pawpaws, the hazlenuts, and the persimmons; and I can feel the thumping rain, upon my head, of hickory nuts and walnuts when we were out in the frosty dawn to scramble for them with the pigs, and the gusts of wind loosed them and sent them down. I know the stain of blackberries, and how pretty it is, and I know the stain of walnut hulls, and how little it minds soap and water, also what grudged experience it had of either of them. I know the taste of maple sap, and when to gather

it, and how to arrange the troughs and the delivery tubes, and how to boil down the juice, and how to hook the sugar after it is made, also how much better hooked sugar tastes than any that is honestly come by, let bigots say what they will. I know how a prize watermelon looks when it is sunning its fat rotundity among pumpkin vines and "sim-blins"; I know how to tell when it is ripe without "plugging" it; I know how inviting it looks when it is cooling itself in a tub of water under the bed, waiting; I know how it looks when it lies on the table in the shel-tered great floor space between house and kitchen, and the children gathered for the sacrifice and their mouths watering; I know the crackling sound it makes when the carv-ing knife enters its end, and I can see the spit fly along in front of the blade as the knife cleaves its way to the other end; I can see its halves fall apart and display the rich red meat and the black seeds, and the heart standing up, a luxury fit for the elect; I know how a boy looks behind a yard-long slice of that melon, and I know how he feels; for I have been there. I know the taste of the watermelon which has been honestly come by, and I know the taste of the watermelon which has been acquired by art. Both taste good, but the experienced know which tastes best. I know the look of green apples and peaches and pears on the trees, and I know how entertaining they are when they are in-side of a person. I know how ripe ones look when they are piled in pyramids under the trees, and how pretty they are and how vivid their colors. I know how a frozen apple looks, in a barrel down cellar in the wintertime, and how hard it is to bite, and how the frost makes the teeth ache, and yet how good it is, notwithstanding. I know the disposition of elderly people to select the specked apples for the children, and I once knew ways to beat the game. I know the look of an apple that is roasting and sizzling on the hearth on a winter's evening, and I know the comfort that comes of eating it hot, along with some sugar and a drench of cream. I know the delicate art and mystery of so cracking hick-ory nuts and walnuts on a flatiron with a hammer that the kernels will be delivered whole, and I know how the nuts, taken in conjunction with winter apples, cider, and doughnuts, make old people's old tales and old jokes sound fresh and crisp and enchanting, and juggle an evening away before you know what went with the time. I know the look of Uncle Dan'l's kitchen as it was on the privileged nights, when I was a child, and I can see the white and black children grouped on the hearth, with the firelight playing on their faces and the shadows flickering upon the walls, clear back toward the cavernous gloom of the rear, and I can hear Uncle Dan'l telling the immortal tales which Uncle Remus Harris was to gather into his book and charm the world with, by and by; and I can feel again the creepy joy which quivered through me when the time for the ghost story was reached—and the sense of regret, too, which came over me, for it was always the last story of the evening and there was nothing between it and the unwelcome bed.

I can remember the bare wooden stairway in my uncle's house, and the turn to the left above the landing, and the rafters and the slanting roof over my bed, and the squares of moonlight on the floor, and the white cold world of snow outside, seen through the curtainless window. I can remember the howling of the wind and the quaking of the house on stormy nights, and how snug and cozy one felt, under the blankets, listening; and how the powdery snow used to sift in, around the sashes, and lie in little ridges on the floor and make the place look chilly in the morning and curb the wild desire to get up—in case there was any. I can remember how very dark that room was, in the dark of the moon, and how packed it was with ghostly stillness when one woke up by accident away in the night, and forgotten sins came flocking out of the secret chambers of the memory and wanted a hearing; and how ill chosen the time seemed for this kind of business; and how dismal was the hoo-hooing of the owl and the wailing of the wolf, sent mourning by on the night wind.

I remember the raging of the rain on that roof, summer nights, and how pleasant it was to lie and listen to it, and enjoy the white splendor of the lightning and the majestic booming and crashing of the thunder. It was a very satisfactory room, and there was a lightning rod which was reachable from the window, an adorable and skittish thing to climb up and down, summer nights, when there were duties on hand of a sort to make privacy desirable.

I remember the 'coon and 'possum hunts, nights, with the negroes, and the long marches through the black gloom of the woods, and the excitement which fired everybody when the distant bay of an experienced dog announced that the game was treed; then the wild scramblings and stumblings through briers and bushes and over roots to get to the spot; then the lighting of a fire and the felling of the tree, the joyful frenzy of the dogs and the negroes, and the weird picture it all made in the red glare—I remember it all well, and the delight that everyone got out of it, except the 'coon.

I remember the pigeon seasons, when the birds would come in millions and cover the trees and by their weight break down the branches. They were clubbed to death with sticks; guns were not necessary and were not used. I remember the squirrel hunts, and prairie-chicken hunts, and wild-turkey hunts, and all that; and how we turned out, mornings, while it was still dark, to go on these expeditions, and how chilly and dismal it was, and how often I regretted that I was well enough to go. A toot on a tin horn brought twice as many dogs as were needed, and in their happiness they raced and scampered about, and knocked small people down, and made no end of unnecessary noise. At the word, they vanished away toward the woods, and we drifted silently after them in the melancholy gloom. But presently the gray dawn stole over the world, the birds piped up, then the sun rose and poured light and comfort all around, everything was fresh and dewy and fragrant, and life was a boon again. After three hours of tramping we arrived back wholesomely tired, overladen with game, very hungry, and just in time for breakfast.

JOHN AUBREY*

Lytton Strachey
(1880–1932)

If one were asked to choose a date for the beginning of the modern world, probably July 15, 1662, would be the best to fix upon. For on that day the Royal Society was founded, and the place of Science in civilisation became a definite and recognized thing. The sun had risen above the horizon; and yet, before that, there had been streaks of light in the sky. The great age of Newton was preceded by a curious twilight period—a period of gestation and preparation, confused, and only dimly conscious of the end towards which it was moving. It might be called, perhaps, the age of Hobbes, whose half-mediaeval, half-modern mind was the dominating influence over intellects which came to maturity in the middle years of the century. Another even more typical, though less eminent, representative of this embryonic generation was John Aubrey (1626–1697). Aubrey was among those chosen by the first President and Council to be the first Fellows of the Royal Society; and he was extremely proud of the distinction. But in reality the scientific movement which gave the Royal Society its significance did not mean very much to him. His mind moved in a circle of ideas which was rapidly becoming obsolete, and which, so long as our civilisation lasts, can never come into existence again.

His life was not a fortunate one. Born a country gentleman, with estates in Brecknockshire, Herefordshire, and Wiltshire, and educated at Trinity College, Oxford, his happy studies at the University were interrupted by the Civil Wars, and his considerable possessions were dissipated in a long series of unsuccessful lawsuits. In 1666, he tells us, 'all my businesses and affaires ran kim kam; nothing tooke effect'; and the words are applicable to the whole of his life. It was

not only luck that was against him; he was by nature an amiable muddler; in love and in literature, no less than in business, it was always the same—'nothing tooke effect.' Neither Madam Jane Codrington, nor 'that incomparable good conditioned gentlewoman, Mris. M. Wiseman, with whom at first sight I was in love,' would smile upon him; and though 'domina Katherina Ryves,' with a dowry of £2,000, was kinder, just as she was about to marry him, she died. He sought distraction abroad, but without success. '1664, in August,' he noted, 'had a terrible fit of the spleen, and piles, at Orleans.' Yet worse was to follow: 'In an ill howre,' he began to make his addresses to Joan Sumner, whose cruelty was more than negative. She had him arrested in Chancery Lane, and for three years pursued him with lawsuits. His ruin followed; all his broad lands vanished; even Easton Piers, the house of his birth, with its terraced gardens, its 'jedeau,' its grotto and 'volant Mercury,' had to be sold; even his books went at last. By 1670 poor Aubrey had lost everything. But then, unexpectedly, happiness descended upon him. Free at last from the struggles of love and law and the tedious responsibilities of property, he found himself in a 'sweet *otium.*' 'I had never quiett, nor anything of happiness till divested of all,' he wrote. 'I was in as much affliction as a mortall could bee, and never quiet till all was gone, and I wholly cast myself on God's providence.'

God's providence, in Aubrey's case, took the form of a circle of kindly friends, who were ready enough to give him food and shelter in town and country, in return for the benefit of his 'most ingeniose conversation.' He would spend the winter in London —often with Sir William Petty or Sir Christopher Wren,—and then, with the spring, he would ride off on a round of visits—to Lord Thanet's in Kent, to the Longs in Wiltshire, to Edmund Wylde in Shropshire—until the autumn came, and he would turn his horse's head back to London. Grumpy Anthony Wood might write him down 'a shiftless person, roving and magotieheaded, and sometimes little better than crazed'; but his

* From *Portraits in Miniature and Other Essays.*

691

boon companions thought otherwise. They relished to the full the extraordinary quantity and the delightful variety of his information, and could never tire of his engaging manner of presenting it. 'My head,' he said himself, 'was always working; never idle, and even travelling did glean som observations, of which I have a collection in folio of 2 quiers of paper and a dust basket, some whereof are to be valued.' His inquiries were indeed indefatigable; he was learned in natural history, geology, Gothic architecture, mineralogy, painting, heraldry; he collected statistics, he was a profound astrologer, and a learned geometrician; he wrote a treatise on education; even the mysteries of cookery did not elude him, and he compiled 'a collection of approved receipts.' Before he died he had written sufficient to fill several volumes; but, characteristically enough, he brought only one book to the point of publication: his *Miscellanies,* in which he briefly discussed such fascinating subjects as 'Apparitions, Impulses, Knockings, Blows Invisible, Prophecies, Marvels, Magic, Transportation in the Air, Visions in a Bevil or Glass, Converse with Angels and Spirits, Corps-Candles in Wales, Glances of Love and Envy, and Second-Sighted Persons in Scotland.' It is in this book, in the chapter of Apparitions, that the sentence occurs which so much delighted Mr. Jonathan Oldbuck of Monkbarns: '*Anno* 1670, not far from *Cirencester,* was an Apparition; Being demanded, whether a good Spirit or a bad, Returned no answer, but disappeared with a curious Perfume and most melodious Twang.'

Certainly the learned Ray was right when he said of his friend that he was 'a little inclinable to credit strange relations.' Yet it would be an error to dismiss Aubrey as a mere superstitious trifler; he was something more interesting than that. His insatiable passion for singular odds and ends had a meaning in it; he was groping towards a scientific ordering of phenomena; but the twilight of his age was too confusing, and he could rarely distinguish between a fact and a fantasy. He was clever enough to understand the Newtonian system, but he was not clever enough to understand that a horoscope was an absurdity; and so, in his crowded curiosity-shop of a brain, astronomy and astrology both found a place, and were given equal values. When fortune favoured him, however, he could make real additions to knowledge. He was the first English archaeologist, and his most remarkable achievement was the discovery of the hitherto unknown Druidical temple of Avebury. Encouraged by Charles II, he made a careful survey of the great stone circle, writing a dissertation upon it and upon Stonehenge, and refuting the theory of Inigo Jones, who, in order to prove that the latter was Roman, had given an entirely factitious account of it. As he rode over the Wiltshire downs, hawking with Colonel Long, he had ample opportunities for these antiquarian investigations. 'Our sport,' he wrote, 'was very good, and in a romantick countrey, for the prospects are noble and vast, the downs stockt with numerous flocks of sheep, the turfe rich and fragrant with thyme and burnet; nor are the nut-brown shepherdesses without their graces. But the flight of the falcons was but a parenthesis to the Colonell's facetious discourse, who was *tam Marti quam Mercurio,** and the Muses did accompany him with his hawkes and spaniells.'

The country was charming; but London too was full of pleasures, and the winter nights passed swiftly with wine and talk. For the company was excellent. There was Robert Hooke 'that invented the Pendulum-Watches, so much more useful than the other watches,' and a calculating machine, and hundreds of other contrivances—'he believes not fewer than a thousand'—and who declared he had forestalled Mr. Newton; and there was Dr. Tonge, who had first taught children to write by means of copper-plates, and left behind him 'two tomes in folio of alchymy'; and Francis Potter, the first to practise the transfusion of blood, who, at 10 o'clock in the morning of December 10, 1625, as he was going upstairs, had discovered 'the mysterie of the Beaste'; and John Pell, the inventor of the division-sign in

* Equally devoted to Mars and Mercury.

arithmetic, who 'haz sayd to me that he did believe that he solved some questions *non sine divino auxilio.'** And then the gentle gossip went back to earlier days—to old Mr. Oughtred, Sir Christopher's master, who 'taught all free,' and was an astrologer, though he confessed 'that he was not satisfied how it came about that one might foretell by the starres, but so it was,' and whose 'wife was a penurious woman, and would not allow him to burne candle after supper, by which meanes many a good notion is lost, and many a problem unsolved'; and so back to a still more remote and bizarre past—to Dr. John Dee, of Queen Elizabeth's time, 'who wore a gowne like an artist's gowne, with hanging sleeves and a slit,' made plates of gold 'by projection,' and 'used to distil egge-shells.'

Aubrey lived on into old age—vague, precise, idle, and busy to the last. His state of life, he felt, was not quite satisfactory. He was happy; but he would have been happier still in some other world. He regretted the monasteries. He wished 'the reformers had been more moderate on that point.' It was 'fitt there should be receptacles and provision for contemplative men'; and 'what a pleasure 'twould have been to have travelled from monastery to monastery!' As it was, he did the next best thing—he travelled from country house to country house. In the summer of 1697, when he was over seventy, as he was riding through Oxford on his way to Lady Long's, he was seized with sudden illness, and his journeying was ended for ever.

In the great mass of papers that he left behind it was hardly to be supposed that there could be anything of permanent value. Most of the antique science was already out of date at his death. But it so happened that Aubrey's appetite for knowledge had carried him into a field of inquiry which, little explored in his own day, attracts the greatest interest in ours. He was an assiduous biographer. Partly to help the ungrateful Anthony Wood in the compilation of his *Athenae Oxonienses,* but chiefly for his own delight, Aubrey was in the habit of jotting down on

scraps of paper every piece of information he could acquire concerning both his own contemporaries and the English worthies of previous generations. He was accurate, he had an unfailing eye for what was interesting, and he possessed—it was almost inevitable in those days—a natural gift of style. The result is that his *Short Lives* (which have been admirably edited for the Clarendon Press by Mr. Andrew Clark) are not only an authority of the highest importance upon seventeenth-century England, but one of the most readable of books. A biography should either be as long as Boswell's or as short as Aubrey's. The method of enormous and elaborate accretion which produced the *Life of Johnson* is excellent, no doubt; but, failing that, let us have no half-measures; let us have the pure essentials—a vivid image, on a page or two, without explanations, transitions, commentaries, or padding. This is what Aubrey gives us; this, and one thing more—a sense of the pleasing, anxious being who, with his odd old alchemy, has transmuted a few handfuls of orts and relics into golden life.

TIN LIZZIE*

John Dos Passos
(1896–   )

"Mr. Ford the automobileer," the feature-writer wrote in 1900,

"Mr. Ford the automobileer began by giving his steed three or four sharp jerks with the lever at the righthand side of the seat; that is, he pulled the lever up and down sharply in order, as he said, to mix air with gasoline and drive the charge into the exploding cylinder. . . . Mr. Ford slipped a small electric switch handle and there followed a puff, puff, puff. . . . The puffing of the machine assumed a higher key. She was flying along about eight miles an hour. The ruts in the road were deep, but the machine certainly

* Not without divine aid.

went with a dreamlike smoothness. There was none of the bumping common even to a streetcar. . . . By this time the boulevard had been reached, and the automobileer, letting a lever fall a little, let her out. Whiz! She picked up speed with infinite rapidity. As she ran on there was a clattering behind, the new noise of the automobile.

For twenty years or more,

ever since he'd left his father's farm when he was sixteen to get a job in a Detroit machineshop, Henry Ford had been nuts about machinery. First it was watches, then he designed a steamtractor, then he built a horseless carriage with an engine adapted from the Otto gasengine he'd read about in *The World of Science,* then a mechanical buggy with a onecylinder fourcycle motor, that would run forward but not back;

at last, in nineteeight, he felt he was far enough along to risk throwing up his job with the Detroit Edison Company, where he'd worked his way up from night fireman to chief engineer, to put all his time into working on a new gasoline engine,

(in the late eighties he'd met Edison at a meeting of electriclight employees in Atlantic City. He'd gone up to Edison after Edison had delivered an address and asked him if he thought gasoline was practical as a motor fuel. Edison had said yes. If Edison said it, it was true. Edison was the great admiration of Henry Ford's life);

and in driving his mechanical buggy, sitting there at the lever jauntily dressed in a tightbuttoned jacket and a high collar and a derby hat, back and forth over the level illpaved streets of Detroit,

scaring the big brewery horses and the skinny trotting horses and the sleekrumped pacers with the motor's loud explosions,

looking for men scatterbrained enough to invest money in a factory for building automobiles.

He was the eldest son of an Irish immigrant who during the Civil War had married the daughter of a prosperous Pennsylvania Dutch farmer and settled down to farming near Dearborn in Wayne County, Michigan;

like plenty of other Americans, young Henry grew up hating the endless sogging through the mud about the chores, the hauling and pitching manure, the kerosene lamps to clean, the irk and sweat and solitude of the farm.

He was a slender, active youngster, a good skater, clever with his hands; what he liked was to tend the machinery and let the others do the heavy work. His mother had told him not to drink, smoke, gamble or go into debt, and he never did.

When he was in his early twenties his father tried to get him back from Detroit, where he was working as mechanic and repairman for the Drydock Engine Company that built engines for steamboats, by giving him forty acres of land.

Young Henry built himself an uptodate square white dwellinghouse with a false mansard roof and married and settled down on the farm,

but he let the hired men do the farming;

he bought himself a buzzsaw and rented a stationary engine and cut the timber off the woodlots.

He was a thrifty young man who never drank or smoked or gambled or coveted his neighbor's wife, but he couldn't stand living on the farm.

He moved to Detroit, and in the brick barn behind his house tinkered for years in his spare time with a mechanical buggy that would be light enough to run over the clayey wagonroads of Wayne County, Michigan.

By 1900 he had a practicable car to promote.

He was forty years old before the Ford Motor Company was started and production began to move.

Speed was the first thing the early automobile manufacturers went after. Races advertised the makes of cars.

Henry Ford himself hung up several records at the track at Grosse Pointe and on the ice on Lake St. Clair. In his 999 he did the mile in thirtynine and fourfifths seconds.

But it had always been his custom to hire others to do the heavy work. The speed he was busy with was speed in production, the records records in efficient output. He hired

Barney Oldfield, a stunt bicyclerider from Salt Lake City, to do the racing for him.

Henry Ford had ideas about other things than the designing of motors, carburetors, magnetos, jigs and fixtures, punches and dies; he had ideas about sales,

that the big money was in economical quantity production, quick turnover, cheap interchangeable easilyreplaced standardized parts;

it wasn't until 1909, after years of arguing with his partners, that Ford put out the first Model T.

Henry Ford was right.

That season he sold more than ten thousand tin lizzies, ten years later he was selling almost a million a year.

In these years the Taylor Plan was stirring up plantmanagers and manufacturers all over the country. Efficiency was the word. The same ingenuity that went into improving the performance of a machine could go into improving the performance of the workmen producing the machine.

In 1913 they established the assemblyline at Ford's. That season the profits were something like twentyfive million dollars, but they had trouble in keeping the men on the job, machinists didn't seem to like it at Ford's.

Henry Ford had ideas about other things than production.

He was the largest automobile manufacturer in the world; he paid high wages; maybe if the steady workers thought they were getting a cut (a very small cut) in the profits, it would give trained men an inducement to stick to their jobs,

wellpaid workers might save enough money to buy a tin lizzie; the first day Ford's announced that cleancut properlymarried American workers who wanted jobs had a chance to make five bucks a day (of course it turned out that there were strings to it; always there were strings to it)

such an enormous crowd waited outside the Highland Park plant

all through the zero January night

that there was a riot when the gates were opened; cops broke heads, jobhunters threw bricks; property, Henry Ford's own property, was destroyed. The company dicks had to turn on the firehose to beat back the crowd.

The American Plan; automotive prosperity seeping down from above; it turned out there were strings to it.

But that five dollars a day

paid to good, clean American workmen

who didn't drink or smoke cigarettes or read or think,

and who didn't commit adultery

and whose wives didn't take in boarders,

made America once more the Yukon of the sweated workers of the world;

made all the tin lizzies and the automotive age, and incidentally,

made Henry Ford the automobileer, the admirer of Edison, the birdlover,

the great American of his time.

But Henry Ford had ideas about other things besides assemblylines and the livinghabits of his employees. He was full of ideas. Instead of going to the city to make his fortune, here was a country boy who'd made his fortune by bringing the city out to the farm. The precepts he'd learned out of McGuffey's Reader, his mother's prejudices and preconceptions, he had preserved clean and unworn as freshprinted bills in the safe in a bank.

He wanted people to know about his ideas, so he bought the *Dearborn Independent* and started a campaign against cigarette-smoking.

When war broke out in Europe, he had ideas about that too. (Suspicion of armymen and soldiering were part of the midwest farm tradition, like thrift, stickativeness, temperance and sharp practice in money matters.) Any intelligent American mechanic could see that if the Europeans hadn't been a lot of ignorant underpaid foreigners who drank, smoked, were loose about women and wasteful in their methods of production, the war could never have happened.

When Rosika Schwimmer broke through the stockade of secretaries and servicemen who surrounded Henry Ford and suggested to him that he could stop the war, he said sure they'd hire a ship and go over and get the boys out of the trenches by Christmas.

He hired a steamboat, the *Oscar II,* and filled it up with pacifists and socialworkers,

to go over to explain to the princelings of Europe

that what they were doing was vicious and silly.

It wasn't his fault that Poor Richard's commonsense no longer rules the world and that most of the pacifists were nuts,

goofy with headlines.

When William Jennings Bryan went over to Hoboken to see him off, somebody handed William Jennings Bryan a squirrel in a cage; William Jennings Bryan made a speech with the squirrel under his arm. Henry Ford threw American Beauty roses to the crowd. The band played *I Didn't Raise My Boy to Be a Soldier.* Practical jokers let loose more squirrels. An eloping couple was married by a platoon of ministers in the saloon, and Mr. Zero, the flophouse humanitarian, who reached the dock too late to sail,

dove into the North River and swam after the boat.

The *Oscar II* was described as a floating Chautauqua; Henry Ford said it felt like a middlewestern village, but by the time they reached Christiansand in Norway, the reporters had kidded him so that he had gotten cold feet and gone to bed. The world was too crazy outside of Wayne County, Michigan. Mrs. Ford and the management sent an Episcopal dean after him who brought him home under wraps,

and the pacifists had to speechify without him.

Two years later Ford's was manufacturing munitions, Eagle boats; Henry Ford was planning oneman tanks, and oneman submarines like the one tried out in the Revolutionary War. He announced to the press that he'd turn over his war profits to the government,

but there's no record that he ever did.

One thing he brought back from his trip was the Protocols of the Elders of Zion.

He started a campaign to enlighten the world in the *Dearborn Independent;* the Jews were why the world wasn't like Wayne County, Michigan, in the old horse and buggy days;

the Jews had started the war, Bolshevism, Darwinism, Marxism, Nietzsche, short skirts and lipstick. They were behind Wall Street and the international bankers, and the whiteslave traffic and the movies and the Supreme Court and ragtime and the illegal liquor business.

Henry Ford denounced the Jews and ran for senator and sued the *Chicago Tribune* for libel,

and was the laughingstock of the kept metropolitan press;

but when the metropolitan bankers tried to horn in on his business

he thoroughly outsmarted them.

In 1918 he had borrowed on notes to buy out his minority stockholders for the picayune sum of seventyfive million dollars.

In February, 1920, he needed cash to pay off some of these notes that were coming due. A banker is supposed to have called on him and offered him every facility if the bankers' representative could be made a member of the board of directors. Henry Ford handed the banker his hat,

and went about raising the money in his own way:

he shipped every car and part he had in his plant to his dealers and demanded immediate cash payment. Let the other fellow do the borrowing had always been a cardinal principle. He shut down production and canceled all orders from the supplyfirms. Many dealers were ruined, many supplyfirms failed, but when he reopened his plant,

he owned it absolutely,

the way a man owns an unmortgaged farm with the taxes paid up.

In 1922 there started the Ford boom for President (high wages, waterpower, industry scattered to the small towns) that was skillfully pricked behind the scenes

by another crackerbarrel philosopher, Calvin Coolidge;

but in 1922 Henry Ford sold one million

three hundred and thirtytwo thousand two hundred and nine tin lizzies; he was the richest man in the world.

Good roads had followed the narrow ruts made in the mud by the Model T. The great automotive boom was on. At Ford's production was improving all the time; less waste, more spotters, strawbosses, stoolpigeons (fifteen minutes for lunch, three minutes to go to the toilet, the Taylorized speedup everywhere, reach under, adjust washer, screw down bolt, shove in cotterpin, reachunder adjustwasher, screwdown bolt, reachunderadjustscrewdownreachunderadjust until every ounce of life was sucked off into production and at night the workmen went home gray shaking husks).

Ford owned every detail of the process from the ore in the hills until the car rolled off the end of the assemblyline under its own power, the plants were rationalized to the last tenthousandth of an inch as measured by the Johansen scale;

in 1926 the production cycle was reduced to eightyone hours from the ore in the mine to the finished salable car proceeding under its own power,

but the Model T was obsolete.

New Era prosperity and the American Plan
(there were strings to it, always there were strings to it)
had killed Tin Lizzie.

Ford's was just one of many automobile plants.

When the stockmarket bubble burst,
Mr. Ford the crackerbarrel philosopher said jubilantly,
"I told you so.
Serves you right for gambling and getting in debt.
The country is sound."
But when the country on cracked shoes, in frayed trousers, belts tightened over hollow bellies,
idle hands cracked and chapped with the cold of that coldest March day of 1932,
started marching from Detroit to Dearborn, asking for work and the American Plan, all they could think of at Ford's was machineguns.

The country was sound, but they mowed the marchers down.

They shot four of them dead.

Henry Ford as an old man
is a passionate antiquarian,
(lives besieged on his father's farm embedded in an estate of thousands of millionaire acres, protected by an army of servicemen, secretaries, secret agents, dicks under orders of an English exprizefighter,
always afraid of the feet in broken shoes on the roads, afraid the gangs will kidnap his grandchildren,
that a crank will shoot him,
that Change and the idle hands out of work will break through the gates and the high fences;
protected by a private army against
the new America of starved children and hollow bellies and cracked shoes stamping on souplines,
that has swallowed up the old thrifty farmlands
of Wayne County, Michigan,
as if they had never been).
Henry Ford as an old man
is a passionate antiquarian.
He rebuilt his father's farmhouse and put it back exactly in the state he remembered it in as a boy. He built a village of museums for buggies, sleighs, coaches, old plows, waterwheels, obsolete models of motorcars. He scoured the country for fiddlers to play old-fashioned squaredances.

Even old taverns he bought and put back into their original shape, as well as Thomas Edison's early laboratories.

When he bought the Wayside Inn near Sudbury, Massachusetts, he had the new highway where the newmodel cars roared and slithered and hissed oilily past (the new noise of the automobile),
moved away from the door,
put back the old bad road,
so that everything might be
the way it used to be,
in the days of horses and buggies.

The Nature and Functions
of Literature

Critical thinking about the kinds of writing we call "literature" has concerned itself with various questions. Some are general and historical. What can we learn about the people of seventeenth-century England, say, from a study of their literature? What is there in the life of a literary artist that will enable us better to understand his productions? How does social change influence literature? And so on.

Other questions have to do with techniques of writing. Are the characters of a particular author or story true to life and convincing? If so, what makes them so? Is the structure of a poem appropriate to the theme? Is the plot of a story well constructed; is its theme significant? Does a certain play have dramatic impact? If so, how is the impact achieved? What is the effect of using symbolic rather than realistic statement? Certain of these questions are raised throughout the text, and you undoubtedly have discussed others in connection with the literature studied. (Or, if your course begins with this section, you will discuss them.)

In this section we are concerned with critical questions of a different type, with what may be called the philosophical (and, to a certain extent, the psychological) significance of literature. How, basically, does literature differ from other forms of verbal communication—from history or philosophy or psychology? What, in short, is the *nature* of literature?

What, too, is the *purpose*—the functions—of literature in the life of Man? Not every serious thinker has thought literature a good thing: Plato would have banished the poets from his ideal republic, and certain groups have considered literary writing harmful unless it contributed directly to the religious experience. Others, in contrast, have looked on literature as the best means for understanding Mankind or for inculcating moral principles; and Shelley went so far as to call poets the "unacknowledged legislators of the world."

It is easy enough to tell what a cake recipe is "good" for—if it is correctly put together, it tells us how to make a cake. But what is a play, a poem, or a story "good" for? Ordinarily, they give us no information we don't already have. Are they merely to let us "escape" from the humdrum of everyday life, to refresh our minds and bodies by taking us away for awhile from the little cares and vexations that press upon us? This, if it can be accomplished, is unquestionably a "good"—but it is something a baseball or football game or an ice show can accomplish. Is pleasant relaxation the sum of the "good" that literature accomplishes?

These considerations, too, are touched on from time to time in the text. Here we have gathered a few more formal statements about the problem. Space limitation prevents our giving more than a few relatively brief statements by outstanding thinkers and writers. We do so in the hope that they will lead you to further investigation. For no mature person, in thinking of literature, will rest until he has formulated some reasoned notion of the nature and functions of an activity which has occupied Man throughout all the centuries of his existence.

From THE REPUBLIC

Plato

(427?–347 B.C.)

[Imitation is dangerous. 595 A]

[Socrates is speaking to Glaucon.]

Certainly there are many other reasons I think of why we were quite right in our organization of the state, and after considering the matter I think we did especially well about poetry.

We refused to admit it because it is imitative, for that it should not be admitted is the more apparent, I think, now that we have distinguished between the various parts of the soul. Between ourselves—for I hope you won't give me away to the tragic poets and the other imitators—all the imitative arts seem to me ruinous to the mental powers of all their hearers who do not have as an antidote the knowledge of what these arts really are.

The truth must be told, though I hesitate because from childhood I have felt a certain love and veneration for Homer. He seems to me to be the chief teacher and leader of all the splendid tragic poets. Still a man should not be respected to the detriment of the truth, so I must explain what I mean.

But first answer a question.

[Imitation explained. 595 C]

Do you understand imitation well enough to tell me what it is? I don't myself understand very well what purpose there is in it.

It's likely that I should know, then, Glaucon answered.

Socrates replied: It wouldn't be strange that you should, since often those with dim vision make out objects more quickly than those with sharp eyes.

That's all very well, said Glaucon, but when you are present I hardly have the courage to tell what I do think; you give your opinion.

Shall we, then, said Socrates, begin our investigation in our usual manner? We are in the habit of putting in the same class all the various things to which we give the same name.

Now let us take any class of things you like. For example, there are a great many chairs and tables.

But only two ideas pertain to these objects, that of chair and that of table.

Well then, don't we say that the maker of either of these things, having the idea in mind, makes the chairs and tables we use and other things in the same way? For certainly none of the cabinet-makers devises the idea itself; how could he?

Now consider by what name you call this maker.

I mean the one who makes everything that each and every one of the handicrafts turns out.

Glaucon said: You are talking about some wonderfully clever man.

Wait a moment, replied Socrates, you must say something stronger than that. For this same being is the maker not merely of all implements, but he makes everything that grows out of the earth and produces all the animals, and himself too, and in addition the earth and the sky and the gods and everything in heaven and under the earth in Hades.

You are talking of a wonderful and wise being, said Glaucon.

Don't you believe it? replied Socrates. Now tell me, on the whole doesn't it seem to you that there is such a maker, or do you think that in one sense there is a maker of all these things and in another sense there is none? Or don't you see that in a sense you yourself can make all these things?

It is not hard; you can make things everywhere and without delay; the quickest way is to take a mirror and move it about, for you would quickly make the sun and anything that is in the sky and the earth and yourself and the other animals and furniture and plants and everything we have been talking about.

Yes, said Glaucon, reflections of them but not the real things.

[The artist's imitation. 596 E]

Good, Socrates answered, you have the notion I want. I think the painter is one of these makers.

You may say that he doesn't really make what he makes, yet in a sense the painter makes a bed, doesn't he, when he makes the picture of a bed?

And what about the cabinet-maker? Yet he doesn't make the idea, which is the real bed, but only one individual bed.

If he doesn't make the bed in its true essence, he doesn't make the real bed, but something like it though not it; and if anyone says that the product of the cabinet-maker gives us essence or being in the full sense of the word, he is in danger of saying what is not true. So we mustn't be astonished if the cabinet-maker's product turns out to be only a shadow of the truth.

Shall we then, try to learn what this imitator really is?

Then there are altogether three beds, one in nature, which we would admit, I think, to be the work of God, for it can hardly be the work of some other being.

Then there is one made by the cabinet-maker.

And one is made by the painter, isn't it?

Then there are painter, cabinet-maker, and God; these three are concerned with three different kinds of bed.

But God, whether because of his will or through some necessity that not more than one bed should be produced in nature, made just one bed, the real bed. But two or more of that sort were not made by God and never will be made.

The reason is that if he had made two, there would be one behind them whose appearance both of the others would have; that would be the real bed, and not the other two.

Since God understood that and wished to be the real creator of the real bed, but not a sort of cabinet-maker who makes an individual bed, he produced in nature one bed.

Shall we then call him the natural creator of it, or by some such name?

But what of the cabinet-maker? Is he not the maker of the bed? And isn't the painter also the creator and maker of one?

Glaucon did not accept this, but answered: Not at all.

Socrates then asked him: But how do you say he is related to the bed?

It seems to me, answered Glaucon, most reasonable to say that he imitates what the others make.

So, said Socrates, you call him who is not in direct contact with nature an imitator.

The same thing is true of the writer of tragedy, for if he is an imitator he also is by nature out of direct touch with the king and the truth, and so are all the other imitators.

So we are in agreement about the imitator. But about the painter; does he attempt to imitate each object as it naturally is?

Shall we not rather say he imitates the works of the artisans?

[Appearance and reality. 598 A]

Does he imitate them as they are or as they appear to be?

If you look at a bed from one side or from the front or in any other way, isn't it different? Or doesn't it really differ, though it appears different?

And isn't it the same about other things?

Now consider this: to what is painting in each instance directed? Does it imitate the thing as it actually is, or the appearance that it presents? Is it not an imitation of phantasy rather than of truth?

Then imitation is far removed from truth and, as it seems, produces things because it gets hold of a little of each object, namely, the image of each. The painter, for example, will paint us a shoemaker, a carpenter, and other workmen, though he does not understand the craft of any of them. And a good painter, if he is allowed to show at a distance his picture of a carpenter, will deceive children and simple men into thinking that it is really a carpenter.

But, my friend, this is the way we must look at such things: If someone tells us he has met a man who understands all the crafts and all sorts of other things, such as an expert in each craft knows, and that there is nothing he doesn't know more exactly than anyone else, we must think our informer a simple fellow who has been misled by encountering some enchanter and imitator. The imitator seems to him to be all-wise because he himself is unable to distinguish between knowledge and ignorance and imitation.

[The poet's knowledge. 598 D]

Then we must next examine tragedy and Homer who is at the head of it, for we hear some say that the tragic writers know all the crafts, and possess all human knowledge pertaining to virtue and vice, and all divine knowledge; they argue that the good poet, if he is to write on subjects he can treat properly, must deal with what he understands; otherwise he cannot write at all. We should find out whether men who argue thus have not encountered imitators who have deceived them, for they do not realize that something intervenes between the imitations they see and the truth itself, and that imitations are easily produced by one who does not know the truth; such productions are phantasms and not realities. Or is there something in their belief, and do good poets really have sound knowledge of the things on which they are popularly supposed to speak well?

Do you think that, if a man were equally able to produce both the thing imitated and the image of it, he would wish to give himself to the production of images and make that activity prominent in his life as the best thing he can do?

In my belief if he truly understood the things he imitates he would much prefer to work in the things themselves rather than in imitations, and would endeavor to leave behind him as monuments many beautiful works of his own; he would prefer to be praised rather than to praise someone else.

[Is Homer a teacher? 599 B]

We need not, then, examine Homer or other poets by asking if any one of them was a physician and not an imitator of the talk of physicians, and if any poet is reported to have cured anyone in antiquity or recently, as Asclepius did, or whether the poet left successors instructed in medicine, as Asclepius did his descendants, nor shall we ask anything about the other arts, but let them go. We shall be satisfied with asking about the greatest and most splendid things Homer undertakes to deal with, namely wars and military affairs and the government of cities and the education of a man, for it is proper to try to learn from him by asking: My dear Homer, if in your knowledge of virtue you are not out of contact with truth, as a mere maker of images according to our definition of the imitator, and if you are in close touch with the truth, and in a position to know what activities make men better or worse individually or in groups, tell us in what city you made improvements in the government, as Lycurgus did in Sparta, and other men in many other cities great and small. What city recognizes that you have been a good lawgiver and have benefited it? Italy and Sicily have Charondas and we Athenians have Solon, but what city acknowledges you?

Can he point to any?

And what war is mentioned as having been skillfully conducted in the time of Homer with him as general or adviser?

But are the works of a wise man attributed to Homer, as many inventions and devices helpful in the crafts and in other activities are said to be the work of Thales of Miletus and Anacharsis of Scythia? But if it is not related that he did anything of a public sort, perhaps Homer when he was alive privately directed the education of various persons who loved to associate with him, and marked out for others a way of life called the Homeric, just as Pythagoras was greatly loved for this, and his followers to this day call their rule of life the Pythagorean and are distinguished from other men by it.

No, Glaucon answered, nothing of the kind is told of Homer. And, Socrates, perhaps Creophylos, the companion of Homer, would appear in matters of education more ridiculous than his name,[1] if the things reported of Homer are true. For when he was alive he was greatly neglected, it is said, by that friend of his.

Yes, so it is said, Socrates answered. But you know, Glaucon, that if Homer really was a person who could train men and make them better, and could speak on such matters not as an imitator but as one with real knowledge, he would certainly have acquired many companions and been loved and honored by them. Protagoras of Abdera and Prodicus of Ceos and many others would hardly have been able to produce such an effect on their associates as to make them suppose themselves unable to manage their houses and cities without using the principles of their teachers, if Protagoras and the others had not taken charge of their education. The pupils of these men love them so greatly for their wisdom that they almost carry them about as in a triumphal procession. But if the contemporaries of Homer and Hesiod had thought they were able to instruct men in virtue, would they have allowed those poets to go about chanting verses? Would they not have clung to them regardless of expense, and forced them to stay with them? And if they could not persuade the poets to stay, would they not have accompanied them anywhere and everywhere, until they were sufficiently instructed?

[1] It means "of the beef-tribe."

[The poets are only imitators. 600 E]

Shall we decide, then, that all the poets beginning with Homer are imitators of images of virtue or of whatever they write about, and do not lay hold of the truth, but, as we just said, the painter, though he does not understand shoemaking, makes what seems to be a shoemaker to those who also do not understand and who judge from colors and gestures?

So, I take it, we shall say that the poet in his words and phrases uses the colors proper for each of the arts; and though he knows only how to imitate, yet to those who are as ignorant as himself he appears really to know. If he speaks of shoemaking, military affairs, or anything else, he seems to speak very well, for his ornaments of meter and rhythm and harmony naturally have great charm. But when the ideas of the poet are stripped of the colors of poetry, you know, I think, how they appear. You must have observed this. Well then, do they seem to you like those faces that have freshness but not beauty, if you happen to see them when they have passed their bloom?

Let us go on to consider this: We said, didn't we, that the poet is an imitator of what he knows nothing about, of a mere appearance? Let us not leave this subject partly thought out, but treat it fully.

The painter, we say, paints reins and a bit. And the harness-maker and the smith make them.

Then does the painter know what reins and bits really are?

Or does the manufacturer, namely, the smith or the harness-maker, know, or does knowledge belong only to the man who understands a bridle?

In my opinion the horseman is the one who knows.

And this holds generally.

I mean that for all such things there are three crafts, those of the user, the maker, and the imitator.

Then the virtue and beauty and correctness of any implement of life and action is determined by nothing else than the need because of which each one is made or brought forth. It must needs be that the user of each is well versed in it and can tell the maker which ones are good or bad for the use he makes of them; a flute-player can tell a flute-maker about the flutes he uses in playing, and will explain how they should be made, and the flute-maker will carry out his instructions.

Then the man who knows will explain about good and bad flutes, and the worker will follow his directions?

Then in this matter the maker will have a right belief about good and bad, since he is associated with the one who knows and is obliged to listen to him; but the one who uses the flute is the man who knows.

But does the imitator from using the thing he paints get to know what is good and what is bad?

Is his knowledge reliable because he is obliged to come in contact with somebody who knows and who gives him directions on what he should paint?

If not, the imitator will neither learn for himself nor be properly taught whether he imitates well or badly.

A fine imitator he will surely be in his knowledge of the things he works on!

So he will imitate without knowing how each thing is good or bad, but what seems excellent to the ignorant rabble—that, it appears, he will imitate.

It seems we agree on two points, then: that the imitator knows nothing worth mentioning of what he imitates, but his imitation is a sort of game and not serious, and all who undertake tragic poetry in iambic poems and in epics are imitators in the full sense of the word.

Can there be any doubt, I said, that this imitation is not in direct contact with truth?

[Protection against the imitator. 602 C]

Now on what part of the being of man does it exercise the power it has?

But I must explain. When you look at the same thing near at hand and from a distance, does it not appear different in size?

And a stick appears crooked when you see it in the water and straight when it is taken out,

and objects appear hollowed or rounded because the vision is deceived by shading, and every sort of confusion is produced in our minds: painting that uses light and shade, in its effect on our easily deluded senses, doesn't fall at all short of witchcraft, nor do sleight-of-hand performances and similar tricks.

But measuring and counting appear to be excellent remedies against such deceptions, so that appearances of greater or smaller or more or less do not control us, but rather the faculty that has counted and measured and even weighed.

This work would be carried on by the part of the soul that can reckon.

And it often happens to this part of the soul that measures and counts that diverse things and equal things may appear larger or smaller than they are, and opposite things seem to agree. And did we not say that it is impossible for the same part of the mind to have diverse beliefs about the same thing?

Then the part of the soul that judges with respect to measure would not be the same as that which judges contrary to measure. But if the soul is to be healthy it must trust to measure and reckoning.

And anything opposed to this would of necessity be one of the worse parts within us. Because I wished you to admit this, I said that painting and imitation generally carry out their work far from the truth and have to do with that part within us that is remote from the truth, and that the two arts are companions and friends of nothing wholesome or true.

So imitation is a wretched thing begetting wretched things on a wretched stock.

Is that true for what we see alone, or for what we hear and call poetry?

If it is true for poetry, we shouldn't trust merely to the likeness of poetry with painting, but should also consider that part of the reason with which the imitation of poetry is concerned, and see whether it is bad or excellent.

[Self-control. 603 C]

Let us proceed in this way: we may say that an imitative art imitates men who are performing either forced or voluntary acts, and thinking that as a result of their acts they are either happy or miserable, and in all these conditions they either lament or rejoice. And there seems to be nothing further. But in all these conditions does a man enjoy harmony of mind? Or, as he was confused in vision and had at one time opposite ideas about the same things, is he confused in his deeds and at war with himself?

But I recollect that it is not now necessary for us to come to a decision about the matter, for in what we have already said we have sufficiently considered the whole subject, and decided that our spirits are full of ten thousand opposed things at the same time. And though that was correct, it now seems necessary to consider what we then omitted.

We think that a reasonable man, when he sees anything happen as a result of chance, such as the loss of a son or something else of greatest consequence, bears such an affliction more easily than others do.

But now let us consider whether he will display no sorrow at all or whether that is impossible and it is more likely that he will show moderate grief.

Now tell me this about him. Do you think he will be more likely to fight with his sorrow and restrain it when he is in the company of his equals or when he is completely alone?

When he is alone, I think he will dare to utter many things he would be ashamed of if anyone should hear him, and he will do many things that he would not like to have anyone see him doing.

Are not, then, reason and law what require him to resist, but emotion what forces him to lament?

But since there is in man an opposite tendency in this matter, we say that there necessarily are two forces within him.

Is not one of these forces ready to obey the prescriptions of the law?

The law says it is a splendid thing to bear the utmost affliction with a calm mind and not to cry out, because one cannot be sure what is good and what is bad in such things, and there is no future advantage in chafing

under them, nor is anything human deserving of great eagerness, and grief hinders us from doing what should be done as quickly as possible in the circumstances. I refer to the need for showing reason about what has happened, just as in playing with dice one should adjust oneself to the outcome of chance, as good sense requires; we should not act like children when they have bumped themselves, for they put their hands on the part that has been struck and waste their time in crying out; but we should train the soul to seek a remedy as quickly as possible and to raise up what is fallen and sickly and dispel laments by remedies.

We agree, then, that the best part of the soul wishes to follow reason.

[Poetry imitates men who lack self-control. 604 D]

But what shall we say of that part of the soul that leads us to remember our sorrow and to complain and revive our lamentations? is it not irrational, lazy, and prone to cowardice? Yet the soul easily vexed is that which is imitated often and in various ways, but the thoughtful and calm man, always levelheaded, is hard to imitate and an imitation of him is not easily understood, especially in a great assembly when all sorts of men are gathered together in a theater, for the imitation of such a man presents qualities outside their experience.

It is clear that the mimetic poet is not naturally inclined to the rational part of the soul and his wisdom is not directed to its satisfaction, if he wishes to be acceptable to the many, but in order to be pleasing in his imitation he deals with the disturbed and unsettled character.

[Imitative poetry is corrupting. 605 A]

We can, then, properly consider him as parallel with the painter, whom he resembles in making things that are not in harmony with the truth; he is also like him in being occupied with another part of the spirit, and not the best part. Hence in justice we should not take him into the city that is to be well ruled, because he stirs up and nourishes and makes strong this bad part of the spirit, and destroys the rational part, just as anyone by making the wicked powerful would betray the city to them, and would destroy those of more insight. We shall say that the imitative poet sets up a badly governed state in the soul of each individual, rejoicing at the stupidity that cannot distinguish great from small but thinks the same things are sometimes large, sometimes small, for the poet makes images and is remote from the truth. But we have not said the worst of poetry. Its capacity for corrupting good citizens, with a very few exceptions,[1] is an exceedingly dangerous quality.

[Pity for the heroes of drama. 605 C]

Still further, when Homer or some other tragic writer imitates one of the heroes in distress, who gets off a long tirade of lamentation or pours forth verses and beats his breast, the strongest of us listen with pleasure, you know; we surrender our spirits to the guidance of the poet and sympathize with the hero, and are eager to praise the author because he so powerfully stirs our feelings. But when affliction comes into our own lives, you know we pride ourselves on conduct of the opposite sort and try to remain calm and self-controlled, as the behavior befitting a man, and think of what we have just praised as suitable only for women. But, when we see a man whose conduct appears to us unworthy and which we would be ashamed of in ourselves, is it proper for us not to censure him but to applaud and praise him? Yet there is one way in which it is not inconsistent.

If you consider that the part of our being we restrain by force in our own affliction is desirous of weeping and pouring out tears until it gets entirely rid of them, as nature urges it to do, you will see that part of us is the very same the poets satisfy and delight. If that portion of the soul best by nature is inadequately controlled by reason and habit,

---

[1] Perhaps the exceptions are the persons mentioned at the beginning of this tenth book of the *Republic* as having an antidote in the knowledge of the true nature of poetry.

it abandons its watch over lamentation on seeing human sufferings that do not immediately afflict itself, as when a man who claims to be good suffers without cause; it then praises and pities the sufferer and feels that it gains something from the spectacle, namely pleasure, which it wouldn't get if it decided to reject the drama completely. I suppose there are not many who can understand that what applies to the sorrows of others applies to their own, for if they give free rein to pity for the characters of tragedy, they will not find it easy to practice restraint in their own sufferings.

[The comic. The emotions. 606 C]

And isn't the same thing true of the comic? You may be ashamed of a thing that causes laughter, but if you hear it in a comic imitation or in private you are much amused and do not hate it as a vile thing, just as was true of pity. Then you permit what formerly you had restrained in yourself by reason, when you wished to laugh at it, because you were afraid of appearing like a buffoon; as a result, having broken down your dignity at the theater, many times in your own affairs you let yourself go as though you were a comic actor.

And with regard to sexual emotions, anger, and all the passions and sorrows and pleasures of the spirit, which we think are always with us, does not the poetic imitation have the same effect on us? It feeds and waters these passions that ought to be dried up, and puts them in command of us when they should be so ruled that we may grow better and happier instead of worse and more vile.

[The poets must be banished. 606 E]

Well then, Glaucon, when you chance on those who praise Homer and say that poet has been the teacher of Hellas, and that he is of value to those who become familiar with him because they can learn to manage and understand human affairs, and that they can live their whole lives according to the instructions they receive from this poet, we should love and honor them as men of high character so far as their powers extend,[1] and should acknowledge that Homer is the greatest of poets and the first of the writers of tragedy, yet we must hold to the belief that hymns to the gods and praises of good men are the only poems that should be admitted to our state. If we do admit the muse who is so sweet with her lyrics and epics, pleasure and pain will rule in our city instead of law and what is generally accepted as right reason.

Now since we are back on the subject of poetry, let us defend ourselves by showing that we were quite right in banishing it from the city for being what it is, for reason compelled it. Let us say to poetry, that she may not impute to us harshness and rudeness, that there is an ancient quarrel between philosophy and poetry, shown by such sayings as that philosophy is a yelping cur howling at its master, and is strong in the silly talk of fools, and that the crowd of pretended wise men is too much for Zeus, and that the philosophers are carefully thinking out how poor they are; these and many others are signs of the ancient enmity of poetry and philosophy. But if poetry and imitation, the bringers of pleasure, have anything to say, let them speak and show that they have a place in a well-ordered state, for we shall listen with delight, being well aware that we are bewitched by them. But it is not right to give up what one looks on as true. Still, my friend, are you not captivated by poetry, especially when you see her as presented by Homer?

Then it is not proper that she should come back to make her defense in a lyric or some other kind of poem?

And we may also permit her defenders, even if they are not poets but merely lovers of poetry, to speak of her without meter, and assert that she is not merely delightful but that she is also profitable to states and human life; and we shall listen like friends. For we shall be the gainers if she not merely appears delightful but also brings us profit.

But if it cannot be done, my dear friend, we shall act like those who are in love but think their love is not to their advantage and force themselves away from it.

We have an inbred love of such poetry nourished in us by education in a splendid state, and shall be glad to look on her as altogether good and true; yet so long as she does not make good her case, we shall as we listen to her keep in mind the argument we have already accepted, as a charm to prevent us from falling again into the childish loves of the multitude. At any rate we know we are not to suppose this sort of poetry admirable because it has attained the truth and is of great worth, but when we listen we must be on guard, as though in fear for the city within our souls, and must observe the laws we have laid down for poetry.

It is a hard struggle, my dear Glaucon, greater than anyone realizes, between good and evil, and we must not allow honor or wealth or any kind of authority or even poetry to make us neglect justice and the other virtues.

From THE POETICS

Aristotle
(384–322 B.C.)

4. [*Origin and development of poetry and its kinds.*] It is clear that the general origin of poetry was due to two causes, each of them part of human nature. Imitation is natural to man from childhood, one of his advantages over the lower animals being this, that he is the most imitative creature in the world, and learns at first by imitation. And it is also natural for all to delight in works of imitation. The truth of this second point is shown by

---

[1] Of this sort was Protagoras, who said: "When the boy knows his letters and can get the meaning of what is written, as before of what was spoken, the teacher puts into his hands for reading, as he sits on a bench in the school-room, the works of good poets and compels him to commit them to memory; in these poems there are many wise sayings and many digressions that give the highest praise to the good men of the past, in order that the boy may be eager to imitate them and seek to be like them" (*Protagoras,* 325–6).

experience: though the objects themselves may be painful to see, we delight to view the most realistic representations of them in art, the forms for example of the lowest animals and of dead bodies. The explanation is to be found in a further fact: to be learning something is the greatest of pleasures not only to the philosopher but also to the rest of mankind, however small their capacity for it; the reason of the delight in seeing the picture is that one is at the same time learning— gathering the meaning of things, e. g., that the man there is so-and-so; for if one has not seen the thing before, one's pleasure will not be in the picture as an imitation of it, but will be due to the execution or colouring or some similar cause. Imitation, then, being natural to us—as also the sense of harmony and rhythm, the metres being obviously species of rhythms—it was through their original aptitude, and by a series of improvements for the most part gradual on their first efforts, that they created poetry out of their improvisations.

Poetry, however, soon broke up into two kinds according to the differences of character in the individual poets; for the graver among them would represent noble actions, and those of noble personages; and the meaner sort the actions of the ignoble. The latter class produced invectives at first, just as others did hymns and panegyrics. We know of no such poem by any of the pre-Homeric poets, though there were probably many such writers among them; instances, however, may be found from Homer downwards, e. g., his *Margites,* and the similar poems of others. In this poetry of invective its natural fitness brought an iambic metre into use; hence our present term "iambic," because it was the metre of their "iambs" or invectives against one another. The result was that the old poets became some of them writers of heroic and others of iambic verse. Homer's position, however, is peculiar: just as he was in the serious style the poet of poets, standing alone not only through the literary excellence, but also through the dramatic character of his imitations, so too he was the first to outline for us the general

forms of Comedy by producing not a dramatic invective, but a dramatic picture of the Ridiculous; his *Margites* in fact stands in the same relation to our comedies as the *Iliad* and *Odyssey* to our tragedies. As soon, however, as Tragedy and Comedy appeared in the field, those naturally drawn to the one line of poetry became writers of comedies instead of iambs, and those naturally drawn to the other, writers of tragedies instead of epics, because these new modes of art were grander and of more esteem than the old.

If it be asked whether Tragedy is now all that it need be in its formative elements, to consider that, and decide it theoretically and in relation to the theatres, is a matter for another inquiry.

It certainly began in improvisations—as did also Comedy; the one originating with the authors of the Dithyramb, the other with those of the phallic songs, which still survive as institutions in many of our cities. And its advance after that was little by little, through their improving on whatever they had before them at each stage. It was in fact only after a long series of changes that the movement of Tragedy stopped on its attaining to its natural form. (1) The number of actors was first increased to two by Aeschylus, who curtailed the business of the Chorus, and made the dialogue, or spoken portion, take the leading part in the play. (2) A third actor and scenery were due to Sophocles. (3) Tragedy acquired also its magnitude. Discarding short stories and a ludicrous diction, through its passing out of its satyric stage, it assumed, though only at a late point in its progress, a tone of dignity; and its metre changed then from trochaic to iambic. The reason for their original use of the trochaic tetrameter was that their poetry was satyric and more connected with dancing than it now is. As soon, however, as a spoken part came in, nature herself found the appropriate metre. The iambic, we know, is the most speakable of metres, as is shown by the fact that we very often fall into it in conversation, whereas we rarely talk hexameters, and only when we depart from the speaking tone of voice. (4) Another change was a plurality of episodes or acts. As for the remaining matters, the superadded embellishments and the account of their introduction, these must be taken as said, as it would probably be a long piece of work to go through the details.

5. [*Comic and Epic poetry.*] As for Comedy, it is (as has been observed) an imitation of men worse than the average; worse, however, not as regards any and every sort of fault, but only as regards one particular kind, the Ridiculous, which is a species of the Ugly. The Ridiculous may be defined as a mistake or deformity not productive of pain or harm to others; the mask, for instance, that excites laughter, is something ugly and distorted without causing pain.

Though the successive changes in Tragedy and their authors are not unknown, we cannot say the same of Comedy; its early stages passed unnoticed, because it was not as yet taken up in a serious way. It was only at a late point in its progress that a chorus of comedians was officially granted by the archon; they used to be mere volunteers. It had also already certain definite forms at the time when the record of those termed comic poets begins. Who it was who supplied it with masks, or prologues, or a plurality of actors and the like, has remained unknown. The invented Fable, or Plot, however, originated in Sicily with Epicharmus and Phormis; of Athenian poets Crates was the first to drop the Comedy of invective and frame stories of a general and nonpersonal nature, in other words, Fables or Plots.

Epic poetry, then, has been seen to agree with Tragedy to this extent, that of being an imitation of serious subjects in a grand kind of verse. It differs from it, however, (1) in that it is in one kind of verse and in narrative form; and (2) in its length—which is due to its action having no fixed limit of time, whereas Tragedy endeavours to keep as far as possible within a single circuit of the sun, or something near that. This, I say, is another point of difference between them, though at first the practice in this respect was just the same in tragedies as in epic poems.

They differ also (3) in their constituents, some being common to both and others peculiar to Tragedy—hence a judge of good and bad in Tragedy is a judge of that in epic poetry also. All the parts of an epic are included in Tragedy; but those of Tragedy are not all of them to be found in the Epic.

6. [*Definition and analysis of Tragedy.*] Reserving hexameter poetry and Comedy for consideration hereafter, let us proceed now to the discussion of Tragedy; before doing so, however, we must gather up the definition resulting from what has been said. A tragedy, then, is the imitation of an action that is serious and also, as having magnitude, complete in itself; in language with pleasurable accessories, each kind brought in separately in the parts of the work; in a dramatic, not in a narrative form; with incidents arousing pity and fear, wherewith to accomplish its catharsis of such emotions. Here by "language with pleasurable accessories" I mean that with rhythm and harmony or song superadded; and by "the kinds separately" I mean that some portions are worked out with verse only, and others in turn with song.

I. As they act the stories, it follows that in the first place the Spectacle (or stage appearance of the actors) must be some part of the whole; and in the second Melody and Diction, these two being the means of their imitation. Here by "Diction" I mean merely this, the composition of the verses; and by "Melody," what is too completely understood to require explanation. But further: the subject represented also is an action; and the action involves agents, who must necessarily have their distinctive qualities both of character and thought, since it is from these that we ascribe certain qualities to their actions. There are in the natural order of things, therefore, two causes, Thought and Character, of their actions, and consequently of their success or failure in their lives. Now the action (that which was done) is represented in the play by the Fable or Plot. The Fable, in our present sense of the term, is simply this, the combination of the incidents, or things done in the story; whereas Character

is what makes us ascribe certain moral qualities to the agents; and Thought is shown in
all they say when proving a particular point
or, it may be, enunciating a general truth.
There are six parts consequently of every
tragedy, as a whole (that is) of such or such
quality, viz., a Fable or Plot, Characters, Diction, Thought, Spectacle, and Melody; two of
them arising from the means, one from the
manner, and three from the objects of the
dramatic imitation; and there is nothing else
besides these six. Of these, its formative elements, then, not a few of the dramatists have
made due use, as every play, one may say, admits of Spectacle, Character, Fable, Diction,
Melody, and Thought.

II. The most important of the six is the
combination of the incidents of the story.
Tragedy is essentially an imitation not of
persons but of action and life, of happiness
and misery. All human happiness or misery
takes the form of action; the end for which
we live is a certain kind of activity, not a
quality. Character gives us qualities, but it is
in our actions—what we do—that we are
happy or the reverse. In a play accordingly
they do not act in order to portray the Characters; they include the Characters for the
sake of the action. So that it is the action in
it, i. e., its Fable or Plot, that is the end and
purpose of the tragedy; and the end is everywhere the chief thing. Besides this, a tragedy
is impossible without action, but there may
be one without Character. The tragedies of
most of the moderns are characterless—a defect common among poets of all kinds, and
with its counterpart in painting in Zeuxis
as compared with Polygnotus; for whereas
the latter is strong in character, the work of
Zeuxis is devoid of it. And again: one may
string together a series of characteristic
speeches of the utmost finish as regards Diction and Thought, and yet fail to produce
the true tragic effect; but one will have
much better success with a tragedy which,
however inferior in these respects, has a
Plot, a combination of incidents, in it. And
again: the most powerful elements of attraction in Tragedy, the Peripeties and Discov-
eries, are parts of the Plot. A further proof

is in the fact that beginners succeed earlier
with the Diction and Characters than with
the construction of a story; and the same
may be said of nearly all the early dramatists.
We maintain, therefore, that the first essential, the life and soul, so to speak, of Tragedy
is the Plot; and that the Characters come
second—compare the parallel in painting,
where the most beautiful colours laid on
without order will not give one the same
pleasure as a simple black-and-white sketch
of a portrait. We maintain that Tragedy is
primarily an imitation of action, and that it
is mainly for the sake of the action that it
imitates the personal agents. Third comes
the element of Thought, i. e., the power of
saying whatever can be said, or what is appropriate to the occasion. This is what, in the
speeches in Tragedy, falls under the arts of
Politics and Rhetoric; for the older poets
make their personages discourse like statesmen, and the modern like rhetoricians. One
must not confuse it with Character. Character in a play is that which reveals the moral
purpose of the agents, i. e., the sort of thing
they seek or avoid, where that is not obvious
—hence there is no room for Character
in a speech on a purely indifferent subject.
Thought, on the other hand, is shown in all
they say when proving or disproving some
particular point, or enunciating some universal proposition. Fourth among the literary
elements is the Diction of the personages,
i.e., as before explained, the expression of
their thoughts in words, which is practically
the same thing with verse as with prose. As
for the two remaining parts, the Melody is
the greatest of the pleasurable accessories of
Tragedy. The Spectacle, though an attraction,
is the least artistic of all the parts, and has
least to do with the art of poetry. The tragic
effect is quite possible without a public performance and actors; and besides, the get-
ting-up of the Spectacle is more a matter for
the costumier than the poet.

7. [*Tragedy: arrangement and length of the
play.*] . . . [L]et us now consider the proper
construction of the Fable or Plot, as that is at
once the first and the most important thing

in Tragedy. We have laid it down that a tragedy is an imitation of an action that is complete in itself, as a whole of some magnitude; for a whole may be of no magnitude to speak of. Now a whole is that which has beginning, middle, and end. A beginning is that which is not itself necessarily after anything else, and which has naturally something else after it; an end is that which is naturally after something itself, either as its necessary or usual consequent, and with nothing else after it; and a middle, that which is by nature after one thing and has also another after it. A well-constructed Plot, therefore, cannot either begin or end at any point one likes; beginning and end in it must be of the forms just described. Again: to be beautiful, a living creature, and every whole made up of parts, must not only present a certain order in its arrangement of parts, but also be of a certain definite magnitude. Beauty is a matter of size and order, and therefore impossible either (1) in a very minute creature, since our perception becomes indistinct as it approaches instantaneity; or (2) in a creature of vast size—one, say, 1000 miles long—as in that case, instead of the object being seen all at once, the unity and wholeness of it is lost to the beholder. Just in the same way, then, as a beautiful whole made up of parts, or a beautiful living creature, must be of some size, but a size to be taken in by the eye, so a story or Plot must be of some length, but of a length to be taken in by the memory. As for the limit of its length, so far as that is relative to public performances and spectators, it does not fall within the theory of poetry. If they had to perform a hundred tragedies, they would be timed by water clocks, as they are said to have been at one period. The limit, however, set by the actual nature of the thing is this: the longer the story, consistently with its being comprehensible as a whole, the finer it is by reason of its magnitude. As a rough general formula, "a length which allows of the hero passing by a series of probable or necessary stages from misfortune to happiness, or from happiness to misfortune," may suffice as a limit for the magnitude of the story.

8. [*Tragedy: Unity of action.*] The Unity of a Plot does not consist, as some suppose, in its having one man as its subject. An infinity of things befall that one man, some of which it is impossible to reduce to unity; and in like manner there are many actions of one man which cannot be made to form one action. One sees, therefore, the mistake of all the poets who have written a *Heracleid,* a *Theseid,* or similar poems; they suppose that, because Heracles was one man, the story also of Heracles must be one story. Homer, however, evidently understood this point quite well, whether by art or instinct, just in the same way as he excels the rest in every other respect. In writing an *Odyssey,* he did not make the poem cover all that ever befell his hero—it befell him, for instance, to get wounded on Parnassus and also to feign madness at the time of the call to arms, but the two incidents had no necessary or probable connexion with one another—instead of doing that, he took as the subject of the *Odyssey,* as also of the *Iliad,* an action with a Unity of the kind we are describing. The truth is that, just as in the other imitative arts one imitation is always of one thing, so in poetry the story, as an imitation of action, must represent one action, a complete whole, with its several incidents so closely connected that the transposal or withdrawal of any one of them will disjoin and dislocate the whole. For that which makes no perceptible difference by its presence or absence is no real part of the whole.

9. [*Tragedy: the probable and universal.*] From what we have said it will be seen that the poet's function is to describe, not the thing that has happened, but a kind of thing that might happen, i. e., what is possible as being probable or necessary. The distinction between historian and poet is not in the one writing prose and the other verse—you might put the work of Herodotus into verse, and it would still be a species of history; it consists really in this, that the one describes the thing that has been, and the other a kind of thing that might be. Hence poetry is something more philosophic and of graver

import than history, since its statements are of the nature rather of universals, whereas those of history are singulars. By a universal statement I mean one as to what such or such a kind of man will probably or necessarily say or do—which is the aim of poetry, though it affixes proper names to the characters; by a singular statement, one as to what, say, Alcibiades did or had done to him. In Comedy this has become clear by this time; it is only when their plot is already made up of probable incidents that they give it a basis of proper names, choosing for the purpose any names that may occur to them, instead of writing like the old iambic poets about particular persons. In Tragedy, however, they still adhere to the historic names; and for this reason: what convinces is the possible; now whereas we are not yet sure as to the possibility of that which has not happened, that which has happened is manifestly possible, else it would not have come to pass. Nevertheless even in Tragedy there are some plays with but one or two known names in them, the rest being inventions; and there are some without a single known name, e. g., Agathon's *Antheus,* in which both incidents and names are of the poet's invention; and it is no less delightful on that account. So that one must not aim at a rigid adherence to the traditional stories on which tragedies are based. It would be absurd, in fact, to do so, as even the known stories are only known to a few, though they are a delight none the less to all.

It is evident from the above that the poet must be more the poet of his stories or Plots than of his verses, inasmuch as he is a poet by virtue of the imitative element in his work, and it is actions that he imitates. And if he should come to take a subject from actual history, he is none the less a poet for that; since some historic occurrences may very well be in the probable and possible order of things; and it is in that aspect of them that he is their poet.

Of simple Plots and actions the episodic are the worst. I call a Plot episodic when there is neither probability nor necessity in the sequence of its episodes. Actions of this sort bad poets construct through their own fault, and good ones on account of the players. His work being for public performance, a good poet often stretches out a Plot beyond its capabilities, and is thus obliged to twist the sequence of incident.

Tragedy, however, is an imitation not only of a complete action, but also of incidents arousing pity and fear. Such incidents have the very greatest effect on the mind when they occur unexpectedly and at the same time in consequence of one another; there is more of the marvellous in them then than if they happened of themselves or by mere chance. Even matters of chance seem most marvellous if there is an appearance of design as it were in them; as for instance the statue of Mitys at Argos killed the author of Mitys' death by falling down on him when a looker-on at a public spectacle; for incidents like that we think to be not without a meaning. A Plot, therefore, of this sort is necessarily finer than others.

.   .   .   .

11. [*Tragedy: Peripety, Discovery, and Suffering.*] A Peripety is the change of the kind described from one state of things within the play to its opposite, and that too in the way we are saying, in the probable or necessary sequence of events; as it is for instance in *Oedipus:* here the opposite state of things is produced by the Messenger, who, coming to gladden Oedipus and to remove his fears as to his mother, reveals the secret of his birth. And in *Lynceus:* just as he is being led off for execution, with Danaus at his side to put him to death, the incidents preceding this bring it about that he is saved and Danaus put to death. A Discovery is, as the very word implies, a change from ignorance to knowledge, and thus to either love or hate, in the personages marked for good or evil fortune. The finest form of Discovery is one attended by Peripeties, like that which goes with the Discovery in *Oedipus.* There are no doubt other forms of it; what we have said may happen in a way in reference to inanimate things, even things of a very casual kind; and it is also possible to discover

whether some one has done or not done something. But the form most directly connected with the Plot and the action of the piece is the first-mentioned. This, with a Peripety, will arouse either pity or fear—actions of that nature being what Tragedy is assumed to represent; and it will also serve to bring about the happy or unhappy ending. The Discovery, then, being of persons, it may be that of one party only to the other, the latter being already known; or both the parties may have to discover themselves. Iphigenia, for instance, was discovered to Orestes by sending the letter; and another Discovery was required to reveal him to Iphigenia.

.   .   .   .

13. [*The tragic hero.*] The next points after what we have said above will be these: (1) What is the poet to aim at, and what is he to avoid, in constructing his Plots? and (2) What are the conditions on which the tragic effect depends?

We assume that, for the finest form of Tragedy, the Plot must be not simple but complex; and further, that it must imitate actions arousing fear and pity, since that is the distinctive function of this kind of imitation. It follows, therefore, that there are three forms of Plot to be avoided. (1) A good man must not be seen passing from happiness to misery, or (2) a bad man from misery to happiness. The first situation is not fear inspiring or piteous, but simply odious to us. The second is the most untragic that can be; it has no one of the requisites of Tragedy; it does not appeal either to the human feeling in us, or to our pity, or to our fears. Nor, on the other hand, should (3) an extremely bad man be seen falling from happiness into misery. Such a story may arouse the human feeling in us, but it will not move us to either pity or fear; pity is occasioned by undeserved misfortune, and fear by that of one like ourselves; so that there will be nothing either piteous or fear inspiring in the situation. There remains, then, the intermediate kind of personage, a man not preeminently virtuous and just, whose misfor-

tune, however, is brought upon him not by vice and depravity but by some error of judgement, of the number of those in the enjoyment of great reputation and prosperity; e. g., Oedipus, Thyestes, and the men of note of similar families. The perfect Plot, accordingly, must have a single, and not (as some tell us) a double issue; the change in the hero's fortunes must be not from misery to happiness, but on the contrary from happiness to misery; and the cause of it must lie not in any depravity, but in some great error on his part; the man himself being either such as we have described, or better, not worse, than that. Fact also confirms our theory. Though the poets began by accepting any tragic story that came to hand, in these days the finest tragedies are always on the story of some few houses, on that of Alcmeon, Oedipus, Orestes, Meleager, Thyestes, Telephus, or any others that may have been involved, as either agents or sufferers, in some deed of horror. The theoretically best tragedy, then, has a Plot of this description. The critics, therefore, are wrong who blame Euripides for taking this line in his tragedies, and giving many of them an unhappy ending. It is, as we have said, the right line to take. The best proof is this: on the stage, and in the public performances, such plays, properly worked out, are seen to be the most truly tragic; and Euripides, even if his execution be faulty in every other point, is seen to be nevertheless the most tragic certainly of the dramatists. After this comes the construction of Plot which some rank first, one with a double story (like the *Odyssey*) and an opposite issue for the good and the bad personages. It is ranked as first only through the weakness of the audiences; the poets merely follow their public, writing as its wishes dictate. But the pleasure here is not that of Tragedy. It belongs rather to Comedy, where the bitterest enemies in the piece (e. g., Orestes and Aegisthus) walk off good friends at the end, with no slaying of any one by any one.

14. [*The tragic deed.*] The tragic fear and pity may be aroused by the Spectacle; but

they may also be aroused by the very structure and incidents of the play—which is the better way and shows the better poet. The Plot in fact should be so framed that, even without seeing the things take place, he who simply hears the account of them shall be filled with horror and pity at the incidents; which is just the effect that the mere recital of the story in *Oedipus* would have on one. To produce this same effect by means of the Spectacle is less artistic, and requires extraneous aid. Those, however, who make use of the Spectacle to put before us that which is merely monstrous and not productive of fear, are wholly out of touch with Tragedy; not every kind of pleasure should be required of a tragedy, but only its own proper pleasure.

The tragic pleasure is that of pity and fear, and the poet has to produce it by a work of imitation; it is clear, therefore, that the causes should be included in the incidents of his story. Let us see, then, what kinds of incident strike one as horrible, or rather as piteous. In a deed of this description the parties must necessarily be either friends, or enemies, or indifferent to one another. Now when enemy does it on enemy, there is nothing to move us to pity either in his doing or in his meditating the deed, except so far as the actual pain of the sufferer is concerned; and the same is true when the parties are indifferent to one another. Whenever the tragic deed, however, is done within the family— when murder or the like is done or meditated by brother on brother, by son on father, by mother on son, or son on mother—these are the situations the poet should seek after. The traditional stories, accordingly, must be kept as they are, e. g., the murder of Clytaemnestra by Orestes and of Eriphyle by Alcmeon. At the same time even with these there is something left to the poet himself; it is for him to devise the right way of treating them. Let us explain more clearly what we mean by "the right way." The deed of horror may be done by the doer knowingly and consciously, as in the old poets, and in Medea's murder of her children in Euripides. Or he may do it, but in ignorance of his relationship, and discover that afterwards, as does the Oedipus in Sophocles. Here the deed is outside the play; but it may be within it, like the act of the Alcmeon in *Astydamas,* or that of the Telegonus in *Ulysses Wounded.* A third possibility is for one meditating some deadly injury to another, in ignorance of his relationship, to make the discovery in time to draw back. These exhaust the possibilities, since the deed must necessarily be either done or not done, and either knowingly or unknowingly.

The worst situation is when the personage is with full knowledge on the point of doing the deed, and leaves it undone. It is odious and also (through the absence of suffering) untragic; hence it is that no one is made to act thus except in some few instances, e. g., Haemon and Creon in *Antigone.* Next after this comes the actual perpetration of the deed meditated. A better situation than that, however, is for the deed to be done in ignorance, and the relationship discovered afterwards, since there is nothing odious in it, and the Discovery will serve to astound us. But the best of all is the last; what we have in *Cresphontes,* for example, where Merope, on the point of slaying her son, recognizes him in time; in *Iphigenia,* where sister and brother are in a like position; and in *Helle,* where the son recognizes his mother, when on the point of giving her up to her enemy.

This will explain why our tragedies are restricted (as we said just now) to such a small number of families. It was accident rather than art that led the poets in quest of subjects to embody this kind of incident in their Plots. They are still obliged, accordingly, to have recourse to the families in which such horrors have occurred.

On the construction of the Plot, and the kind of Plot required for Tragedy, enough has now been said.

15. [*The character of the tragic personages.*] In the Characters there are four points to aim at. First and foremost, that they shall be good. There will be an element of character in the play, if (as has been observed) what a personage says or does reveals a certain moral purpose; and a good element of character, if the purpose so revealed is good. Such good-

ness is possible in every type of personage, even in a woman or a slave, though the one is perhaps an inferior, and the other a wholly worthless being. The second point is to make them appropriate. The Character before us may be, say, manly; but it is not appropriate in a female Character to be manly, or clever. The third is to make them like the reality, which is not the same as their being good and appropriate, in our sense of the term. The fourth is to make them consistent and the same throughout; even if inconsistency be part of the man before one for imitation as presenting that form of character, he should still be consistently inconsistent. We have an instance of baseness of character, not required for the story, in the Menelaus in *Orestes*; of the incongruous and unbefitting in the lamentation of Ulysses in *Scylla,* and in the (clever) speech of Melanippe; and of inconsistency in *Iphigenia at Aulis,* where Iphigenia the suppliant is utterly unlike the later Iphigenia. The right thing, however, is in the Characters just as in the incidents of the play to endeavour always after the necessary or the probable; so that whenever such-and-such a personage says or does such-and-such a thing, it shall be the necessary or probable outcome of his character; and when-ever this incident follows on that, it shall be either the necessary or the probable conse-quence of it. From this one sees (to digress for a moment) that the Dénouement also should arise out of the plot itself, and not de-pend on a stage artifice, as in *Medea,* or in the story of the (arrested) departure of the Greeks in the *Iliad.*

.   .   .   .

From PREFACE TO
LYRICAL BALLADS

William Wordsworth
(1770–1850)

. . . The poet writes under one restriction only, namely, the necessity of giving im-mediate pleasure to a human Being posessed of that information which may be expected from him, not as a lawyer, a physician, a mariner, an astronomer, or a natural philoso-pher, but as a Man. Except this one restric-tion, there is no object standing between the Poet and the image of things; between this, and the Biographer and Historian, there are a thousand.

Nor let this necessity of producing im-mediate pleasure be considered as a degrada-tion of the Poet's art. It is far otherwise. It is an acknowledgment of the beauty of the universe, an acknowledgment the more sin-cere, because not formal, but indirect; it is a task light and easy to him who looks at the world in the spirit of love: further, it is a homage paid to the native and naked dignity of man, to the grand elementary principle of pleasure, by which he knows, and feels, and lives, and moves. We have no sympathy but what is propagated by pleasure: I would not be misunderstood; but where-ever we sym-pathise with pain, it will be found that the sympathy is produced and carried on by sub-tle combinations with pleasure. We have no knowledge, that is, no general principles drawn from the contemplation of particular facts, but what has been built up by pleasure, and exists in us by pleasure alone. The Man of Science, the Chemist and Mathematician, whatever difficulties and disgusts they may have had to struggle with, know and feel this. However painful may be the objects with which the Anatomist's knowledge is connected, he feels that his knowledge is pleasure; and where he has no pleasure he has no knowledge. What then does the Poet? He considers man and the objects that sur-round him as acting and re-acting upon each other, so as to produce an infinite complexity of pain and pleasure; he considers man in his own nature and in his ordinary life as contemplating this with a certain quantity of immediate knowledge, with certain convic-tions, intuitions, and deductions, which from habit acquire the quality of intuitions; he considers him as looking upon this complex scene of ideas and sensations, and finding everywhere objects that immediately excite in him sympathies which, from the necessities of his nature, are accompanied by an over-balance of enjoyment.

To this knowledge which all men carry about with them, and to these sympathies in which, without any other discipline than that of our daily life, we are fitted to take delight, the Poet principally directs his attention.

.   .   .   .

I have said that poetry is the spontaneous overflow of powerful feelings: it takes its origin from emotion recollected in tranquillity: the emotion is contemplated till, by a species of reaction, the tranquillity gradually disappears, and an emotion, kindred to that which was before the subject of contemplation, is gradually produced, and does itself actually exist in the mind. In this mood successful composition generally begins, and in a mood similar to this it is carried on; but the emotion, of whatever kind, and in whatever degree, from various causes, is qualified by various pleasures, so that in describing any passions whatsoever, which are voluntarily described, the mind will, upon the whole, be in a state of enjoyment. . . .

THE LITERATURE OF KNOWLEDGE AND THE LITERATURE OF POWER*

Thomas De Quincey
(1785–1859)

Books . . . do not suggest an idea coextensive and interchangeable with the idea of Literature; since much literature, scenic, forensic, or didactic, (as from lecturers and public orators), may never come into books, and much that *does* come into books may connect itself with no literary interest. But a far more important correction, applicable

* From an essay on the review of *The Works of Alexander Pope, Esq.* by W. Roscoe, Esq. *The North British Review*, August, 1848.

to the common vague idea of literature, is to be sought not so much in a better definition of literature as in a sharper distinction of the two functions which it fulfils. In that great social organ which, collectively, we call literature, there may be distinguished two separate offices that may blend and often *do* so, but capable, severally, of a severe insulation, and naturally fitted for reciprocal repulsion. There is, first, the literature of *knowledge;* and, secondly, the literature of *power.* The function of the first is—to *teach;* the function of the second is—to *move:* the first is a rudder; the second, an oar or a sail. The first speaks to the *mere* discursive understanding; the second speaks ultimately, it may happen, to the higher understanding or reason, but always *through* affections of pleasure and sympathy. Remotely, it may travel towards an object seated in what Lord Bacon calls *dry* light; but, proximately, it does and must operate—else it ceases to be a literature of *power,*—on and through that *humid* light which clothes itself in the mists and glittering *iris* of human passions, desires, and genial emotions. Men have so little reflected on the higher functions of literature as to find it a paradox if one should describe it as a mean or subordinate purpose of books to give information. But this is a paradox only in the sense which makes it honourable to be paradoxical. Whenever we talk in ordinary language of seeking information or gaining knowledge, we understand the words as connected with something of absolute novelty. But it is the grandeur of all truth which *can* occupy a very high place in human interests that it is never absolutely novel to the meanest of minds: it exists eternally by way of germ or latent principle in the lowest as in the highest, needing to be developed, but never to be planted. To be capable of transplantation is the immediate criterion of a truth that ranges on a lower scale. Besides which, there is a rarer thing than truth,— namely, *power,* or deep sympathy with truth. What is the effect, for instance, upon society, of children? By the pity, by the tenderness, and by the peculiar modes of admiration, which connect themselves with the helplessness, with the innocence, and with the simplicity of children, not only are the primal affections stregthened and continually renewed, but the qualities which are dearest in the sight of heaven,—the frailty, for instance, which appeals to forbearance, the innocence which symbolises the heavenly, and the simplicity which is most alien from the worldly,—are kept up in perpetual remembrance, and their ideals are continually refreshed. A purpose of the same nature is answered by the higher literature, viz. the literature of power. What do you learn from "Paradise Lost"? Nothing at all. What do you learn from a cookery-book? Something new, something that you did not know before, in every paragraph. But would you therefore put the wretched cookery-book on a higher level of estimation than the divine poem? What you owe to Milton is not any knowledge, of which a million separate items are still but a million of advancing steps on the same earthly level; what you owe is *power*,—that is, exercise and expansion to your own latent capacity of sympathy with the infinite, where every pulse and each separate influx is a step upwards, a step ascending as upon a Jacob's ladder from earth to mysterious altitudes above the earth. *All* the steps of knowledge, from first to last, carry you further on the same plane, but could never raise you one foot above your ancient level of earth: whereas the very *first* step in power is a flight—is an ascending movement into another element where earth is forgotten.

Were it not that human sensibilities are ventilated and continually called out into exercise by the great phenomena of infancy, or of real life as it moves through chance and change, or of literature as it recombines these elements in the mimicries of poetry, romance, &c., it is certain that, like any animal or power or muscular energy falling into disuse, all such sensibilities would gradually droop and dwindle. It is in relation to these great *moral* capacities of man that the literature of power, as contradistinguished from that of knowledge, lives and has its field of action. It is concerned with what is

highest in man; for the Scriptures themselves never condescended to deal by suggestion or co-operation with the mere discursive understanding: when speaking of man in his intellectual capacity, the Scriptures speak not of the understanding, but of *"the understanding heart,"* making the heart, *i.e.,* the great *intuitive* (or non-discursive) organ, to be the interchangeable formula for man in his highest state of capacity for the infinite. Tragedy, romance, fairy tale, or epopee, all alike restore to man's mind the ideals of justice, of hope, of truth, of mercy, of retribution, which else (left to the support of daily life in its realities) would languish for want of sufficient illustration. What is meant, for instance, by *poetic justice?*—It does not mean a justice that differs by its object from the ordinary justice of human jurisprudence; for then it must be confessedly a very bad kind of justice; but it means a justice that differs from common forensic justice by the degree in which it *attains* its object, a justice that is more omnipotent over its own ends, as dealing—not with the refractory elements of earthly life, but with the elements of its own creation, and with materials flexible to its own purest preconceptions. It is certain that, were it not for the Literature of Power, these ideals would often remain amongst us as mere arid notional forms; whereas, by the creative forces of man put forth in literature, they gain a vernal life of restoration, and germinate into vital activities. The commonest novel, by moving in alliance with human fears and hopes, with human instincts of wrong and right, sustains and quickens those affections. Calling them into action, it rescues them from torpor. And hence the pre-eminency over all authors that merely *teach* of the meanest that *moves,* or that teaches, if at all, indirectly *by* moving. The very highest work that has ever existed in the Literature of Knowledge is but a *provisional* work: a book upon trial and sufferance, and *quamdiu bene se gesserit.** Let its teaching be even partially revised, let it be but expanded,—nay, even let its teaching

* As long as it behaves itself.

be but placed in a better order,—and instantly it is superseded. Whereas the feeblest works in the Literature of Power, surviving at all, survive as finished and unalterable amongst men. For instance, the *Principia* of Sir Isaac Newton was a book *militant* on earth from the first. In all stages of its progress it would have to fight for its existence: 1st, as regards absolute truth; 2dly, when that combat was over, as regards its form or mode of presenting the truth. And as soon as a La Place, or anybody else, builds higher upon the foundations laid by this book, effectually he throws it out of the sunshine into decay and darkness; by weapons won from this book he superannuates and destroys this book, so that soon the name of Newton remains as a mere *nominis umbra,* but his book, as a living power, has transmigrated into other forms. Now, on the contrary, the Iliad, the Prometheus of Æschylus, the Othello or King Lear, the Hamlet or Macbeth, and the Paradise Lost, are not militant, but triumphant for ever as long as the languages exist in which they speak or can be taught to speak. They never *can* transmigrate into new incarnations. To reproduce *these* in new forms, or variations, even if in some things they should be improved, would be to plagiarise. A good steam-engine is properly superseded by a better. But one lovely pastoral valley is not superseded by another, nor a statue of Praxiteles by a statue of Michael Angelo. These things are separated not by imparity, but by disparity. They are not thought of as unequal under the same standard, but as different in *kind,* and, if otherwise equal, as equal under a different standard. Human works of immortal beauty and works of nature in one respect stand on the same footing: they never absolutely repeat each other, never approach so near as not to differ; and they differ not as better and worse, or simply by more and less: they differ by undecipherable and incommunicable differences, that cannot be caught by mimicries, that cannot be reflected in the mirror of copies, that cannot become ponderable in the scales of vulgar comparison.

. . . . At this hour, five hundred years since their creation, the tales of Chaucer, never equalled on this earth for their tenderness, and for life of picturesqueness, are read familiarly by many in the charming language of their natal day, and by others in the modernisations of Dryden, of Pope, and Wordsworth. At this hour, one thousand eight hundred years since their creation, the Pagan tales of Ovid, never equalled on this earth for the gaiety of their movement and the capricious graces of their narrative, are read by all Christendom. This man's people and their monuments are dust; but *he* is alive: he has survived them, as he told us that he had it in his commission to do, by a thousand years; "and *shall* a thousand more."

All the literature of knowledge builds only ground-nests, that are swept away by floods, or confounded by the plough; but the literature of power builds nests in aërial altitudes of temples sacred from violation, or of forests inaccessible to fraud. *This* is a great prerogative of the *power* literature; and it is a greater which lies in the mode of its influence. The *knowledge* literature, like the fashion of this world, passeth away. An Encyclopaedia is its abstract; and, in this respect, it may be taken for its speaking symbol—that before one generation has passed an Encyclopaedia is superannuated; for it speaks through the dead memory and unimpassioned understanding, which have not the repose of higher faculties, but are continually enlarging and varying their phylacteries. But all literature properly so called—literature κατ᾽ἐξοχην,*—for the very same reason that it is so much more durable than the literature of knowledge, is (and by the very same proportion it is) more intense and electrically searching in its impressions. The directions in which the tragedy of this planet has trained our human feelings to play, and the combinations into which the poetry of this planet has thrown our human passions of love and hatred, of admiration and contempt, exercise a power for bad or good over human life that cannot be contemplated, when stretching through many generations, with-

---

* Possessions for eternity.

out a sentiment allied to awe.[1] And of this let every one be assured—that he owes to the impassioned books which he has read many a thousand more of emotions than he can consciously trace back to them. Dim by their origination, these emotions yet arise in him, and mould him through life, like forgotten incidents of his childhood.

[1] The reason why the broad distinctions between the two literatures of power and knowledge so little fix the attention lies in the fact that a vast proportion of books,—history, biography, travels, miscellaneous essays, &c.,—lying in a middle zone, confound these distinctions by interblending them. All that we call "amusement" or "entertainment" is a diluted form of the power belonging to passion, and also a mixed form; and, where threads of direct *instruction* intermingle in the texture with these threads of *power,* this absorption of the duality into one representative *nuance* neutralises the separate perception of either. Fused into a *tertium quid,* or neutral state, they disappear to the popular eye as the repelling forces which, in fact, they are.

ART, PLAY, AND CIVILISATION*

I. A. Richards
(1893–   )

The value of the experiences which we seek from the arts does not lie, so we have insisted, in the exquisiteness of the moment of consciousness; a set of isolated ecstasies is not a sufficient explanation. Its inadequacy is additional evidence that the theories of value and of the mind upon which it rests are defective. We must now consider what wider explanations are made possible by the theory of value and the outline account of mental activity and of communication above indicated. The ground, in part at least, is cleared. What now can be said as to why the arts are important and why good taste and sound criticism are not mere luxuries, trivial excrescences grafted upon an independent civilisation?

* Chapter XXXI of *Principles of Literary Criticism.*

A number of accounts of varying adequacy each in some degree interesting but needing careful interpretation have been put forward. The arts communicate experiences, it has been said, and make states of mind accessible to the many which otherwise would be only possible to few. To this it might be added that the arts are also a means by which experiences arise in the mind of the artist which would never otherwise come about. Both as an occasion for a collectedness and concentration difficult to attain in the ordinary course of life, and as the means by which human effort may acquire a continuity analogous to but more subtle than the continuity of science, the study and practice of the arts can give immensely increased power to the artist, preserving him from that diffusion of his energies which is perhaps his greatest danger. All this is true, but it does not go to the root of the matter.

Again the educational aspect of the arts is constantly being stressed, sometimes in a manner which does them disservice. "Message" hunting—the type of interest which discovers in *Macbeth* the moral that "Honesty is the best policy"; in *Othello* a recommendation to "Look before you leap," in *Hamlet* perhaps a proof that "Procrastination is the Thief of Time," or in *King Lear* an indication that "Your sins will find you out,"[1] in Shelley an exhortation to Idealism, in Browning comfort for the discouraged and assurances as to a future life; but in Donne or Keats no "message"—this mode of interpreting the phrase "a criticism of Life," though to a minute degree on the right lines, is probably more damaging than those entirely erratic theories, of which "Art for Art's sake" is an example, with which we have been more concerned.

None the less but in subtler ways the educational influence of the arts is all-pervasive. We must not overlook bad art in estimating it. "I should be said to insist absurdly on the power of my own confraternity" wrote a novelist of the 19th century "if I were to declare that the bulk of the

[1] Even Coleridge was not exempt from this failing. Cf. his comments on Gloster.

young people in the upper and middle classes receive their moral teaching chiefly from the novels that they read. Mothers would no doubt think of their own sweet teaching; fathers of the examples which they set; and schoolmasters of the excellence of their instructions. Happy is the country which has such mothers, fathers and schoolmasters! But the novelist creeps in closer than the father, closer than the schoolmaster, closer almost than the mother. He is the chosen guide, the tutor whom the young pupil chooses for herself. She retires with him, suspecting no lesson . . . and there she is taught how she shall learn to love; how she shall receive the lover when he comes; how far she should advance to meet the joy; why she should be reticent and not throw herself at once into this new delight."

The influence is also exerted in more indirect ways. There need be, we must remember, no discernible connection or resemblance whatever between the experience due to the work of art and the later behaviour and experience which is modified through it. Without such resemblance the influence may easily be overlooked or denied, but not by anyone who has a sufficient conception of the ways in which attitudes develop. No one who has repeatedly lived through experiences at the level of discrimination and co-ordination presupposed by the greater writers, can ever, when fully "vigilant," be contented with ordinary crudities, though a touch of liver may of course suspend these superior responses. And conversely, keen and vigilant enjoyment of Miss Dell, Mr. Burroughs, Mrs. Wilcox or Mr. Hutchinson, when untouched by doubts or the joys of ironic contemplation, is likely to have as a consequence not only an acceptance of the mediocre in ordinary life, but a blurring and confusion of impulses and a very widespread loss of value.

These remarks apply even more evidently to the Cinema. People do not much imitate what they see upon the screen or what they read of in best-sellers. It would matter little if they did. Such effects would show themselves clearly and the evil would be of a manageable kind. They tend instead to develop stock attitudes and stereotyped ideas, the attitudes and ideas of producers: attitudes and ideas which can be "put across" quickly through a medium that lends itself to crude rather than to sensitive handling. Even a good dramatist's work will tend to be coarser than that of a novelist of equal ability. He has to make his effects more quickly and in a more obvious way. The Cinema suffers still more than the stage from this disability. It has its compensating advantages in the greater demands which it makes of the audience, but hitherto very few producers have been able to turn them to account. Thus the ideas and attitudes with which the "movie fan" becomes familiar tend to be peculiarly clumsy and inapplicable to life. Other causes, connected with the mentality of producers, increase the effect.

The danger lies not in the fact that school-girls are sometimes incited to poke revolvers at taximen, but in much subtler and more insinuating influences. Most films indeed are much more suited to children than to adults, and it is the adults who really suffer from them. No one can intensely and whole-heartedly enjoy and enter into experiences whose fabric is as crude as that of the average super-film without a disorganisation which has its effects in everyday life. The extent to which second-hand experience of a crass and inchoate type is replacing ordinary life offers a threat which has not yet been realised. If a false theory of the severance and disconnection between "aesthetic" and ordinary experience has prevented the value of the arts from being understood, it has also preserved their dangers from recognition.

Those who have attempted to find a place in the whole structure of life for the arts have often made use of the conception of Play; and Groos and Herbert Spencer are famous exponents of the theory. As with so many other Aesthetic Doctrines the opinion that Art is a form of Play may indicate either a very shallow or a very penetrating view. All depends upon the conception of Play which is entertained. Originally the view arose in connection with survival values. Art, it was thought, had little practical value of the obvious kinds, so some indirect means must be found by which it could be thought to be of service. Perhaps, like play, it was a means of harmlessly expending superfluous energy. A more useful contribution was made when the problem of the value of play itself was seriously attacked. The immense practical utility of most forms of play then became evident. Characteristically play is the preparatory organisation and development of impulses. It may easily become too narrowly specialised, and the impulses active may be such as never to receive "serious" exercise. None the less with our present understanding of the amazingly recondite interactions between what appear to be totally different activities of the nervous system, the importance of play is not likely to need much insistence.

There are many human activities which, fortunately or unfortunately as the case may be, are no longer required of or possible to civilised man. Yet their total discontinuance may lead to grave disturbances. For some of these play serves as an opportunity. The view that art provides in some cases an analogous outlet through vicarious experience has naturally been put forward, notably by Mr. Havelock Ellis. "We have lost the orgy, but in its place we have art."[1] If we do not extend the "sublimation" theory too far or try to bring under this Safety-valve heading work with which it has no concern, it may be granted that in some cases the explanation is in place. But the temptation to extend it, and so to misconceive the whole matter, is great.

The objection to the Play Theory, unless very carefully stated, lies in its suggestion that the experiences of Art are in some way incomplete, that they are substitutes, meagre copies of the real thing, well enough for those who cannot obtain better. "The moralising force of Art lies, not in its capacity to present a timid imitation of our experiences, but in its power to go beyond our

experience, satisfying and harmonising the unfulfilled activities of our nature."[2] The Copy View, with the antithesis between Life and Literature which so often accompanies it, is a devastating misconception. Coupled with the suggestion involved by the word "Play," that such things are for the young rather than for the mature, and that Art is something one grows out of, it has a large share of the responsibility for the present state of the Arts and of Criticism. Its only rival in obscuring the issues is its close cousin the Amusement or Relaxation Theory.

The experiences which the arts offer are not obtainable, or but rarely, elsewhere. Would that they were! They are not incomplete; they might better be described as ordinary experiences completed. They are not such that the most adequately equipped person can dispense with them and suffer no loss, and this loss is not momentary, but recurrent and permanent; the best equipped are precisely the people who most value these experiences. Nor is Art, as by way of corollary is sometimes maintained, a thing which had its function in the youth of the world, but with the development of Science becomes obsolete. It may very possibly decline and even disappear, but if it does a biological calamity of the first order will have occurred. Nor again is it something which may be postponed while premillennial man grapples with more immediate problems. The raising of the standard of response is as immediate a problem as any, and the arts are the chief instrument by which it may be raised *or lowered*.

Hitherto we have been concerned chiefly with more or less specific effects of the experiences of the arts, with the effects, upon single definite groups or systems of impulses, of their exercise in these experiences. The Play Theory tends to limit us to these consequences. Important though they are, we must not overlook the more general effects which any well-organised experience produces. They may in certain cases be extraordinarily widespread. Such an apparently irrelevant

[1] Essay on Casanova, in *Affirmations*, p. 115.

[2] *Affirmations*, p. 115.

test as the ability to stand upon one foot without unsteadiness has recently been employed, by Mr. Burt, as an index to mental and especially to emotional organisation. All our activities react upon one another to a prodigious extent in ways which we can only as yet conjecture.

Finer adjustment, clearer and more delicate accommodation or reconciliation of impulses in any one field tends to promote it in others. A step in mathematical accomplishment, other things being equal, facilitates the acquisition of a new turn in ski-ing. Other things are rarely equal it should perhaps be remarked. If this is true even of such special narrowly restricted impulses as are involved in a scientific technique, it is far more evident when the major, the most widespread systems, those active in our responses to human beings and to the exigences of existence, are engaged.

There is abundant evidence that removal of confusion in one sphere of activity tends to be favourable to its removal elsewhere. The ease with which a trained mind approaches a new subject is the plainest example, but equally a person whose ordinary emotional experience is clear, controlled and coherent, is the least likely to be thrown into confusion by an unheard-of predicament. Complications sometimes obscure this effect: a mathematician approaching psychology may attempt to apply methods which are inappropriate, and the sanest people may prove stupid in their dealings with individuals of other races. The specialist, either intellectual or moral, who is helpless outside his own narrow field is a familiar figure in inferior comedy. But what would have to be shown before the principle is invalidated is that, granted equal specialisation, the successful specialist is not better fitted for life in general than his unsuccessful *confrère*. Few people, however, will dispute the assertion that transference of ability frequently occurs although the mode by which it comes about may be obscure.

When very widespread and very fundamental impulses are implicated, where attitudes constantly taken up in ordinary life are aroused, this transference effect may be very marked. Everybody knows the feeling of freedom, of relief, of increased competence and sanity, that follows any reading in which more than usual order and coherence has been given to our responses. We seem to feel that our command of life, our insight into it and our discrimination of its possibilities, is enhanced, even for situations having little or nothing to do with the subject of the reading. It may be a chapter of *Gösta Berling* or of *The ABC of Atoms,* the close of the *Vanity of Human Wishes,* or the opening of *Harry Richmond;* whatever the differences the refreshment is the same. And conversely everybody knows the diminution of energy, the bafflement, the sense of helplessness, which an ill-written, crude, or muddled book, or a badly acted play, will produce, unless the critical task of diagnosis is able to restore equanimity and composure.

Neither the subject nor the closeness of correspondence between the experience and the reader's own situation has any bearing upon these effects. But indeed, to anyone who realises what kind of a thing an experience is, and through what means it comes about, the old antithesis between subject and treatment ceases to be of interest. . . . They are not separable or distinct things and the division is of no service. In this case the effects we are considering depend only upon the kind and degree of organisation which is given to the experiences. If it is at the level of our own best attempts or above it (but not so far above as to be out of reach) we are refreshed. But if our own organisation is broken down, forced to a cruder, a more wasteful level, we are depressed and temporarily incapacitated, not only locally but generally. It is when what we are offered, and inveigled into accepting, is only slightly inferior to our own developed capacity, so that it is no easy matter to see what is wrong, that the effect is greatest. Stuff of an evident and extreme badness is exhilarating rather than depressing when taken from a discriminating standpoint; and there need be nothing snobbish or self-congratulatory in such reading. What is really discomposing and damaging to the critical reader is the mediocre, the work which falls just below his own standards of response. Hence the rage which some feel at the productions of Sir James Barrie, Mr. Locke, or Sir Hall Caine, a rage which work comparatively devoid of merits fails to excite.

These effects are not merely momentary or evanescent; if we would understand the place of the arts in civilisation we must consider them more closely. An improvement of response is the only benefit which anyone can receive, and the degradation, the lowering of a response, is the only calamity. When we take into account not merely the impulses actually concerned in the experience but all the allied groups which thrive or suffer with it, and all the far-reaching effects of success or failure upon activities which may seem to be independent, the fact that some people feel so keenly about the arts is no longer surprising.

Underestimation of the importance of the arts is nearly always due to ignorance of the workings of the mind. Experiences such as these, into which we willingly and wholeheartedly enter, or into which we may be enticed and inveigled, present peculiar opportunities for betrayal. They are the most formative of experiences, because in them the development and systematisation of our impulses goes to the furthest lengths. In ordinary life a thousand considerations prohibit for most of us any complete working out of our response; the range and complexity of the impulse-systems involved is less; the need for action, the comparative uncertainty and vagueness of the situation, the intrusion of accidental irrelevancies, inconvenient temporal spacing—the action being too slow or too fast—all these obscure the issue and prevent the full development of the experience. We have to jump to some rough and ready solution. But in the "imaginative experience" these obstacles are removed. Thus what happens here, what precise stresses, preponderances, conflicts, resolutions and interinanimations, what remote relationships between different systems of impulses arise, what before unapprehended and inexecutable connections are established, is a matter which, we see clearly, may modify all the rest of life. As a chemist's balance to a grocer's scales, so is the mind in the imaginative moment to the mind engaged in ordinary intercourse or practical affairs. The comparison will bear pressing. The results, for good or evil, of the untrammelled response are not lost to us in our usual trafficking.

INDEX
OF
AUTHORS AND TITLES

INDEX OF AUTHORS AND TITLES